D0927067

Psychoanalysis Psychiatry and Law

Psychoanalysis

Psychiatry

and Law

Jay Katz YALE UNIVERSITY

Joseph Goldstein YALE UNIVERSITY

Alan M. Dershowitz HARVARD UNIVERSITY

THE FREE PRESS, NEW YORK

COLLIER-MACMILLAN LIMITED, LONDON

Copyright © 1967 by The Free Press

A DIVISION OF THE MACMILLAN COMPANY

Printed in the United States of America

All rights reserved. No part of this book may be reproduced or transmitted in any form or by any means, electronic or mechanical, including photo-copying, recording, or by any information storage and retrieval system, without permission in writing from the Publisher.

Collier-Macmillan Canada, Ltd., Toronto, Ontario

FIRST PRINTING

The illustrations by Ellen Raskin were adapted from the gargoyles and windows of the Yale Law School.

Library of Congress Catalog Card Number: 65-27757

340.6
K 19 ₚ

102801

To our families present, past, and future

PREFACE

This book grows out of a long and intense collaboration. It is a new effort by lawyers and psychoanalysts to achieve understanding by studying and challenging the experiences, assumptions, and knowledge of their different disciplines. Our collaboration began at Yale with the work of Professor Richard C. Donnelly, who prepared with us early drafts of teaching materials for seminars in Law and Psychiatry. This collaboration extended as well to our students at Yale and Harvard who have contributed to the development and revision of the book's five drafts.

The volume consists of two chapters, each of which has been used in separate seminars. Chapter I, "Psychoanalysis and Law," is designed to present a detailed study of psychoanalytic theory and to explore its relevance, if any, to a wide variety of fundamental legal issues. Here the lawyer is encouraged to view law generally as an ordering process, and to pose questions about its assumptions, procedures, and participants. Chapter II, "Law and Psychiatry," returns the lawyer to his more familiar role as a participant in a particular legal process: the process of invocation, administration, and appraisal of mental health laws.

Chapter I has been designed to be taught by an interdisciplinary team of lawyer and psychoanalyst; Chapter II may be taught solely by someone trained in law. Although Chapter I is not a prerequisite for Chapter II, the order of presentation is prompted by our desire to explore the possible implications of psychoanalytic theory for evaluating the work and assumptions of psychiatry in its encounters with law. Chapter II like Chapter I, has been designed to be taught as a separate seminar or course; it brings together materials from many traditional areas of law as a new area for legal study: problems in the process of mental health administration.* Since this is essentially two books bound in a single volume, we have provided separate general introductions for each chapter rather than a single overall introduction.

The conventions adopted in the organization of this volume follow those initiated in *Criminal Law*:** "The NOTES omit string citations and references to other materials easily located through standard indices. Because they raise important issues, NOTES are printed in the same type as the major problem material. To the extent that this book departs from what might be called [traditional] 'legal' categories, the index provides a means for regrouping the materials in accord with traditional concepts, words, and phrases. In addition, there are three tables of contents: the first provides an over-view of the three major chapters and their parts; the second a detailed analytical breakdown of all the sections, including NOTES;

---

* Because such problems assume particular significance for large concentrations of population and for the poor, Chapter II may be perceived as part of a program of studies in "urban law" or "law and poverty."

** Richard C. Donnelly, Joseph Goldstein, and Richard D. Schwartz, *Criminal Law*. New York: The Free Press (1962).

and the third, which appears at the beginning of each chapter, falls in between these two in degree of comprehensiveness. There are also tables of cases, of authors, and of articles."*

This work has been supported in large measure by a grant from the National Institute of Mental Health to the Yale Law School. In dispensing these and other funds,** Dean Eugene V. Rostow and, more recently, Deans Louis H. Pollak and Ralph Sharpe Brown, of the Yale Law School, and Dean Erwin N. Griswold of the Harvard Law School, have been encouraging partners in this collaboration. We are specially indebted to three wonderful people —David L. Bazelon, Richard C. Donnelly and Anna Freud—who in different ways made significant contributions to this volume. We appreciate greatly, for calling to our attention certain materials and for other assistance, the help of Robert Arnstein, Sidney Blatt, Dale Cameron, Elias Clark, Arthur E. Cohen, Fred Cohen, Nathan Dershowitz, Joseph Freiman, Charles Fried, Lon L. Fuller, Arthur J. Goldberg, Sonja Goldstein, Steven Goodman, Mark De Wolfe Howe, Friedrich Kessler, John Koskinan, Frank Michelman, Paul Nejelski, Lottie Newman, Richard Newman, Neil Peck, Ernst Prelinger, Frederick C. Redlich, Roy Schafer, David Shapiro, Harold Solomon, Alan Stone, Martin Wangh, Robert Weinberg, and Wendy Weinberg.

Though we do not acknowledge them by name, we are grateful to the many other attorneys, doctors, agencies, and court personnel who generously responded to our requests.

We owe much to the staff of the Yale Law Library, particularly to Harry Bitner, Robert E. Brooks, James M. Golden, Isaiah Shein, and Solomon C. Smith and to the staff of the Harvard Law Library, particularly to Robert Doyle, Philip Putnam, and George Strait, all of whom met countless demands with patient and skillful searches.

Among the many students, now lawyers, who played a special role in the preparation of this volume we thank Edmund G. Brown, Jr., Henry Freedman, Clarence Jacobson, Martin Levine, Jack Litman, Harold Nathan, James H. Schink, Stephen Schulhofer, and Robert Winter.

We gratefully acknowledge the generous secretarial help particularly of Helen Minor and also of Joan Cirace, Isabel Malone, Doris Moriarty, and Charlene Rudin in the preparation of many mimeographed versions.

We thank Meira G. Pimsleur for providing us with the Index, Ellen Raskin for her fine drawings, and Emanuel Geltman, W. Carter Hunter, Edward G. McLeroy of The Free Press for their fine editorial work; and finally, we thank Jeremiah Kaplan, George D. McCune, Sidney Solomon, and Valery H. Webb for the sympathetic and skillful direction they gave to the production of this book.

J. K.
J. G.

New Haven, Connecticut   A. M. D.
Cambridge, Massachusetts

* *Ibid.*, at v.
** Grants contributing to this effort were received from the Ford Foundation, the Gralnick Foundation, the Institute of American Freedoms, the Milton Fund of Harvard University, and The Russell Sage Foundation.

Condensed Table of Contents

Analytical Table of Contents

Chapter II
Law and Psychiatry   421
Introduction   422

Part One. PROBLEMS FOR DECISION IN THE CIVIL COMMITMENT PROCESS— THE CASE OF BERTHA RADEK   423

Part Two. TO WHAT EXTENT AND WHY ARE "MENTAL ILLNESS," "DANGEROUSNESS," "NEED FOR TREATMENT," "TREATABILITY" AND "AVAILABILITY OF TREATMENT" RELEVANT TO DECISIONS CONCERNED WITH INSTITUTIONALIZATION AND DEIN-STITUTIONALIZATION? 503

Part Three. TO WHAT EXTENT AND BY WHAT MEANS SHOULD THE STATE SUPERVISE INSTITUTIONS AND STAFF IN THE ADMINISTRATION OF MENTAL HOSPITALS? 633

CHAPTER I

PSYCHOANALYSIS
AND LAW

—Theories of Man

In this Chapter we, as students of law, seek to identify the assumptions reflected in and by law about the nature of man, his motivations, his capacities, and his limitations and to compare them with the assumptions in a single theory of man, psychoanalysis. The materials are designed to present a detailed study of psychoanalytic theory and to explore its relevance, if any, to law. Thus we have interwoven materials from psychoanalysis with problems from many fields of law in order to enable the lawyer to try out another tool in his never-ending jurisprudential task of asking and answering "what are the purposes of law?" and "how may law be promulgated and administered to best serve these purposes?"

"Law," for purposes of this exploration, "may be defined as an essential part of man's reality, a mechanism for moulding and reinforcing controls over himself in relation to others, a process of assigning to some man-made authority, i.e., the STATE, the power to decide why, under what circumstances, to what extent, and by what means man, as a private person, is to be restrained or encouraged in the making and implementing of individual decisions. Law is, in turn, a device for controlling the State—i.e., the individual as official-decisionmaking agent of the State—in the exercise of its power over man. The underlying question always confronting the decisionmakers and those concerned with the study of law is whether, how and to what extent the State should not or should be authorized to intervene in what would otherwise be the private ordering of a man's life. . . .

*　　*　　*

"Law is a continuous and continuing process both for meeting man's need for continuity in the external world through the creation and application of *rule* and *precedent* and at the same time, for meeting man's need for flexibility, growth and development by creating for *precedent* a *counter precedent*, for *rule* a *counter rule* and for *agency of decision* an *agency of review*. Thus, from the community's vantage point, the decisionmaker at every level from the most general to the most specific has and is compelled to make a choice—a choice which hopefully he can exercise with some awareness of the values in issue and of the external and internal pressures at work. . . .

"Since the law is concerned with every aspect of human activity, since its decisions are not rigidly bound by sterile logic, and since the decisionmaker, or in any event, the student of law, must always ask 'What is the purpose of the decision?' and 'What must I learn to make a decision compatible with that purpose?' the work and the findings of many disciplines are not only appropriate but essential sources of data. . . . This is not meant to imply that a lawyer ought indiscriminately to collect data . . . but rather that he first determine what he seeks to do and then pose for himself a series of questions which must be tested by the underlying question: . . . 'In what way would any answer to the question posed be relevant to that which I seek to accomplish?' "*

---

* Goldstein, J.: *Psychoanalysis and Law—A Subject for Study?* Paper read at the Hampstead Child Therapy Clinic, London (1965).

2

The burden of this Chapter is to find a definition, if there be one, of psychoanalysis for law purposes. When we use the term psychoanalysis we mean Freudian psychoanalytic theory. We have decided to make a relatively thorough presentation of one theory of man in order to facilitate an understanding of its methodology, development and conclusions. We have selected Freudian theory for a number of reasons: It is the one with which we are most familiar; it endeavors to construct a systematic theory of human behavior and other theories seem to rest on assumptions derived from it or on challenges to it.*

These materials are not designed to help students of law become professionals in another discipline, but rather to assist them in recognizing the limitations not only of law but of any discipline whose assistance they may seek. They should resist the temptation to engage in what we have come to call "curbstone psychoanalysis," the "diagnosis" of a judge, counsel or party from the limited materials found in a trial transcript or court opinion. Furthermore these materials are not intended to provide an opportunity for teachers to engage students in group "therapy."** To invade the privacy of a student in this way, would be neither educational nor therapeutic. The interpretation of "underlying dynamics" without detailed associations uncovered in a confidential setting suggests a model of the mind and therapy which goes counter to all that psychoanalytic theory intends to convey.

In this effort lawyer and psychoanalyst must be alert to another possible danger. Since psychoanalysis in theory and practice is concerned with individual man and the resolution of his problems in relation to internal and external demands, and since law is primarily concerned with men in groups (and as groups) in terms of societal demands, psychoanalytic generalizations may not apply to law or may be distorted in translation to law. This may not, however, be a real danger for the group is made up of the sum of its parts, i.e., each man as an individual dealing with his reality which is, after all, the subject of both psychoanalysis and law.

Since the legal materials have been selected and ordered to facilitate exploration of their relevance to some particular aspect of psychoanalytic theory, it may be difficult to identify or understand the assumptions about man and law implicit in a given legal document without placing it in an appropriate legal context. In some instances, the legal materials we have selected suggest a context; in other instances, you are asked to provide one on the basis of prior experience. In all instances you should ask "What additional information is required in order to identify and place the issues to be resolved in an appropriate setting?"

Thus it is the purpose of this Chapter to delineate a tentative image of the "law making," "law abiding," and "law breaking" man; and to explore in detail the psychoanalytic theory of man.

---

* We have omitted materials on the clinical theories of psychoanalysis, such as the theory of neurosis and psychosis and the theory of technique.

** *Contra*, Watson, *On the Low Status of the Criminal Bar: Psychological Contributions of the Law School*, 43 Texas L. Rev. 302 (1965).

4

PART ONE

SHOULD LAWYERS SEARCH FOR A PSYCHOLOGICAL IMAGE OF MAN?

In our search for an image of man as reflected in and perceived by law we focus on an single appellate decision construing the United States Constitution and the conscientious objector provisions of the Selective Service Act in relation to a variety of expectations and assumptions about the capacity of individuals to face a threat to life and liberty in fulfilling conflicting obligations to self and to state. In examining this case for this purpose, we pose a series of questions which may be asked about any decision in the process of promulgating, invoking, administering, and appraising law. What is the process and what are its characteristics? Who are participants in the process and what are their characteristics? What images of men do other men have which seem to permit and require them to develop such institutions and symbols as family, government, citizen, constitution, legislature, statute, court, jury, decision, opinion, precedent, justice, religion, freedom, war, army, tax, fault, crime, responsibility, and penalty? What images do men have of judges, attorneys, parties, legislators, and citizens as psychological beings which seem to allow and compel them to assign and carry out their functions?

In examining this case* and the accompanying materials there begins to emerge a picture of man and law that prompts us to ask of psychoanalytic theory: Are there forces in man interacting within him and among men which require the creation of some external authority to administer man in his day-to-day relations with himself and others? Finally we ask why do we, as students of law, study a theory of man, what questions do we pose for it and for what purposes?

---

* In order to preserve every clue to the nature of man reflected in the opinion, this case is reprinted in full.

UNITED STATES v. SEEGER
380 U.S. 163 (1965)

MR. JUSTICE CLARK delivered the opinion of the Court.

These cases involve claims of conscientious objectors under § 6(j) of the Universal Military Training and Service Act, 50 U.S.C.App. § 456(j) (1958 ed.), which exempts from combatant training and service in the armed forces of the United States those persons who by reason of their religious training and belief are conscientiously opposed to participation in war of any form. The cases were consolidated for argument and we consider them together although each involves different facts and circumstances. The parties raise the basic question of the constitutionality of the section which defines the term "religious training and belief," as used in the Act, as "an individual's belief in a relation to a Supreme Being involving duties superior to those arising from any human relation, but [not including] essentially political, sociological, or philosophical views or a merely personal moral code." The constitutional attack is launched under the First Amendment's Establishment and Free Exercise Clauses and is twofold: (1) The section does not exempt nonreligious conscientious objectors; and (2) it discriminates between different forms of religious expression in violation of the Due Process Clause of the Fifth Amendment. Jakobson (No. 51) and Peter (No. 29) also claim that their beliefs come within the meaning of the section. Jakobson claims that he meets the standards of § 6(j) because his opposition to war is based on belief in a Supreme Reality and is therefore an obligation superior to those resulting from man's relationship to his fellow man. Peter contends that his opposition to war derives from his acceptance of the existence of a universal power beyond that of man and that this acceptance in fact constitutes belief in a Supreme Being, qualifying him for exemption. We granted certiorari in each of the cases because of their importance in the administration of the Act.

We have concluded that Congress, in using the expression "Supreme Being" rather than the designation "God," was merely clarifying the meaning of religious training and belief so as to embrace all religions and to exclude essentially political, sociological, or philosophical views. We believe that under this construction, the test of belief "in a relation to a Supreme Being" is whether a given belief that is sincere and meaningful occupies a place in the life of its possessor parallel to that filled by the orthodox belief in God of one who clearly qualifies for the exemption. Where such beliefs have parallel positions in the lives of their respective holders we cannot say that one is "in a relation to a Supreme Being" and the other is not. We have concluded that the beliefs of the objectors in these cases meet these criteria, and, accordingly, we affirm the judgments in Nos. 50 and 51 and reverse the judgment in No. 29.

The Facts in the Cases

No. 50: Seeger was convicted in the District Court for the Southern District of New York of having refused to submit to induction in the armed forces. He was originally classified 1-A in 1953 by his local board, but this classification was changed in 1955 to 2-S (student) and he remained in this status until 1958 when he was reclassified 1-A. He first claimed exemption as a conscientious objector in 1957 after successive annual renewals of his student classification. Although he did not adopt verbatim the printed Selective Service System form, he declared that he was conscientiously opposed to participation in war in any form by reason of his "religious" belief; that he preferred to leave the question as to his belief in a Supreme Being open, "rather than answer 'yes' or 'no' "; that his "skepticism or disbelief in the existence of God" did "not necessarily mean lack of faith in anything whatsoever"; that his was a "belief in and devotion to goodness and virtue for their own sakes, and a religious faith in a purely ethical creed." R. 69-70, 73. He cited such personages as Plato, Aristotle, and Spinoza for support of his ethical belief in intellectual and oral integrity "without belief in God, except in the remotest sense." R. 73. His belief was found to be sincere, honest, and made in good faith; and his conscientious objection to be based upon individual training and belief, both of which included research in religious and cultural fields. Seeger's claim, however, was denied solely because it was not based upon a "belief in a relation to a Supreme Being" as required by § 6(j) of the Act. At trial Seeger's counsel admitted that Seeger's belief was not in relation to a Supreme Being as commonly understood, but contended that he was entitled to the exemption because "under the present law Mr. Seeger's position would also include definitions of religion which have been stated more recently," R. 49, and could be "accommodated" under the definition of religious training and belief in the 1948 Act, R. 53. He was convicted and the Court of Appeals reversed, holding that the Supreme Being requirement of the section distinguished "between internally derived and externally compelled beliefs" and was, therefore, an "impermissible classification" under the Due Process Clause of the Fifth Amendment. 326 F.2d 846.

No. 51: Jakobson was also convicted in the Southern District of New York on a charge of refusing to submit to induction. On his appeal the Court of Appeals reversed on the ground that rejection of his claim may have rested on the factual finding, erroneously made, that he did not believe in a Supreme Being as required by § 6(j). 325 F.2d 409.

Jakobson was originally classified as 1-A in

September, 1953 and enjoyed a student classification until June, 1956. It was not until April, 1958 that he made claim to noncombatant classification (1-A-O) as a conscientious objector. He stated on the Selective Service System form that he believed in a "Supreme Being" who was "Creator of Man" in the sense of being "ultimately responsible for the existence of" man and who was "the Supreme Reality" of which "the existence of man is the *result*." R. 44. (Emphasis in the original.) He explained that his religious and social thinking had developed after much meditation and thought. He had concluded that man must be "partly spiritual" and, therefore, "partly akin to the Supreme Reality"; and that his "most important religious law" was that "no man ought ever to wilfully sacrifice another man's life as a means to any other end * * *." R. 45–46. In December, 1958 he requested a 1-O classification since he felt that participation in any form of military service would involve him in "too many situations and relationships that would be a strain on [his] conscience that [he felt he] must avoid." R. 70. He submitted a long memorandum of "notes on religion" in which he defined religion as the "*sum and essence of one's basic attitudes to the fundamental problems of human existence*," R. 72 (emphasis in the original); he said that he believed in "Godness" which was "the Ultimate Cause for the fact of the Being of the Universe"; that to deny its existence would but deny the existence of the universe because "anything that Is, has an Ultimate Cause for its Being." R. 73. There was a relationship to Godness, he stated, in two directions i.e., "vertically, toward Godness directly," and "horizontally, toward Godness through Mankind and the World." R. 74. He accepted the latter one. The Board classified him 1-A-O and Jakobson appealed. The hearing officer found that the claim was based upon a personal moral code and that he was not sincere in his claim. The Appeal Board classified him 1-A. It did not indicate upon what ground it based its decision, i.e., insincerity or a conclusion that his belief was only a personal moral code. The Court of Appeals reversed, finding that his claim came within the requirements of § 6(j). Because it could not determine whether the Appeal Board had found that Jakobson's beliefs failed to come within the statutory definition, or whether it had concluded that he lacked sincerity, it directed dismissal of the indictment.

No. 29: Forest Britt Peter was convicted in the Northern District of California on a charge of refusing to submit to induction. In his Selective Service System form he stated that he was not a member of a religious sect or organization; he failed to execute section VII of the questionnaire but attached to it a quotation expressing opposition to war, in which he stated that he concurred. In a later form he hedged the question as to his belief in a Supreme Being by saying that it depended on the definition and he appended a statement that he felt it a violation of his moral code to take human life and that he considered this belief superior to his obligation to the state. As to whether his conviction was religious, he quoted with approval Reverend John Haynes Holmes' definition of religion as "the consciousness of some power manifest in nature which helps man in the ordering of his life in harmony with its demands * * * [; it] is the supreme expression of human nature; it is man thinking his highest, feeling his deepest, and living his best." R. 27. The source of his conviction he attributed to reading and meditation "in our democratic American culture, with its values derived from the western religious and philosophical tradition." Ibid. As to his belief in a Supreme Being, Peter stated that he supposed "you could call that a belief in the Supreme Being or God. These just do not happen to be the words I use." R. 11. In 1959 he was classified as 1-A, although there was no evidence in the record that he was not sincere in his beliefs. After his conviction for failure to report for induction the Courts of Appeals, assuming *arguendo* that he was sincere, affirmed, 324 F.2d 173.

Background of § 6(j)

Chief Justice Hughes, in his opinion in *United States* v. *Macintosh*, 283 U.S. 605, (1931), enunciated the rationale behind the long recognition of conscientious objection to participation in war accorded by Congress in our various conscription laws when he declared that "in the forum of conscience, duty to a moral power higher than the state has always been maintained." (Dissenting opinion.) In a similar vein Harlan Fiske Stone, later Chief Justice, drew from the Nation's past when he declared that

> "both morals and sound policy require that the state should not violate the conscience of the individual. All our history gives confirmation to the view that liberty of conscience has a moral and social value which makes it worthy of preservation at the hands of the state. So deep in its significance and vital, indeed, is it to the integrity of man's moral and spiritual nature that nothing short of the self-preservation of the state should warrant its violation; and it may well be questioned whether the state which preserves its life by a settled policy of violation of the conscience of the individual will not in fact ultimately lose it by the process." Stone, The Conscientious Objector, 21 Col.Univ.Q. 253, 269 (1919).

Governmental recognition of the moral dilemma posed for persons of certain religious faiths by the call to arms came early in the history of this country. Various methods of ameliorating their difficulty were adopted by the Colonies, and were later perpetuated in state statutes and constitutions. Thus by the time of the Civil War there existed a state pattern of exempting conscientious objectors on religious grounds. In the Federal Militia Law of 1862 control of conscription was left primarily in the States. However, General Order No. 99, issued pursuant to that Act, provided for striking from the conscription list those who were exempted by the States; it also established a commutation or substitution system fashioned from earlier state enactments. With the Federal Conscription Law of 1863, which enacted the commutation and substitution provisions of General Order No. 99, the Federal Government occupied the field entirely, and in the 1864 Draft Law it extended exemptions to those conscientious objectors who were members of religious denominations opposed to the bearing of arms and who were prohibited from doing so by the articles of faith of their denominations. Selective Service System Monograph No. 11, Conscientious Objection 41 (1950). In that same year the Confederacy exempted certain pacifist sects from military duty. Id., at 46.

The need for conscription did not again arise until World War I. The Draft Act of 1917, 40 Stat. 76, 78, afforded exemptions to conscientious objectors who were affiliated with a "well-recognized religious sect or organization [then] organized and existing and whose existing creed or principles [forbade] its members to participate in war in any form * * *." The Act required that all persons be inducted into the armed service, but allowed the conscientious objectors to perform noncombatant service in capacities designated by the President of the United States. Although the 1917 Act excused religious objectors only, in January, 1918, the Secretary of War instructed that "personal scruples against war" be considered as constituting "conscientious objection." Id., at 54–55. This Act, including its conscientious objector provisions, was upheld against constitutional attack in the Selective Draft Law Cases, [*Arver* v. *United States*] 245 U.S. 366, 389, (1918).

In adopting the 1940 Selective Training and Service Act Congress broadened the exemption afforded in the 1917 Act by making it unnecessary to belong to a pacifist religious sect if the claimant's own opposition to war was based on "religious training and belief." 54 Stat. 889. Those found to be within the exemption were not inducted into the armed services but were assigned to noncombatant service under the supervision of the Selective Service System. The Congress recognized that one might be religious without belonging to an organized church just as surely as minority members of a faith not opposed to war might through religious reading reach a conviction against participation in war. Congress Looks at the Conscientious Objectors 71, 79, 83, 87, 88, 89 (1943). Indeed, the consensus of the witnesses appearing before the congressional committees was that individual belief—rather than membership in a church or sect—determined the duties that God imposed upon a person in his everyday conduct; and that "there is a higher

loyalty than loyalty to this country, loyalty to God." Id., at 29–31. See also the proposals which were made to the Committee but rejected. Id., at 21–23, 82–83, 85. Thus, while shifting the test from membership in such a church to one's individual belief the Congress nevertheless continued its historic practice of excusing from armed service those who believed that they owed an obligation, superior to that due the state, of not participating in war in any form.

Between 1940 and 1948 two courts of appeals[1] held that the phrase "religious training and belief" did not include philosophical, social, or political policy. Then in 1948 the Congress amended the language of the statute and declared that "religious training and belief" was to be defined as "an individual's belief in a relation to a Supreme Being involving duties superior to those arising from any human relation, but [not including] essentially political, sociological, or philosophical views or a merely personal moral code." The only significant mention of this change in the provision appears in the report of the Senate Committee recommending adoption. It said simply this: "This section reenacts substantially the same provisions as were found in subsection 5(g) of the 1940 act. Exemption extends to anyone who, because of religious training and belief in his relation to a Supreme Being, is conscientiously opposed to combatant military service or to both combatant and noncombatant military service. (See *United States* v. *Berman*, 156 F.2d 377, *certiorari* denied, 329 U.S. 795.)" S.Rep.No. 1268, 80th Cong.,2d Sess., 14 U.S.Code Cong. Service 1948, p. 2002.

Interpretation of § 6(*j*)

1. The crux of the problem lies in the phrase "religious training and belief" which Congress has defined as "belief in a relation to a Supreme Being involving duties superior to those arising from any human relation." In assigning meaning to this statutory language we may narrow the inquiry by noting briefly those scruples expressly excepted from the definition. The section excludes those persons who, disavowing religious belief, decide on the basis of essentially political, sociological, or economic considerations that war is wrong and that they will have no part of it. These judgments have historically been reserved for the Government, and in matters which can be said to fall within these areas the conviction of the individual has never been permitted to override that of the state. *United States* v. *Macintosh*, *supra* (dissenting opinion). The statute further excludes those whose opposition to war stems from a "merely personal moral code," a phrase to which we shall have

---

1. See *United States* v. *Kauten*, 133 F.2d 703 (C.A.2d Cir. 1943); *Berman* v. *United States*, 156 F.2d 377 (C.A.9th Cir. 1946).

occasion to turn later in discussing the application of § 6(j) to these cases. We also pause to take note of what is not involved in this litigation. No party claims to be an atheist or attacks the statute on this ground. The question is not, therefore, one between theistic and atheistic beliefs. We do not deal with or intimate any decision on that situation in this case. Nor do the parties claim the monotheistic belief that there is but one God; what they claim (with the possible exception of Seeger who bases his position here not on factual but on purely constitutional grounds) is that they adhere to theism, as opposed to atheism, which is "the belief in the existence of a god or gods; belief in superhuman powers or spiritual agencies in one or many gods."[2] Our question, therefore, is the narrow one: Does the term "Supreme Being" as used in § 6(j) mean the orthodox God or the broader concept of a power or being, or a faith, "to which all else is subordinate or upon which all else is ultimately dependent"? *Webster's New International Dictionary* [Second Edition]. In considering this question we resolve it solely in relation to the language of § 6(j) and not otherwise.

2. Few would quarrel, we think, with the proposition that in no field of human endeavor has the tool of language proved so inadequate in the communication of ideas as it has in dealing with the fundamental questions of man's predicament in life, in death, or in final judgment and retribution. This fact makes the task of discerning the intent of Congress in using the phrase "Supreme Being" a complex one. Nor is it made the easier by the richness and variety of spiritual life in our country. Over 250 sects inhabit our land. Some believe in a purely personal God, some in a supernatural deity; others think of religion as a way of life envisioning as its ultimate goal the day when all men can live together in perfect understanding and peace. There are those who think of God as the depth of our being; others, such as the Buddhists, strive for a state of lasting rest through self-denial and inner purification; in Hindu philosophy, the Supreme Being is the transcendental reality which is truth, knowledge, and bliss. Even those religious groups who have traditionally opposed war in every form have splintered into various denominations: From 1940 to 1947 there were four denominations using the name "Friends," Selective Service System Monograph No. 11, Conscientious Objection 13 (1950); the "Church of the Brethren" was the official name of the oldest and largest church body of four composed of those commonly called Brethren, id., at 11; and the "Mennonite Church" was the largest of seventeen denominations, including the Amish and Hutterites, grouped as "Mennonite bodies" in the 1936 report on the Census of Religious Bodies, id., at 9. This vast panoply of beliefs reveals the magnitude of the problem which

faced the Congress when it set about providing an exemption from armed service. It also emphasizes the care that Congress realized was necessary in the fashioning of an exemption which would be in keeping with its long-established policy of not picking and choosing among religious beliefs.

In spite of the elusive nature of the inquiry, we are not without certain guide lines. In amending the 1940 Act, Congress adopted almost intact the language of Chief Justice Hughes in *United States* v. *Macintosh, supra:*

> "The essence of religion is belief in a relation to *God* involving duties superior to those arising from any human relation." At 633–634 of 283 U.S., (Emphasis supplied).

By comparing the statutory definition with those words, however, it becomes readily apparent that the Congress deliberately broadened them by substituting the phrase "Supreme Being" for the appellation "God." And in so doing it is also significant that Congress did not elaborate on the form or nature of this higher authority which it chose to designate as "Supreme Being." By so refraining it must have had in mind the admonitions of the Chief Justice when he said in the same opinion that even the word "God" had myriad meanings for men of faith:

> "[P]utting aside dogmas with their particular conceptions of deity, freedom of conscience itself implies respect for an innate conviction of paramount duty. The battle for religious liberty has been fought and won with respect to religious beliefs and practices, which are not in conflict with good order, upon the very ground of the supremacy of conscience within its proper field." At 634.

Moreover, the Senate Report on the bill specifically states that § 6(j) was intended to re-enact "substantially the same provisions as were found" in the 1940 Act. That statute, of course, refers to "religious training and belief" without more. Admittedly, all of the parties here purport to base their objection on religious belief. It appears, therefore, that we need only look to this clear statement of congressional intent as set out in the report. Under the 1940 Act it was necessary only to have a conviction based upon religious training and belief; we believe that is all that is required here. Within that phrase would come all sincere religious beliefs which are based upon a power or being, or upon a faith, to which all else is subordinate or upon which all else is ultimately dependent. The test might be stated in these words: A sincere and meaningful belief which occupies in the life of its possessor a place parallel to that filled by the God of those admittedly qualifying for the exemption comes within the statutory definition. This construction avoids imputing to Congress an intent to classify different religious beliefs, exempting some and excluding others, and is in accord with the well-estab-

---

2. See *Webster's New International Dictionary* (Second Edition 1951); *Webster's New Collegiate Dictionary* (1949).

lished congresssional policy of equal treatment for those whose opposition to service is grounded in their religious tenets.

3. The Government takes the position that since *Berman* v. *United States, supra,* was cited in the Senate Report on the 1948 Act, Congress must have desired to adopt the Berman interpretation of what constitutes "religious belief." Such a claim, however, will not bear scrutiny. First, we think it clear that an explicit statement of congressional intent deserves more weight than the parenthetical citation of a case which might stand for a number of things. Congress specifically stated that it intended to re-enact substantially the same provisions as were found in the 1940 Act. Moreover, the history of that Act reveals no evidence of a desire to restrict the concept of religious belief. On the contrary the Chairman of the House Military Affairs Committee which reported out the 1940 exemption provisions stated:

> "We heard the conscientious objectors, and all of their representatives that we could possibly hear, and summing it all up, their whole objection to the bill, aside from their objection to compulsory military training, was based upon the right of conscientious objection and in most instances to the right of ministerial students to continue in their studies, and we have provided ample protection for those classes and those groups." 86 Cong.Rec. 11368 (1940).

During the House debate on the bill, Mr. Faddis of Pennsylvania made the following statement:

> "We have made provision to take care of conscientious objectors. I am sure the committee has had all the sympathy in the world with those who appeared claiming to have religious scruples against rendering military service in its various degrees. Some appeared who had conscientious scruples against handling lethal weapons, but who had no scruples against performing other duties which did not actually bring them into combat. Others appeared who claimed to have conscientious scruples against participating in any of the activities that would go along with the Army. The committee took all of these into consideration and has written a bill which, I believe, will take care of all the reasonable objections of this class of people." 86 Cong. Rec. 11418 (1940).

Thus the history of the Act belies the notion that it was to be restrictive in application and available only to those believing in a traditional God.

As for the citation to Berman, it might mean a number of things. But we think that Congress' action in citing it must be construed in such a way as to make it consistent with its express statement that it meant substantially to re-enact the 1940 provision. As far as we can find, there is not one word to indicate congressional concern over any conflict between Kauten and Berman. Surely, if it thought that two clashing

interpretations as to what amounted to "religious belief" had to be resolved, it would have said so somewhere in its deliberations. Thus, we think that rather than citing Berman for what it said "religious belief" was, Congress cited it for what it said "religious belief" was not. For both Kauten and Berman hold in common the conclusion that exemption must be denied to those whose beliefs are political, social, or philosophical in nature, rather than religious. Both, in fact, denied exemption on that very ground. It seems more likely, therefore, that it was this point which led Congress to cite Berman. The first part of the § 6(j) definition—belief in a relation to a Supreme Being—was indeed set out in Berman, with the exception that the court used the word "God" rather than "Supreme Being." However, as the Government recognizes, Berman took that language word-for-word from Macintosh. Far from requiring a conclusion contrary to the one we reach here, Chief Justice Hughes' opinion, as we have pointed out, supports our interpretation.

Admittedly, the second half of the statutory definition—the rejection of sociological and moral views—was taken directly from Berman. But, as we have noted, this same view was adhered to in *United States* v. *Kauten, supra.* Indeed the Selective Service System has stated its view of the cases' significance in these terms: "The *United States* v. *Kauten* and *Herman Berman* v. *United States* cases ruled that a valid conscientious objector claim to exemption must be based solely on 'religious training and belief' and not on philosophical, political, social, or other grounds * * *." Selective Service System Monograph No. 11, Conscientious Objection, 337 (1950). See *id.,* at 278. That the conclusions of the Selective Service System are not to be taken lightly is evidenced in this statement by Senator Gurney, Chairman of the Senate Armed Services Committee and sponsor of the Senate bill containing the present version of § 6(j):

> "The bill which is now pending follows the 1940 Act, with very few technical amendments, worked out by those in Selective Service who had charge of the conscientious-objector problem during the war." 94 Cong.Rec. 7305 (1948).

Thus we conclude that in enacting § 6(j) Congress simply made explicit what the courts of appeals had correctly found implicit in the 1940 Act. Moreover, it is perfectly reasonable that Congress should have selected Berman for its citation, since this Court denied certiorari in that case, a circumstance not present in Kauten.

Section 6(j), then, is no more than a clarification of the 1940 provision involving only certain "technical amendments," to use the words of Senator Gurney. As such it continues the congressional policy of providing exemption from military service for those whose opposition is based on grounds that can fairly be said to be "religious."[3] To hold otherwise would not only fly in the face of Congress' entire action in the past; it would ignore the historic position of our country on this issue since its founding.

4. Moreover, we believe this construction embraces the ever-broadening understanding of the modern religious community. The eminent Protestant theologian, Dr. Paul Tillich, whose views the Government concedes would come within the statute, identifies God not as a projection "out there" or beyond the skies but as the ground of our very being. The Court of Appeals stated in No. 51 that Jakobson's views "parallel [those of] this eminent theologian rather strikingly." In his book, *Systematic Theology*, Dr. Tillich says:

"'I have written of the God above the God of theism. * * * In such a state [of self-affirmation] the God of both religious and theological language disappears. But something remains, namely, the seriousness of that doubt in which meaning within meaninglessness is affirmed. The source of this affirmation of meaning within meaninglessness, of certitude within doubt, is not the God of traditional theism but the "God above God," the power of being, which works through those who have no name for it, not even the name of God.' 2 *Systematic Theology* 12 (1957)."

Another eminent cleric, the Bishop of Woolwich, John A. T. Robinson, in his book, *Honest to God* (1963), states:

"The Bible speaks of a God 'up there.' No doubt its picture of a three decker universe, of 'the heaven above, the earth beneath, and the waters under the earth,' was once taken quite literally * * * [at p. 11] [Later] in place of a God who is literally or physically 'up there' we have accepted, as part of our mental furniture, a God who is spiritually or metaphysically 'out there.' But now it seems there is no room for him, not merely in the inn, but in the entire universe: For there are no vacant places left. In reality, of course, our new view of the universe has made not the slightest difference * * *. [At 13–14].

"But the idea of a God spiritually or metaphysically 'out there' dies very much harder. Indeed most people would be seriously disturbed by the thought that it should need to die at all. For it *is* their God and they have nothing to put in its place.

---

3. A definition of "religious training and belief" identical to that in § 6(j) is found in § 337 of the Immigration and Nationality Act, 66 Stat. 258, 8 U.S.C. § 1448(a). (1958 ed.). It is noteworthy that in connection with this Act, the Senate Special Subcommittee to Investigate Immigration and Naturalization stated: "The subcommittee realizes and respects the fact that the question of whether or not a person must bear arms in defense of his country may be one which invades the province of religion and personal conscience." Thus, it recommended that an alien not be required to vow to bear arms when he asserted "his opposition to participation in war in any form because of his personal religious training and belief." S.Rep. No. 1515, 81st Cong., 2d Sess., 746.

* * * Everyone of us lives with some mental picture of a God 'out there,' a God who exists above and beyond the world he made, a God 'to' whom we pray and to whom we 'go' when we die [at p. 14]. But the signs are that we are reaching the point at which the whole conception of God 'out there,' which has served us so well since the collapse of the three decker universe is becoming more a hindrance than a help." At 15–16.

The Schema of the recent Ecumenical Council included a most significant declaration on religion.

"The community of all peoples is one. One is their origin, for God made the entire human race to live on all the face of the earth. One, too, is their ultimate end, God. Men expect from the various religions answers to the riddles of the human condition: What is man? What is the meaning and purpose of our lives? What is the moral good and what is sin? What are death, judgment, and retribution after death?

* * *

"Ever since primordial days, numerous peoples have had a certain perception of that hidden power which hovers over the course of things and over the events that make up the lives of men; some have even come to know of a Supreme Being and Father. Religions in an advanced culture have been able to use more refined concepts and a more developed language in their struggle for an answer to man's religious questions.

* * *

"Nothing that is true and holy in these religions is scorned by the Catholic Church. Ceaselessly the Church proclaims Christ, 'the Way, the Truth, and the Life,' in whom God reconciled all things to Himself. The Church regards with sincere reverence those ways of action and of life, precepts and teachings which, although they differ from the ones she sets forth, reflect nonetheless a ray of that Truth which enlightens all men."

Dr. David Saville Muzzey, a leader in the Ethical Culture Movement, states in his book, *Ethics As a Religion* (1951), that "[e]verybody except the avowed atheists (and they are comparatively few) believes in some kind of God," and that "The proper question to ask, therefore, is not the futile one, Do you believe in God? but rather, What *kind* of a God do you believe in?" Dr. Muzzey attempts to answer that question:

"Instead of positing a personal God, whose existence man can neither prove nor disprove, the ethical concept is founded on human experience. It is anthropocentric, not theocentric. Religion, for all the various definitions that have been given of it, must surely mean the devotion of man to the highest ideal that he can conceive. And that ideal is a community of spirits in which the latent moral potentialities of men shall have been elicited by their reciprocal endeavors to cultivate the best in their fellow men. What ultimate reality is we do not know; but we have the faith that expresses itself in the human world as the power which inspires in man moral purposes. [At 95].

*   *   *

"Thus the 'God' that we love is not the figure on the great white throne, but the perfect pattern, envisioned by faith, of humanity as it should be, purged of the evil elements which retard its progress toward 'the knowledge, love, and practice of the right.' " [At 98].

These are but a few of the views that comprise the broad spectrum of religious beliefs found among us. But they demonstrate very clearly the diverse manners in which beliefs, equally paramount in the lives of their possessors, may be articulated. They further reveal the difficulties inherent in placing too narrow a construction on the provisions of § 6(j) and thereby lend conclusive support to the construction which we today find that Congress intended.

5. We recognize the difficulties that have always faced the trier of fact in these cases. We hope that the test that we lay down proves less onerous. The examiner is furnished a standard that permits consideration of criteria with which he has had considerable experience. While the applicant's words may differ, the test is simple of application. It is essentially an objective one, namely, does the claimed belief occupy the same place in the life of the objector as an orthodox belief in God holds in the life of one clearly qualified for exemption?

Moreover, it must be remembered that in resolving these exemption problems one deals with the beliefs of different individuals who will articulate them in a multitude of ways. In such an intensely personal area, of course, the claim of the registrant that his belief is an essential part of a religious faith must be given great weight. Recognition of this was implicit in this language, cited by the Berman court from State v. Amana Society, 109 N.W.894 (1906):

" 'Surely a scheme of life designed to obviate [man's inhumanity to man], and by removing temptations, and all the inducements of ambition and avarice, to nurture the virtues of unselfishness, patience, love, and service, ought not to be denounced as not pertaining to religion *when its devotee regards it as an essential tenet of their* [sic] *religious faith.*' " At 381, 156 F.2d. (Emphasis by the Court of Appeals.)

The validity of what he believes cannot be questioned. Some theologians, and indeed some examiners, might be tempted to question the existence of the registrant's "Supreme Being" or the truth of his concepts. But these are inquiries foreclosed to Government. As Mr. Justice Douglas stated in United States v. Ballard, 322 U.S. 78, 86 (1944): "Men may believe what they cannot prove. They may not be put to the proof of their religious doctrines or beliefs. Religious experiences which are real as life to some may be incomprehensible to others." Local boards and courts in this sense are not free to reject beliefs because they consider them "incomprehensible." Their task is to decide whether the beliefs professed by a registrant are sincerely held and whether they are, in his own scheme of things, religious.

But we hasten to emphasize that while the "truth" of a belief is not open to question, there remains the significant question whether it is "truly held." This is the threshold question of sincerity which must be resolved in every case. It is, of course, a question of fact —a prime consideration to the validity of every claim for exemption as a conscientious objector. The Act provides a comprehensive scheme for assisting the Appeals Board in making this determination, placing at their service the Federal Bureau of Investigation, hearing examiners, and other facilities of the Department of Justice. Finally, we would point out that in Estep v. United States, 327 U.S. 114, (1946), this Court held that:

"The provision making the decisions of the local boards 'final' means to us that Congress chose not to give administrative action under this Act the customary scope of judicial review which obtains under other statutes. It means that the courts are not to weigh the evidence to determine whether the classification made by the local boards was justified. The decisions of the local boards made in conformity with the regulations are final even though they may be erroneous. The question of jurisdiction of the local board is reached only if there is no basis in fact for the classification which it gave the registrant." At 122–123.

Application of § 6(j) to the Instant Case

As we noted earlier, the statutory definition excepts those registrants whose beliefs are based on a "merely personal moral code." The records in these cases, however, show that at no time did any one of the applicants suggest that his objection was based on a "merely personal moral code." Indeed at the outset each of them claimed in his application that his objection was based on a religious belief. We have construed the statutory definition broadly and it follows that any exception to it must be interpreted narrowly. The use by Congress of the words "merely personal" seems to us to restrict the exception to a moral code which is not only personal but which is the sole basis for the registrant's belief and is in no way related to a Supreme Being. It follows, therefore, that if the claimed religious beliefs of the respective registrants in these cases meet the test that we lay down then their objections cannot be based on a "merely personal" moral code.

In Seeger, No. 50, the Court of Appeals failed to find sufficient "externally compelled beliefs." However, it did find that "it would seem impossible to say with assurance that [Seeger] is not bowing to 'external commands' in virtually the same sense as is the objector who defers to the will of a supernatural power." It found little distinction between Jakobson's devotion to a mystical force of "Godness" and Seeger's compulsion to "goodness." Of course, as we have said, the statute does not distinguish between externally and internally derived beliefs. Such a determination would, as the Court of Appeals observed, prove impossible as a practical matter, and we have found that Congress intended no such distinction.

The Court of Appeals also found that there was no question of the applicant's sincerity. He was a product of a devout Roman Catholic home; he was a close student of Quaker beliefs from which he said "much of [his] thought is derived"; he approved of their opposition to war in any form; he devoted his spare hours to the American Friends Service Committee and was assigned to hospital duty.

In summary, Seeger professed "religious belief" and "religious faith." He did not disavow any belief "in a relation to a Supreme Being"; indeed he stated that "the cosmic order does, perhaps, suggest a creative intelligence." He decried the tremendous "spiritual" price man must pay for his willingness to destroy human life. In light of his beliefs and the unquestioned sincerity with which he held them, we think the Board, had it applied the test we propose today, would have granted him the exemption. We think it clear that the beliefs which prompted his objection occupy the same place in his life as the belief in a traditional deity holds in the lives of his friends, the Quakers. We are reminded once more of Dr. Tillich's thoughts:

> "And if that word [God] has not much meaning for you, translate it, and speak of your life, of the source of your being, of your ultimate concern, *of what you take seriously without any reservation.* Perhaps, in order to do so, you must forget everything traditional that you have learned about God. * * *" Tillich, *The Shaking of the Foundations*, 56–57 (1948). (Emphasis supplied.)

It may be that Seeger did not clearly demonstrate what his beliefs were with regard to the usual understanding of the term "Supreme Being." But as we have said Congress did not intend that to be the test. We therefore affirm the judgment in No. 50.

In Jakobson, No. 51, the Court of Appeals found that the registrant demonstrated that his belief as to opposition to war was related to a Supreme Being. We agree and affirm that judgment.

We reach a like conclusion in No. 29. It will be re-

membered that Peter acknowledged "some power manifest in nature * * * the supreme expression" that helps man in ordering his life. As to whether he would call that belief in a Supreme Being, he replied, "You could call that a belief in the Supreme Being or God. Those just do not happen to be words I use." We think that under the test we establish here the Board would grant the exemption to Peter and we therefore reverse the judgment in No. 29. It is so ordered.

Judgments in Nos. 50 and 51 affirmed; judgment in No. 29 reversed.

MR. JUSTICE DOUGLAS, concurring.

If I read the statute differently from the Court, I would have difficulties. For then those who embraced one religious faith rather than another would be subject to penalties; and that kind of discrimination, as we held in *Sherbert* v. *Verner*, 374 U.S. 398, would violate the Free Exercise Clause of the First Amendment. It would also result in a denial of equal protection by preferring some religions over others—an invidious discrimination that would run afoul of the Due Process Clause of the Fifth Amendment. See *Bolling* v. *Sharpe*, 347 U.S. 497.

The legislative history of this Act leaves much in the dark. But it is, in my opinion, not a *tour de force* if we construe the words "Supreme Being" to include the cosmos, as well as an anthropomorphic entity. If it is a *tour de force* so to hold, it is no more so than other instances where we have gone to extremes to construe an Act of Congress to save it from demise on constitutional grounds. In a more extreme case than the present one we said that the words of a statute may be strained "in the candid service of avoiding a serious constitutional doubt." *United States* v. *Rumely*, 345 U.S. 41, 47[4].

The words "a Supreme Being" have no narrow technical meaning in the field of religion. Long before the birth of our Judeo–Christian civilization the idea of God had taken hold in many forms. Mention of only two—Hinduism and Buddhism—illustrates the fluidity and evanescent scope of the concept. In the Hindu *religion* the Supreme Being is conceived in the forms of several cult Deities. The chief of these, which stand for the Hindu Triad, are Brahma, Vishnu, and Siva. Another Deity, and the one most widely worshipped, is Sakti, the Mother Goddess, conceived as power, both destructive and creative. Though Hindu religion encompasses the worship of many Deities, it believes in only one single God, the eternally existent One Being with his manifold attributes and manifestations. This idea is expressed in Rigveda, the earliest sacred text of the Hindus, in verse 46 of a hymn

---

4. And see *Crowell* v. *Benson*, 285 U.S. 22, 62; *Ullman* v. *United States*, 350 U.S. 422, 433; *Ashwander* v. *TVA*, 297 U.S. 288, 341, 348 (concurring opinion).

attributed to the mythical seer Dirghatamas (Rigveda, I, 164):

> "They call it Indra, Mitra, Varuna and Agni
> And also heavenly beautiful Garutman:
> The Real is One, though sages name it variously—
> They call it Agni, Yama, Matarisvan."

See Smart, *Reasons and Faiths* (1958), p. 35, n. 1; 32 Harvard Oriental Series (Lanman ed. 1925), pp. 434–435.

Indian *philosophy*, which comprises several schools of thought, has advanced different theories of the nature of the Supreme Being. According to the Upanisads, Hindu sacred texts, the Supreme Being is described as the power which creates and sustains everything, and to which the created things return upon dissolution. The word which is commonly used in the Upanisads to indicate the Supreme Being is "Brahman." Philosophically, the Supreme Being is the transcendental Reality which is Truth, Knowledge, and Bliss. It is the source of the entire universe. In this aspect Brahman is Isvara, a personal Lord and Creator of the universe, an object of worship. But, in the view of one school of thought, that of Sankara, even this is an imperfect and limited conception of Brahman which must be transcended: to think of Brahman as the Creator of the material word is necessarily to form a concept infected with illusion, or *maya*—which is what the world really is, in highest truth. Ultimately, mystically, Brahman must be understood as without attributes, as *neti neti* (not this, not that). See Smart, *op. cit, supra*, p. 133.

Buddhism—whose advent marked the reform of Hinduism—continued somewhat the same concept. As stated by Nancy Wilson Ross, "God—if I may borrow that word for a moment—the universe, and man are one indissoluble existence, one total whole. Only THIS—capital THIS—is. Anything and everything that appears to us as an individual entity or phenomenon, whether it be a planet or an atom, a mouse or a man, is but a temporary manifestation of THIS in form; every activity that takes place, whether it be birth or death, loving or eating breakfast, is but a temporary manifestation of THIS in activity. When we look at things this way, naturally we cannot believe that each individual person has been endowed with a special and individual soul or self. Each one of us is but a cell, as it were, in the body of the Great Self, a cell that comes into being, performs its functions, and passes away, transformed into another manifestation. Though we have temporary individuality, that temporary, limited individuality is not either a true self or our true self. Our true self is the Great Self; our true body is the Body of Reality, or the Dharmakaya, to give it its technical Buddhist name." *The World of Zen* (1960), p. 18.

Does a Buddhist believe in "God" or a "Supreme Being"? That, of course, depends on how one defines "God," as one eminent student of Buddhism has explained:

> "It has often been suggested that Buddhism is an atheistic system of thought, and this assumption has given rise to quite a number of discussions. Some have claimed that since Buddhism knew no God, it could not be a religion; others that since Buddhism obviously was a religion which knew no God, the belief in God was not essential to religion. These discussions assume that *God* is an unambiguous term, which is by no means the case." Conze, *Buddhism* (1959), pp. 38–39.

Dr. Conze then says that if "God" is taken to mean a personal creator of the universe, then the Buddhist has no interest in the concept. *Id.*, p. 39. But if "God" means something like the state of oneness with God as described by some Christian mystics, then the Buddhist surely believes in "God," since this state is almost indistinguishable from the Buddhist concept of Nirvana, "the Supreme Reality, * * * the eternal, hidden, and incomprehensible Peace." *Id.*, pp. 39–40. And finally, if "God" means one of the many deities in an at least superficially polytheistic religion like Hinduism, then Buddhism tolerates a belief in many Gods: "The Buddhists believe that a faith can be kept alive only if it can be adapted to the mental habits of the average person. In consequence, we find that, in the earlier Scriptures, the deities of Brahmanism are taken for granted and that, later on, the Buddhists adopted the local Gods of any district to which they came." *Id.*, p. 42.

When the present Act was adopted in 1948 we were a nation of Buddhists, Confucianists, and Taoists, as well as Christians. Hawaii, then a territory, was indeed filled with Buddhists, Buddhism being "probably the major faith, if Protestantism and Roman Catholicism are deemed different faiths." Stokes and Pfeffer, *Church and State in the U.S.* (1964), p. 560. Organized Buddhism first came to Hawaii in 1887 when Japanese laborers were brought to work on the plantations. There are now numerous Buddhist sects in Hawaii, and the temple of the Shin sect in Honolulu is said to have the largest congregation of any religious organization in the city. See Mulholland, *Religion in Hawaii* (1961), pp. 44–50.

In the continental United States Buddhism is found "in real strength" in Utah, Arizona, Washington, Oregon, and California. "Most of the Buddhists in the United States are Japanese or Japanese–Americans; however, there are 'English' departments in San Francisco, Los Angeles, and Tacoma." Mead, *Handbook of Denominations* (1961), p. 61. The Buddhist Churches of North America, organized in 1914 as the Buddhist Mission of North America and incorporated under the present name in 1942, represent the Jodo Shinshu Sect of Buddhism in this country. This sect is the only Buddhist group reporting information to the annual *Yearbook of American Churches*. In

1961, the latest year for which figures are available, this group alone had fifty-five churches and an inclusive membership of 60,000; it maintained eighty-nine church schools with a total enrollment of 11,150. *Yearbook of American Churches*, 1965, p. 30. According to one source, the total number of Buddhists of all sects in North America is 171,000. See *World Almanac* (1965), p. 636.

When the Congress spoke in the vague general terms of a Supreme Being I cannot, therefore, assume that it was so parochial as to use the words in the narrow sense urged on us. I would attribute tolerance and sophistication to the Congress, commensurate with the religious complexion of our communities. In sum, I agree with the Court that any person opposed to war on the basis of a sincere belief, which in his life fills the same place as a belief in God fills in the life of an orthodox religionist, is entitled to exemption under the statute. None comes to us an avowedly irreligious person or as an atheist;[5] one, as a sincere believer in "goodness and virtue for their own sakes." His questions and doubts on theological issues, and his wonder, are no more alien to the statutory standard than are the awe-inspired questions of a devout Buddhist.

NOTES

NOTE 1

OLIVECRONA, KARL

Law as Fact*

The rules of law are . . . imperative statements about imaginary actions, rights, duties, etc. [T]hey cannot be defined as anybody's commands. Those who have drafted them or acted as formal lawgivers have not at all acted in such a way as a person who commands. And to those who take cognizance of the rules, the lawgivers are for the most part entirely unknown. They have only the imperative statements as such before them, isolated from the lawgivers, who may have died 100 years ago. Thus the statements function, independent of any person commanding, as guides for people's conduct. For different reasons the patterns of conduct contained in the rules are taken as models for action in real life. The imperatively expressed ideas function as a cause of people's acting in certain ways.

*   *   *

[A]n independent imperative may sometimes be replaced by a sentence which expresses a judgment. In the Decalogue we have, e.g., the imperative statement: "Thou shalt not steal. . . ." Formally, these sentences

give expression to judgments. And we believe that real judgments lie behind them. Seemingly, therefore, we are able to instruct each other about what we shall do, i.e., about our duties. We believe that we have a knowledge of this and that we can impart this knowledge to others, just if it were a question of facts in the surrounding world.

Here a fateful illusion is concealed. We do not impart knowledge by such utterances, we create suggestion in order to influence the mentality and the actions of other people. There is no real judgment behind the sentences. The objective nature of an action is not determined by saying that it should, or should not, be undertaken. What lies behind the sentences is something other than a judgment. It is that, in our mind, an imperative expression is coupled to the idea of an action. This is a *psychological* connection only, though of the utmost importance in social life. But for certain reasons the connection appears to us as existing objectively. Thus we get an illusion of a reality outside the natural world, a reality expressed by this "shall." That is the basis of the idea of the binding force of the law.

*   *   *

In reality, the law of a country consists of an immense mass of ideas concerning human behavior, accumulated during centuries through the contributions of innumerable collaborators. These ideas have been expressed in the imperative form by their originators, especially through formal legislation, and are being preserved in the same form in books of law. The ideas are again and again revived in human minds, accompanied by the imperative expression: "This line of conduct *shall* be taken" or something else to the same effect.

NOTE 2

FULLER, LON L.

The Morality of Law*

I come now to the most important respect in which an observance of the demands of legal morality can serve the broader aims of human life generally. This lies in the view of man implicit in the internal morality of law. [L]egal morality can be said to be neutral over a wide range of ethical issues. It cannot be neutral in its view of man himself. To embark on the enterprise of subjecting human conduct to the governance of rules involves of necessity a commitment to the view that man is, or can become, a responsible agent, capable of understanding and following rules, and answerable for his defaults.

Every departure from the principles of the law's inner morality is an affront to man's dignity as a

5. If he was an atheist, quite different problems would be presented. Cf. *Torcaso* v. *Watkins*, 367 U.S. 488.

* London: Oxford University Press, 1939, (pp. 43–48). Reprinted by permission of Einal Munksgaard, Copenhegan.

* New Haven: Yale University Press, 1964, (pp. 162–65). Reprinted by permission.

responsible agent. To judge his actions by unpublished or retrospective laws, or to order him to do an act that is impossible, is to convey to him your indifference to his powers of self-determination. Conversely, when the view is accepted that man is incapable of responsible action, legal morality loses its reason for being. To judge his actions by unpublished or retrospective laws is no longer an affront, for there is nothing left to affront—indeed, even the verb "to judge" becomes itself incongruous in this context; we no longer judge a man, we act upon him.

Today a whole complex of attitudes, practices, and theories seems to drive us toward a view which denies that man is, or can meaningfully strive to become, a responsible, self-determining center of action. The causes of this development are of the most varied sort; in their motivation they seem to run the gamut from the basest to the most noble.

One stream of influence comes from science, and more particularly from certain doctrinaire schools of thought in the social sciences. Let me allow the eminent psychologist B. F. Skinner at this point to speak for himself:

> If we are to use the methods of science in the field of human affairs, we must assume that behavior is lawful and determined. We must expect to discover that what a man does is the result of specifiable conditions and that once these conditions have been discovered, we can anticipate and to some extent determine his actions. This possibility is offensive to many people. It is opposed to a tradition of long standing which regards man as a free agent . . . no one who is a product of western civilization can [accept the scientific view of human behavior] without a struggle.
>
> The conception of a free, responsible individual is embedded in our language and pervades our practices, codes, and beliefs. Given an example of human behavior, most people can describe it immediately in terms of such a conception. The practice is so natural that it is seldom examined. A scientific formulation, on the other hand, is new and strange.
>
> We do not hold people responsible for their reflexes—for example, for coughing in church. We hold them responsible for their operant behavior—for example, for whispering in church or remaining in church while coughing. But there are variables which are responsible for whispering as well as coughing, and these may be just as inexorable. When we recognize this, we are likely to drop the notion of responsibility altogether and with it the doctrine of free will as an inner causal agent. This may make a great difference in our practices. The doctrine of personal responsibility is associated with certain techniques of controlling behavior—techniques which generate "a sense of responsibility" or point out "an obligation to society." These techniques are relatively ill-adapted to their purpose.[1]

That views like those just quoted represent an overreaching of "science" and are based on a most naive epistemology, does not seem seriously to detract from their appeal. Though no one, including Professor Skinner, really believes them to the extent of adopting them as a consistent basis for action, we recognize that they express a partial truth. By overstating that truth and leaving undefined its proper limits, they encourage an attitude of indifference toward the decay of the concept of responsibility implicit in many developments in the law, most of which certainly do not serve the ends for which Professor Skinner has striven so hard.

For in justice to Professor Skinner it should be noted that he does not simply doubt the validity of the concept of responsibility; he proceeds to construct an alternative mode of social control. Stated in very simple terms he proposes that instead of telling men to be good, we condition them to be good. Whatever the merits or faults of this program, it has no affinity with that of the overworked prosecutor who seeks to simplify his job through laws that will make criminal responsibility independent of any proof of fault or intent.

NOTE 3

HART, HENRY M. JR.

The Aims of the Criminal Law*

. . . Man is a social animal, and the function of law is to enable him to realize his potentialities as a human being through the forms and modes of social organization. It is important to consider how the criminal law serves this ultimate end.

Human beings, of course, realize their potentialities in part through enjoyment of the various satisfactions of human life, both tangible and intangible, which existing social resources and their own individual capacities make available to them. Yet, the social resources of the moment are always limited, and human capacities for enjoyment are limited also. Social resources for providing the satisfactions of life and human capacities for enjoying them, however, are always susceptible of enlargement, so far as we know, without eventual limit. Man realizes his potentialities most significantly in the very process of developing these resources and capacities—by making himself a functioning and participating member of his community, contributing to it as well as drawing from it.

What is crucial in this process is the enlargement of each individual's capacity for effectual and responsible decision. For it is only through personal, self-reliant participation, by trial and error, in the prob-

---

1. *Science and Human Behavior* (1953); the quotations in the text are taken from pp. 6–7, 10, 115–16.

---

* Reprinted by permission from *Law and Contemporary Problems*, Vol. 23, No. 3, 1958, pp. 401, 409–410, published by Duke University School of Law, Durham, N.C.

lems of existence, both personal and social, that the capacity to participate effectively can grow. Man learns wisdom in choosing by being confronted with choices and by being made aware that he must abide the consequences of his choice. In the training of a child in the small circle of the family, this principle is familiar enough. It has the same validity in the training of an adult in the larger circle of the community.

Seen in this light, the criminal law has an obviously significant and, indeed, a fundamental role to play in the effort to create the good society. For it is the criminal law which defines the minimum conditions of man's responsibility to his fellows and holds him to that responsibility. The assertion of social responsibility has value in the treatment even of those who have become criminals. It has far greater value as a stimulus to the great bulk of mankind to abide by the law and to take pride in so abiding.

NOTE 4

MANNHEIM, KARL

Man and Society*

Though reward and punishment are both social incentives, and the rewards for which we strive are socially determined, it is true, nevertheless, that a society which is based chiefly on command and punishment is more brutal than one based on reward. The methods which try to rouse men to act by kindling their desires are much subtler in conception and more sublimated in effect. Their efficiency cannot be rightly assessed by noting the speed of reaction in isolated cases alone. We must also remember that the strain of waiting for orders and the fear of punishment destroy both individual spontaneity and the general power of response, so that these become atrophied in spheres in which they are essential.

NOTE 5

NIETZSCHE, FRIEDRICH

Beyond Good and Evil**

Since at all times, as long as there have been human beings, there have been human herds (clan unions, communities, tribes, nations, states, churches) and very many who obeyed compared with very few who were in command; since, therefore, obedience was the trait best and longest exercised and cultivated among men, one may be justified in assuming that on the average it has become an innate need, a kind of *formal conscience* that bids "thou shalt do something or other absolutely, and absolutely refrain from something or other," in other words, "thou shalt." This

need seeks to satisfy itself and to fill its form with some content. Depending on how strong, impatient, and tense it is, it seizes upon things with little discrimination, like a gross appetite, and accepts whatever meets its ear, whatever any representative of authority (parents, teachers, laws, class prejudices, public opinion) declaims into it. . . . Let us imagine this instinct taking over to its limits: In the end there would be none whatever who could command or be independent; or else all those in command would in the end suffer inwardly from a bad conscience and have to practice a self-deception before they could command, namely pretend that they too are only obeying. . . .

NOTE 6

HOBBES, THOMAS

Leviathan*

Nature hath made men so equal, in the faculties of the body, and mind; as though there be found one man sometimes manifestly stronger in body, or of quicker mind than another; yet when all is reckoned together, the difference between man, and man, is not so considerable, as that one man thereupon claim to himself any benefit, to which another may not pretend, as well as he. For as to the strength of body, the weakest has strength enough to kill the strongest, either by secret machination, or by confederacy with others, that are in the same danger with himself.

And as to the faculties of the mind . . . I find a yet greater equality among men, than that of strength. For prudence, is but experience; which equal time, equally bestows on all men, in those things they equally apply themselves unto. That which may perhaps make such equality incredible, is but a vain conceit of one's own wisdom, which almost all men think they have in a greater degree, than the vulgar; that is, than all men but themsleves, and a few others, whom by fame, or for concurring with themselves, they approve. For such is the nature of men, that howsoever they may acknowledge many others to be more witty, or more eloquent, or more learned; yet they will hardly believe there be so many wise as themsleves; for they see their own wit at hand, and other men's at a distance. But this proveth rather that men are in that point equal, than unequal. For there is not ordinarily a greater sign of the equal distribution of any thing, than that every man is contented with his share.

From this equality of ability, ariseth equality of hope in the attaining of our ends. And therefore if any two men desire the same thing which, nevertheless they cannot both enjoy, they become enemies;

* London: Routledge & Kegan Paul, Ltd., 1948 and New York: Harcourt, Brace & World. Reprinted by permission.
** New York: Macmillan Co., London: George Allen & Unwin, 1923 (pp. 106–107). Reprinted by permission.

* *English Works*, Vol. III, (1889) pp. 110–16. London: J. Bohn.

and in the way to their end, which is principally their own conservation, and sometimes their delectation only, endeavor to destroy, or subdue one another. . . .

*   *   *

[I]n the nature of man, we find three principal causes of quarrel. First, competition; secondly, diffidence; thirdly, glory.

The first, maketh man invade for gain; the second, for safety; and the third, for reputation. . . .

Hereby it is manifest, that during the time men live without a common power to keep them all in awe, they are in that condition which is called war; and such a war, as is of every man, against every man. For WAR, consisteth not in battle only, or the act of fighting; but in a tract of time, wherein the will to contend battle is sufficiently known: And therefore the notion of *time*, is to be considered in the nature of war; as it is in the nature of weather. For as the nature of foul weather, lieth not in a shower or two of rain; but in an inclination thereto of many days together: So the nature of war, consisteth not in actual fighting; but in the known disposition thereto, during all the time there is no assurance to the contrary. All other time is PEACE.

Whatsoever therefore is consequent to a time of war, where every man is enemy to every man; the same is consequent to the time, wherein men live without other security, than what their own strength, and their own invention shall furnish them withal. In such condition, there is no place for industry; because the fruit thereof is uncertain: And consequently no culture of the earth; no navigation, nor use of the commodities that may be imported by sea; no commodious building; no instruments of moving, and removing, such things as require much force; no knowledge of the face of the earth; no account of time; no arts; no letters; no society; and which is worst of all, continual fear, and danger of violent death; and the life of man, solitary, poor, nasty, brutish, and short.

*   *   *

To this war of every man, against every man, this also is consequent; that nothing can be unjust. The notions of right and wrong, justice and injustice have there no place. Where there is no common power, there is no law: where no law, no injustice. Force, and fraud, are in war the two cardinal virtues. Justice, and injustice are none of the faculties neither of the body, nor mind. If they were, they might be in a man that were alone in the world, as well as his senses, and passions. They are qualities, that relate to men in society, not in solitude. It is consequent also to the same condition, that there be no propriety, no dominion, no *mine* and *thine* distinct; but only that to be every man's, that he can get; and for

so long, as he can keep it. And thus much for the ill condition, which man by mere nature is actually placed in; though with a possibility to come out of it, consisting partly in the passions, partly in his reason.

The passions that incline men to peace, are fear of death; desire of such things as are necessary to commodious living; and a hope by their industry to obtain them. And reason suggesteth convenient articles of peace, upon which men may be drawn to agreement. These articles, are they, which otherwise are called the laws of Nature. . . .

NOTE 7

HAND, LEARNED

To Yale Law Graduates (1931)*

It seems to me that the chief obstacle to our success lies not in our powers, were we able to use them but in the make-up of those same selves which remain so little changed amid our new methods and accomplishments. It is our human wills that are at fault, not our minds or our energy. It is possible that we may decide upon another orgy of slaughter and destruction, and while I do not take too seriously the lurid threats of mutual annihilation which one sometimes reads, it is certainly open to doubt how often men may continue to enjoy the pastime of murder, arson, and spoil without lapsing into anarchy and chaos. Nobody can, and nobody today does, feel that security which was the convention at the turn of the last century. We shall succeed in using those powers for a happy future only in case we learn so far to forbear with one another, so much to eschew greed and aggression, that we give ourselves the chance to do what lies within us. The condition of our survival in any but the meagerest existence is our willingness to accomodate ourselves to the conflicting interests of others, to learn to live in a social world.

It is here that we can find a scope and meaning in our work as lawyers which raises it out of the dusty routine of gaining our living. For the law is no more than the formal expression of that tolerable compromise that we call justice, without which the rule of the tooth and claw must prevail. . . .

NOTE 8

FREUD, SIGMUND

Civilization and its Discontents (1930)**

The last, but certainly not the least important, of

* Reprinted from: Dilliard, Irving: *The Spirit of Liberty*, 1960, (p. 87) by permission of Alfred A. Knopf, New York.
** Reprinted from: 21 *The Standard Edition of the Complete Psychological Works of Sigmund Freud*, James Strachey, ed., London: The Hogarth Press and the Institute of Psychoanalysis, 1961, (pp. 94–96, 111–14). Reprinted by permission of Hogarth & W. W. Norton Co.

the characteristic features of civilization remains to be assessed: The manner in which the relationships of men to one another, their total relationships, are regulated—relationships which affect a person as a neighbor, as a source of help, as another person's sexual object, as a member of a family and of a State. Here it is especially difficult to keep clear of particular ideal demands and to see what is civilized in general. Perhaps we may begin by explaining that the element of civilization enters on the scene with the first attempt to regulate these social relationships. If the attempt were not made, the relationships would be subject to the arbitrary will of the individual: That is to say, the physically stronger man would decide them in the sense of his own interests and instinctual impulses. Nothing would be changed in this if this stronger man should in his turn meet someone even stronger than he. Human life in common is only made possible when a majority comes together which is stronger than any separate individual and which remains united against all separate individuals. The power of this community is then set up as "right" in opposition to the power of the individual, which is condemned as "brute force." This replacement of the power of the individual by the power of a community constitutes the decisive step of civilization. The essence of it lies in the fact that the members of the community restrict themselves in their possibilities of satisfaction, whereas the individual knows no such restrictions. The first requisite of civilization, therefore, is that of justice—that is, the assurance that a law once made will not be broken in favor of an individual. This implies nothing as to the ethical value of such a law. The further course of cultural development seems to tend toward making the law no longer an expression of the will of a small community—a caste or a stratum of the population or a racial group—which, in its turn, behaves like a violent individual toward other, and perhaps more numerous, collections of people. The final outcome should be a rule of law to which all—except those who are not capable of entering a community—have contributed by a sacrifice of their instincts, and which leaves no one—again with the same exception—at the mercy of brute force.

The liberty of the individual is no gift of civilization. It was greatest before there was any civilization, though then, it is true, it had for the most part no value, since the individual was scarcely in a position to defend it. The development of civilization imposes restrictions on it, and justice demands that no one shall escape those restrictions. What makes itself felt in a human community as a desire for freedom may be their revolt against some existing injustice, and so may prove favorable to a further development of civilization; it may remain compatible with civilization. But it may also spring from the remains of their original personality, which is still untamed by civilization and may thus become the basis in them of hostility to civilization. The urge for freedom, therefore, is directed against particular forms and demands of civilization or against civilization altogether. It does not seem as though any influence could induce a man to change his nature into a termite's. No doubt he will always defend his claim to individual liberty against the will of the group. A good part of the struggles of mankind center round the single task of finding an expedient accommodation—one that is, that will bring happiness—between this claim of the individual and the cultural claims of the group; and one of the problems that touches the fate of humanity is whether such an accommodation can be reached by means of some particular form of civilization or whether this conflict is irreconcilable.

*   *   *

The . . . truth . . . which people are so ready to disavow, is that men are not gentle creatures who want to be loved, and who at the most can defend themselves if they are attacked; they are, on the contrary, creatures among whose instinctual endowments is to be reckoned a powerful share of aggressiveness. . . .

*   *   *

The communists believe that they have found the path to deliverance from our evils. According to them, man is wholly good and is well-disposed to his neighbor; but the institution of private property has corrupted his nature. The ownership of private wealth gives the individual power, and with it the temptation to ill-treat his neighbor; while the man who is excluded from possesion is bound to rebel in hostility against his oppressor. If private property were abolished, all wealth held in common, and everyone allowed to share in the enjoyment of it, illwill and hostility would disappear among men. Since everyone's needs would be satisfied, no one would have any reason to regard another as his enemy; all would willingly undertake the work that was necessary. I have no concern with any economic criticisms of the communist system; I cannot enquire into whether the abolition of private property is expedient or advantageous. But I am able to recognize that the psychological premises on which the system is based are an untenable illusion. In abolishing private property we deprive the human love of aggression of one of its instruments, certainly a strong one, though certainly not the strongest; but we have in no way altered the differences in power and influence which are misused by aggressiveness, nor have we altered anything in its nature. Aggressiveness was not created by property. It reigned almost without limit in primitive times, when property was still very scanty, and it already shows itself in the nursery almost before property has given up its primal, anal form; it forms the basis of every relation of affection and love among people (with the sinlge exception, perhaps, of the mother's relation to her male child). If we do away with personal rights over material wealth, there still remains prerogative in the field of sexual relationships, which is bound to become the source of the strongest dislike and the most violent hostility among men who in other respects are on an equal footing. If we were to remove this factor, too, by allowing complete freedom of sexual life and thus abolishing the family, the germ-cell of civilization, we cannot, it is true, easily foresee what new paths the development of civilization could take; but one thing we can expect, and that is that this indestructible feature of human nature will follow it there.

It is clearly not easy for men to give up the satisfaction of this inclination to aggression. They do not feel comfortable without it. The advantage which a comparatively small cultural group offers of allowing this instinct an outlet in the form of hostility against intruders is not to be despised. It is always possible to bind together a considerable number of people in love, so long as there are other people left over to receive the manifestations of their aggressiveness. . . .

NOTE 9

FULLER, LON L.

Freedom—A Suggested Analysis*

[F]reedom and order are not antithetical . . . individual freedom, in the sense of a choice among alternatives, can generally be assured only through forms of social order. . . . It is easy to conclude from this that complex systems of order can strike only as the result of some single painful act. . . .

This conclusion would . . . be a dangerous mistake, for some of the most important and complex systems of order we know have come into existence, not by a single act of creation, but through the cumulative effect of countless purposive directions of human effort. Examples of such systems are language, economic markets, scientific theory, the common law, and, on a homelier plane, a footpath through a woodland. These are sometimes referred to as cases of "spontaneous order," but this expression is objectionable in implying that they have come into existence without purposive human effort. In fact . . . they are produced by the coming together of countless individual purposive acts.

*   *   *

The existence of such systems of order arising out of a multitude of individual decisions shows the

---

* *University of Chicago Law School Conference on Jurisprudence*, Conference Series No. 15, (1955), pp. 49–52. Reprinted by permission.

fallacy of assuming that we face the alternative either of leaving things alone, and thus securing freedom at the cost of chaos, or of intervening drastically by some planful legislative act, and thus securing order at the cost of freedom. Legislative fiat is at least as capable of destroying order as it is of creating it.

*   *   *

[I]n arranging the forms of order through which individual choice is given social expression (or in taking steps to preserve the existing forms), we should bear in mind that choice is meaningless without understanding. A gambler at a roulette table has, in a sense, a wide range of choice, embracing, I am told, among other alternatives, thirty-seven different numbers. Yet no one, except a person simple-minded enough to believe in "systems" for beating the banker would regard this as a truly significant choice. Indeed when the player puts his chips on "17," he does not have the sense of choosing; rather, he has the titillation of subjecting himself to the risk of loss or gain without the responsibility for choice. If he has a sense of freedom, it is properly described as freedom from freedom.

When we speak of increasing freedom by expanding the range of choice open to the individual, we do not have in mind the roulette-table kind of freedom. We must intend choice in situations where the citizen knows, or can know, at least approximately the consequences of what he is doing.

*   *   *

The point I wish to make here is that choice is most likely to be informed and intelligent when it is made, as it were, in context—when it relates not to tomorrow's needs but today's, when it compares not one hypothetical good with another but, let us say, two objects standing side-by-side on the same counter.

*   *   *

The great advantage of such systems of social order that are built up by the fitting together of many individual decisions is that those decisions have been reached with reference to specific situations of fact. The words of a language, for example, have come into existence because in some particular context people wanted to say something and needed a word to say it with. Words are not created by someone who thinks they might come in handy on some later occasion.

*   *   *

Imagine a newly settled rural community in which it is apparent that sooner or later a path will be worn through a particular woodland. Suppose the community decides to plan the path in advance. There would be definite advantages in this course. Experts could be brought in. A general view of the whole situation could be obtained that would not be available to any individual wayfarer. What would be lacking would be the contribution of countless small decisions by people actually using the path, the decision for example, of those whose footprints pulled the path slightly to the east so that they might look at a field of daisies, or of those who detoured around a spot generally dry, but unaccountably wet in August.

I hope the figure of the path will not be taken with more seriousness than it is offered. Lest I be accused of romanticizing the problem, I should like to close by relating an actual incident that seems in point.

Through the foresight of the city fathers the Cambridge Common is provided with an elaborate network of paved sidewalks, carefully planned to serve the convenience of any person wishing to traverse the Common from any angle. It was found, however, that at certain points people perversely insisted on walking across the grass. The usual countermeasures were tried, but failed. Now the city is taking down its barriers and its "keep-off-the-grass" signs and is busily engaged in paving the paths cut by trespassing feet. Those who have had experience with the problem of designing forms for the life of the human animal will see here, I believe, a pattern of events that has repeated itself many, many times.

NOTE 10

SIMMEL, GEORG

Sociology*

[A] typical form of subordination [is] subordination neither to an individual nor to a plurality, but to an impersonal, objective principle. The fact that here a real interaction, at least an immediate interaction, is precluded, seems to deprive this form of the element of freedom. The individual who is subordinate to an objective law feels himself determined by it; while he, in turn, in no way determines the law, and has no possibility of reacting to it in a manner which could influence it—quite in contrast to even the most miserable slave, who, in some fashion at least, can still in this sense [interact with] his master. For if one simply does not obey the law, one is, to this extent, not *really* subjected to it; and if one changes the law, one is not subordinate to the old law at all, but is again, in the same entirely unfree manner, subject to the new law. In spite of this, however, for modern [man, with his capacity for an objective view of social relations, and his awareness] of the difference between the spheres of spontaneity and of obedience, subordination to a law which functions as the emanation of impersonal, uninfluenceable powers, is the more dignified situation. . . .

---

* Reprinted with permission of The Free Press, New York, from *The Sociology of Georg Simmel*, K. H. Wolff, ed., p. 250. Copyright 1950 by The Free Press.

NOTE 11

WHITEHEAD, ALFRED N.

Adventures of Ideas*

Routine is the god of every social system; it is the seventh heaven of business, the essential component in the success of every factory, the ideal of every statesman. The social machine should run like clockwork. Every crime should be followed by an arrest, every arrest by a judicial trial, every trial by a conviction, every conviction by a punishment, every punishment by a reformed character. . . .

Now it is the beginning of wisdom to understand that social life is founded upon routine. Unless society is permeated, through and through, with routine, civilization vanishes. So many sociological doctrines, the products of acute intellects, are wrecked by obliviousness to this fundamental sociological truth. Society requires stability, foresight itself presupposes stability, and stability is the product of routine. But there are limits to routine, and it is for the discernment of these limits, and for the provision of the consequent action, that foresight is required.

The two extremes of complete understanding and of complete routine are never realized in human society. But of the two, routine is more fundamental than understanding, that is to say, routine modified by minor flashes of short-range intelligence. Indeed the notion of complete understanding controlling action is an ideal in the clouds, grotesquely at variance with practical life. But we have under our eyes countless examples of societies entirely dominated by routine. The elaborate social organizations of insects appear to be thoroughgoing examples of routine. Such organizations achieve far-reaching, complex purposes: They involve a differentiation of classes, from cows to serfs, from serfs to workers, from workers to warriors, from warriors to janitors, and from janitors to queens. Such organizations have regard to needs in a distant future, especially if the comparatively short space of life of the individual insects is taken into account as the unit of measurement.

These insect societies have been astoundingly successful, so far as concerns survival power. They seem to have a past extending over tens of thousands of years, perhaps of millions of years. It is the greatest of mistakes to believe that it has required the high-grade intelligence of mankind to construct an elaborate social organization. A particular instance of this error is the prevalent assumption that any social routine whose purposes are not obvious to our analysis is thereby to be condemned as foolish. We can observe insects performing elaborate routine actions whose purposes they cannot possibly under-

---

* Cambridge: Cambridge University Press, 1947, (pp. 87–88, 113–16). Reprinted by permission.

stand, which yet are essential either for their own individual survival or for race survival.

But these insect societies have one great characteristic in common. They are not progressive. It is exactly this characteristic that discriminates communities of mankind from communities of insects. Further, this great fact of progressiveness, be it from worse to better, or from better to worse, has become of greater and greater importance in western civilization as we come to modern times. The rate of change has increased even in my lifetime. It is possible that in future ages mankind may relapse into the stage of stable societies. . . .

NOTE 12

Report of the Attorney General's Committee on Poverty and the Administration of Federal Criminal Justice*

American criminal procedure is accusatorial in nature and is founded upon the adversary system. It "presumes" the innocence of the accused. It requires the government to establish the guilt of the defendant beyond reasonable doubt. It imposes procedural regulations on the criminal process by constitutional command. In the modern era it is not always fully understood that the adversary system performs a vital social function and is the product of long historical experience. . . . The adversary system is the institution devised by our legal order for the proper reconciliation of public and private interests in the crucial areas of penal regulation. As such, it makes essential and invaluable contributions to the maintenance of the free society.

The essence of the adversary system is challenge. The survival of our system of criminal justice and the values which it advances depends upon a constant, searching, and creative questioning of official decisions and assertions of authority at all stages of the process. The proper performance of the defense function is thus as vital to the health of the system as the performance of the prosecuting and adjudicatory functions. It follows that insofar as the financial status of the accused impedes vigorous and proper challenges, it constitutes a threat to the viability of the adversary system. . . . Persons suffering such disabilities are incapable of providing the challenges that are indispensable to satisfactory operation of the system. The loss to the interests of accused individuals, occasioned by these failures, are great and apparent. It is also clear that a situation in which persons are required to contest a serious accusation but are denied access to the tools of contest is offensive to fairness and equity. Beyond these considerations, however, is the fact that the conditions produced by the financial incapacity of the accused are detrimental to the proper functioning of the system of justice and that the loss in vitality of the adversary system, thereby occasioned, significantly endangers the basic interests of a free community.

NOTE 13

COHEN, MORRIS R.

The Basis of Contract*

[O]ur modern practices of shaking hands to close a bargain, signing papers, and protesting a note are, like the taking of an oath on assuming office, not only designed to make evidence secure, but are in large part also expressions of the fundamental human need for formality and ceremony, to make sharp distinctions where otherwise lines of demarcation would not be so clearly apprehended.

Ceremonies are the channels that the stream of social life creates by its ceaseless flow through the sands of human circumstance. Psychologically, they are habits; socially, they are customary ways of doing things; and ethically, they have what Jellinek has called the normative power of the actual, that is, they control what we do by creating a standard of respectability or a pattern to which we feel bound to conform. The daily obedience to the act of the government, which is the basis of all political and legal institutions, is thus largely a matter of conformity to established ritual or form of behavior. For the most part, we obey the law or the policeman as a matter of course, without deliberation. The customs of other people seem to us strange and we try to explain them as ceremonies symbolic of things that are familiar or seem useful to us. But many of our own customs can appear to an outsider as equally nonrational rituals that we follow from habit. We may justify them as the sacred vessels through which we obtain the substance of life's goods. But the maintenance of old forms may also be an end in itself to all those to whom change from the familiar is abhorrent.

NOTE 14

MAINE, HENRY S.

Ancient Law**

A general proposition of some value may be advanced with respect to the agencies by which Law is brought into harmony with society. These instrumentalities seem to me to be three in number, Legal Fictions, Equity, and Legislation. . . .

[I] now employ the expression "Legal Fiction" to signify any assumption which conceals, or affects to conceal, the fact that a rule of law has undergone alteration, its letter remaining unchanged, its operation being modified. . . . The *fact* is . . . that the law

---

* Washington, 1963.

* *Law and the Social Order.* New York: Harcourt Brace & World, 1933, (pp. 99–100). Reprinted by permission.
** New York: Charles Scribner, 1864, (pp. 23–28).

has been wholly changed; the *fiction* is that it remains what it always was. It is not difficult to understand why fictions in all their forms are particularly congenial to the infancy of society. They satisfy the desire for improvement, which is not quite wanting, at the same time that they do not offend the superstitious disrelish for change which is always present. At a particular stage of social progress they are invaluable expedients for overcoming the rigidity of law, and, indeed, without one of them, the Fiction of Adoption which permits the family tie to be artificially created, it is difficult to understand how society would ever have escaped from its swaddling-clothes, and taken its first step towards civilization. . . .

The next instrumentality by which the adaptation of law to social wants is carried on I call Equity, meaning by that word any body of rules existing by the side of the original civil law, founded on distinct principles and claiming incidentally to supersede the civil law in virtue of a superior sanctity inherent in those principles. The Equity, whether of the Roman Praetors or of the English Chancellors, differs from the Fictions which in each case preceded it, in that the interference with law is open and avowed. On the other hand, it differs from Legislation, the agent of legal improvement which comes after it, in that its claim to authority is grounded, not on the prerogative of any external person or body, not even on that of the magistrate who enunciates it, but on the special nature of its principles, to which it is alleged that all law ought to conform. The very conception of a set of principles, invested with a higher sacredness than those of the original law and demanding application independently of the consent of any external body, belongs to a much more advanced stage of thought than that to which legal fictions originally suggested themselves.

Legislation, the enactments of a legislature which, whether it take the form of an autocratic prince or of a parliamentary assembly, is the assumed organ of the entire society, is the last of the ameliorating instrumentalities. It differs from Legal Fictions just as Equity differs from them, and it is also distinguished from Equity, as deriving its authority from an external body or person. Its obligatory force is independent of its principles. The legislature, whatever be the actual restraints imposed on it by public opinion, is in theory empowered to impose what obligations it pleases on the members of the community. There is nothing to prevent its legislating in the wantonness of caprice. Legislation may be dictated by equity, if that last word be used to indicate some standard of right and wrong to which its enactments happen to be adjusted; but then these enactments are indebted for their binding force to the authority of the legislature, and not to that of the principles on which the legislature acted; and thus they differ from rules of Equity, in the technical sense of the word, which pretend to a

paramount sacredness entitling them at once to the recognition of the courts even without the concurrence of prince or parliamentary assembly. . . .

NOTE 15

BENTHAM, JEREMY

An Introduction to the Principles of Morals and Legislation*

Nature has placed mankind under the governance of two sovereign masters, *pain* and *pleasure*. It is for them alone to point out what we ought to do, as well as to determine what we shall do. On the one hand the standard of right and wrong, on the other the chain of causes and effects, are fastened to their throne. They govern us in all we do, in all we say, in all we think: Every effort we can make to throw off our subjection, will serve but to demonstrate and confirm it. In words a man may pretend to abjure their empire: But in reality he will remain subject to it all the while. The *principle of utility* recognizes this subjection, and assumes it for the foundation of that system, the object of which is to rear the fabric of felicity by the hands of reason and of law. Systems which attempt to question it, deal in sounds instead of sense, in caprice instead of reason, in darkness instead of light.

But enough of metaphor and declamation: It is not by such means that moral science is to be improved.

The principle of utility is the foundation of the present work: It will be proper therefore at the outset to give an explicit and determinate account of what is meant by it. By the principle of utility is meant that principle which approves or disapproves of every action whatsoever, according to the tendency which it appears to have to augment or diminish the happiness of the party whose interest is in question: Or, what is the same thing in other words, to promote or to oppose that happiness. I say of every action whatsoever; and therefore not only of every action of a private individual, but of every measure of government.

By utility is meant that property in any object, whereby it tends to produce benefit, advantage, pleasure, good, or happiness, (all this in the present case comes to the same thing) or (what comes again to the same thing) to prevent the happening of mischief, pain, evil, or unhappiness to the party whose interest is considered: If that party be the community in general, then the happiness of the community; if a particular individual, then the happiness of that individual.

*   *   *

Has the rectitude of this principle been ever formally contested? It should seem that it had, by those who have not known what they have been meaning.

* New York: Hafner Publishing Co. 1948 (pp. 1–4). Reprinted by permission.

102801

Is it susceptible of any direct proof? It should seem not. For that which is used to prove everything else, cannot itself be proved: A chain of proofs must have their commencement somewhere. To give such proof is as impossible as it is needless.

Not that there is or ever has been that human creature breathing, however stupid or perverse, who has not on many, perhaps on most occasions of his life, deferred to it. By the natural constitution of the human frame, on most occasions of their lives men in general embrace this principle, without thinking of it: If not for the ordering of their own actions, yet for the trying of their own actions, as well as of those of other men. There have been, at the same time, not many, perhaps, even of the most intelligent, who have been disposed to embrace it purely and without reserve. There are even few who have not taken some occasion or other to quarrel with it, either on account of their not understanding always how to apply it, or on account of some prejudice or other which they were afraid to examine into, or could not bear to part with. For such is the stuff that man is made of: In principle and in practice, in a right track and in a wrong one, the rarest of all human qualities is consistency.

NOTE 16

OLMSTEAD v. UNITED STATES
277 U.S. 438, 478 (1927)

BRANDEIS, J. (dissenting):

The makers of our constitution undertook to secure conditions favorable to the pursuit of happiness. They recognized the significance of man's spiritual nature, of his feelings, and of his intellect. They knew that only a part of the pain, pleasure, and satisfactions of life are to be found in material things. They sought to protect Americans in their beliefs, their thoughts, their emotions, and their sensations. They conferred, as against the Government, the right to be let alone—the most comprehensive of rights and the right most valued by civilized men. To protect that right, every unjustifiable intrusion by the Government upon the privacy of the individual, whatever the means employed, must be deemed a violation of the Fourth Amendment. . . .

NOTE 17

BENTHAM, JEREMY

Theory of Legislation*

We come now to the principal object of law—the care of security. That inestimable good, the distinctive index of civilization, is entirely the work of law.

---

* Reprinted from *Rational Basis of Legal Institutions of Property*. New York: Macmillan Co., 1923. (pp. 209–13). Reprinted by permission.

Without law there is no security; and, consequently, no abundance, and not even a certainty of subsistence; and the only equality which can exist in such a state of things is an equality of misery.

*   *   *

Law alone has done that which all the natural sentiments united have not the power to do. Law alone is able to create a fixed and durable possession which merits the name of property. Law alone can accustom men to bow their heads under the yoke of foresight, hard at first to bear, but afterwards light and agreeable. Nothing but law can encourage men to labors superfluous for the present, and which can be enjoyed only in the future.

*   *   *

Law does not say to man, *Labor, and I will reward you;* but it says: *Labor, and I will assure to you the enjoyment of the fruits of your labor—that natural and sufficient recompense which without me you cannot preserve; I will insure it by arresting the hand which may seek to ravish it from you.* If industry creates, it is law which preserves; if at the first moment we owe all to labor, at the second moment, and at every other, we are indebted for everything to law.

To form a precise idea of the extent which ought to be given to the principle of security, we must consider that man is not like the animals, limited to the present, whether as respects suffering or enjoyment; but that he is susceptible of pains and pleasures by anticipation; and that it is not enough to secure him from actual loss, but it is necessary also to guarantee him, as far as possible, against future loss. It is necessary to prolong the idea of his security through all the perspective which his imagination is capable of measuring.

This presentiment, which has so marked an influence upon the fate of man, is called *expectation*. It is hence that we have the power of forming a general plan of conduct; it is hence that the successive instants which compose the duration of life are not like isolated and independent points, but become continuous parts of a whole. *Expectation* is a chain which unites our present existence to our future existence, and which passes beyond us to the generation which is to follow. The sensibility of man extends through all the links of this chain.

The principle of security extends to the maintenance of all these expectations; it requires that events, so far as they depend upon laws, should conform to the expectations which law itself has created.

*   *   *

The better to understand the advantages of law, let us endeavor to form a clear idea of *property*. We shall see that there is no such thing as natural property, and that it is entirely the work of law.

Property is nothing but a basis of expectation; the expectation of deriving certain advantages from a thing which we are said to possess, in consequence of the relation in which we stand toward it.

There is no image, no painting, no visible trait, which can express the relation that constitutes property. It is not material, it is metaphysical; it is a mere conception of the mind.

To have a thing in our hands, to keep it, to make it, to sell it, to work it up into something else; to use it—none of these physical circumstances, nor all united, convey the idea of property. A piece of stuff which is actually in the Indies may belong to me, while the dress I wear may not. The ailment which is incorporated into my very body may belong to another, to whom I am bound to account for it.

The idea of property consists in an established expectation; in the persuasion of being able to draw such or such an advantage from the thing possessed, according to the nature of the case. Now this expectation, this persuasion, can only be the work of law. I cannot count upon the enjoyment of that which I regard as mine, except through the promise of the law which guarantees it to me. It is law alone which permits me to forget my natural weakness. It is only through the protection of law that I am able to inclose a field, and give myself up to its cultivation with the sure though distant hope of harvest.

*   *   *

Property and law are born together, and die together. Before laws were made there was no property; take away laws, and property ceases.

As regards property, security consists in receiving no check, no shock, no derangement to the expectation founded on the laws, of enjoying such and such a portion of good. The legislator owes the greatest respect to this expectation which he has himself produced. When he does not contradict it, he does what is essential to the happiness of society; when he disturbs it, he always produces a proportionate sum of evil.

NOTE 18

BOSANQUET, BERNARD

The Principle of Private Property*

The true reason [for the existence of property] is the recognition of a common good by the members of a society, as realized in each other's lives, for this is the foundation of all rights.

---

* Reprinted from: *Aspects of the Social Problem*, Bosanquet B., ed., New York: Macmillan Co., 1895. (pp. 308–11). Reprinted by permission.

This common good has its existence in the lives of members, each of whom has a conception of himself and of his wellbeing through participation in an organized whole, apart from his particular momentary wants. This permanent conception demands a provision for possible self-satisfaction and possible self-expression, "the means of realizing a will, which is, in possibility, a will for social good." This is quite a different thing from the mere successive removal of wants successively arising, such as satisfies an animal. And in the social institution of property, beginning with the clan, and completed by the developed State, this "realized will," or permanent conception of wellbeing, takes its place as a right—that is to say, as a want socially recognized as demanding fulfilment. Man can only be fully realized as social when he is fully distinguished as individual. In the mere clan he is relatively unfree and unsocial.

We may illustrate this point by contrast with the position of a child in the family. . . . His relation to things has no unity corresponding to his moral nature. No nerve of connection runs through his acts in dealing with the external world. So with his food; he may waste or throw away his food at one meal, he gets nonetheless at the next (unless by way of discipline). He gets what is thought necessary quite apart from all his previous action. So too with his dress. The dress of a young child does not express his own character at all, but that of his mother. If he spoils his things, that makes no difference to him (unless as a punishment); he has what is thought proper for him at every given moment. So with travel, enjoyments, and education up to a certain point. What he is enabled to have and do in no way expresses his own previous action or character, except in as far as he is put in training by his parents for grown-up life. The essence of this position is, that the dealings of such an agent with the world of things do not affect each other, nor form an interdependent whole. He may eat his cake and have it; or he may not eat it and yet not have it. To such an agent the world is miraculous; things are not for him adjusted, organized, contrived; things simply *come* as in a fairy tale. The same is the case with a slave. Life is from hand to mouth; it has as such no totality, no future, and no past.

Now, private property is not simply an arrangement for meeting successive momentary wants as they arise on such a footing as this. It is wholly different in principle, as adult or responsible life differs from child-life, which is irresponsible. It rests on the principle that the inward or moral life cannot be a unity unless the outward life—the dealing with things—is also a unity. In dealing with things this means a causal unity, i.e., that what we do at one time, or in one relation, should affect what we are able to do at another time, or in another relation. . . .

Private property, then, is the unity of life in its external or material form; the result of past dealing with the material world, and the possibility of future dealing with it; the general or universal means of possible action and expression corresponding to the moral self that looks before and after, as opposed to the momentary wants of a child or of an animal. A grown man knows that if he does this he will not be able to do that, and his humanity, his power of organization, and intelligent self-assertion, depend on his knowing it. If he wants to do something in particular ten years hence he must act accordingly today; he must be able in some degree to measure his resources. If he wants to marry he must fit himself to maintain a family; he must look ahead and count the cost, must estimate his competence and his character. That is what makes man different from an animal or a child; he considers his life as a whole, and organizes it as such—that is, with a view to reasonable possibilities, not merely to the passing moment.

NOTE 19

KESSLER, FRIEDRICH AND SHARP, MALCOLM

Cases on Contract*

Within the framework of a free enterprise system the essential prerequisite of contractual liability is volition, that is, consent freely given and not coercion or status. Contract, in this view, is the "meeting place of the ideas of agreement and obligation." As a matter of historical fact, the rise of contract within western civilization reflects the erosion of a status-organized society; contract became, at an ever increasing rate, a tool of change and of growing self-determination and self-assertion. Self-determination during the nineteenth century was regarded as the goal toward which society progressed; the movement of progressive societies, in the words of Sir Henry Maine, is a movement from Status to Contract. "It is through contract that man attains freedom. Although it appears to be the subordination of one man's will to another, the former gains more than he loses."

Nineteenth-century industrial society was a mobile society of small enterprisers, individual merchants, and independent craftsmen. Its dominant current of belief was that individual and cooperative action left unrestrained in family, church, and market would not lessen the freedom and dignity of the individual but would secure the highest possible social justice. The representatives of this school of thought were firmly convinced, to state it somewhat roughly, of the existence of a natural law according to which the individual serving his own interest was also serving the interest of the community. Profits, under this system, could

only be earned by supplying wanted commodities, and freedom of competition would prevent profits from rising unduly. The play of the market, if left to itself, would, therefore, maximize net satisfactions and afford the ideal conditions for the distribution of wealth. . . .

Contract, in this view, is the principle of order *par excellence* and the only legitimate means of social integration in a free society. Translated into legal language this means that in a progressive society all law is ultimately based on contract. And since contract as a social phenomenon is the result of a "coincidence of free choices" on the part of the members of the community, merging their egoistical and altruistic tendencies, a contractual society safeguards its own stability. Contract is an instrument of peace in society. It testifies to the "natural identity of interests" of the members of the community—all the more since, with increasing rationality, man becomes less rather than more egoistic.

NOTE 20

HOLMES, OLIVER W.

Natural Law*

*   *   *

. . . As an arbitrary fact people wish to live, and we say with various degrees of certainty that they can do so only on certain conditions. To do it they must eat and drink. That necessity is absolute. It is a necessity of less degree but practically general that they should live in society. If they live in society, so far as we can see, there are further conditions. Reason working on experience does tell us, no doubt, that if our wish to live continues, we can do it only on those terms. But that seems to me the whole of the matter. I see no *a priori* duty to live with others and in that way, but simply a statement of what I must do if I wish to remain alive. If I do live with others they tell me that I must do and abstain from doing various things or they will put the screws on to me. I believe that they will, and being of the same mind as to their conduct I not only accept the rules but come in time to accept them with sympathy and emotional affirmation and begin to talk about duties and rights. But for legal purposes a right is only the hypostasis of a prophecy—the imagination of a substance supporting the fact that the public force will be brought to bear upon those who do things said to contravene it—just as we talk of the force of gravitation accounting for the conduct of bodies in space. One phrase adds no more than the other to what we know without it. No doubt behind

---

* This is a slightly altered, though authorized, version of a portion of the Introduction to *Cases and Materials on Contracts*. Boston: Little Brown & Co., 1953 (pp. 3–4).

---

* 32 *Harvard L. Rev.*, pp. 40–49. Copyright 1918 by the Harvard Law Review Association.

these legal rights is the fighting will of the subject to maintain them, and the spread of his emotions to the general rules by which they are maintained; but that does not seem to me the same thing as the supposed *a priori* discernment of a duty or the assertion of a pre-existing right. A dog will fight for his bone.

* * *

NOTE 21

HOLMES, OLIVER W.

Speeches*

. . . The law, so far as it depends on learning, is indeed, as it has been called, the government of the living by the dead. To a very considerable extent no doubt it is inevitable that the living should be so governed. The past gives us our vocabulary and fixes the limits of our imagination; we cannot get away from it. There is, too, a peculiar logical pleasure in making manifest the continuity between what we are doing and what has been done before. But the present has a right to govern itself so far as it can; and it ought always to be remembered that historic continuity with the past is not a duty, it is only a necessity.

. . . An ideal system of law should draw its postulates and its legislative justification from science. As it is now, we rely upon tradition, or vague sentiment, or the fact that we never thought of any other way of doing things, as our only warrant for rules which we enforce with as much confidence as if they embodied revealed wisdom. Who here can give reasons of any different kind for believing that half the criminal law does not do more harm than good? Our forms of contract, instead of being made once for all, like a yacht, on lines of least resistance, are accidental relics of early notions, concerning which the learned dispute. How much has reason had to do in deciding how far, if at all, it is expedient for the State to meddle with the domestic relations? And so I might go on through the whole law.

* * *

. . . It is a misfortune if a judge reads his conscious or unconscious sympathy with one side or the other prematurely into the law, and forgets that what seem to him to be first principles are believed by half his fellow men to be wrong. . . . Judges are apt to be naive, simple-minded men, and they need something of Mephistopheles. We too need education in the obvious—to learn to transcend our own convictions and to leave room for much that we hold dear to be done away with short of revolution by the orderly change of law.

---

* Boston: Little, Brown & Co. 1934. (pp. 67–69, 101). Reprinted by permission.

NOTE 22

POUND, ROSCOE

The Administrative Application of Legal Standards*

To be an instrument for conserving values, for eliminating friction in the use of the goods of existence and waste in the enjoyment of them—in other words, in order to secure as many interests as possible with the sacrifice of as few as possible—the administration of justice must have three characteristics. First, it must be free, so far as things human may be, from passion, bias, and prejudice. Second, it must be certain and consistent so that judgments may be foreseen and men may proceed in advance of controversy with assurance as to the outcome of their action. Third, it must be practical; it must be conscious that it is a means towards practical ends; it must not forget that it is dealing with life and all the variations and mutations that make up life, and not with postulates, or with postulates only so far as they are effective means of handling actualities. Hence, if it habitually employs logic to meet the first and the second of these requirements it must have the courage to throw logic overboard upon occasion to meet the requirements of the third. Obviously we cannot wholly satisfy these three requirements in their entirety. As in all other practical situations, we must compromise. But the tendency has been to insist upon some one of them for the time being exclusively and to neglect or ignore the others. Primitive law and the strict law concerned themselves chiefly if not wholly with the first. Above all it was feared that the personal bent of the magistrate would subject one free man to the arbitrary will of another or would affect the granting of the remedies which made up the whole armory of the law. Hence the narrow purpose by which the strict law deliberately constrained itself. It was content to administer the arbitrarily fixed and rigidly settled remedies in a formally consistent and mechanically impartial fashion, in order to maintain the social interest in the general security at all hazards. In the maturity of law, in a commerical society in which the security of acquisitions and the security of transactions, property, and contract, are all important, men were chiefly impressed with the second requirement. Thus they came under the influence of a false principle of certainty, and assuming that there was one paramount interest to secure, sacrificed too much in the endeavor to secure it.

Rigid form, mechanical application of strict rules and inexorable logic, proceeding on the basis of fixed principles and exactly limited conceptions, are the means by which legal systems have sought to attain impartiality and certainty in the administration of

---

* 67 *Reports of the American Bar Association*, 451–452. (1919). Reprinted by permission.

justice. In the stage of the strict law reliance was upon rule and form. Mechanical application of rule and rigid adherence to form admit of no personal bias and give no latitude for differences of individual opinion. Moreover, the process of decision, so conducted, is simple and easy, whereas to go beneath form to substance requires hard thinking and close reasoning. . . .

NOTE 23

FREUND, PAUL A.

Social Justice*

Much of law is designed to avoid the necessity for the judge to reach what Holmes called his "can't helps," his ultimate convictions or values. The force of precedent, the close applicability of statute law, the separation of powers, legal presumptions, statutes of limitations, rules of pleading and evidence, and above all the pragmatic assessments of fact that point to one result whichever ultimate values be assumed, all enable the judge in most cases to stop short of a resort to his personal standards. When these prove unavailing, as is more likely in the case of courts of last resort at the frontiers of the law, and most likely in a supreme constitutional court, the judge necessarily resorts to his own scheme of values. It may therefore be said that the most important thing about a judge is his philosophy; and if it be dangerous for him to have one, it is at all events less dangerous than the self-deception of having none.

NOTE 24

CARDOZO, BENJAMIN N.

The Nature of the Judicial Process**

I have spoken of the forces of which judges avowedly avail to shape the form and content of their judgments. Even these forces are seldom fully in consciousness. They lie so near the surface, however, that their existence and influence are not likely to be disclaimed. But the subject is not exhausted with the recognition of their power. Deep below consciousness are other forces, the likes and the dislikes, the predilections and the prejudices, the complex of instincts and emotions and habits and convictions, which make the man, whether he be litigant or judge. . . . There has been a certain lack of candor in much of the discussion of the theme, or rather perhaps in the refusal to discuss it, as if judges must lose respect and confidence by the reminder that they are subject to human limitations. I do not doubt the grandeur of the conception which lifts them into the realm of pure reason, above and beyond the sweep of perturbing

* Englewood Cliffs, N.J.: Prentice Hall, 1962, (p. 110). Reprinted by permission.
** New Haven: Yale University Press, 1921. (pp. 167–79). Reprinted by permission.

and deflecting forces. Nonetheless . . . they do not stand aloof on these chill and distant heights; and we shall not help the cause of truth by acting and speaking as if they do. The great tides and currents which engulf the rest of men, do not turn aside in their course, and pass the judges by. We like to figure to ourselves the processes of justice as coldly objective and impersonal. The law, conceived of as a real existence, dwelling apart and alone, speaks, through the voices of priests and ministers, the words which they have no choice except to utter. That is an ideal of objective truth toward which every system of jurisprudence tends. It is an ideal of which great publicists and judges have spoken as of something possible to attain. "The judges of the nation," says Montesquieu, "are only the mouths that pronounce the words of the law, inanimate beings, who can moderate neither its force nor its rigor." So Marshal, in *Osborne* v. *Bank* of the United States, 9 Wheat. 738, 866: The judicial department "has no will in any case. . . . Judicial power is never exercised for the purpose of giving effect to the will of the judge; always for the purpose of giving effect to the will of the legislature; or in other words, to the will of the law." It has a lofty sound; it is well and finely said; but it can never be more than partly true. Marshall's own career is a conspicuous illustration of the fact that the ideal is beyond the reach of human faculties to attain. He gave to the constitution of the United States the impress of his own mind; and the form of our constitutional law is what it is, because he molded it while it was still plastic and malleable in the fire of his own intense convictions. At the opposite extreme are the words of the French jurist, Saleilles, in his treatise "De la Personnalité Juridique": "One wills at the beginning the result; one finds the principle afterwards; such is the genesis of all juridical construction. Once accepted, the construction presents itself, doubtless, in the ensemble of legal doctrine, under the opposite aspect. The factors are inverted. The principle appears as an initial cause, from which one has drawn the result which is found deduced from it." I would not put the case thus broadly. So sweeping a statement exaggerates the element of free volition. It ignores the factors of determinism which cabin and confine within narrow bounds the range of unfettered choice. Nonetheless, by its very excess of emphasis, it supplies the needed corrective of an ideal of impossible objectivity. Nearer to the truth, and midway between these extremes, are the words of a man who was not a jurist, but whose intuitions and perceptions were deep and brilliant—the words of President Roosevelt in his message of December 8, 1908, to the Congress of the United States: "The chief lawmakers in our country may be, and often are, the judges, because they are the final seat of authority. Every time they interpret contract, property, vested rights, due process of law, liberty, they necessarily enact into law parts of a system of social philosophy; and as such interpretation is fundamental, they give direction to all lawmaking. The decisions of the courts on economic and social questions depend upon their economic and social philosophy; and for the peaceful progress of our people during the twentieth century we shall owe most to those judges who hold to a twentieth-century economic and social philosophy and not to a long outgrown philosophy, which was itself the product of primitive economic conditions."

I remember that this statement when made, aroused a storm of criticism. It betrayed ignorance, they said, of the nature of the judicial process. The business of the judge, they told us, was to discover objective truth. His own little individuality, his tiny stock of scattered and unco-ordinated philosophies, these, with all his weaknesses and unconscious prejudices, were to be laid aside and forgotten. What did men care for *his* reading of the eternal verities? It was not worth recording. What the world was seeking, was the eternal verities themselves. Far am I from denying that this is, indeed, the goal toward which all of us must strive. Something of Pascal's spirit of self-search and self-reproach must come at moments to the man who finds himself summoned to the duty of shaping the progress of the law. The very breadth and scope of the opportunity to give expression to his finer self, seem to point the accusing finger of disparagement and scorn. What am I that in these great movements onward, this rush and sweep of forces, my petty personality should deflect them by a hairbreadth? Why should the pure light of truth be broken up and impregnated and colored with any element of my being? Such doubts and hesitations besiege one now and again. The truth is, however, that all these inward questionings are born of the hope and desire to transcend the limitations which hedge our human nature. Roosevelt, who knew men, had no illusions on this score. He was not positing an ideal. He was not fixing a goal. He was measuring the powers and the endurance of those by whom the race was to be run. My duty as judge may be to objectify in law, not my own aspirations and convictions and philosophies, but the aspirations and convictions and philosophies of the men and women of my time. Hardly shall I do this well if my own sympathies and beliefs and passionate devotions are with a time that is past. "We shall never be able to flatter ourselves, in any system of judicial interpretation, that we have eliminated altogether the personal measure of the interpreter. In the moral sciences, there is no method or procedure which entirely supplants subjective reason." We may figure the task of the judge, if we please, as the task of a translator, the reading of signs and symbols given from without. Nonetheless, we will not set men to such a task, unless they have absorbed the spirit, and have filled themselves with a love, of the language they must read.

. . . It has been said that "History, like mathematics, is obliged to assume that eccentricities more or less balance each other, so that something remains constant at last." The like is true of the work of courts. The eccentricities of judges balance one another. One judge looks at problems from the point of view of history, another from that of philosophy, another from that of social utility, one is a formalist, another a latitudinarian, one is timorous of change, another dissatisfied with the present; out of the attrition of diverse minds there is beaten something which has a constancy and uniformity and average value greater than its component elements. The same thing is true of the work of juries. I do not mean to suggest that the product in either case does not betray the flaws inherent in its origin. The flaws are there as in every human institution. Because they are not only there but visible, we have faith that they will be corrected. There is no assurance that the rule of the majority will be the expression of perfect reason when embodied in constitution or in statute. We ought not to expect more of it when embodied in the judgments of the courts. The tide rises and falls, but the sands of error crumble.

NOTE 25

HAND, LEARNED

Mr. Justice Cardozo*

The antinomy at the basis of a judge's work has been so often discussed that I can justify no more than a bare restatement of it. His authority and his immunity depend upon the assumption that he speaks with the mouth of others: The momentum of his utterances must be greater than any which his personal reputation and character can command, if it is to do the work assigned to it—if it is to stand against the passionate resentments arising out of the interests he must frustrate. He must pose as a kind of oracle, voicing the dictates of a vague divinity—a communion which reaches far beyond the memory of any now living, and has gathered up a prestige beyond that of any single man. Yet the customary law of English-speaking peoples stands, a structure indubitably made by the hands of generations of judges, each professing to be a pupil, yet each in fact a builder who has contributed his few bricks and his little mortar, often indeed under the illusion that he has added nothing. A judge must manage to escape both horns of this dilemma: He must preserve his authority by cloaking himself in the majesty of an overshadowing past; but he must discover some composition with the dominant trends of his time—at all hazards he must maintain that tolerable continuity without which

* Columbia L. Rev. 9, 52 Harvard L. Rev. 361, 48 Yale L. J 379 (1939). Reprinted by permission.

society dissolves, and men must begin again the weary path up from savagery.

NOTE 26

FRANK, JEROME

Law and the Modern Mind*

Lawyers and judges purport to make large use of precedents; that is, they purport to rely on the conduct of judges in past cases as a means of procuring analogies for action in new cases. But since what was actually decided in the earlier cases is seldom revealed, it is impossible, in a real sense, to rely on these precedents. What the courts in fact do is to manipulate the language of former decisions. They could approximate a system of real precedents only if the judges, in rendering those former decisions, had reported with fidelity the precise steps by which they arrived at their decisions. . . .

The decision of a judge after trying a case is the product of a unique experience. "Of the many things which have been said of the mystery of the judicial process," writes Yntema, "the most salient is that *decision is reached after an emotive experience in which principles and logic play a secondary part*. The function of juristic logic and the principles which it employs seem to be like that of language, to describe the event which has already transpired. These considerations must reveal to us the impotence of general principles to control decision. Vague because of their generality, they mean nothing save what they suggest in the organized experience of one who thinks them, and, because of their vagueness, they only remotely compel the organization of that experience. The important problem . . . is not the formulation of the rule but the ascertainment of the cases to which, and the extent to which, it applies. And this, even if we are seeking uniformity in the administration of justice, will lead us again to the circumstances of the concrete case. . . . The reason why the general principle cannot control is because it does not inform. . . . It should be obvious that when we have observed a recurrent phenomenon in the decisions of the courts, we may appropriately express the classification in a rule. But the rule will be only a mnemonic device, a useful but hollow diagram of what has been. It will be intelligible only if we *relive again the experience of the classifier*."

*   *   *

. . . If and when we have judges trained to observe their own mental processes and such judges with great

particularity set forth in their opinions all the factors which they believe led to their conclusions, a judge in passing on a case may perhaps find it possible, to some considerable extent, intelligently to use as a control or guide, the opinion of another judge announced while passing on another case. But as matters stand, reliance on precedents is illusory because judges can seldom tell precisely what has been theretofore decided.

*   *   *

Perhaps one of the worst aspects of rule-fetishism and veneration for what judges have done in the past is that the judges, in writing their opinions, are constrained to think of themselves altogether too much as if they were addressing posterity. Swayed by the belief that their opinions will serve as precedents and will therefore bind the thought processes of judges in cases which may thereafter arise, they feel obliged to consider excessively not only what has previously been said by other judges but also the future effect of those generalizations which they themselves set forth as explanations of their own decisions. When publishing the rules which are supposed to be the core of their decisions, they thus feel obligated to look too far both backwards and forwards. . . .

Such injustice is particularly tragic because it is based on a hope doomed to futility, a hope of controlling the future. Of course, present problems will be clarified by reference to future ends; but ends, although they have a future bearing, must obtain their significance in present consequences, otherwise those ends lose their significance. For it is the nature of the future that it never arrives. . . .

NOTE 27

HAND, LEARNED

The Bill of Rights*

May I start with some words of my unforgettable master, John Chipman Gray, in his Columbia Lectures on the "Nature and Sources of the Law"? "The difficulties of so-called interpretation arise when the legislature has no meaning at all; when the question which is raised on the statute never occurred to it; when what the judges have to do is, not to determine what the legislature did mean on a point that was not present to its mind, but to guess what it would have intended on a point not present to its mind, had the point been present." I cannot believe that any of us would say that the "meaning" of an utterance is exhausted by the specific content of the utterer's mind at the moment. Do you not all agree with Holmes, J., in repudiating that position which he described as follows: "We see what you are driving

---

* Selections from *Law and the Modern Mind* by Jerome Frank, Copyright 1930, 1933, 1949 by Coward McCann, Inc., copyright 1930 by Brentano's, Inc., are from Anchor Books edition, 1963. Copyright renewed in 1958 by Florence K. Frank. Reprinted by arrangement with the estate of Barbara Frank Kristein.

---

* Cambridge: Harvard University Press, 1953. (pp. 18–19). Reprinted by permission.

at, but you have not said it, and therefore we shall go on as before."[2]

What does a body of men like a legislature "mean" by the words contained in a statute? What "points" are "present" to their minds? Indeed what "points" were common in the minds of a majority of those who voted? These are unanswerable questions. All we know is that a majority has accepted the sequence of words in which the "law" has been couched, and that they expect the judges to decide whether an occasion before them is one of those that the words cover. That is an intricate process made up of many factors; perhaps the single most important one is the general purpose, declared in, or to be imputed to, the command. Gray calls the result a "guess" and indeed it is; but who are we that we should insist upon certainties in a world of no more at best than probabilities? May I break from its setting an epigram of my friend, Bernard Berenson: "In the beginning was the Guess"? Yes, my friends, in the beginning and at the ending let us be content with the "Guess.". . . .

NOTE 28

LASSWELL, HAROLD AND McDOUGAL, MYRES

Legal Education and Public Policy: Professional Training in the Public Interest*

. . . One of the basic manifestations of deference to human beings is to give full weight to the fact that they have minds. People need to be equipped with the knowledge of how democratic doctrines can be justified. They can not be expected to remain loyal to democratic ideals through all the disappointments and disillusionments of life without a deep and enduring factual knowledge of the potentialities of human beings for congenial and productive interpersonal relations. As a means of maintaining a clear and realistic appraisal of human nature, there must be deeply based recognition of the factors governing the formation of human character. No democracy is even approximately genuine until men realize that men *can* be free; and that the laborious work of modern science has provided a nonsentimental foundation for the intuitive confidence with which the poets and prophets of human brotherhood have regarded mankind. Buttressing the aspirations of these sensitive spirits stands the modern arsenal of acts about the benevolent potentialities of human nature, and a secure knowledge of methods by which distorted personality growth can be prevented or cured. Through the further application of methods that have already achieved partial success, we can

provide instruments capable of putting into practice admonitions of the moralists and visions of the dreamers. Without this knowledge, the intuitions of genius are helpless; armed with this knowledge, including knowledge of the means of further knowledge, moral intention becomes steadily more capable of fulfilling itself in reality. There is no rational room for pessimism about the *possibility* of putting morals into practice on the basis of what we know, and know we can know, about the development of human personality. Any form of crippling predestinarianism, based on myths about "heredity," whether of an individual or a race, can be brushed aside.

If democratic forms of power are to be full blooded with reality, the overwhelming mass of mankind must be provided with enough intellectual skill to make a proper evaluation of policy goals and alternatives. These skills include observation and analysis; and analysis implies intellectual tools for the understanding of human relationships. Our basic knowledge must be ever-expanding; this makes necessary an organization of scientific work capable of providing more of what we need to know about the factors that mold man and society. . . .

NOTE 29

BATOR, PAUL

Finality in Criminal Law and Federal Habeas Corpus for State Prisoners*

. . . Repose is a psychological necessity in a secure and active society, and it should be one of the aims—though, let me make explicit, not the sole aim—of a procedural system to devise doctrines which, in the end, do give us repose, do embody the judgment that we have tried hard enough and thus may take it that justice has been done. There comes a point where a procedural system which leaves matters perpetually open no longer reflects humane concern but merely anxiety and a desire for immobility. Somehow, somewhere, we must accept the fact that human institutions are short of infallible; there is reason for a policy which leaves well enough alone and which channels our limited resources of concern toward more productive ends. I want to be careful to stress that I do not counsel a smug acceptance of injustice merely because it is disturbing to worry whether injustice has been done. What I do seek is a general procedural system which does not cater to a perpetual and unreasoned anxiety that there is a possibility that error has been made in every criminal case in the legal system.

---

2. *Johnson* v. *United States*, 163 Fed. 30, 32.

* Reprinted by permission of the Yale Law Journal Co. and Fred B. Rothman & Co. from the *Yale Law Journal*, vol. 52, p. 225 (1943).

* 76 *Harvard L. Rev.* 441, 452–453. Copyright 1963 by the Harvard Law Review Association.

NOTE 30

HOLMES, OLIVER W.

The Common Law and Collected Speeches*

. . . The life of the law has not been logic: it has been experience. The felt necessities of the time, the prevalent moral and political theories, intuitions of public policy, avowed or unconscious, even the prejudices which judges share with their fellow-men, have had a good deal more to do than the syllogism in determining the rules by which men should be governed. The law embodies the story of a nation's development through many centuries, and it cannot be dealt with as if it contained only the axioms and corollaries of a book of mathematics. In order to know what it is, we must know what it has been, and what it tends to become. We must alternately consult history and existing theories of legislation. But the most difficult labor will be to understand the combination of the two into new products at every stage. The substance of the law at any given time pretty nearly corresponds, so far as it goes, with what is then understood to be convenient; but its form and machinery, and the degree to which it is able to work out desired results depend very much upon its past.

The rational study of law is still to a large extent the study of history. History must be a part of the study, because without it we cannot know the precise scope of rules which it is our business to know. It is a part of the rational study, because it is the first step toward an enlightened scepticism, that is, toward a deliberate reconsideration of the worth of those rules. When you get the dragon out of his cave on to the plain and in the daylight, you can count his teeth and claws, and see just what is his strength. . . .

---

* Reprinted from: *The Life of the Law*. John Honnold, ed. New York: Free Press, 1963 (p. 3). Reprinted by permission.

PART TWO

BEGINNING THE SEARCH FOR
A PSYCHOANALYTIC IMAGE OF MAN

Traditionally, psychoanalysts have been concerned with internal controls of human behavior and lawyers with external controls. While this may be a stereotype each has of the other, psychoanalysts and lawyers are, in fact, students of both external and internal controls. The primary emphasis of the materials in the remaining Parts of this Chapter is on psychoanalytic concepts essential to an understanding of man's internal world and its relationship to the external world. An important question is: To what extent are internal mechanisms of control reflected in and affected by the development and efficacy of external controls? In seeking answers to this question we turn to the work of Sigmund Freud. We focus first on unconscious, preconscious, and conscious mental processes and then on the development, structure, dynamics and economics of the psychic apparatus—id, ego, and superego.

Before engaging in a detailed examination of these concepts we introduce them and the techniques which led to their formulation by presenting a clinical study of Elisabeth von R., which Sigmund Freud published in 1892 as his "first full-length analysis of a hysteria," and two encyclopedia articles prepared by Freud some thirty years later, which give a general overview of psychoanalysis.

A.

An Early Clinical Study — 1892

In examining the case of Elisabeth von R. we ask: How does Freud define the problem he faces with his patient; what does he know about her; what does he want to know and why; and what assumptions is he making about the nature of man which prompt him to make these inquiries?

FREUD, SIGMUND

Fraulein Elisabeth von R. (1892)*

In the autumn of 1892 I was asked by a doctor I knew to examine a young lady who had been suffering for more than two years from pains in her legs and who had difficulties in walking. When making this request he added that he thought the case was one of hysteria, though there was no trace of the usual indications of that neurosis. He told me that he knew the family slightly and that during the last few years it had met with many misfortunes and not much happiness. First the patient's father had died, then her mother had had to undergo a serious eye-operation, and soon afterwards a married sister had succumbed to a heart-affection of long standing after a confinement. In all these troubles and in all the sick-nursing involved, the largest share had fallen to our patient.

My first interview with this young woman of twenty-four years of age did not help me to make much further progress in understanding the case. She seemed intelligent and mentally normal and bore her troubles, which interfered with her social life and pleasures, with a cheerful air—the *belle indifférence* of a hysteric, I could not help thinking. She walked with the upper part of her body bent forward, but without making use of any support. Her gait was not of any recognized pathological type, and moreover was by no means strikingly bad. All that was apparent was that she complained of great pain in walking and of being quickly overcome by fatigue both in walking and in standing, and that after a short time she had to rest, which lessened the pains but did not do away with them altogether. The pain was of an indefinite character; I gathered that it was something in the nature of a painful fatigue. A fairly large, ill-defined area of the anterior surface of the right thigh was indicated as the focus of the pains, from which they most often radiated and where they reached their

greatest intensity. In this area the skin and muscles were also particularly sensitive to pressure and pinching (though the prick of a needle was, if anything, met with a certain amount of unconcern). This hyperalgesia of the skin and muscles was not restricted to this area but could be observed more or less over the whole of both legs. The muscles were perhaps even more sensitive to pain than the skin; but there could be no question that the thighs were the parts most sensitive to both these kinds of pain. The motor power of the legs could not be described as small, and the reflexes were of medium strength. There were no other symptoms, so that there was no ground for suspecting the presence of any serious organic affection. The disorder had developed gradually during the previous two years and varied greatly in intensity.

I did not find it easy to arrive at a diagnosis, but I decided for two reasons to assent to the one proposed by my colleague, viz., that it was a case of hysteria. In the first place I was struck by the indefiniteness of all the descriptions of the character of her pains given me by the patient, who was nevertheless a highly intelligent person. A patient suffering from organic pains will, unless he is neurotic in addition, describe them definitely and calmly. He will say, for instance, that they are shooting pains, that they occur at certain intervals, that they extend from this place to that, and that they seem to him to be brought on by one thing or another. . . . Fraulein von R. behaved in quite an opposite way; and we are driven to conclude that, since she nevertheless attached sufficient importance to her symptoms, her attention must be dwelling on something else, of which the pains were only an accessory phenomenon—probably on thoughts and feelings, therefore, which were connected with them.

But there is a second factor which is even more decisively in favor of this view of the pains. If one stimulates an area sensitive to pain in someone with an organic illness or in a neurasthenic [afflicted with "nervous debility"], the patient's face takes on an expression of discomfort or physical pain. Moreover he flinches and draws back from the examination and resists it. In the case of Fraulein von R., however, if one pressed or pinched the hyperalgesic skin and muscles of her legs, her face assumed a peculiar ex-

---

* Reprinted from: Breuer, J. and Freud, S.: *Studies on Hysteria* in 2 *The Standard Edition of the Complete Psychological Works of Sigmund Freud*, James Strachey, ed. London: The Hogarth Press and the Institute of Psychoanalysis, 1955, (pp. 135–75) and Basic Books, Inc., publishers, 1957. Reprinted by permission of Hogarth and Basic Books, Inc.

pression, which was one of pleasure rather than pain. She cried out—and I could not help thinking that it was as though she was having a voluptuous tickling sensation—her face flushed, she threw back her head and shut her eyes and her body bent backwards. None of this was very exaggerated but it was distinctly noticeable, and it could only be reconciled with the view that her disorder was hysterical, and that the stimulation had touched upon a hysterogenic zone.

Her expression of face did not fit in with the pain which was ostensibly set up by the pinching of her muscles and skin; it was probably more in harmony with the subject matter of the thoughts which lay concealed behind the pain and which had been aroused in her by the stimulation of the parts of the body associated with those thoughts. . . .

. . . There were numerous hard fibers in the muscular substance, and these seemed to be especially sensitive. Thus it was probably that an organic change in the muscles of the kind indicated was present and that the neurosis attached itself to this and made it seem of exaggerated importance.

Treatment proceeded on the assumption that the disorder was of this mixed kind. We recommended the continuation of systematic kneading and faradization of the sensitive muscles, regardless of the resulting pain, and I reserved to myself treatment of her legs with high tension electric currents, in order to be able to keep in touch with her. Her question whether she should force herself to walk was answered with a decided "yes."

In this way we brought about a slight improvement. In particular, she seemed to take quite a liking to the painful shocks produced by the high tension apparatus, and the stronger these were the more they seemed to push her own pains into the background. In the meantime my colleague was preparing the ground for psychical treatment, and when, after four weeks of my pretence treatment, I proposed the other method and gave her some account of its procedure and mode of operation, I met with quick understanding and little resistance.

The task on which I now embarked turned out, however, to be one of the hardest that I had ever undertaken, and the difficulty of giving a report upon it is comparable, moreover, with the difficulties that I had then to overcome. For a long time, too, I was unable to grasp the connection between the events in her illness and her actual symptom, which must nevertheless have been caused and determined by that set of experiences.

When one starts upon a cathartic treatment of this kind, the first question one asks oneself is whether the patient herself is aware of the origin and the precipitating cause of her illness. If so, no special technique is required to enable her to reproduce the story of her illness. The interest shown in her by the physician, the understanding of her which he allows her to feel and

the hopes of recovery he holds out to her—all these will decide the patient to yield up her secret. From the beginning it seemed to me probable that Fraulein Elisabeth was conscious of the basis of her illness, that what she had in her consciousness was only a secret and not a foreign body. Looking at her, one could not help thinking of the poet's words:

Das Mäskchen da weissagt verborgnen Sinn.[1]

In the first instance, therefore, I was able to do without hypnosis, with the reservation, however, that I could make use of it later if in the course of her confession material arose to the elucidation of which her memory was unequal. Thus it came about that in this, the first full-length analysis of a hysteria undertaken by me, I arrived at a procedure which I later developed into a regular method and employed deliberately. This procedure was one of clearing away the pathogenic psychical material layer by layer, and we liked to compare it with the technique of excavating a buried city. I would begin by getting the patient to tell me what was known to her and I would carefully note the points at which some train of thought remained obscure or some link in the causal chain seemed to be missing. And afterwards I would penetrate into deeper layers of her memories at these points by carrying out an investigation under hypnosis or by the use of some similar technique. The whole work was, of course, based on the expectation that it would be possible to establish a completely adequate set of determinants for the events concerned. I shall discuss presently the methods used for the deep investigation.

The story which Fraulein Elisabeth told of her illness was a wearisome one, made up of many different painful experiences. While she told it she was not under hypnosis; but I made her lie down and keep her eyes shut, though I made no objection to her occasionally opening them, changing her position, sitting up, and so on. When she was more deeply moved than usual by a part of her story she seemed to fall into a state more or less resembling hypnosis. She would then lie motionless and keep her eyes tightly shut.

I will begin by repeating what emerged as the most superficial layer of her memories. The youngest of three daughters, she was tenderly attached to her parents and spent her youth on their estate in Hungary. Her mother's health was frequently troubled by an affection of the eyes as well as by nervous states. Thus it came about that she found herself drawn into especially intimate contact with her father, a vivacious man of the world, who used to say that this daughter of his took the place of a son and a friend with whom he could exchange thoughts.

1. "Her mask reveals a hidden sense." Adapted from Goethe's *Faust*, Part I (Scene 16).—Nevertheless, it will be seen later that I was mistaken in this.

Although the girl's mind found intellectual stimulation from this relationship with her father, he did not fail to observe that her mental constitution was on that account departing from the ideal which people like to see realized in a girl. He jokingly called her "cheeky" and "cock-sure," and warned her against being too positive in her judgments and against her habit of regardlessly telling people the truth, and he often said she would find it hard to get a husband. She was, in fact, greatly discontented with being a girl. She was full of ambitious plans. She wanted to study or to have a musical training, and she was indignant at the idea of having to sacrifice her inclination and her freedom of judgment by marriage. As it was, she nourished herself on her pride in her father, in the prestige and social position of her family and she jealously guarded everything that was bound up with these advantages. The unselfishness, however, with which she put her mother and elder sisters first, when an occasion arose, reconciled her parents completely to the harsher side of her character.

In view of the girls' ages it was decided that the family should move to the capital, where Elisabeth was able for a short time to enjoy a fuller and gayer life in the home circle. Then, however, the blow fell which destroyed the happiness of the family. Her father had concealed, or had perhaps himself overlooked, a chronic affection of the heart, and he was brought home unconscious one day suffering from a pulmonary oedema. He was nursed for eighteen months, and Elisabeth saw to it that she played the leading part at his sick-bed. She slept in his room, was ready to wake if he called her at night, looked after him during the day, and forced herself to appear cheerful, while he reconciled himself to his hopeless state with uncomplaining resignation. The beginning of her illness must have been connected with this period of nursing, for she remembered that during its last six months she had taken to her bed for a day and a half on account of the pains we have described. She asserted, however, that these pains quickly passed off and had not caused her any uneasiness or attracted her attention. And, in fact, it was not until two years after her father's death that she felt ill and became incapable of walking on account of her pains.

The gap that was caused in the life of this family of four women by her father's death, their social isolation, the breaking-off of so many connections that had promised to bring her interest and enjoyment, her mother's ill-health which was now becoming more marked—all this cast a shadow over the patient's state of feeling; but at the same time it kindled a lively desire in her that her family might soon find something to replace their lost happiness, and led her to concentrate her whole affection and care on the mother who was still living.

When the year of mourning had passed, her elder sister married a gifted and energetic man. He occupied a responsible position and his intellectual powers seemed to promise him a great future. But to his closer acquaintances he exhibited a morbid sensitiveness and an egoistic insistence on his fads; and he was the first in the family circle to venture to show lack of consideration for the old lady. This was more than Elisabeth could bear. She felt called upon to take up the fight against her brother-in-law whenever he gave her occasion, while the other women did not take his temperamental outbursts to heart. It was a painful disappointment to her that the rebuilding of their former family happiness should be thus interrupted; and she could not forgive her married sister for the feminine pliancy with which she persistently avoided taking sides. Elisabeth retained a number of scenes in her memory in this connection, involving complaints, in part not expressed in words, against her first brother-in-law. But her chief reproach against him remained the fact that, for the sake of a prospective promotion, he moved with his small family to a remote town in Austria and thus helped to increase her mother's isolation. On this occasion Elisabeth felt acutely her helplessness, her inability to afford her mother a substitute for the happiness she had lost and the impossibility of carrying out the intention she had formed at her father's death.

The marriage of her second sister seemed to promise a brighter future for the family, for the second brother-in-law, though less outstanding intellectually, was a man after the heart of these cultivated women, brought up as they had been in a school of consideration for others. His behavior reconciled Elisabeth to the institution of marriage and to the thought of the sacrifices it involved. Moreover, the second young couple remained in her mother's neighborhood, and their child became Elisabeth's favorite. Unfortunately another event cast a shadow over the year in which this child was born. The treatment of her mother's eye-trouble necessitated her being kept in a dark room for several weeks, during which Elisabeth was with her. An operation was then pronounced unavoidable. The agitation at this prospect coincided with the preparations for her first brother-in-law's move. At last her mother came through the operation, which was performed by a master hand. The three families were united at a summer holiday resort, and it was hoped that Elisabeth, who had been exhausted by the anxieties of the last few months, would make a complete recovery during what was the first period of freedom from sorrows and fears that the family had enjoyed since her father's death.

It was precisely during this holiday, however, that Elisabeth's pains and locomotor weakness started. She had been to some extent aware of the pains for a short while, but they came on violently for the first time after she had had a warm bath in the bath establishment of the little watering-place. A few days earlier she had been for a long walk—in fact a regular tramp lasting half a day—and this they connected with the appearance of the pains, so that it was easy to take the view that Elisabeth had first been "overtired" and had then "caught cold."

From this time on Elisabeth was the invalid of the family. She was advised by her doctor to devote the rest of the same summer to a course of hydropathic treatment at Gastein [in the Austrian Alps], and she went there with her mother. But a fresh anxiety now arose. Her second sister had become pregnant again and reports of her condition were most unfavorable, so that Elisabeth could hardly make up her mind to travel to Gastein. She and her mother had been there for barely a fortnight when they were called back by the news that her sister, who had now taken to her bed, was in a very bad state.

There followed an agonizing journey, during which Elisabeth was tormented not only by her pains but by dreadful expectations; on their arrival at the station there were signs that led them to fear the worst; and when they entered the sick-room there came the certainty that they had come too late to take their leave of a living person.

Elisabeth suffered not only from the loss of this sister, whom she had dearly loved, but almost as much from the thoughts provoked by her death and the changes which it brought along with it. Her sister had succumbed to an affection of the heart which had been aggravated by her pregnancy. The idea now presented itself that heart disease was inherited from the father's side of the family. It was then recalled that the dead sister had suffered during her early girlhood from chorea accompanied by a mild cardiac disorder. They blamed themselves and the doctors for having permitted the marriage, and it was impossible to spare the unhappy widower the reproach of having endangered his wife's health by bringing on two pregnancies in immediate succession. From that time onward Elisabeth's thoughts were occupied without interruption with the gloomy reflection that when, for once in a way, the rare conditions for a happy marriage had been fulfilled, this happiness should have come to such an end. Furthermore, she saw the collapse once more of all she had desired for her mother. Her widowed brother-in-law was inconsolable and withdrew from his wife's family. It appeared that his own family, which had been estranged from him during his short, happy marriage, thought this was a favorable moment for drawing him back into their own circle. There was no way of preserving the unity that had existed formerly. It was not practicable for him to live with her mother in view of Elisabeth's unmarried state. Since, also, he refused to allow the two women to have the custody of the child, which was the dead woman's only legacy, he gave them occasion for the first time to accuse him of hard-heartedness. Lastly—and this was not the least

distressing fact—a rumor reached Elisabeth that a dispute had arisen between her two brothers-in-law. She could only guess at its cause; it seemed, however, that the widower had put forward financial demands which the other declared were unjustifiable and which, indeed, in view of the mother's present sorrow, he was able to characterize as blackmail of the worst description.

Here, then, was the unhappy story of this proud girl with her longing for love. Unreconciled to her fate, embittered by the failure of all her little schemes for re-establishing the family's former glories, with those she loved dead or gone away or estranged, unready to take refuge in the love of some unknown man—she had lived for eighteen months in almost complete seclusion, with nothing to occupy her but the care of her mother and her own pains.

If we put greater misfortunes on one side and enter into a girl's feelings, we cannot refrain from deep human sympathy with Fraulein Elisabeth. But what shall we say of the purely medical interest of this tale of suffering, of its relations to her painful locomotor weakness, and of the chances of an explanation and cure afforded by our knowledge of these psychical traumas?

As far as the physician was concerned, the patient's confession was at first sight a great disappointment. It was a case history made up of commonplace emotional upheavals, and there was nothing about it to explain why it was particularly from hysteria that she fell ill or why her hysteria took the particular form of a painful abasia [inability to walk]. It threw light neither on the causes nor the specific determination of her hysteria. We might perhaps suppose that the patient had formed an association between her painful mental impressions and the bodily pains which she happened to be experiencing at the same time, and that now, in her life of memories, she was using her physical feelings as a symbol of her mental ones. But it remained unexplained what her motives might have been for making a substitution of this kind and at what moment it had taken place. These, incidentally, were not the kind of questions that physicians were in the habit of raising. We were usually content with the statement that the patient was constitutionally a hysteric, liable to develop hysterical symptoms under the pressure of intense excitations *of whatever kind*.

Her confession seemed to offer even less help toward the cure of her illness than it did toward its explanation. It was not easy to see what beneficent influence Fraulein Elisabeth could derive from recapitulating the tale of her sufferings of recent years —with which all the members of her family were so familiar—to a stranger who received it with only a moderate sympathy. Nor was there any sign of the confession producing a curative effect of this kind. During this first period of her treatment she never failed to repeat that she was still feeling ill and that her pains were as bad as ever; and, when she looked at me as she said this with a sly look of satisfaction at my discomfiture, I could not help being reminded of old Herr von R.'s judgment about his favorite daughter— that she was often "cheeky" and "ill-behaved." But I was obliged to admit that she was in the right.

If I had stopped the patient's psychical treatment at this stage, the case of Fraulein Elisabeth von R. would clearly have thrown no light on the theory of hysteria. But I continued my analysis because I firmly expected that deeper levels of her consciousness would yield an understanding both of the causes and the specific determinants of the hysterical symptoms. I therefore decided to put a direct question to the patient in an enlarged state of consciousness and to ask her what physical impression it had been to which the first emergence of pains in her legs had been attached.

With this end in view I proposed to put the patient into a deep hypnosis. But, unfortunately, I could not help observing that my procedure failed to put her into any state other than the one in which she had made her recital. I was glad enough that on this occasion she refrained from triumphantly protesting: "I'm not asleep, you know; I can't be hypnotized." In this extremity the idea occurred to me of resorting to the advice of applying pressure to the head . . . I carried this out by instructing the patient to report to me faithfully whatever appeared before her inner eye or passed through her memory at the moment of the pressure. She remained silent for a long time and then, on my insistence, admitted that she had thought of an evening on which a young man had seen her home after a party, of the conversation that had taken place between them, and of the feelings with which she had returned home to her father's sick-bed.

This first mention of the young man opened up a new vein of ideas the contents of which I now gradually extracted. It was a question here of a secret, for she had initiated no one, apart from a common friend, into her relations with the young man and the hopes attached to them. He was the son of a family with which they had long been on friendly terms and who lived near their former estate. The young man, who was himself an orphan, was devotedly attached to her father and followed his advice in pursuing his career. He had extended his admiration for her father to the ladies of the family. Numerous recollections of reading together, of exchanging ideas, and of remarks made by him which were repeated to her by other people, bore witness to the gradual growth in her of a conviction that he loved her and understood her and that marriage with him would not involve the sacrifices on her part which she dreaded from marriage in general. Unluckily, he was scarcely any older than herself and was still far from being self-supporting. But she was firmly determined to wait for him.

After her father had fallen seriously ill and she had been so much taken up with looking after him, her meetings with her friend became more and more rare. The evening which she had first remembered represented what had actually been the climax of her feeling; but even then there had been no éclaircissement between them. On that occasion she had allowed herself to be persuaded, by the insistence of her family and of her father himself, to go to a party at which she was likely to meet him. She had wanted to hurry home early but had been pressed to stay and had given way when he promised to see her home. She had never had such warm feelings toward him as while he was accompanying her that evening. But when she arrived home late in this blissful frame of mind, she found her father was worse and reproached herself most bitterly for having sacrificed so much time to her own enjoyment. This was the last time she left her sick father for a whole evening. She seldom met her friend after this. After her father's death the young man seemed to keep away from her out of respect for her sorrow. The course of his life then took him in other directions. She had to familiarize herself by degrees with the thought that his interest in her had been displaced by others and that she had lost him. But this disappointment in her first love still hurt her whenever she thought of him.

It was, therefore, in this relationship and in the scene described above in which it culminated that I could look for the causes of her first hysterical pains. The contrast between the blissful feelings she had allowed herself to enjoy on that occasion and the worsening of her father's state which had met her on her return home constituted a conflict, a situation of incompatibility. The outcome of this conflict was that the erotic idea was repressed from association and the affect attaching to that idea was used to intensify or revive a physical pain which was present simultaneously or shortly before. Thus it was an instance of the mechanism of conversion for the purpose of defence. . . .

A number of comments might, of course, be made at this point. I must emphasize the fact that I did not succeed in establishing from her memory that the conversion took place at the moment of her return home. I therefore looked about for similar experiences during the time she was nursing her father and elicited a number of them. Among these, special prominence attached, on account of their frequent occurrence, to scenes in which, at her father's call, she had jumped out of bed with bare feet in a cold room. I was inclined to attribute some importance to these factors, since in addition to complaining about the pain in her legs she also complained of tormenting sensations of cold. Nevertheless, even here I was unable to get hold of any scene which it was possible to identify as that at which the conversion had occurred. I was inclined for this reason to think that there was a gap in the explanation at this point, until

I recollected that the hysterical pains in the legs had in fact not made their appearance during the period when she was nursing her father. She only remembered a single attack of pain, which had only lasted a day or two and had not attracted her attention. I now directed my inquiries to this first appearance of the pains. I succeeded in reviving the patient's memory of it with certainty. At that very time a relative had visited them and she had been unable to receive him, owing to being laid up in bed. This same man had been unlucky enough, when he visited them again two years later, to find her in bed once more. But in spite of repeated attempts we failed to trace any psychical cause for the first pains. I thought it safe to assume that they had, in fact, appeared without any psychical cause and were a mild rheumatic affection; and I was able to establish that this organic disorder, which was the model copied in her later hysteria, had in any case to be dated before the scene of her being accompanied back from the party. From the nature of things it is nevertheless possible that these pains, being of organic origin, may have persisted for some time to a mitigated degree without being very noticeable. The obscurity due to the fact that the analysis pointed to the occurrence of a conversion of psychical excitation into physical pain though that pain was certainly not perceived at the time in question or remembered afterwards—this is a problem which I hope to be able to solve later on the basis of further considerations and later examples.

The discovery of the reason for the first conversion opened a second, fruitful period of the treatment. The patient surprised me soon afterwards by announcing that she now knew why it was that the pains always radiated from that particular area of the right thigh and were at their most painful there: It was on this place that her father used to rest his leg every morning, while she renewed the bandage round it, for it was badly swollen. This must have happened a good 100 times, yet she had not noticed the connection till now. In this way she gave me the explanation that I needed of the emergence of what was an atypical hysterogenic zone. Further, her painful legs began to "join in the conversation" during our analyses. What I have in mind is the following remarkable fact. As a rule the patient was free from pain when we started work. If, then, by a question or by pressure upon her head I called up a memory, a sensation of pain would make its first appearance, and this was usually so sharp that the patient would give a start and put her hand to the painful spot. The pain that was thus aroused would persist so long as she was under the influence of the memory; it would reach its climax when she was in the act of telling me the essential and decisive part of what she had to communicate, and with the last word of this it would disappear. I came in time to use such pains as a compass to guide me; if she stopped talking but admitted that she still

had a pain, I knew that she had not told me everything, and insisted on her continuing her story till the pain had been talked away. Not until then did I arouse a fresh memory.

During this period of "abreaction" the patient's condition, both physical and mental, made such a striking improvement that I used to say, only half-jokingly, that I was taking away a certain amount of her motives for pain every time and that when I had cleared them all away she would be well. She soon got to the point of being without pain most of the time; she allowed herself to be persuaded to walk about a great deal and to give up her former isolation. In the course of the analysis I sometimes followed the spontaneous fluctuations in her condition; and I sometimes followed my own estimate of the situation when I considered that I had not completely exhausted some portion of the story of her illness.

During this work I made some interesting observations, whose lessons I subsequently found confirmed in treating other patients. As regards the spontaneous fluctuations, in the first place, I found that in fact none had occurred which had not been provoked by association with some contemporary event. On one occasion she had heard of an illness of one of her acquaintances which reminded her of a detail of her father's illness; another time her dead sister's child had been on a visit to them, and its likeness to its mother had stirred up her feelings of grief; and yet another time a letter from her distant sister showed clear evidence of her unfeeling brother-in-law's influence and gave rise to a pain which required her to produce the story of a family scene which she had not yet told me about. Since she never brought up the same precipitating cause of a pain twice over, it seemed that we were justified in supposing that we should in this way exhaust the stock of them; and I, therefore, did not hesitate to get her into situations which were calculated to bring up fresh memories which had not yet reached the surface. For instance, I sent her to visit her sister's grave, and I encouraged her to go to a party at which she might once more come across the friend of her youth.

In the next place, I obtained some insight into the manner of origin of what might be described as a "monosymptomatic" hysteria. For I found that her *right* leg became painful under hypnosis when the discussion turned on her nursing her sick father, on her relations with the friend of her youth, or on other events falling within the first period of her pathogenic experiences; on the other hand, the pain made its appearance in her other, *left*, leg as soon as I stirred up a memory relating to her dead sister or her two brothers-in-law—in short, to an impression from the second half of the story of her illness. Having thus had my attention aroused by the regularity of this relation, I carried my investigation further and formed an impression that this differentiation went still further and that every fresh psychical determinant of painful sensations had become attached to some fresh spot in the painful area of her legs. The original painful spot in her right thigh had related to her nursing her father; the area of pain had extended from this spot to neighboring regions as a result of fresh traumas. Here, therefore, what we were dealing with was not strictly speaking a *single* physical symptom, linked with a variety of mnemic complexes in the mind, but a number of similar symptoms which appeared, on a superficial view, to be merged into one symptom. But I did not pursue further the delimitation of zones of pain corresponding to different psychical determinants, since I found that the patient's attention was directed away from this subject.

I did, however, turn my attention to the way in which the whole symptomatic complex of abasia might have been built up upon these painful zones, and in that connection I asked her various questions, such as what was the origin of her pains in walking, in standing, and in lying down? Some of these questions she answered spontaneously, some under the pressure of my hand. Two things emerged from this. In the first place she divided all the scenes with painful impressions attached to them into groups for me, according as she had experienced them while she was sitting or standing, and so on. For instance, she was *standing* by a door when her father was brought home with his heart attack, and in her fright she stood stock still as though she was rooted to the ground. She went on to add a number of other memories to this first example of fright while she was standing, till she came to the fearful scene in which once again she *stood*, as though spellbound, by her sister's deathbed. This whole chain of memories might be expected to show that there was a legitimate connection between her pains and standing up; and it might indeed be accepted as evidence of an association. But we must bear in mind that another factor must be proved to be present in all these events, one which directed her attention precisely to her standing (or, as the case may be, to her walking, sitting, etc.) and consequently led to conversion. The explanation of her attention taking this direction can scarcely be looked for elsewhere than in the circumstance that walking, standing, and lying are functions and states of those parts of her body which in her case comprised the painful zones, namely, her legs. It was therefore easy in the present case to understand the connection between the astasia–abasia [inability to walk or stand] and the first occurrence of conversion.

Among the episodes which, according to this catalogue, seemed to have made walking painful, one received special prominence: A walk which she had taken at the health resort in the company of a number of other people and which was supposed to have been too long. The details of this episode only

emerged with hesitation and left several riddles unsolved. She had been in a particularly yielding mood, and eagerly joined her party of friends. It was a fine day, not too hot. Her mother stopped at home and her elder sister had already gone away. Her younger sister felt unwell, but did not want to spoil her enjoyment; the brother-in-law began by saying that he would stay with his wife, but afterwards decided to join the party on Elisabeth's account. This scene seemed to have had a great deal to do with the first appearance of the pains, for she remembered being very tired and suffering from violent pain when she returned from the walk. She said, however, that she was not certain whether she had already noticed the pains before this. I pointed out to her that she was unlikely to have undertaken such a long walk if she had had any considerable pains. I asked her what it was in the walk that might have brought on the pain and she gave me the somewhat obscure reply that the contrast between her own loneliness and her sick sister's married happiness (which her brother-in-law's behavior kept constantly before her eyes) had been painful to her.

Another scene, which was very close to the former one in time, played a part in linking the pains with *sitting*. It was a few days later. Her sister and brother-in-law had already left the place. She found herself in a restless, yearning mood. She rose early in the morning and climbed a small hill to a spot which they had often been to together and which afforded a lovely view. She sat down there on a stone bench and gave herself up to her thoughts. These were once again concerned with her loneliness and the fate of her family; and this time she openly confessed to a burning wish that she might be as happy as her sister. She returned from this morning meditation with violent pains, and that same evening had the bath after which the pains made their final and permanent appearance.

It was further shown without any doubt that her pain in walking and standing used, to begin with, to be allayed when she was *lying down*. The pains were not linked to lying down as well until, after hearing the news of her sister's illness, she traveled back from Gastein and was tormented during the night alike by worry about her sister and by raging pains, as she lay, sleepless, stretched out in the railway carriage. And for quite a time after this, lying down was actually more painful to her than walking or standing.

In this way, firstly, the painful region had been extended by the addition of adjacent areas: Every fresh theme which had a pathogenic effect had cathected a new region in the legs; secondly, each of the scenes which made a powerful impression on her had left a trace behind it, bringing about lasting and constantly accumulating cathexis of the various functions of the legs, a linking of these functions with her feelings of pain. But a third mechanism had unmistakably been involved in the building up of her astasia–abasia. The patient ended her description of a whole series of episodes by complaining that they had made the fact of her "standing alone" painful to her. In another series of episodes, which comprised her unsuccessful attempts to establish a new life for her family, she was never tired of repeating that what was painful about them had been her feeling of helplessness, the feeling that she could not "take a single step forward." In view of this, I was forced to suppose that among the influences that went to the building up of her abasia, these reflections of hers played a part; I could not help thinking that the patient had done nothing more nor less than look for a *symbolic* expression of her painful thoughts and that she had found it in the intensification of her sufferings. . . . This psychical mechanism of symbolization did not play a prominent part with Fraulein Elisabeth von R. It did not *create* her abasia. But everything goes to show that the abasia which was already present received considerable reinforcement in this way. Accordingly, this abasia, at the stage of development at which I came across it, was to be equated not only with a functional paralysis based on psychical associations but also with one based on symbolization.

Before I resume my account of the case I will add a few words on the patient's behavior during this second phase of the treatment. Throughout the analysis I made use of the technique of bringing out pictures and ideas by means of pressing on the patient's head, a method, that is, which would be unworkable without the patient's full co-operation and willing attention. Sometimes, indeed, her behavior fulfilled my highest expectations, and during such periods it was surprising with what promptitude the different scenes relating to a given theme emerged in a strictly chronological order. It was as though she were reading a lengthy book of pictures, whose pages were being turned over before her eyes. At other times there seemed to be impediments of whose nature I had no suspicion then. When I pressed her head she would maintain that nothing occurred to her. I would repeat my pressure and tell her to wait, but still nothing appeared. The first few times when this recalcitrance exhibited itself I allowed myself to be led into breaking off the work: It was an unfavorable day; we would try another time. Two observations, however, decided me to alter my attitude. I noticed, in the first place, that the method failed in this way only when I found Elisabeth in a cheerful state and free from pain, never when she was feeling badly. In the second place, that she often made such assertions as that she saw nothing, after she had allowed a long interval to pass during which her tense and preoccupied expression of face nevertheless betrayed the fact that a mental process was taking place in her. I resolved, therefore, to adopt the hypothesis that the procedure never failed: That on every occasion under

the pressure of my hand some idea occurred to Elisabeth or some picture came before her eyes, but that she was not always prepared to communicate it to me, and tried to suppress once more what had been conjured up. I could think of two motives for this concealment. Either she was applying criticism to the idea, which she had no right to do, on the ground of its not being important enough or of its being an irrelevant reply to the questions she had been asked; or she hesitated to produce it because—she found it too disagreeable to tell. I therefore proceeded as though I was completely convinced of the trustworthiness of my technique. I no longer accepted her declaration that nothing had occurred to her, but assured her that something *must* have occurred to her. Perhaps, I said, she had not been sufficiently attentive, in which case I should be glad to repeat my pressure. Or perhaps she thought that her idea was not the right one. This, I told her, was not her affair; she was under an obligation to remain completely objective and say what had come into her head, whether it was appropriate or not. Finally I declared that I knew very well that something *had* occurred to her and that she was concealing it from me; but she would never be free of her pains so long as she concealed anything. By thus insisting, I brought it about that from that time forward my pressure on her head never failed in its effect. I could not but conclude that I had formed a correct opinion of the state of affairs, and I derived from this analysis a literally unqualified reliance on my technique. It often happened that it was not until I had pressed her head three times that she produced a piece of information; but she herself would remark afterwards: "I could have said it to you the first time."—"And why didn't you?"—"I thought it wasn't what was wanted," or "I thought I could avoid it, but it came back each time." In the course of this difficult work I began to attach a deeper significance to the resistance offered by the patient in the reproduction of her memories and to make a careful collection of the occasions on which it was particularly marked.

I have now arrived at the third period of the treatment. The patient was better. She had been mentally relieved and was now capable of successful effort. But her pains had manifestly not been removed; they recurred from time to time, and with all their old severity. This incomplete therapeutic result corresponded to an incompleteness in the analysis. I still did not know exactly at what moment and by what mechanism the pains had originated. During the reproduction of the great variety of scenes in the second period and while I was observing the patient's resistance to telling me about them, I had formed a particular suspicion. I did not venture yet, however, to adopt it as the basis of my further action. But a chance occurrence decided the matter. One day while I was working with the patient, I heard a man's footsteps in the next room and a pleasant voice which seemed to be asking some question. My patient thereupon got up and asked that we might break off for the day: she had heard her brother-in-law arrive and inquire for her. Up to that point she had been free from pain, but after the interruption her facial expression and gait betrayed the sudden emergence of severe pains. My suspicion was strengthened by this and I determined to precipitate the decisive explanation.

I therefore questioned her about the causes and circumstances of the first appearance of the pains. By way of answer her thoughts turned toward her summer visit to the health resort before her journey to Gastein, and a number of scenes turned up once more which had not been treated very completely. She recalled her state of feeling at the time, her exhaustion after her anxieties about her mother's eyesight and after having nursed her at the time of her operation, and her final despair of a lonely girl like her being able to get any enjoyment out of life or achieve anything in it. Till then she had thought herself strong enough to be able to do without the help of a man; but she was now overcome by a sense of her weakness as a woman and by a longing for love in which, to quote her own words, her frozen nature began to melt. In this mood she was deeply affected by her second sister's happy marriage—by seeing with what touching care he looked after her, how they understood each other at a single glance, and how sure they seemed to be of each other. It was no doubt to be regretted that the second pregnancy followed so soon after the first, and her sister knew that this was the reason of her illness; but how willingly she bore it because he was its cause. On the occasion of the walk which was so intimately connected with Elisabeth's pains, her brother-in-law had at first been unwilling to join in it and had wanted to stay by his sick wife. She, however, persuaded him with a look to go with them, because she thought it would give Elisabeth pleasure. Elisabeth remained in his company all through the walk. They discussed every kind of subject, among them the most intimate ones. She found herself in complete agreement with everything he said, and a desire to have a husband like him became very strong in her. Then, a few days later, came the scene on the morning after the departure of her sister and brother-in-law when she made her way to the place with a view, which had been a favorite object of their walks. There *she sat down and dreamt* once again of enjoying such happiness as her sister's and of finding a husband who would know how to capture her heart like this brother-in-law of hers. She was in pain when she stood up, but it passed off once more. It was not until the afternoon, when she had had the warm bath, that the pains broke out, and she was never again free from them. I tried to discover what thoughts were occupying her mind while she was

having the bath; but I learnt only that the bath-house had reminded her of the members of her family who had gone away, because that was the building in which they had stayed.

It had inevitably become clear to me long since what all this was about; but the patient, deep in her bittersweet memories, seemed not to notice the end to which she was steering, and continued to reproduce her recollections. She went on to her visit to Gastein, the anxiety with which she looked forward to every letter, finally the bad news about her sister, the long wait till the evening, which was the first moment at which they could get away from Gastein, then the journey, passed in tormenting uncertainty, and the sleepless night—all of these accompanied by a violent increase in her pains. I asked her whether during the journey she had thought of the grievous possibility which was afterwards realized. She answered that she had carefully avoided the thought, but she believed that her mother had from the beginning expected the worst. Her memories now went on to their arrival in Vienna, the impression made on them by the relatives who met them, the short journey from Vienna to the summer resort in its neighborhood where her sister lived, their reaching there in the evening, the hurried walk through the garden to the door of the small garden house, the silence within and the oppressive darkness; how her brother-in-law was not there to receive them, and how they stood before the bed and looked at her sister as she lay there dead. At that moment of dreadful certainty that her beloved sister was dead without bidding them farewell and without her having eased her last days with her care—at that very moment another thought had shot through Elisabeth's mind, and now forced itself irresistibly upon her once more, like a flash of lightning in the dark: "Now he is free again and I can be his wife."

Everything was now clear. The analyst's labors were richly rewarded. The concepts of the "fending off" of an incompatible idea, of the genesis of hysterical symptoms through the conversion of psychical excitations into something physical and the formation of a separate psychical group through the act of will which led to the fending off—all these things were, in that moment, brought before my eyes in concrete form. Thus and in no other way had things come about in the present case. The girl felt toward her brother-in-law a tenderness whose acceptance into consciousness was resisted by her whole moral being. She succeeded in sparing herself the painful conviction that she loved her sister's husband, by inducing physical pains in herself instead; and it was in the moments when this conviction sought to force itself upon her (on her walk with him, during her morning reverie, in the bath, by her sister's bedside) that her pains had come on, thanks to successful conversion. At the time when I started her treatment the group of ideas relating to her love had already been separated from her knowledge. Otherwise she would never, I think, have agreed to embarking on the treatment. The resistance with which she had repeatedly met the reproduction of scenes which operated traumatically corresponded in fact to the energy with which the incompatible idea had been forced out of her associations.

The period that followed, however, was a hard one for the physician. The recovery of this repressed idea had a shattering effect on the poor girl. She cried aloud when I put the situation drily before her with the words: "So for a long time you had been in love with your brother-in-law." She complained at this moment of the most frightful pains, and made one last desperate effort to reject the explanation: It was not true, I had talked her into it, it *could* not be true, she was incapable of such wickedness, she could never forgive herself for it. It was easy to prove to her that what she herself had told me admitted of no other interpretation. But it was a long time before my two pieces of consolation—that we are not responsible for our feelings, and that her behavior, the fact that she had fallen ill in these circumstances, was sufficient evidence of her moral character—it was a long time before these consolations of mine made any impression on her.

In order to mitigate the patient's sufferings I had now to proceed along more than one path. In the first place I wanted to give her an opportunity of getting rid of the excitation that had been piling up so long, by "abreacting" it. We probed into the first impressions made on her in her relations with her brother-in-law, the beginning of the feelings for him which she had kept unconscious. Here we came across all the little premonitory signs and intuitions of which a fully-grown passion can make so much in retrospect. On his first visit to the house he had taken her for the girl he was to marry and had greeted her before her elder but somewhat insignificant-looking sister. One evening they were carrying on such a lively conversation together and seemed to be getting on so well that his fiancée had interrupted them half-seriously with the remark: "The truth is, you two would have suited each other splendidly." Another time, at a party where they knew nothing of his engagement, the young man was being discussed and a lady criticized a defect in his figure which suggested that he had had a disease of the bones in his childhood. His fiancée herself listened quietly, but Elisabeth flared up and defended the symmetry of her future brother-in-law's figure with a zeal which she herself could not understand. As we worked through these recollections it became clear to Elisabeth that her tender feeling for her brother-in-law had been dormant in her for a long time, perhaps even from the beginning of her acquaintance with him, and had lain concealed all that time behind the mask of mere sisterly affection, which her highly-developed family feeling could enable her to accept as natural.

This process of abreaction certainly did her much good. But I was able to relieve her still more by taking a friendly interest in her present circumstances. With this end in view I arranged for an interview with Frau von R. I found her an understanding and sensitive lady, though her vital spirits had been reduced by her recent misfortunes. I learned from her that on closer examination the charge of unfeeling blackmail which had been brought by the elder brother-in-law against the widower and which had been so painful to Elisabeth had had to be withdrawn. No stain was left on the young man's character. It was a misunderstanding due to the different value which, as can readily be seen, would be attached to money by a business man, to whom money is a tool of his trade, and a civil servant. Nothing more than this remained of the painful episode. I begged her mother from that time forward to tell Elisabeth everything she needed to know, and in the future to give her the opportunity of unburdening her mind to which I should have accustomed her.

I was also, of course, anxious to learn what chance there was that the girl's wish, of which she was now conscious, would come true. Here the prospects were less favorable. Her mother told me that she had long ago guessed Elisabeth's fondness for the young man, though she had not known that the feeling had already been there during her sister's lifetime. No one seeing the two of them together—though, in fact, this had now become a rare event—could doubt the girl's anxiety to please him. But, she told me, neither she (the mother) nor the family advisers were particularly in favor of a marriage. The young man's health was by no means good and had received a fresh set-back from the death of his beloved wife. It was not at all certain, either, that his mental state was yet sufficiently recovered for him to contract a new marriage. This was perhaps why he was behaving with so much reserve; perhaps, too, it was because he was uncertain of his reception and wished to avoid comments that were likely to be made. In view of these reservations on both sides, the solution for which Elisabeth longed was unlikely to be achieved.

I told the girl what I had heard from her mother and had the satisfaction of benefiting her by giving her the explanation of the money affair. On the other hand I encouraged her to face with calmness the uncertainty about the future which it was impossible to clear up. But at this point the approach of summer made it urgent for us to bring the analysis to an end. Her condition was once more improved and there had been no more talk of her pains since we had been investigating their causes. We both had a feeling that we had come to a finish, though I told myself that the abreaction of the love she had so long kept down had not been carried out very fully. I regarded her as cured and pointed out to her that the solution of her difficulties would proceed on its own account now that the path had been opened to it. This she did not dispute. She left Vienna with her mother to meet her eldest sister and her family and to spend the summer together.

I have a few words to add upon the further course of Fraulein Elisabeth von R.'s case. Some weeks after we had separated I received a despairing letter from her mother. At her first attempt, she told me, to discuss her daughter's affairs of the heart with her, the girl had rebelled violently and had since then suffered from severe pains once more. She was indignant with me for having betrayed her secret. She was entirely inaccessible, and the treatment had been a complete failure. What was to be done now? she asked. Elisabeth would have nothing more to do with me. I did not reply to this. It stood to reason that Elisabeth after leaving my care would make one more attempt to reject her mother's intervention and once more take refuge in isolation. But I had a kind of conviction that everything would come right and that the trouble I had taken had not been in vain. Two months later they were back in Vienna, and the colleague to whom I owed the introduction of the case gave me news that Elisabeth felt perfectly well and was behaving as though there was nothing wrong with her, though she still suffered occasionally from slight pains. Several times since then she has sent me similar messages and each time promised to come and see me. But it is a characteristic of the personal relationship which arises in treatments of this kind that she has never done so. As my colleague assures me, she is to be regarded as cured. Her brother-in-law's connection with the family has remained unaltered.

In the spring of 1894 I heard that she was going to a private ball for which I was able to get an invitation, and I did not allow the opportunity to escape me of seeing my former patient whirl past in a lively dance. Since then, by her own inclination, she has married someone unknown to me.

Discussion

I have not always been a psychotherapist. Like other neuropathologists, I was trained to employ local diagnoses and electro-prognosis, and it still strikes me, myself, as strange that the case histories I write should read like short stories and that, as one might say, they lack the serious stamp of science. I must console myself with the reflection that the nature of the subject is evidently responsible for this, rather than any preference of my own. The fact is that local diagnosis and electrical reactions lead nowhere in the study of hysteria, whereas a detailed description of mental processes such as we are accustomed to find in the works of imaginative writers enables me, with the use of a few psychological formulas, to obtain at least some kind of insight into the course of that affection. Case histories of this kind are intended to be judged like psychiatric ones; they have, however, one advantage over the latter, namely an intimate connection between the story of the patient's sufferings and the symptoms of his illness—a connection for which we still search in vain in the biographies of other psychoses.

In reporting the case of Fraulein Elisabeth von R. I have endeavored to weave the explanations which I have been able to give of the case into my description of the course of her recovery. It may perhaps be worthwhile to bring together the important points once more. I have described the patient's character, the features which one meets with so frequently in hysterical people and which there is no excuse for regarding as a consequence of degeneracy: her giftedness, her ambition, her moral sensibility, her excessive demand for love which, to begin with, found satisfaction in her family, and the independence of her nature which went beyond the feminine ideal and found expression in a considerable amount of obstinacy, pugnacity, and reserve. No appreciable hereditary taint, so my colleague told me, could be traced on either side of her family. It is true that her mother suffered for many years from a neurotic depression which had not been investigated; but her mother's brothers and sisters and her father and his family could be regarded as well-balanced people free from nervous trouble. No severe case of neuropsychosis had occurred among her close relatives.

Such was the patient's nature, which was now assailed by painful emotions, beginning with the lowering effect of nursing her beloved father through a long illness.

There are good reasons for the fact that sick-nursing plays such a significant part in the prehistory of cases of hysteria. A number of the factors at work in this are obvious: The disturbance of one's physical health arising from interrupted sleep, the neglect of one's own person, the effect of constant worry on one's vegetative functions. But, in my view, the most important determinant is to be looked for elsewhere. Anyone whose mind is taken up by the hundred and one tasks of sick-nursing which follow one another in endless succession over a period of weeks and months will, on the one hand, adopt a habit of suppressing every sign of his own emotion, and on the other, will soon divert his attention away from his own impressions, since he has neither time nor strength to do justice to them. Thus he will accumulate a mass of impressions which are capable of affect, which are hardly sufficiently perceived, and which, in any case, have not been weakened by abreaction. He is creating material for a "retention hysteria." If the sick person recovers, all these impressions, of course, lose their significance. But if he dies, and the period of mourning sets in, during which the only things that seem to have value are those that relate to the person who has died, these impressions that have not yet been dealt with come into the picture as well; and after a short interval of exhaustion the hysteria, whose seeds were sown during the time of nursing, breaks out.

*   *   *

. . . While she was nursing her father, as we have seen, she for the first time developed a hysterical symptom—a pain in a particular area of her right thigh. It was possible by means of analysis to find an adequate elucidation of the mechanism of the symptom. It happened at a moment when the circle of ideas embracing her duties to her sick father came into conflict with the content of the erotic desire she was feeling at the time. Under the pressure of lively self-reproaches she decided in favor of the former, and in doing so brought about her hysterical pain.

According to the view suggested by the conversion theory of hysteria what happened may be described as follows. She repressed her erotic idea from consciousness and transformed the amount of its effect into physical sensations of pain. It did not become clear whether she was presented with this first conflict on one occasion only or on several; the latter alternative is the more likely. An exactly similar conflict—though of higher ethical significance and even more clearly established by the analysis—developed once more some years later and led to an intensification of the same pains and to an extension beyond their original limits. Once again it was a circle of ideas of an erotic kind that came into conflict with all her moral ideas; for her inclinations centered upon her brother-in-law, and, both during her sister's lifetime and after her death, the thought of being attracted by precisely this man was totally unacceptable to her. The analysis provided detailed information about this conflict, which constituted the central point in the history of the illness. The germs of the patient's feeling for her brother-in-law may have been present for a long time; its development was favored by physical exhaustion owing to more sick-nursing and by moral exhaustion owing to disappointments extending over many years. The coldness of her nature began to yield and she admitted to herself her need for a man's love. During the several weeks which she passed in his company at the health resort her erotic feelings as well as her pains reached their full height.

The analysis, moreover, gave evidence that during the same period the patient was in a special psychical state. The connection of this state with her erotic feelings and her pains seems to make it possible to understand what happened on the lines of the conversion theory. It is, I think, safe to say that at that time the patient did not become clearly conscious of her feelings for her brother-in-law, powerful though they were, except on a few occasions, and then only momentarily. If it had been otherwise, she would also inevitably have become conscious of the contradiction between those feelings and her moral ideas and would have experienced mental torments like those I saw her go through after our analysis. She had no recollection of any such sufferings; she had avoided them. It followed that her feelings themselves did not become clear to her. At that time, as well as during the analysis, her love for her brother-in-law was present in her consciousness like a foreign body, without having entered into relationship with the rest of her ideational life. With regard to these feelings she was in the peculiar situation of knowing and at the same time not knowing—a situation, that is, in which a psychical group was cut off. But this and nothing else is what we mean when we say that these feelings were not clear to her. We do not mean that their consciousness was of a lower quality or of a lesser degree, but that they were cut off from any free associative connection of thought with the rest of the ideational content of her mind.

But how could it have come about that an ideational group with so much emotional emphasis on it was kept so isolated? In general, after all, the part played in association by an idea increases in proportion to the amount of its affect.

We can answer this question if we take into account two facts which we can make use of as being established with certainty. (1) Simultaneously with the formation of this separate psychical group the patient developed her hysterical pains. (2) The patient offered strong resistance to the attempt to bring about an association between the separate psychical group and the rest of the content of her consciousness; and when, in spite of this, the connection was accomplished she felt great psychical pain. Our view of hysteria brings these two facts into relation with the splitting of her consciousness by asserting that the second of them indicates the *motive* for the splitting of consciousness, while the first indicates its *mechanism*. The motive was that of defense, the refusal on the part of the patient's whole ego to come to terms with this ideational group. The mechanism was that of conversion, i.e., in place of the mental pains which she avoided, physical pains made their appearance. In this way a transformation was effected which had the advantage that the patient escaped from an intolerable mental condition; though, it is true, this was at the cost of a psychical abnormality—the splitting of consciousness that came about—and of a physical illness—her pains, on which an astasia-abasia was built up.

I cannot, I must confess, give any hint of how a conversion of this kind is brought about. It is obviously not carried out in the same way as an intentional and voluntary action. It is a process which occurs under the pressure of the motive of defense in someone whose organization—or a temporary modification of it—has a proclivity in that direction.

This theory calls for closer examination. We may ask: What *is* it that turns into physical pain here? A cautious reply would be: Something that might have become, and should have become, *mental* pain. If we venture a little further and try to represent the ideational mechanism in a kind of algebraical picture, we may attribute a certain quota of affect to the ideational complex of these erotic feelings which remained unconscious, and say that this quantity (the quota of affect) is what was converted. It would follow directly from this description that the "unconscious love" would have lost so much of its intensity through a conversion of this kind that it would have been reduced to no more than a weak idea. This reduction of strength would then have been the only thing which made possible the existence of these unconscious feelings as a separate psychical group. The present case, however, is not well fitted to give a clear picture of such a delicate matter. For in this case there was probably only partial conversion; in others it can be shown with likelihood that complete conversion also occurs, and that in it the incompatible idea has in fact been "repressed," as only an idea of very slight intensity can be. The patients concerned declare, after associative connection with the incompatible idea has been established, that their thoughts had not been concerned with it since the appearance of the hysterical symptoms.

I have asserted that on certain occasions, though only for the moment, the patient recognized her love for her brother-in-law consciously. As an example of this we may recall the moment when she was standing by her sister's bed and the thought flashed through her mind: "Now he is free and you can be his wife." I must now consider the significance of these moments in their bearing on our view of the whole neurosis. It seems to me that the concept of a "defense hysteria" in itself implies that at least *one* moment of this kind must have occurred. Consciousness, plainly, does not know in advance when an incompatible idea is going to crop up. The incompatible idea, which, together with its concomitants, is later excluded and forms a separate psychical group, must originally have been in communication with the main stream of thought. Otherwise the conflict which led to their exclusion could not have taken place. It is these moments, then, that are to be described as "traumatic": It is at these moments that conversion takes place, of which the results are the splitting of consciousness and the hysterical symptom. In the case of Fraulein Elisabeth von R. everything points to there having been several such moments—the scenes of the walk, the morning reverie, the bath, and at her sister's bedside. It is even possible that new moments of the same kind happened during the treatment. What makes it possible for there to be *several* of these traumatic moments is that an experience similar to the one which original y introduced the incompatible idea adds fresh excitation to the sep arated psychical

group and so puts a temporary stop to the success of the conversion. The ego is obliged to attend to this sudden flare-up of the idea and to restore the former state of affairs by a further conversion. Fraulein Elisabeth, who was much in her brother-in-law's company, must have been particularly liable to the occurrence of fresh traumas. From the point of view of my present exposition, I should have preferred a case in which the traumatic history lay wholly in the past.

I must now turn to a point which I have described as offering a difficulty to the understanding of this case history. On the evidence of the analysis, I assumed that a first conversion took place while the patient was nursing her father, at the time when her duties as a nurse came into conflict with her erotic desires, and that what happened then was the prototype of the later events in the Alpine health resort which led to the outbreak of the illness. But it appeared from the patient's account that while she was nursing her father and during the time that followed—what I have described as the "first period"—*she had no pains whatever and no locomotor weakness*. It is true that once during her father's illness she was laid up for a few days with pains in her legs, but it remained a question whether this attack was already to be ascribed to hysteria. No causal connection between these first pains and any psychical impression could be traced in the analysis. It is possible, and indeed probable, that what she was suffering from at that time were common rheumatic muscular pains. Moreover, even if we were inclined to suppose that this first attack of pains was the effect of a hysterial conversion as a result of the repudiation of her erotic thoughts at the time, the fact remains that the pains disappeared after only a few days, so that the patient had behaved differently in reality from what she seemed to indicate in the analysis. During her reproduction of what I have called the first period she accompanied all her stories about her father's illness and death, about her impressions of her dealings with her first brother-in-law, and so on, with manifestations of pain, whereas at the time of actually experiencing these impressions she had felt none. Is not this a contradiction which is calculated to reduce very considerably our belief in the explanatory valeu of an analysis such as this?

I believe I can solve this contradiction by assuming that the pains—the products of conversion—did not occur while the patient was experiencing the impressions of the first period, but only after the event, that is, in the second period, while she was reproducing those impressions in her thoughts. That is to say, the conversion did not take place in connection with her impressions when they were fresh, but in conneetion with her memories of them. I even believe that such a course of events is nothing unusual in hysteria and indeed plays a regular part in the genesis of hysterical symptoms. . . .

*　　*　　*

. . . In some of these instances it could be established that the symptom in question had already appeared for a short time after the first trauma and had then passed off, till it was brought on again and stabilized by a succeeding trauma. There is, however, in principle no difference between the symptom appearing in this temporary way after its first provoking cause and its being latent from the first. Indeed, in the great majority of instances we find that a first trauma has left no symptom behind, while a later trauma of the same kind produces a symptom, and yet that the latter could not have come into existence without the co-operation of the earlier provoking cause; nor can it be cleared up without taking all the provoking causes into account.

Stated in terms of the conversion theory, this incontrovertible fact of the summation of traumas and of the preliminary latency of symptoms tells us that conversion can result equally from fresh symptoms and from recollected ones. This hypothesis completely explains the apparent contradiction that we observed between the events of Fraulein Elisabeth von R.'s illness and her analysis. There is no doubt that the continued existence in consciousness of ideas whose affect has not been dealt with can be tolerated by healthy individuals up to a great amount. The view which I have just been putting forward does no more than bring the behavior of hysterical people nearer to that of healthy ones. What we are concerned with is clearly a quantitative factor—the question of how much affective tension of this kind an organism can tolerate. Even a hysteric can retain a certain amount of affect that has not been dealt with; if, owing to the occurrence of similar provoking causes, that amount is increased by summation to a point beyond the subject's tolerance, the impetus to conversion is given. Thus when we say that the construction of hysterical symptoms can proceed on the strength of recollected affects as well as fresh ones, we shall not be making any unfamiliar assertion, but stating something that is almost accepted as a postulate.

I have now discussed the motives and mechanism of this case of hysteria; it remains for me to consider how precisely the hysterical symptom was determined. Why was it that the patient's mental pain came to be represented by pains in the legs rather than elsewhere? The circumstances indicate that this somatic pain was not *created* by the neurosis but merely used, increased, and maintained by it. I may add at once that I have found a similar state of things in almost all the instances of hysterical pains into which I have been able to obtain an insight. There had always been a genuine, organically-founded pain present at the start. It is the commonest and most widespread human pains that seem to be most often chosen to play a part in hysteria: In particular, the periosteal and neuralgic pains accompanying dental disease, the headaches that arise from so many different sources, and, not less often, the rheumatic muscular pains that are so often unrecognized. In the same way I attribute an organic foundation to Fraulein Elisabeth von R.'s first attack of pain which occurred as far back as while she was nursing her father. I obtained no result when I tried to discover a psychical cause for it—and I am inclined, I must confess, to attribute a power of differential diagnosis to my method of evoking concealed memories, provided it is carefully handled. This pain, which was rheumatic in its origin, then became a mnemic symbol of her painful psychical excitations; and this happened, so far as I can see, for more than one reason. The first and no doubt the most important of these reasons was that the pain was present in her consciousness at about the same time as the excitations. In the second place, it was connected, or could be connected, along a number of lines with the ideas in her mind at the time. The pain, indeed, may actually have been a consequence, though only a remote one, of the period of nursing—of the lack of exercise and reduced diet that her duties as a sick-nurse entailed. But the girl had no clear knowledge of this. More importance should probably be attached to the fact that she must have felt the pain during that time at significant moments, for instance, when she sprang out of bed in the cold of winter in response to a call from her father. But what must have had a positively decisive influence on the direction taken by the conversion was another line of associative connection: The fact that on a long succession of days one of her painful legs came into contact with her father's swollen leg while his bandages were being changed. The area on her right leg which was marked out by this contact remained thereafter the focus of her pains and the point from which they radiated. It formed an artificial hysterogenic zone whose origin could in the present case be clearly observed.

If anyone feels astonished at this associative connection between physical pain and psychical affect, on the ground of its being of such a multiple and artificial character, I should reply that this feeling is as little justified as astonishment at the fact that it is the rich people who own the most money. Where there are no such numerous connections a hysterical symptom will not, in fact, be formed; for conversion will find no path open to it. And I can affirm that the example of Fraulein Elisabeth von R. was among the simpler ones as regards its determination. . . .

*　　*　　*

B.

A Theoretical Overview — 1923–26

1.

FREUD, SIGMUND

Psychoanalysis (1923)*

Psychoanalysis is the name (1) of a procedure for the investigation of mental processes which are almost inaccessible in any other way, (2) of a method (based upon that investigation) for the treatment of neurotic disorders, and (3) of a collection of psychological information obtained along those lines, which is gradually being accumulated into a new scientific discipline.

*   *   *

[Psychoanalysis] succeeded in demonstrating that certain common mental acts of normal people, for which no one had hitherto attempted to put forward a psychological explanation, were to be regarded in the same light as the symptoms of neurotics: That is to say, they had a *meaning*, which was unknown to the subject but which could easily be discovered by analytic means. The phenomena in question were such events as the temporary forgetting of familiar words and names, forgetting to carry out prescribed tasks, everyday slips of the tongue and of the pen, misreadings, losses and mislayings of objects, certain errors, instances of apparently accidental self-injury, and finally habitual movements carried out seemingly without intention or in play, tunes hummed "thoughtlessly," and so on. All of these were shorn of their physiological explanation, if any such had ever been attempted, were shown to be strictly determined, and were revealed as an expression of the subject's suppressed intentions or as a result of a clash between two intentions one of which was permanently or temporarily unconscious. The importance of this contribution to psychology was of many kinds. The range of mental determinism was extended by it in an unforeseen manner; the supposed gulf between normal and pathological mental events was narrowed; in many cases a useful insight was afforded into the play of mental forces that must be suspected to lie behind the phenomena. Finally, a class of material was brought to light which is calculated better than any other to stimulate a belief in the existence of unconscious mental acts even in people to whom the hypo-

thesis of something at once mental and unconscious seems strange and even absurd. . . .

*   *   *

. . . A new approach to the depths of mental life was opened when the technique of free association was applied to dreams. . . . By pursuing these associations further we obtain knowledge of thoughts which coincide entirely with the dream but which can be recognized—up to a certain point—as genuine and completely intelligible portions of waking mental activity. Thus the recollected dream emerges as the *manifest dream-content*, in contrast to the *latent dream-thoughts* discovered by interpretation. The process which has transformed the latter into the former, that is to say into "the dream," and which is undone by the work of interpretation, may be called the *"dream-work."*

. . . The unrecognizability, strangeness, and absurdity of the manifest dream are partly the result of the translation of the thoughts into a different, so to say *archaic*, method of expression, but partly the effect of a restrictive, critically disapproving agency in the mind, which does not entirely cease to function during sleep. It is plausible to suppose that the *"dream-censorship,"* which we regard as being responsible in the first instance for the distortion of the dream-thoughts into the manifest dream, is an expression of the same mental forces which during the daytime had held back or *repressed* the unconscious wishful impulse.

[A]nalytic work has shown that the dynamics of the formation of dreams are the same as those of the formation of symptoms. In both cases we find a struggle between two trends, of which one is unconscious and ordinarily repressed and strives toward satisfaction—that is, wish-fulfilment—while the other, belonging probably to the conscious ego, is disapproving and repressive. The outcome of this conflict is a *compromise-formation* (the dream or the symptom) in which both trends have found an incomplete expression. The theoretical importance of this conformity between dreams and symptoms is illuminating. Since dreams are not pathological phenomena, the fact shows that the mental mechanisms which produce the symptoms of illness are equally present in normal mental life, that the same uniform law embraces both the normal and the abnormal and that the findings of research into neurotics or psychotics cannot be without significance for our understanding of the healthy mind.

*   *   *

* Reprinted from: 18 *The Standard Edition of the Complete Psychological Works of Sigmund Freud*, James Strachey, ed. London: The Hogarth Press and the Institute of Pschyoanalysis, 1955. (pp. 235–43). Reprinted by permission of Hogarth and Basic Books, Inc.

2.

FREUD, SIGMUND

Psychoanalysis (1926)*

Psychoanalysis, in its character of depth-psychology, considers mental life from three points of view: the dynamic, the economic, and the topographical.

From the first of these standpoints, the *dynamic* one, psychoanalysis derives all mental processes (apart from the reception of external stimuli) from the interplay of forces, which assist or inhibit one another, combine with one another, enter into compromises with one another, etc. All of these forces are originally in the nature of *instincts*; thus they have an organic origin. They are characterized by possessing an immense (somatic) store of power ("*the compulsion to repeat*"); and they are represented mentally as images or ideas with an affective charge. In psychoanalysis, no less than in other sciences, the theory of the instincts is an obscure subject. An empirical analysis leads to the formulation of two groups of instincts: The so-called "ego-instincts," which are directed toward self-preservation, and the "object-instincts," which are concerned with relations to an external object. The social instincts are not regarded as elementary or irreducible. Theoretical speculation leads to the suspicion that there are two fundamental instincts which lie concealed behind the manifest *ego-instincts and object-instincts*: *namely* (*a*) Eros, the instinct which strives for ever closer union, and (*b*) the instinct of destruction, which leads toward the dissolution of what is living. In psychoanalysis the manifestation of the force of Eros is given the name "*libido*."

From the *economic* standpoint psychoanalysis supposes that the mental representatives of the instincts have a charge (*cathexis*) of definite quantities of energy, and that it is the purpose of the mental apparatus to hinder any damming-up of these energies and to keep as low as possible the total amount of the excitations with which it is loaded. The course of mental processes is automatically regulated by the "*pleasure–unpleasure principle*"; and unpleasure is thus in some way related to an increase of excitation and pleasure to a decrease. In the course of development the original pleasure principle undergoes a modification with reference to the external world, giving place to the "*reality principle*," in accordance with which the mental apparatus learns to postpone the pleasure of satisfaction and to tolerate temporarily feelings of unpleasure.

Topographically, psychoanalysis regards the mental

* Reprinted from: 20 *The Standard Edition of the Complete Psychological Works of Sigmund Freud*, James Strachey, ed. London: The Hogarth Press and the Institute of Psychoanalysis, 1959. (pp. 265–68). Reprinted by permission of Hogarth and Encyclopaedia Britannica.

apparatus as a compound instrument, and endeavors to determine at what points in it the various mental processes take place. According to the most recent psychoanalytic views, the mental apparatus is composed of an "*id*," which is the repository of the instinctual impulses, of an "*ego*," which is the most superficial portion of the id and one which has been modified by the influence of the external world, and of a "*superego*," which develops out of the id, dominates the ego, and represents the inhibitions of instinct that are characteristic of man. The quality of consciousness, too, has a topographical reference; for processes in the id are entirely unconscious, while consciousness is the function of the ego's outermost layer, which is concerned with the perception of the external world.

At this point two observations may be in place. It must not be supposed that these very general ideas are presuppositions upon which the work of psychoanalysis depends. On the contrary, they are its latest conclusions and are "open to revision." Psychoanalysis is founded securely upon the observation of the facts of mental life; and for that very reason its theoretical superstructure is still incomplete and subject to constant alteration. Secondly, there is no reason for surprise that psychoanalysis, which was originally no more than an attempt at explaining pathological mental phenomena, should have developed into a psychology of normal mental life. The justification for this arose with the discovery that the dreams and mistakes ["parapraxes," such as, slips of the tongue, etc.] of normal men have the same mechanism as neurotic symptoms.

The first task of psychoanalysis was the elucidation of nervous disorders. The analytic theory of the neuroses is based on three cornerstones: the recognition of (1) "*repression*," of (2) the importance of the sexual instinct, and of (3) "*transference*."

1. There is a force in the mind which exercises the functions of a censorship, and which excludes from consciousness and from any influence upon action all tendencies which displease it. Such tendencies are described as "repressed." They remain unconscious; and if one attempts to bring them into the patient's consciousness one provokes a "*resistance*." These repressed instinctual impulses, however, have not always become powerless. In many cases they succeed in making their influence felt in the mind by circuitous paths, and the indirect or substitutive satisfactions of repressed impulses thus achieved are what constitute neurotic symptoms.

2. For cultural reasons the most intense repression falls upon the sexual instincts; but it is precisely in connection with them that repression most easily miscarries, so that neurotic symptoms are found to be substitutive satisfactions of repressed sexuality. The belief that in man sexual life begins only at puberty is incorrect. On the contrary, signs of it can be detected from the beginning of extra-uterine exist-

ence; it reaches a first culminating point at or before the fifth year ("early period"), after which it is inhibited or interrupted ("latency period") until the age of puberty, which is the second climax of its development. This diphasic onset of sexual development seems to be distinctive of the genus Homo. All experiences during the first period of childhood are of the greatest importance to the individual, and in combination with his inherited sexual constitution form the dispositions for the subsequent development of character and disease. It is wrong to make sexuality coincide with "genitality." The sexual instincts pass through a complicated course of development, and it is only at the end of it that the "primacy of the genital zones" is attained. Before this there are a number of "pregenital" organizations of the libido—points at which it may become "fixated" and to which, in the event of subsequent repression, it will return ("*regression*"). The infantile fixations of the libido are what determine the form of any later neurosis. Thus the neuroses are to be regarded as inhibitions in the development of the libido. There are no specific causes of nervous disorders; the question whether a conflict finds a healthy solution or leads to a neurotic inhibition of function depends upon quantitative considerations.

*   *   *

3. By "*transference*" is meant a striking peculiarity of neurotics. They develop toward their physician emotional relations, both of an affectionate and hostile character, which are not based upon the actual situation but are derived from their relations to their parents (the Oedipus complex). Transference is a proof of the fact that adults have not overcome their former childish dependence; it coincides with the force which has been named "suggestion"; and it is only by learning to make use of it that the physician is enabled to induce the patient to overcome his internal resistances and do away with his repressions. Thus psychoanalytic treatment acts as a second education of the adult, as a corrective to his education as a child.

NOTE

RAPAPORT, DAVID and GILL, MERTON, M.

The Points of View and Assumptions of Metapsychology*

Freud first used the term metapsychology to

* 40 *The International Journal of Psychoanalysis*, 1959, (pp. 153–59). Reprinted by permission.

indicate that his psychology deals with what is beyond the realm of conscious experience. Later, however, he defined metapsychology as the study of the assumptions upon which the system of psychoanalytic theory is based. . . .

*   *   *

The three metapsychological points of view formulated by Freud—the dynamic, the topographic, and the economic . . . require reassessment.

While the topographical conception of the mental apparatus in terms of the systems *Ucs.*, *Pcs.*, and *Cs.* was superseded by the structural conception in terms of the id, ego, and superego, Freud never explicitly replaced the topographic point of view of metapsychology by a structural one. . . .

Moreover, while the psychoanalytic theory is undoubtedly a genetic psychology, Freud apparently took this so much for granted that he saw no necessity to formulate a genetic point of view of metapsychology. It could be argued that the genetic point of view is not of the same order of abstraction as the three classical points of view, because every genetic proposition in the theory of psychoanalysis involves dynamic, economic, and structural relationships. But this argument fails to distinguish between psychoanalytic propositions on the one hand and metapsychological points of view and assumptions on the other. Even though in various psychoanalytic propositions one or another metapsychological point of view or assumption may be dominant, *all* psychoanalytic propositions involve *all* metapsychological points of view. Only the assumptions of metapsychology are independent from each other.

Finally, since Hartmann's and Erikson's studies of adaptation, it has become clear that psychoanalytic theory has always implied basic assumptions concerning adaptation, though with varying degrees of emphasis. So far, however, we have not had an explicit formulation of these assumptions or of an adaptive point of view in metapsychology. . . .

*   *   *

The genetic point of view demands that the psychoanalytic explanation of any psychological phenomenon include propositions concerning its psychological origin and development.

*   *   *

The adaptive point of view demands that the psychoanalytic explanation of any psychological phenomenon include propositions concerning its relationship to the environment.

PART THREE

ABOUT "NOT KNOWING"—
IS THERE AN UNCONSCIOUS?

We begin our detailed study of psychoanalysis with the unconscious, a concept basic to psychoanalysis as theory and therapy. In studying this concept it may prove useful to bear in mind the following questions which are raised later with regard to problems in law:

To what extent does, can, or should the State take into account the unconscious in the promulgation, invocation, and administration of its laws?

Should the unconscious be taken as a characteristic common to all human activity, and thus deemed of no special significance to decisions in law?

Should the law seek to authorize different responses for the variety of unconscious manifestations in individual human behavior?

Under what, if any, circumstances, should the legal process seek to probe the unconscious of any of its participants?

A.

For Purposes of Psychoanalysis

1.

FREUD, SIGMUND

Introductory Lectures on Psychoanalysis (1916)*

* Reprinted from: 15 *The Standard Edition of the Complete Psychological Works of Sigmund Freud*, James Strachey, ed.

[M]ental processes are in themselves unconscious and . . . of all mental life it is only certain individual acts and portions that are conscious. [P]sychoanalysis

London: The Hogarth Press and the Institute of Psychoanalysis, 1963 (pp. 21–79). Reprinted by permission of George Allen & Unwin, Ltd. and Liveright Publishing Corp, N.Y.

. . . cannot accept the identity of the conscious and the mental. It defines what is mental as processes, such as, feeling, thinking, and willing, and it is obliged to maintain that there is unconscious thinking and unapprehended willing. . . . The question whether we are to make the psychical coincide with the conscious or make it extend further sounds like an empty dispute about words; yet I can assure you that the hypothesis of there being unconscious mental processes paves the way to a decisive new orientation in the world and in science.

*   *   *

We will not start with postulates but with an investigation. Let us choose as its subject certain phenomena which are very common and very familiar but which have been very little examined, and which, since they can be observed in any healthy person, have nothing to do with illnesses. They are what are known as "parapraxes," to which everyone is liable. It may happen, for instance, that a person who intends to say something may use another word instead (a *slip of the tongue*) . . . or he may do the same thing in writing, and may or may not notice what he has done. Or a person may read something, whether in print or manuscript, different from what is actually before his eyes (a *misreading*) . . . or he may hear wrongly something that has been said to him (a *mishearing*). . . . Another group of these phenomena has as its basis *forgetting* . . . not, however, a permanent forgetting but only a temporary one. Thus a person may be unable to get hold of a *name* which he nevertheless knows and which he recognizes at once, or he may forget to carry out an *intention*, though he remembers it later and has thus only forgotten it at that particular moment. In a third group the temporary character is absent—for instance, in the case of *mislaying* . . . when a person has put something somewhere and cannot find it again, or in the precisely analogous case of *losing*. . . . Here we have a forgetting which we treat differently from other kinds of forgetting, one at which we are surprised or annoyed instead of finding it understandable. . . .

*   *   *

Let us now call in someone who knows nothing of psychoanalysis, and ask him how he explains such occurrences. His first reply will certainly be: "Oh. That's not worth explaining: They're just small chance events." What does the fellow mean by this? Is he maintaining that there are occurrences, however small, which drop out of the universal concatenation of events—occurrences which might just as well not happen as happen? If anyone makes a breach of this kind in the determinism of natural events at a single point, it means that he has thrown overboard the whole *Weltanschauung* of science. Even the *Weltanschauung* of religion, we may remind him, be-

haves much more consistently, since it gives an explicit assurance that no sparrow falls from the roof without God's special will. I think our friend will hesitate to draw the logical conclusion from his first reply; he will change his mind and say that after all when he comes to study these things he can find explanations of them. What is in question are small failures of functioning, imperfections in mental activity, whose determinants can be assigned. A man who can usually speak correctly may make a slip of the tongue (1) if he is slightly indisposed and tired, (2) if he is excited, and (3) if he is too much occupied with other things. It is easy to confirm these statements. Slips of the tongue do really occur with particular frequency when one is tired, has a headache or is threatened with migraine. In the same circumstances proper names are easily forgotten. Some people are accustomed to recognize the approach of an attack of migraine when proper names escape them in this way. When we are excited, too, we often make mistakes over words—and over *things* as well, and a "bungled action" follows. Intentions are forgotten and a quantity of other undesigned actions become noticeable if we are absent-minded—that is, properly speaking, if we are concentrated on something else. A familiar example of this absent-mindedness is the professor . . . who leaves his umbrella behind and takes the wrong hat because he is thinking about the problems he is going to deal with in his next book. All of us can recall from our own experience instances of how we can forget intentions we have formed and promises we have made because in the meantime we have had some absorbing experience.

*   *   *

[If] we examine the observations more closely, what we find does not tally entirely with this attention theory of parapraxes, or at least does not follow from it naturally. We discover that parapraxes of this kind and forgetting of this kind occur in people who are *not* fatigued or absent-minded or excited, but who are in all respects in their normal state—unless we choose to ascribe *ex post facto* to the people concerned, purely on account of their parapraxis, an excitement which, however, they themselves do not admit to. Nor can it be simply the case that a function is ensured by an increase in the attention directed upon it and endangered if that attention is reduced. There are a large number of procedures that one carries out purely automatically, with very little attention, but nevertheless performs with complete security. A walker, who scarcely knows where he is going, keeps to the right path for all that, and stops at his destination without having *gone astray*. . . . Or at all events this is so as a rule. An expert pianist strikes the right keys without thinking. He may, of course, make an occasional mistake; but if automatic playing increased the danger of bungling, that danger would be at its greatest for a virtuoso, whose playing, as a result of prolonged practice, has become *entirely* automatic. We know, on the contrary, that many procedures are carried out with quite particular certainty if they are not the object of a specially high degree of attention, and that the mishap of a parapraxis is liable to occur precisely if special importance is attached to correct functioning and there has, therefore, certainly been no distraction of the necessary attention. It could be argued that this is the result of "excitement," but it is difficult to see why the excitement should not on the contrary *increase* the attention directed to what is so earnestly intended. If by a slip of the tongue someone says the opposite of what he intends in an important speech or oral communication, it can scarcely be explained by the psycho-physiological or attention theory.

There are, moreover, a number of small subsidiary phenomena in the case of parapraxes which we do not understand and on which the explanations so far given shed no light. For instance, if we have temporarily forgotten a name, we are annoyed about it, do all we can to remember it, and cannot leave the business alone. Why in such cases do we so extremely seldom succeed in directing our attention, as we are after all anxious to do, to the word which (as we say) is "on the tip of our tongue" and which we recognize at once when we are told it? Or again: There are cases in which the parapraxes multiply, form chains, and replace one another. On a first occasion one has missed an appointment. On the next occasion, when one has firmly decided not to forget *this* time, it turns out that one has made a note of the wrong hour. Or one tries to arrive at a forgotten word by roundabout ways and thereupon a second name escapes one which might have helped one to find the first. If one searches for this second name, a third disappears, and so on. As is well known, the same thing can happen with misprints, which are to be regarded as the parapraxes of the compositor. An obstinate misprint of this kind, so it is said, once slipped into a social-democrat newspaper. Its report of some ceremonial included the words: "Among those present was to be noticed His Highness the *Kornprinz*." Next day an attempt was made at a correction. The paper apologized and said: "We should, of course, have said 'the *Knorprinz*.'"[1] . . .

* * *

[Is] there something, then, that compels me in the particular case to make the slip in one special way, or does it remain a matter of chance, of arbitrary choice, and is the question perhaps one to which no sensible answer at all can be given?

* * *

---

1. [What was intended was the "*Kronprinz* (Crown Prince)". "*Korn*" means "corn" and "*Knorr*" "protuberance."]

The most usual, and at the same time the most striking kind of slips of the tongue . . . are those in which one says the precise opposite of what one intended to say. Here, of course, we are very remote from relations between sounds and the effects of similarity; and instead we can appeal to the fact that contraries have a strong conceptual kinship with each other and stand in a particularly close psychological association with each other. There are historical examples of such occurrences. A president of the Lower House of our Parliament once opened the sitting with the words: "Gentlemen, I take notice that a full quorum of members is present and herewith declare the sitting *closed*."

* * *

[We] examined the conditions under which in general slips of the tongue occur, and afterwards the influences which determine the kind of distortion which the slip produces. But we have so far paid no attention whatever to the *product* of the slip considered by itself, without reference to its origin. If we decide to do so, we are bound in the end to find the courage to say that in a few examples what results from the slip of the tongue has a sense of its own. What do we mean by "has a sense"? That the product of the slip of the tongue may perhaps itself have a right to be regarded as a completely valid psychical act, pursuing an aim of its own, as a statement with a content and significance. So far we have always spoken of "parapraxes [faulty acts]," but it seems now as though sometimes the faulty act was itself quite a *normal* act, which merely took the place of the other act which was the one expected or intended.

The fact of the parapraxis having a sense of its own seems in certain cases evident and unmistakable. When the President of the Lower House with his first words *closed* the sitting instead of opening it, we feel inclined, in view of our knowledge of the circumstances in which the slip of the tongue occurred, to recognize that the parapraxis had a sense. The President expected nothing good of the sitting and would have been glad if he could have brought it to an immediate end. We have no difficulty in pointing to the sense of this slip of the tongue. [Or] we are told that a lady who was well known for her energy remarked on one occasion: "My husband asked his doctor what diet he ought to follow; but the doctor told him he had no need to diet: he could eat and drink what I want." Here again the slip of the tongue has an unmistakable other side to it: It was giving expression to a consistently planned program.

If it turned out . . . that not only a *few* instances of slips of the tongue and of parapraxes in general have a sense, but a considerable number of them, the *sense* of parapraxes, of which we have so far heard nothing, would inevitably become their most interesting feature and would push every other consideration into the background. We should then be able to leave all physiological or psycho-physiological factors on one side and devote ourselves to purely psychological investigations into the sense—that is, the meaning or purpose—of parapraxes. We shall, therefore, make it our business to test this expectation on a considerable number of observations.

*   *   *

[P]arapraxes . . . are not chance events but serious mental acts; they have a sense; they arise from the concurrent action—or perhaps rather, the mutually opposing action—of two different intentions. . . .

*   *   *

[I]s this the explanation of *all* cases of slips of the tongue? I am very much inclined to think so, and my reason is that every time one investigates an instance of a slip of the tongue an explanation of this kind is forthcoming. But it is also true that there is no way of proving that a slip of the tongue cannot occur without this mechanism. It may be so; but theoretically it is a matter of indifference to us, since the conclusions we want to draw for our introduction to psychoanalysis remain, even though—which is certainly not the case—our view holds good of only a minority of cases of slips of the tongue. The next question—whether we may extend our view to other sorts of parapraxis—I will answer in advance with a "yes." . . .

[W]hat significance remains for the factors put forward by the authorities—disturbances of the circulation, fatigue, excitement, absent-mindedness, and the theory of disturbed attention—if we accept the psychical mechanism of slips of the tongue which we have described? . . . The influence on the production of slips of the tongue by physiological dispositions brought about by slight illness, disturbances of the circulation, or states of exhaustion, must be recognized at once; daily and personal experience will convince you of it. But how little they explain! Above all, they are not necessary preconditions of parapraxes. Slips of the tongue are just as possible in perfect health and in a normal state. These somatic factors only serve, therefore, to facilitate and favor the peculiar mental mechanism of slips of the tongue. . . .

*   *   *

[H]ow does one discover the two mutually interfering purposes? You do not realize, probably, what a momentous question this *is*. One of the two, the purpose that is disturbed, is of course unmistakable: The person who makes the slip of the tongue knows it and admits to it. It is only the other, the disturbing purpose, that can give rise to doubt and hesitation. Now, we have already seen, and no doubt you have not forgotten, that in a number of cases this other

purpose is equally evident. It is indicated by the *outcome* of the slip, if only we have the courage to grant that outcome a validity of its own. Take the President of the Lower House, whose slip of the tongue said the contrary of what he intended. It is clear that he wanted to open the sitting, but it is equally clear that he also wanted to close it. That is so obvious that it leaves us nothing to interpret. But in the other cases, in which the disturbing purposes only *distorts* the original one without itself achieving complete expression, how do we arrive at the disturbing purpose from the distortion?

In a first group of cases this is done quite simply and securely—in the same way, in fact, as with the *disturbed* purpose. We get the speaker to give us the information directly. After his slip of the tongue he at once produces the wording which he originally intended. . . .

*   *   *

But if the subject does not himself give us the explanation of the sense of a parapraxis, where are we to find the starting points for our interpretation—the circumstantial evidence? In various directions. In the first place from analogies with phenomena apart from parapraxes: When, for instance, we assert that distorting a name when it occurs as a slip of the tongue has the same insulting sense as a deliberate twisting of a name. Further, from the psychical situation in which the parapraxis occurs, the character of the person who makes the parapraxis, and the impressions which he has received before the parapraxis and to which the parapraxis is perhaps a reaction. What happens as a rule is that the interpretation is carried out according to general principles: To begin with there is only a suspicion, a suggestion for an interpretation, and we then find a confirmation by examining the psychical situation. Sometimes we have to wait for subsequent events as well (which have, as it were, announced themselves by the parapraxis) before our suspicion is confirmed.

I cannot easily give you illustrations of this if I limit myself to the field of slips of the tongue. . . .

But I can give you a large selection of circumstantial evidence of this kind if I pass over to the wide field of the other parapraxes.

If anyone forgets a proper name which is familiar to him normally or if, in spite of all his efforts, he finds it difficult to keep it in mind, it is plausible to suppose that he has something against the person who bears the name so that he prefers not to think of him. . . .

*   *   *

[A] lady inquired from her doctor for news of a common acquaintance, but called her by her maiden name. She had forgotten her friend's married name. She admitted afterwards that she had been very unhappy about the marriage and disliked her friend's husband.

* * *

The forgetting of intentions can in general be traced to an opposing current of thought, which is unwilling to carry out the intention. But this view is not only held by us psychoanalysts; it is the general opinion, accepted by everyone in their daily lives and only denied when it comes to theory. A patron who gives his protégé the excuse of having forgotten his request fails to justify himself. The protégé immediately thinks: "It means nothing to him; it's true he promised, but he doesn't really want to do it." For that reason forgetting is banned in certain circumstances of ordinary life; the distinction between the popular and the psychoanalytic view of the parapraxes seems to have disappeared. Imagine the lady of the house receiving her guest with the words: "What? Have you come today? I'd quite forgotten I invited you for today." Or imagine a young man confessing to his fiancée that he had forgotten to keep their last rendezvous. He will certainly not confess it; he will prefer to invent on the spur of the moment the most improbable obstacles which prevented his appearing at the time and afterwards made it impossible for him to let her know. We all know, too, that in military affairs the excuse of having forgotten something is of no help and is no protection against punishment, and we must all feel that that is justified. Here all at once everyone is united in thinking that a particular parapraxis has a sense and in knowing what that sense is. Why are they not consistent enough to extend this knowledge to the other parapraxes and to admit them fully? . . .

* * *

[Let us] turn to a particularly ambiguous and obscure kind of parapraxis—to losing and mislaying. You will no doubt find it incredible that we ourselves can play an intentional part in what is so often the painful accident of losing something. . . .

Nor will anyone who has sufficiently often experienced the torment of not being able to find something that he himself has put away feel inclined to believe that there is a purpose in mislaying things. Yet instances are far from rare in which the circumstances attendant on the mislaying point to an intention to get rid of the object temporarily or permanently.

Here is the best example, perhaps, of such an occasion. A youngish man told me the following story: "Some years ago there were misunderstandings between me and my wife. I found her too cold, and although I willingly recognized her excellent qualities we lived together without any tender feelings. One day, returning from a walk, she gave me a book which she had bought because she thought it would interest me. I thanked her for this mark of attention, promised to read the book, and put it on one side. After

that I could never find it again. Months passed by, in which I occasionally remembered the lost book and made vain attempts to find it. About six months later my dear mother, who was not living with us, fell ill. My wife left home to nurse her mother-in-law. The patient's condition became serious and gave my wife an opportunity of showing the best side of herself. One evening I returned home full of enthusiasm and gratitude for what my wife had accomplished. I walked up to my desk, and without any definite intention but with a kind of somnambulistic certainty opened one of the drawers. On the very top I found the long-lost book I had mislaid." With the extinction of the motive the mislaying of the object ceased as well.

* * *

. . . The governing condition of these cases, it will be realized, is that the present psychical situation is unknown to us or inaccessible to our inquiries. Our interpretation is consequently no more than a suspicion to which we ourselves do not attach too much importance. Later, however, something happens which shows us how well-justified our interpretation had been. I was once the guest of a young married couple and heard the young woman laughingly describe her latest experience. The day after her return from the honeymoon she had called for her unmarried sister to go shopping with her as she used to do, while her husband went to his business. Suddenly she noticed a gentleman on the other side of the street, and nudging her sister had cried: "Look, there goes Herr L." She had forgotten that this gentleman had been her husband for some weeks. I shuddered as I heard the story, but I did not dare to draw the inference. The little incident only occurred to my mind some years later when the marriage had come to a most unhappy end.

Maeder tells of a lady who, on the eve of her wedding, had forgotten to try on her wedding dress and, to her dressmaker's despair, only remembered it late in the evening. He connects this forgetfulness with the fact that she was soon divorced from her husband. I know a lady now divorced from her husband, who in managing her money affairs frequently signed documents in her maiden name, many years before she in fact resumed it. I know of other women who have lost their wedding rings during the honeymoon, and I know too that the history of their marriages has given a sense to the accident. And now here is one more glaring example, but with a happier ending. The story is told of a famous German chemist that his marriage did not take place, because he forgot the hour of his wedding and went to the laboratory instead of to the church. He was wise enough to be satisfied with a single attempt and died at a great age unmarried.

* * *

. . . We may take it as the outcome of our efforts so far and the basis of our further investigations that parapraxes have a sense. Let me insist once again that I am not asserting—and for our purposes there is no need to do so—that every single parapraxis that occurs has a sense, even though I regard that as probably the case. It is enough for us if we can point to such a sense relatively often in the different forms of parapraxis. Moreover, in this respect these different forms behave differently. Cases of slips of the tongue and of the pen, etc., may occur on a purely physiological basis. I cannot believe that this is so in the types depending on *forgetting* (forgetting names or intentions, mislaying, etc.). It is very probably that there are cases of *losing* which can be regarded as unintended. It is in general true that only a certain proportion of the *errors* that occur in ordinary life can be looked at from our point of view. . . .

*   *   *

Let us pause a moment longer over the assertion that parapraxes are "psychical acts." Does this imply more than what we have said already—that they have a sense? I think not. I think, rather, that the former assertion [that they are psychical acts] is more indefinite and more easily misunderstood. Anything that is observable in mental life may occasionally be described as a mental phenomenon. The question will then be whether the particular mental phenomenon has arisen immediately from somatic, organic, and material influences—in which case its investigation will not be part of psychology—or whether it is derived in the first instance from other mental processes, somewhere behind which the series of organic influences begins. It is this latter situation that we have in view when we describe a phenomenon as a mental process, and for that reason it is more expedient to clothe our assertion in the form: "The phenomenon has a sense." By "sense" we understand "meaning," "intention," "purpose," and "position in a continuous psychical context."

*   *   *

The most interesting questions which we have raised about parapraxes and not yet answered are perhaps these. We have said that parapraxes are the product of mutual interference between two different intentions, of which one may be called the disturbed intention and the other the disturbing one. The disturbed intentions give no occasion for further questions, but concerning the latter we should like to know, first, what sort of intentions emerge as a disturbance to others, and secondly what is the relation of the disturbing intentions to the disturbed ones?

If you will allow me, I will once more take slips of the tongue as representatives of the whole class and I will reply to the second question before the first.

In a slip of the tongue the disturbing intention may be related in its content to the disturbed one, in which case it will contradict it or correct it or supplement it. Or—the more obscure and more interesting case— the content of the disturbing intention may have nothing to do with that of the disturbed one.

We shall have no difficulty in finding evidence of the former relation in instances we already know and in similar ones. In almost every case in which a slip of the tongue reverses the sense, the disturbing intention expresses the contrary to the disturbed one and the parapraxis represents a conflict between two incompatible inclinations. "I declare the sitting opened, but I should prefer it to be already closed" is the sense of the President's slip of the tongue. . . .

*   *   *

The other sort of relation between the two mutually interfering intentions seems puzzling. If the disturbing intention has nothing to do with the disturbed one, where can it have come from and why is it that it makes itself noticeable as a disturbance at this particular point? The observation which can alone give us the answer to this shows that the disturbance arises from a train of thought which has occupied the person concerned a short time before and, whether it has already been expressed in speech or not, produces this subsequent effect. It must in fact, therefore, be described as a perseveration, though not necessarily as the perseveration of spoken words. In this case too an associative link between the disturbing and the disturbed intentions is present; but it does not lie in their content but is artificially constructed, often along extremely forced associative paths.

*   *   *

We can now turn . . . to the main question, which we have long postponed, of what sort of intentions these are, which find expression in this unusual fashion as disturbers of other intentions. Well, they are obviously of very different sorts, among which we must look for the common factor. If we examine a number of examples with this in view, they will soon fall into three groups. The first group contains those cases in which the disturbing purpose is known to the speaker and, moreover, had been noticed by him before he made the slip of the tongue. . . . A second group is made up of other cases in which the disturbing purpose is equally recognized as his by the speaker, but in which he was unaware that it was active in him just before he made the slip. Thus, he accepts our interpretation of his slip, but nevertheless remains to some extent surprised at it. . . . In a third group the interpretation of the disturbing intention is vigorously rejected by the speaker; he not only denies that it was active in him before he made the slip, but seeks to maintain that it is entirely foreign to him. . . .

*   *   *

[W]hat distinguishes these three groups from one another is the differing extent to which the intention is forced back. In the first group the intention is there and makes itself noticed before the speaker's remark; only then is it rejected; and it takes its revenge in the slip of the tongue. In the second group the rejection goes further: The intention has already ceased to be noticeable before the remark is made. Strangely enough, this does not in the least prevent it from playing its part in causing the slip. But this behavior makes it easier for us to explain what happens in the third group. I shall venture to assume that a purpose can also find expression in a parapraxis when it has been forced back and not noticed for a considerable time, for a very long time perhaps, and can for that reason be denied straight out by the speaker. But even if you leave the problem of the third group on one side, you are bound to conclude from the observations we have made in the other cases that *the suppression of the speaker's intention to say something is the indispensable condition for the occurrence of a slip of the tongue.*

[P]arapraxes are the outcome of a compromise: They constitute a half success and a half-failure for each of the two intentions; the intention which is being challenged is neither completely suppressed nor, apart from special cases, carried through quite unscathed. We may conclude that special conditions must prevail in order that an interference or compromise of this kind shall come about, but we can form no conception of what they can be. . . .

*   *   *

An interesting problem attaches to the *practical* importance of slips of the pen. You may perhaps remember the case of a murderer, H., who found the means of obtaining cultures of highly dangerous pathogenic organisms from scientific institutes by representing himself as a bacteriologist. He then used these cultures for the purpose of getting rid of his near connections by this most modern of methods. Now on one occasion this man complained to the directors of one of these institutes that the cultures that had been sent to him were ineffective; but he made a slip of the pen, and instead of writing "in my experiments on mice or guinea pigs" he wrote quite clearly "in my experiments on men." The doctors at the institute were struck by the slip, but, so far as I know, drew no conclusions from it. Well, what do you think? Should not the doctors, on the contrary, have taken the slip of the pen as a confession and started an investigation which would have put an early stop to the murderer's activities? Was not ignorance of our view of parapraxes responsible in this case for an omission

of practical significance? Well, I think a slip of the pen like this would certainly have seemed to me most suspicious; but something of great importance stands in the way of using it as a confession. The matter is not as simple as all that. The slip was certainly a piece of circumstantial evidence; but it was not enough in itself to start an investigation. It is true that the slip of the pen said that he was concerned with thoughts of infecting men, but it did not make it possible to decide whether these thoughts were to be taken as a clear intention to injure or as a fantasy of no practical importance. It is even possible that a man who had made a slip like this would have every subjective justification for denying the fantasy and would repudiate it as something entirely foreign to him. You will understand these possibilities still better when later on we come to consider the distinction between psychical and material reality. But this is another instance of a parapraxis acquiring importance from subsequent events.

*   *   *

The instances of forgetting an intention are in general so uniform and so perspicuous that for that very reason they are of no interest for our investigation. Nevertheless there are two points at which we can learn something new from a study of these parapraxes. Forgetting—that is, failure to carry out—an intention points, as we have said, to a counter-will that is hostile to it. This is no doubt true; but our inquiries show that the counter-will can be of two kinds—direct or indirect. What I mean by the latter will best appear from one or two examples. If a patron forgets to put in a word with a third person on behalf of his *protégé*, this may happen because he is not really very much interested in the *protégé* and therefore has no great desire to speak on his behalf. In any case, that is how the *protégé* will understand the patron's forgetting. But things may be more complicated. The counter-will in the patron against carrying out the intention may come from another direction and may be aimed at quite a different point. It may have nothing to do with the *protégé* but may perhaps be directed against the third person to whom the recommendation was to have been made. So you see from this once more the doubts that stand in the way of a practical application of our interpretations. In spite of the correct interpretation of the forgetting, the *protégé* is in danger of being too distrustful and of doing his patron a grave injustice. Or, supposing someone forgets an appointment which he has promised someone else to keep, the most frequent reason for it will be, no doubt, a direct disinclination to meeting this person. But in such a case analysis might show that the disturbing purpose did not relate to him but was directed against the place at which the meeting was planned to happen and was avoided on account of a distressing memory attaching to it.

Or, again, if someone forgets to post a letter, the counter-purpose may be based on the contents of the letter; but it is by no means out of the question that the letter may be harmless in itself and may only be subject to the counter-purpose because something about it recalls another letter which had been written on some earlier occasion and which offered the counter-will a direct point of attack. It can be said, therefore, that here the counter-will was transferred from the earlier letter, which justified it, to the present one, which it had in fact no grounds for concern about. You see, then, that we must practice restraint and foresight in applying our interpretations, justified as they are: Things that are psychologically equivalent may in practice have a great variety of meanings.

Phenomena such as these last may seem to you most unusual, and you will perhaps be inclined to suppose that an "indirect" counter-will already indicates that the process is a pathological one. But I can assure you that it occurs as well within the limits of what is normal and healthy. Moreover, you should not misunderstand me. I am far from admitting that our analytic interpretations are untrustworthy. The ambiguities in the forgetting of intentions which I have been mentioning exist only so long as we have not made an analysis of the case and are only making our interpretations on the basis of our general assumptions. If we carry out an analysis upon the person in question, we invariably learn with sufficient certainty whether the counter-will is a direct one or what other origin it may have.

The second point I have in mind is this. If in a large majority of instances we find confirmation of the fact that the forgetting of an intention goes back to a counter-will, we grow bold enough to extend the solution to another set of instances in which the person under analysis does not confirm but denies the counter-will we have inferred. Take as examples of this such extremely common events as forgetting to return books one has been lent or to pay bills or debts. We shall venture to insist to the person concerned that an intention exists in him to keep the books and not to pay the debts, while he will deny this intention but will not be able to produce any other explanation of his behavior. Thereupon we shall go on to say that he has this intention but knows nothing about it, but that it is enough for us that it reveals its presence by producing the forgetting in him. He may repeat to us that he has in fact forgotten. You will now recognize the situation as one in which we found ourselves once before. If we want to pursue our interpretations of parapraxes, which have so frequently proved justified, to a consistent conclusion, we are forced to the inescapable hypothesis that there are purposes in people which can become operative without their knowing about them. . . .

*   *   *

NOTES

NOTE 1

FREUD, SIGMUND

The Psychopathology of Everyday Life (1901)*

. . . Does the elucidation . . . of parapraxes and chance actions apply quite generally or only in certain cases? And if the latter, what are the conditions under which it can be called in to explain phenomena that might also have been brought about in another way? In answering this question my experiences leave me in the lurch. I can but utter a warning against supposing that a connection of the kind here demonstrated is only rarely found; for every time I have made the test on myself or on my patients, a connection has been clearly shown to exist just as in the examples reported, or there have at least been good grounds for supposing that it did. It is not surprising if success in finding the hidden meaning of a symptomatic act is not achieved every time, for the magnitude of the internal resistances opposing the solution comes into account as a deciding factor. Equally, it is not possible to interpret every single dream of one's own or of one's patients; to prove that the theory holds good in general it is enough if one can penetrate a part of the way into the hidden connection. It often happens that a dream which proves refractory during an attempt to solve it the next day will allow its secret to be wrested from it a week or a month later, after a real change has come about in the meantime and has reduced the contending psychical values. The same applies to the solving of parapraxes and symptomatic acts. . . .

[W]e must not overlook the fact that repressed thoughts and impulses certainly do not achieve expression in symptomatic acts and parapraxes by their own unaided efforts. The technical possibility for such side-slipping on the part of the innervations must be presented independently; this will then be readily exploited by the intention of the repressed to make itself felt consciously. In the case of verbal parapraxes, detailed investigations by philosophers and philologists have endeavored to determine what are the structural and functional relations that put themselves at the service of such an intention. If we distinguish, among the determinants of parapraxes and symptomatic acts, between the unconscious motive on the one hand and the physiological and psychophysical relations that come to meet it on the other, it remains an open question whether there are, within the range of normality yet other factors that can—like the unconscious motive, and in place of it—create para-

———————
* Reprinted from: 6 *The Standard Edition of the Complete Psychological Works of Sigmund Freud*, James Strachey, ed. London: The Hogarth Press and the Institute of Psychoanalysis, 1963, (pp. 269–71). Reprinted by permission of Ernest Benn, Ltd. and The Macmillan Co.

praxes and symptomatic acts along the lines of these relations. It is not my task to answer this question.

NOTE 2

JONES, ERNEST

The Repression Theory in its Relation to Memory (1915)*

. . . In working with psychoanalysis one finds that the unconscious material in the mind is very much more extensive than might have been surmised, that the assimilative capacity of the complexes, due to the radiation of affect, is very much greater, and that, therefore, the number of associations that are established in the unconscious is simply enormous. That being so, it is extremely difficult, and at present impossible, to set any limits to the extent to which operations characteristically applying to unconscious material, such as repression does, are in action. One is practically never in a position, for instance, to assert that such and such an idea cannot have been associated with any "unpleasant" buried complex, for to be so would necessitate a most searching investigation of all its associations, both conscious and unconscious. It is rather like the question of the alleged destruction or fading of forgotten memories, a negative proposition that it is impossible to prove. One can only say, with considerable emphasis, that the more extensive the investigation the greater is the number of forgotten ideas that prove to be affectively connected with repressed complexes, so that the possibility is at least open that they all are.

NOTE 3

FREUD, SIGMUND

Some Elementary Lessons in Psychoanalysis (1938)**

[I]t is possible in the case of persons in a state of hypnosis to prove experimentally that there are such things as unconscious psychical acts and that consciousness is not an indispensable condition of [psychical] activity. Anyone who has witnessed such an experiment will receive an unforgettable impression and a conviction that can never be shaken. Here is more or less what happens. The doctor enters the hospital ward, puts his umbrella in the corner, hypnotizes one of the patients and says to him: "I'm going out now. When I come in again, you will come

to meet me with my umbrella open and hold it over my head." The doctor and his assistants then leave the ward. As soon as they come back, the patient, who is no longer under hypnosis, carries out exactly the instructions that were given him while he was hypnotized. The doctor questions him: "What's this you're doing? What's the meaning of all this?" The patient is clearly embarrassed. He makes some lame remark such as "I only thought, Doctor, as it's raining outside you'd open your umbrella in the room before you went out." The explanation is obviously quite inadequate and made up on the spur of the moment to offer some sort of motive for his senseless behavior. It is clear to us spectators that he is in ignorance of his real motive. We, however, know what it is, for we were present when the suggestion was made to him which he is now carrying out, while he himself knows nothing of the fact that it is at work in him.

NOTE 4

FREUD, SIGMUND

Introductory Lectures on Psychoanalysis (1916)*

*   *   *

A lady, nearly thirty years of age, who suffered from the most severe obsessional manifestations . . . performed (among others) the following remarkable obsessional action many times a day. She ran from her room into another neighboring one, took up a particular position there beside a table that stood in the middle, rang the bell for her housemaid, sent her on some indifferent errand or let her go without one, and then ran back into her own room. This was certainly not a very distressing symptom, but was nevertheless calculated to excite curiosity. . . . Whenever I asked the patient "Why do you do that? What sense has it?" she answered: "I don't know." But one day, after I had succeeded in defeating a major, fundamental doubt of hers, she suddenly knew the answer and told me what it was that was connected with the obsessional action. More than ten years before, she had married a man very much older than herself, and on the wedding-night he was impotent. Many times during the night he had come running from his room into hers to try once more, but every time without success. Next morning he had said angrily: "I should feel ashamed in front of the housemaid when she makes the bed," took up a bottle of red ink that happened to be in the room and poured its contents over the sheet, but not on the exact place where a stain would have been appropriate. I could

---

* Reprinted from: *Papers on Psychoanalysis*. London: Bailliere, Tindall & Cox, 1920. (p. 117). Reprinted by permission of Bailliere, Tindall & Cassell, Ltd.
** Reprinted from: 23 *The Standard Edition of the Complete Psychological Works of Sigmund Freud*, James Strachey, ed. London: The Hogarth Press and the Institute of Psychoanalysis, 1964. (p. 285) and 2 *Collected Papers of Sigmund Freud*, American edition published by Basic Books, Inc., 1959. Reprinted by permission of Hogarth and Basic Books, Inc.

---

* 16 *The Standard Edition of the Complete Psychological Works of Sigmund Freud*, James Strachey, ed. London: The Hogarth Press and the Institute of Psychoanalysis, 1963 (pp. 261–279). Reprinted by permission of George Allen & Unwin and Liveright Publishing Co.

not understand at first what this recollection had to do with the obsessional action in question; the only resemblance I could find was in the repeated running from one room into the other, and perhaps also in the entrance of the housemaid. My patient then led me up to the table in the second room and showed me a big stain on the tablecloth. She further explained that she took up her position in relation to the table in such a way that the maid who had been sent for could not fail to see the stain. There could no longer be any doubt of the intimate connection between the scene on her wedding-night and her present obsessional action, though all kinds of other things remained to be learnt.

It was clear, in the first place, that the patient was identifying herself with her husband; she was playing his part by imitating his running from one room into the other. Further, to carry on the analogy, we must agree that the bed and the sheet were replaced by the table and the tablecloth. This might seem arbitrary, but surely we have not studied dream-symbolism to no purpose. In dreams too we often find a table which has to be interpreted as a bed. Table and bed together stand for marriage, so that the one can easily take the place of the other.

It already seems proved that the obsessional action had a sense; it appears to have been a representation, a repetition, of the significant scene. But we are not obliged to come to a halt here. If we examine the relation between the two more closely, we shall probably obtain information about something that goes further—about the intention of the obsessional action. Its kernel was obviously the summoning of the housemaid, before whose eyes the patient displayed the stain, in contrast to her husband's remark that he would feel ashamed in front of the maid. Thus he, whose part she was playing, did not feel ashamed in front of the maid; accordingly the stain was in the right place. We see, therefore, that she was not simply repeating the scene, she was continuing and at the same time correcting it; she was putting it right. But by this she was also correcting the other thing, which had been so distressing that night and had made the expedient with the red ink necessary—his impotence. So the obsessional action was saying: "No, it's not true. He had no need to feel ashamed in front of the housemaid; he was not impotent." It represented this wish, in the manner of a dream, as fulfilled in a present-day action; it served the purpose of making her husband superior to his past mishap.

*   *   *

. . . I have described to you how our first patient carried out a senseless obsessional action and how she reported an intimate memory from her past life as having some connection with it: and how afterwards I examined the connection between the two and discovered the intention of the obsessional action from its relation to the memory. But there is one factor which I entirely neglected, though it deserves our fullest attention. However often the patient repeated her obsessional action, she knew nothing of its being derived from the experience she had had. The connection between the two was hidden from her; she could only quite truthfully reply that she did not know what it was that was making her carry out her action. Then suddenly one day, under the influence of the treatment, she succeeded in discovering the connection and reported it to me. But she still knew nothing of the intention with which she was performing the obsessional action—the intention of correcting a distressing portion of the past and of putting her beloved husband in a better light. It took a fairly long time and called for much labour before she understood and admitted to me that such a motive alone could have been the driving force of her obsessional action.

The link with the scene after her unhappy wedding-night and the patient's affectionate motive constituted, taken together, what we have called the "sense" of the obsessional action. But while she was carrying out the obsessional action this sense had been unknown to her in both directions—both its "whence" and its "whither". . . . Mental processes had therefore been at work in her and the obsessional action was the effect of them; she had been aware of this effect in a normal mental fashion, but none of the mental predeterminants of this effect came to the knowledge of her consciousness. She behaved in precisely the same way as a hypnotized subject whom Bernheim had ordered to open an umbrella in the hospital ward five minutes after he woke up. The man carried out this instruction when he was awake, but he could produce no motive for his action. It is a state of affairs of this sort that we have before our eyes when we speak of the existence of *unconscious mental processes*. . . .

. . . We must recognize . . . that these symptoms of obsessional neurosis, these ideas and impulses which emerge one knows not whence, which prove so resistant to every influence from an otherwise normal mind, which give the patient himself the impression of being all-powerful guests from an alien world, immortal beings intruding into the turmoil of mortal life—these symptoms offer the plainest indication of there being a special region of the mind, shut off from the rest. . . . Obsessional ideas and obsessional impulses are not, of course, themselves unconscious, any more than the performance of obsessional actions escapes conscious perception. They would not have become symptoms if they had not forced their way into consciousness. But their physical predeterminants which we infer by means of analysis, the connections into which we insert them by interpretation, are unconscious, at least until we have made them conscious to the patient by the work of analysis.

If, now, you consider further that the state of affairs which we have established in our . . . [case] is confirmed for every symptom of every neurotic illness— that always and everywhere the sense of the symptoms is unknown to the patient and that analysis regularly shows that these symptoms are derivatives of unconscious processes but can, subject to a variety of favorable circumstances, be made conscious—if you consider this, you will understand that in psychoanalysis we cannot do without what is at the same time unconscious and mental, and are accustomed to operate with it as though it were something palpable to the senses. . . . To say it for our ends once again: the possibility of giving a sense to neurotic symptoms by analytic interpretation is an unshakeable proof of the existence—or, if you prefer it, of the necessity for the hypothesis—of unconscious mental processes.

*   *   *

2.

FREUD, SIGMUND

The Ego and the Id (1923)*

The division of the psychical into what is conscious and what is unconscious is the fundamental premise of psychoanalysis; and it alone makes it possible for psychoanalysis to understand the pathological processes in mental life, which are as common as they are important, and to find a place for them in the framework of science. To put it once more, in a different way: Psychoanalysis cannot situate the essence of the psychical in consciousness, but is obliged to regard consciousness as a quality of the psychical, which may be present in addition to other qualities or may be absent.

*   *   *

"Being conscious" is in the first place a purely descriptive term, resting on perception of the most immediate and certain character. Experience goes on to show that a psychical element (for instance, an idea) is not as a rule conscious for a protracted length of time. On the contrary, a state of consciousness is characteristically very transitory; an idea that is conscious now is no longer so a moment later, although it can become so again under certain conditions that are easily brought about. In the interval the idea was—we do not know what. We can say

* Reprinted from: 19 *The Standard Edition of the Complete Psychological Works of Sigmund Freud*, James Strachey, ed. London: The Hogarth Press and the Institute of Psychoanalysis, 1961. (pp. 13–18). Reprinted by permission of Hogarth and W. W. Norton & Co.

that it was *latent*, and by this we mean that it was *capable of becoming conscious* at any time. Or, if we say that it was *unconscious*, we shall also be giving a correct description of it. Here "unconscious" coincides with "latent and capable of becoming conscious." The philosophers would no doubt object: "No, the term "unconscious" is not applicable here; so long as the idea was in a state of latency it was not anything psychical at all." To contradict them at this point would lead to nothing more profitable than a verbal dispute.

But we have arrived at the term or concept of the unconscious along another path, by considering certain experiences in which mental *dynamics* play a part. We have found—that is, we have been obliged to assume—that very powerful mental processes or ideas exist (and here a quantitative or *economic* factor comes into question for the first time) which can produce all the effects in mental life that ordinary ideas do (including effects that can in their turn become conscious as ideas), though they themselves do not become conscious. [A]t this point psychoanalytic theory steps in and asserts that the reason why such ideas cannot become conscious is that a certain force opposes them, that otherwise they could become conscious, and that it would then be apparent how little they differ from other elements which are admittedly psychical. The fact that in the technique of psychoanalysis a means has been found by which the opposing force can be removed and the ideas in question made conscious renders this theory irrefutable. The state in which the ideas existed before being made conscious is called by us *repression*, and we assert that the force which instituted the repression and maintains it is perceived as *resistance* during the work of analysis.

Thus we obtain our concept of the unconscious from the theory of repression. The repressed is the prototype of the unconscious for us. We see, however, that we have two kinds of unconscious—the one which is latent but capable of becoming conscious, and the one which is repressed and which is not, in itself and without more ado, capable of becoming conscious. This piece of insight into psychical dynamics cannot fail to affect terminology and description. The latent, which is unconscious only descriptively, not in the dynamic sense, we call *preconscious*; we restrict the term *unconscious* to the dynamically unconscious repressed; so that now we have three terms, conscious (*Cs.*), preconscious (*Pcs.*), and unconscious (*Ucs.*), whose sense is no longer purely descriptive. The *Pcs.* is presumably a great deal closer to the *Cs.* than is the *Ucs.*, and since we have called the *Ucs.* psychical we shall with even less hesitation call the latent *Pcs.* psychical. . . .

We can now play about comfortably with our three terms, *Cs.*, *Pcs.*, and *Ucs.*, so long as we do not forget that in the descriptive sense there are two kinds of unconscious, but in the dynamic sense only one.[1] For purposes of exposition this distinction can in some cases be ignored, but in others it is of course indispensable. At the same time, we have become more or less accustomed to this ambiguity of the unconscious and have managed pretty well with it. As far as I can see, it is impossible to avoid this ambiguity; the distinction between conscious and unconscious is in the last resort a question of perception, which must be answered "yes" or "no," and the act of perception itself tells us nothing of the reason why a thing is or is not perceived. No one has a right to complain because the actual phenomenon expresses the dynamic factor ambiguously.

*   *   *

1. [Strachey, Alix. *The Descriptive and the Dynamic Unconscious:* On October 28, 1923, a few months after this work appeared, Ferenczi wrote to Freud in these terms: . . . "On p. 13 I find the following: '. . . that in the descriptive sense there are two kinds of unconscious, but in the dynamic sense only one.' Since, however, you write on p. 12 that the latent unconscious is unconscious only descriptively, not in the dynamic sense, I had thought that it was precisely the dynamic line of approach that called for the hypothesis of there being two sorts of *Ucs.,* while description knows only *Cs.* and *Ucs.*"

To this Freud replied on October 30, 1923: ". . . Your question about the passage on p. 13 of *The Ego and the Id* has positively horrified me. What appears there gives a directly opposite sense to p. 12; and in the sentence on p. 13 'descriptive' and 'dynamic' have simply been transposed."

A little consideration of this startling affair suggests, however, that Ferenczi's criticism was based on a misunderstanding and that Freud was over-hasty in accepting it. . . .

We will start off with the first half of Freud's later sentence: "In the descriptive sense there are two kinds of unconscious." The meaning of this seems perfectly clear: The term "unconscious" in its descriptive sense covers two things—the latent unconscious and the repressed unconscious. Freud might, however, have expressed the idea even more clearly. Instead of "two kinds of unconscious" he might have said explicitly that in the descriptive sense there are "two kinds of things that are unconscious." And in fact Ferenczi evidently misunderstood the words: He took them to be saying that the term "descriptively unconscious" had two different *meanings*. This, as he rightly saw, could not be so: The term unconscious, used descriptively, could only have one meaning—that the thing it was applied to was not conscious. In logical terminology, he thought Freud was speaking of the *connotation* of the term whereas he was actually speaking of its *denotation*.

We now proceed to the second half of Freud's later sentence: ". . . but in the dynamic sense [there is] only one [kind of unconscious]." Here again the meaning seems perfectly clear: The term "unconscious" in its dynamic sense covers only one thing—the repressed unconscious. This is once more a statement about the *denotation* of the term; though even if it had been about its *connotation* it would still be true—the term "dynamic unconscious" can only have one meaning. Ferenczi, however, objects to it, on the ground that "it was precisely the dynamic line of approach that called for the hypothesis of there being two sorts of *Ucs.*" Ferenczi was once more misunderstanding Freud. He took him to be saying that if we consider the term "unconscious," bearing dynamic factors in mind, we see that it has only one meaning—which would, of course, have been the opposite of everything that Freud was arguing. Whereas what Freud really meant was that all the things that are unconscious dynamically (i.e., that are repressed) fall into one class. . . . [ibid. at 60–61].]

*   *   *

NOTES

NOTE 1

FREUD, SIGMUND

The Unconscious (1915)*

It would . . . be wrong to imagine that the *Ucs.* remains at rest while the whole work of the mind is performed by the *Pcs.*—that the *Ucs.* is something finished with, a vestigial organ, a residuum from the process of development. It is wrong also to suppose that communication between the two systems is confined to the act of repression, with the *Pcs.* casting everything that seems disturbing to it into the abyss of the *Ucs.* On the contrary, the *Ucs.* is alive and capable of development and maintains a number of other relations with the *Pcs.,* amongst them that of co-operation. In brief, it must be said that the *Ucs.* is continued into what are known as derivatives, that is accessible to the impressions of life, that it constantly influences the *Pcs.,* and is even, for its part, subjected to influences from the *Pcs.*

*   *   *

Among the derivatives of the *Ucs.* instinctual impulses . . . there are some which unite in themselves characters of an opposite kind. On the one hand, they are highly organized, free from self-contradiction, have made use of every acquisition of the system *Cs.* and would hardly be distinguished in our judgment from the formations of that system. On the other hand they are unconscious and are incapable of becoming conscious. Thus *qualitatively* they belong to the system *Pcs.,* but *factually* to the *Ucs.* . . . Of such a nature are those fantasies of normal people as well as of neurotics which we have recognized as preliminary stages in the formation both of dreams and of symptoms and which, in spite of their high degree of organization, remain repressed and therefore cannot become conscious. They draw near to consciousness and remain undisturbed so long as they do not have an intense cathexis, but as soon as they exceed a certain height of cathexis they are thrust back. Substitutive formations, too, are highly organized derivatives of the *Ucs.* of this kind; but these succeed in breaking through into consciousness, when circumstances are favorable—for example, if they happen to join forces with an anticathexis from the *Pcs.*

. . . To consciousness the whole sum of psychical processes presents itself as the realm of the preconscious. A very great part of this preconscious

* Reprinted from: 14 *The Standard Edition of the Complete Psychological Works of Sigmund Freud*, James Strachey, ed. London: The Hogarth Press and the Institute of Psychoanalysis, 1957. (pp. 190–95) and 4 *Collected Papers of Sigmund Freud*, American edition published by Basic Books, Inc., 1959. Reprinted by permission of Hogarth and Basic Books, Inc.

originates in the unconscious, has the character of its derivatives, and is subjected to a censorship before it can become conscious. Another part of the *Pcs.* is capable of becoming conscious without any censorship. Here we come upon a contradiction of an earlier assumption. In discussing the subject of repression we were obliged to place the censorship which is decisive for becoming conscious between the systems *Ucs.* and *Pcs.* Now it becomes probable that there is a censorship between the *Pcs.* and the *Cs.* Nevertheless we shall do well not to regard this complication as a difficulty, but to assume that to every transition from one system to that immediately above it (that is, every advance to a higher stage of psychical organization) there corresponds a new censorship. . . .

The reason for all these difficulties is to be found in the circumstance that the attribute of being conscious, which is the only characteristic of psychical processes that is directly presented to us, is in no way suited to serve as a criterion for the differentiation of systems. Apart from the fact that the conscious is not always conscious but also at times latent, observation has shown that much that shares the characteristics of the system *Pcs.* does not become conscious; and we learn in addition that the act of becoming conscious is dependent on the attention of the *Pcs.* being turned in certain directions. Hence consciousness stands in no simple relation either to the different systems or to repression. The truth is that it is not only the psychically repressed that remains alien to consciousness, but also some of the impulses which dominate our ego—something, therefore, that forms the strongest functional antithesis to the repressed. The more we seek to win our way to a metapsychological view of mental life, the more we must learn to emancipate ourselves from the importance of the symptom of "being conscious."

So long as we still cling to this belief we see our generalizations regularly broken through by exceptions. On the one hand we find that derivatives of the *Ucs.* become conscious as substitutive formations and symptoms—generally, it is true, after having undergone great distortion as compared with the unconscious, though often retaining many characteristics which call for repression. On the other hand, we find that many preconscious formations remain unconscious, though we should have expected that, from their nature, they might very well have become conscious. Probably in the latter case the stronger attraction of the *Ucs.* is asserting itself. We are led to look for the more important distinction as lying, not between the conscious and the preconscious, but between the preconscious and the unconscious. The *Ucs.* is turned back on the frontier of the *Pcs.* by the censorship, but derivatives of the *Ucs.* can circumvent this censorship, achieve a high degree of organization and reach a certain intensity of cathexis in the *Pcs.* When, however, this intensity is exceeded

and they try to force themselves into consciousness, they are recognized as derivatives of the *Ucs.* and are repressed afresh at the new frontier of censorship, between the *Pcs.* and the *Cs.* Thus the first of these censorships is exercised against the *Ucs.* itself, and the second against its *Pcs.* derivatives. One might suppose that in the course of individual development the censorship had taken a step forward.

In psychoanalytic treatment the existence of the second censorship, located between the systems *Pcs.* and *Cs.*, is proved beyond question. We require the patient to form numerous derivatives of the *Ucs.*, we make him pledge himself to overcome the objections of the censorship to these preconscious formations becoming conscious, and by overthrowing *this* censorship, we open up the way to abrogating the repression accomplished by the *earlier* one. To this let us add that the existence of the censorship between the *Pcs.* and the *Cs.* teaches us that becoming conscious is no mere act of perception, but is probably also a *hypercathexis*, a further advance in the psychical organization.

Let us turn to the communications between the *Ucs.* and the other systems, less in order to establish anything new than in order to avoid omitting what is most prominent. At the roots of instinctual activity the systems communicate with one another most extensively. One portion of the processes which are there excited passes through the *Ucs.*, as through a preparatory stage, and reaches the highest psychical development in the *Cs.*; another portion is retained as *Ucs.* But the *Ucs.* is also affected by experiences originating from external perception. Normally all the paths from perception to the *Ucs.* remain open, and only those leading on from the *Ucs.* are subject to blocking by repression.

* * *

The content of the system *Pcs.* (or *Cs.*) is derived partly from instinctual life (through the medium of the *Ucs.*), and partly from perception. It is doubtful how far the processes of this system can exert a direct influence on the *Ucs.*; examination of pathological cases often reveals an almost incredible independence and lack of susceptibility to influence on the part of the *Ucs.* A complete divergence of their trends, a total severence of the two systems, is what above all characterizes a condition of illness. Nevertheless, psychoanalytic treatment is based upon an influencing of the *Ucs.* from the direction of the *Cs.*, and at any rate shows that this, though a laborious task, is not impossible. The derivatives of the *Ucs.* which act as intermediaries between the two systems open the way. . . . But we may safely assume that a spontaneously effected alteration in the *Ucs.* from the direction of the *Cs.* is a difficult and slow process.

Co-operation between a preconscious and an unconscious impulse, even when the latter is intensely repressed, may come about if there is a situation in which the unconscious impulse can act in the same sense as one of the dominant trends. The repression is removed in this instance, and the repressed activity is admitted as a reinforcement of the one intended by the ego. The unconscious becomes ego-syntonic in respect of this single conjunction without any change taking place in its repression apart from this. In this co-operation the influence of the *Ucs.* is un-mistakable: The reinforced tendencies reveal themselves as being nevertheless different from the normal; they make specially perfect functioning possible, and they manifest a resistance in the face of opposition which is similar to that offered, for instance, by ob-sessional symptoms.

The content of the *Ucs.* may be compared with an aboriginal population in the mind. If inherited mental formations exist in the human being—something analogous to instinct in animals—these constitute the nucleus of the *Ucs.* . . .

NOTE 2

FREUD, SIGMUND

The Interpretation of Dreams (1900)*

. . . Becoming conscious is connected with the application of a particular psychical function, that of attention—a function which, as it seems, is only available in a specific quanity, and this may have been diverted from the train of thought in question on to some other purpose. There is another way, too, in which trains of thought of this kind may be withheld from consciousness. The course of our conscious reflections shows us that we follow a particular path in our application of attention. If, as we follow this path, we come upon an idea which will not bear criticism, we break off: We drop the cathexis of attention. Now it seems that the train of thought which has thus been initiated and dropped can con-tinue to spin itself out without attention being turned to it again, unless at some point or other it reaches a specially high degree of intensity which forces atten-tion to it. Thus, if a train of thought is initially re-jected (consciously, perhaps) by a judgment that it is wrong or that it is useless for the immediate intel-lectual purposes in view, the result may be that this train of thought will proceed, unobserved by consciousness. . . .

*   *   *

A train of thought that has been set going . . . in the preconscious may either cease spontaneously or persist. We picture the first of these outcomes as im-plying that the energy attaching to the train of thought is diffused along all the associative paths that radiate from it; this energy sets the whole network of thoughts in a state of excitation which lasts for a certain time and then dies away as the excitation in search of dis-charge becomes transformed into a quiescent cathex-is. . . . Lurking in our preconscious, however, there are other purposive ideas, which are derived from sources in our unconscious and from wishes which are always on the alert. These may take control of the excitation attaching to the group of thoughts which has been left to its own devices, they may establish a connection between it and an unconscious wish, and they may "transfer" to it the energy be-longing to the unconscious wish. Thenceforward the neglected or suppressed train of thought is in a position to persist, though the reinforcement it has received gives it no right of entry into consciousness. We may express this by saying that what has hitherto been a preconscious train of thought has now been "drawn into the unconscious."

NOTE 3

FREUD, SIGMUND

A Note upon the Mystic Writing-Pad (1925)*

If I distrust my memory . . . I am able to supple-ment and guarantee its working by making a note in writing. In that case the surface upon which this note is preserved . . . is as it were a materialized portion of my mnemic apparatus, which I otherwise carry about with me invisible. I have only to bear in mind the place where this "memory" has been deposited and I can then "reproduce" it at any time I like, with the certainty that it will have remained unaltered and so have escaped the possible distortions to which it might have been subjected in my actual memory.

If I want to make full use of this technique for im-proving my mnemic function, I find that there are two different procedures open to me. On the one hand, I can choose a writing surface which will preserve in-tact any note made upon it for an indefinite length of time—for instance, a sheet of paper which I can write upon in ink. I am then in possession of a "permanent memory-trace." The disadvantage of this procedure is that the receptive capacity of the writing surface

* Reprinted from: 5 *The Standard Edition of the Complete Psychological Works of Sigmund Freud*, James Strachey, ed. London: The Hogarth Press and the Institute of Psycho-analysis, 1953. (pp. 593–94). Basic Books, Inc., publishers, 1960. Reprinted by permission of George Allen & Unwin, Ltd. and Basic Books, Inc.

* Reprinted from: 19 *The Standard Edition of the Complete Psychological Works of Sigmund Freud*, James Strachey, ed. London: The Hogarth Press and the Institute of Psycho-analysis, 1961. (pp. 227–32) and 5 *Collected Papers of Sigmund Freud*, American Edition published by Basic Books, Inc., 1959. Reprinted by permission of Hogarth and Basic Books, Inc.

is soon exhausted. The sheet is filled with writing, there is no room on it for any more notes, and I find myself obliged to bring another sheet into use, that has not been written on. Moreover, the advantage of this procedure, the fact that it provides a "permanent trace," may lose its value for me if after a time the note ceases to interest me and I no longer want to "retain it in my memory." The alternative procedure avoids both of these disadvantages. If, for instance, I write with a piece of chalk on a slate, I have a receptive surface which retains its receptive capacity for an unlimited time and the notes upon which can be destroyed as soon as they cease to interest me, without any need for throwing away the writing surface itself. Here the disadvantage is that I cannot preserve a permanent trace. If I want to put some fresh notes on the slate, I must first wipe out the ones which cover it. Thus an unlimited receptive capacity and a retention of permanent traces seem to be mutually exclusive properties in the apparatus which we use as substitutes for our memory: Either the receptive surface must be renewed or the note must be destroyed.

* * *

[S]ome time ago there came upon the market, under the name of the "Mystic Writing Pad," a small contrivance that promises to perform more than the sheet of paper or the slate. It claims to be nothing more than a writing tablet from which notes can be erased by an easy movement of the hand. But if it is examined more closely it will be found that its construction shows a remarkable agreement with my hypothetical structure of our perceptual apparatus and that it can, in fact, provide both an everready receptive surface and permanent traces of the notes that have been made upon it.

The Mystic Pad is a slab of dark-brown resin or wax with a paper edging; over the slab is laid a thin, transparent sheet, the top end of which is firmly secured to the slab while its bottom end rests on it without being fixed to it. This transparent sheet is the more interesting part of the little device. It itself consists of two layers, which can be detached from each other except at their two ends. The upper layer is a transparent piece of celluloid; the lower layer is made of thin translucent waxed paper. When the apparatus is not in use, the lower surface of the waxed paper adheres lightly to the upper surface of the wax slab.

To make use of the Mystic Pad, one writes upon the celluloid portion of the covering sheet which rests on the wax slab. For this purpose no pencil or chalk is necessary, since the writing does not depend on material being deposited on the receptive surface. It is a return to the ancient method of writing on tablets of clay or wax: A pointed stilus scratches

the surface, the depressions upon which constitute the "writing." In the case of the Mystic Pad this scratching is not effected directly, but through the medium of the covering sheet. At the points which the stilus touches, it presses the lower surface of the waxed paper on to the wax slab, and the grooves are visible as dark writing upon the otherwise smooth whitish-gray surface of the celluloid. If one wishes to destroy what has been written, all that is necessary is to raise the double covering sheet from the wax slab by a light pull, starting from the free lower end. The close contact between the waxed paper and the wax slab at the places which have been scratched (upon which the visibility of the writing depended) is thus brought to an end and it does not recur when the two surfaces come together once more. The Mystic Pad is now clear of writing and ready to receive fresh notes.

* * *

If, while the Mystic Pad has writing on it, we cautiously raise the celluloid from the waxed paper, we can see the writing just as clearly on the surface of the latter, and the question may arise why there should be any necessity for the celluloid portion of the cover. Experiment will then show that the thin paper would be very easily crumpled or torn if one were to write directly upon it with the stilus. The layer of celluloid thus acts as protective sheath for the waxed paper, to keep off injurious effects from without. The celluloid is a "protective shield against stimuli"; the layer which actually receives the stimuli is the paper. [T]he perceptual apparatus of our mind consists of two layers, of an external protective shield against stimuli whose task it is to diminish the strength of excitations coming in, and of a surface behind it which receives the stimuli, namely, the system *Pcpt.–Cs.* [Perception–Conscious].

The analogy would not be of much value if it could not be pursued further than this. If we lift the entire covering sheet—both the celluloid and the waxed paper—off the wax slab, the writing vanishes and, as I have already remarked, does not reappear again. The surface of the Mystic Pad is clear of writing and once more capable of receiving impressions. But it is easy to discover that the permanent trace of what was written is retained upon the wax slab itself and is legible in suitable lights. Thus the Pad provides not only a receptive surface that can be used over and over again, like a slate, but also permanent traces of what has been written, like an ordinary paper pad: It solves the problem of combining the two functions *by dividing them between two separate but interrelated component parts or systems.* But this is precisely the way in which, according to the hypothesis which I mentioned just now, our mental apparatus performs its perceptual function. The layer which receives the stimuli—the system *Pcpt.–Cs.*—forms no permanent traces; the foundations of memory come about in other, adjoining, systems.

We need not be disturbed by the fact that in the Mystic Pad no use is made of the permanent traces of the notes that have been received; it is enough that they are present. There must come a point at which the analogy between an auxiliary apparatus of this kind and the organ which is its prototype will cease to apply. It is true, too, that once the writing has been erased, the Mystic Pad cannot "reproduce" it from within; it would be a mystic pad indeed if, like our memory, it could accomplish that. Nonetheless, I do not think it is too far-fetched to compare the celluloid and waxed paper cover with the system *Pcpt.–Cs.* and its protective shield, the wax slab with the unconscious behind them, and the appearance and disappearance of the writing with the flickering-up and passing-away of consciousness in the process of perception.

But I must admit that I am inclined to press the comparison still further. On the Mystic Pad the writing vanishes every time the close contact is broken between the paper which receives the stimulus and the wax slab which preserves the impression. This agrees with . . . my theory . . . that cathectic innervations are sent out and withdrawn in rapid periodic impulses from within into the completely pervious system *Pcpt.–Cs.* So long as that system is cathected in this manner, it receives perceptions (which are accompanied by consciousness) and passes the excitation on to the unconscious mnemic systems; but as soon as the cathexis is withdrawn, consciousness is extinguished and the functioning of the system comes to a standstill. It is as though the unconscious stretches out feelers, through the medium of the system *Pcpt.–Cs.*, toward the external world and hastily withdraws them as soon as they have sampled the excitations coming from it. Thus the interruptions, which in the case of the Mystic Pad have an external origin, were attributed by my hypothesis to the discontinuity in the current of innervation; and the actual breaking of contact which occurs in the Mystic Pad was replaced in my theory by the periodic nonexcitability of the perceptual system. . . .

If we imagine one hand writing upon the surface of the Mystic Writing Pad while another periodically raises its covering sheet from the wax slab, we shall have a concrete representation of the way in which I tried to picture the functioning of the perceptual apparatus of our mind.

NOTE 4

SCHACHTEL, ERNEST G.

Metamorphosis*

. . . Memory as a function of the living personality can be understood only as a capacity for the organization and reconstruction of past experiences and impressions in the service of present needs, fears, and interests. It goes without saying that, just as there is no such thing as impersonal perception and impersonal experience, there is also no impersonal memory. Man perceives and remembers not as a camera reproduces on the film the objects before its lens; the scope and quality of his perceptions and experiences as well as of their reproduction by memory are determined by his individual needs, fears, and interests. This is the more apparent the more significant an experience has been for the person.

With this concept of memory in mind, the puzzling problem of childhood amnesia seems to become more transparent and accessible to understanding. No greater change in the needs of man occurs than that which takes place between early childhood and adulthood. Into this change have gone all the decisive formative influences of the culture transmitted by the parents, laying the fundament of the transformation into the grownup, "useful" member of society from the little heathen, who is helpless but as yet sees nothing wrong with following the pleasure principle completely and immediately and who has an insatiable curiosity and capacity for experience. An explanation of childhood amnesia that takes into account these changes leads to the following tentative hypothesis:

> The categories (or schemata) of adult memory are not suitable receptacles for early childhood experiences and therefore not fit to preserve these experiences and enable their recall. The functional capacity of the conscious, adult memory is usually limited to those types of experience which the adult consciously is aware of and is capable of having.

It is not merely the repression of a specific content, such as early sexual experience, that accounts for the general childhood amnesia; the biologically, culturally, and socially influenced process of memory organization results in the formation of categories (schemata) of memory which are not suitable vehicles to receive and reproduce experiences of the quality and intensity typical of early childhood. . . .

---

* © 1959 by Basic Books, Inc., New York. (p. 284).

B.

For Law Purposes

1.

In Wills

APPEAL OF INGRAHAM
118 Me. 67, 105 Atl. 812 (1919)

DUNN, J.

Robert C. Foster, namesake of his father, distinguished from him as junior, and whose only prospective heir he was, is pretermitted from his father's will, a document executed when the child was less than five years old, and which became operative before he had attained the age of eight years, by its probate in Cumberland county on May 4, 1916.

The question in this case is whether exclusion of the boy from provision of that will was intentional, and not occasioned by mistake, on the part of the testator, a subject of investigation regarding which the will itself is silent.

At the outset, and without scrutiny, the disposition of the estate may seem to be unreasonable and unnatural, even to savor of unjustness; but, under the rule of law applicable, the maker of the will was not bound to have good or any reason for what he did, or, if he had reason to state it. With the wisdom or propriety of his act the law has nothing to do. If adequate and convincing proof, extrinsical the will, shall show that when that instrument was made, the son being present to his mind, the parent purposely ignored him, and otherwise made bestowal of his bounty, then we must hold that the testator's will be done.

In natural and moral law is the basis of the relationship of parent and child. From this source flows the presumption, crystallized in a statute . . . that the omission to provide for a child, or the issue of a deceased child, living when a will is made, is the result of forgetfulness, infirmity, or misapprehension, and not of design. But the presumption is rebuttable. The statute adverted to reads:

> "A child, or the issue of a deceased child, not having any devise in the will, take the share of the testator's estate, which he would have taken if no will had been made, unless it appears that such omission was intentional, or was not occasioned by mistake, or that such child or issue had a due proportion of the estate during the life of the testator."

There is no pretense that Robert C. Foster, Jr., had befitting share of the estate in the lifetime of his father. The sole inquiry of the case is, to repeat, whether omission to provide for him in the will was intentional, and not occasioned by mistake, on the part of his immediate ancestor. The clause, "or was not occasioned by mistake," is introduced in the statute to enforce or give emphasis to the meaning of the preceding word, "intentional," which is the ruling expression. It is written, in *Hurely* v. *O'Sullivan*, 137 Mass. at p. 89, the word "mistake," as here used is not to be construed as meaning such mistake "as would or might have caused the testator to entertain a different intention from that which omission from the will would show, but mistake or accident in the will or in its transcription." It must, in the context, refer to such mistake or mistakes as are likely accidentally to occur in the preparation of a will, as momentary rather than purposed forgetfulness, owing to the distress of the testator, or error, on the part of the scribe or otherwise, in reducing the testator's intention in that behalf to writing, and not to misapprehension or misunderstanding as to matters outside the will, whether of law or of fact. The statute does not state two contingencies in which omission from the will would work to deprive the child of his share, that is to say, an intentional omission and also where, but for a mistake, the testator would not have done that which he intended to do, and actually did. On the contrary, it states one and only one contingency. . . .

In its language the statute is broad enough to embrace all competent evidence tending to prove that such omission was intentional and not occasioned by mistake. . . . Seeking the testator's intention, it is pertinent to inquire, consonantly with the law of evidence, concerning him and his son; the affection, or lack thereof, that subsisted between them; of the motives which may be supposed to have operated with the testator and to have influenced him in the disposition of his property. All the relevant facts and circumstances, including the intention of the testator as he declared it before, at, or after the making of the will, may be shown.

What then of Robert C. Foster, the elder? Of his child and his relation to him, of his property, of its testamentary disposition, and of his intention, as he may have declared it, that concerning? Bred to the law, he came to the bar, and entered upon the practice of the profession at Portland, in partnership with his own father, but he did not especially actively concern himself with the business of the firm. In 1906 he married. The child first born of the marriage died in early infancy. In 1910 his wife left him, taking little

Robert not then two and a half years old, and going to her girlhood home in Illinois. Efforts to bring about reconcilliation between husband and wife, in which both the testator and his parents participated, the one by letters manifesting his better traits and characteristics, and importuning that she return to live with him, the others by personal interviews with the wife, after a journey afar for that purpose were unavailing. A month after the dissociation, the probate court in Cumberland county granted the mother custody and care of the child, to continue throughout his minority. Three or four months later on, while Mr. Foster was absent in Europe, his wife, who previously had returned to Portland, removed her property and effects from what had been the family domicile. Within eight months from that time this court decreed the wife matrimonial divorcement. Promptly thereafter, for the consideration of $5,000 to her paid, she released to her former husband all her interest in his real and personal estate, and exempted him from all liability to provide for, or to contribute to, the support and education of their son, while he had been, and should continue to be, in her custody. Mrs. Foster thereupon permanently removed from Maine. She settled in Illinois, and married again.

From the day that his wife left him until that of his death, Robert Foster never had opportunity to speak to his child. The case ungrudgingly concedes that, while the family lived together, he was an affectionate father, proud of his child, and ambitious for his future. When the boy was taken elsewhere to live, the father's interest in him waned. For Christmas, twenty days from the day on which Robert's mother took her child away from the paternal home, he sent him $5 accompanied by a note couched in the words of a parent's love. On the third anniversary of the child's birth, in the next July, he sent him another present of money. Beyond those gifts, after the separation, he gave him nothing. He made no provision for him or his welfare, excepting the gross payment made to the mother at the time she assumed responsibility for the child's support. Not altogether without foundation in fact, though not entirely based on truth, Mr. Foster was told that his son was known and called by the name of the stepfather. At once his attitude underwent decided change. He abandoned effort to see the boy. He gave away the toy bank in which for him it had been his habit to deposit dimes, assigning as a reason that he never expected to see the child. In the summer of the year of 1912, and once more in the summer of the very next year, the boy visited at the home of a maternal aunt, the site of whose house was a lot of land adjoining, and back of that on which was located the residence of Mr. Foster, in Portland. His attention called to the fact that the lad was at play in the nearby yard, Mr. Foster came from out one room into another, and looked through a window

at him. What passed through his mind and was reflected in his eyes as he contemplated his son was fleeting; but as he gazed he soliloquized, and she who, in other days, had been nurse to that child both in Maine and in Illinois, then, pausing in her housework, during the father's monologue, and herself looking at the boy in the yard, heard the parent say, "They have treated me meanly, and I am through with them." At another time he spoke to his friend and physician, Dr. Gray, already familiar with the estrangement, and told him of his formed intention, his considered and positive purpose, that his property should not go at his death to his former wife or to his child.

After the divorce had been granted and his former wife had gone away from Maine, Mr. Foster remained in and about Portland. In April, 1913, Foster's father, then stricken with the illness that was his last, sent for him, and when he had come, the father said:

> "Robert, I have made my will, giving all my property to you, and your mother has made hers, giving hers to you; now I want you to make yours, so that if anything should happen to you before it does to us that there won't any of your property go into that family (the family of Robert's former wife), but will come back into our family."

And Robert said that he would. Less than a fortnight later, at the law office of the firm, in his father's absence, Robert Foster with his own hand wrote out his will, and then and there executed it. In his will he gave $500 to his housekeeper. The rest of his property, both real and personal, he devised and bequeathed to his father and mother, or to the one of them who should live longer than the other, omitting his child without mention. When he had signed and published the will, and it had been subscribed by the attesting witnesses, he took it to his father, and the latter put it, with his own and Robert's mother's will, in the family safe in the father's home, where, always accessible to the maker, it remained until taken to the court for probate.

Robert C. Foster's property was not the fruit of his own industry. The house that he owned and occupied, and the personal property consisting, additionally to his household effects, of a few bonds and other evidences of indebtedness, of which at the time of the divorcement he was possessed, were gifts to him from his parents. Two years later on, when his father died, the bulk of the father's property passed by will to Robert. He then abandoned the practice of the law, sold his dwelling place, and went to live in an apartment house. He began the study of medicine. A policy of insurance on his life was canceled for the reason, as he stated, that, as his mother, the beneficiary named in his will, already had ample estate of her own, there was no occasion to carry the contract, and the money requisite for premiums thereon might the more conveniently be used by him in defrayment of medical school expenses. At Christmas time in 1915, before his death in March next following, while at home through a recess of the medical school in which he was enrolled as a student, he talked with his mother respecting the disposal of his property in case she outlived him. He told her of a person or two to whom, as expressive of his affection for them, he wished certain of it to be given; he said that he wanted some of it to go to Bowdoin College, of which he was a graduate. But in that solemn conversation, from its beginning to its end, when after the manner of mankind he must have scanned with telescopic vision both the present and the past, and have endeavoured to peer into the mysterious economy of the future, the name of his child never was mentioned. Candid consideration of all the evidence in the case leads irresistibly to the conclusion that soon after the entry of decree on her libel for divorce, and before the making of his will, she who had been Robert C. Foster's wife, and with her the child born to them in wedlock, the disinherison of whom originated this case, together went out of that man's life forever. Afterward he exercised what was his undoubted legal right; he denied his property to him for whose presence on earth he was responsible. The weight of the burden of his executrix and principal beneficiary, herself going down life's steep declivity, would have been greatly lessened had he stated in his will that, touching the omission of devise to the boy, he did what he designed to do. Why he did not say so is conjectural. He may have thought all men would know without his saying. He may have forgotten that the silence of the grave is tongueless. Be that as it may, the conclusion of the court is that the omission and failure on the part of Robert C. Foster to provide in his will for his only living child was intentional, and not occasioned by mistake.

It is conceived by the court to be its duty to set aside and disregard the verdict of the jury. It is neither necessary nor desirable again to send the case to a jury. The mandate to the court below will be that the omission of the appellant's ward from devise in the will of the ward's father, Robert C. Foster, was intentional, and not occasioned by mistake, on the part of the testator. The decree of the probate court denying the petition for the payment to appellants' ward of the same share of the estate of the testator as he would have taken if no will had been made is affirmed. . . .

* * *

NOTES

NOTE 1

IN RE TORREGANO'S ESTATE
54 Cal. 2d 234, 352 P. 2d 505 (1960)

PETERS, JUSTICE

The trial court held that, as a matter of law, plaintiff is not a pretermitted heir of Ernest J. Torregano, deceased.

Torregano, a San Francisco attorney, died on January 18, 1954. His will was dated June 25, 1947 [it] left the bulk of his estate to his brother, Alfred Torregano, the defendant herein. . . .

* * *

Testator, Ernest J. Torregano, was born November 21, 1882, a member of a fairly large Negro family. During 1902 or 1903 he married Viola Perrett, a member of his minstrel troupe, and brought her to live at his mother's house in New Orleans, Louisiana. On February 7, 1904, plaintiff, Gladys Torregano Stevens, was born the issue of such marriage, in the home of her grandmother (decedent's mother). When plaintiff was less than a year old testator (having established his family in a separate residence) took a position as a porter on a railroad train running between New Orleans and San Francisco, California. For the next year or more he continued in such work, residing with his wife and child during the periods of stopover in New Orleans. He then found permanent work in San Francisco, but did not immediately terminate his infrequent visits to his family. Some time after the earthquake and fire of 1906 he took up the study of law, and "commenced to pass for white." During this period, he sent for his brother Alfred, presumably the only other member of his family so capable of "passing," and the two of them ultimately succeeded. Testator ultimately became a successful member of the bar in San Francisco. Prior to 1915 testator had ceased his infrequent visits to New Orleans, but maintained contact with various members of his family by correspondence. During this period, he maintained two addresses in San Francisco, one for a "white" establishment and the other as an address to receive his mail from his colored family. During the year 1915 (or thereabouts), testator's mother and his half-brother, Edgar, visited him in San Francisco. On that occasion testator's mother told him that his wife and daughter, the plaintiff, were dead. On her return to New Orleans, testator's mother told the wife and child that testator was dead. On that date plaintiff was a child of tender years, incapable of producing issue, which testator then knew. The testator never had any other issue. After the date of the visit from his mother there was no further contact (by mail or otherwise) between testator and his wife (Viola) or plaintiff, although there was subsequent contact between testator and at least one of his sisters. On March 15, 1917, testator married Pearl C. Bryant, of Oakland, California, the marriage certificate indicating that he and his parents were white.[1] In 1922 Viola remarried (presumably relying upon the misinformation given to her by testator's mother). Pearl died prior to June 25, 1947.

The will was introduced into evidence. From all of the foregoing facts, including the subsequent re-marriage, the fact that testator was a successful practicing attorney who was versed in the law, and the fact that the will made no specific mention of plaintiff, and, in fact, inferred lack of any issue, there is no doubt that a jury could have found—if such evidence is admissible and relevant under the law—that testator, when executing his will, believed plaintiff to have been dead for many years, and that she had died at a time when she could not possibly have had issue.

Much of the evidence upon which the foregoing statement is based was received over the objection of defendant. He took the attitude that extrinsic evidence was inadmissible. . . .

*   *   *

Our first . . . conclusion is that extrinsic evidence is admissible to prove a testator's *lack* of intent to omit from his will any provision for a presumptive heir.

In contending that evidence *dehors* the will was not admissible herein, respondent relies upon that portion of Probate Code, § 90, which states that a child who is not provided for succeeds to a portion of the estate "unless it appears from the will that such omission is intentional." The quoted phrase specifically bars the introduction of evidence, other than that found on the face of the will, in proving that testator intentionally omitted provision for his child. The significant fact is that the code section makes no reference to the method of proving *lack* of intent to exclude a child. . . .

*   *   *

From a standpoint of reason and common sense, it is obvious, by very definition, that a pretermission can exist only through oversight. It occurs only when there has been an omission to provide, absent an intent to omit. [T]he mistake or accident which caused the testator to omit provision for his child cannot possibly appear from the will itself. Extrinsic evidence for this purpose must be contemplated by the statute. Otherwise pretermission could never be proven.

---

1. No inference of bigamy is to be inferred by reason of this subsequent marriage. No evidence was offered in rebuttal of the testimony from which the jury may have found that testator believed Viola to be dead. On the contrary a legal presumption operates in favor of absence of any intent to commit bigamy. This presumption, together with the fact that he re-married within two years of the date that his mother told him that his wife and child were dead, is convincing evidence that testator believed his mother's statement to be true.

. . . Extrinsic evidence is always admissible for the purpose of proving the circumstances under which a will was executed. . . . In the instant case petitioner produced evidence of relationship and family circumstances from which the jury could have found that for some thirty-two years testator and his daughter each believed the other dead. Should the trier of fact accept that evidence as true, it could further find that the erroneous belief continued to and including the date of making the will. Such evidence is then part of the "circumstances" under which the will was executed, and thus admissible.

Extrinsic evidence is also admissible to explain an ambiguity arising on the face of a will, or to resolve a latent ambiguity which does not so appear. In the instant case the testator declared: "* * * that I am a widower and that I have no children, issue of my marriage"; . . . He also declared that his deceased wife's name was Pearl, and made no mention of a previous wife, or of any issue by such. Granting appellant's right to offer evidence that she is testator's daughter, by a wife named Viola, a latent ambiguity immediately appears, which ambiguity must be resolved by recourse to extrinsic evidence.

*   *   *

Appellant's entire case must rest on the contention that appellant was omitted from the will because the testator thought her dead. If true, that explains rationally his failure to provide for her, absent an intent to disinherit her. Since such a lack of intention could not appear from the face of the will, she is entitled to prove such by resort to extrinsic evidence.

*   *   *

Since its origin as a state, California has continuously protected both spouse and children (and to some extent, grandchildren) from unintentional omission from a share in testator's estate. Such protection, unknown to the common law, has been provided by statute, commencing with the Acts of 1850, continued by various sections of the Civil Code. . . . Thus the Legislature has indicated a continuing policy of guarding against the omission of lineal descendants by reason of oversight, accident, mistake, or unexpected change of condition.

From 1850 to date the courts have announced certain well-settled rules of construction applicable to the objects and interpretation of these statutes. Among these are the following:

1. The sole object of these statutes is to protect children against omission or oversight "which not infrequently arises from * * * the peculiar circumstances under which the will is executed."

2. Neither the pecuniary value, nor the lack thereof, which the child receives, has any effect upon the object of these statutes, the purpose being merely to prevent unintentional omission.

3. Public policy requires that a testator remember his children at the time of making his will.

4. "It is the policy of the law that wife and children must be provided for."

5. The law does not favor the failure to provide for surviving spouse or children.

6. "The heirs of a testator are favored by the policy of the law and cannot be disinherited upon mere conjecture."

7. There is a presumption of law that the failure to name a child or grandchild in a will was unintentional.

8. Although a testator may lawfully disinherit any or all of his natural heirs if he so desires, in order to avoid the operation of the pretermission statutes, an intent to omit provision for testator's child "must appear on the face of the will, and it must appear there from words which indicate such intent directly, or by implication equally as strong. Any other rule would lead to guesses or to inferences merely conjectural, which would be too unsubstantial to base a judgment on."

9. "[B]efore what are considered to be the 'natural rights' of children to share in the inheritance of their immediate ancestors shall be taken away, the intent that they shall not so share must appear upon the face of the will strongly and convincingly."

10. Before a testator may be said to have intentionally omitted his child, it must appear on the face of the will that he had such child in mind at the time of executing the will, and having the child in mind he omitted to provide.

11. A cardinal rule of interpretation, applicable to cases involving pretermission, requires that the court not only look to the clause under scrutiny, but in determining the testator's intent, it interpret that clause in relation to every other expression in the will.

12. In determining the question of intentional omission, more than in any other situation involving the interpretation of wills, the court must be guided by the individual facts of each case, and must not be governed by previous interpretation of similar words or phrases.

* * *

Directly applicable to the case under consideration is the rule that before a testator may be said to have intentionally omitted his child, it must appear on the face of the will that he had such child in mind at the time of executing the will, and having the child in mind he omitted to provide. . . . If a jury may find from the facts herein that Torregano thought appellant dead, he could not be said to have had her in mind for the purpose of excluding her from his estate. One does not disinherit a deceased person.

* * *

Under the circumstances here presented the question of whether or not appellant is a pretermitted heir is one of fact, and the trial court erred in taking it from the jury. Whether appellant is the person she claims to be, whether or not Torregano believed her dead, and whether he intended, under the facts, that the phrase "by relationship or otherwise" should include appellant, are issues which must be determined by the trier of fact. Under the facts of this case such questions are not matters of law.

The judgment is reversed and the cause remanded for a new trial.

NOTE 2

IN RE RAY'S ESTATE
69 Nev. 207, 245 P. 2d 990 (1952)

MERRILL, JUSTICE.

* * *

In 1 Page on Wills, 967, § 526, with reference to the statutory protection of pretermitted heirs, it is stated: "* * * Statutes of this class were originally framed on the theory that a testator who neither provided for his children, nor expressly indicated his intention not to provide for them, must have omitted to provide for them through inadvertence; and that his probable intention could best be enforced by giving the omitted children such share as they would have taken had testator died intestate. They are thus based on the theory of mistake; and, in the cases to which they apply, they reverse the general rule that a testator is presumed to know the contents of his will, and to intend that effect shall be given thereto."

* * *

. . . Indeed, it may well be that, assuming a child was truly forgotten, the statutory provisions are over-liberal. In point of fact as opposed to theory, a child so lightly regarded by the testator and so remotely an object of his bounty as to be completely forgotten, might not reasonably expect to have received a full intestate share had he been remembered. The statute may then be said (in the absence of mistake, fraud, or undue influence) to frustrate testamentary intent more frequently than it may be said fairly and truly to supply it. These considerations, however, would appear to be clearly legislative rather than judicial. . . .

NOTE 3

LUFF v. LUFF
— F.2d — (1966)

* * *

FAHY, CIRCUIT JUDGE: The question is whether the last will and testament of Morris F. Luff, deceased, of whom appellant, Willard J. Luff, is a surviving brother and one of several heirs at law, was impliedly revoked. The will, dated April 7, 1953, provided that testator's entire estate should go to Ruth K. Luff, appellee, who then was his wife. Thereafter they separated. Some five years after the separation she sued for and obtained an absolute divorce upon the ground of five years consecutive separation without cohabitation. A property settlement agreement entered into between the parties during the pendency of the divorce proceeding was made a part of the decree of divorce. There was no child, and neither remarried.

The will was found in testator's apartment after his death. At his request it had been sent to him by his former wife after their divorce. She offered the will for probate. Appellant filed a caveat, and the issue as to the validity of the will came on for trial before judge and jury. Appellant relied entirely upon the divorce and property settlement as impliedly revoking the will. Appellee introduced considerable testimony tending to show that decedent should not be held to have intended to revoke the will. At the close of all the evidence the motion of appellee for a directed verdict in her favor was granted, the will thus being given effect. We reverse, being of opinion that the divorce with property settlement revoked the will by implication of law. . . .

*   *   *

. . . In *Caswell* v. *Kent*, 186 A.2d 581 [582–83] (Me.), decided in 1962, it is stated:

> The majority rule clearly rests on the assumption based upon common knowledge and experience that it is so rare and so unusual for a testator under these circumstances [divorce and property settlement] to desire or intend that his divorced spouse should benefit further under his will, that it is not improper or unreasonable to require that such a testator make that extraordinary desire and intention manifest by a formal republication of his will or by the execution of a new will.

*   *   *

The intention to revoke is imputed and conclusive. It may not be overcome by evidence adduced subsequent to the death of the testator and then relied upon as indicative of an intention that the will should be effective. Inquiry into the state of mind of the testator is confined to that imputed to him by the divorce and property settlement. . . .

> At common law certain changes in the condition and circumstances of the testator worked a revocation by implication, and it was formerly held that this was prima facie only, and open to rebuttal by proof that the testator intended his will to remain, notwithstanding the change in his circumstances. The rule however, by all modern authorities, is that the presumption of law arising from the changed conditions is conclusive, and no evidence is admissible to rebut it. . . .

In re Hall's Estate, 119 N.W. 219, 220. This is the sounder rule, illustrated by the present case. There was evidence of strained relations between testator and appellant, one of his heirs. It was also argued that when at the divorced husband's request his former wife sent the will to him he kept it in a bureau drawer in his apartment where it was found after his death, and that this indicated an intention not to revoke it. Testator is not available to give his version of either of these matters. He has a sister and other brothers besides appellant; and he may have asked his former wife to send the will to him so that it would no longer be in her control. He may have retained it undestroyed as a memento of happier days, or because of indecision. It is safer to rely upon the divorce and carefully composed adjustment of property between the parties, by which the former husband was relieved of further legal obligation to his former wife with respect to his property. While he remained of course free to make additional provision for her if he desired to do so the law should require this to be done anew in a manner provided by statute for valid testamentary disposition.

Reversed and remanded for further proceedings not inconsistent with this opinion.

LEVENTHAL, CIRCUIT JUDGE, *dissenting:* I cannot follow the path taken by my brethren. The point of departure for all of us becomes for me the point of return—the word of the testator executed in full accordance with the statute, witnessed by two adult witnesses. No word written down by ordinary man is more solemn than his last will and testament. The governing legislation not only provided the requirements for the writing to be effective as a testament, but carefully provided that one who wished to revoke his will might do so by written document or destruction of the prior will. Even the untutored who do not know of the statutory provisions are generally aware that their solemn word stands unless destroyed or amended.

*   *   *

. . . In modern society divorce is not only more frequent than it used to be, but increasingly is sought notwithstanding considerable and genuine affection by couples who realize that they have become incompatible, and that their divorce will at least provide the possibility of taking up life anew.

Doubtless many, perhaps most, divorced men desire to disinherit their wives. Doubtless many do so, some even with ceremonial bonfires and whoops of joy. What we are considering, however, is the probable intent of those divorced men who do not destroy their wills. It is fair to observe that people tend to do the things they really want to do, and that inaction generally signifies contentment or at worst indecision.

The procedural record leaves us without findings as to testator's actual intent. Nevertheless, it is fair to conclude that this record suggests a man who was virtually indifferent to if not estranged from his brother, but still sentimental, if not loving, in his thoughts of his former wife. This is relevant precisely because it occurs often enough among divorced men —and presumably still more often among divorced men who do not revoke their wills—that I am not sufficiently convinced of the probable intention of the testators to override their own writings.

* * *

Accepting the doctrine of implied revocation of wills as a judicial exception, it is properly confined, in my view, to such change of circumstance . . . as provides a clear presumption that revocation accords with the testator's intent, and the conviction that revocation is necessary to avoid injustice. In other situations, the premium of certainty bids us pay the price of an occasional injustice where a man forgets his outstanding will or is negligent or inattentive. . . .

* * *

. . . A man who intends to disinherit a divorced wife is more likely to speak up to his counsel at once, and have it taken care of. A man who has decided not to disinherit his divorced wife is less likely to bring the matter up even assuming he is aware of the little-known statutory technique of republication of a will. He may be hesitant to expose and enlarge the wound to his ego by admitting the depth of his affection for the former wife. He may have the hope that a new and more reciprocating object of his affection may yet appear on the scene.

* * *

[W]hen the husband has not found a new spouse and has not destroyed his solemn will and testament, I do not find a clear-cut presumption or injustice which impels me to mandate intestacy in the absence of a legislative expression that this is the consequence of a property settlement.

I respectfully dissent.

2.

In Criminal Procedure

R. v. YOUNG
[1964] 2 All E.R. 480

LORD PARKER, C. J., delivered the following judgment of the court: The appellant was convicted at London Sessions of driving while unfit through drink; it is against that conviction that he now appeals. [I]t was, if one may use the expression, a borderline case, and, indeed, at the conclusion of the evidence, the deputy chairman in fact invited the jury, if they so

desired, to return a verdict of not guilty without proceeding any further; in other words to say that they were not satisfied that the prosecution had proved their case. The foreman intimated that they were not all of that view, and the case proceeded. [The deputy chairman] adjourned on the Friday night having been through the prosecution case, leaving till the Monday morning the continuation of the summing-up dealing in particular with the defence. At the adjournment, he told the jury to go away and be back again on Monday, saying:

"... and you will bear in mind not to say anything to anybody; don't discuss this case, even amongst yourselves; try to forget all about it until Monday morning."

On the Monday morning, the deputy chairman continued and finished his summing-up, and then . . . it appears that the deputy chairman said: "Will you consider your verdict now, members of the jury," and that thereupon the foreman, without consulting any other member of the jury, without so much as a glance at any member of the jury, stood up and said: "We have agreed upon a verdict, we find the accused not guilty—I mean guilty, guilty." The court assumes that the verdict of not guilty just returned was a mere slip of the tongue, but the fact remains that the foreman, without any consultation, stated that they found the appellant guilty. The learned deputy chairman then used words to the effect: "You made up your mind before coming into court" to which the foreman replied: "Yes," and in that connection it is to be observed that the deputy chairman said to the jury after counsel for the appellant had moved in arrest of judgment:

"You see, members of the jury, it is obvious you had decided your decision without hearing what I had to say about the [appellant's] case and after hearing what I said about the prosecution's case."

In the opinion of this court, this verdict cannot stand. It is quite clear that, although the jury had heard all the evidence, had heard speeches for the prosecution and particularly for the defence, yet, unless they were going to find him not guilty, it was their duty before returning a verdict of guilty to listen to what the judge had to say about the defence. It is true that it is a well-known principle of law that, if a foreman gets up and gives a verdict apparently on behalf of all the members of the jury, their assent is conclusively inferred. That the court entirely accepts, but here the assent which is conclusively inferred is the assent of a finding of guilty before the summing-up continued on the Monday morning. The court is quite satisfied that this verdict cannot stand.

* * *

NOTES

NOTE 1

"Not Guilty" Heard Twice—But Verdict is "Guilty"*

Bristol, England

A man waited in the cells here for sentencing on a robbery charge recently after twice having heard the jury foreman pronounce him "Not guilty."

Patrick Brooke, twenty-three years old, and two other men had pleaded innocent to the charge of robbery with violence of a Pakistani shopkeeper.

When the jury foreman announced the verdict of "not guilty," Brooke was released from the dock and strolled smiling across the courtroom.

Then a woman juror protested: "That was not our verdict."

A policeman quickly barred the exit.

The jury went into a ten-minute huddle and the foreman said they had agreed on their verdict on Brooke—again "not guilty."

Again the woman juror objected. "We found him guilty," she said.

The jury went out again and then gave their third and final verdict—"guilty."

NOTE 2

SLOCUM v. U.S.
325 F. 2d 465 (8th Cir. 1963)

SANBORN, CIRCUIT JUDGE.

* * *

The contention of Slocum that "The jury returned an inconsistent verdict and the trial court's method of correction amounted to a denial of appellant's right of reasonable opportunity to have the jury intelligently polled," is not sustained by the record. The record clearly shows that the jury's verdict as to Slocum was a verdict of guilty. It appears that the foreman of the jury inadvertently had signed the form of verdict designed for use if the verdict as to Slocum was "not guilty," but, before returning it into court, drew a line through his signature; that, in reporting the verdicts in open court, the courtroom clerk at first failed to notice the line drawn through the signature of the foreman on the "not guilty" form of verdict, and read that as well as the "guilty" verdict, before discovering his mistake. The trial judge made certain that the jury had found Slocum guilty, by first asking whether the "guilty" verdict which was signed by the foreman was the verdict of all the jurors, and, after having been assured that it was, by polling the jury. There was no uncertainty

* The *New York Times*. Reprinted by permission.

whatever left as to the verdict of the jury with respect to Slocum. . . .

NOTE 3

CURLEY v. UNITED STATES
160 F. 2d 229, 232 (D.C. Cir. 1947)

PRETTYMAN, ASSOCIATE JUSTICE

The functions of the jury include the determination of the credibility of witnesses, the weighing of the evidence, and the drawing of justifiable inferences of fact from proven facts. It is the function of the judge to deny the jury any opportunity to operate beyond its province. The jury may not be permitted to conjecture merely, or to conclude upon pure speculation or from passion, prejudice, or sympathy. The critical point in this boundary is the existence or non existence of a reasonable doubt as to guilt. If the evidence is such that reasonable jurymen must necessarily have such a doubt, the judge must require acquittal, because no other result is permissible within the fixed bounds of jury consideration. But if a reasonable mind might fairly have a reasonable doubt or might fairly not have one, the case is for the jury, and the decision is for the jurors to make. The law recognizes that the scope of a reasonable mind is broad. Its conclusion is not always a point certain, but, upon evidence, may be one of a number of conclusions. Both innocence and guilt beyond reasonable doubt may lie fairly within the limits of reasonable conclusion from given facts.

NOTE 4

UNITED STATES v. FARINA
184 F. 2d 18 (2nd Cir. 1950)

FRANK, CIRCUIT JUDGE (dissenting).

What influences juries, courts seldom know. Indeed, most courts . . . not only do not diligently seek such knowledge but have a general policy of deliberate unwillingness to learn—and usually seal up the only possible sources from which they could learn—what occurred in the jury room. As we recently said, per Judge Learned Hand, this policy stems from awareness that, were the full truth disclosed, it is doubtful whether more than 1 per cent of verdicts could stand.

* * *

[The trial judge told the jury that reasonable] doubt is one which a juror "can give a reason for entertaining." This . . . was matter to which the jurors probably paid close attention, since the important "reasonable doubt" principle is . . . often popularly discussed out of court. The judge's definition of that principle, therefore, most probably impressed the jury.

[This] instruction . . . means that the jurors must not consider any doubt about guilt unless they can articulate, at least to themselves, a sound "reason" for doing so.

Our own judicial experience teaches that sometimes even trial judges have difficulty in rationally explaining the grounds of their decisions. Some trial judges resent any obligation in jury-less cases, where the oral testimony is conflicting, to go beyond publishing laconic, unexplained, judgments. They even object to filing special findings of fact. Some of those judges complain that the formulation of fact findings is too arduous and, more, bound to be artificial. I share the view that, on net balance, that complaint is unjustified. There would be more justification for complaint, if a trial judge were required to reveal, or even to disclose that he himself knew, the "reasons" for his special findings. But there is no such requirement.

Surely, then, we ought not ask a juror, who has nothing like a trial judge's experience and training, not merely to find facts but also to be able to recognize, and to make explicit to himself or the other jurors, the "reason" for joining in a finding of fact or for any intermediate step in his mental processes. Mr. Justice Holmes, speaking for the Supreme Court, said the reasoning of an administrative body need not be thus articulate, since its decision expresses "an intuition of experience which outruns analysis and sums up many unnamed and tangled impressions * * * which may lie beneath consciousness without losing their worth." [Chicago, B. & Q. Ry. Co. v. Babcock, 204 U.S. 585, 598.] We should not exact more of a jury. Accordingly, I think the jurors were badly misinstructed when told they must ignore any doubt which they could "give no reason for entertaining."

My colleagues assume, in effect, that the jurors construed that instruction as would an intelligent law student or lawyer, well versed in the traditional meaning of "reasonable doubt." I cannot go along with that assumption. Far more probably, the jurors thought the judge meant just what he said. One can, then, well imagine that one of the jurors, when in the jury room, impressively remarked to his fellow-jurors: "Remember that the judge especially warned us we must discard any doubt about guilt unless we can 'give a reason' for holding it." So it seems to me not at all improbable that the jurors, acting under this erroneous instruction, and incapable of formulating a rational explanation of a doubt they entertained, concluded that they had the duty to discard a doubt which, had they been properly instructed, would legitimately have yielded an acquittal. The defendants ought not bear the risk that the verdict derived from such an error.

* * *

NOTE 5

LASSWELL, HAROLD D.

Psychopathology and Politics*

. . . On one occasion the judge began to enumerate the three principal alternatives which lay before him in deciding a pending case. He remembered two of them but hesitated several seconds before the third came into his mind. This led him to remember that he had often casually noticed that this third possibility seemed to elude him, although on reflection he felt that it deserved as much attention as the other two. He began spontaneously to relax and report everything that crossed his mind, and produced a long string of catch phrases from law and politics like "freedom of contract," "life, liberty and pursuit of happiness," "freedom of speech and assembly." He presently noted that a picture was forming of one of his old law-school classrooms. He felt that someone was just about to speak to him, and had to resist the temptation to turn around. Then there came across his mind a long series of incidents in which one of his law professors was the principal figure. This teacher was reputed to possess a mastermind and a caustic tongue; and the judge, though he had always wanted to make a great impression on him, had met with no particular success. The professor had a habit of using his most ironic tone of voice when he spoke of "this freedom of contract." Now it happened that the attorney who was arguing for alternative No. 3 before the court pronounced the word "freedom" with unction. This aroused in the judge's mind the ironic tone of the old professor's voice, and this in turn brought back the rather humiliating failure he had been in his efforts to impress the professor. He now exhibited a tendency to repress everything connected with the episode, including the attorney's argument.

3.

In Copyrights

FRED FISHER, INC., v. DILLINGHAM
298 F. 145 (S.D. N.Y. 1924)

Hearing upon bill and answer in a suit upon musical copyright. The composition in question was originally published as instrumental music, in which form it had small success. Later, when published as a song, it gained an enormous vogue, and was sung or played all over the country under the name "Dardanella," but, being of ephemeral quality, had subsided in popularity by the end of 1920. The supposed infringement was a vocal number in the light opera,

* New York: The Free Press, 1960, pp. 35–36. Reprinted by permission of the publisher.

Good Morning, Dearie, composed by the defendant Jerome Kern. The number was called "Kalua," and also attained wide popularity, running into millions of mechanical records and published copies.

There is no similarity between the melodies of the two pieces in any part, but the supposed infringement is in the accompaniment of the chorus or refrain of "Kalua," which has in part an absolute identity with the accompaniment of the verse, though not the chorus, of "Dardanella." This accompaniment introduces the copyright song, and is known in music as an "ostinato," or constantly repeated figure, which produces the effect of a rolling underphrase for the melody, something like the beat of a drum or tom-tom, except that it has a very simple melodic character of its own. It consists of only eight notes, written in two measures and repeated again and again, with no changes, except the variation of a musical fifth in the scale to accommodate itself harmonically to the changes in the melody. Precisely the same eight notes are in the accompaniment to the chorus or refrain of "Kalua," used also as an "ostinato," precisely as they are used in "Dardanella," giving the same effect, and designed, as the composer says, to indicate the booming of a surf upon the beach.

* * *

LEARNED HAND, DISTRICT JUDGE. . . . The copyright to the composition "Dardanella" covered the piece as a whole; there were not several copyrights for each part of it. Nevertheless the plagiarism of any substantial component part, either in melody or accompaniment, would be the proper subject of such a suit as this. To sustain it, however, more must appear than the mere similarity, or even identity, of the supposed infringement with the part in question. In this lies one distinction between a patent and a copyright. One may infringe a patent by the innocent reproduction of the machine patented, but the law imposes no prohibition upon those who, without copying, independently arrive at the precise combination of words or notes which have been copyrighted. The plaintiff therefore concedes that it must show that Kern, the composer, used "Dardanella" as the source of his accompaniment.

The argument is a strong one. Not only is the figure in each piece exactly alike, but it is used in the same way; that is, as an "ostinato" accompaniment. Further, the defendants have been able to discover in earlier popular music neither this figure, nor even any "ostinato" accompaniment whatever. The fact that "Kalua" appeared shortly after "Dardanella" had faded out, and was written by one who had necessarily known it, as a musician knew it, makes it still more hard to assume any independent provenience for "Kalua." Can I suppose that such parallelism could be the result of coincidence only?

Mr. Kern swears that he was quite unconscious of any plagiarism, and on the whole I am disposed to give him the benefit of the doubt. For this I rely, not only upon the impression which he made upon me, but upon the insufficiency of the motive. I cannot agree that the accompaniment was at all as important to the success of "Dardanella" as the plaintiff would ask me to believe. I admit that it was a good bass, and helped; but I think the piece won its success substantially because of the melody. It is, of course, possible that Kern might have lifted it bodily, hoping to escape detection. However, he has an established place among composers of light opera, and has already succeeded more than once. Certainly detection would be a matter of some moment to him. No producer willingly invites the suits which follow musical piracy. Once convicted in such a case, Kern's market might suffer. With the profit small and price high, it seems to me unlikely that he should have set about deliberate plagiarism.

Whether he unconsciously copied the figure, he cannot say, and does not try to. Everything registers somewhere in our memories, and no one can tell what may evoke it. On the whole, my belief is that, in composing the accompaniment to the refrain of "Kalua," Mr. Kern must have followed, probably unconsciously, what he had certainly often heard only a short time before. I cannot really see how else to account for a similarity, which amounts to identity. So to hold I need not reject his testimony that he was unaware of such a borrowing. . . .

On the issue of infringement this conclusion is enough. The point is a new one, but I think it is plain. The author's copyright is an absolute right to prevent others from copying his original collocation of words or notes, and does not depend upon the infringer's good faith. Once it appears that another has in fact used the copyright as the source of his production, he has invaded the author's rights. It is no excuse that in so doing his memory has played him a trick. In an indictment under Copyright Act, § 28 (Comp. St. § 9549), the excuse might be a defense, since the infringement would not be willful; but it is seldom that a tort, as this is, depends upon the purpose of the wrongdoer. Therefore I find with the plaintiff on the issue of infringement.

* * *

. . . As for damages, it seems to me absurd to suggest that it has suffered any injury. "Dardanella" had faded out before "Kalua" appeared; but, if it had been at the peak of its popularity, I do not believe that the accompaniment to the chorus of "Kalua" would have subtracted one copy or one record from its sales. The controversy is "a trivial pother" . . . a mere point of honor, of scarcely more than irritation, involving no substantial interest.

Except that it raises an interesting point of law, it would be a waste of time for every one concerned.

* * *

4.

In Criminal Law

PEOPLE v. GIBSON
92 C.A. 2d 55, 206 P. 2d 375 (Cal. 1949)

WOOD, JUSTICE.

Defendant was charged with the murder of his wife. In a trial by jury, under his plea of not guilty, he was convicted of murder in the first degree, and the punishment was fixed at life imprisonment. . . .

Appellant admits that he killed his wife by cutting her throat with a butcher's boning knife. He contends that the trial court erred as follows: (1) In sustaining objections to his proffered testimony to the effect that before and at the time of the homicide certain matters regarding the character and conduct of his wife were preying on his mind. (2) In sustaining an objection to his offer of proof, by way of a hypothetical question to be asked a psychiatrist, that if such matters were preying on his mind he might then commit homicide without being conscious thereof. . . .

* * *

. . . About three weeks before the homicide Mrs. Gibson had met a Mr. Fricker, aged seventy-eight years, at a dance. In the evening of January 10, 1948, Mrs. Gibson went to a dance with Mr. Fricker. That was the only time they had gone out together. They left the dance about 11:30 P.M. and went in an automobile to a place about one-half block from Mrs. Gibson's apartment, which place was near the entrance to the alley which extended along the brick wall. About midnight they left the automobile there and walked in the alley to the gate in the brick wall. Mrs. Gibson opened the gate and went into the yard. Mr. Fricker remained outside and started to hand to Mrs. Gibson her extra pair of shoes which he had carried as they walked from the automobile. He also tried to kiss Mrs. Gibson, and when he put his head through the gate opening something went over his head, touched his hair, and barely scratched his head. Then he dropped the shoes in the alley and ran about thirty feet. Then as he walked back toward the gate he heard a man inside the wall cursing and saying: "Your are a liar. You told me a damn lie. You are no good. You made me believe I [you] was not here any more and then you are still here." "You don't make be believe I [you] don't work here any more." He then heard a woman shout, "Help." Then suddenly it was quiet, he did not hear anything more, and he left.

Shortly after midnight Mrs. Hellman heard a pounding noise, and upon investigating she found Mrs. Gibson lying on the back porch, bleeding profusely, and with a "horrible gash" in her throat.

* * *

Appellant, a butcher . . . testified that he saw his wife on January 1, 1948, and she told him that she was moving from Mrs. Hellman's place, but she did not tell him where she was going; that thereafter he telephoned to the Hellman residence and someone told him that Mrs. Gibson was not there and had not left a forwarding address . . . that he had also sent her a registered letter, with a request for a return receipt, to Mrs. Hellman's address; that on Saturday, January 10, 1948, his wife told him by telephone that she had left Mrs. Hellman's place on January 1 and had obtained employment in Bel Air, that she could not give him the address because there was no street name, and that she did not know the telephone number; that he asked her in that conversation where he could meet her Sunday morning, and she replied that he should remain in his room Saturday evening and she would telephone him and tell where to meet her; that after he left the market that evening he bought a pint of whisky and took it to his room; that he drank some of the whiskey, lay on the bed and went to sleep; that he was awakened when the landlady came to collect the rent; that he paid her two weeks' rent in advance, and she asked him if he had seen the letter that she had left in his room; that he then saw the registered letter, which he had sent to his wife, lying on the dresser, and it was marked "Refused"; that he then thought it would be a good idea to go to his former residence, the apartment at the rear of Mrs. Hellman's place; that he probably called a taxicab; that he dressed in his better clothes, intending to spend the night there and go to church the next morning; that he finished the bottle of whiskey which he had brought to his room, and when he started to open another bottle of whiskey he could not find his nail file which he customarily used to open bottles; that he then took the knife (the one used in the homicide) from a dresser draw and started to open the bottle with it, and at that time he heard an automobile horn; that he went out to hail the taxicab and ask the driver to wait for him; that he had intended to return to his room before starting on the trip, but the apartment house door closed and locked when he went outside and he did not have his key; that at that time he did not recall "having the knife in my possession"; that he did not know when he put the knife in his pocket; that he got out of the taxicab at the Pacific Electric station in Beverly Hills and went to a café and ordered a drink of whiskey; that he walked from there to his former residence at the rear of Mrs. Hellman's place; that as he approached the place he was a little cautious because he was not sure that his wife was there; that all the blinds in the house were down and the lights in the house were on; that he looked through a crack and saw that some of his wife's things were in the house, and he believed that she was still there; that he knocked on the door but there was no response; that he became worried about his wife because she "never went out at nights that way" in the last year and a half, and because all the windows were closed and there was "only open gas heat in the house, and it was dangerous"; that as he was reaching in his side coat pocket to get a cigarette he "encountered this knife," which was wrapped; that he removed the knife from his pocket, unwrapped it, and threw the paper over the brick wall; that he then cut the screen of the bathroom window with the knife; that he used the knife in trying to push the window open but it did not open, and "the knife bent back"; that he "was getting to feel woozy or wobbly," and being unsteady he leaned against the brick wall and the tree, and he stood "there with my back against the tree, and the wall, kind of wedged in between there so that I could look out the driveway and see my wife when she did arrive"; that while he was in that position he "fell asleep or passed out intoxicated"; that when he awoke he saw his wife with her back and left side toward him, just extending her arms around a man's neck and turning her head sideways, and in turning her head sideways in front of his head she cut off the man's view of appellant; that the man was prevented, by his head, from seeing appellant, "but he [the man], at that time, or prior to that time, when, I don't know—but he had his hands on her buttocks, apparently pulling her towards him," and there "were no shoes in his hands at that time"; that when "I seen him in this position—arms reached, I believe, from him, a step or two removed from him, it seemed as though my best description of it, it was like a toy balloon that was blown up—becoming beyond bounds or out of proportion, only it was like a light, a light bursting, or a light bulb expanding. Everything was a white light. I do remember lunging and striking out at her"; that "That is the last knowledge, the bursting of light, an extreme light or a white light, as you might describe it, that I had any knowledge of it until being in a taxicab on my way home to my residence, and "the next memory I had [after that] was I spoke to the two arresting officers."

*   *   *

[A]ppellant's attorney offered to prove that at the time of the homicide various things were preying on appellant's mind, which things were as follows: That shortly after their marriage he learned that his wife had been a prostitute; that she had absconded with his funds and left him penniless in Louisiana, just prior to the time they were to occupy a new house purchased by him; that she taunted him upon frequent occasions regarding sexual relations she had had with other men; that he had loved her and had always forgiven her transgressions; that he had made her the recipient of many gifts and she was ungrateful and unfaithful; that she had deceived him as to the number of times she had been married and had stated that she had been married twice whereas in fact she had been married seven times; that about midnight on January 10 he observed her in the arms of another man. Then appellant offered to present testimony of a psychiatrist, by way of a hypothetical question based upon the assumption that if said things above mentioned were preying upon the mind of a man, the man might commit homicide without being conscious thereof. The court rejected the offer of proof regarding the things that were preying on appellant's mind, and rejected the offer of the testimony of the psychiatrist. . . . Those rulings of the court were erroneous [but] not prejudicial. The evidence was offered in support of appellant's asserted defense that he committed the act charged without being conscious thereof. Section 26 of the Penal Code provides in part as follows: "All persons are capable of committing crimes except those belonging to the following classes: * * * Five. Persons who committed the act charged without being conscious thereof." According to appellant's own testimony he carried the butcher's boning knife in his overcoat pocket from the place where he was rooming to the home of his wife; that when he found that she was not at home he removed the knife from his pocket, unwrapped it and threw the wrapping paper over the brick wall; that he then stood in a narrow place between the tree and the brick wall so that he could see his wife when she arrived home. Although he testified that "the bursting of light" was the last knowledge he had until he was "in a taxicab on my way home," he also testified that he did "remember lunging and striking out at her." The fact that he knew he lunged and struck at her establishes that he was not unconscious for a while at least after the alleged "bursting of light." In view of that testimony of appellant showing that he was conscious of making the assault, the proffered testimony of the psychiatrist, to the effect that in his opinion there might be circumstances in which a man might commit an assault and might not be conscious thereof, would be practically valueless. It is also to be noted that appellant testified in fine detail as to what he saw when his wife and the man arrived at the place where he was waiting. . . . The period of time from the alleged "bursting of light" to the time he arrived at his home was approximately an hour. Since he testified that he regained consciousness while in a taxicab on the way home, it appears that the period of alleged unconsciousness was less than an hour. A bartender testified that appellant was in the bar late at night and told him that he would not be seeing appellant around there any more—that he (bartender) would be hearing the reason "pretty soon." That incident, indicating consciousness, was before he entered the taxicab to return home. Also he gave the taxicab driver his correct address. Almost immediately after he arrived home he wrote a letter to his relatives stating, in part, "Forgive and forget me this had to come" and "it is the gas chamber for me." In view of the fact that at the time he wrote that letter no one had informed him that he had killed his wife, the statements in the letter that "this had to come" and "it is the gas chamber for me" are wholly contradictory of the theory or assertion that he was not conscious at the time he killed her. The testimony of appellant that he was at the gate when he lunged and struck at her and the fact that blood was outside and inside the apartment and a large pool of blood was in the shower stall indicates that appellant pursued her from the gate to the shower. In order to accept appellant's theory that he became unconscious when his wife was at the gate, a trier of fact would be required to draw the unreasonable conclusion that while he was unconscious he cut her with the knife when she was at the gate and then, while he was still unconscious, pursued her to the shower and there inflicted the fatal cut.

*   *   *

The judgment and the order denying the motion for a new trial are affirmed.

*   *   *

NOTES

NOTE 1

HOLMES, OLIVER W.

The Common Law*

. . . The law takes no account of the infinite varieties of temperament, intellect, and education which make the internal character of a given act so different in different men. It does not attempt to see men as God sees them, for more than one sufficient reason. In the first place, the impossibility of nicely measuring a man's powers and limitations is far clearer than that of ascertaining his knowledge of law, which has been thought to account for what is called the presumption that every man knows the law. But a more satisfactory explanation is, that, when men live in society, a certain average of conduct, a sacrifice of individual peculiarities going beyond a certain point, is necessary to the general welfare. If, for instance, a man is born hasty and awkward, is always having accidents and hurting himself or his neighbors, no doubt his congenital defects will be allowed for in

the courts of Heaven, but his slips are no less troublesome to his neighbors than if they sprang from guilty neglect. His neighbors accordingly require him, at his proper peril, to come up to their standard, and the court which they establish decline to take his personal equation into account.

The rule that the law does, in general, determine liability by blameworthiness, is subject to the limitation that minute differences of character are not allowed for. The law considers, in other words, what would be blameworthy in the average man, the man of ordinary intelligence and prudence, and determines liability by that. If we fall below the level in those gifts, it is our misfortune; so much as that we must have at our peril, for the reasons just given. But he who is intelligent and prudent does not act at his peril, in theory of law. On the contrary, it is only when he fails to exercise the foresight of which he is capable, or exercises it with evil intent, that he is answerable for the consequences.

There are exceptions to the principle that every man is presumed to possess ordinary capacity to avoid harm to his neighbors, which illustrate the rule, and also the moral basis, of liability in general. When a man has a distinct defect of such a nature that all can recognize it as making certain precautions impossible, he will not be held answerable for not taking them. A blind man is not required to see at his peril; and although he is, no doubt, bound to consider his infirmity in regulating his actions, yet if he properly finds himself in a certain situation, the neglect of precautions requiring eyesight would not prevent his recovering for an injury to himself, and, it may be presumed, would not make him liable for injuring another. So it is held that, in cases where he is the plaintiff, an infant of very tender years is only bound to take the precautions of which an infant is capable; the same principle may be cautiously applied where he is defendant. Insanity is a more difficult matter to deal with, and no general rule can be laid down about it. There is no doubt that in many cases a man may be insane, and yet perfectly capable of taking the precautions, and of being influenced by the motives, which the circumstances demand. But if insanity of a pronounced type exists, manifestly incapacitating the sufferer from complying with the rule which he has broken, good sense would require it to be admitted as an excuse.

NOTE 2

WILLIAMS, GLANVILLE L.

Criminal Law*

The discovery of unconscious motivations raises a difficult legal question on the definition of intention.

---

* Boston: Little, Brown & Co., 1881. (pp. 108–9). Reprinted by permission.

* London: Sweet & Maxwell, Ltd., Second Edition, 1961. (pp. 36–38). Reprinted by permission.

Probably unconscious intention is to be ignored for legal purposes (1) because it is difficult to prove satisfactorily, (2) because we have little knowledge of how far the threat of a sanction can influence the unconscious. The most that the law can demand is that socially undesirable wishes should be repressed; it cannot make the individual responsible as for intention if the repressed urge manifests itself in some neurotic symptom which is also of an undesirable nature. Thus: A soldier wishes to escape from the danger of battle, but out of a sense of duty he repressed this striving, which becomes unconscious but manifests itself in a neurotic symptom, such as, paralysis, fainting, or a hysterical fugue. The result may be that initially desired—that he escapes danger; and it is "purposive from the point of view of the patient's personality"; but it is not brought about by conscious intention; it is concealed from awareness; and it is therefore regarded as involuntary.

*   *   *

Again, it is said that dreams frequently express unconscious thoughts and volitions that temporarily become conscious; but a man is not criminally responsible for what he does in a dream. This would be so even if the dream happened to coincide with a conscious desire. D wishes that his wife were dead and considers the possibility of strangling her. One night he dreams that he is carrying out his plan, and actually strangles her in his sleep. This, assuming the facts to be established, is not murder. The *mens rea* of a dream is not a *mens rea* for which a man is punishable; it is only the waking consciousness that involves criminal culpability.

The field of the unconscious is irrelevant to responsibility where it pertains merely to motives, for even conscious motives are ruled out. To illustrate, a man may steal because of an early antagonism to his father, since repressed, which unconsciously leads him to do something of which his father would disapprove. The stealing is deliberate; it is only the motive that belongs to the unconscious. The analysis of neurotic motives is, of course, important in the realm of treatment.

NOTE 3

COMMONWEALTH v. DRUM
58 Penn St. R. 9 (1868)

JUSTICE AGNEW . . .

[I]ntention to kill is the essence of [first degree murder]. Therefore, if an intention to kill exists, it is wilful; if this intention be accompanied by such circumstances as evidence a mind fully conscious of its own purpose and design, it is deliberate; and if sufficient time be afforded to enable the mind fully to frame the design to kill, and to select the instrument, or to frame the plan to carry this design into execu-

tion, it is premeditated. The law fixed upon no length of time as necessary to form the intention to kill, but leaves the existence of a fully formed intent as a fact to be determined by the jury, from all the facts and circumstances in the evidence.

5.

In Family Law

LANG v. LANG
[1955] A.C. 402

*   *   *

The parties were married in South Australia on November 8, 1924. On October 29, 1951, the wife presented a petition to the Supreme Court of Victoria praying for a divorce on the ground that her husband had without just cause or excuse wilfully deserted her and had continued in desertion for three years and upwards.

The appellant denied that he had been guilty of constructive desertion.

*   *   *

LORD PORTER.

. . . The facts are not in dispute. There are in effect concurrent findings that the husband grossly ill-used and insulted his wife over a period of five years and gave her ample justification for leaving him.

The whole and sole question is whether the wife has proved the necessary animus or intent on the part of the husband. How should that animus be ascertained? In particular, (1) is it enough for her to show a course of conduct on the part of the husband which in the eyes of a reasonable man would, by making her life insufferable, be calculated to drive the wife out, the husband's actual intention being immaterial on the footing that every man is presumed to intend the natural and probable consequences of his acts? Or (2) should the objective criterion of the reasonable man's reactions be rejected on the footing that the real question is, did this particular husband (who may not have been reasonable) know that his conduct, if persisted in, would in all human probability result in the wife's departure—it being remembered that it is possible (human nature being what it is) for such knowledge on the husband's part to co-exist with a desire that she should stay, since people often desire a thing but deliberately act in a way which makes that desire unrealizable. Or again (3), should inferences which would naturally be drawn, be wholly disregarded and an intention which would naturally be drawn from the husband's conduct negatived provided there is proved to exist, *de facto*, on his part a genuine desire (however illogical or impossible it may be to square such a desire with his conduct) that the matrimonial union should continue? On this view the husband's desire to maintain the home is conclusive whatever his conduct. All three of these views have found expression in the decided cases.

. . . The material facts are conveniently summarized in the judgment of the Supreme Court of Victoria . . . : "I take up the story in some detail from the respondent's return from the Middle East in 1942. He had been on active service, and that was the time of his return. In a conversation with his son—and the substance of it was repeated to others—he said that thenceforward he was going to be master; and when son asked him whether that meant that he was going to knock his mother about he said that was the only thing she understood. From this time on, I find a series of constant disturbances and acts of violence on his part. There were slaps and punches which he administered to the petitioner on the face and the body. He struck her on occasions with a ruler and with a cane and with a slipper and did this in the undignified way, on occasion, of placing her across his knee and administering punishment in that way. There were bruises put upon her body by these means and the bruises on occasions were seen by other people. He twisted her arms behind her back and so caused her pain, and on occasion he so held the twisted arms in a position that continued for nearly an hour, and when the police arrived, on the summons of one of the children, he was still holding his wife's arms in that position. On two occasions at least he dragged her by the hair into the bathroom and held her under the cold shower. He abused her and he constantly called her a bitch, and there were nightly disturbances created by him, destroying his wife's rest. Now that is a series of incidents and a course of conduct which persisted over several years. She told him on a number of occasions that if he continued that conduct she would have to leave as that conduct was affecting her health. And on one occasion she did leave, and left for some little time. I shall deal with that more particularly, but on another occasion she left and walked the street for the night so that she might not stop in the house."

She separated from him on two occasions, viz., in 1943 and in July, 1948, before they finally parted. On the first occasion she remained away for about two months and was induced to return by promises of amendment, which were, however, promptly and continuously thereafter violated. On some date in July, 1948, he treated her with such violence that, not for the first time, the police had to be invoked. She then asked him to leave, and he did: Returning however, on August 11. On August 13 occurred the culminating incident which caused her finally to leave him. The husband professed to have taken advice from a psychiatric friend as to how he could improve his relations with his wife, and to have been advised to try "Caveman stuff."

It is a little surprising that this suggestion was treated by the husband as a new departure: "Caveman stuff" is not an unfair description for the treatment he had been applying to his wife for years past and which had twice caused her to leave him. However, on August 13, he planned and carried out what he referred to as the "rape of Lucrece"; in the words of the trial judge's finding he "forced sexual intercourse on her in circumstances of calculated and revolting indignity": and told her that he was going to "use her for the same purpose whenever he wanted to and as often as he wanted to." These last words are important. She finally then left and filed her petition, ignoring a number of letters which he wrote begging her to return but not expressing any intention to treat her differently if she did. Her patience was not unnaturally exhausted, and even if he had expressed penitential sentiments it would not have been unreasonable for the wife to doubt their sincerity.

* * *

In the present case the existence of conduct by the husband being of sufficient gravity to constitute the necessary factum, the question is what he intended, or must be taken to have intended, while so conducting himself. Did he intend to bring the matrimonial relations to an end? Let it be supposed that a husband intentionally persists in conduct which the hypothetical reasonable man would think calculated to cause the wife to leave him; is he necessarily guilty of constructive desertion, notwithstanding that he genuinely desires the marriage to survive? If so, evidence of his consistently expressed desire that the wife should stay with him is irrelevant and inadmissible. . . .

In other words, if a man deliberately makes his wife's life unbearable according to an objective standard, i.e., the reasonable man's reactions, is he conclusively presumed to intend to drive her out—the presumption that a man intends the natural and probable consequences of his acts being treated as irrebuttable? . . .

The other view . . . is that no matter how reprehensible has been the husband's behavior, if there is positive and credible evidence negativing any actual intention on his part to end the marriage, the law will not impute such an intention to him.

In Australia . . . in *Moss* v. *Moss* [(1912) 15 C.L.R. 538], on appeal from New South Wales, what has been referred to as the objective test of conduct amounting to constructive desertion was laid down in terms so designed as to make the deserter's actual intentions immaterial if the objective test were justified. If the course of conduct is sufficiently blameworthy and prolonged, the case decides that the law will impute to the guilty party an intention to bring the matrimonial union to an end, whatever his actual or professed desire. Overtures for a reconciliation, for instance, or a genuine *de facto* wish that the wife should stay, will in such a case be overridden by this imputation. . . .

"The matter has been very recently discussed in the High Court in the case of *Baily* v. *Baily* [(1952) 86 C.L.R. 424]. That case makes it plain that the test which has to be applied in these cases is one either of actual intention by the husband to bring the matrimonial relationship to an end or an intention on his part to persist in a course of conduct which any reasonable person would regard as calculated to bring about such a result. It is the second limb of that test which is relied upon in this case, namely, that the facts are such as to show an intention on the husband's part to persist in a course of conduct which any reasonable person would regard as calculated to bring about a rupture in the matrimonial relationship."

. . . *Bain* v. *Bain* [(1923) 33 C.L.R. 317] in substance affirms the same view; though it is a somewhat more complex decision, since it touches expressly on the problem created when there is a clash of intentions, or, if that be strictly impossible, a clash of intention with wish or desire, or aim.

*   *   *

[Consider] the following quotation from *Bain* v. *Bain*: "A man may intend to retain his wife's presence, but also at the same time to pursue a certain line of conduct. If at all hazards he deliberately pursues that line of conduct, his intention to retain his wife's presence is conditional on or subservient to the other intention. If his conduct is such that his wife, as a natural or necessary consequence, is morally coerced into withdrawing, it cannot be said with any truth that the husband intends her to remain. He knows in that case that the result of his deliberate act will be and is his wife's withdrawal, and, therefore, in every real sense he intends that withdrawal."

[The judge] went on to point out that "on countless occasions he must have been in the state of knowing that what he was doing would necessitate her withdrawal. . . ."

*   *   *

In the English decisions there is discernible a similar dualism. The courts . . . certainly use language which suggest that if the respondent desires the partner to remain with him, then the petitioner cannot ever prove constructive desertion. In these cases the court applied a subjective test, viz., the husband's intention. If intention bears the same meaning as desire, this reasoning, when pressed to its logical conclusion, leads to the result that a husband who desires his wife to stay in the matrimonial home simply in order that he may ill-treat her or make her a target for insult, cannot be guilty of constructive desertion. In *Hosegood* v. *Hosegood* [(1960) 66 T.L.R.

(Pt. 1) 735], Denning L. J. . . . conveniently summarizes the two rival strains of English authority in the following passage. He says: "There are at present two schools of thought about constructive desertion. One school says that, in constructive desertion, as in actual desertion, a husband is not to be found guilty, however bad his conduct, unless he had in fact an intention to bring the married life to an end. This school admits that there are many cases where he may be presumed to have that intention. For instance, when a man deliberately makes his wife's life unbearable, he may be presumed to intend to drive her out, because he may be presumed to intend the natural consequences of his acts. But this school says that if in truth the facts negative any intention to bring the married life to an end, the courts should not attribute it to him. For instance, the conduct of an habitual criminal or an habitual drunkard may be so bad that his wife is forced to leave him; but he may be devoted to her, and the last thing he may intend is that she should leave. In such a case this school of thought would hold that there is no desertion: *Boyd* v. *Boyd*. The other school of thought does lip service to the necessity for such an intention, but says that, even if the husband had no intention in fact to bring the married life to an end, yet he is conclusively presumed to intend the natural consequences of his acts: And if his conduct is so bad or so unreasonable that his wife is forced to leave him, he must be presumed to intend her to leave and he is guilty of constructive desertion, however much he may in fact desire her to remain. . . .

. . . "To my mind the views of the first school are logically unanswerable. When people say that a man must be taken to intend the natural consequences of his acts, they fall into error: there is no 'must' about it; it is only 'may'. The presumption of intention is not a proposition of law but a proposition of ordinary good sense. It means this: That, as a man is usually able to foresee what are the natural consequences of his acts, so it is, as a rule, reasonable to infer that he did foresee them and intend them. But, while that is an inference which may be drawn, it is not one which must be drawn. If on all the facts of the case it is not the correct inference, then it should not be drawn."

*   *   *

The difference between the two views is . . . what meaning is to be attached to the word "intention" and what evidence is sufficient to rebut a *prima facie* case.

Prima facie, a man who treats his wife with gross brutality may be presumed to intend the consequences of his acts. Such an inference may indeed be rebutted, but if the only evidence is of continuous cruelty and no rebutting evidence is given, the natural and almost inevitable inference is that the husband intended to drive out the wife. The court is at least entitled, and indeed driven to such an inference unless convincing evidence to the contrary is adduced. In their Lordships' opinion this is the proper approach to the problem, and it must, therefore, be determined whether the natural inference has been rebutted in the present case.

The fact that the question at issue involves a consideration of the effect of the actions of one person upon another adds to the complexities of the case. But, apart from this, the distinction between intention and desire has to be borne in mind. A man may wish one thing and intend another —*Video meliora proboque, Deteriora soquor*—and, indeed, as the High Court have pointed out, a man's intention does not necessarily always remain constant but fluctuates from time to time. Nevertheless, some general principle must be sought and adopted.

But before the question of the rebutting evidence is reached it has first to be determined what is the exact connotation of the word "intention" as used in the relevant cases.

In *Bain* v. *Bain* the High Court visualizes the problem which may arise where the husband appears to be actuated by "intents" which conflict with, or contradict, each other. The answer given is in substance that in such a conjuncture the dominant intention must be ascertained and looked to. . . .

Their Lordships are of opinion that this . . . goes to the root of the matter. But they venture to question whether as a matter of strict terminology a man can be said to entertain conflicting "intentions." A man may well have incompatible desires. He may have an intention which conflicts with a desire, i.e., he may will one thing, and wish another, as when he renounces some cherished article of diet in the interest of health. But "intention" necessarily connotes an element of volition; desire does not. Desires and wishes can exist without any element contributed by the will. What, then, is the legal result where an intention to bring about a particular result (be it proved directly or by inference from conduct) co-exists with a desire that that result should not ensue? That is the substantial point raised by this appeal. The issue may be put more concretely. What legal inference is to be drawn where the whole of a husband's conduct is such that a reasonable man would know—that the particular husband must know—that in all human probability it will result in the departure of the wife from the matrimonial home? Apart from rebutting evidence this, in their Lordships' opinion, is sufficient proof of an intention to disrupt the home: But suppose, further, a husband's hope is that in some way his actions will not produce these natural consequences, that the wife will stay and that the home will not be disrupted. Where a man's own actions are concerned and not their effect on another, the answer is easy. If he desires to resist temptation but yields to it his intention is evidenced by his acts. His better self

is, it may be, overborne, yet in the end his intention is to yield. Where, however, the effect of his actions upon other people is concerned and there is no certainty but only a high degree of probability as to what the result will be, is a court to say that if he did entertain an unjustified hope that his wife would stay, the intention normally to be inferred from his acts is rebutted, and is the correct conclusion that he did not intend to drive her out? In their Lordships' opinion no such conclusion is justified. If the husband knows the probable result of his acts and persists in them, in spite of warning that the wife will be compelled to leave the home, and indeed, as in the present case, has expressed an intention of continuing his conduct and never indicated any intention of amendment, that is enough however passionately he may desire or request that she should remain. His intention is to act as he did, whatever the consequences, though he may hope and desire that they will not produce their probable effect.

To say that is not enough unless he knows that separation must inevitably result from his actions is to ask too much. Men's actions and judgments are not founded upon certainty—in most cases certainty is unascertainable—but on probabilities. No doubt a high degree of probability is required, but no more.

With these considerations in mind, can it be said that the appellant has rebutted the natural inference, which would be drawn from his acts if no countervailing testimony was given? In their Lordships' opinion no sufficient ground has been given for rejecting the findings of the High Court.

. . . They found, and, as their Lordships think, were entitled to find, that the appellant must have known that what he was doing would necessitate her withdrawal if she acted as any reasonable creature would. Such a find, if warranted, is in their Lordships' opinion decisive of the case, and . . . there is in their view ample ground for coming to the conclusion that the appellant must have recognized the gravity of the effect of his behavior though he hoped and desired that it might not have its natural result.

* * *

[F]or the reasons they have indicated, their Lordships will humbly advise Her Majesty to dismiss the appeal.

NOTE

Royal Commission Report on Capital Punishment*

[O]ther witnesses . . . thought it would be most dangerous to provide that "mercy killings" should not be murder, because it would be impossible to de-

* London: Her Majesty's Stationery Office, Cmd. 8932 September 1953. (pp. 63–64).

fine a category which could not be seriously abused. Such a definition could only be in terms of the motive of the offender, but both English and Scottish law have always eschewed definitions in terms of motive, which is notoriously difficult to establish and cannot, like intent, be inferred from a person's overt actions. Moreover, it was agreed by almost all witnesses, including those who thought that there would be no real difficulty in discriminating between genuine and spurious suicide pacts, that, even if such a definition could be devised, it would in practice often prove extremely difficult to distinguish killings where the motive was merciful from those where it was not. How, for example, were the jury to decide whether a daughter had killed her invalid father from compassion, from a desire for material gain, from a natural wish to bring to an end a trying period of her life, or from a combination of motives?

WHAT IS THE PSYCHOANALYTIC THEORY OF THE HUMAN MIND?— THE STRUCTURE, DYNAMICS, ECONOMICS, AND DEVELOPMENT OF ID, EGO, AND SUPEREGO*

In the previous Part we studied the topographic theory and its distinctions between conscious, preconscious, and unconscious. In 1923, Freud noted, "In the further course of psycho-analytic work, these distinctions proved inadequate and, for practical purposes, insufficient. This has become clear in more ways than one; but the decisive instance is as follows. We have formed the idea that in each individual there is a coherent organization of mental processes; and we call this his *ego*. It is to this ego that consciousness is attached; the ego controls the approaches to motility—that is, to the discharge of excitations into the external world; it is the mental agency which supervises all its own constituent processes, and which goes to sleep at night, though even then it exercises the censorship on dreams. From this ego proceed the repressions, too, by means of which it is sought to exclude certain trends in the mind not merely from consciousness but also from other forms of effectiveness and activity. In analysis these trends which have been shut out stand in opposition to the ego, and the analysis is faced with

---

* For materials on adaptation, see Part Six.

the task of removing the resistances which the ego displays against concerning itself with the repressed. Now we find during analysis that, when we put certain tasks before the patient, he gets into difficulties; his associations fail when they should be coming near the repressed. We then tell him that he is dominated by a resistance; but he is quite unaware of the fact, and, even if he guesses from his unpleasurable feelings that a resistance is now at work in him, he does not know what it is or how to describe it. Since, however, there can be no question but that this resistance emanates from his ego and belongs to it, we find ourselves in an unforeseen situation. We have come upon something in the ego itself which is also unconscious, which behaves exactly like the repressed—that is, which produces powerful effects without itself being conscious and which requires special work before it can be made conscious. From the point of view of analytic practice, the consequence of this discovery is that we land in endless obscurities and difficulties if we keep to our habitual forms of expression and try, for instance, to derive neuroses from a conflict between the conscious and the unconscious. We shall have to substitute for this antithesis another, taken from our insight into the structural conditions of the mind—the antithesis between the coherent ego and the repressed which is split off from it.

"For our conception of the unconscious, however, the consequences of our discovery are even more important. Dynamic considerations caused us to make our first correction; our insight into the structure of the mind leads to the second. We recognize that the *Ucs.* does not coincide with the repressed; it is still true that all that is repressed is *Ucs.*, but not all that is *Ucs.* is repressed. A part of the ego, too—and Heaven knows how important a part—may be *Ucs.*, undoubtedly is *Ucs.* And this *Ucs.* belonging to the ego is not latent like the *Pcs.*; for if it were, it could not be activated without becoming *Cs.*, and the process of making it conscious would not encounter such great difficulties. When we find ourselves thus confronted by the necessity of postulating a third *Ucs.*, which is not repressed, we must admit that the characteristic of being unconscious begins to lose significance for us. It becomes a quality which can have many meanings, a quality which we are unable to make, as we should have hoped to do, the basis of far-reaching and inevitable conclusions. . . ."[1]

In this Part we study those forces which Freud came to conceptualize in a structural theory as id, ego, and superego. "To the oldest of these physical provinces or agencies we give the name of *id*. It contains everything that is inherited, that is present at birth, that is laid down in the constitution—above all, therefore, the instincts, which originate from the somatic organization and which find a first psychical expression here [in the id] in forms unknown to us.

"Under the influence of the real external world around us, one portion of the id has undergone a special development. From what was originally a cortical layer, equipped with the organs for receiving stimuli and with arrangements for acting as a protective shield against stimuli, a special organization has arisen which henceforward acts as an intermediary between the id and the external world. To this region of our mind we have given the name of *ego*.

"*Here are the principal characteristics of the ego.* In consequence of the pre-established connection between sense perception and muscular action, the ego has voluntary movement at its command. It has the task of self-preservation. As regards *external* events, it performs that task by becoming aware of stimuli, by storing up experiences about them (in the memory), by avoiding excessively strong stimuli (through flight), by dealing with moderate stimuli (through adap-

---

1. Reprinted from: *The Ego and the Id* (1923), 19 *The Standard Edition of the Complete Psychological Works of Sigmund Freud*, James Strachey, ed. London: The Hogarth Press and the Institute of Psychoanalysis, 1961. (pp. 16–18). Reprinted by permission of Hogarth and W. W. Norton & Co.

tation) and finally by learning to bring about expedient changes in the external world to its own advantage (through activity). As regards *internal* events, in relation to the id, it performs that task by gaining control over the demands of the instincts, by deciding whether they are to be allowed satisfaction, by postponing that satisfaction to times and circumstances favorable in the external world or by suppressing their excitations entirely. . . .

"The long period of childhood, during which the growing human being lives in dependence on his parents, leaves behind it as a precipitate the formation in his ego of a special agency in which this parental influence is prolonged. It has received the name of *superego*. In so far as this superego is differentiated from the ego or is opposed to it, it constitutes a third power which the ego must take into account."[1]

We interrupt the presentation of id, ego, and superego by inserting problems for decision in law. While doing so, we share Waelder's view that "the conceptions id, ego, and superego [should not be] used . . . in the sense of sharply distinguished parts of the personality. [T]hese elements are to be conceived as different factors evidenced in each psychic act of the adult human. The individual actions and fantasies have each their ego, their id, and their superego phase. . . ."[2]

It may be useful while studying the theory of id, ego, and superego to bear in mind the following questions:

Does law develop out of a recognition, express or implied, that id out of control would destroy us as individuals and as a society?

Does law rest on the assumption that man has both an ego and a superego which require nutriment for the control of id?

Does law, though a part of reality, develop as do ego and superego, out of a continuous interaction with id and reality?

Before examining in detail these concepts we turn to one of the basic data of psychoanalysis, the dream. We have selected Freud's own dream about his patient, Irma—the "first dream ever subjected to an exhaustive psychoanalytic interpretation."

---

1. Reprinted from: *An Outline of Psychoanalysis* (1938), 23 *The Standard Edition of the Complete Psychological Works of Sigmund Freud*, James Strachey, ed. London: The Hogarth Press and the Institute of Psychoanalysis, 1964. (pp. 145–46). Reprinted by permission of Hogarth and W. W. Norton & Co.

2. Waelder, R.: "The Principles of Multiple Functions," 5 *Psychoanalytic Quarterly* 61 (1936). Reprinted by permission.

A.

A Dream—A Clue to the Human Mind

FREUD, SIGMUND

The Interpretation of Dreams (1900)*

Preamble

During the summer of 1895 I had been giving psychoanalytic treatment to a young lady who was on

* Reprinted from: 4 *The Standard Edition of the Complete Psychological Works of Sigmund Freud*, James Strachey, ed. London: The Hogarth Press and the Institute of Psychoanalysis, 1953. (pp. 106–21) and Basic Books, Inc., Publishers, 1957. Reprinted by permission of George Allen & Unwin and Basic Books, Inc.

very friendly terms with me and my family. It will be readily understood that a mixed relationship such as this may be a source of many disturbed feelings in a physician and particularly in a psychotherapist. While the physician's personal interest is greater, his authority is less; any failure would bring a threat to the old-established friendship with the patient's family. This treatment had ended in a partial success; the patient was relieved of her hysterical anxiety but did not lose all her somatic symptoms. At that time I was not quite clear in my mind as to the criteria indicating that a hysterical case history was finally closed, and I proposed a solution to the patient which she seemed unwilling to accept. While we were thus at variance, we had broken off the treatment for the summer vacation. One day I had a visit from a junior colleague, one of my oldest friends, who had been staying with my patient, Irma, and her family at their country resort. I asked him how he had found her and he answered: "She's better, but not quite well." I was conscious that my friend Otto's words, or the tone in which he spoke them, annoyed me. I fancied I detected a reproof in them, such as to the effect that I had promised the patient too much; and, whether rightly or wrongly, I attributed the supposed fact of Otto's siding against me to the influence of my patient's relatives, who, as it seemed to me, had never looked with favor on the treatment. However, my disagreeable impression was not clear to me and I gave no outward sign of it. The same evening I wrote out Irma's case history, with the idea of giving it to Dr. M. (a common friend who was at that time the leading figure in our circle) in order to justify myself. That night (or more probably the next morning) I had the following dream, which I noted down immediately after waking.

Dream of July 23–24, 1895

A large hall—numerous guests, whom we were receiving. Among them was Irma. I at once took her on one side, as though to answer her letter and to reproach her for not having accepted my "solution" yet. I said to her: "If you still get pains, it's really only your fault." She replied: "If you only knew what pains I've got now in my throat and stomach and abdomen —it's choking me"—I was alarmed and looked at her. She looked pale and puffy. I thought to myself that after all I must be missing some organic trouble. I took her to the window and looked down her throat, and she showed signs of recalcitrance, like women with artificial dentures. I thought to myself that there was really no need for her to do that. She then opened her mouth properly and on the right I found a big white patch; at another place I saw extensive whitish grey scabs upon some remarkable curly structures which were evidently modeled on the turbinal bones of the nose. I at once called in Dr. M., and he repeated the examination and confirmed it. . . . Dr. M. looked quite different from usual; he was very pale, he walked with a limp, and his chin was clean-shaven. . . . My friend Otto was now standing beside her as well, and my friend Leopold was percussing her through her bodice and saying: "She has a dull area low down on the left." He also indicated that a portion of the skin on the left shoulder was infiltrated. (I noticed this, just as he did, in spite of her dress.) . . . M. said: "There's no doubt it's an infection, but no matter; dysentery will supervene and the toxin will be eliminated." . . . We were directly aware, too, of the origin of the infection. Not long before, when she was feeling unwell, my friend Otto had given her an injection of a preparation of propyl, propyls . . . propionic acid . . . trimethylamin (and I saw before me the formula for this printed in heavy type). . . . Injections of that sort ought not to be made so thoughtlessly. . . . And probably the syringe had not been clean.

This dream has one advantage over many others. It was immediately clear what events of the previous day provided its starting-point. My preamble makes that plain. The news which Otto had given me of Irma's condition and the case history which I had been engaged in writing till far into the night continued to occupy my mental activity even after I was asleep. Nevertheless, no one who had only read the preamble and the content of the dream itself could have the slightest notion of what the dream meant. I myself had no notion. I was astonished at the symptoms of which Irma complained to me in the dream, since they were not the same as those for which I had treated her. I smiled at the senseless idea of an injection of propionic acid and at Dr. M's consoling reflections. Toward its end the dream seemed to me to be more obscure and compressed than it was at the beginning. In order to discover the meaning of all this it was necessary to undertake a detailed analysis.

Analysis

The hall—numerous guests, whom we were receiving. We were spending that summer at Bellevue, a house standing by itself on one of the hills adjoining the Kahlenberg. The house had formerly been designed as a place of entertainment and its reception rooms were in consequence unusually lofty and hall-like. It was at Bellevue that I had the dream, a few days before my wife's birthday. On the previous day my wife had told me that she expected that a number of friends, including Irma, would be coming out to visit us on her birthday. My dream was thus anticipating this occasion: It was my wife's birthday and a number of guests, including Irma, were being received by us in the large hall at Bellevue.

I reproached Irma for not having accepted my solution; I said: "If you still get pains, it's your own fault." I might have said this to her in waking life, and I may actually have done so. It was my view at that time (though I have since recognized it as a wrong one) that my task was fulfilled when I had informed a patient of the hidden meaning of his symptoms: I considered that I was not responsible for whether he accepted the solution or not—though this was what success depended on. I owe it to this mistake, which I have now fortunately corrected, that my life was made easier at a time when, in spite of all my inevitable ignorance, I was expected to produce therapeutic successes. I noticed, however, that the words which I spoke to Irma in the dream showed that I was specially anxious not to be responsible for the pains which she still had. If they were her fault they could not be mine. Could it be that the purpose of the dream lay in this direction?

Irma's complaint: Pains in her throat and abdomen and stomach; it was choking her. Pains in the stomach were among my patient's symptoms but were not very prominent; she complained more of feelings of nausea and disgust. Pains in the throat and abdomen and constriction of the throat played scarcely any part in her illness. I wondered why I decided upon this choice of symptoms in the dream but could not think of an explanation at the moment.

She looked pale and puffy. My patient always had a rosy complexion. I began to suspect that someone else was being substituted for her.

I was alarmed at the idea that I had missed an organic illness. This, as may well be believed, is a perpetual source of anxiety to a specialist whose practice is almost limited to neurotic patients and who is in the habit of attributing to hysteria a great number of symptoms which other physicians treat as organic. On the other hand, a faint doubt crept into my mind—from where, I could not tell—that my alarm was not entirely genuine. If Irma's pains had an organic basis, once again I could not be held responsible for curing them; my treatment only set out to get rid of *hysterical* pains. It occurred to me, in fact, that I was actually *wishing* that there had been a wrong diagnosis; for, if so, the blame for my lack of success would also have been got rid of.

I took her to the window to look down her throat. She showed some recalcitrance, like women with false teeth. I thought to myself that really there was no need for her to do that. I had never had any occasion to examine Irma's oral cavity. What happened in the dream reminded me of an examination I had carried out some time before of a governess: At a first glance she had seemed a picture of youthful beauty, but when it came to opening her mouth she had taken measures to conceal her plates. This led to recollections of other medical examinations and of little secrets revealed in the course of them—to the satisfaction of neither party. "*There was really no need for her to do that*" was no doubt intended in the first place as a compliment to Irma; but I suspected that it had another meaning besides. (If one carries out an analysis attentively, one gets a feeling of whether or not one has exhausted all the background thoughts that are to be expected.) The way in which Irma stood by the window suddenly reminded me of another experience. Irma had an intimate woman friend of whom I had a very high opinion. When I visited this lady one evening I had found her by a window in the situation reproduced in the dream, and her physician, the same Dr. M., had pronounced that she had a diphtheritic membrane. The figure of Dr. M. and the membrane reappear later in the dream. It now occured to me that for the last few months I had had every reason to suppose that this other lady was also a hysteric. Indeed, Irma herself had betrayed the fact to me. What did I know of her condition? One thing

precisely: That, like my Irma of the dream, she suffered from hysterical choking. So in the dream I had replaced my patient by her friend. I now recollected that I had often played with the idea that she too might ask me to relieve her of her symptoms. I myself, however, had thought this unlikely, since she was of a very reserved nature. She was *recalcitrant*, as was shown in the dream. Another reason was that *there was no need for her to do it:* she had so far shown herself strong enough to master her condition without outside help. There still remained a few features that I could not attach either to Irma or to her friend: *pale; puffy; false teeth.* The false teeth took me to the governess whom I have already mentioned; I now felt inclined to be satisfied with *bad* teeth. I then thought of someone else to whom these features might be alluding. She again was not one of my patients, nor should I have liked to have her as a patient, since I had noticed that she was bashful in my presence and I could not think she would make an amenable patient. She was usually pale, and once, while she had been in specially good health, she had looked puffy.[1] Thus I had been comparing my patient Irma with two other people who would also have been recalcitrant to treatment. What could the reason have been for my having exchanged her in the dream for her friend? Perhaps it was that I should have *liked* to exchange her: Either I felt more sympathetic toward her friend or had a higher opinion of her intelligence. For Irma seemed to me foolish because she had not accepted my solution. Her friend would have been wiser, that is to say she would have yielded sooner. She would then have *opened her mouth properly,* and have told me more than Irma.[2]

What I saw in her throat: A white patch and turbinal bones with scabs on them. The white patch reminded me of diphtheritis and so of Irma's friend, but also of a serious illness of my eldest daughter's almost two years earlier and of the fright I had had in those anxious days. The scabs on the turbinal bones recalled a worry about my own state of health. I was making frequent use of cocaine at that time to reduce some troublesome nasal swellings, and I had heard a few days earlier that one of my women patients who

---

1. The still unexplained complaint about *pains in the abdomen* could also be traced back to this third figure. The person in question was, of course, my own wife; the pains in the abdomen reminded me of one of the occasions on which I had noticed her bashfulness. I was forced to admit to myself that I was not treating either Irma or my wife very kindly in this dream; but it should be observed by way of excuse that I was measuring them both by the standard of the good and amenable patient.

2. I had a feeling that the interpretation of this part of the dream was not carried far enough to make it possible to follow the whole of its concealed meaning. If I had pursued, my comparison between the three women, it would have taken me far afield.—There is at least one spot in every dream at which it is unplumable—a navel, as it were, that is its point of contact with the unknown.

had followed my example had developed an extensive necrosis of the nasal mucous membrane. I had been the first to recommend the use of cocaine, in 1885, and this recommendation had brought serious reproaches down on me. The misuse of that drug had hastened the death of a dear friend of mine. This had been before 1895 [the date of the dream].

I at once called in Dr. M., and he repeated the examination. This simply corresponded to the position occupied by M. in our circle. But the "*at once*" was sufficiently striking to require a special explanation. It reminded me of a tragic event in my practice. I had on one occasion produced a severe toxic state in a woman patient by repeatedly prescribing what was at that time regarded as a harmless remedy (sulphonal), and had hurriedly turned for assistance and support to my experienced senior colleague. There was a subsidiary detail which confirmed the idea that I had this incident in mind. My patient—who succumbed to the poison—had the same name as my eldest daughter. It had never occurred to me before, but it struck me now almost like an act of retribution on the part of destiny. It was as though the replacement of one person by another was to be continued in another sense: This Mathilde for that Mathilde, an eye for an eye and a tooth for a tooth. It seemed as if I had been collecting all the occasions which I could bring up against myself as evidence of lack of medical conscientiousness.

Dr. M. was pale, had a clean-shaven chin, and walked with a limp. This was true to the extent that his unhealthy appearance often caused his friends anxiety. The two other features could only apply to someone else. I thought of my elder brother, who lives abroad, who is clean-shaven and whom, if I remembered right, the M. of the dream closely resembled. We had had news a few days earlier that he was walking with a limp owing to an arthritic affection of his hip. There must, I reflected, have been some reason for my fusing into one the two figures in the dream. I then remembered that I had a similar reason for being in an ill humor with each of them: They had both rejected a certain suggestion I had recently laid before them.

My friend Otto was now standing beside the patient and my friend Leopold was examining her and indicated that there was a dull area low down on the left. My friend Leopold was also a physician and a relative of Otto's. Since they both specialized in the same branch of medicine, it was their fate to be in competition with each other, and comparisons were constantly being drawn between them. Both of them acted as my assistants for years while I was still in charge of the neurological out-patients' department of a children's hospital. Scenes such as the one represented in the dream used often to occur there. While I was discussing the diagnosis of a case with Otto, Leopold would be examining the child once more and

would make an unexpected contribution to our decision. The difference between their characters was like that between the bailiff Brasig and his friend Karl: One was distinguished for his quickness, while the other was slow but sure. If in the dream I was contrasting Otto with the prudent Leopold, I was evidently doing so to the advantage of the latter. The comparison was similar to the one between my disobedient patient Irma and the friend whom I regarded as wiser than she was. I now perceived another of the lines along which the chain of thought in the dream branched off: From the sick child to the children's hospital. *The dull area low down on the left* seemed to me to agree in every detail with one particular case in which Leopold had struck me by his thoroughness. I also had a vague notion of something in the nature of a metastatic affection; but this may also have been a reference to the patient whom I should have liked to have in the place of Irma. So far as I had been able to judge, she had produced an imitation of a tuberculosis

A portion of the skin on the left shoulder was infiltrated. I saw at once that this was the rheumatism in my shoulder, which I invariably notice if I sit up late into the night. Moreover, the wording in the dream was most ambiguous: "*I noticed this, just as he did. . . .*" I noticed it in my own body, that is. I was struck, too, by the unusual phrasing: "A portion of the skin was infiltrated." We are in the habit of speaking of "a left upper posterior infiltration," and this would refer to the lung and so once more to tuberculosis.

In spite of her dress. This was in any case only an interpolation. We naturally used to examine the children in the hospital undressed: And this would be a contrast to the manner in which adult female patients have to be examined. I remembered that it was said of a celebrated clinician that he never made a physical examination of his patients except through their clothes. Further than this I could not see. Frankly, I had no desire to penetrate more deeply at this point.

Dr. M. said: "*It's an infection, but no matter. Dysentery will supervene and the toxin will be eliminated.*" At first this struck me as ridiculous. But nevertheless, like all the rest, it had to be carefully analyzed. When I came to look at it more closely it seemed to have some sort of meaning all the same. What I discovered in the patient was a local diphtheritis. I remembered from the time of my daughter's illness a discussion on diphtheritis and diphtheria, the latter being the general infection that arises from the local diphtheritis. Leopold indicated the presence of a general infection of this kind from the existence of a dull area, which might thus be regarded as a metastitic focus. I seemed to think, it is true, that metastases like this do not in fact occur with diphtheria: It made me think rather of pyaemia.

No matter. This was intended as a consolation. It

seemed to fit into the context as follows. The content of the preceding part of the dream had been that my patient's pains were due to a severe organic affection. I had a feeling that I was only trying in that way to shift the blame from myself. Psychological treatment could not be held responsible for the persistence of diphtheritic pains. Nevertheless, I had a sense of awkwardness at having invented such a severe illness for Irma simply in order to clear myself. It looked so cruel. Thus I was in need of an assurance that all would be well in the end, and it seemed to me that to have put the consolation into the mouth precisely of Dr. M. had not been a bad choice. But here I was taking up a superior attitude toward the dream, and this itself required explanation.

And why was the consolation so nonsensical?

Dysentery. There seemed to be some remote theoretical notion that morbid matter can be eliminated through the bowels. Could it be that I was trying to make fun of Dr. M's fertility in producing far-fetched explanations and making unexpected pathological connections? Something else now occurred to me in relation to dysentery. A few months earlier I had taken on the case of a young man with remarkable difficulties associated with defecating, who had been treated by other physicians as a case of "anaemia accompanied by malnutrition." I had recognized it as a hysteria, but had been unwilling to try him with my psychotherapeutic treatment and had sent him on a sea voyage. Some days before, I had had a despairing letter from him from Egypt, saying that he had had a fresh attack there which a doctor had declared was dysentery. I suspected that the diagnosis was an error on the part of an ignorant practitioner who had allowed himself to be taken in by the hysteria. But I could not help reproaching myself for having put my patient in a situation in which he might have contracted some organic trouble on top of his hysterical intestinal disorder. Moreover, "dysentery" sounds not unlike "diphtheria"—a word of ill omen which did not occur in the dream.[1]

Yes, I thought to myself, I must have been making fun of Dr. M. with the consoling prognosis "Dysentery will supervene, etc.": For it came back to me that, years before, he himself had told an amusing story of a similar kind about another doctor. Dr. M. had been called in by him for consultation over a patient who was seriously ill, and had felt obliged to point out, in view of the very optimistic view taken by his colleague, that he had found albumen in the patient's urine. The other, however, was not in the least put out: "*No matter,*" he had said, "the albumen will soon be eliminated!"—I could no longer feel any doubt, therefore, that this part of the dream was expressing derision at physicians who are ignorant of

hysteria. And, as though to confirm this, a further idea crossed my mind: "Does Dr. M. realize that the symptoms in his patient (Irma's friend) which give grounds for fearing tuberculosis also have a hysterical basis? Has he spotted this hysteria or has he been taken in by it?"

But what could be my motive for treating this friend of mine so badly? That was a very simple matter. Dr. M. was just as little in agreement with my "solution" as Irma herself. So I had already revenged myself in this dream on two people: On Irma with the words "If you still get pains, it's your own fault," and on Dr. M. by the wording of the nonsensical consolation that I put into his mouth.

We were directly aware of the origin of the infection. This direct knowledge in the dream was remarkable. Only just before we had had no knowledge of it, for the infection was only revealed by Leopold.

When she was feeling unwell, my friend Otto had given her an injection. Otto had in fact told me that during his short stay with Irma's family he had been called in to a neighboring hotel to give an injection to someone who had suddenly felt unwell. These injections reminded me once more of my unfortunate friend who had poisoned himself with cocaine. I had advised him to use the drug internally [i.e. orally] only, while morphia was being withdrawn; but he had at once given himself cocaine *injections*.

A preparation of propyl . . . propyls . . . propionic acid. How could I have come to think of this? During the previous evening, before I wrote out the case history and had the dream, my wife had opened a bottle of liqueur, on which the word "Ananas"[3] appeared and which was a gift from our friend Otto: For he has a habit of making presents on every possible occasion. It was to be hoped, I thought to myself, that some day he would find a wife to cure him of the habit. This liqueur gave off such a strong smell of fusel oil that I refused to touch it. My wife suggested our giving the bottle to the servants, but I—with even greater prudence—vetoed the suggestion, adding in a philanthropic spirit that there was no need for *them* to be poisoned either. The smell of fusel oil (amyl . . .) evidently stirred up in my mind a recollection of the whole series—propyl, methyl, and so on—and this accounted for the propyl preparation in the dream. It is true that I carried out a substitution in the process: I dreamt of propyl after having smelt amyl. But substitutions of this kind are perhaps legitimate in organic chemistry.

Trimethylamin. I saw the chemical formula of this substance in my dream, which bears witness to a great effort on the part of my memory. Moreover, the formula was printed in heavy type, as though there had been a desire to lay emphasis on some part of the

---

1. The German words *Dysenterie* and *Diphtherie* are more alike than the English ones.

3. I must add that the sound of the word "Ananas" bears a remarkable resemblance to that of my patient Irma's family name.

context as being of quite special importance. What was it, then, to which my attention was to be directed in this way by trimethylamin? It was to a conversation with another friend who had for many years been familiar with all my writings during the period of their gestation, just as I had been with his. He had at that time confided some ideas to me on the subject of the chemistry of the sexual processes, and had mentioned among other things that he believed that one of the products of sexual metabolism was trimethylamin. Thus this substance led me to sexuality, the factor to which I attributed the greatest importance in the origin of the nervous disorders which it was my aim to cure. My patient Irma was a young widow; if I wanted to find an excuse for the failure of my treatment in her case, what I could best appeal to would no doubt be this fact of her widowhood, which her friends would be so glad to see changed. And how strangely, I thought to myself, a dream like this is put together! The other woman, whom I had as a patient in the dream instead of Irma, was also a young widow.

I began to guess why the formula for trimethylamin had been so prominent in the dream. So many important subjects converged upon that one word. Trimethylamin was an allusion not only to the immensely powerful factor of sexuality, but also to a person whose agreement I recalled with satisfaction whenever I felt isolated in my opinions. Surely this friend who played so large a part in my life must appear again elsewhere in these trains of thought. Yes. For he had a special knowledge of the consequences of affections of the nose and its accessory cavities; and he had drawn scientific attention to some very remarkable connections between the turbinal bones and the female organs of sex. (Cf. the three curly structures in Irma's throat.) I had had Irma examined by him to see whether her gastric pains might be of nasal origin. But he suffered himself from suppurative rhinitis, which caused me anxiety; and no doubt there was an allusion to this in the pyaemia which vaguely came into my mind in connection with the metastases in the dream.

Injections of that sort ought not to be made so thoughtlessly. Here an accusation of thoughtlessness was being made directly against my friend Otto. I seemed to remember thinking something of the same kind that afternoon when his words and looks had appeared to show that he was siding against me. It had been some such notion as: "How easily his thoughts are influenced. How thoughtlessly he jumps to conclusions!"—Apart from this, this sentence in the dream reminded me once more of my dead friend who had so hastily resorted to cocaine injections. As I have said, I had never contemplated the drug being given by injection. I noticed too that in accusing Otto of thoughtlessness in handling chemical substances I was once more touching upon the story of the unfortunate Mathilde, which gave grounds for the same accusa-

tion against myself. Here I was evidently collecting instances of my conscientiousness, but also of the reverse.

And probably the syringe had not been clean. This was yet another accusation against Otto, but derived from a different source. I had happened the day before to meet the son of an old lady of eighty-two, to whom I had to give an injection of morphia twice a day. At the moment she was in the country and he told me that she was suffering from phlebitis. I had at once thought it must be an infiltration caused by a dirty syringe. I was proud of the fact that in two years I had not caused a single infiltration; I took constant pains to be sure that the syringe was clean. In short, I was conscientious. The phlebitis brought me back once more to my wife, who had suffered from thrombosis during one of her pregnancies; and now three similar situations came to my recollection involving my wife, Irma, and the dead Mathilde. The identity of these situations had evidently enabled me to substitute the three figures for one another in the dream.

I have now completed the interpretation of the dream. While I was carrying it out I had some difficulty in keeping at bay all the ideas which were bound to be provided by a comparison between the content of the dream and the concealed thoughts lying behind it. And in the meantime the "meaning" of the dream was borne in upon me. I became aware of an intention which was carried into effect by the dream and which must have been my motive for dreaming it. The dream fulfilled certain wishes which were started in me by the events of the previous evening (the news given me by Otto and my writing out of the case history). The conclusion of the dream, that is to say, was that I was not responsible for the persistence of Irma's pains, but that Otto was. Otto had in fact annoyed me by his remarks about Irma's incomplete cure, and the dream gave me my revenge by throwing the reproach back on to him. The dream acquitted me of the responsibility for Irma's condition by showing that it was due to other factors—it produced a whole series of reasons. The dream represented a particular state of affairs as I should have wished it to be. *Thus its content was the fulfilment of a wish and its motive was a wish.*

Thus much leapt to the eyes. But many of the details of the dream also became intelligible to me from the point of view of wish fulfilment. Not only did I revenge myself on Otto for being too hasty in taking sides against me by representing him as being too hasty in his medical treatment (in giving the injection); but I also revenged myself on him for giving me the bad liqueur which had an aroma of fusel oil. And in the dream I found an expression which united the two reproaches: The injection was of a preparation of propyl. This did not satisfy me and I pursued my revenge further by contrasting him with his more trustworthy competitor. I seemed to be saying: "I like *him* better than *you.*" But Otto was not the only person to suffer from the vials of my wrath. I took revenge as well on my disobedient patient by exchanging her for one who was wiser and less recalcitrant. Nor did I allow Dr. M. to escape the consequences of his contradiction but showed him by means of a clear allusion that he was an ignoramus on the subject. ("*Dysentery will supervene*, etc.") Indeed I seemed to be appealing from him to someone else with greater knowledge (to my friend who had told me of trimethylamin) just as I had turned from Irma to her friend and from Otto to Leopold. "Take these people away! Give me three others of my choice instead! Then I shall be free of these undeserved reproaches!" The groundlessness of the reproaches was proved for me in the dream in the most elaborate fashion. *I* was not to blame for Irma's pains, since she herself was to blame for them by refusing to accept my solution. *I* was not concerned with Irma's pains, since they were of an organic nature and quite incurable by psychological treatment. Irma's pains could be satisfactorily explained by her widowhood (cf. the trimethylamin) which *I* had no means of altering. Irma's pains had been caused by Otto giving her an incautious injection of an unsuitable drug—a thing *I* should never have done. Irma's pains were the result of an injection with a dirty needle, like my old lady's phlebitis—whereas *I* never did any harm with my injections. I noticed, it is true, that these explanations of Irma's pains (which agreed in exculpating me) were not entirely consistent with one another, and indeed that they were mutually exclusive. The whole plea—for the dream was nothing else—reminded one vividly of the defense put forward by the man who was charged by one of his neighbors with having given him back a borrowed kettle in a damaged condition. The defendant asserted first, that he had given it back undamaged; secondly, that the kettle had a hole in it when he borrowed it; and thirdly, that he had never borrowed a kettle from his neighbor at all. So much the better: If only a single one of these three lines of defense were to be accepted as valid, the man would have to be acquitted.

Certain other themes played a part in the dream, which were not so obviously connected with my exculpation from Irma's illness: My daughter's illness and that of my patient who bore the same name, the injurious effect of cocaine, the disorder of my patient who was traveling in Egypt, my concern about my wife's health and about that of my brother and of Dr. M., my own physical ailments, my anxiety about my absent friend who suffered from suppurative rhinitis. But when I came to consider all of these, they could all be collected into a single group of ideas and labeled, as it were, "concern about my own and other people's health—professional conscientiousness." I called to mind the obscure disagreeable impression I had had when Otto brought me the news of Irma's condition. This group of thoughts that played a part

in the dream enabled me retrospectively to put this transient impression into words. It was as though he had said to me: "You don't take your medical duties seriously enough. You're not conscientious; you don't carry out what you've undertaken." Thereupon, this group of thoughts seemed to have put itself at my disposal, so that I could produce evidence of how highly conscientious I was, of how deeply I was concerned about the health of my relations, my friends, and my patients. It was a noteworthy fact that this material also included some disagreeable memories, which supported my friend Otto's accusation rather than my own vindication. The material was, as one might say, impartial; but nevertheless there was an unmistakable connection between this more extensive group of thoughts which underlay the dream and the narrower subject of the dream which gave rise to the wish to be innocent of Irma's illness.

I will not pretend that I have completely uncovered the meaning of this dream or that its interpretation is without a gap. I could spend much more time over it, derive further information from it and discuss fresh problems raised by it. I myself know the points from which further trains of thought could be followed. But considerations which arise in the case of every dream of my own restrain me from pursuing my interpretative work. If anyone should feel tempted to express a hasty condemnation of my reticence, I would advise him to make the experiment of being franker than I am. For the moment I am satisfied with the achievement of this one piece of fresh knowledge. If we adopt the method of interpreting dreams which I have indicated here, we shall find that dreams really have a meaning and are far from being the expression of a fragmentary activity of the brain, as the authorities have claimed. *When the work of interpretation has been completed, we perceive that a dream is the fulfilment of a wish.*

NOTE

FREUD, SIGMUND

The Interpretation of Dreams (1900)*

. . . We have accepted the idea that the reason why dreams are invariably wish fulfilments is that they are products of the system *Ucs.*, whose activity knows no other aim than the fulfilment of wishes and which has at its command no other forces than wishful impulses. If we insist, for even a moment longer, upon our right to base such far-reaching psychological speculations

* Reprinted from: 5 *The Standard Edition of the Complete Psychological Works of Sigmund Freud*, James Strachey, ed. London: The Hogarth Press and the Institute of Psychoanalysis, 1953. (pp. 568–70) and Basic Books, Inc., Publishers, 1957. Reprinted by permission of George Allen & Unwin and Basic Books, Inc.

upon the interpretation of dreams, we are in duty bound to prove that those speculations have enabled us to insert dreams into a nexus which can include other psychical structures as well. If such a thing as a system *Ucs.* exists (or something analogous to it for the purposes of our discussion), dreams cannot be its only manifestation; every dream may be a wish fulfilment, but apart from dreams there must be other forms of abnormal wish fulfilments. And it is a fact that the theory governing all psychoneurotic symptoms culminates in a single proposition, which asserts that *they too are to be regarded as fulfilments of unconscious wishes.*[1] Our explanation makes the dream only the first member of a class which is of the greatest significance to psychiatrists and an understanding of which implies the solution of the purely psychological side of the problem of psychiatry.[2]

The other members of this class of wish fulfilments —hysterical symptoms, for instance—possess one essential characteristic, however, which I cannot discover in dreams. . . . A symptom is not merely the expression of a realized unconscious wish; a wish from the preconscious which is fulfilled by the same symptom must also be present. So that the symptom will have *at least* two determinants, one arising from

each of the systems involved in the conflict. As in the case of dreams, there are no limits to the further determinants that may be present—to the "overdetermination" of the symptoms. The determinant which does not arise from the *Ucs.* is invariably, so far as I know, a train of thought reacting against the unconscious wish—a self-punishment, for instance. I can therefore make the quite general assertion that *a hysterical symptom develops only where the fulfilments of two opposing wishes, arising each from a different psychical system, are able to converge in a single expression.* . . . Examples would serve very little purpose here, since nothing but an exhaustive elucidation of the complications involved could carry conviction. I will, therefore, leave my assertion to stand for itself and only quote an example in order to make the point clear, and not to carry conviction. In one of my women patients, then, hysterical vomiting turned out to be on the one hand the fulfilment of an unconscious fantasy dating from her puberty—of a wish, that is, that she might be continuously pregnant and have innumerable children, with a further wish, added later, that she might have them by as many men as possible. A powerful defensive impulse had sprung up against this unbridled wish. And, since the patient might lose her figure and her good looks as a result of her vomiting, and so might cease to be attractive to anyone, the symptom was acceptable to the punitive train of thought as well; and since it was permitted by both sides it could become a reality. . . .

---

1. Or more correctly, one portion of the sympton corresponds to the unconscious wish fulfilment and another portion to the mental structure reacting against the wish.

2. As Hughlings Jackson said: "Find out all about dreams and you will have found out all about insanity."

B.

Id

1.

FREUD, SIGMUND

Three Essays on the Theory of Sexuality (1905)*

The fact of the existence of sexual needs in human beings and animals is expressed in biology by the assumption of a "sexual instinct," on the analogy of the instinct of nutrition, that is, of hunger. Everyday language possesses no counterpart to the word "hunger," but science makes use of the word "libido" for that purpose.

Popular opinion has quite definite ideas about the nature and characteristics of this sexual instinct. It is generally understood to be absent in childhood, to set

* Reprinted from: 7 *The Standard Edition of the Complete Psychological Works of Sigmund Freud*, James Strachey, ed. London: The Hogarth Press and the Institute of Psychoanalysis, 1953. (pp. 135–208) and *Studies on Hysteria*, Basic Books, Inc., Publishers, 1957. Reprinted by permission of Hogarth and Basic Books, Inc.

in at the time of puberty in connection with the process of coming to maturity and to be revealed in the manifestations of an irresistible attraction exercised by one sex upon the other; while its aim is presumed to be sexual union, or at all events actions leading in that direction. We have every reason to believe, however, that these views give a very false picture of the true situation. If we look into them more closely we shall find that they contain a number of errors, inaccuracies, and hasty conclusions.

I shall at this point introduce two technical terms. Let us call the person from whom sexual attraction proceeds the *sexual object* and the act toward which the instinct tends the *sexual aim.* . . .

* * *

The normal sexual aim is regarded as being the union of the genitals in the act known as copulation, which leads to a release of the sexual tension and a temporary extinction of the sexual instinct—a satisfaction analogous to the sating of hunger. But even in the most normal sexual process we may detect rudiments which, if they had developed, would have led to the deviations described as "perversions." For there are certain intermediate relations to the sexual object, such as touching and looking at it, which lie on the road toward copulation and are recognized as being preliminary sexual aims. On the one hand these activities are themselves accompanied by pleasure, and on the other hand they intensify the excitation, which should persist until the final sexual aim is attained. Moreover, the kiss, one particular contact of this kind, between the mucous membrane of the lips of the two people concerned, is held in high sexual esteem among many nations (including the most highly civilized ones), in spite of the fact that the parts of the body involved do not form part of the sexual apparatus but constitute the entrance to the digestive tract. Here, then, are factors which provide a point of contact between the perversions and normal sexual life and which can also serve as a basis for their classification. Perversions are sexual activities which either (a) extend, in an anatomical sense, beyond the regions of the body that are designed for sexual union, or (b) linger over the intermediate relations to the sexual object which should normally be traversed rapidly on the path toward the final sexual aim.

*   *   *

[I]nfantile amnesia, which turns everyone's childhood into something like a prehistoric epoch and conceals from him the beginnings of his own sexual life, is responsible for the fact that in general no importance is attached to childhood in the development at sexual life. . . .

The Period of Sexual Latency in Childhood and its Interruptions

*   *   *

There seems no doubt that germs of sexual impulses are already present in the newborn child and that these continue to develop for a time, but are then overtaken by a progressive process of suppression; this in turn is itself interrupted by periodical advances in sexual development or may be held up by individual peculiarities. Nothing is known for certain concerning the regularity and periodicity of this oscillating course of development. It seems, however, that the sexual life of children usually emerges in a form accessible to observation round about the third or fourth year of life.

It is during this period of total or only partial latency that are built up the mental forces which are later to impede the course of the sexual instinct and, like dams, restrict its flow—disgust, feelings of shame, and the claims of aesthetic and moral ideals. One gets an impression from civilized children that the construction of these dams is a product of education,

and no doubt education has much to do with it. But in reality this development is organically determined and fixed by heredity, and it can occasionally occur without any help at all from education. Education will not be trespassing beyond its appropriate domain if it limits itself to following the lines which have already been laid down organically and to impressing them somewhat more clearly and deeply.

What is it that goes to the making of these constructions which are so important for the growth of a civilized and normal individual? They probably emerge at the cost of the infantile sexual impulses themselves. Thus the activity of those impulses does not cease even during this period of latency, though their energy is diverted, wholly or in great part, from their sexual use and directed to other ends. Historians of civilization appear to be at one in assuming that powerful components are acquired for every kind of cultural achievement by this diversion of sexual instinctual forces from sexual aims and their direction to new ones—a process which deserves the name of "sublimation." To this we would add, accordingly, that the same process plays a part in the development of the individual and we would place its beginning in the period of sexual latency of childhood.

It is possible further to form some idea of the mechanism of this process of sublimation. On the one hand, it would seem, the sexual impulses cannot be utilized during these years of childhood, since the reproductive functions have been deferred—a fact which constitutes the main feature of the period of latency. On the other hand, these impulses would seem in themselves to be perverse—that is, to arise from erotogenic zones and to derive their activity from instincts which, in view of the direction of the subject's development, can only arouse unpleasurable feelings. They consequently evoke opposing mental forces (reacting impulses) which, in order to suppress this unpleasure effectively, build up the mental dams . . . disgust, shame, and morality.

We must not deceive ourselves as to the hypothetical nature and insufficient clarity of our knowledge concerning the processes of the infantile period of latency or deferment; but we shall be on firmer ground in pointing out that such an application of infantile sexuality represents an educational ideal from which individual development usually diverges at some point and often to a considerable degree. From time to time a fragmentary manifestation of sexuality which has evaded sublimation may break through; or some sexual activity may persist through the whole duration of the latency period until the sexual instinct emerges with greater intensity at puberty. Insofar as educators pay any attention at all to infantile sexuality, they behave exactly as though they shared our views as to the construction of the moral defensive forces at the cost of sexuality, and as though they knew that sexual activity makes a child ineducable: For they stigmatize every sexual manifestation by children as a "vice," without being able to do much against it. . . .

The Manifestations of Infantile Sexuality

For reasons which will appear later, I shall take thumb sucking (or sensual sucking) as a sample of the sexual manifestations of childhood. . . .

Thumb sucking appears already in early infancy and may continue into maturity, or even persist all through life. It consists in the rhythmic repetition of a sucking contact by the mouth (or lips). There is no question of the purpose of this procedure being the taking of nourishment. A portion of the lip itself, the tongue, or any other part of the skin within reach— even the big toe—may be taken as the object upon which this sucking is carried out. In this connection a grasping instinct may appear and may manifest itself as a simultaneous rhythmic tugging at the lobes of the ears or a catching hold of some part of another person (as a rule the ear) for the same purpose. Sensual sucking involves a complete absorption of the attention and leads either to sleep or even to a motor reaction in the nature of an orgasm. It is not infrequently combined with rubbing some sensitive part of the body such as the breast or the external genitalia. Many children proceed by this path from sucking to masturbation.

. . . In the nursery, sucking is often classed along with the other kinds of sexual "naughtiness" of children. This view has been most energetically repudiated by numbers of pediatricians and nerve specialists, though this is no doubt partly due to a confusion between "sexual" and "genital." Their objection raises a difficult question and one which cannot be evaded: What is the general characteristic which enables us to recognize the sexual manifestations of children? The concatenation of phenomena into which we have been given an insight by psychoanalytic investigation justifies us, in my opinion, in regarding thumb sucking as a sexual manifestation and in choosing it for our study of the essential features of infantile sexual activity.

We are in duty bound to make a thorough examination of this example. It must be insisted that the most striking feature of this sexual activity is that the instinct is not directed toward other people, but obtains satisfaction from the subject's own body. It is "autoerotic." . . .

Furthermore, it is clear that the behavior of a child who indulges in thumb sucking is determined by a search for some pleasure which has already been experienced and is now remembered. In the simplest case he proceeds to find this satisfaction by sucking rhythmically at some part of the skin or mucous membrane. It is also easy to guess the occasions on which the child had his first experiences of the pleasure which he is now striving to renew. It was the child's first and most vital activity, his sucking at his mother's breast, or at substitutes for it, that must have familiarized him with this pleasure. The child's lips, in our view, behave like an erotogenic zone, and no doubt stimulation by the warm flow of milk is the cause of the pleasurable sensation. The satisfaction of the erotogenic zone is associated, in the first instance, with the satisfaction of the need for nourishment. To begin with, sexual activity attaches itself to functions serving the purpose of self-preservation and does not become independent of them until later. No one who has seen a baby sinking back satiated from the breast and falling asleep with flushed cheeks and a blissful smile can escape the reflection that this picture persists as a prototype of the expression of sexual satisfaction in later life. The need for repeating the sexual satisfaction now becomes detached from the need for taking nourishment—a separation which becomes inevitable when the teeth appear and food is no longer taken in only by sucking, but is also chewed up. The child does not make use of an extraneous body for his sucking, but prefers a part of his own skin because it is more convenient, because it makes him independent of the external world, which he is not yet able to control, and because in that way he provides himself, as it were, with a second erotogenic zone, though one of an inferior kind. The inferiority of this second region is among the reasons why at a later date he seeks the corresponding part—the lips—of another person. ("It's a pity I can't kiss myself," he seems to be saying.)

It is not every child who sucks in this way. It may be assumed that those children do so in whom there is a constitutional intensification of the erotogenic significance of the labial region. If that significance persists, these same children when they are grown up will become epicures in kissing, will be inclined to perverse kissing, or, if males, will have a powerful motive for drinking and smoking. If, however, repression ensues, they will feel disgust at food and will produce hysterical vomiting. The repression extends to the nutritional instinct owing to the dual purpose served by the labial zone. Many of my women patients who suffer from disturbances of eating, *globus hystericus*, constriction of the throat and vomiting, have indulged energetically in sucking during their childhood.

Our study of thumb sucking or sensual sucking has already given us the three essential characteristics of an infantile sexual manifestation. At its origin it attaches itself to one of the vital somatic functions; it has as yet no sexual object, and is thus autoerotic; and its sexual aim is dominated by an erotogenic zone. It is to be anticipated that these characteristics will be found to apply equally to most of the other activities of the infantile sexual instincts.

The Sexual Aim of Infantile Sexuality

The example of thumb sucking shows us still more

about what constitutes an erotogenic zone. It is a part of the skin or mucous membrane in which stimuli of a certain sort evoke a feeling of pleasure possessing a particular quality. There can be no doubt that the stimuli which produce the pleasure are governed by special conditions, though we do not know what those are. A rhythmic character must play a part among them and the analogy of tickling is forced upon our notice. It seems less certain whether the character of the pleasurable feeling evoked by the stimulus should be described as a "specific" one—a "specific" quality in which the sexual factor would precisely lie. Psychology is still so much in the dark in questions of pleasure and unpleasure that the most cautious assumption is the one most to be recommended. . . .

The character of erotogenicity can be attached to some parts of the body in a particularly marked way. There are predestined erotogenic zones, as is shown by the example of sucking. The same example, however, also shows us that any other part of the skin or mucous membrane can take over the functions of an erotogenic zone, and must, therefore, have some aptitude in that direction. Thus the quality of the stimulus has more to do with producing the pleasurable feeling than has the nature of the part of the body concerned. A child who is indulging in sensual sucking searches about his body and chooses some part of it to suck—a part which is afterwards preferred by him from force of habit; if he happens to hit upon one of the predestined regions (such as the nipples or genitals) no doubt it retains the preference. A precisely analogous tendency to displacement is also found in the symptomatology of hysteria. In that neurosis repression affects most of all the actual genital zones and these transmit their susceptibility to stimulation to other erotogenic zones (normally neglected in adult life), which then behave exactly like genitals. But besides this, precisely as in the case of sucking, any other part of the body can acquire the same susceptibility to stimulation as is possessed by the genitals and can become an erotogenic zone. . . .

The sexual aim of the infantile instinct consists in obtaining satisfaction by means of an appropriate stimulation of the erotogenic zone which has been selected in one way or another. This satisfaction must have been previously experienced in order to have left behind a need for its repetition; and we may expect that nature will have made safe provisions so that this experience of satisfaction shall not be left to chance. We have already learnt what the contrivance is that fulfils this purpose in the case of the labial zone: It is the simultaneous connection which links this part of the body with the taking in of food. . . . We can, therefore, formulate a sexual aim in another way: It consists in replacing the projected sensation of stimulation in the erotogenic zone by an external stimulus which removes that sensation by producing a feeling of satisfaction. This external stimulus will usually consist in some kind of manipulation that is analogous to the sucking.

*   *   *

Masturbatory Sexual Manifestations

It must come as a great relief to find that, when once we have understood the nature of the instinct arising from a single one of the erotogenic zones, we shall have very little more to learn of the sexual activity of children. The clearest distinctions as between one zone and another concern the nature of the contrivance necessary for satisfying the instinct; in the case of the labial zone it consisted of sucking, and this has to be replaced by other muscular actions according to the position and nature of the other zones.

Like the labial zone, the anal zone is well suited by its position to act as a medium through which sexuality may attach itself to other somatic functions. It is to be presumed that the erotogenic significance of this part of the body is very great from the first. We learn with some astonishment from psychoanalysis of the transmutations normally undergone by the sexual excitations arising from this zone and of the frequency with which it retains a considerable amount of susceptibility to genital stimulation throughout life. The intestinal disturbances which are so common in childhood see to it that the zone shall not lack intense excitations. Intestinal catarrhs at the tenderest age make children "nervy," as people say, and in cases of later neurotic illness they have a determining influence on the symptoms in which the neurosis is expressed, and they put at its disposal the whole range of intestinal disturbances. . . .

Children who are making use of the susceptibility to erotogenic stimulation of the anal zone betray themselves by holding back their stool till its accumulation brings about violent muscular contractions and, as it passes through the anus, is able to produce powerful stimulation of the mucous membrane. In so doing it must no doubt cause not only painful but also highly pleasurable sensations. One of the clearest signs of subsequent eccentricity or nervousness is to be seen when a baby obstinately refuses to empty his bowels when he is put on the pot—that is, when his nurse wants him to—and holds back that function till he himself chooses to exercise it. He is naturally not concerned with dirtying the bed, he is only anxious not to miss the subsidiary pleasure attached to defecating. Educators are once more right when they describe children who keep the process back as "naughty."

The contents of the bowels, which act as a stimulating mass upon a sexually sensitive portion of mucous membrane, behave like forerunners of another organ, which is destined to come into action after the phase of childhood. But they have other important meanings for the infant. They are clearly treated as a part of the infant's own body and represent his first "gift": by producing them he can express his active compliance with his environment and, by witholding them, his disobedience. From being a "gift" they later come to acquire the meaning of "baby"—for babies, according to one of the sexual theories of children, are acquired by eating and are born through the bowels.

The retention of the fecal mass, which is thus carried out intentionally by the child to begin with, in order to serve, as it were, as a masturbatory stimulus upon the anal zone or to be employed in his relation to the people looking after him, is also one of the roots of the constipation which is so common among neuropaths. Further, the whole significance of the anal zone is reflected in the fact that few neurotics are to be found without their special scatological practices, ceremonies, and so on, which they carefully keep secret.

*   *   *

Among the erotogenic zones that form part of the child's body there is one which certainly does not play the opening part, and which cannot be the vehicle of the oldest sexual impulses, but which is destined to great things in the future. In both male and female children it is brought into connection with micturition (in the glans and clitoris) and in the former is enclosed in a pouch of mucous membrane, so that there can be no lack of stimulation of it by secretions which may give an early start to sexual excitation. The sexual activities of this erotogenic zone, which forms part of the sexual organs proper, are the beginning of what is later to become "normal" sexual life. The anatomical situation of this region, the secretions in which it is bathed, the washing and rubbing to which it is subjected in the course of a child's toilet, as well as accidental stimulation . . . make it inevitable that the pleasurable feeling which this part of the body is capable of producing should be noticed by children even during their earliest infancy, and should give rise to a need for its repetition. If we consider this whole range of contrivances and bear in mind that both making a mess and measures for keeping clean are bound to operate in much the same way, it is scarcely possible to avoid the conclusion that the foundations for the future primacy over sexual activity exercised by this erotogenic zone are established by early infantile masturbation, which scarcely a single individual escapes. The action which disposes of the stimulus and brings about satisfaction consists in a rubbing movement with the hand or in the application of pressure (no doubt on the lines of a pre-existing reflex) either from the hand or by bringing the thighs together. This last method is by far the more common in the case of girls. The preference for the hand which is shown by boys is already evidence of the important contribution which the instinct for mastery is destined to make to masculine sexual activity.

It will be in the interests of clarity if I say at once that three phases of infantile masturbation are to be distinguished. The first of these belongs to early infancy, and the second to the brief efflorescence of sexual activity about the fourth year of life; only the third phase corresponds to pubertal masturbation, which is often the only kind taken into account.

The masturbation of early infancy seems to disappear after a short time; but it may persist uninterruptedly until puberty, and this would constitute the first great deviation from the course of development laid down for civilized men. At some point of childhood after early infancy, as a rule before the fourth year, the sexual instinct belonging to the genital zone usually revives and persists again for a time until it is once more suppressed, or it may continue without interruption. This second phase of infantile sexual activity may assume a variety of different forms which can only be determined by a precise analysis of individual cases. But all its details leave behind the deepest (unconscious) impressions in the subject's memory, determine the development of his character, if he is to remain healthy, and the symptomatology of his neurosis, if he is to fall ill after puberty. In the latter case we find that this sexual period has been forgotten and that the conscious memories that bear witness to it have been displaced. . . .

During the years of childhood with which I am now dealing, the sexual excitation of early infancy returns, either as a centrally determined tickling stimulus which seeks satisfaction in masturbation, or as a process in the nature of a nocturnal emission which, like the nocturnal emissions of adult years, achieves satisfaction without the help of any action by the subject. The latter case is the more frequent with girls and in the second half of childhood; its determinants are not entirely intelligible and often, though not invariably, it seems to be conditioned by a period of earlier *active* masturbation. The symptoms of these sexual manifestations are scanty; they are mostly displayed on behalf of the still undeveloped sexual apparatus by the *urinary* apparatus, which thus acts, as it were, as the former's trustee. Most of the so-called bladder disorders of this period are sexual disturbances: Nocturnal enuresis, unless it represents an epileptic fit, corresponds to a nocturnal emission.

The reappearance of sexual activity is determined by internal causes and external contingencies, both of which can be guessed in cases of neurotic illness from the form taken by their symptoms and can be discovered with certainty by psychoanalytic investigation. I shall have to speak presently of the internal causes; great and lasting importance attaches at this period to the accidental *external* contingencies. In the foreground we find the effects of seduction, which treats a child as a sexual object prematurely and teaches him, in highly emotional circumstances, how to obtain satisfaction from his genital zones, a satisfaction which he is then usually obliged to repeat again and again by masturbation. An influence of this kind may originate either from adults or from other children. . . . Obviously seduction is not required in order to arouse a child's sexual life; that can also come about spontaneously from internal causes.

*   *   *

Moreover, the effects of seduction do not help to reveal the early history of the sexual instinct; they rather confuse our view of it by presenting children prematurely with a sexual object for which the infantile sexual instinct at first shows no need. It must, however, be admitted that infantile sexual life, in spite of the preponderating dominance of erotogenic zones, exhibits components which from the very first involve other people as sexual objects. Such are the instincts of scopophilia, exhibitionism, and cruelty, which appear in a sense independently of erotogenic zones; these instincts do not enter into intimate relations with genital life until later, but are already to be observed in childhood as independent impulses, distinct in the first instance from erotogenic sexual activity. Small children are essentially without shame, and at some periods of their earliest years show an unmistakable satisfaction in exposing their bodies, with especial emphasis on the sexual parts. The counterpart of this supposedly perverse inclination, curiosity to see other people's genitals, probably does not become manifest until somewhat later in childhood, when the obstacle set up by a sense of shame has already reached a certain degree of development. Under the influence of seduction the scopophilic perversion can attain great importance in the sexual life of a child. But my researches into the early years of normal people, as well as of neurotic patients, force me to the conclusion that scopophilia can also appear in children as a spontaneous manifestation. Small children whose attention has once been drawn—as a rule by masturbation—to their own genitals usually take the further step without help from outside and develop a lively interest in the genitals of their playmates. Since opportunities for satisfying curiosity of this kind usually occur only in the course of satisfying the two kinds of need for excretion, children of this kind turn into *voyeurs*, eager spectators of the processes of micturition and defecation. When repression of these inclinations sets in, the desire to see other people's genitals (whether of their own or the opposite sex) persists as a tormenting compulsion, which in some cases of neurosis later affords the strongest motive force for the formation of symptoms.

The cruel component of the sexual instinct develops in childhood even more independently of the sexual activities that are attached to erotogenic zones. Cruelty in general comes easily to the childish nature, since the obstacle that brings the instinct for mastery to a halt at another person's pain—namely a capacity for pity—is developed relatively late. The fundamental psychological analysis of this instinct has, as we know, not yet been satisfactorily achieved. It may be assumed that the impulse of cruelty arises from the instinct for mastery and appears at a period of sexual life at which the genitals have not yet taken over their later role. It then dominates a phase of sexual life which we shall later describe as a pregenital organization. . . .

The Sexual Researches of Childhood

At about the same time as the sexual life of children reaches its first peak, between the ages of three and five, they also begin to show signs of the activity which may be ascribed to the instinct for knowledge or research. This instinct cannot be counted among the elementary instinctual components, nor can it be classed as exclusively belonging to sexuality. Its activity corresponds on the one hand to a sublimated manner of obtaining mastery, while on the other hand it makes use of the energy of scopophilia. Its relations to sexual life, however, are of particular importance, since we have learnt from psychoanalysis that the instinct for knowledge in children is attracted unexpectedly early and intensively to sexual problems and is in fact possibly first aroused by them.

It is not by theoretical interests but by practical ones that activities of research are set going in children. The threat to the bases of a child's existence offered by the discovery or the suspicion of the arrival of a new baby and the fear that he may, as a result of it, cease to be cared for and loved, make him thoughtful and clear-sighted. And this history of the instinct's origin is in line with the fact that the first problem with which it deals is not the question of the distinction between the sexes but the riddle of where babies come from. . . . On the contrary, the existence of two sexes does not to begin with arouse any difficulties or doubts in children. It is self-evident to a male child that a genital like his own is to be attributed to everyone he knows, and he cannot make its absence tally with his picture of these other people.

This conviction is energetically maintained by boys, is obstinately defended against the contradictions which soon result from observation, and is only abandoned after severe internal struggles (the castration complex). . . .

The assumption that all human beings have the same (male) form of genital is the first of the many remarkable and momentous sexual theories of children. . . .

Little girls do not resort to denial of this kind when they see that boys' genitals are formed differently from their own. They are ready to recognize them immediately and are overcome by envy for the penis—an envy culminating in the wish, which is so important in its consequences, to be boys themselves.

*   *   *

The Phases of Development of the Sexual Organization

The characteristics of infantile sexual life which we have hitherto emphasized are the facts that it is essentially autoerotic (i.e., that it finds its object in the infant's own body) and that its individual component instincts are upon the whole disconnected and independent of one another in their search for pleasure. The final outcome of sexual development lies in what is known as the normal sexual life of the adult, in which the pursuit of pleasure comes under the sway of the reproductive function and in which the component instincts, under the primacy of a single erotogenic zone, form a firm organization directed toward a sexual aim attached to some extraneous sexual object.

The study, with the help of psychoanalysis, of the inhibitions and disturbances of this process of development enables us to recognize abortive beginnings and preliminary stages of a firm organization of the component instincts such as this—preliminary stages which themselves constitute a sexual regime of a sort. These phases of sexual organization are normally passed through smoothly, without giving more than a hint of their existence. It is only in pathological cases that they become active and recognizable to superficial observation.

We shall give the name of "pregenital" to organizations of sexual life in which the genital zones have not yet taken over their predominant part. We have hitherto identified two such organizations, which almost seem as though they were harking back to early animal forms of life.

The first of these is the oral or, as it might be called, cannibalistic pregenital sexual organization. Here sexual activity has not yet been separated from the ingestion of food; nor are opposite currents within the activity differentiated. The *object* of both activities is the same; the sexual *aim* consists in the incorporation of the object—the prototype of a process which, in the form of identification, is later to play such an important psychological part. A relic of this constructed phase of organization, which is forced upon our notice by pathology, may be seen in thumb sucking, in which the sexual activity, detached from the nutritive activity, has substituted for the extraneous object one situated in the subject's own body.

A second pregenital phase is that of the sadistic-anal organization. Here the opposition between two currents, which runs through all sexual life, is already developed: They cannot yet, however, be described as "masculine" and "feminine," but only as "active" and "passive." The *activity* is put into operation by the instinct for mastery through the agency of the somatic musculature; the organ which, more than any other, represents the *passive* sexual aim is the erotogenic mucous membrane of the anus. Both of these currents have objects, which, however, are not identical. Alongside these, other component instincts operate in an autoerotic manner. In this phase, therefore, sexual polarity and an extraneous object are already observable. But organization and subordination to the reproductive function are still absent.

This form of sexual organization can persist throughout life and can permanently attract a large portion of sexual activity to itself. The predominance in it of sadism and the cloacal part played by the anal zone give it a quite peculiarly archaic coloring. It is further characterized by the fact that in it the opposing pairs of instincts are developed to an approximately equal extent, a state of affairs described by Bleuler's happily chosen term "ambivalence."

The assumption of the existence of pregenital organizations of sexual life is based on the analysis of the neuroses, and without a knowledge of them can scarcely be appreciated. Further analytic investigation may be expected to provide us with far more information on the structure and development of the normal sexual function.

In order to complete our picture of infantile sexual life, we must also suppose that the choice of an object, such as we have shown to be characteristic of the pubertal phase of development, has already frequently or habitually been effected during the years of childhood: That is to say, the whole of the sexual currents have become directed toward a single person in relation to whom they seek to achieve their aims. This then is the closest approximation possible in childhood to the final form taken by sexual life after puberty. The only difference lies in the fact that in childhood the combination of the component instincts and their subordination under the primacy of the genitals have been effected only very incompletely or not at all. Thus the establishment of that primacy in the service of reproduction is the last phase through which the organization of sexuality passes.

It may be regarded as typical of the choice of an object that the process is diphasic, that is, that it occurs in two waves. The first of these begins between the ages of two and five, and is brought to a halt or to a retreat by the latency period; it is characterized by the infantile nature of the sexual aims. The second wave sets in with puberty and determines the final outcome of sexual life.

Although the diphasic nature of object choice comes down in essentials to no more than the operation of the latency period, it is of the highest importance in regard to disturbances of that final outcome. The resultants of infantile object choice are carried over into the later period. They either persist as such or are revived at the actual time of puberty. But as a consequence of the repression which has developed between the two phases they prove unutilizable. Their sexual aims have become mitigated and they now represent what may be described as the "affectionate current" of sexual life. Only psychoanalytic investigation can show that behind this affection, admiration and respect there lie concealed the old sexual longings of the infantile component instincts which have now become unserviceable. The object choice of the pubertal period is obliged to dispense with the objects of childhood and to start afresh as a "sensual current." Should these two currents fail to converge, the result is often that one of the ideals of sexual life, the focusing of all desires upon a single object, will be unattainable.

*   *   *

The Transformations of Puberty

With the arrival of puberty, changes set in which are destined to give infantile sexual life its final, normal shape. The sexual instinct has hitherto been predominantly autoerotic; it now finds a sexual object. Its activity has hitherto been derived from a number of separate instincts and erotogenic zones, which, independently of one another, have pursued a certain sort of pleasure as their sole sexual aim. Now, however, a new sexual aim appears, and all the component instincts combine to attain it, while the erotogenic zones become subordinated to the primacy of the genital zone. . . . A normal sexual life is only assured by an exact convergence of the affectionate current and the sensual current, both being directed toward the sexual object and sexual aim. (The former, the affectionate current, comprises what remains over of the infantile efflorescence of sexuality.) It is like the completion of a tunnel which has been driven through a hill from both directions.

The new sexual aim in men consists in the discharge of the sexual products. The earlier one, the attainment of pleasure, is by no means alien to it; on the contrary, the highest degree of pleasure is attached to this final act of the sexual process. The sexual instinct is now subordinated to the reproductive function; it becomes so to say, altruistic. If this transformation is to succeed, the original dispositions and all the other characteristics of the instincts must be taken into account in the process. Just as on any other occasion on which the organism should by rights make new combinations and adjustments leading to complicated mechanisms, here too there are possibilities of pathological disorders if these new arrangements are not carried out. Every pathological disorder of sexual life is rightly to be regarded as an inhibition in development.

2.

FREUD, SIGMUND

Instincts and their Vicissitudes (1915)*

We have often heard it maintained that sciences should be built up on clear and sharply defined basic concepts. In actual fact no science, not even the most exact, begins with such definitions. The true beginning of scientific activity consists rather in describing phenomena and then in proceeding to group, classify, and correlate them. Even at the stage of description it is not possible to avoid applying certain abstract ideas to the material in hand, ideas derived from somewhere or other but certainly not from the new observations alone. Such ideas—which will later become the basis concepts of the science—are still more indispensable as the material is further worked over. They must at first necessarily possess some degree of indefiniteness; there can be no question of any clear delimitation of their content. So long as they remain in this condition, we come to an understanding about their meaning by making repeated references to the material of observation from which they appear to have been derived, but upon which, in fact, they have been imposed. Thus, strictly speaking, they are in the nature of conventions—although everything depends on their not being arbitrarily chosen but determined by their having significant relations to the empirical material, relations that we seem to sense before we can clearly recognize and demonstrate them. It is only after more thorough investigation of the field of observation that we are able to formulate its basic scientific concepts with increased precision, and progressively so to modify them that they become serviceable and consistent over a wide area. Then, indeed, the time may have come to confine them in definitions. The advance of knowledge, however, does not tolerate any rigidity even in definitions. . . .

A conventional basic concept of this kind, which at the moment is still somewhat obscure but which is indispensable to us in psychology, is that of an "instinct."[1] Let us try to give a content to it by approaching it from different angles.

---

* Reprinted from: 14 *The Standard Edition of the Complete Psychological Works of Sigmund Freud*, James Strachey, ed. London: The Hogarth Press and the Institute of Psychoanalysis, 1957. (pp. 117–25) and *Collected Papers of Sigmund Freud*, American Edition, published by Basic Books, Inc., 1959. Reprinted by permission of Hogarth and Basic Books, Inc.

1. It should be remarked by way of preface that here . . . the English word "instinct" stands for the German "*Trieb*." . . . The word "instinct" is . . . not used here in the sense which seems at the moment to be the most current among biologists. But Freud shows in the course of this paper the meaning which he attaches to the word so translated. . . .

There is, however, an ambiguity in Freud's use of the term "*Trieb*" ("instinct") and "*Triebreprasentanz*" ("instinctual

First, from the angle of *physiology*. This has given us the concept of a "stimulus" and the pattern of the reflex arc, according to which a stimulus applied to living tissue (nervous substance) *from* the outside is discharged by action *to* the outside. This action is expedient insofar as it withdraws the stimulated substance from the influence of the stimulus, removes it out of its range of operation.

What is the relation of "instinct" to "stimulus"? There is nothing to prevent our subsuming the concept of "instinct" under that of "stimulus" and saying that an instinct is a stimulus applied to the mind. But we are immediately set on our guard against *equating* instinct and mental stimulus. There are obviously other stimuli to the mind besides those of an instinctual kind, stimuli which behave far more like physiological ones. For example, when a strong light falls on the eye, it is not an instinctual stimulus. . . .

[A]n instinctual stimulus does not arise from the external world but from within the organism itself. For this reason it operates differently upon the mind and different actions are necessary in order to remove it. Further, all that is essential in a stimulus is covered if we assume that it operates with a single impact, so that it can be disposed of by a single expedient action. A typical instance of this is motor flight from the source of stimulation. These impacts may, of

course, be repeated and summated, but that makes no difference to our notion of the process and to the conditions for the removal of the stimulus. An instinct, on the other hand, never operates as a force giving a *momentary* impact but always as a *constant* one. Moreover, since it impinges not from without but from within the organism, no flight can avail against it. A better term for an instinctual stimulus is a "need." What does away with a need is "satisfaction." This can be attained only by an appropriate ("adequate") alteration of the internal source of stimulation.

*   *   *

. . . In the course of this discussion, however, we cannot fail to be struck by something that obliges us to make a further admission. In order to guide us in dealing with the field of psychological phenomena, we do not merely apply certain conventions to our empirical material as basic *concepts*; we also make use of a number of complicated *postulates*. We have already alluded to the most important of these, and all we need now do is to state it expressly. This postulate is of a biological nature, and makes use of the concept of "purpose" (or perhaps of expediency) and runs as follows: The nervous system is an apparatus which has the function of getting rid of the stimuli that reach it, or of reducing them to the lowest possible level; or which, if it were feasible, would maintain itself in an altogether unstimulated condition.[2] Let us for the present not take exception to the indefiniteness of this idea and let us assign to the nervous system the task—speaking in general terms—of *mastering stimuli*. We then see how greatly the simple pattern of the physiological reflex is complicated by the introduction of instincts. External stimuli impose only the single task of withdrawing from them; this is accomplished by muscular movements, one of which eventually achieves that aim and thereafter, being the expedient movement, becomes a hereditary disposition. Instinctual stimuli, which originates from within the organism, cannot be dealt with by this mechanism. Thus they make far higher demands on the nervous system and cause it to undertake involved and interconnected activities by which the external world is so changed as to afford satisfaction to the internal source of stimulation. . . .

When we further find that the activity of even the most highly developed mental apparatus is subject to the pleasure principle, i.e., is automatically regulated by feelings belonging to the pleasure–unpleasure series, we can hardly reject the further hypothesis that these feelings reflect the manner in which the process of mastering stimuli takes place—certainly in the sense that unpleasurable feelings are connected with an increase and pleasurable feelings with a de-

---

representative") to which, for the sake of clearer understanding, attention must be drawn. [H]e describes an instinct as "a concept on the frontier between the mental and the somatic . . . the psychical representative of the stimuli originating from within the organism and reaching the mind." . . . Some years earlier . . . he wrote of instinct as "the concept on the frontier between the somatic and the mental . . . the psychical representative of organic forces." And again, in a passage probably written a few months before the present paper . . . he wrote of instinct as "the psychical representative of an endosomatic, continuously flowing source of stimulation . . . a concept lying on the frontier between the mental and the physical." These three accounts seem to make it plain that Freud was drawing no distinction between an instinct and its "physical representative." He was apparently regarding the instinct itself as the psychical representative of somatic forces. If now, however, we turn to the later papers in this series, we seem to find him drawing a very sharp distinction between the instinct and its psychical representative. This is perhaps shown most clearly in a passage in "The Unconscious": "An instinct can never become an object of consciousness—only the idea [*Vorstellung*] that represents the instinct can. Even in the unconscious, moreover, an instinct cannot be represented otherwise than by an idea. . . . When we nevertheless speak of an unconscious instinctual impulse or of a repressed instinctual impulse . . . we can only mean an instinctual impulse the ideational representative of which is unconscious." This same view appears in many other passages. . . . Both of these apparently differing views of the nature of an instinct are to be found elsewhere in Freud's later writings, though the second predominates. It may be, however, that the contradiction is more apparent than real, and that its solution lies precisely in the ambiguity of the concept itself—a frontier concept between the physical and the mental.

[Editor's Note. Reprinted from: 14 *The Standard Edition of the Complete Psychological Works of Sigmund Freud.* James Strachey, ed. London: The Hogarth Press and the Institute of Psychoanalysis, 1957. (pp. 111–13).]

---

2. This is the "principle of constancy."

crease of stimulus. We will, however, carefully pre-serve this assumption in its present highly indefinite form, until we succeed, if that is possible, in discover-ing what sort of relation exists between pleasure and unpleasure, on the one hand, and fluctuations in the amounts of stimulus affecting mental life, on the other. It is certain that many very various relations of this kind, and not very simple ones, are possible.[3]

If now we apply ourselves to considering mental life from a *biological* point of view, an "instinct" appears to us as a concept on the frontier between the mental and the somatic, as the psychical repre-sentative of the stimuli originating from within the organism and reaching the mind, as a measure of the demand made upon the mind for work in conse-quence of its connection with the body.

We are now in a position to discuss certain terms which are used in reference to the concept of an instinct—for example, its "pressure," its "aim," its "object," and its "source."

By the pressure [*Drang*] of an instinct we under-stand its motor factor, the amount of force or the measure of the demand for work which it represents. The characteristic of exercising pressure is common to all instincts; it is in fact their very essence. Every instinct is a piece of activity; if we speak loosely of passive instincts, we can only mean instincts whose *aim* is passive.

---

3. It will be seen that two principles are here involved. One of these is the "principle of constancy." It is stated again in *Beyond the Pleasure Principle*, Chapter I, as follows: "The mental apparatus endeavors to keep the quantity of excitation present in it as low as possible or at least to keep it constant." For this principle Freud, in the same work, adopted the term "Nirvana principle." The second principle involved is the "pleasure principle," stated at the beginning of the paragraph to which this note is appended. It, too, is restated in *Beyond the Pleasure Principle:* "The course taken by mental events is automatically regulated by the pleasure principle. . . . [That course] takes a direction such that its final outcome coincides with . . . an avoidance of unpleasure or a production of plea-sure." Freud seems to have assumed to begin with that these two principles were closely correlated and even identical. . . . In the passage in the text above, however, a doubt appears to be expressed as to the completeness of the correlation between the two principles. This doubt is carried further in *Beyond the Pleasure Principle* and is discussed at some length in "The Economic Problem of Masochism." Freud there argues that the two principles cannot be identical, since there are un-questionably states of increasing tension which are pleasurable (e.g., sexual excitement), and he goes on to suggest (what had already been hinted at in the two passages in *Beyond the Pleasure Principle* just referred to) that the pleasurable or un-pleasurable quality of a state may be related to a *temporal* characteristic (or rhythm) of the changes in the quantity of excitation present. He concludes that in any case the two principles must not be regarded as identical: The pleasure principle is a *modification* of the Nirvana principle. The Nirvana principle, he maintains, is to be attributed to the "death instinct," and its modification into the pleasure principle is due to the influence of the "life instinct" or libido.

The aim [*Ziel*] of an instinct is in every instance satisfaction, which can only be obtained by removing the state of stimulation at the source of the instinct. But although the ultimate aim of each instinct re-mains unchangeable, there may yet be different paths leading to the same ultimate aim; so that an instinct may be found to have various nearer or intermediate aims, which are combined or interchanged with one another. Experience permits us also to speak of in-stincts which are "inhibited in their aim," in the case of processes which are allowed to make some advance toward instinctual satisfaction but are then inhibited or deflected. We may suppose that even processes of this kind involve a partial satisfaction.

The object [*Objekt*] of an instinct is the thing in regard to which or through which the instinct is able to achieve its aim. It is what is most variable about an instinct and is not originally connected with it, but becomes assigned to it only in consequence of being peculiarly fitted to make satisfaction possible. The object is not necessarily something extraneous: It may equally well be a part of the subject's own body. It may be changed any number of times in the course of the vicissitudes which the instinct undergoes during its existence; and highly important parts are played by this displacement of instinct. It may happen that the same object serves for the satisfaction of several instincts simultaneously. . . . A particularly close attachment of the instinct to its object is dis-tinguished by the term "fixation." This frequently occurs at very early periods of the development of an instinct and puts an end to its mobility through its intense opposition to detachment.

By the source [*Quelle*] of an instinct is meant the somatic process which occurs in an organ or part of the body and whose stimulus is represented in mental life by an instinct. We do not know whether this pro-cess is invariably of a chemical nature or whether it may also correspond to the release of other, e.g., mechanical, forces. The study of the sources of in-stincts lies outside the scope of psychology. Although instincts are wholly determined by their origin in a somatic source, in mental life we know them only by their aims. An exact knowledge of the sources of an instinct is not invariably necessary for purposes of psychological investigation; sometimes its source may be inferred from its aim.

Are we to suppose that the different instincts which originate in the body and operate on the mind are also distinguished by different *qualities*, and that that is why they behave in qualitatively different ways in mental life? This supposition does not seem to be justified; we are much more likely to find the simpler assumption sufficient—that the instincts are all quali-tatively alike and owe the effect they make only to the amount of excitation they carry, or perhaps, in ad-dition, to certain functions of that quantity. What distinguishes from one another the mental effects produced by the various instincts may be traced to the difference in their sources. . . .

What instincts should we suppose there are, and how many? There is obviously a wide opportunity here for arbitrary choice. No objection can be made to anyone's employing the concept of an instinct of play or of destruction or of gregariousness, when the subject matter demands it and the limitations of psychological analysis allow of it. Nevertheless, we should not neglect to ask ourselves whether instinctual motives like these, which are so highly specialized on the one hand, do not admit of further dissection in accordance with the *sources* of the instinct, so that only primal instincts—those which cannot be further dissected—can lay claim to importance.

I have proposed that two groups of such primal instincts should be distinguished: the *ego*, or *self-preservative*, instincts and the *sexual* instincts. But this supposition has not the status of a necessary postulate, as has, for instance, our assumption about the biological purpose of the mental apparatus; it is merely a working hypothesis, to be retained only so long as it proves useful, and it will make little difference to the results of our work of description and classification if it is replaced by another. The occasion for this hypothesis arose in the course of the evolution of psychoanalysis, which was first employed upon the psychoneuroses, or, more precisely, upon the group described as "transference neuroses" (hysteria and obsessional neurosis); these showed that at the root of all such affections there is to be found a conflict between the claims of sexuality and those of the ego. It is always possible that an exhaustive study of the other neurotic affections (especially of the narcissistic psychoneuroses, the schizophrenias) may oblige us to alter this formula and to make a different classification of the primal instincts. But for the present we do not know of any such formula, nor have we met with any argument unfavorable to drawing this contrast between sexual and ego instincts.

I am altogether doubtful whether any decisive pointers for the differentiation and classification of the instincts can be arrived at on the basis of working over the psychological material. This working over seems rather itself to call for the application to the material of definite assumptions concerning instinctual life, and it would be a desirable thing if those assumptions could be taken from some other branch of knowledge and carried over to psychology. . . .

Since a study of instinctual life from the direction of consciousness presents almost insuperable difficulties, the principal source of our knowledge remains the psychoanalytic investigation of mental disturbances. Psychoanalysis, however, in consequence of the course taken by its development, has hitherto been able to give us information of a fairly satisfactory nature only about the *sexual* instincts; for it is precisely that group which alone can be observed in isolation, as it were, in the psychoneuroses. . . .

* * *

3.

FREUD, SIGMUND

Civilization and Its Discontents (1930)*

. . . Of all the slowly developed parts of analytic theory, the theory of the instincts is the one that has felt its way the most painfully forward. And yet that theory was so indispensable to the whole structure that something had to be put in its place. In what was at first my utter perplexity, I took as my starting point a saying of the poet-philosopher, Schiller, that "hunger and love are what moves the world." Hunger could be taken to represent the instincts which aim at preserving the individual; while love strives after objects, and its chief function, favored in every way by nature, is the preservation of the species. Thus, to begin with, ego instincts and object instincts confronted each other. It was to denote the energy of the latter and only the latter instincts that I introduced the term "libido." Thus the antithesis was between the ego instincts and the "libidinal" instincts of love (in its widest sense) which were directed to an object. One of these object instincts, the sadistic instinct, stood out from the rest, it is true, in that its aim was so very far from being loving. Moreover, it was obviously in some respects attached to the ego instincts: It could not hide its close affinity with instincts of mastery which have no libidinal purpose. But these discrepancies were got over; after all, sadism was clearly a part of sexual life, in the activities of which affection could be replaced by cruelty. Neurosis was regarded as the outcome of a struggle between the interest of self-preservation and the demands of the libido, a struggle in which the ego had been victorious but at the price of severe sufferings and renunciations.

Every analyst will admit that even today this view has not the sound of a long-discarded error. Nevertheless, alterations in it became essential, as our inquiries advanced from the repressed to the repressing forces, from the object instincts to the ego. The decisive step forward was the introduction of the concept of narcissism—that is to say, the discovery that

* Reprinted from: 21 *The Standard Edition of the Complete Psychological Works of Sigmund Freud*, James Strachey, ed. London: The Hogarth Press and the Institute of Psychoanalysis, 1961. (pp. 117–22). Reprinted by permission of Hogarth and W. W. Norton & Co.

the ego itself is cathected with libido, that the ego, indeed, is the libido's original home, and remains to some extent its headquarters. This narcissistic libido turns toward objects, and thus becomes object libido; and it can change back into narcissistic libido once more. . . . [T]he concept of libido was endangered. Since the ego instincts, too, were libidinal, it seemed for a time inevitable that we should make libido coincide with instinctual energy in general, as C. G. Jung had already advocated earlier. Nevertheless, there still remained in me a kind of conviction, for which I was not as yet able to find reasons, that the instincts could not all be of the same kind. My next step was taken in *Beyond the Pleasure Principle* when the compulsion to repeat and the conservative character of instinctual life first attracted my attention. Starting from speculations on the beginning of life and from biological parallels, I drew the conclusion that, besides the instinct to preserve living substance and to join it into ever larger units, there must exist another, contrary instinct seeking to dissolve those units and to bring them back to their primeval, inorganic state. That is to say, as well as Eros there was an instinct of death. The phenomena of life could be explained from the concurrent or mutually opposing action of these two instincts. It was not easy, however, to demonstrate the activities of this supposed death instinct. The manifestations of Eros were conspicuous and noisy enough. It might be assumed that the death instinct operated silently within the organism toward its dissolution, but that, of course, was no proof. A more fruitful idea was that a portion of the instinct is diverted toward the external world and comes to light as an instinct of aggressiveness and destructiveness. In this way the instinct itself could be pressed into the service of Eros, in that the organism was destroying some other thing, whether animate or inanimate, instead of destroying its own self. Conversely, any restriction of this aggressiveness directed outward would be bound to increase the self-destruction, which is in any case proceeding. At the same time one can suspect from this example that the two kinds of instinct seldom—perhaps never—appear in isolation from each other, but are alloyed with each other in varying and very different proportions and so become unrecognizable to our judgment. In sadism, long since known to us as a component instinct of sexuality, we should have before us a particularly strong alloy of this kind between trends of love and the destructive instinct; while its counterpart, masochism, would be a union between destructiveness directed inward and sexuality—a union which makes what is otherwise an imperceptible trend into a conspicuous and tangible one.

The assumption of the existence of an instinct of death or destruction has met with resistance even in analytic circles; I am aware that there is a frequent inclination rather to ascribe whatever is dangerous and hostile in love to an original bipolarity in its own nature. To begin with it was only tentatively that I put forward the views I have developed here, but in the course of time they have gained such a hold upon me that I can no longer think in any other way. To my mind, they are far more serviceable from a theoretical standpoint than any other possible ones; they provide that simplification, without either ignoring or doing violence to the facts, for which we strive in scientific work. I know that in sadism and masochism we have always seen before us manifestations of the destructive instinct (directed outward and inward), strongly alloyed with erotism; but I can no longer understand how we can have overlooked the ubiquity of nonerotic aggressivity and destructiveness and can have failed to give it its due place in our interpretation of life. (The desire for destruction when it is directed *inward* mostly eludes our perception, of course, unless it is tinged with erotism). . . .

The name "libido" can once more be used to denote the manifestations of the power of Eros in order to distinguish them from the energy of the death instinct. It must be confessed that we have much greater difficulty in grasping that instinct; we can only suspect it, as it were, as something in the background behind Eros, and it escapes detection unless its presence is betrayed by its being alloyed with Eros. It is in sadism, where the death instinct twists the erotic aim in its own sense and yet at the same time fully satisfies the erotic urge, that we succeed in obtaining the clearest insight into its nature and its relation to Eros. But even where it emerges without any sexual purpose, in the blindest fury of destructiveness, we cannot fail to recognize that the satisfaction of the instinct is accompanied by an extraordinarily high degree of narcissistic enjoyment, owing to its presenting the ego with a fulfilment of the latter's old wishes for omnipotence. The instinct of destruction, moderated and tamed, and, as it were, inhibited in its aim, must, when it is directed toward objects, provide the ego with the satisfaction of its vital needs and with control over nature. Since the assumption of the existence of the instinct is mainly based on theoretical grounds, we must also admit that it is not entirely proof against theoretical objections. But this is how things appear to us now, in the present state of our knowledge; future research and reflection will no doubt bring further light which will decide the matter.

. . . I adopt the standpoint, therefore, that the inclination to aggression is an original, self-subsisting instinctual disposition in man. . . . This aggressive instinct is the derivative and the main representative of the death instinct which we have found alongside of Eros and which shares world dominion with it. . . .

4.

FREUD, SIGMUND

Beyond the Pleasure Principle (1920)*

In the theory of psychoanalysis we have no hesitation in assuming that the course taken by mental events is automatically regulated by the pleasure principle. We believe, that is to say, that the course of those events is invariably set in motion by an unpleasurable tension, and that it takes a direction such that its final outcome coincides with a lowering of that tension—that is, with an avoidance of unpleasure or a production of pleasure. . . .

. . . We have decided to relate pleasure and unpleasure to the quantity of excitation that is present in the mind but is not in any way "bound"; and to relate them in such a manner that unpleasure corresponds to an *increase* in the quantity of excitation and pleasure to a *diminution*. What we are implying by this is not a simple relation between the strength of the feelings of pleasure and unpleasure and the corresponding modifications in the quantity of excitation; least of all—in view of all we have been taught by psychophysiology—are we suggesting any directly proportional ratio: The factor that determines the feeling is probably the amount of increase or diminution in the quantity of excitation *in a given period of time*. Experiment might possibly play a part here; but it is not advisable for us analysts to go into the problem further so long as our way is not pointed by quite definite observations.

* * *

The facts which have caused us to believe in the dominance of the pleasure principle in mental life also find expression in the hypothesis that the mental apparatus endeavors to keep the quantity of excitation present in it as low as possible or at least to keep it constant. This latter hypothesis is only another way of stating the pleasure principle; for if the work of the mental apparatus is directed toward keeping the quantity of excitation low, then anything that is calculated to increase that quanity is bound to be felt as adverse to the functioning of the apparatus, that is as unpleasurable. The pleasure principle follows from the principle of constancy: Actually the latter principle was inferred from the facts which forced us to adopt the pleasure principle. . . .

It must be pointed out, however, that strictly speaking it is incorrect to talk of the dominance of the pleasure principle over the course of mental processes. If such a dominance existed, the immense majority of our mental processes would have to be

* Reprinted from: 18 *The Standard Edition of the Complete Psychological Works of Sigmund Freud*, James Strachey, ed. London: The Hogarth Press and the Institute of Psycho-analysis, 1955. (pp. 7–56). Reprinted by permission of Hogarth and Liveright Publishing Co.

accompanied by pleasure or to lead to pleasure, whereas universal experience completely contradicts any such conclusion. The most that can be said, therefore, is that there exists in the mind a strong *tendency* toward the pleasure principle, but that that tendency is opposed by certain other forces or circumstances, so that the final outcome cannot always be in harmony with the tendency toward pleasure. . . .

If we turn now to the question of what circumstances are able to prevent the pleasure principle from being carried into effect, we find ourselves once more on secure and well-trodden ground and, in framing our answer, we have at our disposal a rich fund of analytic experience.

The first example of the pleasure principle being inhibited in this way is a familiar one which occurs with regularity. We know that the pleasure principle is proper to a *primary* method of working on the part of the mental apparatus, but that, from the point of view of the self-preservation of the organism among the difficulties of the external world, it is from the very outset inefficient and even highly dangerous. Under the influence of the ego's instincts of self-preservation, the pleasure principle is replaced by the *reality principle*. This latter principle does not abandon the intention of ultimately obtaining pleasure, but it nevertheless demands and carries into effect the postponement of satisfaction, the abandonment of a number of possibilities of gaining satisfaction and the temporary toleration of unpleasure as a step on the long indirect road to pleasure. The pleasure principle long persists, however, as the method of working employed by the sexual instincts, which are so hard to "educate," and, starting from those instincts, or in the ego itself, it often succeeds in overcoming the reality principle, to the detriment of the organism as a whole.

There can be no doubt, however, that the replacement of the pleasure principle by the reality principle can only be made responsible for a small number, and by no means the most intense, of unpleasurable experiences. Another occasion of the release of unpleasure, which occurs with no less regularity, is to be found in the conflicts and dissensions that take place in the mental apparatus while the ego is passing through its development into more highly composite organizations. Almost all the energy with which the apparatus is filled arises from its innate instinctual impulses. But these are not all allowed to reach the same phases of development. In the course of things it happens again and again that individual instincts or parts of instincts turn out to be incompatible in their aims or demands with the remaining ones, which are able to combine into the inclusive unity of the ego. The former are then split off from this unity by the process of repression, held back at lower levels of psychical development, and cut off, to begin with, from the possibility of satisfaction. If they succeed subsequently, as can so easily happen with repressed sexual instincts, in struggling through, by roundabout paths, to a direct or to a substitutive satisfaction, that event, which would in other cases have been an opportunity for pleasure, is felt by the ego as unpleasure. As a consequence of the old conflict which ended in repression, a new breach has occurred in the pleasure principle at the very time when certain instincts were endeavoring, in accordance with the principle, to obtain fresh pleasure. The details of the process by which repression turns a possibility of pleasure into a source of unpleasure are not yet clearly understood or cannot be clearly represented; but there is no doubt that all neurotic unpleasure is of that kind—pleasure that cannot be felt as such.

The two sources of unpleasure which I have just indicated are very far from covering the majority of our unpleasurable experiences. But as regards the remainder it can be asserted with some show of justification that their presence does not contradict the dominance of the pleasure principle. Most of the unpleasure that we experience is *perceptual* unpleasure. It may be perception of pressure by unsatisfied instincts; or it may be external perception which is either distressing in itself or which excites unpleasurable expectations in the mental apparatus—that is, which is recognized by it as a "danger." The reaction to these instinctual demands and threats of danger, a reaction which constitutes the proper activity of the mental apparatus, can then be directed in a correct manner by the pleasure principle or the reality principle by which the former is modified. . . .

*   *   *

At this point I propose to . . . examine the method of working employed by the mental apparatus in one of its earliest *normal* activities—I mean in children's play.

. . . I have been able, through a chance opportunity which presented itself, to throw some light upon the first game played by a little boy of one-and-a-half and invented by himself. It was more than a mere fleeting observation, for I lived under the same roof as the child and his parents for some weeks, and it was some time before I discovered the meaning of the puzzling activity which he constantly repeated.

The child was not at all precocious in his intellectual development. At the age of one-and-a-half he could say only a few comprehensible words; he could also make use of a number of sounds which expressed a meaning intelligible to those around him. He was, however, on good terms with his parents and their one servant girl, and tributes were paid to his being a "good boy." He did not disturb his parents at night, he conscientiously obeyed orders not to touch certain things or go into certain rooms, and above all he never cried when his mother left him for a few hours. At the same time, he was greatly attached to his mother, who had not only fed him herself but had also looked after him without any outside help. This good little boy, however, had an occasional disturbing habit of taking any small objects he could get hold of and throwing them away from him into a corner, under the bed, and so on, so that hunting for his toys and picking them up was often quite a business. As he did this he gave vent to a loud, long-drawn-out "o-o-o-o," accompanied by an expression of interest and satisfaction. His mother and the writer of the present account were agreed in thinking that this was not a mere interjection but represented the German word "*fort*" ["gone"]. I eventually realized that it was a game and that the only use he made of any of his toys was to play "gone" with them. One day I made an observation which confirmed my view. The child had a wooden reel with a piece of string tied round it. It never occurred to him to pull it along the floor behind him, for instance, and play at its being a carriage. What he did was to hold the reel by the string and very skilfully throw it over the edge of his curtained cot, so that it disappeared into it, at the same time uttering his expressive "o-o-o-o." He then pulled the reel out of the cot again by the string and hailed its reappearance with a joyful "*da*" ["there"]. This, then, was the complete game—disappearance and return. As a rule one only witnessed its first act, which was repeated untiringly as a game in itself, though there is no doubt that the greater pleasure was attached to the second act.

The interpretation of the game then became obvious. It was related to the child's great cultural achievement—the instinctual renunciation (that is, the renunciation of instinctual satisfaction) which he had made in allowing his mother to go away without protesting. He compensated himself for this, as it were, by himself staging the disappearance and return of the objects within his reach. It is of course a matter of indifference from the point of view of judging the effective nature of the game whether the child invented it himself or took it over on some outside suggestion. Our interest is directed to another point. The child cannot possibly have felt his mother's departure as something agreeable or even indifferent. How then does his repetition of this distressing experience as a game fit in with the pleasure principle? It may perhaps be said in reply that her departure had to be enacted as a necessary preliminary to her joyful return, and that it was in the latter that lay the true purpose of the game. But against this must be counted the observed fact that the first act, that of departure, was staged as a game in itself and far more frequently than the episode in its entirety, with its pleasurable ending.

No certain decision can be reached from the analysis of a single case like this. On an unprejudiced view one gets an impression that the child turned his experience into a game from another motive. At the outset he was in a *passive* situation—he was overpowered by the experience; but, by repeating it, unpleasurable though it was, as a game, he took on an *active* part. These efforts might be put down to an instinct for mastery that was acting independently of whether the memory was in itself pleasurable or not. But still another interpretation may be attempted. Throwing away the object so that it was "gone" might satisfy an impulse of the child's, which was suppressed in his actual life, to revenge himself on his mother for going away from him. In that case it would have a defiant meaning: "All right, then, go away! I don't need you. I'm sending you away myself." A year later, the same boy whom I had observed at his first game used to take a toy, if he was angry with it, and throw it on the floor, exclaiming: "Go to the fwont!" He had heard at that time that his absent father was "at the front," and was far from regretting his absence; on the contrary he made it quite clear that he had no desire to be disturbed in his sole possession of his mother. We know of other children who liked to express similar hostile impulses by throwing away objects instead of persons. We are, therefore, left in doubt as to whether the impulse to work over in the mind some overpowering experience so as to make onself master of it can find expression as a primary event, and independently of the pleasure principle. For, in the case we have been discussing, the child may, after all, only have been able to repeat his unpleasant experience in play because the repetition carried along with it a yield of pleasure of another sort but nonetheless a direct one.

Nor shall we be helped in our hesitation between these two views by further considering children's play. It is clear that in their play children repeat everything that has made a great impression on them in real life, and that in doing so they abreact the strength of the impression and, as one might put it, make themselves master of the situation. But on the other hand it is obvious that all their play is influenced by a wish that dominates them the whole time —the wish to be grownup and to be able to do what grown-up people do. It can also be observed that the unpleasurable nature of an experience does not always unsuit it for play. If the doctor looks down a child's throat or carries out some small operation on him, we may be quite sure that these frightening experiences will be the subject of the next game; but we must not in that connection overlook the fact that there is a yield of pleasure from another source. As the child passes over from the passivity of the experience to the activity of the game, he hands on the disagreeable experience to one of his playmates and in this way revenges himself on a substitute.

*   *   *

. . . Psychoanalysis was . . . first and foremost an art of interpreting. Since this did not solve the therapeutic problem, a further aim quickly came in view: To oblige the patient to confirm the analyst's construction from his own memory. In that endeavor the chief emphasis lay upon the patient's resistances: The art consisted now in uncovering these as quickly as possible, in pointing them out to the patient and in inducing him by human influence—this was where suggestion operating as "transference" played its part—to abandon his resistances.

But it became ever clearer that the aim which had been set up—the aim that what was unconscious should become conscious—is not completely attainable by that method. The patient cannot remember the whole of what is repressed in him, and what he cannot remember may be precisely the essential part of it. Thus he acquires no sense of conviction of the correctness of the construction that has been communicated to him. He is obliged to *repeat* the repressed material as a contemporary experience instead of, as the physician would prefer to see, *remembering* it as something belonging to the past. These reproductions, which emerge with such unwished-for exactitude, always have as their subject some portion of infantile sexual life—of the Oedipus complex, that is, and its derivatives; and they are invariably acted out in the sphere of the transference, of the patient's relation to the physician. When things have reached this stage, it may be said that the earlier neurosis has now been replaced by a fresh, "transference neurosis." It has been the physician's endeavour to keep this transference neurosis within the narrowest limits: To force as much as possible into the channel of memory and to allow as little as possible to emerge as repetition. The ratio between what is remembered and what is reproduced varies from case to case. The physician cannot as a rule spare his patient this phase of the treatment, He must get him to re-experience some portion of his forgotten life, but must see to it, on the other hand, that the patient retains some degree of aloofness, which will enable him, in spite of everything, to recognize that what appears to be reality is in fact only a reflection of a forgotten past. If this can be successfully achieved, the patient's sense of conviction is won, together with the therapeutic success that is dependent on it.

In order to make it easier to understand this "compulsion to repeat," which emerges during the psychoanalytic treatment of neurotics, we must above all get rid of the mistaken notion that what we are dealing with in our struggle against resistances is resistance on the part of the *unconscious*. The unconscious— that is to say, the "repressed"—offers no resistance whatever to the efforts of the treatment. Indeed, it itself has no other endeavor than to break through the pressure weighing down on it and force its way either to consciousness or to a discharge through some real action. Resistance during treatment arises from the same higher strata and systems of the mind which originally carried out repression. But the fact that, as we knew from experience, the motives of the resistances, and indeed the resistances themselves, are unconscious at first during the treatment, is a hint to us that we should correct a shortcoming in our terminology. We shall avoid a lack of clarity if we make our contrast not between the conscious and the unconscious but between the coherent *ego* and the *repressed*. It is certain that much of the ego is itself unconscious, and notably what we may describe as its nucleus; only a small part of it is covered by the term "preconscious." Having replaced a purely descriptive terminology by one which is systematic or dynamic, we can say that the patient's resistance arises from his ego, and we then at once perceive that the compulsion to repeat must be ascribed to the unconscious repressed. It seems probable that the compulsion can only express itself after the work of treatment has gone halfway to meet it and has loosened the repression.

There is no doubt that the resistance of the conscious and unconscious ego operates under the sway of the pleasure principle: It seeks to avoid the unpleasure which would be produced by the liberation of the repressed. *Our* efforts, on the other hand, are directed toward procuring the toleration of that unpleasure by an appeal to the reality principle. But how is the compulsion to repeat—the manifestation of the power of the repressed—related to the pleasure principle? It is clear that the greater part of what is re-experienced under the compulsion to repeat must cause the ego unpleasure, since it brings to light activities of repressed instinctual impulses. That, however, is unpleasure of a kind we have already considered and does not contradict the pleasure principle: Unpleasure for one system and simultaneously satisfaction for the other. But we come now to a new and remarkable fact, namely that the compulsion to repeat also recalls from the past experiences which include no possibility of pleasure, and which can never, even long ago, have brought satisfaction even to instinctual impulses which have since been repressed.

* * *

The early efflorescence of infantile sexual life is doomed to extinction because its wishes are incompatible with reality and with the inadequate stage of development which the child has reached. That efflorescence comes to an end in the most distressing circumstances and to the accompaniment of the most painful feelings. Loss of love and failure leave behind them a permanent injury to self-regard in the form of a narcissistic scar which . . . contributes more than anything to the "sense of inferiority" which is so common in neurotics. The child's sexual researches, on which limits are imposed by his physical development, lead to no satisfactory conclusion; hence such later complaints as "I can't accomplish anything; I can't succeed in anything." The tie of affection, which binds the child as a rule to the parent of the opposite sex, succumbs to disappointment, to a vain expectation of satisfaction or to jealousy over the birth of a new baby—unmistakable proof of the infidelity of the object of the child's affections. His own attempt to make a baby himself, carried out with tragic seriousness, fails shamefully. The lessening amount of affection he receives, the increasing demands of education, hard words and an occasional punishment—these show him at last the full extent to which he has been scorned. These are a few typical and constantly recurring instances of the ways in which the love characteristic of the age of childhood is brought to a conclusion.

Patients repeat all of these unwanted situations and painful emotions in the transference and revive them with the greatest ingenuity. They seek to bring about the interruption of the treatment while it is still incomplete; they contrive once more to feel themselves scorned, to oblige the physician to speak severely to them and treat them coldly; they discover appropriate objects for their jealousy; instead of the passionately desired baby of their childhood, they produce a plan or a promise of some grand present—which turns out as a rule to be no less unreal. None of these things can have produced pleasure in the past, and it might be supposed that they would cause less unpleasure today if they emerged as memories or dreams instead of taking the form of fresh experiences. They are of course the activities of instincts intended to lead to satisfaction; but no lesson has been learnt from the old experience of these activities having led instead only to unpleasure. In spite of that, they are repeated, under pressure of a compulsion.

What psychoanalysis reveals in the transference phenomena of neurotics can also be observed in the lives of some normal people. The impression they give is of being pursued by a malignant fate or possessed by some "demonic" power; but psychoanalysis has always taken the view that their fate is for the most part arranged by themselves and determined by early infantile influences. The compulsion which is here in evidence differs in no way from the compulsion to repeat which we have found in neurotics, even though the people we are now considering have never shown any signs of dealing with a neurotic conflict by producing symptoms. Thus we have come across people all of whose human relationships have the same outcome: Such as the benefactor who is abandoned in anger after a time by each of his protégés, however much they may otherwise differ from one another, and who thus seems doomed to taste all the bitterness of ingratitude; or the man whose friendships all end in betrayal by his friend; or the man who time after time in the course of his life raises someone else into a position of great private or public authority and then, after a certain interval, himself upsets that authority and replaces him by a new one; or, again, the lover each of whose love affairs with a woman passes through the same phases and reaches the same conclusion. This "perpetual recurrence of the same thing" causes us no astonishment when it relates to *active* behavior on the part of the person concerned and when we can discern in him an essential character trait which always remains the same and which is compelled to find expression in a repetition of the same experiences. We are much more impressed by cases where the subject appears to have a *passive* experience, over which he has no influence, but in which he meets with a repetition of the same fatality. There is the case, for instance, of the woman who married three successive husbands each of whom fell ill soon afterwards and had to be nursed by her on their deathbeds. . . .

If we take into account observations such as these, based upon behavior in the transference and upon the life histories of men and women, we shall find courage to assume that there really does exist in the mind a compulsion to repeat which overrides the pleasure principle. . . .

*   *   *

. . . Enough is left unexplained to justify the hypothesis of a compulsion to repeat—something that seems more primitive, more elementary, more instinctual than the pleasure principle which it overrides. But if a compulsion to repeat *does* operate in the mind, we should be glad to know something about it, to learn what function it corresponds to, under what conditions it can emerge and what its relation is to the pleasure principle—to which, after all, we have hitherto ascribed dominance over the course of the processes of excitation in mental life.

*   *   *

NOTES

NOTE 1

FREUD, SIGMUND

The Unconscious (1915)*

[T]he antithesis of conscious and unconscious is not applicable to instincts. An instinct can never become an object of consciousness—only the idea that represents the instinct can. Even in the unconscious, moreover, an instinct cannot be represen-

* Reprinted from: 14 *The Standard Edition of the Complete Psychological Works of Sigmund Freud*, James Strachey, ed. London: The Hogarth Press and the Institute of Psychoanalysis, 1957. (pp. 177–84) and 4 *Collected Papers of Sigmund Freud*, American Edition, published by Basic Books, Inc., 1959. Reprinted by permission of Hogarth and Basic Books, Inc.

ted otherwise than by an idea. If the instinct did not attach itself to an idea or manifest itself as an affective state, we could know nothing about it. When we nevertheless speak of an unconscious instinctual impulse or of a repressed instinctual impulse, the looseness of phraseology is a harmless one. We can only mean an instinctual impulse the ideational representative of which is unconscious, for nothing else comes into consideration.

We should expect the answer to the question about unconscious feelings, emotions and affects to be just as easily given. It is surely of the essence of an emotion that we should be aware of it, i.e., that it should become known to consciousness. Thus the possibility of the attribute of unconsciousness would be completely excluded as far as emotions, feelings and affects are concerned. But in psychoanalytic practice we are accustomed to speak of unconscious love, hate, anger, etc., and find it impossible to avoid even the strange conjunction, "unconscious consciousness of guilt," or a paradoxical "unconscious anxiety." Is there more meaning in the use of these terms than there is in speaking of "unconscious instincts"?

The two cases are in fact not on all fours. In the first place, it may happen that an affective or emotional impulse is perceived, but misconstrued. Owing to the repression of its proper representative it has been forced to become connected with another idea, and is now regarded by consciousness as the manifestation of that idea. If we restore the true connection, we call the original affective impulse an "unconscious" one. Yet its affect was never unconscious; all that had happened was that its *idea* had undergone repression. In general, the use of the terms "unconscious affect" and "unconscious emotion" has reference to the vicissitudes undergone, in consequence of repression, by the quantitative factor in the instinctual impulse. We know that three such vicissitudes are possible: Either the affect remains, wholly or in part, as it is; or it is transformed into a qualitatively different quota of affect, above all into anxiety; or it is suppressed, i.e., it is prevented from developing at all. . . . We know, too, that to suppress the development of affect is the true aim of repression and that its work is incomplete if this aim is not achieved. In every instance where repression has succeeded in inhibiting the development of affects, we term those affects (which we restore when we undo the work of repression) "unconscious." Thus it cannot be denied that the use of the terms in question is consistent; but in comparison with unconscious ideas there is the important difference that unconscious ideas continue to exist after repression as actual structures in the system *Ucs.*, whereas all that corresponds in that system to unconscious affects is a potential beginning which is prevented from developing. Strictly speaking, then, and although no fault can be found with the linguistic usage, there are no unconscious affects as there are unconscious ideas. But there may very well be in the system *Ucs.* affective structures which, like others, become conscious. The whole difference arises from the fact that ideas are cathexes—basically of memory traces—while affects and emotions correspond to processes of discharge, the final manifestations of which are perceived as feelings. In the present state of our knowledge of affects and emotions we cannot express this difference more clearly.

It is of special interest to us to have established the fact that repression can succeed in inhibiting an instinctual impulse from being turned into a manifestation of affect. This shows us that the system *Cs.* normally controls affectivity as well as access to motility; and it enhances the importance of repression, since it shows that repression results not only in withholding things from consciousness, but also in preventing the development of affect and the setting off of muscular activity. Conversely, too, we may say that as long as the system *Cs.* controls affectivity and motility, the mental condition of the person in question is spoken of as normal. Nevertheless, there is an unmistakable difference in the relation of the controlling system to the two contiguous processes of discharge. Whereas the control by the *Cs.* over voluntary motility is firmly rooted, regularly withstands the onslaught of neurosis, and only breaks down in psychosis, control by the *Cs.* over the development of affects is less secure. . . .

* * *

Let us make a tentative effort to give a metapsychological description of the process of repression. . . . Here we may replace "cathexis" by "libido," because, as we know, it is the vicissitudes of *sexual* impulses with which we shall be dealing.

In anxiety hysteria[1] a first phase of the process is frequently overlooked, and may perhaps be in fact missed out; on careful observation, however, it can be clearly discerned. It consists in anxiety appearing without the subject knowing what he is afraid of. We must suppose that there was present in the *Ucs.* some love impulse demanding to be transposed into the system *Pcs.*; but the cathexis directed to it from the latter system has drawn back from the impulse (as though in an attempt at flight) and the unconscious libidinal cathexis of the rejected idea has been discharged in the form of anxiety.

On the occasion of a repetition (if there should be one) of this process, a first step is taken in the direction of mastering the unwelcome development of anxiety. The [*Pcs.*] cathexis that has taken flight attaches itself to a substitutive idea which, on the one hand, is connected by association with the rejected idea, and, on the other, has escaped repression by reason of its remoteness from that idea. This substitutive idea—a "substitute by displacement"—permits the still uninhibitable development of anxiety to be rationalized. It now plays the part of an anticathexis for the system *Cs.* (*Pcs.*), by securing it against an emergence in the *Cs.* of the repressed idea. On the other hand it is, or acts as if it were, the point of departure for the release of the anxiety affect, which has now really become quite uninhibitable. Clinical observation shows, for instance, that a child suffering from an animal phobia experiences anxiety under two kinds of conditions: In the first place, when his repressed love impulse becomes intensified and, in the second, when he perceives the animal he is afraid of. The substitutive idea acts in the one instance as a point at which there is a passage across from the system *Ucs.* to the system *Cs.*, and, in the other instance, as a self-sufficing source for the release of anxiety. The extending dominance of the system *Cs.* usually manifests itself in the fact that the first of these two modes of excitation of the substitutive idea gives place more and more to the second. The child may perhaps end by behaving as though he had no predilection whatever toward his father but had become quite free from him, and as though his fear of the animal was a real fear—except that this fear of the animal, fed as such a fear is from an unconscious instinctual source, proves obdurate and exaggerated in the face of all influences brought to bear from the system *Cs.*, and thereby betrays its derivation from the system *Ucs.* In the second phase of anxiety hysteria, therefore, the anticathexis from the system *Cs.* had led to substitute formation.

Soon the same mechanism finds a fresh application. The process of repression, as we know, is not yet completed, and it finds a further aim in the task of inhibiting the development of the anxiety which

1. The instinctual impulse subjected to repression [in an animal phobia] is a libidinal attitude toward the father, coupled with fear of him. After repression, this impulse vanishes out of consciousness: The father does not appear in it as an object of libido. As a substitute for him we find in a corresponding place some animal which is more or less fitted to be an object of anxiety. The formation of the substitute for the ideational portion [of the instinctual representative] has come about by *displacement* along a chain of connections which is determined in a particular way. The quantitative portion has not vanished, but has been transformed into anxiety. The result is fear of a wolf, instead of a demand for love from the father. The categories here employed are of course not enough to supply an adequate explanation of even the simplest case of psychoneurosis: There are always other considerations to be taken into account. A repression such as occurs in an animal phobia must be described as radically unsuccessful. All that it has done is to remove and replace the idea; it has failed altogether in sparing unpleasure. And for this reason, too, the work of the neurosis does not cease. It proceeds to a second phase, in order to attain its immediate and more important purpose. What follows is an attempt at flight—the formation of the *phobia proper*, of a number of avoidances which are intended to prevent a release of the anxiety. [*Ibid.* at p. 155].

arises from the substitute. This is achieved by the whole of the associated environment of the substitutive idea being cathected with special intensity, so that it can display a high degree of sensibility to excitation. Excitation of any point in this outer structure must inevitably, on account of its connection with the substitutive idea, give rise to a slight development of anxiety; and this is now used as a signal to inhibit, by means of a fresh flight on the part of the [*Pcs.*] cathexis, the further progress of the development of anxiety. The further away the sensitive and vigilant anticathexes are situated from the feared substitute, the more precisely can the mechanism function which is designed to isolate the substitutive idea and to protect it from fresh excitations. These precautions naturally only guard against excitations which approach the substitutive idea from outside, through perception; they never guard against instinctual excitation, which reaches the substitutive idea from the direction of its link with the repressed idea. Thus the precautions do not begin to operate till the substitute has satisfactorily taken over representation of the repressed, and they can never operate with complete reliability. With each increase of instinctual excitation the protecting rampart round the substitutive idea must be shifted a little further outward. The whole construction, which is set up in an analogous way in the other neuroses, is termed a *phobia*. The flight from a conscious cathexis of the substitutive idea is manifested in the avoidances, renunciations, and prohibitions by which we recognize anxiety hysteria.

Surveying the whole process, we may say that the third phase repeats the work of the second on an ampler scale. The system *Cs.* now protects itself against the activation of the substitutive idea by an anticathexis of its environment, just as previously it had secured itself against the emergence of the repressed idea by a cathexis of the substitutive idea. In this way the formation of substitutes by displacement has been further continued. We must also add that the system *Cs.* had earlier only one small area at which the repressed instinctual impulse could break through, namely, the substitutive idea; but that ultimately this *enclave* of unconscious influence extends to the whole phobic outer structure. Further, we may lay stress on the interesting consideration that by means of the whole defensive mechanism thus set in action a projection outward of the instinctual danger has been achieved. The ego behaves as if the danger of a development of anxiety threatened it not from the direction of an instinctual impulse but from the direction of a perception, and it is thus enabled to react against this external danger with the attempts at flight represented by phobic avoidances. In this process repression is successful in one particular: The release of anxiety can to some extent be dammed up, but only at a heavy sacrifice of personal freedom. Attempts at flight from the demands of instinct are, however, in general useless, and, in spite of everything, the result of phobic flight remains unsatisfactory.

NOTE 2

STERBA, RICHARD

Introduction to the Psychoanalytic Theory of the Libido*

In order to understand . . . object relationships a term must be explained which is constantly employed in psychoanalytic literature, that of object-cathexis. Cathexis signifies an accumulation of psychic energy in any one part of the psychic apparatus. Our sense organs receive innumerable perceptions and stimuli from every individual object in the outside world and these are experienced intensely if our interest in the object is intense. Intra-physically, these perceptions form a unity of the ideas and memories which were experienced in connection with the stimulating object in the outside world. This intrapsychic unity of ideas and memories is termed the object representation. The psychic relations, changes of attitude, increase or decrease of interest, briefly, the processes of "cathexis with psychic energy," take place on the object representation. Some of these processes are expressed in the relationship with the real object in the outside world. A great many, however, remain in the interior of the psychic apparatus; even the varying intensity of interest resulting from the perceptions received from the object in the outside world is not immediately expressed in action towards the object; it is first expressed in feelings and thoughts, according to the increase or decrease in the cathexis of the object representation. An object relationship may never even be expressed to the object. A man may fall in love with an actress whom he has never seen off the screen or stage, the actress may be unaware of her admirer's existence, nevertheless he has effected an object relationship because the object representation of the actress, which is within his mind, has been cathected or charged with libido. It is easy to understand that countless psychic processes can occur in the idea and memory-unit we have of a person— which is called the object-representation—without a corresponding real action in the outside world; it is clear also that often there could be no such action, because interior and exterior inhibitions prevent the psychic process from being transformed into action towards the real object. [The] processes of psychic energy cathexis occur on the object-representation, independently of the real object or person, although they may be released by the behavior of the latter; few are transformed into real actions towards the

* New York: *Nervous and Mental Disease Monographs*, 1947. (pp. 37–38). Reprinted by permission.

object. Briefly, object-cathexis means a charging of the object-representation with psychic energy derived from the various instinctual sources.

NOTE 3

JACOBSON, EDITH

The Self and the Object World*

[W]e may visualize an initial psychoeconomic state, characterized by a low level of tension and by a general, diffuse dispersion of as yet undifferentiated psychophysiological energy within the primal, structurally also undifferentiated self. Under the influence of both, of intrinsic factors and of external stimuli, the undifferentiated forces would then begin to develop into the libidinal and aggressive psychic drives with which the id is endowed. During the embryonal and also predominantly during the earliest infantile stage, most of this undifferentiated energy of the primal self is diffusely discharged in small amounts on the inside at first exclusively through physiological channels. But after birth the pregenital erogenous zones and, to an increasing degree, the whole sensory and motor systems, the "primary autonomous" core of the future ego, become periodically hypercathected; processes of drive discharge toward the outside begin to develop, which become observable in pregenital (sexual and aggressive) activity and in biologically prepatterned, primitive affectomotor and instinctive reflex motor reactions, easily recognizable as the forerunners of feeling, thinking, and of motor and other ego functions. In the course of structural differentiation the libidinal and aggressive drives would undergo processes of fusion and partial neutralization. These neutralized drives, together with part of the libidinal and aggressive drives, would become vested in the new systems, the ego and the superego, and could be utilized for the building up of emotional and thought processes and the corresponding ego and superego functions.

5.

HARTMANN, HEINZ, KRIS, ERNST, and LOEWENSTEIN, RUDOLPH M.

Notes on the Theory of Aggression**

*   *   *

The variety of aims of the sexual impulses are well known. The aims of aggression are generally considered to be less diversified. In this sense one is wont to contrast the plasticity of libido to the

rigidity of aggression. We should like to supplement this traditional view by an alternative: It seems that the plasticity of aggression manifests itself in the control of the body, in the control of reality, and in the formation of psychic structure, areas that will in part be later discussed in greater detail.

What should we assume the aims of aggression to be? It has been said that they consist in total destruction of objects, animate or inanimate, and that all attempts to be "satisfied with less," with battle with or domination of the object, or with its disappearance imply restrictions of the original aims. It seems that at the present stage in the development of psychoanalytic hypotheses the question as to the specific aims of the aggressive drive cannot be answered; nor is a definite answer essential. However, it seems possible to distinguish between degrees of discharge of aggressive tension. The aims of aggression could then be classified according to the degree of discharge they allow for and according to the means utilized in discharge.

In emphasizing the relation of instinctual drive to discharge of energy, the similarities and differences of aim inhibition with libido and with aggression become evident. Libidinal impulses may be aim inhibited under two conditions: The inhibition may be temporary, may induce an accessory and preparatory stage of impulse completion; or it may substitute for the uninhibited action. In the first case discharge is delayed but under certain conditions mounting pleasure is experienced; in the second case, in which behaviour is permanently aim inhibited, there occurs, in addition to the damming up of libido, substitute formation or sublimation.

As far as ego and superego impose modifications on both instinctual drives, conditions with libido and aggression tend to be similar. In the case of aggression, however, modification of aims is imposed by an additional reason of particular and paramount importance: The unmodified aggressive impulse threatens the existence of the object and the investment of the object with libido acts as its protection. Through a simultaneous cathexis with libido the aims of aggression are modified. This modification may be brought about in two different ways: By the mere coexistence of two investments, leading to the prevalence of libido over aggression; and by the fusion of both instinctual drives. In discussing types of ambivalence we will later refer to this difference. The fact, however, that the ultimate aims of aggression are more frequently modified by libido than those of libido by aggression may well be thought to be connected with the genetic importance of the love object for the survival of the individual.

In rounding off our discussion it seems appropriate to enumerate four types of conflict through which the aims of aggression are modified. (1) Aggression and libido may be involved in conflict when the cathexis

---

* New York: International Universities Press, Inc., 1964. (pp. 14–15). Reprinted by permission.

** 3–4 *The Psychoanalytic Study of the Child*, 1949. (pp. 12–25·. Reprinted by permission of International Universities Press, Inc.

of both drives is vested in the same object (instinctual conflict). (2) The reaction of the object to attempts at completion of aggressive acts may endanger the individual (conflict with reality). (3) This danger may be anticipated by the ego, which is in part already identified with the object, and the ego might be opposed to the completion of aggressive acts (structural conflict, involving the ego). (4) The conflict may involve moral values (structural conflict, involving the superego).

*   *   *

Here we select four types of processes which *modify* the impact of aggression. This modification is achieved: (1) by displacement of aggression to other objects; (2) by restriction of the aims of the aggressive impulses; (3) by sublimation of aggressive energy; and (4) through the influences of libido mentioned above; one of these influences operating as "fusion." These processes are frequently interdependent; in clinical observation they cannot always be separated. Parallel modifications of libidinal impulses are well known. However, their relevance is greater where aggression is concerned, since the "full" discharge of aggressive energy endanger the objects, whereas the full discharge of libido, however dangerous it may be, does not threaten the existence of the object itself.

Displacement of cathexis is, one might say, the simplest of the four processes. The object, Freud said, "is the most variable thing about a drive and is not originally connected with it but becomes attached to it only in consequence of being peculiarly fitted to provide satisfaction" (1915). The role of displacement of libido and its vicissitudes have been much discussed in psychoanalysis; less data have been accumulated in relation to aggression. Of all processes discussed here, it is the one that does not of necessity limit the discharge of aggression itself; full discharge is not excluded, if the substitute object is conveniently chosen, particularly if it is inanimate. It is here that both reality and structural organizations are to be taken into account. They determine occasions, intensity, and forms of aggressive action and organize the hierarchy of motivation.

The problem of "man in search of a target" is familiar not only from clinical observations, from the daily life of the child, but—as Freud had seen—from the vicissitudes of our social organization itself: One might say that social conflict is exploited by the manipulation of masses to provide the individual group member with an enemy whom he eagerly accepts as target of aggression, thus using social tension for the displacement of individual tension.

Since often the ultimate aims of aggression cannot be reached, modification of aggression must be largely entrusted to the other methods enumerated above.

Little is known about the conditions of fusion and diffusion of aggression and libido, and no new theoretical problems seem to arise in relation to the restriction of aims of aggression. However, it seems necessary to discuss briefly the sublimation of aggressive energy.

Here we touch upon a gap in Freud's presentation. . . . He introduced the idea of sublimation of libido, i.e., of a transformation of libido in neutralized energy, which contributes to the constitution of permanent object relations and to the forming of a psychic structure; then, as soon as psychic structure exists, this energy is at the disposal of the ego and superego; but Freud did not in sufficient detail elaborate the implications of the idea of the neutralization of aggressive energy.

We are inclined to consider the contribution of neutralized aggressive energy to the equipment of ego and superego to be at least as important as that of libido. Aggression is dangerous because it involves the individual in conflicts that are difficult if not impossible to solve, since they threaten the very object on whom man depends; but in a sublimated form aggressive energy can be integrated into the structure of ego and superego. Libido, on the other hand, can be fully discharged and can therefore be linked more closely to the object.

We should like to go one step further: The formation of a permanent object relation is, as has been shown elsewhere, dependent on the capacity of the individual to bear frustration; no permanent object relation, or no true constitution of a love object could be achieved without this capacity. We now add another condition: Such permanent object relation is also dependent on the sublimation of aggression. And if we here return to the concept of fusion of instincts it seems suggestive to assume that partial neutralization of drive energy establishes favorable conditions for the fusion of (residual) libido and especially of (residual) aggression.

The assumption regarding the sublimation of aggressive energy also sheds new light on one of the central problems of Freud's theory of aggression, i.e., the problem of self-destruction. If in order to divert aggression from another object the self is adopted as substitute object, the safety of the individual may be threatened. "A person in a fit of rage often demonstrates the transition from the checking of aggression to self-destructiveness by turning his aggressiveness against himself: He tears his hair or beats his face with his fists—treatment which he would evidently have preferred to apply to someone else."

But this simple example is part of a more far-reaching, if speculative, consideration. Aggression in the form of self-destructiveness constitutes a serious threat for the individual's survival, ". . . it at length succeeds in doing this individual to death." Freud here implicitly refers to his speculation on the death instinct. An impressive array of clinical studies published since 1939 tends to confirm the validity of his considerations: Studies of various psychosomatic conditions seem to converge in the finding that internalized aggression plays a relevant role in the etiology of illness.

However clinically important the assumptions concerning the internalization of aggression are, we cannot, in establishing general hypotheses on the vicissitudes of aggression, be satisfied with the dichotomy of self-destructive and externalized aggression. Not all internalized aggression leads the way to destruction of the self, no more than all internalized libidinal energy leads necessarily to self-infatuation. Freud was used to comparing the relation between narcissism and object love to that between self-destruction and destruction of the object. This analogy might have contributed to his assumption of self-destruction as of the primary form of aggression, to be compared to primary narcissism. However, he omitted to extend the parallel to other aspects which are relevant for the context of this paper. He neglected to take account of the fact that he had established a more complex concept of narcissism, which includes not only "self-love" but also other cathexes of the self; one of the forms of these cathexes is the cathexis of the ego with neutralized libido. Similarly we assume the existence of a neutralized "de-aggressivized" psychic energy, that does not lead to self-destruction but supplies ego and superego with motor power and equips particularly the ego for its function in action. On the basis of this assumption we may venture to say that if in the balance between libido and aggression a shift toward aggression takes place, such shift need not necessarily interfere with the individuals emotional stability.

We have said that the ego helps to modify aggression by directing it to substitute objects, by restriction, and by sublimation. On the other hand, it is well known that internalization of aggression is an essential condition for the formation of the superego, and that once the superego is formed, modified aggression is used by the superego in its relation to the ego. But what appears as displacement, restriction, or sublimation, considered in relation to the id and to discharge of aggressive energy, is, if we take into account the total personality and its position in social reality, a most important prerequisite of mental integration and of mastery of the environment.

The relation of aggression to the ego organization is not exhausted with these remarks. It is specific in various other ways. Aggression is closely linked to the apparatus of the ego, specifically to the muscular apparatus, the function of which is, as indicated above, more essential for the discharge of aggressive than of libidinal tension. Once the ego exists as a functioning organization the relation between aggression and the skeletal musculature implies a particularly close tie between the ego and aggression since this organization normally controls motility.

Musculature and motility, apparatuses for the discharge of aggression, contribute decisively to the differentiation between self and environment and, through action, to the differentiation of the environment itself. The environment in turn invites action and determines specific areas of action; it thus offers opportunities for the discharge of particular modes of aggression and their individual modifications.

The methods to be used in action develop *pari passu* with the apparatus of the ego, and the general scope of ego functions. Where aggression is involved means and ends are more highly differentiated than where libido is involved. The variety in the relation of means and ends as far as aggression is concerned can be considered a counterpart to the variety in the aims of sexuality.

These means and ends comprehend a development that has led from the use of the body itself to its extensions by the tools of modern technology and to the "conquest of nature." It seems that their importance led Freud to retain the assumption concerning the identity of ego drives and aggression, even at a time when his definition of the structural organization already implied that the controls of means and ends are to be considered as important functions of the ego as a system.

Objective danger is one situation that allows for and invites the discharge of aggression. . . .

*   *   *

Aggressive energy not discharged in flight may be internalized. It may be used as cathexis of the superego and be the source of guilt feelings; internalization may also lead to neutralization of aggressive energy in the ego without interfering with the integrity of the individual; if it is internalized (in the ego) without neutralization the incentive to some kind of self-destruction may exist. It will be important to clarify in the future the conditions under which these different solutions occur. While much seems to depend on the nature of the reality situation, particularly on the gravity of the danger, and on vicissitudes of the aggressive drive in the individual's previous life, a decisive part is played by the structure of the ego and superego. Tentatively we are inclined to assume that the capacity to neutralize large quantities of aggression may constitute one of the criteria of "ego strength" or of the high capacity of the ego for integration. Alternatively, the internalization of nonneutralized aggressive energy in the ego may be the hallmark of a weak, or eventually of a masochistic, ego.

These various outcomes can be exemplified in one particular type of danger situation: The position of the defeated toward the victor. The defeated might wait for the opportunity to defeat in turn the victor.

In that case one cannot even speak of internalization but of suspension of the aggressive response. The neutralization of the internalized aggressive energy might lead to a modification of the superego demands: Victory or aggression might be devaluated, and a moral victory over the physical victor might be ultimately achieved. Or, the defeated might feel guilty for the defeat. Internalization without neutralization leads to some kind of self-destructive attitude. If the latter is libidinized, the attitude of the defeated will be that of pleasurable submission, or what could be called the mentality of the slave; the defeated will renounce his superego for the superego of his master. Then we can speak of masochism of the ego in relation to the superego. It might safely be presumed that the latter situation occurs when in childhood, before the formation of the superego, a strong passive attachment to the father prevailed which becomes the pattern of the relation of the ego to the superego. Alternatively, if a strong superego has been formed, guilt feelings will dominate the picture.

*   *   *

6.

FREUD, SIGMUND

An Outline of Psychoanalysis (1938)*

The sole prevailing quality in the id is that of being unconscious. Id and unconscious are as intimately linked as ego and preconscious: Indeed, in the former case the connection is even more exclusive. If we look back at the developmental history of an individual and of his psychical apparatus, we shall be able to perceive an important distinction in the id. Originally, to be sure, everything was id; the ego was developed out of the id by the continual influence of the external world. In the course of this slow development certain of the contents of the id were transformed into the preconscious state and so taken into the ego; others of its contents remained in the id unchanged, as its scarcely accessible nucleus. During this development, however, the young and feeble ego put back into the unconscious state some of the material it had already taken in, dropped it, and behaved in the same way to some fresh impressions which it *might* have taken in, so that these, having been rejected, could leave a trace only in the id. In consideration of its origin we speak of this latter portion of the id as *the repressed*. It is of little importance that we are not always able to draw a sharp line between these two categories of contents in the

* Reprinted from: 23 *The Standard Edition of the Complete Psychological Works of Sigmund Freud*. London: The Hogarth Press and the Institute of Psychoanalysis, 1964. (pp. 163–69, 197–98). Reprinted by permission of Hogarth and W. W. Norton & Co.

id. They coincide approximately with the distinction between what was innately present originally and what was acquired in the course of the ego's development.

Having now decided upon the topographical dissection of the psychical apparatus into an ego and an id, with which the difference in quality between preconscious runs parallel, and having agreed that this quality is to be regarded only as an *indication* of the difference and not as its essence, a further question faces us. What, if this is so, is the true nature of the state which is revealed in the id by the quality of being unconscious and in the ego by that of being preconscious and in what does the difference between them consist?

But of that we know nothing. And the profound obscurity of the background of our ignorance is scarcely illuminated by a few glimmers of insight. Here we have approached the still shrouded secret of the nature of the psychical. We assume, as other natural sciences have led us to expect, that in mental life some kind of energy is at work; but we have nothing to go upon which will enable us to come nearer to a knowledge of it by analogies with other forms of energy. We seem to recognize that nervous or psychical energy occurs in two forms, one freely mobile and another, by comparison, bound; we speak of cathexes and hypercathexes of psychical material, and even venture to suppose that a hypercathexis brings about a kind of synthesis of different processes—a synthesis in the course of which free energy is transformed into bound energy. Further than this we have not advanced. At any rate, we hold firmly to the view that the distinction between the unconscious and the preconscious state lies in dynamic relations of this kind, which would explain how it is that, whether spontaneously or with our assistance, the one can be changed into the other.

Behind all these uncertainties, however, there lies one new fact, whose discovery we owe to psychoanalytic research. We have found that processes in the unconscious or in the id obey different laws from those in the preconscious ego. We name these laws in their totality the *primary process*, in contrast to the *secondary process* which governs the course of events in the preconscious, in the ego. . . .

*   *   *

The evidence of the share taken by the unconscious id in the formation of dreams is abundant and convincing. (*a*) Memory is far more comprehensive in dreams than in waking life. Dreams bring up recollections which the dreamer has forgotten, which are inaccessible to him when he is awake. (*b*) Dreams make an unrestricted use of linguistic symbols, the meaning of which is for the most part unknown to the dreamer. Our experience, however, enables us to confirm their sense. They probably originate from earlier phases in the development of speech. (*c*) Memory very often reproduces in dreams impressions from the dreamer's early childhood of which we can definitely assert not only that they had been forgotten but that they had become unconscious owing to repression. That explains the help—usually indispensable—given us by dreams in the attempts we make during the analytic treatment of neuroses to reconstruct the dreamer's early life. (*d*) Furthermore, dreams bring to light material which cannot have originated either from the dreamer's adult life or from his forgotten childhood. We are obliged to regard it as part of the *archaic heritage* which a child brings with him into the world, before any experiences of his own, influenced by the experiences of his ancestors. We find the counterpart of this phylogenetic material in the earliest human legends and in surviving customs. Thus dreams constitute a source of human prehistory which is not to be despised.

But what makes dreams so invaluable in giving us insight is the circumstance that, when the unconscious material makes its way into the ego, it brings its own modes of working along with it. This means that the preconscious thoughts in which the unconscious material has found its expression are handled in the course of the dream work as though they were unconscious portions of the id; and, in the case of the alternative method of dream formation, the preconscious thoughts which have obtained reinforcement from an unconscious instinctual impulse are brought down to the unconscious state. It is only in this way that we learn the laws which govern the passage of events in the unconscious and the respects in which they differ from the rules that are familiar to us in waking thought. Thus the dream work is essentially an instance of the unconscious working over of preconscious thought processes. To take an analogy from history: Invading conquerors govern a conquered country, not according to the judicial system which they find in force there, but according to their own. It is, however, an unmistakable fact that the outcome of the dream work is a compromise. The ego organization is not yet paralyzed, and its influence is to be seen in the distortion imposed on the unconscious material and in what are often very ineffective attempts at giving the total result a form not too unacceptable to the ego (*secondary revision*). In our analogy this would be an expression of the continued resistance of the defeated people.

The laws that govern the passage of events in the unconscious, which come to light in this manner, are remarkable enough and suffice to explain most of what seems strange to us about dreams. Above all there is a striking tendency to *condensation*, an inclination to form fresh unities out of elements which in our waking thought we should certainly have kept separate. As a consequence of this, a single element of the manifest dream often stands for a whole number of latent dream thoughts as though it were a combined allusion to all of them; and in general the compass of the manifest dream is extraordinarily small in comparison with the wealth of material from which it has sprung. Another peculiarity of the dream work, not entirely independent of the former one, is the ease with which psychical intensities (cathexes) are *displaced* from one element to another, so that it often happens that an element which was of little importance in the dream thoughts appears as the clearest and accordingly most important feature of the manifest dream, and, vice versa, that essential elements of the dream thoughts are represented in the manifest dream only by slight allusions. Moreover, as a rule the existence of quite insignificant points in common between two elements is enough to allow the dream work to replace one by the other in all further operations. It will easily be imagined how greatly these mechanisms of condensation and displacement can increase the difficulty of interpreting a dream and of revealing the relations between the manifest dream and the latent dream thoughts. From the evidence of the existence of these two tendencies to condensation and displacement our theory infers that in the unconscious id the energy is in a freely mobile state and that the id sets more store by the possibility of discharging quantities of excitation than by any other consideration; and our theory makes use of these two peculiarities in defining the character of the primary process we have attributed to the id.

The study of the dream work has taught us many other characteristics of the processes in the unconscious which are as remarkable as they are important; but we must only mention a few of them here. The governing rules of logic carry no weight in the unconscious; it might be called the Realm of the Illogical. Urges with contrary aims exist side by side in the unconscious without any need arising for an adjustment between them. Either they have no influence whatever on each other, or, if they have, no decision is reached, but a compromise comes about which is nonsensical since it embraces mutually incompatible details. With this is connected the fact that contraries are not kept apart but treated as though they were identical, so that in the manifest dream any element may also have the meaning of its opposite. Certain philologists have found that the same held good in the most ancient languages and that contraries such as "strong–weak", "light–dark," and "high–deep" were originally expressed by the same roots, until two different modifications of the primitive word distinguished between the two meanings. Residues of this original double meaning seem to have survived even in a highly developed language like Latin in its use of words such as "*altus*" ("high'. and "deep") and "*sacer*" ("sacred" and "infamous"))'

*   *   *

The core of our being, then, is formed by the obscure *id*, which has no direct communication with the external world and is accessible even to our own knowledge only through the medium of another agency. Within this id the organic *instincts* operate, which are themselves compounded of fusions of two primal forces (Eros and destructiveness) in varying proportions and are differentiated from one another by their relation to organs or systems of organs. The one and only urge of these instincts is toward satisfaction, which is expected to arise from certain changes in the organs with the help of objects in the external world. But immediate and unheeding satisfaction of the instincts, such as the id demands, would often lead to perilous conflicts with the external world and to extinction. The id knows no solicitude about ensuring survival and no anxiety; or it would perhaps be more correct to say that, though it can generate the sensory elements of anxiety, it cannot make use of them. The processes which are possible in and between the assumed psychical elements in the id (the *primary process*) differ widely from those which are familiar to us through conscious perception in our intellectual and emotional life; nor are they subject to the critical restrictions of logic, which repudiates some of these processes as invalid and seeks to undo them.

The id, cut off from the external world, has a world of perception of its own. It detects with extraordinary acuteness certain changes in its interior, especially oscillations in the tension of its instinctual needs, and these changes become conscious as feelings in the pleasure–unpleasure series. It is hard to say, to be sure, by what means and with the help of what sensory terminal organs these perceptions come about. But it is an established fact that self-perceptions—coenaesthetic feelings and feelings of pleasure–unpleasure—govern the passage of events in the id with despotic force. The id obeys the inexorable pleasure principle. But not the id alone. It seems that the activity of the other psychical agencies too is able to modify the pleasure principle but not to nullify it; and it remains a question of the highest theoretical importance, and one that has not yet been answered, when and how it is ever possible for the pleasure principle to be overcome. . . .

NOTE

FREUD, SIGMUND

New Introductory Lectures on Psychoanalysis (1933)*

[T]he id . . . is the dark, inaccessible part of our personality; what little we know of it we have learnt

---

* Reprinted from: 22 *The Standard Edition of the Complete Psychological Works of Sigmund Freud*, James Strachey, ed. London: The Hogarth Press and the Institute of Psychoanalysis, 1964. (pp. 73–75). Reprinted by permission of Hogarth and W. W. Norton & Co.

from our study of the dream work and of the construction of neurotic symptoms, and most of that is of a negative character and can be described only as a contrast to the ego. We approach the id with analogies: We call it a chaos, a cauldron full of seething excitations. We picture it as being open at its end to somatic influences, and as there taking up into itself instinctual needs which find their psychical expression in it, but we cannot say in what substratum. It is filled with energy reaching it from the instincts, but it has no organization, produces no collective will, but only a striving to bring about the satisfaction of the instinctual needs subject to the observance of the pleasure principle. The logical laws of thought do not apply in the id, and this is true above all of the law of contradiction. Contrary impulses exist side by side, without cancelling each other out or diminishing each other: At the most they may converge to form compromises under the dominating economic pressure toward the discharge of energy. There is nothing in the id that could be compared with negation; and we perceive with surprise an exception to the philosophical theorem that space and time are necessary forms of our mental acts. There is nothing in the id that corresponds to the idea of time; there is no recognition of the passage of time, and—a thing that is most remarkable and awaits consideration in philosophical thought—no alteration in its mental processes is produced by the passage of time. Wishful impulses which have never passed beyond the id, but impressions, too, which have been sunk into the id by repression, are virtually immortal; after the passage of decades they behave as though they had just occurred. They can only be recognized as belonging to the past, can only lose their importance and be deprived of their cathexis of energy, when they have been made conscious by the work of analysis, and it is on this that the therapeutic effect of analytic treatment rests to no small extent.

Again and again I have had the impression that we have made too little theoretical use of this fact, established beyond any doubt, of the unalterability by time of the repressed. This seems to offer an approach to the most profound discoveries. Nor, unfortunately, have I myself made any progress here.

The id of course knows no judgments of value: No good and evil, no morality. The economic or, if you prefer, the quantitative factor, which is intimately linked to the pleasure principle, dominates all its processes. Instinctual cathexes seeking discharge —that, in our view, is all there is in the id. It even seems that the energy of these instinctual impulses is in a state different from that in the other regions of the mind, far more mobile and capable of discharge; otherwise the displacements and condensations would not occur which are characteristic of the id and which so completely disregard the *quality* of what is cathected—what in the ego we should call an idea.

We would give much to understand more about these things! You can see, incidentally, that we are in a position to attribute to the id characteristics other than that of its being unconscious, and you can recognize the possibility of portions of the ego and superego being unconscious without possessing the same primitive and irrational characteristics.

7.

SOME PROBLEMS IN THE LAW OF INSURANCE, TORTS, AND CRIMES

a.   UNITED STATES NATIONAL BANK v.
        UNDERWRITERS AT LLOYD'S
        239 Or. 298, 396 P.2d 765 (1964)

O'CONNELL, JUSTICE.

This is an action to recover $100,000 under a certificate of accidental death insurance issued by the defendants. The insured died of a gunshot wound. Defendants appeal from a judgment entered on a verdict for plaintiff, the executor of the insured.

The issue at trial was whether the insured, Marion Mark Powell, died as a result of accidental bodily injury or as a result of suicide. . . .

*   *   *

The defendants' fifth assignment of error attacks the following instruction to which exception was duly taken:

> "I instruct you that the law never presumes that one accused of committing a suicide is guilty thereof. The presumption is against suicide. . . ."

*   *   *

The presumption against suicide is a presumption based upon a "fact" that has probative value. The "fact" is not formally adduced as evidence, but is derived from the generally accepted assumption, judicially noticed, that there is a human revulsion against suicide. From this psychological fact it is assumed that when a violent death is shown to have occurred and the evidence does not establish the cause of death as suicide or accident, it is more probable than not that death resulted from an accident. Stated statistically, it is assumed that of all the violent deaths which occur the greater number result from accidents rather than suicide.

The jury should be informed that it is entitled to use this generality as a basis for reasoning that, since there is a normal human revulsion against suicide generally, the deceased in the particular case before it also experienced the revulsion and, therefore, did not take his own life. The jury should be told that the presumption expresses a *generality* only, i.e., that humans do not *ordinarily* take their own lives. The

presumption does not purport to describe the state of mind of all persons in every circumstance. In the particular case before it the jury is free to conclude from the evidence adduced that the deceased overcame the normal revulsion against suicide.

There is a preliminary question of whether we should even recognize the existence of a presumption against suicide in the present case. . . . The critics of the presumption rely upon statistics showing that a majority of deaths resulting from gunshot wounds not inflicted by third persons are motivated by suicide.[1] On the basis of these statistics it is contended that a presumption against suicide should not be recognized where death occurs under such circumstances.

The suggestion that the presumption against suicide be abolished in these circumstances does not appeal to us. Assuming that the statistics accurately represent the percentages of death by accident and suicide, it will seldom be clear where a particular case falls within the fact grouping upon which the statistics are based. Where death results from wounds not inflicted by another person, the circumstances may vary considerably as to the place, motive, and other *indicia*, sometimes pointing to suicide and sometimes pointing to accident. If the facts point more strongly to accident than suicide, certainly there is no reason why the plaintiff should not be entitled to have the benefit of the presumption simply because the case falls into the category constituting the basis for the statistics. The trial judge, and eventually the appellate court, would be confronted with the task of deciding in each case whether or not the facts justified the recognition of the presumption. It is preferable to recognize the presumption, informing the jury that it is merely a broad generalization as to human reaction to suicide, and permit the opponent to weaken or destroy the inference by showing that in the facts of the particular case the evidence points the other way.

Those who would reject the presumption against suicide in the case of self-inflicted gunshot wounds rely upon statistics taken from the public records. It is quite probable that one could rummage through other records and find data running counter to many other presumptions based upon a general probability. When are we permitted to assume that these statistics are trustworthy? Obviously the statistics represent purely hearsay statements. Moreover, the raw statistics do not tell us what data was used in making the tabulation separating cases of suicide from cases of accident. This court is divided on the

---

1. E.g., Statistics taken from the public records of the Vital Statistics Section of the Oregon State Board of Health show that in 1962, of 157 firearm deaths (excluding homicides), 127 were attributable to suicides. In 1961, there were 110 suicides out of 132 firearm deaths; in 1960 the proportion was 129 out of 147.

question of whether there is evidence to support a verdict of suicide in the present case. How does the Board of Health classify the present case? It could be classified either way, depending upon whether one accepts the view taken by the jury or the view taken by the dissent in this case. Until the matter is fully adjudicated the case must be placed in a third category of unclassified cases. But the public statistics make only two classifications which do not reveal how the doubtful cases are resolved for the purposes of the classification. It is our conclusion that the presumption against suicide is applicable to the facts of the present case and that the jury should be made aware of the existence of the presumption.

*   *   *

Nothing that we have said should be taken to mean that the jury should not be instructed on the effect of the presumption against suicide. We hold only that the instruction should not describe the presumption as standing until the jury is satisfied that it has been overcome by evidence to the contrary. The jury should be told that there is a presumption against suicide. The basis for the presumption should be explained, i.e., the normal human revulsion against taking one's own life. It would be proper to explain to the jury that it may infer that because people normally do not take their own lives because of this instinct for self-preservation, the deceased did not take his own life in the case before it. The jury should be told that the improbability of suicide is to be treated as any other evidentiary fact and that the presumption does not endow the fact upon which it is based with any special value for evidentiary purposes. . . .

*   *   *

Defendants contend that error was committed in sustaining plaintiff's objection to an offer of proof in which Dr. Shanklin, a psychiatrist, expressed his opinion with respect to the emotional state of persons prior to committing suicide. The evidence developed by plaintiff tended to show that Powell was a person well adjusted to his surroundings; that he was happy and with no apparent reason for committing suicide. The offer of proof purported to show that suicides sometimes occur when a person is not despondent. Dr. Shanklin testified as follows:

"They [suicides] don't necessarily occur in the depths of despondency. Speaking generally, in other levels of retardation you will see your great peak of suicides as the improvement begins. This is the pattern, so that the behavior the day before or week before, even though it is quite jolly and socially correct, appropriate in all respects—this is of no moment in deciding whether or not this particular act was suicide or accident."

If this is a statement simply that some people commit suicide even though immediately preceding it they manifest a jolly spirit and correct social attitude, the testimony does not inform the members of the jury of anything they would not already know from their general observation. If the witness was purporting to tell the jury that in certain cases in which a person's condition is improving there is a pattern of suicide in spite of an outward appearance of jollity, the statement is too vague and not sufficiently related to Powell's condition.

This court is unable to discern from testimony what scientific phenomenon the witness was attempting to describe or how it relates to the particular death in this case, and we do not think the jury was in any better position to do so. The trial court refused to accept the offer of proof on the ground that it dealt with a matter within the province of the jury and that it was "too speculative." Apparently the trial court interpreted the testimony as we do. We hold that there was no abuse of discretion in rejecting the offer of proof.

The judgment is affirmed.

b.   COMSTOCK v. WILSON
          257 N.Y. 231, 177 N.E. 431 (1931)

*   *   *

LEHMAN, J.

Plaintiff's automobile, in which the plaintiff's testatrix was a passenger, came into collision with an automobile operated by the defendant. The collision caused some noise or "grating sound." The left fender of plaintiff's car was loosened from the running board. The plaintiff's testatrix stepped from the automobile and started to write down the defendant's name and license number. While doing so, she fainted and fell to the sidewalk, fracturing her skull. All this occurred within a few minutes after the accident. She lived about twenty minutes after the fall. The plaintiff, claiming that the death of his testatrix was the result of defendant's negligence, has recovered judgment for $5,000 against her.

The trial judge submitted to the jury, as a question of fact, whether the alleged negligence of the defendant was the proximate cause of the death of plaintiff's testatrix. He refused the defendant's request to charge that, "if the jury find that the deceased at the time of the collision sustained only shock or fright, without physical injury, they must find for the defendant." The defendant appealed to the Appellate Division from an order denying her motion for a new trial, and the Appellate Division in granting leave to appeal from its order of affirmance has certified the question whether it was error for the trial court to refuse the defendant's request to charge. . . .

*   *   *

. . . Mental suffering or disturbance, even without

consequences of physical injury, may in fact constitute actual damage; nevertheless the courts generally do not regard it as such damage as gives rise to a cause of action, though it be the direct result of the careless act. Whether the true explanation of that conclusion lies in an historical conception of injury or in supposed considerations of public policy may for the present be put aside. In either event the reason fails where fright or nervous shock causes visible physical injury. . . .

*   *   *

[W]here there has been a physical impact, even though slight, accompanied by shock, there may be a recovery for damages to health caused by the shock even though that shock was the result produced by the impact and fright concurrently. . . .

The courts in such case attempt no differentiation between the direct physical injury caused by the impact and the damage caused by the fright, even where the fright preceded the impact. The result may seem at times anomalous, for the direct physical injury may be insignificant in relation to the damages consequent upon the fright. That anomaly did not escape the keen mind of Mr. Justice Holmes. "As has been explained repeatedly, it is an arbitrary exception, based upon a notion of what is practicable, that prevents a recovery for visible illness resulting from nervous shock alone. *Spade* v. *Lynn & Boston R. R.*, 168 Mass. 285. . . . But when there has been a battery and the nervous shock results from the same wrongful management as the battery, it is at least equally impracticable to go further and to inquire whether the shock comes through the battery or along with it. Even were it otherwise, recognizing as we must the logic in favor of the plaintiff when a remedy is denied because the only immediate wrong was a shock to the nerves, we think that when the reality of the cause is guaranteed by proof of a substantial battery of the person there is no occasion to press further the exception to general rules." *Homans* v. *Boston Elevated Ry. Co.*, 180 Mass., 456.

[T]he courts [have] decided that for practical reasons there is ordinarily no duty to exercise care to avoid causing mental disturbance, and no legal right to mental security. Serious consequences from mere mental disturbance unaccompanied by physical shock cannot be anticipated, and no person is bound to be alert to avert a danger that foresight does not disclose. The conclusion is fortified by the practical consideration that where there has been no physical contact, there is danger that fictitious claims may be fabricated. Therefore, where no wrong was claimed other than a mental disturbance, the courts refused to sanction a recovery for the consequences of that disturbance. Here there was more. The defendant should have foreseen that a collision with the car in which plaintiff's testatrix was a passenger would cause injury to the passengers. She did collide with the car

through lack of care, and she did cause injury to the plaintiff's testatrix. That injury was not confined to fright. The fright was only a link in the chain of causation between collision and fractured skull. The collision itself, the consequent jar to the passengers in the car, was a battery and an invasion of their legal right. Their cause of action is complete when they suffered consequent damages.

*   *   *

Judgment affirmed.

NOTES

NOTE 1

FREUD, SIGMUND

Beyond the Pleasure Principle (1920)*

A condition has long been known and described which occurs after severe mechanical concussions, railway disasters, and other accidents involving a risk of life; it has been given the name of "traumatic neurosis." The terrible war which has just ended gave rise to a great number of illnesses of this kind, but it at least put an end to the temptation to attribute the cause of the disorder to organic lesions of the nervous system brought about by mechanical force. The symptomatic picture presented by traumatic neurosis approaches that of hysteria in the wealth of its similar motor symptoms, but surpasses it as a rule in its strongly marked signs of subjective ailment (in which it resembles hypochondria or melancholia) as well as in the evidence it gives of a far more comprehensive general enfeeblement and disturbance of the mental capacities. No complete explanation has yet been reached either of war neuroses or of the traumatic neuroses of peace. In the case of the war neuroses, the fact that the same symptoms sometimes came about without the intervention of any gross mechanical force seemed at once enlightening and bewildering. In the case of the ordinary traumatic neuroses two characteristics emerge prominently: First, that the chief weight in their causation seems to rest upon the factor of surprise, of fright; and secondly, that a wound or injury inflicted simultaneously works as a rule *against* the development of a neurosis. . . .

*   *   *

[The fact] that a gross physical injury caused simultaneously by the trauma diminishes the chances that a neurosis will develop, becomes intelligible if one bears in mind two facts which have been stressed by

---

* Reprinted from: 18 *The Standard Edition of the Complete Psychological Works of Sigmund Freud*, James Strachey, ed. London: The Hogarth Press and the Institute of Psychoanalysis, 1955. (pp. 12, 33). Reprinted by permission of Hogarth and Liveright Publishing Co.

psychoanalytic research: Firstly, that mechanical agitation must be recognized as one of the sources of sexual excitation, and secondly, that painful and feverish illnesses exercise a powerful effect, so long as they last, on the distribution of libido. Thus, on the one hand, the mechanical violence of the trauma would liberate a quantity of sexual excitation which, owing to the lack of preparation for anxiety, would have a traumatic effect; but, on the other hand, the simultaneous physical injury, by calling for a narcissistic hypercathexis of the injured organ, would bind the excess of excitation. It is also well known, though the libido theory has not yet made sufficient use of the fact, that such severe disorders in the distribution of libido as melancholia are temporarily brought to an end by intercurrent organic illness, and indeed that even a fully developed condition of *dementia praecox* is capable of a temporary remission in these same circumstances.

NOTE 2

LA PORTE v. ASSOCIATED INDEPENDENTS, INC.
163 So. 2d 267 (Fla. 1964)

Action against an employer for malicious killing of plaintiff's pet dog through the wrongful act of its employee, a garbage collector. . .

*   *   *

THOMAS, JUSTICE.

. . . The plaintiff, was awarded a verdict of $2,000 compensatory damages and $1,000 punitive damages. . . .

*   *   *

The respondent is a corporation engaged in the business of collecting garbage. Among its customers was the petitioner. Early one morning, while the petitioner was occupied in the preparation of breakfast, a garbage collector came for the refuse. The petitioner had tethered her pet, a miniature dachshund, Heidi, outside the house and beyond reach of the garbage can. Heidi was pedigreed and had been purchased two years before. She saw the garbage man empty the can and hurl it in the direction of the dog. Upon hearing her pet yelp, the petitioner went outside to find Heidi injured. The collector laughed and left. Heidi expired from the blow.

In the afternoon petitioner consulted a physician who later testified that she was upset to the point of marked hysteria and in such a plight that she could not recount the experience coherently. The doctor testified also that he had been treating her for nervousness for the past two years. But there is no need to pursue the matter of the effect of Heidi's demise upon her nervous system.

The narrow point for decision is whether or not the element of mental suffering was properly submitted to the jury for their consideration in assessing damages. . . .

*   *   *

In [*Kirksey* v. *Jernigan*, 45 So. 2d 188] it was shown that an undertaker had possessed and embalmed the body of a child without authority of the parent and had refused to surrender the body until a fee for the embalming was paid. The action of the parent for compensatory and punitive damages was dismissed in the trial court. The Supreme Court reversed the judgment and undertook to distinguish cases involving mental suffering from intentional or malicious torts and those in which mental suffering may have resulted from negligent acts. This court acknowledged its commitment to the rule that there could be no recovery for mental pain unconnected with physical hurt in an action arising from "negligent breach of a contract [when] simple negligence [was] involved."

The court then remarked that the rule would not, however, be extended to cases purely in tort "where the wrongful act is such as * * * reasonably [to] imply malice," or when from "great indifference to the persons, property, or rights of others, such malice will be imputed as would justify the assessment of exemplary or punitive damages."

It is to us obvious from the facts we have related that the act performed by the representative of the respondent was malicious and demonstrated an extreme indifference to the rights of the petitioner. Having this view we think there was no prohibition of punitive damages under the rule just cited relative to awarding compensation for mental pain, as would be the case if there had been physical injury, resulting only from simple negligence. . . .

. . . The restriction of the loss of a pet to its intrinsic value in circumstances such as the ones before us is a principle we cannot accept. Without indulging in a discussion of the affinity between "sentimental value" and "mental suffering," we feel that the affection of a master for his dog is a very real thing and that the malicious destruction of the pet provides an element of damage for which the owner should recover, irrespective of the value of the animal because of its special training such as a Seeing Eye dog or sheep dog.

The respondent tried to distinguish between the Kirksey case, *supra*, and the instant one on two bases, namely, that in the former the body of a child was involved and in the latter a dog; that in the former there was a personal transaction between the undertaker and complainant while in the latter there was none since the garbage gatherer "did not even know the plaintiff was anywhere within sight, nor had he ever met her or seen the dog previously." As to the first of these we hasten to say that the anguish resulting from the mishandling of the body of a child cannot be equated to the grief from the loss of a dog but that does not imply that mental suffering from the loss of a pet dog, even one less an aristocrat than Heidi, is nothing at all. As for the matter of contact between the miscreant and the injured person, the attempted distinction is just too fine for us to accept.

* * *

The judgment of the trial court is reinstated.

c.   STATE v. WHITE
60 Wash. 2d 551, 374 P. 2d 942 (1962),
Cert. Denied 375 U.S. 883(1963)

DONWORTH, JUDGE.

Appellant was charged, by Information, with committing two murders alleged to have been committed at different times and places on the same day. . . .

* * *

The State's evidence . . . included appellant's signed confession . . . in which he described the beating of Mrs. Jumper (whom he had never seen before) as follows:

> ". . . As I was passing the laundry room, I looked in and noticed a white woman doing something with some clothes. She was either folding or hanging up clothes. I decided to go into the laundry room to use the head. The woman had her back to me as I entered the door and was standing over by one of the dryers. I walked pass [*sic*] the woman into the back and tried the door to the head but it was locked. I then turned around and started back out. When I got even with the woman I just punched her with my fist knocking off her glasses and knocking her to the floor. The glasses slid across the floor to a spot near the door. The woman wasn't knocked unconscious by my blow and she grabbed me around the legs and by one hand. I then lifted her up off the floor real fast and fairly high so that her legs flew up in the air. I then dropped her and her head hit the cement floor before the rest of her body. The woman still wasn't unconscious and was trying to get up. I then picked her up and took her back into a small storage room. I laid her down on the cement floor on her back with her head toward the door. She still wasn't unconscious so I hit her three or four times with my fists in her face. She didn't move anymore then except she sort of raised her arm and I removed her watch and ring. I then started to leave but then came back to where she was lying. I had earlier torn off her panties and had ripped her dress so when I got back into the room I had sexual intercourse with her. I had intercourse with her for about a minute but did not reach a climax. I would describe this woman as being about forty-five or forty-six years of age with grayish black hair and with a stocky build. . . .

* * *

. . . There was substantial evidence from which the jury could have found that appellant could not control his own behavior. . . .

[H]e, by the testimony of his witnesses and by documentary proof, presented to the jury a compre-

hensive history of his life from the time he was four months old until the date of trial.

This evidence showed the frustration that appellant experienced in his relationship with his foster mother who alternately was indulgent with him and then angrily rejected him completely.

Appellant introduced in evidence many reports and other documents relating to his experiences at various schools he attended and correctional institutions to which he was sent. Among these was the report of the Ryther Child Center, to which he was referred at the age of fourteen years for psychiatric treatment. While at Ryther, a complete psychiatric and psychological work-up was done on appellant in 1951. Dr. Charles A. Maugham, who did the evaluation, concluded that appellant would end up either in prison or in a State hospital if not treated.

Ryther could not control appellant, and it was decided to transfer him to a setting which could better protect him and the community. He was transferred to Luther Burbank School. It was far from ideal, but there were no better facilities available. The records of the Seattle Public Schools Guidance Service show his experiences during his year at the Luther Burbank School for Boys, after which he was paroled to his mother. Two months later he was remanded to the Juvenile Court and was sent to the State institution for boys at Chehalis, and from there to the forestry camp. Thereafter, appellant joined the Army and served overseas. He contracted syphilis, and after getting into considerable trouble, was separated from the service with an undesirable discharge. On appellant's return from the Army to his home in Seattle, he soon got into further difficulty with the law and was sentenced to the Monroe Reformatory. Up until this time he had had a record of burglaries, fighting, larceny, prowling, riding in stolen cars, and auto thefts. He was released on parole in March, 1959, and returned to Seattle. His parole officer testified that, in June, 1959, he assaulted his foster mother and threatened to burn her house down. He also testified that, during this period, appellant made serious attempts to obtain employment but failed to get a job because of the parole officer's heavy case load and the reluctance of employers to hire parolees. He said that appellant had violated his parole in several respects but he was not sent back to the reformatory, although he had asked the parole officer to lock him up because he did not think he could get along if he remained at liberty.

In summary, then, appellant's history is a history of lack of control. First, his parents failed to control him. The situation is summarized by Abram Kardiner, "When the State Brings Up the Child," *Saturday Review*, August, 26, 1961:

> "* * * Eventually the child comes to recognize the parents as the benevolent mediator between his weak self and what would otherwise be a hostile world.

This leads, first, to the idealization of the parent and to an enhancement of his authority to impose discipline, and ultimately to the development of what we call conscience. Should this pattern fail to occur, the only remaining implement of social control is fear of punishment, which must rest either on institutional pressures or on the police. The absence of the usual attitudes toward the parent, for whatever reason, creates a child with an emotional deficiency that may well make him socially ineducable."

Next, our institutions did not provide the necessary controls. Due to inadequate facilities, appellant was released, time after time, to make room for others.

Appellant called as expert witnesses a psychologist [who] . . . stated that, in his opinion, at the time the crimes charged occurred, [appellant] did not have the will or the power to resist emotional impulses.

*   *   *

. . . It is contended that if a man does not have control over his own behavior, he has no free will and cannot be blamed for his misbehavior. Therefore, the interests of both society and the individual defendant would best be served if such a defendant were not held criminally responsible for his actions. It is the latter part of this contention that we feel merits full consideration.

*   *   *

. . . In *Commonwealth* v. *Woodhouse*, 401 Pa. 242, 164 A. 2d 98 (1960), the court said:

"[S]upposing the power to resist is only impaired, would this prove irresponsibility? All men are subject to strong urges of various descriptions. Would this reduce 'Irresistible Impulse' to something that is not psychopathic at all? Others suggest that it is impossible, in any particular case, to say that an impulse was irresistible; all that can be said is that the impulse did not appear to have been successfully resisted. 'The difficulty of distinguishing between uncontrolled impulse and the impulse that is not controlled would take too fertile a dialectorial field.' Henderson, *Psychiatry and the Criminal Law*, 4 Psychiatric q. 103; Hamblen Smith, *Psychology and the Criminal*, 179."

*   *   *

Conviction confirmed.

NOTES

NOTE 1

R. v. BYRNE
[1960] 3 All E.R. 1

LORD PARKER, C. J. . . . The appellant was convicted of murder before STABLE, J., at Birmingham Assizes and sentenced to imprisonment for life. The victim was a young woman whom he strangled in the Y.W.C.A. hostel, and after her death he committed horrifying mutilations on her dead body. The facts as to the killing were not disputed, and were admitted in a long statement made by the appellant. The only defense was that in killing his victim the appellant was suffering from diminished responsibility as defined by sec. 2 of the Homicide Act, 1957, and was accordingly guilty, not of murder, but of manslaughter.

Three medical witnesses were called by the defense, the senior medical officer at Birmingham prison and two specialists in psychological medicine. Their uncontradicted evidence was that the appellant was a sexual psychopath, that he suffered from abnormality of mind, as, indeed, was abundantly clear from the other evidence in the case, and that such abnormality of mind arose from a condition of arrested or retarded development of mind or inherent causes. The nature of the abnormality of mind of a sexual psychopath, according to the medical evidence, is that he suffers from violent perverted sexual desires which he finds it difficult or impossible to control. Save when under the influence of his perverted sexual desires, he may be normal. All three doctors were of opinion that the killing was done under the influence of his perverted sexual desires, and, although all three were of opinion that he was not insane in the technical sense of insanity laid down in the rules in *M'Naghten's Case* (1), it was their view that his sexual psychopathy could properly be described as partial insanity.

In his summing up the learned judge, after summarizing the medical evidence, gave to the jury a direction of law, on the correctness of which this appeal turns. He told the jury that, if on the evidence they came to the conclusion that the facts could be fairly summarized as follows:

"(i) from an early age [the appellant] has been subject to these perverted, violent desires and in some cases has indulged his desires; (ii) the impulse or urge of these desires is stronger than the normal impulse or urge of sex to such an extent that the subject finds it very difficult or perhaps impossible in some cases to resist putting the desire into practice; (iii) the act of killing this girl was done under such impulse or urge; and, (iv) setting aside these sexual addictions and practices, [the appellant] was normal in every other respect."

—those facts, with nothing more, would not bring a case within the section and "do not constitute such abnormality of mind as substantially to impair a man's mental responsibility for his acts." He went on to say:

"In other words, mental affliction is one thing. The section is there to protect them. The section is not there to give protection where there is nothing else than what is vicious and depraved."

*   *   *

[I]n a case where the abnormality of mind is one

which affects the accused's self-control, the step between "he did not resist his impulse" and "he could not resist his impulse" is, as the evidence in this case shows, one which is incapable of scientific proof. *A fortiori*, there is no scientific measurement of the degree of difficulty which an abnormal person finds in controlling his impulses. These problems, which in the present state of medical knowledge are scientifically insoluble, the jury can only approach in a broad, commonsense way. . . .

*   *   *

NOTE 2

KING v. COGDON

Supreme Court of Victoria 1950 (unreported)*

*   *   *

Mrs. Cogdon was charged with the murder of her only child, a daughter called Pat, aged nineteen. . . . Describing the relationship between Pat and her mother, Mr. Cogdon testified: "I don't think a mother could have thought any more of her daughter. I think she absolutely adored her." On the conscious level, at least, there was no reason to doubt Mrs. Cogdon's deep attachment to her daughter.

To the charge of murdering Pat, Mrs. Cogdon pleaded not guilty. Her story, though somewhat bizarre, was not seriously challenged by the Crown. . . . She told how, on the night before her daughter's death she had dreamt that their house was full of spiders and that these spiders were crawling all over Pat. In her sleep, Mrs. Cogdon left the bed she shared with her husband, went into Pat's room and awakened to find herself violently brushing at Pat's face, presumably to remove the spiders. This woke Pat. Mrs. Cogdon told her she was just tucking her in. At the trial, she testified that she still believed, as she had been told, that the occupants of a nearby house bred spiders as a hobby, preparing nests for them behind the pictures on their walls. It was these spiders which in her dreams had invaded their home and attacked Pat. There had also been a previous dream in which ghosts had sat at the end of Mrs. Cogdon's bed and she had said to them, "Well, you have come to take Pattie." It does not seem fanciful to accept the psychological explanation of these spiders and ghosts as the projections of Mrs. Cogdon's subconscious hostility toward her daughter; a hostility which was itself rooted in Mrs. Cogdon's own early life and marital relationship.

* Reprinted from: Morris, Norval: *Somnombulistic Homicide—Ghosts, Spiders, and North Koreans*, Res. Judicatae V: 29 (1951). Reprinted by permission.

The morning after the spider dream she told her doctor of it. He gave her a sedative and, because of the dream and certain previous difficulties she had reported, discussed the possibility of psychiatric treatment. That evening Mrs. Cogdon suggested to her husband that he attend his lodge meeting. [W]hile Pat was having a bath preparatory to retiring, Mrs. Cogdon went into her room, put a hot water bottle in the bed, turned back the bedclothes, and placed a glass of hot milk beside the bed ready for Pat. She then went to bed herself. There was some desultory conversation between them about the war in Korea, and just before she put out her light Pat called out to her mother, "Mum, don't be so silly worrying about the war, it's not on our front door step yet."

Mrs. Cogdon went to sleep. She dreamt that "the war was all around the house," that the soldiers were in Pat's room, and that one soldier was on the bed attacking Pat. This was all of the dream that she could later recapture. Her first "waking" memory was of running from Pat's room, out of the house to the home of her sister who lived next door. When her sister opened the front door Mrs. Cogdon fell into her arms crying, "I think I've hurt Pattie."

In fact Mrs. Cogdon had, in her somnambulistic state, left her bed, fetched an axe from the woodheap, entered Pat's room, and struck her two accurate forceful blows on the head with the blade of the axe, thus killing her.

Mrs. Cogdon's story was supported by the evidence of her physician, a psychiatrist, and a psychologist. [T]he psychologist and the psychiatrist concurred in hinting that the emotional motivation lay in an acute conflict situation in her relations with her own parents; that during marital life she suffered very great sexual frustration; and that she overcompensated for her own frustration by overprotection of her daughter. Her exaggerated solicitude for her daughter was a conscious expression of her subconscious emotional hostility to her, and the dream ghosts, spiders, and Korean soldiers were projections of that aggression. . . .

At all events the jury believed Mrs. Cogdon's story, and regarded the presumption that the natural consequences of her acts were intended as being completely rebutted by her account of her mental state at the time of the killing, and by the unanimous support given to it by the medical and psychological evidence . . . she was acquitted because the act of killing itself was not, in law, regarded as her act at all. . . .

*   *   *

. . . Mrs. Cogdon escapes basically because of the state of her consciousness; not because she had no conscious intention or rational motive to kill, a state she shares with many convicted murderers. She was "asleep": had she been "awake" her only defense would have been one of insanity. . . .

But the difference between being "asleep" and "awake" is not absolute. Consciousness is not like a light, either off or on; it is a finely graded scale ranging from death to the extreme awareness of the artist. Indeed, with the electroencephalograph we can even chart certain variations of consciousness between people, and in one person at different times. Had Mrs. Cogdon been "awake," that is, just a little more conscious, a little more aware of her actions, then her act may have had to be regarded as "voluntary." The line is an extremely fine one, as is shown by the fact that in and during her dream Mrs. Cogdon was "aware" of the axe, her daughter and the soldiers. Not unexpectedly, she could not remember this part of the dream, for within us we struggle to repress such profoundly disturbing and shocking memory traces. Thus we all dream, but some, for various reasons, remember more than others. Nor would Mrs. Cogdon's position have been legally different even if she could have then recalled all the dream, including the killing, Her exculpation lay not in the state of her memory but in her inability to bring into consciousness her emotional motivations, and consequently her diminished awareness of the deed.

Why is it, then, that we so firmly reject "irresistible impulse" as a valid defense? Admittedly it is difficult to establish, but so is the voluntary or involuntary quality of an act. One motivated by an "irresistible impulse" is "aware" and "conscious" of it, is "awake," and therefore his action is "voluntary," even if for him it is an impulse he can no more arrest than could Canute arrest the sea. That he can resist it the law affirms, or at least will punish him as if he could, and this despite the fact that modern psychology is inexplorably based on the belief that our actions are emotionally determined. Cheerfully we accept lack of consciousness of action as proof of its involuntary character, but indignantly reject lack of ability to control an action of which the actor is conscious as a proof of the same thing. Perhaps it is that we don't believe that there is an "irresistible impulse" (if indeed this term is not itself a truism to the logical determinist—every impulse not resisted being subjectively irresistible when considered in the setting of the personality of the actor and the environment of the act), but this disbelief is possibly only another way of stating that we have all experienced dreams, and semi-waking not-fully-conscious states when the alarm continues to ring in the morning, but have not experienced other sudden dissociated states of greatly reduced consciousness—we therefore deny their existence.

*   *   *

NOTE 3

FISHER, CHARLES

Psychoanalytic Implications of Recent Research on Sleep and Dreaming*

[D]reaming is associated with a very marked loss of muscle tone, of interest because of its bearing on the problem of motor paralysis during sleep. As early as "The Project," Freud stated, "Dreams are devoid of motor discharge and, for the most part, of motor elements. We are paralysed in dreams. . . ."

Freud's idea that motor discharge is blocked at the spinal level has been confirmed by recent work. Hodes and Dement reported an abolition of electrically induced reflexes in the leg during REMPs [rapid eye movement periods].[1] Their results indicate that during REMPs descending suprasegmental reflexes act to suppress an evoked spinal reflex. Their data are consistent with other evidence suggesting a significant over-all reduction of activity of spinal elements during REMPs, e.g., loss of muscle tone in animals and man. It appears that the organism is held to its resting place in the face of the marked internal activation associated with dreaming sleep because the brain blocks the peripheral manifestations of its own activity. The loss of muscle tone makes muscular movement impossible, and, looked at teleologically, one may think of this loss as a mechanism which insures the organism against acting out the dream. . . .

NOTE 4

FREUD, SIGMUND

Moral Responsibility for the Content of Dreams (1923)**

*   *   *

. . . Must one assume responsibility for the content of one's dreams? . . . Obviously one must hold oneself responsible for the evil impulses of one's dreams. What else is one to do with them? Unless the content of the dream (rightly understood) is inspired by alien

* 13 *J. American Psychoanalytic Association* 1965 (pp. 204–205). Reprinted by permission.

1. The dream-sleep cycle refers to the periodic emergence of phases of dreaming (REM) and nondreaming (NREM) sleep. These cyclic changes can be observed through continuous all-night recordings of EEG, REMs, and other physiological measurements. . . . It is certain that the occurrence of REMs is not an artifact of the recording method; nor is it due to the fact that the subject is observed under laboratory conditions. The REMs can be seen through the closed eyelids and have been noted many times in persons sleeping under their usual home conditions.

** Reprinted from: 19 *The Standard Edition of the Complete Psychological Works of Sigmund Freud.* John Strachey, ed. London: The Hogarth Press and the Institute of Psychoanalysis, 1961. (pp. 132–34). Reprinted by permission of Hogarth and Basic Books, Inc.

spirits, it is a part of my own being. If I seek to classify the impulses that are present in me according to social standards into good and bad, I must assume responsibility for both sorts; and if, in defense, I say that what is unknown, unconscious, and repressed in me is not my "ego," then I shall not be basing my position upon psychoanalysis, I shall not have accepted its conclusions—and I shall perhaps be taught better by the criticisms of my fellow men, by the disturbances in my actions and the confusion of my feelings. I shall perhaps learn that what I am disavowing not only "is" in me but sometimes "acts" from out of me as well.

It is true that in the metapsychological sense this bad repressed content does not belong to my "ego"— that is, assuming that I am a morally blameless individual—but to an "id" upon which my ego is seated. But this ego developed out of the id, it forms with it a single biological unit, it is only a specially modified peripheral portion of it, and it is subject to the influences and obeys the suggestions that arise from the id. For any vital purpose, a separation of the ego from the id would be a hopeless undertaking.

Moreover, if I were to give way to my moral pride and tried to decree that for purposes of moral valuation I might disregard the evil in the id and need not make my ego responsible for it, what use would that be to me? Experience shows me that I nevertheless *do* take the responsibility, that I am somehow compelled to do so. Psychoanalysis has made us familiar with a pathological condition, obsessional neurosis, in which the poor ego feels itself responsible for all sorts of evil impulses of which it knows nothing, impulses which are brought up against it in consciousness but which it is unable to acknowledge. Something of this is present in every normal person. It is a remarkable fact that the more moral he is the more sensitive is his "conscience." It is just as though we could say that the healthier a man is, the more liable he is to contagions and to the effects of injuries. This is no doubt because conscience is itself a reaction formation against the evil that is perceived in the id. The more strongly the latter is suppressed, the more active is the conscience.

The ethical narcissism of humanity should rest content with the knowledge that the fact of distortion in dreams, as well as the existence of anxiety dreams and punishment dreams, afford just as clear evidence of his *moral* nature as dream interpretation gives of the existence and strength of his *evil* nature. If anyone is dissatisfied with this and would like to be "better" than he was created, let him see whether he can attain anything more in life than hypocrisy or inhibition.

The physician will leave it to the jurist to construct for social purposes a responsibility that is artificially limited to the metapsychological ego. It is notorious that the greatest difficulties are encountered by the attempts to derive from such a construction practical consequences which are not in contradiction to human feelings.

NOTE 5

INBAU, FRED E. and REID, JOHN E.

Criminal Interrogation and Confessions*

If a subject will admit that he had "thought" about committing the offense in question, this fact is suggestive of his guilt. It is well, therefore, to inquire about such thoughts. For instance, the subject may be asked whether he ever thought about taking the missing money, or about holding-up the particular victim of a robbery, or of forcing himself upon a particular rape victim, or even about committing *any* offense of the type under investigation. A response of "No" is the characteristic answer of an innocent subject, for even though the idea may have flashed through his mind he would not have given it any further consideration. On the other hand, a guilty person is much more likely to say "Yes," although, to be sure, he is apt to add "but not seriously."

In utilizing this technique, if the interrogator does not receive an acknowledgment of having thought about committing the offense or one similar to it, he should then say: "The reason I'm asking you if you ever thought about doing this is because if you ever did, then that may account for the fact that your looks and appearances are giving the impression that you're not telling the truth." A guilty person is apt to try to explain away this impression by admitting that he had thought about doing the act in question or one similar to it. An innocent person will usually persist in his denial of any such thinking.

Once a subject admits having thought about the offense, or about a similar one, the interrogator should ask him to tell about the kind and frequency of such thoughts. If the thoughts went as far as plans or preparation, then the interrogator should become even more secure in his belief of the subject's guilt. The interrogator may then say: "Joe, this thinking finally got to a point where in one of your weakest moments (or when you were under the most pressure) you gave in. Right?"

In some case situations such as the investigation of a sex-motivated murder, a subject may be asked, "Have you ever dreamed about doing something like this?" Such a question was asked by one of us during the interrogation of a subject suspected of a sex-motivated murder in which the offender had decapitated the victim and taken further sexual liberties with the dead body. He admitted that he had dreamed about "placing naked women into a knife machine." Thereupon, the interrogator asked him to give the full details of the dream. Then, after further interrogation the subject admitted his guilt, and his confession was fully substantiated by such evidence as the finding of

* Baltimore: The Williams & Wilkins Co., 1962. (pp. 101–102). Reprinted by permission.

the girl's wrist watch at the place where the subject stated he had thrown it.

Although the foregoing case is a very unique one in our experience, perhaps further case situations of a similar nature may establish a relationship between the capacity to dream of such conduct and the doing of the act in question, which is comparable to the relationship we have found to exist in many cases between the thinking of certain criminal conduct and the actual commission of the act.

NOTE 6

STATE v. ANDERSON
137 N.W. 2d 781 (Minn. 1965)

OTIS, JUSTICE

Defendant appeals from a conviction for committing incest with his 17-year-old daughter. The incidents constituting the crime are alleged by the daughter to have occurred over a period of 5 years, during which time with infrequent exceptions the father, daughter, her two brothers, a sister, and stepmother were living together in close proximity in the same farmhouse. The daughter charges that the acts complained of took place in rooms immediately adjacent to a central kitchen at times when the stepmother was physically present in the home. Nevertheless, there was no corroborative evidence, direct or circumstantial, to prove that the father actually had relations with her on any specific occasion, let alone "practically every night" as the daughter testified. She charged that the intercourse occurred in her bedroom, her father's bedroom, and in the living room. Yet there was no testimony by either the stepmother, the brothers, or the sister that any of them entertained the slightest suspicion that defendant was guilty of such misconduct during the period it is alleged to have occurred. At most, the stepmother, who was divorced from the defendant at the time of trial, stated she had seen the father improperly fondle his daughter and in her presence enter the daughter's bedroom when she was bathing. The sons not only contradicted this testimony but categorically denied a charge by the daughter that her father had exposed himself in their presence or had made obscene references to their comparative manliness.

This matter represents a classic conflict between a frustrated daughter and an unduly strict father. The record discloses that the father's suspicion that his daughter was having illicit relations with a neighbor boy was subsequently confirmed by a brother. In a fit of anger, the father struck her. A few weeks later, she left home, provoking from him an intemperate and vindictive letter accusing her of promiscuity. The fact that she was thus stung by the treatment she had received, considered in the light of a mental or emotional instability which shortly thereafter prompted her confinement for psychiatric treatment, tends to discredit her testimony to a point where, in our opinion, there must be a new trial.

Apart from the fact that the father had remarried before his divorce was final and as a result was convicted of bigamy, the evidence discloses no prior record whatever of any sexual aberration or any other history reflecting on his character. During all of this 5-year period when the daughter claims her father had intercourse with her "practically every night," she made no complaint to her friends, her teachers, her stepmother, her brothers, her aunts, or any other relative in whom it would be natural to confide, notwithstanding the fact she knew "it wasn't right" and testified she "fought back." Her testimony indicates that no measures whatever were taken to prevent conception, yet she never became pregnant. Nor did the State produce any medical testimony to prove through a physical examination that the daughter had ever previously had sexual intercourse with anyone.

1. The problems inherent in cases of this kind have not been better stated than by Mr. Justice Mitchell in *State* v. *Connelly*, 57 Minn. 482, 485, 59 N.W. 479, 481:

> "* * * There is no rule of law which forbids a jury to convict of rape on the uncorroborated evidence of the prosecutrix, provided they are satisfied beyond a reasonable doubt of the truth of her testimony. But the courts have always recognized the danger of convicting on her uncorroborated evidence, for, in the language of Lord Hale, '*it is an accusation easily made, hard to be proved, and still harder to be disproved by one ever so innocent.*'
>
> "Where the testimony of the prosecutrix is uncorroborated, and bears some intrinsic evidence of improbability, courts have sometimes refused even to submit it to the jury. In some states, corroborating evidence is required by statute.
>
> "Where the charge is true, there will almost always be some corroborating evidence, such as injury to the person or clothing of the prosecutrix, or the fact that she made complaint as soon as practicable, and without unreasonable delay. While the rule requiring immediate complaint is not inflexible, yet the unexplained failure to do so is always considered a very important fact. It is so natural as to be almost inevitable that a female upon whom the crime has been committed will make immediate complaint, if she have a mother or other confidential friend to whom she can make it. The rule is founded upon the laws of human nature. * * *

> *   *   *

> "*The crime is so abhorrent that, to some minds, to charge a person with it, raises a presumption of guilt. It is human nature to incline to the story of the female, especially if a young girl.* But, while virtue and veracity are the rule with them, yet even young girls, like older females, sometimes concoct an untruthful story to conceal a lapse from virtue.
>
> "Hence all the authorities agree that this is a crime requiring special scrutiny by the jury, and a careful

weighing of the evidence and all remote and near circumstances and probabilities in cases where the testimony of the female is not corroborated, and especially where the testimony is at all improbable or suspicious." (Italics supplied.)

In recognition of the role which psychological factors play in provoking charges of sexual misconduct, there is a marked trend on the part of many courts and legislatures to insist on corroboration in prosecutions for such offenses.

The considerations which have prompted these safeguards have been thoroughly considered by Dean Wigmore in 3 Wigmore, Evidence (3 ed.) § 924a, to which we have made passing reference in *State* v. *Wulff*, 194 Minn. 271, 274, 260 N.W. 515, 516:

> "* * * Modern psychiatrists have amply studied the behavior of errant young girls and women coming before the courts in all sorts of cases. Their psychic complexes are multifarious, distorted partly by inherent defects, partly by diseased derangements or abnormal instincts, partly by bad social environment, partly by temporary physiological or emotional conditions. One form taken by these complexes is that of contriving false charges of sexual offences by men. The unchaste (let us call it) mentality finds incidental but direct expression in the narration of imaginary sex-incidents of which the narrator is the heroine or the victim. On the surface the narration is straightforward and convincing. *The real victim, however, too often in such cases is the innocent man; for the respect and sympathy naturally felt by any tribunal for a wronged female helps to give easy credit to such a plausible tale.*" (Italics supplied.)

Dean Wigmore in support of his views quotes the following from Dr. Karl A. Menninger (p. 463):

> "Every girl who enters a plausible but unproved story of rape should be required to have a psychiatric examination. As you know, I have elsewhere expressed myself publicly as favoring the psychiatric examination of criminals and those charged with crime, and I agree with you that this should be extended to include some of the individuals who make criminal charges, not only of rape but also of malpractice and other personal attacks. The reason I think that rape in particular belongs in this category is one well known to psychologists, namely, that fantasies of being raped are exceedingly common in women, indeed one may almost say that they are probably universal. By this I mean that most women, if we may judge from our clinical experience, entertain more or less consciously at one time or another fleeting fantasies or fears that they are being or will be attacked by a man. Of course, the normal woman who has such a fantasy does not confuse it with reality, *but it is so easy for some neurotic individuals to translate their fantasies into actual beliefs and memory falsifications that I think a safeguard should certainly be placed upon this type of criminal charge.*" (Italics supplied.)

2. In an atmosphere as highly charged with emotion as the prosecution of a father for violating his daughter, where the corroboration is as deficient as in this case, we consider an incident in which the clerk of the court wept openly in the presence of the jury as a matter of serious consequence. While ordinarily it would probably not be sufficient to warrant a new trial, considered with what we regard as inadequate proof of the crime, we find it constitutes substantial prejudice.

We have held in a long line of cases that where this court entertains grave doubt as to defendant's guilt the interests of justice require that there be a new trial. This is such a case. We believe a conviction under the circumstances recited can only be sustained upon clear and convincing evidence which we find lacking in this record. . . .

Reversed and new trial granted.

NOTE 7

DEUTSCH, HELENE

The Psychology of Women*

We meet girls who, although normal and well adjusted in all other respects, write love letters to themselves, not merely in order to boast about these missives to their friends, but to endow their fantasies with some degree of reality. Lying serves the double purpose of discharging tensions arising from the excessive demands made on one's fantasy life and of protecting oneself from actual realization. What essentially distinguishes such fantasies (pseudology) from daydreams is that they are communicated to others as real happenings. The imaginary gratifications of ambitious or erotic desires—consummated without regard for external reality—that are the principal content of daydreams, also supply material for pseudology. Just as the daydream is sometimes limited to a modest mitigation of some undesirable situation, while at other times it is a fantastic creation in utter contradiction to reality, so the content of pseudology varies from trite love affairs or petty satisfactions of vanity to complicated romantic adventures. Like the daydreamer, the pseudologist fulfils his wishes by inventing lies, and always places himself in the center of his fantasy.

There is, however, one essential difference between the two. While daydreamers are characterized by bashful secrecy broken only rarely to intimate friends, pseudologists importune others with their fantasies, which they relate as real events. In this, their purpose is usually to achieve the satisfaction inherent in the act of communication—one of their motives is obviously the revelation of the fantasy carefully concealed by daydreamers.

Daydreamers, further, are inclined to regard their fantasies as true, and this is part of their pleasure. But

---

* New York: Grune & Stratton, 1945, (Vol. I, pp. 123–27, 256–57). Reprinted by permission.

the pseudologists' longing for reality seems to be much more intense—intense enough for them to represent products of their imagination as truth even to other people.

The following case is a good illustration of this point. A girl undergoes a remarkable experience between the ages of thirteen and seventeen. She is an attractive girl, intelligent and of ardent temperament. She does not lack opportunities for amorous relations, but always avoids them with the greatest reserve. A high-school boy of about seventeen, rather unattractive, whom she knows only by sight, becomes the hero of her erotic fantasies. These have an extremely passionate character—consuming kisses, ardent embraces, sexual ecstasies, the young girl's imagination creating everything that reality can give to a sexually mature woman. She becomes so absorbed in this fantasy that in her seclusion she leads a life full of joys and sorrows: Her eyes are often swollen with tears because her lover turns out to be tyrannical, covers her with abuse, and even beats her; then, overflowing with love, he brings her flowers that actually she buys herself. She manages to get a picture of him and on it she writes a loving dedication in her own hand, distorted for the purpose. She has dates with him in forbidden places, they become secretly engaged, etc. For three years she keeps a detailed diary about all these imaginary experiences; when her lover goes away she continues her relations with him by writing him letters that she never mails, and to which she replies herself.

What interests us in this case is the fact that she tells everyone about these mysterious relations, representing them as real, so that she exposes herself to unpleasantness and punishment; when reprimanded, she always admits contritely not that she is lying, but that she is still involved in the forbidden relationship. Her descriptions are so convincing that no one doubts the truth of them, even though the innocent boy has denied having any relations with her.

As we have said, this girl had every opportunity to experience in reality what she invented pseudologically. But she had several motives for preferring the latter course. The fact that her erotic life consisted in fantasies woven around a chosen object is . . . normal for a girl in the pubescent stage. . . . In her choice she was determined by her unconscious attitude toward her brother; this too is a regressive although normal determinant of erotic choice. The regressive nature of adolescent fantasies is manifested in the fact that as a rule the real objects that are chosen strongly resemble earlier objects—that is to say, father or brother. Under the impact of puberty our pseudologic girl tries to center her longing on a real object, but succeeds only partially. She chooses one object after the model of her brother, but she is incapable of a real love relation. The kind of relation she wants must be imaginary, not real. The girl strictly avoided every

opportunity to become acquainted with the hero of her fantasies. She preferred the fantasy; in it her brother, to whom she was unconsciously faithful, and her real object could merge. In her childhood she had had various real experiences with her brother that were preserved in her unconscious and that at a given moment were revived with all the force of a fresh experience. The old experience was attributed to the new object, and former reality endowed the present love fantasy with a real character.

This resurrection of snatches of remembered real events distinguishes pseudology from more normal puberty fantasies. Fenichel rightly notes that pseudology is a special method of negating reality. During puberty every reality that might gratify sexual wishes may appear dangerous, and a regression to fantasy or pseudology takes place. Pseudology is used as a defense; the adolescent girl takes her fantasy for reality in order to renounce a reality that she regards as perhaps more dangerous.

Another form of escape from a present that is unsatisfactory or conceals dangers is the postponement of realization. Young girls indulge in detailed plans for the future that they think up alone or with appropriate collaborators. These plans vary from the most trite and prosaic pictures to the most fantastic and impossible. Many a young girl debates in her own mind the most insignificant fixture in the kitchen of her future home, before the slightest chance of marriage has presented itself. Others see themselves eloping under the most romantic circumstances and build splendid castles in the air for their future residences. The erotic plans vary between being desired with burning passion and suffering poignantly for the sake of the imaginary lover.

However, absorption in daydreams is also not without its dangers, and the young girl tries to tear herself away from these experiences. Often she takes the same path she took during prepuberty to liberate herself from childhood dependency. She turns actively toward reality and under normal conditions succeeds in achieving a compromise. In this case, reality must contain a sufficient amount of pleasure elements, must offer sufficient gratification, and be interesting enough to compete with her fantasies. But this step into reality does not always succeed. In the first place, the outside world opposes the desire for sexual pleasure in adolescence and thrusts the girl back into her dreams. In the second place, the imaginary world is often so full and rich that reality is in comparison pale and unsatisfactory. In such cases colorful fantasy is preferred to gray reality. We have also seen that the fear of real fulfillment, which makes fantasy appear a less dangerous refuge, also drives the girl away from reality.

In many girls the orientation toward reality takes a form that easily creates new problems. For instance, I have met young girls who, because of a fear of passive sexual experiences, plunged into intense sexual activity. They tried to overcome fear by the tested method of "active intervention," but the experiences they themselves provoked usually weighed upon them just as heavily, and their fear only changed its content. The fear of fulfilling sexual wishes is replaced by guilty self-reproach for having too rashly overruled sexual inhibitions.

*   *   *

We learn—often even without deeper analytic investigation—that rape fantasies are variants of the seduction fantasies so familiar to us in the lying accounts of hysterical women patients. Both rape and seduction fantasies are deliberately passed on to other persons as true, and they have the typical pseudologic character we found in the more romantic and fantastic lies of puberty. That is, they draw their appearance of truth from the fact that underlying them is a real but repressed experience. It is precisely rape fantasies that often have such irresistible verisimilitude that even the most experienced judges are misled in trials of innocent men accused of rape by hysterical women. My own experience of accounts by white women of rape by Negroes (who are often subjected to terrible penalties as a result of these accusations) has convinced me that many fantastic stories are produced by the masochistic yearnings of these women. Freud calls attention to the fact that hysterical patients often speak of having been seduced by their fathers, and that the same seduction fantasy sometimes involves the mother. He thinks that seduction by the mother—as contrasted with that by the father—"has a real basis, for the mother, who took care of her child's body, must actually have aroused pleasure sensations in the genitals."

NOTE 8

RUSSELL, BERTRAND

Roads to Freedom*

. . . Anarchists maintain that the criminal is manufactured by bad social conditions and would disappear in such a world as they aim at creating. No doubt there is a great measure of truth in this view. There would be little motive to robbery, for example, in an Anarchist world, unless it were organized on a large scale by a body of men bent on upsetting the Anarchist régime. It may also be conceded that impulses toward criminal violence could be very largely eliminated by a better education. But all such contentions, it seems to me, have their limitations. To take an extreme case, we cannot suppose that there would be no lunatics in an Anarchist community, and some of these lunatics would, no doubt, be homicidal.

* London: George Allen & Unwin Ltd., 1918. (pp. 127–36). Reprinted by permission.

Probably no one would argue that they ought to be left at liberty. But there are no sharp lines in nature: From the homicidal lunatic to the sane man of violent passions there is a continuous gradation. Even in the most perfect community there will be men and women, otherwise sane, who will feel an impulse to commit murder from jealousy. These are now usually restrained by the fear of punishment, but if this fear were removed, such murders would probably become much more common, as may be seen from the present behavior of certain soldiers on leave. Moreover, certain kinds of conduct arouse public hostility, and would almost inevitably lead to lynching, if no other recognized method of punishment existed. There is in most men a certain natural vindictiveness, not always directed against the worst members of the community. . . .

The conclusion which appears to be forced upon us is that the Anarchist ideal of a community in which no acts are forbidden by law is not, at any rate for the present, compatible with the stability of such a world as the Anarchists desire. In order to obtain and preserve a world resembling as closely as possible that at which they aim, it will still be necessary that some acts should be forbidden by law. We may put the chief of these under three heads:

*   *   *

1. *Theft.* It is true that in an Anarchist world there will be no destitution, and therefore no thefts motived by starvation. But such thefts are at present by no means the most considerable, or the most harmful. The system of rationing, which is to be applied to luxuries, will leave many men with fewer luxuries than they might desire. It will give opportunities for peculation by those who are in control of the public stores, and it will leave the possibility of appropriating such valuable objects of art as would naturally be preserved in public museums. It may be contended that such forms of theft would be prevented by public opinion. But public opinion is not greatly operative upon an individual unless it is the opinion of his own group. A group of men combined for purposes of theft might readily defy the public opinion of the majority unless that public opinion made itself effective by the use of force against them. . . .

2. *Crimes of violence.* Cruelty to children, crimes of jealousy, rape, and so forth, are almost certain to occur in any society to some extent. The prevention of such acts is essential to the existence of freedom for the weak. If nothing were done to hinder them, it is to be feared that the customs of a society would gradually become rougher, and that acts which are now rare would cease to be so. If Anarchists are right in maintaining that the existence of such an economic system as they desire would prevent the commission of crimes of this kind, the laws forbidding them would

no longer come into operation, and would do no harm to liberty. If, on the other hand, the impulse to such actions persisted, it would be necessary that steps should be taken to restrain men from indulging it.

3. The third class of difficulties is much the most serious, and involves much the most drastic interference with liberty. I do not see how a private army could be tolerated within an Anarchist community, and I do not see how it could be prevented except by a general prohibition of carrying arms. If there were no such prohibition, rival parties would organize rival forces, and civil war would result. Yet, if there is such a prohibition, it cannot well be carried out without a very considerable interference with individual liberty. No doubt, after a time, the idea of using violence to achieve a political object might die down, as the practice of duelling has done. But such changes of habit and outlook are facilitated by legal prohibition, and would hardly come about without it. . . .

C.
Ego

1.

FREUD, SIGMUND

New Introductory Lectures on Psychoanalysis (1933)*

We can best arrive at the characteristics of the actual ego, insofar as it can be distinguished from the id and from the superego, by examining its relations to the outermost superficial portion of the mental apparatus, which we describe as the system *Pcpt.–Cs.* This system is turned toward the external world, it is the medium for the perceptions arising thence, and during its functioning the phenomenon of consciousness arises in it. It is the sense organ of the entire apparatus; moreover it is receptive not only to excitations from outside but also to those arising from the interior of the mind. We need scarcely look for a justification of the view that the ego is that portion of the id which was modified by the proximity and influence of the external world, which is adapted for the reception of stimuli and as a protective shield against stimuli, comparable to the cortical layer by which a small piece of living substance is surrounded. The relation to the external world has become the decisive factor for the ego; it has taken on the task of representing the external world to the id—fortunately for the id, which could not escape destruction if, in its blind efforts for the satisfaction of its instincts, it disregarded that supreme external power. In accomplishing this function, the ego must observe the external world, must lay down an accurate picture of it in the memory traces of its perceptions, and by its exercise of the function of "reality testing" must put aside whatever in this picture of the external world is an addition derived from internal sources of excitation. The ego controls the approaches to motility under the id's orders; but between a need and an action it has interposed a postponement in the form of the activity of thought, during which it makes use of the mnemic residues of experience. In that way it has dethroned the pleasure principle which dominates the course of events in the id without any restriction and has replaced it by the reality principle, which promises more certainty and greater success.

The relation to time, which is so hard to describe, is also introduced into the ego by the perceptual system; it can scarcely be doubted that the mode of operation of that system is what provides the origin of the idea of time. But what distinguishes the ego from the id quite especially is a tendency to synthesis in its contents, to a combination and unification in its mental processes which are totally lacking in the id. . . . It alone produces the high degree of organization which the ego needs for its best achievements. The ego develops from perceiving the instincts to controlling them; but this last is only achieved by the [psychical] representative of the instinct being allotted its proper place in a considerable assemblage, by its being taken up into a coherent context. To adopt a popular mode of speaking, we might say that the ego stands for reason and good sense while the id stands for the untamed passions.

So far we have allowed ourselves to be impressed by the merits and capabilities of the ego; it is now time to consider the other side as well. The ego is after all only a portion of the id, a portion that has been expediently modified by the proximity of the external world with its threat of danger. From a dynamic point of view it is weak, it has borrowed its energies from the id, and we are not entirely without insight into the methods—we might call them dodges—by which it extracts further amounts of energy from the id. One such method, for instance, is by identifying itself with actual or abandoned objects. The object cathexes spring from the instinctual demands of the id. The ego has in the first instance to take note of

* Reprinted from: 22 *The Standard Edition of the Complete Psychological Works of Sigmund Freud*, James Strachey, ed. London: The Hogarth Press and the Institute of Psychoanalysis, 1964. (pp. 75–80). Reprinted by permission of Hogarth and W. W. Norton & Co.

them. But by identifying itself with the object it recommends itself to the id in place of the object and seeks to divert the id's libido on to itself. We have already seen that in the course of its life the ego takes into itself a large number of precipitates like this of former object cathexes. The ego must on the whole carry out the id's intentions, it fulfils its task by finding out the circumstances in which those intentions can best be achieved. The ego's relation to the id might be compared with that of a rider to his horse. The horse supplies the locomotive energy, while the rider has the privilege of deciding on the goal and of guiding the powerful animal's movement. But only too often there arises between the ego and the id the not precisely ideal situation of the rider being obliged to guide the horse along the path by which it itself wants to go.

There is one portion of the id from which the ego has separated itself by resistances due to repression. But the repression is not carried over into the id: The repressed merges into the remainder of the id.

We are warned by a proverb against serving two masters at the same time. The poor ego has things even worse: It serves three severe masters and does what it can to bring their claims and demands into harmony with one another. These claims are always divergent and often seem incompatible. No wonder that the ego so often fails in its task. Its three tyrannical masters are the external world, the superego, and the id. When we follow the ego's efforts to satisfy them simultaneously—or rather, to obey them simultaneously—we cannot feel any regret at having personified this ego and having set it up as a separate organism. It feels hemmed in on three sides, threatened by three kinds of danger, to which, if it is hard pressed, it reacts by generating anxiety. Owing to its origin from the experiences of the perceptual system, it is earmarked for representing the demands of the external world, but it strives, too, to be a loyal servant of the id, to remain on good terms with it, to recommend itself to it as an object and to attract its libido to itself. In its attempts to mediate between the id and reality, it is often obliged to cloak the *Ucs.* commands of the id with its own *Pcs.* rationalizations, to conceal the id's conflicts with reality, to profess, with diplomatic disingenuousness, to be taking notice of reality even when the id has remained rigid and unyielding. On the other hand it is observed at every step it takes by the strict superego, which lays down definite standards for its conduct, without taking any account of its difficulties from the direction of the id and the external world, and which, if those standards are not obeyed, punishes it with tense feelings of inferiority and of guilt. Thus the ego, driven by the id, confined by the superego, repulsed by reality, struggles to master its economic task of bringing about harmony among the forces and influences working in and upon it; and we can understand how it is that so often we cannot suppress a cry: "Life is

not easy!" If the ego is obliged to admit its weakness, it breaks out in anxiety—realistic anxiety regarding the external world, moral anxiety regarding the superego, and neurotic anxiety regarding the strength of the passions in the id.

I should like to portray the structural relations of the mental personality, as I have described them to you, in the unassuming sketch which I now present you with:

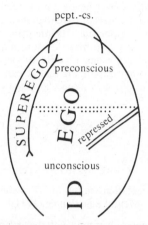

As you see here, the superego merges into the id; indeed, as heir to the Oedipus complex it has intimate relations with the id; it is more remote than the ego from the perceptual system. The id has intercourse with the external world only through the ego—at least, according to this diagram. It is certainly hard to say today how far the drawing is correct. In one respect it is undoubtedly not. The space occupied by the unconscious id ought to have been incomparably greater than that of the ego or the preconscious. I must ask you to correct it in your thoughts.

. . . In thinking of this division of the personality into an ego, a superego, and an id, you will not, of course, have pictured sharp frontiers like the artificial ones drawn in political geography. We cannot do justice to the characteristics of the mind by linear outlines like those in a drawing or in primitive painting, but rather by areas of color melting into one another as they are presented by modern artists. After making the separation we must allow what we have separated to merge together once more. You must not judge too harshly a first attempt at giving a pictorial representation of something so intangible as psychical processes. It is highly probable that the development of these divisions is subject to great variations in different individuals; it is possible that in the course of actual functioning they may change and go through a temporary phase of involution. Particularly in the case of what is phylogenetically the last and most delicate of these divisions—the differentiation between the ego and the superego—something of the sort seems to be true. There is no question but that the same thing results from psychical illness. It is easy to imagine, too, that certain mystical practices may succeed in upsetting the normal relations between the different regions of the mind, so that, for instance, perception may be able to grasp happenings in the depths of the ego and in the id which were otherwise inaccessible to it. It may safely be doubted, however, whether this road will lead us to the ultimate truths from which salvation is to be expected. Nevertheless it may be admitted that the therapeutic efforts of psychoanalysis have chosen a similar line of approach. Its intention is, indeed, to strengthen the ego, to make it more independent of the superego, to widen its field of perception and enlarge its organization, so that it can appropriate fresh portions of the id. Where id was, there ego shall be. . . .

NOTES

NOTE 1

FREUD, SIGMUND

Formulations on the Two Principles of Mental Functioning (1911)*

[W]e are now confronted with the task of investigating the development of the relation of neurotics and of mankind in general to reality, and in this way of bringing the psychological significance of the real external world into the structure of our theories.

In the psychology which is founded on psychoanalysis we have become accustomed to taking as our starting point the unconscious mental processes, with the peculiarities of which we have become acquainted through analysis. We consider these to be the older, primary processes, the residues of a phase of development in which they were the only kind of mental process. The governing purpose obeyed by these primary processes is easy to recognize; it is described as the pleasure-unpleasure [Lust-Unlust] principle, or more shortly the pleasure principle. These processes strive toward gaining pleasure; psychical activity draws back from any event which might arouse unpleasure. (Here we have repression.) Our dreams at night and our waking tendency to tear ourselves away from distressing impressions are remnants of the dominance of this principle and proofs of its power.

[T]he state of psychical rest was originally disturbed by the peremptory demands of internal needs. When this happened, whatever was thought of (wished for) was simply presented in a hallucinatory manner, just as still happens today with our dream thoughts every

night.[1] It was only the nonoccurrence of the expected satisfaction, the disappointment experienced, that led to the abandonment of this attempt at satisfaction by means of hallucination. Instead of it, the psychical apparatus had to decide to form a conception of the real circumstances in the external world and to endeavor to make a real alteration in them. A new principle of mental functioning was thus introduced; what was presented in the mind was no longer what was agreeable but what was real, even if it happened to be disagreeable. This setting up of the *reality principle* proved to be a momentous step.

1. In the first place, the new demands made a succession of adaptations necessary in the psychical apparatus, which, owing to our insufficient or uncertain knowledge, we can only retail very cursorily.

The increased significance of external reality heightened the importance, too, of the sense organs that are directed toward that external world, and of the *consciousness* attached to them. Consciousness now learned to comprehend sensory qualities in addition to the qualities of pleasure and unpleasure which hitherto had alone been of interest to it. A special function was instituted which had periodically to search the external world, in order that its data might be familiar already if an urgent internal need should arise—the function of *attention*. Its activity meets the sense impressions halfway, instead of awaiting their appearance. At the same time, probably, a system of *notation* was introduced, whose task it was to lay down the results of this periodical activity of consciousness—a part of what we call *memory*.

The place of repression, which excluded from cathexis as productive of unpleasure some of the emerging ideas, was taken by an *impartial passing of judgment*, which had to decide whether a given idea was true or false—that is, whether it was in agreement with reality or not—the decision being determined by making a comparison with the memory traces of reality.

A new function was now allotted to motor discharge, which, under the dominance of the pleasure principle, had served as a means of unburdening the mental apparatus of accretions of stimuli, and which had carried out this task by sending innervations into the interior of the body (leading to expressive movements and the play of features and to manifestations of affect). Motor discharge was now employed in the appropriate alteration of reality; it was converted into *action*.

Restraint upon motor discharge (upon action), which then became necessary, was provided by means of the process of *thinking*, which was developed

* Reprinted from: 12 *The Standard Edition of the Complete Psychological Works of Sigmund Freud*, James Strachey, ed. London: The Hogarth Press and the Institute of Psychoanalysis, 1958. (pp. 218-23). Reprinted by permission of Hogarth and Basic Books, Inc.

1. The state of sleep is able to re-establish the likeness of mental life as it was before the recognition of reality, because a prerequisite of sleep is a deliberate rejection of reality (the wish to sleep).

from the presentation of ideas. Thinking was endowed with characteristics which made it possible for the mental apparatus to tolerate an increased tension of stimulus while the process of discharge was postponed. It is essentially an experimental kind of acting, accompanied by displacement of relatively small quantities of cathexis together with less expenditure (discharge) of them. For this purpose the conversion of freely displaceable cathexes into "bound" cathexes was necessary, and this was brought about by means of raising the level of the whole cathectic process. It is probable that thinking was originally unconscious, insofar as it went beyond mere ideational presentations and was directed to the relations between impressions of objects, and that it did not acquire further qualities, perceptible to consciousness, until it became connected with verbal residues.

2. A general tendency of our mental apparatus, which can be traced back to the economic principle of saving expenditure [of energy], seems to find expression in the tenacity with which we hold on to the sources of pleasure at our disposal, and in the difficulty with which we renounce them. With the introduction of the reality principle one species of thought activity was split off; it was kept free from reality testing and remained subordinated to the pleasure principle alone. This activity is *fantasying*, which begins already in children's play, and later, continued as *daydreaming*, abandons dependence on real objects.

3. The supersession of the pleasure principle by the reality principle, with all the psychical consequences involved, which is here schematically condensed into a single sentence, is not in fact accomplished all at once; nor does it take place simultaneously all along the line. For while this development is going on in the ego instincts, the sexual instincts become detached from them in a very significant way. The sexual instincts behave autoerotically at first; they obtain their satisfaction in the subject's own body and therefore do not find themselves in the situation of frustration which was what necessitated the institution of the reality principle; and when, later on, the process of finding an object begins, it is soon interrupted by the long period of latency, which delays sexual development until puberty. These two factors—autoerotism and the latency period—have as their result that the sexual instinct is held up in its psychical development and remains far longer under the dominance of the pleasure principle, from which in many people it is never able to withdraw.

In consequence of these conditions, a closer connection arises, on the one hand, between the sexual instinct and fantasy and, on the other hand, between the ego instincts and the activities of consciousness. Both in healthy and in neurotic people this connection strikes us as very intimate, although the considerations of genetic psychology which have just been put forward lead us to recognize it as a *secondary* one. The continuance of autoerotism is what makes it possible to retain for so long the easier momentary and imaginary satisfaction in relation to the sexual object in place of real satisfaction, which calls for effort and postponement. In the realm of fantasy, repression remains all powerful; it brings about the inhibition of ideas *in statu nascendi* before they can be noticed by consciousness, if their cathexis is likely to occasion a release of unpleasure. This is the weak spot in our psychical organization; and it can be employed to bring back under the dominance of the pleasure principle thought processes which had already become rational. An essential part of the psychical disposition to neurosis thus lies in the delay in educating the sexual instincts to pay regard to reality and, as a corollary, in the conditions which make this delay possible.

4. Just as the pleasure ego can do nothing but *wish*, work for a yield of pleasure, and avoid unpleasure, so the reality ego need do nothing but strive for what is *useful* and guard itself against damage. Actually the substitution of the reality principle for the pleasure principle implies no deposing of the pleasure principle, but only a safeguarding of it. A momentary pleasure, uncertain in its results, is given up, but only in order to gain along the new path an assured pleasure at a later time. . . .

NOTE 2

HARTMANN, HEINZ

Notes on the Reality Principle*

In our literature, two meanings are currently attached to the term reality principle. Used in one sense, it indicates a tendency to take into account in an adaptive way, in perception, thinking, and action, whatever we consider the "real" features of an object or a situation. But in another, maybe we could say, narrower sense, we refer primarily to the case in which it represents a tendency to wrest our activities from the immediate need for discharge inherent in the pleasure principle. It is in this sense that we speak of the reality principle as the natural opponent, or at least modifier, of the pleasure principle. This poses a problem. One cannot state in a general way that reality-syntonic behavior curtails pleasure. This would be a quite illegitimate generalization, and not only because—as Freud repeatedly emphasized . . . —behavior under the guidance of the reality principle is aimed at gaining, in a new way, assured pleasure at a later stage, while giving up momentary pleasure. In this case, its timing determines whether or not discharge is reality syntonic. But beyond this con-

* 11 *The Psychoanalytic Study of the Child*, 1956. (pp. 33–35). Reprinted by permission of International Universities Press, New York.

sideration of expected or assured gains, there is also the fact that the activities of the functions that constitute the reality principle can be pleasurable in themselves. I remind you at this point of the pleasurable potentialities of sublimated activities. Organized thought or action, in which postponement is of the essence, can become a source of pleasure. While this, at first sight, seems to complicate things, there is no way of denying it; indeed, it becomes perfectly clear if we think of the reality principle in terms of ego functions. If I have emphasized here the double meaning of the term reality principle, it was in order to forestall possible misunderstandings; failure to note the double meaning has occasionally led to a misrepresentation of Freud's thinking on the subject. In opposing reality principle and pleasure principle, he certainly did not mean to negate the pleasures we derive from the world outside; and he repeatedly commented on the advantages the ego provides for instinctual gratifications, aside from its different role as an opponent of the drives.

Freud emphasized, as I reminded you before, the importance of situations of frustration in the development of the reality principle. The assumption that in the hypothetical case of continuous and full gratification the objectivating and anticipating functions would be badly impaired is, indeed, quite convincing. But we should also consider here the thought first expressed, I think, by Anna Freud, that the postponement or control of discharge is one of the essential features of the human ego from its beginnings; it is probably an essential feature already of its forerunners, before the ego as a system of personality has been fully established. We should also consider what is, I think, a necessary assumption, that the child is born with a certain degree of preadaptiveness; that is to say, the apparatus of perception, memory, mobility, etc., which help us to deal with reality are, in a primitive form, already present at birth; later they will mature and develop in constant interaction, of course, with experience; you know that the very system to which we attribute these functions, the ego, is also our organ of learning. What I have said is to the point here, because it means that some preparedness for dealing with reality precedes those experiences Freud referred to in the passage quoted.

NOTE 3

JACOBSON, EDITH

The Self and the Object World*

The earliest infantile stage is represented by the mother-child unit. Of course, this situation cannot yet be described in terms of identification, which is a process or the result of a process.

*New York: International Universities Press, Inc., 1964. (pp. 38–69). Reprinted by permission.

I have repeatedly stated that at first the infant can probably hardly discriminate between his own pleasurable sensations and the objects from which they are derived. Only when the perceptive functions have sufficiently matured can gratifications or frustrations become associated with the object. . . . Induced by . . . repeated unpleasurable experiences of frustration and separation from the love object, fantasies of (total) incorporation of the gratifying object begin to arise, expressive of wishes to re-establish the lost unit. This desire probably never ceases to play a part in our emotional life. Even normally, the experience of physical merging and of an "identity" of pleasure in the sexual act may harbor elements of happiness derived from the feeling of return to the lost, original union with the mother. The original intensity and survival of such wishes justifies Bowlby's stress on the significant role of separation anxiety, which appears about the sixth or seventh month.

These earliest wishful fantasies of merging and being one with the mother (breast) are certainly the foundation on which all object relations as well as all future types of identification are built.

Let us view these fantasies more closely in connection with the child's instinctual activities at the age of about three months, when he is already able to perceive the love object, or at least part objects, as different from himself. Whenever he is fed by his mother or is physically close to her body, his wishful fantasies of complete reunion with the mother by means of (oral and visual, respiratory, skin) incorporation will be gratified. Hence, with the achievement of gratification, his images of the self and of the love object will temporarily merge, only to be severed again with the increase of instinctual needs and experiences of hunger, frustration, and real separation, which are apt to arouse aggressive and libidinal desires.

Thus the hungry infant's longing for food, libidinal gratifications, and physical merging with the mother, which is the precursor of future object relations, is also the origin of the first, primitive type of identification, an identification achieved by refusion of self and object images. This refusion of self and object images will be accompanied by a temporary weakening of the perceptive functions and hence by a return from the level of beginning ego formation to an earlier, less differentiated state.

This type of identification plays a predominant role in the mental life of the baby throughout the preoedipal and early oedipal phase, and to some extent even later. . . . induced in the service of the ego do not normally weaken the boundaries between the images of self and objects, whereas in the early infantile stage such firm boundaries have not yet been established. And as long as those fantasy and feeling identifications coexist and collaborate with mature personal relations and firmly established ego and superego identifications, they will not in any way affect a person's feelings of identity.

Child analysts seem to agree that up to the age of three, conscious fantasies of merging with love objects are within the margin of normal development. . . . [E]ven far beyond the preoedipal period the unconscious self and object images tend rapidly to vary, separate, and merge again. Even when the child has progressed to a full awareness of himself and of his love objects as individual entities, his dependency on the mother for the satisfaction of most of his instinctual needs and the execution of his ego functions is still bound to prevent the complete separation of maternal and self images. Instinctual gratifications, physical and emotional closeness, the support, protection, and guidance offered by the mother, all tend to join them again and again; so that in general the maternal (and paternal) image will continue for some years to be only an extension of the child's image of his self, or vice versa. This is what lends the child's relationship to his mother such "narcissistic" qualities. His involvement in the mother is of dramatic intensity. But even when she is no longer exclusively a need-gratifying object but has become the object of touching affection, the baby, as yet unable to love in the sense of caring for others, is still mainly concerned with his own precious self. Even though he must and does adjust to the parental attitudes, he cannot understand and respect the parental needs, unless they serve his own or are in accordance with them.

Whereas the above-described fantasies of fusion with the love object are rooted in the child's symbiotic interrelationship with the mother, a more active type of primitive identification develops from his increasing efforts to imitate the love objects. Fenichel described the close connections and interrelations between the still predominantly receptive infantile fantasies of this period and the imitations of the love objects which begin in the first year of life but already require the participation of the motor apparatus. Since these imitations originate in the close, empathic ties between mother and child, they probably emerge from what we may call primitive affective identifications. The fact that the mother is able directly to induce affects in the baby by way of her own affective expression . . . is well known, but difficult to explain. Observations on infants leave little doubt that the child very early begins to perceive, to respond to, and to imitate the gestures, the inflections of voice, and other visible and audible affective manifestations of the mother. I have already spoken of the mutual "tuning in" of the mother's and child's discharge patterns, and discussed how the mother's interplay with the infant stimulates and prepares his awakening emotional life and his ego functions. We may surmise that the child's imitation of parental emotional expression arises on this basis and that early reciprocal affecto-motor identifications between mother and child precede and usher in the child's imitations of the parents' functional activities.

The child's expanding motor activities, his learning to walk and to talk and to behave like the parents, his cleanliness training, which is expressive of a beginning instinctual control—all these accomplishments certainly mark the progress of ego formation. But his playful imitations of what the parents do are at first only forerunners of true ego identifications, just as his beginning reaction formations are but the precursors of superego formation. In fact, we must not speak of ego identifications before the child begins to develop ego attitudes and character traits taken over from the parents, and before he manifests true ego interests and practices meaningful ego functions guided by their example and their demands.

In the beginning the baby's imitations of the mother, of her gestures, her behavior, her actions, are indeed only formal "as if" activities without awareness of their meaning, founded merely on the close links of empathy with the mother. It is not yet their essential goal to achieve a real likeness to the love objects. At this stage the child is still apt to believe that imitating the mother, "playing mother," means being or becoming the mother. Such magic, illusory fantasies indicate how much the child wants to maintain the mother as a part of himself and to adhere to the primitive aim of merging with her without distinction and consideration of the external and his own, inner reality.

The main progress manifests itself in the child's growing desire to achieve this goal no longer only through sensual gratifications and physical closeness with the love object but also by activity of his own. However, his insufficient capacity for perception of reality still permits him to join and to expand his images of objects and self in accordance with his wishful, magic fantasies, regardless of the love objects' and his own limitations.

This is the period of constant cathectic shifts and changes, to which I have already referred above. Libido and aggression are continuously turned from the love object to the self and vice versa, or also from one object to the other, while self and object images as well as images of different objects undergo temporary fusions and separate and join again. Simultaneously, there is a tendency to cathect one such composite image unit with libido only, while all the aggression is directed to another one, until ambivalence can be tolerated. These cathectic processes are reflected in introjective and projective mechanisms based on the child's unconscious fantasies of incorporation and ejection of the love object. At this stage the child displays submissive, clinging, following attitudes or behavior alternating with temporary grandiose ideas showing his "magic participation" in the parents' omnipotence. There are erratic vacillations between attitudes of passive, helpless dependency on the omnipotent mother and active, aggressive strivings for self expansion and a powerful control over the love objects.

* * *

The increasingly contradictory, either passive-submissive or active-aggressive behavior of the child during the preoedipal and early oedipal period goes hand in hand, of course, with his ambivalent emotional fluctuations between loving and trusting admiration of his omnipotent parents and disappointed, distrustful depreciation of his love objects. The magic fantasy world of the preoedipal child is only gradually relinquished; its remnants certainly survive the oedipal period. . . .

* * *

As the child enters his second year of life, changes in the nature of his relations to the object world set in, which are indicative of his gradual transition from the early infantile symbiotic phase to the stage of individuation and of beginning secondary ego autonomy. They mark the introduction into the psychic organization of a new time category, the concept of the future. Moreover, they presuppose the ability to distinguish single physical and mental features of the love objects, to compare and to perceive differences between objects—animate and inanimate—as well as between the objects and the self. When the child has advanced to this point, his narcissistic strivings begin to take a new turn: their aims change. Expressive of the child's rapid body growth and the growth of his ego, ambitious strivings develop which no longer revolve exclusively about wishes to control magically the love objects on which he depends. In their stead, ambitious efforts for realistic achievements can be observed, which seem in part to be independent of the child's instinctual needs. But under the influence of his instinctual conflicts these strivings soon become highly charged with aggressive energy and find increasing expression in competitive struggles with admired, powerful love objects, in particular with his rivals. As these trends develop, the child's desires to remain part of his love objects, or to make them part of his own self, will slowly recede and give way to wishes for realistic likeness with them. This goal can be achieved by virtue of selective identifications, based on mechanisms of "partial introjection."

Evidently, this new and advanced type of identifications represents a compromise between the child's need to retain the symbiotic situation, to depend and lean on the need-gratifying, protective, and supportive love objects, and opposing tendencies to loosen the symbiotic ties by way of aggressive, narcissistic expansion and independent ego functioning. Under the influence of oedipal rivalry, this conflict will reach its first climax toward the end of

the oedipal period and will then be resolved by superego formation. But it will be intensely revived during adolescence, and come to its final peak and find its definite solution in the adolescent's rupture of his oedipal ties and the establishment of ego and superego autonomy.

To return to the preoedipal child, it seems that his identifications with the mother, both as the aggressor and as the person who imposes instinctual restrictions, pave the way to these new processes of identification. In contrast to his magic fantasies of fusion and his primitive affective identifications and merely formal imitations, they have a meaningful content and a realistic aim. Such an aim can be reached by way of deep-seated modifications of the ego, which now really assumes certain characteristics of the admired object.

This presupposes a new stage in the development of the self images: the distinction between realistic and wishful self images. In fact, the ego cannot acquire a realistic likeness to the love object unless admired traits of this object become enduringly introjected into the child's wishful self images. These wishful self images thus become expressive of both: of the child's own ambitions, of his own strivings for narcissistic expansion and ego growth, and of admired characteristics of his love objects. In so far as the realistic self representations become a mirror of the ego, they now begin to reflect the traits actually taken over from the object of identification, so that a likeness between object and self images can now be experienced on a realistic basis. This new step in the development of the self images and the growing distinction between wishful and realistic images of the self are so meaningful because they are a prerequisite for the establishment of ego ideal and ego goals, i.e., of realistic goals regarding the future. . . .

* * *

Whereas the child's wishful self images increasingly give him direction by pointing to potential changes in the future, his representations of the actual self point to his present state and to the past stages in his development. Thus their differentiation must strengthen the feeling of selfsameness in spite of continuous changes.

Of course, the child will be protected from relapses into the world of magic fantasies of fusions and early infantile types of identifications to the extent to which he succeeds in building up true object relations which no longer display the narcissistic qualities described above. This again presupposes the constitution of well-defined self representations separated by distinct, firm boundaries from the likewise realistic representations of his love objects.

However, I cannot follow up the fascinating interplay between these developmental processes without first trying to derive some orientation from a preliminary schematic survey. Its sole purpose is to correlate the various stages of energic and structural differentiation to the constitution and cathexis of object and self representations, and to the corresponding ideational, affective, and functional development.

We may visualize the process of structural and energic differentiation as passing through the following infantile stages:

1. The primal (embryonal) condition of diffuse dispersion of undifferentiated drive energy in the unstructured "primal" psychophysiological self; discharge occurs predominantly by silent physiological processes.

2. With birth, growing cathexis of the perception and memory systems, of the motor apparatus and of the pregenital erogenous zones sets in; pleasurable and unpleasurable sensations begin to be perceived and become attached to, though still confused with, beginning outside perceptions. Energic differentiation occurs; libidinal and aggressive cathectic gathering poles are formed around nuclei of as yet unorganized and disconnected memory traces. Discharge to the outside begins by way of primitive, biologically prepatterned (instinctive) reactions to internal and external stimuli. Affective organ language develops.

3a. The stage of beginning structural differentiation and ego formation. Pleasure principle and "primary process" prevail. Unconscious (early preoedipal) fantasy life, pregenital sexual and affectomotor activity begin to develop, although affective organ language is still predominant. Multiple, rapidly changing and not yet clearly distinguished part images of love objects and body part images are formed and linked up with the memory traces of past pleasure-unpleasure experiences and become vested with libidinal and aggressive forces. Corresponding affect components arise; impulsive affectomotor reactions to external and internal stimuli change in quick sequence, reflecting the variability of unconscious imagery, the cathectic fluidity, and the tendency to immediate drive discharge; signal affects begin to become effective.

3b. When the child learns to walk and talk and acquires urinary and bowel control, a more organized stage sets in. Object and self awareness grows, perception and organization of memory traces expand. The object imagery gradually extends to the surrounding animate and inanimate world. Language symbols, functional motor activity, and reality testing develop. But magic animistic fantasy life, preverbal at first, predominates and remains concentrated on the mother until preoedipal and later oedipal triangle configurations shape up. Object constancy develops. Specific affect qualities and more sustained emotional states come into being, influenced by increasing formation of countercathexes.

4. Infantile sexuality reaches its climax; fusion and neutralization of sexual and aggressive drives has set in. Thought processes are organized, functional motor activity and object relations develop rapidly. Accordingly, single affects begin to merge into compound fusions. Emotional and instinctual control is being established; tension tolerance increases. Preponderance of libido and enduring libidinal object investments develop. As tender attachements grow and affects become attached to ego functions, awareness of self begins to extend to awareness of emotional and thought processes, of ego attitudes and ego functions. A concept of the self as an entity that has continuity and direction is formed. Reality principle and "secondary" process become more dominant. Signal anxiety (castration fear) exerts a drastic influence on repression and countercathectic formations.

5. Drive neutralization is greatly enhanced by superego formation; the latency period begins. Physical and mental activities make rapid progress; conceptual thinking develops and expands; maturation and structural organization of ideational and emotional processes advance with the growing ability of the ego to bind down psychic energy in enduring cathexes; increasingly realistic preconscious representations of the animate and inanimate, concrete and abstract object world are formed, and can be stabilized by their firm and lasting cathexis with libidinal, aggressive, and neutralized forces. The superego establishes a lasting and dominant control over the cathexis of the self representations. Superego fear becomes the leading affect signal. In the process of final taming, repatterning, modification, and organization of the affects under the influence of the superego, enduring feelings and feeling states develop on a large scale as an expression of the ego's state and reactivity. The subtle differentiation of the emotional qualities proceeds hand in hand with an increasing awareness of the qualities of emotional experiences. These changes and the establishment of physical, intellectual, and moral achievement standards enhance the experience of a consistent self that maintains its continuity despite changes.

We know, of course, that the most influential factor in the child's development is the child-parent relationship, whose part in the building up of the ego we may summarize briefly as follows. Parental influences stimulate the growth of the ego and support the control, partial inhibition, partial fusion, neutralization and utilization of sexual and aggressive drives in the service of the ego and of "secondary"-process functioning. Thus they contribute greatly to the psychosexual development and the maturation of feelings, thinking, acting, and the sense of reality, and promote the establishment of aim-inhibited personal and social relations and of solid identifications with the love objects in the ego and superego. In general, they promote the child's gradual individuation and his advance from the psychobiologically determined dependency situation to independent ego activity spreading out to social, cultural, and eventually ego-syntonic sexual pursuits.

Even though we are sufficiently familiar with the parental influence on infantile development, we must at least focus on certain aspects of it which are significant in the present context. To be sure, the goal of education as I outlined it above can be reached only in an atmosphere of parental love and care, with sufficient libidinal stimulation and gratification. Since it promotes the establishment of stable, enduring libidinal cathexes both of the objects and of the self, parental love is the best guarantee for the development of object and self constancy, of healthy social and love relations, and of lasting identifications, and hence for a normal ego and superego formation. However, the instinctual and emotional frustrations and prohibitions, combined with parental demands and stimulation of social and cultural pursuits, also make significant contributions to the development of an effective, independently functioning, and self-reliant ego.

They teach the child to relinquish not only his preoedipal and oedipal sexual drives but also his early infantile magic expectance of support, protection, and wish fulfillment from without. On his way to this goal, the child passes through experiences of continual deprivations, hurt, frustration, and disappointments in his parents, which arouse intense feelings of ambivalence. Although dangerous, the child's ambivalence conflicts can be utilized by the ego for very constructive purposes. We remember that at first the child wants to take in what he likes and to spit out what he dislikes; to ascribe to his self what is pleasant and to the "strange" outside object what is unpleasant. In other words, he tends to turn aggression toward the frustrating objects and libido toward the self. Hence frustrations, demands, and restrictions, within normal bounds, reinforce in principle the process of discovery and distinction of objects and self; they throw the child back upon his resources and stimulate progressive forms of identification with the parents, which open the road to realistic independent achievements. Enhancing the narcissistic endowment of his ego, they promote the eventual establishment of secondary ego and superego autonomy.

Yet overgratifications, no less than severe frustrations, tend to induce regressive fantasies of reunion between self and love object. Constant overgratification or excessive frustration may therefore delay the child in establishing firm boundaries between the objects and the self, and hence may interfere with ego and superego formation and with the normal process of individuation. . . .

*   *   *

[T]he small child's fantasies of fusion with his love objects are expressive of the early infantile situation, in which he must actually borrow the mother's ego for his own need fulfillments. If this situation is maintained for an unduly long period, the child's object relations may remain fixated forever at this primitive narcissistic level. This may be caused by unfavorable parental attitudes of a narcissistic, masochistic, or hostile, neglectful, overdepriving, or overgratifying and overprotective nature. But it may also be the result of a constitutional weakness, deficiency, or retarded maturation of the infantile ego, which may compel the child to lean heavily on the mother's ego for need gratification, support or control. The normal child seems to show the first signs of awareness of a "non-I" (Spitz) around the age of three months. Precisely how the development of self imagery and of self awareness proceeds from then on is a question which is difficult to answer, at least with regard to the first year of life. At any rate, to the extent to which the child begins to cathect and employ the executive organs of his own body and to acquire the physical and mental functions that will turn him into an autonomous, independent human being in his own right, he will be ready to develop the outlines of his future identity and, concomitantly, to build up advanced forms of personal interrelations and identifications.

In general, about the age of two or two and a half years the child's ego maturation, his ability to walk and to talk, the ever-widening scope of his perceptive and locomotor functions, his increasing manual accomplishments, his weaning and cleanliness training, etc., have advanced enough to bring about the startling discovery of his own identity, the experience of "I am I." It must be understood that this discovery does not imply that the child has already built up an enduring, consistent concept of his self as an entity. This concept undergoes many changes, and induces an increasing feeling of direction and continuity as the psychic organization grows, becomes differentiated, structured, organized and reorganized, until maturity is reached.

The child's discovery of his identity occurs in the wake of important changes in his relations to his first love objects—changes which contribute a great deal to his individuation and his awakening sense of identity. From the observation of early infantile and psychotic imagery we may infer that in the child's first object images—apart from their projective features—perceptions of different objects probably become merged into varying image composites. But, significantly, the child, already at the age of about eight months, sometimes even earlier, begins to distinguish different objects: his mother from his father, from the nurse, from strangers, etc. The distinction between objects can probably proceed more rapidly and consistently than the distinction between self and objects, because perception of the external world is easier than self perception and, besides, because the child normally has less instinctual motivation for a fusion between different objects than for a re-merging with his mother. In fact, the child's insatiable instinctual appetites stimulate his ability to discriminate between persons who may offer him supplementary gratifications and those who bar his way to need fulfillment. In any case, the beginning constitution of boundaries between images of different objects ushers in the development of specific and different relations to his various love objects. Concomitantly the child's first envy and rivalry conflicts take shape, conflicts which have a decisive influence on the processes under discussion.

At this point Greenacre's statement on identity, referring to likenesses with others and to differences from them, begins to become pertinent. Of course, experiences of likeness are bound to arise from the child's close intimacy with his mother and, as Greenacre stresses, will be favored by the mutual affective identifications between mother and child, to which I referred above. But what about the experiences of differences, which are a prerequisite for the development of identity feelings?

We know that by the end of the first year, the little boy or girl begins to show definite aquisitiveness, possessiveness, and manifestations of envy. To be sure, these ambivalent acquisitive wishes and the child's oral envy, which soon induce intense feelings of rivalry toward the father, siblings, and other objects, are the strongest incentive for his first comparisons. They teach him to distinguish, first, between his needs, his gratifications, and his frustrations; then between his and others' gratifications, and between his belongings and those of others. Passing through many frustrations, disappointments, failures, and corresponding hostile experiences of envy, rivalry and competition, the child eventually learns the difference between wishful and more or less realistic self and object images. Thus, not only the loving but also the hostile components of the infantile self- and object-directed strivings furnish the fuel that enables the child to develop his feeling of identity and the testing of external and inner reality, and on this basis to build up his identifications and object relations. This again calls attention to the significant role of aggression in these developmental processes. . . .

At first the child's acquisitive strivings are of course concentrated on his mother. But as soon as he discovers that he has rivals, he begins to displace the envious hostile impulses provoked by his frustrations from the mother onto these rivals. Projecting his own instinctual desires onto them, the child now wants to acquire what they possess and apparently received from the mother. From wanting the same gratifications and possessions as the rival, there is only a short but decisive step to looking for likeness and wanting likeness with him. Increasing love and admiration for the superior and also gratifying rival will reinforce this quest. However, frustration, hostility, and envy will compel the child also to take cognizance of such differences as may be responsible for his frustrations and shortcomings.

We noted above that the child's need to keep the "good," gratifying love object as part of himself, and to spit out and rid himself of the "bad," frustrating objects, tends to throw him on his own resources, to increase the narcissistic endowment of his ego, and to stimulate ambitious strivings for narcissistic expansion and independent accomplishments. Now we may add that his feelings of envy and rivalry, while arousing desires for likeness, will propel him more forcefully toward delineations from his rivals than toward distinction from his main love object, the mother. Moreover, these feelings will promote his discrimination between such rival objects.

The mother-infant relationship must certainly be regarded as the matrix of identity formation, but the child's individuation which depends so greatly on separation from the object and on the discovery of differences soon gains momentum from his more ambivalent relations to his rivals than from his close intimacy with his mother. Of course this simplifies matters considerably, since the child displays envy and rivalry feelings toward the mother as well, to the extent to which he develops closeness with his father and other rivals.

So far I have described how the child's finding of his identity, although dependent on the maturational growth of his ego, gains tremendous support from his beginning emotional relations to his first love objects and especially from his preoedipal envy and rivalry conflicts. I shall now focus on the influence which the child's identity feelings exercise upon his object relations and identifications. We realize that the discovery of his identity, which is so greatly promoted by aggressive forces, is a prerequisite for his gradual transition from the stage of primitive fusions and identifications with his love objects to the level of true object relations and of only partial and selective identifications with them. In fact, the child cannot establish emotional investments in other persons as objects which are different from his own self until he is able to experience his own identity; and since active strivings to acquire likenesses to others are also motivated by the discovery of differences from them, these strivings cannot develop either until the child has become aware of such differences.

Considering the infantile cathectic conditions, we realize, moreover, that enduring selective identification processes, which follow a steady course and direction and alter the structure of the ego consistently, cannot set in before the child's object-libidinal and narcissistic strivings have advanced to a certain level. The initially continuous vacillations between self- and object-directed cathexes and between the different object cathexes must have sufficiently subsided to permit comparatively lasting emotional investments in both: in objects and in the self. Such stable investments can only develop in the wake of processes of unification and consolidation of the object and self images. These processes call on the libidinal resources of the child, which are the indispensable ferment needed to forge "total" concepts from the opposing images of good and bad love objects and of a good and bad self.

I mentioned above the child's inclination to displace hostility from the mother to his rivals. Facilitating the gradual fusion of good and bad maternal images into a unified "good" but also sometimes "bad" mother, these shifts certainly assist the development of tension tolerance and of those feelings of pleasurable anticipation which introduce the category of time and secure the establishment of lasting emotional relations with the mother, i.e., of object constancy. This implies that the development of personal relations with the mother precedes the acceptance of rival figures as total ("good" and also "bad") persons. This second step is not an easy achievement for the child. It must wait until his intense ambivalence toward the rival gradually subsides under the influence of reactive libidinal strivings, and his love wins out over the hostile, envious, jealous, derogatory feelings. The increasing prevalence of libidinal over aggressive investments concomitantly builds up the libidinal endowment of the self images, which is a precondition for the achievement of normal self esteem and for the formation of a unified concept of the self. Since the latter represents a decisive step in the development of identity feelings, this again underscores the all-important role of the libidinal forces in this process, and hence of the mother's love which helps to generate them.

I have emphasized the child's earlier delineation from the hated rivals, which soon promotes the development of his sense of identity more than does his closeness to the mother. Considering the identifications, in contrast to the object relations, it appears that this factor also tends more easily to induce partial identifications with rivals than with the main love object. To be sure, from an early age on, one can also observe identifications which appear to be induced primarily and predominantly by libidinal wishes to maintain, if not union, at least the utmost closeness with the love object, by virtue of actually becoming like it. Such identifications seem to arise directly from the child's earliest fantasy and feeling identifications with the mother rather than from instinctual conflicts. For this reason they hardly bear the imprint of the child's sexual and ambivalence struggles and do not

become an important tool for his defenses. Predominantly centered about the main love object, such identifications can still be observed in adults, in situations of close intimacy, such as, e.g., between marital partners who may ultimately resemble each other physically, emotionally, ideationally, and in their behavior.

In general, though, the infantile identification processes become increasingly centered about rival figures. [E]nduring selective identifications with the predominant rival, the father, cannot be established before the child's loving feelings toward him are sufficiently strengthened to permit relations with him, too, as with a total "good and bad" person. In fact, the better the totality of other persons and of the self can be experienced, the more easily can the distinction, the perception of the differences between one's own self and others be tolerated, and likeness not only discovered but accepted, desired, and acquired.

This implies that the establishment of object and self constancy must be regarded as a very important prerequisite for both a healthy process of identification and normal superego formation. Conversely, the development of moral standards supports this merging of "good" and "bad" object and self images into concepts of total "good and also bad" persons and a total "good and also bad" self.

While this re-emphasizes the role of love in the establishment of sound identifications, they will forever reflect the inherent ambivalence to which they owe their existence. Indeed, any kind of identification implies: "I don't need you; if you don't want to do it for me, I can do it myself; and if you don't want to give it to me, I can give it to myself." While identifications thus display the child's touching dependency on his parents, they bring him closer step by step to the state of independence and to the time when the parents will become dispensable. Moreover, the selectivity of identifications increasingly express the child's rebellious struggle for the development and maintenance of his own independent identity, since it means: "In this respect I like you and want to be like you, but in other respects I don't like you and don't want to be like you; I want to be different, in fact myself."

The process of consolidation of self and object representations advances hand in hand with processes of increasing drive fusion and drive neutralization under the influence of ego formation. Just as discrimination between external objects precedes the distinction between them and one's own self, the experience of other persons' totality develops earlier than the concept of a unified self. In fact, the formation of such a concept depends not only on the child's libidinal investment in himself but on the general growth of the ego that leads to organization and coordination, correlation and interaction of sensory, instinctual, emotional experiences with ideational processes and with the perceptive and executive functions.

*   *   *

[T]he processes of identification . . . begin to show direction and to become more enduring, more consistent and more selective, to the extent to which libidinal development makes progress and personal relations become stable and specified. [O]nly by becoming enduring, selective, and consistent, can identifications gradually be integrated, become part of the ego, permanently modify its structure, and support the organization and stabilization of the ego's defense system. This advances ego formation and the establishment of secondary ego autonomy and concomitantly the process of identity formation to the point where the child becomes aware of having a coherent self that has continuity and remains the same despite and in the midst of changes. Here the different influence on the feeling of identity of such enduring identifications with objects, as compared to primitive fantasy and feeling identifications, becomes apparent. Only the identifications which originate in enduring emotional object investments, and which result in gradual, consistent structural changes showing a definite direction, can fortify the inner feeling of continuity of the self. It is the proper balance between libido and aggression on which the success or failure of these processes depends. . . . identifications break down simultaneously. Both may eventually be replaced by fusions with objects, which, involving fantasies of destroying them or being destroyed by them, may lead to experiences of *Weltuntergang* and loss of identity. We find in such patients fears of accepting and acquiring likenesses to others, in conjunction with an inability to perceive and tolerate differences from them, and to relate to them as to separate and different individuals. Likeness and difference are equally frightening, because likeness threatens to destroy the self and difference the object.

The role of libido as against that of aggression in such regressive fusions between self and objects becomes evident from a comparison between experiences of ecstasy in normal persons and fusion experiences in psychotics. Since normal experiences of ecstasy do not aim at destruction but are founded on a fantasy of libidinal union between self and object world, they result in a transitory sense of self expansion and the feeling that the self and the world are rich. Such experiences of merging, which may briefly transform the images of the self and the object world into a fantasy unit vested with libidinal forces, permit an immediate re-establishment of the boundaries between them. By contrast, pathological regressive fusions caused by severe aggression may result in an irreparable breakdown of these boundaries and hence of the self and object representations.

NOTE 4

SCHAFER, ROY

Regression in the Service of the Ego: The Relevance of a Psychoanalytic Concept for Personality Assessment*

[W]e must consider the distinction introduced by Freud between the primary process and the secondary process. The primary process, which is genetically and formally the more primitive, operates with un-neutralized drive energies, and its regulative principle is tension reduction (the pleasure principle); it strives toward immediate discharge of energy accumulations by a direct route and through the mechanisms of displacement, condensation, substitute formation, and symbolization. The secondary process operates by the principle of least effort; its energies are relatively neutralized, i.e., relatively bound in motives and structures of a highly socialized nature, and freely available for whichever ego activities of the moment may require energic support; it is oriented toward objective reality; it follows the safest course toward the sought-for object in reality, using delays of impulse, detours, and experimental action in thought, until the suitable object and modes of action have been found.

The contrast between primary process and secondary process may be detailed further. *Thinking*, under the domination of the primary process, tends to be unreflective, timeless, and concrete; under the domination of the secondary process, thinking is reflective, shows time perspective, and uses abstract concepts corresponding to reality relations. Concerning *memory* in particular, domination by the primary process means that memories available are organized around the imperative drive or drives, while other memories, not relevant to immediate drive pressures, are unavailable; the contrast to this is conceptual and reality-oriented organization of memories and their free availability, depending on the needs of the real—external as well as internal—situation. Concerning *perception*, the contrast is one of drive selectivity and organization, disregard of total external context, and

* Reprinted from: Lindzey, G. ed.: *Assessment of Human Motives.* New York: Holt, Rinehart & Winston, Inc., 1958. (pp. 123–25). Reprinted by permission.

diffuse, physiognomic, and animistic formal characteristics on the primary side, and, on the secondary side, adaptive selectivity and organization, boundness by objective context, and articulated, stable formal characteristics. From the standpoint of *affects*, primary process involves diffuse, unmodulated affects and affect storms limited in their variability, while secondary process involves articulated, varied, and subtly blended affects. From the standpoint of *motility*, primary-process domination implies rapid spilling over into action and participation, and often grossness of action (as in convulsive laughter), while secondary-process domination implies restrained and modulated motility (as in the smile or the free laugh). Looked at from the standpoint of the *self*, primary-process functioning tends to eliminate the boundaries and inner coherence of the self so that what is thought and what is real are confused, the wish is equivalent to the deed, fantasies are events, and past ego states are present contradictory selves; secondary-process functioning maintains the boundaries and coherence of the self in these respects. From the standpoint of *defense*, the contrast is one of weakness (consciousness overwhelmed by normally unconscious impulses, affects, and fantasies) versus strength. From the standpoint of the *ego ideal*, the contrast is one of megalomanic, unattainable, infantile conceptions versus conceptions relatively more regulated by reality testing or realistic considerations of the possible rather than the exalted. From the standpoint of the superego, the contrast is one of archaic severity versus closeness to the ego. From the standpoint of the *ego as a whole*, the contrast is one of passivity versus activity, respectively, discharge of impulse occurring relatively independently of the ego, or the ego being unable to modify the damming up of impulses by its countercathectic energy distributions versus impulses being discharged by means of the ego's controlling and executive apparatuses or being merely postponed in their discharge by controlling and defensive ego functions. . . .

In psychoanalytic discussions the contrasts listed above have often been presented in terms of id versus ego or the system Unconscious versus the systems Preconscious and Conscious. They have been stressed in the study of such phenomena as dreams; extreme fatigue; states of emotional excitement; schizophrenia; altered states of consciousness, such as, fugues, amnesias, intoxications, and deliria; preliterate cultures; and the behavior of the infant and young child. . . . Obviously, the contrasts drawn represent ideal polar positions. Any specific behavior must be assessed in terms of its relative position with respect to these poles or in terms of the particular admixture of primary and secondary processes in it. There are all degrees of transition.

*   *   *

2.

FREUD, ANNA

The Ego and the Mechanisms of Defense (1936)*

The id, the ego, and the superego in self-perception— We all know that the three psychic institutions vary greatly in their accessibility to observation. Our knowledge of the id—which was formerly called the system *Ucs.*—can be acquired only through the derivatives which make their way into the systems *Pcs.* and *Cs.* If within the id a state of calm and satisfaction prevails, so that there is no occasion for any instinctual impulse to invade the ego in search of gratification and there to produce feelings of tension and "pain," we can learn nothing of the id contents. It follows, at least theoretically, that the id is not under all conditions open to observation.

The situation is, of course, different in the case of the superego. Its contents are for the most part conscious and so can be directly arrived at by endopsychical perception. Nevertheless, our picture of the superego always tends to become hazy when harmonious relations exist between it and the ego. We then say that the two coincide, i.e., at such moments the superego is not perceptible as a separate institution either to the subject himself or to an outside observer. Its outlines become clear only when it confronts the ego with hostility or at least with criticism. The superego, like the id, becomes perceptible in the state which it produces within the ego: For instance, when its criticism evokes a sense of guilt.

The ego as observer.—Now this means that the proper field for our observation is always the ego. It is, so to speak, the medium through which we try to get a picture of the other two institutions.

When the relations between the two neighboring powers—ego and id—are peaceful, the former fulfils to admiration its role of observing the latter. Different instinctual impulses are perpetually forcing their way from the id into the ego, where they gain access to the motor apparatus, by means of which they obtain gratification. In favorable cases the ego does not object to the intruder but puts its own energies at the other's disposal and confines itself to perceiving; it notes the onset of the instinctual impulse, the heightening of tension, and the feelings of "pain" by which this is accompanied and, finally, the relief from tension when gratification is experienced. Observation of the whole process gives us a clear and undistorted picture of the instinctual impulse concerned, of the quantity of libido with which it is cathected, and the aim which it pursues. The ego, if it assents to the impulse, does not enter into the picture at all.

Unfortunately the passing of instinctual impulses

* New York: International Universities Press, Inc., 1946, (pp. 5–129). Reprinted by permission.

from one institution to the other may be the signal for all manner of conflicts, with the inevitable result that observation of the id is interrupted. On their way to gratification the id impulses must pass through the territory of the ego and here they are in an alien atmosphere. In the id the so-called "primary process" prevails; there is no synthesis of ideas, affects are liable to displacement, opposites are not mutually exclusive and may even coincide, and condensation occurs as a matter of course. The sovereign principle which governs the psychic processes is that of obtaining pleasure. In the ego, on the contrary, the association of ideas is subject to strict conditions, to which we apply the comprehensive term "secondary process"; further, the instinctual impulses can no longer seek gratification without more ado—they are required to respect the demands of reality and, more than that, to conform to ethical and moral laws by which the superego seeks to control the behavior of the ego. Hence these impulses run the risk of incurring the displeasure of institutions essentially alien to them. They are exposed to criticism and rejection and have to submit to every kind of modification. Peaceful relations between the neighboring powers are at an end. The instinctual impulses continue to pursue their aims with their own peculiar tenacity and energy, and they make hostile incursions into the ego, in the hope of overthrowing it by a surprise attack. The ego on its side becomes suspicious; it proceeds to counterattack and to invade the territory of the id. Its purpose is to put the instincts permanently out of action by means of appropriate defensive measures, designed to secure its own boundaries.

The picture of these processes transmitted to us by means of the ego's faculty of observation is more confused but at the same time much more valuable. It shows us two psychic institutions in action at one and the same moment. No longer do we see an undistorted id impulse but an id impulse modified by some defensive measure on the part of the ego. The task of the analytic observer is to split up the picture, representing as it does a compromise between the separate institutions, into its component parts: the id, the ego and, it may be, the superego.

Inroads by the id and by the ego considered as material for observation.—In all this we are struck by the fact that the inroads from the one side and from the other are by no means equally valuable from the point of view of observation. All the defensive measures of the ego against the id are carried out silently and invisibly. The most that we can ever do is to reconstruct them in retrospect: we can never really witness them in operation. This statement applies, for instance, to successful repression. The ego knows nothing of it; we are aware of it only subsequently, when it becomes apparent that something is missing. I mean by this that, when we try to form an objective judgment about a particular individual, we realize

that certain id impulses are absent which we should expect to make their appearance in the ego in pursuit of gratification. If they never emerge at all, we can only assume that access to the ego is permanently denied to them, i.e., that they have succumbed to repression. But this tells us nothing of the process of repression itself.

The same is true of successful reaction formation, which is one of the most important measures adopted by the ego as a permanent protection against the id. Such formations appear almost unheralded in the ego in the course of a child's development. We cannot always say that the ego's attention had previously been focused on the particular contrary instinctual impulse which the reaction formation replaces. As a rule, the ego knows nothing of the rejection of the impulse or of the whole conflict which has resulted in the implanting of the new characteristic. Analytic observers might easily take it for a spontaneous development of the ego, were it not that definite indications of obsessional exaggeration suggest that it is of the nature of a reaction and that it conceals a long-standing conflict. Here again, observation of the particular mode of defense does not reveal anything of the process by which it has been evolved.

We note that all the important information which we have acquired has been arrived at by the study of inroads from the opposite side, namely, from the id to the ego. The obscurity of a successful repression is only equalled by the transparency of the repressive process when the movement is reversed, i.e., when the repressed material returns, as may be observed in neurosis. Here we can trace every stage in the conflict between the instinctual impulse and the ego's defense. Similarly, reaction formation can best be studied when such formations are in process of disintegration. In such a case the id's inroad takes the form of a reinforcement of the libidinal cathexis of the primitive instinctual impulse, which the reaction formation concealed. This enables the impulse to force its way into consciousness and, for a time, instinctual impulse and reaction formation are visible within the ego side-by-side. Owing to another function of the ego—its tendency to synthesis—this condition of affairs, which is particularly favorable for analytic observation, lasts only for a few moments at a time. Then a fresh conflict arises between id derivative and ego activity, a conflict to decide which of the two is to keep the upper hand or what compromise they will adopt. If through reinforcement of its energic cathexis the defense set up by the ego is successful, the invading force from the id is routed and peace reigns once more in the psyche—a situation most unfruitful for our observations.

*   *   *

[M]any beginners in analysis have an idea that it is

essential to succeed in inducing their patients really and invariably to give all their associations without modification or inhibition, i.e., to obey implicitly the fundamental rule of analysis. But, even if this ideal were realized, it would not represent an advance, for after all it would simply mean the conjuring up again of the now obsolete situation of hypnosis, with its one-sided concentration on the part of the physician upon the id. Fortunately for analysis such docility in the patient is in practice impossible. The fundamental rule can never be followed beyond a certain point. The ego keeps silence for a time and the id derivatives make use of this pause to force their way into consciousness. The analyst hastens to catch their utterances. Then the ego bestirs itself again, repudiates the attitude of passive tolerance which it has been compelled to assume and by means of one or other of its customary defense mechanisms intervenes in the flow of associations. The patient transgresses the fundamental rule of analysis, or, as we say, he puts up "resistances." This means that the inroad of the id into the ego has given place to a counterattack by the ego upon the id. The observer's attention is now diverted from the associations to the resistance, i.e., from the content of the id to the activity of the ego. The analyst has an opportunity of witnessing, then and there, the putting into operation by the latter of one of those defensive measures against the id, which I have already described and which are so obscure, and it now behoves him to make it the object of his investigation. He then notes that with this change of object the situation in the analysis has suddenly changed. In analyzing the id he is assisted by the spontaneous tendency of the id derivatives to rise to the surface: His exertions and the strivings of the material which he is trying to analyze are similarly directed. In the analysis of the ego's defensive operations there is, of course, no such community of aim. The unconscious elements in the ego have no inclination to become conscious and derive no advantage from so doing. Hence any piece of ego analysis is much less satisfactory than the analysis of the id. It has to proceed by circuitous paths, it cannot follow out the ego activity directly, the only possibility is to reconstruct it from its influence on the patient's associations. From the nature of the effect produced—whether it be omission, reversal, displacement of meaning, etc.—we hope to discover what kind of defense the ego has employed in its intervention. So it is the analyst's business first of all to recognize the defence mechanism. When he has done this, he has accomplished a piece of ego analysis. His next task is to undo what has been done by the defense, i.e., to find out and restore to its place that which has been omitted through repression, to rectify displacements and to bring that which has been isolated back into its true context. When he has re-established the severed connections, he turns his attention once more from the analysis of the ego to that of the id.

We see then that what concerns us is not simply the enforcement of the fundamental rule of analysis for its own sake but the conflict to which this gives rise. It is only when observation is focused now on the id and now on the ego and the direction of interest is twofold, extending to both sides of the human being whom we have before us, that we can speak of *psychoanalysis.* . . .

The various other means employed in analytic technique can now be classified without difficulty, according as the attention of the observer is directed to one side or the other.

Interpretation of dreams.—The situation when we are interpreting our patient's dreams and when we are listening to his free associations is the same. The dreamer's psychic state differs little from that of the patient during the analytic hour. When he obeys the fundamental rule of analysis he voluntarily suspends the function of the ego; in the dreamer this suspension takes place automatically under the influence of sleep. The patient is made to lie at rest on the analyst's couch, in order that he may have no opportunity to gratify his instinctual wishes in action; similarly, in sleep, the motor system is brought to a standstill. And the effect of the censorship, the translation of latent dream thoughts into manifest dream content, with the distortions, condensations, displacements, reversals, and omissions which this involves, corresponds to the distortions which take place in the associations under the pressure of some resistance. Dream interpretation, then, assists us in our investigation of the id, insofar as it is successful in bringing to light latent dream thoughts (id content), and in our investigation of the ego institutions and their defensive operations, insofar as it enables us to reconstruct the measures adopted by the censor from their effect upon the dream thoughts.

*   *   *

Parapraxes.—From time to time we obtain further glimpses of the unconscious in another way, in those irruptions of the id which are known as parapraxes. As we know, these irruptions are not confined to the analytic situation. They may occur at any time when, in some special circumstances, the vigilance of the ego is relaxed or diverted and an unconscious impulse (again owing to some special circumstances) is suddenly reinforced. . . .

Transference.—The same theoretical distinction between observation of the id on the one hand and observation of the ego on the other may be drawn in the case of that which is perhaps the most powerful instrument in the analyst's hand: The interpretation of the transference. By transference we mean all those impulses experienced by the patient in his relation with the analyst which are not newly created by the objective analytic situation but have their source in early—indeed, the very earliest—object relations and are now merely revived under the influence of the repetition compulsion. Because these impulses are repetitions and not new creations they are of incomparable value as a means of information about the patient's past affective experiences. We shall see that we can distinguish different types of transference phenomena according to the degree of their complexity.

(a) Transference of libidinal impulses.—The first type of transference is extremely simple. The patient finds himself disturbed in his relation to the analyst by passionate emotions, e.g., love, hate, jealousy, and anxiety, which do not seem to be justified by the facts of the actual situation. The patient himself resists these emotions and feels ashamed, humiliated, and so forth, when they manifest themselves against his will. Often it is only by insisting on the fundamental rule of analysis that we succeed in forcing a passage for them to conscious expression. Further investigation reveals the true character of these affects—they are irruptions of the id. They have their source in old affective constellations, such as the Oedipus and the castration complex, and they become comprehensible and indeed are justified if we disengage them from the analytic situation and insert them into some infantile affective situation. When thus put back into their proper place, they help us to fill up an amnestic gap in the patient's past and provide us with fresh information about his infantile instinctual and affective life. Generally he is quite willing to co-operate with us in our interpretation, for he himself feels that the transferred affective impulse is an intrusive foreign body. By putting it back into its place in the past we release him from an impulse in the present which is alien to his ego. . . .

(b) Transference of defense.—The case alters when we come to the second type of transference. The repetition compulsion, which dominates the patient in the analytic situation, extends not only to former id impulses but equally to former defensive measures against the instincts. Thus he not only transfers undistorted infantile id impulses, which become subject to a censorship on the part of the adult ego secondarily and not until they force their way to conscious expression; he transfers also id impulses in all those forms of distortion which took shape while he was still in infancy. It may happen in extreme cases that the instinctual impulse itself never enters into the transference at all but only the specific defense adopted by the ego against some positive or negative attitude of the libido, as, for instance, the reaction of flight from a positive love fixation in latent female homosexuality or the submissive, feminine-masochistic attitude, to which Wilhelm Reich has called attention in male patients whose relations to their fathers were once characterized by aggression. . . . If

we succeed in retracing the path followed by the instinct in its various transformations, the gain in the analysis is two-fold. The transference phenomenon which we have interpreted falls into two parts, both of which have their origin in the past: A libidinal or aggressive element, which belongs to the id, and a defense mechanism, which we must attribute to the ego—in the most instructive cases to the ego of the same infantile period in which the id impulse first arose. Not only do we fill in a gap in the patient's memory of his instinctual life, as we may also do when interpreting the first, simple type of transference, but we acquire information which completes and fills in the gaps in the history of his ego development or, to put it another way, the history of the transformations through which his instincts have passed.

*   *   *

. . . Only the analysis of the ego's unconscious defensive operations can enable us to reconstruct the transformations which the instincts have undergone. Without a knowledge of these we may, indeed, discover much about the contents of the repressed instinctual wishes and fantasies, but we shall learn little or nothing about the vicissitudes through which they have passed and the various ways in which they enter into the structure of the personality.

*   *   *

The relation of the ego to the analytic method.— . . . It is the task of the analyst to bring into consciousness that which is unconscious, no matter to which psychic institution it belongs. He directs his attention equally and objectively to the unconscious elements in all three institutions. To put it in another way, when he sets about the work of enlightenment he takes his stand at a point equidistant from the id, the ego, and the superego.

*   *   *

Psychoanalytical theory and the mechanisms of defense.—The term "defense," . . . is the earliest representative of the dynamic standpoint in psychoanalytical theory. . . .

*   *   *

. . . In his work on the theory of instinct [Freud] describes the processes of turning against the self and reversal, and these he designates as "vicissitudes of instinct." From the point of view of the ego these two latter mechanisms also must come under the heading of methods of defense, for every vicissitude to which the instincts are liable has its origin in some ego activity. Were it not for the intervention of the ego or of those external forces which the ego represents, every instinct would know only one fate—that of gratification. To these nine methods of defense, which are very familiar in the practice and have been exhaustively described in the theoretical writings of psychoanalysis (regression, repression, reaction formation, isolation, undoing, projection, introjection, turning against the self, and reversal), we must add a tenth, which pertains rather to the study of the normal than to that of neurosis: sublimation, or displacement of instinctual aims.

So far as we know at present, the ego has these ten different methods at its disposal in its conflicts with instinctual representatives and affects. It is the task of the practicing analyst to discover how far these methods prove effective in the processes of ego resistance and symptom formation which he has the opportunity of observing in individuals.

A comparison of the results achieved by the different mechanisms in individual cases.—I will take as an illustration the case of a young woman employed in an institution for children. She was the middle child in a number of brothers and sisters. Throughout childhood she suffered from passionate penis envy, relating to her elder and her younger brother, and from jealousy, which was repeatedly excited by her mother's successive pregnancies. Finally, envy and jealousy combined in a fierce hostility to her mother. But, since the child's love fixation was no less strong than her hatred, a violent defensive conflict with her negative impulses succeeded an initial period of uninhibited unruliness and naughtiness. She dreaded lest the manifestation of her hate should cause her to lose her mother's love, of which she could not bear to be deprived. She also dreaded that her mother would punish her and she criticized herself most severely for her prohibited longings for revenge. As she entered upon the period of latency, this anxiety situation and conflict of conscience became more and more acute and her ego tried to master her impulses in various ways. In order to solve the problem of ambivalence she displaced outward one side of her ambivalent feeling. Her mother continued to be a love object, but, from that time on, there was always in the girl's life a second important person of the female sex, whom she hated violently. This eased matters: Her hatred of the more remote object was not visited with the sense of guilt so mercilessly as was her hatred of her mother. But even the displaced hatred was a source of much suffering. As time went on, it was plain that this first displacement was inadequate as a means of mastering the situation.

The little girl's ego now resorted to a second mechanism. It turned inward the hatred, which hitherto had related exclusively to other people. The child tortured herself with self-accusations and feelings of inferiority and, throughout childhood and adolescence right into adult life, she did everything she could to put herself at a disadvantage and injure her interests, always surrendering her own wishes to the demands made on her by others. To all outward

appearance she had become masochistic since adopting this method of defense.

But this measure, too, proved inadequate as a means of mastering the situation. The patient then entered on a process of projection. The hatred which she had felt for female love objects or their substitutes was transformed into the conviction that she herself was hated, slighted, or persecuted by them. Her ego thus found relief from the sense of guilt. The naughty child, who cherished wicked feelings against the people around her, underwent metamorphosis into the victim of cruelty, neglect, and persecution. But the use of this mechanism left upon her character a permanent paranoid imprint, which was a source of very great difficulty to her both in youth and adult years.

The patient was quite grown up when she came to be analyzed. She was not regarded as ill by those who knew her, but her sufferings were acute. In spite of all the energy which her ego had expended upon its defense she had not succeeded in really mastering her anxiety and sense of guilt. On any occasion when her envy, jealousy, and hatred were in danger of activation, she invariably had recourse to all her defense mechanisms. But her emotional conflicts never came to any issue which could set her ego at rest and, apart from this, the final result of all her struggles was meager in the extreme. She succeeded in maintaining the fiction that she loved her mother, but she felt herself to be full of hatred and on this account she despised and mistrusted herself. She did not succeed in preserving the sense of being loved; it had been destroyed by the mechanism of projection. Nor did she succeed in escaping the punishments which she had feared in childhood; by turning her aggressive impulses inward she inflicted upon herself all the suffering which she had formerly anticipated in the form of punishment by her mother. The three mechanisms of which she had made use could not prevent her ego from being in a perpetual state of uneasy tension and vigilance, nor relieve it of the exaggerated demands made upon it and the sense of acute torment from which it suffered.

Let us compare these processes with the corresponding relations in hysteria or obsessional neurosis. We will assume that the problem is the same in each case: How to master that hatred of the mother which springs from penis envy. Hysteria solves it by means of repression. The hatred of the mother is obliterated from consciousness and any possible derivatives which seek entry into the ego are vigorously warded off. The aggressive impulses associated with hatred and the sexual impulses associated with penis envy may be transformed into bodily symptoms, if the patient possesses the capacity for conversion and somatic conditions are favorable. In other cases the ego protects itself against the reactivation of the original conflict by developing a phobia and avoiding the occasions of trouble. It imposes restrictions upon its activity, thus evading any situation which might lead to a return of the repressed impulses.

In obsessional neurosis, as in hysteria, hatred of the mother and penis envy are in the first instance repressed. Subsequently the ego secures itself against their return by means of reaction formations. A child who has been aggressive toward her mother develops an excessive tenderness toward her and is worried about her safety; envy and jealousy are transformed into unselfishness and thoughtfulness for others. By instituting obsessional ceremonials and various precautionary measures she protects the beloved persons from any outbreak of her aggressive impulses, while by means of a moral code of exaggerated strictness she checks the manifestation of her sexual impulses.

A child who masters her infantile conflicts in the hysterical or obsessional manner here described presents a more pathological picture than the patient whose case we first considered. The repression which has taken place has deprived such children of the control of part of their affective life. The original relation to the mother and brothers and the important relation to their own femininity have been withdrawn from further conscious assimilation and have become obsessively and irrevocably fixed in the reactive alteration undergone by the ego. A great part of their activity is consumed in maintaining the anticathexes which are designed subsequently to secure the repression, and this loss of energy is apparent in the inhibition and curtailment of other vital activities. But the ego of the child who has solved her conflicts by means of repression, with all its pathological sequels, is at peace. It suffers secondarily through the consequences of the neurosis which repression has brought upon it. But it has, at least within the limits of the conversion hysteria or obsessional neurosis, bound its anxiety, disposed of its sense of guilt, and gratified its ideas of punishment. The difference is that, if the ego employs repression, the formation of symptoms relieves it of the task of mastering its conflicts, while, if it employs the other defensive methods, it still has to deal with the problem.

In practice, the use of repression as distinct from other defensive methods is less common than a combination in one and the same individual of the two techniques. This is well illustrated by the history of a patient who also suffered in very early childhood from acute penis envy, in her case in relation to her father. The sexual fantasies of this phase reached their climax in the wish to bite off her father's penis. At this point the ego set up its defense. The shocking idea was repressed. It was replaced by its opposite—a general disinclination to bite, which soon developed into a difficulty in eating, accompanied by hysterical feelings of disgust. One part of the prohibited impulse—that represented by the oral fantasy—had now been mastered. But the aggressive content, i.e., the wish to rob her father or a father substitute, remained in con-

sciousness for a time, until, as the superego developed, the ego's moral sense repudiated this impulse. By means of a mechanism of displacement, which I shall discuss more fully later, the urge to rob was transformed into a peculiar kind of contentedness and unassumingness. We see that the two successive methods of defense produced a substratum of hysteria and, superimposed on this, a specific ego modification, not in itself of a pathological character.

The impression conveyed by these examples is confirmed when we examine in detail the effect of the different defence mechanisms in other cases. Theoretically, repression may be subsumed under the general concept of defense and placed side by side with the other specific methods. Nevertheless, from the point of view of efficacy it occupies a unique position in comparison with the rest. In terms of quantity it accomplishes more than they, that is to say, it is capable of mastering powerful instinctual impulses, in face of which the other defensive measures are quite ineffective. It acts once only, though the anticathexis, effected to secure the repression, is a permanent institution demanding a constant expenditure of energy. The other mechanisms, on the contrary, have to be brought into operation again whenever there is an accession of instinctual energy. But repression is not only the most efficacious, it is also the most dangerous, mechanism. The dissociation from the ego entailed by the withdrawal of consciousness from whole tracts of instinctual and affective life may destroy the integrity of the personality for good and all. Thus repression becomes the basis of compromise formation and neurosis. The consequences of the other defensive methods are not less serious but, even when they assume an acute form, they remain more within the limits of the normal. They manifest themselves in innumerable transformations, distortions, and deformities of the ego, which are in part the accompaniment of and in part substitutes for neurosis.

Suggestions for a chronological classification.— Even when we have accorded to repression its exceptional position among the ego's methods of defense, we still feel as regards the rest that we are including under a single heading a number of heterogeneous phenomena. Methods such as that of isolation and undoing stand side-by-side with genuine instinctual processes, such as, regression, reversal, and turning against the self. Some of these serve to master large quantities of instinct or affect, others only small quantities. The considerations which determine the ego's choice of mechanism remain uncertain. Perhaps repression is pre-eminently of value in combating sexual wishes, while other methods can more readily be employed against instinctual forces of a different kind, in particular, against aggressive impulses. Or it may be that these other methods have only to complete what repression has left undone or to deal with such prohibited ideas as return to consciousness when repression fails. Or possibly each defense mechanism is first evolved in order to master some specific instinctual urge and so is associated with a particular phase of infantile development.

The appendix to *Inhibitions, Symptoms, and Anxiety* . . . contains a provisional answer to these suggestions. "It may well be that before its sharp cleavage into an ego and an id, and before the formation of a superego, the mental apparatus makes use of different methods of defense from those which it employs after it has attained these levels of organization." This may be expanded as follows. Repression consists in the withholding or expulsion of an idea or affect from the conscious ego. It is meaningless to speak of repression where the ego is still merged with the id. Similarly we might suppose that projection and introjection were methods which depended on the differentiation of the ego from the outside world. The expulsion of ideas or affects from the ego and their relegation to the outside world would be a relief to the ego, only when it had learnt to distinguish itself from that world. Or again, introjection from the outside world into the ego could not be said to have the effect of enriching the latter unless there were already a clear differentiation between that which belonged to the one and that which belonged to the other. But the situation is by no means so simple. In the case of projection and introjection the first beginnings are much more obscure. Sublimation, i.e., the displacement of the instinctual aim in conformity with higher social values, presupposes the acceptance or at least the knowledge of such values, that is to say, presupposes the existence of the superego. Accordingly, the defense mechanisms of repression and sublimation could not be employed until relatively late in the process of development, while the position in time which we shall assign to projection and introjection depends upon the theoretical standpoint which happens to be adopted. Such processes as regression, reversal, or turning round upon the self are probably independent of the stage which the psychic structure has reached and as old as the instincts themselves, or at least as old as the conflict between instinctual impulses and any hindrance which they may encounter on their way to gratification. We should not be surprised to find that these are the very earliest defense mechanisms employed by the ego.

But this suggested chronological classification does not accord with our experience that the earliest manifestations of neurosis which we observe in young children are hysterical symptoms, of whose connection with repression there can be no doubt; on the other hand, the genuine masochistic phenomena, which result from the turning round of the instinct upon the self, are very rarely met with in earliest childhood. According to the theory of the English school of analysis, introjection and projection, which

in our view should be assigned to the period after the ego has been differentiated from the outside world, are the very processes by which the structure of the ego is developed and but for which differentiation would never have taken place. These differences of opinion bring home to us the fact that the chronology of psychic processes is still one of the most obscure fields of analytical theory. We have a good illustration of this in the disputed question of when the individual superego is actually formed. So a classification of the defense mechanisms according to position in time inevitably partakes of all the doubt and uncertainty which even today attach to chronological pronouncements in analysis. It will probably be best to abandon the attempt so to classify them and, instead, to study in detail the situations which call forth the defensive reactions.

The instinctual dangers against which the ego defends itself are always the same, but its reasons for feeling a particular irruption of instinct to be dangerous may vary.

Motives for the defense against instincts: (a) superego anxiety in the neuroses of adults.—The defensive situation with which we have been longest familiar in analysis and of which our knowledge is most thorough is that which forms the basis of neurosis in adults. The position here is that some instinctual wish seeks to enter consciousness and with the help of the ego to attain gratification. The latter would not be adverse from admitting it but the superego protests. The ego submits to the higher institution and obediently enters into a struggle against the instinctual impulse, with all the consequences which such a struggle entails. The characteristic point about this process is that the ego itself does not regard the impulse which it is fighting as in the least dangerous. The motive which prompts the defense is not originally its own. The instinct is regarded as dangerous because the superego prohibits its gratification and, if it achieves its aim, it will certainly stir up trouble between the ego and the superego. Hence the ego of the adult neurotic fears the instincts because it fears the superego. Its defense is motivated by superego anxiety.

So long as our attention is confined to the defense against instinct set up by adult neurotics we shall regard the superego as a redoubtable force. It appears in the light of the author of all neurosis. It is the mischief maker which prevents the ego's coming to a friendly understanding with the instincts. It sets up an ideal standard, according to which sexuality is prohibited and aggression pronounced to be antisocial. It demands a degree of sexual renunciation and restriction of aggression which is incompatible with psychic health. The ego is completely deprived of its independence and reduced to the status of an instrument for the execution of the superego's wishes; the result is that it becomes hostile to instinct and incapable of enjoyment. . . .

(b) objective anxiety in infantile neurosis.—The study of defense in infantile neurosis teaches us that the superego is by no means an indispensable factor in the formation of the neuroses. Adult neurotics seek to ward off their sexual and aggressive wishes in order not to come into conflict with the superego. Little children treat their instinctual impulses in the same way in order not to transgress their parents' prohibitions. The ego of a little child, like that of an adult, does not combat the instincts of its own accord; its defense is not prompted by its feelings in the matter. It regards the instincts as dangerous because those who bring the child up have forbidden their gratification and an irruption of instinct entails restrictions and the infliction or threat of punishment. Castration anxiety produces in young children the same result as that produced in adult neurotics by anxiety of conscience; the infantile ego fears the instincts because it fears the outside world. Its defense against them is motivated by dread of the outside world, i.e., by objective anxiety.

When we discover that objective anxiety causes the infantile ego to develop the same probias, obsessional neuroses, hysterical symptoms, and neurotic traits as occur in adults in consequence of their superego anxiety, the power of that institution naturally sinks in our estimation. We realize that what we ascribed to it should really have been put down simply to the anxiety itself. In the formation of neurosis it seems to be a matter of indifference to what that anxiety relates. The crucial point is that, whether it be dread of the outside world or dread of the superego, it is the anxiety which sets the defensive process going. The symptoms which enter consciousness as the ultimate result of this process do not enable us to determine which type of anxiety in the ego has produced them.

If we study this second defense situation—defense against the instincts from the motive of objective anxiety—we shall form a high estimate of the influence which the outside world exerts over children and accordingly we shall once more conceive hopes of an effective prophylaxis of neurosis. It is pointed out that little children nowadays suffer from a degree of objective anxiety which is quite unnecessary. The punishments which they fear may be inflicted upon them, if they gratify their instincts, are for the most part altogether obsolete in our present stage of civilization. Castration is no longer practiced in retribution for prohibited sexual indulgence nor are acts of aggression punished by mutilation. But, all the same, there is still in our educational methods a faint resemblance to the barbaric punishments of earlier times, just enough to arouse some dim apprehensions and fears, residues handed on by inheritance. Optimists take the point of view that it should be possible to avoid these remote suggestions of threats of castration and measures of violence, even now adumbrated, if not in the disciplinary methods

actually employed, at least in the manner and voice of adults. Those who hold this view hope that the connection between modern education and these age-old fears of punishment may be finally severed. Surely, they say, the child's objective anxiety would then diminish and a radical change would take place in the relation between his ego and his instincts, which would mean the final cutting away of much of the ground from under infantile neurosis.

(c) instinctual anxiety (dread of the strength of the instincts).—As before, however, psychoanalytic experience destroys the prospect of an effective prophylaxis. The human ego by its very nature is never a promising soil for the unhampered gratification of instinct. I mean by this that the ego is friendly to the instincts, only so long as it is itself but little differentiated from the id. When it has evolved from the primary to the secondary process, from the pleasure principle to the reality principle, it has become, as I have already shown, alien territory to the instincts. Its mistrust of their demands is always present but, under normal conditions, hardly noticeable. It is lost sight of in the much more tumultuous warfare waged within its domain by the superego and the outside world against the impulses of the id. But, if the ego feels itself abandoned by these protective higher powers or if the demands of the instinctual impulses become excessive, its mute hostility to instinct is intensified to the point of anxiety. "What it is that the ego fears either from an external or from a libidinal danger cannot be specified; we know that it is in the nature of an overthrow or of extinction, but it is not determined by analysis." Robert Walder describes it as "the danger that the ego's whole organization may be destroyed or submerged." The effect of the anxiety experienced by the ego because of the strength of the instincts is the same as that produced by the superego anxiety or the objective anxiety which so far we have been studying. Defense mechanisms are brought into operation against the instincts, with all the familiar results in the formation of neuroses and neurotic characteristics. In children the defense thus prompted can best be studied in cases where great pains have been taken by means of education on analytical lines and by therapeutic analysis to remove those occasions for objective anxiety and anxiety of conscience which otherwise tend to conceal it. In later life we can see it in full force whenever a sudden accession of instinctual energy threatens to upset the balance of the psychic institutions, as is normally the case, owing to physiological changes, at puberty and the climacteric and occurs for pathological reasons at the beginning of one of the periodic advances which occur in psychosis.

Further motives for the defense against instinct.—To these three powerful motives for the defense against instinct (superego anxiety, objective anxiety, anxiety due to the strength of the instincts) must be added those which in later life spring from the ego's need for synthesis. The adult ego requires some sort of harmony between its impulses, and so there arises a series of conflicts of which Alexander has given a full account. They are conflicts between opposite tendencies, such as homosexuality and heterosexuality, passivity and activity, etc. Which of two opposing impulses is warded off or admitted or what compromise is arrived at between them is again determined in the individual case by the amount of energy with which each is cathected.

The first two of the motives for defense which we have so far studied (superego anxiety and objective anxiety) have, besides, a source in common. If the instinct could achieve gratification in spite of opposition by the superego or the outside world, the result would, indeed, be primarily pleasure but secondarily "pain," either in consequence of the sense of guilt emanating from the unconscious or of the punishments inflicted by the outside world. Hence, when instinctual gratification is warded off from one or other of these two motives, the defense is undertaken in accordance with the reality principle. Its main purpose is to avoid this secondary pain.

Motives for the defense against affects.—Precisely the same reasons as prompt the ego's defense against the instincts underlie its defense against affects. Whenever it seeks to defend itself against instinctual impulses from one of the motives which I have indicated, it is obliged to ward off also the affects associated with the instinctual process. The nature of the affects in question is immaterial: they may be pleasurable, painful or dangerous to the ego. It makes no difference, for the ego is never allowed to experience them exactly as they are. If an affect is associated with a prohibited instinctual process, its fate is decided in advance. The fact that it is so associated suffices to put the ego on guard against it.

So far, the reasons for the defense against affect lie quite simply in the conflict between ego and instinct. There is, however, another and more primitive relation between the ego and the affects which has no counterpart in that of the ego to the instincts. Instinctual gratification is always primarily something pleasurable. But an affect may be primarily pleasurable or painful, according to its nature. If the ego has nothing to object to in a particular instinctual process and so does not ward off an affect on that ground, its attitude toward it will be determined entirely by the pleasure principle: It will welcome pleasurable affects and defend itself against painful ones. Indeed, even if owing to the repression of an instinct the ego is impelled by anxiety and a sense of guilt to defend itself against the accompanying affect, we can still see traces of selection in accordance with the pleasure principle. It is all the more ready to ward off affects associated with prohibited sexual impulses if these affects happen to be distressing, e.g., pain, longing,

mourning. On the other hand, it may resist a prohibition somewhat longer in the case of positive affects, simply because they are pleasurable, or may sometimes be persuaded to tolerate them for a short time when they make a sudden irruption into consciousness.

*   *   *

The defensive methods so far discovered by analysis all serve a single purpose—that of assisting the ego in its struggle with its instinctual life. They are motivated by the three principal types of anxiety to which the ego is exposed—instinctual anxiety, objective anxiety and anxiety of conscience. In addition, the mere struggle of conflicting impulses suffices to set the defense mechanisms in motion.

Psychoanalytic investigation of the problems of defense has developed in the following way: Beginning with the conflicts between the id and the ego institutions (as exemplified in hysteria, obsessional neurosis, etc.), it passed on to the struggle between the ego and the superego (in melancholia) and then proceeded to the study of the conflicts between the ego and the outside world (cf. the infantile animal phobia discussed in *Inhibitions, Symptoms, and Anxiety*). In all these situations of conflict the ego is seeking to repudiate a part of its own id. Thus the institution which sets up the defense and the invading force which is warded off are always the same; the variable factors are the motives which impel the ego to resort to defensive measures. Ultimately all such measures are designed to secure the ego and to save it from experiencing "pain."

Now the ego does not defend itself only against the "pain" arising from within. In the same early period in which it becomes acquainted with dangerous internal instinctual stimuli it experiences also "pain" which has its source in the outside world. The ego is in close contact with that world, from which it borrows its love objects and derives those impressions which its perception registers and its intelligence assimilates. The greater the importance of the outside world as a source of pleasure and interest, the more opportunity is there to experience "pain" from that quarter. A little child's ego lives as yet in accordance with the pleasure principle; it is a long time before it is trained to bear "pain." During this period the individual is still too weak to oppose the outside world actively, to defend himself against it by means of physical force or to modify it in accordance with his own will; as a rule the child is too helpless physically to take to flight and his understanding is as yet too limited for him to see the inevitable in the light of reason and submit to it. In this period of immaturity and dependence the ego, besides making efforts to master instinctual stimuli, endeavors in all kinds of ways to defend itself against the objective "pain" and dangers which menace it.

*   *   *

It is comparatively easy to discover the defence mechanisms to which the ego habitually resorts, so long as each is employed separately and only in conflict with some specific danger. When we find denial, we know that it is a reaction to external danger; when repression takes place, the ego is struggling with instinctual stimuli. The strong outward resemblance between inhibition and ego restriction makes it less certain whether these processes are part of an external or an internal conflict. The matter is still more intricate when defensive measures are combined or when the same mechanism is employed sometimes against an internal and sometimes against an external force. We have an excellent illustration of both these complications in the process of identification. Since it is one of the factors in the development of the superego, it contributes to the mastery of instinct. But, as I hope to show in what follows, there are occasions when it combines with other mechanisms to form one of the ego's most potent weapons in its dealings with external objects which arouse its anxiety.

August Aichhorn relates that, when he was giving advice on a Child Guidance Committee, he had to deal with the case of a boy at an elementary school, who was brought to him because of a habit of making faces. The master complained that the boy's behavior, if he were blamed or reproved, was quite abnormal. On such occasions he made faces which caused the whole class to burst out laughing. The master's view was that either the boy was consciously making fun of him or else the twitching of his face must be due to some kind of tic. His report was at once corroborated, for the boy began to make faces during the consultation, but, when master, pupil, and psychologist were together, the situation was explained. Observing the two attentively, Aichhorn saw that the boy's grimaces were simply a caricature of the angry expression of the teacher and that, when he had to face a scolding by the latter, he tried to master his anxiety by involuntarily imitating him. The boy identified himself with the teacher's anger and copied his expression as he spoke, though the imitation was not recognized. Through his grimaces he was assimilating himself to or identifying himself with the dreaded external object.

[A] little girl who tried by means of magic gestures to get over the mortification associated with her penis envy . . . was purposely and consciously making use of a mechanism to which the boy resorted involuntarily. At home she was afraid to cross the hall in the dark, because she had a dread of seeing ghosts. Suddenly, however, she hit on a device which enabled her to do it: She would run across the hall, making all sorts of peculiar gestures as she went. Before long, she triumphantly told her little brother the secret of how she had got over her anxiety. "There's no need to be afraid in the hall," she said, "you just have to pretend that you're the ghost who might meet you." This shows that her magic gestures represented the movements which she imagined that ghosts would make.

We might be inclined to regard this kind of conduct as an idiosyncrasy in the two children whose cases I have quoted, but it is really one of the most natural and widespread modes of behavior on the part of the primitive ego and has long been familiar to those who have made a study of primitive methods of invoking and exorcizing spirits and of primitive religious ceremonies. Moreover, there are many children's games in which through the metamorphosis of the subject into a dreaded object anxiety is converted into pleasurable security. Here is another angle from which to study the games of impersonation which children love to play.

Now the physical imitation of an antagonist represents the assimilation of only one part of a composite anxiety experience. We learn from observation that the other elements have also to be mastered.

[A] six-year-old patient . . . had to pay a series of visits to a dentist. At first everything went splendidly; the treatment did not hurt him and he was triumphant and made merry over the idea of anyone's being afraid of the dentist. But there came a time when my little patient arrived at my house in an extremely bad temper. The dentist had just hurt him. He was cross and unfriendly and vented his feelings on the things in my room. His first victim was a piece of india rubber. He wanted me to give it to him and, when I refused, he took a knife and tried to cut it in half. Next, he coveted a large ball of string. He wanted me to give him that too and painted me a vivid picture of what a good lead it would make for his animals. When I refused to give him the whole ball, he took the knife again and secured a large piece of the string. But he did not use it; instead, he began after a few minutes to cut it into tiny pieces. Finally he threw away the string too, turned his attention to some pencils and went on indefatigably sharpening them, breaking off the points and sharpening them again. It would not be correct to say that he was playing at "dentists." There was no actual impersonation of the dentist. The child was identifying himself not with the person of the aggressor but with his aggression.

On another occasion this little boy came to me just after he had had a slight accident. He had been joining in an outdoor game at school and had run full tilt against the fist of the games master, which the latter happened to be holding up in front of him. My little patient's lip was bleeding and his face tear-stained, and he tried to conceal both facts by putting up his hand as a screen. I endeavored to comfort and reassure him. He was in a woebegone condition when he left me, but next day he appeared holding himself very erect and dressed in full armor. On his head he wore a military cap and he had a toy sword at his side and a pistol in his hand. When he saw my surprise at this transformation, he simply said, "I just wanted to have these things on when I was playing with you." He did not, however, play; instead, he sat down and wrote a letter to his mother: "Dear Mummy, please, please, please, please send me the pocketknife you promised me and don't wait till Easter!" Here again we cannot say that, in order to master the anxiety experience of the previous day, he was impersonating the teacher with whom he had collided. Nor, in this instance, was he imitating the latter's aggression. The weapons and armor, being manly attributes, evidently symbolized the teacher's strength and, like the attributes of the father in the animal fantasies, helped the child to identify himself with the masculinity of the adult and so to defend himself against narcissistic mortification or actual mishaps.

The examples which I have so far cited illustrate a process with which we are quite familiar. A child introjects some characteristic of an anxiety object and so assimilates an anxiety experience which he has just undergone. Here, the mechanism of identification or introjection is combined with a second important mechanism. By impersonating the aggressor, assuming his attributes or imitating his aggression, the child transforms himself from the person threatened into the person who makes the threat. In *Beyond the Pleasure Principle* the significance of this change from the passive to the active role as a means of assimilating unpleasant or traumatic experiences in infancy is discussed in detail. "If a doctor examines a child's throat or performs a small operation, the alarming experience will quite certainly be made the subject of the next game, but in this the pleasure gain from another source cannot be overlooked. In passing from the passivity of experience to the activity of play the child applies to his playfellow the unpleasant occurrence that befell himself and so avenges himself on the person of this proxy." What is true of play is equally true of other behavior in children. In the case of the boy who made faces and the little girl who practiced magic it is not clear what finally became of the threat with which they identified themselves, but in the other little boy's ill temper the aggression taken over from the dentist and the games master was directed against the world at large.

*   *   *

Jenny Wälder has given a vivid picture of this process in a five-year-old boy whom she treated. When his analysis was about to touch on the material connected with masturbation and the fantasies associated with it, this little boy, who was usually shy and inhibited, became fiercely aggressive. His habitually passive attitude disappeared and there was no trace left of his feminine characteristics. In the analytic hour he pretended to be a roaring lion and attacked the analyst. He carried a rod about with him and

played at "Krampus," i.e., he laid about him with it on the stairs, in his own house, and in my room. His grandmother and mother complained that he tried to strike them in the face. His mother's uneasiness reached its climax when he took to brandishing kitchen knives. Analysis showed that the child's aggressiveness could not be construed as indicating that some inhibition on his instinctual impulses had been lifted. The release of his masculine tendencies was still a long way off. He was simply suffering from anxiety. The bringing into consciousness and the necessary confession of his former and recent sexual activities aroused in him the expectation of punishment. According to his experience, grown-up people were angry when they discovered a child indulging in such practices. They shouted at him, checked him sharply with a box on the ears or beat him with a rod; perhaps they would even cut off some part of him with a knife. When my little patient assumed the active role, roaring like a lion and laying about him with the rod and the knife, he was dramatizing and forestalling the punishment which he feared. He had introjected the aggression of the adults in whose eyes he felt guilty and, having exchanged the passive for the active part, he directed his own aggressive acts against those same people. Every time that he found himself on the verge of communicating to me what he regarded as dangerous material, his aggressiveness increased. But directly his forbidden thoughts and feelings broke through and had been discussed and interpreted, he felt no further need of the "Krampus" rod, which till then he had constantly carried about with him, and he left it at my house. His compulsion to beat other people disappeared simultaneously with his anxious expectation of being beaten himself.

In "identification with the aggressor" we recognize a by no means uncommon stage in the normal development of the superego. When the two boys whose cases I have just described identified themselves with their elders' threats of punishment, they were taking an important step toward the formation of that institution: They were internalizing other people's criticisms of their behavior. When a child constantly repeats this process of internalization and introjects the qualities of those responsible for his upbringing, making their characteristics and opinions his own, he is all the time providing material from which the superego may take shape. But at this point children are not quite wholehearted in acknowledging that institution. The internalized criticism is not as yet immediately transformed into self-criticism. As we have seen in the examples which I have given, it is dissociated from the child's own reprehensible activity and turned back on the outside world. By means of a new defensive process identification with the aggressor is succeeded by an active assault on the outside world.

Here is a more complicated example, which will

perhaps throw light on this new development in the defensive process. A certain boy, when his Oedipus complex was at its height, employed this particular mechanism to master his fixation to his mother. His happy relations with her were disturbed by outbursts of resentment. He would unbraid her passionately and on all sorts of grounds, but one mysterious accusation invariably recurred: He persistently complained of her curiosity. It is easy to see the first step in the working over of his prohibited affects. In his fantasy his mother knew of his libidinal feeling for her and indignantly rejected his advances. Her indignation was actively reproduced in his own fits of resentment against her. In contrast to Jenny Wälder's patient, however, he did not reproach her on general grounds but on the specific ground of curiosity. Analysis showed that this curiosity was an element not in his mother's instinctual life but in his own. Of all the component instincts which entered into his relation with her his scopophilic impulse was the most difficult to master. The reversal of roles was complete. He assumed his mother's indignation and, in exchange, ascribed to her his own curiosity.

* * *

[A] young patient used periodically to have fits of violent aggressiveness. I myself, her parents, and other people in less close relation with her were almost equally the objects of her resentment. There were two things in particular of which she constantly complained. First, during these phases she always had the feeling that people were keeping from her some secret which everybody knew but herself, and she was tormented by the desire to find out what it was. Secondly, she felt deeply disappointed by the shortcomings of all her friends. [T]he periods in which the patient kept back material coincided with those in which she complained of secretiveness in the analyst, so this patient's aggressive phases set in automatically whenever her repressed masturbation fantasies, of which she herself was unaware, were about to emerge into consciousness. Her strictures on her love objects corresponded to the blame which she expected from them because of her masturbation in childhood. She identified herself fully with this condemnation and turned it back upon the outside world. The secret which everybody kept from her was the secret of her own masturbation, which she kept not only from others but from herself. Here again, the patient's aggressiveness corresponded to that of other people and their "secret" was a reflection of her own repression.

These . . . examples have given us some idea of the origin of this particular phase in the development of the function of the superego. Even when the external criticism has been introjected, the threat of punishment and the offence committed have not as yet been connected up in the patient's mind. The moment the criticism is internalized, the offence is externalized. This means that the mechanism of identification with the aggressor is supplemented by another defensive measure, namely, the projection of guilt.

An ego which with the aid of the defense mechanism of projection develops along this particular line introjects the authorities to whose criticism it is exposed and incorporates them in the superego. It is then able to project its prohibited impulses outward. Its intolerance of other people is prior to its severity toward itself. It learns what is regarded as blameworthy but protects itself by means of this defense mechanism from unpleasant self-criticism. Vehement indignation at someone else's wrong doing is the precursor of and substitute for guilty feelings on its own account. Its indignation increases automatically when the perception of its own guilt is imminent. This stage in the development of the superego is a kind of preliminary phase of morality. True morality begins when the internalized criticism, now embodied in the standard exacted by the superego, coincides with the ego's perception of its own fault. From that moment, the severity of the superego is turned inward instead of outward and the subject becomes less intolerant of other people. But, when once it has reached this stage in its development, the ego has to endure the more acute "pain" occasioned by self-criticism and the sense of guilt.

It is possible that a number of people remain arrested at the intermediate stage in the development of the superego and never quite complete the internalization of the critical process. Although perceiving their own guilt, they continue to be peculiarly aggressive in their attitude to other people. In such cases the behavior of the superego toward others is as ruthless as that of the superego toward the patient's own ego in melancholia. Perhaps when the evolution of the superego is thus inhibited it indicates an abortive beginning of the development of melancholic states.

NOTES

NOTE 1

BIBRING, GRETE L., DWYER, THOMAS F., HUNTINGTON, DOROTHY S., AND VALENSTEIN, ARTHUR, F.

Glossary of Defenses*

This glossary is not intended to be a definitive classification of defenses. Defensive activities of the ego include not only specifically describable unconscious mechanisms but also complex unconscious functional

* Reprinted from: *A Study of the Psychological Processes in Pregnancy and of the Earliest Mother–Child Relationship.* 16 *The Psychoanalytic Study of the Child,* 1961. (pp. 62–71). Reprinted by permission of International Universities Press, New York.

responses which are more or less specific and recurrent and yet of a defensive nature. It appears that there is a continuum of defensive measures making up the defensive organization of the ego. The extremes can be readily distinguished from each other, but there is an indeterminate middle range which defies exact specification regarding those defensive functions which justify explicit specification as defense mechanisms, and those more complex measures made up of various combinations and sequence of defense mechanisms and admixtures of other ego functions. However, they are so closely related to those relatively irreducible defense mechanisms as to justify inclusion in a tabulation of defenses.

In recording our defenses, we were constantly aware of the fact that a variety of classificatory problems emerged: for example, basic and complex, pure and composite, including the greater or lesser admixture of instinctual elements, ubiquitous and specifically determined, archaic, and mature. This will be elaborated in further publications. At this point we decided to include on an experiential basis in the generally accepted catalogue some defensive measures peculiar to and characteristic for individual patients, and to divide the list in this glossary into two groups:

1. Basic (first order)
2. Complex (second order)[1]

However this might seem arbitrary, the arrangement is a tentative one, not meant to suggest mutual exclusiveness, but only the more or less quality of basic irreducibility, and complex synthesis of various ego-defensive functions. Reserved for future publication must be the problem of classification, the relationship of defenses to symptom formation, as well as considerations concerning the dual aspect of defenses, namely, the warding off of anxieties in relation to unconscious conflict; and second, the actively autonomous, adaptive function in the service of constructive, maturational, progressive growth and mastery of the drives.

*   *   *

Acting out: Serves as a resistance against conscious recognition of an impulse. The unconscious fantasy, involving objects, is lived out impulsively in behavior. Acting out is ego syntonic and involves more the gratification of the impulse, whether sexual or aggressive, than the prohibition against it, thus differentiating it from a symptom. Acting out may occur through the omitting or impulsive exaggeration of a normally adjustive, appropriate behavior, or it may be behavior which is contrary to established modes.

_____
[1. These have been omitted.]

Behavior is called acting out if it disrupts social adjustment.

Affectualization: The overemphasis on and the excessive use of the emotional aspects of issues in order to avoid the rational understanding and appreciation of them. Feeling is unconsciously intensified for purposes of defense.

Avoidance: An active turning away from conflict-laden thoughts, objects or experiences.

Blocking: An inhibition, usually temporary in nature, of affects especially, but possibly also thinking and impulses. It is a dynamic defensive process which comes close to repression in its effect. However, it is briefer, often with a dawning awareness of tension, resulting from the holding back of the affect, thought, or impulse to act.

Control through thinking: The use of the thought process in a compelling way to defend against acute emergent anxieties. It is characterized by a need to know all the details, to quite a complete extent. The content of the frightening situation is not primarily drained of anxieties, but through extended anticipatory familiarization with the danger, an attempt is made to prepare oneself and thus lessen the anxiety.

Denial: Denial accomplishes the negation of awareness in conscious terms of existing perceptions of inner or outer stimuli. Literally seeing but refusing to acknowledge what one sees or hearing and negating what is actually heard are expressions of denial and exemplify the close relationship of denial to sensory experience. It is to be distinguished from avoidance which is manifested, for example, by the actual closing of the eyes or the refusal to look. Denial plays its part as an important defense with respect to experience in the spheres of action, affects, and thought. In contrast to repression, which is immediately concerned with drive discharge, denial is closer to the perceptual system, whether it operates with regard to the external world, the environment, or the internal world, the self. Denial may be made more effective through exaggeration, negation, fantasy formation, or displacement.

1. *Denial by exaggeration:* A particular and often encountered response which exactly exaggerates, often in a caricatured way, the element which is laden with anxiety, to the point that it becomes apparently "foolish" and unreal.

2. *Denial through fantasy:* Denial is sometimes characteristically supported by the elaboration of fantasy which supplants certain anxiety-laden elements with more reassuring considerations. For example, "dreams of glory" may supplant and support a denial of either actual ineffectiveness or helplessness, or a sense of inadequacy.

Desexualization: A change in the quality of an instinctual impulse but not its object. It signifies a neutralization of the libinidal or aggressive cathexis of the object.

Detachment: The withdrawal of a libidinal or aggressive cathexis from an object. It usually is associated with elements of isolation and splitting off.

Displacement: As a defense mechanism involves a purposeful unconscious shifting from one object to another in the interest of solving a conflict. Although the object is changed, the instinctual nature of the impulse and its aim remain the same.

Intellectualization: Based on thinking as a special and limited variety of doing—the control of affects and impulses through thinking them instead of experiencing them. Intellectualization is a systematic overdoing of thinking, deprived of its affect, in order to defend against anxiety attributable to an unacceptable impulse. It is the thinking process, defensively directed against and replacing emotion and impulse. In that thinking has been in one sense defined as experimental action in small and contained degree, intellectualization restricts the individual to the realm of testing.

Introjection: Has as its prototype oral incorporation, which has libidinal as well as significant aggressive components. Introjection is similar to incorporation in that it is also close to the oral part drive, but it further connotes a specific defense and early ego functioning. Introjection specifies the perceiving and treating of that which is in fact outside as if it were inside one's self. Through introjection, an attempt is made to obliterate the existence of a separation between self and object.

Isolation: The intrapsychic separation of affect from content. Isolation is a *splitting off* process followed by three possibilities: (1) the idea is repressed, (2) the affect is repressed, (3) neither the idea nor the affect is repressed, but once separated the affect is displaced to a different or substitute thought. Isolation refers to "loss" of affect, whereas "emptying of content" refers to "loss" of the idea through repression, suppression, or distraction. *Compartmentalization* is a specialized form of isolation in which there is a keeping apart of sets of ideas or affects one from another.

Magical thinking: The treating of thinking as if it were doing; "thinking or wishing makes it so." In the discrimination of thought and action, reality testing is given up. Magical thinking is used illogically as a way of avoiding danger or fulfilling needs. It comes close to rituals. Animism and superstitions are manifestations of magical thinking.

Projection: The perceiving and treating of certain unacceptable inner impulses and their derivatives as if they were outside the self. The impulses may arise in the id, or activity of the superego may be so reflected, as, for example, in a hallucinated recrimination.

Rationalization: Attitudes, beliefs, or behavior which otherwise might be unacceptable may be justified by the incorrect application of a truth, or the invention of a convincing fallacy.

Reaction formation: The management of unacceptable impulses by permitting the expression of the impulse in an exactly antithetical form; in effect the expression of the unacceptable impulse in the negative. Reaction formation may be a temporarily invoked defense mechanism, but on the basis of a persistent instinctual conflict, it may become imbedded in the developing ego structure in the form of a character trait on a relatively permanent level.

Regression: (1) A return to a previous stage of functioning to avoid the anxieties and hostilities involved in later stages; a re-establishment of an earlier stage where conflict is less. As a purposive way of handling a specific conflictual situation, regression is a defense and an ego mechanism. It is a "way out" and, as it were, a flight into earlier modes of adjustment. (2) A return to earlier points of fixation marking modes of behavior that had been given up. This could well be an outcome of a breakdown of equilibrium at a later phase of development. It implies a conservative biological principle of adjustment, namely: The constant trend to attain instinctual gratification in one way or another and to return always and ever to earlier modes of doing so whenever more specialized and later developed modes fail. In this sense, regression is the outcome of instinctual biological trends.

Repression: Repression occupies a central position in the organization of the defensive measures and mechanisms of the ego. In almost every instance of defensive activity, repression plays a part in insuring the effectiveness of the various defenses. Repression is uniquely related to, and predominantly directed against, specific instinctual impulses.

In the historical evolution of the concept of repression, its special role in warding off unacceptable instinctual manifestations was recognized. In this regard, it is to be distinguished from all other defenses in its singular position in rendering these manifestations unconscious in the dynamic, economic, and structural sense. With the introduction of a systematic ego psychology, the concept of repression gained a new significance with regard to its effect on ego functioning. Much of ego function is in itself unconscious, in particular the operation of the entire defensive organization of the ego. Repression is the paramount mechanism through which this unconscious ego state is maintained, and the activity of the various defenses kept at an unconscious level. As an unanswered theoretical problem, there remains the unique relationship of repression to instinctual drive on the one hand, and its dynamic role with regard to the unconscious ego state on the other hand. As a consequence, the concept of repression is in need of fuller clarification, with special regard to its role in the interrelationship of ego and id, and of drive and ego function. It is our impression on the basis of clinical experience that the instinctual element implicit in defensive activity seems to be more emphatically repressed in the sense of unconsciousness [*Ucs.*] than the ego-functional element [*Ucs.→Pcs.*].

Restriction of ego function: The unconsciously determined limitation or renunciation of specific ego functions, singly or in combination, to avoid anxiety arising out of conflict with instinctual trends, with the superego, or with environmental forces or figures. Restriction of ego function may be relatively benign, involving little interference with overall ego effectiveness. Often, however, it becomes structuralized in the form of substantial inhibition of ego functioning, sometimes to so pathological an extent as to become symptom. (However, this touches upon the unsettled theoretical issue of the relationship between defense and symptom, and instinctualization of ego function.)

Somatization: The defensive conversion of psychic derivatives into bodily symptoms.

Sublimation: The gratification of an impulse whose goal is retained but whose aim, or aim and object, is changed from a socially objectionable one to a socially valued one. Libidinal sublimation involves the inhibition of the manifest sexual aspect and thus the renunciation of direct sexual gratification. There are, then, two aspects involved in the complex process of gratification through sublimation: (1) for the sexual drives, a desexualization as far as consciousness is concerned, and (2) the placing of a value judgment: replacing the aim, or aim and object, with something valued by the superego or society. There is a question, not yet answered, of whether a sublimation may be maintained exclusively, or only relatively, as a secondary autonomous function, on the basis of ego gratification. It seems that a sublimation remains supported, however slightly, by the original instinctual impulse, which is still active at an unconscious level.

Turning against the self: The turning back upon the self of an impulse directed against an object. This usually refers to an aggressive impulse, but may also refer to turning of libidinal feelings toward the self rather than toward an object. Turning against the self is displacement into one's self, but it is that singular displacement of using one's self as the object.

Undoing: Balancing or canceling out an unacceptable action, affect, or thought by a subsequent action, affect, or thought in contradictory terms.

Withdrawal: The removal of interest or affect from an object. There are two facets of withdrawal: (1) withdrawal occasioned by anxiety attributable to conflict were the interest to be maintained, and (2) withdrawal initiated by increased narcissistic requirements, as, for example, in times of illness or crisis such as pregnancy, etc.

NOTE 2

FREUD, SIGMUND

Inhibitions, Symptoms and Anxiety (1926)*

[A] sympton is a sign of, and a substitute for, an instinctual satisfaction which has remained in abeyance; it is a consequence of the process of repression. Repression proceeds from the ego when the latter—it may be at the behest of the superego—refuses to associate itself with an instinctual cathexis which has been aroused in the id. The ego is able by means of repression to keep the idea which is the vehicle of the reprehensible impulse from becoming conscious. Analysis shows that the idea often persists as an unconscious formation.

So far everything seems clear; but we soon come upon difficulties which have not as yet been solved. Up till now our account of what occurs in repression has laid great stress on this point of exclusion from consciousness. But it has left other points open to uncertainty. One question that arose was, what happened to the instinctual impulse which had been activated in the id and which sought satisfaction? The answer was an indirect one. It was that owing to the process of repression the pleasure that would have been expected from satisfaction had been transformed into unpleasure. But we were then faced with the problem of how the satisfaction of an instinct could produce unpleasure. The whole matter can be clarified, I think, if we commit ourselves to the definite statement that as a result of repression the intended course of the excitatory process in the id does not occur at all; the ego succeeds in inhibiting or deflecting it. . . . At the same time this view implies a concession to the ego that it can exert a very extensive influence over processes in the id, and we

---

* Reprinted from: 20 *The Standard Edition of the Complete Psychological Works of Sigmund Freud*, James Strachey, ed. London: The Hogarth Press and the Institute of Psychoanalysis, 1959, (pp. 91–93). Reprinted by permission of Hogarth and W. W. Norton & Co.

shall have to find out in what way it is able to develop such surprising powers.

It seems to me that the ego obtains this influence in virtue of its intimate connections with the perceptual system—connections which, as we know, constitute its essence and provide the basis of its differentiation from the id. The function of this system, which we have called *Pcpt.–Cs.*, is bound up with the phenomenon of consciousness. It receives excitations not only from outside but from within, and endeavors, by means of the sensations of pleasure and unpleasure which reach it from these quarters, to direct the course of mental events in accordance with the pleasure principle. We are very apt to think of the ego as powerless against the id; but when it is opposed to an instinctual process in the id it has only to give a "*signal of unpleasure*" in order to attain its object with the aid of that almost omnipotent institution, the pleasure principle. To take this situation by itself for a moment, we can illustrate it by an example from another field. Let us imagine a country in which a certain small faction objects to a proposed measure the passage of which would have the support of the masses. This minority obtains command of the press and by its help manipulates the supreme arbiter, "public opinion," and so succeeds in preventing the measure from being passed.

But this explanation opens up fresh problems. Where does the energy come from which is employed for giving the signal of unpleasure? Here we may be assisted by the idea that a defense against an unwelcome *internal* process will be modeled upon the defense adopted against an *external* stimulus, that the ego wards off internal and external dangers alike along identical lines. In the case of external danger the organism has recourse to attempts at flight. The first thing it does is to withdraw cathexis from the perception of the dangerous object; later on it discovers that it is a better plan to perform muscular movements of such a sort as will render perception of the dangerous object impossible even in the absense of any refusal to perceive it—that it is a better plan, that is, to remove itself from the sphere of danger. Repression is an equivalent of this attempt at flight. The ego withdraws its (preconscious) cathexis from the instinctual representative that is to be repressed and uses that cathexis for the purpose of releasing unpleasure (anxiety). The problem of how anxiety arises in connection with repression may be no simple one; but we may legitimately hold firmly to the idea that the ego is the actual seat of anxiety. . . .

This brings us to a further question: How is it possible, from an economic point of view, for a mere process of withdrawal and discharge, like the withdrawing of a preconscious ego cathexis, to produce unpleasure or anxiety, seeing that, according to our assumptions, unpleasure and anxiety can only arise as a result of an *increase* in cathexis? The reply is that this causal sequence should not be explained from an economic point of view. Anxiety is not newly created in repression; it is reproduced as an affective state in accordance with an already existing mnemic image. If we go further and inquire into the origin of that anxiety—and of affects in general—we shall be leaving the realm of pure psychology and entering the borderland of physiology. Affective states have become incorporated in the mind as precipitates of primeval traumatic experiences, and when a similar situation occurs they are revived like mnemic symbols. . . .

[M]ost of the repressions with which we have to deal in our therapeutic work are cases of *after* pressure. They presuppose the operation of earlier, *primal repressions* which exert an attraction on the more recent situation. Far too little is known as yet about the background and preliminary stages of repression. There is a danger of overestimating the part played in repression by the superego. We cannot at present say whether it is perhaps the emergence of the superego which provides the line of demarcation between primal repression and after pressure. At any rate, the earliest outbreaks of anxiety, which are of a very intense kind, occur before the superego has become differentiated. It is highly probable that the immediate precipitating causes of primal repressions are quantitative factors such as an excessive degree of excitation and the breaking through of the protective shield against stimuli.

This mention of the protective shield sounds a note which recalls to us the fact that repression occurs in two different situations—namely, when an undesirable instinctual impulse is aroused by some external perception, and when it arises internally without any such provocation. . . . But the protective shield exists only in regard to external stimuli, not in regard to internal instinctual demands.

So long as we direct our attention to the ego's attempt at flight we shall get no nearer to the subject of symptom formation. A symptom arises from an instinctual impulse which has been detrimentally affected by repression. If the ego, by making use of the signal of unpleasure, attains its object of completely suppressing the instinctual impulse, we learn nothing of how this has happened. We can only find out about it from those cases in which repression must be described as having to a greater or less extent failed. In this event the position, generally speaking, is that the instinctual impulse has found a substitute in spite of repression, but a substitute which is very much reduced, displaced, and inhibited and which is no longer recognizable as a satisfaction. And when the substitutive impulse is carried out there is no sensation of pleasure; its carrying out has, instead, the quality of a compulsion.

In thus degrading a process of satisfaction to a symptom, repression displays its power in a further respect. The substitutive process is prevented, if possible, from finding discharge through motility; and even if this cannot be done, the process is forced to expend itself in making alterations in the subject's own body and is not permitted to impinge upon the external world. It must not be transformed into action. For, as we know, in repression the ego is operating under the influence of external reality and therefore it debars the substitutive process from having any effect upon that reality.

Just as the ego controls the path to action in regard to the external world, so it controls access to consciousness. In repression it exercises its power in both directions, acting in the one manner upon the instinctual impulse itself and in the other upon the [physical] representative of that impulse. At this point it is relevant to ask how I can reconcile this acknowledgment of the might of the ego with the description of its position which I gave in *The Ego and the Id*. In that book I drew a picture of its dependent relationship to the id and to the superego and revealed how powerless and apprehensive it was in regard to both and with what an effort it maintained its show of superiority over them. This view has been widely echoed in psychoanalytic literature. Many writers have laid much stress on the weakness of the ego in relation to the id and of our rational elements in the face of the demonic forces within us; and they display a strong tendency to make what I have said into a cornerstone of a psychoanalytic *Weltanschauung*. Yet surely the psychoanalyst, with his knowledge of the way in which repression works, should, of all people, be restrained from adopting such an extreme and one-sided view.

*   *   *

. . . The apparent contradiction is due to our having taken abstractions too rigidly and attended exclusively now to the one side and now to the other of what is in fact a complicated state of affairs. We were justified, I think, in dividing the ego from the id, for there are certain considerations which necessitate that step. On the other hand the ego is identical with the id, and is merely a specially differentiated part of it. If we think of this part by itself in contradistinction to the whole, or if a real split has occurred between the two, the weakness of the ego becomes apparent. But if the ego remains bound up with the id and indistinguishable from it, then it displays its strength. The same is true of the relation between the ego and the superego. In many situations the two are merged; and as a rule we can only distinguish one from the other when there is a tension or conflict between them. In repression the decisive fact is that the ego is an organization and the id is not. The ego is, indeed, the organized portion of the id. We should be quite wrong if we pictured the ego and the id as two opposing camps and if we supposed that, when the ego tries to suppress a part of the id by means of repression, the remainder of the id comes to the rescue of the endangered part and measures its strength with the ego. This may often be what happens, but it is certainly not the initial situation in repression. As a rule the instinctual impulse which is to be repressed remains isolated. Although the act of repression demonstrates the strength of the ego, in one particular it reveals the ego's powerlessness and how impervious to influence are the separate instinctual impulses of the id. For the mental process which has been turned into a symptom owing to repression now maintains its existence outside the organization of the ego and independently of it. Indeed, it is not that process alone but all its derivatives which enjoy, as it were, this same privilege of extraterritoriality; and whenever they come into associative contact with a part of the ego organization, it is not at all certain that they will not draw that part over to themselves and thus enlarge themselves at the expense of the ego. An analogy with which we have long been familiar compared a symptom to a foreign body which was keeping up a constant succession of stimuli and reactions in the tissue in which it was embedded. It does sometimes happen that the defensive struggle against an unwelcome instinctual impulse is brought to an end with the formation of a symptom. As far as can be seen, this is most often possible in hysterical conversion. But usually the outcome is different. The initial act of repression is followed by a tedious or interminable sequel in which the struggle against the instinctual impulse is prolonged into a struggle against the symptom.

In this secondary defensive struggle the ego presents two faces with contradictory expressions. The one line of behavior it adopts springs from the fact that its very nature obliges it to make what must be regarded as an attempt at restoration or reconciliation. The ego is an organization. It is based on the maintenance of free intercourse and of the possibility of reciprocal influence between all its parts. Its desexualized energy still shows traces of its origin in its impulse to bind together and unify, and this necessity to synthesize grows stronger in proportion as the strength of the ego increases. It is therefore only natural that the ego should try to prevent symptoms from remaining isolated and alien by using every possible method to bind them to itself in one way or another, and to incorporate them into its organization by means of those bonds. As we know, a tendency of this kind is already operative in the very act of forming a symptom. A classical instance of this are those hysterical symptoms which have been shown to be a compromise between the need for satisfaction and the need for punishment. Such symptoms participate in the ego from the very beginning, since they fulfil a requirement of the superego, while on the other hand they represent positions occupied by the repressed and points at which an irruption has been made by it into the ego organization. They are a kind of frontier station with a mixed garrison. . . . The ego now proceeds to behave as though it recognized that the sympton had come to stay and that the only thing to do was to accept the situation in good part and draw as much advantage from it as possible. It makes an adaptation to the sympton—to this piece of the internal world which is alien to it—just as it normally does to the real external world. It can always find plenty of opportunities for doing so. The presence of a symptom may entail a certain impairment of capacity, and this can be exploited to appease some demand on the part of the superego or to refuse some claim from the external world. In this way the symptom gradually comes to be the representative of important interests; it is found to be useful in asserting the position of the self and becomes more and more closely merged with the ego and more and more indispensable to it. It is only very rarely that the physical process of "healing" round a foreign body follows such a course as this. There is a danger, too, of exaggerating the importance of a secondary adaptation of this kind to a symptom, and of saying that the ego has created the symptom merely in order to enjoy its advantages. It would be equally true to say that a man who had lost his leg in the war had got it shot away so that he might thenceforward live on his pension without having to do any more work.

In obsessional neurosis and paranoia the forms which the symptoms assume become very valuable to the ego because they obtain for it, not certain advantages, but a narcissistic satisfaction which it would otherwise be without. The systems which the obsessional neurotic constructs flatter his self-love by making him feel that he is better than other people because he is specially cleanly or specially conscientious. The delusional constructions of the paranoic offer to his acute perceptive and imaginative powers a field of activity which he could not easily find elsewhere.

All of this results in what is familiar to us as the "(secondary) gain from illness" which follows a neurosis. This gain comes to the assistance of the ego in its endeavor to incorporate the symptom and increases the symptom's fixation. When the analyst tries subsequently to help the ego in its struggle against the symptom, he finds that these conciliatory bonds between ego and symptom operate on the side of the resistances and that they are not easy to loosen.

The two lines of behavior which the ego adopts toward the symptom are in fact directly opposed to each other. For the other line is less friendly in character, since it continues in the direction of repression. Nevertheless the ego, it appears, cannot be accused of inconsistency. Being of a peaceable disposition it would like to incorporate the symptom and make it part of itself. It is from the symptom itself that the

trouble comes. For the symptom, being the true substitute for and derivative of the repressed impulse, carries on the role of the latter; it continually renews its demands for satisfaction and thus obliges the ego in its turn to give the signal of unpleasure and put itself in a posture of defense.

The secondary defensive struggle against the symptom takes many shapes. It is fought out on different fields and makes use of a variety of methods. . . .

NOTE 3

SEITZ, PHILIP F.

Experiments in the Substitution of Symptoms by Hypnosis*

The patient was a forty-one-year-old white, single man. He was referred for psychiatric study by a neurologist in a Veterans Hospital. The chief complaint was a coarse, parkinsonian-like tremor of the hands and forearms. The patient had been in a Veterans Hospital for two years because of this symptom. Until the referring neurologist suspected the presence of hysteria, the diagnosis had been postencephalitic parkinsonism.

The history of the present illness revealed that the patient had been well, except for "sick headaches" four times a year, until he entered the Army in 1942. At that time he developed influenza, had a temperature of 106°F., and was in a hospital for one week. He was rehospitalized about one month later because of stomach pains, chills, and fever. This hospitalization lasted for almost three months, following which he was discharged from the service for medical reasons.

In 1943, after discharge from the service, he entered a Veterans Hospital and was found to have a duodenal ulcer. This condition was treated medically and the patient's symptoms improved. However, he still had abdominal pain occasionally, and had epigastric soreness most of the time. In 1946 he had a "nervous breakdown" during which he alternated between crying and "wild hysterical spells." He also had an exacerbation of stomach cramps and pain at that time. He was unable to work for about four months, following which he returned to his job as an auto mechanic.

In 1948, two years prior to the present study, he developed the parkinsonian-like tremor of his hands and forearms. He could remember no unusual emotional disturbances associated with onset of the tremor. He claimed that one day, while lying on a couch thinking of nothing in particular, his hands and arms began trembling. (In later interviews, he underwent an intense abreaction of feelings connec-

---

* 15 *Psychosomatic Medicine*, 1953. (pp. 405–9). Reprinted by permission.

ted with an experience which occurred the day preceding onset of his tremor. The incident was a fight with his boss. In a fit of anger, his boss called him a "son of a bitch" and a "mother fucker." The patient went out of control and tried to strangle the man. He was prevented from killing the boss by other employees. Within twenty-four hours after this fight the tremor began.)

[D]iagnostic interviewing revealed the following: The presenting symptom was a rapid, coarse, jerking of the hands and forearms in an oblique direction from above and near his body to downward and away from his body. The frequency of the tremor was approximately five times a second. The hands were held in a half-flexed, grasping position. No "pill-rolling" of the thumb and fingers was present. The tremor was absent during sleep. (In later interviews the symbolic meaning of this tremor was brought out clearly. The tremor represented a rapid alternation between reaching out to strangle and drawing back to inhibit the homicidal impulse.) Several other symptoms were elicited in the review of systems. He had "sick headaches," followed by stiff neck, several times a year. He had difficulty concentrating, occasionally saw spots before his eyes, and was hard of hearing in his left ear. In high places he experienced marked vertigo. He had hemorrhoids, was sometimes short of breath without exertion, and often experienced fluttering and pain in his heart. He had frequency of urination and difficulty in starting his urinary stream. He denied any difficulty with sexual potency, but said that he had no interest in sex.

He was the only child of American-born parents in a small midwestern town. His father, who was seventy-one years old, had been a miner and was retired following an injury to his back in the mines. The patient referred to his father as "Daddy," and described him as "an average man who neither smoked nor drank." The patient was unable to describe his relationship to his father, and consistently denied any conflict with him. His mother, who was also seventy-one, had mild rheumatism. He described her, as he did his father, as an idealized person free of any faults. He referred to her as "Mommy." Information concerning the patient's infancy and childhood was meager, since he said he could remember nothing about it. He insisted that he had a "perfect childhood." He was always very close to his mother. "She made over me a lot—still does, in fact." He did average work in school, but was always somewhat shy and timid socially. He could remember no close friends at any time in his life. In high school he had no dates because girls never interested him. He denied masturbation or any other sexual activities. He had lived with his parents his entire life, except for the short time he was away in the Army and the periods of hospitalization.

After finishing high school, he attended a teachers' college for one year. At that time he suffered a broken arm in an automobile accident, and received a considerable amount of money as a legal settlement for his injury. He spent the money to pay off the mortgage on his parents' home, and lost interest in completing his college work. He worked as an auto mechanic, changing jobs frequently, during the next twenty years. Since his discharge from the service he had worked only sporadically. He had no friends, and spent most of his time driving around the small town in which he lived.

The patient was a short, stocky man with hair greying at the temples. His face was ruddy, his expression bland and indifferent. He sat on the edge of his chair with his tremulous hands and arms extended in front of him. At times he gripped the arms of the chair; but the tremor became more marked when he did this, so he would re-extend them in front of himself. He spoke in a rather childlike and naive manner. He was excessively courteous and ingratiating. At all times during the interviews he was alert and interested, answering questions quickly and to the point. The stream of thought was logical, coherent, and relevant. His mood was neither elevated nor depressed, affect was appropriate and content of thought revealed no special preoccupations. Large memory gaps, especially for childhood, were present. Otherwise the sensorium was clear.

The diagnostic impression following initial interviewing was "conversion reaction, hysterical tremor of hands and arms, in a schizoid character." Psychological tests support this diagnosis. On the basis of psychiatric interviewing, the hysterical tremor was formulated dynamically as a symbolic expression and inhibition of patricidal impulses having oedipal origin.

In view of the schizoid character disturbance, the investigator was uncertain regarding the feasibility of hypnotic symptom manipulations in this patient. The history had revealed that on at least one previous occasion, homicidal impulses had burst out of repression; and, in a dissociated state, the patient had almost committed murder. The hysterical symptom of tremor, therefore, acted as a defense against a not too well compensated psychotic reaction. However, the neurotic defense had become stabilized over a two-year period, and several other symptomatic defenses (such as headache, hysterical deafness, and chest pain) were present. These features suggested that hypnotic symptom manipulation might be done safely, since other symptomatic defenses were already available.

The patient was seen for psychotherapeutic interviews at weekly intervals. During these appointments, approximately thirty minutes were devoted to interviewing the patient in a waking state, and the other half hour to hypnotic studies. The patient was readily hypnotizable, achieving deep somnambulistic trances for which he was spontaneously amnesic. Reliving of the fight with his boss was induced hypnotically by telling him to remember what happened just before his tremor developed. Although the subsequent abreaction was intense, it was not out of control. This finding further supported the impression that hypnotic symptom substitution would be safely possible. The investigator decided to proceed very cautiously with hypnotic experiments in symptom substitution.

Experiment 1

During a deep hypnotic trance the patient was told that the jerking of his hands and arms would be absent upon awakening. No substitute symptom was suggested, since the aim of this experiment was to determine what symptom would replace the tremor spontaneously. Following the trance the tremor was absent; but in its place the patient now exhibited marked torticollis, with his head twisted far to the left, and his eyes turned to the left. The patient was rehypnotized and asked what his thoughts were in connection with the "wry neck." His associations were about hanging, his neck being broken by hanging, strangulation, and his head being twisted off. A symbolic connection between the original conversion symptom and the spontaneous substitute symptom was readily apparent in this experiment. The original symptom defensively expressed the impulse to strangle. The substitute symptom dramatized masochistically the talion punishment of being strangled by hanging. Attention is called to the fact that, in this first experiment, the substitute symptom, like the original conversion reaction, found expression in the voluntary muscular organ system.

Experiment 2

In a later interview, the patient was hypnotized and told that the tremor would be absent when he awakened. No substitute symptom was suggested, but he was told that "wry neck" would also not occur posthypnotically. The aim of this procedure was to determine what other symptoms could replace the original conversion reaction. Upon awakening from the trance the tremor was absent, and torticollis did not develop. This time he became very pale, sweat stood out on his brow, and he began to gag, choke, and vomit. When he was rehypnotized and asked to tell his thoughts about this reaction his associations were: Being choked, gagging, and his throat being blocked. Once again, the substitute symptoms appeared to have a symbolic relationship to the original conversion reaction.

The original symptom of tremor defensively expressed phallic-aggressive impulses through voluntary muscular activity. In this second experiment, the replacement symptoms were vegetative reactions which involved a shift toward the interior of the body, and were expressed principally in oral terms. The "psychodynamic equivalence" of the symptoms must,

therefore, involve relationships in terms of regressive depth, as well as in terms of symbolism. Expressed in another way, the relationships between "equivalent symptoms" may be vertical as well as horizontal. The first replacement symptom (torticollis) was dynamically related to the original conversion reaction by virtue of symbolic similarity; but both were phallic level activities expressed through the voluntary muscular system (horizontal equivalence). The second replacement symptoms (gagging–choking–vomiting) were symbolically related to the original conversion reaction, but at a deeper regressive level, expressed through vegetative activities in the upper gastrointestinal tract (vertical equivalence). The alternation between gastrointestinal and frankly hysterical symptoms in this patient's past history may be explained by this concept.

Experiment 3

On another occasion the patient was again hypnotized and told that his tremor would be absent posthypnotically. No substitute symptom was suggested, but the patient was instructed that neither the "wry neck" nor gagging, choking, and vomiting would occur. The purpose of this experiment was to investigate still other spontaneous substitutes for the original conversion reaction. Following the trance, the tremor was absent. The patient complained of severe headache, which he described as a "bursting pressure" in his head. He was rehypnotized and asked to talk about his thoughts in connection with the headache. His associations were about strangulation, his circulation cut off, throbbing in his head, and pressure building up to the bursting point. A relationship between the original conversion reaction and the replacement symptom was again apparent.

In this experiment, the spontaneous substitute symptom involved a shift into the head. According to a theory proposed by Kepecs, the ascent of symptoms into the head is associated with unconscious feelings and impulses which are approaching awareness or action. The results of the next experiment appear to support Kepecs' concept.

Experiment 4

Only one further hypnotic experiment was conducted in this case, for reasons which will be evident. The same procedure as outlined above was followed, the purpose being to elicit still other spontaneous substitute symptoms. Following the trance, the tremor was absent; and, as had been suggested, the previous substitute symptoms did not develop. This time the patient exhibited a dazed facial expression posthypnotically. He shook his head a few times as if to clear it, then arose from his chair and advanced toward the investigator. His hands were outstretched in a grasping position toward the investigator's throat. He was rehypnotized quickly and told to go back and sit down, which he did. The final hypnotic instructions were that when he awakened he would again have the tremor, and that through further treatment he would find healthier solutions to his problems. Following this trance the tremor was present, and no further hypnotic experiments were attempted. In this instance, the replacement symptom was a psychotic dissociated state in which the impulse to strangle was acted out.

In this series of experiments, the original conversion reaction affecting the hands and arms was replaced successively by substitute symptoms which involved first the neck, then the upper gastrointestinal tract, then within the head itself, and finally acting out of the patricidal impulse. These findings suggest, in line with Kepecs' observations and hypotheses, that shifts in symptoms toward the head may indicate that ego-alien impulses and feelings are nearing awareness or action. In the present case, the third replacement symptom of "bursting pressure in the head" appears to have presaged the impending dissociated state and acting out.

The results of these investigations also suggest that this experimental method involves certain dangers which must be anticipated and controlled. The principal complication to be avoided is hypnotic removal of symptoms which defend against potentially psychotic dissociative reactions. Attention is also called to the fact that all four replacement reactions in this case were previously present in the patient's repertoire of symptoms. For a number of years he had had "sick headaches," followed by "stiff neck." His first three hypnotically induced substitute symptoms were torticollis, upper gastrointestinal symptoms, and headache. The fourth replacement symptom—dissociated acting out of the patricidal impulse—had occurred two years previously, in association with onset of his tremor. These observations suggest that substitute symptoms tend to draw upon the patient's previous symptomatic defenses. According to this concept, the types of symptoms which a patient might develop during treatment or in the future should be predictable, to some extent, in terms of the past history of psychogenic symptoms.

NOTE 4

HARTMANN, HEINZ

Notes on the Theory of Sublimation*

The most common definition refers to sublimation as a deflection of the sexual drives from instinctual aims to aims which are socially or culturally more acceptable or valued. There may also be a change of objects. In this definition, sublimation is actually a

---

* Reprinted from: Hartmann, H. *Essays in Ego Psychology.* New York: International Universities Press, 1964. (pp. 216–36). Reprinted by permission.

special case of displacement, special in the sense that it includes only those displacements that lead to the substitution of worthy aims. The advantage of this approach was that it clearly stated that the highest achievements of man—art, science, religion—may have and often do have their origin in libidinal tendencies. But some authors, e.g., Bernfeld and Sterba, have objected to this definition, pointing out quite correctly that it is always questionable to include value judgments in the definition of a mental process—which, of course, does not mean that the function of valuation cannot be made the object of empirical studies. At any rate, on the basis of such a definition every inquiry into the relations between sublimation and the creation of values rests more or less on a *petitio principii.*

It was, therefore, a reasonable suggestion to eliminate the element of value judgment and to speak of ego-syntonic aims (Bernfeld). This important emendation still left many questions unanswered. We are used to saying that in sublimation ego aims are substituted for instinctual aims, which may be accompanied by a change of objects. But is it really true that it depends only on the aims (and objects) whether or not we can speak of sublimated activities? Here we meet the problem of the relations between sublimation and sexualization. Some definitions of sublimation leave open the question what the differences between the two processes are; or rather, they forget to make this distinction. Clinically, we know that sexualization of ego functions, beyond a certain limit, interferes with proper functioning, while in a large field of human activities successful functioning depends on sublimation.

In the case of sexualization, we often say that an ego function has, mostly unconsciously, been invested with a "sexual meaning"; I remind you also of certain forms of inhibition which may ensue. However, this concept of "meaning" is in need of clarification. Obviously, in the case of sublimation, too, we may find unconscious genetic determinants of a sexual character. One could try to relate the differences between sublimation and sexualization to the preponderance of the secondary or the primary process; to the degree to which the functions in question are, or are not, realitysyntonic; to whether suppression of the function can lead to anxiety; to how likely it is that the ego activity changes into direct instinctual gratification, and so on.

[I]t seems that a clear presentation of this problem calls for the introduction of metapsychological concepts. And for the purpose of this discussion we will retain the fact that basing the concept of sublimation on the aims of behavior only will of necessity fall short of a satisfactory definition.

*   *   *

In *The Ego and the Id* Freud equates desexualization and sublimation; and thought processes are quite generally subsumed under sublimation. Somewhat later he stated—again quite generally—that the ego works with desexualized energy. . . . Freud did not systematically synchronize the concept of sublimation with the new level of his psychological thinking; but his later statements imply fundamental changes which ought to be spelled out and challenge further development. Here the stage is reached at which sublimation, as other psychoanalytic concepts before, refers to a psychological process, this process being a change in the mode of energy, away from an instinctual and toward a noninstinctual mode. This formulation eliminates the doubts concerning earlier concepts of sublimation that did not account for the clinically essential differences between sublimation and sexualization. Moreover, we see the relations between displacement and sublimation in a new light; not only the aims are (usually) changed in sublimation, but also the mode of the cathexis is. It is even likely that the same aim of the ego may be pursued at times with less, at times with more, sublimated energy; this can be studied in the play of children and in other developmentally relevant ego activities.

The process of sublimation can be linked with several mechanisms, of which displacement is only one. I just mention identification, whose importance in this respect has often been emphasized by Freud and many others. Even more important, the correlation between change of mode of energies, on the one hand, and change of aims or objects, on the other hand, has again become a topic of empirical research, being no longer prejudged, as it was, by too narrow a definition. On this basis, the role of sublimation in the formation of objects, particularly constant objects, can be hypothesized. Freud approached this subject in speaking of the "tender" or "aim-deflected" strivings toward an object and thought that "if we want," we could consider them as a "beginning" of sublimatory processes. I suppose we could assign them their place as one of the many shades of neutralization in the continuum from fully instinctual to fully neutralized energy, a subject we shall have to deal with later.

That all ego functions are fed by desexualized or sublimated energy (later we will say: by neutralized energy), is indeed only the last touch Freud gave his gradually evolving ideas on the ego, which step by step emphasized its importance in the mental economy. It is with this turn in his theory formation that the problems which sublimation poses become essential for our metapsychological understanding of the ego. If we agree with Freud's later proposition, we will tend to see in sublimation not a more or less occasional happening but rather a continuous process, which, of course, does not exclude temporary increases or decreases in sublimatory activities. This hypothesis will, of course, also be one more reason for us, and a decisive one, no longer to limit the study of

sublimation to culturally or socially valuable achievements only. . . .

* * *

. . . We have accepted Freud's idea that sublimation of libido is a process by which the ego is provided with energy appropriate to its special needs; that is, the energies the ego uses for its specific functions are as a rule not instinctual, they are desexualized. But is there a parallel to this with aggressive energy? I assume . . . that the mode of the aggressive energies too can be changed, in a way comparable to desexualization. It also appears that this desaggressivized energy is no less important for the formation and the function of the ego than is desexualized libido. This, then, implies that self-destruction is not the only alternative to aggression being turned outward; neutralization is another alternative. If desexualization is really correlated with defusion of instincts the possible dangers inherent in such defusion could still be counteracted, as long as the capacity to neutralize aggression is unimpaired. If we further assume that self-preservation is, in man, to a considerable degree a function of the ego, we will come to the conclusion that it is actually dependent on neutralization.

We call neutralization the change of both libidinal and aggressive energy away from the instinctual and toward a noninstinctual mode.[1] The process of neutralization is essential in what we usually call sublimation, and it is mostly this aspect I am dealing with in this paper. But what is the relation of the two terms? There are several terminological possibilities. We may continue to speak of sublimation only in the case where neutralization of libido is involved, because this is the way it was meant by Freud and is still dominant in analytic literature. One may also use the

---

1. This term has occasionally been interpreted as referring to instinctual energy somewhere in between libido and aggression. But this is at variance with the term as we use it here. Also, "neutralization" does not mean instinct fusion—though the two processes may be interrelated. In Freud's work one occasionally finds the word *neutralisieren* (to neutralize); e.g., "as a result of the combination of unicellular organisms into multicellular forms of life, the death instinct of the single cell can successfully be neutralized," or "libido . . . serves to neutralize the destructive impulses which are simultaneously present." However, this word is not defined by Freud as a technical term, but rather is used as interchangeable with a number of other words. At any rate, it is clear that its use does not coincide with "neutralization" as defined above. In another context Freud speaks of "*indifferente Energie*," which is assumed to be "desexualized libido" and "sublimated energy." "*Indifferente Energie*" is rendered by the translator of the *Standard Edition* as "neutral energy." Still what Freud describes in that passage is in some respects but not fully identical with either "neutralized energy" or "primary ego energy," in the sense in which these concepts are used here. The latter concepts are closer to what is a later and clearly different hypothesis advanced by Freud (it has been widely neglected in analytic literature): The general assumption that the ego works with desexualized energy.

word sublimation for the desinstinctualization of both aggression and libido, making it a synonym of neutralization. An alternative suggestion would reserve the term for the change of aims, often associated with neutralization. Again, the term is sometimes used for the nondefensive, in contradistinction to the defensive, ego functions, and for their aims and cathexis. This question of nomenclature cannot be too important in itself and, for the purpose of my presentation, a decision between these alternatives does not seem necessary. What I want to remind you of here is just that much of what I said before about "sublimation" refers to the process now defined as "neutralization." In what follows you will see from the context where I speak of this process and where I refer to other aspects often associated with the concept of sublimation.

Beyond emphasizing the central position of the process of neutralization in general in the build-up of the ego, and in its differentiation from the id, a certain number of more specific hypotheses are necessary to organize and clarify our thinking on the great variety of phenomena we have in mind in speaking of ego functions. In what follows, I shall, then, attempt to develop some such propositions based upon Freud's statements quoted above, on the desinstinctualized character of the mode of energy used by the ego. It is, of course, in elaborating the implications of these propositions, and their applications with respect to specific problems, that their usefulness will have to be tested.

The question is often discussed in analytic literature whether moral masochism, or play, or any number of phenomena "are" or "are not" sublimations. But this is not just an either–or question. I think, it comes closer to observable facts if we speak, as I suggested, not just of two modes of energy of each drive: instinctual or neutralized. Both clinical experience and theory point to the probability that there exists a continuum of gradations of energy, from the fully instinctual to the fully neutralized mode. . . .

If we accept this proposition, the next problem would then be what degrees of neutralization are commonly used for certain ego activities. Individual differences, differences as to situation and developmental level, must of course be considered. But some generalizations may be hypothesized. To draw my example from aggression: There is the unmitigated form of free aggression; the aggression the superego uses in its relations to the ego is already partly modified; even further removed from instinctual energy is the one the ego . . . employs in countercathexis—but it is still aggression and also retains that element of aggression, "fight"; we find the highest degree of neutralization of aggression in nondefensive ego activities. It is not unlikely that differences between instinctual and neutralized energy go mostly parallel with the differences between primary and secondary

processes. This would mean that in this respect, too, transitory phases have to be considered.

* * *

Once the ego has accumulated a reservoir of neutralized energy of its own, it will—in interaction with the outer and inner world—develop aims and functions whose cathexis can be derived from this reservoir, which means that they have not always to depend on *ad hoc* neutralizations. Stating this more completely and with reference to the relationships of the ego and the id (here I do not want to broaden this statement to include the interactions with the superego), we may say: The ego accepts some instinctual tendencies and helps them toward gratification, without change of aims or of the mode of energy involved. In other cases, it will substitute ego aims for aims of the id. This can be done in a variety of ways. The ego aims may lie in the direction of id tendencies; they may be opposed to them (countercathexis); the third group are those nondefensive aims the ego, as I just said, sets itself in the course of development. Ego aims will normally be fed by neutralized energy and achieve a certain amount of secondary autonomy. But ego aims may, under certain conditions, also be cathected with instinctual energy—the case we call sexualization and aggressivization. In the first case, in which these aims use neutralized energy, the energy is either drawn from *ad hoc* acts of neutralization, or provided by the reservoir of neutralized energy at the ego's disposal.

We see that the ego gradually gains a comparative independence from immediate outside or inside pressure, a fact that one is used to considering (though usually not in this terminology) as a general trend in human development. Thus we may say that while displacements partly determine the directions neutralization takes, it is also true that neutralization can lead displacements, because, as a rule, different degrees of neutralization are not equally well suited for all aims and functions of the ego. . . .

There are considerable variations in this respect also from one individual to the other. And in the same individual the level of neutralization, as to one specific function, is not constant. It seems, furthermore, that neutralization of libidinal and of aggressive energy varies independently—or rather partly independently. . . .

* * *

. . . Sublimation has often been described as a defense mechanism, and it is true that it represents one of the most efficient means to deal with "danger" threatening from the drives. Thus it can be used as defense, though it is not always and often not only defense, as it takes care, economically speaking, of the nondefensive functions of the ego too. I may add that even where it serves defense, sublimation is hardly a "mechanism" in the usual sense. If we compare it with other defensive measures, there is also this difference that the change of instinctual to neutralized energy forms at least one element of its definition, thus setting sublimation apart from other defense methods, the concept of none of which refers to a change in the mode of energy. We may say that the process of neutralization in itself, and in general, can serve defensive purposes, far beyond the more special case in which certain shades of neutralized aggression are used in countercathexis.

* * *

From what I said, it already clearly appears that neutralization (the change of the purely instinctual strivings into a mode of energy more appropriate to the functions of the ego, together with the delay of immediate instinctual discharge, the control by the ego) plays a decisive part in the mastery of reality. The formation of constant and independent objects, the institution of the reality principle, with all its aspects, thinking, action, intentionality, all depend on neutralization. According to Hart, it is a compromise between instinct and reality. As I said before, if we accept Freud's statement that self-preservation, in man, is mostly taken care of by the ego, we come to understand neutralization also as a powerful help to this central biological aspect of man, not as its opponent as it has occasionally been described. Besides reality testing and the mechanisms of adaptation, the integrating (or synthetic, or organizing) functions share in the maintenance of self-preservation; and they too are not purely instinctual in character but mostly belong to those that work with neutralized energy, though they may be in part genetically traceable to the instincts, as are other neutralizations.

* * *

NOTE 5

KNIGHT, ROBERT P.

Introjection, Projection, and Identification*

The question comes up . . . whether or not these mechanisms [of defense], by definition unconscious, can actually be conscious or partly conscious. Recognizing that the fundamental process or pattern is unconscious, I believe that there can be various degrees of conscious awareness of or insight into what is going on. When I say, "If I were you, I would do so and so," or when I speak of putting myself in someone else's place, I am, for the time being, orienting my relationship to the object in question so that temporary identification with him results through the

* 9 *The Psychoanalytic Quarterly*, 1940 (p. 338). Reprinted by permission.

projection of my own feelings onto him and possibly also my introjection of him. The adage, "Set a thief to catch a thief," and the observation that a successful criminal might make a successful detective, or vice versa, may be explained from this same point of view. The success of either thief or detective in outwitting the other is based on his capacity to project his own countertendencies onto and thus identify himself with the other. Perhaps it might be more accurate to view the resulting identification as a more or less conscious affair and still regard the elementary processes by which it is achieved, projection and introjection, as unconscious mechanisms operating in response to the conscious wish or need to identify with another.

3.

FREUD, SIGMUND

Analysis Terminable and Interminable (1937)*

* * *

If we ask what is the source of the great variety of kinds and degrees of alteration of the ego, we cannot escape the first obvious alternative, that such alterations are either congenital or acquired. Of these, the second sort will be the easier to treat. If they are acquired, it will certainly have been in the course of development, starting from the first years of life. For the ego has to try from the very outset to fulfil its task of mediating between its id and the external world in the service of the pleasure principle, and to protect the id from the dangers of the external world. If, in the course of these efforts, the ego learns to adopt a defensive attitude toward its own id as well and to treat the latter's instinctual demands as external dangers, this happens, at any rate in part, because it understands that a satisfaction of instinct would lead to conflicts with the external world. Thereafter, under the influence of education, the ego grows accustomed to removing the scene of the fight from outside to within and to mastering the *internal* danger before it has become an *external* one; and probably it is most often right in doing so. During this fight on two fronts—later there will be a third front as well—the ego makes use of various procedures for fulfilling its task, which, to put it in general terms, is to avoid danger, anxiety, and unpleasure. We call these procedures *"mechanisms of defense."* Our knowledge of them is not yet sufficiently complete. . . .

It was from one of these mechanisms, repression,[1]

* Reprinted from: 23 *The Standard Edition of the Complete Psychological Works of Sigmund Freud*, James Strachey, ed. London: The Hogarth Press and the Institute of Psychoanalysis, 1964. (pp. 235–43). Reprinted by permission of Hogarth and Basic Books.

1. All repressions take place in early childhood; they are primitive defensive measures taken by the immature, feeble ego. In later years no fresh repressions are carried out; but

that the study of neurotic processes took its whole start. There was never any doubt that repression was not the only procedure which the ego could employ for its purposes. Nevertheless, repression is something quite peculiar and is more sharply differentiated from the other mechanisms than they are from one another. I should like to make this relation to the other mechanisms clear by an analogy, though I know that in these matters analogies never carry us very far. Let us imagine what might have happened to a book, at a time when books were not printed in editions but were written out individually. We will suppose that a book of this kind contained statements which in later times were regarded as undesirable. . . . At the present day, the only defensive mechanism to which the official censorship could resort would be to confiscate and destroy every copy of the whole edition. At that time, however, various methods were used for making the book innocuous. One way would be for the offending passages to be thickly crossed through so that they were illegible. In that case they could not be transcribed, and the next copyist of the book would produce a text which was unexceptionable but which had gaps in certain passages, and so might be unintelligible in them. Another way, however, if the authorities were not satisfied with this, but wanted also to conceal any indication that the text had been mutilated, would be for them to proceed to distort the text. Single words would be left out or replaced by others, and new sentences interpolated. Best of all, the whole passage would be erased and a new one which said exactly the opposite put in its place. The next transcriber could then produce a text that aroused no suspicion but which was falsified. It no longer contained what the author wanted to say; and it is highly probable that the corrections had not been made in the direction of truth.

If the analogy is not pursued too strictly, we may say that repression has the same relation to the other methods of defense as omission has to distortion of the text, and we may discover in the different forms of this falsification parallels to the variety of ways in which the ego is altered. An attempt may be made to

the old ones persist, and their services continue to be made use of by the ego for mastering the instincts. New conflicts are disposed of by what we call "after-repression." We may apply to these infantile repressions our general statement that repressions depend absolutely and entirely on the relative strength of the forces involved and that they cannot hold out against an increase in the strength of the instincts. Analysis, however, enables the ego, which has attained greater maturity and strength, to undertake a revision of these old repressions; a few are demolished, while others are recognized but constructed afresh out of more solid material. These new dams are of quite a different degree of firmness from the earlier ones; we may be confident that they will not give way so easily before a rising flood of instinctual strength. Thus the real achievement of analytic therapy would be the subsequent correction of the original process of repression, a correction which puts an end to the dominance of the quantitative factor. [Ibid. at p. 227.]

raise the objection that the analogy goes wrong in an essential point, for the distortion of a text is the work of a tendentious censorship, no counterpart to which is to be found in the development of the ego. But this is not so; for a tendentious purpose of this kind is to a great extent represented by the compelling force of the pleasure principle. The psychical apparatus is intolerant of unpleasure; it has to fend it off at all costs, and if the perception of reality entails unpleasure, that perception—that is, the truth—must be sacrificed. Where external dangers are concerned, the individual can help himself for some time by flight and by avoiding the situation of danger, until he is strong enough later on to remove the threat by actively altering reality. But one cannot flee from oneself; flight is no help against internal dangers. And for that reason the defensive mechanisms of the ego are condemned to falsify one's internal perception and to give one only an imperfect and distorted picture of one's id. In its relations to the id, therefore, the ego is paralyzed by its restrictions or blinded by its errors; and the result of this in the sphere of psychical events can only be compared to being out walking in a country one does not know and without having a good pair of legs.

The mechanisms of defense serve the purpose of keeping off dangers. It cannot be disputed that they are successful in this; and it is doubtful whether the ego could do without them altogether during its development. But it is also certain that they may become dangers themselves. It sometimes turns out that the ego has paid too high a price for the services they render it. The dynamic expenditure necessary for maintaining them, and the restrictions of the ego which they almost invariably entail, prove a heavy burden on the psychical economy. Moreover, these mechanisms are not relinquished after they have assisted the ego during the difficult years of its development. No one individual, of course, makes use of all the possible mechanisms of defense. Each person uses no more than a selection of them. But these become fixated in his ego. They become regular modes of reaction of his character, which are repeated throughout his life whenever a situation occurs that is similar to the original one. This turns them into infantilisms, and they share the fate of so many institutions which attempt to keep themselves in existence after the time of their usefulness has passed. "*Vernunft wird Unsinn, Wohltat Plage*" as the poet complains.[2] The adult's ego, with its increased strength, continues to defend itself against dangers which no longer exist in reality; indeed, it finds itself compelled to seek out those situations in reality which can serve as an approximate substitute for the original danger, so as to be able to justify, in relation to them, its maintaining its habitual modes of reaction. Thus we can easily understand

2. "Reason becomes unreason, kindness torment." Goethe, *Faust*, Part I, Scene 4.

how the defensive mechanisms, by bringing about an ever more extensive alienation from the external world and a permanent weakening of the ego, pave the way for, and encourage, the outbreak of neurosis.

. . . During the treatment our therapeutic work is constantly swinging backward and forward like a pendulum between a piece of id-analysis and a piece of ego-analysis. In the one case we want to make something from the id conscious, in the other we want to correct something in the ego. The crux of the matter is that the defensive mechanisms directed against former danger recur in the treatment as *resistances* against recovery. It follows from this that the ego treats recovery itself as a new danger.

The therapeutic effect depends on making conscious what is repressed, in the widest sense of the word, in the id. We prepare the way for this making conscious by interpretations and constructions, but we have interpreted only for ourselves not for the patient so long as the ego holds on to its earlier defenses and does not give up its resistances. Now these resistances, although they belong to the ego, are nevertheless unconscious and in some sense separated off within the ego. The analyst recognizes them more easily than he does the hidden material in the id. One might suppose that it would be sufficient to treat them like portions of the id and, by making them conscious, bring them into connection with the rest of the ego. In this way, we should suppose, one half of the task of analysis would be accomplished; we should not reckon on meeting with a resistance against the uncovering of resistances. But what happens is this. During the work on the resistances the ego withdraws —with a greater or less degree of seriousness—from the agreement on which the analytic situation is founded. The ego ceases to support our efforts at uncovering the id; it opposes them, disobeys the fundamental rule of analysis, and allows no further derivatives of the repressed to emerge. We cannot expect the patient to have a strong conviction of the curative power of analysis. He may have brought along with him a certain amount of confidence in his analyst, which will be strengthened to an effective point by the factors of the positive transference which will be aroused in him. Under the influence of the unpleasurable impulses which he feels as a result of the fresh activation of his defensive conflicts, negative transferences may now gain the upper hand and completely annul the analytic situation. The patient now regards the analyst as no more than a stranger who is making disagreeable demands on him, and he behaves toward him exactly like a child who does not like the stranger and does not believe anything he says. If the analyst tries to explain to the patient one of the distortions made by him for the purposes of defense, and to correct it, he finds him uncomprehending and inaccessible to sound arguments. Thus we see

that there *is* a resistance against the uncovering of resistances, and the defensive mechanisms really do deserve the name which we gave them originally, before they had been more closely examined. They are resistances not only to the making conscious of contents of the id, but also to the analysis as a whole, and thus to recovery.

The effect brought about in the ego by the defenses can rightly be described as an "alteration of the ego" if by that we understand a deviation from the fiction of a normal ego which would guarantee unshakable loyalty to the work of analysis. It is easy, then, to accept the fact, shown by daily experience, that the outcome of an analytic treatment depends essentially on the strength and on the depth of root of these resistances that bring about an alteration of the ego. . . .

The next question we come to is whether every alteration of the ego—in our sense of the term—is acquired during the defensive struggles of the earliest years. There can be no doubt about the answer. We have no reason to dispute the existence and importance of original, innate distinguishing characteristics of the ego. This is made certain by the single fact that each person makes a selection from the possible mechanisms of defense, that he always uses only a few of them and always the same ones. This would seem to indicate that each ego is endowed from the first with individual dispositions and trends, though it is true that we cannot specify their nature or what determines them. Moreover, we know that we must not exaggerate the difference between inherited and acquired characters into an antithesis; what was acquired by our forefathers certainly forms an important part of what we inherit. When we speak of an "archaic heritage" we are usually thinking only of the id and we seem to assume that at the beginning of the individual's life no ego is as yet in existence. But we shall not overlook the fact that id and ego are originally one; nor does it imply any mystical overvaluation of heredity if we think it credible that, even before the ego has come into existence, the lines of development, trends, and reactions which it will later exhibit are already laid down for it. The psychological peculiarities of families, races, and nations, even in their attitude to analysis, allow of no other explanation. Indeed, more than this: Analytic experience has forced on us a conviction that even particular psychical contents, such as symbolism, have no other sources than hereditary transmission, and researches in various fields of social anthropology make it plausible to suppose that other, equally specialized precipitates left by early human development are also present in the archaic heritage.

With the recognition that the properties of the ego which we meet with in the form of resistances can equally well be determined by heredity as acquired in defensive struggles, the topographical distinction between what is ego and what is id loses much of its value for our investigation. If we advance a step further in our analytic experience, we come upon resistances of another kind, which we can no longer localize and which seem to depend on fundamental conditions in the mental apparatus. I can only give a few examples of this type of resistance; the whole field of inquiry is still bewilderingly strange and insufficiently explored. We come across people, for instance, to whom we should be inclined to attribute a special "adhesiveness of the libido." The processes which the treatment sets in motion in them are so much slower than in other people because, apparently, they cannot make up their minds to detach libidinal cathexes from one object and displace them onto another, although we can discover no special reason for this cathectic loyalty. One meets with the opposite type of person, too, in whom the libido seems particularly mobile; it enters readily upon the new cathexes suggested by analysis, abandoning its former ones in exchange for them. The difference between the two types is comparable to the one felt by a sculptor, according to whether he works in hard stone or soft clay. Unfortunately, in this second type the results of analysis often turn out to be very impermanent: The new cathexes are soon given up once more, and we have an impression, not of having worked in clay, but of having written on water. . . .

In another group of cases we are surprised by an attitude in our patients which can only be put down to a depletion of the plasticity, the capacity for change and further development, which we should ordinarily expect. We are, it is true, prepared to find in analysis a certain amount of psychical inertia. When the work of analysis has opened up new paths for an instinctual impulse, we almost invariably observe that the impulse does not enter upon them without marked hesitation. We have called this behavior, perhaps not quite correctly, "resistance from the id." But with the patients I here have in mind, all the mental processes, relationships, and distributions of force are unchangeable, fixed and rigid. One finds the same thing in very old people, in which case it is explained as being due to what is described as force of habit or an exhaustion of receptivity—a kind of psychical entropy. But we are dealing here with people who are still young. Our theoretical knowledge does not seem adequate to give a correct explanation of such types. Probably some temporal characteristics are concerned—some alterations of a rhythm of development in psychical life which we have not yet appreciated.

In yet another group of cases the distinguishing characteristics of the ego, which are to be held responsible as sources of resistance against analytic treatment and as impediments to therapeutic success, may spring from different and deeper roots. Here we are dealing with the ultimate things which psycho-logical research can learn about: The behavior of the two primal instincts, their distribution, mingling, and defusion—things which we cannot think of as being confined to a single province of the mental apparatus, the id, the ego, or the superego. No stronger impression arises from the resistances during the work of analysis than of there being a force which is defending itself by every possible means against recovery and which is absolutely resolved to hold onto illness and suffering. One portion of this force has been recognized by us, undoubtedly with justice, as the sense of guilt and need for punishment, and has been localized by us in the ego's relation to the superego. But this is only the portion of it which is, as it were, psychically bound by the superego and thus becomes recognizable; other quotas of the same force, whether bound or free, may be at work in other, unspecified places. If we take into consideration the total picture made up of the phenomena of masochism immanent in so many people, the negative therapeutic reaction and the sense of guilt found in so many neurotics, we shall no longer be able to adhere to the belief that mental events are exclusively governed by the desire for pleasure. These phenomena are mistakable indications of the presence of a power in mental life which we call the instinct of aggression or of destruction according to its aims, and which we trace back to the original death instinct of living matter. It is not a question of an antithesis between an optimistic and a pessimistic theory of life. Only by the concurrent or mutually opposing action of the two primal instincts—Eros and the death instinct—never by one or the other alone, can we explain the rich multiplicity of the phenomena of life.

How parts of these two classes of instincts combine to fulfil the various vital functions, under what conditions such combinations grow looser or break up, to what disturbances these changes correspond, and with what feelings the perceptual scale of the pleasure principle replies to them—these are problems whose elucidation would be the most rewarding achievement of psychological research. For the moment we must bow to the superiority of the forces against which we see our efforts come to nothing. . . .

4.

WAELDER, ROBERT

The Principle of Multiple Function: Observations on Overdetermination*

. . . The ego always faces problems and seeks to find their solution. Each of man's actions has in every case to pass through the ego and is thus an attempt to solve a problem. Even in the extreme case of an action carried out under the pressure of impulse which may

* 5 *The Psychoanalytic Quarterly*, 1936. (pp. 46–52). Reprinted by permission.

seem at first to be driven purely by the instincts, the ego contributes its part; the imperatively appearing demand for satisfaction is that problem proposed to the ego, the resulting action is the means to the solution of that problem.

If it is correct to designate the scheme of the processes in the ego as the attempted solution of problems, then we must further ask ourselves what those problems are to whose solution the ego is consecrated, in which characteristic types, respectively, can the manifold content of these actual appearing problems be classified. Some will clearly be those coming to the ego from without, or those which are placed before the ego by factors foreign to it, as, for instance, in the example of the impulsive action of the instinct. How many of such possible problems exist can be gathered by realizing how many agencies the ego faces. There is first the id, the world of the instincts which approaches the ego with its claims; then there is the outside world with its demands on the individual; there is, finally, in growing proportions from a certain time forward in the development of the individual, the superego with its commands and prohibitions. They all demand something and they all place the ego before the problem of finding ways and means to meet those demands, that is, the problem of finding attempted solutions. In addition, we would consider as a fourth problem that which imposes itself on the ego through the compulsion to repeat. Although it is customary in psychoanalysis to consider the compulsion to repeat as part of the id (its lowermost layer), it nevertheless seems to us propitious to distinguish between the claims of those impulses which require concrete gratification and the demands of the tendencies to repeat and continue former actions, even those which are unpleasant, or, more correctly, to distinguish between these two sides of the instinctive impulse, without the intention in so doing to give a more far-reaching opinion concerning the status of the compulsion to repeat. If we are permitted to speak in this connection of the compulsion to repeat as of an agency of its own, the ego appears to be solicited by concrete problems from four directions: From the outside world, from the compulsion to repeat, from the id, and from the superego.

However, the role of the ego is not limited to this passivity alone. The situation is by no means so simple, the ego has more to do than merely to take orders and care for their execution. Rather, it develops toward the outer world, as well as toward the other agencies in man himself, its own peculiar activity. This activity may be characterized as striving to hold its own, and beyond this to assimilate in organic growth the outer world as well as the other agencies within the individual. This activity of the ego is first noticed in the ego's contact with the outer world. But it seems that also in its contact with the instinctual life there exists from the very beginning this trend to

co-ordinate itself with its central steering—a fact which seems to be proven in that the ego experiences each excessive *crescendo* of the instinctual forces as danger for itself and independently of any consequences menacing from the outside, a danger to be destroyed and its organization overwhelmed. Evidently, the ego has then also an active trend toward the instinctual life, a disposition to dominate or, more correctly, to incorporate it into its organization. The fact that there is a similar disposition of the ego toward the impulse to repeat, that the ego uses repetitions imposed on it by this deep-rooted disposition in order to overcome the menacing drives, has been emphasized by Freud from the very beginning when he introduced the concept of the compulsion to repeat. In the real occurrence of the repetitions it is difficult to distinguish in how far the ego is subject to the compulsion from behind and in how far it uses it as a means to overcome the psychic experience; these two sides of the actual repetition can be separated only by abstraction. Furthermore, it would be fairly easy to illustrate by way of example that the ego also contains a similar tendency in its relationship to the superego.

The function of the ego is, therefore, not limited to finding attempted solutions for problems which are placed before it by the outer world, by the compulsion to repeat, by the id, by the superego, but in addition it assigns to *itself* definite problems, such as overcoming the other agencies or joining them to its organization by active assimilation. There are, then, eight problems whose solution is attempted by the ego: Four of these are assigned to the ego and the other four the ego assigns to itself. Or, even, better there are eight *groups* of problems, since what we have termed as problems contains in each instance a *group* of problems. (For example, the problem of instinctual gratification assigned by the id naturally contains as many problems as there are instincts seeking gratification.) Thus, the occurrences within the ego can be described as distinct attempted solutions; man's ego is characterized through a number of specific methods of solution.

It appears now as if our psychic life were directed by a general principle which we may name the principle of multiple function. According to this principle no attempted solution of a problem is possible which is not of such a type that it does not at the same time, in some way or other, represent an attempted solution of *other* problems. Consequently, each psychic act can and must be conceived in every case as a simultaneous attempted solution of all eight problems, although it may be more successful as an attempted solution of one particular problem than of another.

In a consideration of this principle, it first occurs to us that it is fundamentally impossible that any sort of an attempted solution could answer to a like degree and with equal success all eight problems, for these problems are of inconsistent character. Above all, the problems of the first group which are assigned to the ego are at variance with those of the second which the ego assigns to itself. For instance, instinct gratification is at variance with instinct control, and fulfilment of the commands of the superego is in opposition to the assimilating victory over the superego. As a rule, there will be still other contrasts between the problems, as for instance between those of the id and those of the outer world or of the superego. And, finally, other possible variances are to be found within a problem group, as for instance when opposing impulses demand gratification, opposing superego demands occur in definite conflict rising against the claims of the not less contradictory outer world, etc. The whole complex of the problems whose solution is constantly attempted by the ego is consequently inconsistent in three directions and a complete simultaneous solution of these eight problems is impossible. The character of each psychic act is thus proven to be a compromise, as psychoanalysis first discovered in the case of the neurotic symptom, which is a compromise between instinct and the defense against it. Perhaps this affords us a possible clue to the understanding of that sense of perpetual contradiction and feeling of dissatisfaction which, apart from neurosis, is common to all human beings.

It is thus fundamentally impossible for any psychic act to be to the same extent and with equal success an attempted solution for all and each of the several problems. If it is a necessary conclusion that under the principle of multiple function an attempted solution solves one problem with more success than the other, then we can understand the unique position of all psychic acts which approach such a far-reaching solution. This is in the first place true of the act of love if it is to combine completeness of physical gratification with a happy relationship. Fulfilment of the instinctual need, the deepest repetition impulse, a satisfaction of the demand of the superego, and the claims of reality are all contained therein as well as the redemption and the self-discovery of the ego in face of all those realities. It appears now that the unique importance of the act of love in the psychic household is to be understood as that psychic act which comes nearest to a complete solution of all the contradictory problems of the ego. Consequently, if each psychic act is in some way—no matter how imperfectly—an attempted solution of all other problems which are found in the ego, this is only possible because each psychic act is of multiple meaning. If perchance the work on a machine which in the first place is an attempted solution of the adjustment to the outer world, becomes even imperfectly an instinctual gratification, this is possible only because the work on the machine has in addition some other meaning. In other words: A multiple meaning corresponds to a multiple function.

These considerations bring us in close touch with one of the oldest and most familiar concepts of psychoanalysis—over-determination. It is over-determination which as one of the most fundamental concepts of psychoanalysis most clearly distinguishes it from other psychological schools. This concept was introduced into psychoanalysis, as a result of empirical observation, first as something accidental which might or perhaps might not exist in a world more or less replete with diversity. Where it appeared, over-determination was explained by the fact that a psychic trend alone was not yet equivalent to psychic effectiveness and that only the conjunction of several trends would, so to speak, exceed the boundary value of psychic effectiveness. It is clear that this conception has been built up in analogy to those of the older neurology and that it shows a logical difficulty: There can be a complete determination—natural science knows the concept of the necessary and adequate causes—and as long as one remains within the sphere of natural science, it is difficult to understand in how far an occurrence should be determined more than adequately. In mathematics over-determination is even nonsensical: A triangle is adequately determined by three determining components; it is over-determined by four, i.e., in general, impossible. In psychoanalysis over-determination meets further a practical difficulty: In psychoanalytical application, psychoanalytical hermeneutics, the introduction of the concept of over-determination yields neither a guiding point nor a boundary for the expected reconstructions; over-determination opens onto infinity, as it were, and there is no principle of psychoanalytical hermeneutics that can set down any sort of postulate as to how far over-determination reaches and when it may be considered exhausted.

The principle of multiple function is perhaps in a position to meet all these difficulties. It is free from faults in logic for it no longer affirms that a psychic act is determined beyond its own complete determination, but only that it must have more than one sense, that even if initiated as an attempted solution for one definite problem, it must also, at the same time and in some way, be an attempted solution for other specific problems. The whole phenomenon of the multiple function and of the multiple meaning of each psychic act, then, is not—in analogy to the older neurology—to be understood through any sort of conception of a summation of stimuli and threshold values, but—parallel to the concepts of newer neurology and biology—is to be understood as the expression of the collective function of the total organism. Since the organism always reacts in its entirety and since all these problems are constantly living within it, each attempted solution of a problem must be conjointly determined, modified, and arranged through the existence and the working of the other, until it can serve, even if imperfectly, as an attempted solution for all these problems and thus necessarily preserve its multiple meaning. There is nothing of the happenchance in this procedure which may appear in one case and not in another; it naturally follows from the structure of the psychic organism. Finally, we have now a definite guide for psychoanalytic hermeneutics. The multiple meaning of a psychic act is clearly exhausted if it is interpreted as an attempted solution for all eight problems or, more correctly expressed, for the problems of all eight groups. The multiple meaning naturally has not ceased to be infinite, but there are certain directions marked out in this infinity. The valency which must be attributed to these various meanings is certainly not affected.

5.

REICH, ANNIE

A Character Formation Representing the Integration of Unusual Conflict Solutions into the Ego Structure*

These notes represent some material from the analysis of an obsessional character which lends itself well, I believe, to illustrate the complex interaction between the many factors that have a bearing upon character development. It points up the interaction between the drives and the ego, environmental influences, peculiarities of the object relationships, and the role of the superego, which finally result in the complicated structure of the human personality. However, my presentation will neglect the constitutional element because I am unable to shed specific light on it, although it may have been present in this case. In general it is likely, for instance, that such factors influence the choice of particular conflict solution, speed of development and particular structure of the ego. A preponderance of particular drives, etc., may to a large extent be constitutionally conditioned; but it also may be the result of identification with important childhood objects characterized by the same instinctual strivings. Thus in my case there was a prevalence of sadomasochistic drives and conflicts in both parents as well as in the patient. It is impossible to determine whether the constitutional element or the impact of the parental influences represent the decisive factor. There may frequently be an interaction of both determinants.

The example I have chosen concerns a man who by himself and his environment was considered "normal"; a rather meaningless concept, reflecting sociocultural value connotations. But he was unencumbered by circumscribed symptoms and was capable of functioning well enough with regard to

---

* 13 *The Psychoanalytic Study of the Child*, 1958. (pp. 309–23). Reprinted by permission of International Universities Press, New York.

work, sexual performance, adjustment to love objects, and to society in general. Only the deeper scrutiny of analysis disclosed peculiarities in his behavior, due to a prevalence of inhibition and reaction formation that blocked a more productive and gratifying use of his energies.

His history, as will be shown, reveals an abundance of traumatic situations, difficult conflicts, and a preponderance of regressed pregenital and sadomasochistic strivings. Conditions for the formation of good object relations and healthy identifications were far from favorable. Nevertheless, the all-over result of this complicated development was an amazingly positive, one might say ego-syntonic one. Important sublimations were formed, libidinal strivings found acceptable forms of expression. Lasting object relationships were established.

It is my feeling in general that we do not really or fully understand what makes such a successful character development under difficult circumstances possible. To my knowledge, there is not much in psychoanalytic literature that is concerned with special study of the prerequisites and conditions of favorable character development. To understand these conditions in a special situation may contribute toward a more general understanding of the problem.

Roger V. was in his forties, a successful psychologist in an academic position, happily married, and the father of three nice teen-age boys. He was a man of above-average endowment, keen intelligence, and a particularly astute faculty of psychological observation. He was well established in his field, although not as outstanding as he would have wished to be; loved by his family, well liked by his friends. His behavior was a tiny bit stiff, his way of talking a shade circumstantial. He was utterly reliable, a solid citizen, the "Rock of Gibraltar" in his group. He was a little overconscientious, too well-intentioned—maybe one could best describe it as too "virtuous." He came to analysis because he felt, with justification, that he was not living up to his potentialities, that he should have been more productive in his work.

In the analysis, the reasons for this insufficient productivity became clear. Roger lived too much in doing his "duty"; he was too much concerned with other people's welfare. He not only had to strive during his long working hours to be "helpful" to others (students, colleagues, etc.); but when he came home he had to devote himself completely to his family, had to have time for the special needs and wishes of each, listen to every worry and concern of his wife, supervise the boys' homework, try to "help" them to "cope with their problems." On top of all this, he had to spend an inordinate amount of time on household chores, walking the dog, doing small repairs, etc. In more ways than one, he was also strictly a "do-it-yourself" man, as will be shown later. It was important to be able to do everything by himself, without having to call in outside help. His behavior had accustomed his wife and children to rely on him and to be much more dependent on his manifold assistance than was good for them.

The most disconcerting of Roger's self-imposed duties, however, was to concern himself with his parents and to see or at least telephone them very frequently. He had to make constant and futile, but very burdensome attempts to "straighten them out." His mother was a masochistically complaining, aggressive, demanding, depressed person, forever in strife with her husband, whom she accused of being inconsiderate and brutal. They were continually involved in bickering and scenes. The father was a masculine, active, but rather primitive, crude, and not very bright man. Lacking in understanding, he provoked the mother by inconsiderate behavior, in reaction to which she would masochistically egg him on to further attacks. The father was mostly interested in the financial success of his business, but was not unkind to Roger.

Since early years Roger had endeavored to "make his parents happy" by showing them how to be happy, how to live in a more reasonable way. Already as a young child he was his parents' mainstay; he was treated as though he were the parent and they the children who were entitled to receive his constant support. Only in a financial way had the father, a successful engineer, been of help when Roger was younger. The mother, a little more sophisticated, was proud of her son and ambitious for him, but for her own purposes. Always dissatisfied with her lot, unhappy in her marriage, feeling damaged and deprived, she sought to use him as an antidote against her narcissistic injuries. At the same time, she wanted him to remain tied to her and was jealous of his accomplishments.

As mentioned before, Roger's complaints were justified. That his excessive "kindness" and concern for others took up too much of his time was obvious. But beyond this, something else interfered with the full concentration on his own work. There was a twofold motive for this inhibition. To work for himself appeared inordinately selfish. He had to shrink back from the success to which he aspired, and which would put him in the limelight. Such exhibition was intolerable to him because it implied standing out above others, a victory that would cruelly wound his rivals. Here the warded-off, competitive hostility clearly shone through his self-sacrificing kindness. The second reason was his feeling that real success and a full life in the world of his scientific interests would destroy the bond between him and his parents; not only by reducing the time he devoted to them, but by bringing into focus the disparity between his life and theirs, between his accomplishments and their crude primitivity. Thus he would lose these most important objects of his childhood, a prospect that filled him

with "deep sadness." He preferred to maintain his compulsive "goodness."

His position as friend and helper of the parents was the pattern after which virtually all his other relationships were modeled. He tried to help everybody to behave reasonably, thereby giving "nourishment" and "strength" to others. The deeper meaning of this wish and of the compulsion to imbue mankind with reason will be discussed later. The same pattern was evident even in his sexual behavior to his wife. There was no conspicuous disturbance of functioning, but a complete focus on gratifying his partner, entirely subordinating his needs to her wishes, which interfered with his full pleasure and abandonment.

Freud said that a person's sexual life serves as a pattern for his life in general. In the course of Roger's analysis it emerged that his muting of sexual pleasure as a consequence of reactive overconcern for the partner, was in fact paralleled by interferences of similar kind casting a certain pall on his interests, his object relationships, indeed on all contacts with reality. He recognized that he was always in a state of watchfulness with regard to himself. He could not just let himself go when talking, lest some "nonsense" might emerge. Nothing could be done with full spontaneity, because he constantly had to "control" himself lest some unacceptable, selfish, aggressive, infantile sexual strivings might break through.

Besides this reactive behavior, however, there was a difficulty of a different kind. Bent though he was on being helpful to people, he always felt some abstractedness while with them; he was never quite present. During his analysis he learned to understand that what distracted him in such situations was a continual preoccupation with fantasies which absorbed a large part of his libidinous interest.

Thus there were, one might say, two sides to the coin: A stream of "subterranean" fantasies, so to speak—not completely repressed, but kept in a state of isolation—and the more conscious efforts to keep the danger in check. This can be described as a typical obsessional behavior pattern. As a result, Roger, lived in a lasting state of inner loneliness and isolation, which represented the antithesis to the deepest aims of his fantasies.

On the surface, the content of this fantasy world was "pure" and "innocent" enough. It was precisely a yearning to escape from such isolation. He longed for closeness with his love objects, for a closeness that would reach the utmost degree. He dreamed of some kind of fusion with another being, some kind of mystic communion. This almost religious daydream proved to be multilayered. It contained elements from all instinctual levels, and in all of them danger was inherent that had to be warded off. The final form in which it appeared, of a melting together with the beloved object, related to earliest oral aims which had been regressively revived; hence it was closest to Roger's conscious awareness. The oral fantasies served to ward off later and even less acceptable desires. He would stress that he had to think of the "communion with his beloved ones" in terms of "taking in," "feeding," "melting," because anything else was more objectionable.

These "melting-together" fantasies were based on pleasant memories about his relationship with his mother; on sensations of being taken care of when sick, of being bathed in warm water by her until a relatively advanced age. Impressions of heat and cold were highly sexualized and experienced as a completely pleasurable, passive dissolving with or within the mother. But even this passive, nondestructive relationship with the mother could not be enjoyed for a greater length of time. She had been an anxious person, inclined to be overconcerned about any illness of the boy, and her anxiety about her own intactness had thus been transmitted to him. He felt that she liked to keep him a baby and, by infantilizing him, interfered with his growing up. She insisted that he could not do anything on his own, not get dressed, tie his shoe laces, go anywhere by himself, etc. She wanted to make him helpless and keep him close, like a part of her body. But he could not trust his mother; there was a feeling that in this helpless state she would hurt him. She was wont to ridicule him for being sick so much, which was felt by her as an injury and a special burden to herself. A particular memory stood out of being hungry after play, when he was very little, and wanting something to eat; his mother kept him waiting for his meal, and he fainted. Somehow the sensation of blacking out reflected the negative, highly unpleasant form of giving up his identity, of dissolving into the mother, due to being starved by her. The mother thus was experienced as cruel and murderous. It became obvious that on the deepest level his fantasy of fusion with the mother meant mutual devouring: To be eaten up by the mother.

The reaction against this unacceptable passive surrender was strengthened by the fact that the oral wishes overlaid later, even more unacceptable, anal and phallic ones; the anxieties appropriate to these levels were fused with the oral dangers. Hence the oral escape proved of no avail.

His regressive trend into orality was rooted in countless traumatic experiences of witnessing the continual sadomasochistic play between the parents. Various primal-scene observations were interpreted by the boy as rape and violence. Believing his father's sexual approaches to be responsible for his mother's constant complaints about her suffering and for her accusations that "pieces" were being brutally "torn out" of her, he thought that she was left bleeding, injured, and defective forever. The observations stirred up intense excitement and the wish to participate in the savage sexual experience alternately as the active and the passive partner; yet the child would shrink back, in horror, from playing the role of the cruel castrator. He was aware, furthermore, that the parental love play had something to do with the production of babies, which likewise meant cruel injury to the mother. In her vehement complaints she would accuse both father *and* son for having done this terrible thing to her, so that by Roger's birth she was damaged forever and ever.

Moreover, the primal-scene experiences probably occurred at a very early age when the pregenital phases, still far from being outgrown, were easily subject to regressive revival. In these very regressed fantasies about the parental sexual activities, everything was confused. Male and female role could no longer be distinguished. Either partner could act as aggressor or victim. In violent, tumultuous fights, either partner would tear the other to pieces and incorporate him in any one of various ways; via the genital, anus, or mouth, via hands or legs or skin. As the result of this gruesome conjugation, after having gone through some kind of digestive union, the baby would emerge via any of the body openings. Phallus, feces, and baby were confused in these fantasies. Mouth, anus, genitals merged into one cloaca. Anal, oral, and genital sadistic concepts flowed together. The whole body, the penis, the scybalum were being digested, to be ejected again anally or orally.

The "union" with his beloved—which in beautiful and pure, near-religious disguise remained the center of his fantasy life—thus represented a terrible, complete annihilation of the love object. I shall later discuss in what form the longing for this experience could be preserved and made innocuous.

The fantasy of mutual devouring was so horrifying that it had to vanish from the boy's conscious thought. Its slightly less regressed derivatives, however, remained conscious and filled him with anxiety. He had a fantasy, for instance, in which sexual union with the mother took the form of falling into her vagina as into a bottomless cavern; here his concern about the mother's lack of a penis was obviously merged with his fear of being devoured. Because of the deep confusion about phallic and anal wishes, he had the feeling that his mother treated his penis as she treated his anal productions, as something objectionable and disgusting. The final outcome of his by now phallic-oedipal wishes consisted in the fantasies of uniting with the mother in a violent love play, of "tearing pieces" out of her with his phallus, which represented an aggressive tool for the purpose of producing babies. Forced to withdraw from the active-sadistic role, in which like the father he was the cruel castrator, he visualized himself as being *invaded or penetrated* by the mother, a fantasy that was also related to frequent enemas administered by her.

It is likely, although this was not fully clarified by the analysis, that the fantasy about passive penetration by the mother covered an even more terrifying one with regard to the father. At any event, the danger of passivity left important traces in his character structure, which will be discussed later.

The passive fantasy was extremely frightening, since it left him in the position of the castrated mother. To avoid this terrible danger he resorted regressively to another, again active, form of anality which was to prove greatly significant. The phallic-sadistic elements of the fantasy were given up, and a shift of libidinal interest occurred from the dangerous love object to the self. The child fantasied that he was giving birth anally to many babies by cutting or tearing a long column of feces into many small pieces with his anus, at will. The anus had become a female organ: A big, black hole—a cloaca—like the cavern into which he had feared to fall. In addition, it also represented a mouth equipped with sharp teeth. In this fantasy, however, he was strong, active, *creative*, and quite on his own, completely independent of the dangerous love object. Thus, a new feature emerged here which was to become very important in his later makeup: For the first time, he was a "do-it-yourself" person.

Furthermore, this represented a partial narcissistic withdrawal. He could love and fertilize himself in manifold, not only anal, ways. Thus he could establish a "union with himself," avoiding danger and annihilation.

This narcissistic withdrawal, however, was not the only method by which Roger tried to cope with the phallic-sadistic strivings which in their active as well as their passive variety were completely unacceptable. It seems that a toning down from sadistic to exhibitionistic wishes took place, which made it possible to preserve the phallic drives in a predominantly exhibitionistic form: Exhibition as wooing of the mother and competition with the father. But this, too, was felt to be extremely destructive and had to be modified.

Soon the child's exhibitionistic wishes became divested of their directly phallic quality. Phallic activity appeared only in an already regressed, passive form. There were early games with the mother, in which she would fondle his naked body while he lay on a pillow, waiting to be dressed. He remembered her caressing hands, and how he would stretch his whole body with pleasure. In this memory and in the resulting fantasies, the erect phallus was replaced by the whole, stretched-out body being passively caressed; violence, penetration, invasion, tearing, etc., were carefully excluded.

As I just mentioned, exhibitionistic fantasies were apparently the most acceptable ones at the height of infantile sexuality. The thorough inhibition of aggressive-phallic urges, combined with the need for compensatory undoing of castration anxiety, restricted the boy to what might be called a "phallic passivity." To be looked at and admired, without actively doing anything, were the most permissible aims at this time. They were to remain important throughout life, and we shall come back to the imprint thus left on his character structure.

The most significant immediate consequence of this phallic passivity was the absence of any open genital masturbatory activity in childhood; masturbation equivalents in the form of tongue sucking and hair twiddling took its place. But more striking—to anticipate the later history—is the fact that there was no open masturbation in puberty; he merely would indulge in prolonged fantasies, without any manual manipulation. (Masturbation started only after the age of nineteen, when adult sexual experiences with girls had already taken place.) An important incident contributed to this pattern. When he was fourteen, at the height of pubertal development, his mother had to undergo an operation. It stirred up all the old memories about her being injured and castrated, which strengthened the defensive forces so that the step into masturbatory activity was made impossible. Indeed, the repression of active-sexual drives was so thorough as to forestall any intense struggle against temptation to masturbate. After that time he detached himself from his family to some degree, becoming interested in school and intellectual achievements. The addiction to fantasies took the place of masturbation.

But let us return to Roger's childhood. Attempts to break through his passivity seemed to have received a decisive blow by an event, at the age of six, which seriously impeded the budding tendency toward identification with the active-aggressive father and hence the development in the direction of an active-masculine sexuality and character structure. At that time the mother threatened to leave her husband and to take Roger with her, a threat to which the boy reacted with profound fright. Fully aware by then of his mother's helpless and neurotic behavior, he saw his father as a brutal, but strong person without whom they would both be lost. His mother was offering him the chance, so to speak, to step into the father's shoes. Yet he felt so frightened, weak, and in danger of starving, that he had to forgo his wish to play an active role with her, but had to cling to the father who alone could sustain them both. His castration anxiety thus was clad in oral terms: Both he and the mother were weak and "defective," needing "strength and nourishment" from the father.

The impact of this traumatic episode effected a final turning away from the original instinctual aims; and a rigid superego was established whose most preeminent demand was *not* to be like the aggressive, sexual parents. Important defenses were mobilized, among which powerful reaction formations stood out.

When Roger later learned from other boys about sexual intercourse, he found it revolting. It meant "invading other people's privacy," "violating their dignity." From then on, he had to control himself in order to make sure that he would not indulge in any "savage, infantile, sexual orgies." What had to be warded off most severely were the active-aggressive, phallic urges. He escaped from them into the already well-prepatterned, passive position, which, however, was equally unbearable.

But this was not all. At that period he started his attempts to re-educate his parents, to reconcile them and induce them to live without violence and strife. Obviously he tried to extend his own reaction formations to them, to wean them away from sexuality too. He became moralistic, and at the same time mature beyond his age. Looking back on himself later, he was to remark: "I was already an old man as a child." He began to become the support of his parents, to give "strength and nourishment" to them. A reversal thus had set in. What he originally had needed to receive from the parents, he now gave to them. Whereas they had incessantly stirred up his unruly desires, he helped them to control themselves. He bestowed oral gratification upon them, in a symbolic way, to undo starvation and castration.

By this behavior he likewise undid the dangers of passivity. Henceforth compelled to ward off any passive longing, he could not accept help from anyone, ask for anything, etc. Instead he adopted the strictly "do-it-yourself" attitude traceable to early fantasies about anal-parthenogenetic procreation. Removing himself to a large degree from objects, he now took pride in fulfilling his own and other people's needs by himself alone. The gratification afforded by this pattern was a narcissistic one. In his masturbation fantasy about "union with himself" the deepest core of the pattern was demonstrated most clearly. Its bearing on the problem of "creativity," which drove him into analysis, will be discussed later.

We see that Roger has succeeded in *becoming active again*, but in a nonsexual, nonaggressive way. He now enjoyed building, improving, rescuing others, being rational and constructive. Here he was identified with the feeding mother, the strong and protective father. He had achieved to cleanse the parental figures of their unacceptable, sexual traits, and to reconstruct them within himself in an idealized form. This idealized and internalized image of the united parents, with whom he thus identified, represented an aspect of his superego that could, in contrast to the negative one I described before, be called an ego ideal. An intense form of gratification resulted from living up to this ideal in a large degree. He could vest himself in this way with a good deal of the libidinal cathexis originally directed toward the parents, which yielded a considerable feeling of narcissistic pride.

By being the savior and helper he succeeded also in winning praise and admiration from his objects, so that a nonsexual behavior could replace and gratify the repressed wish to win the mother via phallic exhibition. Thus by being "constructive" he achieved a new form of "union"; again, highly gratifying with a narcissistic undertone. And indeed, by being admirable and outstanding, he fulfilled his mother's deep, narcissistic need: He was magnificent, perfect. She gloated in the glory of her son. His greatness was the only means by which her defects, her castration, could be cured. He was part of her; her penis. Thus through his success the longing for mystic union was fulfilled.

I mentioned at the outset that Roger was highly accomplished in his work and generally successful in the role of confidant and altruistic friend. Obviously this success was based not alone upon his own emotional needs, but equally on his ability to understand other people's problems: on his astute, intuitive psychological insight. The coincidence of these two factors raised his behavior from the level of a purely neurotic activity to that of a true sublimation.

The genesis of his psychological propensity was significant. It represented yet another method of substitution for the unattainable sexual union with the infantile love objects. That from his wishes for direct participation in the sadomasochistic love play he withdrew into seeing, understanding, thinking, was as decisive as the retreat into exhibitionism. This shift from action to thinking is generally of moment for the development of obsessional characters and, when successful, constitutes an avenue toward important sublimations. In Roger's case its aggressive-libidinal origin could be clearly discerned. Giving up his dangerous objects, he had turned his interest upon himself. Here, too, he "did it himself" and established "the union" with himself.

What this really meant was strikingly demonstrated by his behavior in the analysis. To avoid being analyzed by me, which for him implied all the dangers pointed out before, Roger analyzed himself. This self-analytical action, which he could perform amazingly well, was based upon a very special capacity for self-observation and introspection that had existed long before his contact with analysis. His "communion with himself" had taken the form of a constant self-observation and rumination about himself. By introspection he "penetrated" himself, "invaded" his own "privacy." This self-centered and very acute psychological interest thus had the character of a substitute activity replacing the masturbation from which he so conspicuously refrained. During his adolescent years it was pursued while sitting on the toilet, where to his mother's annoyance he would stay for a very long time.

Thinking about himself represented the desexualized version of exhibiting and at the same time looking at himself. It was thus a derivative of the forbidden phallic wish to show his erection to the mother, and to be looked at and caressed by her. He was simultaneously playing both roles here. Furthermore, the act of looking at himself with "sharp eyes" and with "penetrating understanding" corresponded to an aggressive, phallic attack against himself (the sharp eye representing a penis substitute). Thus in a symbolic form he was simultaneously active and passive, sadistic and masochistic. This again made him independent of the object, yielded narcissistic gratification, and removed him from infantile dangers.

This transmutation was particularly successful due to the sublimated character of the thinking and observing process. Roger's capability to make correct observations had developed at an early age when his mother, extending her anxieties about herself to the child, would anxiously observe him with regard to health and intactness. In identification with his mother he observed and admired himself, thereby undoing her feeling of castration and his own. Quite early his faculty of observation and understanding had become a very keen one, of which he could be proud, as the mother was proud of him. Later on, it came to be extended from himself to other persons; from being able to become aware of his own feeling, he developed an ability to sense what was going on in others.

The libidinal undercurrents of Roger's interest in observing and understanding never interfered with the quality of his performance. He succeeded in developing reality-syntonic capacities for thinking in general and for specifically psychological comprehension. Notwithstanding their closeness to the instinctual sources, there was never an intrusion of one sphere into the other, never a lowering of the standard of his reality testing.

Reality testing is a function of the ego. Yet it seems to me that in this particular situation the superego was involved. Roger, in spite of his rigid defenses, had easy access to his fantasy life; but it was of paramount importance for him to be able to keep reality apart from fantasy. His constant stress upon the "rational" revealed him as being on guard against an intrusion of fantasies. Thus, "rational thinking" and "objective observation" had the character of a super-ego demand.

This intellectual ability, which played an important role in Roger's professional work, demonstrates nicely how a sublimation is composed of two factors; one of them being a securely desexualized ego component, while the other stems from and merges with the world of instincts. According to Hartmann, irreversibility may be considered the most important characteristic of a true sublimation. Roger's psychological propensities were never in danger of reverting to infantile fantasies. And yet, as I described in the beginning, he could not always make as full use of them as should have been possible.

In the course of his analysis it became clear that, at the deepest level, real and unencumbered intellectual productivity represented the gratification of fundamental infantile fantasies for Roger: It meant creating babies with the mother, fulfilling the longing for fusion with her. But in these fantasies he had taken over the maternal role as well; he now was the object, producing children with himself. Creativity thus represented complete narcissistic fulfilment. It was here that the inhibition took place.

Nevertheless, in view of his history, it seems quite striking that Roger was not sicker. We frequently encounter patients suffering from far more severe pathology, whose childhood histories appear much less traumatic. Likewise remarkable is the absence of childhood objects with whom he could identify directly for the purpose of superego formation, without restoring to idealization or having to take exclusively the converse of the parental figures as his model. Yet he succeeded singularly well in developing defenses the results of which could be used in such constructive form for ego purposes and could be integrated as character traits into the structure of the ego.

A number of factors may have contributed to this success.

1. As has been variously indicated, in spite of all conflicts and anxieties there was a basic identification with the active-masculine father figure. After puberty this became positively influenced and strengthened by the example of a young cousin and some masculine, active friends.

2. Roger's capability of melting together defensive patterns with slightly modified instinctual gratification was an unusual one. We have seen that in his case the psychological interest as well as the altruistic behavior pattern was by no means founded exclusively upon reaction formation, but contained a considerable amount of transformed libidinal drive. It may be due to this factor that he remained free of more disturbing pathological symptoms. His ability to fit his adult sexual life into the frame of the curing-healing-giving compulsion may have preserved him from more serious potency disturbances and allowed him to achieve a substantial degree of sexual gratification despite the heavy burden of his early experiences.

3. The considerable ego strength here displayed, particularly the success of the synthetic function in integrating the wealth of pregenital fantasies into the realm of the ego, might be explainable by the assumption that the ego could continually draw energy from the id, neutralizing it and using it for its own aims. One might say that the ego possessed a particular capacity for sublimation, based on the one hand upon

the solid structure of his defenses, and on the other hand upon this free line of access to the id.

4. Furthermore, his ability to solve his problems in a "constructive" way seems to have been rooted in some element of magic thinking, of preserved omnipotence. It was as though these regressively revived features of a primitive ego could be mobilized *at will* for purposes of reconstruction.

6.

SOME PROBLEMS IN THE LAW OF CRIMES AND EVIDENCE

a.
STATE v. DAMMS
9 Wis. 2d 183, 100 N.W. 2d 592 (1960)

*   *   *

The defendant Ralph Damms was charged by information with the offense of attempt to commit murder in the first degree. . . . The jury found the defendant guilty as charged, and the defendant was sentenced to imprisonment . . . for a term of not more than ten years. . . .

. . . Prior to the date of the alleged crime, Marjory Damms, wife of the defendant, had instituted an action for divorce against him and the parties lived apart. She was thirty-nine years and he thirty-three years of age. Marjory Damms was also estranged from her mother, Mrs. Laura Grant.

That morning, a little before eight o'clock, Damms drove his automobile to the vicinity in Milwaukee where he knew Mrs. Damms would take the bus to go to work. He saw her walking along the sidewalk, stopped, and induced her to enter the car by falsely stating that Mrs. Grant was ill and dying. They drove to Mrs. Grant's home. Mrs. Damms then discovered that her mother was up and about and not seriously ill. Nevertheless, the two Damms remained there nearly two hours conversing and drinking coffee. Apparently it was the intention of Damms to induce a reconciliation between mother and daughter, hoping it would result in one between himself and his wife, but not much progress was achieved in such direction.

At the conclusion of the conversation Mrs. Damms expressed the wish to phone for a taxicab to take her to work. Damms insisted on her getting into his car, and said he would drive her to work. They again entered his car but instead of driving south towards her place of employment, he drove in the opposite direction. Some conversation was had in which he stated that it was possible for a person to die quickly and not be able to make amends for anything done in the past, and referred to the possibility of "judgment day" occurring suddenly. Mrs. Damms' testimony as to what then took place is as follows: "When he

was telling me about this being judgment day, he pulled a cardboard box from under the seat of the car and brought it up to the seat and opened it up and took a gun out of a paper bag. [He] aimed it at my side and he said, 'This is to show you I'm not kidding.' I tried to quiet him down. He said he wasn't fooling. I said if it was just a matter of my saying to my mother that everything was all right, we could go back and I would tell her that."

They did return to Mrs. Grant's home and Mrs. Damms went inside and Damms stayed outside. In a few minutes he went inside and asked Mrs. Damms to leave with him. Mrs. Grant requested that they leave quietly so as not to attract the attention of the neighbors. They again got into the car and . . . Damms stated to Mrs. Damms that he was taking her "up north" for a few days, the apparent purpose of which was to effect a reconciliation between them. As they approached a roadside restaurant, he asked her if she would like something to eat. She replied that she wasn't hungry but would drink some coffee. Damms then drove the car off the highway beside the restaurant and parked it with the front facing, and in close proximity to, the restaurant wall.

Damms then asked Mrs. Damms how much money she had with her and she said "a couple of dollars." He then requested to see her checkbook and she refused to give it to him. A quarrel ensued between them. Mrs. Damms opened the car door and started to run around the restaurant building screaming, "Help!" Damms pursued her with the pistol in his hand. Mrs. Damms' cries for help attracted the attention of the persons inside the restaurant, including two officers of the State Traffic Patrol who were eating their lunch. One officer rushed out of the front door and the other the rear door. In the meantime, Mrs. Damms had run nearly around three sides of the building. In seeking to avoid colliding with a child, who was in her path, she turned, slipped and fell. Damms crouched down, held the pistol at her head, and pulled the trigger, but nothing happened. He then exclaimed, "It won't fire. It won't fire."

Damms testified that at the time he pulled the trigger the gun was pointing down at the ground and not at Mrs. Damms' head. However, the two traffic patrol officers both testified that Damms had the gun pointed directly at her head when he pulled the trigger. The officers placed Damms under arrest. They found that the pistol was unloaded. The clip holding the cartridges, which clip is inserted in the butt of the gun to load it, they found in the cardboard box in Damms' car together with a box of cartridges.

That afternoon, Damms was questioned by a deputy sheriff at the Waukesha County jail, and a clerk in the sheriff's office typed out the questions and Damms' answers as they were given. Damms later read over such typed statement of questions and answers, but refused to sign it. In such statement

Damms stated that he thought the gun was loaded at the time of the alleged attempt to murder. Both the deputy sheriff and the undersheriff testified that Damms had stated to them that he thought the gun was loaded. On the other hand, Damms testified at the trial that he knew at the time of the alleged attempt that the pistol was not loaded.

*   *   *

CURRIE, JUSTICE.

The two questions raised on this appeal are:
1. Did the fact, that it was impossible for the accused to have committed the act of murder because the gun was unloaded, preclude his conviction of the offense of attempt to commit murder?
2. Assuming that the foregoing question is answered in the negative, does the evidence establish the guilt of the accused beyond a reasonable doubt?
Sec. 939.32(2), Stats., provides as follows:

"An attempt to commit a crime requires that the actor have an intent to perform acts and attain a result which, if accomplished, would constitute such crime and that he does acts toward the commission of the crime which demonstrate unequivocally, under all the circumstances, that he formed that intent and would commit the crime *except for the intervention of* another person or *some other extraneous factor.*" (Italics supplied.)

The issue with respect to the first of the aforestated two questions boils down to whether the impossibility of accomplishment due to the gun being unloaded falls within the statutory words, "except for the intervention of * * * some other extraneous factor." We conclude that it does.

*   *   *

In an article in 1956 *Wisconsin Law Review*, 350, 364, by Assistant Attorney General Platz, who was one of the authors of the new criminal code, explaining such code, he points out that "attempt" is defined therein in a more intelligible fashion than by using such tests as "beyond mere preparation," "*locus poenitentiae*" (the place at which the actor may repent and withdraw), or "dangerous proximity to success." Quoting the author (ibid, footnote at p. 364):

"Emphasis upon the dangerous propensities of the actor as shown by his conduct, rather than upon how close he came to succeeding, is more appropriate to the purposes of the criminal law to protect society and reform offenders or render them temporarily harmless."

Robert H. Skilton, in an article entitled, "The Requisite Act in a Criminal Attempt (1937)," 3 *University of Pittsburgh Law Review* 308, 314, advances the view, that impossibility to cause death because of the attempt to fire a defective weapon at a person, does not prevent the conviction of the actor of the crime of attempted murder:

"[If] the defendant does not know that the gun he fires at B is defective, he is guilty of an attempt to kill B, even though his actions under the circumstances given never come near to killing B. * * * The possibility of the success of the defendant's enterprise need only be an apparent possibility to the defendant, and not an actual possibility."

*   *   *

Sound public policy would seem to support the majority view that impossibility not apparent to the actor should not absolve him from the offense of attempt to commit the crime he intended. An unequivocal act accompanied by intent should be sufficient to constitute a criminal attempt. Insofar as the actor knows, he has done everything necessary to insure the commission of the crime intended, and he should not escape punishment because of the fortuitous circumstance that by reason of some fact unknown to him it was impossible to effectuate the intended result.

*   *   *

It is our considered judgment that the fact, that the gun was unloaded when Damms pointed it at his wife's head and pulled the trigger, did not absolve him of the offense charged, if he actually thought at the time that it was loaded.

*   *   *

The jury undoubtedly believed the testimony of the deputy sheriff and undersheriff that Damms told them on the day of the act that he thought the gun was loaded. This is also substantiated by the written statement constituting a transcript of his answers given in his interrogation at the county jail on the same day. The gun itself, which is an exhibit in the record, is the strongest piece of evidence in favor of Damms' present contention that he at all times knew the gun was unloaded. Practically the entire bottom end of the butt of the pistol is open. Such opening is caused by the absence of the clip into which the cartridges must be inserted in order to load the pistol. This readily demonstrates to anyone looking at the gun that it could not be loaded. Because the unloaded gun with this large opening in the butt was an exhibit which went to the jury room, we must assume that the jury examined the gun and duly considered it in arriving at their verdict.

We are not prepared to hold that the jury could not come to the reasonable conclusion that, because of Damms' condition of excitement when he grabbed the gun and pursued his wife, he so grasped it as not to see the opening in the end of the butt which would have unmistakenly informed him that the gun was unloaded. Having so concluded, they could rightfully disregard Damms' testimony given at the trial that he knew the pistol was unloaded.

Judgment affirmed.

*   *   *

DIETERICH, JUSTICE (dissenting).

*   *   *

The issue raised on this appeal: Could the defendant be convicted of murder, under sec. 939.32(2), Stats., when it was impossible for the defendant to have caused the death of anyone because the gun or pistol involved was unloaded?

*   *   *

In view of the statute, the question . . . is whether the impossibility of accomplishment due to the pistol being unloaded falls within the statutory words *"except for the intervention of * * * or some other extraneous factor,"* it does not.

In interpreting the statute we must look to the ordinary meaning of words. *Webster's New International Dictionary* defines "extraneous" as not belonging to or dependent upon a thing, * * * originated or coming from without.

The plain distinct meaning of the statute is: A person must form an intent to commit a particular crime and this intent must be coupled with sufficient preparation on his part and with overt acts from which it can be determined clearly, surely, and absolutely the crime would be committed except for the intervention of some independent thing or something originating or coming from someone or something over which the actor has no control.

As an example—if the defendant actor had formed an intent to kill someone, had in his possession a loaded pistol, pulled the trigger while his intended victim was within range and the pistol did not fire because the bullet or cartridge in the chamber was defective or because someone unknown to the actor had removed the cartridges or bullets or because of any other thing happening which happening or thing was beyond the control of the actor, the actor could be guilty. But when as in the present case (as disclosed by the testimony) the defendant had never loaded the pistol, although having ample opportunity to do so, then he had never completed performance of the act essential to kill someone, through the means of pulling the trigger of the pistol. This act, of loading the pistol, or using a loaded pistol, was dependent on the defendant himself. It was in no way an extraneous factor since by definition an extraneous factor is one which originates or comes from without.

Under the majority opinion the interpretations of the statute are if a person points an unloaded gun (pistol) at someone, knowing it to be unloaded and pulls the trigger, he can be found guilty of an attempt to commit murder. This type of reasoning I cannot agree with.

He could be guilty of some offense, but not attempt to commit murder. If a person uses a pistol as a bludgeon and had struck someone, but was prevented from killing his victim because he (the actor) suffered a heart attack at that moment, the illness would be an extraneous factor within the statute and the actor could be found guilty of attempt to commit murder, provided the necessary intent was proved.

In this case, there is no doubt that the pistol was not loaded. The defendant testified that it had never been loaded or fired. The following steps must be taken before the weapon would be capable of killing.

*   *   *

A. To load pistol requires pulling of slide operating around barrel toward holder or operator of pistol.

B. After pulling slide to rear, safety latch is pushed into place by operator of pistol to hold pistol in position for loading.

C. A spring lock is located at one side of opening of magazine located at the bottom grip or butt of gun.

D. This spring is pulled back and the clip is inserted into magazine or bottom of pistol and closes the bottom of the grip or butt of the pistol.

E. The recoil or release of the safety latch on the slide loads the chamber of the pistol and it is now ready to fire or be used as a pistol.

The law judges intent objectively. It is impossible to peer into a man's mind particularly long after the act has been committed.

Viewing objectively the physical salient facts, it was the defendant who put the gun, clip, and cartridges under the car seat. It was he, same defendant, who took the pistol out of the box without taking clip or cartridges. It is plain he told the truth—he knew the gun would not fire—nobody else knew that so well. In fact his exclamation was "It won't fire. It won't fire." The real intent showed up objectively in those calm moments while driving around the county with his wife for two hours, making two visits with her at her mother's home, and drinking coffee at the home. He could have loaded the pistol while staying on the outside at his mother-in-law's home on his second trip, if he intended to use the pistol to kill, but he did not do this required act.

The majority states: "The gun itself, which is an exhibit in the record, is the strongest piece of evidence in favor of Damms' present contention that he at all times knew the gun was unloaded. Practically the entire bottom end of the butt of the pistol is open. * * * This readily demonstrates to anyone looking at the gun that it could not be loaded." They are so correct.

The defendant had the pistol in his hand several times before chasing his wife at the restaurant and it was his pistol. He, no doubt, had examined this pistol at various times during his period of ownership—unless he was devoid of all sense of touch and feeling in his hands and fingers it would be impossible for him not to be aware or know that the pistol was unloaded. He could feel the hole in the bottom of the butt, and this on at least two separate occasions for he handled the pistol by taking it out of the box and showing it to his wife before he took her back to her mother's home the second time, and prior to chasing her at the restaurant.

Objective evidence here raises reasonable doubt of intent to attempt murder. It negatives intent to kill. The defendant would have loaded the pistol had he intended to kill or murder or used it as a bludgeon.

*   *   *

The Assistant Attorney General contends and states in his brief:

"In the instant case, the failure of the attempt was due to lack of bullets in the gun but a loaded magazine was in the car. If defendant had not been prevented by the intervention of the two police officers, or possibly someone else, or conceivably by the flight of his wife from the scene, he could have returned to the car, loaded the gun, and killed her. Under all the circumstances the jury were justified in concluding that that is what he would have done, but for the intervention."

If that conclusion is correct, and juries are allowed to convict persons based on speculation of what *might* have been done, we will have seriously and maybe permanently, curtailed the basic rights of our citizenry to be tried only on the basis of proven facts.

I cannot agree with his contention or conclusion.

The total inadequacy of the means (in this case the unloaded gun or pistol) in the manner intended to commit the overt act of murder, precludes a finding of guilty of the crime charged . . .

NOTES

NOTE 1

AMERICAN LAW INSTITUTE
MODEL PENAL CODE*

. . . The literature and decisions dealing with the definition of a criminal attempt reflect ambivalence as to how far the governing criterion should be found in the dangerousness of the actor's conduct, measured by objective standards, and how far in the dangerousness of the actor, as a person manifesting a firm disposition to commit a crime. Both criteria may lead, of course, to the same disposition of a concrete case. When they do not, we think . . . that the proper focus of attention is the actor's disposition. . . . Needless to say, we are in full agreement that the

* *Tentative Draft No.* 10. Copyright 1960. Reprinted with the permission of The American Law Institute.

law must be concerned with conduct, not with evil thoughts alone. The question is what conduct, when engaged in with a purpose to commit a crime or to advance toward the attainment of a criminal objective, should suffice to constitute a criminal attempt?

In fashioning an answer we must keep in mind that in attempt . . . it is not intrinsic to the actor's conduct that he has disclosed his criminal design to someone else; nor is there any natural line that is suggested by the situation—like utterance or agreement. The law must deal with the problem presented by a single individual and must address itself to conduct that may fall anywhere upon a graded scale from early preparation to the final effort to commit the crime.

We think, therefore, that it is useful to begin with any conduct designed to effect or to advance toward the attainment of the criminal objective and to ask when it ought *not* to be regarded as a crime, either because it does not adequately manifest the dangerousness of the actor or on other overriding grounds of social policy. . . .

NOTE 2

EAGAN v. STATE
58 Wyo. 167, 128 P. 2d 215 (1942)

BLUME, JUSTICE.

. . . Dan Eagan killed his wife, Catherine, by shooting her through the neck with a revolver. The place of the homicide was in the basement apartment occupied by the couple. . . . The State charged Eagan with first degree murder. His defense alleged an accidental shooting. The jury found him guilty of murder in the second degree . . .

Defendant, an attorney at law then engaged in practice at Casper, had been married [to the deceased for] five years.

There was no eyewitness to the shooting other than the defendant himself. . . .

Defendant testified that on December 11, 1940, he was at his office during the day. . . . Upon arrival at home, he had a drink of whiskey and his wife a bottle of beer. . . . The defendant, his wife and daughter, and the maid, had dinner together. After dinner, the maid went to a show. Eagan's wife washed the dishes, while he went to his workshop in the basement to work on a gunstock. He testified at this point that he had a hobby of guns . . . While he was working on the gunstock, as above mentioned, his daughter was in and out of his workroom a number of times. At about 7:30 defendant's wife came into the workroom, sat on a bench, and talked with him for a time in an apparently amicable conversation. His wife then left, to put their daughter to bed . . . Some time during the evening, the exact time not appearing, she brought the pint of whiskey above mentioned into the gunroom and the evidence is to the effect that the pint was consumed between them during the course of the evening. After a time, the wife left the gunroom and went back into the bedroom of the basement apartment. Defendant finished what he wanted to do that evening and himself went into the bedroom, stopping at his gun-cabinet and taking therefrom the revolver with which the killing was done, and three shells (loaded cartridges) which fitted the gun. "As to the reason I took this gun from the cabinet and the shells—the gun had not been working properly . . ."

His wife was either in the room then, or entered immediately after. She got a pillow and laid down in front of the fire. For a time, duration not stated, deceased and defendant talked, he examining the gun and manipulating its mechanism, she lying down in front of the fire. "I had conversation with Catherine after she came into the room. As to what it was about —one thing was about the gun. I ejected one shell from it to show her that it didn't unload or load like hers. * * * When I ejected the shell from this gun, she was lying down in front of the fire. She was looking at me. * * * [I] had been working the mechanism to see how it was centering, looking down * * * I had to get the gun so I could see down there to see the shine of that cap to see if it was on center, and I turned it a number of times * * * and as I worked to bring it around here in the light, it went off." . . . "When I cocked the gun, I pulled the hammer back, and at the same time I did so I pulled the trigger back. * * * I don't know how the gun happened to fire. It all happened so quickly, and, like any accident, it just went off."

While he stated that everything "was confused," he testified that deceased toppled over, evidently backward toward the exerciser. . . . Defendant testified that he lifted her from this position, saw the wound, and immediately laid her on the floor in front of and with her head toward the stove, in the position in which other witnesses first saw her. He . . . called Doctor Henderson . . .

When Doctor Henderson arrived, the four-year-old child was asleep in bed and did not wake up. The defendant was kneeling beside the deceased and begged her to open her eyes. According to the coroner, who arrived shortly thereafter, the defendant was greatly shocked. The gun, when Doctor Henderson came, was lying on the floor. The defendant picked it up, apparently placed it on the table, and somewhat later in the evening, stating that he "couldn't stand it," apparently reached for the gun as though to kill himself, but was prevented by the coroner and officers who had arrived by that time. . . .

A firearms expert . . . stated that . . . tests show that while the weapon was defective, there was "nothing inherent in the design of this type of gun to permit * * * a discharge of this firearm without pulling the trigger in the usual manner. * * * The gun had three cocks, and occasionally would go off at the half cock. Ordinarily the gun could not be discharged, from the tests, without pulling the trigger at full cock, and with a pressure of seven to eight pounds." He testified that the result of a series of tests made to determine the distance the gun was held from the person of the deceased showed that "the gun was held from five to seven inches from the object." The sheriff of Natrona County, corroborating the defendant to that extent, testified that to see whether the gun would center, the best way would be to have the thumb on the hammer and a finger on the trigger. The witness Murray, however, testified that that was not a safe procedure.

*　　*　　*

Testimony was introduced to show the conduct of the defendant toward the deceased. It was shown that they were separated for two months between March and May, 1939, but that they thereafter became reconciled. In July, 1939 . . . he struck his wife on the head with his hand, and later kicked the back of the front seat of the car several times (she sitting in front and he in the back), so that it knocked her against the windshield and the dashboard. The defendant did not deny this, though he attempted to soften the testimony. [At a] New Year's Eve party . . . defendant came up, infuriated about something, asked his wife "Where in the hell have you been, you chippy-chasing son of a bitch?" His wife said nothing, and the defendant then said "Say something, you son of a bitch, or I will knock you down." Witness thought that he was going to strike her; she interfered, and he told her that it was a family affair, but turned and went off, the deceased soon following. The defendant denied this occurrence. . . . [In July or August of 1940, the deceased] and her husband got into an argument. He put his hands on the neck of the deceased, as to choke her, and shook her. Witness stayed at the house till one o'clock that night. Defendant took her home, and apologized for his action. The next morning she and the defendant and deceased went out riding and apparently everything was pleasant between defendant and deceased. . . . [O]n December 10, 1940, the day before the deceased was killed, the defendant . . . and the deceased [went for] a drink at the Elks Club. They went into the cocktail lounge. In talking the subject of Christmas gifts came up, and deceased . . . looked at her and said "How would you like a nice fresh divorce for Christmas?" and she said "I would like it." Everything before and after these remarks was pleasant between them. Defendant testified that they were joking.

*　　*　　*

Defendant testified that he and the deceased took . . . hunting trips in the fall. . . .

*　　*　　*

It is contended that the evidence is not sufficient to sustain the verdict herein, particularly in that it is insufficient to show malice. That is the important question in this case.

*   *   *

We turn then to consider the facts and circumstances immediately connected with the homicide, in the light of these rules of law. It may be that the full truth still lies hidden within the breast of the defendant alone. . . .

It was shown that the defendant's right thumb was out of joint, making it not unlikely to weaken it in holding the hammer of the gun, hence perhaps contributing to the accidental discharge of it. . . . The prosecuting attorney argued to the jury that since defendant had knowledge of this condition at the time of the homicide, it was criminal to handle the gun the way he claimed. That must be conceded, particularly in view of his knowledge of firearms, but it does not necessarily show an intent to kill, and is not, we think, inconsistent with the claim of accident . . . A striking fact herein is the place where the deceased was shot. If the bullet had entered the neck a fraction of an inch further back, it would, in all probability, have caused but a flesh wound, not fatal. It would seem that if the defendant had intended to kill the deceased, he would never have taken the chance of shooting her in the place where she was shot, but would have selected a surer place. Excluding possibilities, this fact would seem to show the State's theory to be wrong. . . .

That leaves for consideration the conduct of the defendant toward the deceased. If the defendant is guilty of murder, we ought to be able to find a motive. Motive, it is true, is not essential but it would seem that the absence in this case should have considerable influence in determining the degree of guilt. Malice is essential; it must be shown beyond a reasonable doubt, and as stated in *State* v. *Sorrentino*, the term "implies a wicked condition of mind while the homicide is committed; a mind, we may say, committing the very act willfully." And it would seem, in view of the fact that the relationship between the defendant and deceased was laid bare, we should be able to find malice therefrom, if it was present in this case. The contention that the defendant is guilty of murder seems to sum up in this: That he wanted to get rid of his wife. When the point at issue is stated thus, we can, we think, perceive the probative effect of the testimony to be now considered more clearly. Malice was attempted to be shown by introducing testimony of previous quarrels and difficulties between defendant and deceased. We may concede that they were all competent to be shown, but the probative effect thereof must be determined from all the facts and circumstances shown in the case. . . . These difficulties would have shown motive, and perhaps malice, if the deceased had killed the de-

fendant, but the reverse is not so clear. It was shown that the parties separated for two months in the early part of 1939 from March to May, and then became reconciled. Instead of showing malice and motive, and intent to kill, the reverse would seem to be true, for the reconciliation was voluntary and apparently gladly made by the defendant, as well as deceased. It was shown that some time in 1939 the defendant slapped his wife, with others present. For a man to slap a woman, let alone his wife, is not permissible under the spirit of American chivalry, and this fact, stressed in the argument to the jury, had undoubtedly much to do in bringing about the verdict in this case. But of course, to slap her, even with malice, is one thing; to kill her with malice is another. . . .

The incident on New Year's Eve of 1939 is, perhaps, the worst and most inexcusable incident shown in the record, illustrating the conduct of the defendant. . . . While the testimony does not show it, judging from the drinking habits of the defendant, the occasion, and the fact that intoxicating liquors were served at the place, we have no doubt that he was drunk. Even then, the testimony would be of probative effect, if followed by similar conduct. . . . It is altogether probable that the defendant was right in stating that he and his wife were joking when . . . he asked how she would like a nice fresh divorce, and she stated "I would like it." If, perchance, it were to be considered as serious, it would show, we think, the contrary of what the State contends. If he wanted to get rid of her, and he was able to do so by a divorce, with her consent, as the statement implied, it seems hardly credible that, instead, he would resort to murder. Divorces are frequent and comparatively easily obtained under the laws of this State, leaving little room for the desire or necessity for murder where both parties consent. [The] hunting trips, moreover, would seem to have afforded a much better opportunity for killing her and for a claim that it was accidental, than to kill her in the house and make that claim. . . . Furthermore, there is not the slightest indication in the record that there was "another woman" in the case, which might have given the defendant a motive for killing his wife and getting rid of her. Neither is there any indication that defendant was jealous or had cause to be jealous of any relations of deceased with other men, or that, after the reconciliation, he had any fear or cause to fear that deceased would leave him, which might have influenced him in the commission of a crime. Defendant and deceased had a little daughter, of whom defendant was very fond. He knew that she needed a mother, which would have a tendency to cause him to hesitate to get rid of the latter by murder.

After a most painstaking examination of the record before us, and consideration of the questions involved herein, we have, regrettable as the terrible tragedy was, and hesitant as we are to interfere with the verdict of the jury, come to the conclusion under the rules of law . . . and the facts, that the defendant was clearly guilty of criminal carelessness, or, at least, that there was ample evidence for the jury to so find. There is, however, such serious doubt as to the defendant's guilt of a greater crime, that the jury should have resolved that doubt in his favor; that, accordingly, the verdict of the jury should be set aside as to murder in the second degree, but sustained as to manslaughter, included in the former; that the judgment herein should be set aside, and that the trial court should cause the defendant to be brought before it, and resentence him for manslaughter. It is so ordered.

NOTE 3

OHIO v. NEBB
THE COURT OF COMMON PLEAS
OF FRANKLIN COUNTY, OHIO
Docket No. 39,540 (June 8, 1962)

[*Proceedings and Testimony*]

of Dr. T. R. Huxtable, Jr. on Voir Dire Examination.

*   *   *

BY MR. TYACK [for defendant]:

Q. Will you please state your name? A. Dr. T. R. Huxtable, Jr. * * * I am a psychiatrist. Medical doctor, specializing in psychiatry.

*   *   *

Q. Doctor, would the statements made by a person under hypnosis, with medical certainty, reasonable medical certainty, be held to be a truthful, correct statement? A. I would say yes.

*   *   *

Q. . . . to what extent does that person have any control over his statements made under hypnosis? A. Usually none; the statements you get usually are fact. I would have to qualify that, in certain types of mental disorders, this may not be true but, generally speaking, using the hypnosis, or pentothal or amytal, or what is commonly referred to as "truth serums," you get the facts.

*   *   *

Q. . . . To what extent would a person under hypnosis be subjected to a power of suggestion, so to speak, by either the hypnosis or the person interrogating the person? A. Well, the person is subject to a great deal of power of suggestion. But taking—if I were to place a person under hypnosis and suggest to them that in the posthypnotic state they will experience such and such a feeling, I do this; but if you place a patient under hypnosis for the purpose of finding out the true facts of what he feels and what he thinks, this is a different thing. We are not using the matter of suggestion here. We are using simply a matter of trying to find out what is fact and what is fiction. That is entirely different from the posthypnotic suggestion where you give the patient the suggestion that they are going to do so and so and so and so. This we don't do when we are trying to find out exactly what is going on.

*   *   *

BY MR. ALLISON [for the State]:

Q. Now, Doctor, is it possible for any given—for a given subject to absolutely convince himself over a period of months or years that something which didn't happen actually did happen, or vice versa, and then maintain that statement under hypnosis? A. I don't think so.

Q. Would you say that it is impossible? A. Yes.

*   *   *

Q. Isn't it a fact, Doctor, while sodium amytal or pentothal is frequently referred to as truth serum, this is absolutely a misnomer; what it does is relax the conscious mind and let the unconscious mind bring forth matters which the conscious mind have relegated so deep into the background that consciously a person does not remember them? A. True.

Q. And does hypnosis produce the same end result? A. Yes.

Q. In other words, Doctor, a person in a true hypnotic trance—when a person is in a true hypnotic trance and I were to ask him questions, I am talking to his unconscious mind, not his conscious mind, is that correct? A. You are talking to the unconscious and partially to the conscious, but without any restrictions.

Q. Now, Doctor, I have one further question. Is it possible that a subject could have suffered a traumatic shock so severe that even the unconscious would not recall the details of what happened? A. I don't think so.

Q. Doctor, is it possible that an emotional block could preclude a subject from totally recalling? A. In a conscious level, yes, but in the unconscious state under hypnosis I don't think so. I have never seen it. . . .

*   *   *

Thereupon, the defendant, Arthur C. Nebb, was placed in a hypnotic state by Dr. Huxtable, and the following proceedings were had:

*   *   *

MR. ALLISON: Arthur, what time did you first go to your house that night?

MR. NEBB: I don't know the time.

MR. ALLISON: Was it dark yet?

MR. NEBB: Yes.

*   *   *

MR. ALLISON: Now, what did you do after you got there and parked the car?

MR. NEBB: I seen Nelson and Camelia from the car. Nelson was putting on his coat, and Bernice was sitting on the studio couch at the door. Nelson and Camelia came out the door and walked down the driveway, and they went across the street.

I started to get out of the car, and I got my coat— and they come out of their driveway and their lights hit me.

*   *   *

MR. ALLISON: . . . What happened after the lights hit you? . . .

MR. NEBB: I got out of the car . . . and as I got closer to the house I looked in the doorway, and my wife was standing up, and she reached out and a hand —a hand reached in hers and a man stood up. * * * She kissed him, and she caught him by the hand and they walked into the dining room. I didn't see them any more. . . . So I went to the window, and they was in the bedroom . . .

DR. HUXTABLE: What happened then? . . .

MR. NEBB: I seen her take off her clothes and pants, and he took off hers and he took off his'n, and she got into bed. I had to—I had to get help.

DR. HUXTABLE: Why?

MR. NEBB: I wanted somebody to see it.

MR. ALLISON: What did you do, Arthur?

MR. NEBB: I went back and got in the car and I drove to Jesse Oliver's home. . . . I went on in and I got there, I went in there, and Jesse, his wife was in there, and I told him . . . to follow me. . . .

MR. ALLISON: Before you left Jesse Oliver's house, what did you say about killing both of them?

MR. NEBB: Killing both of them?

DR. HUXTABLE: What did you say to Jesse?

MR. NEBB: I told Jesse to—that I caught them in the bed, and for him to . . . follow me.

MR. ALLISON: Did you tell him you ought to kill them both, or ought to get them both, kill them both, anything along that line?

DR. HUXTABLE: Answer Mr. Allison, Arthur.

MR. NEBB: Yeah.

DR. HUXTABLE: What did you say?

MR. NEBB: I said "I got them both."

*   *   *

DR. HUXTABLE: Did you say anything that night to Jesse Oliver about killing both of them?

MR. NEBB: No.

DR. HUXTABLE: Why did he say you did?

MR. NEBB: I don't know. I said, "I got them both." They was in bed together.

MR. ALLISON: Arthur, could you have said that you ought to get them both?

MR. NEBB: No.

*   *   *

DR. HUXTABLE: Arthur, Mr. Oliver said you came to see him and you said, "I've got them both together," that you wanted him to come as a witness. Then you said to Oliver "I ought to kill them both," or "I'm going to kill them both." Remember saying that? What did you say? What did you say?

MR. NEBB: I ought to—I ought to kill them both?

DR. HUXTABLE: Did you say that? Did you say that? Arthur?

MR. NEBB: Yes.

*   *   *

DR. HUXTABLE: You got in the car and went back to your house; what did you go back for?

MR. NEBB: I wanted to catch them in the bed together.

MR. ALLISON: Did you think Jesse Oliver was following you?

MR. NEBB: Yes.

MR. ALLISON: Did you wait for him when you got there?

MR. NEBB: No.

MR. ALLISON: Why did you take the gun with you when you went back to the house, Arthur?

MR. NEBB: The gun was under the seat.

DR. HUXTABLE: But you took it with you?

MR. ALLISON: When you got out of your truck you took the gun with you. Why did you do it? Why did you take the gun with you?

MR. NEBB: To hold them in the bed.

*   *   *

MR. ALLISON: Were they in the bed when you got there, Arthur?

MR. NEBB: No.

MR. ALLISON: What did you do when you walked in the door, Arthur?

MR. NEBB: When I walked in the door I was surprised. I seen Camelia and Nelson on the couch, and I had the gun in my hand—

MR. ALLISON: Which hand, Arthur?

MR. NEBB: My right.

MR. ALLISON: Will he do physical things that I tell him to? Arthur, point the finger of your right hand like you had the gun. Hold your hand like you were holding the gun.

DR. HUXTABLE: Hold your right hand out there like you were holding the gun, just exactly the way you pointed it when you went in the house. Go ahead.

(Mr. Nebb complied.)

DR. HUXTABLE: Which way were you facing?

MR. ALLISON: Stand up, Arthur, and do it.

DR. HUXTABLE: Arthur, stand up. Open your eyes. Stand up. You are all right, stand up. Show them exactly how you did it. Go ahead. Stand up, you are all right.

(Mr. Nebb stood up.)

DR. HUXTABLE: You walked in the house with the

gun in your hand. Show us how you went in and how you held it.

MR. NEBB: Went in the house—

DR. HUXTABLE: Look in the direction you pointed it. Show us how you pointed it.

MR. NEBB: Like this. . . . I seen Nelson go for the living room and Bernice hollered, "What's the matter?" and Camelia jumped up, and just then Bernice jumped and grabbed me and the gun fired.

DR. HUXTABLE: Stand up. You are all right.

MR. NEBB: Fired.

DR. HUXTABLE: You are all right.

MR. NEBB: And I fired again.

DR. HUXTABLE: How many times?

MR. NEBB: I fired again.

DR. HUXTABLE: How many times?

MR. NEBB: Again.

DR. HUXTABLE: What you see here is a reliving of the emotional reaction at the time this took place.

MR. NEBB: She went down.

DR. HUXTABLE: What did you do? How many times did you fire. How many times? How many times?

MR. NEBB: Five. Five. Five.

DR. HUXTABLE: You are all right. Stand up. You want to sit down on the chair? Open your eyes. Get in the chair again. Sit down. What did you do then?

MR. NEBB: I thought she was dead. Camelia kept hollering at me and everything drained out of me.

DR. HUXTABLE: Arthur, when you drove back from Jesse Oliver's in that car, were you going back to kill Bernice?

MR. NEBB: No, I wanted to get back there and see who he was.

MR. ALLISON: Were you going to kill him, Arthur?

MR. NEBB: No, I didn't want to hurt anybody, I just wanted to—

MR. ALLISON: Arthur, when you got back from Georgia did you tell me you intended to kill her?

MR. NEBB: I believe I would have killed her if Camelia wouldn't have hollered, if Camelia hadn't have hollered I would have killed her because I—

MR. ALLISON: Did you tell me you intended to kill her, Arthur? When you got back from Georgia, when we were in the Sheriff's office, did you tell me that you intended to kill her?

DR. HUXTABLE: Answer Mr. Allison, Arthur.

MR. NEBB: I believe I did make that statement to you, but—

MR. ALLISON: You made it two or three times, didn't you, Arthur, that you intended to kill her?

MR. NEBB: I—not two or three times.

MR. ALLISON: Why did you tell me that night that you intended to kill her?

MR. NEBB: Because I—in my mind, I believe I would have killed her if Camelia hadn't have hollered, because after the gun went off I couldn't stop myself.

* * *

MR. ALLISON: Now, where was the man when you went in the house with the gun? Where was the other man?

MR. NEBB: The other man?

MR. ALLISON: Yes.

MR. NEBB: I didn't see him. I guess he was in the bedroom or the kitchen. I didn't see him.

MR. ALLISON: Why did you raise the gun and fire over Bernice's head?

MR. NEBB: I didn't raise the gun. Bernice grabbed the gun.

MR. ALLISON: How did she grab it, Arthur?

MR. NEBB: When she jumped up I fell backward and hit the door casing. When I fell backward, she'd turned me loose and running from me and—

MR. ALLISON: Is that when you started shooting at her?

MR. NEBB: The shot—the shot I fired at her, I don't know if I pulled the trigger when my arm hit the casing as I went backward.

MR. ALLISON: Was it a revolver, Arthur, or an automatic pistol?

MR. NEBB: A revolver.

MR. ALLISON: Did you cock it before you went in the house?

MR. NEBB: No.

MR. ALLISON: Was the hammer back?

MR. NEBB: No.

MR. ALLISON: What did you do with that gun, Arthur? Where is the gun now?

MR. NEBB: I dropped it.

MR. ALLISON: Dropped it where? You didn't drop it in the house, Arthur. Where did you drop it?

MR. NEBB: I did. I did drop it in the house.

MR. ALLISON: Doctor, could you pursue this particular thing with him?

DR. HUXTABLE: Where is the gun, Arthur?

MR. ALLISON: If he can tell me where the gun is I'll buy the story.

DR. HUXTABLE: Where is the gun, Arthur?

MR. ALLISON: Because I've looked for it pretty good.

DR. HUXTABLE: Arthur, answer me. Where is the gun? What did you do with it?

MR. NEBB: The gun's there in the house.

DR. HUXTABLE: It's not there, Arthur. Where is it? Where is it?

MR. NEBB: It's got to be there! I left it right there.

* * *

MR. ALLISON: What name did you call your wife that night, Arthur?

DR. HUXTABLE: Arthur.

MR. ALLISON: Did you call her a bad name?

DR. HUXTABLE: Arthur, answer. What did you call her? Come on now, what did you call her?

MR. NEBB: Yes.

DR. HUXTABLE: What did you call her, Arthur?

MR. NEBB: "You bitch, how could you do this to me?"

*   *   *

MR. ALLISON: When you said to your wife, "You bitch, how could you do this to me?" where was the man sitting?

MR. NEBB: The man—I didn't—I didn't see any man.

MR. ALLISON: Are you sure, Arthur?

MR. NEBB: When I said—

MR. ALLISON: Think hard, real hard. You are right there and Bernice is sitting on the davenport, and a man is beside her.

MR. NEBB: When I said, "bitch," I was over her. I didn't say that when she was at the studio couch. I was over her.

MR. ALLISON: You mean after you had already shot her? Is when you said that?

MR. NEBB: Yes.

MR. ALLISON: Did you see the man laying there when you went out the door, Arthur?

MR. NEBB: No, I didn't see no man at all.

MR. ALLISON: When did you first find out you had killed the man, Arthur?

DR. HUXTABLE: Come on, Arthur. Speak up. Answer Mr. Allison.

MR. NEBB: Jesse Oliver told me when I called him.

MR. ALLISON: Why did you keep shooting at your wife after she fell down, Arthur?

MR. NEBB: I don't know. The trigger kept—kept going. I couldn't stop.

MR. ALLISON: Your finger had to pull the trigger, didn't it? The trigger didn't go by itself that way, did it? Your finger had to pull it.

MR. NEBB: Yes.

*   *   *

MR. ALLISON: Did you want to see her dead, Arthur?

MR. NEBB: No. No, I didn't want to see her dead. I wanted to go back if she'd take me back.

*   *   *

DR. HUXTABLE: Arthur, I'm going to count to three. You are going to wake up . . . one, two, three. Wide awake. . . .

*   *   *

MR. TYACK: How are you doing, Arthur?

MR. NEBB: I don't know.

THE COURT: This case will stand in recess until 1:30 this afternoon.

Friday Afternoon Session

*   *   *

Thereupon, at 2:40 o'clock P.M. the trial of the aforesaid cause resumed and the following proceedings were had.

THE COURT: Mr. Allison.

MR. ALLISON: If the Court please, at this time the State will move to amend the indictment and delete from the indictment the words "purposely" and "of deliberate premeditated malice," and substituting therefor the word "unlawfully."

THE COURT: Is there any objection to this, Mr. Tyack?

MR. TYACK: No, sir.

THE COURT: The indictment will be so amended. * * * What is your plea to this charge?

MR. NEBB: Guilty.

THE COURT: Is there a question in your mind about this one, Mr. Nebb?

MR. NEBB: I carried the gun in there, sir.

*   *   *

THE COURT: You carried the gun in there. That's right. Now, do I correctly understand as to the indictment in the other case, as amended, leaving out the words "purposely and of premeditated malice," and substituting the word "unlawfully," you did kill Estel Stepp, you wish to change your plea to the lesser crime?

MR. NEBB: I am guilty.

THE COURT: You plead guilty to the lesser crime of manslaughter that is involved there. Is there a question in your mind about that. . . .

*   *   *

MR. NEBB: No, sir.

*   *   *

NOTE 4

FREUD, SIGMUND

Five Lectures on Psychoanalysis (1909)*

It is only if you exclude hypnosis that you can observe resistances and repressions and form an adequate idea of the truly pathogenic course of events. Hypnosis conceals the resistance and renders a certain area of the mind accessible; but, as against this, it builds up the resistance at the frontiers of this area into a wall that makes everything beyond it inaccessible.

* Reprinted from: 11 *The Standard Edition of the Complete Psychological Works of Sigmund Freud*, James Strachey, ed. London: The Hogarth Press and the Institute of Psychoanalysis, 1957. (p. 26). Reprinted by permission of Hogarth and Liveright Publishing Co.

NOTE 5

DESSION, GEORGE H.; FREEDMEN, LAWRENCE Z.;
DONNELLY, RICHARD C.; AND
REDLICH, FREDRICK C.

Drug-Induced Revelation and
Criminal Investigation*

[E]xperimental and clinical findings indicate that only individuals who have conscious and unconscious reasons for doing so are inclined to confess and yield to interrogation under drug influence. On the other hand, some are able to withhold information and some, especially character neurotics, are able to lie. Others are so suggestible they will describe, in response to suggestive questioning, behavior which never in fact occurred. . . . But drugs are not "truth sera." They lessen inhibitions to verbalization and stimulate unrepressed expression not only of fact but of fancy and suggestion as well. Thus the material produced is not "truth" in the sense that it conforms to empirical fact. . . .

b.   **Testimony of Rudolf Hess***

Q. Do you prefer to testify in English or in German? A. In German.

Q. What is your full name? A. Rudolf Hess.

Q. What was your last official position? A. Unfortunately, this already comes into a period which I cannot remember any more. I am suffering from loss of memory, and the doctor has told me that this is a frequent occurrence, especially in time of war, but that there is some chance that my memory will return. There are many cases where I cannot even remember what happened ten or fourteen days ago.

Q. What period is it that you cannot remember? A. Anything longer than, say ten or fourteen days ago. It has frequently happened that I met gentlemen I could not even remember their faces when I saw them again. It is terrible. Yesterday I was told by a doctor, or maybe it was a clerk over there, that it happens sometimes that people don't even know their own names any more, and he said that possibly by a shock it would suddenly all return again. This is terrible for me, and everything depends on it for me because I will have to defend myself in the trial which is going to come soon. There is nobody to defend me if I cannot do it myself.

Q. You mean that you cannot even remember what

* Reprinted by permission of the Yale Law Journal Company and Fred B. Rothman and Company from the *Yale Law Journal*, vol. 62, pp. 315, 319 (1953).
** Excerpts from testimony of Rudolf Hess, taken at Nurenberg, Germany, October 9, 1945, 1045–1215, 1430–1510, 1700–1707, by Col. John H. Amen, IGD, OUSCC. *International Military Trials Nurenberg*, Supp. B. 1154–72 (1948).

your last official position was in Germany? A. No. I have no idea. It is just like a fog.

Q. Do you remember that you used to be in Germany? A. Well, I think that that is self-understood, because I have been told so repeatedly, but I don't remember just where I was and not even in what house I was. It has all disappeared. It is gone.

*   *   *

Q. Why don't you like the Jews? A. If I had to explain that to you in detail, I am again facing nothing. I only know that this is deeply within me.

Q. How do you remember that you don't like them? A. When the name "Jew" is mentioned, something stirs in me, which is dislike, or that they are not sympathetic to me, or rather that I have no sympathies for them. I cannot explain it in detail.

Q. You cannot recall any reason why you shouldn't like them? A. No.

*   *   *

Q. Do you believe that Germany was justified in conducting this recent war? A. I cannot give you an answer to that, because the circumstances are—not any of the circumstances are in my memory.

Q. So perhaps they were wrong, and perhaps they were right; is that it? A. Yes. That depends entirely upon the situation, which I don't know.

Q. When did you first learn that the Fuehrer was dead? A. That I don't know.

Q. Do you know whether he is dead or not? A. Well, that is a term to me, so to speak. I don't know why it is a term, but if I looked at the picture of the Fuehrer, which was hanging in front of me, I knew that he was dead.

Q. You knew he was dead from looking at his picture? A. That was a thought association, just that the Fuehrer is dead. That is all.

Q. Where did you get that thought? A. That I don't know.

*   *   *

First Reunion with Old Friends and Associates[1]

COL. AMEN: Your name is Rudolf Hess?

RUDOLF HESS: Yes.

COL. AMEN: Will you look over here to the right to this gentleman here.

RUDOLF HESS: At him? (Pointing to Hermann Goering).

COL. AMEN: Yes.

HERMANN GOERING: Don't you know me?

RUDOLF HESS: Who are you?

HERMANN GOERING: You ought to know me. We have been together for years.

1. This confrontation was made in order to test the genuineness of Hess' claimed amnesia.

RUDOLF HESS: That must have been the same time as the book that was submitted to me this morning. I have lost my memory for some time, especially now before the trial. It is terrible, and the doctor tells me that it is going to come back.

HERMANN GOERING: Don't you know me? You don't recognize me?

RUDOLF HESS: Not personally, but I remember your name.

HERMANN GOERING: But we talked a lot together.

RUDOLF HESS: We were together; that must have been the case. That must have been so. As the Deputy of the Fuehrer all the time in that position, I must have met the other high personalities like you, but I cannot remember anyone, to the best of my will.

HERMANN GOERING: Listen, Hess, I was the Supreme Commander of the Luftwaffe, and you flew to England in one of my planes. Don't you remember that I was the Supreme Commander of the Luftwaffe. First I was a Field Marshal, and later a Reichmarshal at a meeting of the Reichstag while you were present; don't you remember that?

RUDOLF HESS: No.

HERMANN GOERING: Do you remember that the Fuehrer, at a meeting of the Reichstag, announced in the Reichstag that if something happened to him, that I would be his successor, and if something happened to me, you were to be my successor? Don't you remember that?

RUDOLF HESS: No.

HERMANN GOERING: You don't remember that? We two discussed that very long afterwards.

RUDOLF HESS: This is terrible. If the doctors wouldn't assure me time and time again that my memory would return some day, I would be driven to desperation.

HERMANN GOERING: Don't you remember that I visited your family and your wife? I saw you and your wife together repeatedly. You also visited my family with your wife.

RUDOLF HESS: This is all a fog, behind which everything has disappeared; everything that happened in that time.

HERMANN GOERING: Do you remember that I lived just outside Berlin, in a great house in the forest, at Karinhall; don't you remember that you came there many times? Do you remember that we were together at Obersalzberg with the Fuehrer, where you have been for years, near Berchtesgaden?

RUDOLF HESS: I have been there for years?

HERMANN GOERING: Yes, for years, even before the acquisition of power.

RUDOLF HESS: That means nothing to me.

HERMANN GOERING: Hess, remember all the way back to 1923, at that time when I was the leader of the S.A., that you led one of my S.A. troops in Munich already for me before 1923? Do you remember that we together made the *putsch* in Munich?

RUDOLF HESS: The *putsch* in Munich was already mentioned this morning.

HERMANN GOERING: Do you remember that you arrested the Minister?

RUDOLF HESS: I arrested the Minister?

HERMANN GOERING: Yes.

RUDOLF HESS: I seem to have a pretty involved past, according to that.

HERMANN GOERING: I am just calling the most glaring things to your attention. Do you remember the beginning of the year 1933, and that we took over the government then, and that you got the central political office from the Fuehrer, and that we discussed it for a long time?

RUDOLF HESS: No.

HERMANN GOERING: You also told me that you wanted to become a member of the government, and I told you that I would try to help you. Do you remember that you moved to the Wilhemstrasse, into the palace which really belonged to me, as the Prime Minister of Prussia, but I enabled you to live there?

RUDOLF HESS: I don't know.

HERMANN GOERING: I visited you many times, and I handed it to you so you would have a house in Berlin. I turned the house over to you for your benefit.

RUDOLF HESS: I have been told that everything will come back at one time by a shock.

HERMANN GOERING: Just a moment. Do you remember Mr. Messerschmitt? You were well acquainted with him. He constructed all our fighter planes, and he also gave you the plane that I refused to give you, the plane with which you flew to England. Mr. Messerschmitt gave that to you behind my back.

RUDOLF HESS: No; that is all black. That is all black. That is all blacked out. It is all beyond fourteen days, and everything then I have a slight memory, and nothing exact. They told me that people who suffered heavily in the war would get attacks like that.

HERMANN GOERING: Do you remember that the war started—

RUDOLF HESS: I know that there was a war, but I don't know how it came about.

HERMANN GOERING: Do you remember that you flew in a plane, you yourself, in this war, flew to England?

RUDOLF HESS: No.

HERMANN GOERING: You used a Messerschmitt plane. Do you remember that you wrote a long letter to the Fuehrer?

RUDOLF HESS: About what?

HERMANN GOERING: What you were going to do in England, that you were going to bring about peace.

RUDOLF HESS: I have no idea of it.

HERMANN GOERING: I have come to the end. I cannot ask him any more.

*   *   *

Advantage or Disadvantage of Loss of Memory Before Trial

Q. When did you get this idea of losing your memory? A. I don't know. It is a fact that I don't have it now.

Q. I say, when did you get the idea that it would be the smart thing to lose it? A. I don't quite understand that. You mean to say by that that I thought it might be a good idea to lose my memory and then deceive you like that?

Q. Yes. That is just what I mean. A. Well, I can only say that that is not true.

Q. Well, it might be very helpful in connection with the coming proceedings, might it not? A. Well, how could it be helpful?

Q. Well, if you don't remember anything that you were implicated in, it would be more difficult to, perhaps, prove it. A. Well, take the book, for instance, that you showed me yesterday. I don't see what benefit I could derive from losing my memory there.

Q. Oh, no, but, for instance, when you directed the murder of various people, which you did. A. I did that?

Q. Yes. So the witnesses say. A. You mean that because I can't remember it, the witnesses are less creditable?

Q. Oh, somewhat. A. Or, do you mean because I am lying?

Q. To make people feel sorry for you also. A. On the contrary, I don't understand that. If I give the appearance that I lost my memory, then people will not like me, and it might influence the trial in such a way that I will get a worse judgment.

Q. Well, all I was interested in was finding out when it was that you got the idea of doing that. A. Well, if I tell you that I never had any such idea, I can't tell you when I got it.

Q. So you think, for purposes of the trial, you would be better off to have your memory than to have lost it; is that right? A. There is one thing that I can do in the coming trial, and that is to fight with everything I have for my own skin, and the only instrument I have to fight with is my brain and my memory.

Q. Well, your brain is just as good now as it ever was, isn't it? A. Well, how does it help me, though, if my brain is working all right and if I don't have any memory; if I can't confront a witness with facts?

Q. Well, it doesn't, of course, if you really haven't got any memory left. A. Then I must ask the gentleman again why he thinks, or for what reason he thinks, I am doing this. Does he think I am so childish, or so naive, that I think I could improve my position with that?

Q. I'm not quite sure why you are. A. Yes. Well, that is just it, and that is why I am asking you, because I am much less sure why I should have any advantage from it.

Q. Well, Goering thinks that maybe he can help you get it back again in the near future. A. I don't know what I can give him. Whether I can give him a decoration or a medal later, I don't know; but whatever I can give to him, I willingly will give to him.

Q. Well, we will let him try. A. Well, I am only grateful for that.

Q. That is all for now.

NOTES

NOTE 1

KATZ, JAY

On Primary Gain and Secondary Gain*

Primary gain . . . has been defined as the gains accruing to an individual from the relief of guilt and anxiety through symptom formation as well as from the disguised instinct gratification present in the symptom. . . .

Primary gain, if defined only from the vantage point of relief from anxiety and guilt, represents a purely intrapsychic process which is unconsciously elaborated and has no referent in external events. . . . However, if instinct gratification through symptom formation is included in the definition of primary gain, interaction with the external world . . . must be considered as an aspect of the primary gain.

The conciseness and precision in the definition of primary gain does not apply to secondary gain. . . .

*   *   *

Alexander . . . stresses the advantages subsequent to symptom formation in his formulation of secondary gain, but then he has second thoughts:

> Being incapacitated by illness may have certain advantages. Among the most transparent is financial compensation for accidents. Illness may serve also as a legitimate excuse to avoid unpleasant duties and discard pressing responsibilities. It provokes sympathy and attention and assures the sufferers a privileged position. These advantages retard recovery and make therapy particularly difficult.
>
> *They are secondary consequences of neurotic illness* and do not belong to its dynamic structure or to the motivation which produces neurosis. This is particularly true of financial compensation for accidents. It is, however, extremely difficult to draw a sharp line between earlier dependent longings of patients and their secondary exploitation of illness to satisfy passive dependent needs. . . .

The concept of secondary gain must be applied with great precaution. Any adult person who prefers support from others to the productive use of his own

---

* 18 *The Psychoanalytic Study of the Child*, 1963 (25–31, 39–40). Reprinted by permission.

powers is unduly dependent. This infantile trait is always a significant, and frequently the most significant, factor in his neurosis. The important consideration is that the emotional and financial gains derived from illness contribute to the prolongation of illness. . . .

Alexander brings genetic propositions ("infantile traits, earlier dependent longings") to the discussion of secondary gain. But he addresses himself primarily to the impact of reality factors without sorting them out. Illness, for example, may result in a partial regression to an earlier developmental level and thus alter patterns of interaction with significant persons in the environment. Here secondary gain will be affected by the degree of regression and the responsiveness of the environment. Then there is the reality of society which provides compensations for injuries and illnesses. In the context of such social reality the question arises whether the "exploitation of illness" may not for particular patients represent a "better" adaptation to reality than they had previously been able to make. To answer such questions, criteria for adaptation and maladaptation are needed. One of the difficulties with Alexander's formulation is that he postulates both that secondary gain does not "belong to the dynamic structure of the neurosis" and that there is a relationship "between earlier dependent longings . . . and . . . secondary exploitation of illness." Alexander is aware of the problem—"no sharp line can be drawn."

* * *

It is striking throughout most of the literature on primary and secondary gain that, while "gain" or "advantage" is part of both definitions, different though unarticulated connotations are given to these words. What is the difference between the "value" the neurosis has after its development (secondary gain) from the "value" inherent in its development (primary gain)? Why does a patient "prefer to keep his neurosis"? Is it only, or at all, related to the secondary gains? May this not be too superficial an interpretation of the "obvious" use to which symptoms are put? Is it not possible that the resistance to give up the neurosis represents, at least in part, a further defensive effort by the ego to protect the individual from a re-emergence of the dreaded *id* impulses (primary gain) which initially led to symptom formation? . . .

* * *

The word "advantage" itself adds to the confusion since it carries the connotation of increased "profit" and "leverage" and, therefore, its use can easily hide unarticulated value judgments. And in labeling one aspect of the symptom picture as bringing advantages, the concomitant disadvantages usually receive insufficient attention. In addition, the impact of other mental mechanisms which may come into play, e.g.,

regression, are not sufficiently considered. For example, is the "advantage" the discarding of pressing responsibilities, the expectation of financial compensations, or the attempt at integration at a regressed level? Here all the disadvantageous manifestations of the ego's inability to cope with both the inner and outer world at a higher developmental level must also be included in the analysis. . . .

* * *

From the vantage point of optimal functioning, a neurotic symptom initially leads to a maladaptation, yet the picture may change. Hartmann, for example, points out that "an attitude which arose originally in the service of defense against an instinctual drive may, in the course of time, become an independent structure and . . . through a change of function turn a means into a goal in its own right". . . . While Hartmann's concept of change of function refers to such issues as ego autonomy, it possibly can be analogized to the fate of a symptom. The symptom's instinct component may be defended against (neutralized") so effectively and the symptom may turn out to be so useful to an adaptation of a particular individual to a particular environment, that one could speak here too of a means having been turned "into a goal in its own right." Thus in the life history of secondary gains, due to their constant interaction with mental structures and the outside world, many changes may occur.

For example, Erikson . . . has stressed that at times, especially in adolescence, it may be necessary for a person temporarily to become a patient in order to take time out before he commits himself to an adult role. How the environment meets this situation will be crucial for the integration of the individual. Thus a symptom may allow a person to find, for a while, a much-needed identity as a patient. Also, if members of a family accept the patient's symptoms, or in fact have unwittingly helped to bring them out for neurotic reasons of their own, then such symptoms may eventually allow the patient an adaptation to his neurotic environment. And if removal from such an environment is impossible, the adaptive values may be considerable. If society through provisions for workmen's compensation, welfare funds, and large insurance settlements creates an environment where there may be advantages to being sick for at least certain people, the extent to which illness becomes a "fitting into" the environment requires much further scrutiny. Surely social structure influences the adaptive possibilities of a particular form of behavior. While a descriptive approach to the study of secondary gain has been able to list the "advantages" which a patient derives from his illness, it has tended to overlook the adaptive aspects of such advantages. Such an approach has also contributed to an insulation of "gains" from their genetic and dynamic setting and, instead, has tended to view them almost as independent goals. The concept of adaptation suggests that the "advantages through illness" are the result of complex mutual regulations between the individual and society—of more or less successful and unsuccessful attempts by patients to find an appropriate niche in their environment.

*   *   *

NOTE 2

COLEMAN v. COKER
204 Tenn. 310, 321 S.W. 2d 540 (1959)

BURNETT, JUSTICE

This is a workmen's compensation case. . . . The trial judge found that the death of the employee arose out of and in the course of his employment and thus awarded compensation to the widow. . . .

. . . Coleman employed Joe Richard Coker, a carpenter, shortly before August 29, 1957. Coker had only been employed a few days before his death. . . . He, at the time of his employment, was asked no questions nor made no representations as to his previous physical disabilities. On the date of the death it is found by the trial judge that the man died of a heart attack which was due to aggravation by strain, effort, and exertion of his work, of this pre-existing condition. . . .

The plaintiff in error in this appeal [alleges that] the court erred in not dismissing the suit because the deceased's death was brought about by reason of the willful misconduct of the deceased "in refusing to follow his doctor's instructions."

*   *   *

[T]he deceased had had angina pectoris for a period of at least three years prior to his death. For approximately eighteen months he knew he had this heart condition. The doctor had advised him against doing carpentry work and this advice, it would be gathered from the proof, was given him some eighteen months prior to this attack. This doctor had prescribed diet, rest, the use of certain medical tablets and warned against strenuous exertion and this of course is the usual prescription in such cases. Along with the further statement the doctor says that he thought it best for this patient to abstain from the use of alcohol. The record shows that Mr. Coker did comply with this advice on all these matters except the continuing of his work as a trim carpenter. Even though this was advised against by the doctor he did not specifically forbid him to do so. As we read the record no such precise order was given. It does not appear that the doctor with the full knowledge of the fact that Mr. Coker was continuing to work, ever warned him against working, and it does not appear that he ever in unequivocal terms brought home to this man the fact that in doing his usual work he was placing himself in imminent peril.

At any rate this man worked at different intervals over a period of eighteen months prior to his death, after being advised of his condition and he had gotten along reasonably well during that time and there is nothing as far as the record shows that on the day in question he was doing anything different from what he had been doing off and on for the last eighteen months. He of course might have forgotten that a year and one-half before the doctor had warned him against such work. The fact that he had engaged in this during this time was certainly sufficient to take the fact away from his immediate consciousness that he was in immediate danger.

As we see it at the most this was not a willful act on the part of the deceased, it was certainly inadvertence and a mistake of judgment as it turned out, but inadvertence or mistake of judgment or negligence, or even gross negligence, fall far short of being willful misconduct under the authorities. . . .

*   *   *

Affirmed.

NOTE 3

BETTELHEIM, BRUNO

The Informed Heart*

The universal success of the *Diary of Anne Frank* suggests how much the tendency to deny is still with us, while her story itself demonstrates how such denial can hasten our own destruction. It is an onerous task to take apart such a humane and moving story, arousing so much compassion for gentle Anne Frank. But I believe that its worldwide acclaim cannot be explained unless we recognize our wish to forget the gas chambers and to glorify attitudes of extreme privatization, of continuing to hold onto attitudes as usual even in a holocaust. Exactly because their going on with private life as usual brought destruction did it have to be glorified; in that way we could overlook the essential fact of how destructive it can be under extreme social circumstances.

While the Franks were making their preparations for going passively into hiding, thousands of other Jews in Holland and elsewhere in Europe were trying to escape to the free world, the better to survive or to be able to fight their executioners. Others who could not do so went underground—not simply to hide from the S.S., waiting passively, without preparation for flight, for the day when they would be caught —but to fight the Germans, and with it for humanity. All the Franks wanted was to go on with life as nearly as possible in the usual fashion.

* Reprinted with permission of The Free Press and Thames & Hudson Ltd. Copyright © 1960 by The Free Press.

Little Anne, too, wanted only to go on with life as usual, and nobody can blame her. But hers was certainly not a necessary fate, much less a heroic one; it was a senseless fate. The Franks could have faced the facts and survived, as did many Jews living in Holland. Anne could have had a good chance to survive, as did many Jewish children in Holland. But for that she would have had to be separated from her parents and gone to live with a Dutch family as their own child.

Everybody who recognized the obvious knew that the hardest way to go underground was to do it as a family; that to hide as a family made detection by the S.S. most likely. The Franks, with their excellent connections among gentile Dutch families should have had an easy time hiding out singly, each with a different family. But instead of planning for this, the main principle of their planning was to continue as much as possible with the kind of family life they were accustomed to. Any other course would have meant not merely giving up the beloved family life, but also accepting as reality man's inhumanity to man. Most of all it would have forced them to accept that going on with life as usual was not an absolute value, but can sometimes be the most destructive of all attitudes.

There is little doubt that the Franks, who were able to provide themselves with so much, could have provided themselves with a gun or two had they wished. They could have shot down at least one or two of the "green police" who came for them. There was no surplus of such police. The loss of an S.S. with every Jew arrested would have noticeably hindered the functioning of the police state. The fate of the Franks wouldn't have been any different, because they all died anyway except for Anne's father, though he hardly meant to pay for his survival with the extermination of his whole family. But they could have sold their lives dearly instead of walking to their death.

There is good reason why the so successful play ends with Anne stating her belief in the good in all men. What is denied is the importance of accepting the gas chambers as real so that never again will they exist. If all men are basically good, if going on with intimate family living no matter what else is what is to be most admired, then indeed we can all go on with life as usual and forget about Auschwitz. Except that Anne Frank died because her parents could not get themselves to believe in Auschwitz. And her story found wide acclaim because for us too, it denies implicitly that Auschwitz ever existed. If all men are good, there was never an Auschwitz.

[S]ubmitting to the total state leads to a disintegration of what once seemed a well-integrated personality, plus a return to many infantile attitudes. [P]erhaps a theoretical speculation may be helpful. Years ago Freud postulated two opposite tendencies:

The life instincts, which he called eros or sex, and the destructive tendencies, which he named the death instinct. The more mature the person becomes, the more he should be able to "fuse" these two opposing tendencies, making the resultant "ego" energy available for the task of meeting and shaping reality.

The more immature the person, the more these tendencies are apt to push the total personality, at one moment in one direction, at the next moment in the other. Thus the so-called childlike friendliness of some primitive people, followed in the next moment by extreme "thoughtless" cruelty. But the disintegration, or perhaps one should better say the "defusion" of ego energy under extreme stress—at one moment into pure destructive tendencies ("Let it be over, no matter how"), at the next moment into irrational life tendencies ("Let's get something to eat now, even if it means death in short order")—was only one aspect of man's primitivization in the total state. Another was engaging in infantile thought processes such as wishful thinking in place of a more mature evaluation of reality, and an infantile disregard for the possibility of death. These led many to think that they of all others would be spared and survive, and many more to simply disbelieve in the possibility of their own death. Not believing in its possibility, they did not prepare for it, including no preparation for how to defend their lives even when death became inescapable. Defending their lives before such time might have hastened their death. So up to a point, this "rolling with the punches" that the enemy dealt out was protective of life. But beyond that point it was destructive of both one's own life and that of others whose survival might be more certain too if one risked one's own life. The trouble is that the longer one "rolls" with the punches, the more likely it becomes that one will no longer have the strength to resist when death becomes imminent, particularly if this yielding to the enemy is accompanied not by an inner strengthening of the personality (which it would require) but an inner disintegration.

Those who did not deny validity to death, who neither denied nor repressed its possibility, who embraced no childish belief in their indestructibility, were those who prepared for it in time as a real possibility. It meant risking one's life for a self-chosen purpose and in doing do, saving one's own life or that of others, or both. When Jews in Germany were restricted to their homes, those who did not allow inertia to take over used the imposing of such restrictions as a warning that it was high time to go underground, join the resistance movement, provide themselves with forged papers, etc., if they had not done so long ago. Most of them survived.

An example out of the lives of some distant relatives of mine may further illustrate. Early in the war, a young man living in a small Hungarian town banded together with a number of other Jews and they prepared themselves for what to do when the Germans invaded. As soon as the Nazis imposed curfew on the Jews, his group left for Budapest since the bigger the city, the better the chances for escaping detection. There, similar groups from other towns converged and joined those of Budapest. From among them they selected typically "Aryan" looking men who, equipped with false papers, immediately joined the Hungarian S.S. so as to be able to warn of impending actions, to report in advance when a particular district would be searched, etc.

This worked so well that most of the groups survived intact. But they had also equipped themselves with small arms, so that when detected they could put up enough of a fight for the majority to escape while a few would die fighting to gain time for the escape. A few of the Jews who had joined the S.S. were discovered and immediately shot, probably a death preferable to one in the gas chambers. But even among their special group the majority survived, hiding within the S.S. up to the last moment.

My young relative was unable to convince some members of his family to go with him when he left. Three times, at tremendous risk to himself he returned, pointing out first the growing persecution of the Jews, later the fact that their transport to the gas chambers had already begun. He could not convince them to move out of their homes, to leave their possessions. On each visit he pleaded more desperately, on each visit he found them less willing or able to listen to him, much less able to take action. It was as if each time they were more on their way to the crematoria where they all in fact died.

On each visit his family clung more desperately to the old living arrangements, the possessions they had accumulated over a lifetime. It was like a parallel process in which their life energies were drained away while their possessions seemed to give them a pseudosecurity to replace the real assurance that no longer came from planning for their lives. Again like children, they preferred to cling desperately to some objects in which they had invested all the meaning they could no longer find in their lives. As they withdrew from the fight for survival, their lives began to reside more and more in these dead objects and the persons in them died piece by piece, little object by little object.

In Buchenwald, I talked to hundreds of German Jewish prisoners who were brought there in the fall of 1938. I asked them why they had not left Germany because of the utterly degrading conditions they were subjected to. Their answer was: "How could we leave? It would have meant giving up our homes, our places of business." Their earthly possessions had so taken possession of them that they could not move; instead of using them, they were run by them.

How the investing of possessions with one's life energy made people see piece by piece is also evident in the court of the Nazi attitude toward Jews. At the time of the first boycott of Jewish stores the whole external goal of the Nazis was the possessions of the Jews. They even let Jews take some of them out of the country if they would just go, leaving the bulk of their possessions behind. For a long time the intention of the Nazis, and of their first discriminatory laws, was to force undesirable minorities, including Jews, into emigration. Only when this did not work was the extermination policy instituted, though it also followed the inner logic of the Nazi racial ideology. But one wonders if the notion that millions of Jews (and later foreign nationals) would submit to extermination did not also result from seeing how much degradation they would accept without fighting back. The persecution of the Jews worsened, slow step by slow step, when no violent resistance occurred. It may have been Jewish acceptance, without fight, of ever harsher discrimination and degradation that first gave the S.S. the idea that they could be gotten to the point where they would walk to the gas chambers on their own.

Most Jews in Poland who did not believe in business as usual survived World War II. As the Germans approached, they left everything behind and fled to Russia, much as many of them distrusted the Soviet system. But there, while perhaps citizens of a second order, they were at least accepted as human beings. Those who stayed on to continue business as usual moved toward their own destruction and perished. Thus in the deepest sense the walk to the gas chamber was only the last consequence of a philosophy of business as usual; a last step in no longer defying the death instinct, which might also be called the principle of inertia. Because the first step was taken long before one entered the death camp.

True, the same suicidal behavior has another meaning. It means that man can be pushed so far and no further; that beyond a certain point he chooses death to an inhuman existence. But the initial step toward this terrible choice was inertia.

Those who give in to it, who have withdrawn all vital energy from the world, can no longer act with initiative, and are threatened by it in others. They can no longer accept reality for what it is; having grown infantile, they see it only in the infantile perspective of a wishful denial of what is too unpleasant, of a wishful belief in their personal immortality. All this is dramatically illustrated in an experience of Lengyel's. She reports that although she and her fellow prisoners lived just a few hundred yards from the crematoria and the gas chambers and knew what they were all about, yet after months most prisoners denied knowledge of them. Realization of their true situation might have helped them to save either the life they were going to lose anyway, or the lives of others. But that realization they could not afford. When Lengyel and many other prisoners were selected to be sent to the gas chambers, they did not try to break away, as she successfully did. Worse, the first time she tried it, some of the fellow prisoners selected with her for the gas chambers called the supervisors, telling them she was trying to get away. Lengyel desperately asks the question: "How was it possible that people denied the existence of the gas chambers when all day long they saw the crematoria burning and smelled the odor of burning flesh? How come they preferred not to believe in the extermination just to prevent themselves from fighting for their very own lives?" She offers no explanation except that they begrudged anyone who might save himself from the common fate, because they lacked enough courage to risk action themselves. I believe they did it because they had given up their will to live, had permitted their death tendencies to flood them. As a result they now identified more closely with the S.S. who were devoting themselves to destruction, than to those fellow prisoners who still had a grip on life and hence managed to escape death.

When prisoners began to serve their executioners, to help them speed the death of their own kind, things had gone beyond simple inertia. By then, death instinct running rampant had been added to inertia. Those who tried to serve their executioners in what were once their civilian capacities were merely continuing if not business, then life as usual. Whereby they opened the door to their death.

Lengyel speaks of a Dr. Mengele, S.S. physician at Auschwitz, in a typical example of the "business as usual" attitude that enabled some prisoners, and certainly the S.S., to retain whatever inner balance they could despite what they were doing. She describes how Dr. Mengele took all correct medical precautions during childbirth, rigorously observing all aseptic principles, cutting the umbilical cord with greatest care, etc. But only half an hour later he sent mother and infant to be burned in the crematorium.

*   *   *

[T]he story of the extermination camps shows that even in such an overpowering environment, certain defenses do offer some protection, most important of which is understanding what goes on in oneself, and

why. With enough understanding, the individual does not fool himself into believing that with every adjustment he makes he is protecting himself. He is able to recognize that much that on the surface seems protective, is actually self-destructive. A most extreme example were those prisoners who volunteered to work in the gas chambers hoping it would somehow save their lives. All of them were killed after a short time. But many of them died sooner, and after weeks of a more horrible life, than might have been true if they had not volunteered.

*   *   *

Perhaps [one] rare instance, an example of supreme self-assertion, can shed light on the question. Once, a group of naked prisoners about to enter the gas chamber stood lined up in front of it. In some way the commanding S.S. officer learned that one of the women prisoners had been a dancer. So he ordered her to dance for him. She did, and as she danced, she approached him, seized his gun, and shot him down. She too was immediately shot to death.

But isn't it probable that despite the grotesque setting in which she danced, dancing made her once again a person? Dancing, she was singled out as an individual, asked to perform in what had once been her chosen vocation. No longer was she a number, a nameless, depersonalized prisoner, but the dancer she used to be. Transformed, however momentarily, she responded like her old self, destroying the enemy bent on her destruction, even if she had to die in the process.

Despite the hundreds of thousands of living dead men who moved quietly to their graves, this one example, and there were several like her, shows that in an instant the old personality can be regained, its destruction undone, once we decide on our own that we wish to cease being units in a system. Exercising the last freedom that not even the concentration camp could take away—to decide how one wishes to think and feel about the conditions of one's life—this dancer threw off her real prison. This she could do because she was willing to risk her life to achieve autonomy once more. If we do that, then if we cannot live, at least we die as men.

D.
Superego

1.

FREUD, SIGMUND

The Interpretation of Dreams (1900)*

[H]ow are we to explain [a child's] death wishes against his parents, who surround him with love and fulfil his needs and whose preservation that same egoism should lead him to desire?

A solution of this difficulty is afforded by the observation that dreams of the death of parents apply with preponderant frequency to the parent who is of the same sex as the dreamer: That men, that is, dream mostly of their father's death and women of their mother's. I cannot pretend that this is universally so, but the preponderance in the direction I have indicated is so evident that it requires to be explained by a factor of general importance. It is as though—to put it bluntly—a sexual preference were making itself felt at an early age: As though boys regarded their fathers and girls their mothers as their rivals in love, whose elimination could not fail to be to their advantage.

Before this idea is rejected as a monstrous one, it is as well in this case, too, to consider the real relations obtaining—this time between parents and children. We must distinguish between what the cultural standards of filial piety demand of this relation and what everyday observation shows it in fact to be. More than one occasion for hostility lies concealed in the relation between parents and children—a relation which affords the most ample opportunities for wishes to arise which cannot pass the censorship.

Let us consider first the relation between father and son. The sanctity which we attribute to the rules laid down in the Decalogue has, I think, blunted our powers of perceiving the real facts. We seem scarcely to venture to observe that the majority of mankind disobey the Fifth Commandment. Alike in the lowest and in the highest strata of human society filial piety is wont to give way to other interests. The obscure information which is brought to us by mythology and legend from the primeval ages of human society gives an unpleasing picture of the father's despotic power and of the ruthlessness with

* Reprinted from: 4 *The Standard Edition of the Complete Psychological Works of Sigmund Freud*, James Strachey, ed. London: The Hogarth Press and the Institute of Psychoanalysis, 1953. (pp. 255–64) and Basic Books, Inc., Publishers, 1960. Reprinted by permission of George Allen & Unwin, Ltd. and Basic Books, Inc.

which he made use of it. Kronos devoured his children, just as the wild boar devours the sow's litter; while Zeus emasculated his father and made himself ruler in his place. The more unrestricted was the rule of the father in the ancient family, the more must the son, as his destined successor, have found himself in the position of an enemy, and the more impatient must he have been to become ruler himself through his father's death. Even in our middle-class families fathers are as a rule inclined to refuse their sons independence and the means necessary to secure it and thus to foster the growth of the germ of hostility which is inherent in their relation. A physician will often be in a position to notice how a son's grief at the loss of his father cannot suppress his satisfaction at having at length won his freedom. In our society today fathers are apt to cling desperately to what is left of a now sadly antiquated *potestas patris familias*; and an author who, like Ibsen, brings the immemorial struggle between fathers and sons into prominence in his writings may be certain of producing his effect.

Occasions for conflict between a daughter and her mother arise when the daughter begins to grow up and long for sexual liberty, but finds herself under her mother's tutelage; while the mother, on the other hand, is warned by her daughter's growth that the time has come when she herself must abandon her claims to sexual satisfaction.

All of this is patent to the eyes of everyone. But it does not help us in our endeavor to explain dreams of a parent's death in people whose piety toward their parents has long been unimpeachably established. Previous discussions, moreover, will have prepared us to learn that the death wish against parents dates back to earliest childhood.

This supposition is confirmed with a certainty beyond all doubt in the case of psychoneurotics when they are subjected to analysis. We learn from them that a child's sexual wishes—if in their embryonic stage they deserve to be so described—awaken very early, and that a girl's first affection is for her father and a boy's first childish desires are for his mother. Accordingly, the father becomes a disturbing rival to the boy and the mother to the girl. . . . The parents too give evidence as a rule of sexual partiality: A natural predilection usually sees to it that a man tends to spoil his little daughters, while his wife takes her sons' part; though both of them, where their judgment is not disturbed by the magic of sex, keep a strict eye upon their children's education. The child is very well aware of this partiality and turns against that one of his parents who is opposed to showing it. Being loved by an adult does not merely bring a child the satisfaction of a special need; it also means that he will get what he wants in every other respect as well. Thus he will be following his own sexual instinct and at the same time giving fresh strength to the inclination shown by his parents if his choice between them falls in with theirs.

The signs of these infantile preferences are for the most part overlooked; yet some of them are to be observed even after the first years of childhood. An eight-year-old girl of my acquaintance, if her mother is called away from the table, makes use of the occasion to proclaim herself her successor: "*I'm* going to be Mummy now. Do you want some more greens, Karl? Well, help yourself, then!" and so on. A particularly gifted and lively girl of four, in whom this piece of child psychology is especially transparent, declared quite openly: "Mummy can go away now. Then Daddy must marry me and I'll be his wife." Such a wish occurring in a child is not in the least inconsistent with her being tenderly attached to her mother. If a little boy is allowed to sleep beside his mother when his father is away from home, but has to go back to the nursery and to someone of whom he is far less fond as soon as his father returns, he may easily begin to form a wish that his father should *always* be away, so that he himself could keep his place beside his dear, lovely Mummy. One obvious way of attaining this wish would be if his father were dead; for the child has learnt one thing by experience—namely that "dead" people, such as Grandaddy, are always away and never come back.

Though observations of this kind on small children fit in perfectly with the interpretation I have proposed, they do not carry such complete conviction as is forced upon the physician by psychoanalyses of adult neurotics. In the latter case dreams of the sort we are considering are introduced into the analysis in such a context that it is impossible to avoid interpreting them as *wishful* dreams.

One day one of my women patients was in a distressed and tearful mood. "I don't want ever to see my relations again," she said, "they must think me horrible." She then went on, with almost no transition, to say that she remembered a dream, though of course she had no idea what it meant. When she was four years old she had a dream that *a lynx or fox was walking on the roof; then something had fallen down or she had fallen down; and then her mother was carried out of the house dead*—and she wept bitterly. I told her that this dream must mean that when she was a child she had wished she could see her mother dead, and that it must be on account of the dream that she felt her relations must think her horrible. I had scarcely said this when she produced some material which threw light on the dream. "Lynx-eye" was a term of abuse that had been thrown at her by a street

urchin when she was a very small child. When she was three years old, a tile off the roof had fallen on her mother's head and made it bleed violently.

I once had an opportunity of making a detailed study of a young woman who passed through a variety of psychical conditions. Her illness began with a state of confusional excitement during which she displayed a quite special aversion to her mother, hitting and abusing her whenever she came near her bed, while at the same period she was docile and affectionate toward a sister who was many years her senior. This was followed by a state in which she was lucid but somewhat apathetic and suffered from badly disturbed sleep. It was during this phase that I began treating her and analyzing her dreams. An immense number of these dreams were concerned, with a greater or less degree of disguise, with the death of her mother: At one time she would be attending an old woman's funeral, at another she and her sister would be sitting at table dressed in mourning. There could be no question as to the meaning of these dreams. As her condition improved still further, hysterical phobias developed. The most tormenting of these was a fear that something might have happened to her mother. She was obliged to hurry home, wherever she might be, to convince herself that her mother was still alive. This case, taken in conjunction with what I had learnt from other sources, was highly instructive: It exhibited, translated as it were into different languages, the various ways in which the psychical apparatus reacted to one and the same exciting idea. In the confusional state, in which, as I believe, the second psychical agency was overwhelmed by the normally suppressed first one, her unconscious hostility to her mother found a powerful *motor* expression. When the calmer condition set in, when the rebellion was suppressed and the domination of the censorship re-established, the only region left open in which her hostility could realize the wish for her mother's death was that of dreaming. When a normal state was still more firmly established, it led to the production of her exaggerated worry about her mother as a hysterical counterreaction and defensive phenomenon. In view of this it is no longer hard to understand why hysterical girls are so often attached to their mothers with such exaggerated affection.

* * *

In my experience, which is already extensive, the chief part in the mental lives of all children who later become psychoneurotics is played by their parents. Being in love with the one parent and hating the other are among the essential constituents of the stock of psychical impulses which is formed at that time and which is of such importance in determining the symptoms of the later neurosis. It is not my belief, however, that psychoneurotics differ sharply in this respect from other human beings who remain normal—that they are able, that is, to create something absolutely new and peculiar to themselves. It is far more probable—and this is confirmed by occasional observations on normal children—that they are only distinguished by exhibiting on a magnified scale feelings of love and hatred to their parents which occur less obviously and less intensely in the minds of most children.

This discovery is confirmed by a legend that has come down to us from classical antiquity: A legend whose profound and universal power to move can only be understood if the hypothesis I have put forward in regard to the psychology of children has an equally universal validity. What I have in mind is the legend of King Oedipus and Sophocles' drama which bears his name.

Oedipus, son of Laïus, King of Thebes, and of Jocasta, was exposed as an infant because an oracle had warned Laïus that the still unborn child would be his father's murderer. The child was rescued, and grew up as a prince in an alien court, until, in doubts as to his origin, he too questioned the oracle and was warned to avoid his home since he was destined to murder his father and take his mother in marriage. On the road leading away from what he believed was his home, he met King Laïus and slew him in a sudden quarrel. He came next to Thebes and solved the riddle set him by the Sphinx who barred his way. Out of gratitude the Thebans made him their king and gave him Jocasta's hand in marriage. He reigned long in peace and honor, and she who, unknown to him, was his mother bore him two sons and two daughters. Then at last a plague broke out and the Thebans made inquiry once more of the oracle. It is at this point that Sophocles' tragedy opens. The messengers bring back the reply that the plague will cease when the murderer of Laïus has been driven from the land.

> But he, where is he? Where shall now be read
> The fading record of this ancient guilt?

The action of the play consists in nothing other than the process of revealing, with cunning delays and ever-mounting excitement—a process that can be likened to the work of a psychoanalysis—that Oedipus himself is the murderer of Laïus, but further that he is the son of the murdered man and of Jocasta. Appalled at the abomination which he has unwittingly perpetrated, Oedipus blinds himself and forsakes his home. The oracle has been fulfilled.

Oedipus Rex is what is known as a tragedy of destiny. Its tragic effect is said to lie in the contrast between the supreme will of the gods and the vain attempts of mankind to escape the evil that threatens them. The lesson which, it is said, the deeply moved spectator should learn from the tragedy is submission to the divine will and realization of his own impot-

ence. Modern dramatists have accordingly tried to achieve a similar tragic effect by weaving the same contrast into a plot invented by themselves. But the spectators have looked on unmoved while a curse or an oracle was fulfilled in spite of all the efforts of some innocent man: Later tragedies of destiny have failed in their effect.

If *Oedipus Rex* moves a modern audience no less than it did the contemporary Greek one, the explanation can only be that its effect does not lie in the contrast between destiny and human will, but is to be looked for in the particular nature of the material on which that contrast is exemplified. There must be something which makes a voice within us ready to recognize the compelling force of destiny in the *Oedipus*. . . . His destiny moves us only because it might have been ours—because the oracle laid the same curse upon us before our birth as upon him. It is the fate of all of us, perhaps, to direct our first sexual impulse toward our mother and our first hatred and our first murderous wish against our father. Our dreams convince us that that is so. King Oedipus, who slew his father Laïus and married his mother Jocasta, merely shows us the fulfilment of our own childhood wishes. But, more fortunate than he, we have meanwhile succeeded, insofar as we have not become psychoneurotics, in detaching our sexual impulses from our mothers and in forgetting our jealousy of our fathers. Here is one in whom these primeval wishes of our childhood have been fulfilled, and we shrink back from him with the whole force of the repression by which those wishes have since that time been held down within us. While the poet, as he unravels the past, brings to light the guilt of Oedipus, he is at the same time compelling us to recognize our own inner minds, in which those same impulses, though suppressed, are still to be found. The contrast with which the closing Chorus leaves us confronted—

> . . . Fix on Oedipus your eyes,
> Who resolved the dark enigma, noblest champion and
> most wise.
> Like a star his envied fortune mounted beaming far
> and wide:
> Now he sinks in seas of anguish, whelmed beneath a
> raging tide. . . .

—strikes as a warning at ourselves and our pride, at us who since our childhood have grown so wise and so mighty in our own eyes. Like Oedipus, we live in ignorance of these wishes, repugnant to morality, which have been forced upon us by Nature, and after their revelation we may all of us well seek to close our eyes to the scenes of our childhood.

There is an unmistakable indication in the text of Sophocles' tragedy itself that the legend of Oedipus sprang from some primeval dream material which had its content the distressing disturbance of a child's relation to his parents owing to the first stirrings of sexuality. At a point when Oedipus, though he is not yet enlightened, has begun to feel troubled by his recollection of the oracle, Jocasta consoles him by referring to a dream which many people dream, though, as she thinks, it has no meaning:

> Many a man ere now in dreams hath lain
> With her who bare him. He hath least annoy
> Who with such omens troubleth not his mind.

Today, just as then, many men dream of having sexual relations with their mothers, and speak of the fact with indignation and astonishment. It is clearly the key to the tragedy and the complement to the dream of the dreamer's father being dead. The story of Oedipus is the reaction of the imagination to these two typical dreams. And just as these dreams, when dreamt by adults, are accompanied by feelings of repulsion, so too the legend must include horror and self-punishment. Its further modification originates once again in a misconceived secondary revision of the material, which has sought to exploit it for theological purposes. The attempt to harmonize divine omnipotence with human responsibility must naturally fail in connection with this subject matter just as with any other.

2.

FREUD, SIGMUND

New Introductory Lectures on Psychoanalysis (1933)*

We describe one group of . . . patients as suffering from delusions of being observed. They complain to us that perpetually, and down to their most intimate actions, they are being molested by the observation of unknown powers—presumably persons—and that in hallucinations they hear these persons reporting the outcome of their observation: "Now he's going to say this, now he's dressing to go out" and so on. Observation of this sort is not yet the same thing as persecution, but it is not far from it; it presupposes that people distrust them, and expect to catch them carrying out forbidden actions for which they would be punished. How would it be if these insane people were right, if in each of us there is present in his ego an agency like this which observes and threatens to punish, and which in them has merely become sharply divided from their ego and mistakenly displaced into external reality?

I cannot tell whether the same thing will happen to you as to me. Ever since, under the powerful impression of this clinical picture, I formed the idea that the separation of the observing agency from the rest of the ego might be a regular feature of the ego's struc-

_____
* Reprinted from: 22 *The Standard Edition of the Complete Psychological Works of Sigmund Freud*, James Strachey, ed. London: The Hogarth Press and the Institute of Psychoanalysis, 1964. (pp. 60–69, 109). Reprinted by permission of Hogarth and W. W. Norton & Co.

ture, that idea has never left me, and I was driven to investigate the further characteristics and connections of the agency which was thus separated off. The next step is quickly taken. The content of the delusions of being observed already suggests that the observing is only a preparation for judging and punishing, and we accordingly guess that another function of this agency must be what we call our conscience. There is scarcely anything else in us that we so regularly separate from our ego and so easily set over against it as precisely our conscience. I feel an inclination to do something that I think will give me pleasure, but I abandon it on the ground that my conscience does not allow it. Or I have let myself be persuaded by too great an expectation of pleasure into doing something to which the voice of conscience has objected and after the deed my conscience punishes me with distressing reproaches and causes me to feel remorse for the deed. I might simply say that the special agency which I am beginning to distinguish in the ego is conscience. But it is more prudent to keep the agency as something independent and to suppose that conscience is one of its functions and that self-observation, which is an essential preliminary to the judging activity of conscience, is another of them. And since when we recognize that something has a separate existence we give it a name of its own, from this time forward I will describe this agency in the ego as the "*superego*."

I am now prepared to hear you ask me scornfully whether our ego-psychology comes down to nothing more than taking commonly used abstractions literally and in a crude sense, and transforming them from concepts into things—by which not much would be gained. To this I would reply that in ego-psychology it will be difficult to escape what is universally known; it will rather be a question of new ways of looking at things and new ways of arranging them than of new discoveries. . . .

Hardly have we familiarized ourselves with the idea of a superego like this which enjoys a certain degree of autonomy, follows its own intentions, and is independent of the ego for its supply of energy, than a clinical picture forces itself on our notice which throws a striking light on the severity of this agency and indeed its cruelty, and on its changing relations to the ego. I am thinking of the condition of melancholia, or, more precisely, of melancholic attacks, which you too will have heard plenty about, even if you are not psychiatrists. The most striking feature of this illness, of whose causation and mechanism we know much too little, is the way in which the superego—"conscience," you may call it, quietly—treats the ego. While a melancholic can, like other people, show a greater or lesser degree of severity to himself in his healthy periods, during a melancholic attack his superego becomes over severe, abuses the poor ego, humiliates it and ill-treats it, threatens it with the direst punishments, reproaches it for actions in the remotest past which had been taken lightly at the time—as though it had spent the whole interval in collecting accusations and had only been waiting for its present access of strength in order to bring them up and make a condemnatory judgment on their basis. The superego applies the strictest moral standard to the helpless ego which is at its mercy; in general it represents the claims of morality, and we realize all at once that our moral sense of guilt is the expression of the tension between the ego and the superego. It is a most remarkable experience to see morality, which is supposed to have been given us by God and thus deeply implanted in us, functioning [in these patients] as a periodic phenomenon. For after a certain number of months the whole moral fuss is over, the criticism of the superego is silent, the ego is rehabilitated and again enjoys all the rights of man till the next attack. In some forms of the disease, indeed, something of a contrary sort occurs in the intervals; the ego finds itself in a blissful state of intoxication, it celebrates a triumph, as though the superego had lost all its strength or had melted into the ego; and this liberated, manic ego permits itself a truly uninhibited satisfaction of all its appetites. Here are happenings rich in unsolved riddles!

No doubt you will expect me to give you more than a mere illustration when I inform you that we have found out all kinds of things about the formation of the superego—that is to say, about the origin of conscience. . . . Even if conscience is something "within us," yet it is not so from the first. In this it is a real contrast to sexual life, which is in fact there from the beginning of life and not only a later addition. But, as is well known, young children are amoral and possess no internal inhibitions against their impulses striving for pleasure. The part which is later taken on by the superego is played to begin with by an external power, by parental authority. Parental influence governs the child by offering proofs of love and by threatening punishments which are signs to the child of loss of love and are bound to be feared on their own account. This realistic anxiety is the precursor of the later moral anxiety. So long as it is dominant there is no need to talk of a superego and of a conscience. It is only subsequently that the secondary situation develops (which we are all too ready to regard as the normal one), where the external restraint is internalized and the superego takes the place of the parental agency and observes, directs, and threatens the ego in exactly the same way as earlier the parents did with the child.

The superego, which thus takes over the power, function, and even the methods of the parental agency is, however, not merely its successor but actually the legitimate heir of its body. It proceeds directly out of it, we shall learn presently by what process. First, however, we must dwell upon a discrepancy between the two. The superego seems to have made a one-sided choice and to have picked out only the parents' strictness and severity, their prohibiting and punitive function, whereas their loving care seems not to have been taken over and maintained. If the parents have really enforced their authority with severity we can easily understand the child's in turn developing a severe superego. But, contrary to our expectation, experience shows that the superego can acquire the same characteristic of relentless severity even if the upbringing had been mild and kindly and had so far as possible avoided threats and punishments. . . .[1]

I cannot tell you as much as I should like about the metamorphosis of the parental relationship into the superego, partly because that process is so complicated that an account of it will not fit into the framework of an introductory course of lectures such as I am trying to give you, but partly also because we ourselves do not feel sure that we understand it completely. So you must be content with the sketch that follows.

The basis of the process is what is called an "identification"—that is to say, the assimilation of one ego to another one, as a result of which the first ego behaves like the second in certain respects, imitates it, and in a sense takes it up into itself. Identification has been not unsuitably compared with the oral, cannibalistic incorporation of the other person. It is a very important form of attachment to someone else, probably the very first, and not the same thing as the choice of an object. The difference between the two can be expressed in some such way as this. If a boy identifies himself with his father, he wants to *be like* his father; if he makes him the object of his choice, he wants to *have* him, to possess him. In the first case his ego is altered on the model of his father; in the second case that is not necessary. Identification and object choice are to a large extent independent of each other; it is, however, possible to identify oneself with someone whom, for instance, one has taken as a sexual object, and to alter one's ego on his model. It is said that the influencing of the ego by the sexual object occurs particularly often with women and is characteristic of femininity. I must already have spoken to you in my earlier lectures of what is by far the most instructive relation between identification and object choice. It can be observed equally easily in children and adults, in normal as in sick people. If one has lost an object or has been obliged to give it up, one often compensates oneself

1. There is no doubt that, when the superego was first instituted, in equipping that agency use was made of the piece of the child's aggressiveness toward his parents for which he was unable to effect a discharge outward on account of his erotic fixation as well as of external difficulties; and for that reason the severity of the superego need not simply correspond to the strictness of the upbringing. . . .

by identifying oneself with it and by setting it up once more in one's ego, so that here object choice regresses, as it were, to identification.

I myself am far from satisfied with these remarks on identification; but it will be enough if you can grant me that the installation of the superego can be described as a successful instance of identification with the parental agency. The fact that speaks decisively for this view is that this new creation of a superior agency within the ego is most intimately linked with the destiny of the Oedipus complex, so that the superego appears as the heir of that emotional attachment which is of such importance for childhood. With his abandonment of the Oedipus complex a child must, as we can see, renounce the intense object cathexes which he has deposited with his parents, and it is as a compensation for this loss of objects that there is such a strong intensification of the identifications with his parents which have probably long been present in his ego. Identifications of this kind as precipitates of object cathexes that have been given up will be repeated often enough later in the child's life; but it is entirely in accordance with the emotional importance of this first instance of such a transformation that a special place in the ego should be found for its outcome. Close investigation has shown us, too, that the superego is stunted in its strength and growth if the surmounting of the Oedipus complex is only incompletely successful. In the course of development the superego also takes on the influences of those who have stepped into the place of parents—educators, teachers, people chosen as ideal models. Normally it departs more and more from the original parental figures; it becomes, so to say, more impersonal. Nor must it be forgotten that a child has a different estimate of its parents at different periods of its life. At the time at which the Oedipus complex gives place to the superego they are something quite magnificent; but later they lose much of this. Identifications then come about with these later parents as well, and indeed they regularly make important contributions to the formation of character; but in that case they only affect the ego, they no longer influence the superego, which has been determined by the earliest parental imagos.

I hope you have already formed an impression that the hypothesis of the superego really describes a structural relation and is not merely a personification of some such abstraction as that of conscience. One more important function remains to be mentioned which we attribute to this superego. It is also the vehicle of the ego ideal by which the ego measures itself, which it emulates, and whose demand for ever greater perfection it strives to fulfil. There is no doubt that this ego ideal is the precipitate of the old picture of the parents, the expression of admiration for the perfection which the child then attributed to them.

*   *   *

. . . We have allotted [the superego] functions of self-observation, of conscience, and of [maintaining] the ideal. It follows from what we have said about its origin that it presupposes an immensely important biological fact and a fateful psychological one: Namely, the human child's long dependence on its parents and the Oedipus complex, both of which, again, are intimately interconnected. The superego is the representative for us of every moral restriction, the advocate of a striving toward perfection—it is, in short, as much as we have been able to grasp psychologically of what is described as the higher side of human life. Since it itself goes back to the influence of parents, educators, and so on, we learn still more of its significance if we turn to those who are its sources. As a rule parents and authorities analogous to them follow the precepts of their own superegos in educating children. Whatever understanding their ego may have come to with their superego, they are severe and exacting in educating children. They have forgotten the difficulties of their own childhood and they are glad to be able now to identify themselves fully with their own parents who in the past laid such severe restrictions upon them. Thus a child's superego is in fact constructed on the model not of its parents but of its parents' superego; the contents which fill it are the same and it becomes the vehicle of tradition and of all the time-resisting judgments of value which have propagated themselves in this manner from generation to generation. You may easily guess what important assistance taking the superego into account will give us in our understanding of the social behavior of mankind—in the problem of delinquency, for instance—and perhaps even what practical hints on education. It seems likely that what are known as materialistic views of history sin in underestimating this factor. They brush it aside with the remark that human "idealogies" are nothing other than the product and superstructure of their contemporary economic conditions. That is true, but very probably not the whole truth. Mankind never lives entirely in the present. The past, the tradition of the race and of the people, lives on in the ideologies of the superego, and yields only slowly to the influences of the present and to new changes; and so long as it operates through the superego it plays a powerful part in human life, independently of economic conditions.

*   *   *

Now, however, another problem awaits us—at the opposite end of the ego, as we might put it. It is presented to us by an observation during the work of analysis, an observation which is actually a very old one. As not infrequently happens, it has taken a long time to come to the point of appreciating its importance. The whole theory of psychoanalysis is, as you know, in fact built up on the perception of the resistance offered to us by the patient when we attempt to make his unconscious conscious to him. The objective sign of this resistance is that his associations fail or depart widely from the topic that is being dealt with. He may also recognize the resistance *subjectively* by the fact that he has distressing feelings when he approaches the topic. But this last sign may also be absent. We then say to the patient that we infer from his behavior that he is now in a state of resistance; and he replies that he knows nothing of that, and is only aware that his associations have become more difficult. It turns out that we were right; but in that case his resistance was unconscious too, just as unconscious as the repressed, at the lifting of which we were working. We should long ago have asked the question: From what part of his mind does an unconscious resistance like this arise? The beginner in psychoanalysis will be ready at once with the answer: It is, of course, the resistance of the unconscious. An ambiguous and unserviceable answer! If it means that the resistance arises from the repressed, we must rejoin: Certainly not! We must rather attribute to the repressed a strong upward drive, an impulsion to break through into consciousness. The resistance can only be a manifestation of the ego, which originally put the repression into force and now wishes to maintain it. That, moreover, is the view we always took. Since we have come to assume a special agency in the ego, the superego, which represents demands of a restrictive and rejecting character, we may say that repression is the work of this superego and that it is carried out either by itself or by the ego in obedience to its orders. If then we are met by the case of the resistance in analysis not being conscious to the patient, this means either that in quite important situations the superego and the ego can operate unconsciously, or—and this would be still more important—that portions of both of them, the ego and the superego themselves, are unconscious. In both cases we have to reckon with the disagreeable discovery that on the one hand (super-) ego and conscious and on the other hand repressed and unconscious are far from coinciding.

3.

FREUD, SIGMUND

The Ego and the Id (1923)*

. . . The intricacy of the problem [of origin of the ego ideal] is due to two factors: The triangular character of the Oedipus situation and the constitutional bisexuality of each individual.

In its simplified form the case of a male child may

be described as follows. At a very early age the little boy develops an object cathexis for his mother, which originally related to the mother's breast and is the prototype of an object choice on the anaclitic model; the boy deals with his father by identifying himself with him. For a time these two relationships proceed side-by-side, until the boy's sexual wishes in regard to his mother become more intense and his father is perceived as an obstacle to them; from this the Oedipus complex originates. His identification with his father then takes on a hostile coloring and changes into a wish to get rid of his father in order to take his place with his mother. Henceforward his relation to his father is ambivalent; it seems as if the ambivalence inherent in the identification from the beginning had become manifest. An ambivalent attitude to his father and an object relation of a solely affectionate kind to his mother make up the content of the simple positive Oedipus complex in a boy.

Along with the demolition of the Oedipus complex, the boy's object cathexis of his mother must be given up. Its place may be filled by one of two things: Either an identification with his mother or an intensification of his identification with his father. We are accustomed to regard the latter outcome as the more normal; it permits the affectionate relation to the mother to be in a measure retained. In this way the dissolution of the Oedipus complex would consolidate the masculinity in a boy's character. In a precisely analogous way, the outcome of the Oedipus attitude in a little girl may be an intensification of her identification with her mother (or the setting up of such an identification for the first time)—a result which will fix the child's feminine character.

These identifications are not what we should have expected, since they do not introduce the abandoned object into the ego; but this alternative outcome may also occur, and is easier to observe in girls than in boys. Analysis very often shows that a little girl, after she has had to relinquish her father as a love object, will bring her masculinity into prominence and identify herself with her father (that is, with the object which has been lost), instead of with her mother. This will clearly depend on whether the masculinity in her disposition—whatever that may consist in—is strong enough.

It would appear, therefore, that in both sexes the relative strength of the masculine and feminine sexual dispositions is what determines whether the outcome of the Oedipus situation shall be an identification with the father or with the mother. This is one of the ways in which bisexuality takes a hand in the subsequent vicissitudes of the Oedipus complex. The other way is even more important. For one gets an impression that the simple Oedipus complex is by no means its commonest form, but rather represents a simplification or schematization which, to be sure, is often enough justified for practical purposes. Closer

* Reprinted from: 19 *The Standard Edition of the Complete Psychological Works of Sigmund Freud*, James Strachey, ed. London: The Hogarth Press and the Institute of Psychoanalysis, 1961 (pp. 31–39, 48–55). Reprinted by permission of Hogarth and W. W. Norton & Co.

study usually discloses the more complete Oedipus complex, which is twofold, positive and negative, and is due to the bisexuality originally present in children: That is to say, a boy has not merely an ambivalent attitude toward his father and an affectionate object choice toward his mother, but at the same time he also behaves like a girl and displays an affectionate feminine attitude to his father and a corresponding jealousy and hostility toward his mother. It is this complicating element introduced by bisexuality that makes it so difficult to obtain a clear view of the facts in connection with the earliest object choices and identifications, and still more difficult to describe them intelligibly. It may even be that the ambivalence displayed in the relations to the parents should be attributed entirely to bisexuality and that it is not, as I have represented above, developed out of identification in consequence of rivalry.

In my opinion it is advisable in general, and quite especially where neurotics are concerned, to assume the existence of the complete Oedipus complex. Analytic experience then shows that in a number of cases one or the other constituent disappears, except for barely distinguishable traces; so that the result is a series with the normal positive Oedipus complex at one end and the inverted negative one at the other, while its intermediate members exhibit the complete form with one or other of its two components preponderating. At the dissolution of the Oedipus complex the four trends of which it consists will group themselves in such a way as to produce a father identification and a mother identification. The father identification will preserve the object relation to the mother which belonged to the positive complex and will at the same time replace the object relation to the father which belonged to the inverted complex: And the same will be true, *mutatis mutandis*, of the mother identification. The relative intensity of the two identifications in any individual will reflect the preponderance in him of one or other of the two sexual dispositions.

The broad general outcome of the sexual phase dominated by the Oedipus complex may, therefore, be taken to be the forming of a precipitate in the ego, consisting of these two identifications in some way united with each other. This modification of the ego retains its special position; it confronts the other contents of the ego as an ego ideal or superego.

The superego is, however, not simply a residue of the earliest object choices of the id; it also represents an energetic reaction formation against those choices. Its relation to the ego is not exhausted by the precept: "You *ought to be* like this (like your father)." It also comprises the prohibition: "You *may not be* like this (like your father)—that is, you may not do all that he does; some things are his prerogative." This double aspect of the ego ideal derives from the fact that the ego ideal had the task of repressing the Oedipus com-

plex; indeed, it is to that revolutionary event that it owes its existence. Clearly the repression of the Oedipus complex was no easy task. The child's parents, and especially his father, were perceived as the obstacle to a realization of his Oedipus wishes; so his infantile ego fortified itself for the carrying out of the repression by erecting this same obstacle within itself. It borrowed strength to do this, so to speak, from the father, and this loan was an extraordinarily momentous act. The superego retains the character of the father, while the more powerful the Oedipus complex was and the more rapidly it succumbed to repression (under the influence of authority, religious teaching, schooling, and reading), the stricter will be the domination of the superego over the ego later on—in the form of conscience or perhaps of an unconscious sense of guilt. I shall presently bring forward a suggestion about the source of its power to dominate in this way—the source, that is, of its compulsive character which manifests itself in the form of a categorical imperative.

If we consider once more the origin of the superego as we have described it, we shall recognize that it is the outcome of two highly important factors, one of a biological and the other of a historical nature: Namely, the lengthy duration in man of his childhood helplessness and dependence, and the fact of his Oedipus complex, the repression of which we have shown to be connected with the interruption of libidinal development by the latency period and so with the diphasic onset of man's sexual life. . . . We see, then, that the differentiation of the superego from the ego is no matter of chance; it represents the most important characteristics of the development both of the individual and of the species; indeed, by giving permanent expression to the influence of the parents it perpetuates the existence of the factors to which it owes its origin.

*   *   *

The ego ideal is, therefore, the heir of the Oedipus complex, and thus it is also the expression of the most powerful impulses and most important libidinal vicissitudes of the id. By setting up this ego ideal, the ego has mastered the Oedipus complex and at the same time placed itself in subjection to the id. Whereas the ego is essentially the representative of the external world, of reality, the superego stands in contrast to it as the representative of the internal world, of the id. Conflicts between the ego and the ideal will, as we are now prepared to find, ultimately reflect the contrast between what is real and what is psychical, between the external world and the internal world.

Through the forming of the ideal, what biology and the vicissitudes of the human species have created in the id and left behind in it is taken over by the ego and re-experienced in relation to itself as an individual.

Owing to the way in which the ego ideal is formed, it has the most abundant links with the phylogenetic acquisition of each individual—his archaic heritage. What has belonged to the lowest part of the mental life of each of us is changed, through the formation of the ideal, into what is highest in the human mind by our scale of values. . . .

It is easy to show that the ego ideal answers to everything that is expected of the higher nature of man. As a substitute for a longing for the father, it contains the germ from which all religions have evolved. The self-judgment which declares that the ego falls short of its ideal produces the religious sense of humility to which the believer appeals in his longing. As a child grows up, the role of father is carried on by teachers and others in authority; their injunctions and prohibitions remain powerful in the ego ideal and continue, in the form of conscience, to exercise the moral censorship. The tension between the demands of conscience and the actual performances of the ego is experienced as a sense of guilt. Social feelings rest on identifications with other people, on the basis of having the same ego ideal.

*   *   *

The way in which the superego came into being explains how it is that the early conflicts of the ego with the object cathexes of the id can be continued in conflicts with their heir, the superego. If the ego has not succeeded in properly mastering the Oedipus complex, the energic cathexis of the latter, springing from the id, will come into operation once more in the reaction formation of the ego ideal. The abundant communication between the ideal and these *Ucs.* instinctual impulses solves the puzzle of how it is that the ideal itself can to a great extent remain unconscious and inaccessible to the ego. The struggle which once raged in the deepest strata of the mind, and was not brought to an end by rapid sublimation and identification, is now continued in a higher region. . . .

*   *   *

[T]he ego is formed to a great extent out of identifications which take the place of abandoned cathexes by the id; that the first of these identifications always behave as a special agency in the ego and stand apart from the ego in the form of a superego, while later on, as it grows stronger, the ego may become more resistant to the influences of such identifications. The superego owes its special position in the ego, or in relation to the ego, to a factor which must be considered from two sides: On the one hand it was the first identification and one which took place while the ego was still feeble, and on the other hand it is the heir to the Oedipus complex and has thus introduced the most momentous objects into the ego. The superego's relation to the later alterations of the ego is roughly similar to that of the primary sexual phase of childhood to later sexual life after puberty. Although it is accessible to all later influences, it nevertheless preserves throughout life the character given to it by its derivation from the father complex—namely, the capacity to stand apart from the ego and to master it. It is a memorial of the former weakness and dependence of the ego, and the mature ego remains subject to its domination. As the child was once under a compulsion to obey its parents, so the ego submits to the categorical imperative of its superego.

But the derivation of the superego from the first object cathexes of the id, from the Oedipus complex, signifies even more for it. This derivation, as we have already shown, brings it into relation with the phylogenetic acquisitions of the id and makes it a reincarnation of former ego structures which have left their precipitates behind in the id. Thus the superego is always close to the id and can act as its representative *vis-à-vis* the ego. It reaches deep down into the id and for that reason is further from consciousness than the ego is.

We shall best appreciate these relations by turning to certain clinical facts, which have long since lost their novelty but which still await theoretical discussion.

There are certain people who behave in a quite peculiar fashion during the work of analysis. When one speaks hopefully to them or expresses satisfaction with the progress of the treatment, they show signs of discontent and their condition invariably becomes worse. One begins by regarding this as defiance and as an attempt to prove their superiority to the physician, but later one comes to take a deeper and juster view. One becomes convinced, not only that such people cannot endure any praise or appreciation, but that they react inversely to the progress of the treatment. Every partial solution that ought to result, and in other people does result, in an improvement or a temporary suspension of symptoms produces in them for the time being an exacerbation of their illness; they get worse during the treatment instead of getting better. They exhibit what is known as a "negative therapeutic reaction."

There is no doubt that there is something in these people that sets itself against their recovery, and its approach is dreaded as though it were a danger. We are accustomed to say that the need for illness has got the upper hand in them over the desire for recovery. If we analyze this resistance in the usual way—then, even after allowance has been made for an attitude of defiance toward the physician and for fixation to the various forms of gain from illness, the greater part of it is still left over; and this reveals itself as the most powerful of all obstacles to recovery, more powerful than the familiar ones of narcissistic inaccessibility, a negative attitude toward the physician and clinging to the gain from illness.

In the end we come to see that we are dealing with what may be called a "moral" factor, a sense of guilt, which is finding its satisfaction in the illness and refuses to give up the punishment of suffering. We shall be right in regarding this disheartening explanation as final. But as far as the patient is concerned this sense of guilt is dumb; it does not tell him he is guilty; he does not feel guilty, he feels ill. This sense of guilt expresses itself only as a resistance to recovery which it is extremely difficult to overcome. It is also particularly difficult to convince the patient that this motive lies behind his continuing to be ill; he holds fast to the more obvious explanation that treatment by analysis is not the right remedy for his case.

The description we have given applies to the most extreme instances of this state of affairs, but in a lesser measure this factor has to be reckoned with in very many cases, perhaps in all comparatively severe cases of neurosis. In fact it may be precisely this element in the situation, the attitude of the ego ideal, that determines the severity of a neurotic illness. We shall not hesitate, therefore, to discuss rather more fully the way in which the sense of guilt expresses itself under different conditions.

An interpretation of the normal, conscious sense of guilt (conscience) presents no difficulties; it is based on the tension between the ego and the ego ideal and is the expression of a condemnation of the ego by its critical agency. The feelings of inferiority so well known in neurotics are presumably not far removed from it. In two very familiar maladies the sense of guilt is over-strongly conscious; in them the ego ideal displays particular severity and often rages against the ego in a cruel fashion. The attitude of the ego ideal in these two conditions, obsessional neurosis and melancholia, presents, alongside of this similarity, differences that are no less significant.

In certain forms of obsessional neurosis the sense of guilt is over noisy but cannot justify itself to the ego. Consequently the patient's ego rebels against the imputation of guilt and seeks the physician's support in repudiating it. It would be folly to acquiesce in this, for to do so would have no effect. Analysis eventually shows that the superego is being influenced by processes that have remained unknown to the ego. It is possible to discover the repressed impulses which are really at the bottom of the sense of guilt. Thus in this case the superego knew more than the ego about the unconscious id.

In melancholia the impression that the superego has obtained a hold upon consciousness is even stronger. But here the ego ventures no objection; it admits its guilt and submits to the punishment. We understand the difference. In obsessional neurosis what were in question were objectionable impulses which remained outside the ego, while in melancholia the object to which the superego's wrath applies has been taken into the ego through identification.

It is certainly not clear why the sense of guilt reaches such an extraordinary strength in these two neurotic disorders; but the main problem presented in this state of affairs lies in another direction. We shall postpone discussion of it until we have dealt with the other cases in which the sense of guilt remains unconscious.

It is essentially in hysteria and in states of a hysterical type that this is found. Here the mechanism by which the sense of guilt remains unconscious is easy to discover. The hysterical ego fends off a distressing perception with which the criticisms of its superego threaten it, in the same way in which it is in the habit of fending off an unendurable object cathexis—by an act of repression. It is the ego, therefore, that is responsible for the sense of guilt remaining unconscious. We know that as a rule the ego carries out repressions in the service and at the behest of its superego; but this is a case in which it has turned the same weapon against its harsh taskmaster. In obsessional neurosis, as we know, the phenomena of reaction formation predominate; but here [in hysteria] the ego succeeds only in keeping at a distance the material to which the sense of guilt refers.

One may go further and venture the hypothesis that a great part of the sense of guilt must normally remain unconscious, because the origin of conscience is intimately connected with the Oedipus complex, which belongs to the unconscious. If anyone were inclined to put forward the paradoxical proposition that the normal man is not only far more immoral than he believes but also far more moral than he knows, psychoanalysis, on whose findings the first half of the assertion rests, would have no objection to raise against the second half.

*   *   *

The question which we put off answering runs as follows: How is it that the superego manifests itself essentially as a sense of guilt (or rather, as criticism—for the sense of guilt is the perception in the ego answering to this criticism) and moreover develops such extraordinary harshness and severity toward the ego? If we turn to melancholia first, we find that the excessively strong superego which has obtained a hold upon consciousness rages against the ego with merciless violence, as if it had taken possession of the whole of the sadism available in the person concerned. Following our view of sadism, we should say that the destructive component had entrenched itself in the superego and turned against the ego. What is now holding sway in the superego is, as it were, a pure culture of the death instinct, and in fact it often enough succeeds in driving the ego into death, if the latter does not fend off its tyrant in time by the change round into mania.

*   *   *

The dangerous death instincts are dealt with in the individual in various ways: In part they are rendered harmless by being fused with erotic components, in part they are diverted toward the external world in the form of aggression, while to a large extent they undoubtedly continue their internal work inhindered. How is it then that in melancholia the superego can become a kind of gathering place for the death instincts?

From the point of view of instinctual control, of morality, it may be said of the id that it is totally nonmoral, of the ego that it strives to be moral, and of the superego that it can be supermoral and then become as cruel as only the id can be. It is remarkable that the more a man checks his aggressiveness toward the exterior the more severe—that is, aggressive —he becomes in his ego ideal. The ordinary view sees the situation the other way round: The standard set up by the ego ideal seems to be the motive for the suppression of aggressiveness. The fact remains, however, as we have stated it: The more a man controls his aggressiveness, the more intense becomes his ideal's inclination to aggressiveness against his ego. It is like a displacement, a turning round upon his own ego. But even ordinary normal morality has a harshly restraining, cruelly prohibiting quality. It is from this, indeed, that the conception arises of a higher being who deals out punishment inexorably.

I cannot go further in my consideration of these questions without introducing a fresh hypothesis. The superego arises, as we know, from an identification with the father taken as a model. Every such identification is in the nature of a desexualization or even of a sublimation. It now seems as though when a transformation of this kind takes place, an instinctual defusion occurs at the same time. After sublimation the erotic component no longer has the power to bind the whole of the destructiveness that was combined with it, and this is released in the form of an inclination to aggression and destruction. This defusion would be the source of the general character of harshness and cruelty exhibited by the ideal—its dictatorial "Thou shalt."

4.

FREUD, SIGMUND

The Dissolution of the Oedipus Complex (1924)*

To an ever-increasing extent the Oedipus complex reveals its importance as the central phenomenon of the sexual period of early childhood. After that, its dissolution takes place; it succumbs to repression, as

* Reprinted from: 19 *The Standard Edition of the Complete Psychological Works of Sigmund Freud*, James Strachey, ed. London: The Hogarth Press and the Institute of Psychoanalysis, 1961. (pp. 173–79) and 2 *Collected Papers of Sigmund Freud*, American Edition, published by Basic Books, Inc., 1959. Reprinted by permission of Hogarth and Basic Books, Inc.

we say, and is followed by the latency period. It has not yet become clear, however, what it is that brings about its destruction. Analyses seem to show that it is the experience of painful disappointments. The little girl likes to regard herself as what her father loves above all else; but the time comes when she has to endure a harsh punishment from him and she is cast out of her fool's paradise. The boy regards his mother as his own property; but he finds one day that she has transferred her love and solicitude to a new arrival. Reflection must deepen our sense of the importance of those influences, for it will emphasize the fact that distressing experiences of this sort, which act in opposition to the content of the complex, are inevitable. Even when no special events occur, like those we have mentioned as examples, the absence of the satisfaction hoped for, the continued denial of the desired baby, must in the end lead the small lover to turn away from his hopeless longing. In this way the Oedipus complex would go to its destruction from its lack of success, from the effects of its internal impossibility.

Another view is that the Oedipus complex must collapse because the time has come for its disintegration, just as the milk teeth fall out when the permanent ones begin to grow. Although the majority of human beings go through the Oedipus complex as an individual experience, it is nevertheless a phenomenon which is determined and laid down by heredity and which is bound to pass away according to program when the next preordained phase of development sets in. This being so, it is of no great importance what the occasions are which allow this to happen, or indeed, whether any such occasions can be discovered at all.

The justice of both these views cannot be disputed. Moreover, they are compatible. There is room for the ontogenetic view side-by-side with the more far-reaching phylogenetic one. It is also true that even at birth the whole individual is destined to die, and perhaps his organic disposition may already contain the indication of what he is to die from. Nevertheless, it remains of interest to follow out how this innate program is carried out and in what way accidental noxae exploit his disposition.

We have lately been made more clearly aware than before that a child's sexual development advances to a certain phase at which the genital organ has already taken over the leading role. But this genital is the male one only, or, more correctly, the penis; the female genital has remained undiscovered. This phallic phase, which is contemporaneous with the Oedipus complex, does not develop further to the definitive genital organization, but is submerged, and is succeeded by the latency period. Its termination, however, takes place in a typical manner and in conjunction with events that are of regular recurrence.

When the (male) child's interest turns to his genitals

he betrays the fact by manipulating them frequently; and he finds that the adults do not approve of this behavior. More or less plainly, more or less brutally, a threat is pronounced that this part of him which he values so highly will be taken away from him. Usually it is from women that the threat emanates; very often they seek to strengthen their authority by a reference to the father or the doctor, who, so they say, will carry out the punishment. In a number of cases the women will themselves mitigate the threat in a symbolic manner by telling the child that what is to be removed is not his genital, which actually plays a passive part, but his hand, which is the active culprit. It happens particularly often that the little boy is threatened with castration, not because he plays with his penis with his hand, but because he wets his bed every night and cannot be got to be clean. Those in charge of him behave as if this nocturnal incontinence was the result and the proof of his being unduly concerned with his penis, and they are probably right. In any case, long-continued bed wetting is to be equated with the emissions of adults. It is an expression of the same excitation of the genitals which has impelled the child to masturbate at this period.

Now it is my view that what brings about the destruction of the child's phallic genital organization is this threat of castration. Not immediately, it is true, and not without other influences being brought to bear as well. For to begin with the boy does not believe in the threat or obey it in the least. Psychoanalysis has recently attached importance to two experiences which all children go through and which, it is suggested, prepare them for the loss of highly valued parts of the body. These experiences are the withdrawal of the mother's breast—at first intermittently and later for good—and the daily demand on them to give up the contents of the bowel. But there is no evidence to show that, when the threat of castration takes place, those experiences have any effect. It is not until a *fresh* experience comes his way that the child begins to reckon with the possibility of being castrated, and then only hesitatingly and unwillingly, and not without making efforts to depreciate the significance of something he has himself observed.

The observation which finally breaks down his unbelief is the sight of the female genitals. Sooner or later the child, who is so proud of his possession of a penis, has a view of the genital region of a little girl, and cannot help being convinced of the absence of a penis in a creature who is so like himself. With this, the loss of his own penis becomes imaginable, and the threat of castration takes its deferred effect.

We should not be as short sighted as the person in charge of the child who threatens him with castration, and we must not overlook the fact that at this time masturbation by no means represents the whole of his sexual life. As can be clearly shown, he stands in the Oedipus attitude to his parents; his masturbation is only a genital discharge of the sexual excitation belonging to the complex, and throughout his later years will owe its importance to that relationship. The Oedipus complex offered the child two possibilities of satisfaction, an active and a passive one. He could put himself in his father's place in a masculine fashion and have intercourse with his mother as his father did, in which case he would soon have felt the latter as a hindrance; or he might want to take the place of his mother and be loved by his father, in which case his mother would become superfluous. The child may have had only very vague notions as to what constitutes a satisfying erotic intercourse; but certainly the penis must play a part in it, for the sensations in his own organ were evidence of that. So far he had had no occasion to doubt that women possessed a penis. But now his acceptance of the possibility of castration, his recognition that women were castrated, made an end of both possible ways of obtaining satisfaction from the Oedipus complex. For both of them entailed the loss of his penis—the masculine one as a resulting punishment and the feminine one as a precondition. If the satisfaction of love in the field of the Oedipus complex is to cost the child his penis, a conflict is bound to arise between his narcissistic interest in that part of his body and the libidinal cathexis of his parental objects. In this conflict the first of these forces normally triumphs: The child's ego turns away from the Oedipus complex.

I have described elsewhere how this turning away takes place. The object cathexes are given up and replaced by identifications. The authority of the father or the parents is introjected into the ego, and there it forms the nucleus of the superego, which takes over the severity of the father and perpetuates his prohibition against incest, and so secures the ego from the return of the libidinal object cathexis. The libidinal trends belonging to the Oedipus complex are in part desexualized and sublimated (a thing which probably happens with every transformation into an identification) and in part inhibited in their aim and changed into impulses of affection. The whole process has, on the one hand, preserved the genital organ—has averted the danger of its loss—and, on the other, has paralyzed it—has removed its function. This process ushers in the latency period, which now interrupts the child's sexual development.

I see no reason for denying the name of a "repression" to the ego's turning away from the Oedipus complex, although later repressions come about for the most part with the participation of the superego, which in this case is only just being formed. But the process we have described is more than a repression. It is equivalent, if it is ideally carried out, to a destruction and an abolition of the complex. We may plausibly assume that we have here come upon the borderline—never a very sharply drawn one—between the normal and the pathological. If the ego has in fact not achieved much more than a *repression* of the complex, the latter persists in an unconscious state in the id and will later manifest its pathogenic effect.

Analytic observation enables us to recognize or guess these connections between the phallic organization, the Oedipus complex, the threat of castration, the formation of the superego, and the latency period. These connections justify the statement that the destruction of the Oedipus complex is brought about by the threat of castration. But this does not dispose of the problem; there is room for a theoretical speculation which may upset the results we have come to or put them in a new light. Before we start along this new path, however, we must turn to a question which has arisen in the course of this discussion and has so far been left on one side. The process which has been described refers, as has been expressly said, to male children only. How does the corresponding development take place in little girls?

At this point our material—for some incomprehensible reason—becomes far more obscure and full of gaps. The female sex, too, develops an Oedipus complex, a superego, and a latency period. May we also attribute a phallic organization and a castration complex to it? The answer is in the affirmative; but these things cannot be the same as they are in boys. Here the feminist demand for equal rights for the sexes does not take us far, for the morphological distinction is bound to find expression in differences of psychical development. "Anatomy is Destiny," to vary a saying of Napoleon's. The little girl's clitoris behaves just like a penis to begin with; but, when she makes a comparison with a playfellow of the other sex, she perceives that she has "come off badly" and she feels this as a wrong done to her and as a ground for inferiority. For a while still she consoles herself with the expectation that later on, when she grows older, she will acquire just as big an appendage as the boy's. Here the masculinity complex of women branches off. A female child, however, does not understand her lack of a penis as being a sex character; she explains it by assuming that at some earlier date she had possessed an equally large organ and had then lost it by castration. She seems not to extend this inference from herself to other, adult females, but, entirely on the lies of the phallic phase, to regard them as possessing large and complete—that is to say, male—genitals. The essential difference thus comes about that the girl accepts castration as an accomplished fact, whereas the boy fears the possibility of its occurrence.

The fear of castration being thus excluded in the little girl, a powerful motive also drops out for the setting up of a superego and for the breaking off of the infantile genital organization. In her, far more than in the boy, these changes seem to be the result of upbringing and of intimidation from outside which threatens her with a loss of love. The girl's Oedipus complex is much simpler than that of the small bearer of the penis; in my experience, it seldom goes beyond the taking of her mother's place and the adopting of a feminine attitude toward her father. Renunciation of the penis is not tolerated by the girl without some attempt at compensation. She slips—along the line of a symbolic equation, one might say—from the penis to a baby. Her Oedipus complex culminates in a desire, which is long retained, to receive a baby from her father as a gift—to bear him a child. One has an impression that the Oedipus complex is then gradually given up because this wish is never fulfilled. The two wishes—to possess a penis and a child—remain strongly cathected in the unconscious and help to prepare the female creature for her later sexual role. The comparatively lesser strength of the sadistic contribution to her sexual instinct, which we may no doubt connect with the stunted growth of her penis, makes it easier in her case for the direct sexual trends to be transformed into aim-inhibited trends of an affectionate kind. It must be admitted, however, that in general our insight into these developmental processes in girls is unsatisfactory, incomplete, and vague.

I have no doubt that the chronological and causal relations described here between the Oedipus complex, sexual intimidation (the threat of castration), the formation of the superego, and the beginning of the latency period are of a typical kind; but I do not wish to assert that this type is the only possible one. Variations in the chronological order and in the linking up of these events are bound to have a very important bearing on the development of the individual.

NOTES

NOTE 1

WAELDER, ROBERT

The Problem of the Genesis of Psychical Conflict in Earliest Infancy*

*   *   *

A little girl of three years old whose upbringing had presented no difficulty in her first year and little serious difficulty in her second and third years, suddenly began to show signs of trouble. She was heard one day saying to herself, "Mummy has smashed me up." At about the same time it happened that when her mother was drying her after her bath the little girl displayed great anxiety every time the mother approached her genitals with the towel.

*   *   *

* 18 *International Journal of Psychoanalysis*, 1937. (pp. 453–59). Reprinted by permission.

Some months before this episode, this child and a sister a year older than herself had seen a little boy naked when they were playing on the beach. Probably this was the first time that they had noticed the difference between the sexes. The elder sister, at that time three years and three months old, reacted immediately and very definitely; the younger at first showed no reaction. We are not here concerned with the reactions of the older child; I will merely say that for a long time she was occupied in working over this experience and several times discussed it with her mother in the presence of her younger sister. Thus we are inclined to suppose that the latter's reactions, as manifested in the incident I have described, were part of the castration complex and that her complaint that her mother had injured her was the familiar accusation, of which Freud has told us, that the mother was to blame for the little girl's lack of a penis. We shall soon see the further material by which this interpretation is borne out.

*   *   *

. . . It happened that, at about the same time that she made the remark I have recorded and displayed anxiety lest her mother should touch her genitals, the children's father went into the nursery and tried to shake hands with them. The younger of the two refused to give him her hand, saying, "I won't give you my hand, I will only give you my finger." When her father asked in amazement why she did so, she replied, using her own childish terms, that it was because he had a penis and "a little bag." (Her knowledge of the scrotum could only have been derived from the incident on the beach several months previously; it had never been mentioned in the conversations between her elder sister and the grownups.) It is true that she only said this once. Only a few hours later, when her father, hoping to elicit the same reply, again asked her to give him her hand, she refused, as she had done before, but gave as her reason, "because you've got an apron." The displacement had been made with extraordinary rapidity, within a few hours. (The fact that she had turned her father into a woman is another story.)

From that time on, certain difficulties arose which might perhaps be called symptoms. At meals the child did not want to have her meat cut up and wished to take all her food only in large pieces, not divided up in any way, so that in fact it was impossible for her to eat them. For instance, she would not allow anyone to break off a piece of cake for her, and so forth. A dog which she knew was once brought to see her when it had just been shaved and the effect was to give her a shock. She became more and more preoccupied with the idea of "big and little" until she could think of nothing else. The rivalry in relation to her elder sister, which had long ago been allayed, broke out again. The younger child constantly thought about

how much older her sister was and how soon she could catch her up. She fantasied that she was big and her sister little and invented a game in which she was the mother and her elder sister the baby. She took a great delight in this game. Anyone who entered the nursery was immediately scrutinized as to his or her height, and at night she would beg grownups to sit beside her cot, using the phrase that "big" X (man or woman, as the case might be) was to sit beside her. Spectacles worn by adults were for her an object of the liveliest interest, and at one time, whenever her father, who wore glasses, approached her, she immediately began to talk about them and to investigate them, refusing to talk about anything else. She also evolved a theory that she had once been big and had only just become little.

Now I think that all this material goes to prove that everything I have related represented attempts on the child's part to work over her castration complex by methods familiar to us in our female patients. . . .

The little girl also developed a transitory symptom in the shape of a tic. On one occasion she took hold of her nose and asked if it was a big one. This gesture very soon became a tic: Every moment she put her fingers to her nose. At this point her mother intervened with an interpretation and gave a suitable explanation that nothing had been taken away from the child, that all boys and men were from their birth like the little friend whom she had observed, that all girls and woman, including her mother, were like herself and that the one form was just as nice as the other and that some day she would have children. At first this interpretation had no effect, but its effect was instantaneous when it was repeated by the other child, the sister a year older than herself. The tic vanished the same day.

Finally the child developed a habit of blaming her mother for everything disagreeable which happened. If she dropped anything, it was her mother's fault, although the latter was often nowhere near: She should have looked after her better. The same explanation applies here—the child was reproaching her mother, who was really "to blame for everything," seeing that she had not borne the little girl as a boy. Matters went on thus for some months, when the episode occurred for the sake of which I have chosen this example.

One night the mother was awakened by the child's crying and saying that "it had blown on her tummy." As the child was partly uncovered, the mother at first thought that she felt cold. But the little girl went on to say that she had wanted to bite her genitals and that then it blew. So it was a question of a dream and of one which, in comparison with most of the dreams of children of this age, had been much distorted. The mother soothed the child for the moment and suggested that she should go to sleep and that the next day they would talk about it.

The next morning the mother asked the child to tell her the dream again. She learnt another detail: There was a man at the window whose face was smashed and he had a piece of bread in his hand. The man mustn't come into the room.

The mother asked about the astonishing dream element that the child had wanted to bite her own genitals. The little girl said (naturally using her childish words) "The genitals were big, the genitals were little." She then stood up, blew out her abdomen and said, "It blew like that."

* * *

The mother's intimate knowledge of every detail in the child's life enabled her to understand the situation immediately from the little girl's words and gestures. In the last few months she had manifested acute anxiety. In her nursery, as in that of many other children, there were toy baloons which could be blown up. Sometimes, if one blew too hard, a balloon burst. The child had displayed great anxiety when trying to blow one up herself and when her nursery governess did so. Often the little girl would cry out that they ought not to do it, the balloon would burst. When she herself tried to blow it up she was awkward about it and held the mouthpiece, which was made of soft rubber, between her teeth instead of between her lips, so that she generally did not succeed. She had been told not to bite it and then it would go better. It must be noted that a balloon in a collapsed condition, the rubber bladder with a tube-shaped mouthpiece, really does look very much like a penis with the scrotum.

The mother's knowledge of this detail enabled her to understand a fragment of the dream. The dream thought obviously was that the child wanted to blow up her own genitals and make them big like those of the little boy and that she was seized with anxiety lest they should burst. This explained the other dream fragment: that it had "blown on her tummy." Thus the biting could hardly be described as aggression: It simply indicated what she did to her balloon.

The mother interpreted this fragment to the child, telling her that she had been afraid of her genitals bursting if they were blown up. The child replied, "But they have burst already," thus betraying the fantasy that her genitals had once been blown up, had burst, and so had arrived at their present miserable condition. It was plain that in her fantasy her mother was to blame.

The detail of the man with the smashed face and a piece of bread in his hand, who was at the window and must not come into the room was explained as follows. On their daily walks the children used to meet a cripple, who begged for bread. This experience supplies another proof of the possibility of being broken up: "He must not come into the room."

Upon the mother's interpretation the child's face lighted up, proving that her mother was right and that really a certain amount of material had been released. Remembering the psychoanalytical success of the elder sister, which I have already recorded, and the generally recognized fact that children are specially impressed by what other children tell them, the mother repeated her interpretation and explanation in another form. On the child's asking whether she also had dreams and begging her to tell one she recounted an imaginary dream of her own. She said she had dreamt of a little girl who cried bitterly because she was a girl and who thought that her mother had once blown her up and that then she had burst and now was smashed. But a great crowd of children told her that she was not smashed but just as nice looking as boys were. The mother described the conversation between the little girl and the other children, in which the little girl was finally convinced, and how she was now quite contented. The child followed this story with a delighted smile, indicating a sense of relief.

This does not by any means exhaust the meanings of the dream. On the previous day (not for the first time) the little girl had heard it said that children were once inside their mothers' body. She had, of course, long known about pregnancy; some time before, she had had a married nurse who became pregnant and remained in service for a time. The children had known that she was going to have a baby and, later on, she had brought it to see them. Thus the dream was concerned with the dangers of feminine existence: Not only had her own originally male genital burst, but if she ever had a baby, she would be in danger of the same fate.

* * *

NOTE 2

FREUD, SIGMUND

Notes upon a Case of Obsessional Neurosis (1909)*

In psychoanalyses we frequently come across occurrences . . . dating back to the earliest years of the patient's childhood, in which his infantile sexual activity appears to reach its climax and often comes to a catastrophic end owing to some misfortune or punishment. Such occurrences are apt to appear in a shadowy way in dreams. Often they will become so clear that the analyst thinks he has a firm hold of them, and will nevertheless evade any final elucidation; and unless he proceeds with the greatest skill and caution

* Reprinted from: 10 *The Standard Edition of the Complete Psychological Works of Sigmund Freud*, James Strachey, ed. London: The Hogarth Press and the Institute of Psychoanalysis, 1955. (pp. 206–7). Reprinted by permission of Hogarth and Basic Books, Inc.

he may be compelled to leave it undecided whether the scene in question actually took place or not. It will help to put us upon the right track in interpreting it, if we recognize that more than one version of the scene (each often differing greatly from the other) may be detected in the patient's unconscious fantasies. If we do not wish to go astray in our judgment of their historical reality, we must above all bear in mind that people's "childhood memories" are only consolidated at a later period, usually at the age of puberty; and that this involves a complicated process of remodeling, analogous in every way to the process by which a nation constructs legends about its early history. It at once becomes evident that in his fantasies about his infancy the individual as he grows up *endeavors to efface the recollection of his autoerotic activities;* and this he does by exalting their memory traces to the level of object love, just as a real historian will view the past in the light of the present. This explains why these fantasies abound in seductions and assaults, where the facts will have been confined to autoerotic activities and the caresses or punishments that stimulated them. Furthermore, it becomes clear that in constructing fantasies about his childhood the individual *sexualizes his memories;* that is, he brings commonplace experiences into relation with his sexual activity, and extends his sexual interest to them—though in doing this he is probably following upon the traces of a really existing connection. [I]t is not my intention in these remarks to detract from the importance which I have hitherto attached to infantile sexuality by reducing it to nothing more than sexual interest at the age of puberty....

NOTE 3

HARTMANN, HEINZ and KRIS, ERNST

The Genetic Approach in Psychoanalysis*

[I]n most cases in which Freud introduces phylogenetic propositions, ontogenetic propositions could be carried one step further. For instance, Freud argues that the intensity of the fear of castration experienced by the male child in our civilization is unaccountable if we consider it as a reaction to the actual threats to which the boy is being exposed in the phallic phase; only the memory of the race will explain it. To this we are inclined to reply with Freud's own arguments. While in many cases the child in our civilization is no longer being threatened with castration, the intensity of the veiled aggression of the adult against the child may still produce the same effect. One might say that there always is "castration" in the air. Adults who restrict the little boy act according to patterns rooted in their own upbringing. However symbolic or dist-

ant from actual castration their threats might be, they are likely to be interpreted by the little boy in terms of his own experiences. The tumescent penis with which he responds in erotic excitement, that strange phenomenon of a change in a part of his body that proves to be largely independent of his control, leads him to react not to the manifest content but rather to the latent meaning of the restriction with which his strivings for mother, sister, or girl playmate meet. And then, what he may have seen frequently before, the genitals of the little girl, acquire a new meaning as evidence and corroboration of that fear. However, the intensity of fear is not only linked to his present experience, but also to similar experiences in his past. The dreaded retaliation of the environment revives memories of similar anxieties when desires for other gratifications were predominant and when the supreme fear was not that of being castrated but that of not being loved. . . .

NOTE 4

FLUGEL, J. C.

Man, Morals and Society*

[T]he growth of the superego is a relatively slow process, the beginnings of which can be traced back to the earliest stages of an individual's psychological development. There are two characteristics of these earliest stages that are of special importance from our present point of view. In the first place the very young child has not yet formed any clear distinction between himself and his environment; in the second place his impulses are highly ambivalent, i.e., are compounded of love and aggression to a degree and with an intimacy of fusion that are seldom to be found in later life. This last statement requires, however, some slight qualification, inasmuch as in Klein's view indeed the baby finds all stimuli painful during the first few weeks of life, and therefore reacts to them with the infantile equivalent of hate. In these early days he had, we must presume, not yet got used to the new and far more varied surroundings to which he has been transferred from the homogeneous and protective environment of the womb. He then gradually learns that some stimuli satisfy his needs and are not mere disturbances of his would-be Nirvana state; such stimuli he comes to love and enjoy. But the very young child, with no more than a minimal appreciation of time, is unable to bear tension; he does not possess the knowledge, so consoling to older human beings, that loss, frustration, pain, and discomfort are usually but temporary and will be followed by relief. Consequently a very small change in the situation (e.g., a less comfortable posture or pressure of

* 1 *The Psychoanalytic Study of the Child,* 1945. (pp. 21–22). Reprinted by permission of International Universities Press, New York.

* New York: International Universities Press, 1945. (pp. 108–19). Reprinted by permission of International Universities Press and Gerald Duckworth & Co., Ltd.

his clothes, a less easy grasp of the nipple or a less ready flow of milk) will convert a pleasant satisfying stimulus into an unpleasant dissatisfying one. Thus the child can both love and hate the same objects in rapid succession or alternation, and his love and hate alike tend to work on the all-or-nothing principle—there are not the qualifications and quantitative variations that are found in later life.

At the same time, . . . the child has not learnt the distinction—later of such far-reaching import—between the self and the not-self. He does not clearly recognize the difference between a disagreeable outer stimulus and an unpleasant tension in himself (such as that caused by being cold, wet, or hungry). Everything connected with a state of tension, e.g., his own hunger sensations on the one hand and the breast that does not easily supply milk on the other, are regarded as "bad" in the same way; just as the feeling of satisfied hunger and the satisfying nipple are regarded as "good" in the same way.

Associated with this fundamental absence of the distinction between the subjective and the objective, between the self and the not-self, are two further confusions of detail with important consequences. There is no adequate distinction between sensations and their accompanying feelings and impulses, nor —more important still—between these feelings and impulses and the associated outer objects. In other words the child does not distinguish between the cognitive and orectic aspects of his own experience, nor between his own orexis and the outer world. Thus the sensations of hunger are not separated from the distress and anger aroused by these sensations, nor is anger, with its accompanying tendency to suck or bite aggressively, separated from the mother's breast which is failing to satisfy the hunger—and similarly in other situations. When distress is not alleviated and unsatisfied desire persists, the child begins to feel overwhelmed by his own inner tension, and it is this condition which gives rise to what psychoanalysts have sometimes described as fear of the instincts (i.e., of uncontrollable instinctual tension). . . . A vivid impression of the way in which the infant can come to feel threatened and overmastered by its own aggressiveness is conveyed, for instance, by Riviere: "The child is overwhelmed by choking and suffocating; its eyes are blinded with tears, its ears deafened, its throat sore; its bowels gripe, its evacuations burn it." Thus the child's autogenous aggression, the biological purpose of which, as manifested for instance in crying, is no doubt to get others to relieve its needs, may threaten to destroy its owner, and it is the impotence of the child in face of the mounting tension which makes uncontrolled and unrelieved aggression appear as a situation of acute danger. If at these earliest stages there is at the same time no clear distinction between such distressful and alarming inner conditions and the associated outer objects or circumstances, it is easy to see that the first step has been taken toward the creation of an outer "bogy" of ill-defined but intense and almost unimaginable evilness.

A later and more definite step in the same direction occurs as soon as the mechanism of projection comes into play. The origins of this mechanism—of such immense importance to mental development and, especially in later life, to psychopathology—are perhaps to be found in the primal lack of distinction between the self and the not-self. In any case, however, when the distinction does actually begin to be drawn, the line of demarcation is not logical or consistent and the not-self will include many elements (both of "badness" and "goodness") which a more experienced and sophisticated mind would unhesitatingly consider to be subjective and to belong to the person's own inner orectic life. Soon, however, other tendencies (our understanding of which admittedly still leaves much to be desired) begin to exercise a more selective influence in leading the child to ascribe some of his own experiences to the outer world and thus to cause projection. The most important factor in this selective influence (and here psychoanalysts are in pretty general agreement) is the attempt to identify pleasure with the self and unpleasure with the not-self. Many harmful and painful stimuli come from the outer world; the satisfactory way of dealing with them, as the child gradually learns, is to remove the stimuli or to remove himself from them. A "bad" thing that falls into the not-self category can very often be dealt with in this way; hence there arises a very natural endeavor to place it in this category and thus to establish a correspondence on the one hand of the "good" and pleasant with the self, and on the other of the "bad" and unpleasant with the not-self. Unfortunately not all "good" or "bad" things really fall into these respective categories, so that the attempt necessarily predisposes to delusions and unrealism; it is in fact a manifestation of Freud's "pleasure principle." Nevertheless, the impulse to divide the universe of "good" and "bad" along these lines is so strong that it is only corrected slowly and with difficulty, and throughout life the tendency to project the evil in ourselves is a constant menace to our true appreciation of reality. Anyhow, in the early stages of his life the child has in his desire to achieve this correspondence a strong motive for projecting his own painful feelings and the accompanying aggressive desires upon the outer world—and most naturally of course upon the outer objects or persons that are, in virtue of temporal and spatial contiguity, associated with these feelings. In this way the outer bogies become natural recipients, representatives, or incarnations of the infant's own distressful states and hostile tendencies, and reality becomes distorted in a way that is at once both pessimistic and grotesque.

The qualities projected on to the bogies depend upon the stage of development at which projection occurs, in much the same way as the manifestations of sado–masochism depend upon the level concerned. Thus at the earliest or oral stage the projected figures suck, bite, tear, or rend; at the anal or urethral levels they are liable to flood the world with filth or water, or indulge in other forms of widespread and fierce destructiveness; while at the phallic level they castrate, mutilate, and maim—all of these stages finding expression not only in individual childish fantasy but in frequently recurring themes of fairy tale and myth. Projections of this type are responsible for the weirder forms of childish phobias, which people the world with strange and sinister figures liable, as it seems to the child, to attack him in queer, malignant, and terrifying ways.

At the stage at which the earliest projections occur there is, according to Klein, as yet no full and clear appreciation of persons as such. The child has not yet learnt to recognize his mother as a permanent complex organic unity; at first it will for instance only distinguish the nipple and then the breast as an "object" of the outer world, even this being moreover an object that is intimately connected with, and therefore still to some extent confused with, his own weal or woe. It is thus at first the breast or other parts of the body, rather than whole and complete persons, upon which the infant's own aggressive tendencies are projected.

*   *   *

At the age of two to three months, when, according to Klein, the child begins to perceive its mother as a person, his impulses are still at the aggressive-ambivalent stage. He wants ("cannibalistically") to incorporate the nipple and the breast, and later to consume the contents of the mother's body (this last being perhaps one of the most startling of Klein's discoveries). The attitudes characteristic of this stage, carrying over to later periods with fuller understanding, give rise to the notions of sucking out, biting, tearing, or otherwise destroying these contents—which may be regarded in some aspects as "good" (e.g., as milk) but in other aspects as "bad" (e.g., faeces, or an undesired and hated rival in the form of an unborn baby). These impulses, crude in form and often intensely hostile in nature, are projected on to the mother as a person, so that there arises the notion of a fierce mother figure who is in her turn prepared to bite, tear, rend, destroy, and eviscerate. Thus the projection of the child's own aggressiveness may create a quite fantastic notion of the cruelty and severity of the parents, in comparison with which their real tendencies to express anger or impatience or to administer punishment sink into insignificance. Some writers, e.g., Ernest Jones, have been so impressed with this element of aggression that is projected on to the parents that they have been tempted to think that the parents' real aggressiveness

is a comparatively negligible factor and that, such as it is, it is often "exploited" by the child, as affording a convenient "rationalization" of his own fantastic fears, themselves due to a projection of his own aggression. . . .

*   *   *

It is clear that the parent figure (or at earlier stages the "object") thus introjected is a figure very different from the real parent, inasmuch as it is endowed with all the crude and primitive aggressiveness of the young child himself. In this way then, it would appear, does the superego acquire its more alarming and barbaric features. Here we have the true origin of the harshness and severity of the superego which, from the start of its investigations in this direction, had been among the most astonishing and disconcerting discoveries of psychoanalysis. As we have already said, the formation of the superego, according to Klein and her school, is very far from being a single process connected with a particular stage or event of psychological history (e.g., the passing of the Oedipus complex). It results rather from a long series of introjections carried on through a long period of time, and thus bears the marks of many different developmental levels. And between each process of introjection there occurs a corresponding process of projection. . . .

. . . Feeling that he has incorporated a "bad" object (or one that is to some extent "bad"), the child is impelled to deal with the unpleasant and dangerous situation thus created. He does so by projecting the "bad" object upon the parent and thus attempting to re-establish the equations good = self, bad = outer world. This is followed in turn by a new introjection. But although the projected object is, as we have seen, a grossly distorted one, it is, nevertheless, to some extent modified by the real qualities of the outer object, which in the vast majority of cases are, of course, far less alarming than the imagined qualities derived from the child's own crude aggressiveness; real parents, though they may sometimes express anger and impatience, may slap and scold, may be preoccupied or negligent, do not bite, tear, devour, or otherwise destroy. To the extent that the distorted idea of the parent has been affected by these real qualities, the reintrojected image will be less terrifying than it was before its projection. In this way a benign cycle of events may be established and the introjected parent that is the primitive superego gradually grows less savage and grotesque and more adapted to reality.

This process of what might perhaps be called the taming or civilizing of the primitive superego is aided and complicated by two further factors, which for the sake of simplicity we have hitherto left out of account, but which make the picture we are asked to form of the growth of the superego rather less fearsome and macabre than it might so far have appeared.

In the first place there tends to come about a fusion of the originally incompatible and contradictory notions of good and bad objects. We have seen that the child, with little or no appreciation of time and of the inevitable periodic recurrence of needs and satisfactions, tends to experience feelings on the all-or-nothing principle. In moments of satisfaction everything is well, and the breast—and later the mother—is an entirely good object, the prototype perhaps of the fairy godmother or genie who fulfils all wishes completely and instantaneously. At moments of dissatisfaction the child feels that all is lost, that he is overwhelmed by his distress, and that the object or parent is entirely bad, hostile, and frustrating. Thus the child builds up two opposite but equally distorted pictures of the parents. Gradually, however, the two pictures begin to fuse and interpenetrate. The bad parent is seen as not utterly hostile or vindictive. The good parent does not gratify every wish immediately; on the contrary, by imposing restraints upon the child's own aggressiveness, he (or, more often, she) can afford some measure of reassurance and protection even in the very act of frustration. Thus there gradually arises the notion, to which we have already referred, of what Isaacs calls the "good-strict" parent, one on whose superior strength and power of control the child can rely when he feels the danger of being overwhelmed by his own instincts. Since frustration may thus also give protection, it may in certain cases bring a welcome feeling of security and relief rather than an increased sense of overpowering and devastating need. Insofar as this attitude of the parent is itself introjected in the growing superego, the superego begins to be welcomed as a source of strength within the individual which shields him from the consequences of his own unbridled passions. In Riviere's words, "the feeling that 'I am an uncontrolled bundle of unpleasant and dangerous impulses toward myself and others' leads to 'I have somebody like my good helping mother inside me, who will watch over me and never allow me to go too far, who will save me and herself from serious danger.' " Here then we get some further light upon the more beneficent aspects of the superego, aspects of which in our later considerations we have perhaps tended to lose sight.

The second complicating factor is one on which Klein in particular has laid much stress. The young child not only possesses extremely aggressive impulses but has no clear idea of the limitations of his own powers. On the contrary, in virtue of what Freud in quite early days of psychoanalysis had called the "omnipotence of thought," he feels that his destructive impulses are only too liable to achieve their aim and that the breast or the loving, helping mother has probably been destroyed beyond repair. Any external real withdrawal of love, help, or presence is apt to be interpreted in this sense. With the loss of the good external object, the child feels that he has also lost the corresponding good internal object that he had acquired, or can acquire, through introjection. Confronted with a catastrophic situation of this kind, the child resorts to attempts at reparation or restitution; he tries to make good the damage he has done. For the most part he can only do this in more or less symbolic form, and indeed in the play techniques devised by Klein and others such attempts at reparation are often to be observed. Moreover, the impulse of reparation thus started is one that tends to persist throughout life. It is seen at work in many obsessional symptoms (in which indeed there may be an alternation of symbolically destructive and symbolically restitutive thoughts and actions, as in the very clear case reported by Fenichel of a boy who constantly muttered a prayer for his mother's return to health and then slapped his mouth to annul the effect of what he had just said). Above all it enters as an important element into many of the phenomena usually classified as sublimations, and in this way contributes very greatly to human culture. In the ability to carry out creative and constructive work men find the most satisfactory means of reassurance and of assuaging guilt. It is, Isaacs suggests, one of the greatest tragedies of early life that just when the child's need to make good is so urgent, his powers of doing something creative are so limited and his capacity for causing destruction and disorder so relatively great. . . .

NOTE 5

SCHAFER, ROY

The Loving and Beloved Superego in Freud's Structural Theory*

*   *   *

Freud clearly saw the laying down of the superego as a decisive factor in preparing the child to fit into and participate in the civilized community. When he spoke of society's accomplishing in a few years of childhood training what has taken many ages for civilization to achieve, he recognized the adaptive aspect of the superego and society's stake in it. The superego is as important a carrier and protector of cultural continuity as the ego; in fact, it is obviously the more conservative of the two in content and resistance to change. In *Group Psychology*, pursuing his discussions in *Totem and Taboo*, Freud pointed out how social conscience and the sense of duty grow out of the mastery of sibling rivalry, and in *The Ego and the Id* he clearly set forth how the establishment of the superego preserves object relations. The ad-

*15 *The Psychoanalytic Study of the Child*, 1960. (pp. 163, 183–85, 181–88). Reprinted by permission of International Universities Press, New York.

vances of civilization, the binding of men together in social organizations are founded on the sense of guilt.

It is here that we should consider in some detail Freud's point that in rearing their children, parents are "glad to be able to identify fully at last with their own parents"; they then repeat their own parents' severe and exacting pattern with the result that the superego of the child is not built on the parents' egos, but on their superegos. From the adaptive point of view, the meaning seems to be this: The parent provides, in the form of his superego, a pre-established structure for his child to adopt so that the child will not have to accomplish anew all the cultural achievements in the history of his group. A considerable psychic saving is involved for the child. The child takes over or internalizes this "parental function." He thereby becomes father to himself and acquires basic equipment for later becoming psychological father of his children. By introjecting the parental superego, he also establishes a motivational base for learning and perfecting a certain moral, protective, and comforting know-how. This know-how is part of being grown up. In this process the child is additionally helped to meet his ego ideal, as described above, and subsequently to feel worthy of love. And in being prepared for life in the community he is put in the position of being able to find, engage, and use alternative or modified real models and object relations such as he needs to complete his development. As Freud pointed out, the neurotic with his defective superego is, by contrast, asocial and cut off from the great institutions of society.

Obviously, this line of thought indicates the necessity of examining the parent's superego in order to understand the child's. Much will depend on how right or conflict free the parent feels in his role of moral guide, how much he can genuinely and realistically act "in the divine conviction of doing the right thing." Insofar as his superego is immature, hostile, and distant from his ego, it will produce disruptions in crucial parent–child interactions, in particular those interactions concerning the child's budding instinctual and ego expressions. It is under these conditions that we might expect the child to develop an Oedipus complex, both masculine and feminine, that is especially difficult to relinquish, and consequently a severe superego. I have in mind here Freud's view that it is the strength of the Oedipus complex and its incomplete resolution that underlie the severity of the superego. In other words, severity of superego function testifies to the inadequacy of superego formation. It is, therefore, no great jump to recognize that disturbance in the parental superego plays a double role in disturbing the child's superego development: It exaggerates the Oedipal conflict and provides a faulty model for dealing with it. In this way, superego pathology is perpetuated.

To extrapolate further, when the parent has a healthy superego and is relatively unambivalent in exercising parental superego functions, he furnishes the child with an adaptive model for the internal as well as external disposition of love and aggression. If nothing else, he expresses some of his inevitable aggressiveness toward his child in the form of useful moral guidance and restriction. Both by imposing meaningful limits on behavior and by administering real punishment, the parent corrects the terrifying archaic fantasies of punishment introduced by the child in his struggle with his own impulses. As a result, the child will experience less alienation from real objects, less damming up of impulses, less devious discharge or sudden eruption, and less sense of guilt and need for punishment.

Parental gentleness and leniency form no obstacle to the child's forming a critical superego, as Freud well knew. And while he did not say in so many words that the child needs a parental superego of optimal strength in order to live and develop, he did say that the ego needs the superego's love to live, and by that he implied the child's vital need for a healthy parental superego to introject. Furthermore, by rigid permissiveness, as we well know, a parent often attempts to deny the tension between his ego and superego; in this he is bound to fail for his unconscious superego will express itself in countless subtle though powerful ways and the child will take over this ill-concealed superego. Unconflicted gentleness is likely to go hand in hand with unconflicted firmness.

*   *   *

. . . There is a loving and beloved aspect of the superego. It represents the loved and admired Oedipal and preoedipal parents who provide love, protection, comfort, and guidance, who embody and transmit certain ideals and moral structures more or less representative of their society, and who, even in their punishing activities, provide needed expressions of parental care, contact, and love. The maturing child will identify himself with these parental aspects. The identification will take place partly by way of imitative primary identification and partly by way of identification for purposes of mastering the Oedipal crisis. The former comes under the heading of ego identification primarily, the latter under the heading of superego identification primarily. By means of this identification the child ultimately attains the position of being able to love, protect, comfort, and guide himself and his children after him, and of doing so according to relatively ego-syntonic, culture-syntonic, and impersonal sets of ideals and moral standards. . . .

. . . The superego is not the reservoir and inner channel of hatred alone. . . .

In the hostile aspect of the superego, object hate is turned around and transformed into self-hate; in the benign aspect of the superego it is object love which is turned around and transformed into that aspect of self-love or narcissism felt as pride and security in relation to society and destiny as well as one's own conscience and ideals. The superego builds and upholds as well as splits and tears down, just as the ego does.

In these conclusions the ego and superego remain, as Freud meant them to, the mind's two great structures for the disposition of love and hate. . . .

NOTE 6

FREUD, SIGMUND

Civilization and its Discontents (1930)*

. . . What means does civilization employ in order to inhibit the aggressiveness which opposes it, to make it harmless, to get rid of it, perhaps? . . . This we can study in the history of the development of the individual. What happens in him to render his desire for aggression innocuous? Something very remarkable, which we should never have guessed and which is, nevertheless, quite obvious. His aggressiveness is introjected, internalized; it is, in point of fact, sent back to where it came from—that is, it is directed toward his own ego. There it is taken over by a portion of the ego, which sets itself over against the rest of the ego as superego, and which now, in the form of "conscience," is ready to put into action against the ego the same harsh aggressiveness that the ego would have liked to satisfy upon other, extraneous individuals. The tension between the harsh superego and the ego that is subjected to it, is called by us the sense of guilt; it expresses itself as a need for punishment. Civilization, therefore, obtains mastery over the individual's dangerous desire for aggression by weakening and disarming it and by setting up an agency within him to watch over it, like a garrison in a conquered city.

[I]f we ask how a person comes to have a sense of guilt, we arrive at an answer which cannot be disputed: a person feels guilty (devout people would say "sinful") when he has done something which he knows to be "bad." But then we notice how little this answer tells us. Perhaps, after some hesitation, we shall add that even when a person has not actually *done* the bad thing but has only recognized in himself an *intention* to do it, he may regard himself as guilty; and the question then arises of why the intention is regarded as equal to the deed. Both cases, however, presuppose that one had already recognized that what is bad is reprehensible, is something that must not be carried out. How is this judgment arrived at? We may reject the existence of an original, as it

were natural, capacity to distinguish good from bad. What is bad is often not at all what is injurious or dangerous to the ego; on the contrary, it may be something which is desirable and enjoyable to the ego. Here, therefore, there is an extraneous influence at work, and it is this that decides what is to be called good or bad. Since a person's own feelings would not have led him along this path, he must have had a motive for submitting to this extraneous influence. Such a motive is easily discovered in his helplessness and his dependence on other people, and it can best be designated as fear of loss of love. If he loses the love of another person upon whom he is dependent, he also ceases to be protected from a variety of dangers. Above all, he is exposed to the danger that this stronger person will show his superiority in the form of punishment. At the beginning, therefore, what is bad is whatever causes one to be threatened with loss of love. For fear of that loss, one must avoid it. This, too, is the reason why it makes little difference whether one has already done the bad thing or only intends to do it. In either case the danger only sets in if and when the authority discovers it, and in either case the authority would behave in the same way.

This state of mind is called a "bad conscience"; but actually it does not deserve this name, for at this stage the sense of guilt is clearly only a fear of loss of love, "social" anxiety. In small children it can never be anything else, but in many adults, too, it has only changed to the extent that the place of the father or the two parents is taken by the larger human community. Consequently, such people habitually allow themselves to do any bad thing which promises them enjoyment, so long as they are sure that the authority will not know anything about it or cannot blame them for it; they are afraid only of being found out. Present-day society has to reckon in general with this state of mind.

A great change takes place only when the authority is internalized through the establishment of a superego. The phenomena of conscience then reach a higher stage. Actually, it is not until now that we should speak of conscience or a sense of guilt. At this point, too, the fear of being found out comes to an end; the distinction, moreover, between doing something bad and wishing to do it disappears entirely, since nothing can be hidden from the superego, not even thoughts. It is true that the seriousness of the situation from a real point of view has passed away, for the new authority, the superego, has no motive that we know of for ill-treating the ego, with which it is intimately bound up; but genetic influence, which leads to the survival of what is past and has been surmounted, makes itself felt in the fact that fundamentally things remain as they were at the beginning. The superego torments the sinful ego with the same feeling of anxiety and is on the watch for opportunities of getting it punished by the external world.

* Reprinted from: 21 *The Standard Edition of the Complete Psychological Works of Sigmund Freud*, James Strachey, ed. London: The Hogarth Press and the Institute of Psychoanalysis, 1961. (pp. 123–33, 136–37). Reprinted by permission of Hogarth and W. W. Norton & Co.

At this second stage of development, the conscience exhibits a peculiarity which was absent from the first stage and which is no longer easy to account for. For the more virtuous a man is, the more severe and distrustful is its behavior, so that ultimately it is precisely those people who have carried saintliness furthest who reproach themselves with the worst sinfulness. This means that virtue forfeits some part of its promised reward; the docile and continent ego does not enjoy the trust of its mentor, and strives in vain, it would seem, to acquire it. The objection will at once be made that these difficulties are artificial ones, and it will be said that a stricter and more vigilant conscience is precisely the hallmark of a moral man. Moreover, when saints call themselves sinners, they are not so wrong, considering the temptations to instinctual satisfaction to which they are exposed in a specially high degree—since, as is well known, temptations are merely increased by constant frustration, whereas an occasional satisfaction of them causes them to diminish, at least for the time being. The field of ethics, which is so full of problems, presents us with another fact: namely that ill luck—that is, external frustration—so greatly enhances the power of the conscience in the superego. As long as things go well with a man, his conscience is lenient and lets the ego do all sorts of things; but when misfortune befalls him, he searches his soul, acknowledges his sinfulness, heightens the demands of his conscience, imposes abstinences on himself and punishes himself with penances. Whole peoples have behaved in this way, and still do. This, however, is easily explained by the original infantile stage of conscience, which, as we see, is not given up after the introjection into the superego, but persists alongside of it and behind it. Fate is regarded as a substitute for the parental agency. If a man is unfortunate it means that he is no longer loved by this highest power; and, threatened by such a loss of love, he once more bows to the parental representative in his superego—a representative whom, in his days of good fortune, he was ready to neglect. . . .

Thus we know of two origins of the sense of guilt: One arising from fear of an authority, and the other, later on, arising from fear of the superego. The first insists upon a renunciation of instinctual satisfactions; the second, as well as doing this, presses for punishment, since the continuance of the forbidden wishes cannot be concealed from the superego. We have also learned how the severity of the superego—the demands of conscience—is to be understood. It is simply a continuation of the severity of the external authority, to which it has succeeded and which it has in part replaced. We now see in what relationship the renunciation of instinct stands to the sense of guilt. Originally, renunciation of instinct was the result of fear of an external authority: One renounced one's satisfactions in order not to lose its love. If one has

carried out this renunciation, one is, as it were, quits with the authority and no sense of guilt should remain. But with fear of the superego the case is different. Here, instinctual renunciation is not enough, for the wish persists and cannot be concealed from the superego. Thus, in spite of the renunciation that has been made, a sense of guilt comes about. This constitutes a great economic disadvantage in the erection of a superego, or, as we may put it, in the formation of a conscience. Instinctual renunciation now no longer has a completely liberating effect; virtuous continence is no longer rewarded with the assurance of love. A threatened external unhappiness —loss of love and punishment on the part of the external authority—has been exchanged for a permanent internal unhappiness, for the tension of the sense of guilt.

These interrelations are so complicated and at the same time so important that, at the risk of repeating myself, I shall approach them from yet another angle. The chronological sequence, then, would be as follows. First comes renunciation of instinct owing to fear of aggression by the *external* authority. (This is, of course, what fear of the loss of love amounts to, for love is a protection against this punitive aggression.) After that comes the erection of an *internal* authority, and reununciation of instinct owing to fear of it—owing to fear of conscience. In this second situation bad intentions are equated with bad actions, and hence come a sense of guilt and a need for punishment. The aggressiveness of conscience keeps up the aggressiveness of the authority. So far things have no doubt been made clear; but where does this leave room for the reinforcing influence of misfortune (of renunciation imposed from without) and for the extraordinary severity of conscience in the best and most tractable people? We have already explained both these peculiarities of conscience, but we probably still have an impression that those explanations do not go to the bottom of the matter, and leave a residue still unexplained. And here at last an idea comes in which belongs entirely to psychoanalysis and which is foreign to people's ordinary way of thinking. This idea is of a sort which enables us to understand why the subject matter was bound to seem so confused and obscure to us. For it tells us that conscience (or more correctly, the anxiety which later becomes conscience) is indeed the cause of instinctual renunciation to begin with, but that later the relationship is reversed. Every renunciation of instinct now becomes a dynamic source of conscience and every fresh renunciation increases the latter's severity and intolerance. If we could only bring it better into harmony with what we already know about the history of the origin of conscience, we should be tempted to defend the paradoxical statement that conscience is the result of instinctual renunciation, or that instinctual renunciation (imposed on us from without) creates conscience, which then demands further instinctual renunciation.

The contradiction between this statement and what we have previously said about the genesis of conscience is in point of fact not so very great, and we see a way of further reducing it. In order to make our exposition easier, let us take as our example the aggressive instinct, and let us assume that the renunciation in question is always a renunciation of aggression. (This, of course, is only to be taken as a temporary assumption.) The effect of instinctual renunciation on the conscience then is that every piece of aggression whose satisfaction the subject gives up is taken over by the superego and increases the latter's aggressiveness (against the ego). This does not harmonize well with the view that the original aggressiveness of conscience is a continuance of the severity of the external authority and therefore has nothing to do with renunciation. But the discrepancy is removed if we postulate a different derivation for this first instalment of the superego's aggressivity. A considerable amount of aggressiveness must be developed in the child against the authority which prevents him from having his first, but nonetheless his most important, satisfactions, whatever the kind of instinctual deprivation that is demanded of him may be; but he is obliged to renounce the satisfaction of this revengeful aggressiveness. He finds his way out of this economically difficult situation with the help of familiar mechanisms. By means of identification he takes the unattackable authority into himself. The authority now turns into his superego and enters into possession of all the aggressiveness which a child would have liked to exercise against it. The child's ego has to content itself with the unhappy role of the authority—the father—who has been thus degraded. Here, as so often, the [real] situation is reversed: "If I were the father and you were the child, I should treat you badly." The relationship between the superego and the ego is a return, distorted by a wish, of the real relationships between the ego, as yet undivided, and an external object. That is typical, too. But the essential difference is that the original severity of the superego does not—or does not so much—represent the severity which one has experienced from it [the object], or which one attributes to it; it represents rather one's own aggressiveness toward it. If this is correct, we may assert truly that in the beginning conscience arises through the suppression of an aggressive impulse, and that it is subsequently reinforced by fresh suppressions of the same kind.

Which of these two views is correct? The earlier one, which genetically seemed so unassailable, or the newer one, which rounds off the theory in such a welcome fashion? Clearly, and by the evidence, too, of direct observations, both are justified. They do not contradict each other, and they even coincide at one point, for the child's revengeful aggressiveness will be in part determined by the amount of punitive aggression which he expects from his father. Experience shows, however, that the severity of the superego which a child develops in no way corresponds to the severity of treatment which he has himself met with. The severity of the former seems to be independent of that of the latter. A child who has been very leniently brought up can acquire a very strict conscience. But it would also be wrong to exaggerate this independence; it is not difficult to convince oneself that severity of upbringing does also exert a strong influence on the formation of the child's superego. What it amounts to is that in the formation of the superego and the emergence of a conscience innate constitutional factors and influences from the real environment act in combination. This is not at all surprising; on the contrary, it is a universal etiological condition for all such processes.

*   *   *

[I]t may not be superfluous to elucidate the meaning of a few words such as "superego," "conscience," "sense of guilt," "need for punishment," and "remorse," which we have often, perhaps, used too loosely and interchangeably. They all relate to the same state of affairs, but denote different aspects of it. The superego is an agency which has been inferred by us, and conscience is a function which we ascribe, among other functions, to that agency. This function consists in keeping a watch over the actions and intentions of the ego and judging them, in exercising a censorship. The sense of guilt, the harshness of the superego, is thus the same thing as the severity of the conscience. It is the perception which the ego has of being watched over in this way, the assessment of the tension between its own strivings and the demands of the superego. The fear of this critical agency (a fear which is at the bottom of the whole relationship), the need for punishment, is an instinctual manifestation on the part of the ego, which has become masochistic under the influence of a sadistic superego; it is a portion, that is to say, of the instinct toward internal destruction present in the ego, employed for forming an erotic attachment to the superego. We ought not to speak of a conscience until a superego is demonstrably present. As to a sense of guilt, we must admit that it is in existence before the superego, and therefore before conscience, too. At that time it is the immediate expression of fear of the external authority, a recognition of the tension between the ego and that authority. It is the direct derivative of the conflict between the need for the authority's love and the urge toward instinctual satisfaction, whose inhibition produces the inclination to aggression. The superimposition of these two strata of the sense of guilt— one coming from fear of the *external* authority, the other from fear of the *internal* authority—has hampered our insight into the position of conscience in a number of ways. Remorse is a general term for the ego's reaction in a case of sense of guilt. It contains, in little altered form, the sensory material of the anxiety which is operating behind the sense of guilt; it is itself a punishment and can include the need for punishment. Thus remorse, too, can be older than conscience.

NOTE 7

FREUD, SIGMUND

Criminals from a Sense of Guilt (1916)*

In telling me about their early youth, particularly before puberty, people who have afterward often become very respectable have informed me of forbidden actions which they committed at that time— such as thefts, frauds, and even arson. I was in the habit of dismissing these statements with the comment that we are familiar with the weakness of moral inhibitions at that period of life, and I made no attempt to find a place for them in any more significant context. But eventually I was led to make a more thorough study of such incidents by some glaring and more accessible cases in which the misdeeds were committed while the patients were actually under my treatment, and were no longer so youthful. Analytic work then brought the surprising discovery that such deeds were done principally because they were forbidden, and because their execution was accompanied by mental relief for their doer. He was suffering from an oppressive feeling of guilt, of which he did not know the origin, and after he had committed a misdeed this oppression was mitigated. His sense of guilt was at least attached to something.

Paradoxical as it may sound, I must maintain that the sense of guilt was present before the misdeed, that it did not arise from it, but conversely—the misdeed arose from the sense of guilt. These people might justly be described as criminals from a sense of guilt. The pre-existence of the guilty feeling had of course been demonstrated by a whole set of other manifestations and effects.

But scientific work is not satisfied with the establishment of a curious fact. There are two further questions to answer: What is the origin of this obscure sense of guilt before the deed, and is it probable that this kind of causation plays any considerable part in human crime?

An examination of the first question held out the promise of bringing us information about the source of mankind's sense of guilt in general. The invariable outcome of analytic work was to show that this ob-

scure sense of guilt derived from the Oedipus complex and was a reaction to the two great criminal intentions of killing the father and having sexual relations with the mother. In comparison with these two, the crimes committed in order to fix the sense of guilt to something came as a relief to the sufferers. We must remember in this connection that parricide and incest with the mother are the two great human crimes, the only ones which, as such, are pursued and abhorred in primitive communities. And we must remember, too, how close other investigations have brought us to the hypothesis that the conscience of mankind, which now appears as an inherited mental force, was acquired in connection with the Oedipus complex.

In order to answer the second question we must go beyond the scope of psychoanalytic work. With children it is easy to observe that they are often "naughty" on purpose to provoke punishment, and are quiet and contented after they have been punished. Later analytic investigation can often put us on the track of the guilty feeling which induced them to seek punishment. Among adult criminals we must no doubt except those who commit crimes without any sense of guilt, who have either developed no moral inhibitions or who, in their conflict with society, consider themselves justified in their action. But as regards the majority of other criminals, those for whom punitive measures are really designed, such a motivation for crime might very well be taken into consideration; it might throw light on some obscure points in the psychology of the criminal, and furnish punishment with a new psychological basis.

*   *   *

5.

SANDLER, JOSEPH

On the Concept of Superego*

*   *   *

The development of the ego, from the earliest weeks of life onward, is marked by the construction, within the mind of the child, of organized frames of reference or *schemata* which subserve adaptation. These *schemata* or mental models revolve at first around experiences of need satisfaction, and no distinction is made by the child between sensations which arise from inside its own body and those which occur as a result of the activities of the mother. With development, these *schemata* gradually extend to include aspects of the external world other than those

---

* Reprinted from: 14 *The Standard Edition of the Complete Psychological Works of Sigmund Freud*, James Strachey, ed. London: The Hogarth Press and the Institute of Psychoanalysis, 1957. (pp. 332–33). Reprinted by permission of Hogarth and Basic Books, Inc.

* 15 *The Psychoanalytic Study of the Child*, 1960. (pp. 145–59). Reprinted by permission of International Universities Press, New York.

intimately associated with immediate need satisfaction. Essentially they enable the child to assess the properties of the outer world with increasing efficiency, and to predict the pleasurable or unpleasurable consequences of his behavior.

The term *internalization* has been used in regard to these processes, but as its current usage is such as to include processes of introjection and identification as well, it seems preferable to think in terms of an *organizing activity* to describe the construction of these inner models. The concept of an organizing activity seems a particularly appropriate one as the *schemata* of the child embrace not only data gained through sensory impressions arising from the outer world, but sense data (including affect data) arising from instinctual tensions as well. In addition, it will be necessary, as I hope to show later, to *contrast* organizing activities with those of introjection and identification, and to dissociate them from processes of "taking in" traditionally associated with oral instinctual aims. Indeed, organizing is primary to and must precede introjection and identification, in the sense in which these latter two processes will be used in this presentation. One can neither identify with nor introject aspects of another person unless one's ego has previously constructed some sort of mental model of that person. . . .

Organizing activity begins to occur extremely early in life, from the moment when the child's experience of the present can be said to be modified by what has been experienced in the past; from the moment sensations begin to be transformed into percepts, however primitive these percepts may be; from the moment that differential cathexis of aspects of the child's world can be said to occur. Clearly, it is those experiences which are directly concerned with need satisfaction that are first registered and organized by the child, under the dominance of the pleasure principle, and the child's first models of the world (and the term "world" includes, of course, the child's own body) are extremely scanty, primitive, and self-centered. . . .

Organizing activity is much more than the mere taking in of impressions from the outside, but is intimately connected with the development of all organized ego functions and secondary processes. It includes the construction of frames of reference, *schemata*, and all the techniques by which the child controls his perceptions (arising from the id or the outside world) and activities. It includes also the development of ego functions such as memory, thinking, imagination, and the capacity for purposive action, functions which in turn foster further organizing activity. Part of the child's inner world consists of models of his objects (or aspects of his objects) and of the self, models[1] which are com-

posites and abstractions created[2] by the child out of its multiple experiences. The self-*schema* can also be classed as a type of object *schema*, cathected by instinctual energy as are the other object models of the child.

In the normal child, object relationships develop out of the child's first experiences of satisfaction and dissatisfaction, and their development is associated, in the inner world of the child, with the construction of a libidinally cathected mother schema or imago, although this is limited at first to qualities of experience associated by the child with need satisfaction. Initially these need-satisfying experiences are not differentiated from the self, but as time goes on a distinct mother *schema* is organized. It consists, in essence, of a set of expectations relating to the mother's appearance and activities, and when the mother conforms to these expectations (which vary according to the state of instinctual tension within the child), the child experiences satisfaction. When the mother's behavior does not in fact correspond to the cathected internal mother imago, the child experiences frustration, unpleasure, and anger. Later the response of the child becomes more and more removed from the original gratifying situations, so that the presence of the mother, or even the knowledge of the mother's readiness to attend to the child, becomes a source of satisfaction in itself.

The internal imago of the mother is thus not a substitute for an object relationship, but is itself an indispensable part of the relationship. Without it no object relationship (in the psychological sense) exists. It is not in itself a source of real gratification to the child, although it may temporarily achieve a diminution of an instinctual tension through hallucination. The real source of gratification is the mother or any other object who can conform to the child's mother *schema*.

The child's inner world enables him to distinguish, localize, and interpret his sensory impressions; but it also functions to provide him with warning or guiding signals which regulate his behavior. Thus his developing body *schema* gives him a means of identifying sensations and experiences in his own body, and also assists him to co-ordinate his bodily activities, as, for example, in learning to walk. Similarly his mother and father *schemata* gradually enable him to recognize and interpret the activities of his parents, and at the same time allow him to predict what behavior will evoke their love and approval, and what their disapproval, and to control

---

1. The use of the term *"schema"* or *"model"* in this context by no means implies a static conception. The "models" are, in a sense, "working models," and include all the sequences of behavior on the part of the object which can be predicted by the child on the basis of its past experiences.

2. The term "introjection," which has been used to describe this process, is reserved in this paper for a very special sort of ego activity, a mechanism which is associated with unique and important changes in the disposition of instinctual energies.

his behavior accordingly. I want to draw particular attention to these two functions of the child's inner world, the function of *representing* and the function of *guiding*, for they will ultimately be reflected in that specialized part of the inner world which later becomes the superego.

The growth of the inner world goes hand in hand with the partial abandonment of the pleasure principle in favor of the reality principle. The notion of "reality" in this context includes the reactions of the parents to the child's behavior, and no essential distinction can be made till relatively late in development between the "real world" as adults know it and the culturally determined or idiosyncratic commands, wishes, and precepts of the parents. There is as yet no distinction in kind between frustrations imposed by the parents and those which are a consequence of the resistance of other aspects of the "real world" to the demands of the child. Indeed, the child gains much of its knowledge of the properties of the real world, with consequent benefit to ego development, through parental interpretations of reality. It is largely through the agency of the parents that the reality principle replaces the pleasure principle.

Now we know that the needs of the child progress from the need for bodily satisfaction and comfort to a need to feel loved in a variety of other ways as well. With increasing discrimination between the self and other *schemata*, the child comes to realize that his early pleasurable, narcissistic state of union with the mother is threatened. He suffers a lowering of the level of libidinal cathexis of the self, with consequent narcissistic depletion, and, as Freud puts it (1914), he needs to restore the state of "a real happy love [which] corresponds to the primal condition in which object-libido and ego-libido [we would now say self-cathexis] cannot be distinguished."

The child's many attempts to restore this original narcissistic state provide an enormous impetus to ego development. Freud (1914) says: "The development of the ego consists in a departure from primary narcissism and gives rise to a vigorous attempt to recover that state."[3]

---

3. The problem of what it means to "feel loved," or to "restore narcissistic cathexis," is one which has as yet been insufficiently explored. What the child is attempting to restore is an affective state of well-being which we can correlate, in terms of energy, with the level of narcissistic cathexis of the self. Initially this affective state, which normally forms a background to everyday experience, must be the state of bodily well-being which the infant experiences when his instinctual needs have been satisfied (as distinct from the pleasure in their satisfaction). This affective state later becomes localized in the self, and we see aspects of it in feelings of self-esteem as well as in normal background feelings of safety. The maintenance of this *central effective state* is perhaps the most powerful motive for ego development, and we must regard the young child (and later the adult) as seeking well-being as well as pleasure-seeking; the two are by no means the same and in analysis we can often observe a conflict between the two.

The child has a number of techniques at its disposal for the restoration of this original state of well-being, and of these I want to consider only two which are relevant here:

1. *Obedience* to and compliance with the demands of the parents.

2. *Identification* with and imitation of the parents.

The term *identification*, which refers both to a process and to the end product of that process, has been used by psychoanalysts in a variety of ways, and attempts to differentiate ego identifications from superego identifications have led to much confusion. In the present formulation the term will be used only in respect of identifications which modify the ego; so-called superego identifications will be seen as a combination of *introjection* on the one hand, and a corresponding "ego" identification on the other.

The observation of very young children has taught us that identifications with parents and others are an aspect of normal development, and that identification is by no means always a substitute for an object relationship, nor is it always used defensively. Transient identifications may later become a permanent feature of the child's personality, but the capacity to make temporary identifications remains after childhood, and is a particular feature of adolescence. We can define identification by saying that it represents a process of modifying the self-*schema* on the basis of a present or past perception of an object, and that such modification may be temporary or permanent, whole or partial, ego enriching or ego restrictive, depending on what is identified with and whether the need for such an identification is of short or long duration.

Whereas in primary identification the child fuses or confuses the rudimentary *schema* of the self with that of another person, so that the distinction between self and not-self does not exist, in secondary identification the self-*schema* is modified so that it becomes *like* that of the object, and some of the libidinal cathexis of the object is transferred to the self. . . .

Identification is a means of feeling the same as the admired and idealized object, and therefore at one with it; and, as Freud has pointed out, it can exist side-by-side with object relationships. If we recall the joy with which the very young child imitates, consciously or unconsciously, a parent or an older sibling, we can see that identification represents an important technique whereby the child feels loved and obtains an inner state of well-being. We might say that the esteem in which the omnipotent and admired object is held is duplicated in the self and gives rise to self-esteem. The child feels at one with the object and close to it, and temporarily regains the feeling of happiness which he experienced during the earliest days of life. Identificatory behavior is further reinforced by the love, approval, and praise of the real object, and it is quite striking to observe the extent to which the education of the child progresses through the reward, not only of feeling omnipotent like the idealized parent, but also through the very positive signs of love and approval granted by parents and educators to the child. The sources of "feeling loved," and of self-esteem, are the real figures in the child's environment; and in these first years identificatory behavior is directed by the child toward enhancing, via these real figures, his feeling of inner well-being.

Identification may also be used for the purposes of defense, particularly where the child is faced with a problem of resolving a conflict between its need for an object's love and its hostility to that object. In the familiar "identification with the aggressor" the child deals with his fear of a threatening person by identifying with his omnipotent, powerful, and terrifying qualities. It may also be called into play in an attempt to deal with a loss or a withdrawal from a loving object. In this latter case it is usually accompanied by an introjection of the object, a process which I shall discuss presently; but identification is not the same as introjection as it will be defined here, and the distinction between the two is, as we shall see, of supreme importance in understanding the formation of the superego.

The two *techniques* of restoring a feeling of being loved (of increasing the level of libidinal cathexis of the self) which I have mentioned, identification and obedience, make use of the two functions of the child's parental *schemata* . . . the function of representing and the function of guiding, respectively. But the mechanisms of identification and obedience by no means operate in isolation from each other. In many activities the child obtains what amounts to a double gain through behaving in such a way as to identify with the parents and at the same time obey their wishes. Thus the toddler who seriously washes his hands after playing with dirt gains both from "doing what mother wants" and from "being like mother."

What develops in the ego of the child in the pre-oedipal years is an organization which reflects the idealized and desirable qualities of the parents on the one hand and which prompts the child to suitable object-related behavior on the other (behavior, that is, which will gain for the child a feeling of being loved). It contains approving and permissive as well as prohibiting and restraining features. It is not yet a structure (in the sense in which Freud used the term in *The Ego and the Id*), for the introjection of parental authority which will elevate it to autonomous super-ego status has not yet taken place. It is a preautonomous superego *schema*, a "plan" for the later superego. It is a sort of undergraduate superego which only works under the supervision of the parents, and is a differentiated part of the child's own "reality," influenced as is all the child's inner world by instinctual drives and fantasies. It has not yet gained a license for independent practice, so to speak, and it will only do so with the decisive introjections which go with the resolution of Oedipal conflict. What might appear to be conflict between ego and "super-ego" in the preoedipal stages is based on the child's predictions, often distorted, of parental reaction.

We know that the child's view of his parents is objective only to a limited degree. His parental *schemata* will be colored by his fantasies, and in particular by the projection of unwanted qualities of his own onto them. The child may not be able to tolerate the aggressive and sadistic parts of his self, and transfers these features from one part of his inner world to another—from his model of his self to his model of his parents. In this sense, projection is the opposite of identification.

The warning signal of impending punishment or loss of love provided by the preautonomous superego *schema* does not yet deserve the name of guilt, though the affective state it produces in the ego may be identical with that which we refer to as guilt, later in the child's development.

I do not need to describe here the ways in which the child's conflict between his instinctual urges and his need to preserve his narcissism are intensified when the child enters the phallic stage. His positive and negative Oedipus complexes, the ambivalence inherent in them, the impossibility of really fulfilling his instinctual wishes, the fear of punishment and castration (which is correlated with a father image distorted by the projection of the child's own aggression)—all of these combine to create a situation of unbearable tension in the child. During the phallic phase the superego *schema* is much elaborated and modified, although it will always bear the stamp of his pregenital relationships to his parents. This *schema*, not yet the superego, has the function of representing (albeit in a distorted way) the admired and feared qualities of the parents. But it also functions to indicate to the ego which piece of behavior will evoke the love and admiration of the parents, and which will cause their displeasure, with consequent lowering of the narcissistic level in the self.

We link the development of the superego proper with the resolution of the Oedipus complex. Freud regarded this development not only as the outcome of Oedipal conflict, but also as the very means whereby the child effects a resolution of this conflict. The superego is formed, as Freud puts it, as a precipitate within the ego, and its formation is correlated with a partial and relative reduction of interest in and dependence on the real parents. The major source of self-esteem is no longer the real parents, but the superego. *Introjection* of the parents has taken place, and a structure has been formed which did not exist in this form before.

At this point it is necessary to indicate the meaning given to the term introjection in this context; for, after all, have not the functions which we call super-ego previously existed in the mind of the child in the shape of the parental *schemata*? What distinguishes the introject from the internal *schema* is precisely the capacity of the introject to substitute, in whole or in part, for the real object as a source of narcissistic gratification. This implies that the introject must somehow be developed out of the *schema*, crystallized and structuralized within the ego, so that it can be given the power to satisfy, and be felt by the ego to be a sufficient substitute for the objects. The construction of an introject is thus the sequel of a complete or partial dissolution of the relationship to the real object. Through introjection the *relationship* to the object is maintained and perpetuated, but the real object is no longer so vital to the relationship. It follows that what is introjected is neither the personality nor the behavior of the parents, but their *authority*. . . .

With this elevation of the superego *schema* to autonomous status—with its structuralization, in the sense described by Freud in *The Ego and the Id* (1923)—what was previously experienced as the threat of parental disapproval becomes guilt, though the affective experience is probably the same in both; and an essential component of this affective state is the drop in self-esteem. This differentiates guilt from anxiety, and links it with feelings of inferiority and inadequacy as well as with the affect which is experienced in pathological states of depression. An *opposite* and equally important affective state is also experienced by the ego, a state which occurs when the ego and superego are functioning together in a smooth and harmonious fashion; that is, when the feeling of being loved is restored by the approval of the superego. Perhaps this is best described as a state of mental comfort and well-being, of *eupathy*. It is the counterpart of the affect experienced by the child when his parents show signs of approval and pleasure at his performance, when the earliest state of being at one with his mother is temporarily regained. It is related to the affective background of self-confidence and self-assurance, as well as to the pathological state of mania.

Freud has described the way in which both super-ego formation and identification are associated with a desexualization of the child's libidinal aims, and with an instinctual defusion. This defusion enables the child to retain his tender feelings toward his parents, and to divert his destructive urges into his now structuralized *schema* of parental attributes and behavior—that is, into his superego. The degree to which his hostile wishes cannot find expression through his ego will determine the degree of severity or even savagery of his superego. This may occur to such a degree that the superego may be a much-distorted representative of the real parents of childhood. In this way, as Freud has frequently pointed out, the superego is also a representative of the id, in close and constant touch with it.

There has been a strong tendency in psychoanalytic writings to overlook the very positive side of the child's relationship to his superego; a relation based on the fact that it can also be a splendid source of love and well-being. It functions to approve as well as to disapprove; and the relative understressing by psychoanalysts of the former may be due to the fact that they are primarily concerned as therapists, rather than as educators, with situations of conflict and inner disharmony.

It will be noticed that superego formation has been linked throughout with introjection, and has been separated conceptually from processes of identification. That the reinforcement of identifications with the parents is something which occurs concurrently with superego formation and progression into latency, is something which cannot be questioned. Freud himself did not always distinguish identification with the parents, particularly with the father, from their introjection and the consequent setting up of an internal authority which can act in opposition to the ego; but in view of recent developments, particularly the increasing theoretical importance of the concept of "self," such a distinction appears to be essential.

Identification is a technique whereby the self is modified so that it corresponds, to a greater or lesser extent, with an object as perceived by the ego. The model for the ego may be a real person, or an introject. Thus we have a state of affairs in which the ego can use its capacity for identification to obtain a libidinal gain through being at one either with another person who is idealized or feared (or both), or through feeling at one with the introject which contains a representation of the behavior, appearance, and attitudes of the parents. Thus we can replace the notion of superego identification with that of *identification with the introject*.[4] It changes and modifies the *content* of the self, but does not result in the formation of psychic structure. Where ego and superego work together harmoniously, the harmony may be achieved by such an identification on the part of the ego, and also by direct obedience to or compliance with superego precepts and demands. This harmonious working together does not represent a merging of the superego into the self (which we see in manic states and which is associated with primary identification), but a modification of the self on the basis of a model of the idealized qualities of the parents, or their demands and prohibitions, as embodied in the superego. Furthermore, if the child can both identify with and obey the introjected parents at one and the same time (as in the example

---

4. Anna Freud has suggested that this is essentially similar to the mechanism of identification with the aggressor.

I gave earlier of the child washing his hands "to be like mother" and "to please mother"), a double gain is effected.

We can also see, particularly in the course of an analysis, how guilt feelings may be dealt with by identification with the introject, an identification which shows itself through the adoption of a strict and moralizing attitude to another. The child who tells a doll or the analyst not to be naughty deals with his feelings of guilt and gains a feeling of well-being by identifying with the critical aspects of his superego, projecting his self-imago onto another. In this extremely common mechanism there is also a double gain. We know that those who most vocally proclaim moral precepts are often those who feel most guilty about their own unconscious wish to do that which they criticize in others.

That dependence on the superego is so long lasting, and often results in more or less permanent changes in the ego, is a reflection of the child's dependence on his real parents as a source of narcissistic gain in the earliest years of life. But the superego is only supported by the ego as long as it functions, in its turn, to support the ego; and situations do exist in which the ego can and will totally disregard the standards and precepts of the superego, if it can gain a sufficient quantity of narcissistic support elsewhere. We see this impressive phenomenon in the striking changes in ideals, character, and morality which may result from the donning of a uniform and the feeling of identity with a group. If narcissistic support is available in sufficient quantity from an identification with the ideals of a group, or with the ideals of a leader, then the superego may be completely disregarded, and its functions taken over by the group ideals, precepts, and behavior. If these group ideals permit a direct gratification of instinctual wishes, then a complete character transformation may occur; and the extent to which the superego can be abandoned in this way is evident in the appalling atrocities committed by the Nazis before and during the last war. Changes in morality can sometimes be seen when a person becomes much loved by another; the superego is then not as necessary as before as a provider of love and as a source of well-being.

Many examples exist in ordinary life of the way in which group morality and group ideals may replace personal morality; these include religious conversion, and the gang formation and hero worship of adolescence. In psychotherapy or in analysis, the supporting role of the analyst, who may be invested with the authority of the parents, can permit the ego's dependence on its superego to be sufficiently reduced to enable forbidden and repressed material to be brought into consciousness and inner conflict worked through.

Similar phenomena occur when the feeling of well-being in the self can be obtained by means of drugs, and drug addiction can then replace what might be termed normal superego addiction. Indeed, the superego has been facetiously defined as that part of the mental apparatus which is soluble in alcohol.

Anna Freud has pointed out that the establishment of the superego does not entirely remove the child's dependence on the real parents and parental figures as a source of love, and when we speak of the latency child's independence we use a relative term. To some extent this reliance on others as a source of self-esteem persists throughout life, and we all know how the support and reassurance of a friend can mitigate unhappiness in oneself.

*   *   *

In its dealings with its superego the ego may involve other persons as well. It may do so when it has the need to force others to reinforce the superego through the provocation of approval, forgiveness, or punishment. In so-called superego projection (or externalization), we can observe an attempt by the ego to restore the existence of the original superego objects in the external world. In one sense, this is an attempt at regression, and it is particularly fostered by the analytic situation, where it appears in the form of a superego transference. The involvement of others in superego conflict also appears in moral masochism. (When the ego has a masochistic attitude to the superego, this is a reflection of an earlier masochistic tie to the parents.)

The problem of delinquent behavior has been studied by Aichhorn and other psychoanalysts, and it does seem that their findings, particularly in relation to the superego, can be integrated into the conceptual framework outlined in this paper. This applies in particular to the well-known distinction between those who are delinquent because of the introjection of a delinquent parental morality, those whose delinquency is a result of structural faults in the superego, and those neurotic delinquents who are hounded by an inordinate sense of guilt.

. . . The basic ideas expressed here are to be found in Freud's paper "On Narcissism," and it is precisely the role of narcissism in the development and function of the superego which needs to be stressed. Threats to the narcissistic cathexis of the self exist from birth, and stem from the interaction of the instinctual life of the child, in both its libidinal and aggressive aspects, with the demands and frustrations of the real world. The factors which ultimately determine the superego operate from the beginning, yet what we tend to call superego precursors are an integral part of the development of the ego itself; the superego as a structure comes into existence only with the resolution of the Oedipus complex. And although it is often the agent of pain and destruction, its existence appears to be brought about by the child's attempts to transform paradise lost into paradise regained.

Freud sums up the function of the superego, appropriately in the last chapter of his last book, *An Outline of Psychoanalysis* (1938), as follows. He says:

The torments caused by the reproaches of conscience correspond precisely to a child's dread of losing his parents' love, a dread which has been replaced in him by the moral agency. On the other hand, if the ego has successfully resisted a temptation to do something that would be objectionable to the superego, it feels its self-respect raised and its pride increased as though it had made some precious acquisition. In this way the superego continues to act the role of an external world toward the ego, although it has become part of the internal world. During the whole of a man's later life it represents the influence of his childhood, of the care and education given to him by his parents, of his dependence on them—of the childhood which is so greatly prolonged in human beings by a common family life. And in all of this what is operating is not only the personal qualities of these parents but also everything that produced a determining effect upon them themselves, the tastes and standards of the social class in which they live, and the characteristics and traditions of the race from which they spring [pp. 122–23].

*   *   *

6.

CAMERON, NORMAN

Introjection, Reprojection, and Hallucination in the Interaction between Schizophrenic Patient and Therapist*

*   *   *

The patient, Grace L., a native of Cincinnati, when referred to me, was a twenty-five-year-old single graduate student in the humanities at a coeducational college. She was living what seemed outwardly an effectual life, qualifying each year for a scholarship, and carrying a part-time job as well. She sought intensive therapy on the advice of her college psychiatrist, who had seen her once a week for three months, and now felt that she needed more time than he could spare. In her initial interview with me she complained of feeling tired and discouraged, of being in continual conflict over marriage and a career, of feeling shy and inadequate in relation to others, and of sleepwalking. She seemed vivacious, direct, anxious, and mildly perplexed. Apart from the sleepwalking and mild perplexity there was nothing to suggest the severity of what lay behind the complaints.

As therapy proceeded a graver clinical picture soon

---

* 42 *International Journal of Psychoanalysis*, 1961. (pp. 86–92). Reprinted by permission.

emerged. In spite of her outward effectual show, the patient was continually assailed internally by critical and accusing voices; she had serious difficulties in distinguishing between external and internal reality, and between herself and others; and she sometimes could not decide if she had been awake or asleep during what another person would have unhesitatingly called a dream. She called many of her experiences "strange," "weird," "fantastic," and "grotesque"—which they were—and she sometimes said that she herself could not understand what she was saying.

At the same time this intelligent and verbally gifted young woman was able to give spontaneous descriptions of her regressive and often archaic experiences with fidelity, undistorted by psychological sophistication. Her only contact with psychological science had been a one-semester college course which she said was "mostly about eye-movements and color vision," and had bored her. It is striking that throughout therapy she kept at her daily work successfully, first as a graduate student and then in a responsible teaching and supervising job. As time went on it became obvious that, as Freud has formulated it, the patient was "in revolt" against primitive superego attacks from which she attempted with therapeutic help to liberate herself.

Incorporation and Use of Therapist Attitudes

It was my consistent experience with this sensitive, traumatized, resentful but superficially compliant person that she throve on firmness and bluntness in her therapist. Firmness gave her inner stability and bluntness gave her trust. The four clinical episodes which I have chosen to illustrate the incorporation and use of therapist attitudes all show this. Two of them also include unmistakable expressions of introjected material in manifest dreams. One is in the form of an hallucinated command, which ties up with her use of hallucination to be described in a later section. Here are the episodes.

Episode 1. In this episode the change in attitude was consciously experienced and immediate. Early in therapy, at the end of an hour filled with archaic material, the patient asked for a change in the time of the next hour, which I refused. She protested that she had something important to do in college at the assigned time. I told her that she would have to choose which was more important to her. She left, saying petulantly that, all right, she would come.

Next time she began the hour by saying that the preceding session had been a milestone. "The whole hour seemed to be leading up to the end of the hour. When you stood firm that was a milestone, too. I've never really chosen before. Growing up is discovering what is most important. When I said to change it around, it would have been like slapping you in the face," if the change had been allowed. This experience was followed by marked reduction in her flippancy toward her own behavior, and an attitude of increased confidence in and respect for the seriousness of therapy. These changed attitudes, with the usual ups and downs, remained permanent.

Episode 2. Here the patient did not consciously recognize the source of her change in attitude; but the relationship is no less clear. Near the beginning of one hour Grace became infuriated with me over a blunt comment. She carried on an angry tirade, calling me names and listing grievances against me. I told her there might be some truth in what she said, but that my comment still stood. Toward the end of the hour her anger subsided. Four days later this usually timid patient, who had never been able to endure serious criticism, reported that an angry teacher had made a public attack upon her supervisory methods. "She was so excited about it! And I was trying to find out what there was in what she wanted to say. I was encouraging her to be difficult instead of just smoothing things over." For some reason, she said, she was not afraid of "disappearing" this time, as she had always done previously under similar circumstances.

The use Grace made of my incorporated strength is obvious. If I could take her tongue-lashing without becoming defensive or giving ground, she could stand fast in the face of another's attack. If I did not wither and disintegrate under her assault—a fear she sometimes consciously experienced and directly expressed—she need not fear disintegration herself from a verbal barrage. If I could concede that there might be some truth contained in her angry talk, she could dare to take a detached attitude under comparable circumstances, and try to "find out what there was" in what the excited woman wanted to say. The general process of testing limits went on continually; but this change also grew into an enduring ego attitude.

Episode 3. Here an introjected command is used by the patient four months afterward in a manifest dream. The command was originally given by the therapist under the following circumstances. During one therapeutic hour the patient became increasingly apathetic and incoherent, finally lapsing into almost inaudible mumbling and then silence. I said, "Sit up!" and getting no response said it again louder. She sat up looking dazed, and said, "I feel funny, queasy." She soon regained contact and lay down of her own accord, saying, "I'll feel better lying down." The hour proceeded uneventfully.

Here is the dream four months later. "I was bleeding myself for a good cause that I didn't know what it was. I was holding a bottle up and filling it with blood. I was getting weaker and weaker (she felt she was dying) and somebody said, 'Sit up!' I sat up in bed (actually) feeling weak and woozy. There was nobody around, and somebody said, 'Lie down again! If you sit up the blood will *really* run

out!' So I lay down and I wanted to put all that blood back again. The dream just stopped."

To rescue herself in a dream of gradual death, we see the patient using the same command that I had once used to bring her out of a catatonic-like state. It will be noticed that even the sense of her own statements made in the same long past therapeutic hour ("I feel funny, queasy" and "I'll feel better lying down now") are also rendered, though less literally, in her manifest dream context.

Episode 4. The last episode illustrates the incorporation and use of therapist anger, which appears first as effective resistance to parental aggression, and later as a temper tantrum in a manifest dream. The background was the family's unflagging opposition to therapy, expressed in an endless succession of attempts at interference. There were, for example, repeated protestations to Grace that she was "too normal" to spend all this time on herself "in introspection." Then a letter came containing the pious hope that she would not "land up in a mental institution" because of therapy. An attempt was made to get "confidential" information directly from me without the patient's knowledge. Finally, Grace received a special delivery letter warning her to get out of my hands at once.

The situation by this time had reached a point where the patient was becoming dangerously disturbed, caught between a desperate need for help and her extreme fear of the family, of their telephone conversations, their letters, and their hallucinated voices. She said, "I feel I'm walking on the edge of a precipice and I'll fall in any minute now; this (therapy) is my last hope." She spoke openly of suicide.

The day after the special delivery letter came it was decided to intervene vigorously. In the next hour, when the patient again expressed despair over the family's aggressive opposition, I said angrily that this was deliberate interference and I would not stand for it. I said that I refused to go on unless we were free from this constant interruption, and she could decide whether she wanted to go on or not. The day before she had remarked that, if I said so, she would not go home to Cincinnati this summer at all, probably hoping for my intervention then. I told her now, still angrily, that I would consider her going home an interruption of therapy, and for all I cared she could tell her family this.

Grace said next day that I had frightened her by my anger. Otherwise she made no direct reference to the hour. Three days later, however, she wrote a letter home, on her own initiative and without telling me beforehand, that disposed of both the question of continuing in therapy and of going home—at least for several months. I do not know what she wrote; but her whole attitude became firm and decisive, and her anxiety decreased dramatically. The immediate effect of her incorporating my open aggression was a spontaneous, decisive, and aggressive handling of a situation in which she had previously been helpless. The night after she sent the letter home she had the following dream, in which my angry outburst appears as her own, and at the same time a scarcely veiled Oedipal situation is depicted.

"I was at the (student) health service and you were my doctor. There was a woman with blonde hair. She was cold and aloof. She said it was the end of the year and she wondered if I'd mind changing doctors. I had a temper tantrum. I stamped my feet, jumped up and down, yelled and ran around the room. There was a catalogue and I tore it to shreds. I was damn mad. I know what it means—instead of taking everything I'm mad as hops!" Later in the hour the patient made the classic negation, "It was not my mother," and added for good measure, "It had nothing to do with my father."

Here normal overt anger was used as a deliberate technical intervention to turn the tide of an internal battle that threatened to disintegrate the patient and drive her to suicide. The anger the therapist expressed was genuine anger; only the timing of its overt release was deliberate. Had the anger been mere simulation, this intuitively sensitive patient would only have been driven to further desperation, by finding deception where she needed trust. It will become clear in what follows that the patient was vividly aware of significant changes taking place in her internal economy.

Vicissitudes of Internal Objects and Introjection of the Therapist

In this section I shall give a clinical description of the vicissitudes of internal objects and of the introjected therapist image, and in an ensuing section attempt to discuss their significance. In my description I shall observe the following topical sequence:

1. The operation of a concrete personified internal mother image, which functioned as a primitive superego, and of another internal critic which the patient called the *No-girl*.

2. The clear emergence of the hallucinated mother's voice, disowned and projected by the patient as part of a regressive attempt at ego reorganization.

3. The appearance of my hallucinated voice in a moment of crisis, some months after a number of my attitudes in therapy had been incorporated; its use as a replacement for the mother's voice; and the subsequent fading away of the mother's hallucinated voice.

4. Return of the mother's voice during a period of deprivation (sudden hospitalization of the therapist), and its final disappearance.

5. Introjection of the therapist image and use of this introject to further the process of forming new partial identifications.

6. The brief appearance of a male *Nay-sayer* during a period when all voices had been absent for some time.

7. The final return of critical female voices immediately following a severe experience of unexpected maternal rejection.

1. *The Mother and the No-girl.* In most of the first hundred hours of therapy the patient included some form of complaint that her mother was continually interfering with her life. The complaints sounded like memories of petty nagging in childhood—mainly about being neat, clean, and tidy, showing good manners at the table, not leaving clothes lying about, etc.—plus current urgings to pay more attention to her appearance and to plan for marrying. In view of the fact that some of these urgings were actually included in current letters, and during visits home, I did not realize at first that this continual interference came also from an internal nagging presence, sometimes a voice, sometimes a more indefinite but still personified influence. Early in therapy the patient expressed irritation over all this, but no real anger. Her anger was openly expressed from the start toward a less clearly personified presence which the patient called an "internal critic."

In the nineteenth hour Grace for the first time spoke frankly of hearing a voice. This was the voice of the "internal critic." It did nothing but criticize her, so she named it the *No-girl*. Its function seemed to be restricted to the patient's current behavior when she was with other people, and never in relation to being neat, clean, and tidy, having good table manners, not leaving clothes about, etc. It said such things as, "Oh yes you did! You were noisy and tried to be the center of attention. You were silly and unladylike. Cut it out—you can do it. Control yourself!" The patient said bitterly, "If I'd been quiet as a mouse, I *swear* I don't know what she'd have said; but it would've been wrong!" The *No-girl*'s criticism, she said, "leads to a complete paralysis of the emotions. I go on acting as if nothing's happened, but I do everything wrong then, and I don't have any fun any more."

The patient tried various ways of handling the *No-girl* which she described in therapy. "I'm trying to disown her, to dissociate myself from her. She's so mean and hateful all the time. Sometimes at a party I'd like to push her over into a corner and cover her up and have a good time. But you could get divided, and then what would I be!" She began a kind of reality testing. She would string along a series of incidents in which she had actually done diametrically opposite things in social situations. But even so, the *No-girl* called every one of them wrong. The outcome of these reality testing attempts seemed to the patient to make her situation hopeless. Actually they helped to rid her of this internal tyrant which, along with the personified mother image, had ruled her most of her life.

Next Grace began asking the opinions of people actually present about this or that social behavior, during a card game or a coffee break, or during a dinner party. She always asked about something related to what the *No-girl* was attacking her for at the time, although she made it appear to her friends as if it were merely a question of what behavior would be correct under such and such circumstances. She discovered by this means that, while usually the attacks were unjust, sometimes the *No-girl* turned out to be "sounding a perfectly normal warning." As the patient carried on this form of reality testing the *No-girl* gradually faded, while more realistic self-criticism began to take over. The situation became complicated, however, by the emergence of the mother's hallucinated voice, seeming now to come from the outside.

2. *The Mother's Voice Outside.* In the 150th hour Grace said that her mother had been giving her "the third degree all the time by word of mouth" for several weeks. This hallucination was obviously a new and startling experience for her. Since she had been hearing voices internally for fifteen years or more, it seemed to be the clear projection of the voice, coming apparently from without, that now impressed her. The serious attempt she made to understand this new phenomenon rings true.

"I hear the sound of her actual voice; it isn't just thinking to myself. It's outside me like over there in the corner. I think her part of me is being externalized. It's still there but it's becoming more obvious that it *is* her, and not me. I'm becoming more independent from her. Instead of rules and regulations" —i.e., instead of having a more abstract, impersonal superego—"she's kept on being part of me. I followed it as my conscience; and now it's more obvious that it *is* mother's voice and not *my* voice. I think what will happen is her voice will become more audible and disappear. I thought it would be the opposite. But it's becoming altogether audible, as if she's standing there and separate from me. It's as if mother were right in the room all the time, watching everything I did." We shall return to the hypothesis contained in this statement of hers when we come to the discussion.

The patient made two other interesting observations about the voice. One was that the energy of her "conscience machine" comes from her mother. The occasion was a shift in the maternal image hallucinated. Grace was living temporarily with an elderly woman; and she hallucinated this woman's face and voice telling her to tidy up. She said, "Now it's Mrs. X's voice, but I think the energy comes from my mother. This is the energy because my mother has said these things. I've no reason to think Mrs. X cares. *This conscience machine goes on grinding it out; but the energy of this machine comes from my mother.*"

The second observation she made was that she had much less trouble distinguishing between herself and her mother's voice when they were in conflict than when they were in agreement. She said, "I have a hard time distinguishing when I agree with her. If I disagree I can say, 'Shut up! I don't care!' But when I agree I can't tell if I'm being obedient to her voice or to myself." This experience seems to equate the hallucinated voice with a primitive superego function. Freud, in discussing the normal mature relation of ego and superego, wrote that "as a rule we can distinguish them only when a state of tension, a conflict between them, has arisen." Again a psychotic experience throws a relatively obscure early relationship into contemporary bold relief.

3. *The Therapist's Voice Hallucinated.* My voice was first hallucinated early in the second year when another direct attempt was made to get the patient home against her wishes, five months after the family interference had been stopped. This time a letter from her mother, enclosing a sizable check, told Grace of a big family reunion. It also revealed that the mother had found out about a teachers' meeting in Cincinnati at the same time, which the patient would ordinarily have attended. Grace was furious. She was in financial distress and she would have liked very much to be a part of the family reunion. But because she recognized the coercion in her mother's maneuvering, she stuck by an earlier decision and did not go. She had to take an interurban bus trip before she could come to me for her next hour, so she put the case before me in imagination, arguing it logically, point by point. Suddenly she heard my voice saying out loud, "I know you're really angry with your mother. Why don't you *say* so!" Now she began arguing with me out loud; but I insisted on repeating exactly the same thing, no matter what she said. Finally she gave up and began laughing. Here is her account.

"I wasn't angry with you for saying that; I knew you had to. I was bent on telling you I don't *have* to be angry. It's gone beyond that. I suppose I couldn't have been *so* secure or I wouldn't have minded that your voice kept coming back. I understand the goal is the independent personality arranging a way of establishing limits of yourself. You have to show people they can't invade your limits like that" (i.e., as her mother had just tried to do). "When you've *made* boundaries you don't need to get angry. I know where I stand. I'm right and they're wrong. I guess that's one more step from indifference to compassion. Why did I keep hearing your voice? It was a new point of reference. It felt *good* to argue with you; and you got into such a ridiculous position, like a broken record."

From this point on, my voice gained in importance while the mother's faded. There was some confusion at first. For example, once when I made a critical comment Grace asked me if I had actually said it, because it sounded like her mother's voice. Usually, she said, she differentiated on the basis of my tone of voice, manner, and actions—in which she included my general demeanor just before and after she lay down. By way of illustration she mimicked her mother's voice, and then mine, saying the same words. She was obviously engaged in another form of reality testing. A week after my voice appeared on the bus, she spoke of having got rid of her mother's; and a month later she remarked that she had not heard it for a long time. It did come back, but only once in its original form.

4. *Return and Final Disappearance of the Mother's Voice.* Unfortunately, three months after my voice appeared I was suddenly hospitalized with an acutely herniated intervertebral disc. Surgery was finally required, and I was kept from my office for nearly four months. During this period the patient held together well, but critical voices reappeared. She said upon my return, "I count on you to be an ally against my critical self. She ran wild while you were away, criticizing me all the time and making me do things, pushing me. I guess she's a sort of amalgam of my mother and my sister. She used to be my mother. I don't think she really is any more."

A month later Grace began hearing the voice of young Mrs. Y, with whom she was temporarily living, just as she had heard Mrs. X a year earlier. When alone, the patient could hear Mrs. Y talking about her to other women, expressing surprise at her ineptness and ignorance in housekeeping matters. Also, Grace said, "I have little conversations with her. I don't know that she has any existence. *She's a sort of a form of my mother*, because I know mother better than her. It's really my mother saying inane things that Mrs. Y says or I imagine, but so obviously not true that I say 'Too bad! I don't care!' Mother doesn't know the real me!" Soon after this the whole family returned to the attacks in hallucinated form when she bought a car she needed. Their harangue lasted ten days—"a whole chorus of voices"—and then for five months she made no allusion to family voices, although some form of internal critic was still active.

Just before the patient left for the Christmas holidays, and when she was very fatigued, her mother's voice reappeared clearly for a day, reproaching her for lying in bed late, but also saying, with unwonted sympathy, that she was working too hard. Next, back in Cincinnati, she experienced unprecedented good relationships with her mother. The mother even recounted intimately shared things from Grace's early childhood, which made the patient feel happy, such as having let her feel the baby kicking when the mother was pregnant. At the same time there was the old complaint that whenever Grace tried to talk about her current life, interests, and hopes, she met only silence from her mother or an abrupt change of topic.

The patient said on her return that this "creature" who criticized her must represent her mother; but the mother's voice as such never came back. Within two weeks she said her hate for her mother had all gone; and she began expressing affection instead. There was a corresponding change in the tone of the mother's letters. Throughout the ensuing year Grace developed more and more realistic attitudes, recognizing her mother's many positive contributions to her personality structure, as well as the fact that her mother's failings seemed more the result of defect than of conscious malice. Outspoken expressions of pride in her mother as a woman emerged, along with increasing attention to her own femininity. Evidently, with the vanishing of the dangerous mother image, it became possible for the patient to intensify her identification with the external manifestations of the good mother in her actual mother's behavior and appearance.

5. *Introjection of the Therapist.* Running parallel with the return and final disappearance of the mother's voice there was evidence from time to time that my hallucinated voice was also active in the patient's internal economy. Occasionally Grace reported something it had said. She was having arguments with it, like the ones she had had with Mrs. X and Mrs. Y, but more or less in keeping with my actual attitudes. Once when something she quoted me as having said turned out to be her own thought, she said impatiently, "It's the same thing." During my four months' absence my voice did oppose the critics; but without reinforcement from my actual presence it could not prevail against them. "I couldn't find you at the center of my affection," she said, "I couldn't have that in me or with me. You were a strong ally against this person; you went away and she got the best of me."

During the next seven months there were occasional comments like, "I keep hearing you"; but Grace did not volunteer any content, or indicate whether my voice was experienced as inside or outside. It seemed therapeutically contraindicated for me to inquire. However, on the day before the final appearance of the mother's voice (i.e., just before the patient went home for Christmas), she made her first unmistakable statement of having introjected the therapist, which merits quotation in detail.

"I resent you. *It's because you're inside me that I resent you. I've taken you inside. It's the internal you that makes me mad.* Everything I do I have to tell you. Whether it's good or bad I have to come and tell you. I wanted to just have that evening and feel as I wanted to about it. But you had to pass judgment on it. I can remember when it happened. I was closing the garage door and you were suddenly there.

Not your voice—I don't have hallucinations or anything like that. But you were there just the same; and we had an argument. You said, 'You went ahead and did exactly the same thing you did before!' and I said, 'I didn't! It was different!' I don't want to make this sound too neurotic; but I'm aware that you're involved, and it can't ever be simple any more I don't mean you're always critical; but you were this time, and I didn't agree. Sometimes you say positive things, or seem to have a positive attitude—because it isn't your voice. Sometimes it is and sometimes it isn't—or I don't know if it is. This sounds all very strange; but that's the way it is. I'm sorry, that's the best I can describe it."

A month later—and incidentally a week after saying that her hatred for her mother had gone—the patient reported arguing with me over her coming late and thus shortening her hour with me. Again introjection at a primitive level is obvious, as well as a clear recognition that my voice had now replaced her mother's.

"I've been arguing with you all morning before I came. You said, 'You're late.' I said, 'I know I'm late. I got tied up and couldn't get here earlier.' 'Why didn't you *start* sooner?' 'I *did* think I'd started early enough, but that damn car got stuck.' 'Why didn't you get up sooner?' 'I was tired.' 'Why didn't you got to bed earlier?' I shut up at this point. I just wasn't going to have you run my life. I've got something else besides you in my life. *You take the place of my mother—your voice. I don't know why I took your voice in.* You're not mad or nasty, just unpleasant, making me feel foolish and not letting me run my own life. I know you're not doing this at all. It must be the old Witch;[1] but not really. She doesn't say, '*Why didn't you get up earlier?*' (inquiring voice). "She says, '*Why didn't you get up earlier!*' " (nasty, attacking voice). "It's distinctive. I hate her! That's why I make her into you."

From this point on there was no further mention of my voice; and for a year—the fourth year of therapy—there was nothing said about female voices or the female "internal critic." A few times the patient said that what used to be her mother's voice was herself. Once she heard the male voice of her principal, "a voice that was not quite a voice," reproaching her for not working harder. She remarked, "It's really my voice talking to myself; but he gets into the form of it." She spoke of experiencing "a great pulling together, a feeling of wholeness, not just *trying* to be but *being*." She added that she was not hearing voices any more and did not miss them.

6. *The Male Nay-sayer.* Four weeks later a male

Nay-sayer put in a brief appearance. The patient spoke about him in three successive hours and never alluded to him afterward. He first appeared suddenly as a disapproving voice during a Parent-Teachers' Association meeting when the patient's teaching methods were being criticized. Grace merely said that after a certain criticism the Nay-sayer was there for the rest of the evening.

The next night he appeared in a manifest dream, as her garage mechanic, who kept reproaching her for not taking better care of her car. "This time," she related, "I didn't say, 'Yes, I've done all these things. I'm very sorry.' I just said, 'Haven't you heard about a God that forgives?' I said it out loud; I was sitting up in bed. But he knew things about me and kept piling them up, throwing past sins in my face. I said, 'Haven't you heard about a God that takes care of people who sin because they don't know any better?' In the dream I said they would be forgiven —the things I've done without knowing, which plague me. You don't have to resurrect them all up in order to be forgiven for them."

"The Nay-sayer," she said, "is definitely a man. It's a man accusing, or the masculine part of myself or integrated—no, I'm not making myself clear. He has a function that can't be denied, a part in the whole person. It's a man for me, a lot of rational and masculine characteristics, always fierce and sharp and aggravating. Men aren't always those things. It must be the picture of a man I had. My father wasn't like that at all. It's all tangled up. I don't want to be a man; so he can just be outside of me. I've discovered that a man can also be compassionate and still be a man."

The next therapeutic hour followed a weekend, during which the patient had been pondering over the problem of why the Nay-sayer was a man. She said nothing new excepting a comment that she might have thought her mother was a man, when she was a child, since she had never been afraid of her father. She then spoke for the first time for years about her childhood fear of "that terrible siren in the night" when the fire engines went by. The Nay-sayer was never mentioned again. His probable dynamic significance will be discussed later.

7. *Maternal Rejection and the Return of Critical Female Voices.* After a year's absence the critical, attacking female voices came back suddenly, immediately after a severe, unexpected experience of maternal rebuff. The patient went home for the Christmas holidays. She fully expected a warm welcome because her Thanksgiving visit home had been successful, and there had been an affectionate exchange of letters for several months. The moment she got home, however, she noticed that her mother seemed "miles and miles away, just like that first Christmas," i.e., three years earlier.

---

1. The Witch was one name used by the patient to refer to her internal critic that seemed to have replaced the *No-girl* and the mother.

The climax of frustration came one evening when she made a direct appeal to her mother to listen to her plans and hopes for the future. Her mother paid no attention to her; she just went on reading a magazine. Even the father, a peaceable man, remonstrated with the mother over her ignoring Grace, but without result. So the patient talked about her plans and hopes to her father; but she felt sure her mother was listening behind the magazine. There were other unhappy incidents, and the patient finally left home feeling rejected, humiliated, angry, and, as she expressed it, "emptied out."

Back in her own apartment, the patient got a cool reception from her landlady. She jumped to the conclusion that this was because she had left the place in a mess. The next day she could "hear two women's voices being catty" about her housekeeping; and later on the internal critic which she called the *Witch* came back, keeping up a running fire of nasty, critical, disparaging comment. This whole incident was obviously a setback, and a sign that some of the advances made during therapy were still unstable.

There were also encouraging signs. For one thing, the patient recognized the unreality of the two women's voices before coming to her first post-holiday hour; and for another, the internal mother and the mother's voice did not return as such. It will be recalled that the internal mother, unmistakably personified, was prominent throughout the first year and a half of therapy; and it had probably been active for many years before. The *Witch* was always a much less personified entity than the internal mother, and less personified even than the *No-girl*. I assumed, therefore, that by no means all the ground gained had been lost. The fact remains, however, that this primitive level of self-control and self-criticism persisted; the critical, attacking female voice did not again disappear.

The setback necessitated a review of the patient's decision, made three months earlier, to leave therapy the following spring and take a position she greatly wanted in Seattle, where she also had good friends. During the ensuing month there were no signs of progressive ego disorganization and, excepting for the return of the *Witch*, the archaic material that came up was no different from what had been intermittently present during the preceding year of maximal improvement. Moreover, much of the good relationship with mother and the home was apparently restored through a reasonably affectionate correspondence. It was decided that the wisest thing would be not to attempt any interference with the patient's plans, in which she had frankly included the recognition that she might need further therapeutic help where she was going. Therapy was accordingly terminated by mutual agreement on the date originally set.

*   *   *

7.

SOME PROBLEMS IN THE LAW OF EVIDENCE AND CRIMES

a.   MILLER v. UNITED STATES
320 F.2d 767 (D.C. Cir. 1963)

BAZELON, CHIEF JUDGE.

[Appellant's robbery] conviction rested on the testimony of the complaining witness, Cornell Watson. In its brief the Government described this testimony as follows:

"* * * Watson testified that . . . he was *en route* home from work and boarding a bus at 7th and Florida Avenue, Northwest in the District of Columbia. His wallet . . . was in his left hip pocket at the time. As he was boarding the bus he felt a slight jostle and subsequently discovered his wallet was missing. As a result of a conversation with persons on the bus [The record indicates that he was told that 'they had observed two people running down Florida Avenue and had gotten off * * *.'] Watson got off the bus . . . into an alley. Upon entering the alley Watson observed four or five men, including the appellant, who was looking through a wallet described by Watson as belonging to him, and the one he had on his person prior to boarding the bus. Watson yelled, 'Hey, that's my wallet. Give it back to me,' and gave chase to the appellant who ran away still holding the wallet. The chase lasted a number of blocks and suddenly appellant stopped and came back toward Watson who caught hold of him. Watson testified that he asked appellant for his wallet and appellant replied, 'Here, man, take this dollar and my ring and I will go back and get your wallet.' Watson took the dollar and about that time Police Officer Mitchell appeared and took appellant into custody. During the ensuing excitement an unknown citizen returned Watson's wallet to him. Watson testified he did not see anyone take his wallet or see anyone throw it away."

*   *   *

The Government sought to link appellant to the alleged crime by inferences of guilt from . . . flight.

*   *   *

Two factual assumptions underlie the legal relationship between flight and guilt: (1) that one who flees shortly after a criminal act is committed or when he is accused of committing it does so because he feels some guilt concerning that act; and (2) that one who feels some guilt concerning an act has committed that act.[1] Both assumptions purport to rest on common experience, not moral principles.

1. Wigmore puts it as follows: "There are two processes or inferences involved,—from conduct to consciousness of guilt, and then from consciousness of guilt to the guilty deed." 1 Wigmore on Evidence § 173 (1940).

The first assumption . . . has been subjected to a good deal of judicial criticism, on the ground that, in fact, common experience does not support it.

*   *   *

. . . In *Alberty* v. *United States*, 162 U.S. 499, 511 . . . the Court . . . noted that

"it is not universally true that a man, who is conscious that he has done wrong, 'will pursue a certain course not in harmony with the conduct of a man who is conscious of having done an act which is innocent, right, and proper'; since it is a matter of common knowledge that men who are entirely innocent do sometimes fly from the scene of a crime through fear of being apprehended as the guilty parties, or from an unwillingness to appear as witnesses. Nor is it true as an accepted axiom of criminal law that 'the wicked flee when no man pursueth, but the righteous are as bold as a lion.' Innocent men sometimes hesitate to confront a jury—not necessarily because they fear that the jury will not protect them, but because they do not wish their names to appear in connection with criminal acts, are humiliated at being obliged to incur the popular odium of an arrest and trial, or because they do not wish to be put to the annoyance or expense of defending themselves."[2]

*   *   *

This chorus of judicial caution, however, has been limited to the first assumption that one who flees shortly after a criminal act is committed or when he is accused of committing it feels some guilt concerning that act. It has not been extended to the second assumption that one who feels some guilt concerning an act has committed that act. Courts and commentators have commonly accepted this second assumption without criticism. Wigmore summarizes the judicial attitude by saying that this assumption "gives rise to no dispute * * *."

"The commission of a crime leaves usually upon the consciousness a moral impression which is characteristic. The innocent man is without it; the guilty man usually has it. Its evidential value has never been doubted. The inference from consciousness of guilt to 'guilty' is always available in evidence. It is a most powerful one, because the only other hypothesis conceivable is the rare one that the person's consciousness is caused by a delusion, and not by the actual doing of the act." 1 *Wigmore on Evidence* § 173 (1940).

Thus, although some courts recognize that flight may be prompted by something other than feelings of guilt, judicial opinion seems to assume that if flight is prompted by feelings of guilt, the accused is certainly the guilty doer.

---

2. See also *Cooper* v. *United States*, 94 U.S. App. D.C. 343, 218 F. 2d 39 (1954), wherein Judge Prettyman observed for this court that a certain circumstance "is explained by terrorized innocence as well as by a sense of guilt. After all, innocent people caught in a web of circumstances frequently become terror-stricken."

But available empirical data suggest the wisdom of caution concerning this assumption. Many years ago Sigmund Freud warned the legal profession:

"You may be led astray * * * by a neurotic who reacts as though he were guilty even though he is innocent—because a lurking sense of guilt already in him assimilates the accusation made against him on this particular occasion. You must not regard this possibility as an idle one; you have only to think of the nursery, where you can often observe it. It sometimes happens that a child who has been accused of a misdeed denied the accusation, but at the same time weeps like a sinner who has been caught. You might think that the child lies, even while it asserts its innocence; but this need not be so. The child is really not guilty of the specific misdeed of which he is being accused, but he is guilty of a similar misdemeanor of which you know nothing and of which you do not accuse him. He therefore quite truly denies his guilt in the one case, but in doing so betrays his sense of guilt with regard to the other. The adult neurotic behaves in this and in many other ways just as the child does. People of this kind are often to be met, and it is indeed a question whether your technique will succeed in distinguishing such self-accused persons from those who are really guilty." *Collected Papers* (1959), Vol. 2, p. 13.

The observation that feelings of guilt may be present without actual guilt in so-called normal as well as neurotic people has been made by many recognized scholars and is a significant factor in the contemporary view of the dynamics of human behavior.

It is not suggested that guilt feelings may not reflect actual guilt, but only that they do not always reflect it, and that Wigmore's commonly accepted opinion that "guilty consciousness" is "the strongest evidence * * * that the person is indeed the guilty doer," should not be elevated to an immutable principle either of law or human behavior.

When evidence of flight has been introduced into a case, in my opinion the trial court should, if requested, explain to the jury, in appropriate language, that flight does not necessarily reflect feelings of guilt, and that feelings of guilt, which are present in many innocent people, do not necessarily reflect actual guilt. This explanation may help the jury to understand and follow the instruction which should then be given, that they are not to presume guilt from flight; that they may, but need not, consider flight as one circumstance tending to show feelings of guilt; and that they may, but need not, consider feelings of guilt as evidence tending to show actual guilt.

*   *   *

BURGER, CIRCUIT JUDGE (dissenting).

*   *   *

. . . Fact issues and the reasonable inferences from accepted fact are for juries—not judges—in criminal trials and if we trust the jury system we do not need to attempt to guide every detail of jury deliberations. Let alone with a minimum of basic instruction juries can infuse the law with a sense of reality and can temper judicial technicality with the leaven of the common experience and community conscience. We should not attempt to limit the scope of jury deliberations by telling jurors to ignore their own experience and common sense, and in a case like the one before us, denigrate other evidence in the case which plainly suggests that flight was indeed indicative of guilt.

The desire to minimize if not eliminate flight as a source of reasonable inferences represents a futile attempt to require jurors to "unring the bell" of their individual and collective experiences. . . . The "fuller instructions regarding flight" urged by Judge BAZELON may be appropriate to a philosophical interchange between judges, lawyers, and experts in psychology, but they are totally unnecessary to a jury and add nothing whatever to what the instruction conveyed to the jury. . . .[3]

At best jurors get only a few general impressions from the trial judge's charge. I think it is fair to say that they understand such concepts as presumptions of innocence, burden of proof, criminal intent and credibility. Beyond these fundamentals and description of the specific elements of a particular crime, most instructions probably become confusing and blur the juror's recollection of the really vital elements of the charge.

NOTE

DEARMAN, H. B. and SMITH, B. M.

Unconscious Motivation and the Polygraph Test*

A young bank vice-president was referred to the senior author by his employer, the president of the

---

3. The full instruction on flight was as follows:

"There is a further doctrine of law that becomes pertinent in this case, and that is the testimony of the complaining witness, Cornell Watson, that the defendant fled from the alley where he was first confronted and ran for a period of several blocks. This brings into the case a *presumption* or an element of consideration which hinges around the principle that flight may be considered by jurors as evidence of guilt. In other words, you are entitled to draw from testimony which you accept as credible a conclusion that flight on the part of a defendant was or is evidence of guilt. You are instructed, however, as a matter of law that flight means not merely a leaving, but means a leaving under a consciousness of guilt and for the purpose of evading arrest. Therefore, if you find that the defendant's conduct was induced by fear of arrest, then it is a flight from justice and you may consider it as a circumstance indicating guilt. If, on the other hand, the defendant has explained his presence at the point where he said he was first accosted by the complaining witness to your complete satisfaction, then the element of flight is not a factor to be considered by you." [*Ibid.* at 769–70.]

* 119 *American Journal of Psychiatry*, 1963. (pp. 1017–18). Reprinted by permission.

bank, because a lie-detector examiner had alleged that the man had stolen money from the bank. A complete audit of the books had revealed no losses, and the president, expressing great confidence in his employee's integrity, wanted to "get to the truth of the matter." . . .

* * *

The essential details of the case are here summarized:

The patient, a white, married, twenty-seven-year-old man was the only child of parents of average economic status. When he was seven, his parents were divorced ("because the father drank too much"), and he and his mother lived with her parents until he was thirteen when the mother remarried. The boy and his stepfather did not get along very well, but he lived at home until he graduated, in the upper third of his class, from high school. He went to college primarily "to get away from home," flunked his first year, but settled down and earned his degree. In his second year of college he met the girl he was to marry two and one-half years later. They have one child. He went to work for his present employer shortly after graduating from college and was rapidly promoted to vice-president and manager of a branch bank.

On the occasion of the "routine" polygraph test by the examiner from the bank's detective agency, the patient showed a "violent" reaction to the question, "Have you ever stolen any money from the bank or its customers?" And positive responses to other questions concerning the bank. He also showed a positive reaction to the supposedly neutral question, "Do you drink coffee?" The patient was very upset by his failure to "clear the polygraph" and admitted to some minor misuse of bank funds, such as including parking fees on his expense account. The polygraph test was administered again, and again he "failed to clear." The patient confessed to the polygraph examiner that maybe his worry about personal problems, which he discussed with the interrogator, accounted for the positive reaction, so a third polygraph test was made. Again the interpretation was that the patient was lying and had stolen money. A final polygraph test was done in an effort to pinpoint the amount of money involved. The machine indicated that he showed peak reactions at $800 and at $1,100. The patient was thoroughly confused because he could not remember taking any such sums. However, since he had been convinced that he couldn't "fool the machine," he signed a confession that he had taken $1,000 and told how he must have done it. The books were audited, and it was discovered not only that he had not used the method that he had stated but that no shortage of that amount had occurred in his branch since he had been employed there.

As a result of this dilemma, the patient was referred

for examination. In the course of the seven hours of psychiatric examination (including a two-hour sodium amytal interview) and subsequent psycho-therapeutic interviews, the following relevant material emerged:

(1.) The patient had strongly ambivalent feelings toward his mother. She had divorced his father and seven years later married a man with whom he did not "get along." In the interim the patient felt neglected by his mother and developed positive feelings for his grandparents. He also felt that some of his mother's behavior toward him was somewhat seductive. (2.) The patient's wife was two years his senior, and she had previously been married and divorced. His wife was very similar to his mother in many respects. (3.) His wife and his mother were both "customers of the bank." (4.) He had been involved in financial affairs with his wife and his mother to the extent of approximately $800 and $1,100 and about which he felt somewhat guilty. (5.) In a number of instances he unconsciously identified wife with mother. His unconscious hostility for his mother was apparently the motivating force for a number of incidents (including wrecking her car and for which one of the sums mentioned above was involved).

It will be remembered that the question on the polygraph examination that evoked the most violent reaction was, "Have you ever stolen any money from the bank or its customers?" It seemed reasonable to assume that the patient was responding to the "customers" part of the question inasmuch as he identified his wife and mother as customers and inasmuch as he felt guilty about financial transactions that he had had with each of them.

In order to test this assumption, an independent polygraph examiner (a woman) was employed. She was given no background information prior to her examination of the patient. She was asked to give the exact questions used by the original interrogator and an additional set of five questions in which "bank," "customers of the bank," and "wife and mother" were separated.

This interrogator's interpretation of her findings prior to learning the background of the case was that the patient was lying and that he was guilty of theft. A careful examination of the polygraph records shows, however, that only in those questions in which the word "customers" appeared did the patient consistently show emotional reactivity on the polygraph record. On the basis of this evidence, it was concluded that the assumption made above of the patient's identification of wife-mother-customers was responsible for his emotional reaction.

It is interesting to note, however, that at the time of the polygraph examination, even though this material was conscious, it still evoked autonomic responses. It is of further interest that the positive response accompanying a truthful "yes" to the question, "Do you drink coffee?" was apparently due to his mother's prohibition of coffee during the patient's childhood.

b.   UNITED STATES v. POLLARD
                171 F. Supp. 474 (E.D. Mich. 1959)

LEVIN, DISTRICT JUDGE.

The defendant, having waived indictment, the Government instituted this prosecution on a three-count information charging him . . . with attempted robbery. . . .

On arraignment, the accused pleaded guilty. . . . Subsequently, upon advice of counsel, he moved to set aside the guilty pleas on the ground that he was insane at the time he committed the acts upon which the prosecution was based. The Court, with the acquiescence of the Government, permitted the defendant to withdraw his guilty plea, and a plea of not guilty was entered. . . .

Prior to trial, I was advised that a psychiatric report of a psychiatrist retained by the defendant indicated that the defendant was, at the time of the offenses, suffering from a diseased mind which produced an irresistible impulse to commit the criminal acts. . . .

The defendant elected to be tried by the Court without a jury. During the trial, the following facts appeared:

The defendant is an intelligent, twenty-nine-year-old man. In 1949, he married and, during the next four years, three sons and a daughter were born of this marriage. He was apparently a well-adjusted, happy, family man. In 1952, he became a member of the Police Department of the City of Detroit and continued to work as a policeman until he was apprehended for the acts for which he is now being prosecuted. In April, 1956, his wife and infant daughter were brutally killed in an unprovoked attack by a drunken neighbor.

On May 21, 1958, one day before he remarried, at about 11:00 A.M., defendant entered the 24th-Michigan Branch of the Detroit Bank & Trust Company. He paused for a few moments to look over the bank and then proceeded to an enclosure in which a bank official was at work. He told the official, whom he believed to be the manager, that he wanted to open a savings account. He then walked through a swinging gate into the enclosure, sat down at the desk, pulled out a gun and pointed it at the official. He ordered the official to call a teller. When the teller arrived, the defendant handed a brown paper grocery bag to him and told him to fill it with money. While it was being filled, defendant kept the bank official covered. The teller filled the bag with money as ordered and turned it over to the defendant. Thereupon, defendant ordered the bank official to accompany him to the exit. As both the defendant and bank official approached the exit, the official suddenly wrapped his arms around the defendant, who then dropped the bag and fled from the bank and escaped.

About 4:00 P.M., on the same day, he entered the Chene-Medbury Branch of the Bank of the Commonwealth and walked to a railing behind which a bank employee was sitting. He pointed his gun at the man and told him to sit quietly. The employee, however, did not obey this order but instead raised an alarm, whereupon the defendant ran from the bank and again escaped.

[A]fter his abortive attempts to rob the two banks, he decided to rob a third bank and actually proceeded on the same day to an unnamed bank he had selected but decided not to make the attempt when he discovered that the bank was "too wide open"— had too much window area so that the possibility of apprehension was enhanced.

On June 3, at about 3:00 P.M., the defendant entered the Woodrow Wilson-Davison Branch of the Bank of the Commonwealth and went directly to an enclosure behind which a male and female employee were sitting at desks facing each other. Defendant held his gun under a jacket which he carried over his right arm. He ordered the woman employee to come out from behind the railing. In doing so, she grasped the edge of her desk. Defendant, in the belief that she may have pushed an alarm button, decided to leave but ordered the woman to accompany him out of the bank. When they reached the street, he told her to walk ahead of him, but not to attract attention. Defendant noticed a police car approaching the bank and waited until it passed him, then ran across an empty lot to his car and again escaped.

On June 11, 1958, he attempted to hold up a grocery market. He was thwarted in the attempt when the proprietor screamed and, becoming frightened, the defendant fled. In so doing, he abandoned his automobile in back of the market where he had parked it during the holdup attempt. Routinely, this car was placed under surveillance and later when the defendant, dressed in his Detroit Police Officer's uniform, attempted to get in it, he was arrested by detectives of the Detroit Police Force.

After his apprehension, the defendant confessed to eleven other robberies, or attempted robberies.

The three psychiatrists who submitted the written reports, all qualified and respected members of their profession, testified that in their opinion the defendant, at the time he committed the criminal acts, knew the difference between right and wrong and knew that the acts he committed were wrong but was suffering from a "traumatic neurosis" or "dissociative reaction," characterized by moods of depression and severe feelings of guilt, induced by the traumatic effect of the death of his wife and child and his belief that he was responsible for their deaths because by his absence from home he left them exposed to the actions of the crazed, drunken neighbor. They further stated that he had an unconscious desire to be punished by society to expiate these guilt feelings and that the governing power of his mind was so destroyed or impaired that he was unable to resist the commission of the criminal acts. In their opinion, however, the defendant was not then, nor is he now, psychotic or committable to a mental institution.

Three of defendant's fellow police officers, called as defense witnesses, testified that during the period in which the defendant committed the criminal acts he had a tendency to be late for work; that at times he was despondent; and that he occasionally seemed to be lost in thought and did not promptly respond to questions directed to him. One of the officers testified that on one occasion, he repeatedly beat the steering wheel of the police car in which they were riding, while at the same time reiterating the name of his murdered wife. However, none of them found his conduct or moods to be of such consequence that they believed it necessary to report the defendant to a superior officer.

Defendant's present wife, who impressed me as an intelligent person, testified that on two occasions defendant suddenly, and for no reason apparent to her, lapsed into crying spells and that he talked to her once or twice about committing suicide. She also testified that during one such period of depression he pointed a gun at himself; that she became frightened and called the police; that the police came, relieved him of his gun, and took him to the precinct police station; and that after his release he appeared jovial and acted as if nothing had happened. Defendant's brother-in-law stated that the defendant had always been a very happy person but that he became noticeably despondent after the death of his wife and child and expressed a desire to commit suicide because he now no longer had a reason for living.

A police lieutenant of the Detroit Police Department testified that the defendant's police work, during the period with which we are now concerned, as evidenced by his efficiency rating and his written duty reports, was, if anything, more effective than his service prior to the death of his wife.

*   *   *

The psychiatrists . . . testified that the defendant suffered from severe feelings of depression and guilt; and that in their opinion he had an irresistible impulse to commit criminal acts, an unconscious desire to be apprehended and punished; and that he geared his behavior to the accomplishment of this end. However, his entire pattern of conduct during the period of his criminal activities militates against this conclusion. His conscious desire not to be apprehended and punished was demonstrably greater than his unconscious desire to the contrary. After his apprehension, despite searching interrogation for over five hours by Detroit police officers and by agents of the Federal Bureau of Investigation, he denied any participation in criminal conduct of any kind. It was only after he was positively identified by bank personnel that he finally admitted that he did attempt to perpetrate the bank robberies. I asked one of the psychiatrists to explain this apparent inconsistency. In answer to my question, he stated that although the defendant had an unconscious desire to be apprehended and punished, when the possibility of apprehension became direct and immediate, the more dominating desire for self-preservation asserted itself. This explanation may have merit if applied to individual acts. However, the validity of a theory that attempts to explain the behavior of a person must be determined in light of that person's entire behavioral pattern and not with reference to isolated acts which are extracted from that pattern. The defendant's pattern of behavior of May 21, 1958, discloses that the desire for self-preservation was not fleeting and momentary but continuing, consistent, and dominant. What, then, becomes of the theory of irresistible impulse? Looking to the events of that day, I am asked to believe, first, that the defendant, acting pursuant to an irresistible impulse, selected a bank site to rob, entered the bank to accomplish that end, purposely failed in the attempt, and when the end he sought, apprehension, was in view, escaped because of the dominance, at the moment of ultimate accomplishment, of the stronger drive for self-preservation. I must then believe that when the defendant knew he was apparently free from detection, his compulsive state reasserted itself and that he again went through the steps of planning, abortive attempt, and escape. And if I acquiesce in this theory, what other psychiatric theory explains his subsequent conduct—his plan to rob a third unnamed bank and the rejection of that plan because of his subjective belief that the possibility of apprehension would be too great? If the theory remains the same, then it appears that in the latter case, the fear of apprehension and punishment tipped "the scales enough to make resistible an impulse otherwise irresistible." Guttmacher and Weihofen, *Psychiatry and the Law*, p. 413. It is a logical inference that, in reality, the other robbery attempts were made as the result of impulses that the defendant did not choose voluntarily to resist because, to him, the possibility of success outweighed the likelihood of detection which is in essence a motivation for all criminal conduct. The impulse being resistible, the defendant is accountable for his criminal conduct.

. . . Admittedly, motivations may be mixed. However, all the facts have clearly established that defendant's criminal activity was planned to satisfy an extrinsic need by a reasoned but anti-social method. The defendant had financial problems of varying degrees of intensity throughout his life. He had financial difficulties during his first marriage. He was now embarking upon a second marriage. He was about to undertake the responsibility of supporting not only a wife and himself, but also four children, three of them the product of his first marriage. In statements given to agents of the Federal Bureau of Investigation admitting his criminal activity, he stated: "Inasmuch as I was about to marry my second wife, I decided that I would not lead the same type of financially insecure life that I led with my first wife. I needed about $5,000 in order to buy a house. My only purpose in deciding to rob a bank was to obtain $5,000 and if I obtained the money, I did not intend to continue robbing." Defendant's entire pattern of conduct was consistent with this expressed motivation.

Life does not always proceed on an even keel. Periods of depression, feelings of guilt and inadequacy are experienced by many of us. Defendant was a devoted husband and loving father. His feelings of despondency and depression induced by the brutal killing of his wife and infant daughter were not unnatural. How else the defendant should have reacted to his tragic loss I am not told. His conduct throughout this crucial period did not cause any concern among his colleagues. All stated unequivocally that in their opinion he was sane. Significant also is the fact that his present wife married him on May 22, 1958, after a year of courtship. It is a permissible inference that defendant's conduct relative to his mental condition, as related by her, did not suggest to her that the defendant was insane.

I am satisfied beyond a reasonable doubt that the defendant committed the acts for which he is now charged and that when he committed them he was legally sane.

I, therefore, adjudge the defendant guilty of the three counts of the information.

NOTES

NOTE 1

POLLARD v. UNITED STATES
282 F. 2d 450, 460 (6th Cir. 1960)

MCALLISTER, CHIEF JUDGE

*   *   *

[A]cts that appear rational are not to be taken by the factfinder as evidence of sanity, where all of the other evidence in the case is proof of a defendant's mental unsoundness.

[I]n the Report of the Neuropsychiatric Staff Conference of the Medical Center for Federal Prisoners, it was pointed out that the attempted robberies by Pollard were bizarre and ineffectively planned and executed; that when he tried to leave one bank, he ordered a bank official to follow behind him instead of ahead of him, which resulted in his being caught from behind and barely escaping after a struggle, during which he dropped the paper bag of money he had collected; that on the various occasions of his attempted robberies, he would suddenly enter a bank that he had never seen before, without prior knowledge of the arrangement of the premises, or of the personnel. Taken in consideration with all of the other factors, such conduct, on the part of a highly intelligent police officer with a knowledge of how crimes are committed, has about it nothing of sanity.

*   *   *

It is emphasized by the Government that Pollard was motivated to attempt the bank robberies because of his need for financial security. . . .

The claimed motivation seems pointless. . . . His second wife, at the time of her marriage to him, had money of her own—enough to pay her own bills, and take care of her daughter with the money which was paid for support by her former husband. . . . She considered herself to be relatively comfortable financially. Between the time of Pollard's arrest on June 11, 1958, and his trial, she had, herself, paid off about $700 in bills that he had owed. Pollard's financial condition could not be considered a reasonable motivation for his attempted bank robberies. As far as income went, he was much better off than most other policemen and if such a financial condition could be considered a reasonable motivation for Pollard's attempted robberies, every other policeman in the department would have had twice the motivation to commit such crimes as Pollard had.

*   *   *

[T]he judgment of the District Court is set aside and the case remanded for further proceedings. . . .

NOTE 2

ALEXANDER, FRANZ

Fundamentals of Psychoanalysis*

One of the most fundamental principles of psychodynamics is that all human acts are overdetermined and motivated by a number of conflicting motives. A philanthropist may give money for a cancer hospital because his wife died of cancer, because he wants to do something for the community from which his wealth originated, because he desires prominence, because he wants to relieve guilt feelings caused by ruthless business methods, and also because he wishes to satisfy an interest in humanity. The correct answer to such questions as "Why did you help your friend?" is not "I did it out of loyalty and not because I wanted to be superior to him," but "I helped him because of loyalty *and* because I wanted to be superior to him *and* because I felt under obligation to him *and* because I hoped that at some other time he might help me." Most likely there are still several other reasons. Not "either . . . or" but "both . . . and" is the formula for human acts.

Rationalization means selecting the most acceptable from a complex of mixed motives to explain behavior. This permits the repression of other alien motives. Since the selected motives are suitable to the act, the unacceptable ones may be overlooked or denied. It is by no means correct to define rationalization as the invention of necessarily nonexistent motives; it is usually an arbitrary selection which passes speciously for the whole.

Obviously rationalization is a powerful aid in repressing unacceptable motives and is probably the most common defense measure of the ego.

* New York: W. W. Norton Co., 1948. (pp. 108–9). Reprinted by permission.

E.

Should Law Ask: Is Psychoanalysis a Science?

1.

NAGEL, ERNEST

Methodological Issues in Psychoanalytic Theory*

[P]sychoanalytic theory is intended to be a theory of human behavior in the same sense of "theory" that, for example, the molecular theory of gases is a set of assumptions which systematizes, explains, and predicts certain observable phenomena of gases.

* Reprinted from: *Psychoanalysis, Scientific Method and Philosophy*, Hook, Sidney (ed.). New York: New York University Press, 1959. (pp. 38–55). Reprinted by permission.

Accordingly, [we may] evaluate the merits of Freudian theory by standards of intellectual cogency similar to those we employ in judging theories in other areas of positive science. It would of course be absurdly pedantic to apply to Freudian theory the yardstick of rigor and precision current in mathematical and experimental physics. Proper allowance must certainly be made for the notorious difficulties encountered in all inquiries into distinctively human behavior, and for what is perhaps an inevitable fuzziness of all generalizations about human conduct. Nevertheless . . . no apology is required for raising substantially the same kinds of issues of fact and logic concerning

Freudian theory that are pertinent to a general examination of the cognitive worth and standing of a theory in the natural or social sciences.

*   *   *

Freudian theory maintains, and I think rightly so, that it is not possible to account for most human conduct exclusively in terms either of manifest human traits or of conscious motives and intentions. Accordingly, the theory introduces a number of assumptions containing terms that ostensibly refer to matters neither manifest nor conscious, and that are not explicitly definable by way of what is manifest and conscious. In so far as Freudian theory employs notions of this kind which do not describe anything observable (let me call such notions "theoretical" ones for the sake of brevity), the theory is quite like the molecular theory of gases or the gene theory of heredity. I do not think, therefore, that there is any substance in those criticisms of Freudian theory which object to the theory *merely* on the ground that it uses theoretical notions.

(a) My first difficulty with Freudian theory nevertheless is generated by the fact that while it is unobjectionable for a theory to be couched in terms of theoretical notions, the theory does not seem to me to satisfy two requirements which any theory must satisfy if it is to be capable of empirical validation. I must state these requirements briefly. In the first place, it must be possible to deduce determinate consequences from the assumptions of theory, so that one can decide on the basis of logical considerations, and prior to the examination of any empirical data, whether or not an alleged consequence of the theory is indeed implied by the latter. For unless this requirement is fulfilled, the theory has no definite content, and questions as to what the theory asserts cannot be settled except by recourse to some privileged authority or arbitrary caprice. In the second place, even though the theoretical notions are not explicitly defined by way of overt empirical procedures and observable traits of things, nevertheless at least *some* theoretical notions must be *tied down* to *fairly definite and unambiguously specified* observable materials, by way of rules of procedure variously called "correspondence rules," "co-ordinating definitions," and "operational definitions." For if this condition is not satisfied, the theory can have no determinate consequences upon *empirical* subject matter. An immediate corollary to these requirements is that since a consistent theory cannot imply two incompatible consequences, a credible theory must not only be *confirmed* by observational evidence, but it must also be capable of being *negated* by such evidence. In short, a theory must not be formulated in such a manner that it can always be construed and manipulated so as to explain whatever the actual facts are, no matter whether controlled observation shows one state of affairs to obtain or its opposite.

In respect to both of these requirements, however, Freudian theory in general, and the metapsychology in particular, seem to me to suffer from serious shortcomings. I lack the time to argue the matter at length, and some examples must suffice to illustrate the nature of my difficulties.

[A]mong the energic principles [that constitute metapsychology are] the following two: "The drives [in particular "sexuality" and "aggression"] are the main sources of energy in the mental apparatus"; and, secondly, "The regulations of energies in the mental apparatus follows the pleasure principle ['the tendency to immediate discharge'] the reality principle [i.e., 'considerations of reality'] derived from it under the influence of ego-development, and a tendency to keep the level of excitation constant, or at a minimum." Now is it really possible to deduce from these assumptions, even when they are conjoined with the remaining ones, any *determinate* conclusions in the familiar sense of "deduce"? For example, can one conclude anything even as to the general conditions under which the sexual drive will discharge its "energy," rather than (to use Freud's own locutions) combine with the aggressive drive to form a "compromise" or have its "level of excitation" raised because of "considerations of reality"? My question is not whether, *after* the theoretical general conditions for such alternatives have been ascertained in some independent manner, it is possible to assign corresponding "degrees of strength" to the drives and the restraining influence of the ego, so that the alleged "conclusions" will then in effect be *explicitly* contained in the premises. It is, I take it, no great feat to play the role of Epimetheus. My query is whether such conclusions can be deduced from the theory *prior* to knowing just what consequences the theory must have if it is to be in agreement with assumed matters of fact.

I will not conceal my doubts about the possibility of obtaining such conclusions from the theory, although I admit that all sorts of things may be *suggested* by its assumptions. The reason for my doubts is that the theory is stated in language so vague and metaphorical that almost anything appears to be compatible with it. I am not objecting to the use of metaphors *per se*, for I am fully aware of the great heuristic values of metaphors and analogies in the construction and development of theories in all departments of science. My point is the different one that in Freudian theory metaphors are employed without even half-way definite rules for expanding them, and that in consequence admitted metaphors such as "energy" or "level of excitation" have no specific content and can be filled in to suit one's fancy. In short, Freudian formulations seem to me to have so much "open texture," to be so loose in statement, that while they are unquestionably suggestive, it is well-nigh impossible to decide whether what is thus suggested is genuinely implied by the theory or whether it is related to the latter only by the circumstance that someone *happens* to associate one with the other. . . .

. . . Now I agree that if aggressive drive is taken to be the independent theoretical variable in a given case, there is no necessary incompatibility between maintaining, on the one hand, that a certain intensity of the drive in an individual is manifested by overtly aggressive behavior, and also maintaining, on the other hand, that other intensities of the drive in that individual are manifested by excessive kindness in his conduct. For the differences in overt behavior may be accounted for in terms of different intensities in the drive, perhaps in conjunction with additional stipulated differences. What is by no means clear, however, is that the allegedly different intensities of the drive are not postulated *ad hoc* and *ex post facto*, and that without *antecedent* knowledge of just how a given individual will behave, relatively unambiguous statements about his overt behavior can nevertheless be deduced from the hypotheses of the theory when appropriate initial conditions are supplied.

In any event, there is an uncomfortable ambiguity in the way the theoretical notion of aggressive drive appears to be associated with observable behavior. This ambiguity is equally present in the rules of correspondence for the notion of sexual drive, which is sometimes co-ordinated with almost any form of *sensuality*. A similar lack of even moderate precision can be noted in the correspondence rules Freud seems to have proposed for the theoretical notions of the id, the ego and the superego. [It] will be instructive to consider briefly the co-ordinating definitions Freud appears to have had in mind for them. According to him, the id represents the influence of heredity, the superego corresponds to the moral standards of society, and the ego represents the accidental and current events of an individual's own experience. I construe this account as an attempt to provide "operational definitions" for these theoretical notions. If I am right in this assumption, one cannot help being impressed by the extraordinary vagueness of the correspondence rules. Just how is one to distinguish in the gross behavior of an individual those features which are responses, for example, to the impact of current events, from those features which are the outcome of social pressures? It seems to me that in general the distinctions are enormously vague, and that the line between them can be drawn only in an arbitrary manner. Even if one overlooks the imprecise way in which the theoretical notions are themselves specified, it is difficult to see how conclusions about manifest behavior—ostensibly deduced from metapsychology on the basis of such rules of correspondence—can be anything but the products of a large measure of arbitrary decision.

*　　*　　*

[One is] led to inquire further whether there are any statements which . . . are unmistakable instances of deduction from Freudian theory, or whether the theory has the remarkable feature that a statement can be shown to be a theorem only if it is first accepted as a postulate. Do any of the familiar Freudian theses, such as those about infantile sexuality and sexual development, frustration and aggression, or totemism and social taboos, follow logically from the theory, when suitable assumptions not identical with those theses are added to the theory? More generally, what is the logical relation of Freudian metapsychology to any of the more specific Freudian contentions? I do not believe straightforward replies to such questions can be given . . . But if this is so, there is surely good ground for the suspicion that Freudian theory can always be so manipulated that it escapes refutation no matter what the well-established facts may be.

(b) . . . The theory is intended to explain human behavior on the cardinal assumption that all conduct is *motivated* or *wish-fulfilling*. But since most of our conduct is not in fact *consciously* motivated, the theory postulates the complex "mental apparatus" . . . which includes under various names what are in some sense *unconscious* motives or wishes. As I understand Freudian theory . . . these unconscious motives, wishes, drives, urges and intentions must be regarded as "psychic" or "mental processes," as "purposive ideas" which are directed toward definite "aims" or "objects," and not simply as latent somatic dispositions possessing no *specific goals*. Indeed, if these unconscious drives were not strongly analogous to conscious motives and wishes, the claim that psychoanalytic theory explains human conduct in motivational terms would be difficult to make out and would perhaps collapse. On the other hand, these unconscious motives have an enduring character and tenacious attachment to specific objectives that conscious wishes do not exhibit. Indeed, in Freudian theory a thwarted wish of early childhood, directed toward some person, may not completely vanish, but may enjoy a repressed existence in the unconscious, and continue to operate in identical form into the present even though that person has long since died. In consequence, there is an important failure of analogy between conscious motives and unconscious mental processes, so that it is only by a radical shift in the customary meanings of such words as "motive" and "wish" that Freudian theory can be said to offer an explanation of human conduct in terms of motivations and wish-fulfillments.

This comment would perhaps be calling attention only to a relatively verbal matter, were it not for the fact that the unconscious mechanism postulated to account for human conduct is emphatically said to be a *psychical* or *mental* apparatus which is endowed with all the customary attributes of substantiality and causal agency. As is well known, Freud hoped that this mental apparatus would eventually be identified with physiological processes in the body; and he himself observed that the question whether the unconscious processes he postulated are to be conceived as mental or as physical can easily become a war of words. Nevertheless, he not only insisted that the apparatus of metapsychology is *mental*, but also described its parts as if they were things struggling with one another or with the external world. He admitted that the assumption of unconscious mental activity was in a sense an extension of that primitive animism which attributes a consciousness to the things around us, even though he noted that the mental, like the physical, may "in reality" not be what "it appears to us to be." And he repeatedly talked of the id, the ego and the superego as inhabited by drives charged with energies, acting like forces, and in some cases immutably directed toward quite specific objects. "*Psychic reality*," he once vigorously asserted, "is a special form of existence which must not be confounded with *material* reality." . . .

It is certainly tempting to read all this as just metaphorical language, a convenient and dramatically suggestive way of talking about some of the complex but still unknown detailed mechanisms of the body. On this reading of Freudian theory, its assumptions would be formulations of the relations between, and the teleological organization of, various latent capacities and dispositions of the human organism. Accordingly, its "motivational" explanations of human conduct would then not differ in kind, though they would differ in not specifying the detailed mechanisms involved, from teleological explanations of the behavior of such teleologically organized (or "feed-back") systems as an engine provided with a governor or the human body as a self-regulative structure for the maintenance of its internal temperature.

However, such a reading is difficult to carry through if one is to make consistent sense of the theory, in part because of the characterization the theory gives of many drives as immutably fixed to specific objectives, but in larger measure because of the causal powers the theory ascribes to its theoretical entities. If these causal ascriptions are themselves construed figuratively, I cannot make ends meet in understanding the theory as a supposedly "dynamic" account of human personality and conduct. On the other hand, if those ascriptions are taken seriously (i.e., more or less literally), then on the suggested reading of the rest of the theory the latter would in effect be asserting what is to me the unintelligible doctrine that various *modes of organization* of human activities are the *causes* of those activities.

* * *

I come to the second group of questions, those dealing with the nature of the evidence for Freudian theory. There appear to be three major types of such evidence: clinical data, obtained from patients in psychoanalytic interviews; experimental findings in psychological laboratories; and anthropological information gathered by studies of primitive and advanced societies. Since the clinical evidence is regarded by psychoanalysts as by far the most important type . . . I shall devote the remainder of my comments to it. For the sake of the record I think I ought nevertheless to state my conviction, although without supporting reasons, that even when the best face is put on the experimental and anthropological evidence the available data do not uniformly support Freudian theory. Some of this evidence can certainly be construed as being favorable to, or at any rate compatible with, the theory; but some of the evidence is decidely negative.

The psychoanalytic interview (or method) is the distinctive procedure used by analysts for arriving at psychoanalytic hypotheses, for obtaining evidence for or against such hypotheses, and for effecting therapies. . . . As everyone knows, the aim of the psychoanalytic interview is to discover the causes of a patient's neurosis or psychosis, on the assumption that his present condition is the manifestation of internal conflicts produced by an unfulfilled but repressed "wish" of early childhood, which is still operative in the unconscious and which is usually ,sexual in character. Briefly stated, the method of ascertaining such alleged causes consists in having the subject engage in "free association" narration of his conscious thoughts, until the "latent meaning" of his fragmentary recollections of childhood experiences—i.e., the frustrated but suppressed wish that is the source of his present difficulties—is uncovered by the "interpretations" which the analyst places upon what is told him. Accordingly, the crucial issue is how such interpretations are established as valid.

Judging by what analysts themselves say on this question, the grounds for regarding an interpretation as sound are its coherence (or compatibility) with all the things disclosed by the patient in the interview, its acceptance by the patient, and (at least in some cases) the improvement in the condition of the patient when he accepts the interpretation and so recognizes the alleged source of his troubles. Now although the probative worth of such evidence has been frequently challenged, and some of its defects have been acknowledged even by psychoanalysts, I have never come across adequate answers to what seem to me grave criticisms. In the hope of eliciting better answers, permit me therefore to enumerate the difficulties, however familiar they may be, that I regard as important.

(a) Only passing mention need be made of the circumstance that although in the interview the analyst is supposedly a "passive" auditor of the "free association" narration by the subject, in point of fact the analyst does direct the course of the narrative. This by itself does not necessarily impair the evidential worth of the outcome, for even in the most meticulously conducted laboratory experiment the experimenter intervenes to obtain the data he is after. There is nevertheless the difficulty that in the nature of the case the full extent of the analyst's intervention is not a matter that is open to public scrutiny, so that by and large one has only his own testimony as to what transpires in the consulting room. It is perhaps unnecessary to say that this is not a question about the personal integrity of psychoanalytic practitioners. The point is the fundamental one that no matter how firmly we may resolve to make explicit our biases, no human being is aware of all of them, and that objectivity in science is achieved through the criticism of publicly accessible material by a community of independent inquirers. . . .

Moreover, unless data are obtained under carefully standardized circumstances, or under different circumstances whose dependence on known variables is nevertheless established, even an extensive collection of data is an unreliable basis for inference. To be sure, analysts apparently do attempt to institute standard conditions for the conduct of interviews. But there is not much information available on the extent to which the standardization is actually enforced, or whether it relates to more than what may be superficial matters.

(b) The mere coherence of an interpretation with the data supplied by a subject seems to me to carry little weight as evidence for its truth, especially if more than one such coherent interpretation can be given, whether within the general framework of Freudian metapsychology or on the basis of quite different assumptions. I have read enough of the analytic literature to have been impressed by the ingenuity with which the reported data of various cases are made to dovetail into psychoanalytic interpretations. Nevertheless, I am also familiar with the fact that analysts themselves sometimes differ in their diagnoses of the same case; and I have little doubt myself that for every ingenious interpretation of a case, another one no less superficially plausible can be invented. Accordingly, even if we waive the important point . . . that the analyst may base his interpretation not on *all* the information given by the patient, but on an unwittingly biased selection of the data, the question remains whether there is any objective way of deciding between alternative interpretations.

[T]wo such ways [have been suggested]. One of them is the making of successful predictions, the other is the use of established laws based on experience with various types of patients. I want to consider each of these briefly.

(c) What sorts of predictions can be made by an analyst? [A]part from therapeutic prognoses, which for the moment I will ignore, the only kinds of predictions I have found mentioned in the relevant literature refer to the reactions of the patient. Thus, Ernst Kris cites as examples of such predictable reactions "the reactions of acknowledgment to any interpretation given, for instance, that of sudden insight combined with the production of confirmatory details or substitute reactions of a variety of kinds," such as the recall by the subject of past experiences which he was previously unable to remember. However, neither the *acceptance* of a given interpretation by a subject, nor his *claim* to a sudden insight into the alleged source of his difficulties, seems to me to constitute, by itself, a critical confirmation of the interpretation. For the interpretation does not, as such, predict either its own acceptance by the subject or the insight claimed by him; and in any event it is pertinent to ask how often an interpretation of a certain kind when proposed to comparable subjects is neither accepted by the subjects nor accompanied by a sense of illumination about themselves. Nor is it clear why the mere say-so of a patient that he now understands the source of his difficulties is competent evidence for the assumption that the alleged source is indeed the actual source. There have been countless numbers of people throughout human history who have believed quite sincerely that their successes or failures could be attributed to various things they did or did not do or that were done to them; nevertheless, most of such beliefs have subsequently been shown to be baseless. Why is not this lesson of human experience relevant for assessing the analogous claims of psychoanalytic subjects?

Moreover, as Kris himself notes, the improvement in recall which sometimes follows the presentation of an interpretation must not be assumed to "produce" the recall: the interpretation can be viewed only as a *help* to better recall. Even with this reservation, however, one is begging the question in supposing that it is the *specific content* of an interpretation, as distinct from the over-all directed prodding of the subject's memory that takes place during the interview, that accounts for the improved recall. More generally, the changes in various symptoms which the patient exhibits as the interview progresses do not constitute critical evidence for an *interpretation*, unless it can be shown that such changes are not produced by some combination of factors for which the interview as a whole is responsible. There is at any rate some ground for the suspicion that the interpretations are frequently imposed on data which are themselves manufactured by the psychoanalytic method. Can an adult who is recalling childhood experiences remember them as he actually experienced them, or does he report them in terms of ideas which carry the burden of much of his later experience, including the experience of a psychoanalytic interview? Is an adult "regressing" to a childish attitude who, in order to recapture a childhood experience, may find it necessary to put himself into a childish frame of mind? I do not pretend to know the answers to such questions. But neither am I convinced that adequate attention has been paid to them by most analysts.

(d) [Psychoanalysts are] not very explicit about [the] second suggested way of supplying an objective support for an interpretation, namely, by the use of established laws in developmental psychology. [They seem to be saying] that different types of neurotic personality can be distinguished, and that each type is in fact associated with a fairly distinctive kind of childhood traumatic experience. Accordingly, once the analyst has determined by way of the interview to which type his patient belongs, his interpretation is supported by an appeal to the corresponding law. Now I agree that such a procedure would make an interpretation prima facie credible, if indeed there are well-established regularities of the kind indicated. Nevertheless, though I am not in the position to question the claim that there are such regularities, I would like to be clearer about their nature. In the first place, do the regularities hold between manifest neurotic symptoms and the *allegations* patients belonging to a certain type make concerning their childhood experiences, or between neurotic symptoms and *actual childhood experiences* whose occurrence has been ascertained independently of the subjects' memories of them? If it is the former, the evidential value of such a regularity for a given interpretation is dubious, for reasons too obvious to need explicit mention.

But in the second place, and on either alternative, the fact that some event or attribute B occurs with a certain relative frequency p when some other event or attribute A occurs, is not sufficient to show that A and B are significantly related—unless there is further evidence that the relative frequency of B in the absence of A, or the relative frequency of the non-occurrence of B in the presence of A, is markedly different from p. Thus, the fact that many men who have certain kinds of traumatic experiences in childhood develop into neurotic adults does not establish a causal relation between the two, if there is about the same proportion of men who undergo similar childhood experiences but develop into reasonably normal adults. In short, data must be analyzed so as to make possible comparisons on the basis of some *control* group, if they are to constitute cogent evidence for a causal inference. The introduction of such controls is the *minimum* requirement for the reliable interpretation and use of empirical data. I am therefore not impressed by [the] assertion that psychoanalytic

interpretations are based on a great wealth of observations, for it is not the sheer *quantity* of data that is of moment but their probative strength. I am not aware, however, that analysts have in fact subjected their clinical data to systematic and critical statistical scrutiny. I have not read everything that Freud wrote, and I may be doing him an injustice in supposing that he cannot be rightly accused of having made such a scrutiny. But at any rate I have not found in the books of his I have read, in some of which he announced what he regarded as important changes in his theoretical views because of fresh clinical evidence, that these changes were controlled by the elementary logical principle to which I have just been calling attention.

(e) This is a convenient place to say a few words about the evidence supplied for Freudian theory by psychoanalytic therapy. I agree . . . that the adequacy of the theory should not be *equated* with the success of its therapy. Nevertheless, the evidence from the latter is not surely irrelevant to the former. Unfortunately, information about the effectiveness of Freudian therapy is notoriously difficult to obtain, and I am in any case not sufficiently familiar with whatever material is available to have a reasoned opinion about it. . . .

(f) There is one final point I wish to make. Psychoanalytic interpretations frequently assert that the present difficulties of a patient have their source in an unfulfilled wish of early childhood, which persists in self-identical manner and produces discord in the unconscious stratum of mentality. It is pertinent to ask, therefore, what is the evidence for the tacit assumption that none of the events that have transpired since that early traumatic experience need be considered in accounting for the patient's present neurosis. For even if one grants that such a childhood experience is an indispensable condition for an adult neurosis, the assumption that the repressed wish has continued to operate essentially unmodified in the subject's unconscious, despite the countless number of more proximate happenings in the subject's life, cannot be accepted as a matter of course. If I understand correctly the import of investigations such as those on the impact of thirst on cognition, to which Dr. Hartmann refers, they are not only irrelevant for establishing this assumption, but point in the opposite direction. Indeed, the available evidence on the influence of education and cultural conditioning upon the development of human personality casts serious doubt on that assumption. Without this assumption, however, the clinical data obtained in psychoanalytic interviews do not confirm the typical interpretations that, were they sound, would support Freudian theory.

A possible rejoinder to the difficulties I have been raising is that despite the dubious character of the evidence for Freudian theory, it is the only theory we do possess that explains in a systematic way an extensive domain of important phenomena. To such a comment I can only reply that this is indeed most unfortunate if true, but that nonetheless the imaginative sweep of a set of ideas does not confer factual validity upon them. I do not minimize the importance of having *some* theory, even a dubious one, if it helps to open up fresh areas of investigation and if it is a source of fruitful ideas for the conduct of controlled inquiry. I certainly acknowledge the great service Freud and his school have rendered in directing attention to neglected aspects of human behavior, and in contributing a large number of suggestive notions which have leavened and broadened the scope of psychological, medical and anthropological inquiry. But on the Freudian theory itself, as a body of doctrine for which factual validity can be reasonably claimed, I can only echo the Scottish verdict: Not proven.

2.

WAELDER, ROBERT

Psychoanalysis, Scientific Method, and Philosophy*

*   *   *

There was much discussion whether psychoanalysis could be called "scientific" or whether it was a candidate for future scientific status with something like a learner's permit—a "protoscience"—or whether it was "more like phrenology, chiropractic or Christian Science" . . . Several speakers felt that psychoanalytic theories were sufficiently ambiguous so that any kind of experience could be taken as confirming them and that psychoanalysts had not supplied adequate evidence for their theories wherever they are unambiguous. . . .

The evidence that psychoanalysts are asked to supply should consist of experiments or adequate statistics, undertaken on the material of sense perceptions; no allowance is being made for the kind of reasoning that we all apply in historical matters, or for the data of introspection or empathy. The condemnation of psychoanalysis for the failure to apply such evidence ranged from the fairly urbane indictment . . . that the "verdict" is "not proven," to considerably less urbane statements . . . "As a set of hypotheses [psychoanalysis] was a great achievement fifty years ago; as no more than a set of hypotheses it is a great disgrace today." This contributor seemed to advocate legal or other action against the practice of psychoanalysis; after pointing out that "experimental design in this area is difficult" but "far from . . . impossible" he stated that "we have the resources, the need and the absolute moral obligation to execute such experiments before encouraging *or condoning*

* 10 *J. American Psychoanalytic Association*, 1962. (pp. 622–636). Reprinted by permission.

the further practice of psychoanalysis" (italics mine).

Against verbal assault of this kind, the defenders of psychoanalysis took two positions: they either tried to point out that evidence of the kind requested by the critics did, in fact, exist, but was very complex and therefore difficult to present to the public in full; or they argued that psychoanalysis was still a young science; when given more time, such evidence would eventually be forthcoming.

Before entering into consideration of this issue, a digression on exactitude in science may be permitted. The so-called exact sciences, particularly physics and chemistry, have been able to make quantitative predictions of a high degree of accuracy, and this intellectual achievement—apart from any question of practical application—has rightly been the marvel of the modern world. It means no diminution for the genius of the great men who built the edifice of the exact sciences to reflect on the conditions which have made this exactness possible. It seems to me that there are four conditions prerequisite for such exactness:

1. In order to be able to provide exact proof, the events which we study must be contemporary; they must happen right here and now, and they must be repeated over and over again, either spontaneously like the movements of the stars, or they must be capable of being repeated at will. Whenever the object of our study lies in the past—of the universe as in cosmology, of the earth as in geology, of animal life as in palaeontology, of human events as in archaeology and history, of an individual life as in the rules of evidence in a case of law—the direct evidence cannot be supplied. All that we have is some form of indirect, or circumstantial, evidence.

In the natural sciences, the theory of evolution through natural selection is a case in point. It is generally looked upon as a scientific theory, and as one of the major scientific achievements of modern time. Yet, direct evidence can only be said to exist for very small evolutionary changes due to the differential survival of micromutations; e.g., the change from a strain of rabbits that is almost always killed by myxomatosis to a strain that is fairly resistant to it; or the daily changes of micro-organisms in response to the introduction of antibiotics. But there is, of course, no such evidence for macromutations and megamutations with which the theory of evolution stands and falls.

Charles Singer, the great historian of science, once commented on this situation as follows: "Evolution is perhaps unique among major scientific theories in that the appeal for its acceptance is not that there is any evidence for it but that any other proposed interpretation of the data is wholly incredible."

But is evolution really unique in this respect? On what else do we base our belief that there lived, in the late fifteenth and early sixteenth centuries, a seafarer named Christopher Columbus who wanted to find a Western sea route to the Indies, was commissioned for his journey by Ferdinand of Aragon and Isabella of Castile, and discovered America in the process? All this rests on reports of various kinds, and reports can be mistaken or mendacious; no reproduction of the events is possible. But we accept these reports as true in their main outline—after having subjected them to exacting criticism according to what the historians call the "historic method"—because it is enormously unlikely that so many reports from different and apparently independent sources should fit so well together unless they all derived from the same real events; in short, we accept the story of Columbus "because any other proposed interpretation of the data is wholly incredible." The same is true when the criminal investigator tries to reconstruct a crime on the basis of confessions, testimony of witnesses, or circumstantial evidence, or a combination of them; we are satisfied that this reconstruction is correct when any alternate interpretation is utterly incredible.

This consideration is also the basis for the deciphering of a script—or indeed for the very assumption that certain frequently recurrent designs on stone, or clay, or parchment are characters of a script and not, e.g., mere decorations—for the deciphering of an enemy code, or the reconstruction of an ancient, forgotten language. These are all historical interpretations because what is reconstructed is the meaning of a sign for those who put it there, or how an ancient people spoke. There is no complete evidence that this was so; we cannot conjure it up and listen. It might all be a delusion, a vast edifice of interlocking errors—except for the fact that *the reconstructions fit an enormous mass of data from many sources* and that the probability of this all being a matter of coincidence is so infinitesimal as to be negligible.

* * *

2. In order to be able to make exact statements about cause-effect relationships, it is necessary that the variables of a subject be *loosely coupled*, so that it is possible to study the effect of a single variable alone, or at least to study not more than two or three variables at a time. Where the variables are very closely coupled, so that whenever one variable changes, a host of others change simultaneously, conclusive evidence as to cause and effect is very difficult to come by, as is the case in all biological sciences.

3. Then there is a special case of this factor which deserves special attention. It must be possible to assume that the subject matter under study does not significantly change during the investigation, i.e., that nature is holding still long enough for the examination to be finished. If this is not the case, we are faced with a new unknown in our material.

This condition is not always met in the study of living organisms, e.g., a virus may change its virulence quickly. In our own field, the living patient before us is changing constantly. The psychoneuroses seem to have changed since the early days of psychoanalysis, with simple and rather transparent cases of *grande hystérie* retreating from sophisticated urban quarters and being reported from backwaters only; and, in general, with repression, the simple form of defense, giving way to more complicated mechanisms.

This point is of particular importance whenever "evidence" would require very time-consuming research. Not only may programs of this kind be impractical, they may be theoretically unsound because we have no right to assume that the world does not evolve in the meantime.

4. Finally, very exact answers to questions can often be given if the subjects with which we deal are very small in relation to ourselves and to all things that matter to us. In that case, what we care about practically is not what happens to these small individual units but merely what happens to large aggregates of them. In this case, probability considerations may give us all the information we need.

All these conditions prevail in physics and chemistry, and they contribute to making these disciplines as admirably exact as they are. They do not exist in many other disciplines, particularly not in the biological and social sciences. The physicist deals only with contemporary, reproducible events. There are questions which can be asked about the past of a physical system—e.g., the past of the surface of the earth—but the disciplines that ask such questions are no longer called physics. The physicist keeps his record of exactitude clean simply by relegating such questions to other disciplines.

The coupling of variables in the subject matter of physics is happily loose. And the possibility of historical change can be neglected in inanimate nature; the laws of gravitation and the gravitational constant are apparently the same today as they were at the time of Ptolemy. If inanimate things should change their characteristics at all, there is every reason to assume that the change is too slow to be noticeable in historical time. As has already been pointed out, this assumption cannot be made for living matter.

Finally, those events in which we have a practical stake involve large agglomerations of particles, and statistical treatment is therefore adequate for our needs. In the latter respect, the exactitude of physics as compared with that of other disciplines rests again not on the actual power of foresight but on the nature of the questions asked. Physics shows up so much better than, say, medicine, because simpler questions are presented to it.

* * *

It is, of course, different with the matters with which psychoanalysis deals. Our subject matter lies partly in the past—the life history of a person. Even when we deal with "contemporary" events it is often a matter of dealing with the recent past—e.g., an anxiety attack just before the hour, a dream of last night, a family quarrel over the week end—and in this sense historical. All variables are closely interrelated; we have no chance of observing the change of one without the simultaneous change of many others. Our subject is changing while we are working with him, is maturing or declining, and is assimilating experience in the process of living. We are definitely interested in an individual and his destiny and not content with statistical answers. For all these reasons, the prospects of exactness are not too good.

In their efforts to justify psychoanalysis in terms of the standards of the "exact sciences," psychoanalysts often make claims for the possibility of prediction in psychoanalysis which do not seem well founded to me. For example, Arlow gave as an instance of prediction his experience with a patient whose meticulously detailed answers to questions in the initial interview permitted him to predict that certain other characteristics, such as monetary acquisitiveness and a particular emphasis on cleanliness, would also be present. This is certainly true, but it is not the kind of prediction that those who consider prediction the touchstone of science have in mind. For what Arlow has done was to infer from the observation of certain symptoms of the obsessive-compulsive character the existence of other traits of this type. It is the same as if a doctor made a diagnosis on the basis of some symptoms and now felt certain that other, as yet unobserved, symptoms of the disease would be there, too. *Ex ungue leonem*—you can tell the lion from the claw; if the hunter in the jungle sees a lion's paw through the foliage, he can "predict" that the lion's body will be there, too. But what we mean by prediction in science is more than that: it is not only that certain features always occur together, so that from the existence of some we can infer the existence of others, but that we are able to foresee *future changes* of the situation; or, in medical language, that we have prognosis and not merely diagnosis.

The power of prediction, in this sense, is actually not very great in psychoanalysis and is not likely ever to become very great, for reasons which were pointed out by Freud: our ignorance of the quantitative factor which makes it impossible to predict the outcome in the case of conflict.

*   *   *

I have discussed at some length the advantages that are enjoyed by physics and chemistry. But not all the advantages are on one side, nor all the disadvantages on the other. There is another aspect of the matter, which has not yet been touched upon. The kind of evidence that I have so far considered and that psychoanalysis has been asked by its critics to supply is exclusively outside evidence, i.e., evidence of the kind required for statements about atoms and molecules and physical matters in general. It overlooks the fact that we have one source of knowledge about psychic events that is completely lacking in matters of the physical world, viz., *introspection* and its equivalent in the observation of human beings, which, for the purposes of this discussion, I propose to call *empathy*.

It is very difficult, perhaps impossible, to prove by mere outside evidence even so simple a statement as this: John is deeply in love with Mary. It is desperately difficult to find clear criteria to distinguish deep love from more shallow relationships, or from make-believe, or self-deception. But is it really necessary? Are introspection and empathy not sources of information too, *not infallible*, to be sure, *but not negligible* either? And if the very tight coupling of many variables and the fact that we are vitally interested not only in the statistical behavior of large aggregates but in the behavior of individual entities—if these conditions are disadvantages in our discipline as compared with physics and chemistry, one must hold against them the great advantage, not enjoyed by the latter sciences, that we know much about our subject through introspection and empathy, a source not open to the physicist or the chemist.

The story of the ugly duckling is well known. Other ducks called him ugly and looked down on him until it turned out that he was not a misfit of a duckling but a specimen of another, beautiful kind of bird, a swan. Psychoanalysis, largely, though by no means entirely, a matter of introspection and empathy, is treated as though it were a purely physicalistic discipline, and scolded and berated for its deficiencies as such. It is time to understand that the ugly duckling is not a duckling at all.

The interpretations offered by the psychoanalyst to his patient point out inner connections that can be fully experienced. Of course, any individual interpretation that is suggested in the course of an analysis may or may not be correct; the patient may or may not accept it, and his acceptance or rejection may be caused by realistic estimates or by emotional prejudices. But as analysis proceeds, mistaken interpretations will gradually wither away, inaccurate or incomplete interpretations will gradually be amended or completed, and emotional prejudices of the patient will gradually be overcome. In a successful analysis, the patient eventually becomes aware of the previously unconscious elements in his neurosis: he can fully feel and experience how his neurotic symptoms grew out of the conflicts of which he is now conscious; and he can fully feel and experience how facing up to these conflicts dispels the symptoms and, as Freud put it, "transforms neurotic suffering into everyday misery"; and how flinching will bring the symptoms back again. There are patients who, at a late stage of their analysis or after its termination, can virtually make and unmake their previous symptoms at will.

These conditions are obviously difficult to envisage for those who have never experienced them, either in themselves or in the close observation of others; hence the clamor for a proof that would be convincing for *them*, too, without experience of this kind.

The speakers in the Symposium, as laymen in general, talked of "cure" of a neurosis in the sense in which an attack of common cold is cured: all symptoms of the disease disappear. There are cures of this kind in psychoanalysis, particularly in the case of those who can work out a completely satisfactory solution of their conflicts. But in many instances, "cure" is not a completely stable equilibrium; it needs eternal vigilance, like freedom. The new equilibrium is more like that of a high Gothic structure, needing constant repair, than like that of a Roman basilica. The symptoms will recur or threaten to recur, but the patient has learned to deal with them through self-analysis.

A person of great intelligence and sound judgment, with little formal schooling, who had undergone analytic treatment for a psychoneurosis (anxiety hysteria) wrote about eight months after termination of his analysis: "It is not easy adjusting to independence. . . . However, with a great deal of effort I have been able to arrive at a degree of self-honesty that eliminates the anxiety I occasionally feel threatened by." This is a beautiful account of the situation; symptoms threaten again, but this graduate of analysis is able each time to solve them by self-analysis, so that the threatening symptoms are dissipated again.

Whenever a psychoanalyst is satisfied that he has untied the Gordian knot of a neurosis and has correctly understood its dynamics and its psychogenesis, his confidence is based on two kinds of data, one of outside observation of events, the other of the patient's self-observation. The first is the experience, repeated countless times during the working-through period of the analysis and again countless times during the person's later life, that this particular interpretation, or set of interpretations, and no other, can dispel the symptoms when they reappear, that they alone are the key that opens the lock; because particularly in the more serious neurosis of long standing, successful analytic therapy often does not bring about an ideal "cure" in the sense of our utopian desires, a traceless disappearance of disturbances without any price to be paid for it, but rather the ability to conquer them and to maintain a good, though contrived rather than stable, balance by vigilance and effort.

Then, as is well described in the above-quoted words of a former patient, there is an inner experience; what had been unconscious can now be consciously felt. To be sure, it is not always immediately available but can be felt if a real effort is made.

It is interesting and noteworthy that the only *practitioner* of an exact science who participated in this Symposium, the physicist Percy W. Bridgman (Harvard University), was also the only one among the nonanalytic speakers who had a clear realization of the role of inner experience in psychoanalysis. ". . . some of the features," he said in a very brief but meaty comment, "which distinguish psychoanalysis from other disciplines can be explained by the prominent role that introspection plays. This role is fundamental, because without the introspectional report that the analyst is able to draw from the patient some of the basic concepts of the analyst are merely verbal constructs. . . ."

*   *   *

Several speakers in this Symposium contended that psychoanalytic theory is so vague and ambiguous that whatever the facts may be, the psychoanalyst can always, by some twist, claim them as a corroboration of his theory.

These ideas about psychoanalysis seem to be based partly on the concept of overcompensation, or reaction formation, and partly on the concept of resistance. Since it is possible, according to psychoanalytic theory, that a reaction formation against an instinctual drive has taken place—e.g., solicitude for every living creature as a reaction formation against cruelty —the analyst can now, so our critics think, attribute both aggressiveness and kindness to the aggressive drives, the former as a direction expression, the latter as an overcompensation, and claim that his theory of aggressive drives is corroborated if he meets with savagery or if he meets with kindness—in fact by any kind of behavior.

Since the idea of compensation is not limited to psychoanalysis, this argument is rather widely applicable. There is, for example, the theory of immunity, according to which an organism that has gone through an infectious disease thereby often acquires immunity against it. Applying the argument of our critics, we might say that this is circular reasoning, too; for if a person falls ill, one can attribute it to invasion by a parasitic organism, and if he does not fall ill, one can attribute it to immunity acquired in consequence of such an invasion. If this is not the same argument, I wish to be shown the difference. The critic, in both instances, attacks a grotesque distortion of what the theory in question actually says.

In quite the same way, these critics seem to think, the psychoanalyst evaluates the response of his patient to his interpretations. If the patient accepts the interpretations offered by his analyst, the analyst will consider them thereby proved; if the patient rejects them, the analyst will take this as resistance and will in turn claim that the resistance proves his interpretations to be correct. Life is thus very simple for an analyst; his ground rules are: heads I win, tails you lose.

The argument probably stems from Freud's statement that there is no "No" in the unconscious; it is, of course, spurious. It is not true that in psychoanalysis, both acceptance and rejection of an interpretation are taken as corroborations. On the contrary, *neither* the acceptance *nor* the rejection of an interpretation by the patient indicates that the interpretation is or is not correct. Freud expressed himself on this point without any ambiguity, and since the myth of self-serving circular reasoning has a tenacious life, a full quotation of Freud's statement on this point may be made.[1]

> A plain "Yes" from a patient is by no means unambiguous. It can indeed signify that he recognizes the correctness of the construction that has been presented to him; but it can also be meaningless, or can even deserve to be described as "hypocritical," since it may be convenient for his resistance to make use of an assent in such circumstances in order to prolong the concealment of a truth that has not been discovered. The "Yes" has no value unless it is followed by indirect confirmations, unless the patient, immediately after his "Yes," produces new memories which complete and extend the construction. Only in such an event do we consider that the "Yes" has dealt completely with the subject under discussion.
>
> A "No" from a person in analysis is no more unambiguous than a "Yes," and is indeed of even less value. In some rare cases it turns out to be the expression of a legitimate dissent. Far more frequently it expresses a resistance which may have been evoked by the subject-matter of the construction that has been put forward but which may just as easily have arisen from some other factor in the complex analytic situation. Thus, a patient's "No" is no evidence of the correctness of a construction, though it is perfectly compatible with it.

[A] new ornament to the old argument [is] the proposition that in empirical science as different from dogmatic revelation, it must be possible to state, for every hypothesis, what kind of observations would, if they were made, disprove the hypothesis.

This proposition is, of course, unchallengeable. For instance, we believe that procreation in mammals depends on the fertilization of the egg by the sperm; but a clearly established case of parthenogenesis would show that the sperm is not an absolutely necessary condition and the statement would have to be discarded or qualified. Since every empirical theory is based on a set of observations (A), the observation of (non-A) would disprove the theory. It does not matter how unlikely (non-A) may be; all that matters is that it is *thinkable;* if no set of observations is thinkable that would disprove a proposition, what we have is not a scientific theory but a prejudice or a paranoid system.

By this test, psychoanalytic theories can easily qualify as empirical theories. In any *individual* analysis, the hypotheses which are formed in earlier stages of the analysis are often disproved and almost always modified in the further courses of events as more and more facts become known. *General* theories that have been distilled from countless theories about individual cases could all be disproved by the appearance of appropriate material, e.g., the theory that repression, or an equivalent mechanism, is a *conditio sine qua non* of psychoneurosis would be disproved by presenting a case of hysteria, phobia, or obsessional neurosis in which, as far as can be determined, all inner conflicts have never ceased to be fully accessible to consciousness and no repression of any part or aspect of them be detected.

* * *

Ernest Nagel pointed out that psychoanalysis sees all behavior as motivated, and since not all behavior is consciously motivated, the theory introduces unconscious motives: "these unconscious motives, wishes, drives, urges and intentions must be regarded as 'psychic' or 'mental processes.' " On the other hand, Nagel points out, these unconscious mental processes are really different from conscious motives; e.g., unconscious wishes may be directed toward a dead person while conscious wishes are not. Here Professor Nagel finds a contradiction in the theory; on the one hand, unconscious wishes are believed to be psychic forces, hence like conscious ones; on the other hand, they are not like them because they may desire what we consciously do not: ". . . there is an important failure of analogy between conscious motives and unconscious mental processes, so that it is only by a radical shift in the customary meanings of such words as 'motive' and 'wish' that Freudian theory can be said to offer an explanation of human conduct in terms of motivations and wish-fulfillments." In short, since psychoanalysis claims that one can unconsciously wish things that a sane mind recognizes as impossible of fulfillment, it follows, according to Nagel, that Freud's unconscious is not a psychic thing at all.

The problem that proved so disturbing to Professor Nagel seems easy enough to solve. The unconscious as seen by Freud is a psychic phenomenon; true, our concept of what is psychic does stem from our conscious experience, but it need not simply be identical with it; *not every characteristic of adult conscious life need necessarily enter into our concept of what is "physic."* Some of these characteristics may be considered to be accidental rather than essential, and the high degree of integration and reality adjustment of our adult thinking is one of those accidentals. The definition which I have suggested on another occasion might take care of this "difficulty": "Freud's basic discovery was that of an effective unconscious psychic life, the contents of which are not funda-

---

1. The quoted statement deals with constructions, i.e., historical interpretations with a considerable element of conjectural restoration of lacunae of memory; but the words apply just as well to all kinds of interpretation.

mentally different from those of consciousness, though closer to the infantile than the adult mind"— *not fundamentally different*, but not necessarily identical.

By his difficulty of accepting the unconscious as something psychic because it does not show *all* the characteristics of the conscious mind of an adult at its most highly integrated, Professor Nagel has deprived himself of the possibility of understanding the fundamental point of psychoanalytic therapy, namely, the fact that psychoanalytic therapy is based on this very difference between the conscious and the unconscious mind—the contents of the former being in contact with each other, including the perceptions of the outside world, while the contents of the latter are isolated. Repression, which makes psychic content unconscious, thereby also protects it from the wear and tear of life, and the forces of adjustment begin to work again as soon as repression has been lifted and the unconscious content has entered consciousness.

* * *

NOTE

HOSPERS, JOHN

Philosophy and Psychoanalysis*

* * *

1. The charge [is] often made . . . that psychoanalytic theory is defective because . . . one and the same fact is made to prove two opposite things. I believe that this charge is unfounded, and would like to refer to [an example] to illustrate this.

"If the patient is aggressive, this may be taken as an indication that he really *is* aggressive; on the other hand, it may be taken as an indication of the opposite, that he is really passive and that the aggressiveness is only a defense against the passivity."

This is taken as an example of an empirical fact that is (erroneously, the philosophers believe) used to confirm two opposed hypotheses. But it is the philosophers who are in error: (i) While I agree that the same fact cannot *prove* (conclusively establish) two different hypotheses, the same fact can *confirm* (count

* Reprinted from: *Psychoanalysis, Scientific Method and Philosophy*, Hook, Sidney (ed.). New York: New York University Press, 1959. (pp. 339–342). Reprinted by permission.

toward establishing) two different hypotheses, depending on what the *other* facts are. The smile on a person's face may indicate that the person is friendly, but it may also indicate that he is unfriendly; to know which it was we might have to examine his behavior over a considerable period. His smile might reveal a genuine friendly feeling, but it might be a mask concealing hatred or resentment. How absurd it would be to argue: "A smile is taken on one occasion to indicate friendliness and on another occasion to prove unfriendliness. But it is fallacious to take one and the same empirical phenomenon sometimes to confirm one hypothesis and sometimes to confirm its opposite." . . .

. . . (ii) in the example of aggressive behavior, it is *not* "the same fact" that is taken to confirm two opposed hypotheses; for the behavioral manifestations in the two cases are really very different. They are similar enough for both to be called "aggressiveness," and people who are not very observant may mistake the one for the other, but the analyst wouldn't be worth his salt who could not distinguish the one kind from the other in a person's behavior. "Real" aggression is stirred into action only when there is genuine provocation from the outside world; neurotic aggression (pseudo-aggression, as it is called) is unconsciously *self-provoked*. Real aggression is roughly proportionate to the degree of provocation; pseudo-aggression lashes out at the slightest provocation, real or imaginary. Real aggression is used to harm the aggressor and to protect oneself; pseudo-aggression damages the aggressor (and according to the psychoanalysts, this is its unconscious aim, since this is the effect that it unerringly achieves). Real aggression is used only in self-defense or for personal gain; neurotic aggression is used indiscriminately, against an innocent bystander as much as against a real offender. Real aggression is ordinarily timed so as to wait till the enemy is vulnerable; pseudo-aggression is "trigger-happy"—it is characterized by an inability to wait. (Explanation: since it is used as a defense against psychic masochism, and since the reproach of psychic masochism is constantly made, the defense is also constant, and cannot wait until the enemy is vulnerable.) The theory of psychic dynamics underlying these cases would take many pages to explain; but in any case the fallacy that is charged is not committed here. What is required is an astute observation of many kinds of behavioral detail. . . .

* * *

F.

Are the Topographic and Structural Theories Compatible?

1.

ARLOW, JACOB A. and BRENNER, CHARLES

Psychoanalytic Concepts and the Structural Theory*

[I]t is our conviction that the topographic and the structural theories are neither compatible nor interchangeable. We maintain that it is actually disadvantageous to use the terms of the two theories interchangeably and to speak of the id, the ego, and the superego in one breath and of the unconscious, the preconscious, and the conscious in the next, a practice which . . . is so widespread among analysts as to be nearly universal.

The two theories, in fact, which are so similar in many respects, are so different in others as to be incompatible with one another. Nor are these differences of minor importance. On the contrary, they have principally to do with the topic of unconscious mental conflict, an area of vital importance in psychoanalysis.

[T]he structural theory is the more satisfactory of the two. It is distinctly superior to the topographic one. For this reason it has largely replaced the topographic theory, often to a greater degree than has been explicitly realized. It is, we feel, the theory which psychoanalysts should apply to the understanding of all mental phenomena.

* * *

Freud very early introduced the concept of a mental or psychic apparatus, whose function it is to deal with the energies of the mind by binding or discharging them. . . . In the metapsychological papers of 1915 . . . the psychic apparatus was conceived of as comprising three systems, called the Unconscious (*Ucs.*), the Preconscious (*Pcs.*), and the Conscious (*Cs.*) or Perceptual–Conscious (*Pcpt.–Cs.*), respectively, of which the systems *Pcs.* and *Cs.* were sometimes grouped together as the system *Cs.–Pcs.* because of the intimate functional relationship between them. The three systems, *Ucs.*, *Pcs.*, and *Cs.*, were often referred to as regions of the mind, and it is for this reason that the theory of the psychic apparatus which includes them is generally known as the topographic one.

In 1923, in *The Ego and the Id*, Freud introduced

* New York: International Universities Press, 1964. (pp. 3–42, 84–102). Reprinted by permission.

major conceptual changes and a new terminology into the psychoanalytic theory of the psychic apparatus. . . . He discarded the idea of dividing the psychic apparatus according to the accessibility or inaccessibility of its various elements to consciousness. Instead he proposed to distinguish two systems within the mind which he called the id and the ego. The ego was further subdivided by distinguishing within it a particular group of mutually related functions to be called the superego. Because these innovations were of a major order, their introduction is usually signalized by calling Freud's second theory of the psychic apparatus by a new name: the structural theory.

It is customary, therefore, to distinguish between two psychoanalytic theories of the psychic apparatus of which the one, the topographic theory, divides the apparatus into systems on the basis of the criterion: accessible to consciousness v. inaccessible to consciousness, while the other, the structural theory, divides it on the basis: inner world (manifestations of the instinctual drives) v. outer world (external environment).

It is important to realize that the distinction between these two theories and the nomenclature which marks that distinction are essentially matters of generally accepted custom and convenience. The structural and topographic theories were never named as such and presented by Freud in finished or "final" form. They are groups of related ideas within the area of psychoanalytic theory which have never been precisely delineated. That is, no one has ever said explicitly which parts of psychoanalytic theory prior to 1923 were to be included within the term "topographic theory" nor which parts after 1923 were to be understood as comprising the structural theory. It has simply been understood in a general way that each theory comprises a group of related ideas having to do particularly with the nature and functioning of what Freud called the mental apparatus.

* * *

The Topographic Theory

* * *

. . . [W]e wish to emphasize the following: That the central idea of the topographic theory is that the psychic apparatus can be divided into systems on the basis of their relationship to consciousness. As regards mental conflict, what is of prime importance in the topographic theory is whether the wish which gives rise to conflict is or is not accessible to consciousness. Freud himself made this clear. In "The Unconscious" he mentioned the possibility of an alternative basis for dividing the mental apparatus and rejected it because, he said, whether a particular mental element is conscious or not is the starting point of our investigations as analysts. He maintained that we must therefore hold to it as a guide to our theoretical formulations. It is worth noting, parenthetically, that the alternative basis which Freud rejected in 1915 was precisely the one which he eventually adopted in 1923 as the central idea of the structural theory. We can see here clearly one of the basic differences between the topographic and the structural theory. . . . [W]e may proceed to present the topographic theory in more detail.

Just a few words of definition. (1) The amount of mental energy invested in a mental process or representation is called its cathexis. (2) The aspect of mental functioning which has to do with the amount of mental energy involved in any particular mental phenomenon is called the economic (i.e., quantitative) aspect of that phenomenon. (3) We have . . . defined mental energy itself as deriving from the instinctual drives and as impelling the mind to activity. It is assumed that instinctual gratification results in a discharge of mental energy and that mental activity of whatever sort is accompanied by a transfer or flow of mental energy.

*   *   *

The System Ucs.

[T]he system Ucs. is defined by the fact that its elements are (1) inaccessible to consciousness. In addition it is characterized (2) by a particular mode of functioning, known as the primary process; (3) by the nonverbal nature of its memory traces; (4) by the fact that it is incapable of any form of mentation other than to wish, i.e., by the fact that it operates according to the pleasure principle; (5) by its relation to the instinctual life; and (6) by its generally infantile character.

*   *   *

Primary Process. Thus far we have discussed the relationship between the systems Ucs. and Pcs. in spatial terms, as though each were a region of the mind which could be physically and spatially distinguished from the other. This is a convenient fiction for many purposes. Indeed it is responsible for the very name of the theory, since "topographic" means "having to do with the configuration of an area." However, even in 1900 Freud made it clear that the systems of the mind he proposed to distinguish cannot be thought of as different localities except in a

figurative sense. . . . He explained that the proper way to define the systems Ucs. and Pcs. is in terms of energy discharge and potential. The system Ucs., for example, is properly defined as comprising those mental elements and processes which function according to the primary process. The systems Pcs. and Cs. by the same token comprise whatever in the mind functions according to the secondary process. Since we are at the moment concerned with a description of the system Ucs., the question for us to answer here is: "What is the primary process?"

The primary process is so called because it is the earlier of the two modes of mental functioning which are distinguished by the topographic theory. In early childhood, when the system Ucs. comprises nearly the whole of the mental apparatus, its mode of operation is the only mode of functioning of the mind. Not until later does a different mode of functioning, to be called the secondary process, appear. The words "primary" and "secondary" have only this temporal, developmental connotation. They are not intended to convey any idea of relative importance. In fact, the secondary process is assumed to become dominant eventually in the normal adult.

The principal feature of the primary process is a tendency to the complete discharge of mental energies without delay. Thus cathexes of mental energy subject to the primary process press continuously for discharge. This may be observed, for example, in connection with the instinctual wishes of early childhood, when the primary process holds undisputed sway over the mind. It is easy to see how imperiously such wishes demand gratification. The same imperious demand for gratification characterizes instinctual demands within the system Ucs. throughout life.

Two other characteristics of the primary process are (a) that cathexes of mental energy which follow the primary process are readily displaced, or highly mobile, and (b) that such cathexes are readily condensed. The clinical observations which lend support to these assumptions are the following. When one is able to trace back to their origins the consequences of the operation of the primary process, i.e., when one is able to analyze a neurotic symptom, a dream, a joke, or a parapraxis, one often discovers that in the course of formation of the symptom, dream, etc., ideas and images have substituted one for the other with an ease and freedom quite different from what one is used to in ordinary, conscious thinking. Such observations are accounted for by the concept of ready displaceability of cathexes. Cathexes pass easily from one idea or image to another. They are highly mobile. In addition, one discovers from such analyses that many ideas are often represented by a single thought or image. That is, the cathexes originally distributed over many mental elements have become condensed on a single element.

*   *   *

The System Pcs.

1. The system *Pcs.* comprises those elements of the mind which are accessible to consciousness. For an element of the system *Ucs.* to become conscious, it must first become preconscious. This it does . . . by becoming joined to the corresponding word traces. Thus elements of the system *Pcs.*, and in particular memory traces which belong to that system, are verbal in nature.

2. The censor between the systems *Ucs.* and *Pcs.* is a part of or one of the functions of the latter system. If the censor withdraws the word cathexis from a memory trace of the system *Pcs.*, that memory trace is repressed and is thenceforth part of the system *Ucs.* If the censor withholds cathexis from an element of the system *Ucs.*, that element must remain part of the system *Ucs.* It is likewise repressed. If, on the other hand, the censor permits an element of the system *Ucs.* to be cathected by the energy of the corresponding word memory, that element becomes a part of the system *Pcs.* and is thus accessible to consciousness.

3. The system *Pcs.* is not present from birth. It begins to develop in childhood, and as the individual grows to adulthood the system *Pcs.* gradually achieves ascendancy in the functioning of the mind. Because it is a secondary development in mental life, the mode of functioning which is characteristic of the system *Pcs.* is called the secondary process. The principal difference between the secondary and the primary processes is this: Mental energy which follows the primary process presses for immediate discharge, i.e., wishes of the system *Ucs.* strive for immediate gratification. On the other hand, mental energy which follows the secondary process can be bound, i.e., its discharge can be delayed temporarily or even, perhaps, indefinitely. In other words, wishes of instinctual origin which have gained access to the system *Pcs.* still press for gratification, but gratification may be postponed for a longer or shorter time in accordance with external realities, with the individual's own moral standards, etc. The system *Ucs.*, like the infant, is interested only in immediate gratification. The system *Pcs.*, a product of adulthood, is realistic, willing to wait, able to control its instinctual wishes.

4. The influence of realistic considerations upon the functioning of the system *Pcs.* is formulated as a regulatory principle of the mind, called the reality principle. The system *Ucs.* operates solely according to what is called the pleasure–unpleasure principle, or, more simply, the pleasure principle. According to this principle, the system *Ucs.* operates solely to avoid unpleasure and to achieve pleasure. It will be noted that this is identical with the earlier statement that in the system *Ucs.*, instinctual energy seeks prompt and complete discharge. The system *Pcs.*, on the other hand, though it too follows the pleasure principle, does so only with modifications. It delays the pleasurable discharge of instinctual energy in accordance with the dictates of reality, of conscience, of logic, etc. Thus the capacity to bind cathexes is intimately connected with the functioning of the reality principle, just as mobility of cathexes subserves the pleasure principle.

5. The binding of mental energy and the consequent delay in its discharge which characterize the functioning of the system *Pcs.* results in a higher cathectic level within the system *Pcs.* as a whole than exists in the system *Ucs.* in which mental energy is discharged as quickly as possible. Mental energy builds up within the system *Pcs.* much as water will be stored up behind a dam that prevents it from flowing away freely and promptly. The fact that the system *Pcs.* has such stored-up mental energy available to it permits it to function in a more precise and discriminating way than can the system *Ucs.* In particular, it can engage in that type of trial action that we call thought. In doing so it can solve problems without the great expenditure of mental energy that would be required by full action on a trial-and-error basis. It can accomplish the same result by expending a relatively very small amount of mental energy in thinking. Thus the functioning of the system *Pcs.* is more precise, more discriminating, and expends less mental energy than does the functioning of the system *Ucs.*

The System Cs.

We have already noted the close relationship between the system *Cs.* and the system *Pcs.* This is a relationship that develops *pari passu* with the development of the system *Pcs.* The tendency is for conscious awareness to be limited to (1) sensations due to stimuli from the outer word, and (2) events, i.e., thoughts, memories, emotions, etc., within the system *Pcs.* In other words, the normal waking adult is not directly conscious of anything going on in the system *Ucs.* As far as what is going on within his own mind is concerned, he can be conscious only of what is going on in the system *Pcs.* Elements of that system can be made conscious by being cathected by the system *Cs.* This cathexis is called the cathexis of attention. Elements of the system *Ucs.* cannot ordinarily be cathected by the system *Cs.*, that is, they cannot attract or receive the cathexis of attention. They must first become preconscious by being joined with the corresponding word trace. Thus, for an element of the system *Ucs.* to become conscious it must receive an additional cathexis or hypercathexis from two sources. First it must be cathected by the system *Pcs.*, i.e., it must receive the word cathexis that belongs to it; and second it must receive attention cathexis from the system *Cs.* Exceptions to this rule are to be found in dreaming, in jokes, and above all in neurotic symptom formation. Thus, for example, an obsessional idea does not become conscious by first being cathected by the system *Pcs*. On the contrary, it becomes conscious despite every effort on the part of the censor of the system *Pcs*. to repress it.

The system *Cs*., in addition to perceiving what goes on within the mind and in the outer world, has the function of controlling voluntary motor activity. Since the system *Pcs*., as we have noted, normally controls access to the system *Cs*., it follows that it is the system *Pcs*. which normally has control of external perception, of action, and of conscious awareness. It maintains its control by means of the intersystemic censor, i.e., by repression, and in this sense the censor is the guardian of mental health. . . .

This outline of the functions of the systems *Ucs*., *Pcs*., and *Cs*., as well as of the relations of the three systems with one another will suffice for our present purpose. We have attempted to pay particular attention in the course of our outline to the explanations offered by the topographic theory for the clinically observable data concerning intrapsychic conflict, since, as we shall see, it was precisely in this area that Freud eventually found the topographic theory to be inadequate.

Freud's Criticisms of the Topographic Theory

* * *

What were the clinical data which convinced Freud that the explanation which the topographic theory offers of intrapsychic conflict is unsatisfactory? What were the observations that convinced him of the need to revise the topographic theory into what we know as the structural one?

The two observations which Freud emphasized in *The Ego and the Id* were (1) that in neurotic conflicts the forces within the mind which oppose the sexual wishes in question are by no means always readily accessible to consciousness; and (2) that a need for punishment likewise may often be quite inaccessible to consciousness, or accessible to it only with great difficulty.

* * *

1. At the close of the first chapter of *The Ego and the Id* Freud illustrated the fact that anti-instinctual forces within the mind are often inaccessible to consciousness by the following example. When an unconscious wish becomes active in the mind of a patient in analysis as he is lying on the couch, it ordinarily makes itself known through its influence on his associations. If the wish is not a repressed one, the patient will express it more and more directly and will soon become himself aware of it. If, however, the wish is a repressed one, instead of expressing his wish more directly and becoming aware of it, at a certain point the patient will fall silent or change the

subject. It is clear to the analyst that the patient is resisting talking about the repressed wish. The patient himself, however, is quite unaware that he is trying to avoid saying something or to avoid thinking about something, i.e., that he is engaged in repressing a wish which, if he did not repress it, would become conscious. Moreover, it requires special work on the part of both the analyst and the patient before the patient can become aware that he is in fact resisting something, work which today we subsume under the heading of defense analysis, or, more generally, of ego analysis.

These facts are easy to observe and familiar to all analysts. What implications do they have for theory? In what way or ways do they contradict the topographic theory?

The contradiction is this. According to the topographic theory, the repressing agency of the mind is the censor of the system *Pcs*. Since it belongs to that system it should, by definition, be readily accessible to consciousness. The topographic theory makes no provision for the fact that mental forces which are responsible for repression can be inaccessible to consciousness, or accessible to it only with the help of analytic work. On the contrary, as we have seen, according to the topographic theory, anything active in the mind which is inaccessible to consciousness and which can be made conscious only by analysis must belong to the system *Ucs*. It could not possibly belong to the system *Pcs*. By the same token, still according to the topographic theory, it cannot be an anti-instinctual or repressing element of the mind. It must be a repressed sexual wish. Here then is a clear contradiction between fact and theory. Theory says that whatever is inaccessible to consciousness must be a repressed, sexual wish of the system *Ucs*. The fact is, however, that an anti-instinctual, repressing mental activity of the mind may be inaccessible to consciousness as well.

. . . If the mind is divided into systems on the basis of accessibility to consciousness, then mental conflict cannot be described as a conflict between two systems of the mind, i.e., between the systems *Ucs*. and *Pcs*. What is inaccessible to consciousness is not identical with what is instinctual. It includes at least some of what is anti-instinctual as well. What is important to realize in all this is that Freud considered the decisive reason for discarding the topographic theory to be the recognition that it did not offer an adequate explanation of mental conflict. It seems as though he reasoned in this way. As clinicians we see that the centrally important factor in mental life is conflict. In conflict one group of mental functions or tendencies is in opposition to another group. Any theory we have of the mental apparatus must give this fact first place. If we are to divide the mental apparatus into separate parts, the division must be along the lines of cleavage which are apparent in conflict; otherwise our theoretical division is of no use to us just where we need it the most in our practice. What we need in our practice is a theory that will help us to understand, to study, and to treat situations of intrapsychic conflict. Unless a theory takes conflict as its starting point therefore, it is not likely to be of much use to us.

2. The second of the two observations in *The Ego and the Id* which runs counter to the ideas of the topographic theory and which required a change in that theory is that a need or tendency to punish one-self may be inaccessible to consciousness. According to the topographic theory, a moral trend, such as a need for punishment, should be a part of the system *Pcs.*, should be arrayed with the anti-instinctual forces of the mind in situations of conflict over sexual wishes, and should, by those tokens, be readily accessible to consciousness. To find that a need for punishment may be quite inaccessible to consciousness therefore raises all the objections to the topographic theory that we have just discussed in connection with unconscious repressive forces in general.

However, there is an additional problem in connection with a need for punishment which is inaccessible to consciousness. Freud pointed out that hysterical patients may actually repress self-punitive tendencies. . . .

What this means is that intrapsychic conflict does not consist only of conflict between sexual wishes on the one hand and anti-instinctual forces on the other. There can also be conflicts between a need for punishment on the one hand and counterforces, e.g., repression, on the other hand. Moreover, these conflicts can be of pathogenic significance and may consequently require analysis in the therapeutic situation, analysis which today we should call superego analysis.

Conflicts of this sort cannot be satisfactorily accounted for within the conceptual framework of the topographic theory except by assuming that they occur within the system *Pcs.* Even then, however, one could not explain the fact that they are inaccessible to consciousness without analytic work, something which, by definition, ought to assign them to the system *Ucs.*

*　　*　　*

The Structural Theory

*　　*　　*

. . . The structural theory was intended to achieve the correspondence which the topographic theory lacks. It divides the mind in accordance with Freud's experience as to which mental functions are generally allied with one another in situations of mental conflict and which are opposed to one another. Thus

the major division of the mind is into two parts. One part, called the id, is directly related to the instinctual drives, while the other part, called the ego, is more coherent and more organized. It regulates or opposes the drives, mediating between them and the demands of the external world. This division corresponds to what one can observe of how the mind functions in situations of conflict over an instinctual drive. On the one side in such a conflict is the instinctual wish with its associated fantasies and memories. On the other side are the anti-instinctual forces of the mind, both moral and defensive. The structural theory makes a second division within the ego itself, separating from the rest of the ego those functions which may be called the moral ones. They are called the superego. This division corresponds to those conflicts over self-punitive trends which we noted. . . .

The structural theory then divides the mind into three groups of functions called the id, the ego, and the superego. The division is made in such a way that the principal sorts of mental conflicts with which we are familiar can be described as occurring between id on the one hand and ego and superego on the other, or between ego and superego. Each group of functions is often called a mental structure, whence the name, the structural theory. . . .

The Id

The id consists of the mental representatives of the instinctual drives. As such it is the great source of mental energy for the whole of the mental apparatus. The wishes of the id press for gratification and in so doing they impel the functions of the ego to action. As we shall see when we come to discuss the ego, this action may be of various kinds. The point is that the impulse and the energy for the ego come from the id.

The energy of the id is assumed to be of two kinds, in accordance with the dual instinct theory: Aggressive energy, deriving from the aggressive instinct, and libido deriving from the erotic instinct. Since these two kinds of energy are assumed to be never wholly separate from each other but rather to be always fused, though in varying proportions, the cathexes of the instinctual wishes and fantasies of the id are partly aggressive and partly libidinal. That is to say, however destructive, cruel, and aggressive a particular fantasy or action may be, analysis will show it aims at some degree of erotic gratification as well. By the same token, no matter how loving and tender a fantasy or action may be, if it can be analyzed, analysis will show that there is at the same time some element of aggressive energy which is also being discharged.

The cathexes of the id are mobile and press for immediate and rapid discharge. Thus displacement and condensation characterize id processes, without, however, being limited to them. . . . A demand for immediate gratification likewise characterizes the id. This corresponds to the tendency of id cathexes to press for prompt and rapid discharge.

The Ego

At the beginning of life the whole of the mental apparatus functions in the way just described as characteristic for the id. The mind of the infant is concerned solely with the task of discharging as promptly as possible the mobile cathexes of instinctual origin which energize it. Certain parts of the mind are of particular importance in executing this task, namely, the parts which subserve the functions of perception and of motor action. In other words, the infant achieves instinctual gratification with the help of his ability (1) to perceive the opportunities for gratification in his environment, e.g., an object to suck; and (2) to exploit those opportunities or physically to alter his environment, i.e., in the example just given, to bring the object he has perceived to his mouth. These perceptual and executant parts of the mind form the nucleus of the developing ego as the infant matures. Freud's formulation of this relationship between id and ego was that at the beginning of life the id comprises the whole of the mind and that the ego represents that part of the mind which develops under the impact of sensory stimuli from the outer world. According to this formulation, the ego is, figuratively speaking, the differentiated, cortical layer of the id, the part of the id which is in contact with the outer world. Hartmann has since suggested that it is more appropriate to think of the infant's mind as an undifferentiated matrix which in the course of development differentiates into an executant part, the ego, and an energizing part, the id. This alternative formulation takes into account in a more explicit way the fact that the sensory and motor apparatuses of the body, as well as the mental functions of perception and motor action from which the ego later develops, are distinguishable even at the beginning of life from the instinctual drives and their activities, just as the ego is later distinguishable from the id. In any case, it is clear that the early relationship between the id and the developing ego is that the latter is the executant for the former by virtue of being the part of the mind which achieves and maintains contact with the outer world.

The role which the ego plays in mental life is one which develops gradually. At first the ego is represented by a group of sensory and motor functions which act as the dutiful servants of the id and as its ambassadors to the outside world, so to speak. After a few years a marked change has taken place. In addition to its original role as executant for the id drives, the ego is able to exercise at least a modicum of control over instinctual wishes and may even oppose them directly in situations of conflict by using such measures as repression. The precise ways in which this change comes about are not easy to specify in detail. . . . It seems certain that many factors are involved in the development of the ego into a coherent organization of mental functions. One of these factors is maturation of the nervous system. Without it even so basically important a function as voluntary motor control, for example, could not develop, since we know that the corticospinal tracts become myelinated and able to function only some months after birth. For many other ego functions as well, the nervous system must mature postnatally before the mental activity in question becomes possible. Equally indispensable to normal ego development are what we call good early object relations. By this we mean a set of experiences with the persons of his environment which afford the infant gratification and frustration in suitable or favorable proportions. The effect of such object relations is manifold as far as ego development is concerned. Among other things they are important for the vitally significant identifications which result from them. A particularly significant step in ego development is the acquisition of language, a process which results in an incalculable facilitation of thought, as Freud remarked. The gradual acquisition of the ability to test reality, i.e., to distinguish between environmental fact and inner fantasy, should also be mentioned in connection with ego development, as should the acquisition of a store of memories and the gradual achievement of motor control. The capacity to delay the process of instinctual discharge is an attribute of ego functioning which also deserves special mention because of its general importance in the way the ego operates. Freud considered it to be the one attribute which most characteristically distinguishes ego from id. In particular, it is of special importance in the development of thinking, an ego function which Freud described as trial action, i.e., a delay in the discharge of all but a small amount of available mental energy.

All of these factors, and many others, are of very great importance in ego development, but the factor which is of crucial importance in the development of *conflict* between ego and id, and in the ability of the ego to oppose the instinctual drives, is anxiety. The relation between anxiety and conflict may be summarized as follows. We have observed earlier that the accumulation of instinctual energy within the mind produces unpleasure and leads to mental activity which is directed toward discharging the energy in question or toward binding it. If, however, the amount of instinctual energy which has accumulated is too great for the mental apparatus to deal with it either by binding it or by discharging it, a state of intense unpleasure results. Freud called such an event a traumatic event and the resultant state a traumatic state. He identified the emotion which accompanies a traumatic state of anxiety. Traumatic states are most apt to occur in infancy and in early childhood when the ability of the mental apparatus to bind and to discharge energy efficiently and without outside help is not yet well developed. Later on, as the ego develops, the individual's capacity to deal with large amounts of mental energy increases greatly.

*   *   *

The way in which anxiety makes it possible for the ego to oppose an instinctual wish is this. Once the ego has reacted to an instinctual wish with anxiety, the pleasure principle comes into operation. As Freud emphasized, this principle dominates the operation of the child's mind. It compels the ego to oppose the wish which gave rise to anxiety (the anticipation of intense unpleasure) rather than to gratify it. Thus it is anxiety which is responsible for the appearance of conflict between id and ego in the course of every child's development. It is important to bear in mind that conflicts of this sort are not to be thought of as necessarily abnormal or pathological. On the contrary, while they play a fundamentally important role in pathological mental processes such as neurotic symptoms, they are also inevitable and significant factors in normal mental development and functioning.

The means which the ego employs to oppose id wishes are called defenses. Each is set in action by anxiety, i.e., each has as its aim to diminish or to avoid anxiety. Any means at the ego's command may be used as a defense. Thus, for example, heterosexuality may be used as a defense against homosexual wishes, or vice versa. Among the better known defenses are repression, isolation, undoing, reaction formation, denial, projection, identification, the substitution of oneself for an external instinctual object, and vice versa.

To sum up what we have just said about anxiety, conflict, and defense, (1) there are typical fears which motivate the institution of anti-instinctual defenses by the ego; (2) defenses are of many kinds; and (3) the consequences of conflict may be either normal or pathological. They include character traits, sublimations, and individual sexual patterns or preferences as well as such consequences of conflict as permanent blocking of an instinctual derivative (successful defense) and neurotic symptom formation (unsuccessful defense).

Let us turn now to other aspects of ego functioning.

Ego cathexes may be either mobile or bound. Mobility of cathexis is characteristic of ego functioning in infancy and in early childhood, as well as of those situations in later life in which ego functions are closely allied with id impulses and act as their executants, i.e., facilitate their discharge. An example of such a situation is sexual intercourse and orgasm. The capacity to bind mental energy increases as the child matures, reaching a maximum in adult life. It is closely associated with deinstinctualization or neutralization of mental energy by which is meant deflection of energy from its original, instinctual, pleasure-seeking aims and utilization of it for ego functions which have no directly instinctual quality. An example is the mental energy used for speech. When the little child is in the process of learning to speak, he derives obvious pleasure from the mere activity of speaking or even of prattling. In later life, however, speaking is not ordinarily pleasurable in itself. It is an activity under the control of the ego which can be used in the service of the functions and aims of the ego, whether these aims are instinctual and pleasure-seeking or not. Among the ways by which energy can be neutralized and made available for ego activities, sublimation and identification occupy important places.

There is no complete list of ego functions. However, any attempt to formulate such a list would have to include the following: (1) consciousness; (2) sense perception; (3) the perception and expression of affect; (4) thought; (5) control of motor action; (6) memory; (7) language; (8) defense mechanisms and defensive activity in general; (9) control, regulation, and binding of instinctual energy; (10) the integrative and harmonizing function; (11) reality testing; and (12) the capacity to inhibit or suspend the operation of any of these functions and to regress to a primitive level of functioning. Thought processes of the ego vary from logical, realistic, problem-solving to unrealistic, nonverbal daydreaming.

The Superego

The superego may be defined as the group of mental functions which have to do with ideal aspirations and with moral commands and prohibitions. It owes its origin as an organized division of the mind to identification with parental figures, in particular to identification with their ethical and moral aspects. This identification is primarily a consequence of the violent mental conflicts of the phallic, Oedipal phase of development. It is in fact one of the most important consequences of the Oedipal phase.

Usually it is the Oedipal rival who is the principal source of the identifications which comprise the nucleus of the superego. Thus the little boy identifies with the father, who, at least in the child's fantasy, threatens to castrate and send him away forever in retaliation for the child's Oedipal wish to displace and castrate his father. By internalizing his father's threat and making it a part of his own mind, i.e., by identifying with this aspect of his father, the boy becomes more able to institute defenses against and thus to control his frightening incestuous and parricidal wishes. At the same time the identification gratifies the instinctual wish to share in the father's fantasied (sexual) omnipotence by merging with him, e.g., via a fantasy of oral incorporation.

One of the most striking characteristics of the superego and one which is particularly impressive in the pathological situations with which the analyst deals clinically is its cruel, relentless, and even destructive attitude toward the individual of whose mind it is a part. This is particularly apparent in depressed patients, in patients with obsessional neuroses, and in those patients whose mental lives are dominated by a need for punishment. Freud explained the aggressive or destructive nature of superego functioning as a consequence of identification. He postulated that identification results in a partial defusion of mental energy into libido and aggressive energy. In the case of superego formation, the aggressive energy which is liberated in this way becomes available to the superego and accounts for the superego's cruelty and destructiveness.

Freud conceived of the superego as a specialized part of the ego. It resembles the rest of the ego in that some of its elements are readily accessible to consciousness while others are not. It also resembles the rest of the ego in that superego ideation can vary from what is logical, consistent, and mature to what is primitive and infantile.

Superego activity may be manifest in a variety of ways. It may regulate ego activities and particularly the ego's anti-instinctual, defensive activities in accordance with its moral standards. In such a case there is harmony between ego and superego. In other cases there may not be complete harmony between the two. In such instances the superego functions so as to give rise to a feeling of guilt within the ego, or a feeling of remorse, or a desire to do penance or to make restitution. At other times it may motivate an individual to punish himself without knowing why he does so, or even, in many cases, without knowing that he is doing so.

Final Comment

Two important aspects of the structural theory are the emphasis which it places on the genetic or developmental aspect of mental functioning and what Waelder called the principle of multiple functioning.

According to the structural theory, those mental functions which are called the ego, which normally form a coherent and integrated whole, and which may be in conflict with either the id or the superego, develop from the apparatuses of the mind which have to do with an individual's response to the world about him. Thus the ego may be characterized in either of two ways. (1) It may be defined as a group of functions of the mind which are usually associated with one another in situations of mental conflict; or (2) it may be defined as the group of mental functions which in one way or another have to do with mediating between the demands of the id and those of the

outer world. The structural theory calls explicit attention to the genetic relationship between ego functions in later life and those of infancy and childhood. It particularly emphasizes the effects of early conflicts on later ego functions. The importance of such genetic relationships in practical analytic work is especially apparent with respect to the understanding of anxiety and defense in cases of pathogenic conflict in later life.

The superego likewise is defined in the structural theory on a genetic basis as well as on a functional one. From the latter point of view it may be defined as the group of mental functions having to do with ideal aspirations and with moral prohibitions. From the former, it is definable as the consequence of certain Oedipal identifications, namely, of identification with the moral aspect of the parents. Here again the structural theory's emphasis on the genetic point of view is of very great practical importance in actual analytic work with patients.

As for multiple function, according to the structural theory, any product of mental activity is invariably multiply determined. This is true whether the product is a thought, an action, a fantasy, or a symptom. Whatever it may be, it is the outcome of a mutual interaction among tendencies of id, ego, and superego. At times these tendencies reinforce one another, at other times they cooperate, at still other times they oppose one another. In any case, each contributes its share to the final outcome.

The Primary and Secondary Processes

[W]e propose to evaluate another set of psychoanalytic concepts in the light of the transition from the topographic to the structural theory. These concepts are primary and secondary processes.

As pointed out . . . the assumption that there are two types of mental functioning, one called the primary process and the other the secondary process, is an integral part of the topographic theory. We wish to emphasize that this assumption is one that has to do essentially with mental energies. It constitutes one of the fundamental aspects of psychoanalysis as a dynamic psychology, a psychology which uses energic principles. Freud's purpose in dividing mental activities on the basis of whether they function according to the primary or secondary process was to offer a satisfactory explanation of what happens to the energy of an unconscious instinctual impulse from the time of its initiation in the system *Ucs.* to its final expression as a conscious mental experience. It enabled him to bring together various mental phenomena on the basis of the degree of mobility of cathexis by which each could be characterized. Such divergent phenomena as dreams, neurotic symptoms, jokes, and parapraxes could be understood to share the common feature of a high degree of mobility of cathexis. Ordinary, rational thought, on the other hand, was related to mental cathexes which were bound, or relatively immobile.

The concepts of primary and secondary process are closely related in the topographic theory to the idea of regression, specifically to systemic and genetic regression. Systemic regression implies the re-emergent dominance of the system *Ucs.*, together with a reversion to types of wishes and mental activity characteristic of the earliest periods of life. With this regression there is a shift to primary-process functioning.

The primary process is the type of mental functioning characteristic of the system *Ucs.* It is also the manner in which the mind functions during the earliest period of life before the system *Pcs.* comes into being. It is for this reason that it is called primary.

The fundamental characteristic of the primary process is the tendency for instinctual cathexes to press for full and rapid discharge. Full discharge of cathexes results in feelings of pleasure or the cessation of feelings of unpleasure. The high degree of mobility which is the hallmark of the primary process is in keeping with the pleasure principle which holds sway in the system *Ucs.* Roughly stated, discharge equals pleasure and pleasure is the only concern of the system *Ucs.* Nothing in the system *Ucs.* impedes the tendency toward full and rapid discharge of cathexes. Any object or avenue of discharge can be used for that purpose regardless of the demands of morality or considerations of causality, logic, and reality. The ultimate goal of the primary-process tendency is, according to Freud, to achieve a set of perceptions which is identical with earlier sensory experiences that had been accompanied by pleasurable gratification. . . . What is implied in this tendency is the notion that the achievement of such an identity of perception is the equivalent of a complete or massive discharge of drive cathexes. Other activities, such as thinking, for example, imply a lesser discharge of instinctual tension.

The clinical phenomena which illustrate the primary process tendency are those which are characterized by the mechanisms of displacement and condensation. This type of mobility of cathexes was important in the explanation of the origin of dreams in the topographic theory. . . .

The secondary process is the mode of functioning typical for the system *Pcs.* Like the system *Pcs.* itself, this quality of mental functioning is a later acquisition of the mind. The secondary process results from the impact of reality and of the environment upon the developing mental apparatus. It reflects the effects of experiences of mastering frustration, of being rewarded by important objects in the environment, and of socially determined moral precepts. From the energic point of view, the tendency of the secondary process is to delay, modify, tone down, or oppose the discharge of the drive cathexes. Presumably, according to the topographic theory, this is made possible by the greater energic potential of the system *Pcs.*

The fundamental characteristic of the secondary process is stability of cathexes. Secondary-process cathexes are "bound" by the process of being attached to word and object representations which are fixed and constant. A freely mobile displacement of cathexes or the condensation of many cathexes onto one mental element is not ordinarily possible. One word or object may not be substituted so readily for another, nor may a part of an object be used to represent the whole. When cathexes are bound in such a manner, when words and objects come to have fixed relationships, logic and causality become possible. Thus the laws of syntax, freedom from contradiction, and realistic temporal relations become part of secondary-process activity. The binding of drive cathexes to fixed word and object representations is an essential step in the development of the reality principle. It serves the end of making it possible to achieve realistic gratification and thus becomes an important element in the process of adaptation.

Thus we can see that according to the topographic theory, there are two fundamentally different types of mental activity. Mental activity in the system *Ucs.* is characterized by mobile cathexes and follows the laws of the primary process. Mental activity in the systems *Pcs.* and *Cs.* is characterized by bound cathexes and follows the laws of the secondary process.

Considerable obscurity and confusion have surrounded the concept of the primary process. It is perhaps one of the most difficult of psychoanalytic ideas to grasp. The reasons for this confusion are not hard to find. The term has been employed in many ways. Freud himself used the concept of primary process in the sense just given. In the literature of psychoanalysis, however, the term primary process has often been used as synonymous with irrational or unrealistic thought or fantasy. It has come to mean unconscious mental activity in general. By the same token the term secondary process has been used to mean ordinary rational thinking, instead of being used, as Freud used it, to refer to the binding of cathexes. It is the binding of cathexes (the secondary process) which makes rational thought and realistic action possible, according to the topographic theory, just as it is the mobility of cathexes (primary process) which leads to condensation and displacement.

We may now turn to a consideration of the problems involved in transferring the terms primary and secondary process to the conceptual framework of the structural theory. . . . We have already emphasized that these two concepts were of basic importance in the topographic theory. Do they also require some revision in order to be consonant with the rest of the structural theory, or can they be carried over unchanged, as is sometimes assumed? If revision is necessary, how much is required and what must it be?

Let us begin by taking note of Freud's discussion of this problem. In *The Interpretation of Dreams* (1900) he stated that the system *Ucs.* is composed solely of freely mobile cathexes seeking discharge. The system *Pcs.*, on the other hand, has definite, fixed, and stable representations for words and objects. Fifteen years later, in his paper on "The Unconscious" (1915) Freud took cognizance of certain difficulties in this point of view. The stumbling block was to be found in the existence of repressed, unconscious fantasies. Because they are not readily accessible to consciousness and because they produce derivatives which indicate the impulsiveness of their nature and the mobility of their cathexes, such fantasies, in the topographic hypothesis, should be considered portions of the system *Ucs.* On the other hand, because such fantasies are made up of definite verbal concepts and object representations and because they demonstrate features of the secondary process, such fantasies should be considered part of the system *Pcs.* Freud wrote:

> Among the derivatives of the *Ucs.* instinctual impulses . . . there are some which unite in themselves characters of an opposite kind. On the one hand, they are highly organized, free from self-contradiction, have made use of every acquisition of the system *Cs.* and would hardly be distinguished by our ordinary judgment from the formations of that system. On the other hand they are unconscious and incapable of becoming conscious. Thus *qualitatively* they belong to the system *Pcs.*, but *factually* to the *Ucs.* . . . Of such a nature are those fantasies of normal people as well as of neurotics which we have recognized as preliminary stages in the formation both of dreams and of symptoms and which, in spite of their high degree of organization, remain repressed and therefore cannot become conscious. . . . Substitutive formations, too, are highly organized derivatives of the *Ucs.* of this kind; but these succeed in breaking through into consciousness, when circumstances are favorable—for example, if they happen to join forces with an anticathexis from the *Pcs.*
>
> [Further in the same essay, Freud wrote:] The reason for all these difficulties is to be found in the circumstance that the attribute of being conscious, which is the only characteristic of psychical processes that is directly presented to us, is in no way suited to serve as a criterion for the differentiation of systems. Apart from the fact that the conscious is not always conscious but also at times latent, observation has shown that much that shares the characteristics of the system *Pcs.* does not become conscious; . . . Hence consciousness stands in no simple relation either to the different systems or to repression. The truth is that it is not the only psychically repressed that remains alien to consciousness, but also some

of the impulses which dominate our ego—something, therefore, that forms the strongest functional antithesis to the repressed.

We see from these quotations that as early as 1915, Freud recognized that secondary-process phenomena may be associated with elements of the system *Ucs.* In other words, the simple statement that the system *Ucs.* operates according to the primary process and the system *Pcs.* operates according to the secondary process required modification. The dichotomy—*Ucs.*-primary process, *Pcs.*-secondary process—a fundamental feature of the topographic theory, does not hold up. The awareness of this contradiction within the topographic theory was one of the factors which stimulated Freud to study the possibility for instituting a new frame of reference for psychoanalysis. The structural theory was the outcome of this study.

How then should the terms primary process and secondary process be understood within the framework of the structural hypothesis? Primary process, we suggest, should be used to refer to mobility of instinctual cathexes and their tendency to rapid discharge. This was Freud's original formulation of the concept. Mobility of cathexes becomes manifest pre-eminently in those phenomena which demonstrate the effect of displacement and condensation of drive cathexes. Examples of high degrees of cathectic mobility are readily available in the analysis of dreams. It is this quality which accounts for the absurdities and contradictions which one finds in dreams. When cathectic energies are easily shifted from realistically appropriate objects to inappropriate ones, causal relationships and logic and temporal sequences are inevitably overthrown. The effect is that of complete disregard for reality. Strictly speaking, the characteristics just mentioned are the end results of mobility of cathexes. They are the effects of the primary process, not the primary process itself, as noted earlier.

If we utilize this definition of the primary process within the framework of the structural theory, we should make the following points which are basic. . . .

1. The activities of the ego and superego as well as those of the id may be characterized by the primary process.

2. Primary-process tendencies remain active throughout life. Mature mental functioning does not imply a complete suppression or cessation of such activity.

3. Primary-process phenomena are not necessarily pathological, nor are they always maladaptive.

4. No sharp line of distinction can be drawn between those phenomena in which cathexes are firmly bound (secondary process) and those phenomena in which cathexes are highly mobile (primary process). There is instead a continuum of phenomena which demonstrate varying degrees of mobility of cathexis.

The difference between primary and secondary process is actually a quantitative one indicating the degree of mobility of cathexes. It reflects the growing ability of the ego to regulate cathectic discharge.

5. Primary and secondary processes are not identical with thinking. Mobility of cathexes is a broader concept which is intended to encompass other phenomena in addition to thinking. At any moment thinking may be characterized by a greater or lesser component of mobile cathexes (primary process).

6. The close association between timelessness and primary process should be re-examined.

Let us consider each one of these points seriatim:

1. The first point in our list stated that primary-process functioning is a tendency of mental life in general. It may characterize the activity of the superego and the ego as well as the id. The special connection between rapid mobility of cathexes and the functioning of the id is well known and has been commented upon repeatedly. No illustration of this fact need be presented here. Certain observations, however, concerning the superego and the ego are in order.

That superego function may show the hallmark of the primary process should come as no surprise. The energic investment of the superego is instinctual. Its drive endowment is primarily aggressive. Freud noted, accordingly, that the superego in many respects is closer to the id than it is to the ego. By this he referred to the fact that the superego's demands for self-punishment may press upon the ego as urgently, as insistently, and as irrationally as any libidinal wish of the id. The self-destructive and self-punitive tendencies observed in patients suffering from psychotic depressions illustrate this statement.

There is, however, less dramatic, but equally impressive evidence of the fact that the functions of the superego may show the effects of high mobility of cathexes. Eidelberg pointed this out in connection with the analysis of parapraxes, especially certain slips of the tongue. Many slips of the tongue are based upon the breakthrough into speech of elements which betray the speaker, elements which expose him to shame, humiliation, and even defeat. Slips of this kind often constitute unintended confessions of guilt. They serve the interests of the superego. Like other parapraxes their mechanism is dependent on a high degree of mobility of cathexes. This mobility is manifested in the mechanisms of displacements and condensation, so typical of the primary mode of mental functioning. Examples of *ego* activities which function according to the primary process will be given later.

2. There is, of course, nothing new in the statement that primary-process tendencies remain active throughout life. In the context of the *topographic* hypothesis, however, the appearance of phenomena characterized by a high degree of cathectic mobility signifies the breakthrough into conscious mental functioning of elements of the system *Ucs*. It indicates an irruption of repressed, archaic, libidinal, childhood wishes which disregard reality and which are maladaptive or comical in their effects. As mentioned earlier . . . this formulation is in conflict with many facts of clinical experience. The structural hypothesis offers a framework which is free of these contradictions.

During the earliest phases of life the psychic apparatus functions according to the primary process; that is to say, its activity is characterized by a very high degree of cathectic mobility. This may be recognized in the tendency toward immediate or very rapid discharge of drive cathexes. From the outset, therefore, the psychic apparatus is under the complete domination of the pleasure principle.

With the development of the ego, however, this situation begins to change. According to Anna Freud, the core of the ego as an organized system may be said to reside in its role of inhibiting or suppressing the discharge of instinctual cathexes. [O]ne can postulate a general tendency in the direction of an increasing capacity of the ego to master the discharge of drive cathexes. This mastery, however, does not always take the form of suppression or opposition. As executant of the psychic apparatus the ego facilitates and makes possible drive discharge. It does so with due regard for demands of reality and the superego. In addition, the ego "tames" or "neutralizes" drive energy for its own purposes. Some ego functions, however, may be carried out with unneutralized drive energy. Kris has called attention to a very important group of ego functions which have in common the initiation by the ego of regressive mental functioning. Essentially, these are phenomena in which more primitive patterns of mental activity emerge. They are activities which are characterized by high cathectic mobility, yet they emerge in a context which could hardly be considered pathological. Thus we can see that mental activity according to the primary process is characteristic not only of early childhood and of pathological phenomena but also of adult ego activities which may be normal and adaptive.

3. The fact that primary-process phenomena are not necessarily pathological and that they are not always maladaptive follows quite logically from the considerations mentioned in the preceding paragraph. The literature of psychoanalysis which deals with creative thinking, scientific discovery, and artistic experiences is replete with examples in which new insights and realistic advances resulted from mental activity which was characterized by a high degree of mobility of the cathectic investment of mental representations. Play activity, the enjoyment of art, and psychoanalytic therapy are other examples of activities in which primary process may characterize an adaptive activity. If we follow the structural hypo-

thesis consistently, we can see that it is not the influence of unconscious mental activity alone, nor the fact that its energic investment is very mobile, which determines whether or not an activity is pathological.

4. According to the structural theory and the principle of multiple function, any mental activity represents the result of the integration by the ego of the demands of the various agencies of the mind. In addition, the ego takes into account the individual's relationship to reality. A wide and varied range of mental activities may result from this integrative effort. These activities demonstrate many different patterns of cathectic mobility. In some instances one may observe a high degree of cathectic mobility, in other instances the opposite may be the case. In between is a broad spectrum of activities or functions which demonstrate varying degrees of cathectic mobility. Artistic creativity is of course one of the richest areas from which examples may be drawn to illustrate this point. Some artistic sublimations are carried out in a controlled, neutral fashion indicating a high level of ego mastery. They depend upon stable patterns of cathectic discharge. Other equally successful artistic activities are carried out in a manner which makes it appear that the ego has been overwhelmed. The artist experiences the creative urge in a passive manner, flooded by a plethora of impressions, thoughts, and images. In such cases ego control is intact even though the regression of function may have been considerable and the patterns of cathectic discharge very rapid.

The following clinical fragment illustrates a sublimation which was carried out under conditions of rapid cathectic discharge. Although clearly dependent upon primary-process functioning, the sublimation of the instinctual energies involved was both realistic and adaptive. This material is from the analysis of a young married woman suffering from hysteria. She was frigid. The analytic material revealed that she had the idea that without a penis orgasm is impossible. Her unconscious conflict centered about her wish to possess by force and to enjoy the use of her father's penis. Her father was a very successful and powerful man. He had done brilliantly in his own profession, in hobbies, in sports, and in various business ventures. The patient had considerable artistic talent. During the analysis she began to devote this talent to the decoration of her new home. Unconsciously her house represented her body, and decorating it had the significance of correcting the ugliness of being without a penis. Her concern over furnishing and decorating her house was soon drawn into the unconscious conflict over the wish to seize her father's phallus. At every phase of the decorating of her house she wanted to obtain from her father money, furniture, wood, or some other item which she could use to adorn her home. In the midst of one

such experience she reported the following episode:

She was sitting in bed one morning sipping coffee and smoking a cigarette. She was thinking of how to furnish one of the rooms. She decided she needed a certain kind of desk but could not afford it. "Perhaps," she thought, "my father would give me one if I were to ask him. Better yet, I'll make one myself. But I have no wood. I could ask my father for some wood, but he has used all the cherry wood in his own home." She dismissed the thought of turning to her father.

At this point she felt her thoughts coming with increasing speed and intensity; they seemed to be rapidly getting out of control. All sorts of ideas flooded in on her. She thought of various ways of combining wood, plastic, iron, and other materials to make the desk she desired. By this time the tempo of her thoughts was so rapid that she seemed to have no control over them. She was seized by a sense of overwhelming excitement. At the apex of these feelings, according to the patient, "Suddenly I got the idea that it would be possible to reconvert an old double wardrobe into a desk. The idea just clicked. It flooded me like a tremendous burst from within. When the thought reached my mind and I saw that this was it, I lost all control. I began to scream my husband's name at the top of my voice. I screamed it again and again. They [husband and the children] came running into the room. From the way I was screaming they thought something had happened, something was wrong. I could not control it. I kept shouting, 'I have it, I have it!' As soon as I saw them I began to babble away a mile a minute how I was going to redesign the desk, how I would arrange the drawers, how much it would cost, where I would put it, etc. I couldn't stop talking. I was getting more and more out of breath. Finally the excitement seemed to wear off, almost suddenly. The tension left me, I felt relaxed. I felt all in. I was tired. I was completely spent."

In relating this experience during the session, the patient realized what she had not been aware of at the time of the experience, namely, that the mounting crescendo, the creative idea coming at the apex of excitement, and the uncontrollable outpouring of feeling with a subsequent relaxation and desire to sleep all recapitulated the sequence of events in an orgasm. The patient had a creative spell which simulated orgasm. She was not at all conscious of any sexual feeling. This is an example of an ego activity—artistic creation—being carried out successfully and consciously according to the pattern of primary-process discharge.

5. What is the relationship of primary process . . . to thinking? In the light of what has been said so far it should be clear that in the framework of the structural theory, the primary process is not considered as a form of thinking. It is a mental process which is involved in some instances of thinking. If

we are consistent in our terminology and if we define the primary process in terms of high mobility of cathexes, we must conclude that the concept of the primary process is broader than thinking. Thinking is an ego function, partly autonomous in origin and richly influenced by the vicissitudes of the drives. Thinking, like other ego functions, e.g., perception, may become a vehicle for drive discharge. Under such circumstances its functioning may be characterized by varying degrees of cathectic mobility depending upon the interaction of forces in the ego as described earlier. Thinking characterized by highly mobile cathexes need not be unrealistic or maladaptive. Whether it is or not depends very much on the element of ego control. On the contrary, the ability to give free reign to primary-process tendencies often plays an important adaptive role in thinking which is used in problem solving and scientific creativeness. Conversely, the inability to give free reign to primary-process tendencies in thinking may, under certain circumstances, be maladaptive. Such an inability may interfere with certain types of work, play, and with psychoanalytic treatment.

Since rapid cathectic discharge is not always pathological, its juxtaposition and opposition to the concept of secondary-process thinking as rational, adaptive, and reality oriented, a concept inherited from the topographic theory, is no longer significant. It would seem advantageous to conceptualization in psychoanalysis if one dropped the term "secondary process" when it is used synonymously with conscious thinking and simply referred to thinking as thinking.

Functions of the ego, other than thinking, may be involved in rapid cathectic discharge and operate according to the primary process. This consideration has a bearing on hallucinations and dreams. A few observations concerning the function of perception and its relation to mobility of cathexes will be discussed now.

Ordinarily, perception is regarded as an autonomous ego function. Under certain conditions, however, and for relatively brief periods, the function of perception may become a vehicle for the discharge of drive cathexes and accordingly may operate under the influence of highly mobile cathexes. Part of what is considered the sensitivity of the artist may be ascribed to this phenomenon. His perception of the external world is often fraught with the potential for rapid, mobile discharge of drive cathexes. This tendency is present in all individuals in varying degrees. Study of the conditions under which one experiences illusions or distortions of reality like *déjà vu* or distortions of time sense demonstrates how tensions from the drives may utilize the data of perception in order to effect rapid cathectic discharge.

*   *   *

6. In the topographic theory disturbances in the sense of time have been described as characteristic of the system *Ucs.* and the primary process. This idea stems from two sources in that theory. First it stems from the fact that one of the striking characteristics of dreams is the complete disregard of temporal relations. The statement has been made that in the system *Ucs.*, where the primary process reigns supreme, there is no sense of time. The second source of the notion of the timelessness of the primary process derives from the fact that during treatment, in analyzing the wishes behind dreams, symptoms, and other mental products, one keeps encountering in their pristine form, vital and unchanged, the long-forgotten wishes of childhood. Since the evidence for the existence of these wishes becomes manifest during treatment in association with phenomena which demonstrate primary-process tendencies, the notion of the timelessness of the system *Ucs.* developed. Loewenstein has reported the contents of his correspondence with Freud concerning the concept of the timelessness of the system *Ucs.* In response to Lowenstein's criticism, Freud answered that he intended this expression to relate only to the fact that unconscious wishes persist and remain active until they are made conscious, at which time through the process of association and reality testing they can be correlated with reality.

According to the structural theory, the conceptualization of time depends upon the maturation and development of the ego during childhood. For the first several years of life the child has no concept of time or an inadequate one. Those phenomena (dreams, symptoms) which in a large measure derive from infantile sources often reflect the little child's inadequate or absent sense of time.

Clinical distortions of the sense of time are not directly related to primary-process mobility of cathexis. Such feelings as time seeming to stand still or that a very long period seemed to have been lived through in what was actually a very short space of time, the feeling that one is a child again, the feeling of having experienced a particular situation at an earlier time, etc., are phenomena which result from intrapsychic conflict. They are related to specific fantasies in which ideas involving time play an important part. They are not simply a direct consequence of primary-process mobility of cathexis. This point may be illustrated in the following clinical examples.

On the Monday following Father's Day, a young woman patient began her session by stating that she felt 100 years had passed since the previous session on Friday. Her association to this statement led to the fairy tale "Sleeping Beauty." The patient concentrated on two themes. First, that all the occupants of the palace had not died but had only been asleep for 100 years. Second, that the prince who awakened her belonged to another generation. He had not yet been born at the time when the princess fell under the magical spell. Further associations concerned her being glad to see the analyst after the weekend and longings for her dead father. This patient felt guilty because she blamed herself for her father's untimely death. The "Sleeping Beauty" fairy tale contained elements which corresponded to several important wishes of the patient, a self-punitive wish to change places with her father, a wish to be reunited with him, a wish to bring him back to life, and finally a typical Oedipal wish of breaching the time and incest barrier by marrying someone of another generation. Her temporarily distorted sense of time was connected with the fantasy of being the sleeping beauty.

Another patient reported the following experience which took place when his mother's death from cancer was imminent. He kept waking up early in the morning long before his customary time for rising. Each time he looked at the clock and reached the reassuring conclusion that he could return safely to sleep, there was still lots of time. In his associations he revealed that he had a fantasy of magically extending the duration of each minute in order to prolong his mother's life or, more accurately, to delay the moment of her death.

Summary

In this section we have made the following points:

1. The concepts of primary and secondary process should be defined in terms of varying degrees of mobility of cathexes. There is a continuum of phenomena demonstrating more or less mobility of cathexes.

2. The regulation of cathectic discharge is a function of the ego. This function may be affected by many factors.

3. No sharp line of demarcation can be drawn between primary- and secondary-process phenomena.

4. Phenomena characterized by rapid cathectic discharge are not necessarily pathological, nor are they always maladaptive. Regressions in the service of the ego constitute important illustrations of this thesis.

5. Patterns of rapid discharge of cathexes may mark the operations of the id, ego, and superego.

6. Primary and secondary processes are not identical with thinking.

7. Functions other than thinking, dreaming, and symptom formation may become involved in patterns of high cathectic mobility.

8. The concept of time appears only gradually in the course of the maturation of the growing child's ego functions. Clinical disturbances of the sense of time result from intrapsychic conflict. They are related to fantasies in which ideas about time play an important part. They are not simply a consequence of primary-process mobility of cathexes.

NOTES

NOTE 1

GILL, MERTON M.

Topography and Systems in Psychoanalytic Theory*

*   *   *

The structural theory, however great or small its difference from the topographic theory, brought new problems. The separation of the repressed and the repressing into two different systems obscured the similarity between them which is suggested by the fact that they are both dynamically unconscious. Worse, however, is that the structural theory too has built-in contradictions. First, since primary-process functioning is found in the unconscious defenses attributed to the ego, then either some of the defenses cannot really belong to the ego, or the ego does not operate entirely according to the secondary process. Second, the conception of the id as totally without structure is inconsistent with Freud's statements that the id includes ideas, memories, symbols, and mechanisms. The inevitable conclusion is, therefore, that the ego is in part less structured than it is usually considered to be, while the id is more structured than it is usually considered to be and does not all function with totally uninhibited energy. Id and ego are thus brought closer together, a conclusion which is in line with important trends in analytic theory, both past and present. Freud repeatedly warned against too strict delimitations of id and ego. . . .

The obvious next step is to apply to the conceptions of id and ego the many recent suggestions to the effect that the mental apparatus must be conceptualized in terms of hierarchies and continuities rather than sharp divisions. Pleasure and reality principles, primary and secondary process, free energy and inhibited energy, unconsciousness and preconsciousness—all these represent continua. The present assumption is that they represent degrees rather than extremes. Kris expresses this point of view, though he does not refer to the pleasure and reality principles, as follows:

> The difference between preconscious and unconscious mental processes, however, is explained by assumptions concerning the nature of the prevalent psychic energy: Unconscious processes use mobile psychic energy; preconscious processes bound energy. [The situation is probably more complex than this simple equating suggests.] The two degrees of mobility correspond to two types of discharge characterized as the primary and secondary processes. We are thus faced with the delimitation between the id and the ego. Note that two sets of assumptions are here suggested by Freud (the types of en-

* New York: International Universities Press, *Psychological Issues*, Vol. 3, No. 9, 1963. (pp. 140–47). Reprinted by permission.

ergy, free and bound, and the types of discharge, the primary and secondary process) to account for the same events; the formulation in terms of energy permits differentiations in degree, in shading; the formulation in terms of process states extremes. [Why is it not possible to state both in degrees?] Hypotheses of transitions between extremes seem to me . . . preferable.[1]

It seems clear that the logical conclusion we must reach is that since these characteristics of the id and ego are on *continua*, the id and ego themselves are also on a *continuum*.

Not only are the psychic systems *continua*, but the ideal poles at both ends are a fiction. Freud expressed himself on the primary-process pole aspect of the *continuum* in 1900: "It is true that, so far as we know, no psychical apparatus exists which possesses a primary process only and that such an apparatus is to that extent a theoretical fiction." He also said, in effect, that an apparatus operating purely by the secondary process is a fiction: " . . . thinking must aim at freeing itself more and more from exclusive regulation by the unpleasure principle and at restricting the development of affect in thought activity to the minimum required for acting as a signal." This minimal but essential affect development can be stated, from other points of view, as minimal employment of the pleasure principle, of the primary process, of the "id." In suggesting that it can be called the "id" aspect of behavior—to which the objection could be raised that the affect concerned might be a high-level derivative—I am hinting at one possible redefinition of the id, the issue to which I now turn.

First, an "abstraction" should be distinguished from a "fiction." Id, ego, and superego, however defined, are conceptual abstractions. But if an abstraction is so defined as to violate what are regarded as matters of fact, it becomes a fiction. A purely primary-process apparatus is inconceivable because a force must be somehow confined, and the confining must be itself a structure. Rapaport expressed this concept in terms of "thresholds." As for a purely secondary-process apparatus, it is both inconceivable and undesirable in Freud's view of the development of the human psychic apparatus.

1. Kris also describes another *continuum*—that of degrees of hypercathexis which nevertheless do not result in consciousness. He says: "It is generally assumed that preconscious thought processes become conscious by hypercathexis. We now realize that there are various degrees of hypercathexis. If energy is diverted from the perceiving function of the ego to fantasy, this in itself may not lead to consciousness but simply to an intensification of the preconscious process." Rapaport has also spoken of various degrees and kinds of hypercathexis, but saw them as leading not to intensification of preconscious processes but rather to different states of consciousness or varieties of conscious experience. I have explained why I think the *continuum* of unconscious to preconscious should be defined in descriptive terms as the degree of difficulty in gaining access to consciousness.

My demonstration of primary-process functioning in the ego, of the necessity for the id to have some structure if it is not to be a fiction, and the resulting conception of the id and ego as a *continuum* make it necessary to propose a definition of id and ego and to describe their relationship.

The conception of the id as unstructured is a reflection of the fact that it is considered as an exclusively motivational concept, while the ego includes motives, counterforces, and adaptive mechanisms. An exclusively motivational concept is not consistent with the current view of the psychic apparatus as a hierarchy of motivations and structures—the latter including both those which inhibit and those which facilitate discharge—with both motivations and structures existing at all levels of the hierarchy. It is not, in fact, even consistent with some of Freud's own hypotheses, such as his description of the mechanisms that serve as defense before the organization of the ego—primitive structures in the id, in this case inhibiting ones. It may be that the conception of the id as including such primitive inhibiting structures has been delayed because these are in fact conceptualized as the superego, a separate system, whereas in the ego both motive and counterstructure are attributed to the same system. Such a conclusion would explain why in *The Ego and the Id* Freud discussed how the superego is unconscious, rather than how the defenses are unconscious, and it would be consistent with Freud's statements that the superego is closer to the id than it is to the ego. I have little doubt that the conception of the superego would be clarified by this conclusion, although how fully it would clarify the formal position of the superego in the psychic hierarchy is another matter.

With the foregoing considerations in mind, it is possible to envisage at least three definitions of id and ego.[2]

1. All motives—of whatever level of the hierarchy—could be called "id" and all counterforces and discharge structures "ego." Such a definition would run into the difficulty of labeling as "id" highly derivative motives and affects. By way of a concept I advanced recently it could be argued that all behavior has id and ego aspects while still preserving the designation "id" for primitive motives alone. Only primitive motives would be called "id," but all behavior would be considered as occurring in a "nest" of motives, with the manifest behavior being a result of a particular motive which, in a wider context, subserves a more primitive motive, which in a still wider context subserves a still more primitive motive, perhaps always ultimately a motive primitive enough to be called "id." Such a scheme would not be inconsistent with

2. I will not deal specifically with the superego in discussing these three possibilities but will assume that it would be provisionally included in the scheme, as I mentioned above, as a primitive system of defense.

the theory of the relative autonomy of derivative motives. However, against such a definition is the fact that, unless there are compelling reasons to the contrary, the restriction of id to primitive motivation is such a well-established conception it probably is desirable that motivation beyond the primitive drive level be conceptualized as belonging to the ego.

2. The id could be defined as a chaos of completely free, uninhibited, and uncontrolled energy. In such a view the id has no structure and is therefore a fiction. I am not, of course, suggesting that because a concept is a fiction it may not have scientific value, but only that it should be recognized as such and that this particular fiction should not be mistaken for a structural concept.[3]

If the id were regarded as such a fiction, the conception of the mental apparatus would be reduced to the ego. The ego would be seen as a complex multi-layered apparatus, parts of which function chiefly but not entirely by the primary process, while other parts are organized primarily by the secondary process. It is important to realize that the ego is actually regarded as such a system no matter how the id is conceptualized. Even if we include primitive mechanisms and structure in our view of the id, the ego still remains a complex, hierarchically-ordered apparatus varying from primary to secondary processes, from primitive to highly organized structures, from motives little removed from primitive drive to motives which are secondarily autonomous, from dynamically unconscious mental contents to those which have ready access to consciousness. This conception of the ego is the one which is already recognized in the psychoanalytic literature.

Another way of stating the conception that the ego is a complex multileveled apparatus would be to say that it includes a series of censorships, the most primitive of which lies between ego and id. Such a formulation is in effect the same as that of a hierarchy of defense. While Freud did say that to every advance to a higher stage of mental organization there corresponds a new censorship, it has rarely been explicitly stated that these censorships are *within* the ego.[4]

3. A third possible definition of id and ego and their relationship is that the id is the most primitive level of a *continuum*, but a level at which there is already some advance toward secondary-process organization, some reality principle, some structure. The ego would differ from the one described in the second definition in that it would not include the most primitive levels: These would be called id. The problem of defining a demarcation between id and ego in such a conception would remain difficult, but is no more than a restatement of Freud's conception that the ego shades into the id. In the undefined "border" region one might classify id and ego aspects of particular behaviors in relation to other behaviors. In this range of the *continuum*, behavior would be called "id" in relation to behavior higher in the hierarchy but "ego" in relation to behavior lower. This conception parallels that of the layering of impulse-defense units I discussed earlier.

What definition shall we choose? Let us first remind ourselves that the separation of id and ego was designed to solve the fourth difficulty of the topographic conception—that the repressed and the repressing had been put into the same system, the *Ucs.* Freud, impressed by the problem of controlling the impulses, conceptualized this as a conflict which necessitated locating the two parties to the conflict in different systems. The fact that we must continue to make this conceptual distinction between impulse and impulse restraint draws us toward his kind of solution, but there is no methodological imperative for our doing so.

The last two definitions which I have proposed have the advantage of conceptualizing drive and drive restraints as functionally inseparable and as aspects of behavior. . . . The last two definitions have the further advantage of making it easier to conceptualize the functional inseparability of motive and discharge structure as well as of motive and inhibiting structure. The first definition would, like the present structural scheme, again separate drive, drive restraint, and drive discharge. [I] believe that it is better to conceptualize drive, drive restraint, and drive discharge together.

The choice between the last two definitions I would resolve in favor of the third because it does less violence to the present conception of the id—by which I mean the id as it is actually presented, rather than as it is conceptualized in the theory. I favor, then, a definition in which id and ego are conceived of as a hierarchical continuum of forces and structures existing at all levels of the hierarchy.

Such a solution argues that Freud's resolution of the fourth difficulty of the topographic systems was not a good one because, by putting force into one

---

3. In such a scheme the definition of the id might follow one of Freud's definitions of instinctual drive as nonmental, and become the congeries of instinctual drives insofar as they exist outside the psychic apparatus.

4. Glover is the exception: "A more elaborate differentiation of superego structure will, however, involve a closer study of the *relation of different ego systems to consciousness.* . . . In this connection it may be remembered that Freud was prepared to postulate the existence of a series of censorships lying between the repression barrier and perceptual consciousness, that is to say, operating at different levels of the preconscious system up to and including the margins of consciousness."

See also Jones, who describes the same concept in his discussion of the stratification of affect in the mental apparatus and again thus: ". . . the inhibiting tendencies as being distributed, in a streaming fashion, throughout the whole mind,

conscious as well as unconscious, increasing in strength, however, as one proceeds from the level of consciousness to the lowest layers of the unconscious."

system and counterforce into another, it obscured the existence of a hierarchy of force–counterforce integrations, and, while conceptualizing counterforce in structural terms, did not do the same for force. The recognition of this hierarchy, furthermore, makes it clear that, on any particular level of the hierarchy, force and counterforce, despite their antithesis, show similarities in mode of functioning, energy employed, and energy regulated.

NOTE 2

RAPAPORT, DAVID

The Structure of Psychoanalytic Theory*

Let us take the words of a man who utters the sentence, "Now things are becoming queer," and let us provide the context from which psychoanalytic theory will adduce its explanation of this verbal behavior:

This behavior occurred in the course of a discussion in a group—The other members responded to it with consternation—The man was bewildered by this response—Later he found out that he had said "queer" and not "clear" as he had intended to do, and as he thought he had done—He was embarrassed by this discovery—The discussion concerned a mismanagement of the group's affairs—The subject's utterance followed an explanation by the chairman of the group—The chairman attributed the mismanagement to a misunderstanding by the treasurer of an instruction given by him, and not to any malicious intent—The chairman commanded the unquestioned respect of the group and also wielded considerable power otherwise.

In terms of common-sense psychology, we are dealing here with a slip of the tongue.

In descriptive terms: The subject's conscious intention was to agree with the chairman's explanation. He did not carry out this intention, but instead expressed himself in a way that caused consternation; he was unaware both of not having carried out his intention, and of his consternation-arousing utterance. When he was told what he had said, he became embarrassed.

In terms of a data language: The independent variable (conscious intention) determined a value of the dependent variable (verbal utterance of agreement and conscious awareness of it). However, an intervening variable determined another value of the action component of the dependent variable (dissenting, consternation-arousing verbal utterance). The intervening variable left the conscious-awareness component of the dependent variable unaltered. A second intervening variable (external reality: infor-

* Reprinted from: *Psychology: A Study of a Science*, Vol. 3, S. Koch, ed. Copyright © 1959. McGraw-Hill Book Co. (pp. 116–20). Used by permission.

mation) altered the conscious-awareness component of the dependent variable and determined its affective aspect (embarrassment).

This formulation is not "neutral": It implies that the independent variable is a "motivation" (intention). Indeed, even the descriptive terms imply this. Before Freud, at least the common-sense term "slip of the tongue" was neutral, but it is not neutral now. Let us attempt a crude associationist formulation, to show that data languages are inseparable from construct languages and thus cannot be neutral: The chairman's explanation was associated in the subject to an approving verbal statement; the subject's actual response, however, was linked to the chairman's explanation by stronger associative bonds; the clash of the two associative complexes resulted in a compromise in which one of the complexes determined the awareness, while the other determined the verbal response of the subject.

In terms of psychoanalytic construct language: The subject's conscious intention is referred to a socially adaptive ego interest. The failure to carry out the intention is referred to an id motivation. The unawareness of the failure is referred to an unconscious ego motivation conflicting with this id motivation. The unawareness of the actual verbal expression used is referred both to the unconscious (id) motivation which was expressed, and to the unconscious ego controls (defenses) which, though they failed to prevent the use of the ego's executive apparatus by the id motivation, succeed in preventing its access to consciousness (compromise). The acute embarrassment is referred to the affect manifestation of the clash between the unconscious motivations and the restored ego control.

Let us take a closer look at the concepts involved. The unawareness is obviously the reference of the descriptive concept unconscious. It is likewise obvious that the intent to say "clear" is a conscious motive. But it is an inference that this motive is a force and it is a further inference that saying "queer" indicates the presence of another, unconscious, force. It is a still further inference that a third force is also involved which prevents conscious awareness both of the failure of the conscious intention and the success of the unconscious intention. It is yet a further inference that the latter two forces conflicted and reached a compromise, indicated both by the "clang" similarity of the words "clear" and "queer," and by the fact that the unconscious force attained control of the executive apparatus but did not gain access to consciousness. Thus we see that some of the concepts involved here are close to the observations, while others are at increasing distance from them.

In clinical inferences, the distance between observations and concepts may seem even greater. The clinician may infer, for instance, that the slip pertains to the ancient triangle formed by the subject, his older brother, and father, which was reactivated by the triangular situation of the subject, treasurer, and chairman. He may even go further and infer that homoerotic and aggressive drives involved in jealousy are the unconscious forces which conflict here with the ego's defenses against them and interfere with ego interests.

No wonder psychologists gained the impression that the relation of psychoanalytic concepts and theories to observations is distant and arbitrary. But is this impression accurate? Let us suppose that our subject volunteers for a free-association session, and his associations cluster around the treasurer and the chairman, rather than around the interests of the group. Will we then be justified in inferring that the agent behind the word "queer" is an unconscious force directed toward the treasurer and the chairman? Let us suppose further that the subject's associations not only corroborate that this unconscious force is an aggressive drive, but identify it as being of a jealous–suspicious variety. Let us finally assume that, in the course of these associations, the subject comes to realize that he actually has had filial feelings toward the chairman and vague, poorly understood feelings of irritation with the treasurer, akin to those he used to feel toward his brother, and thereby he specifies that the unconscious force pertains to the subject–brother–father triangle.

True, in this sequence the concepts (unconscious, unconscious impulse, unconscious hostile impulse, unconscious hostile and libidinal impulse, unconscious hostile and libidinal infantile impulse) are increasingly remote from the slip of the tongue which is the original observation. But the associations, too, are observations and the increasingly remote concepts are introduced in reference to these additional observations. Thus, the distance between observations and concepts is not as great as it seems on first sight. But there still remains a difficulty: The relationship of each more remote concept to the corresponding additional observation presupposes the less remote concepts. For instance, without assuming that the unawareness of the subject is a referent of the descriptive concept unconscious and without assuming the unconsciously motivated character of the slip, it would make no sense to infer that the subject's associations specify the pertinence of the aggressive impulse (indicated by the slip) to the treasurer and the chairman.

This relationship between observations and concepts is common to all sciences: *Observations demonstrate theoretical relationships only to those who already conceive of the observed in terms of the theory's concepts.* But the psychologist seems to overlook this truism when it comes to psychoanalysis. This oversight is so common that the lack of systematic treatments of the theory alone cannot account for it.

There must be other reasons, and a few of these will be conjectured:

The psychologist is accustomed to explicit—and, indeed, operational—definitions of concepts and is wary of psychoanalysis' definitions of concepts. He suspects that the mutual implications of its concepts hide a vicious circle. In the lack of a systematic statement of the theory, we can sympathize with his wariness, but we must keep in mind that in physics nobody would think of asking for an explicit definition of energy that did not involve the concept of work (which in turn involves the concepts of path and force, which in turn involve mass and acceleration, which in turn involve time and velocity, which in turn involve space and time). . . .

The clinical psychoanalyst is deft and nonchalant in using concepts at a great distance from the observations. For instance, he may conjecture from the word "queer" what *might* be involved in this slip, bypassing the intervening observations (e.g., associations) and concepts. It may be a well-supported conjecture, if the patient's previous productions converge on it; or it may be a poorly supported one, if the analyst is more imaginative than careful. It may even help the patient to insight if it is conveyed to him. But a *conjecture* it remains until the patient's associations or other productions confirm it. Some such conjectures are supported by so much experience, and pertain to relationships so common, that they are *almost* certain. These are particularly prone to turn into cliches, to give the outsider the impression of arbitrariness of an uncanny "second sight," and to oversimplify the complexity of the theoretical relationships even in the psychoanalyst's mind. Actually the psychoanalyst's use of these may not differ from an electrician's use of technical terms and repair or construction procedures without his referring to or even being aware of their theoretical implications. When the rules of thumb of clinical psychoanalysis are equated with the theory of psychoanalysis, the observations and concepts which bridge the gap between the basic concepts and the initial observations are inevitably overlooked.

2.

SOME PROBLEMS IN THE LAW OF PATENTS, COMMUNICATIONS, AND CONTRACTS

a.   CORRIGAN, ROBERT E. et al.

Apparatus for Producing Visual Stimulation

Filed May 7, 1958; Granted October 30, 1962; Application No. 3,060,795

The present invention relates to apparatus for producing visual stimulation at levels of awareness below that ability of an observer to report the stimulus verbally. More particularly, the present invention relates to apparatus for imparting useful information to an observer by subconscious stimulation and subsequently resulting in conscious purposive behavior of said observer without his awareness of the basis for such behavior, said apparatus comprising means for stimulating said observer below his conscious recognition level without said observer being consciously aware of any change in his environmental and physical status to impart information to said observer at said subconscious recognition level and said observer subsequently utilizing said information at the conscious recognition level.

No efforts have heretofore been directed to imparting useful information to an individual by stimulation solely below the conscious recognition level, i.e., prior to the individual's ability to verbally report stimuli. Prior workers in the general field utilized subconscious stimulation only preliminarily and always continued through to conscious recognition, thus positively changing the environmental and physical status of the individual upon whom the process was being applied.

Contrary to the above, the present invention depends upon the proved fact that humans are endowed with at least two levels of response, (1) the nonverbally reportable levels of awareness that establish that point at which stimuli will be verbally reportable, and (2) conscious awareness, i.e., the ability to report verbally the world around us.

A great amount of experimental work has been conducted in order to conclusively establish the fact that the foregoing two levels of response do exist. In carrying out these experiments, various types of apparatus as well as various media of application, were used. For example, the experiments can be carried out by means of the tachistoscope, television, motion pictures, magic lantern devices, controlled flash procedures used with signs, controlled temporal increase and decrease of brilliance of a sign, and/or combinations of the foregoing with appropriate auditory stimulation, e.g., radio, telephone, and phonograph.

The above noted media can be used in various fields of endeavor. As will be appreciated from a more complete consideration of the invention, among the fields to which the said invention is best applied, are (1) medicine, psychiatry, and psychology (as a diagnostic and therapeutic tool); (2) education (as an aid in teaching at all levels and, in particular, as a rehabilitative auxiliary in, for example, juvenile delinquency); (3) advertising and marketing (as point-of-sale advertising technique and as mass-advertising process); (4) propaganda and psychological warfare (conditioning civilian and military personnel, enemy aliens, prisoners of war, or opposing forces or civilian population) and to counter "brainwashing"; and (5) enhancement of motion pictures.

Our invention is particularly applicable to motion picture and television presentation. In this regard, it can be appreciated that the average individual is far more likely to come into contact with such media in the course of his everyday life. Accordingly, the apparatus utilized by us in practicing our invention has been primarily concerned with the motion picture and television field.

With the above in mind, the principal object of the present invention is to provide apparatus for the production of visual stimulation at levels of awareness below that ability of an observer to report the stimulus verbally, in order to induce selective perception resulting in selective overt response.

A more specific object of the invention is to provide apparatus for imparting useful information to an observer by subconscious stimulation and subsequently resulting in conscious purposive behavior of said observer without his awareness of the basis for such behavior, said apparatus comprising means for stimulating said observer below his conscious recognition level without said observer being consciously aware of any change in his environment and physical status to impart information to said observer at his subconscious recognition level and said observer subsequently utilizing said information at the conscious recognition level.

A further object of the invention is to provide means as described heretofore whereby information is projected on a screen at such a temporal speed and/or light intensity as to make the image of this information imperceptible to the human eye, but, nevertheless, perceptible to the subconscious level of awareness, i.e., subliminal, and thereafter utilizing this information at the conscious recognition level of the human mind.

Another object of this invention is to provide means for imparting useful information to an observer by subconscious stimulation, said observer subsequently using the said information, said means comprising means for stimulating said observer below his conscious recognition level without said observer being consciously aware of any change in his environment and physical status to impart information to said observer at his subconscious recognition level, coincidentally (i.e., continuously or in an interleaved fashion) imparting consciously recognizable information to said observer, and said observer thereafter utilizing the subconsciously presented information at the conscious recognition level.

An additional object of this invention is to provide means for producing a subconscious response in a human being, said response being later utilized in the conscious recognition level of said human being, said means comprising at least one motion picture projector adapted to project both subliminal and supraliminal (consciously recognizable) information on a motion picture screen at predetermined levels of frequency presentation and light intensity.

NOTES

NOTE 1

CORRIGAN, ROBERT, E. et al.

Communications from the Examiner (1958–60)*

*   *   *

Claims 1–21 are . . . rejected as being against public policy. To work upon the subconscious mind of an unsuspecting, involuntary individual appears to be conducive to mental unrest and physical deterioration. . . .

*   *   *

Claims 1–33 are rejected as drawn to subject matter not within the statutory classes. The claims recite steps of affecting the human senses and thus come into the category of mental steps. The claims do not recite an act or acts performed upon subject matter to be transformed to a different state or thing. The concept of stimulating a conscious person with subliminal information, visual or otherwise, is not considered to be a tangible act but is something mental and within the will of said conscious person. Dealings with nervous systems and with eye retinas no doubt would result in discoveries but are of existing laws of nature and are not patentable—*Funk Brothers Seed Co.* v. *Kalo Inoculant Co.*, 76 U.S.P.Q. 280, 333 U.S. 127. As stated in *Greenewalt* v. *Stanley Co.* 1932 CD 535, 54 F(2d) 195, "We do not find authority in the law for the issuance of a patent for results dependent upon such intangible, illusory, and non-material things as emotional or aesthetic reactions." Applicants' methods are presented for educational, propaganda, medical, and advertising purposes. In *ex parte* Turner 1894 CD 36 claims to a method of advertising were not allowed on the ground that no physical effect would be produced and the only result would be a state of mind, amounting to a predisposition, and ending there unless the reader wills otherwise. It is obvious that applicants' methods result in a state of mind.

*   *   *

Claims 4, 5 are rejected as unpatentable since they rely on everyday phenomena of nature. Each person in his environment is subject to vibratory waves which are supraliminally sensed and to other waves which are subliminally impressed on the person's senses. For example, in walking along a city sidewalk the eyes and ears of a person will receive all gradations of light and sound vibrations. Obviously some of these vibrations will be below the threshold of recognition, i.e., subliminal, due to distance away of the source or due to intervening objects. Naturally there is predetermined information in all the vibratory waves reaching a person from his environment. It is well settled that phenomena of nature are not patentable.

NOTE 2

BEDFORD v. HUNT
1 Mas. (1817)

STORY, J. . . . . No person is entitled to a patent under the act of Congress, unless he has invented some new and useful art, machine, manufacture, or composition of matter, not known or used before.

By useful invention, in the statute, is meant such a one as may be applied to some beneficial use in society, in contradistinction to an invention, which is injurious to the morals, the health, or the good order of society. It is not necessary to establish, that the invention is of such general utility, as to supersede all other inventions now in practice to accomplish the same purpose. It is sufficient, that it has no noxious or mischievous tendency, that it may be applied to practical uses, and that so far as it is applied, it is salutary. If its practical utility be very limited, it will follow, that it will be of little or no profit to the inventor; and if it be trifling, it will sink into utter neglect. The law, however, does not look to the degree of utility; it simply requires, that it shall be capable of use, and that the use is such as sound morals and policy do not discountenance or prohibit. . . .

NOTE 3

DELIER, ANTHONY W.

Walker on Patents (1937)*

With respect to the invention of Colt's revolver, it is perhaps true that it was injurious to the morals, and injurious to the health, and injurious to the good order of society. That instrument of death may have been injurious to morals, in tending to tempt and to promote the gratification of private revenge. It may have been injurious to health, in that it is very liable to accidental discharge, and to thereby cause wounds, and even homicide. It may also have been injurious to good order, especially in the newer parts of the country, because it facilitates and increases private warfare among frontiersmen. On the other hand, the revolver, by furnishing a ready means of self-defense, may sometimes have promoted morals and health and good order. By what tests, therefore, is utility to be determined in such cases? Is it to be done by balancing the good functions with the evil functions? Or is everything useful within the meaning of the law, if it is used, or is designed and adapted to be used, to accomplish a good result, though in fact it is

---

* U.S. Department of Commerce, Patent Office. Serial Nos. 590,868; 733,713.

* New York: Baker, Voorhis and Co., 1937, Vol. I, (pp. 317–18). Reprinted by permission.

oftener used, or is as well or even better adapted to be used, to accomplish a bad one? Or is utility negatived by the mere fact that the thing in question is sometimes injurious to morals, or to health, or to good order? . . .

b.   New Jersey Assembly

Concurrent Resolution No. 33 Creating Commission To Study Subliminal Projection (1958)*

A CONCURRENT RESOLUTION creating a legislative commission to study the operation of and effect upon the health and welfare of the people of New Jersey by the proposed new mass advertising medium known as "subliminal projection" or "hidden message advertising."

* * *

WHEREAS, Such subconscious motivation is beyond the control of reason and may have a deleterious effect upon the health and welfare of the citizens of the State; and

WHEREAS, The economy of the State might be seriously disturbed by such hidden stimuli; and

WHEREAS, There is grave danger of the misuse of such a device to influence the thinking of our citizens while they are unconscious of any pressure being exerted upon their minds; now, therefore,

BE IT RESOLVED by the General Assembly of the State of New Jersey (the Senate concurring):

There is hereby created a commission.

. . . to study the operation of the device known as "subliminal projection" and to ascertain the effects of this advertising medium upon the health and welfare of the citizens of New Jersey and upon the economy of the State. The commission shall, if the results of its study shall indicate the desirability therefor, propose such legislation to regulate or ban the use of this "hidden message advertising" as may be necessary to guard the health and welfare of the citizens of New Jersey and to maintain a stable economy for the State. . . .

* * *

c. Public Hearing before the Commission (1959)**

ASSEMBLYWOMAN MILDRED BARRY HUGHES (Chairman): This public hearing is now declared open.

* * *

The first one to be heard this morning will be Dr. Bush.

---

* State of New Jersey: *Final Report of the Commission to Study Subliminal Projection*, May, 1959.

** Hearing held at Assembly Chamber, State House, Trenton, New Jersey.

[i]

DR. CLIFFORD BUSH

DR. CLIFFORD BUSH: I am . . . Chairman of the Education Department at Newark State College.

* * *

My interest, outside of the laboratory, is simply this: If an individual can be influenced through subliminal perception, without his awareness, are we not infringing upon his right in a free society to make choices of his own free will? . . .

* * *

[ii]

DR. ZYGMUNT A. PIOTROWSKI

DR. ZYGMUNT A. PIOTROWSKI: . . . I am . . . Clinical Professor of psychology and a member of the Department of Psychiatry at the Jefferson Medical College in Philadelphia.

* * *

The term "subliminal projection" means the projection of visual stimuli—words, pictures, other figures—onto a screen in such a manner that while they are not consciously perceived or recognized by the observer, they influence his thoughts or actions. Experiments have proved that subliminal perception, i.e., perception without awareness, exists. Daily experience shows that subliminal perception is occurring all the time. Perhaps one of the most telling and simple examples is the man who falls asleep while listening to the radio or looking at television and wakes up the moment someone turns the radio off: In this case, a sudden reduction of subliminal auditory stimulation wakes the man up because—without being aware of it—the sleeper interpreted the sudden stoppage of sound as a marked change in his immediate environment. When we perceive anything specific, we attach meaning to it. And any meaningful change in the environment subliminally perceived or supraliminally perceived may cause a very definite reaction on the part of the person.

It is an incontrovertible fact that one can perceive subliminally, i.e., without being aware that one perceives, and that an experimenter can deliberately cause others to perceive subliminally. On the other hand, we do not know enough about the exact effects of subliminal projection of visual or auditory stimuli in radio or television. We do know that all people do not react in the same way to consciously or unconsciously perceived stimuli. In the last forty years, we have learned that there are great differences among individuals in their reactions to vague, indeterminate, or subliminal stimuli.

One experimental finding seems rather well established. It has been shown that words frequently used, both in print and in spoken language, are recognized more easily and readily than unfamiliar words which are heard and read infrequently. Thus, the rare word or picture is not recognized as readily as the familiar word and picture. It would follow that hidden advertising would not be an efficient way of introducing a new product. However, once a product is generally known, the best way of advertising it is through repetition of its name or trademark through supraliminal or ordinary advertising. . . .

As far as I could ascertain, no competent investigation of the effect of subliminal projection through television or radio has been published. However, our knowledge about visual subliminal perception makes it doubtful that the so-called hidden message advertising would be very effective. Incidentally, the current measurement of the effects of any form of advertising is very inaccurate, unsystematic, impressionistic, and unscientific. Therefore, at present, it would be most difficult to prove the efficacy of subliminal advertising.

There would be one advantage of hidden advertising, namely, programs would not be interrupted by sales talks and visual sales displays. But, there might be one great disadvantage, that is, the fear of being influenced against one's best judgment and against one's conscious will. People might develop the suspicion that they are being manipulated without knowing about it.

It is interesting to inquire why subliminal projection, the effectiveness of which remains unproved, has caused concern among some of us. A possible explanation of this concern may be that some people are disturbed by hidden or subliminal messages in television because they think this technique might be misused for undesirable social, political, or other purposes. We have no evidence to evaluate this tentative explanation. We do know, however, that at times some groups of people get quite disturbed even by imaginary fears, especially if they suspect that someone might take advantage of them.

If I were convinced that there is no serious fear of disturbing people by the idea of hidden or subliminal television messages, I would suggest that subliminal projection be ignored. However, as there seems to be some danger that subliminal projection is or may be misunderstood, its influence grossly exaggerated . . . I would propose that subliminal television projection be regulated in the sense that programs with subliminal projection be identified as such, and that the content of the messages—verbal or pictorial—undergo the same regulations which now apply to any radio or television messages.

*   *   *

CHAIRMAN HUGHES: . . . Do you feel that, if this technique were perfected over the coming years, it might be more effective even as a medium of control or of influence?

DR. PIOTROWSKI: Yes. Well, in the first place, as a matter of fact, we are subjected to subliminal projection all the time. When you are traveling on a train or by car, you don't see what the billboards have said, consciously,—you may have picked up something, that you ought to buy this or that product. In other words, subliminal projection, by television, would not be anything unique. It's just putting it where it has not been before. But it is there all the time. It has been from the beginning of time. If you read a newspaper in a very haphazard way; many people have taught themselves not to listen consciously to talk during intermissions of good musical programs— well, that's subliminal projection. The moment the man stops talking, they hear it and tune the radio louder. Subliminal projection is a fact of life. It's there all the time. I mean, it's futile to think that you can do away with it. If you walk on the sidewalk, if you're absent-minded,—after all, many absent-minded professors get home without being killed, which means that they use subliminal projection to avoid dangers. I mean, this is something that, I think, ought to be considered to put the whole matter into a proper proportion. I, personally, feel that if one group uses subliminal projection, another one would use it too. As long as you give people a choice, that's all right. I would be against, perhaps, one group trying to perfect it. I mean, that would, of course, be a possible danger; although we really can't tell. There is a great difference between posthypnotic suggestion and subliminal projection. In posthypnotic suggestion, the patient who is being hypnotized concentrates all the attention he has on you. The essence of hypnosis is that everything else is disregarded, except the words of the hypnotizer. It's a pretty different process from what is attempted in the hidden message advertising. There, after all, you are going to see something else, and that hidden message is only part. It does not force itself upon the attention of the viewer or the listener. It's an entirely different process. . . .

There is also a psychological problem. The more passive part of humanity is more likely to be influenced by this than the more active ones. You see, people who are very active do not respond to stimulation that is against their wishes; the more passive people, on the whole, are more perceptive of that sort of thing because their lives are not too well organized. So that, if there is any damage, so to speak, it would be in the most passive group of population, which is passive and, consequently, it does not much affect.

*   *   *

CHAIRMAN HUGHES: I think that no State, at the moment, has any law, and I think this is the first State that is doing a very complete study on the matter. . . .

*   *   *

SENATOR MCCAY: Doctor, I gathered from your last

answer . . . that you don't have too great a fear that brainwashing might take place as a result of subliminal projection.

DR. PIOTROWSKI: I doubt it very much. . . . Well, I don't know that this Chamber is the right place to say it but Princeton University, the Undergraduate School, made a very simple experiment. They used the stereopticon. It's subliminal projection in the sense that when you look at the stereopticon and have two different pictures, not two slightly different photographs of one but two different ones, you first see one because one eye dominates the process of conscious perception. For example, the students there were shown a very properly dressed lady on one picture, and an actress in a very gay theatre in another picture. Most of the students saw the very properly dressed lady, and the other one emerged very slowly. So here is proof that young men in their twenties respond to the stimulus to which they were accustomed, first.

Another study . . . showed, for example, that the more manly students reacted to subliminal perception very differently from the more studious and, let's say, the more withdrawn young men. Therefore, the personality of the viewer has a great deal to do with the effect that subliminal projection may have.

SENATOR MCCAY: I gather that your main concern is that there be a warning that a person or persons are being subjected to subliminal projection, so as to protect their rights.

DR. PIOTROWSKI: Yes. I think that would probably kill any desire on the part of advertisers to use it, because the other firms can say, "Look, he has to use hidden messages. What does he have to hide?" And I think, if you adopt such a rule that you allow it, then it ought to be stated—whenever hidden messages are used that fact ought to be stated with the program, printed in special program booklets or newspaper advertising. I think that would drive any advertiser away from it.

*   *   *

DR. KELLY: . . . In your opinion, would the identification of the program effectively allay the fears of this anxious element of our population, or would it increase the fears?

DR. PIOTROWSKI: I am thinking of what Orson Welles did, was it twenty or twenty-five years ago, when he terrified so many people into getting into their cars and driving in all directions when the war threatened. I think the more serious the reputation of the television or radio station, the more likely it is to affect the people. They would say that if people so serious as these engage into it, they must have a very serious reason, and when it's hidden you don't offer it directly enough.

. . . [T]he essence of anxiety is the fear of the unknown and, therefore, it is natural that you must invoke anxiety in many because by definition a hidden message is a message of unknown content. . . .

*   *   *

MR. WIRTHS: . . . I remember someone once saying that where it was used on a screen in a movie house, and maybe it would say "Eat peanuts," to stimulate peanut sales, by the time the person acted on it they might go back and get a glass of water or wash their hands or something. Is this kind of interpretation sort of a basic thing?

DR. PIOTROWSKI: Oh, very definitely. I mean, this is one of the most basic and completely uncontrovertible facts—that human reactions, the vaguer the stimulus, the less definite it is, the greater variety of reactions you get from a group of people.

MR. WIRTHS: Well, suppose you had a very precise one. Suppose someone kept flashing on the screen in a motion picture, in a subliminal fashion, the word "Kill, kill, kill," would that person be likely to go out and kill or might they interpret it to go home and kiss their baby?

DR. PIOTROWSKI: Well, this is speculation because we haven't examined the fact yet. Posthypnotic suggestion here might be compared with it because such experiments were done. I think if you deal with a very disturbed psychotic patient—I don't think that 99 per cent of society would go out and kill but among the remaining 1 per cent if there was one who was very disturbed, that might possibly lead to this action, provided the patient has been thinking about it anyway. And, you see, if he reads a newspaper and reads about a murder, that is the same suggestion. You see, when you have a known murder, which is very well described in newspapers, you are going to have, usually, a series of other ones.

My point is that this is not unique, that you get a lot of suggestions from all sources, but one shouldn't take this out of context and treat this as something unique, of which there are no competitor phenomena in other parts of our life. Most people would not respond to it.

MR. WIRTHS: Well, let me ask you this question, along the same line: Suppose someone were interested in influencing our population to embrace communism, would it be more effective to have some secret messages over the course of a fifteen-minute program or would it be more effective to hire the usual type of orator and have him harangue a crowd of people for fifteen minutes on the subject and try to sell them by persuasion?

DR. PIOTROWSKI: Oh, a good haranguing would be much more effective. I have no doubt about that, no question about that. Not that such an experiment was performed but we have enough of the essentials of the situation tested that I am sure of that conclusion.

MR. WIRTHS: In other words, then, what you are

saying is that the *supra* stimuli is so much more effective than the subliminal—

DR. PIOTROWSKI: Yes.

*   *   *

[*iii*]

DR. BERTRAM VOGEL

CHAIRMAN HUGHES: . . . Will you give your full name and title?

DR. BERTRAM VOGEL: I'm Dr. Bertram Vogel, Doctor of Philosophy. I'm a Clinical Psychologist. I'm an Associate Professor of Psychology at Newark State College. . . .

*   *   *

MR. WIRTHS: . . . If we were to decide that it was necessary to regulate this technique, how would we establish a cutting-off point, as to when something was subliminal and when it was supraliminal?

DR. VOGEL: Well, ideally, you would have to test each individual and determine what his particular threshold was. This is one of the difficulties, obviously. For example, if somebody were going to do this in a moving picture house, he wouldn't have that opportunity, he wouldn't be able to do this. It's impractical. In a laboratory, one can. I can take my subjects and run them again, again, and again, and determine what is their, generally speaking, average threshold. So, I have some idea to run something below that, and I have some evidence. In a moving picture house, I would imagine, or somewhere on a screen, you might get a few individuals who would actually see this. It wouldn't be subliminal to them unless the subliminality of the exposure was tremendous; in other words, unless it was really way down and quite subliminal. I doubt that it would be desirable for a projectionist to set it that low because then he might really go way below the subliminal into an area where really there's no chance to perceive it at all.

*   *   *

CHAIRMAN HUGHES: Doctor, . . . suppose we were dealing with emotions—love, hate, envy, that kind of thing—and the newspapers and magazines and all of the other media had been geared to arouse controversy in certain areas and possibly direct antagonism toward specific minority groups, and this kind of thing were added to it, subliminally—would that be effective enough, do you think, to trigger action or would it merely add to the whole effect?

*   *   *

DR. VOGEL: [T]his would again depend upon the individual needs of the individual, because he will always be sensitive. He will be sensitive to things that involve his own needs, one way or another,

negatively or positively. Now, you can't make me go out and kill somebody. I'm just not going to do that, see? But on the other hand, if I have certain very strong prejudices and let's say I sat on them for a long time, they are easily touched off. It doesn't take much. Then I'm much more sensitive to this kind of stimulation and I might—well, I might do something, because this is in keeping with my personality structure.

*   *   *

[*iv*]

DR. ROBERT E. CORRIGAN

DR. ROBERT E. CORRIGAN: Madam Chairman, members of the Commission: My name is Dr. Robert E. Corrigan. I am the present Vice-president of Psychological Research and Development of Precon Process and Equipment Corporation, New Orleans, Louisiana. . . . Prior to this, I worked as a Senior Research Psychologist in Mandeville, Louisiana, in the hospital there, a diagnostic center, and it was at this hospital and at the Department of Psychiatry and Neurology at Tulane University that I started the initial research projects in preconscious communication which will be reported.

Approximately eighteen months ago, newspapers and magazines introduced to the public a new term and a new concept—*Subliminal Perception*—or—*Subliminal Communication*. . . .

The immediate response by the press to this concept was one of apprehension. The central theme of hundreds of published articles was that a means of advertising had been developed which was capable of selectively influencing individuals and groups without their ability to control their decisions or wishes in response to the message presented.

*   *   *

. . . "Can this thing make me do something I don't want to do—and don't know I'm doing?," "Can it make me buy something I don't want?," "Can it make me vote for a nonpreferred candidate?."

No one has answered these questions based on systematic research results and with a meaningful explanation of the perceptual processes involved. So the public and most members of the press continue to think of this medium of communication with fear and as a threat. I will provide for you today the necessary research data to answer these questions.

The *primary* issue to resolve is the basic fear that information which one cannot consciously "see" or "hear" *somehow* will influence the general public to react in a manner which is contrary to their normal likes and dislikes. This emotional reaction has been based almost entirely on conjecture and opinion with little factual information. The result of this reaction is a prevailing "tag" which defines preconscious communication as the process with the ability to coerce individuals and groups to react in a specified manner *without* their control or volition.

*   *   *

The reason for this meeting today is to review evidence in evaluating the potentials of preconscious communications in terms of its *effectiveness* in eliciting responses by individual and groups. My presence here could be interpreted as playing the role of defense attorney presenting evidence in the case for preconscious communication. I would rather that my role be established as a scientist—as one of a team who has completed nine years' work in developing this medium of communication. I would rather that the data obtained from the research program speak for itself; that this data resolve the questions asked by critics of preconscious communication; and, that this data more clearly define the future role of preconscious communication in society.

*   *   *

. . . I would like to discuss the reasons for substituting the terms *preconscious perception* or *communication* for the term subliminal. The word subliminal is derived from the Latin word *limin*—meaning threshold. Combining the prefix *sub* to the word *limin* provides the word subliminal—meaning below the threshold of conscious recognition.

The concept of the threshold is a statistical one. It is only a measure of performance. It in no way is directed toward or applied in the explanation of behavioral changes. The preconscious threshold is most commonly defined in terms of physical values (intensity and/or duration) at which the desired response is obtained from an observer at least half the time. The word *response* in this definition means the ability of an observer to consciously recognize and to correctly tell what information is being presented.

The conscious threshold value varies from person to person for each sense, and, within each person from moment to moment, from day to day, for types of information, for types of personalities, and so forth. Thus the precise strength of stimulation required to produce preconscious perception is not a constant; it depends upon the conditions of the moment and upon the particular observer. In a discussion of experimental factors we are directly concerned with threshold values, as we are the physical techniques used in obtaining these thresholds—such as the means of projecting visual information or transmitting audio information. These measures of performance only provide us the basis for interpreting changes in behavior.

However from the point of view of *application* of experimental results we are not concerned with threshold values directly but behavioral changes when information is *always* presented below the level or threshold of conscious recognition. In this framework we are *only* concerned with perception or communication *prior* to conscious awareness— namely preconscious perception or communication. We therefore, are concerned directly with the *effectiveness* of preconscious communication and the preconscious perceptual processes which are involved.

. . . The first and most obvious question is: "*What is preconscious communication?*" It is the process whereby individuals and groups can be presented with visual and auditory information without their being consciously aware of exposure to this information but to which they make a selective response. This can be accomplished at present in motion pictures, television, radio, audio-communication systems and point-of-display devices. Every person is constantly perceiving things around him which he cannot *recall* "seeing" or "hearing." Yet, information received in this manner is constantly influencing his conduct.

In discussing preconscious communication we are discussing a medium of communication like those which are already known. The great difference is the discovery that we can react at levels of sensitivity which we had thought were impossible.

The individual responds to preconscious information in exactly the same manner as he does to visual information *above* the threshold of conscious awareness. He responds in a controlled, purposive manner. The individual is, as with all other forms of communication, responding in terms of his prevailing likes and dislikes. He is his own "censor"—for preconscious and conscious material alike.

The second pertinent question is: "*What are the basic principles by which preconscious perception works?*" An exact statement of the basic principles by which preconscious perception works is not definable at this time. Over the years, however, psychologists have accumulated clinical and experimental evidence which indicates that individuals are endowed with two levels of mental activity. One level defined as consciousness is *characterized* by one's ability to recall and to discuss immediately the world around him. The other type, defined as *preconsciousness* (that is below the level of conscious awareness) relates to mental activity which one is unable to immediately recall or discuss. The evidence, however, indicates that these two levels of mental activity are constantly functioning and interacting.

Of significance is clinical evidence indicating that a large share of mental activity which determines our responses is accomplished *without* conscious awareness. Often we do not "see" or "hear" things we do not wish to. In other cases we may distort things so that we are not required to recognize them in their true light. In our everyday contacts we are constantly attempting to influence people around us by means of sounds and movements we are not conscious of making. Correspondingly, we all make some unconscious use of the cues presented to us by others.

Responding *without* conscious awareness is not magical, but, rather, is a *normal*, *active*, and *purposeful* reaction.

Next—"*What are the facts showing the validity of preconscious communication?*" . . . The consensus of experimental results and professional expert opinion is that preconscious communication can influence behavior. One overview of preconscious perception by psychologists from the University of Michigan presents "summative statements and conclusions based upon what seems to be sufficient evidence and consensus in the literature."

Numerous experiments are reported which show essentially the same results, namely, that even when subjects have zero confidence in their judgments they can discriminate between preconscious stimuli reliably (though not perfectly). It was shown that in all cases the reliability of the subjects' judgments increases directly with the intensity of the stimulus. As to whether preconscious communication can produce any but the most simple modifications in behavior— the Michigan group in their survey reported that "evidence suggests that subjects may either (a) 'learn' certain preconscious presented stimuli, or (b) make use of preconscious reinforcers either to *learn* or *strengthen* a previously learned response."

Other data presented have shown that certain "psychological states" such as need, value, conflict, and defense may also significantly influence thresholds of conscious awareness. Thus through the process of selective perception one can be motivated to respond differently based on the emotional tone or meaningfulness of the preconscious information presented. While much is yet to be done to establish the most efficient method for using this medium of communication, the research results demonstrate that individuals respond to preconscious stimulation in an active, purposeful manner.

The research program by our organization was designed to determine the basic principles explaining the operation of preconscious perception, and the conditions under which it works best.

. . . The objective of the research was to determine if individuals react to different classes of preconscious cues prior to their ability to consciously report any stimulus. Words, which differed in emotional meaning, were "flashed" on a screen at such a fast speed that no one could report seeing anything. During succeeding trials, the flashing speed was slowed down to that point where a person could correctly report the word. In order to provide a physical response at various levels of awareness up to the point of correct recognition, each individual was required to perform

an additional task. This consisted of depressing a mechanical lever following each "flash." The words presented to each individual were of three types: *neutral words*, such as apple, river; *words with emotional meaning*, such as death, blood; and *words which are culturally taboo*. The results of these tests were as follows:

First: In order to obtain correct recognition of emotional and taboo words it was necessary to *slow down* the "flashing" speed. We found it took subjects two to three times longer to report the emotional and taboo words.

Second: An analysis of unique patterns in the hand depressions of the mechanical lever following each "flash" at different levels of awareness showed that subjects were responding selectively and differently to the three classes of words. Reliable differences in physical responses were established *even prior* to their ability to consciously report the *most* neutral word. Thus even at "flashing" speeds when no word could be consciously recognized, individuals were obviously perceiving and reacting to the content of the preconscious information. These results, in conjunction with the striking differences in recognition thresholds for the three classes of words, showed conclusively that the threatening words were being "censored" and "resisted" prior to conscious awareness.

The most significant outcome of the initial research was data supporting the hypothesis that individuals are endowed with a capability of receiving visual information at levels of which they are unaware, namely, preconscious levels of awareness. Further the evidence indicates that subjects evaluate the content of this information at these levels and selectively respond prior to their ability to report verbally the information perceived.

These data would support the hypothesis, therefore, that a hierarchy of levels of perception exists. It was also indicated that response processes at levels of which individuals are unaware influence and direct, in part, behavior which has been defined as "conscious," i.e., directly observable and reportable by an individual.

Two further experiments were carried out to test the validity of these experimental results. Two hypotheses were presented: (1) that if the initial data were valid, then an individual could be taught a new response at levels of which he is unaware; and (2) information presented below levels of awareness (preconsciously) can be used by subjects to solve problems more efficiently.

In the second experiment, subjects were taught to learn a new response to the neutral words (examples —apple, stove, river) which were in the dissertation. Individuals initially were "flashed" the neutral words only at preconscious levels of awareness. Following each flash the subject was given an electric shock to the palm of the hand. It was quite an electric shock, believe me. The object of this "shocking" procedure was to associate the effects of the painful "shock" stimulus to the neutral word. Following this conditioning period, the "shock-associated" words were "flashed" on a screen at slower and slower speeds until the subject could consciously report them. If the threshold for conscious recognition were to increase, as was observed for emotional words in the initial project, it would be apparent that individuals had discriminated, recognized, and had reacted selectively to learn a new response at levels of preconscious awareness.

*   *   *

The experimental results . . . indicate that this conditioning effect was actually the case. Results of this study demonstrated conclusively that subjects can be taught to respond selectively to visual information, and to learn a new response to these stimuli at preconscious levels of awareness. . . .

These results suggested the functioning of intellectual or cognitive processes of discrimination, evaluation, and organization at the preconscious levels of awareness.

The third experiment was performed to test the validity of this latter point. In the third experiment we showed that individuals can use visual information presented preconsciously to solve problems more efficiently. The problem solving task was to decipher a series of anagrams in the shortest time possible. An anagram consists of a series of letters presented in a jumbled order, which, when properly arranged, spell a particular word. One group of subjects were presented the answers to problems below conscious awareness before being presented the problem to solve. Another group was presented the same problems without being given the solution preconsciously. The results were most striking. . . . (Slide projected on screen.) When the answers to problems were visually presented preconsciously prior to problem solution, the problem-time solution was decreased by 15 to 46 per cent, depending on the difficulty of the problem.

The data presented for all three experiments demonstrated conclusively:

1. That visual information presented at preconscious levels of awareness is discriminated, recognized, and reacted to by individuals in terms of their prevailing likes and dislikes. Information of negative content is resisted and rejected; information of positive content is more readily accepted.

2. That the process of responding to preconscious information is an active, purposeful, and normal function.

3. That depending on the conditions of presentation individuals can be taught new responses at pre-

conscious levels of awareness, and equally well can use information to solve problems more efficiently.

The combined results indicate not only the capability of stimulating subjects at preconscious levels of awareness resulting in selective response, but that this information is, in every case, discriminated, recognized, evaluated, and responded to in terms of the individual's predisposition to respond. This predisposition to respond is based on the meaningfulness of the information in terms of prevailing likes and dislikes of the individual. He is, therefore, as in all other media of conscious communication (that is, above the level of conscious awareness) his own censor. He cannot be manipulated or changed by merely being presented information which he cannot immediately consciously report. The point is the individual does "see" in the sense of perceiving the information at preconscious levels of awareness and reacts selectively depending on his individual will or volition.

In 1954 we attempted to determine the basic principles by which preconscious information affects groups of subjects in the medium of motion pictures. Based on previous research results we thought that:

A. Presenting a symbol with positive appeal would result in an increased acceptance of an entertainment program—and accordingly, presenting a negative or less positive message would result in a partial rejection of the entertainment program. This would be the case if individuals are truly censoring and monitoring visual information at preconscious levels of awareness.

And the second point we had was—

B. The more positive appeal of the preconscious message, the greater the probability of its being consciously selected at a later time—without the subject being aware that he had been presented the symbol. This conclusion is based on research data which show that individuals resist recognition of information they dislike or prefer less.

To test the validity of these concepts eleven groups were presented one of three geometric symbols which differed in degree of positive appeal. These symbols were: a triangle, a circle, and a square. Symbols were selected to minimize the problem of meaning and interpretation among subjects.

Groups of subjects were shown a movie, a Woody Woodpecker cartoon, without knowing that visual information was being presented preconsciously. Following the cartoon they were asked to state whether they liked, felt neutral toward, or disliked the movie. Then they were presented the series of three symbols for conscious visual inspection. Subjects were requested to select "that one which appeals to you the most." The latter procedure was carried out to determine whether individuals would select that particular symbol presented to them preconsciously in conjunction with the cartoon.

The results of this experiment were most significant:

A. It was found that the conscious preference value for the geometric symbols was in a ratio of 3:2:1 for the triangle, circle, and square, respectively. Translated into English, it means that the triangle was the most preferred, the circle in between, and the square least of all on a ratio of 3 to 2 to 1.

B. The percentage of each symbol group who stated they liked or disliked the movie changed directly according to the defined preference order for the individual symbols.

*   *   *

In summary, the research results in this initial experiment with motion pictures indicated conclusively that individuals are actively responding to preconscious information presented with the movie according to its positive or negative meaning to the individual and that the degree of positive or negative appeal associated with preconscious visual information can determine the effectiveness of conscious selection at a later time.

*   *   *

[W]e will move on to the [next] question which is "What are the possible fields of application with preconscious communication?" Our initial research program in this medium of communication was in the areas of education, training, and psychopathology. It is in these areas where it is believed that the preconscious communications will prove to be most effective.

Let's talk about the first area "Education and Training."

The problems of the educator and that of a training director have much in common. On one hand they must provide a broad and comprehensive program to prepare each individual for the specific job required in terms of skills and knowledges. On the other hand, because of increasing numbers of individuals to be taught and the shortage of teaching personnel, less time is possible for individual attention. These two factors, coupled with the increased demands of job complexity and specialized knowledge for the industrial or scholastic student makes it mandatory to develop teaching techniques which, while reducing individual trial-and-error in the learning process, will result in increased positive motivation by the learner, and further result in increased retention and effectiveness of application.

The research results for visual and auditory preconscious communication indicate the possibility of providing subtle cues which are discriminated without the conscious awareness of the individual. It has been shown that individuals learn new associations at preconscious levels of awareness; that they can use preconscious cues to strengthen a previously learned response; and that they can be motivated to respond based on the meaningfulness of the preconscious information presented. Combining preconscious visual and auditory cues in conjunction with consciously presented materials can provide a teaching tool for group instruction which can increase significantly the efficiency of the learning process under more controlled, systematic conditions. The use of preconscious cues can make it possible to present effective subtle directions and points of emphasis to derive or select the proper method of approach needed to solve a particular problem or more firmly integrate a training principle. Combining this technique with selected symbolism to increase the psychological impact of the conscious level material can more systematically increase the positive reaction and participation by the individual student or trainee. Thus, what is provided by incorporating preconscious communication is more efficient selective perception of the "things" to be learned, and greater motivational impact for the learning and application of the material presented.

An example of how the various Precon devices can be used in the development of a training, educational, or psychological program is well represented in a discussion of the application of preconscious communication in the development of safety attitudes in industrial plants. . . . I [once] presented a formal address entitled, "What is Subliminal Communication? How Can It Affect Safety Attitudes?" The following excerpts from this address, while specific to the concept of industrial safety programs, is readily generalized to other sociological problems in training and education. I quote:

"The establishment of a program for the purpose of training personnel to be safety conscious (or for any other specific purpose in this area) must be oriented specifically to the development of defined attitudes. Initially a systematic and comprehensive series of conferences in conjunction with motion pictures and/or television is desirable to present the concepts in a systematic manner. This is a much more effective means of informing and directing the trainees than is chance and casual learning.

"The real problem in creating positive safety attitudes is twofold: (a) presenting defined safety concepts and (b) convincing employees of the value of safety measures and procedures. Once information has been given to employees, still further education is necessary to make sure that they believe as well as know that certain practices are unsafe.

"In reality, since only the maladjusted individual is likely to hurt himself voluntarily, it is a function of the degree of meaningfulness and awareness associated with safety concepts. The degree of carefulness of the ordinary employee is determined by (1) what he knows of safe and unsafe practices, (2) how important he thinks it is to follow his knowledge on the subject, and if he remembers the implications of unsafe acts and the appropriate safe practices to be followed.

"Preconscious group stimulation would be incorporated with motion pictures, television, and audio-communication devices (1) to systematically increase and establish the proper motivational set necessary to convince each individual of the personal and group threat involved and (2) to increase the efficiency of selection of specific training points to be learned and retained. This can result in increasing the strength and efficiency of communication transmission—and the resulting concept formation of safety attitudes.

"Assume that the initial training courses have resulted in the development of truly dynamic safety attitudes, that is, truly digested safety principles and personal appreciation of the implications of unsafe and careless working habits. The final effort still remains to follow up on the job to reinforce the principles learned and to remind the employee in an effective manner of safety practices to be followed. This is the ultimate criterion since it is only at this point where the accident in question can occur. It is at this junction where point-of-display and audio-communication devices will play a major role, to remind the employee of safety attitudes already learned, and to provide information to reinforce the personal implications of an unsafe act to self and others.

"Several studies reported in the literature have shown that the more familiar a subject is with the preconscious stimulus he is to perceive, the more rapidly he perceives it. We interpret these studies to mean that unfamiliar stimuli or information may be ineffective when presented preconsciously, even though familiar messages may 'get through.' It is imperative, therefore, that the point-of-display devices provide a continuous dynamic preconscious reminder on the job. The materials presented by way of placards and posters must have specific meaning to the individuals based on materials learned in the initial and refresher courses. One application of preconscious point-of-display devices has been tested. The results indicate a significant change in behavior based on the material presented preconsciously.

"What is of most importance, however, is the realization that preconscious communication techniques can be continuously provided (1) to assist in the initial establishment of selected safety concepts, (2) to help a student or trainee to realize, believe in, and be convinced of the implications of unsafe acts, and (3) to remind and reinforce on the job the motivation to apply the safety concepts already learned and appreciated."

While talking about safety attitudes, we can think of the total application here of the various medias and devices by inserting words and thinking in other frames of reference.

A further area of immediate interest in the application of preconscious communication for education and training is with teaching machines, training devices, and training simulators. The present complexity of weapon systems required for our national defense increases significantly the need for more efficient techniques for on-the-job training. The same problem is encountered in industry and in educational institutions to increase the effectiveness of training and teaching programs.

*   *   *

. . . It is important . . . to direct ourselves immediately to the question: "What about the question of 'brainwashing' with preconscious communication?" We have shown that the preconscious mind of an individual is actively monitoring and evaluating information presented at the preconscious levels of awareness and is responding to this material in terms of one's prevailing likes and dislikes, even though the viewer is unable to report "seeing" the material presented. This reaction is completely contrary to the "brainwashing" concept which implies a passive role by an observer in the perceptual process, and one which results in his performing a specific response without his direct control.

It is obvious, therefore, that the safeguards for the use of Precon in any application are "built in" for each individual observer. He is his own censor. He is the first one to satisfy before a positive reaction to advertising can be accomplished. As such, the person to be most concerned is the advertiser himself. The advertiser must be certain that he presents visual material of the highest caliber (both for entertainment and the Precon information). To be positively associated, the information must be acceptable to the general public in that it shall in no way infringe upon the moral or social standards of audiences.

*   *   *

Now the other areas—one of the immediate applications of the Precon Process is in the field of motion picture and television entertainment. The Precon Process would be used to increase the entertainment value of programs by providing preconscious information to enhance the psychological moods or trends of the material. . . . This would stimulate more active participation by audiences, thereby increasing the positive appeal and sense of enjoyment.

*   *   *

. . . Before we return to the formal statement here, if I may, a statement was made by Mr. Breen from *Life* magazine who was in New Orleans looking over all this equipment. He said, "After looking at all this in two days' review, you know preconscious communication isn't very complex. It is about as complex as getting peanut butter off the roof of your mouth." He said, "Now if you have peanut butter on the roof of your mouth, there are three ways to get it off. You can kind of blow it off or try and suck it in or you can put it on the end of your finger. Now there are three ways to get it off the end of your finger. You can snap your finger, and that's not very good, or you can rub it on something, and that's not very good, or you can put it back on the roof of your mouth. Now there are three ways of getting it off the roof of your mouth." (Laughter.)

Now to get back to the formal statement, the seventh and final question to be answered is: "How do the research results presented apply to the primary issues involved in the legislative act before this assembly?"

* * *

The processes of preconscious perception are complex. It has been demonstrated that the response of an individual depends on his preference value for consciously presented material (film), on his preference value for the preconscious stimulus, and the combination of both. The effectiveness of preconscious stimulation in terms of direct conscious response is directly associated with the established preference value for the consciously presented material with which the subliminal stimulus is presented, and the preference value for the preconscious material. The greater the preference value for the conscious level material, the preconscious information, or both combined, the greater the probability of selecting the subliminal stimulus *at a later time*.

An analogy drawn from the research results might be that—"Preconscious to conscious, and conscious to preconscious, involves a two-way track, along which, in both directions, are screening devices, signal lights, and early warning radars." The entire system is under the control and direction of the individual at all times. The method of operation is based on the prevailing needs and attitudes of the individual controller in all phases of operation.

The specific points presented in the Legislative bill before this assembly are expressed as follows:

"Hidden Message Advertising" Bill

The study of a proposed new mass advertising medium known as "subliminal projection" or "hidden message advertising" has been authorized by the adoption of New Jersey Assembly Concurrent Resolution No. 33. According to the resolution the device would permit the advertising of a product without the conscious knowledge of the prospective buyer, and, such subconscious activation is beyond the control of reason and may have a deleterious effect upon the health and welfare of citizens of New Jersey. The resolution further provides that the com-

mission authorized to study this medium shall, if the results indicate its desirability, propose legislation to regulate or ban the use of "hidden message advertising."

I have attempted to pose three questions and their appropriate answers which may assist you in determining your course of action.

Question A. Is the use of preconscious communication beyond the control of reason of observers when used with television, motion pictures, or other media for advertising or other purposes?

Answer A. In no case is the use of preconscious communication beyond "the control of reason" of observers when used with television, motion pictures, or other media for advertising or other purposes. It is assumed that the term "control of reason" in this context refers to the ability of preconscious communication to force an individual to respond in a predetermined way without his direct control and volition. The results of a nine-year research program prove conclusively that an individual, as an "integrated" individual, *does* respond to preconscious communication in a *normal, controlled,* and *purposive* manner *based on his prevailing likes and dislikes.* The individual is his own "censor"—for preconscious and conscious material alike. The *only* difference between preconscious and conscious stimulation is that in the first case the individual is reacting to information at a level of sensitivity which previously was not considered possible.

Question B. May not the use of preconscious communication with television, motion pictures, or other media have a deleterious effect upon the health and welfare of the citizens of New Jersey.

Answer B. In no case may the use of preconscious communication with television, motion pictures, or other media have a deleterious effect upon the health and welfare of the citizens of New Jersey. Preconscious communication is no different in class, function, or degree of effectiveness than any other existing media of communication. The only basic difference is the physical levels of intensity and duration by which this information is presented. In the case of preconscious communication the message is presented as a "whisper" rather than a "shout." In the sociological applications for the fields of education, training, and pyschiatry the ability to "whisper" can be most effective by increasing the process of selective perception while principles to be learned are being presented. Thus rather than deleterious, a significant tool is provided to enhance and increase the effectiveness of information transmission resulting in increased effectiveness in the efficiency of the learning process. The authenticity of this concept can be more directly indicated by the research and development sponsorship presently in progress by university, medical, governmental, and industrial agencies cited.

In the commercial advertising application, the same may be said. Rather than deleterious, the citizen of New Jersey can be provided advertising messages along with television entertainment without disrupting the continuity of their enjoyment. I believe that most would agree that advertising must be present in television programs in order to pay the bill for programs presented. Being their own "censors" TV viewers will accept or reject an advertising message based on their likes and dislikes. They can in no way be coerced into performing or doing anything against their will using preconscious communication.

Question C. Should legislation be proposed to regulate or ban the use of preconscious communication in advertising or other media?

Answer C. At present all media of communication are carefully regulated by Federal and State agencies for television and radio commercial applications. The same degree of regulation must certainly apply for the use of the new preconscious communication. The regulation of preconscious communication must not be set apart from other classes of communication and treated as something completely different and apart in terms of effectiveness or characteristic. Removing the erroneous emotional accusations associated with the use of preconscious communication is the first major step in accomplishing this goal. The methods for monitoring and controlling the preconscious material to be used can then proceed in a logical constructive manner. This is the technique for evaluating all conscious level media of communication and should apply equally for preconscious communication.

The basic requirement for banning preconscious communication is if it is dangerous or potentially harmful. The research results presented today prove conclusively that this is not the case. The perceptual rules for perceiving, evaluating, and responding to both conscious and preconscious material are identical.

d.   **New Jersey**

Final Report of the Commission To Study Subliminal Projection (1959)*

The commission finds that an evaluation of the materials and information submitted to it for study, the demonstrations given and the testimony heard at the public hearing indicate that there is no clear-cut evidence as to the effectiveness of influence through subliminal processes except that, at best, they are marginal. The bulk of the evidence submitted as the result of laboratory experiment was almost completely negative. However, the Commission hesitates to rely on the results of such experimentation as

* State of New Jersey, May 1959.

final and authoritative. It believes that, at present, the evidence on both sides of the question is primarily conjectural.

The Commission believes it unfortunate that the publicity attendant upon the original public announcement was fraught with emotion and the initial reaction approached hysteria, for it is felt that the evidence is conclusive that subliminal influence at its present stage of development is not determinative and, therefore, there is no cause for public alarm.

In fairness to the two companies with whom the Commission has had contact it should be pointed out that neither claims for its process the ability to determine thoughts and actions. In any commercial application of the technique each has stated that its process is but a means to supplement the stronger, more common methods used to influence public attitudes and actions.

However, despite varying opinions as to the effectiveness of subliminal influences, the body of evidence received indicates agreement that, effective or not, there is perception below the threshold of awareness. This evidence alone is sufficient to cause legislative recognition of the technique in the protection of the public right of privacy. Precedence has been established to prohibit supraliminal attempts to influence a "captive audience" and it is felt that the same principle applies to subliminal influence regardless of effectiveness or the lack of awareness.

The Commission feels that so little is really known, at present, about the human mind and human behavior that it would be unwise to assume the final answer has been written. Research into the development of more effective methods and techniques for influencing individual and group attitudes and actions is being carried on at this writing and, undoubtedly, will continue to be carried on in the foreseeable future. It is not beyond the realm of possibility that future developments may cause us to abandon many of our present theories. For this reason the Commission is inclined to accept evidence on both sides as having integrity.

It also finds that the emotional reaction to proposed commercial, political, and ideological use and misuse of the technique has tended to overshadow its possible use in the fields of education and psychotherapy. Although its value in these fields has not been proven, there is some evidence that it may provide a supplemental aid to existing methods. In view of this fact, an absolute prohibition of its use would be irresponsible.

*   *   *

RECOMMENDATIONS

In an area so lacking in definite boundaries as that of influences of human behavior the Commission believes any legislative action taken must be general in nature. It further believes that the subject matter which may be used in commercial, political, or ideological ways is already covered adequately by existing laws.

However, the Commission does feel that there is two-fold legislative responsibility, protection of the right of privacy and protection of the public from fear of exploitation. It believes that the harmful effects of any technique surrounded by an "aura of mystery," engendered by careful publicity, in a field not adequately understood by the general public may be far greater than the true efficiency of the technique would warrant.

Therefore, the Commission recommends that a degree of potential effectiveness for subliminal influence be recognized and that legislation be enacted to regulate the use of the technique of subliminal projection by whatever name it may be called. The Commission recommends that the use of subliminal messages, by word or symbol, in any public place for any reason whatsoever be contingent upon the prior public announcement that it is being used and the public display of the entire body of material to be used. . . .

NOTES

NOTE 1

NEW JERSEY

A Bill Concerning Disorderly Persons (1959)*

BE IT ENACTED *by the Senate and General Assembly of the State of New Jersey:*

Any person who, in any public place uses or permits the use by word or symbol, of a subliminal message or messages without having made immediately prior to such use a public announcement thereof and a public display of the entire body of the material to be so used, is a disorderly person. For the purposes of this act a "subliminal message" is defined as a communication projected below the threshold of human awareness.

NOTE 2

KLEIN, GEORGE S.

Consciousness in Psychoanalytic Theory: Some Implications for Current Research in Perception**

[R]*egistration* must be distinguished from the different *experiential qualities* in which we may be aware of things and of events. The processes respon-

* Introduced May 18, 1959 by Assemblywoman Hughes and Assemblyman Rutherfurd.
** 7 *Journal American Psychoanalytic Association*, 20–7, (1959). Reprinted by permission of International Universities Press, New York.

sible for phenomenal registration seem to be independent of those which govern attention deployment —the means by which we become aware of things in a distinctive quality. Registration and perception would seem to involve distinct processes. Furthermore, the attributes of objects which are potentially registerable without awareness are, as far as we can tell now, at least as varied as the object qualities which we are able to perceive in "waking states," perhaps more so. . . . An object or an event is actually an aggregate of multiple units: surface properties, movements, relations, and causal properties. If we think of an object as an array of such units and relationships, it is conceivable that certain of an object's properties will be perceived (one will be perceptually aware of them), while others may register but not be perceived. Judging from the scanty evidence at hand concerning the possibilities of registrations without awareness, it is possible that in the "waking state" a wide variety of the surface qualities, relationships, and units comprising things are potentially registerable.

Experimental evidence suggests quite extraordinary efficiency in this registration. The structuring process that accomplishes it apparently picks up a great deal, concerns itself in awareness with but little, and in action with still less. Registration is much less selective than would appear from the immediate concerns of observable action and reaction. . . . It is advantageous then to distinguish registration from perception.

A second point must be stressed. Perception is a distinct quality, e.g., the experience of being in contact with "things as they are." We must assume, then, that for a registration to be experienced as a *perception* it must be endowed with an additional and distinctive cathectic quality. Freud spoke of *perceptual cathexis* which can raise an idea to perceptual intensity. This sharpens the issue, and the mystery, of course, of how much is registered and by what mechanism, and how such incidental registrations may acquire the quality of perception; what determines whether the experienced registration will be "recovered" in the form of an image or of a percept or in some nonideational matrix altogether, such as an action. In short, while attention cathexis would seem to be a necessary condition for perceptions to occur, it seems not to be a sufficient condition since there are other qualitatively distinct modes in which objects may present themselves in awareness.

*   *   *

[R]egistrations not accessible as perceptions in the "waking state" are recoverable as *perceptions* in a *dream*, while in the "waking state" such registrations appear to be recoverable mainly through a different quality of awareness—in an image. In the "waking state," perceptions reflect schemata that are adaptively consonant with reality, a fact less conducive to primary process transformation. Imagery in the "waking state" is evidently subject to disciplining reality schema to a lesser degree than perception.

The fact that registrations can take different presentational forms in awareness—either as images or as perceptions—raises interesting questions about the relative advantages of different states of consciousness for the recovery of subliminal stimulations. In the "waking state," subliminal registrations seem less amenable to voluntary *recall* and do not emerge directly as percepts; recovery of subliminal input *does* seem to be more easily achieved, however, by asking subjects to image. Dreams, hypnosis, hypnagogic, and mescaline states perhaps enable a relatively undifferentiated slice of registered experience to be re-experienced with an intensity which in the usual "waking states" can be accomplished only if one has the capacity for eidetic imagery. As reality contact and reality requirements are minimized, so attention cathexis can be deployed to registrations, and they can be brought to awareness in a *passive, eidetic-like* manner. It is possible that all ways of minimizing reality-adaptive intentions, e.g., by reducing postural supports for discrimination, by inducing distractions, by producing a state of passive receptiveness in which thoughts "take over" the subject in contrast to an active, attentive condition which is conducive to "producing" thoughts, etc., may facilitate emergence of subliminally registered contents in general and in *perceptual* form in particular.

In considering the kinds of transformations to which incidental registrations are subject in the "waking state" and the vicissitudes of awareness from one state of consciousness to another, we touch upon matters that concern inventive and creative thinking. Someone's observation that to create a new order you have to destroy a familiar one seems to me a good characterization of inventive and creative thought. Awareness in the ordinary work day paradoxically serves an efficient and sensitizing and yet blinding function. Were this not so, our lives would have little stability. For the most part, conceptual contact with the objects, places, and events we encounter takes place at the lowest common denominator of identity. The conceptual schema which dominate cognition in our jobs, our relationships with others, our encounters with objects have a proven utility; we therefore have a stake in them and we prefer to cling to them—as a principle of efficiency and economy. The thought forms dominating awareness provide us, at the least, with a relatively unchanging and *persisting* world of things—an unchanging background for the effective *control* of things. But the reality-adaptive schema which ordinarily guide awareness can well hinder sensitivity to an "unfamiliar" form and to transformed ideas, by the very fact that their main function is not to promote discovery but to buttress predictability—to

provide insurance against the irregular and the unfamiliar.

Certain forms of creative endeavor and innovations may require a bypassing of the well-trodden scheme of the "waking state." For instance, it is well known that artists surmount the established laws of constancy in order to "see" new forms or latent forms in objects. . . .

* * *

. . . It would seem that the traditional summary of responsiveness to stimulation, based on the narrow perspective of events in the "waking state" of the laboratory requires revision. The sequence seems rather to be: The organism's sensory surfaces are stimulated; registration occurs; followed by a cognitive recruitment of this registered stimulation to various conceptual schema; leading to an *emergence* of the reaction, partly in a particular mode of awareness (perception or imaging), partly on other behavioral levels, and partly via motor facilitations of the various conceptual schema.

* * *

Novel problems are brought into focus by bringing psychoanalytic conceptions to bear upon the data I have reported. There is the question of what is potentially registerable outside awareness. At the present time there seem to be indications that a large variety of thing-properties are potentially registerable. Are they all equally registerable outside awareness? Furthermore, which of the variety of registrations reach the status of *persisting* ideas of things? Do they all achieve "trace" representation? What are the conditions of persistence? Evidently many unit formations of objects acquire some phenomenal structure. But can it be said that they have thereby become "memories"? If some do and some do not, what are the rules of elimination? While a wide range of registerable thing-qualities is suggested by the results I have mentioned, the conditions of such registration and their persistence are by no means well understood. In the apparent immediacy of our perceptual awareness, the problem is not an obvious one. The basic question is: When in the immediate workings of the eye—at what state of the integrative activity of the receiving mechanism—does an impingement become a registration and the registration in turn converted to the quality of a percept, memory, or image?

NOTE 3

PINE, FRED

The Bearing of Psychoanalytic Theory on Selected Issues in Research on Marginal Stimuli*

A major basis for the recent surge of interest in the

* 138 *The Journal of Nervous and Mental Disease*, 1964, (pp. 205–19). Reprinted by permission of Williams & Wilkens Co., Baltimore.

effects of marginal stimuli (subliminal, incidental, or partially seen) has been the hope that research in that area would permit experimentally controlled study of thought processes outside of awareness. The hope has been expressed that the study of such thought processes would indirectly help clarify the contribution that consciousness itself makes to thinking. The formulations in much of this research have grown out of psychoanalytic theory. . . .

The studies to be discussed utilize several different kinds of "marginal" stimuli. There are those involving stimuli (typically visual) that are so dim, so brief, or so quickly followed by a more intense ("masking") stimulus that subjects can report no (or only minimal) perceptual cues from the experience. There are those . . . that use stimuli that are partially seen; typically, they are flashed on a screen at a duration such that the subject can report having seen some but not all of the details. And finally, there are those studies using stimuli well above the perceptual threshold but experienced by the subject as incidental to what he is doing.

What do such stimuli have in common? In one way or another, each bypasses the mechanisms that usually govern the intake of supraliminal and adaptively relevant stimuli. These latter are, metaphorically speaking, ordinarily "grasped" by attention (experienced in awareness) and "put to use" (or put aside as irrelevant) in accord with the adaptive intentions momentarily guiding behavior. Such percepts are included in ordinary waking thought. For example, a hunger-relevant stimulus (say, a stomach contraction or a verbal or pictorial reminder of food) will, at mealtime, lead to a chain of thoughts, coordinated with actions, culminating in realistic pursuit of appropriate gratification—food. In contrast, the marginal stimuli in the studies under discussion here are either too weak to be perceived or too irrelevant to command much attention. One theoretical question is whether (and under what circumstances) such stimuli follow a course through the mental apparatus that is different from the course followed by supraliminal and adaptively relevant stimuli.

*   *   *

The studies under review demonstrate a central phenomenon which may be called unintentionality. A range of effects, direct and indirect, has been obtained.

Unintentionality: Studies in this area by and large have something else in common besides the marginal status of the stimuli used; that is, the "indirectness" of the response through which the impact of the stimulus is gauged. While the subject may be asked whether he can recall the stimulus, direct recall or recognition are *not* the most relevant responses for gauging the effects under study here. . . . The essential response common to the studies reviewed here is an indirect one. Subjects are asked to report any image, dream, or story that comes to mind, or to describe some new stimulus, or to make a drawing; they are *not* given any instruction to include the marginal stimulus (or related material) in these responses. . . . In many of these experiments, when the subject has little or no awareness of the stimulus, or when intrusions from the stimulus that appear in the response are only symbolically or otherwise indirectly related to the initial stimulus . . . the subject can presumably have no awareness of the use that he may be making of the stimulus in the formation of his experimental response.

Thus, the basic phenomenon is that marginal stimuli affect subsequent thoughts unintentionally, as it were; the effect appears in the subject's productions without his *actively* producing it. For example, Smith *et al.* presented either the word "happy" or the word "angry" subliminally and then had the subjects describe a (supraliminal) picture of a face that was affectively neutral. Subjects tended to describe the face in accord with the "suggestion" of the stimulus word; but they *did not know* that they were doing so. They were unaware of the determining influence of the stimulus. Contrast this to a situation in which awareness of the stimulus is unequivocal, as in the following (hypothetical) instruction: "I am going to show you the picture of a person who is ordinarily quite happy; I want you to describe his face." What would happen? The subject *may or may not* be influenced by the suggestion, but in any event he will usually *know* whether or not he is using it. With above-threshold, adaptively relevant stimuli we can choose and select, using or rejecting what we will. But the marginal stimulus affects subsequent cognitive productions without the subject's intending it to do so.

It is this unintentionality in the subject's use of the stimulus that differentiates the marginal stimulation studies from those in the area of incidental learning. . . .

In a wide diversity of studies the essential finding is the unintended inclusion of marginal stimuli in one or another cognitive product given as a response some time subsequent to the presentation of the stimulus. In some experiments the effect of the stimulus has been gauged by its intrusion into images; in others, into stories, dreams, drawings, face descriptions, memory, pseudo "recognition," and word associations. In all of these, the subject's use of the stimulus was unintentional; that is, use of the stimulus was not specifically encouraged by the experimenter and, in most instances at least, the subject was not aware that he was using the stimulus. . . .

The effects, although unintended by the subject, are typically neither bizarre nor inappropriate. The stimuli do not emerge in hallucinatory, symptomatic, or parapraxic form. Rather, they are incorporated in some cognitive product that is evoked for experimental purposes. In this way they are much like those "indifferent" daytime perceptions that find their way into the manifest content of the dream. The fact that the effects of the stimulus *do* get integrated into some cognitive production indicates that some cognitive work is going on; in spite of the apparent passivity of the unintentional use of the stimulus, some controlling and guiding mechanisms are apparently active with regard to the marginally received stimulus. Specification of the directive and organizing processes that can utilize even stimuli outside of awareness is one of the challenges to research in this area.

The range of effects: The reported effects of marginal stimuli can be grouped very loosely as either indirectly or directly related to the initial stimulus.

* * *

To illustrate indirect effects: In an earlier study stimuli were presented to subjects incidentally by broadcasting them through a wall from a room adjoining the experimental room. Subjects experienced them as irrelevant noise. The two stimulus passages had each been constructed to emphasize certain symbolic qualities: A description of a cow emphasizing its oral-passive aspect and a description of a hook emphasizing its phallic-aggressive aspect. Effects of the stimuli in stories subsequently told by the subjects were predominantly indirect. Indirect effects included, for example, an increase in passive and nurturant human relationships—not an increase in cowlike content.

* * *

At least two studies are particularly striking for the directness of the effects obtained. Zuckerman superimposed the phrases "write more" or "don't write" on Thematic Apperception Test pictures about which the subjects were to write stories; superimposition was by a flash at a duration such that the stimulus was subliminal. The resulting stories were longer or shorter, respectively, following subliminal stimulation. The effect was quite "sensible," much like everyday thought and behavior that is guided by realistic cues. Again, however, it must be emphasized that the effect was *unintentional* from the subjects' standpoint; they did not know that they were influenced by the stimulus. Unintentionality of the effect is as characteristic of the studies reporting direct effects as of those reporting indirect ones. A further interesting point in Zuckerman's study is that, in a group where the "write more" and "don't write" stimuli were presented *supraliminally*, no consistent effect was obtained. This is not surprising; a supraliminal stimulus can be taken or left, used as appropriate or discarded as irrelevant. Once intentions come into play *vis-à-vis* the stimulus, individual tendencies toward compliance, negativism, or autonomy also come into play.

* * *

These, then, are some of the basic phenomena— an effect in the form of an unintended intrusion of the marginal stimulus onto subsequent cognitive productions, at times more direct (and akin to effects that might be obtained in ordinary waking thought) and at times more indirect (and in some ways reminiscent of primary process). These phenomena seem reasonably well established in laboratory studies. Comparable phenomena are common enough in everyday experience: A response, unawares, to some sound in another room or to some fleeting visual impression; the suggestion that gets drawn into our thinking, directly or indirectly, without our awareness of its source; the incorporation of briefly attended impressions of the day into the fabric of the dream at night. To some extent these phenomena have now been brought into the laboratory where they can be studied in systematic ways.

* * *

The phenomenon requiring explanation is that a marginal stimulus re-emerges in subsequent cognitive productions in a way unintended by the subject. Why the re-emergence? And how can we account for its varying forms? Some conception of a force is useful in explaining the unintended impact of the marginal stimulus. . . .

The psychoanalytic conception of the role of day residues in dreams provides a useful parallel for the experimental work on marginal stimuli. . . . The dream, like the derivatives of marginal stimuli described above, is presented into awareness without the individual's intending or willing it. The dream may be conceived as the rise to hallucinatory vividness of certain thought contents under the momentum of an infantile wish. Such wishes are not expressed directly in the dream. Through the distorting effect of the dream work, and the need for disguise to satisfy the demands of censorship (and thus to avoid anxiety), wishes undergo transformations and emerge in the more or less acceptable forms of the manifest (experienced) dream. Thoughts and stimuli of the day (day's residue) may have various roles in the dream. The day's residue not only may stimulate a wish but may serve as an effective disguise, for, if the residue is itself affectively neutral it can better elude censorship. Such affectively neutral residues, which have been in the periphery of attention, may become invested with drive cathexis and serve to represent the drive in the dream; this is so particularly because they were peripheral and had not been committed to other explicit meanings and thoughts. The act of dreaming is itself conceived of as a partial discharge of the wish tension. . . .

A parallel model for the workings of marginal stimuli in the studies under review would assume that drive provides the force for the re-emergence of the derivatives of the marginal stimulus. Such an explanation might run as follows: Marginal stimuli, given the fact that (by definition) they bypass the processing and coding mechanisms that govern consciously received and relevant stimuli, must make contact with some other functional systems if they are to have any impact at all on behavior. These stimuli, either not available for or not relevant to adaptive thought or action, may be invested with drive cathexis; that is, like the day's residue in the dream, they become the cognitive representations of the drive. As the drive presses for discharge, these contents are pushed forward into awareness . . . partial discharge of the drive tension is achieved through this representation in awareness. Having been invested with drive energies, however, the content of the initial marginal stimulus may be subject to distortions by the censorship and by a working over of the content by the primary process (symbolization, displacement, and the like). Thus, the later re-emergence of the stimulus (unintended by the subject, and motivated by the drive) may either be in a form quite distant from the initial stimulus input or close to it.

*   *   *

The conditions under which a marginal stimulus will make contact with drives, and the consequences of such contact, also require study. Thought processes outside of awareness are not necessarily more drive related than thought processes in awareness. A stimulus, registered but not experienced in awareness, does not by that fact alone make contact with drives. A variety of integrative processes are carried on outside of awareness; for example: (1) "reminiscence" in memory (increased memory after a delay); (2) problem solving . . . (there are indicators of progress towards problem solution that antecede subject's awareness of solution); and (3) the preconscious incubation that precedes creative insight. Drives may be involved in all of these, but the questions remain: What level of drive? And how are the drives organized? And how is rational thinking maintained in the presence of drives? The same questions apply for the effects of marginal stimuli. These effects, too, are mediated by drives, but by no means at the expense of the subject's adaptive performance of the experimental task. And what are the consequences when a stimulus somehow is invested with drive cathexis? In one study that used a moderately threatening drive-related incidental stimulus, there seemed to be an inhibition of derivatives related to the stimulus in subsequent stories. While this may suggest defensive and drive-related cognitive activity, it suggests equally that recovery is not necessarily *enhanced* by inclusion of the stimulus in a drive schema. The implications of such a linkage to drives for recovery of the initial stimulus remain to be studied in detail.

*   *   *

The marginal stimulus intrudes in various forms upon subsequent response tasks—at times quite directly and at times only indirectly related to the initial stimulus input. What intervening thought process or processes must be inferred to account for the range of effects obtained?

On the basis of the predictable but indirect derivatives of the marginal stimuli reported in several studies, it may be postulated that some lawful, but nonrational or nonlogical, thought process mediated the alteration from initial stimulus to ultimate effect. The nature of the more direct derivatives suggests the workings of a thought process akin to our ordinary, accurate, reality-oriented waking thought. . . .

*   *   *

Some Determinants of the Specific Effect

Just what kind of pathway will be followed in any one case, and thus whether more direct or more indirect effects of the marginal stimulus will emerge in the response, is something that we still know very little about. . . . What determines which effects will appear?

To begin with, the specific stimulus selected for study has an important limiting role. One kind of indirect effect, for example, an effect symbolically related to the initial stimulus, has been reported most clearly for so-called drive stimuli. Whether drive-related stimuli can make contact with a wider range of drives and thought streams in the person than more neutral stimuli, or whether we simply have a theory that helps us identify symbolic expressions of drive (but not of various neutral stimuli), is uncertain. . . .

*   *   *

One other factor apparently having some determining influence on the kind of effect that a marginal stimulus will have is the subject's state of consciousness; in the experimental situation, this varies with his particular intentions and expectations. . . . Is it possible that the kind of thinking that goes on *in awareness* (at the moment of stimulus input, of response output, or both) can to some degree influence the nature of the thought stream in which the marginal stimulus will be implicated *outside of awareness*?

Gardner discusses this point in some detail around the question of the " 'fate' of registrations [of marginal stimuli] in relation to the state of awareness the person is in." Gardner's thinking, as well as my own earlier speculations, gives consideration to an affirmative answer to the question above. That is, it may be that the introduction of a stimulus when the person is in a dream or reverie state . . . may lead to quite a different impact from the introduction of the stimulus when the subject is in an alert, adaptive state. . . .

*   *   *

Under what conditions will a stimulus, itself only

in the periphery of awareness, or derivatives of that stimulus, penetrate into conscious thoughts? What are the conditions for greater or less effects of the marginal stimulus?

Suggestive analogues to the situation of the marginal stimulation studies are abundant. Consider the psychoanalytic situation, for example. For the patient lying on the couch, not facing the psychoanalyst and not required to communicate any *particular* content, there is a day-in and day-out monotony to the visual field and a diminution of the need for focused and adaptive communications and behaviors. Under these conditions, thoughts that are ordinarily outside of awareness (preconscious or unconscious) rise into awareness and are presented as free associations. Or take creative inspiration. Creative individuals have again and again described the sudden rise into consciousness of a creative solution in conditions of relative ease, when their thoughts were free to drift and when the demands of reality were relaxed. Or again, take the situation of the sensory deprivation experiment. There, given a subject who is deprived of the ordinary variations of the stimulus field and who is asked to do nothing in particular, thought contents and even modes of thinking that are ordinarily denied access to awareness will often be experienced.

In each of these situations, the individual's thoughts are not measured against some external criterion of right–wrong or adaptive–maladaptive; in Klein's terms, there is no orientation on the part of the subject toward an "effective appraisal of reality." Nor are the materials that go to make up the thoughts immediately available in the external field or in the subject's consciousness. He not only *can* feel free to allow hunches, passing thoughts, and the like into awareness, but in fact *must* draw to a much larger extent than usual upon his inner experiences to create thoughts. Under such conditions, kinds of thought content ordinarily outside of awareness are experienced and may be reported. Rapaport's remarks on the competition of stimuli for attention hypercathexis in effect summarize these phenomena. The more external stimuli and adaptive tasks demand attention, the less is attention directed to internal events. The exclusion from awareness of intrusive and irrelevant external stimuli and of personal memories and wishes when adaptive demands need to be met is in fact a major achievement of thought. Freud's concept of a stimulus barrier against a flood of stimulation, and additionally, his concept of the censorship of tabooed wishes and thoughts, reflect his early attempts to deal with this phenomenon.

In the studies of marginal stimuli, then, the following general hypothesis may be suggested: The re-emergence (in the response) of a marginal stimulus or its derivatives will be greater the more passing thoughts are experienced as ideas to be utilized rather

than excluded, and the less the bases for a response are immediately available in the subject's conscious thoughts or in the stimulus field. . . .

A variety of studies bear on this general proposition, and generally give supportive data:

1. In a pair of experiments by Goldberg and Fiss and by Fiss *et al.*, as well as in a study by Goldstein and Barthol, subliminal stimuli were shown to have effects on imaginative processes (image and story production) but not on reality-testing processes (discrimination of stimuli). When the subject is free to draw upon inner experience to produce a response, the effect of the stimulus comes through. The Goldstein and Barthol study adds a further point. Stories based on blurred pictures (from the Thematic Apperception Test) included more derivatives of the initial subliminal stimulus than stories based on clearly delineated pictures. Thus, when the materials for response were less immediately available in the field (the blurred picture giving fewer story cues), peripheral thoughts activated by the marginal stimulus had a better chance of inclusion in the story.

2. Greater effects of marginal stimuli have also been reported under conditions of relaxation. . . .

3. Certain massive organismic stresses may decrease the degree to which nonconscious content is kept from awareness, much like the role of relaxation in studies referred to above and the role of diminished ego activity during sleep that makes the emergence of unconscious material possible in dreams. . . .

4. Finally, a recent study by Eagle on some personality characteristics of subjects showing strong effects of subliminal stimuli suggests that a responsiveness to and readiness to use subtle internal cues enhances the effect of marginal stimuli. Two of the personality syndromes that he finds to be correlated with a greater effect of his subliminal stimuli— "receptiveness to inner cues" and "cognitive and affective openness" (v. constriction)—are directly to the point here. . . .

There is considerable support, then, for the hypothesis that the emergence of derivatives of the marginal stimulus is enhanced in a person or in a state wherein fleeting thoughts can be utilized rather than excluded, and where the bases for response are not immediately available in consciousness or in the external field . . . even if this generalization continues to hold, it raises as many questions as it settles. For the thought contents that derive from the marginal stimulus and that emerge from outside of awareness do so without producing anxiety and disruption, and the subject can return at will to thinking that is more actively guided in the direction of adaptation and communication. Thus, the problems of the maintenance of ego control even in the face of some degree of ego passivity arise. Whether or not these problems can be studied experimentally with the tool of marginal stimuli remains to be determined.

NOTE 4

POLLAK v. PUBLIC UTILITIES COMMISSION

191 F.2d 450 (D.C. Cir. 1951)
rev'd 343 U.S. 451 (1952)

EDGERTON, Circuit Judge.

Appellee Capital Transit Company (Transit) operates streetcars and buses in the District of Columbia. In 1948 Transit made a contract with appellee Washington Transit Radio, Inc., (Radio) by which Radio was to instal and maintain loudspeakers in Transit vehicles and provide broadcasts at least eight hours daily except Sunday. . . .

Though Transit and Radio call the broadcasts "music as you ride," they include not only music but also "commercials, announcements, and time signals." The contract permits six minutes of "commercial announcements" per hour. These vary from fifteen to thirty-five seconds in length and are usually scheduled about once in five minutes, though the interval varies.

*   *   *

Transit passengers commonly have to hear the broadcasts whether they want to or not.[1] . . .

*   *   *

. . . Short of imprisonment, the only way to compel a man's attention for many minutes is to bombard him with sound that he cannot ignore in a place where he must be. The law of nuisance protects him at home. At home or at work, the constitutional question has not arisen because the government has taken no part in forcing people to listen. Until radio was developed and someone realized that the passengers of a transportation monopoly are a captive audience, there was no profitable way of forcing people to listen while they travel between home and work or on necessary errands. Exploitation of this audience through assault on the unavertible sense of hearing is a new phenomenon. It raises "issues that were not implied in the means of communication known or contemplated by Franklin and Jefferson and Madison." But the Bill of Rights, as appellants say in their brief, can keep up with anything an advertising man or an electronics engineer can think of. . . .

If Transit obliged its passengers to read what it liked or get off the car, invasion of their freedom would be obvious. Transit obliges them to hear what it likes or get off the car. Freedom of attention, which forced listening destroys, is a part of liberty essential to individuals and to society. . . .

*   *   *

---

1. Appellants' supplementary application to the Commission for rehearing contains a physicist's affidavit explaining in technical terms that "the ear hears plainly at its low sound level what the meter does not detect at its high sound level."

Of course freedom from forced listening, like other freedoms, is not absolute. No doubt the government may compel attention, as it may forbid speech, in exceptional circumstances. But a deprivation of liberty to which the government is a party is unconstitutional when it is "arbitrary or without reasonable relation to some purpose within the competency of the state to effect." *Meyer* v. *State of Nebraska*, 262 U.S. 390, 400, 43 S.Ct. 625, 627, 67 L.Ed. 1042. Forcing Transit passengers to hear these broadcasts has no reasonable relation to any such purpose. Some discomforts may perhaps be inevitable incidents of mass transportation, but forced listening is neither incidental nor inevitable. It deprives the appellants and other passengers who object to the broadcasts of their liberty for the private use of Transit, Radio, and passengers who like the broadcasts. This loss of freedom of attention is the more serious because many people have little time to read, consider, or discuss what they like, or to relax. The record makes it plain that the loss is a serious injury to many passengers. They suffer not only the discomfort of hearing what they dislike but a sense of outrage at being compelled to hear whatever Transit and Radio choose.

*   *   *

NOTE 5

HILL v. BAXTER
[1958] 1 All E. R. 193

LORD GODDARD, C. J.: This Special Case . . . concerns two informations preferred against the respondent, the first for the dangerous driving of a motor vehicle . . . and the second for failing to conform to a Halt sign. . . . The facts found by the justices are that at 10:45 P.M. on the evening of April 12 this year the respondent drove a motor van along Springfield Road, Brighton, in a westerly direction and where the road crosses Beaconsfield Road he ignored an illuminated Halt sign, drove across the road junction at a fast speed and came into collision with a car which was being driven northward in Beaconsfield Road. The respondent's van then carried on for a short distance and overturned. A police constable arrived and found the respondent in a dazed condition and at the hospital to which he was taken said:

> "I remember being in Preston Circus going to Withdean. I don't remember anything else until I was searching for my glasses. I don't know what happened."

The justices found that to be in Springfield Road on the way to Withdean from Preston Circus involved a substantial and unnecessary detour but that the respondent must have exercised skill in driving in order to reach Springfield Road by whatever route he took. The justices apparently accepted the respondent's evidence and found that he remembered nothing from the time when he was at Preston Circus until the accident had happened. They were of opinion that the respondent was not conscious of what he was doing after leaving Preston Circus and to this finding they add the words "with the implication that he was not capable of forming any intention as to his manner of driving." They dismissed the informations. . . .

*   *   *

The first thing to be remembered is that the statute contains an absolute prohibition against driving dangerously or ignoring Halt signs. No question of mens rea enters into the offence; it is no answer to a charge under those sections to say "I did not mean to drive dangerously" or "I did not notice the Halt sign." The justices' finding, that the respondent was not capable of forming any intention as to the manner of driving, is really immaterial. What they evidently meant was that the respondent was in a state of automation. But he was driving and, as the Case finds, exercising some skill, and undoubtedly the onus of proving that he was in a state of automation must be on him. This is . . . a rule of the law of evidence that the onus of proving a fact which must be exclusively within the knowledge of a party lies on him who asserts it. This no doubt is subject to the qualification that where an onus is on the defendant in a criminal case the burden is not as high as it is on a prosecutor. The main contention before us on the part of the appellant was that there was no evidence on which the justices could find that the respondent was in a state of automatism or whatever term may be applied to someone performing acts in a state of unconsciousness. There was in fact no evidence except that of the respondent, and, while the justices were entitled to believe him, his evidence shows nothing except that after the accident he cannot remember what took place after he left Preston Circus. This is quite consistent with being overcome with sleep or at least drowsiness. That drivers do fall asleep is a not uncommon cause of serious road accidents and it would be impossible as well as disastrous to hold that falling asleep at the wheel was any defence to a charge of dangerous driving. If a driver finds that he is getting sleepy he must stop. . . .

*   *   *

PEARSON, J.:

*   *   *

The importance of the finding that he was driving with skill is the necessary implication that he was controlling the car and directing its movements. Therefore, he was driving, and his driving was dangerous. Therefore the offence was committed and there is no evidence to support the acquittal. The facts proved show that the respondent was driving

and driving dangerously, and if the burden of proof was on the defence they failed to prove an extraordinary mischance rendering it impossible for the respondent to control the van and direct its movements. I agree with the proposed order.

*   *   *

NOTE 6

HARBOURN v. KATZ DRUG COMPANY
318 S. W. 2d 226 (Mo. 1958)

STOCKARD, COMMISSIONER.

Appellants, Katz Drug Company and Harold D. Clifton, have appealed from a judgment in favor of Elva Mae Harbourn in the amount of $9,500 for personal injuries sustained when she fell over the platform of a scale located in one of the Katz stores. . . .

*   *   *

Defendants place considerable emphasis on [the following] testimony given by plaintiff. . . .

"Q. Did you see the scale as you approached the doors to leave the store, did you see a scale sitting there between the doors? A. I knew the scales were there—yes, I saw the scales."

*   *   *

"Q. So after you saw the scales at the candy counter and as you walked toward the door, then you momentarily forgot about the scales and fell over them, is that correct, ma'am? A. I was looking straight at the door to see if anyone was coming in.
"Q. Well, you did momentarily forget about the scales, did you, ma'am? A. I thought they were setting in a wall.

*   *   *

"Q. All of it. But the scales were plainly visible, were they, ma'am? A. Yes."

*   *   *

Defendants . . . contend that plaintiff's evidence establishes that she was contributorily negligent as a matter of law. Particular reliance is placed on . . . numerous cases to the effect that where a duty to look exists, the failure to see what is plainly visible constitutes contributory negligence as a matter of law. . . . However, this argument overlooks the fact that under the peculiar facts of this case the presence of the scale did not alone constitute the condition involving an unusual risk, and plaintiff did not know, and we cannot say she should have known, that the north set of doors were locked and that upon reaching them she would have to change her expected course of travel. . . . Therefore, the question is whether she was contributorily negligent as a matter of law in falling over the scale, which she admittedly saw as she approached the doors but momentarily forgot when she unexpectedly encountered the locked set of north doors.

It is unquestionably correct, and properly so, that generally an invitee who is aware of a dangerous condition cannot impose liability on the possessor of property because he momentarily forgot about it and was injured. . . . "Circumstances may [however] exist under which forgetfulness or inattention to a known danger may be consistent with the exercise of ordinary care, as where the situation requires one to give undivided attention to other matters, or is such as to produce hurry or confusion, or where conditions arise suddenly which are calculated to divert one's attention momentarily from the danger." 65 C.J.S. Negligence § 120, pp. 726–727. . . . Common experience teaches us that not all of our past mental impressions are carried into present consciousness, and when plaintiff saw the scale as she approached the doors, she saw only an object not inherently dangerous and which was not in or near her expected path. In leaving the store in the manner intended she had no reason whatever to be concerned about a scale located outside of her intended path. Under these particular circumstances it would be a jury question whether or not plaintiff was negligent, that is, whether or not her forgetfulness was "induced by some sudden and adequate disturbing cause," 38 Am. Jur., Negligence, § 187, when she suddenly found the north set of doors locked and turned to go to the unlocked doors and then momentarily forgot in the resulting confusion that she had previously seen the scale located where she then intended to travel in order to get to the south set of doors and leave the store. . . .

*   *   *

The judgment is reversed. . . .

NOTE 7

RESTATEMENT OF THE LAW 2d,
TORTS §289 (1965)*

Recognizing Existence of Risk

The actor is required to recognize that his conduct involves a risk of causing an invasion of another's interest if a reasonable man would do so while exercising

(a) such attention, perception of the circumstances, memory, knowledge of other pertinent matters, intelligence, and judgment as a reasonable man would have; and

(b) such superior attention, perception, memory, knowledge, intelligence, and judgment as the actor himself has.

* Copyright 1965. Reprinted with the permission of The American Law Institute.

Comment:

e. *Perception.* The actor must exercise the perception of a reasonable man under like circumstances. This means that he must to a reasonable degree make use of his senses to become aware of his surroundings, and of any danger involved in them. He must see what is visible, hear what is audible, and the like, where a reasonable man would do so. Due allowance must be made for distractions and other influences which would affect a reasonable man under the circumstances.

ILLUSTRATION:

3. A, driving an automobile, approaches an intersection where B, a pedestrian, is crossing the street. B is plainly visible, and a reasonable man in A's position would see him. Although A is looking ahead, he is preoccupied, and does not see B and runs into him, injuring B. A is negligent.

f. *Memory.* The elements of memory which are of principal importance in enabling the actor to perceive the circumstances surrounding him, are

1. Fixation, by which a sense impression is fixed in the memory for future use. This depends upon the nature of the phenomenon observed, principally its striking character or its recognizable importance as a fact upon which the safety of the actor or others may in the future depend.

2. Retentiveness, by which a past sense impression is retained for future use.

In both these particulars, the actor's memory must be equal to that of the reasonable man; that is, he must possess a memory which is sufficiently acute and retentive to secure that present realization of past impressions which is essential to the safety of himself and others. Again due allowance must be made for distractions and other influences which would affect a reasonable man under like circumstances.

ILLUSTRATION:

4. A is driving an automobile in the dusk along a road. He approaches an intersection of a cross road which is so hidden by a high hedge that it is impossible for an approaching motorist to see it. A does not realize that this intersection exists and therefore fails to blow his horn or take the precautions which a reasonable man knowing of the intersection would take. A is not negligent if he has never driven over this road before, or if he has driven over it on only one or two occasions, having no reason to believe that he would be required to drive over it again in the near future. He is negligent if he has constantly driven over the road and therefore should have fixed and retained in his memory the location of the intersection, or if he has driven over the road before, knowing that in the near future he will probably drive over it again in the dark.

*   *   *

NOTE 8

SHERMAN v. UNITED STATES
356 U.S. 369 (1958)

MR. CHIEF JUSTICE WARREN . . .

The issue before us is whether petitioner's conviction should be set aside on the ground that as a matter of law the defense of entrapment was established. . . .

In late August 1951, Kalchinian, a government informer, first met petitioner at a doctor's office where apparently both were being treated to be cured of narcotics addiction. Several accidental meetings followed, either at the doctor's office or at the pharmacy where both filled their prescriptions from the doctor. From mere greetings, conversation progressed to a discussion of mutual experiences and problems, including their attempts to overcome addiction to narcotics. Finally Kalchinian asked petitioner if he knew of a good source of narcotics. He asked petitioner to supply him with a source because he was not responding to treatment. From the first, petitioner tried to avoid the issue. Not until after a number of repetitions of the request, predicated on Kalchinian's presumed suffering, did petitioner finally acquiesce. . . .

At the trial the factual issue was whether the informer had convinced an otherwise unwilling person to commit a criminal act or whether petitioner was already predisposed to commit the act and exhibited only the natural hesitancy of one acquainted with the narcotics trade. The issue of entrapment went to the jury. . . .

. . . The function of law enforcement is the prevention of crime and the apprehension of criminals. Manifestly, that function does not include the manufacturing of crime. Criminal activity is such that stealth and strategy are necessary weapons in the arsenal of the police officer. However, "A different question is presented when the criminal design originates with the officials of the Government, and they implant in the mind of an innocent person the disposition to commit the alleged offense and induce its commission in order that they may prosecute." 287 U.S., at 442. Then stealth and strategy become as objectionable police methods as the coerced confession and the unlawful search. Congress could not have intended that its statutes were to be enforced by tempting innocent persons into violation.

However, the fact that government agents "merely afford opportunities or facilities for the commission of the offense does not" constitute entrapment. Entrapment occurs only when the criminal conduct was "the product of the *creative* activity" of law-enforcement officials. (Emphasis supplied.) See 287 U.S., at 441, 451. To determine whether entrapment has been established, a line must be drawn between the trap for the unwary innocent and the trap for the unwary criminal. . . . On the one hand, at trial the accused may examine the conduct of the government agent; and on the other hand, the accused will be subjected to an "appropriate and searching inquiry into his own conduct and predisposition" as bearing on his claim of innocence. See 287 U.S., at 451.

We conclude from the evidence that entrapment was established as a matter of law. In so holding, we are not choosing between conflicting witnesses, nor judging credibility. . . . We reach our conclusion from the undisputed testimony of the prosecution's witnesses.

It is patently clear that petitioner was induced by Kalchinian. The informer himself testified that, believing petitioner to be undergoing a cure for narcotics addiction, he nonetheless sought to persuade petitioner to obtain for him a source of narcotics. In Kalchinian's own words we are told of the accidental, yet recurring, meetings, the ensuing conversations concerning mutual experiences in regard to narcotics addiction, and then of Kalchinian's resort to sympathy. One request was not enough, for Kalchinian tells us that additional ones were necessary to overcome, first, petitioner's refusal, then his evasiveness, and then his hesitancy in order to achieve capitulation. Kalchinian not only procured a source of narcotics but apparently also induced petitioner to return to the habit. Finally, assured of a catch, Kalchinian informed the authorities so that they could close the net. The Government cannot disown Kalchinian and insist it is not responsible for his actions. Although he was not being paid, Kalchinian was an active government informer who had but recently been the instigator of at least two other prosecutions. . . . In his testimony the federal agent in charge of the case admitted that he never bothered to question Kalchinian about the way he had made contact with petitioner. The Government cannot make such use of an informer and then claim disassociation through ignorance.

*   *   *

The case at bar illustrates an evil which the defense of entrapment is designed to overcome. The government informer entices someone attempting to avoid narcotics not only into carrying out an illegal sale but also into returning to the habit of use. Selecting the proper time, the informer then tells the government agent. The setup is accepted by the agent without even a question as to the manner in which the informer encountered the seller. Thus the Government plays on the weaknesses of an innocent party and beguiles him into committing crimes which he otherwise would not have attempted. Law enforcement does not require methods such as this.

*   *   *

NOTE 9

KUBIE, LAWRENCE S.

Implications for Legal Procedure of the Fallibility of Human Memory*

* * *

A recent study was made of the process of supervision in psychotherapy and of the value of tape recordings for conducting supervision and studying the psychotherapeutic process. It was pointed out that we run counter to everything which we have learned about the processes of the memory when we expect a student conducting therapy to recall with precision what happened during a therapeutic session and to reproduce the session undistorted in a subsequent meeting with his supervisor. It is asking him to record and to recall without bias both sides of a rapid and free interchange in which he is a participant and not merely an observer, in which his own complex emotions are intricately involved, and in which he needs constantly to demonstrate his ability not merely to observe but also to guide that which he is observing and to predict that which is to come. In other words, he is asked to be a carefully disciplined pilot, a free reactor, a participant, an observer, a recorder, and an objective recounter, all without screening or bias. The patent absurdity of this demand was the starting point for the studies which were made with tape recordings.

In one seminar a young psychiatrist reported that in a previous session his patient had suddenly asked that the recording machine be turned off because he was about to divulge some material which was particularly painful. The seminar group discussed the possible reasons for this, basing the discussion on their knowledge of the patient gained in previous meetings. To check the accuracy of their speculations the group suggested that the five or ten minutes of the therapeutic interview just preceding and following the interruption of the recording be played back. To the blank astonishment of the young psychiatrist and of the group as a whole, they heard the psychiatrist himself make the suggestion to the patient that the recording be interrupted. Of this fact the psychiatrist had not the slightest recollection. Yet from the material that preceded the interruption it became clear that the psychiatrist's intuition had served him well. He had sensed the patient's mounting tension. He had realized the need for some gestures of special consideration and privacy. The patient had responded with relief and after a few minutes had apparently suggested that the recording be resumed. Nevertheless, the psychiatrist had felt anxious lest he be criticized for his action; out of this anxiety had come the

unconscious reversal of his memory of events and of the roles which he and the patient had played.

* * *

NOTE 10

SIMON, HERBERT A.

Administrative Behavior*

. . . If authority were evidenced entirely in the acceptance of explicit commands, or in the resolution of disagreements, its presence or absence in any relationship could be sought in the presence or absence of these tangible concomitants. But it is equally possible for obedience to anticipate commands. The subordinate may, and is expected to, ask himself "How would my superior wish me to behave under these circumstances?" Under such circumstances, authority is implemented by a subsequent review of completed actions, rather than a prior command. Further, the more obedient the subordinate, the less tangible will be the evidences of authority. For authority will need to be exercised only to reverse an incorrect decision.

This phenomenon has been pointed out by Freidrich, who calls it a "rule of anticipated reactions." It affords a striking example of the manner in which expectations and anticipations govern human behavior, and the difficulties which result from this for the analysis of human institutions. The difficulty in determining authority relations because of the operation of the rule of anticipated reactions is common to all "power" situations. . . .

NOTE 11

AMERICAN LAW INSTITUTE

A Model Code of Pre-arraignment Procedure**

* * *

The requirement that the arrested person be informed that what he says is being recorded raises a difficult question. It seems likely that there are many people who will be reluctant to speak if they know their words are being recorded. This may be true even of persons who would not be inhibited by the knowledge that what they were saying was being reduced to writing or will be testified to in court by the officers present.

But for many people, greater willingness to talk when they believe no recording is being made stems from an inability to understand the link between what is happening in the police station and what will happen in court and afterwards. In a system which

---

* 108 *University of Pennsylvania Law Review*, 59, 60–61. (1959). Reprinted by permission.

* New York: The Macmillan Co., 2nd ed., 1957. (pp. 129–30). Reprinted by permission.
** Tentative Draft No. 1. Copyright 1966. Reprinted with permission of The American Law Institute.

permits questioning of some persons before they have their lawyers present, it seems to the Reporters that there is a special obligation not to mislead suspects about the seriousness of their situation. It is for this reason that disclosure is required, even though it is recognized that it may sometimes make questioning less effective. Also, there may be some cases where disclosure of the fact of recording will make questioning more effective, because some persons may talk more freely when there is no risk that what they say will be misquoted.

NOTE 12

FREUD, SIGMUND

Recommendations to Physicians Practising Psychoanalysis (1912)*

The technique [of psychoanalysis] is a very simple one. [I]t rejects the use of any special expedient (even that of taking notes). It consists simply in not directing one's notice to anything in particular and in maintaining the same "evenly-suspended attention" . . . in the face of all that one hears. In this way we spare ourselves a strain on our attention which could not in any way be kept up for several hours daily, and we avoid a danger which is inseparable from the exercise of deliberate attention. For as soon as anyone deliberately concentrates his attention to a certain degree, he begins to select from the material before him; one point will be fixed in his mind with particular clearness and some other will be correspondingly disregarded, and in making this selection he will be following his expectations or inclinations. This, however, is precisely what must not be done. In making the selection, if he follows his expectations he is in danger of never finding anything but what he already knows; and if he follows his inclinations he will certainly falsify what he may perceive. It must not be forgotten that the things one hears are for the most part things whose meaning is only recognized later on.

It will be seen that the rule of giving equal notice to everything is the necessary counterpart to the demand made on the patient that he should communicate everything that occurs to him without criticism or selection. If the doctor behaves otherwise, he is throwing away most of the advantage which results from the patient's obeying the "fundamental rule of psychoanalysis." The rule for the doctor may be expressed: "He should withhold all conscious influences from his capacity to attend, and give himself over completely to his 'unconscious memory.'" Or,

to put it purely in terms of technique: "He should simply listen, and not bother about whether he is keeping anything in mind."

What is achieved in this manner will be sufficient for all requirements during the treatment. Those elements of the material which already form a connected context will be at the doctor's conscious disposal; the rest, as yet unconnected and chaotic disorder, seems at first to be submerged, but rises readily into recollection as soon as the patient brings up something new to which it can be related and by which it can be continued. The undeserved compliment of having "a remarkably good memory" which the patient pays one when one reproduces some detail after a year and a day can then be accepted with a smile, whereas a conscious determination to recollect the point would probably have resulted in failure.

Mistakes in this process of remembering occur only at times and places at which one is disturbed by some personal consideration . . . that is, when one has fallen seriously below the standard of an ideal analyst. Confusion with material brought up by other patients occurs very rarely. . . .

I cannot advise the taking of full notes, the keeping of a shorthand record, etc., during analytic sessions. Apart from the unfavorable impressions which this makes on some patients, the same considerations as have been advanced with regard to attention apply here too. A detrimental selection from the material will necessarily be made as one writes the notes or shorthand, and part of one's own mental activity is tied up in this way, which would be better employed in interpreting what one has heard. No objection can be raised to making exceptions to this rule in the case of dates, the text of dreams, or particular noteworthy events which can easily be detached from their context and are suitable for independent use as instances. But I am not in the habit of doing this either. As regards instances, I write them down from memory in the evening after work is over. . . .

*   *   *

It is easy to see upon what aim the different rules I have brought forward converge. They are all intended to create for the doctor a counterpart to the "fundamental rule of psychoanalysis" which is laid down for the patient. Just as the patient must relate everything that his self-observation can detect, and keep back all the logical and affective objections that seek to induce him to make a selection from among them, so the doctor must put himself in a position to make use of everything he is told for the purposes of interpretation and of recognizing the concealed unconscious material without substituting a censorship of his own for the selection that the patient has forgone. To put it in a formula: He must turn his own unconscious like a receptive organ toward the transmitting unconscious of the patient. He must adjust himself

---

* Reprinted from: 12 *The Standard Edition of the Complete Psychological Works of Sigmund Freud*, James Strachey, ed. London: The Hogarth Press and the Institute of Psycho-analysis, 1958. (pp. 111–16) and *Studies on Hysteria*, Basic Books, Inc., publishers, 1957. Reprinted by permission of Hogarth and Basic Books, Inc.

to the patient as a telephone receiver is adjusted to the transmitting microphone. Just as the receiver converts back into soundwaves the electric oscillations in the telephone line which were set up by sound waves, so the doctor's unconscious is able, from the derivatives of the unconscious which are communicated to him, to reconstruct that unconscious, which has determined the patient's free associations.

NOTE 13

DURST v. SUPERIOR COURT
222 Cal. App. 2d 447 35 Cal. Rptr. 143 (1964)

FOX, PRESIDING JUSTICE.

Petitioner seeks a writ of prohibition to prohibit his examination by a medical expert ordered by the court . . . unless the petitioner is permitted to have his counsel and a court reporter present at such examination.

Petitioner, an attorney . . . claims that as the result of injuries sustained in an automobile accident on December 5, 1957, he has developed a psychosis which has rendered him totally disabled, entitling him to disability payments for the remainder of his life.

*   *   *

In denying the petitioner's requests the court said, in part: . . .

"It may not be said here that there will be 'no disinterested person present to report, or later to testify to what occurred during the examination.' Dr. Brill is being appointed by the court because he is disinterested, impartial and qualified. His primary function is to report to the court as to what occurred during the examination and his findings as a result thereof. Therefore, the rights of plaintiff will be adequately protected without the presence of counsel or a reporter."

*   *   *

The trial court was correct in its conclusion that the cases relied upon by the petitioner were not authority for the proposition that the court must allow presence of counsel and a reporter.

*   *   *

[In these cases] the court was discussing a physical examination and there were no compelling reasons why persons should be excluded from the examination. In contrast, the instant case involves a psychiatric examination whose subjective nature requires an atmosphere that is conductive to freedom of expression on the part of the examinee. In this connection Dr. Brill submitted an affidavit in which he stated: "That if declarant's psychiatric examination and report is to be effective the patient must not be distracted by the presence of other persons during the examination. That if the patient knows his statements

are being recorded, he will be on the defensive, and such statements will be reserved and not completely objective.

"THAT if declarant is to make a neutral, unbiased, and objective psychiatric examination of patient, it is necessary that such examination not be hampered by verbatim recording of statements made or by the presence of other distracting influences or persons."

*   *   *

The conditions under which such an examination, as is here contemplated, may be made by a court-appointed expert necessarily rest within the sound discretion of the judge making the appointment. In the instant case the trial judge remarked that "[i]n considering plaintiff's request, I have not been unmindful of the rather unusual medical problem involved. . . ." The judge then concluded that ". . . in my opinion it would detract from the ability of the psychiatrist to conduct a meaningful examination to have counsel or a reporter present." . . .

From the foregoing it is clear that the court did not abuse its discretion in making the order here under attack.

*   *   *

NOTE 14

C.A.B. AIRCRAFT ACCIDENT REPORT
No. 1-0038 (Jan. 6, 1960)

At approximately 2356 E.S.T., on February 3, 1959, an American Airlines Lockheed Electra aircraft crashed into the East River while attempting an instrument approach to runway 22 at La Guardia Airport.

*   *   *

The Board believes that a premature descent below landing minimums was the result of preoccupation of the crew on particular aspects of the aircraft and its environment to the neglect of essential flight instrument references for altitudes and height above the approach surface. . . .

*   *   *

In rejecting the possibility of dual and simultaneous altimeter error the Board must, as a consequence, reject portions of the testimony of one or both flight crew members. Considering that the flight crew members received physical injuries and that they were also under great emotional stress, such questioning of their testimony has a rational basis. Under such circumstances, the Board has frequently found that the recollection, particularly of events immediately preceding an accident, is very difficult and often erroneous. Furthermore, we are mindful of the natural human tendency to assume conformance with standard operating procedures to fill in the voids or hazy areas of one's memory. . . .

*   *   *

e. EMBRY v. HARGADINE-McKITTRICK DRY
GOODS CO.

127 Mo. App. 383, 105 S.W. 777 (1907)

* * *

GOODE, J. . . . The appellant was an employee of the respondent company under a written contract to expire December 15, 1903, at a salary of $2,000 per annum. . . .

Appellant contends that on December 23, 1903, he was re-engaged by respondent, through its president, Thos. H. McKittrick, for another year at the same compensation and for the same duties stipulated in his previous written contract. On March 1, 1904, he was discharged. . .

The respondent company contends that its president never re-employed appellant after the termination of his written contract, and hence that it had a right to discharge him when it chose. . . .

Appellant testified: That several times prior to the termination of his written contract on December 15, 1903, he had endeavored to get an understanding with McKittrick for another year, but had been put off from time to time. That on December 23rd, eight days after the expiration of said contract, he called on McKittrick, in the latter's office, and said to him that as appellant's written employment had lapsed eight days before, and as there were only a few days between then and the 1st of January in which to seek employment with other firms, if respondent wished to retain his services longer he must have a contract for another year, or he would quit respondent's service then and there. That he had been put off twice before and wanted an understanding or contract at once so that he could go ahead without worry. That McKittrick asked him how he was getting along in his department, and appellant said he was very busy, as they were in the height of the season getting men out—had about 110 salesmen on the line and others in preparation. That McKittrick then said: "Go ahead, you're all right. Get your men out, and don't let that worry you." That appellant took McKittrick at his word and worked until February 15th without any question in his mind. . . .

McKittrick denied this conversation as related by appellant, and said that, when accosted by the latter on December 23rd, he (McKittrick) was working on his books in order to get out a report for a stockholders' meeting, and, when appellant said if he did not get a contract he would leave, that he (McKittrick) said: "Mr. Embry, I am just getting ready for the stockholders' meeting to-morrow. I have no time to take it up now. I have told you before I would not take it up until I had these matters out of the way. You will have to see me at a later time. I said 'Go back upstairs and get your men out on the road.' I may have asked him one or two other questions relative to the department, I don't remember. The whole conversation did not take more than a minute."

* * *

It is assigned for error that the court required the jury, in order to return a verdict for appellant, not only to find the conversation occurred as appellant swore, but that both parties intended by such conversation to contract with each other for plaintiff's employment for the year from December 1903, at a salary of $2,000. . . . [I]t remains to determine . . . whether the formation of a contract by what, according to Embry, was said, depended on the intention of both Embry and McKittrick. Or, to put the question more precisely: Did what was said constitute a contract of re-employment on the previous terms irrespective of the intention or purposes of McKittrick?

Judical opinion and elementary treatises abound in statements of the rule that to constitute a contract there must be a meeting of the minds of the parties, and both must agree to the same thing in the same sense. Generally speaking, this may be true; but it is not literally or universally true. That is to say, the inner intention of parties to a conversation subsequently alleged to create a contract cannot either make a contract of what transpired, or prevent one from arising, if the words used were sufficient to constitute a contract. In so far as their intention is an influential element, it is only such intention as the words or acts of the parties indicate; not one secretly cherished which is inconsistent with those words or acts. . . .

* * *

[W]e hold that, though McKittrick may not have intended to employ Embry by what transpired between them according to the latter's testimony, yet if what McKittrick said would have been taken by a reasonable man to be an employment, and Embry so understood it, it constituted a valid contract of employment for the ensuing year.

* * *

The judgment is reversed. . .

NOTES

NOTE 1

HOTCHKISS v. NATIONAL CITY BANK OF NEW YORK

200 F. 287, 293 (S.D.N.Y. 1911); aff'd, 201 F. 664 (2d Cir. 1912); aff'd, 231 U.S. 50 (1913)

LEARNED HAND, J. A contract has, strictly speaking, nothing to do with the personal or individual intent of the parties. A contract is an obligation attached by the mere force of law to certain acts of the parties, usually words which ordinarily accompany and represent a known intent. If, however, it were proved by twenty bishops that either party, when he used the words, intended something else than the usual meaning which the law imposes upon them, he would still be held, unless there were some mutual mistake, or something else of the sort. Of course, if it appear by other words, or acts, of the parties, that they attribute a peculiar meaning to such words as they use in the contract that meaning will prevail, but only by virtue of the other words, and not because of their unexpressed intent.

NOTE 2

CORBIN, ARTHUR

Treatise on the Law of Contracts*

*   *   *

There has been a good deal of discussion with respect to two so-called theories of contract, known as the "objective theory" and the "subjective theory." By the first, it is argued that a valid contract is created by agreement in expression, the subjective intention of the parties being immaterial. By the second, it is argued that a contract is not created unless there is agreement in intention, properly expressed. . . .

As usually understood, the "objective theory" is based upon a great illusion—the illusion that words, either singly or in combination, have a "meaning" that is independent of the persons who use them. It is crudely supposed that words have a "true," or "legal," meaning (described as "objective"), one that all persons of whatever race, origin, or education are bound to know, and in accordance with which the law requires them to perform and to accept performance. Words, oral or written, are merely a medium by which one person attempts to convey his thoughts to another person. They are merely audible sounds or visible sights. It is individual men who have "meanings" which they try to convey to others by the use of words; and it is individual men who receive "meanings" by reason of words used by others. . . .

*   *   *

NOTE 3

TAYLOR v. CALDWELL
In the Queen's Bench, 1863.

3 Best & S. 826. (Q.B. 1863)

BLACKBURN, J. [P]laintiffs and defendants had . . . entered into a contract by which the defendants agree to let the plaintiffs have the use of The Surrey Gardens and Music Hall on four days then to come. . .

*   *   *

After the making of the agreement, and before the first day on which a concert was to be given, the Hall was destroyed by fire. This destruction, we must take it on the evidence, was without the fault of either party, and was so complete that in consequence the concerts could not be given as intended. And the question we have to decide is whether, under these circumstances, the loss which the plaintiffs have sustained is to fall upon the defendants. . . . The parties when framing their agreement evidently had not present to their minds the possibility of such a disaster, and have made no express stipulation with reference to it, so that the answer to the question must depend upon the general rules of law applicable to such a contract.

[W]here, from the nature of the contract, it appears that the parties must from the beginning have known that it could not be fulfilled unless when the time for the fulfilment of the contract arrived some particular specified thing continued to exist, so that, when entering into the contract, they must have contemplated such continuing existence as the foundation of what was to be done; there, in the absence of any express or implied warranty that the thing shall exist, the contract is not to be construed as a positive contract, but as subject to an implied condition that the parties shall be excused in case, before breach, performance becomes impossible from the perishing of the thing without default of the contractor.

There seems little doubt that this implication tends to further the great object of making the legal construction such as to fulfill the intention of those who entered into the contract. For in the course of affairs men in making such contracts in general would, if it were brought to their minds, say that there should be such a condition. . . .

*   *   *

. . . In the present case, looking at the whole contract, we find that the parties contracted on the basis of the continued existence of the Music Hall at the time when the concerts were to be given, that being essential to their performance.

We think, therefore, that the Music Hall having ceased to exist, without fault of either party, both parties are excused, the plaintiffs from taking the gardens and paying the money, the defendants from performing their promise to give the use of the Hall and gardens and other things. . . .

NOTE 4

FULLER, LON L. and BRAUCHER, ROBERT

Basic Contract Law*

In *Taylor* v. *Caldwell* the court says that when

---

* St. Paul, Minn.: West Publishing Co., 1963. (Vol. I, § 106). Reprinted by permission.

* St. Paul, Minn.: West & Co. 1964. (pp. 554–559). Reprinted by permission.

framing their agreement the parties "had not present to their minds the possibility" of a disaster affecting the Music Hall, and concludes that the parties "must have contemplated" the "continuing existence" of the Hall "as the foundation" of their agreement.

Is there a contradiction here? The court seems to say that the parties did not think of the possibility of the Hall's burning and therefore assumed it would not burn. But how can the parties assume that no fire will occur, when the possibility of a fire was never present to their minds? If this possibility was not present to their minds, would it not be more accurate to say that they assumed nothing about a fire, either that it would or would not occur?

The difficulty here does not lie in any dispute about psychological fact, but in the inappropriateness of the language ordinarily used to describe certain elementary psychological truths. Words like "intention," "assumption," "expectation" and "understanding" all seem to imply a *conscious* state involving an awareness of alternatives and a deliberate choice among them. It is, however, plain that there is a psychological state which can be described as a "tacit assumption" that does not involve a consciousness of alternatives. The absent-minded professor stepping from his office into the hall as he reads a book "assumes" that the floor of the hall will be there to receive him. His conduct is conditioned and directed by this assumption, even though the possibility that the floor has been removed does not "occur" to him, that is, is not present in his conscious mental processes.

*   *   *

[W]here parties have entered a contract an unexpected obstacle to performance may operate disruptively in varying degrees. To a man who has contracted to carry goods by truck over a route traversing a mountain pass, a landslide filling the pass may be a very disruptive and unexpected event. The man who originally contracted to build the roadway through the mountains might view the same event occurring during the course of construction as a temporary setback and a challenge to his resourcefulness. The man who contracts to deliver goods a year from now at a price now fixed certainly "takes into account" the possibility of some fluctuation in price levels, but may feel that a ten-fold inflation was contrary to an "assumption" or "expectation" that price variations would occur within the "normal" range, and that this expectation was "the foundation of the agreement."

Underlying questions of this sort, and indeed, underlying much of contract law generally, are certain basic problems of psychology that have never been satisfactorily solved. We speak constantly of things that were "intended" or "assumed" without having a clear conception of the psychological processes involved in "intending" and "assuming." The lawyer or judge who turns to psychology for help in dealing with these problems is likely to be disappointed.

*   *   *

The various schools stemming from Freud performed a great service by dramatizing the fact that the determinants of human conduct are not to be identified with consciousness. Where the introspective psychologists tended to assume that all behavior is consciously directed except automatisms and absent-minded acts, the psychoanalytic school made it clear that many acts are performed in quest of goals of which the actor is himself ignorant. At the same time, it is fairly obvious that this branch of psychological theory offers no direct help in dealing with the problem under discussion in this note. This problem lies somewhere between the superficial layer of consciousness and the dark inner recesses of the human psyche probed by the psychoanalysts.

*   *   *

In spite of hopeful beginnings promising a more comprehensive psychological treatment of human behavior, for the time being the only methods available for dealing with problems like that raised by *Taylor* v. *Caldwell* are essentially those resting on intuition and introspection. We "just know" that the burning of a music hall violates a tacit assumption of the parties who executed a contract for hiring it; we "just know" that a two per cent increase in the price of beans does not violate a tacit assumption underlying a contract to deliver a ton of beans for a fixed price.

*   *   *

It should be observed that there are three general limitations on the relevance of psychological fact to the decision of legal controversies beside that already discussed, namely, that psychology has not, in many instances, developed methods capable of answering the questions the law proposes. The *first* of these limitations lies in the fact that it is often wise in the law deliberately to disregard the actual intent ("conscious" or "unconscious") of the party participating in the transaction. In many instances the standard applied by the law is not "subjective" but "objective"; we ask, not what this defendant actually intended, but what the plaintiff reasonably supposed him to intend, or what a reasonable person in the position of the plaintiff would have supposed him to intend. Throughout the law of contracts and torts there is a wavering between the "internal" and the "external" approach to these questions, and unfortunately the courts and writers are not very articulate about the principles on the basis of which choice between these approaches is made.

When the law asks what this particular party "intended" or "expected" in this particular situation, psychological fact is directly relevant; when it asks what a "reasonably prudent man" would have "intended" or "expected," it is less directly so. However, an adoption of the "objective" standard does not make psychological fact completely irrelevant. In such a case we are, as it were, applying the truths of psychology hypothetically, and the more we can learn about the human animal and his motivation, the more effectively can we construct standards of "reasonable" behavior and "reasonable" expectations.

A *second* general limitation on the relevance of psychological truth to legal problems lies in the fact that the law has two rather antithetical tasks with respect to human behavior: (1) that of adjusting its rules to the expectations and intentions of "reasonable" men, and (2) that of disciplining human behavior and guiding it into proper channels. . . .

The law has always to weigh against the advantages of conforming to the laymen's assumptions, the advantages of reshaping and clarifying those assumptions. If it were true, for example, that laymen generally regard the ceremony of "shaking on it" as creating a binding contract, the law might still have ample grounds for refusing to adopt the same view, if this ceremony does not adequately guard against the dangers legal formalities are intended to avert. . . .

[T]he law is partly taking the human animal as he is now conditioned, and attempting to supply him with "behavior supports" in the form of rules that will enable him, without retraining, to perform efficiently and avoid collision with his fellows. At the same time, the law undertakes in innumerable ways to retrain him, and this it cannot do without introducing some disruption into his accustomed ways. It is because the law follows these somewhat contradictory goals that we get many of the puzzling antinomies of the law of contracts: "The purpose of the law of contracts is to carry out the intention of the parties, yet we may interpret a written contract in a way that violates the intention of both parties to it." . . . "The purpose of interpretation is to ascertain the intention of the parties, yet we know that the parties do not 'intend' in terms of the legal categories imposed on their relationship."

*   *   *

G.
The Total Personality

1.

RAPAPORT, DAVID

The Autonomy of the Ego*

An old Jewish story illustrates some of the fundamental issues encountered by psychoanalytic ego psychology. There was an Eastern king who heard about Moses. He heard that Moses was a leader of men, a good man, a wise man, and he wished to meet him. But Moses, busy wandering forty years in the desert, couldn't come. So the king sent his painters to Moses and they brought back a picture of him. The king called his phrenologists and astrologists and asked them, "What kind of man is this?" They went into a huddle and came out with a report which read: This is a cruel, greedy, self-seeking, dishonest man. The king was puzzled, He said, "Either my painters do not know how to paint or there is no such science as astrology or phrenology." To decide this dilemma, he went to see Moses and after seeing him he cried out, "There is no such science as astrology, or phrenology." When Moses heard this he was surprised and asked the king what he meant. The king explained, but Moses only shook his head and said, "No. Your phrenologists and astrologists are right. That's what I was made of! I fought against it and that's how I became what I am."

This story is a good allegory of the first encounter of psychoanalysis with ego psychology. It speaks of the recognition that there are other things to a human being besides the drives. Psychoanalysis at first assumed that these other things were defensive structures which were born of conflict. But ego psychology did not stop at this point. Let us raise a few questions about the Moses story and see what kind of problems ego psychology had to face afterward.

First, what does it mean: "I fought against it?" On the "fought" we can easily agree: That means *conflict*. But what conflicted? The old conception which prevailed before the advent of ego psychology was a conflict of drives with the censor. After the concept of the ego was already coined, it was assumed that the ego and id conflicted, and yet we learn that the ego itself was born out of conflict. So the first problem that budding ego psychology met was: How are the participants of the conflict to be conceived of? This is one of the points I propose to discuss.

* 15 *Bulletin of the Menninger Clinic*, 113–23 (1951). Reprinted by permission.

The second question is: If he "fought against it" and became what he was, what happened to that which he "was made of?" Did it vanish? The Bible says that Moses was not quite the holy man without spot. When he was told to touch the rock, he hit it. He acted as if *he* were doing the wonders and not the Lord. When he descended from Mount Sinai, after communing with the Lord, and saw the golden calf and the erring of his people, he went into a violent rage and broke the Tablets.

This much is already clear: Even though Moses, by his struggle, became somebody very different from the stuff he "was made of," in moments of strain, that grandiose, competitive, raging, immodest stuff of which he was made, and which the astrologists and phrenologists saw in his features, made its appearance in his behavior. We realize that this is how it always happens in psychological life. So we need not be concerned that we may be accused of forgetting . . . the persistence underneath of what the struggle seems to have conquered, when we speak of what someone became by a struggle against his impulses, that is, when we deal with the *function* of the ego. We do not forget, even if our emphasis is on the ego, that Moses was not altogether "holy" though he fought against the "unholy" things within him which we nowadays call impulses and drives.

There is yet a third question: How is it possible for the ego to let something that it has conquered come through, as it did in the case of Moses in the Tablet and the Rock episode?

*   *   *

Our first question as to the nature of the autonomy of the ego was: If the ego grows on conflict, how are we to conceive of the participants of this original conflict? Note the circularity: The ego is both born out of the conflict, and party to the conflict. How can we explain this seeming contradiction? The answer can be seen in the study of infants, in the individual differences between infants, which are present from the very beginning of development, suggesting inborn personality determinants *in nuce*. It may be seen in one of Freud's last papers "Analysis Terminable and Interminable," in which he directly postulates inborn, inherited ego factors. It can be seen also when we consider that after all psychology has found some general laws of perception, memory, and learning which show some interindividual consistency. Let us forget for a moment that we would want to restudy these three functions from the point of view of psychoanalytic ego psychology, and that in recent studies these interindividually consistent laws have yielded individual differences and gained a new meaning. Whatever interindividual consistency there is in these functions shows that these apparatuses of perception, memory, and motility, are inborn and characteristic of the species and the biological in-

dividual, before they become expressive of conflict and experience. Memory, perception, and motility have already been existing and functioning before conflict ever occurred. Here then we see apparatuses which antedate conflict, and become the core of ego development. Indeed we know that these apparatuses may remain, in many cases, outside of conflict later on also. It is thus that a patient on the verge of psychosis, totally helpless to deal with his problems, and torn in every respect, may nevertheless display on the couch, or in the interview, or in testing, an amazingly accurate memory, or sensitive perception, or perfection of motility.

It was Heinz Hartmann who gave the first systematic evaluation of the role of these apparatuses in ego development. He labeled the autonomy of these apparatuses "primary autonomy." The functions which are at any given time outside of the range of conflict he conceptualized as belonging to the conflict-free ego sphere. From the role of this primary autonomy in ego development, he concluded that our usual conception that the id pre-exists the ego is inadequate, that there must be a period in human individual development in which what will later be the ego, and what will later be the id, coexist, as yet undifferentiated from each other; and that it is by the differentiation from an initial undifferentiated phase that both the ego and the id arise.

Psychologists concerned with the psychology of development, and biologists concerned with instincts, have recognized something like this. . . . Biologists . . . have recognized that domestication alters instinct behavior. The rigid co-ordination of drive tension and goal, so clear, for example, in insects, is lost in the course of domestication. It was . . . Hartmann who clarified this issue, concluding that in the human individual, drives are not as adaptive and reality attuned as they are in the animal; the id is reality distant, while animal instincts are primary guarantees of survival by virtue of the strict co-ordination of drive tension and drive object.

The inborn ego apparatuses, and their integration into the ego—which, just like the id, develops from an originally undifferentiated matrix by differentiation—provide the way out of the paradox described above. Yet, without an additional consideration, the answer to the question, "What conflicted with the drives?" may not be clear. We must remember that the motor, perceptual, and memory apparatuses, as well as other inborn apparatuses such as those of affect expression, stimulus barrier, etc., have definite thresholds which are their *structural characteristics*. These *structural characteristics* will set limits to the discharge of drive tension, that is to the pleasure principle, even when the need-satisfying object is present, and even before drive discharge is prevented by the absence of the need-satisfying object. The very nature of structure will always prevent total discharge of tension. The existence of inborn structural elements in the undifferentiated phase may be what precipitates developmentally the differentiation of it into the ego and the id. The developing ego then integrates these structural apparatuses and represents their discharge-limiting and -regulating function in forms usually described as defenses. These are the foundations of the primary autonomy of the ego.

There is, however, more to ego autonomy, and to get a closer view of this "more," and get closer to the answer to our second question, let us turn to Freud's model of primitive psychic function. According to this model, when drive tension rises and the need-satisfying object is absent, instead of the tension discharge which would occur were the need-satisfying object—say the breast—present, a new distribution of tensions—that is, energies—occurs. We describe this new energy distribution by saying that the drive which cannot be satisfied, is repressed. Metapsychologically we formulate repression thus: A counter-cathexis is pitted against the cathexis (energy charge) of the repressed drive.

This is not only a model of instinct vicissitude, but also one of the development of the ego. The counter-cathexis reflects a reality fact: The unavailability of the need-satisfying object. The model thus represents the internalization of reality, which is one of the crucial characteristics and functions of the ego. This internalization is not only a modification of the distribution of drive cathexes by the impact of reality, but also a crucial step in the development of thought organization. Instead of drive discharge, prevented first by the absence of the object and later by repression, there arise on the one hand, affect discharge observed as affect expression, on the other, ideational representations, in the form of wish-fulfilling, hallucinatory images. In the illusions of people on the verge of starvation or dehydration, and in the hallucinations of schizophrenics, we have phenomena substantiating the heuristic value of this model.

Reality is then internalized and represented in the psychic apparatus, not only by the countercathexis of repression, but also by the arising ideational representation, and indirectly even by the affect discharge. The countercathexis of repression is only one of the countercathectic energy distributions which arise in this fashion. Every defense mechanism we observe, corresponds to such a countercathectic energy distribution. Each of these is a new apparatus of the ego, added to the already discussed inborn ego apparatuses. They, arising in the course of the differentiation process of the ego and the id from the undifferentiated phase, also serve to control drive discharge. These defensive apparatuses come to our attention in the form of motivations of behavior, such as denial, avoidance, altruism, honesty, etc. These motivating forces, too, are relatively autonomous, and constitute what "more" there is besides

inborn autonomous apparatuses to ego autonomy. They are what Moses referred to in the story saying: "That's how I became what I am."

To demonstrate to ourselves the autonomy of these defensive apparatuses (secondary autonomy), let us take another look at their development. There was a clash between drive need and reality. Out of this clash arose controlling apparatuses. Some of these, once they arose as emergent organizations, became relatively independent from the source of their origin. How do we know? We know that in our therapeutic work we encounter defenses which we do not manage to break down even in many years of analysis. You could counter this with, "That is no proof. More and better analysis would have penetrated these!" Possibly. But the very fact of difficulty in analysis bespeaks relative autonomy.

But there is more telling evidence for this autonomy than the pragmatic consideration just advanced. We have known from reconstructions in psychoanalysis for many years that many altruistic, aesthetic, and antiviolence motivations are somehow related to reaction formations against impulses of the anal-sadistic phase. Anna Freud reported that they observed in their Hempstead Nurseries that children who displayed, in a particularly blatant fashion, behavior characteristic of the anal-sadistic phase, became later on very benign, nice youngsters, with keen liking for people and animals, and with a sharp aversion to cruelty. . . .

To generalize this point: What came about as a result of conflict, sooner or later may become independent of the conflict, may become relatively autonomous. This becomes particularly clear in studying thought processes: . . . I do not believe that any prolonged study of thought in various psychiatric disorders can leave anyone without the strongest impression that the secondary process once established shows such persistence against the onslaughts of conflict, and against the return of the repressed primary process, that it can be understood in no other way but by assuming that this is not due only to those apparatuses involved in thought (perception, memory) which have primary autonomy, but also to the persisting autonomy of apparatuses which have attained secondary autonomy.

But here we have come to the answer to our second question. While it is true that apparatuses of primary autonomy tend to *remain* such and to persist in the conflict-free ego sphere, and while defensive apparatuses born of conflict may become autonomous, and may function in the conflict-free sphere, and tend to retain their autonomy against the onslaught of conflict—nevertheless secondary and even primary autonomy is *relative*, and these apparatuses, too, may and do get involved or reinvolved in conflict. To give an extreme example: Motility, in spite of its primary autonomy, is involved in conflict in all hysterical motor disorders and schizophrenic motor mannerisms.

In other words, we have to conclude that the autonomy of the ego we are talking about, though it is a most impressive guarantee of independence from instinctual drives, of reality testing, and of social adaptation, is only relative, and may appear so impressive only because without it we would be entirely at the mercy of our impulses. Yet there are in every one of us some functions and structures, the autonomy of which proves irreversible in the course of our life history. . . .

Superimposed on the original drive cathexes, new organizations of energy arise which, owing to processes of binding or neutralization, do not abide any more by the rule of the primary process, which is tension-level-lowering discharge at all costs. That is, the pleasure principle is superseded by the reality principle, by postponement of discharge, by detour, by experimental operation with small quantities of energy. These processes of binding or neutralization which progressively transform the discharge-bent drive energy to a system-bound form seem to play a crucial role in the development of defensive apparatuses (secondary autonomy), and their motivations. Keeping this in mind, let us see whether we can obtain some kind of an answer to our third question about the occasional failure of the ego to bind the forbidden impulses.

To make my point concrete I want to refer to a group of borderline cases, all of whom survived, as it were, on counterphobic defenses. Reckless wild tricks, fearlessness, apparent self-sufficiency, rebelliousness, denial of needs (including need for help), contempt and hate for all who show "weakness," were outstanding characteristics of them all. They were "independent" in the extreme, because they wished and feared dependence in the extreme. In some of these I have seen the dire effects of a direct interpretation of the aggressive meaning of their "independence," in the form of catatonic excitement. I have seen some of them run away when overactive therapy brought positive transference prematurely to a head, thus bringing on an overwhelming threat to their independence. I have seen some of them, however, where a profound respect for the independence and dignity of man permeated the therapeutic atmosphere and where the analysis of the counterphobic defense was extremely gradual and did not call in question independence as a value and motivation. The autonomy of the value motivation was not attacked when the conflict-involved counterphobic defense was analyzed. In some cases therapeutic failure may be due to a lack of autonomy of the "independence striving" as a value motivation, it being just one subordinate aspect of the conflict expressed in the counterphobic defense; in others it may be due to the therapist's neglect to distinguish between the autonomous value-motivation aspect, and the conflict-laden, defensive aspect of the same psychic formation.

The tentative answer to the third of the questions raised is: That autonomy, particularly secondary autonomy, is always relative, and the onslaught of drive motivations, especially when unchecked by therapeutic help or when aided by overzealous therapeutic moves, may reverse autonomy and bring about a regressed, psychotic state in which the patient is, to a far-reaching extent, at the mercy of his drive impulses. The higher-level autonomous motivations are, as it were, dissolved, and the allies the therapist usually counts on—spontaneity and synthesis—are absent. Thus we can see that the issue of ego autonomy is not merely a theoretical problem but also a practical one of therapy, particularly in borderline and psychotic cases.

What was conquered by Moses in his struggle lurks there, always ready to make an attempt to recoup its old ground. If it succeeds—we are faced with a psychosis. This recoup is rarely complete—all ego autonomy is hardly ever suspended—yet a sufficient part of this autonomy may be dissolved to warn us that the therapist of such a borderline case should respect and foster all autonomous ego functions to avoid their crumbling.

2.

RAPAPORT, DAVID

The Theory of Ego Autonomy: A Generalization*

My purpose is to bring up to date the summary of the theory of ego autonomy which I presented in 1950. . . .

To open up the issues, I will contrast the Berkeleian view of man with the Cartesian [Descartes]. In the Berkeleian view, the outside world is the creation of man's imagination. In this solipsistic view, man is totally *independent* of the environment, and totally *dependent* on the forces and images residing within him: He cannot envisage an external world independent of these inner forces. In turn, he need not come to terms with the outside world: Since that world is created by forces inherent in man, he is a priori in harmony with it. In the Cartesian world, on the other hand, man is born as a clean slate upon which experience writes. No forces or images exist in man except for those which arise from the impingements of the outside world. In this world, man is totally *dependent* on and in harmony with the outside world. In turn, he is totally *independent* from, i.e., autono-

* 22 *Bulletin of the Menninger Clinic* 13–32 (1958). Reprinted by permission.

mous from, internal forces, which in this conception do not exist.[1]

Observation confirms neither of these views. It shows that while man's behavior *is* determined by drive forces which originate in him, it is not totally at their mercy since it has a certain independence from them. We refer to this independence as *the autonomy of the ego from the id*. The most common observation which necessitated this conception was the responsiveness and relevance of behavior to external reality. But this dependence of behavior on the external world and on experience is not complete either. Man can interpose delay and thought not only between instinctual promptings and action, modifying and even indefinitely postponing drive discharge, he can likewise modify and postpone his reaction to external stimulation. This independence of behavior from external stimulation we will refer to as *the autonomy of the ego from external reality*. Since the ego is never completely independent from the id nor from external reality, we always speak about *relative* autonomy.

My previous discussion of autonomy focused on the relative independence of behavior from internal drive forces. *The* great discovery of psychoanalysis was the existence of these unconscious forces. It took quite a while to realize that this discovery does not compel us to embrace a solipsistic theory in which a chimney is primarily a phallic symbol and only secondarily the means for letting smoke out of the house. It was some time before we began to take account of the chimney as a smokestack, because these realistic meanings were not the focus of our early interests. However, after psychoanalysis extended its scope to the study of the ego, it became possible and indeed necessary to create conceptual tools to deal with these realistic meanings and their role in behavior. This led to the study of the ego's relative autonomy from the id, the guarantee of our relatively even and solid relationship to the outside world.

*   *   *

. . . I have another story to illuminate the autonomy of the ego from external reality. "A king returned to his capital followed by his victorious army. The band played and his horse, the army, the people, all moved in step with the rhythm. The king, amazed, contemplated the power of music. Suddenly he noticed a man who walked out of step and slowly fell behind. The king, deeply impressed, sent for the man, and told him: 'I never saw a man as strong as you are. The music enthralled everybody except you. Where do you get the strength to resist it?' The man answered, 'I was pondering, and that gave me the strength.' "[2]

1. This sketch of Berkeley's and Descartes' views is oversimplified. Neither actually held such an extreme view. . . .

2. The story actually does not end here. The man tells the

In other words, it is possible for man to maintain relative autonomy, i.e., a degree of independence, from his environment. This relative autonomy of man from his environment is the subject of the following discussion.

Though the conception of the relative autonomy of the ego from the id readjusted the position of the id concept in psychoanalytic theory, it did not dispense with the theory of the id nor did it even alter it radically. Likewise, the theory of the ego's relative autonomy from the environment eliminates neither the theory of the ego's autonomy from the id, nor the theory of the id. In fact, far from being rendered superfluous, our theories of the id, of the ego in general, and of the autonomous ego in particular, may appear in a new light and some of the gaps in our knowledge of them may be bridged by developing the theory of the ego's *relative* autonomy from the environment.

There is actually nothing radically new in what follows. To the medical man, it is a commonplace that nonliving matter cannot escape the impact of its environment and its reactions are strictly (or statistically) predictable, but that organisms can escape such impacts, can avoid responding to them, and when they respond, they can do so in a variety of alternative (vicarious) ways. Man's simultaneous relative dependence on and independence from his environment is an issue well within the biological tradition. While psychoanalytic theory, in general, has had a biological cast from the beginning, this did not extend to its consideration of the environment's role in determining behavior.

Our task is to seek the answers to two questions: What are the guarantees of the ego's autonomy from the environment? How is the autonomy of the ego from the environment related to the autonomy of the ego from the id?

To approach the first question I will review the guarantees of the ego's relative autonomy from the id. That autonomy is guaranteed by ego apparatuses of primary and secondary autonomy.

We no longer assume that the ego arises from the id, but rather that the ego and the id both arise by differentiation from a common undifferentiated matrix, in which the apparatuses that differentiate into the ego's means of orientation, of reality testing,

king of two even stronger men. " 'The first was so strong that when he wanted it, the sun was only *sun* for him, the moon only *moon*, the wind only *wind*, and the mountain only *mountain*, and they meant nothing else to him.' (The exclusion of 'connotative enrichment' is a mechanism of obsessive-compulsive character formation and pathology). The king asked, 'What happened to this man?' 'He built a high wall around himself,' was the answer. But the second man was even stronger: 'He was equally benign to all people, beautiful or ugly, rich or poor. He gave the best advice to the kings and princes, but they didn't listen. He was thought to be self-seeking; and far across the Gobi Desert, Confucius died, alone, old, and in misery.' "

and of action, are already present, These, termed *apparatuses of primary autonomy*, serve drive gratification and enter conflict as independent ego factors. They are the memory apparatus, the motor apparatus, the perceptual apparatuses, and the threshold apparatuses (including the drive- and affect-discharge thresholds). They are evolutionary givens which, by virtue of their long history of selection and modification, have become the primary guarantees of the organism's "fitting in" with (adaptedness to) its environment. In other words, the primary guarantees of the ego's autonomy from the id seem to be the very apparatuses which guarantee the organism's adaptedness to the environment.

The *apparatuses of secondary autonomy* arise either from instinctual modes and vicissitudes, as these become "estranged" from their instinctual sources, or from defensive structures formed in the process of conflict solution, as these undergo a "change of function" and become apparatuses serving adaptation. In other words, the apparatuses of secondary autonomy are not "innate" but arise from "experience." Thus this second guarantee of ego autonomy also involves reality relations. While it is obvious that without relationships to a real external environment we would be solipsistic beings, a long detour was necessary before we could see clearly that the autonomy of the ego from the id—our safeguard against solipsism—is guaranteed by these innate and acquired apparatuses which keep us attuned to our environment.

Now to the guarantees of the ego's autonomy from the environment.

[P]sychoanalytic observations and theory indicate that the instinctual drives are the causal agents and *ultimate guarantees* of the survival of the (pathological and normal) behavior forms which are countermanded by the environment. The evidence amassed by clinical psychoanalysis for this causal role of drives in the persistence of all symptoms and many character traits is overwhelming.

There seems to be equally good evidence that cognitive organizations, ego interests, values, ideals, ego identity and superego influences—all of which are relatively autonomous from the drives—also play a causal role in the persistence of many behavior forms. However, since the autonomy of these is secondary, they may be regarded as only *proximal guarantees* of the ego's autonomy from the environment.

* 　 * 　 *

. . . That the drives (e.g., sex, hunger), which at peak tension may cause enslavement to the environment should be the *ultimate guarantees* of the autonomy from the environment, is a paradox, which however—as I will attempt to show later on—can be resolved.

Man's constitutionally given drive equipment appears to be the *ultimate* (primary) *guarantee* of the ego's autonomy from the environment, that is, its safeguard against stimulus-response slavery. But this autonomy too has *proximal* (secondary) *guarantees:* Namely, higher-order superego and ego structures as well as the motivations pertaining to them. Like the ego's autonomy from the id, its autonomy from the environment also is only relative.

Thus, while the *ultimate guarantees of the ego's autonomy from the id* are man's constitutionally given apparatuses of reality relatedness, the *ultimate guarantees of the ego's autonomy from the environment* are man's constitutionally given drives.

To approach the relationship between the two autonomies, let us examine the conditions which interfere with either or both.

Three examples will illustrate the conditions in which the ego's autonomy from the id is impaired. *First*, there are periods of development in which the drives are intensified and threaten this autonomy of the ego. In puberty, the intensified drives interfere with ego autonomy so extensively that the ego combats them with—among other defenses—intellectualization, which is perhaps the most powerful means of enlisting environmental reality and the apparatuses of memory and thought against the encroachments of the id. The adolescent's subjectivity, his rebellion against his environment and his seclusiveness, as well as the converse of these—for instance his striving for intellectual understanding and objectivity and the quest for all-embracing companionship—indicate the pubertal intensification of id forces and the consequent decrease of the ego's autonomy. The climacteric (both male and female) often involves a similar loss of ego autonomy.

Some recent experiments will serve as the *second* example. Hebb and his students put subjects into a sound-proof, blacked-out room, in which restraints minimized tactile and kinesthetic sensations. They made two important observations: (a) the subjects experienced autistic fantasies, and a decrease of their ability to pursue ordered sequences of thought; (b) repetitive verbal information given to the subjects —against the background of the stimulus-void— attained such an impact on their minds that some of them came to experience it as "truth," that is, this experience approached delusional intensity and persevered for several weeks. . . . Thus stimulus deprivation too is a condition which may interfere with this autonomy.

Our *third* example is the hypnotic state. A common technique of inducing hypnosis is to make the subject concentrate on something and thus in effect to reduce the intake of other external stimulation. The hypnotist further interferes with attention to external stimulation by pouring forth a steady patter. These measures pre-empt the attention cathexes available, and interfere not only with stimulus intake but also with organized, logical, reality-oriented thinking. Thus both the outside and inside sources of signals—which subserve reality orientation and support the ego's autonomy—are blocked. The result—in hypnotizable people—is a regressive state in which the countercathectic barriers differentiating ego and id processes become fluid; images, ideas, and fantasies representing id contents rise to consciousness, and the sense of voluntariness disappears. In the lack of other stimulation which could serve as a comparison, pivot, or means of reality testing, the utterances of the hypnotist attain a great impact just like the repetitive information droned at the subject in Hebb's room. The reduction of reality relationships to a single interpersonal relationship, in hypnosis, impairs the ego's autonomy from the id.

Disregarding for the moment the subject's increased susceptibility to the information given in Hebb's room and by the hypnotist, we will consider only the interferences with the ego's autonomy from the id in these . . . examples.

The generally held assumption that ego structures (controls, defenses, as well as the means used in reality testing and action) are stable, and altered only by major disorders, is amply justified by the continuity of character and behavior, as well as by the great "resistance" these structures offer to therapeutic intervention. The very concept "structure" implies a slow rate of change in comparison to processes of drive-tension accumulation and discharge. Yet Hebb's . . . experiments suggest that these structures depend upon stimulation for their stability, or to use Piaget's terms, they require stimulation as nutriment for their maintenance. When such stimulus nutriment is not available, the effectiveness of these structures in controlling id impulses may be impaired, and some of the ego's autonomy from the id may be surrendered. The example of hypnotic induction seems to corroborate this inference, and the interference of intensified drives with ego autonomy may be considered as due to drive representations commanding attention and thus pre-empting the attention cathexes necessary for effective intake of stimulus nutriment. The interference of passionate love and deep mourning with the ego's autonomy and reality testing are familiar phenomena, and the work of mourning appears to be the actual process of overcoming the state of absorption which militates against the intake of stimulus nutriment. Without assuming that ego structures (other than those of primary autonomy) need stimulus nutriment for their autonomous effectiveness and even for their maintenance, the very process of therapy would be inconceivable.

We have long known this dependence on nutriment of certain structures, e.g., those underlying the conscious superego. When a man pulls up stakes and moves far away where his past is not known, he is subject to temptations: In the course of his sea voyage, the mutt he left behind may grow into a Saint Bernard, or the painting by a local amateur which he owned may turn into a Rembrandt. The superego is a persistent structure, but its conscious parts seem to require stimulus nutriment. In the lack of nutriment it becomes prone to compromise and corruption, and the greater their extent, the more mercilessly does the unconscious superego exact its pound of flesh: The unconscious sense of guilt. The maintenance of conscience seems to require the continuous input of the nourishment readily provided by a stable, traditional environment in which the individual is born, grows up, and ends his life; that is, the stimulus of the presence, opinions, and memories of the "others" who have always known him and always will. We seem to choose the social bonds of marriage, friendship, *etc.*, to secure that familiar (paternal, maternal) pattern of stimulation which we need as nutriment for our various superego and ego structures (for example, those which underlie our values and ideologies).

Now, some examples of interference with the ego's autonomy from the environment:

* * *

[T]ake the procedures lumped together under the term "brainwashing." Instead of reviewing the literature, I will discuss Orwell's *Nineteen Eighty-Four*, in which the writers' intuition epitomizes the means used by most "brainwashing" procedures to bring the individual to the point where the ego's autonomy from the environment is surrendered. The aim of these procedures is not just to force a false *confession* of guilt, but rather to bring about a *profession* of, or a *conversion* to, a particular view and a *belief* in the "facts" pertaining to it.

In the world of *Nineteen Eighty-Four*, the individual is robbed of his privacy, the environment invades it: Whenever the individual is alone he is watched through "telescreens"; whenever he is not driven by his work, he is driven by the "telescreen," which constantly bombards him with information and with instructions which he *must* obey. The language is so simplified that it can convey only factual information and orders; it carries no implications, connotations, allusions, or individual expression. Memory is undermined: When the political alliances of the state change, the books and newspaper files are destroyed and replaced by a revised version which fits the new circumstances. Finally, the fear of unknown but horrible punishment is kept constant. The lack of unobserved privacy coupled with the steady shower of information and orders, the lack of personal expression, the changing records which attack even the continuity vouchsafed by memory, and the mortal fear of punishment, are the means by which the world of *Nineteen Eighty-Four* robs the individual ego of its autonomy and turns the person into an automaton at the command of the environment. *Nineteen Eighty-Four* is an overdrawn caricature of our own world and a good montage of "brainwashing" procedures. The individual rebellion which Orwell describes has its roots in a yearning for tenderness, love, and sex, which—as I suggested above—are *ultimate* guarantees of the ego's autonomy from the environment. *Nineteen Eighty-Four* is fiction, but its implications are corroborated by the evidence available concerning "brainwashing," which indicates that the measures summarized above are potent means for impairing the ego's autonomy from the environment.

[Another] example, Bettelheim's paper "Individual and Mass Behavior in Extreme Situations," will stand here for all the literature on concentration camps and on Nazi methods of mass psychology. Its study shows that in concentration camps two overlapping sets of conditions interfere with autonomy from the environment, both of which—though not discussed above—obtain to varying degrees in "brainwashing" situations also.

The first set of conditions includes extreme needfulness (hunger, cold, *etc.*) and danger, as well as an attack on the inmates' "identity." In extreme needfulness and danger, the drives—which are otherwise the *ultimate guarantees* of this autonomy—endow drive-satisfying objects with a power the effect of which amounts to slavery and surrender of autonomy. The attack on identity (operating through identification with the aggressor, dependence on arbitrary authority akin to the dependence of childhood, and absence of all encomia of status and other supports of identity) impairs the *proximal guarantees* of autonomy.

The second set of conditions includes curtailment of information and stimulation (though less stringent than in Hebb's room), and against the background of this stimulus void, a steady stream of humiliating, degrading and guilt-arousing information (akin in its role to the repetitive information of the Hebb room and to the hypnotist's patter). The deprivation contributes to the surrender of autonomy both by enhancing needfulness and by providing the background for the steady and overwhelming impact of the environment.

Thus the outstanding conditions which impair the ego's autonomy from the environment are: (1) massive intrapsychic blocking of the instinctual drives which are the *ultimate guarantees* of this autonomy; (2) maximized needfulness, danger, and fear which enlist the drives (usually the guarantees of this autonomy) to prompt surrender of autonomy; (3) lack of privacy, deprivation of stimulus nutriment, memorial, and verbal supports, all of which seem to be necessary for the maintenance of the structures (thought structures, values, ideologies, identity)

which are the *proximal guarantees* of this autonomy; (4) a steady stream of instructions and information which, in the lack of other stimulus nutriment, attain such power that they have the ego completely at their mercy.

Just as with the guarantees of autonomy from the id, neither the *ultimate* nor the *proximal* guarantees of autonomy from the environment are absolute. Both autonomies require external and/or drive stimulation of a specific intensity and quality for maintenance and effectiveness.[3]

We are now ready to examine the relations between the ego's two autonomies. In hypnotic states (as well as in Hebb's room) both autonomy from the id and from the environment are impaired. How are such impairments related to each other?

A consideration of certain aspects of compulsive and obsessional disorders may serve to clarify the relationships. What follows is only an *ex parte* consideration of these conditions, a supplement to, not a substitute for, the knowledge we have of them. One of the concomitants of obsessive-compulsive conditions is an increased elaboration of the secondary process. This elaboration has two aspects: On the one hand, it provides means for the defenses of intellectualization and isolation; on the other hand it enables intensified observation and logical analysis to substitute for affective and ideational signals, those natural regulators of judgment and decision which are suppressed by obsessive-compulsive defenses.

Obsessive-compulsive defense thus maximizes the ego's autonomy from the id, but it does so at the cost of an ever-increasing impairment of the ego's autonomy from the environment: The suppression of affective and ideational cues of drive origin renders the ego's judgments and decisions increasingly dependent on external cues. Hence the infirmness of convictions and gullibility of certain obsessive people, but also—as a reaction formation—the blind and rigid clinging to a view once it has been adopted. An extreme form of the obsessive's lack of internal steering is his paralyzing doubt, which may border on the stimulus slavery of the catatonic conditions discussed above. But while the ego's autonomy from the environment is reduced, another development also takes place. The drives and their representations,

---

3. Independently, both Heinz Hartmann and Bruno Bettelheim (personal communications) pointed out to me that this treatment of the autonomies deals exclusively with the problem of "autonomy from" (i.e., freedom from) drives and environment, while the crucial specific clinical and general psychological problem is that of the "freedom to . . ." implied in these autonomies. I agree with them: The crucial task is the study of the autonomous ego motivations, the ego's methods of setting its goals and the ego's capability to give free reign to and to execute derivative id motivations. My aim in this paper is, however, merely to clarify the elements of the theory of autonomies.

whose access to motility and consciousness was so strenuously barred, invade "objective" reality by infiltrating the very thought processes and logic which were elaborated to curb them, and succeed in filling the person's perception and thought with magic and animism.

Thus maximizing the ego's autonomy from the id reduces the ego's autonomy from the environment and results in stimulus slavery. Conversely, the reduction of the ego's autonomy from the id (as by the intensification of drives) results in a loss of touch with reality, which amounts to a maximized autonomy from the environment. In turn, maximizing the ego's autonomy from the environment (as in stimulus deprivation) results in a reduction of the ego's autonomy from the id; and the reduction of the ego's autonomy from the environment may result in a maximized autonomy from the id. But can such maximized or minimized autonomy of the ego, either in relation to the id or in relation to the environment, still be considered autonomy in the proper sense of the word?

Let us examine, for instance, stimulus deprivation as maximized autonomy. It is not that the ego's autonomy from the environment reaches its maximum, but rather that the ego has to make do with an environment which provides insufficient stimulus nutriment for its structures. Stimulus deprivation provides a test of the limits of the ego's autonomy from the environment. Examination of the other instances of "maximized" or "minimized" autonomy leads to similar conclusions.

Yet these extreme instances provide good models for the relationships of the autonomies. They show that the ego's autonomy from the id may be impaired either when its necessary dependence on the environment is excessively increased, or when environmental support is excessively decreased. Likewise, the ego's autonomy from the environment may be impaired when either its necessary independence from or its necessary dependence on the id becomes excessive. Since these autonomies are always relative, their extremes are never reached. Hence, a further implication of the relativity of the autonomies is: Only a relative autonomy of the ego from the id— that is, only autonomy within the optimal range—is compatible with a relative—that is, optimal—autonomy of the ego from the environment, and vice versa. This conclusion is consistent with the one reached in our discussion of the autonomy guarantees. Since reality relations guarantee autonomy from the id, excessive autonomy from the environment must impair the autonomy from the id; and since drives are the ultimate guarantees of the autonomy from the environment, an excessive autonomy from the id must impair the autonomy from the environment.

Whether the treatment of these issues in terms of autonomies and their relations is more useful than a treatment in terms of the dependence on (or distance from) id and environment, remains to be seen.

*　　*　　*

The concept of nutriment is derived from Piaget. According to him, "structures of intelligence" arise by differentiation from constitutionally given sensorimotor coordinations, but require stimulus nutriment to do so. So far no evidence exists to clarify the relationship between Piaget's structures and those structures which psychoanalytic theory has conceptualized. But since our considerations suggest that psychoanalytic "structures" require stimulus nutriment for their *maintenance* and *effectiveness*, the question arises: Does the *development* as well as the maintenance and effectiveness of psychoanalytic "structures" require stimulus nutriment?

[T]he concentration camp and brainwashing procedures [do not] bank primarily on the withdrawal of this elementary stimulus nutriment, though they have used that too as an anxiliary technique. The concentration camp removes first of all the nutriment of the structures underlying dignity, self-respect, and identity. The aim of brainwashing is to remove the nutriment for the structures which underlie beliefs, political convictions, ideology, social and personal allegiances, and ultimately identity. These differences point to what psychoanalysis has already discovered about defenses, controls, etc., namely that psychological structures form a complex hierarchy within the psychic apparatus. Moreover, these differences suggest that the structures on each hierarchic level may require a different nutriment, ranging from simple, minimally organized sensory stimulations, to those complex experiences which a society provides to maintain, in its individuals, ideological beliefs and identities compatible with that society.

*　　*　　*

[W]e must at least touch on the crucial observation that structures can persist and remain effective even when deprived of external stimulus nutriment. What are the facts and how are they to be explained?

. . . Persistence in spite of deprivation is a hallmark of autonomy. Since autonomy is relative, long-range persistence despite deprivation needs further explanation. It is known that people have spent years in solitary confinement without suffering striking impairments of either of the ego autonomies, and that people have maintained their ego autonomy in spite of "brainwashing," though of these only a few have survived to tell the tale. There is the familiar figure of the Englishman who, totally isolated from the setting which would provide the natural nutriment for his proprieties, traditions, outlook, and values, maintains these essentially unchanged in the solitude of the jungle or the desert. Last but not least, clinical and therapeutic observation shows that defenses (in the form of both character traits and symptoms) may survive without tangible environmental nourishment, or where the person has to "provoke" nourishment from the environment.

This survival of defense structures without external stimulus nutriment is understood by psychoanalysis: These structures are maintained, ultimately, by internal (drive) stimulus nutriment. Clinical evidence shows that values, ideologies, and even more complex structures (like identity) too may be maintained by drive nutriment, to the degree to which they are part of a defensive system. The explanation of the maintenance of such higher order ego structures in instances of solitary confinement seems at first glance equally obvious: The method of survival seems to be a deliberate application of physical and mental exercise to prevent weakening of ego autonomy and drifting into fearful or wishful daydreaming, or into mindless, empty surrender. This deliberate application has taken various forms: Physical exercise, a chronological review of past life, mental arithmetic, solving all sorts of other problems, dictionary making in several languages, or reviewing other kinds of knowledge.

But what, in these cases, is the intrapsychic source of this deliberate application, which is the *proximal provider* of stimulus nutriment? We cannot seek this source in the ultimate drive nutriment because, as we have seen, in extreme deprivation situations, drive nutriment tends to abet surrender of the autonomy from the environment. Not would it do to seek the source simply in *ego identity:* Though the major attack of such confinements is on ego identity, and stronger ego identities will persist better, to locate the source of stimulus nutriment *solely* and without further analysis in ego identity would amount to a vicious circle.

The reports of the unscathed survivors of solitary confinement reveal little about the internal source of nutriment. More suggestive are the reports of people whose autonomy from either the id or the environment was on the brink of destruction, but was restored at the last moment by what might be described as a conversion experience. While we are far from a full understanding of conversion experiences, what we do know about them, and what we can infer from these reports, points primarily to the superego, but also to ego interests and ego identity as the sources of voluntary application.

Tentatively, then, it may be assumed that in certain people strikingly, but probably in all people to some degree, external stimulus nutriment may be replaced by internal nutriment. This nutriment may take the form of various deliberate activities, whose motivations (i.e., the *ultimate* source of the nourishment) may be drives, superego, ego identity or ego interests, depending on the structure involved. Hartmann

made it plausible that we have to assume the existence of intrasystemic conflicts within the ego; likewise it may become necessary to assume intrasystemic cooperation of forces by which one substructure of the ego would give rise to ego forces which, by initiating (motor or thought) activity, would provide stimulus nutriment to other substructures, enabling them to function and to give rise to their own brand of ego interests, which in turn would initiate activity providing stimulus nutriment for yet other ego substructures. Indeed it seems probable that closed circles of such mutually sustaining structures can persist— within those limits which show up ultimately as the *relativity* of autonomy. Since various structures require different external stimulus nutriment, it is likely that each requires a different kind of internal nutriment also.

*   *   *

Summing up, the organism is endowed by evolution with apparatuses which prepare it for contact with its environment, but its behavior is not a slave of this environment since it is also endowed with drives which rise from its organization, and are the ultimate guarantees against stimulus slavery. In turn, the organism's behavior is not simply the expression of these internal forces, since the very apparatuses through which the organism is in contact with its environment are the ultimate guarantees against drive slavery. These autonomies have proximal guarantees also, in intrapsychic structures. The balance of these mutually controlling factors does not depend on the outcome of their chance interactions, but is controlled by the laws of the epigenetic sequence, termed autonomous ego development.

Both kinds of protective intrapsychic structures are essential components of the ego's structure and organization and the behavior attributes, conceptualized as ego autonomies, are characteristics of this ego structure and organization. These structures need nutriment for their development, maintenance, and effectiveness, and their ultimate nutriments are drive stimuli on the one hand and external stimuli on the other. But such nutriment is also provided by other ego structures and by the motivations arising from them, and the more autonomous the ego, the more the nutriment is provided from these internal sources. But this "proportionality" obtains only within an optimal range, since ego autonomy from the id and ego autonomy from the environment mutually guarantee each other only within an optimal range. Maximization or minimization of either disrupts their balance. Thus these autonomies are always relative. In terms of the story with which I introduced our problem, the strength which makes a man independent from reality stimulation tends to lead him to build an impenetrable wall around himself.

The ego's autonomy may be defined in terms of ego activity, and impairment of autonomy in terms of ego passivity. The old adage, that freedom is the acceptance of the restraints of the law, returns to us here with renewed significance. The elementary phenomenology from which we started seems to have led us into the very center of metapsychological considerations.

3.

HARTMANN, HEINZ

Ego Psychology and the Problem of Adaptation (1939) *

. . . The normal human being is free neither of problems nor of conflicts. Conflicts are part of the human condition. Naturally, conflicts have a different range and intensity in pathological than in normal cases. The antitheses, pathological versus normal, defense-born versus not-defense-born (or: development resulting from conflict versus conflict-free development) do not coincide: The former contrasts disturbance with achievement, the latter contrasts conflict with the absence of conflict. A "successful" defense may amount to a "failure" in achievement and vice versa. . . .

* * *

. . . We know how conflicts and taboos involving instinctual drives may hamper intellectual development, temporarily or permanently. On the other hand, Anna Freud has shown that intellectualization may serve as a defense against instinctual danger in puberty, representing an attempt to master the instinctual drive by indirect means. But this process has another, reality-oriented aspect also, showing that this mechanism of defense against instinctual drives may at the same time be regarded as an adaptation process. It is in this sense that Anna Freud says: "Instinctual danger makes human beings intelligent." We are entitled to ask: What determines the choice of just this means of instinctual drive mastery? and what determines the extent of intellectualization a person will use? We are familiar with part of these certainly complex interrelationships: For example, with the developmental significance of early infantile attempts at solutions. We may, however, safely assume an autonomous intelligence factor which, as an independent variable, codetermines the choice and success of the defensive process. Though we are not completely ignorant about these matters, we do not have a systematic knowledge of them. Learning to think and learning in general are independent biological functions which exist alongside, and in part independent of, instinctual drives and defenses.

* New York. International Universities Press, Inc., 1958. (pp. 12–32). Reprinted by permission.

Ordered thinking is always directly or indirectly reality oriented. When a defense against instinctual drives results in heightened intellectual achievements, this shows that certain forms of conflict solution may involve biological guarantees of an adaptation process to external reality. This does not hold for all defense processes, of course, but it does hold for intellectualization even outside of pubertal development. "This intellectualization of instinctual life, the attempt to lay hold on the instinctual processes by connecting them with ideas which can be dealt with in consciousness, is one of the most general, earliest, and most necessary acquirements of the human ego. We regard it not as an activity of the ego, but as one of its indispensable components."

Thus the description of this phenomenon as a defense does not fully define it. The definition must also include its reality-oriented and adaptation-facilitating characteristics and regulations. More generally, we are interested in what manner and to what extent is defense indirectly regulated by those ego functions which are not currently involved in the conflict. After all, mental development is not simply the outcome of the struggle with instinctual drives, with love objects, with the superego, and so on. For instance, we have reason to assume that this development is served by apparatuses which function from the beginning of life; . . . memory, associations, and so on, are functions which cannot possibly be derived from the ego's relationships to instinctual drives or love objects, but are rather *prerequisites* of our conception of these and of their development.

In judging the success of a defense we will inquire not only into the fate of the instinctual drive and the protection afforded to the ego, but also—more than before—into its effects on the ego functions not directly involved in the conflict. The concepts of ego strength, ego weakness, ego restriction, etc., are all related to this realm, but they remain nebulous as long as the specific ego functions involved are not studied in detail. Ego strength—though it manifests itself strikingly in the struggles of the conflict sphere—cannot be defined solely in terms of that borderland of the ego which is involved in the conflict. . . .

* * *

It is possible, and even probable, that the relationship to reality is learned by way of *detours*. There are avenues of reality adaptation which, at first, certainly lead away from the real situation. The function of play is a good example, that is, its actual role in human development rather than any teleological theories about it. Another example is the auxiliary function of fantasy in the learning process: Though fantasy always implies an initial turning away from a real situation, it can also be a preparation for reality and may lead to a better mastery of it. Fantasy may fulfill a synthetic function by provisionally connecting our needs and goals with possible ways of realizing them. It is well known that there are fantasies which, while they remove man from external reality, open up for him his internal reality. The basic facts of mental life were the contents of such "fantasies" long before psychoanalysis made them amenable to scientific investigation. The primary function of these fantasies is autoplastic[4] rather than alloplastic;[5] but we should be the last to deny the general importance of increased insight into intrapsychic life, and its particular importance in the mastery of the external world.

I must point out that *knowledge of reality* is not synonymous with *adaptation to reality*. But more about this later on. This, too, is an example of the already mentioned necessity to separate the different aspects of adaptation. The situation appears paradoxical: Taking our point of departure from pathology, from the psychology of neuroses and psychoses, we come to overestimate the positive developmental significance of the shortest pathways to reality, and it is only when we set out from the problem of reality adaptation that we recognize the positive value of the detour through fantasy. Yet, actually, it is the same phenomenon which, considered first from one and then from the other point of view, attains positive or negative emphasis. From the first point of view "positive" means "neurosis prevention"; from the second, it means "general furtherance of adaptation." Only a premature and one-sided evaluation could disregard this essential unity. For a long time psychoanalysis had no occasion to deal with that other aspect of these processes which belongs to the realm of normal psychology, but is, naturally, not understood by nonpsychoanalytic normal psychology.

Denial is based on flight, and *avoidance* even more clearly so. Anna Freud has shown us how they both result in ego restriction. But avoidance of the environment in which difficulties are encountered—and its positive correlate, the search for one which offers easier and better possibilities for action—is also a most effective adaptation process (which, by the way, transcends the common antithesis of autoplastic and alloplastic adaptations). The search for a favorable environment among those available (and likewise for the most favorable of the possible functions) should probably be given a far more central position among adaptation processes—in the broader sense—than is customary. . . .

*   *   *

[T]he application of psychoanalysis to the social sciences . . . I think demonstrates particularly clearly that the concept of adaptation is indispensable to our theory and that the conflict-free ego sphere must be included in our studies. . . . Psychoanalysis and sociology have different centers of interest; many problems relevant in sociology are peripheral in psychoanalysis. Sociology centers on social action, on success or failure in the tasks set by society (i.e., tasks of adaptation); and is interested in the psychology of conflicts, the fate of aggressive and libidinal impulses, etc., only in so far as these are manifested in social behavior. What matters in sociology is man as an achiever (in the broadest sense of this word); it studies primarily what the mental apparatus achieves, and only indirectly how it masters its difficulties. For psychology, both conflict and achievement are indispensable points of view. The application of psychoanalysis to sociology co-ordinates these two points of view. We hope that the study of the conflict-free ego sphere and of its functions—and the further exploration of the problem of adaptation—will open up the no-man's land between sociology and psychoanalysis and thus extend the contribution of psychoanalysis to the social sciences. . . .

*   *   *

The consideration of the conflict-free ego sphere leads us to the functions which are more or less closely related to the tasks of reality mastery, that is, *adaptation*. Now adaptation—though we do not discuss its implications frequently or thoroughly—is a central concept of psychoanalysis, because many of our problems, when pursued far enough, converge on it. The concept of adaptation, though it appears simple, implies (or if crudely used, conceals) a great many problems. . . .

Generally speaking, we call a man well adapted if his productivity, his ability to enjoy life, and his mental equilibrium are undisturbed. In turn, we occasionally encounter statements ascribing any failure to a lack of adaptation. Such statements are meaningless because they overlook the relationship implied in the concept of adaptation, and thus beg the question: What makes a person succeed or fail in a given situation? The degree of adaptiveness can only be determined with reference to environmental situations (average expectable—i.e., typical—situations, or on the average not expectable—i.e., atypical—situations). . . .

The concept of adaptation has the most varied connotations in biology, and it has no precise definition in psychoanalysis either. For decades it was a cherished—perhaps all too cherished—concept of the biological sciences, but recently it has been frequently criticized and rejected. The observation underlying the concept "adaptation" is that living organisms patently "fit" into their environment. Thus, adaptation is primarily a reciprocal relationship between the organism and its environment. "Where the real functions, determined jointly by the organism's whole mechanism and by its environment, are favorable for its survival, there a relationship of

---

4. Effecting intrapsychic changes.
5. Effecting environmental changes.

adaptation obtains between that organism and its environment." We may distinguish between a *state of adaptedness* which obtains between the organism and its environment, and the *process of adaptation* which brings that state about. We may say that the entire development of these processes brings about a relationship, between the genotype and the environment, which is favorable for survival. A state of adaptedness may refer to the present and to the future. The process of adaptation always implies reference to a future condition. . . . Psychoanalysis enables us to discern those processes which by directly and actively changing either the environment or the person bring about a state of adaptedness between the individual and his environment; and to investigate the relationships between the preformed means of human adaptedness and these adaptation processes. We will clarify matters if we assume that adaptation (speaking now mainly about man) is guaranteed, in both its grosser and finer aspects, on the one hand by man's primary equipment and the maturation of his apparatuses, and on the other hand by those ego-regulated actions which (using this equipment) counteract the disturbances in, and actively improve the person's relationship to, the environment. Man's existing relation to the environment codetermines which of the reactions he is capable of will be used in this process, and also which of the reactions used will predominate. The potentialities and the factual limitations of adaptation processes are already implied here.

*   *   *

[W]e must also keep in mind the phenomenon of "change of function," the role of which in mental life and particularly in the development of the ego seems to be very great, and behind which, genetically, there is always a particularly interesting bit of history. The conception of change of function is familiar in psychoanalysis: A behavior form which originated in a certain realm of life may, in the course of development, appear in an entirely different realm and role. An attitude which arose originally in the service of defense against an instinctual drive may, in the course of time, become an independent structure, in which case the instinctual drive merely triggers this automatized apparatus . . . but, as long as the automatization is not controverted, does not determine the details of its action. Such an apparatus may, as a relatively independent structure, come to serve other functions (adaptation, synthesis, etc.); it may also— and this is genetically of even broader significance— through a change of function turn from a means into a goal in its own right. . . .

Adaptation may come about by changes which the individual effects in his environment (use of tools, technology in the widest sense of the word, etc.), as well as by appropriate changes in his psychophysical system. Here Freud's concepts of alloplastic and autoplastic change are apposite. Animals, too, change their environment actively and purposefully, for example, by building nests and dens. A broad range of alloplastic adaptations is, however, available only to man. Two processes may be involved here: Human action adapts the environment to human functions, and then the human being adapts (secondarily) to the environment which he has helped to create. Learning to act alloplastically is certainly one of the outstanding tasks of human development; yet alloplastic action is actually not always adaptive, nor is autoplastic action always unadaptive. It is often a higher ego function which decides whether an alloplastic or an autoplastic action—and in either case, what specific alteration—is appropriate in a given situation. Actually, however, instinctual drives and related factors always play a role too. Furthermore, the choice of the preferred means of adaptation may also be described crudely in typological terms. A third form of adaptation, neither quite independent from nor quite identical with the alloplastic and autoplastic forms, is the choice of a new environment which is advantageous for the functioning of the organism. . . .

Individual adaptation—our sole concern so far— may clash with the adaptation of the species. At breeding time other "spheres of function" recede and the individual becomes helpless against attack. Some species survive by virtue of their fecundity, while their individuals are poorly equipped for self-preservation. Many species display mutual assistance; in these the adaptation of the species and individual self-preservation clearly dovetail. Thus the adaptation of the individual and of the species are often but not always incompatible. Similar conditions exist in human society also, and psychoanalysis must take them into account when it deals with social matters. In setting therapeutic goals the individual's interests will generally outrank society's, but this will no longer hold when we have broadened our point of view to include the needs of society. Conversely, an individual's natural characteristics which do not coincide with his own interests, etc., may be important for society. This is certainly true for the existing societies; whether it must remain true for all ideal forms of society can well be left an unanswered question.

*   *   *

The processes of adaptation are influenced both by constitution and external environment, and more directly determined by the ontogenetic phase of the organism. This developmental-historical factor in the process of adaptation has been particularly stressed by psychoanalysis. The term "historical reaction basis" seems applicable to it. Man does not come to terms with his environment anew in every generation; his relation to the environment is guaranteed by—besides the factors of heredity—an evolution peculiar to man, namely, the influence of tradition and the survival of the works of man. We take over from others (prototypes, tradition) a great many of our methods for solving problems. . . . The works of man objectify the methods he has discovered for solving problems and thereby become factors of continuity, so that man lives, so to speak, in past generations as well as in his own. Thus arises a network of identifications and ideal formations which is of great significance for the forms and ways of adaptation. Freud has shown the important role of the superego in this process. . . . But the ego, too, has its share in building tradition. Whether these traditional methods of solution are rigid or modifiable depends on a great many individual and social factors. . . .

What is the structure of the external world to which the human organism adapts? At this point we cannot separate biological from social conceptions. . . . The first social relations of the child are crucial for the maintenance of his biological equilibrium also. It is for this reason that man's first object relations became our main concern in psychoanalysis. Thus the task of man to adapt to man is present from the very beginning of life. Furthermore, man adapts to an environment part of which has not, but part of which has already been molded by his kind and himself. Man not only adapts to the community but also actively participates in creating the conditions to which he must adapt. Man's environment is molded increasingly by man himself. Thus the crucial adaptation man has to make is to the social structure, and his collaboration in building it. This adaptation may be viewed in various of its aspects and from various points of view; here we are focusing on the fact that the structure of society, the process of division of labor, and the social locus of the individual codetermine the possibilities of adaptation and also regulate in part the elaboration of instinctual drives and the development of the ego. The structure of society decides (particularly—but not exclusively—through its effect on education) which forms of behavior shall have the greatest adaptive chance. Each situation will require different (some more, and some less specialized) forms of behavior, achievements, forms of life, and equilibria. We may describe the fact that the social structure determines, at least in part, the adaptive chances of a particular form of behavior, by the term *social compliance*, coined in analogy to "somatic compliance." Social compliance is a special form of the environmental "compliance" which is implied by the concept of adaptation. This social compliance plays a role not only on the development of neurosis, psychopathy, and criminality (though it by no means suffices to explain them) but also in normal development and particularly in the earliest social organization of the child's environment. It is a special instance of social compliance when society, so to speak, corrects an adaptation disturbance: Individual propensities which amount to disturbances of adaptation in one social group or locus may fulfil a socially essential function in another. It is often overlooked that the degree of need gratification and particularly the possibilities for development afforded by a given social order may not have parallel influences on the child and on the adult. It may not be superfluous to mention again that by adaptation we do not mean only passive submission to the goals of society, but also active collaboration on them and attempts to change them.

4.

HARTMANN, HEINZ and KRIS, ERNST

The Genetic Approach in Psychoanalysis*

The word "psychoanalysis" is commonly used to designate three things: A therapeutic technique, which we here call "psychoanalytic therapy," an observational method to which we here refer as "the psychoanalytic interview," and a body of hypotheses for which we here reserve the term "psychoanalysis." Two groups of hypotheses will be discussed: Some dealing with dynamic and some dealing with genetic propositions. The former are concerned with the interaction and the conflicts of forces within the individual and with their reaction to the external world, at any given time or during brief time spans. The genetic propositions describe how any condition under observation has grown out of an individual's past, and extended throughout his total life span. Representative examples of dynamic propositions are those concerned with defense against danger and reaction to frustration. Genetic propositions state how these reactions come into being and are used in the course of an individual's life.

Psychiatrists, social workers, and even social scientists base their findings frequently on a study of the past of the individual; however, in doing so, they need not have and frequently do not have genetic propositions in mind. The case record, that invaluable tool of modern medical and social exploration, or the psychiatric interview, may reveal that a conflict, a symptom, or a pattern of behavior have occurred before. In using dynamic propositions the psychiatrist may reduce what appeared as a series of incomparable instances into a sequence of similar situations; when such regularity becomes perceivable, decisive progress will have been made. Thus we find the man who tends to drop his effort whenever in love or work an

---

* 1 *The Psychoanalytic Study of the Child*, 11–29 (1945). Reprinted by permission of International Universities Press, New York.

immediate competitor appears. This insight, however, is not gained with any genetic proposition in mind. The finding establishes that an individual reacts similarly under similar conditions; in competition of a certain intensity he prefers retreat to continued pursuit of the goal in order to avoid what he experiences as fear and/or guilt.

If the investigator is guided by genetic propositions he will take such findings as a basis upon which to establish a causal relationship between the individual's retreat pattern in conflict situations and earlier experiences, in which the pattern was gradually formed. Experience in this context need not mean a single event but, more often, a constellation in an individual's early life that may have lasted for a stretch of time; no one isolated constellation need be meant, but rather the sequence of many that overlap in time and space. The expression "forming a pattern" does not only refer to a single trait, a symptom that is, as it were, attached to or superimposed upon the structure of the personality, but also to this structure itself. Investigators who follow the lead of genetic propositions will inquire when retreat from competition was "learned" or adopted as a solution; why, when the competitors were father or sibling, that conflict was solved by retreat, and what experiences had formed parts or earlier stages of the pattern long before the coincidence of situation and response was established. This pattern was learned through failure. The genetic propositions trace the way not only to earlier situations, in which similar behavior was displayed, but to situations in which different behavior was at least attempted: The attack against the rival and its failure in response to parental disapproval or to feelings of guilt. And thus new areas open for the application of genetic propositions: When aggression was barred, why was it turned against the self and not against other objects or toward other activities?

The two types of propositions represent two aspects in the approach of psychoanalysis. The first is concerned with human behavior in a given situation; the second with the explanation of this behavior by an investigation of its origin. This investigation regularly leads back to events that partly cannot be remembered, and tends to embrace periods of life when experiences could not be formulated in verbal symbols.

The forecast of human behavior that psychoanalysis can make is best, when based on both dynamic and genetic propositions. . . .

*   *   *

The genetic approach in psychoanalysis does not deal only with anamnestic data, nor does it intend to show only "how the past is contained in the present." Genetic propositions describe why, in past situations of conflict, a specific solution was adopted;

why the one was retained and the other dropped, and what causal relation exists between these solutions and later developments. Genetic propositions refer to the fact that in an adult's behavior, anxiety may be induced by paradoxically out-dated conditions and they explain why these conditions may still exercise influence. However, in speaking of the similarity of conditions eliciting anxiety we do not speak of an identity of situations. The man who retreats from competition in order to avoid murderous impulses against the man at the next desk, and a child who may experience similar impulses toward a newly born sibling do not live through the same situations. The various parts of the personality of the adult have undergone fundamental changes. Thus for instance, the appraisal of objective danger is clearly different with adult and child. In fact, the whole area to which a cross-sectional analysis of the adult's and the child's situation would refer is fundamentally different. But one part of the adult's personality behaves as if no change had occurred: It has, as psychoanalysts put it, not participated in the development. . . .

The genetic propositions of psychoanalysis have grown out of empirical work. Not only did Freud draw attention to a large number of hitherto unknown facts concerning earliest childhood; but he soon was impressed by rules in the genetic relationship of psychological phenomena. The elements that constitute this relationship are "over-determined," interdependent, and their complexity has in many instances not yet been sufficiently structured in a logical sense. The genetic propositions, however, made it possible to establish typical sequences in development and to trace individual behavior historically to its origins. As a consequence, psychoanalysis has adopted a preference to characterize psychological phenomena according to their position in the process of development. In the psychoanalytic study of personality, character traits are not grouped according to their similarity in a descriptive sense, but rather according to their common genetic roots. Examples in kind are the "oral" and "anal" characters. Here the procedure of psychoanalysis resembles that of biology in those cases where biological classification is based upon genetics. . . .

Why have such classifications been adopted? What is the reason for the emphasis upon genetic propositions in this context? In order to simplify an extremely complex problem we start with an example: Experience has shown that details of behavior that in a cross-sectional analysis appear indistinguishable may clearly be differentiated by genetic investigation. Conversely, details of behavior that in cross-sectional analysis appear different and are actually opposite may have grown out of the same root, and may justify the same prognosis. Pacifism may in one case be a reaction formation to the wish to attack and in the other an expression of fear of being attacked by a superior enemy. Extreme aggressiveness may be in one case the reaction to fear and its concealment, in the other, the direct expression of sadistic wishes. These are distinctions that the genetic methods permit us to establish. What appears to be similar behavior with the individuals when seen in the cross-section can be differentiated when we take account of its genesis. If we are able to indicate the position of such behavior in the longitudinal section what appeared as similar behavior gains in each individual case a very different meaning. It is here that we rely upon the genetic propositions especially when dealing with what has been called the central areas of personality; only the genetic propositions permit us to make perceivable the drives that a behavior detail represents, their direction, their intensity, and their structural interconnection.

*   *   *

In summarizing what is explicitly and implicitly contained in Freud's concept as far as genetic propositions are concerned, we suggest the following formulation. In the life of each individual crucial situations occur. They may be due predominantly to external events or they may be due predominantly to predispositions in the individual which then may invest insignificant situations with high significance. In order to assess the predispositions of an individual that meet those crucial situations, the data in every case would have to refer to his total past. For a considerable time the reference to the instinctual demands dominated the discussions of these predispositions and the functions of the ego were either incompletely described or the description was limited to that of mechanisms of defense at its disposal. Though at the present it is generally realized that the realm of the ego is wider, clinical and theoretical discussions are not conducted on the same level. While there is no hesitation to refer in clinical description to the capacities with which an individual is equipped in coping with pressures of many kinds at any stage of his development, this point of view is comparatively new in theoretical discussions.

If we turn to the ego as the psychic system that controls perception and motility, achieves solutions, and directs actions, we have to insist on distinctions that seemed irrelevant when Freud first formulated his genetic propositions. A number of functions of the ego related to the apparatus at its disposal develop largely outside of the reach of psychic conflict; Hartmann actually speaks of a sphere of the ego free from conflict. These functions gain for our discussion a specific importance since they exercise a considerable influence as independent factors; they determine together with other factors what mechanism of defense an individual adopts and with what results, or what substitute goals he adopts for his instinctual desires. However, this distinction between pyschological pro-

cesses predominantly dependent on biological maturation, and others predominantly dependent on influences of the environment, to which we here refer as "development," is not limited to ego psychology. The growth of the teeth and of the muscular sphincter control are according to Freud influential in determining the progress from one phase of libidinal development to the other; but these maturational sequences determine also the sequence of experiences that owe their special character to one or the other of the libidinal phases. Similarly, the maturation of the apparatus of motility or perception exercises influence on the progress of the general development of the ego—an area of problems which however has not yet been sufficiently clarified. Seen against this background, one of the most general findings of psychoanalysis which by now seems self-evident, gains a specific importance. This finding asserts that the importance of an actual experience through which a child lives, and the direction this experience may give to his life largely depend on the specific phase of the child's development. This is the reason why a superficial collection of anamnestic data concerning an individual's childhood is frequently misleading. The question is not that at some time in childhood a tonsillectomy was performed or that a child was left in hospital care, but under what conditions and when these events took place. The coincidence of hospitalization and the fear of loss of love, that of tonsillectomy and fear of castration, thus the coincidence of predisposition and experience, are the decisive points.

Many of the child's experiences that are uncovered by psychoanalytic therapy are of such specific importance; i.e., many of them are traumatic. However, others of which the memory is recovered by the patient or which are reconstructed by the analyst do not concern experiences that in themselves necessarily had a decisive causal or formative effect, and yet such experiences are of considerable importance for genetic investigation: they are "signs," indicating important changes in the child's life and they impress us as symptoms of his general development. . . .

*   *   *

We now define more closely the crucial situations in an individual's development: There are typical phases of conflict, either between drives with opposite goals or between drives and the ego structure, which regularly occur in both normal and abnormal development. They may be brought about mainly by maturation, when new demands or new tasks are brought into the individual's reach, or they may mainly be brought about by demands and influences of the environment, such as those regularly occurring in every human being's life. The crucial phases of maturation and of development actually coincide to a large extent; at which points they coincide, and at which lines cross each other, will to a considerable degree depend on cultural factors.

If we include these cultural factors it will become evident that however rich and manifold the data are on which psychoanalysis bases its views of the child's development, these data are on the whole not sufficient to allow for the full and detailed formulation of genetic propositions. In other words, it is essential to supplement the data supplied by the psychoanalytic interview with data established by other observational methods; there seems little doubt that in enlarging the set of data we shall approximate the postulate that the genetic propositions of psychoanalysis should be verified.

* * *

. . . This goal could best be achieved by the constant interaction of two observational methods, psychoanalysis and observation of life histories, which we here call the retrospective and prospective method. The method of retrospective research has been established by the technique of psychoanalytic therapy; the methods of prospective research have been elaborated by psychiatrists, psychologists, and anthropologists. The relationship of both observational methods is manifold: The retrospective method was in the past in a position to direct attention to new areas in the child's life, which have gradually been investigated by observers with various kinds of observational skills; there is no reason to assume that this function of pointing to the essential is exhausted. The retrospective method, however, can do more: It can establish interconnections between experiences that are bound to escape observers who have less intimate insight; it is here that child analysis may well be expected to play a part. There are, on the other hand, areas of problems in child development that have found little attention in psychoanalysis—or where the access remains unsatisfactory: Examples of the former are those achievements of the ego that are independent of conflict; examples of the latter are the experiences of the preverbal stage of child development. Psychoanalysis is witness to the importance of this stage for the future; child observation, however, will have to tell the tale of these eventful years.

5.

KRAMER, PAUL

On Discovering One's Identity*

The prolonged analysis of a very ill patient provided an opportunity to reconstruct in some detail early experiences pertaining to the discovery of one's

* 10 *The Psychoanalytic Study of the Child*, 1955 (pp. 47–74). Reprinted by permission of International Universities Press, New York.

own ego, or rather of those segments of the ego that embody the sense of one's identity. The term identity is used to denote the awareness of one's self as an entity separate and distinct from one's environment, specifically, earliest environment. The intention of this presentation is the demonstration of factors that stimulated an accelerated and precocious development of the sense of identity, and to trace how the forced discovery, having proved an experience of traumatic significance, led to a faulty ego development of an unusual nature, and to certain pathological consequences for the total personality of the patient.

Whether or not this contribution to ego pathography adds in some measure to our understanding of normal ego development is not to be determined on the basis of the study of only one case, though some related questions appear to merit further inquiry. The material may be considered in the light of the old problem of the relationship between ego development controlled by inherited factors, and that stimulated by the variable aspects of necessity, but generalizations should be deferred until additional information has been collected, including particularly that to be gained from the analytic study of children.

Since the observations contained little fundamentally new or unexpected findings, no review of the pertinent literature was attempted. The study is presented because of the relative scarcity of published clinical material of this nature, though theoretical considerations are numerous. The material was obtained in the course of an analysis of several years' duration, though it is mainly concerned with problems and phenomena which dominated a stage of the treatment lasting somewhat longer than two years. I have not attempted to organize the analytic material in a logically consistent sequence, but have chosen a collection of examples from the patient's material germane to the main topic of the report. They will be presented in the approximate order of their appearance in the course of the analysis. This order did not always correspond chronologically to the actuality of the patient's childhood.

The familiar tendency of analytic material to emerge in fragments, sometimes separated by months, should be borne in mind. The paper was written largely from memory, with the help of auxiliary mnemonic devices, such as short key notes made at irregular intervals in the course of the treatment.

The patient, a middle-aged man, had been suffering for many years from a variety of diffuse anxiety symptoms. Predominant and most disturbing were his agoraphobia and claustrophobia. He could neither leave familiar surroundings, such as his home and his office, nor could he stay without severe anxiety in a room other than one familiar to him. He was forever concerned with the question whether and how he would be able to leave the room. When in his car, he could extend his travels to the limit of a few miles from his home, but then he was constantly worried about the condition of the engine, the tires, and about other mechanical possibilities of damage to the car which might leave him stranded. He was for years unable to describe his anxiety or to give an account of what he feared. All he could say was that he was plagued by a terrifying feeling expressed in the words, "I can't make it." He was able to add nothing further for a very long time.

After some years of work the patient finally began to reproduce in detail, in acting, in dreaming, and in fantasy, those early infantile experiences which were underlying his symptoms. Memories reaching back into the first three years of life began to emerge, at first in the form of his reliving strange sensations and bewildering experiences, in everyday life and in the transference. Eventually those were transformed into memories, though the patient had much difficulty in verbalizing them. This was true particularly of those early experiences, to be described, which seem to have occurred while he was still inarticulate—in fact, while he was just learning to speak. He was at the time between one and three years of age. During the part of the treatment period with which this paper is concerned, the patient was wont to enter the analyst's room with a seemingly unrelated word or a sentence on his lips. This then became a central point around which an important infantile experience could be reconstructed. I shall give a few examples. Once the patient came into my room repeating the words "Upside down, upside down!" He did not know where the expression came from, nor why he used it, but mentioned that all morning this expression had compulsively pushed itself into his awareness. He also felt dizzy, and objects moved strangely, scintillating in a snakelike fashion, in front of his eyes. He was frightened, and expected one of his severe anxiety attacks to develop. He barely managed to come to the analytic session. After describing all this with great tension, and after he had for some time remained anxiously sitting on the edge of the couch, he stretched out and relaxed. Then he suddenly recognized an image of a tree in a pool of water, upside down, and his own image, also upside down in the water. He then recalled the origin of the scene he described. There was indeed a little creek passing behind the house in which he lived when he was less than two years old, and he recalled the feeling of wonderment and some anxiety on seeing his image so reversed in the water. He recalled reaching for it and causing the water to ripple. The image became distorted, and this puzzled and frightened him. The changes in the image because of the rippling water were re-experienced by him in the form of the scintillating distor-

tion of objects this morning. He remembered further that at the same time in life he observed his own shadow, tried to grasp it with his hands, and was frightened by its change of shape and disappearance as he bent down to touch it.

On another occasion the patient came with the statement, forcefully and repeatedly expressed, "I saw myself!" Again the words impressed themselves on his mind with great force. He had a feeling of conviction, which he could not explain, that this expression was connected in an important manner with his anxieties. Some days later he added some words to the sentence, and it now was: "I saw myself and I got frightened." By way of involved association chains, and experiences of great weakness, smallness, and helplessness, vividly felt by him in every life situation and in the analytic hours during those days, he arrived finally at a distinct and emotionally highly charged series of memories, here to be recounted in the approximate order of their emergence, though, as already mentioned, it may not be the order of their occurrence in the actuality of his early childhood.

He saw himself looking up toward his mother and becoming aware of her large abdomen. She was at the time pregnant with his brother, who was born when he was twenty months old. He reached for her, called and cried, apparently wishing to be lifted and carried. Instead, the mother stepped back out of his reach and addressed him in a firm fashion. A feeling of great helplessness and an awareness of his smallness and weakness overcame the child at that moment. It was instructive to observe how all this was re-enacted in the present. A characteristic example follows: On the day on which this memory emerged I had as usual greeted him at the door of the waiting room. He was sitting there with a deep frown on his face, looking perplexed and unhappy. His arms were spread away from his body in an awkward manner. On seeing me his face lit up, he rose rapidly to his feet and came toward me. He later reported, along with the already mentioned reference to the sentence, "I saw myself and I was frightened," that he had been feeling weak and faint all day. He had a headache, his eyes were burning, his throat was dry, and he had felt an odd tension around his mouth. He was also aware of a momentary feeling of great relief when he saw me coming toward him. When on the couch, all symptoms disappeared, to his amazement. He explained later that he could no longer reproduce them because "mother" was here and he did not have to cry and feel weak, unhappy, and anxious. He then said, after a few moments, that he had a sudden feeling which he expressed as "You are not there." He felt himself on the verge of an attack of anxiety but prevented its emergence by looking at me and convincing himself that I was there. It became evident that this experience was one of many through which the child recognized to his painful disappointment that he and mother were separate entities and that he had no control over her. Thus the experience of discovering his self proved a painful, in fact, as I shall endeavor to show later in this study, a traumatic experience. It seems that in consequence of the discovery that he had no control over his mother, he made other disturbing and thwarting discoveries, which further accentuated his feeling described later as "I saw myself and I got frightened." We succeeded in reconstructing many episodes relating to such experiences. He recalled that he awakened more than once because of hunger and because of being wet. He called his mother by crying loudly. She did not come. The child became enraged because of her failure to appear and finally screamed in a fit of rage and frustration until nearly exhausted. At this stage he found himself unable to stop his screaming and sobbing. He suddenly perceived the rage itself as separate from himself, and as something he could not control. This experience caused a feeling of panic to rise in him. His feeling of weakness in controlling his environment was augmented by his helplessness in mastering happenings within himself.

On a later occasion the patient reported a sensation, rather than a sentence, intruding itself on his consciousness. He felt himself, to use his own words, "stepping out of the analyst's body," more precisely, from his legs. It was as if he were a child barely reaching above the analyst's knees, emerging to walk a few steps on his own, only to get frightened and anxious to return and merge with the analyst again, but finding himself unable to do so and then becoming terror-stricken. As this illusion was analytically investigated, the person of the analyst was replaced by that of his father, and finally, by that of his mother. During this time many sensations and fragments of fantasies appeared, indicative of the child's early concept of seeing himself and his mother as an inseparable entity.

The beginnings of discovery of the self seemed stimulated by occurrences which were, on the one hand, passively endured painful sensations, and on the other, active attempts to increase the range of his functions. Our evidence indicated that this period of ego finding occurred at the time when he was learning to walk, that is, when he was a little over a year old. During our work on this material, the patient experienced sensations which could readily be interpreted as those of a child learning to walk, exuberant at his success, and frightened by failure. The patient forced himself to take longer and longer walks away from his home, set himself goals, one, two, or three streets away and insisted on going by himself, rather than with his wife, as was his previous custom. He found himself glancing back anxiously as if to see whether she watched him. He looked for support toward the walls of the buildings, toward lampposts; he felt dizzy; his knees were faltering; he had sensations of falling forward, and found himself impelled to spread his arms ahead of him to break the fall. On reaching his goal he was bathed in perspiration, anxious, but also secretly elated. The comparison with the child learning to walk was his own and was not suggested to him by me. During the same time he described thoughts of being able to get up from the chair in the waiting room by himself, and said that he felt his hands lifting in a helpless manner toward me and his face turning up as if to appeal to the mother (analyst) to help him or raise him. I had on many occasions observed what he described quite clearly.

At times the patient spoke of a strange and disturbing feeling of deadness involving all of his body except the organ or limb that was active at the moment. For instance, he was aware of feeling only his eyes when he was looking at something, or his hands when he touched something with them, or his mouth when he tasted food. These sensations led to memories that as a young child he had known similar feelings. He recalled a time when he could feel only his face when he cried, only his penis when he urinated, only his eyes when he looked at his mother, while the rest of his body felt numb or absent. This was a very bewildering and frightening sensation. Still later he explained that during the same period of childhood he felt only those parts of his body as alive that were in direct touch with his mother. He once said: "Only that part of me lived through which mother's love flowed into me."

An important and unsuspected aspect of his castration anxiety found its explanation in connection with these experiences. He reported that at one time in childhood he felt his penis alive only when he masturbated. The mother's prohibition of the masturbation removed the feeling (of life) from the penis. It felt dead, absent. On that basis he developed vaguely formulated, but intensely felt fears that his mother could render him dead, altogether, at her will. Once again the feeling of helplessness contributed to the awareness of his separate and feeble identity as contrasted with that of his mother.

During the same period of treatment he reported that for months he had been relying on seeing a woman working in his office building at a certain desk whenever he passed through the hall on the way to or from his own place of work. When on occasions she was not at the accustomed place, he found himself looking for her frantically, and asked desperately, "Is she there, is she there?" On such occasions his mouth became dry, his throat sore, his voice hoarse, his eyes burned, and he had diffuse pains in his chest and in the muscles of his arms. Shortly before the symptom subsided, and following his discovery of its infantile predecessor, he added that at times he had a taste of sour milk in his mouth or, as he eventually described it, a taste of "burped-up milk." This whole set of reactions proved to be almost an exact repetition of his sensations and feelings in very early childhood when he found himself alone, with his mother gone, and not responding to his frantic calls. His eyes burned with tears, he was hoarse, his throat was sore, his mouth was dry from crying, and his muscles ached from the exertion.

The patient throughout life had been extremely preoccupied with a morbid concern over food. He was forever finding its taste peculiar and was convinced of it being spoiled. He discarded huge quantities of food which he thought unfit for consumption, to the great annoyance of his wife. He insisted that the members of the family refrain from eating food which he declared spoiled. One day he reported a short dream: "Mother is away, I am in the kitchen and out of my mouth some brown stuff flows into the basin." In the course of his associations he launched into the description of an experience which he told with absolute conviction of its reality, although it must have occurred, in keeping with his memory of the locale of the occurrence, when he was less than two years old. He saw himself on the floor, and as he said, not only playing with his feces (something which he had reported on previous occasions), but also eating them. He described his mother's coming upon him and angrily reprimanding him. Moreover, she forced him to swallow a huge quantity of what he believes must have been castor oil. Then he recalled the resulting explosive bowel movements and the feelings of great weakness, emptiness, and near collapse that followed them. He had the sensation that the stool and urine would never stop flowing and "that he would turn inside out." He retained from this, and from other experiences of that time, the feeling that the mother did not wish him to keep anything for himself, that all he had belonged to her, and that whatever he kept he had stolen from her. This ideation played a large role at a somewhat later stage of his development when it gave a distinctive color to his castration anxiety. The castration threat was experienced as coming from the mother before it was related to the father, and was felt with no less intensity than that later ascribed by him to the father. After the memory emerged he reported that a few days earlier he and his family had gone to his favorite restaurant. He ordered oysters—a dish for which the restaurant is particularly well known. But this time he could not eat them. They had a distinctly fecal odor. He refused the oysters and tried a salad with his favorite dressing. It tasted like castor oil. Though intellectually convinced that the food was perfect and in spite of his observing that it was enjoyed greatly by the other family members, he found himself unable to eat it. The following day another of the sentences, which we had come to recognize as heralding the emergence of early infantile material, appeared in his mind. This time the words were, "How weak I am." They proved to refer to the state of weakness and emptiness following castor oil treatment. He described vividly the state of despair connected with the recognition of how little he was able to control the actions of his own body, how weak he was in comparison with his mother, who had such absolute control over him and could force him, magically, as he thought, to experience most unpleasant and frightening sensations.

Perhaps a year after the castor oil treatment there occurred an episode of illness referred to in the family tradition as his "appendicitis." He recalls intense abdominal pain and a feeling of great thirst. This culminated in nausea and vomiting, after which he felt well. Analysis brought forth the information that he was at that time preoccupied with the idea that if only he could manage to hold back his stool and to abstain from eating and drinking,[1] he then would be strong like the mother, and like all grownups, since weakness was already identified with inability to control his bowels. He did indeed refuse food and drink and became severely constipated. It was the resulting condition that was suspected to have been an appendicitis. It appears probable that the threat of a possible operation induced him to give up this particular behavior pattern.

I should like to interpolate an explanatory statement which may be germane. The condensed description may have created the impression that the patient experienced his childhood reactions, feelings, and sensations in the manner of an adult observer and reported them in an articulate, precise manner. Nothing could be further from the truth. Many days, weeks, or months of patient work often passed between the first appearance of one of the sentences mentioned or some other symptom and its final explanation. Though his native intelligence was of a very high order, the patient was an unsophisticated and nonintellectual man, completely unfamiliar with psychoanalytic literature, whose rough background and limited education had in no way prepared him for intellectual and theoretical analytic constructions. His memories and reconstructions appeared slowly and often in fragmentary fashion, but nearly always as spontaneous productions of his own. When com-

---

1. This material was introduced by another of his "headline" sentences. This time the phrase was "stooling and sucking."

plete, they emerged with much emotion and an inner conviction of their truth. Many of the states of feeling he reported were quite foreign to my experience and could not have been constructed by me. In fact, I had learned that attempts on my part to introduce interpretations in accordance with my thinking sometimes delayed the clarification of the material. When the patient felt my skepticism he was restless and resentful, and his confidence appeared shaken until the mistake was cleared and he eventually supplied the memory material underlying a particular symptom. As a rule, the symptom then disappeared.

One day the patient spoke with great feeling of the intense empathy he felt with a child lost in a crowd or in a store. He experienced the feelings of the child in this situation with the most painful vividness and realism. The bewilderment, anxiety, the longing for the mother were felt by him as if his own. While speaking of this he recalled distinctly that as a child he often had the feeling, "I am so small I will get lost because mother won't see me." Therefore not only to see the mother but to be seen by her was important to the child, and later to the adult, when a mother figure substituted for the original.

A few weeks later, the patient once again presented us with a phrase that emerged into his consciousness with insistent force. The phrase was "Up and down, up and down." Its meaning was completely puzzling to him. The emergence of this phrase was accompanied by the sensation that objects in his field of vision moved up and down, and also by the uncomfortable, though vague sensations in his body. The patient spoke about certain preferences in food, such as his wish that his oatmeal contain small lumps rather than be completely fluid. Then came a feeling of dislike for liquids in general and for water in particular, and memories emerged of protesting and crying because he was given water rather than milk or semisolid foods when he was a very small child. Finally he added the construction, supported by fragments of memory, of being held on his father's shoulder and "burped," and rocked up and down to stop his crying. He described the feeling of seeing objects bouncing in front of his eyes without knowing what the objects were. He had not yet learned to name them or to recognize their function. Again though much of this was construction, it was accompanied by a feeling of conviction of its correctness.

In another few weeks the patient reported that "something about noise" kept coming into his mind. All he could say at first was that he had the feeling that the noise had something to do with the feeling which he described as "How weak I am." Two days later while taking an afternoon nap he was startled out of his sleep by a tremendous crash. He jumped up in terror and asked his son what crashed, only to be told that nothing had. However, it seems that the son had sneezed. That same day the vision of turning railroad wheels with sparks flying from them came to him, and then there appeared the memory of a time when he suffered from a childhood disease, probably measles, and was lying in a darkened room. Toward evening the shades were raised and the windows opened. They lived at the time in an apartment above his father's shop. The windows in his room were level with an elevated railway structure. He was periodically startled and badly frightened by the noise of the passing trains, and fascinated by the sight of the turning wheels throwing sparks when the brakes were applied. He called for his mother, but she did not come to him. They lived in that apartment when he was twenty-two months old. He remembered further the feeling of having played happily with a young aunt a few days before his illness. Then he found himself sick, very uncomfortable and unhappy, unable to see the favorite aunt. The patient said: "Talking of being weak, that's when I really saw myself. I could not get mother to come to me, and I could not throw the sickness off." He emphasized the last part of the statement. Again, the experience of remaining alone when frightened, and the simultaneous occurrence in his physical being of events beyond his power to control, the discomfort of the illness, contributed to the painful awakening of his self-awareness. An earlier, and more significant incident of similar character is to be described shortly.

Among the patient's many and frequently changing symptoms were several sets of complaints outstanding in terms of their persistence and the intense emotional and intellectual preoccupation which the patient devoted to them. One of these symptom complexes involved his eyes. He suffered frequently from a suddenly occurring disturbance of vision which he described as "streaks of lightning" appearing before his eyes and interfering with his vision. This was originally accompanied by a sensation of shock, of dizziness, a feeling of sudden weakness and of inner emptiness, and a fear of utter collapse. The patient further reported the sensation that things were forever flying into his eyes, but when he examined the eye, or had his physician examine it, nothing was ever to be found. For the longest time the derivation of these symptoms remained hypothetical. It was easy to observe that they occurred when the patient was troubled by someone leaving his vicinity. He himself associated it with the reaction of rage at the departing person. This explanation was undoubtedly partially correct, but it left many questions unanswered.

One day the patient came to the hour in a state of

acute panic. His secretary was leaving for her vacation the next day. He felt paralyzed by fear, anticipated a "breakdown," and felt helpless with rage and frustration. He also had the eye symptoms described above, and was convinced that some foreign body had flown into his eye. In his associations he suddenly saw a picture of a breast being pushed at him. No, he corrected himself, it pulls away, and he cannot stop it. He then spoke of a feeling of hunger and weakness, and of his having a "weaker magic" than the breast. On the following days the patient continued to express sensations of hunger and of confused helplessness. He spoke of a fear of dying, and of his concern over the painfulness of the slow passage of time. "How will I stand it till the evening. I feel hollow and cold inside. I have to go five days[2] without food. I shall die of hunger." Resentment and rage were also prominent in his feelings. Further work made it appear very probable that the patient was indeed re-experiencing, in his eye symptoms and in the accompanying anxious sensations of weakness, hunger, frustration, and rage, reactions to which as an infant he had become subject when he had been weaned or, at any rate, when his mother suddenly had taken him off the breast. We had learned that this did happen fairly often during his infancy because of her having to attend to the store while she was nursing him. She had interrupted the nursing many times under such circumstances. It appears likely that on pathways whose nature must of necessity remain speculative, the sudden increase of tension and of the level of discomfort upon the abrupt withdrawal of the breast expressed itself in a sensation of shock with certain visual manifestations, later appearing as the "streaks of lightning" before his eyes. Perhaps it is more correct to say that the shock may not as much have caused the visual impressions repeated in the symptoms, but that these impressions, having been in some unknown way connected with the catastrophic events producing the shock, became invested with the affective qualities related originally to the distressing experiences.[3] The time factor involved seems important in these considerations: I mean, the suddenness of the traumatic occurrences, the necessity for an adjustment to a frustration more rapid than it was possible for the infant to accomplish. Nor was it possible for him to absorb and neutralize the stimuli causing his discomfort as rapidly as they invaded the imperfect, indeed the still embryonic, ego organization. During the working through period of this material the patient voiced complaints of too much being expected from

him, of his being pushed too fast, and of things being expected before he was ready for them.

It seems that the early experience of abrupt removal from the breast were telescoped together with another set of very early traumata that have now to be described. Together with the weaning they are perhaps the earliest in the series of experiences leading to the discovery of the patient's identity.

In the course of his treatment the patient often complained of a number of uncomfortable symptoms which tended to make their appearance simultaneously. He felt feverish (the patient was forever taking his temperature), and his muscles ached. He felt distress in his chest, a burning in his throat, and was subject to an unpleasant cough. As usual, numerous medical examinations failed to reveal a sufficient organic cause for the patient's complaints. The symptoms made their appearance when a separation from a significant person had occurred in the patient's life, or when he was threatened by such a separation in a way which he feared he could not control. It was also conspicuous that on several occasions a separation accompanied by these symptoms was followed by an estrangement from the object. It was henceforth viewed with a lack of trust, and, in fact, with deep suspicion. We shall return later to this particular circumstance.

In the course of once again relating the complaints just mentioned, the patient added that he had an unfamiliar bitter taste in his mouth and had to "burp" repeatedly. He corrected himself to "I mean belch." He said, "I wonder whether that's the medicine they gave me when I had the double pneumonia." He had sporadically alluded to this illness without ascribing it much significance. Family tradition had it that at the age of certainly less than eighteen months, perhaps as early as nine months, he had suffered seriously from what was termed "double pneumonia." He was repeatedly told that he had nearly died at the time. A connection between his symptoms and the early illness was suspected. We were at first inclined to regard such an assumption with skepticism until, when reporting the recurrence of the same set of symptoms on a later occasion, the patient mentioned that he was disturbed lately by sudden variations in his state of consciousness, a vagueness and absent-mindedness not characteristic of him, and by contradictory rapidly alternating feelings of attraction and repulsion toward his wife. He could find no cause for these vacillations and not even a rationalization offered itself to his puzzled mind.

The analytic study of these symptoms convinced us that they were indeed related to the early illness, the "double pneumonia," and that his uncomfortable sensations and the strange changes in his ego

---

2. The duration of the secretary's absence.

3. It is hardly necessary to emphasize the fact that the eye symptoms of the patient were highly overdetermined, deriving genetically and dynamically from several sources. Here only the factors germane to the topic of this study are considered.

feeling and in his relations to the people around him represented a repetition of his experiences at the time of the early illness. The material pointed to the fact that the baby may have reacted to the discomfort of the illness with the expectation that the agency which he did not yet at this time perceive as distinct from himself, and which in the past had promptly removed unpleasant stimuli will do so again. But this time the expectation was not fulfilled and the infant discovered painfully that this agency, the mother, was not a part of, but separated from him, and not subject to his wishes; moreover, that she must have had hostile intentions toward him, or else why should she have withdrawn from him, and ceased to alleviate his discomfort; and further, that he had no capacity to influence this discomfort, in terms of removal of the pain within him, or in removing himself from the sources of his pain. The responsibility for his discomfort he now ascribed to the "newly separated" hostile mother. "Mother did not help me out. She did not want me," was a frequent lament of the patient at this time. It was brought forth with great intensity of feeling. I am unable to convey the expression of despair and anguish contained in the patient's behavior and words. During the same period the thought appeared in his mind: "I don't own the house, the house owns me." The thought proved to reflect the recognition of the infant that it was not he who controlled the all-powerful mother, but she who controlled him.

It is self-evident that the occurrence of logical thought sequences and constructions is not assumed to have taken place in the infant in the form we have descriptively used here. The description intends no more than to convey in words preverbal affective reactions, which appear to represent early stages of the formation of an ego. The matrix from which this process of ego formation took its course, the "nucleus" of the ego, we assume to have existed in some as yet undefined form before its onset.

I am inclined to see in the patient's grave early illness, along with the other early experiences described, an important predisposing factor for the development of his particularly intractable neurosis. The forcible and sudden, rather than gradual, interruption of his unity with his mother, and the infant's "interpretation" of this event as a consequence of the mother's hostile intent, led to a burst of precocious development, an accelerated and premature formation of an ego extremely narrow in scope and limited in its capacity for further growth. On the basis of an ego so impaired, the development of a malignant neurotic pattern took place. Some details of this process are to be described in the following part of this study.

At one time, well along in his treatment, the patient began to refer to a part of himself as "the little man." He also resorted to expressions like "the little king," and "the little lord," to describe the same aspect of his personality, but the "little man" remained the one most frequently used. Distinct from the rest of his personality, the "little man" first came into evidence in the analysis when the patient became aware of the resistance which this part of him offered to the treatment and to the analyst. He, the "little man," mocked and ridiculed the interpretations and suggestions made by the analyst. He seemed most obstinately determined to prevent improvement in the patient's condition. The "little man" was suspicious and distrusted the analyst and engaged in "snickering behind his back." One day the patient exclaimed in anger: "There is a Goddamn little man in me that keeps laughing at you while you talk." From then on the patient habitually used this expression to describe a part of himself which he perceived as sharply distinct from the rest of his personality.

We learned that a correct interpretation often resulted in the "little man's" secretly laughing at our expense—"The little man now laughs," the patient was wont to say, in a low voice, with an expression of listening to something within himself.

It gradually became quite clear that the "little man's" activity was by no means limited to the analytical situation. He objected sharply to the patient's attempts to transgress the limits of his self-imposed restrictions on walking and traveling. He did not want the patient to become friendly with anyone and insisted that the patient trust no one. The enjoyment of pleasure and gratification, of rest and peace, was categorically prohibited by the "little man." "He won't let me live," became a frequent phrase with which the patient described the relationship of this part of himself to the rest of his personality. The obstructive and interfering influence of this "little man" was most evident when the patient was about to obtain pleasure or experience an improvement of his condition, or when he attempted to make use of a freedom of movement otherwise restricted.

Superficially this appears like the description of a primitive, archaic, and harsh superego. Further study revealed that indeed primitive superego features and the "little man" were overlapping. But fundamentally this phenomenon appeared to be an isolated part of the ego, an area of condensed narcissistic reaction to the early perception of the patient's own weakness and helplessness. It seems that a mobilization of narcissistic ego resources occurred under the impact of the painful discoveries of the child's helplessness, and that these resources became condensed into an ego area which from then on acted as the "little man." This ego segment did not at first contain identifications in terms of those that enter into the superego formation, though such identifications later became added to it. It remained an isolated ego element, continuing to lead a sort of autonomous existence. At times it utilized the superego content that adhered to it, or overlapped with it, for its purposes. For instance, guilt feelings were used to enforce behavior conforming to the "little man's" demands.

One day the patient sat up with a disturbed expression on his face and declared "we are missing something, we are missing the guilt. What makes me knock myself down like that? It must be because I am guilty." Further study made obvious that he had no reason for guilt, nor did he really feel it, but that he felt compelled by his "little man" to find some means to prevent the rest of his person from enjoying a particular situation, a situation implying greater mobility and some pleasure. In this connection the patient once expressed the idea that it could not be true that the hold which the "little man" had on him was a result of a deep guilt, as he, the patient, had often thought. When he discussed fantasies about his having stolen the mother's breast, so that she could not feed the other children, it occurred to him that if he could prove that he did not steal the breast, he would free himself of the "little man." But then he recognized that this was not so. He realized that such a proof of his innocence would indeed deprive the "little man" of a particular weapon, by means of which he exercised his control over the patient, but by no means free the patient from his pervading influence.

To return to the situation offering pleasure and mobility, it became clear in the analysis, that such situations reawakened ancient fears of venturing too far away from the mother (mother substitute), with the corresponding idea that he will not find his way back. When that happened the "little man" became active and began to interfere with the patient's activities. The "little man" took over, in a distorted fashion, the function which the mother fulfilled before the patient discovered himself as being separate from her. Nevertheless, it is dubious whether this occurred on the basis of a true identification that takes place following an object loss, since, at that stage, the mother had not yet been perceived as an object but as a part of himself. What he lost was to him a protecting and supporting part of himself, whereupon he proceeded to mobilize the remaining resources into the "little man" figure, from now on entrusted with the protective functions which until then were an integral component of the mother not yet separated. The establishment of the "little man" in the ego in effect denied the earliest experience of separation from the mother. When discussing the early disturbances of his relationship to his mother, the patient used to say: "The little man took over mother's job

when my brother was born," and "The little man kept on where mother left off, that's why I won't give him up." Once the patient remarked with great emphasis, "When mother was with me I didn't know that I existed, when she was not there I realized that I existed, I felt myself as myself, and that was a frightening thought. . . . That is how I felt this morning when N. was not in the office."

As the different stages of libido development passed and the child was subjected to traumata peculiar to each, they lent specific features to the "little man." Moreover, it seems that this ego segment also actively attracted libidinal energy to itself as if deliberately hoarding such libidinal cathexes to increase its power. Most impressive was the contribution of the anal-sadistic phase to the libido reservoir of the "little man" and hence to the character and demeanor of the ego part so named. The patient spent many weeks re-experiencing it in the transference, remembering details of and elaborating on his early childhood relationship to the bowel function and his fantasies regarding his stools at that period. He became vividly cognizant of the magic and omnipotent powers which he ascribed to the stool in childhood. At one time while speaking about the relationship between the "little man" and the fantasies of the omnipotent stool, he said: "The magic stool and the little man merged and became one. They took each other as partners." This spontaneous description graphically bore witness to the manner in which the ego segment of the "little man" drew to itself anal-sadistic libidinal energy.

Of interest for the genesis of the patient's dominant symptom, his agoraphobia, was his identification of the process of awakening, which was often accompanied by much anxiety, with being eliminated as feces from the mother's body. On the basis of slowly emerging memories the patient suggested that this particular fantasy may have originated in infancy when he awakened and found himself covered with feces which had become cold and irritating. The waking anxiety itself was described by him as very much like the anxiety of his agoraphobic attacks. In this context it should be added that he also equated falling asleep with merging with the mother's breast. He reported fantasies and hypnagogic hallucinations in which he saw himself "falling into mother's breast." Waking up was undoubtedly an anal birth for the unconscious of the patient, and falling asleep a reunion with the mother. Both processes were consequently often associated with anxiety, the first with fear of separation, the second with the dread of total merging with the mother. They were therefore opposed by the "little man," who, in a certain sense, offered himself to the rest of the ego as a mother equivalent from whom separation was never to occur, and the union with whom was not to result in the cessation of individual existence. This ego element consequently sought to draw all libidinal energies unto itself, instead of allowing them to flow over to other objects. We shall return later to these features of the "little man" phenomenon, and shall also refer to the manner in which the separation from him was perceived and elaborated on the phallic level, as castration anxiety, and in which the "little man" became invested with phallic-narcissistic libido and significance.

As a consequence of the fact that the "little man" so voraciously appropriated libidinal energy during all stages of libidinal development, there occurred a sharp increase of secondary narcissistic cathexis, with resulting diminution of the available libido for true object relationships. This was poignantly expressed by the patient in his frequent complaint: "The little man won't let me love," paralleling the already mentioned reproach that "The little man won't let me *live*."

Two childhood experiences, one reconstructed on the basis of analytic material and the other clearly remembered on the basis of reconstruction, had greatly contributed to the process of development and final crystalization of the phenomenon of the "little man."

At an advanced stage of the analysis, on an occasion when the patient for the first time in many years permitted his wife to leave town for a few days, he experienced the following sequence of events. For some days before his wife's trip, he complained about a painful swelling of his legs. During her absence he called me a number of times to report his concern because of a violent bout of diarrhea and cramps. In fact, he believed he had observed a bit of blood and mucus in the stool. For some reason he felt impelled to check his weight. He discovered with surprise and concern that he had lost some six pounds within a few days, or so he believed. He was worried lest a pathological growth might have caused some obstruction in his bowels. He was nauseated and was troubled by a strong urge to vomit, though he did not do so. He felt bloated and could tolerate only soft-boiled eggs as food. The analysis of these events and sensations led to the patient's recognition that he had re-enacted in these few days his experience at an age of twenty months when the brother next to him in age was born. In fact, he reproduced his observations of his mother's pregnancy and delivery in great detail. Their living conditions at the time made it very probable that he could have made such observations in detail. He also recalled that in the period immediately following he felt what he today described as a constant rage against the mother and the newborn child. His memories, though uncertain, indicated that he had reacted to his brother's birth, and to the corresponding change in his mother's attitude, with a giving up of the already acquired capacity to con-

trol his bowel function. He soiled himself occasionally to the great discontent of his mother, who insisted on early training and on scrupulous cleanliness.

A phase of negative behavior toward the mother seems to have followed immediately afterwards. The patient described a feeling of estrangement from the mother in this period and stated definitely, "That is when the little man got quite a boost, right then at that time."

The second experience, eventually clearly remembered, was as follows. Once again he introduced the subject by a phrase that appeared suddenly in his mind, without immediately evident relationship to the current material. The phrase was —"Pleasure and death," and later, "Pleasure is death."

He recalled pictures of a tall vase with some evergreens in it, then a procession which he recognized as a funeral, and finally the picture of a dead man in a casket. It then emerged that when he was about three, his mother had surprised him masturbating and had sharply reprimanded him for it. "She gave me hell," he said. On the afternoon of the same day she took him to a funeral, where he saw a dead man for the first time in his life. He recalled being bewildered by everything he observed and asking his mother repeatedly why people wanted to die. He could not remember his mother's answer, but it became clear to him that he had assumed that death was an action of will, and that since one wanted to do only things that were pleasurable, dying people must have wished to die. Although he did not recall what his mother said to him, he knew that his belief was shattered by her reply, and that he came away with the feeling that death was the ultimate punishment for forbidden pleasure, and not a pleasure in itself. He suspected that he took his mother's explanation to be a threat of death to him, if he were to continue the forbidden masturbatory activity. Since he believed his mother had the power of life and death over him he took her threat seriously. Our material indicated that he did not give up masturbation, but that with the help of the by-now formed ego segment, the "little man," he obstinately continued, at least for a time, masturbatory practices. However, he carefully concealed them from his mother, and developed the philosophy that a crime is one only when one fails to get away with it.

It is of interest to pursue further the effect which the different stages of libido development had on the character of the "little man" phenomenon. The review shows, not unexpectedly, that characteristics of each stage were grafted upon this ego segment, and when fully developed, the "little man," like the patient's manifest character, possessed such features as oral greed, anal obstinancy, and phallic narcissism. These features did not appear fused together, nor were they consistently displayed by the "little man." On the contrary, they were readily forsaken and appeared to slide off, as it were, whenever the justification for the "little man's" existence was challenged. The patient might, for instance, be involved in a stubborn argument, insisting on some minor habit or custom in his office or his home, or he might be engaged in the boastful exposition of his success in business, and carry on this account with great abandon. But if it happened that in the course of such episodes a reference to a trip, or to someone's leaving the patient's vicinity occurred, then there followed immediately a sudden and complete change of mood and attitude on the part of the patient. He gave up his vehement argument, or stopped his self-confident boasting and became preoccupied with the thought, "I cannot make it." At the time when he began to perceive the functioning of the "little man" in him, this thought was accompanied by the feeling that it was the "little man" calling him to order, and warning him to observe his self-imposed limitations. Such observations were very frequent, though it is difficult to convey in description the impressive ease with which the derivatives of the various stages of libido development were drawn to and again shed by the "little man." They had clearly not been integrated in a permanent manner into the total ego organization.

Of great interest is the relationship of the "little man" to anxiety. It appears that when the function of developing anxiety was used to produce a signal for the danger of loss of love, or loss of object relationships, it was experienced by the ego components other than the "little man." On the other hand, situations where anxiety signaled a danger from an unduly powerful, or rapidly increasing instinctual tension, or when the threat was one directly affecting the body of the patient, the anxiety was experienced by the ego part which he called his "little man." The ego development as reconstructed from the patient's history makes this division understandable. The "little man" formed no object relationships,[4] and was in fact established in an effort to make such relationships unnecessary. It will be remembered that the separation of the "little man" from the rest of the ego occurred as part of the discovery of the patient's separateness from his mother, at a stage when the mother was not yet felt as an external object, but was perceived as one with the child. These experiences were accompanied by painful sensations within the infant, such as hunger, the discomfort and pain of childhood diseases, uncontrollable outbursts of temper, and various unpleasant bodily reactions to which I have referred previously. The observation was

therefore not unexpected that anxiety from similar sources, i.e., from threats to the bodily self, or from increased instinctual tension, continued to be called forth and acted upon by the "little man," whereas the anxiety signaling the threat of object loss or loss of love was actuated and perceived by the rest of the ego capable of object relationships. Though there was a distinct difference in the patient's manifest experience of the two kinds of anxiety, this difference does not lend itself to easy description. The overlapping of the two, and the fact that the anxiety in the "little man" part of the ego was frequently provoked by an initial anxious reaction in the ego proper offer obstacles to a clear differentiation.

The "little man's" anxiety seemed indeed to have a more consuming character, and often deserved the term panic. It contained the fear of personal dissolution, of total collapse, and the patient was utterly helpless when under its spell. In late stages of the analysis he described these particular emotions correctly as a fear of his own feelings. He referred to the primitive untamed emotions of his early childhood and their successors in his unconscious. He said: "My feelings must appear goofy, crazy, to the adult."

This anxiety was called forth, as mentioned, by threats to the patient's bodily integrity, and by the dangers of instinctual tension. In addition, the same reaction resulted, whenever the "little man" was confronted with evidence of omnipotence other than his own, or "more powerful" than his own. For example, upon hearing of someone else's illness or death, the patient experienced the anxiety described above. This was in keeping with the observation that the "little man" had become established in an almost automatic, reflex-like manner, in response to the perception of his own weak and helpless self, i.e., as a compensatory narcissistic reaction to the impairment of the feeling of infantile omnipotence.

In contrast, the anxiety felt by the patient's ego proper seemed pale and not dramatic. Since the ego's mature object relationships were in themselves inconspicuous, their loss, while damaging, caused no effects such as called forth by the threats to the security of the "little man." Were it not for certain observations, now to be reported, we might not have become cognizant of the fact that two kinds of anxiety were experienced by the patient in two psychic localities within the ego. A number of the patient's self-observations indicated clearly that often while the patient was in the throes of great anxiety, the "little man" in him experienced no anxiety, but felt triumphant. This reaction occurred when the anxiety attack was occasioned by the threat of object loss, for instance, when a friend was leaving town, or the analyst announced a forthcoming interruption of the treatment. At times, while experiencing a spell of acute anxiety during the analytic hour, the patient

---

4. In the sense of an investment of genital, or aim-inhibited libidinal energy in the object.

was wont to say: "The little man smiles"; or "The little man now laughs." Yet, the patient was undeniably very troubled by anxiety. It was obviously the rest of his ego, distinct from the "little man," that experienced the anxious affect. It is significant that the anxiety in these instances lacked the deeply disruptive character of the near-panic states experienced by the patient when the "little man's" position and security were threatened. The "objects" whose loss threatened the ego in these instances were contemporary objects of the ego proper, not of the "little man." The latter's object, of course, was but one, himself, or the mother as a part of himself. Only the danger of separation from *that* object and from its symbolic representatives, the patient's home, office, or car, and his wife, evoked a stormy, incapacitating anxiety reaction in the "little man," a reaction which in turn badly frightened the ego proper. The ego, one felt, then found itself in the position of a bewildered, shocked, and completely helpless onlooker.

The triumphant reaction of the "little man" when not he but the ego proper felt anxiety, became intelligible in terms of the self-preservative function of this ego segment. It felt triumphant when it had succeeded in asserting its domination over the ego, and in preventing it from risking a repetition of early traumatic experiences occasioned by the removal of objects conceived as part of himself. The patient directly stated that it was as if the "little man" were saying to him, "I warned you to beware of becoming attached to that person, now that you come to depend on him, he is leaving you. . . . You must love no one but me. . . ."

The acute phobic state reactivated the "memory" of the sensations and feelings at the very moment of the traumatic separation, and by means of the development of the anxiety affect warned against the threatening repetition of that experience. It was the successful avoidance of a repetition of the trauma that provided the basis for the triumphant feeling of the "little man," whose very creation was the first act of mastery of the trauma by at least a part of the ego. This was accomplished by a rift in the infantile ego which remained present throughout life. When the so-achieved mastery was in danger of failing, the "little man" experienced anxiety of catastrophic intensity. The patient eventually learned to distinguish between the "little man" and his ego proper. The acquisition of the capacity to make that distinction was therapeutically of considerable importance for the patient.

The consequences of the division in the patient's ego were, of course, not limited to the experiences of anxiety but extended to other ego functions and ego attitudes. For instance, the patient's relationships to the same object regularly contained sets of characteristics, at times contradictory, attributable to the "little man" in him, and to the ego proper. The

patient's manifest attitudes to others depended on the proportion in which the "little man" and the rest of his ego determined the quality and quantity of libido attached to the object. The acquisitiveness of the "little man" in regard to libidinous energies in general restricted the ego in relating genital and aim-inhibited libido to objects. On the other hand, the "little man," dominated by the time and circumstances of his coming into being, and the aims of his continuing existence, directed only pregenital libidinous energies to the same object. Thus the picture of the patient's object relationships was characterized by an obtrusive component, the "little man's" pregenital attitudes, and a much less conspicuous contribution from the ego proper.

I must elaborate on a significant feature of the patient's object relationships, to which I have repeatedly, if briefly alluded. I mean the "little man's" fateful attitude of obstinate enmity toward objects in general. We saw in this trait a manifestation of the fundamental narcissistic position of the "little man," of the wish to maintain the illusion of his omnipotence, and of the striving to protect the patient from the risk of abandonment by his objects.

I referred in the first part of this study to the mistrust and suspicion engendered in the patient when in his infancy the mother failed to alleviate his suffering during a grave illness. We suggested then that he had interpreted this failure as a consequence of the mother's hostile intent. The eminently characteristic tendency of the "little man" to mock and ridicule everybody, so conspicuous in the transference, may well have been rooted in the experiences during that early and dangerous illness.

We further recognized in the "little man's" animosity toward objects evidence that this ego part was invested mainly with pregenital narcissistic, and especially, anal-sadistic libido quantities. The analysis revealed an additional significant motivation for the refusal of the "little man" to permit to the ego the establishment and cultivation of object relationships.

During one period of the analysis the patient was troubled by strange sensations that occurred while he engaged in free associations concerning the analyst. Whenever he was affectionately inclined toward the analyst, he felt as if his whole person was "flowing together" with that of the analyst and becoming one with him, and as if he himself was about to disappear in part, or even completely. This feeling was very vividly perceived by the patient. His description of it was clearly expressive of a profound reaction and certainly not just an allegorical allusion to a libidinous impulse. He was deeply frightened by the bewildering experiences, and made visible efforts to shake himself free from them. It was during that period of the analysis that he spoke also of the sensations of "walking out" of the analyst's body, mentioned previously in a different connection. In the course of dealing with this material, the patient gave much biographical information, illustrating the continuance in his unconscious of childhood fantasies of his belonging to his mother, who, he felt, owned not only his body and its contents, his stools, but also his thoughts, and his feelings. He was but a temporarily separated part of her, existing by her grace, and at any time subject to be reunited with her. The notion of mutual cannibalistic incorporation and the projection of his own wishes to incorporate and dominate the mother contributed to the determinants of this fantasy.

The patient's life was replete with examples of his continuous struggle to retain an identity of his own, and of his endless protest against being owned and dominated by his mother. He was compelled to engage in never ceasing clashes with her in actual life. He enacted similar conflicts with a series of mother substitutes, and in fact, with all objects, including those of only passing significance for him. The main feature of his argument was regularly the accusation that the person failed to show him due consideration, kindness, or love, and instead endeavored to dominate, exploit and "take over" the patient completely. The transference situation offered many opportunities to examine this conflict of the patient. The immediately obvious, perhaps self-evident meanings of the patient's complaint—the projection of his own wishes to dominate the mother substitutes on the very figures he wanted to control, and the identification with his in fact possessive and dominating mother—were important, but not the only determinants of his reactions. It was also the transference situation, of which an illuminating example was quoted above, that eventually provided us with a further narcissistic derivation of the patient's compulsive behavior pattern. It stemmed in the main from his unconscious conviction, supported by the corresponding unconscious wish, that a "complete" object relationship was identical with the re-establishment of the ego state that existed before the separation from the mother, i.e., before the birth of the "little man." Consequently, it was the narcissism of this ego segment, intent on self-preservation, that rebelled against the development of object relationships. In the last sense, the formation of such a relationship meant fusion with the object, and the forsaking of personal existence as an identity of his own. This was clearly an unacceptable fate, both for the narcissism of the ego, most richly centered in the "little man," and for the latter's illusion of omnipotence.

We must return briefly to one of the "little man's" primary aims, and his perhaps most important function, i.e., his efforts at restoration of the lost early infantile omnipotence and the continuous protection and preservation of it. This aim was in direct conflict with the tendency to preserve the patient's personal identity. Re-establishment of the omnipotence was most completely accomplished by total reunion with the mother. The sense of omnipotence was essentially the ego feeling that existed before the awareness of his separateness from the mother arose in the patient. A characteristic statement of the patient was: "For a moment I felt real omnipotent today—with you sitting there, and no one else around, I felt I had you all to myself! The little man was king! But then I got anxious again. . . ." Since that total reunion was unacceptable to the ego, compromise solutions had to be found.

It was illuminating to observe how the patient had succeeded in establishing himself as unquestioned and absolute master of household and business, though he was unaware of his efforts in that regard until late in the course of his analysis. His behavior bore the mark of a person who tolerated no opposition and who surrounded himself with people too weak to oppose him effectively, thus creating the illusion of his omnipotence. But simultaneously, the means the patient used to support his omnipotent position were those of the naively peremptory, yet feeble child rather than those of a masterful man. He alternately wooed the allegiance and good will of his friends and employees with gifts and favors, and strove to make them as totally dependent on him as he felt dependent on them, and at other times ordered them about, expecting complete and immediate obedience. He tolerated opposition with poor grace, and punished it sooner or later. The development of anxiety, and his general discomfort when someone in his vicinity departed, though consciously painful, gave him a welcome excuse to demand their constant presence and subservience to his wishes. It was a typical and frequent occurrence that he asked me, "Shall I let him go?" referring to a prospective departure of an employee, or a relative. His tone of voice implied categorically that he took his right to prohibit the departure for granted, and made no distinction between his power to enforce obedience to such prohibitions and the right to exercise his power. Needless to say that he was forever feeling exploited, misused, and inadequately appreciated by the people around him. He justified his insistence on their loyalty and devotion by constantly pointing to the generous treatment which they received from him. These protestations concealed poorly his possessive and autocratically dominating attitude, an attitude which reflected the persistence in him, unchanged, of the purely narcissistic object relationships of the pregenital child, particularly that at the height of the anal-sadistic phase of development, when the belief in one's omnipotence seems to enjoy a last powerful upsurge before being gradually eroded by the combined pressure of reality and of the growing intellect.

The very formation of the isolated ego part of the "little man" was to some degree a successful effort at restoration, and the continued existence of this ego element a successful preservation, by way of structuralization, of the sense of omnipotence lost in childhood. The price paid for this success by the personality of the patient was clearly a heavy one, as so often it is, when, to borrow a description from Freud, a prehistoric ego structure remains preserved as a fossil in the body of the ego, alien to its more advanced and differentiated elements.

At the danger of appearing redundant I should like to refer once more in broad outline to the development of the "little man" ego element.

The process of the separation of the "little man" from the rest of the ego appears to have taken place gradually in earliest childhood, and was concluded around the patient's third year of life. It seems to have completed the development of an ego identity within him. A succession of narcissistic injuries on every level of early development resulted in the loss of the feeling of infantile omnipotence, and marked dramatically the child's helplessness toward external influences (the mother's behavior toward his needs) and internal events (hunger, affective reactions, control of body functions and of disease). Thus was brought home to the child his separateness from the powerful mother, and the recognition of his own identity as feeble and vulnerable was forced upon him. Compensatorily, a separate structure in the patient's ego was erected, and this proved of fateful significance in the development of his personality and for the whole pattern of his life henceforth.

But have we not spent altogether too much effort to contrive the existence of an ego structure which is in reality nothing but the familiar result of an identification with the denying, controlling, and directing mother? I believe that the answer to this question is definitely negative. Our observations have shown conclusively that the "little man" became established primarily before the mother existed as a separate entity, and identification with her occurred only later, after she had become an object distinct from himself. Undoubtedly many features of the mother were then added to the image of the "little man."

In later years identifications with a few beloved objects, who had offered him affection but had later disappeared from his life, were also added to the image of the "little man," so that the patient on occasion could say, "The little man is all the people that loved me and went away and died." It goes without saying, that with the advent of the phallic stage, the "little man" also acquired a superimposed phallic narcissistic significance.

An illuminating example will illustrate this, and supplement the discussion of the large contribution which this particular process made to the structure of the patient's phobic fears of dissolution, when separated from mother surrogates.

In the course of the treatment there appeared memories of his observing his mother undressed and noting her genitalia. This at first seems to have made little impression on the child, though he was puzzled by the appearance of a "dark spot" where he expected to see the penis. It seems that he waited for the reappearance of the penis, thinking that it had "gone" but would return. There was also evidence of other explanatory attempts which he made to himself at the time, such as that the penis was hidden inside or that it would grow. Then, perhaps a year or more after the initial observation, there seemed to have taken place a shocking realization that the penis would never return to the mother. The circumstances of this discovery remained obscure, but there was evidence that it may have been connected with the observation of a primal scene. The patient said, "My fear of going outside started right there." He came to the conclusion that he must have decided that he in his entirety could disappear and remain "gone," as he had convinced himself that his mother's penis had vanished, never to return.

It became clear that he had identified with the missing penis of his mother, and eventually incorporated this identification into the structure of the "little man," not unlike the fetishist who rebuilds the woman's lost phallus in his fetish. It appeared evident from the previously reported material that this identification with the penis was grafted on an already preformed ego structure, which at this point drew to itself additional, now phallic narcissistic, libidinal energies.

This personification of the primitive narcissistic ego seemed a depository of what in terms of early psychoanalytic theory was described as the ego instincts of self-preservation. The "little man" was indeed almost omnipotent in his practical invincibility. He defended this position by avoiding all instinctual dangers, which in effect perpetuated the illness, and by enslaving a mother substitute, the patient's wife, whom he had succeeded in making so utterly dependent upon himself, that he could be certain of her being available at his command at all times. The isolated existence of this ego segment interfered with the development of a properly integrated ego, and impaired its function of synthesis. In this fashion there came to exist a house divided within the ego itself, and the total effect was that of a weak, helpless, impoverished, and limited ego, even though actually a part of it, the "little man," gave every evidence of possessing great power. Here it was not only the superego that opposed the ego as harsh taskmaster, but an isolated part of the ego itself that was not the result of an identification with the parents, but a segment split off in consequence of the necessity to sustain life with a support suddenly lost. It evolved not out of lost object relationships, as in superego formation proper, but in response to the discovery of one's own weakness. The "little man" represented no moral standards and no ego ideal to be followed. "The little man has no conscience," the patient said on several occasions. He had no regard for, and no relationships to, objects other than those devoted to self-preservation. It cannot be truly said that the "little man" followed the pleasure principle, the *gaining* of pleasure not being one of his objectives. On the contrary, the "little man" objected sharply whenever the patient sought pleasure, or was tempted by the prospect of pleasure. A beautiful spring day invited a walk or ride in the country, very much loved by the patient. Promptly anxiety, tension, and varying physical symptoms developed, as if to warn the patient to resist the temptation. In fact, no price was too high to keep the patient under the "little man's" domination. "The little man," the patient said, "will rather let me die than enjoy myself, or get well." This statement appeared at first at variance with our realization that the "little man's" function was to preserve the patient's life. The discrepancy was resolved when we understood that indeed, from the point of view of the pleasure-seeking id, the "little man" wanted it to "die," i.e., to forsake all striving for pleasure, while at the same time, from the point of view of the ego, the "little man" strove to keep the patient alive, since to him pleasure had the ultimate meaning of death. He once said: "The little man won't let me *live* [i.e., pleasurably], but keeps me *alive*, in a jail."

On the other hand, it was not entirely correct to assume that the "little man" was unable to or did not experience pleasure. Though not engaged in seeking the experience of pleasure as such, for its own sake, he was capable of a sense of pleasurable gratification when his aims were realized. At times, when he succeeded in asserting his will, against the wishes of others, i.e., when he exercised his omnipotence, the intensity of this pleasure rose to that of a feeling of triumph. Only too often the "others" included the patient's own personality as distinct from the "little man" himself. A sadistic tinge was unmistakably and almost invariably present in the "little man's" experience of pleasure. This is not an astonishing finding. As we have seen, the ego part termed his "little man" by the patient, became definitely isolated, and thus prevented from further development, at the height of the anal-sadistic stage of libidinal development, a circumstance which readily accounted for many of the "little man's," and consequently of the patient's, conspicuous characteristics.

Insofar as the "little man's" concern was self-preservation one could describe his functioning as a perversion of obedience to the reality principle, since normal functioning implies modification of the pleasure principle to correspond with realistic conditions, and not the complete forsaking of all pleasure. The patient once reported the memory that at one time early in childhood, he became absolutely determined that "he will never let it happen to him again." He said he "made an oath" to that extent. Months later the meaning of this oath became clear. It received its clarification when we had reviewed in detail the beginnings of the "little man." It represented the determination to protect himself from the feeling of weakness, helplessness, and rage which accompanied the discovery of his identity, the labor pains, as it were, at the birth of his self-awareness as a person separate from his mother, and the reaction to the loss of the feeling of infantile omnipotence.

It is self-evident that I have in this discussion limited myself to an emphasis on the development of ego identity and its role in the pattern of the patient's character and symptomatology. Many other factors not referred to entered into the structure of his highly overdetermined symptoms. To mention but a few important matters, pregenital fantasies of cannibalistic incorporation, and of the reverse, i.e., fantasies of being devoured by the mother, played a conspicuous role in his case. The patient's analysis also taught me that the familiar interpretation of walking as symbolic of sexual intercourse with the mother, and the role of the originally strong pleasure in movement (Abraham), had to be qualified in his case. It was not a genital sexual intercourse, but an anal-sadistic destructive sexual attack, that was symbolized by his walking. It was particularly prohibited, and consequently productive of anxiety because of its archaic destructive character. Pregnancy and birth fantasies as well as destructive wishes against the pregnant mother and the children in her (the patient was the second oldest of eight) were also prominent. However, I believe that equally significant factors in regard to the impairment of his total functioning were undoubtedly those described in terms of his earliest ego development.

I have attempted to demonstrate the beginnings of the development of a sense of personal identity in early childhood, as it could be reconstructed in the analysis of a middle-aged man. This development was, in the case of my patient, a painful process initiated by events of a traumatic nature, and was not successful in its results. The cause for the failure can, as always, be found only in a combination of components, with their relative proportion to each other remaining indefinite. It is impossible to exclude constitutional factors. One of these may be seen in an inherent disproportion between the intensity of instinctual drives and the capacity for their mastery. Early frustrations, the mother's impatient attitude, the discrepancies between her demands for the child's maturation and the infant's innate ability for growth, were other factors involved. A factor of perhaps paramount significance is to be seen in the consequences of the patient's debilitating organic disease in early infancy. This traumatic event undoubtedly initiated, indeed enforced a process of partial ego maturation at an age earlier, and a rate of speed greater than was natural to the infant.[5] We believe to recognize in this latter circumstance, i.e., the necessity for adaptation at a speed exceeding the infant's capacity, an important factor among those causing development deviating from the normal. Thus, necessity instead of providing a stimulating factor became a traumatic influence on the ego development.

In all of the patient's later life, his character, his behavior patterns, and the symptomatology of his neurosis showed the influence of two mutually contradictory tendencies. The desire to unite again with the mother, to prevent forever her separating from him, and to insure the persistence of the feeling of infantile omnipotence based on a not yet interrupted unity with the mother—all these represented one set of paramount motivations in his life. The other was an equally intense effort to forestall such a complete reunion with the mother, to prevent the loss of identity, and the personal death involved in total reunion with her. In consequences of the traumatic circumstances of the discovery of the child's painful separateness from the mother, an ego segment, the "little man," was isolated from the rest of the personality. One of the main functions of this separate structure remained through life the task to prevent either one or the other of the above-mentioned tendencies from gaining the upper hand, and from threatening the individual's existence, either through final separation from the mother, or through merging with her.

Stated differently, the task of the separated ego segment was to realize the motivations mentioned above as fully as possible, yet without permitting the life-threatening total reunion with the mother. The establishment of the separate ego entity, and, with it, the development of the severe neurosis, thus may be said to have secured the patient's life, at the cost of a crippling inhibition of the ego's freedom of movement, a far-reaching renunciation of instinctual gratifications, and the occurrence, through life, of attacks of paralyzing anxiety.

6.

ERIKSON, ERIK H.

Childhood and Society*

As an introduction to a review of Freud's theories concerning the infantile organism as a powerhouse

of sexual and aggressive energies, let me now present observations on two children who seemed strangely deadlocked in combat with their own bowels. As we try to understand the social implications of the eliminative and other body apertures, it will be necessary to reserve judgment regarding the children studied and the symptoms observed. The symptoms seem odd; the children are not. For good physiological reasons the bowels are farthest away from the zone which is our prime interpersonal mediator, namely the face. Well-trained adults dismiss the bowels, if they function well, as the nonsocial backside of things. Yet for this very reason bowel dysfunction lends itself to confused reflection and to secret response. In adults this problem is hidden behind somatic complaints; in children it appears in what seem to be merely willful habits.

Ann, a girl of four, enters the office, half gently pulled, half firmly pushed by her worried mother. While she does not resist or object, her face is pale and sullen, her eyes have a blank and inward look, and she sucks vigorously on her thumb.

I have been informed of Ann's trouble. She seems to be losing her usual resiliance; in one way she is much too babyish, in another much too serious, too unchildlike. When she does express exuberance, it is of an explosive kind which soon turns to silliness. But her most annoying habit is that of holding on to her bowel movements when requested to relinquish them, and then of stubbornly depositing them in her bed during the night, or rather in the early morning just before her sleepy mother can catch her. Reprimands are borne silently and in reverie behind which lurks obvious despair. This despair seems recently to have increased following an accident in which she was knocked down by an automobile. The damage to her body is only superficial, but she has withdrawn even further from the reach of parental communication and control.

Once inside the office the child lets go of the mother's hand and walks into my room with the automatic obedience of a prisoner who no longer has a will of his own. In my playroom she stands in a corner, sucking tensely on her thumb and paying only a very reserved kind of attention to me.

* * *

The child indicates clearly that I will not get anything out of her. To her growing surprise and relief, however, I do not ask her any questions; I do not even tell her that I am her friend and that she should trust me. Instead I start to build a simple block house on the floor. There is a living room; a kitchen; a bedroom with a little girl in a bed and a woman standing close by her; a bathroom with the door open; and

5. A stubborn ego resistance in the treatment stemmed from the patient's anxious opposition to the timing and the speed of changes which, he thought, were expected of him.

* Reprinted from *Childhood and Society*, 2nd Edition,

revised and enlarged by Erik H. Erikson. By permission of W. W. Norton & Co., Inc. Copyright 1950 © 1963 by W. W. Norton & Co., Inc.

a garage with a man standing next to a car. This arrangement suggests, of course, the regular morning hour when the mother tries to pick the little girl up "on time," while the father gets ready to leave the house.

Our patient, increasingly fascinated with this wordless statement of a problem, suddenly goes into action. She relinquishes her thumb to make space for a broad and toothy grin. Her face flushes and she runs over to the toy scene. With a mighty kick she disposes of the woman doll; she bangs the bathroom door shut, and she hurries to the toy shelf to get three shiny cars, which she puts into the garage beside the man. She has answered my "question": She, indeed, does not wish the toy girl to give to her mother what is her mother's, and she is eager to give to her father more than he could ask for.

I am still pondering over the power of her aggressive exuberance when she, in turn, seems suddenly overpowered by an entirely different set of emotions. She bursts into tears and into a desperate whimper, "Where is my mummy?" In panicky haste she takes a handful of pencils from my desk and runs out into the waiting room. Pressing the pencils into her mother's hand, she sits down close to her. The thumb goes back into the mouth, the child's face becomes uncommunicative, and I can see the game is over. The mother wants to give the pencils back to me, but I indicate that I do not need them today. Mother and child leave.

Half an hour later the telephone rings. They have hardly reached home when the little girl asks her mother whether she may see me again that same day. Tomorrow is not nearly enough. She insists with signs of despair that the mother call me immediately for an appointment the same day so that she may return the pencils. I must assure the child over the phone that I appreciate her intentions but that she is quite welcome to keep the pencils until the next day.

The next day, at the appointed time, Ann sits beside her mother in the waiting room. In the one hand she holds the pencils, unable to give them to me. In the other she clutches a small object. She shows no inclination to come with me. It suddenly becomes quite noticeable that she has soiled herself. As she is picked up to be taken to the bathroom, the pencils fall to the floor and with them the object from the other hand. It is a tiny toy dog, one of whose legs has been broken off.

I must add here the information that at this time a neighbor's dog plays a significant role in the child's life. This dog soils too; but he is beaten for it, and the child is not. And the dog, too, has recently been knocked down by a car; but he has lost a leg. Her friend in the animal world, then, is much like herself, only more so; and he is much worse off. Does she expect (or maybe even wish) to be punished likewise?

I have now described the circumstances of a play episode and of an infantile symptom. I shall not go further here into the relativities and relevances which led up to the described situation; nor shall I relate how the deadlock was finally resolved in work with parents and child. I appreciate and share the regret of many a reader that we are not able here to pursue the therapeutic process and, in fact, the passing of this infantile crisis. Instead I must ask the reader to accept this story as a "specimen" and to analyze it with me.

The little girl had not come of her own free will. She had merely let herself be brought by the very mother against whom, as everything indicated, her sullenness was directed. Once in my room, my quiet play apparently had made her forget for a moment that her mother was outside. What she would not have been able to say in words in many hours she could express in a few minutes of nonverbal communication: She "hated" her mother and she "loved" her father. Having expressed this, however, she must have experienced what Adam did when he heard God's voice: "Adam, where art thou?" She was compelled to atone for her deed, for she loved her mother too and needed her. In her very panic, however, she did compulsively what ambivalent people always do: In turning to make amends to one person they "inadvertently" do harm to another. So she took my pencils to appease the mother, and then wanted to force the mother to help her make restitution.

The next day her eagerness to conciliate me is paralyzed. I think I had become the tempter who makes children confess in unguarded moments what nobody should know or say. Children often have such a reaction after an initial admission of secret thoughts. What if I told her mother? What if her mother refused to bring her back to me so she could modify and qualify her unguarded acts? So she refused to act altogether, and let her symptom speak.

Soiling represents a sphincter conflict, an anal and urethral problem. This aspect of the matter we shall call the zonal aspect, because it concerns a *body zone*. On closer review, however, it becomes clear that this child's behavior, even where it is not anal in a zonal sense, has the quality of a sphincter problem. One may almost say that the whole little girl acts like a multiple sphincter. In her facial expression, as well as in her emotional communication, she closes up most of the time, to open up rarely and spasmodically. As we offer her a toy situation so that she may reveal and commit herself in its "unreality," she performs two acts: She closes, in vigorous defiance, the bathroom door of the toy house, and she gives in manic glee three shiny cars to the father doll. More and more deeply involved in the opposition of the simple modalities of taking and giving, she gives to the mother what she took from me and then wants desperately to return to me what she has given to her mother. Back again, her tense little hands hold pencils and toy tight, yet drop them abruptly, as equally suddenly the sphincters proper release their contents.

Obviously then, this little girl, unable to master the problem of how to give without taking (maybe how to love her father without robbing her mother) falls back on an automatic alternation of retentive and eliminative acts. This alternation of holding on and letting go, of withholding and giving, of opening up and closing up, we shall call the *mode* aspect of the matter. The anal-urethral sphincters, then, are the anatomic models for the *retentive* and *eliminative* modes, which, in turn, can characterize a great variety of behaviors, all of which, according to a now widespread clinical habit (and I mean bad habit) would be referred to as "anal."

A similar relationship between a zone and a mode can be seen in this child's moments of most pronounced babyishness. She becomes all mouth and thumb, as if a milk of consolation were flowing through this contact of her very own body parts. She is now "oral." But upon uncoiling from this withdrawal into herself, the young lady can become quite animated indeed, kicking the doll and grasping the cars with a flushed face and a throaty laugh. From the retentive-eliminative position then, an avenue of regression seems to lead further inward (isolation) and backward (regression), while a progressive and aggressive avenue leads outward and forward, toward an initiative which, however, immediately causes guilt. This, then, circumscribes the kind of aggravated crisis in which a child and a family may need help.

. . . In order to demonstrate further the systematic relationship between zones and modes, I shall describe a second episode, concerning a little boy.

I had been told that Peter was retaining his bowel movements, first for a few days at a time, but more recently up to a week. I was urged to hurry when, in addition to a week's supply of fecal matter, Peter had incorporated and retained a large enema in his small, four-year-old body. He looked miserable, and when he thought nobody watched him he leaned his bloated abdomen against a wall for support.

His pediatrician had come to the conclusion that this feat could not have been accomplished without energetic support from the emotional side, although he suspected what was later revealed by X-ray, namely that the boy indeed had by then an enlarged colon. While a tendency toward colonic expansion may initially have contributed to the creation of the symptom, the child was now undoubtedly paralyzed by a conflict which he was unable to verbalize. The local physiological condition was to be taken care of later by diet and exercise. First it seemed necessary to understand the conflict and to establish communication with the boy as quickly as possible so that his co-operation might be obtained.

It has been my custom before deciding to take on a family problem to have a meal with the family in their home. I was introduced to my prospective little patient as an acquaintance of the parents who wanted to come and meet the whole family. The little boy was one of those children who make me question the wisdom of any effort at disguise. "Aren't dreams wonderful?" he said to me in a decidedly artificial tone as we sat down to lunch. While his older brothers ate heartily and quickly and then took to the woods behind the house, he improvised almost feverishly a series of playful statements which, as will be clear presently, revealed his dominant and disturbing fantasy. It is characteristic of the ambivalent aspect of sphincter problems that the patients surrender almost obsessively the very secret which is so strenuously retained in their bowels. I shall list here some of Peter's dreamy statements and my silent reflections upon them.

"I wish I had a little elephant right here in my house. But then it would grow and grow and burst the house."—The boy is eating at the moment. His intestinal bulk is growing to the bursting point.

"Look at that bee—it wants to get at the sugar in my stomach."—"Sugar" sounds euphemistic, but it does transmit the thought that he has something valuable in his stomach and that somebody wants to get at it.

"I had a bad dream. Some monkeys climbed up and down the house and tried to get in to me."—The bees wanted to get at the sugar in his stomach: Now the monkeys want to get at him in his house. Increasing food in his stomach—growing baby elephant in the house—bees after sugar in his stomach —monkeys after him in the house.

After lunch coffee was served in the garden. Peter sat down underneath a garden table, pulled the chairs in toward himself as if barricading himself, and said, "Now I am in my tent and the bees can't get at me." —Again he is inside an enclosure, endangered by intrusive animals.

He then climbed out and showed me to his room. I admired his books and said, "Show me the picture you like best in the book you like best." Without hesitation he produced an illustration showing a gingerbread man floating in water toward the open mouth of a swimming wolf. Excitedly he said, "The wolf is going to eat the gingerbread man, but it won't hurt the gingerbread man because [loudly] *he's not alive*, and food can't feel it when you eat it!" I thoroughly agreed with him, reflecting in the meantime that the boy's playful sayings converged on the idea that whatever he had accumulated in his stomach was alive and in danger of either "bursting" him or of being hurt. I asked him to show me the picture he liked next best in any of the other books. He immediately went after a book called "The Little Engine That Could" and looked for a page which showed a smoke-puffing train going into a tunnel, while on the next page it comes out of it—its funnel *not smoking*. "You see," he said, "the train went into the tunnel and in the dark tunnel it *went dead*!" Something alive went into a dark passage and came out dead. I no longer doubted that this little boy had a fantasy that he was filled with something precious and alive; that if he kept it, it would burst him and that if he released it, it might come out hurt or dead. In other words, he was pregnant.

The patient needed immediate help, by interpretation. I want to make it clear that I do not approve of imposing sexual enlightenment on unsuspecting children before a reliable relationship has been established. Here, however, I felt "surgical" action was called for. I came back to his love for little elephants and suggested that we draw elephants. After we had reached a certain proficiency in drawing all the outer appointments and appendages of an elephant lady and of a couple of elephant babies, I asked whether he knew where the elephant babies came from. Tensely he said he did not, although I had the impression that he merely wanted to lead me on. So I drew as well as I could a cross section of the elephant lady and of her inner compartments, making it quite clear that there were two exits, one for the bowels and one for the babies. "This," I said, "some children do not know. They think that the bowel movements and the babies come out of the same opening in animals and in women." Before I could expand on the dangers which one could infer from such misunderstood conditions, he very excitedly told me that when his mother had carried him she had had to wear a belt which kept him from falling out of her when she sat on the toilet; and that he had proved too big for her opening so she had to have a cut made in her stomach to let him out. I had not known that he had been born by cesarean section, but I drew him a diagram of a woman, setting him straight on what he remembered of his mother's explanations. I added that it seemed to me that he thought he, too, could have babies, that while this was impossible in reality it was important to understand the reason for his fantasy; that, as he might have heard, I made it my business to understand children's thoughts and that, if he wished, I would come back the next day to continue our conversation. He did wish; and he had a superhuman bowel movement after I left.

There was no doubt, then, that once having bloated his abdomen with retained fecal matter this boy thought he might be pregnant and was afraid to let go lest he hurt himself or "the baby." But what had made him retain in the first place? What had caused in him an emotional conflict at this time which found its expression in bowel retention and a pregnancy fantasy?

The boy's father gave me a key to one immediate "cause" of the deadlock. "You know," he said, "that

boy begins to look just like Myrtle." "Who is Myrtle?" "She was his nurse for two years; she left three months ago." "Shortly before his symptoms became so much worse?" "Yes."

Peter, then, has lost an important person in his life: his nurse. A soft-spoken Oriental girl with a gentle touch, she had been his main comfort for years because his parents were out often, both pursuing professional careers. In recent months he had taken to attacking the nurse in a roughhousing way, and the girl had seemed to accept and quietly enjoy his decidedly "male" approach. In the nurse's homeland such behavior is not only not unusual, it is the rule. But there it makes sense, as part of the whole culture. Peter's mother, so she admitted, could not quite suppress a feeling that there was something essentially wrong about the boy's sudden maleness and about the way it was permitted to manifest itself; and, indeed, it did not quite fit *her* culture. She became alerted to the problem of having her boy brought up by a foreigner, and she decided to take over herself.

Thus it was during a period of budding, provoked, and disapproved masculinity that the nurse left. Whether she left or was sent away hardly mattered to the child. What mattered was that he lived in a social class which provides paid mother substitutes from a different race or class. Seen from the children's point of view this poses a number of problems. If you like your ersatz mother, your mother will leave you more often and with a better conscience. If you mildly dislike her, your mother will leave you with mild regret. If you dislike her very much and can provoke convincing incidents, your mother will send her away—only to hire somebody like her or worse. And if you happen to like her very much in your own way or in her own way, your mother will surely send her away sooner or later.

In Peter's case, insult was added to injury by a letter from the nurse, who had heard of his condition and who was now trying her best to explain to him why she had left. She had originally told him that she was leaving in order to marry and was going to have a baby of her own. This had been bad enough in view of the boy's feelings for her. Now she informed him that she had taken another job instead. "You see," she explained, "I always move on to another family when the child in my care becomes too big. I like best to tend babies." It was then that something happened to the boy. He had tried to be a big boy. His father had been of little help because he was frequently absent, preoccupied with a business which was too complicated to explain to his son. His mother had indicated that male behavior in the form provoked or condoned by the nurse was unacceptable behavior. The nurse liked babies better.

So he "regressed." He became babyish and dependent, and in desperation, lest he lose more, *he held on*. This he had done before. Long ago, as a baby, he had demonstrated his first stubbornness by holding food in his mouth. Later, put on the toilet and told not to get up until he had finished, he did not finish and he did not get up until his mother gave up. Now he held on to his bowels—and to much more, for he also became tight-lipped, expressionless, and rigid. All of this, of course, was one symptom with a variety of related meanings. The simplest meaning was: I am holding on to what I have got and I am not going to move, either forward or backward. But as we saw from his play, the object of his holding on could be interpreted in a variety of ways. Apparently at first, believing the nurse to be pregnant, he tried to hold on to her by becoming the nurse and by pretending that he was pregnant too. His general regression, at the same time, demonstrated that he, too, was a baby and thus as small as any child the nurse might have turned to. Freud called this the *overdetermination* of the meaning of a symptom. The overdetermining items, however, are always systematically related: The boy identifies with *both partners of a lost relationship;* he is the nurse who is now with child and he is the baby whom she likes to tend. Identifications which result from losses are like that. In mourning, we become the lost person *and* we become again the person we were when the relationship was at its prime. This makes for much seemingly contradictory symptomatology.

Yet, we can see that here *retention* is the mode and the eliminative tract the model zone used to dramatize holding back, holding on, and holding in. But once it looked and felt as if he did indeed have the equivalent of a baby in him, he remembered what his mother had said about birth and about the danger of birth to mother and child. He could not let go.

The interpretation of this fear to him resulted in a dramatic improvement which released the immediate discomfort and danger and brought out the boy's inhibited autonomy and boyish initiative. But only a combination of dietetic and gymnastic work as well as interviews with mother and child could finally overcome a number of milder setbacks.

LIBIDO AND AGGRESSION

We are now acquainted with two pathological episodes, one in the life of a girl and one in that of a boy. These incidents were chosen because of their clear and observable structures. But what kinds of laws can account for such happenings?

Freud and the early psychoanalysts first pointed to the psychologically uncharted regions of the body's orifices as zones of vital importance for emotional health and illness. To be sure, their theories were based on the observation of adult patients, and it may be worth while to indicate briefly in what way an adult patient observed in psychoanalysis may offer an analogy to what we have seen in our child patients.

An adult's neurotic "anality" may, for example, express itself in a ritualistic overconcern with his bowel functions, under the guise of meticulous hygiene, or a general need for absolute order, cleanliness, and punctuality. In other words, he would seem to be anti-anal rather than anal; he would be averse to either prolonged retention or careless elimination. But his very anti-anal avoidances would make him at the end spend more thought and energy on anal matters than, say, an ordinary person with a mild tendency toward the enjoyment or repudiation of bowel satisfactions. Such a patient's conflict over the modes of retention and elimination might express itself in a general over-restraint, now firmly entrenched in his character. He would not be able to let go: He would allot his time, his money, and his affection (in whatever order) only under carefully ritualized conditions and at appointed times. Psychoanalysis, however, would reveal that, more or less consciously, he entertains peculiarly messy fantasies and violently hostile wishes of total elimination against selected individuals, especially those close to him who by necessity are forced to make demands on his inner treasures. In other words, he would reveal himself as highly ambivalent in his loves, and often as quite unaware of the fact that the many arbitrary rights and wrongs which guard his personal restraints constitute at the same time autocratic attempts at controlling others. While his deeds of passive and retentive hostility often remain unrecognizable to him and to his intended victims, he would be constantly compelled to undo, to make amends, to atone for something done in fact or fantasy. But like our little girl after she had tried to balance her withholdings and givings, he would only find himself in ever deeper conflicts. And like her, the adult compulsive would, deep down, have a stubborn wish for punishment because to his conscience—and he has a peculiarly severe conscience—it seems easier to be punished than to harbor secret hate and go free. It seems easier because his egocentric hate has made him mistrust the redeeming features of mutuality. Thus, what in the child is still free for manifold expression and amelioration in the adult has become fixed character.

In the reconstructed early history of such cases Freud regularly found crises of the kind demonstrated *in statu nascendi* by our child patients. We owe to him the first consistent theory which took systematic account of the tragedies and comedies which center in the apertures of the body. He created this theory by cutting through the hypocrisy and artificial forgetfulness of his time which kept all of man's "lower" functions in the realms of shame, of questionable wit, and of morbid imagination. He was forced to conclude that the nature of these tragedies and comedies was sexual, and as such he determined to describe them. For he found that neurotics and perverts are not only infantile in their attitudes toward their fellow men, but also regularly impaired in their genital sexuality and given to overt or covert gratifications and comforts from other than genital body zones. Moreover, their sexual impairment and their social infantility are all systematically related to their early childhood and particularly to clashes between the impulses of their infantile bodies and the inexorable training methods of their parents. He concluded that during successive stages of childhood zones providing special gratification were endowed with *libido*, a pleasure-seeking energy which before Freud had received official and scientific recognition as *sexual* only when it became *genital* at the conclusion of childhood. Mature genital sexuality, he concluded, is the end product of an infantile sexual development, which he consequently called *pregenitality*. Thus, the kind of compulsive neurotic whom we have just described was to Freud an individual who although overtly anti-anal, was unconsciously *fixated* on or partially *regressed* to a stage of infantile sexuality called the *anal-sadistic* stage.

Similarly, other emotional afflictions prove to be fixations or regressions to other infantile zones and stages.

Addicts, for example, depend, as the baby once did, on the incorporation by mouth or skin of substances which make them feel both physically satiated and emotionally restored. But they are not aware that they yearn to be babies again. Only as they whine and boast and challenge are their disappointed and babyish souls revealed.

Manic-depressive patients, on the other hand, feel hopelessly empty, without substance; or full of something bad and hostile that needs to be destroyed; or again, so permeated with sudden goodness that their sense of power and exuberance knows no bounds and accepts no limitations. Yet they do not know either the source or the nature of all these inner goodnesses and badnesses.

Hysterics, if they are women, act as if strangely victimized, attacked and revolted by things and yet fascinated by them: While genitally frigid, they are preoccupied with events which, on analysis, dramatize the woman's inceptive role. They are unconsciously obsessed with their sexual role, although (or because) it became unacceptable far back in childhood.

All these tormented people, then, whether addicted, depressed, or inhibited, have somehow failed to integrate one or another of the infantile stages, and they defend themselves against these infantile patterns—stubbornly, wastefully, unsuccessfully.

On the other hand, for each omission by repression there is a corresponding commission by perversion. There are those adults who, far from disguising the original infantile pattern, receive the most complete sexual gratification they are capable of from stimulation received or given by the mouth. There are those who prefer the anus to other orifices which lend themselves to intercourse. And there are perverts who above all want to gaze at the genitals or display their own; and those who want to use them, impulsively and promiscuously, for the mere sadistic "making" of other human beings.

Having at last understood the systematic relationship between sexual acts unconsciously desired by neurotics and acts overtly committed by perverts, Freud proceeded to erect the edifice of his libido theory. *Libido*, then, is that sexual energy with which zones other than the genital are endowed in childhood and which enhances with specific pleasures such vital functions as the intake of food, the regulation of the bowels, and the motion of the limbs. Only after a certain schedule of such pregenital uses of libido is successfully resolved does the child's sexuality graduate to a short-lived infantile genitality, which must immediately become more or less "latent," transformed, and deflected. For the genital machinery is still immature; and the first objects of immature sexual desire are forever barred by universal incest taboos.

As to the remnants of pregenital desires, all cultures permit to a degree some kinds of nongenital sexual play which should be called perversion only if they tend to replace and crowd out the dominance of genuine genitality. A significant amount of the pregenital libido, however, is *sublimated*—i.e., is diverted from sexual to nonsexual aims. Thus a measure of infantile curiosity concerning the "doings" in the mother's body may reinforce man's eagerness to understand the workings of machines and of test tubes; or he may eagerly absorb the "milk of wisdom" where he once desired more tangible fluids from more sensuous containers; or he may collect all kinds of things in all kinds of boxes instead of overloading his colon. In pregenital trends which are *repressed*, instead of outgrown, sublimated, or admitted to sex play, Freud saw the most important source of neurotic tension.

Most successful sublimations are, of course, part and parcel of cultural trends and become unrecognizable as sexual derivatives. Only where the preoccupation appears to be too strenuous, too bizarre, too monomanic, can its "sexual" origin be recognized in adults; but at that point the sublimation is on the verge of breaking up—and it was probably faulty at the beginning. It is here that Freud, the physician, became a critic of his Victorian age. Society, so he concluded, is too blindly autocratic in demanding impossible feats of sublimation from her children. True, some sexual energy can and must be sublimated; society depends on it. Therefore, by all means, render unto society that which is society's; but first render unto the child that libidinal vitality which makes worthwhile sublimations possible.

Only those who specialize in the extreme intricacies of mental disturbances and of ordinary mental quirks can fully appreciate what clear and unifying light was thrown into these dark recesses by the theory of a libido, of a mobile sexual energy which contributes to the "highest" as well as to the "lowest" forms of human endeavor—and often to both at the same time.

. . . To Freud . . . it was a genital idea, not a genital organ, which had become dissociated from its goal, causing blocking in the libidinal supply to the genitals (frigidity). The libidinal supply could be converted and displaced along the pathway of some symbolic association with infantile zones and modes.

A retching throat, then, may express defensive ejection above, warding off repressed genital hunger below. To express the fact that libidinization withdrawn from the genitals thus manifests itself elsewhere, Freud used the thermodynamic language of his day, the language of the preservation and transformation of energy. The result was that much that was meant to be a working hypothesis appeared to be making concrete claims which neither observation nor experiment could even attempt to substantiate.

Great innovators always speak in the analogies and parables of their day. Freud, too, had to have the courage to accept and to work with what he himself called his "mythology." True insight survives its first formulation.

. . . Early psychoanalysis . . . describes human motivation as if libido were the prime substance, individual egos being mere defensive buffers and vulnerable layers between this substance and a vague surrounding "outer world" of arbitrary and hostile social conventions.

. . . By delineating the life of the libido, Freud expanded our theoretical acumen as well as our therapeutic effectiveness over all those impairments of individual and group life which stem from the meaningless mismanagement of sensuality. It was clear to him, and it becomes clearer to us—who deal with new areas of the mind (ego), with different kinds of patients (children, psychotics), with new applications of psychoanalysis (society)—that we must search for the proper place of the libido theory in the totality of human life. While we must continue to study the life cycles of individuals by delineating the possible vicissitudes of their libido, we must become sensitive to the danger of forcing living persons into the role of marionettes of a mythical Eros—to the gain of neither therapy nor theory.

Freud the investigator, in turn, went beyond Freud the doctor. He did more than explain and cure pathology. Being by training a developmental physiologist, Freud showed that sexuality develops in stages, a growth which he firmly linked with all epigenetic development.

* * *

From the point of view of the individual child's "libido economy" . . . we would say that in our two patients the rate and the sequence of budding impulses had been disturbed: They were stuck on the theme of anal retention and elimination like a phonograph record with a faulty groove. They repeatedly regressed to babyish themes and repeatedly failed in their attempts to advance to the next theme, the management of their love for significant people of the opposite sex. Ann's love for her father was suggested by the great release of manic joy when she gave three shiny cars to the toy father; while in Peter's case his phallic behavior toward the nurse had immediately preceded the pathogenic events. The libido theory would suggest that the rectal expulsion in the one case and the colonic accumulation in the other had at one time given these children sexual pleasure which they were now trying to regain—only that their by now faulty brake system made them regress further and faster than anticipated. Yet, no longer being innocent infants enjoying as yet untrained bowels, these children apparently indulged in fantasies of expelling hated persons (remember how Ann kicked the mother doll) and retaining loved ones; while the effect of what they did, in all its terrifying consequences, constituted a sadistic triumph over the parent who wished to control them. There is no doubt that there was triumph as well as fear in the eyes of that little girl when she sat in her mess in the early morning and watched her mother come in; and there was a quiet satisfaction in the boy's remote face even when he was manifestly bloated and uncomfortable. But the poor mothers knew from short and intensely painful experiment that to react to the child's tyranny with angry methods would only make things worse. For say what you wish, these children loved and wanted to be loved and they very much preferred the joy of accomplishment to the triumph of hateful failure. Do not mistake a child for his symptom.

Here some would say that children when undergoing such experiences are at the mercy of that second primeval power the assumption of which followed the concept of the libido in the psychoanalytic system—namely, an instinct of destruction, of death. I shall not be able to discuss this problem here, because it is essentially a philosophical one, based on Freud's original commitment to a mythology of primeval instincts. His nomenclature and the discussion which ensued have blurred the clinical study of a force which will be seen to pervade much of our material without finding essential clarification; I refer to the *rage* which is aroused whenever action vital to the individual's sense of mastery is prevented or inhibited. What becomes of such rage when it, in turn, must be suppressed and what its contributions are to man's irrational enmity and eagerness to destroy, is obviously one of the most fateful questions facing psychology.

In order to determine more concretely what kinds of forces are operative in a given clinical situation, it may be more profitable to ask what it is that we are called upon to accomplish. Maybe by clarifying our function in the situation we can come to grips with the forces which we are trying to understand. I would say it is our task to re-establish a mutuality of functioning between the child patient and his parents so that instead of a number of fruitless, painful, and destructive attempts at controlling one another, a mutual regulation is established which restores self-control in both child and parent.

*　　*　　*

What we must try to chart . . . is the approximate sequence of stages when according to clinical and common knowledge the nervous excitability as well as the co-ordination of the "erogenous" organs and the selective reactivity of significant people in the environment are apt to produce decisive encounters.

7.

ERIKSON, ERIK H.

Growth and Crises of the "Healthy Personality"*

The psychoanalyst knows relatively more about the dynamic and cure of the disturbances which he treats daily than about the prevention of such disturbances. He must remember, too, that the prevention and even the cure of disease only foster the necessary condition for health. A person who is not sick is not necessarily healthy in every sense of the word. Health implies a state of surplus energy, vitality, and awareness. In regard to physical well-being, it is understood that the presence of health is more than the absence of disease, although widespread epidemiological prevention is necessary to keep people alive and free from disease. It is a strange fact in our civilization . . . that the expert on mental disease is being forced, often not so very much against his will, into the role of the expert on mental health. But in the long run we want to do more than immunize our children against neurotic suffering. Prevention, based on what we know about disease, is only a necessary beginning. Strictly speaking, we cannot even be sure

* Reprinted from Kluckhohn, C. et al.: *Personality in Nature, Society, and Culture*, (1955), pp. 185–225. New York: Alfred A. Knopf. Used with the permission of the Josiah Macy, Jr. Foundation.

that we know what causes neurotic suffering until we have an idea of the nature of real health. This we have only begun to investigate.

*　　*　　*

I consider it my task to approach the matter of the healthy personality from the genetic point of view: How does a healthy personality grow or, as it were, accrue from the successive stages of increasing capacity to master life's outer and inner tasks and dangers?

I

ON HEALTH AND GROWTH

Whenever we try to understand growth, it is well to remember the *epigenetic principle* which is derived from the growth of organisms *in utero*. Somewhat generalized, this principle states that anything that grows has a *ground plan*, and that out of this ground plan the *parts* arise, each part having its *time* of special ascendancy, until all parts have arisen to form a *functioning whole*. . . . At birth the baby leaves the chemical exchange of the womb for the social exchange system of his society, where his gradually increasing capacities meet the opportunities and limitations of his culture. How the maturing organism continues to unfold, not by developing new organs, but by a prescribed sequence of locomotor, sensory, and social capacities, is described in the child-development literature. Psychoanalysis has given us an understanding of the more idiosyncratic experiences, and especially the inner conflicts, which constitute the manner in which an individual becomes a distinct personality. But here, too, it is important to realize that in the sequence of his most personal experiences the healthy child, given a reasonable amount of guidance, can be trusted to obey inner laws of development, laws which create a *succession of potentialities for a significant interaction* with those who tend him. While such interaction varies from culture to culture, it must remain within the *proper rate and the proper sequence* which govern the *growth of a personality* as well as that of an organism. . . . Personality can be said to develop according to steps predetermined in the human organism's readiness to be driven toward, to be aware of, and to interact with, a widening social radius, beginning with the dim image of a mother and ending with mankind, or at any rate that segment of mankind which "counts" in the particular individual's life.

It is for this reason that, in the presentation of stages in the development of the personality, we employ an *epigenetic diagram* analogous to one previously employed for an analysis of Freud's psychosexual stages. It is, in fact, the purpose of this presentation to bridge the theory of infantile sexuality (without repeating it here in detail), and our knowledge of the child's physical and social growth within his family and the social structure. . . .

[E]ach item of the healthy personality to be discussed is systematically related to all others, and . . . they all depend on the proper development at the proper time of each item; and . . . each item exists in some form before "its" decisive and critical time normally arrives.

* * *

If I say, for example, that a sense of *basic trust* is the first component of mental health to develop in life, a *sense of autonomous will* the second, and a *sense of initiative* the third, the purpose of the diagram may become clearer.

First Stage (about first year)	BASIC TRUST	Earlier form of AUTONOMY	Earlier form of INITIATIVE
Second Stage (about second and third years)	Later form of BASIC TRUST	AUTONOMY	Earlier form of INITIATIVE
Third Stage (about fourth and fifth years)	Later form of BASIC TRUST	Later form of AUTONOMY	INITIATIVE

This diagrammatic statement . . . is meant to express a number of fundamental relations that exist among the three components, as well as a few fundamental facts for each.

Each comes to its ascendance, meets its crisis, and finds its lasting solution (in ways to be presently described in detail) toward the end of the stages mentioned. However, this does not mean that they begin there nor that they end there. All of them begin with the beginning, in some form, although we do not make a point of this fact, and we shall not confuse things by calling these components different names at earlier or later stages. A baby may show something like "autonomy" from the beginning, for example, in the particular way in which he angrily tries to wriggle his head free when tightly held. However, under normal conditions, it is not until the second year that he begins to experience the whole *critical alternative between being an autonomous creature and being a dependent one;* and it is not until then that he is ready for a *decisive encounter* with his environment, an environment which, in turn, feels called upon to convey to him its *particular ideas and concepts of autonomy and coercion* in ways decisively contributing to the character, the efficiency, and the health of his personality in his culture.

It is this *encounter*, together with the resulting crisis, which is to be described for each stage. Each stage becomes a *crisis* because incipient growth and awareness in a significant part-function goes together with a shift in instinctual energy and yet causes specific vulnerability in that part. One of the most difficult questions to decide, therefore, is whether or not a child at a given stage is weak or strong. Perhaps it would be best to say that he is always vulnerable in some respects and completely oblivious and insensitive in others, but that at the same time he is unbelievably persistent in the same respects in which he is vulnerable. It must be added that the smallest baby's weakness gives him power; out of his very dependence and weakness he makes signs to which his environment (if it is guided well by a responsiveness based both on instinctive and traditional patterns) is peculiarly sensitive. A baby's presence exerts a consistent and persistent domination over the outer and inner lives of every member of a household. Because these members must reorient themselves to accommodate his presence, they must also grow as individuals and as a group. It is as true to say that babies control and bring up their families as it is to say the converse. A family can bring up a baby only by being brought up by him. His growth consists of a series of challenges to them to serve his newly developing potentialities for social interaction.

Because of a radical *change in perspective*, each successive step is also a potential crisis. There is, at the beginning of life, the most radical change of all: from intrauterine to extrauterine life. But in postnatal existence, too, such radical adjustments of perspective as lying relaxed, sitting firmly, and running fast must all be accomplished in their own good time. In adult life they exist side by side; but adults "regress" along the familiar path: when tired by running (running after one thing or another) we sit down to rest and eat, and lie down to sleep. The interpersonal perspective, too, changes rapidly in early life, and often radically, as is testified by the proximity in time of such opposites as "not letting mother out of sight" and "wanting to be independent." As we proceed, it may seem to the reader as if we, too, were changing our perspective, as if even our conceptual approach changed from stage to stage; but this is to a large extent determined by the very different *capacities* which use different *opportunities* to become full-grown components of the ever new configuration that is the growing personality. In describing this growth and its crises as a development of a series of alternative basic attitudes, we take recourse to such terms as "a sense of autonomy," or "a sense of doubt." Like a "sense of health" or a "sense of not being well," such senses pervade surface and depth, consciousness and the unconscious. They are ways of experience, accessible to introspection; ways of behaving, observable by others; and objective inner states determinable by test and analysis. It is important to keep these three dimensions in mind, as we proceed.

II

BASIC TRUST VERSUS BASIC MISTRUST

1

For the first component of a healthy personality I nominate a sense of *basic trust*, which I think is an attitude toward oneself and the world derived from the experiences of the first year of life. By "trust" I mean what is commonly implied in reasonable trustfulness as far as others are concerned and a simple sense of trustworthiness as far as oneself is concerned. When I say "basic," I mean that neither this component nor any of those that follow are, either in childhood or in adulthood, especially conscious. In fact, all of these criteria, when developed in childhood and when integrated in adulthood, blend into the total personality. Their crises in childhood, however, and their impairment in adulthood are clearly circumscribed.

In *adults* the impairment of basic trust is expressed in a *basic mistrust* (which pervades much of what in psychiatry is called schizophrenia or paranoia). It characterizes individuals who withdraw into themselves in particular ways when at odds with themselves and with others. These ways, which often are not obvious, are more strikingly represented by individuals who regress into psychotic states in which they sometimes close up, refusing food and comfort and becoming oblivious to companionship. Insofar as we hope to assist them with psychotherapy, we must try to reach them again in specific ways in order to convince them that they can trust the world and that they can trust themselves.

It is from the knowledge of such radical regressions and of the deepest and most infantile layers in our not-so-sick patients that we have learned to regard basic trust as the cornerstone of a healthy personality. Let us see what justifies our placing the crisis and the ascendancy of this component at the beginning of life.

As the newborn is separated from his symbiosis with the mother's body, his inborn and more or less co-ordinated ability to take in by mouth meets the breasts' and the mother's and the society's more or less co-ordinated ability and intention to feed him and to welcome him. At this point he lives through, and loves with, his mouth; and the mother lives through, and loves with, her breasts.

For the mother this is a late and complicated accomplishment, highly dependent on her development as a woman; on her unconscious attitude toward the child; on the way she has lived through pregnancy and delivery; on her and her community's attitude toward the act of nursing—and on the response of the newborn. To him the mouth is the focus of a general first approach to life—the *incorporative* approach. In present-day psychiatry this stage is therefore usually referred to as the "oral" stage. Yet it is clear that, in addition to the overwhelming need for food, a baby is, or soon becomes, receptive in many other respects. As he is willing and able to suck on appropriate objects and to swallow whatever appropriate fluids they emit, he is soon also willing and able to "take in" with his eyes whatever enters his visual field. His tactual senses, too, seem to "take in" what feels good. In this sense, then, one could speak of an "*incorporative stage*," one in which he is, relatively speaking, receptive to what he is being offered. Yet many babies are sensitive and vulnerable, too. In order to ensure that their first experience in this world may not only keep them alive but also help them to co-ordinate their sensitive breathing and their metabolic and circulatory rhythms, we must see to it that we deliver to their senses stimuli as well as food in the proper intensity and at the right time; otherwise their willingness to accept may change abruptly into diffuse defense.

Now, while it is quite clear what *must* happen to keep a baby alive (the minimum supply necessary) and what *must not* happen, least he be physically damaged or chronically upset (the maximum early frustration tolerable), there is increasing leeway in regard to what *may* happen; and different cultures make extensive use of their prerogatives to decide what they consider workable and insist upon calling necessary. Some people think that a baby, lest he scratch his own eyes out, must necessarily be swaddled completely for the better part of the day and throughout the greater part of the first year; also, that he should be rocked or fed whenever he whimpers. Others think that he should feel the freedom of his kicking limbs as early as possible, but also that he, as a matter of course, be forced to cry "please" for his meals until he literally gets blue in the face. All of this depends on the culture's general aim and system. The writer has known some old American Indians who bitterly decried the way in which we often let our small babies cry because we believe that "it will make their lungs strong." No wonder (these Indians said) that the white man, after such an initial reception, seems to be in a hurry to get to the "next world." But the same Indians spoke proudly of the way their infants (breast fed into the second year) become blue in the face with fury when thumped on the head for "biting" the mother's nipples; here the Indians, in turn, believed that "it's going to make good hunters of them."

There seems to be some intrinsic wisdom, some unconscious planning, and much superstition in the seemingly arbitrary varieties of child training: what is "good for the child," what *may* happen to him, depends on what he is supposed to become and where. We shall come back to this.

The simplest and the earliest social modality is "to get," not in the sense of "go and get," but in that of receiving and accepting what is given; and this sounds easier than it is. For the groping and unstable newborn's organism learns this modality only as he learns to regulate his readiness to get with the methods of a mother who, in turn, will permit him to co-ordinate his means of getting as she develops and co-ordinates her means of giving. The mutuality of relaxation thus developed is of prime importance for the first experience of friendly otherness: from psychoanalysis one receives the impression that in thus *getting what is given*, and in learning to *get somebody to do* for him what he wishes to have done, the baby also develops the necessary ground to *get to be* the giver, to "identify" with her.

Where this mutual regulation fails, the situation falls apart into a variety of attempts to control by duress rather than by reciprocity. The baby will try to get by random activity what he cannot get by central suction; he will activate himself into exhaustion or he will find his thumb and damn the world. The mother's reaction may be to try to control matters by nervously changing hours, formulas, and procedures. One cannot be sure what this does to a baby; but it certainly is our clinical impression that in some sensitive individuals (or in individuals whose early frustration was never compensated for) such a situation can be a model for a radical disturbance in their relationship to the "world," to "people," and especially to loved or otherwise significant people.

There are ways of maintaining reciprocity by giving to the baby what he can get through good artificial nipples and other forms of feeding and by making up for what is missed orally through the satisfaction of other than oral receptors: his pleasure in being held, warmed, smiled at, talked to, rocked, and so forth. Besides such "horizontal" compensation (compensation during the same stage of development) there are many "longitudinal" compensations in life: compensations emerging from later stages of the life cycle.

During the "second oral" stage the ability and the pleasure in a more active and more directed incorporative approach ripens. The teeth develop and with them the pleasure in biting *on* hard things, in biting *through* things, and in biting *off* things. This *active incorporative* mode characterizes a variety of other activities (as did the first incorporative mode). The eyes, first part of a passive system of accepting impressions as they come along, have now learned to focus, to isolate, to "grasp"objects from the vaguer background and to follow them. The organs of hearing similarly have learned to discern significant sounds, to localize them, and to guide an appropriate change in position (lifting and turning the head, lifting and turning the upper body). The arms have learned to reach out determinedly and the hands to grasp firmly. As will be noted, we are more interested here in the overall *configuration* and *integration* of

developing approaches to the world than in the *first appearance of specific abilities.* . . .

With all of this a number of interpersonal patterns are established which center in the social modality of *taking* and *holding on to* things—things which are more or less freely offered and given, and things which have more or less a tendency to slip away. As the baby learns to change positions, to roll over, and very gradually to establish himself on the throne of his sedentary kingdom, he must perfect the mechanisms of grasping and appropriating, holding and chewing all that is within his reach.

The *crisis* of the oral stage (during the second part of the first year) is difficult to assess and more difficult to verify. It seems to consist of the coincidence in time of three developments: (1) a physiological one; namely, the general tension associated with a more violent drive to incorporate, appropriate, and observe more actively (a tension to which is added the discomfort of "teething" and other changes in the oral machinery); (2) a psychological one; namely, the infant's increasing awareness of himself as a distinct person; and (3) an environmental one; namely, the mother's apparent turning away from the baby toward pursuits which she had given up during late pregnancy and postnatal care. These pursuits include her full return to conjugal intimacy and may soon lead to a new pregnancy.

Where breast feeding lasts into the biting stage (and, generally speaking, this has been the rule) it is now necessary to learn how to continue sucking without biting, so that the mother may not withdraw the nipple in pain or anger. Our clinical work indicates that this point in the individual's early history provides him with some sense of basic loss, leaving the general impression that once upon a time one's unity with a maternal matrix was destroyed. Weaning, therefore, should not mean sudden loss of the breast and loss of the mother's reassuring presence too, unless, of course, other women can be depended upon to sound and feel much like the mother. A drastic loss of accustomed mother love without proper substitution at this time can lead (under otherwise aggravating conditions) to acute infantile depression or to a mild but chronic state of mourning which may give a depressive undertone to the whole remainder of life. But even under more favorable circumstances, this state seems to introduce into the psychic life a sense of division and a dim but universal nostalgia for a lost paradise.

It is against the combination of these impressions of having been deprived, of having been divided, and of having been abandoned, all of which leave a residue of basic mistrust, that basic trust must be established and maintained.

2

What we here call "trust" coincides with what Dr.

Therese Benedek has called "confidence." If I prefer the word "trust," it is because there is more naivete and more mutuality in it; an infant can be said to be trusting, but it would be assuming too much to say that he "has confidence." The general state of trust, furthermore, implies not only that one has learned to rely on the sameness and continuity of the outer providers but also that one may trust oneself and the capacity of one's own organs to cope with urges; that one is able to consider oneself trustworthy enough so that the providers will not need to be on guard or to leave.

In the psychiatric literature we find frequent references to an "oral character," which is a characterological deviation based on the unsolved conflicts of this stage and which expresses itself in more or less pathological and irrational ways of approaching the world (either too pessimistically or too optimistically) from the sense of being helpless and dependent (or from the sense) of being greedy and grasping, or worse. Wherever oral pessimism becomes dominant and exclusive, infantile fears, such as that of "being left empty," or simply of "being left," and also of being "starved of stimulation," can be discerned definitely in the depressive forms of "being empty" and of "being no good." Such fears, in turn, can give orality that particular avaricious quality which in psychiatry is called "oral sadism," that is, a cruel need to get and to take in ways harmful to others. But there is an optimistic oral character, too, one which has learned to make giving and receiving the most important thing in life; and there is "orality" as a normal substratum in all individuals, a lasting residum, of this first period of dependency on powerful providers. It normally expresses itself in our dependencies and nostalgias, and in our all too hopeful and all too hopeless states.

The pathology and irrationality of these trends depend entirely on the degree to which they are integrated with the rest of the personality (unity of personality) and the degree to which they fit into the general cultural pattern and use approved interpersonal techniques for their expression. The integration of the oral stage with all the following ones results in a combination of faith and realism.

Here, as elsewhere, we must, therefore, consider as a topic for discussion the expression of *infantile urges* in *cultural patterns* which one may (or may not) consider a pathological deviation in the total economic or moral system of a culture or a nation. One could speak, for example, of the invigorating belief in "chance," that traditional prerogative of American trust in one's own resourcefulness and in Fate's store of good intentions. This belief, at times, can be seen to degenerate in large-scale gambling; or in "taking chances" in the form of an arbitrary and often suicidal provocation of Fate; or in the insistence that one has not only the right to an equal chance but also the privilege of being preferred over all others who have invested in the same general enterprise. In a similar way all the pleasant reassurances which can be derived (especially in good company) from old and new taste sensations, from inhaling and imbibing, from munching and swallowing and digesting, can turn into mass addictions neither expressive of, nor conducive to, the kind of basic trust which we have in mind.

Here we are obviously touching on phenomena the analysis of which would call for a comprehensive approach both to personality and to culture. This would be true also for an epidemiological approach to the problem of the oral character, the schizoid character, and the mental diseases seemingly expressive of an underlying weakness in oral reassurance and basic trust.

A related problem for discussion is the belief (reflected in much of the contemporary obstetric and pediatric concern with the methods of child care) that the establishment of a basic sense of trust in earliest childhood makes adult individuals less dependent on mild or malignant forms of addiction, on self-delusion, and on the needs for avaricious appropriation. Of this, little is known; and the question remains whether healthy orality makes for a healthy culture or a healthy culture makes for healthy orality, or both.

At any rate the psychiatrists, obstetricians, pediatricians, and anthropologists, to whom the writer feels closest, today would agree that *the firm establishment of enduring patterns for the balance of basic trust over basic mistrust* is the first task of the budding personality and therefore first of all a task for maternal care. But it must be said that *the amount of trust* derived from earliest infantile experience does not seem to depend on absolute *quantities of food or demonstrations of love* but rather on the *quality* of the maternal relationship. Mothers create a sense of trust in their children by that kind of administration which in its quality combines sensitive care of the baby's individual needs and a firm sense of personal trustworthiness within the trusted framework of their community's life style. (This forms the basis in the child for a sense of identity which will later combine a sense of being "all right," of being oneself, and of becoming what other people trust one will become.) Parents must not only have certain ways of guiding by prohibition and permission; they must also be able to represent to the child a deep, an almost somatic conviction that there is a meaning to what they are doing. In this sense a traditional system of child care can be said to be a factor making for trust, even where certain items of that tradition, taken singly, may seem unnecessarily cruel. Here much depends on whether such items are inflicted on the child by the parent in the firm traditional belief that this is the only way to do things or whether the parent misuses his administration of the baby and the child in order to work off anger, alleviate fear, or win an argument, with the child or with somebody else (her mother, her husband, her doctor, or her priest). This latter kind of situation we shall refer to as the parental *exploitation of the inequality* between adult and child.

In times of change—and what other times are there, in our memory?—one generation differs so much from another that items of tradition often become disturbances. Conflicts between mother's ways, and one's own self-made ways, conflicts between the expert's advice and mother's ways, and conflicts between the expert's authority and one's own self-willed ways may disturb a mother's trust in herself. Furthermore, all the mass transformations in American life (immigration, migration, and Americanization; industrialization, urbanization, mechanization, and others) are apt to disturb young mothers in those tasks which are so simple yet so far-reaching. . . .

III

AUTONOMY VERSUS SHAME AND DOUBT

1

A survey of some of the items discussed in Dr. Spock's book under the major headings "The One-Year-Old" and "Managing Young Children" will enable those of us who, at this time, do not have such inquisitive creatures in our homes to remember our skirmishes, our victories, and our defeats:

196. Feeling his oats.
197. The passion to explore.
199. He gets more dependent and more independent at the same time.
203. Arranging the house for a wandering baby.
204. Avoiding accidents.
      Now's the time to put poisons out of reach.
206. How do you make him leave certain things alone?
207. Dropping and throwing things.
255. Children learn to control their own aggressive feelings.
256. Biting humans.
261. Keeping bedtime happy.
264. The small child who won't stay in bed at night.

My selection is intended to convey the inventory and range of problems described, though I cannot review here either the doctor's excellent advice or his good balance in depicting the remarkable ease and matter-of-factness with which the nursery may be governed at this as at any other stage. Nevertheless, there is an indication of the sinister forces which are leashed and unleashed, especially in the guerilla warfare of unequal wills; for the child is often unequal to his own violent drives, and parent and child unequal to each other.

The over-all significance of this stage lies in the maturation of the muscle system, the consequent ability (and doubly felt inability) to co-ordinate a number of highly conflicting action patterns such as "holding on" and "letting go," and the enormous value with which the still highly dependent child begins to endow his autonomous will.

Whereas psychoanalysis has enriched our vocabulary with the word "orality" to designate the importance of the mouth in the first year, it has added the term "anality" to include the particular pleasureableness and willfulness which attaches to the eliminative organs at one or another period at this stage. The whole procedure of evacuating the bowels and the bladder as completely as possible is, of course, enhanced from the beginning by a premium of "feeling good" which says in effect, "well done." This premium, at the beginning of life, must make up for quite frequent discomfort and tension suffered as the bowels learn to do their daily work. Two developments gradually give these "anal" experiences the necessary volume; the arrival of better formed stool and the general co-ordination of the muscle system which permits the development of voluntary release, of dropping and throwing away. This new dimension of approach to things, however, is not restricted to the sphincters. A general ability, indeed, a violent need, develops to drop and to throw away and to alternate witholding and expelling at will.

As far as anality proper is concerned, at this point everything depends on whether the cultural environment wants to make something of it. There are cultures where the parents ignore anal behavior and leave it to older children to lead the toddler out to the bushes so that his compliance in this matter may coincide with his wish to imitate the bigger ones. Our Western civilization, and especially certain classes within it, have chosen to take the matter more seriously. It is here where the machine age has added the ideal of a mechanically trained, faultlessly functioning, and always clean, punctual, and deodorized body. In addition it has been more or less consciously assumed that early and rigorous training is absolutely necessary for the kind of personality which will function efficiently in a mechanized world which says "time is money" and which calls for orderliness, punctuality, and thrift. Indications are that in this, we have gone too far; that we have assumed that a child is an animal which must be broken or a machine which must be set and tuned—while, in fact, human virtues can grow only by steps. At any rate our clinical work suggests that the neurotics of our time include the "over compulsive" type, who is stingy, retentive, and meticulous in matters of affection, time, and money, as well as in matters concerning his bowels. Also, bowel and bladder training has become the most obviously disturbing items of child training in wide circles of our society.

What, then, makes the anal problem potentially important and difficult?

The anal zone lends itself more than any other to the expression of stubborn self-insistence on contradictory impulses because, for one thing, it is the model zone for two conflicting modes which must become alternating; namely, *retention* and *elimination*. Furthermore, the sphincters are only part of the muscle system with its general ambiguity of rigidity and relaxation, of flexion and extension. This whole stage, then, becomes a battle for *autonomy*. For as he gets ready to stand on his feet more firmly, the infant delineates his world as "I" and "you," "me" and "mine." Every mother knows how astonishingly pliable a child may be at this stage, if and when he has made the decision that he *wants* to do what he is supposed to do. It is impossible, however, to find a reliable formula for making him want to do just that. Every mother knows how lovingly a child at this stage will snuggle and how ruthlessly he will suddenly try to push the adult away. At the same time the child is apt both to hoard things and to discard them, to cling to possessions and to throw them out of the windows of houses and vehicles. All of these seemingly contradictory tendencies, then, we include under the formula of the retentive eliminative modes.

The matter of mutual regulation between adult and child now faces its severest test. If outer control by too rigid or too early training insists on robbing the child of his attempt *gradually* to control his bowels and other functions willingly and by his free choice, he will again be faced with a double rebellion and a double defeat. Powerless in his own body (sometimes afraid of his bowels) and powerless outside, he will again be forced to seek satisfaction and control either by regression or by fake progression. In other words, he will return to an earlier, oral control, that is, by sucking his thumb and becoming whiny and demanding; or he will become hostile and willful, often using his feces (and, later, dirty words) as ersatz ammunition; or he will pretend an autonomy and an ability to do without anybody to lean on which he has by no means really gained.

This stage, therefore, becomes decisive for the ratio between love and hate, for that between co-operation and willfulness, and for that between the freedom of self-expression and its suppression. From a sense of *self-control without loss of self-esteem* comes a lasting sense of autonomy and pride; from a sense of muscular and anal impotence, of loss of self-control, and of parental over-control comes a lasting sense of doubt and shame.

To develop autonomy, a firmly developed and a convincingly continued stage of early trust is necessary. The infant must come to feel that basic faith in himself and in the world (which is the lasting treasure saved from the conflicts of the oral stage) will not be jeopardized by this sudden violent wish to have a choice, to appropriate demandingly, and to eliminate stubbornly. *Firmness* must protect him against the potential anarchy of his as yet untrained sense of discrimination, his inability to hold on and to let go with circumspection. Yet his environment must back him up in his wish to "stand on his own feet" lest he be overcome by that sense of having exposed himself prematurely and foolishly which we call shame, or that secondary mistrust, that looking back after a double-take, which we call doubt.

Shame is an infantile emotion insufficiently studied. Shame supposes that one is completely exposed and conscious of being looked at—in a word, self-conscious. One is visible and not ready to be visible; that is why we dream of shame as a situation in which we are stared at in a condition of incomplete dress, in night attire, "with one's pants down." Shame is early expressed in an impulse to bury one's face, or to sink, right then and there, into the ground. This potentiality is abundantly utilized in the educational method of "shaming" used so exclusively by some primitive peoples, where it supplants the often more destructive sense of guilt to be discussed later. The destructiveness of shaming is balanced in some civilizations by devices for "saving face." Shaming exploits an increasing sense of being small, which paradoxically develops as the child stands up and as his awareness permits him to note the relative measures of size and power.

Too much shaming does not result in a sense of propriety but in a secret determination to try to get away with things when unseen, if, indeed, it does not result in deliberate shamelessness. There is an impressive American ballad in which a murderer to be hanged on the gallows before the eyes of the community, instead of feeling appropriately afraid or ashamed, begins to berate the onlookers, ending every salvo of defiance with the words, "God damn your eyes." Many a small child, when shamed beyond endurance, may be in a mood (although not in possession of either the courage or the words) to express defiance in similar terms. What I mean by this sinister reference is that there is a limit to a child's and an adult's individual endurance in the face of demands which force him to consider himself, his body, his needs, and his wishes as evil and dirty, and to believe, without bitter doubt, in the infallibility of those who pass such judgment. Occasionally he may be apt to turn things around, to become secretly oblivious to the opinions of others, and to consider as evil only the fact that they exist: his chance will come when they are gone, or when he can leave them.

*   *   *

To repeat: muscular maturation sets the stage for experimentation with two simultaneous sets of social modalites—*holding on* and *letting go*. As is the case with all these modalities, their basic conflicts can lead in the end either to hostile or to benign expectations and attitudes. Thus, "to hold" can become a destructive and cruel retaining or restraining, and it can become a pattern of care: "to have and to hold." To "let go," too, can turn into an inimical letting loose of destructive forces, or it can become a relaxed "to let pass" and "to let be." Culturally speaking these modalities are neither good nor bad; their value depends on whether their hostile implications are turned against an enemy or a fellow man—or against the self.

2

But it is time to return from these considerations of the abnormal to a study of the headings which transmit the practical and benevolent advice of the children's doctor. They all add up to this: be firm and tolerant with the child at this stage, and he will be firm and tolerant with himself. He will feel pride in being an autonomous person; he will grant autonomy to others; and now and again he will even let himself get away with something.

Why, then, if we know how, do we not tell parents in detail what to do to develop this intrinsic, this genuine autonomy? The answer is: because when it comes to human values, nobody knows how to fabricate or manage the fabrication of the genuine article. . . . Actually, we are learning only gradually what exactly *not* to do with *what kind* of children at *what age.*

*　　*　　*

There are, of course, a few matters of necessary avoidance which become clear from our basic epigenetic point of view. It will be remembered that every new development carries with it its own specific vulnerability. For example, at around eight months the child seems to be somehow more aware, as it were, of his self; this prepares him for the impending sense of autonomy. At the same time he becomes more cognizant of his mother's features and presence. Sudden or prolonged separation from his mother at that time apparently can cause a sensitive child to experience an aggravation of the experience of division and abandonment, arousing violent anxiety and withdrawal. Again, in the first quarter of the second year, if everything has gone well, the infant just begins to become aware of . . . autonomy. . . . The introduction of bowel training at this time may cause him to resist with all his strength and determination, because he seems to feel that his budding will is being "broken." To avoid this feeling is certainly more important than to insist on his being trained just then because there is a time for the ascendancy of autonomy and there is a time for the sacrifice of autonomy; but obviously the time for a meaningful sacrifice is *after* one has acquired and reinforced a core of autonomy and has also

acquired more insight. The more exact localization in time of the most critical growth periods of the personality is becoming established only now. . . . Often what happened could not have been avoided; and usually the unavoidable cause of trouble is not one thing but the coincidence in time of many changes which upset the child's orientation. He may have been involved in a special growth period when the family moved to a new place. Perhaps he was forced to begin learning words all over again when the grandmother who had taught him his first words suddenly died. This event may have necessitated a trip on the part of the mother, which exhausted her because she happened to be pregnant at the time, and so forth. . . .

*　　*　　*

As was the case with "oral" personality, the compulsive personality (often referred to as "anal" in the psychiatric literature) has its normal aspects and its abnormal exaggerations. If well integrated with other compensatory traits, some compulsiveness is useful in the administration of matters in which order, punctuality, and cleanliness are essential. The question is always whether we remain the masters of the rules by which we want to make things more manageable (not more complicated) or whether the rules master the ruler. But it often happens, in the individual as well as in group life, that the letter of the rules kills the spirit which created them.

3

If I may seemingly digress here, it becomes apparent that the basic need of the individual for a delineation of his autonomy in the adult order of things is taken care of by the system of "law and order," be it the simple distribution of privileges and duties in a small tribe or in the complicated system of a modern state. Political organization assigns with the power of government certain privileges of leadership and certain obligations of conduct; while it assigns to the ruled certain obligations of compliance and certain privileges of remaining autonomous and self-determining. Where this whole matter becomes blurred, however, the matter of individual autonomy becomes an issue of mental health, as well as one of political reorientation. Where large numbers of people have been prepared in childhood to expect from life a high degree of personal autonomy, pride, and rich opportunities for those who are ready to grasp them, and then in later life find themselves ruled by superhuman organizations and machinery too intricate to understand, the result may be deep chronic disappointment not conducive to healthy personalities. . . . For the sense of autonomy in the child (a sense richly fostered in American childhood in general) must be backed up by the preservation in economic and political life of a high sense of autonomy and of initiative, both of which in some classes and regions are challenged by the complication and mechanization of modern life. . . .

[T]he sense of autonomy, which arises, or should arise, in the second stage of childhood, is fostered by a handling of the small individual which expresses a sense of dignity and independence on the part of the parents and a confident expectation that the kind of autonomy fostered earlier will not be frustrated later. This, in turn, necessitates a relationship of parent to parent, of parent to employer, and of parent to government which reaffirms the parent's essential dignity regardless of his social position. It is important to dwell on this point because much of the shame and doubt, much of the indignity and uncertainty which is aroused in children is an expression of the parents' frustrations in marriage, in work, and in citizenship.

IV

INITIATIVE VERSUS GUILT

1

Having found a firm solution of his problem of autonomy, the child of four and five is faced with the next step—and with the next crisis. Being firmly convinced that he *is* a person, the child must now find out *what kind* of a person he is going to be. And here he hitches his wagon to nothing less than a star: he wants to be like his parents, who to him appear very powerful and very beautiful, although quite unreasonably dangerous. He "identifies with them," that is, he plays with the idea of how it would be to be them. Three strong developments help at this stage, yet also serve to bring the child closer to his crisis: (1) he learns to move around more freely and more violently and therefore establishes a wider and, so it seems to him, an unlimited radius of goals; (2) his sense of language becomes perfected to the point where he understands and can ask about many things just enough to misunderstand them thoroughly; and (3) both language and locomotion permit him to expand his imagination over so many things that he cannot avoid frightening himself with what he himself has dreamed and thought up. Nevertheless, out of all this he must emerge with a sense of unbroken initiative as a basis for a high and yet realistic sense of ambition and independence.

One may ask here—one may, indeed—what are the criteria for such an unbroken sense of initiative? The criteria for all the senses discussed here are the same: a crisis, beset with fears, or at least a general anxiousness or tension, seems to be resolved in that the child suddenly seems to "grow together" both psychologically and physically. He seems to be "more himself," more loving and relaxed and brighter in his judgment (such as it is at this stage). Most of all, he

seems to be, as it were, self-activated; he is in the free possession of a certain surplus of energy which permits him to forget failures quickly and to approach what seems desirable (even if it also seems dangerous) with undiminished and better aimed effort. In this way the child and his parents face the next crisis much better prepared.

We are now approaching the end of the third year, when walking is getting to be a thing of ease, or vigor. The books tell us that a child "can walk" much before this; but from the point of view of personality development he cannot really walk as long as he is only able to accomplish the feat more or less well, with more or fewer props, for short spans of time. He has made walking and running an item in his sphere of mastery when gravity is felt to be *within*, when he can forget that he is doing the walking and instead can find out what he can do *with it*. Only then do his legs become an unconscious part of him instead of being an external and still unreliable ambulatory appendix. Only then will he find out with advantage what he now *may* do, along with what he *can* do.

*   *   *

. . . He is ready to visualize himself as being as big as the perambulating grownups. He begins to make comparisons and is apt to develop untiring curiosity about difference in sizes in general (and later of sexual parts in particular). He tries to comprehend possible future roles, or at any rate to understand what roles are worth imitating. More immediately, he can now associate with those of his own age. Under the guidance of older children or special women guardians, he gradually enters into the infantile politics of nursery school, street corner, and barnyard. His learning now is eminently intrusive and vigorous: it leads away from his own limitations and into future possibilities.

The *intrusive mode*, dominating much of the behavior of this stage, characterizes a variety of configurationally "similar" activities and fantasies. These include the intrusion into other bodies by physical attack; the intrusion into other people's ears and minds by aggressive talking; the intrusion into space by vigorous locomotion; the intrusion into the unknown by consuming curiosity.

This is also the stage of infantile sexual curiosity, genital excitability, and occasional preoccupation and overconcern with sexual matters. This "genitality" is, of course, rudimentary, a mere promise of things to come; often it is hardly noticeable as such. If not specifically provoked into precocious manifestation by especially strict and pointed prohibitions ("If you touch it, the doctor will cut it off") or special customs (such as sex play in groups), it is apt to lead to no more than a series of fascinating experiences which soon become frightening and pointless enough to be repressed during the ascendancy of that human speciality which Freud called the "latency" period, that is, the long physiological delay separating infantile sexuality (which in animals is followed by maturity) and physical sexual maturation.

The sexual orientation of the boy is focused on the phallus and its sensations, purposes, and meanings. While erections undoubtedly occur earlier (either reflexively or in response to things and people who make the child feel intensively), a focused interest may now develop in the genitalia of both sexes, as well as an urge to perform playful sex acts, or at least acts of sexual investigation. The increased locomotor mastery and the pride in being big now and *almost* as good as father and mother receives its severest setback in the clear fact that in the genital sphere one is vastly inferior; furthermore it receives an additional setback in the fact that not even in the distant future is one ever going to be father in sexual relationship to mother, or mother in sexual relationship to father. The very deep emotional consequences of this insight make up what Freud has called the Oedipus complex.

Psychoanalysis verifies the simple conclusion that boys attach their first genital affection to the maternal adults who have otherwise given comfort to their bodies and that they develop their first sexual rivalry against the persons who are the sexual owners of those maternal persons. The little girl, in turn, becomes attached to her father and other important men and jealous of her mother, a development which may cause her much anxiety, for it seems to block her retreat to that self-same mother, while it makes the mother's disapproval ever so much more magically dangerous because unconsciously "deserved."

Girls often have a difficult time at this stage, because they observe sooner or later that, although their locomotor, mental, and social intrusiveness is increased equally with, and is as adequate as, that of the boys, thus permitting them to become perfect tomboys, they lack one item: the penis. While the boy has this visible, erectable, and comprehensible organ to which he can attach dreams of adult bigness, the girl's clitoris only poorly sustains dreams of sexual equality. She does not even have breasts as analogously tangible tokens of her future; her maternal drives are relegated to play fantasy or baby tending. On the other hand, where mothers dominate households, the boy, in turn, can develop a sense of inadequacy because he learns at this stage that while a boy can do well in play and work, he will never boss the house, the mother, and the older sisters. His mother and sisters, in fact, might get even with him for vast doubts in themselves by making him feel that a boy (with his snails and puppy-dog tails) is really an inferior if not a repulsive creature. Both the girl and the boy are now extraordinarily appreciative of any convincing promise of the fact that someday they will be as good as father or mother—perhaps better; and they are grateful for sexual enlightenment, a little at

a time, and patiently repeated later. Where the necessities of economic life and the simplicity of its social plan make the male and female roles and their specific powers and rewards comprehensible, the early misgivings about sexual differences are, of course, more easily integrated in the culture's design for the differentiation of sexual roles.

This stage, then, adds to the inventory of basic social modalities in both sexes that of "making" in the older and today slangier sense of "being on the make." There is no simpler, stronger word to match the social modalities previously enumerated. The word suggests enjoyment of competition, insistence on goal, pleasure of conquest. In the boy the emphasis remains on "making" by head-on attack; in the girl it sooner or later changes to "making" by making herself attractive and endearing. The child thus develops the prerequisites for *masculine* and *feminine initiative*, that is, for the selection of social goals and perseverance in approaching them. Thus the stage is all set for entrance into life, except that life must first be school life. Fortunately, or unfortunately, the child here represses many of his fondest hopes and most energetic wishes. His exuberant imagination is tamed and he learns the necessary self-restraint and the necessary interest in impersonal things—even the three R's. This often demands a change of personality that is sometimes too drastic for the good of the child. This change is not only a result of education but also of an inner reorientation, and it is based on a biological fact (the delay of sexual maturation) and a psychological one (the repression of childhood wishes). For those sinister Oedipus wishes (so simply and so trustingly expressed in the boy's assurance that he will marry mother and make her proud of him, and in the girls' that she will marry father and take much better care of him), in consequence of vastly increased imagination and, as it were, the intoxication of increased locomotor powers, seem to lead to secret fantasies of terrifying proportions. The consequence is a deep sense of guilt—a strange sense, for it forever seems to imply that the individual has committed crimes and deeds which, after all, were not only not committed but also would have been biologically quite impossible.

While the struggle for autonomy at its worst concentrated on keeping rivals out, and was therefore more an expression of *jealous rage* most often directed against encroachments by *younger* siblings, initiative brings with it, *anticipatory rivalry* with those who were there first and who may, therefore, occupy with their superior equipment the field towards which one's initiative is directed. Jealousy and rivalry, those often embittered and yet essentially futile attempts at demarcating a sphere of unquestioned privilege, now come to a climax in a final contest for a favored position with one of the parents; the inevitable and necessary failure leads to guilt and anxiety. The child indulges in fantasies of being a giant and a tiger, but in his dreams he runs in terror for dear life. This, then, is the stage of fear for life and limb, including the fear of losing (or on the part of the girl the conviction that she may have lost) the male genital as punishment for the fantasies attached to infantile genital excitement.

All of this may seem strange to readers who have only seen the sunnier side of childhood and have not recognized the potential powerhouse of destructive drives which can be aroused and temporarily buried at this stage, only to contribute later to the inner arsenal of destructiveness which is ever ready to be used when opportunity provokes it. By using the words "potential," "provoke" and "opportunity," I mean to emphasize that there is little in these inner developments which cannot be harnessed to constructive and peaceful initiative if only we learn to understand the conflicts and anxieties of childhood and the importance of childhood for mankind. But if we should choose to overlook or belittle the phenomena of childhood, or to regard them as "cute" (even as the individual forgets the best and the worst dreams of his childhood), we shall forever overlook one of the eternal sources of human anxiety and strife.

2

It is at this stage of initiative that the great governor of initiative, namely, *conscience*, becomes firmly established. The child now feels not only ashamed when found out but also afraid of being found out. He now hears, as it were, God's voice without seeing God. Moreover, he begins automatically to feel guilty even for mere thoughts and for deeds which nobody has watched. This is the cornerstone of morality in the individual sense. But from the point of view of mental health, we must point out that if this great achievement is overburdened by all too eager adults, it can be bad for the spirit and for morality itself. For the conscience of the child *can* be primitive, cruel, and uncompromising, as may be observed in instances where children learn to constrict themselves to the point of overall inhibition; where they develop an obedience more literal than the one the parent wishes to exact; or where they develop deep regression and lasting resentments because the parents themselves do not seem to live up to the new conscience which they have fostered in the child. One of the deepest conflicts in life is the hate for a parent who served as the model and the executor of the conscience but who (in some form) was found trying to "get away with" the very transgressions which the child can no longer tolerate in himself. These transgressions often are the natural outcome of the existing inequality between parent and child. Often, however, they represent a thoughtless exploitation of such inequality; with the result that the child comes to feel that the whole matter is not one of universal goodness but of

arbitrary power. The suspiciousness and evasiveness which is thus mixed in with the all-or-nothing quality of the superego, that organ of tradition, makes moralistic man a great potential danger to himself and to his fellow men. It is as if morality, to him, became synonymous and vindictiveness and with the suppression of others.

It is necessary to point to the source of such moralism (not to be mistaken for morality) in the child of this age because infantile moralism is a stage to be lived through and worked through. The consequences of the guilt aroused at this stage (guilt expressed in a deep-seated conviction that the child as such, or drive as such, is essentially bad) often do not show until much later, when conflicts over iniative may find expression in a self-restriction which keeps an individual from living up to his inner capacities or to the powers of his imagination and feeling if not in sexual impotence or frigidity. All of this, of course, may in turn be "over-compensated" in a great show of tireless initiative, in a quality of "go-at-itiveness" at all cost. This many adults overdo to a point where they can never relax when they feel that their worth as people consists entirely in *what they are doing* or rather in *what they are going to do next*, and not in what they are, as individuals. The strain consequently developed in their bodies, which are always "on the go," with the engine racing, even at moments of rest, is a powerful contribution to the much-discussed psychosomatic diseases of our time.

Here I must admit again to psychopathological bias, and say again that we must learn to look beyond pathology. Pathology is only the sign that valuable human resources are being neglected, that they have been neglected first of all in childhood. Well-meaning, well-guided, and well-trained parents in a functioning cultural and economic system can certainly help their children through this and any other stage with much energy to spare.

The problem is again one of mutual regulation. Where the child, now so ready to overrestrict himself, can gradually develop a sense of paternal responsibility, where he can gain some insight into the institutions, functions, and roles which will permit his responsible participation as an adult, he will soon find pleasurable accomplishment in wielding tools and weapons, in manipulating meaningful toys, and in taking responsibility for himself and for younger children.

For such is the wisdom of the ground plan that at no time is the individual more ready to learn quickly and avidly, to become big in the sense of sharing obligation and performance rather than power, in the sense of *making things, instead of "making" people*, than during this period of his development. He is also eager and able to combine with other children for the purpose of constructing and planning, instead of trying to boss and coerce them; and he is able and willing to profit fully by the association with teachers and ideal prototypes.

Parents often do not realize why some children suddenly seem to think less of them and seem to attach themselves to teachers, to the parents of other children, or to people representing occupations which the child can grasp: firemen and policemen, gardeners and plumbers. The point is that children do not wish to be reminded of the principal inequality with the parent of the same sex. They remain identified with this same parent; but for the present they look for opportunities where superficial identification seems to promise a field of initiative without too much conflict or guilt.

Often, however (and this seems more typical of the American home than of any other in the world), the child can be guided by the parent himself into a second, a more realistic identification based on the spirit of equality experienced in doing things together. In connection with comprehensible technical tasks, a companionship may develop between father and son, an experience of essential *equality in worth*, in spite of the *inequality in time schedules*. Such companionship is a lasting treasure not only for parent and child but for mankind, which so sorely needs an alleviation of all those hidden hatreds which stem from the exploitation of weakness of mere size or schedule.

Only a combination of early prevention and alleviation of hatred and guilt in the growing being, and the consequent handling of hatred in the free collaboration of people who feel *equal in worth although different in kind or function or age*, permits a peaceful cultivation of initiative, a truly free sense of enterprise. And the word "enterprise" was deliberately chosen. For a comparative view of child training suggests that it is the prevalent economic ideal, or some of its modifications, which is transmitted to the child at the time when, in identification with his parent, he applies the dreams of early childhood to the as yet dim goals of an active adult life.

v

INDUSTRY VERSUS INFERIORITY

1

One might say that personality at the first stage crystallizes around the conviction "I am what I am given," and that of the second, "I am what I will." The third can be characterized by, "I am what I can imagine I will be." We must now approach the fourth: "I am what I learn." The child now wants to be shown how to get busy with something and how to be busy with others.

[L]iterate people with more specialized careers, must prepare the child by teaching him things which first of all make him literate. He is then given the widest possible basic education for the greatest number of possible careers. The greater the specialization, the more indistinct the goal of initiative becomes; and the more complicated the social reality is, the vaguer the father's and mother's role in it appears to be. Between childhood and adulthood, then, our children go to school; and school seems to be a world all by itself, with its own goals and limitations, its achievements and disappointments.

Grammar school education has swung back and forth between the extreme of making early school life an extension of grim adulthood by emphasizing self-restraint and a strict sense of duty in doing what one is *told* to do, and the other extreme of making it an extension of the natural tendency in childhood to find out by playing, to learn what one must do by doing steps which one *likes* to do. Both methods work for some children at times but not for all children at all times. The first trend, if carried to the extreme, exploits a tendency on the part of the preschool and grammar-school child to become entirely dependent on prescribed duties. He thus learns much that is absolutely necessary and he develops an unshakable sense of duty; but he may never unlearn again an unnecessary and costly self-restraint with which he may later make his own life and other people's lives miserable, and in fact spoil his own children's natural desire to learn and to work. The second trend, when carried to an extreme, leads not only to the well-known popular objection that children do not learn anything any more but also to such feelings in children as are expressed in the by now famous remark of a metropolitan child who apprehensively asked one morning: "Teacher, *must* we do today what we *want* to do?" Nothing could better express the fact that children at this age *do* like to be mildly coerced into the adventure of finding out that one can learn to accomplish things which one would never have thought of by oneself, things which owe their attractiveness to the very fact that they are *not* the product of play and fantasy but the product of reality, practicality, and logic; things which thus provide a token sense of participation in the world of adults. In discussions of this kind it is common to say that one must steer a middle course between play and work, between childhood and adulthood, between old-fashioned and progressive education. It is always easy (and it seems entirely satisfactory to one's critics) to say that one plans to steer a middle course, but in practice it often leads to a course charted by avoidances rather than zestful goals. . . .

*   *   *

What is infantile play? [I]t is not the equivalent of adult play, . . . it is not recreation. The playing adult steps sideward into another, an artificial reality; the playing child advances forward to new stages of real mastery. This new mastery is not restricted to the technical mastery of toys and *things*; it also includes an infantile way of mastering *experience* by meditating, experimenting, planning, and sharing.

2

While all children at times need to be left alone in solitary play (or later in the company of books and radio, motion pictures and video, all of which, like the fairy tales of old, at least *sometimes* seem to convey what fits the needs of the infantile mind), and while all children need their hours and days of make-believe in games, they all, sooner or later, become dissatisfied and disgruntled without a sense of being useful, without a sense of being able to make things and make them well and even perfectly: this is what I call the *sense of industry*. Without this, the best entertained child soon acts exploited. It is as if he knows and his society knows that now that he is psychologically already a rudimentary parent, he must begin to be somewhat of a worker and potential provider before becoming a biological parent. With the oncoming latency period, then, the normally advanced child forgets, or rather "sublimates" (that is, applies to more useful pursuits and approved goals) the necessity of "making" people by direct attack or the desire to become papa and mamma in a hurry: he now learns to win recognition by producing things. He develops industry, that is, he adjusts himself to the inorganic laws of the tool world. He can become an eager and absorbed unit of a productive situation. To bring a productive situation to completion is an aim which gradually supersedes the whim and wishes of his idiosyncratic drives and personal disappointments. As he once untiringly strove to walk well, and to throw things away well, he now wants to make things well. He develops the pleasure of work completion by steady attention and persevering diligence.

The danger at this stage is the development of a sense of *inadequacy and inferiority*. This may be caused by an insufficient solution of the preceding conflict: he may still want his mummy more than knowledge; he may still rather be the baby at home than the big child in school; he still compares himself with his father, and the comparison arouses a sense of guilt as well as a sense of anatomical inferiority. Family life (small family) may not have prepared him for school life, or school life may fail to sustain the promises of earlier stages in that nothing that he has learned to do well already seems to count one bit with the teacher. And then, again, he may be potentially able to excel in ways which are dormant and which, if not evoked now, may develop late or never.

* * *

[R]egarding the period of a developing sense of industry. I have referred to outer hindrances but not to any crisis (except a deferred inferiority crisis) coming from the inventory of basic human drives. This stage differs from the others in that it does not consist of a swing from a violent inner upheaval to a new mastery. The reason why Freud called it the latency stage is that violent drives are normally dormant at that time. But it is only a lull before the storm of puberty.

On the other hand, this is socially a most decisive stage: since industry involves doing things beside and with others, a first sense of division of labor and of equality of opportunity develops at this time. When a child begins to feel that it is the color of his skin, the background of his parents, or the cost of his clothes rather than his wish and his will to learn which will decide his social worth, lasting harm may ensue for the *sense of identity*, to which we must now turn.

VI

IDENTITY VERSUS SELF-DIFFUSION

1

With the establishment of a good relationship to the world of skills and to those who teach and share the new skills, childhood proper comes to an end. Youth begins. But in puberty and adolescence all sameness and continuities relied on earlier are questioned again because of a rapidity of body growth which equals that of early childhood and because of the entirely new addition of physical genital maturity. The growing and developing youths, faced with this physiological revolution within them, are now primarily concerned with attempts at consolidating their social roles. They are sometimes morbidly, often curiously, preoccupied with what they appear to be in the eyes of others as compared with what they feel they are and with the question of how to connect the earlier cultivated roles and skills with the ideal prototypes of the day. In their search for a new sense of continuity and sameness, some adolescents have to refight many of the crises of earlier years, and they are never ready to install lasting idols and ideals as guardians of a final identity.

The integration now taking place in the form of the ego identity is more than the sum of the childhood identifications. It is the inner capital accured from all those experiences of each successive stage, when successful identifications led to a successful alignment of the individual's *basic drives* with his *endowment* and his *opportunities*. In psychoanalysis we ascribe such successful alignments to "ego synthesis"; this writer has tried to demonstrate that the ego values accrued in childhood culminate in what he has called *a sense of ego identity*. The sense of ego identity, then, is the accrued confidence that one's ability to maintain inner sameness and continuity (one's ego in the psychological sense) is matched by the sameness and continuity of one's meaning for others.

To go back into early childhood once more: a child who has just found himself able to walk, more or less coaxed or ignored by those around him, seems driven to repeat the act for the pure enjoyment of functioning and out of the need to master and perfect a newly initiated function. But he also acts under the immediate awareness of the new status and stature of "one who can wak," although different peoples and different people may express this according to a great variety of expectations: "one who will go far," "one who will be able to stand on his own feet," "one who will be upright," "one who must be watched because he might go too far," or sometimes "one who will surely fall." At any rate, to become "one who can walk" is one of the many steps in child development which suddenly give an experience of physical mastery and of cultural meaning, of pleasure in activity and of social prestige; it thus is one building stone of self-esteem. This self-esteem, confirmed at the end of the major crises, as outlined here, grows to be a conviction that one is learning effective steps toward a tangible future, that one is developing a defined personality within a social reality which one understands. The growing child must, at every step, derive a vitalizing sense of reality from the awareness that his individual way of mastering experience is a successful varient of the way other people around him master experience and recognize such mastery.

In this, children cannot be fooled by empty praise and condescending encouragement. They may have to accept artificial bolstering of their self-esteem in lieu of something better, but what I call their accruing ego identity gains real strength only from wholehearted and consistent recognition of real accomplishment, that is, achievement that has meaning in their culture.

A child has quite a number of opportunities to identify himself, more or less experimentally, with habits, traits, occupations, and ideas of real or fictitious people of either sex. Certain crises force him to make radical selections. However, this historical era in which he lives offers only a limited number of socially meaningful models for workable combinations of identification fragments. Their usefulness depends on the way in which they simultaneously meet the requirements of his maturational stage and his habits of adjustment. But should a child feel that the environment tries to deprive him too radically of all the forms of expression which permit him to develop and to integrate the next step in his ego identity he will defend it with the astonishing strength encountered in animals who are suddenly forced to defend their lives. Indeed, in the social jungle of human existence there is no feeling of being alive without a sense of ego identity. To understand this would be to understand the trouble of adolescents better, especially the trouble of all those who cannot just be "nice" boys and girls, but are desperately seeking for a satisfactory sense of belonging, be it in cliques and gangs here in our country or in inspiring mass movements in others.

The ego identity develops out of a gradual integration of all identifications, but here, if anywhere, the whole has a different quality than the sum of its parts. It is the integration of the whole, not the quality or strength of the parts, which makes the difference. . . .

*   *   *

The emerging ego identity, then, bridges the early childhood stages, when the body and the parent images were given their specific meanings, and the later stages, when a variety of social roles become available and increasingly coercive. A lasting ego identity cannot begin to exist without the trust of the first oral stage; it cannot be completed without a promise of fulfillment which from the dominant image of adhulthood reaches down into the baby's beginnings and which creates at every step an accruing sense of ego strength.

2

The danger of this stage is *role diffusion*; as Biff puts it in Arthur Miller's *The Death of a Salesman*, "I just can't take hold, Mom, I can't take hold of some kind of a life." Where such a dilemma is based on a strong previous doubt of one's ethnic and sexual identify, delinquent and outright psychotic incidents are not uncommon. Youth after youth, bewildered by some assumed role, a role forced on him by the inexorable standardization of American adolescence, runs away in one form or another: leaving schools and jobs, staying out all night, or withdrawing into bizarre and inaccessible moods. Once "delinquent," his greatest need, and often his only salvation, is the refusal on the part of older youths, advisers, and judiciary personnel to type him further by pat diagnoses and social judgments which ignore the special dynamic conditions of adolescence. For if diagnosed and treated correctly, seemingly psychotic and criminal incidents do not in adolescence have the same fatal significance which they have at other ages. Yet many a youth, finding that the authorities expect him to be "a bum" or "a queer," or "off the beam," perversely obliges by becoming just that.

In general it is primarily the inability to settle on an occupational identity which disturbs young people. To keep themselves together they temporarily over-identify, to the point of apparent complete loss of identity, with the heroes of cliques and crowds. On the other hand, they become remarkably clannish, intolerant, and cruel in their exclusion of others who are "different," in skin color or cultural background, in tastes and gifts, and often in entirely petty aspects of dress and gesture arbitrarily selected as *the* signs of an in-grouper or out-grouper. It is important to understand (which does not mean condone or participate in) such intolerance as the necessary *defense against a sense of self-diffusion*, which is unavoidable at a time of life when the body changes its proportions radically, when genital maturity floods body and imagination with all manner of drives, when intimacy with the other sex approaches and is, on occasion, forced on the youngster, and when life lies before one with a variety of conflicting possibilities and choices. Adolescents help one another temporarily through such discomfort by forming cliques and by stereotyping themselves, their ideals, and their enemies.

*   *   *

[I]t is . . . important to understand this in order to treat the intolerance of our adolescents at home with understanding and guidance rather than with verbal stereotypes or prohibitions. It is difficult to be tolerant if deep down you are not quite sure that you are a man (or a woman), that you will ever grow together again and be attractive, that you will be able to master your drives, that you really know who you are, that you know what you want to be, that you know what you look like to others, and that you will know how to make the right decisions without, once for all, committing yourself to the wrong friend, girl, or career.

*   *   *

Democracy in a country like America poses special problems in that it insists on self-made identities ready to grasp many changes and ready to adjust to changing necessities of booms and busts, of peace and war, of migration and determined sedentary life. Our democracy, furthermore, must present the adolescent with ideals which can be shared by youths of many backgrounds and which emphasize autonomy in the from of independence and initiative in the form of enterprise. These promises, in turn, are not easy to fulfill in increasingly complex and centralized systems of economic and political organization, systems which, if geared to war, must automatically neglect the "self-made" identities of millions of individuals and put them where they are most needed. This is hard on young Americans, not because (or perhaps not only because) they are precious and willful, but because their whole upbringing, and therefore the development of a healthy personality, depends on a certain degree of choice, a certain hope for an individual chance, and a certain conviction in freedom of self-determination.

[W]e must bend every effort to present our young men and women, again faced with dislocation and the horror of war, with the tangible and trustworthy promise of opportunities for a rededication to the life for which the country's history, as well as their own childhood, has prepared them. Among the tasks of national defense, this one must not be forgotten.

. . . In searching for the counterpart and development of identity in social life, one confronts the problem of ideology and aristocracy. Here we use the word in its widest possible sense connoting the conviction that the best people rule and that that rule as defined in one's society develops the best in people. In order not to become cynically or apathetically lost, youths in search of an identity must somewhere be able to convince themselves that those who succeed acquire not only the conviction that they have proven to be better than others, but also the obligation of being the best, that is, of personifying the nation's ideals. . . .

VII

THREE STAGES OF ADULTHOOD

1

Intimacy and Distantiation vs. Self-Absorption

Here childhood and youth come to an end; life, so the saying goes, begins: by which we mean work or study for a specified career, sociability with the other sex, and in time, marriage and a family of one's own. But it is only after a reasonable sense of identity has been established that real *intimacy* with the other sex (or, for that matter, with any other person or even with oneself) is possible. Sexual intimacy is only part of what I have in mind, for it is obvious that sexual intimacies do not always wait for the ability to develop a true and mutual psychological intimacy with another person. What I have in mind is that late-adolescent need for a kind of fusion with the essence of other people. The youth who is not sure of his identity shies away from interpersonal intimacy; but the surer he becomes of himself, the more he seeks it in the forms of friendship, combat, leadership, love, and inspiration. There is a kind of adolescent attachment between boy and girl which is often mistaken either for mere sexual attraction or for love. Except where the mores demand heterosexual behavior, such attachment is often devoted to an attempt at arriving at a definition of one's identity by talking things over endlessly, by confessing what one feels like and what the other seems like, and by discussing plans, wishes, and expectations. Where a youth does not accomplish such intimate relation with others—and, I would add, with his own inner resources—in late adolescence or early adulthood, he may either isolate himself and find, at best, highly stereotyped and formal interpersonal relations (formal in the sense of lacking in spontaneity, warmth, and real exchange of fellowship), or he must seek them in repeated attempts and repeated failures. Unfortunately, many young people marry under such circumstances, hoping to find themselves in finding one another; but alas, the early obligation to act in a defined way, as mates and as parents, disturbs them in the completion of this work on themselves. Obviously, a change of mate is rarely the answer, but rather some wisely guided insight into the fact that the condition of a true twoness is that one must first become oneself.

The counterpart of intimacy is *distantiation:* the readiness to repudiate, to isolate, and, if necessary, to destroy those forces and people whose essence seems dangerous to one's own. This more mature and more efficient repudiation (it is utilized and exploited in politics and in war) is an outgrowth of the blinder prejudices which during the struggle for an identity differentiate sharply and cruelly between the familiar and the foreign. At first, intimate, competitive and combative relations are experienced with and against the selfsame people. Gradually, a polarization occurs along the lines of the competitive encounter, the sexual embrace, and various forms of incisive combat.

Freud was once asked what he thought a normal person should be able to do well. The questioner probably expected a complicated, a "deep" answer. But Freud is reported to have said, *"Lieben und arbeiten"* (to love and to work). It pays to ponder on this simple formula, it gets deeper as you think about it. For when Freud said "love," he meant the expansiveness of generosity as well as genital love; when he said love *and* work, he meant a general productiveness which would not preoccupy the individual to the extent that his right or capacity to be a sexual and a loving being would be lost. Thus we may ponder but we cannot improve on the formula, which includes the doctor's prescription for human dignity—and for democratic living.

Psychiatry, in recent years, has emphasized *genitality* as one of the chief signs of a healthy personality. Genitality is the potential capacity to develop orgastic potency in relation to a loved partner of the opposite sex. Orgastic potency here means not the discharge of sex products in the sense of Kinsey's "outlets" but heterosexual mutuality, with full genital sensitivity and with an over-all discharge of tension from the whole body. This is a rather concrete way of saying something about a process which we really do not understand. But the idea clearly is that the experience of the climactic mutuality of orgasm provides a supreme example of the mutual regulation of complicated patterns and in some way appeases the potential rages caused by the daily evidence of the oppositeness of male and female, of fact and fancy, of love and hate, of work and play. Satsifactory sex relations make sex less obsessive and sadistic control superfluous. . . .

2

Generativity vs. Stagnation

The problem of genitality is intimately related to the seventh criterion of mental health, which concerns parenthood. Sexual mates who find, or are on the way to finding, true genitality in their relations will soon wish (if, indeed, developments wait for the express wish) to combine their personalities and energies in the care of common offspring. The pervasive development underlying this wish I have termed *generativity*, because it concerns the establishment (by way of genitality and genes) of the next generation. No other fashionable term, such as creativity or productivity, seems to me to convey the necessary idea. Generativity is primarily the interest in establishing and guiding the next generation, although there are people who, from misfortune or because of special and genuine gifts in other directions, do not apply this drive to offspring but to other forms of altruistic concern and of creativity, which may absorb their kind of parental responsibility. The principal thing is to realize that this is a stage of the growth of the healthy personality and that where such enrichment fails altogether, regression from generativity to an obsessive need for pseudo-intimacy takes place, often with a pervading sense of stagnation and interpersonal improverishment. Individuals who do not develop generativity often begin to indulge themselves as if they were their own one and only child. The mere fact of having or even wanting children does not, of course, involve generativity; in fact the majority of young parents seen in child-guidance work suffer, it seems, from the retardation of or inability to develop this stage. The reasons are often to be found in early childhood impressions; in faulty identifications with parents; in excessive self-love based on a too strenuously self-made personality; and finally (and here we return to the beginnings) in the lack of some faith, some "belief in the species," which would make a child appear to be a welcome trust of the community.

3

Integrity vs. Despair and Disgust

Only he who in some way has taken care of things and people and has adapted himself to the triumphs and disappointments adherent to being, by necessity, the originator of others and the generator of things and ideas—only he may gradually grow the fruit of the seven stages, I know no better word for it than integrity. Lacking a clear definition, I shall point to a few attributes of this state of mind. It is the acceptance of one's own and only life cycle and of the people who have become significant to it as something that had to be and that, by necessity, permitted of no substitutions. It thus means a new, a different love of one's parents, free of the wish that they should have been different, and an acceptance of the fact that one's life is one's own responsibility. It is a sense of comradeship with men and women of distant times and of different pursuits, who have created orders and objects and sayings conveying human dignity and love. Although aware of the relativity of all the various life styles which have given meaning to human striving, the possessor of integrity is ready to defend the dignity of his own life style against all physical and economic threats. For he knows that an individual life is the accidental coincidence of but one life cycle with but one segment of history; and that for him all human integrity stands and falls with the one style of integrity of which he partakes.

[T]he lack or loss of this accrued ego integration is signified by despair and an often unconscious fear of death: the one and only life cycle is not accepted as the ultimate of life. Despair expresses the feeling that the time is short, too short for the attempt to start another life and to try out alternate roads to integrity. Such a despair is often hidden behind a show of disgust, a misanthropy, or a chronic contemptuous displeasure with particular institutions and particular people—a disgust and a displeasure which (where not allied with constructive ideas and a life of co-operation) only signify the individual's contempt of himself.

*   *   *

VIII

CONCLUSION

. . . To develop a child with a health personality, a parent must be a genuine person in a genuine milieu. This, today, is difficult because rapid changes in the milieu often make it hard to know whether one must be genuine *against* a changing milieu or whether one may hope for a chance to do one's bit in the way of bettering or stabilizing conditions. It is difficult, also, because in a changing world we are trying out—we must try out—new ways. To bring up children in personal and tolerant ways, based on information and education rather than on tradition, is a very new way: it exposes parents to many additional insecurities, which are temporarily increased by psychiatry (and by such products of psychiatric thinking as the present paper). Psychiatric thinking sees the world so full of dangers that it is hard to relax one's caution at every step. I, too, have pointed to more dangers than to constructive avenues of action. Perhaps we can hope that this is only an indication that we are progressing through one stage of learning. When a man learns how to drive he must become conscious of all the things that *might* happen; and he must learn to hear and see and read all the danger signals on his dashboard and along the road. Yet he may hope that some day, when he has outgrown this stage of learning, he will be able to glide with the greatest of ease through the landscape, enjoying the view with the confident knowledge that he will react to signs of mechanical trouble or road obstruction with automatic and effective speed.

. . . In order to ban autocracy, exploitation, and inequality in the world, we must first realize that the first inequalities in life is that of child and adult.

Human childhood is long, so that parents and schools may have time to accept the child's personality in trust and to help it to be human in the best sense known to us. This long childhood exposes the child to grave anxieties and to a lasting sense of insecurity which, if unduly and senselessly intensified, persists in the adult in the form of vague anxiety—anxiety which, in turn, contributes specifically to the tension of personal, political, and even international life. This long childhood exposes adults to the temptation of thoughtlessly and often cruelly exploiting the child's dependence by making him pay the psychological debts owed to us by others, by making him the victim of tensions which we will not, or dare not, correct in ourselves or in our surroundings. We have learned not to stunt a child's growing body with child labor; we must now learn not to break his growing spirit by making him the victim of our anxieties.

If we will only learn to let live, the plan for growth is all there.

NOTES

NOTE 1

ERIKSON, ERIK H.

Youth and the Life Cycle*

Question: Are there any points about your concepts of psychosocial development which you would now like to stress in the light of what you have heard about how they have been interpreted during the past decade in the training of professional persons and through them of parents and future parents?

*   *   *

There has been a tendency here and there to turn the eight stages into a sort of rosary of achievement, a device for counting the fruits of each stage—trust, autonomy, initiative, and so forth—as though each were achieved as a permanent trait. People of this bent are apt to leave out the negative counterparts of each stage, as if the healthy personality had permanently conquered these hazards. The fact is that the healthy personality must reconquer them continuously in the same way that the body's metabolism resists decay. All that we learn are certain fundamental means and mechanisms for retaining and regaining mastery. Life is a sequence not only of development but also of accidental crises. It is hardest to take when both types of crisis coincide.

In each crisis, under favorable conditions, the positive is likely to outbalance the negative, and each reintegration builds strength for the next crisis. But the negative is always with us to some degree in the

* Reprinted from: *Children*, Vol. 7, p. 43, (March–April 1960). U.S. Department of Health, Education, and Welfare, Social Security Administration, Children's Bureau. Reprinted by permission.

form of a measure of infantile anxiety, fear of abandonment—a residue of immaturity carried throughout life, which is perhaps the price man has to pay for a childhood long enough to permit him to be the learning and the teaching animal, and thus to achieve his particular mastery of reality.

* * *

In our one-family culture (supported by pediatricians and psychiatrists who exclusively emphasize the mother–child relationship) we tend to lose sight of the fact that other people besides parents are important to youth. Too often we ask only where a given youth came from and what he once was, and not also where he was going, and who was ready to receive him and his intentions and his specific gifts. Thus we have movements to punish parents for the transgressions of their children, ignoring all the other persons and environmental factors that entered into the production of a young person's unacceptable behavior and failed to offer support to his positive search.

* * *

NOTE 2

FREUD, ANNA

Regression as a Principle in Mental Development*

Developmental lines and their disharmonies are not responsible in themselves for all the complexities which arise in childhood, especially not for all the obstacles and arrests which hinder its smooth course.

That there is progressive growth from the state of immaturity to maturity, along lines which are prescribed innately, but influenced and shaped at every step by environmental conditions, is a notion with which we are familiar from the processes of growth on the organic side where the anatomical, physiological, and neurological processes are in constant flux. What we are used to seeing in the body is that growth proceeds in a straightforward, progressive line until adulthood is reached, invalidated only by severe intervening illness or injury and, finally, by the destructive, involutionary processes of old age.

There is no doubt that a similar progressive move underlies psychical development, i.e., that also in the unfolding of drive action, impulses, affects, reason, and mortality, the individual sets out on specifically prescribed paths and, subject to environmental circumstances, pursues them to their conclusion. But the analogy between the two fields does not carry further than this point. While on the physical side, normally progressive development is the only innate force in operation, on the psychical side we have to count invariably with a second, additional set of

* 27 *Bulletin of the Menninger Clinic*, 1963. (pp. 128–39). Reprinted by permission.

influences which work in the opposite direction, namely with fixations and regressions. It is only the recognition of both movements, progressive and regressive ones, and of the interactions between them that leads to satisfactory explanations of the happenings on the developmental lines. . . .

* * *

[R]egression can occur in all three parts of the personality structure, in the id, as well as in the ego and superego; and that it can concern psychical content as well as methods of functioning; that *temporal* regression happens in regard to aim-directed impulses, object representations and fantasy content; *topographical* and *formal* regression in the ego functions, the secondary thought processes, and the reality principle.

Regression in Drive and Libido Development

Most closely studied in analysis is temporal regression in drive and libido development. What is affected here on the one hand is the choice of objects and the relations to them with consequent returns to those of earliest significance and the most infantile expressions of dependence. On the other hand, the drive organization is affected as a whole and returns to earlier pregenital levels and the aggressive manifestations co-ordinated with them are brought about. Regression in this respect is considered as based on a specific characteristic of drive development, namely on the fact that while libido and aggression move forward from one level to the next and cathect the objects which serve satisfaction on each stage, no station on the way is ever fully outgrown as it is on the organic side. While one part of the drive energy is on a forward course, other portions of it, of varying quantity, remain behind, tied to earlier aims and objects and create the so-called *fixation points.* . . . Fixation points may be caused by any type of traumatic experience, by either excessive frustration or excessive gratification on any of these levels and may exist with different degrees of awareness and consciousness, or repression and unconsciousness attached to them. For the developmental outcome, this is less important than the fact that for whatever cause and in either state they have the function of binding and retaining drive energies and that thereby they impoverish later drive functioning and object relations.

Fixations and regressions have been regarded always as interdependent. By virtue of their very existence and according to the measure of libido and aggression with which they are cathected, the fixation points exert a constant retrograde pull on drive activity, an attraction which makes itself felt during all early development and in maturity.

The intricacies of *sexual* regression can be shown best in any clinical instance which is dissected and described in detail, although the statements concerning them are usually unduly abbreviated and therefore incomplete. Thus, it is not enough to say that a boy on the phallic-oedipal level under the impact of castration anxiety "has regressed to the anal or oral phase." What has to be described additionally is the form, scope, and significance of the regressive movement which has taken place. The statement may mean in its simplest form no more than that the boy has retreated from rivalry with the father and from the fantasy of possessing the Oedipal mother and has reactivated his pre-oedipal conception of her with the corresponding clinging, demanding, torturing attitudes, while otherwise everything remains the same: That he continues to regard her as a whole person in her own right and continues to discharge the anal and oral excitations connected with her in the act of phallic masturbation. Or, the same statement may imply that regression has affected also the level of object relatedness itself. In that case, object constancy is given up and what is revived are the anaclitic (or part-object) attitudes: The personal importance of the love object becomes overshadowed again by the importance of satisfying a component instinct, a relationship which is normal for the toddler period but which—at later ages and in maturity—produces shallowness and promiscuity in object relations. There is a third possibility that regression may include also the method of discharging sexual excitement; where this happens, phallic masturbation disappears altogether and is replaced by impulses to eat, to drink, to urinate, or to defecate at the height of excitation.

The most serious manifestations are those, obviously, where all three forms of sexual regression (of object, aim, and method of discharge) occur simultaneously.

*   *   *

Temporary Ego Regressions in Normal Development

The backward moves which occur in every child's normal development of functioning are well known to all those who deal with young children and their upbringing in practical capacities. By the latter, regression of function is taken for granted as a common characteristic of infantile behavior.

Actually, when studied in detail, regressive tendencies can be shown to occur with regard to all the important achievements of the child: In the ego functions of control of motility, reality testing, integration, speech; in the acquisition of bowel and bladder control; in the secondary thought processes and mastery of anxiety; in the elements of social adaptation such as frustration tolerance, impulse control, manners; in superego demands such as honesty, or fairness in dealings with others. In all these respects, an individual child's capacity to function on a comparatively high level is no guarantee that the performance will be stable and continuous. On the contrary: Occasional returns to more infantile

behavior have to be taken as a normal sign. Thus, nonsense talk and even babbling have a rightful place in the child's life, alongside rational speech and alternating with it. Clean toilet habits are not acquired at one go but take the long back-and-forth way through an interminable series of successes, relapses, accidents. Constructive play with toys alternates with messing, destructiveness, and erotic body play. Social adaptation is interrupted periodically by reversals to pure egoism. In fact, what we regard as surprising are not the relapses but occasional sudden achievements and advances. Such moves forward may occur with regard to feeding where they take the form of a sudden refusal of the breast and transition to bottle, spoon, or cup, or from liquids to solids; or at later ages a sudden relinquishing of food fads. They are known to happen with regard to habits such as a sudden giving up of thumb sucking or of a transitional object, or fixed sleeping arrangements. In toilet training, instances are known of almost instantaneous changeover from wetting and soiling to bladder and bowel control; with regard to aggression, its almost overnight disappearance with changeover to shy, restrained, diffident behavior. But convenient as such transformations may be for the child's environment, the diagnostician views them with suspicion and ascribes them not to the ordinary flow of progressive development, but to traumatic influences and anxieties which hasten its normal course unduly. According to experience, the slow method of trial and error, progression, and temporary reversal, is more appropriate to healthy psychical growth.

*   *   *

[B]eneficent aspect of regression refers only to those instances where the process is temporary and spontaneously reversible. Impairment of function due to tiredness then disappears automatically after rest or sleep; if due to frustration, pain, distress, the age-adequate drive positions or methods of ego functioning reinstate themselves as soon as the cause of strain has been removed, or, at least, soon afterward.

But it would be unduly optimistic on our part to expect such a favorable turn of events in the large majority of cases. It happens just as often, especially after traumatic distresses, anxieties, or illnesses, that regressions, once embarked on, become permanent; the drive energies then remain deflected from their age-adequate aims, and ego or superego functions remain impaired, so that any further progressive development is severely damaged. Where this happens, regression ceases to be a beneficent factor in normal development and becomes a pathogenic agent. Unluckily, in our clinical appraisal of regressions as ongoing processes, it is almost impossible to detect whether in a given child's case the dangerous step from temporary to permanent regression has been taken already or whether spontaneous re-instatement of formerly reached levels can be expected still. Personally, I know of no criteria for this so far, even though the whole assessment of the child's normality and abnormality may depend on the distinction.

Structural Considerations

This leaves us with a further point which, so far as the structural aspects of the child's picture are concerned, is perhaps the most important one.

Where regressions are at all permanent, it is obvious that the various agencies within the structure (id, ego, superego) have to come to terms with each other on the basis of the impairments which have taken place. It is precisely these after effects of regression which have decisive repercussions for the personality and which have to be considered.

I take then, first, those instances where regression attacks primarily the ego and superego functions and lowers them permanently. Where this happens we can see invariably that the id derivatives are affected in their turn. Less control is exercised over them by the regressed ego and this results in disturbances in the demarcation line between id and ego and, with it, in impulsive behavior, in break-throughs of affect and in general irruptions of id content and irrationality into the child's consciousness and rational behavior.

We take as the next possibility that regression starts on the side of the id derivatives and affects primarily libido and aggression. This may lead to two wholly different clinical results:

(a) One is that ego and superego give in to the regressive pull exerted by the happenings on the side of the drives and react with regression of their own, i.e., with a lowering of standards and demands. Where this happens, internal conflict between the ego and id is avoided, the drives remain ego-syntonic, but the child's total personality is affected as such, and its whole level is lowered in a retrograde, more infantile direction. Due to the comparative weakness of the immature ego such a spread of regression to both sides of the personality may be more characteristic for childhood than it is for adulthood (although I do not believe that it is wholly absent from the latter). I think it is safe to say that the resulting clinical pictures depend on the intensity of regression on both sides, on the selections of the parts of drive and ego which do regress and, finally, on the interaction between id and ego at the lowered level at which they come to rest. However that may be, it seems to me that many pictures of infantilism, some of the nontypical disturbances, many of the so-called borderline cases have to be included in this category.

(b) On the other hand, there are those other children whose ego and superego are better organized and

stand firm in the face of regressed drive activity. Their functions have reached probably in many respects what we call, with Hartmann, a secondary ego autonomy, i.e., a measure of independence of the id. Instead of condoning the primitive sexual and aggressive fantasies and impulses which arise after return to the fixation points, they are horrified by them, develop anxiety and under the pressure of anxiety, first defense, then compromise and symptom formation. In short, they develop the internal conflicts which lead to the familiar picture of the infantile neurosis. The anxiety hysterias, phobias, pavor nocturnus, the obsessions, rituals, ceremonials, most traumatic disturbances, inhibitions, and character neuroses belong in this category.

Regression and the Developmental Lines

To return to the concept of developmental lines which I introduced at the beginning of this paper:

Once we accept regression as a normal process, we accept also that movement along these lines is in the nature of a two-way traffic. During the whole period of growth, then, it has to be considered legitimate for children to revert periodically, to lose controls again after they have been established, to reinstate early sleeping and feeding patterns (for example in illness), to seek shelter and protection (especially in anxiety and distress) by returning to early forms of being protected and comforted in the symbiotic and pre-Oedipal mother relationship (especially at bedtime). Far from interfering with forward development, it will be beneficial for its freedom if the way back is not blocked altogether by environmental disapproval and by internal repressions and restrictions.

To the disequilibrium in the child's personality which is caused by development on the various lines progressing toward maturity at different speeds, we have to add now the unevennesses which are due to regressions of the different elements of the structure and of their combinations. On this basis it becomes easier to understand why there is so much deviation from straightforward growth and from the average picture of a hypothetically "normal" child. With the interactions between progression and regression being as complex as they are, the disharmonies, imbalances, and intricacies of development, in short the *variations of normality*, become innumerable.

NOTE 3

WANGH, MARTIN

National Socialism and the Genocide of the Jews*

Germany, together with other Christian as well as Moslem lands, has had a long history of anti-Semitism. A vast amount has been written on the

* 45 *International Journal of Psychoanalysis*, 386, 389–95 (1964). Reprinted by permission.

subject. Religious . . . economic . . . and political . . . explanations vie with and supplement each other. Yet do they suffice to elucidate the degeneration of "ordinary" anti-Semitism into Nazi anti-Semitism? Can they make comprehensible the regression from all humanitarian values which occurred in Nazi anti-Semitism? How could a nation abandon all Western cultural inhibitions against human sacrifice, slavery, and even cannibalism? And how could the individual members of the elite guards, the executants of the planned and ruthless genocide of the Jews, avoid all feelings of abhorrence and loathing for the deeds they were committing? No one of the three categories of explanations hitherto offered and just enumerated seems sufficient by itself. Even taken together, the aetiological foundations which they uncover seem as though they might well have resulted in little more than a renewed social exclusion of and a stricter economic discrimination against the Jews.

[T]he question remains: What made an effective number of Germans willing to believe the Nazi propaganda, what made them willing to accept and even to execute the so-called "final solution of the Jewish question"? Surely in those years it was not the churchgoers, either Catholic or Protestant—for their numbers as well as the numbers of those who worshipped in the synagogue had considerably diminished—surely it was not they who were in the Swastika vanguard. The teaching that the Jews were Judases or Christ-killers was less rather than more stressed during the twenties than it had been in the preceding centuries. Thus we certainly cannot speak of a religious exacerbation of anti-Semitism. Nor was there any special emphasis on anti-Semitism from the side of the organized proletariat. Is its cause to be found, then, in the humiliation of the lower middle classes? It seems to be a fact, as mentioned above, that during the initial stages of the expansion of the Nazi party a large percentage of its followers were members of this class, a class which at this time was in danger of losing its identity within the social structure. But would not simply a compensating social humiliation of the Jews have been sufficient? Why, one may ask, were the young men who formed the core of the storm troopers and who finally became executors of the sadistic plans so affected by the status problem of their families that they acceded to the regressive temptations with such enthusiasm? Had the causes been solely economic and social, they would have led logically to economic and social recriminations. But there was no logic in Nazi anti-Semitism. On the contrary, it employed the most disparate and contradictory accusations. That is precisely why it grew. It was irrational, and because it was irrational, it could harbor all kinds of suppressed impulses and, moreover, promise them discharge in action.

The leaders of the Nazi movement, and its older members, belonged to the generation of war veterans who, Simmel (1946, p. 74) says, are often particularly receptive to anti-Semitic propaganda. The soldier who has grown accustomed to handing his superego over to the officer has the difficult task, on returning home, "of accepting again in its entirety the responsibility for his emotions and his actions and of suppressing and repressing his aggressive and destructive tendencies." It is obvious that the murderers of the "Feme" and their Nazi successors were unsuccessful in this endeavor. No one, least of all they themselves, recognized that their constant preoccupation with the question of war guilt was a way of warding off not only the reproach of the Allies, but also the reproach within themselves, a reproach which was constantly exacerbated by their continuing aggression. Thorough psychological studies of these people would undoubtedly reveal that their brooding over war guilt was largely determined by personal childhood experience. . . .

But a disturbed person, no matter how good an orator he may be, does not produce a mass movement. Its success will depend on the character of the listeners who will follow him. There is undoubtedly a reciprocal interdependence between the personality of a leader and the group which chooses him as their leader. . . . Horkheimer writes: "Basic traits of hatred are identical all over," adding that "sociopolitical tendencies determine whether or not they become overt." Now if we agree that a certain group chooses a certain leader who proclaims hatred, then we assume that there is a greater readiness to hate in members of this group. . . . We are, in fact, forced to the conclusion that the persons in the group who have chosen this leader must have a certain similarity with him. They must react to guilt and fear with defence mechanisms similar to those of the leader. . . . The question is not only whether impulses have changed, but whether the capacity of the ego and the character of the superego have changed in such a manner that these id impulses are met with a weakened capacity for control and with regressive defensive measures. To fathom anti-Semitic attitudes in this manner requires genetic and dynamic research into the handling of conflicts in early childhood. . . .

[I] wish to submit the hypothesis that [the *decisive* mass of the followers] were young men affected by the events of their childhood and early adolescence in such a way as to promote a fixation on sado-masochistic fantasies and on specific defences directed against them; and that under the renewed external crisis regression to this fixation level occurred. At the beginning of the thirties there was in Germany an effective number of youths whose psychological structure was such that they had an affinity with those leaders and so could become the executors of their regressive, sadistic projects, so blatantly proclaimed in *Mein Kampf*.

In 1930, at the decisive turning point between

adolescence and manhood, an entire generation stood hungry, bewildered, and distressed in the breadlines of the unemployed. It is important to remember at this point that in the significant years 1930 to 1933, three million young people reached voting age in Germany —over 6 per cent of the electorate (Shirer, 1960)— and that these same three million new voters had all been very young children in 1914, when the First World War began. Not all of them flocked immediately to the lure of the Swastika. But it is not correct to assume therefore that the young S.S. men represented simply the ordinary percentage of psychopaths that every generation produces in every nation. On the contrary, there is general agreement that the core of the S.S. and S.A. was furnished by average young men of the lower middle class, which, as we said, lived in greatest fear of losing its status and separate identity in the depression. The demonstration of military power by the uniformed youth of this class had a snowballing effect upon the rest of the population—whose sensitivity to the same causative factors was lesser only in degree.

To sum up, I suggest that these youthful followers of the Nazi movement reacted regressively to the fear produced by the economic depression of 1930 because their childhood years were encompassed by the First World War and its aftermath. At that time their egos and superegos were subjected to peculiarly noxious psychological influences: To the psychological effect of the father's prolonged absence and his defeat as a soldier, to his failure to protect the family from economic misery, and to the continuous and heightened anxiety of the mothers throughout this time. I suggest that the anxiety occurring as they were entering manhood *re-evoked in these young followers a previous anxiety, experienced in childhood* under a similar constellation of disappointment in the manhood of a father unable to protect the family from the threat of status loss and from physical misery. This very similarity mobilized once again the regressive patterns of defence which had been used in childhood against such anxiety.

I suggest, then, that the economic and social stresses of 1930 to 1933 reawakened in the youth of this generation the anxiety previously experienced in the years 1917 to 1920. And once again, the lower middle class was particularly imperilled by déclassement and unaccustomed poverty. Its mothers, the wives of the soldiers then at war, had with the increase of poverty felt especially exposed to social degradation. Their anxiety had in turn disturbed object stability in their small children and had sharpened class consciousness in their older offspring.

We must also consider what the prolonged absence of the father, even taken by itself, meant for the formation of the superego and the development of the sense of identity of these children. The tendency to react to an absent father with a splitting of emotions about him is important here. Moreover, official war propaganda always lends affirmation and direction to this kind of defence: The father is glorified and all bad traits (and critical memories) are ascribed to the enemy. The enemy is wholly black and diabolical. Need I underline the obvious renewal of this image splitting in the thirties in the deification of the Führer and the infernalization of the Jew? Furthermore: If the fantasy life of the child even in normal times is filled with his slaughter and death, how much more intense and less correctable by reality are such fantasies when the father has gone to war? All these factors are true, of course, for both sides—victor and vanquished. The Oedipal conflict is sharpened for the sons left alone with their mothers and their castration anxiety is thereby increased. But how much more was this anxiety exacerbated by the famine which began in Germany in 1917, since prolonged hunger stimulates oral regression and magnifies fantasies of physical destruction to gigantic dimensions! When the defeat came in 1918, followed by economic calamity, the Oedipal dilemma for the German boy was further intensified. If it is not easy to cede one's place next to the mother even to a victorious returning father, how much more difficult is it when the father does not appear to deserve this renunciation! Defeat, starvation, revolution, inflation—all these served only to prove to the son of the lower middle class that his so emphatically autocratic father was incapable of protecting the family.

What of the defensive measures available to the young sons against such guilt and anxiety-provoking ideas? Of course, there can be and are myriads of individual variations. But should we not expect that the experience of fears common to so many also aroused common defensive measures? Let us begin with the famine—surely we can assume that it led to the mobilization of unconscious wishes for a return to the mother–child units, that it put oral needs in the foreground, and that it stimulated the use of defence mechanisms appropriate to this early ego phase.

Consonant with such regression is the increased use of the mechanism of projection. It springs from the primitive peripherization of irritant stimuli; and, in the interpersonal setting, it has the purpose of retaining the love object threatened by aggression born of frustration. It denies this aggression against its object. It claims to be good and demands: Love me and hate the enemy; he is the aggressive one. Two decades later, the sado-masochistic fantasies and the splitting bred by these circumstances found their way back to consciousness in the storm troopers' wooing of the Führer and in the refrain of his song: "Jewish blood must squirt off the knife." The public admission of these crude fantasies was facilitated by the fact that so many young people responded to the renewed anxiety with like regression. The restraining force of guilt is always minimized when impulses are so broadly shared.

Other infantile instinctual and defensive sources were enhancing the need to march about in uniformed groups. To wear a uniform revived the image of the glorified father who had gone out to war and helped to erase that of those who returned defeated. More than any whose fathers had done military service in peacetime, this uncertain generation needed to proclaim its masculinity by wearing a uniform. And yet by far the greatest part of this very generation of German youth was denied this identification and wish fulfilment because of the sharply limited numbers permitted to the Reichswehr.

German education has always made subordination to authority a prime ideal. During the war, the corresponding wish to follow was greatly intensified by the longing for the absent father. The longing for him—shared with the mother—led to extraordinarily exacerbated childish, homosexual wishes. Proof that they had persisted into adult life was given wide publicity by Hitler himself, in the Röhm episode. The homosexual component undoubtedly loomed large in the Nazi movement. On the other hand, just this very love for the father demanded the most energetic denial and repression of gleeful ideas concerning his degradation. We can recognize this need in the reaction formation of superpatriotism and in the extraordinary willingness for subordination to authority. Therefore, even such coarse propaganda slogans (copied from Italian Fascist slogans, where they had been effective for not too dissimilar reasons) as "Shut Up," "Attention," "Obey," could have a magnetic and hypnotic effect on these youths. Some of their latent homosexual tension was relieved through this submission to a deified, *untouchable* leader. In addition, in childhood, too, the increase of homosexual leanings had offered a way out of the Oedipal conflict, heightened as it was for these sons who had remained alone with their mothers. The woman, in these circumstances, is rejected and the incestuous wish is ascribed to someone else. This composite defense became clearly discernible in the attitude of the Nazis both toward women and toward Jews: Women were regarded as brood machines, and the Jews were persecuted as defilers of the race, i.e., incestuous criminals. . . .

One may ask at this point, how was it that, at a time when feminism was expanding everywhere, the young German woman permitted herself to be relegated to such a humiliating position; not only permitted it, but accepted it with passionate dedication to the Führer. First of all, the factors which fostered enthusiastic submission to the authoritarian and idealized father by the sons were also valid for the nostalgic daughters. Further, in the face of the pronounced homosexuality of her male partner, the young German woman had to give up all effort to win rights for herself as a woman. She had to abandon all feminine, coquettish resistance, and, by wearing a uniform herself also, adopt a reassuring, pseudo-phallic identity. It is also likely that many of the mothers, brought up under the dictum "Kinder, Kirche, Küche" were inadequate for the role which their husbands' prolonged absence assigned to them and that they were more punitive towards their sons than they would otherwise have been. The passive-masochistic inclinations which this fostered reinforced in later life the tendency to submit preferably to a man, because of the greater castration anxiety aroused by submission to a woman.

Prolonged absence of a parent is always regarded by the child as a rejection. His futile longing, mixed with causality-supplying masochistic fantasy, produces feelings of unworthiness and humiliation. He then frequently projects the derivatives of those feelings on to someone else. The young generation of which we speak here, orphaned, temporarily or permanently, during childhood, did just that. It rid itself of its own suicidal depression by displacing self-humiliation and self-contempt on to the Jews and other supposedly inferior peoples, thereby ultimately converting suicide into genocide.

Children brought up under such stress have a low tension tolerance. Their weakened egos are prone to seek relief through action. The need for impulsive action and the need for organized re-enactment combined will follow inexorably along the path of childhood patterns. The wish to rehabilitate, through imitation, or to avenge the father is thus established in childhood. This repetition compulsion is probably also the basis for the common conviction that each generation has to experience its own war. Moreover, in postwar Germany, denial of and self-delusion about the defeat was actually promoted by education. The teaching of war history stopped in most instances with an account of the early victories in the East.

The urge to march around in uniformed groups was felt in all strata of this German postwar generation. Proletarian youth, too, in the beginning of the great depression, rid itself of its tensions in this manner—it also marched and was, after a fashion, uniformed. But it had an enemy, solid and rationalized, the capitalist, who, moreover, had also been the enemy for its fathers. The more rationalized enmity is, the less need it be bloodthirsty and magical. The youth of the lower middle class, however, was in a somewhat different situation, having to cope with two additional stresses: The threatened loss of identity as a class and the greater difficulty in achieving identity as an individual in relation to a more autocratic father.

As I have said, the external calamity of the thirties rekindled the anxiety of the war and postwar years and at the same time reawakened the magic, illogical, sadistic defensive methods of childhood. The former wartime enemy, while denounced, was, in fact, for the time being unassailable. Instead, the stranger within, the Jew, was substituted for him and all aggressive methods of defense against fear could be applied to him with impunity. "The Jews are our misfortune" replaced all bothersome self-examination and justified the weakened ego's compelling need for regressive action. And through the regressive, sadistic, military re-enactment the internalized image of the glorified, protective father was restored. These, then, were some of the vicissitudes that had taken place within the ego of this generation, but its superego functions were also distorted.

The receptivity to Nazi propaganda advocating the use of regressive ego defences had been immensely increased because the superego of the generation in question had been structured under the influence of war propaganda which actually praises sadistic action and fosters the dichotomy "idealization vilification." With the end of the war, the superego of this generation had been further undermined by an exaggeration of the cynicism that normally occurs in adolescence (Loewenstein, 1951), because the young sons of the defeated fathers countered the feeling of guilt caused by their glee over this defeat, by depreciating *all* moral values. As these were essentially tied to the Judaeo-Christian religious teachings this process enhanced the previous and contemporary diminution of religious affiliations. This cynicism toward all moral values is finally most blatantly revealed in the young storm troopers' ruthless adherence to the Nazi dictum: The end justifies the means.

It was, therefore, by a catastrophic concatenation of circumstances that in 1930 an acute external calamity encountered a generation whose premorbid disposition was most sensitive. The numerous individual psychoses which otherwise threatened were warded off by a mass psychosis or, one may add, a trend toward delinquent gang formation was channelled into paramilitary political action groups. . . .

. . . My main objective has been to point (*a*) to the ego and superego debility which occurred in a whole generation, through the impact of prolonged, anxiety-arousing experiences in childhood; and (*b*) to the revival of regressive ideation, defences, and actions under the impact of a stress renewed at the critical moment of life when the adolescent turns to manhood. The happenings of 1917 to 1920 thus cast their shadows ahead on to those of the thirties, not only politically and economically, but also in the depth of individual psychology.

Should this genetic, psychological reasoning concerning the outbreak of Nazism prove to be correct, it must give us cause to be alert in the near future. In 1960, a statistical study by Wilkins demonstrated that English children who were between three and five years of age during the worst war years showed a 40 per cent higher crime rate in their eighth, and from their seventeenth to twentieth years than the corresponding youth of the years of peace. Throughout Europe—and perhaps in a measure in the U.S.A., too—groups of young people are now reaching the age of political effectiveness who were born or brought up under conditions of extreme distress and peril and who, because of this, share the inability to bear up well under stress. A generation is now coming of political age whose ego defences are predisposed to regression and whose superego values are vulnerable. May not the young people of this generation, under the pressure of another economic depression, again become the victims of an unconscious repetition compulsion? Will they not want to do what their fathers did or to avenge what, in fact or allegedly, has been done to their fathers? So long as there is prosperity, the roads to regression will not open so easily; but what will happen if renewed economic and social fears are added to the ever-present war tensions? . . .

*   *   *

8.

SOME PROBLEMS IN THE LAW OF CRIMES, THE MILITARY, INSURANCE, AND JUVENILE CUSTODY

a.   STATE v. SIKORA
          44 N.J. 453, 210 A.2d 193 (1965)

FRANCIS, J.

Defendant Walter J. Sikora shot and killed Douglas Hooey in the early morning of January 15, 1962. . . .

*   *   *

At the time of trial Sikora was 36 years of age, five feet, six inches tall and weighed 116 pounds. He had had an unfortunate childhood. His earliest recollection was of living in a Catholic Home in Bergen County when about five or six years old. He never had any visitors there, as the other children did, and he was lonesome and unhappy. At age seven the Child Welfare Board placed him in a foster home in Northvale, New Jersey. There he claims he was beaten and ran away. On being brought back he refused to stay and was transferred to an orphanage. After a few months there he was sent to the Hackensack Children's Home where he remained for about a year. Over the next few years he was in three foster homes. He was unhappy and received beatings for bedwetting. In the third home he was locked in his room for two weeks after which he ran away again. When picked up by the police he was sent to the Hackensack Child Welfare Home. He was then 15 years old. While there he said he was confined to an isolation room for a week at a time. At 16 years he was transferred and allowed to work in a bakery, but was made to work so hard he ran away again. Then he was committed to James-burg Boys Home where he got along fairly well and remained for about a year. Thereafter the authorities put him to work on a dairy farm in the area. He claimed the hours of work were from 4:00 a.m. to 7:00 or 7:30 p.m., for which he was paid $1 per week and room and board. Later he received $2 weekly. Permission was given to leave the farm and join the Merchant Marine when he was about 19 years old.

After three and one-half years he left the Merchant Marine and came to live in Paterson, New Jersey, where he remained, except for Army service, until this crime was committed. The Army drafted him in 1955 and he was in service until February 1957. He was discharged at his own request "under honor-able conditions." He told some of the psychiatrists who testified at this trial that intoxication and over-staying of leave played a part in his discharge. He was unhappy in the Army because he was 30 years of age when drafted and he had to serve and work with 18- and 19-year-old boys.

Sikora returned to Paterson in February 1957. While there he worked as a general laborer, doing carpentry and painting until 1959 when he became employed in refrigeration and air conditioning in-stallation. While engaged in the latter work, he had living quarters over his employer's shop. This re-mained his official residence until the shooting.

Sikora has never married and the companionship of women was infrequent. Most of his free time was spent alone and in nearby taverns where, apparently, he consumed large quantities of beer. In May 1959 while in a tavern he met a woman who was about 15 years older than he. About three months later, he moved into her apartment and lived with her as man and wife until December 29, 1961. They got along very well and after a time agreed to marry when they had saved a fixed amount of money. Subsequently while intoxicated, he was "rolled" and his savings stolen. This caused friction between them and both began to drink heavily. On December 28, 1961, they had an argument in the course of which Sikora literally turned her apartment "upside down." She had him arrested the next day and he was fined and ordered to leave her home. He did so, returning his belongings to the quarters over his employer's shop. (He was receiving unemployment compensation at the time, having been laid off during December.)

After the separation he telephoned her daily but she refused to speak to him. This upset him greatly. According to the defense psychiatric testimony at the trial, his relationship with her was a markedly de-pendent one, she being the dominant and aggressive party. He continued to frequent the D & D Tavern, a neighborhood establishment where he had first met her. On Friday, January 12, 1962, according to his testimony, he attempted suicide at home by taking a large quantity of pills. The attempt was unsuccessful and he awoke about Sunday noon, January 14, sick but not seriously affected by the experience.

In the early afternoon of that day he wrote his erstwhile girl friend a letter and placed it in her mail-box. He made no effort to go into her apartment. Shortly thereafter he made a telephone call to her which was answered by a male voice, and he then went to the D & D Tavern. This was about 4:30 p.m. While drinking beer he noticed Douglas Hooey there. He had known Hooey casually as a frequenter of the tavern for about two years. Apparently he had had a flare-up with his female friend a short time previous over Hooey.

Sikora visited with a male friend in the tavern until about 9:30 p.m. when the friend left. Thereafter Sikora sat alone at the bar, and on several occasions Hooey would brush by him poking an elbow into his back. Then Hooey would stand nearby and grin, but Sikora had no words with him. On one occasion he overheard Hooey make a disparaging remark about the availability of Sikora's girl friend now that they had broken up. Between 11:00 and 12:00 p.m., after he had consumed 25 to 30 glasses of beer, he testified he was suddenly attacked by Hooey and two or three of his friends, badly beaten and kicked, and then thrown out of the tavern onto the sidewalk. When he arose he was cut and bleeding about the face, head and hands. (The State contended his hands were cut when he broke the glass panel of the door in attempting to re-enter the tavern.)

He walked home, entered his employer's shop, called the police and reported the incident. In a few minutes the police car appeared and he described what had occurred, asking that they accompany him back to the tavern. They declined unless he would ride to police headquarters and sign a complaint. On his refusal and declination of their offer to take him to the hospital, the officers departed.

Sikora went upstairs to his apartment and lay on the bed thinking of what had happened to him and his difficulty with his female friend. While there (according to his testimony) he conceived the idea of killing himself. He said he was crying, and mixed up, and he took from its hiding place an automatic pistol which he had bought during his Merchant Marine service. The gun was fully loaded with eight shells in the clip and one in the chamber. He took the safety off and sat on the bed, but on second thought changed his mind about suicide, and decided to return to the tavern first to talk to Hooey about the fight. The gun had never been fired in the years he owned it. He left his building and went across the street to a shed and test-fired it until it was empty. Then he went back to his apartment, walked part way up the stairs, stopped and reloaded the gun with nine bullets. He took the bullets from a box containing over 50 of them which he had put in his pocket at the time he picked up the gun in his bedroom. According to his testimony, while reloading the gun he thought of the men who had assaulted him in the tavern. Then he "just lost his head" and started for the tavern to talk to Hooey and find out the reason for the attack. In this connection it may be noted that after the homicide and Sikora's arrest, police officers found in his apartment a bloodstained piece of paper on which he had written, "The first bullet is for Doug and the second is for Stella Miller." Although there was some equivocation in his confession, which admittedly was voluntarily given, and in his testimony as to when the note was written, the evidence suggests very strongly that it was written before he armed himself and left his apartment to return to the tavern in search of Hooey.

On leaving the apartment, he put the gun in his waist belt and zippered up his jacket far enough to hide it. Thinking there would be a number of persons in the tavern, he decided to use the alleyway entrance, and endeavor to get Hooey out that door so as to talk to him about the assault. As he neared the tavern he saw the lights go out, and he decided not to go in. It was about 3:00 a.m. which, apparently, is closing time. But as he passed the door he heard a woman remark in profane language that he was the one who had been beaten up earlier. Looking back he saw Hooey coming out the tavern door. Hooey asked, "What the hell are you doing here?" Sikora testified he replied he wanted to find out why he had been beaten up. Both Hooey and the woman started to walk towards him, whereupon he drew the gun and told Hooey not to come closer. Hooey kept coming and Sikora began to back up, repeating his warning. Sikora said Hooey was grinning, and asked if Sikora thought "the thing will shoot." Sikora replied Hooey was "liable to find out" if he did not stop coming forward. Sikora knew the safety catch on the gun was off. There was an intersecting street a short distance from the tavern and Sikora was backing toward it. He stepped off the curb into the street with Hooey approaching him. At this time he fired and four shots entered Hooey's head and body killing him. Then he ran across the street, looked back and fired the gun in the air, shouting as he did, "All you bastards stay back."

From the scene of the killing he went to his girlfriend's house and rang the bell. There was no answer, so he kicked in the door. Not finding her at home he left and returned to his own apartment. Before departing, however, he attempted to retrieve from her mailbox the letter he had deposited there the previous afternoon. After getting it part way out of the box, he decided against taking it and pushed it back. Later the police found bloody finger marks on it. At his apartment he lay on the bed expecting the police to arrive in a short time. He reloaded the gun (he said) with the intention of shooting himself.

About ten minutes later when the police appeared, the intention had not been executed.

The above factual outline represents the substance of Sikora's testimony and his voluntary confession. The confession, which fills 51 pages of the trial transcript, was signed in the early afternoon of the day of the shooting. It reveals a comprehensive recollection of the circumstances before and at the time of the fatal event. The psychiatrists who testified for the State and defense received very much the same history from Sikora at the time of their examinations. The State contended that the facts in their totality demonstrated beyond a reasonable doubt that the defendant had committed a premeditated, deliberate and wilful killing and was therefore guilty of murder in the first degree.

No defense of insanity was interposed. All the psychiatrists agreed Sikora was legally sane before and at the time of the shooting....

* * *

Dr. Galen specializes in psychiatry and psychoanalysis. He received his M.D. degree in 1949. In addition to postgraduate work in neurology and psychiatry, he had three years of training as a psychoanalyst. This last training, he said, dealt with psychodynamics on a very detailed and sophisticated level. It taught him that people are a product of their own life history, their own genetic patterns, and that they all react differently under the stresses of their daily lives. As a result of his study and experience, he believes that mental disturbance and disorder, as distinguished from objective disease, are merely gradients, that people range from being essentially normal, perceiving the world substantially in its normal appearance, all the way to marked distortion of the thinking mechanism, and between the two extremes is a rather jagged line which is prone to and open to many variations. In short, all human behavior is distributed upon an infinite spectrum of fine gradations, there being no all or none in human dynamics. It is his view that mental disorder is one degree of an indeterminate line between gross disorganization and normal functioning, and it is often impossible to say at what point on the line a particular person is functioning at a given time. Mental illness or disorder in this context is a relative term as he sees it; it is disorganization of the personality which causes a person to react in a specific way to a specific kind of stress in a way characteristic for him.

Psychodynamics is the study of what makes a man "tick." In effect the doctor said its purpose is to seek an explanation of an individual's mental condition at a given time in terms of his lifelong emotional development; to relate his questioned conduct and its accompanying emotional symptoms to their long antecedent, predetermining factors. In appearing as a witness, Dr. Galen indicated his function was to help the court understand "the dynamics of what happened to this man with this particular history at this particular time in his life." It was not his place as a psychiatrist to consider the premeditation aspect of murder in terms of right or wrong or good or evil. Evil is a philosophical concept. In his view the psychodynamic psychiatrist cannot consider the aspect of first degree murder which in law requires the conceiving of a design to kill in terms of evil, or evil intent. These moral judgments are best left to the courts to decide. Such a physician deals with the problem in a scientific way by applying his knowledge of the "way people operate," his knowledge of stress and "the way people react to particular kinds of stress, based on their personality disorganization." He feels "somewhat medieval in talking about evil." Basically Dr. Galen's thesis is that man is a helpless victim of his genes and his lifelong environment; that unconscious forces from within dictate the individual's behavior without his being able to alter it.

By way of illustrating the area of psychodynamics under discussion, Dr. Galen referred to a physician friend who, while driving on a public highway, was cut off by another motorist.

> "[T]his man who is a professional man knows clearly, in a general way, right from wrong, good from evil, if we want to get into that old controversy, but this man chased the car who cut him off and finally cut the car off that cut him off. Now, at this particular time, when he was behaving in this way, which was really endangering his life, endangering the lives of other people, although he was sane at the time, he was acting in an irrational manner with a disturbance of his consciousness; and consciousness is a very difficult thing to define and understand unless one sees it as a dynamic."

The impression conveyed by this illustration is that under Dr. Galen's view of the dynamic relationship between the conscious and the unconscious, if his friend had killed someone with his car while pursuing the motorist who had offended him, he should not be held to criminal responsibility because he set out on the chase as the result of unconscious rather than conscious motivation. The idea seems to be that every deed, no matter how quickly executed, is never fully the result of the apparent immediate cause, and must be judged according to the probable unconscious motivations of an individual with the actor's lifelong history. Therefore, if in the opinion of the psychodynamically oriented psychiatrist, the deed, when evaluated against a background of the individual's life history, was probably produced by unconscious rather than conscious motivations, there was no *mens rea*, no criminal intent, and therefore no criminal guilt. In his view the conduct must be considered as having been conditioned by internal and external forces quite beyond the actor's control.

As we have indicated above, when Dr. Galen made his examination about four months after the homicide for about one and three-quarter hours, he obtained substantially the history detailed above. Sikora had a clear recollection of his previous life and of the events of the fatal night, and he was able to give the doctor a step-by-step account of the circumstances of the shooting. On the basis of the history, it was his opinion that at the time of the crime (and perhaps all his adult life) Sikora was suffering from a personality disorder of a passive-dependent type, with aggressive features. This kind of disorder is a function of his personality "which is his way of dealing with himself and with life and with people and with stress." He found no evidence of any overt hallucinations, delusions or ideas of reference; nor any evidence of organic mental disease. The accused's insight and judgment were consonant with his education, emotional status and intellect; he was "estimated" to have a normal to dull-normal level of intelligence....

*   *   *

According to Dr. Galen, tensions had been building up in Sikora, particularly since his female friend rejected him. When he was humiliated in the tavern by the remarks about her availability for other men because she had broken with him, and then physically beaten by Hooey and his companions, the tensions mounted to the point where they represented a situation in life with which he felt unable to cope. So he began to act in an automatic way; the manner in which a person with his personality inadequacy would characteristically act. He responded to the stress in the way which inevitably would be his way of dealing with that kind of stress. He reacted automatically in the fashion of Dr. Galen's physician friend when he was cut off by another motorist.... The beating administered by Hooey in the tavern precipitated the disorganization of his personality to the extent that from then on he probably "acted in at least a semi-automatic way, and probably an automatic way."

The doctor went on to say that from the defendant's course of conduct it could be seen that he was acting in an automatic way "rather than being totally aware of his environment, and the situation...." Although the state was not completely an automatic one there were "strong elements of automatism" present. He was not "fully conscious of his activities" and not "completely aware" of what he was doing. The stress to which he had been subjected had distorted his personality disorder, the kind of man life had made him, when subjected to that stress prevented him from "seeing reality, or premeditating or forming a rational opinion of what is going on in his life." He had been confronted with a situation and reacted with conduct which was his characteristic way of dealing with the particular kind of stress. As the doctor put it in answer to defense counsel's question:

"You may react to someone cutting you off on the highway in a different way than the Prosecutor may. It has to do with your personality. It has to do with your way of dealing with this kind of stress."

In short the doctor opined that the circumstances to which Sikora had been subjected imposed on his personality disorder a stress that impaired or removed his ability consciously to premeditate or weigh a design to kill. The tension was so great that he could handle it only by an automatic reaction motivated by the predetermined influence of his unconscious. Plainly the doctor meant that Sikora's response was not a voluntary exercise of his free will. The stress was such as to distort his mechanisms. During the various actions Sikora took leading up to the killing, which so clearly indicate conception, deliberation and execution of a plan to kill, he was thinking but the thinking was automatic; it was simply subconscious thinking or reaction; it was not conscious thinking. The doctor said Sikora's anxieties at the time were of such a nature that conceivably, his reaction in that automatic way and the commission of the homicide, actually prevented a further disorganization of his personality. The killing, said the doctor, was "a rational murder" but "everything this man did was irrational," and engaged in when he could not conceive the design to kill. . . .

The question now presented is whether psychiatric evidence of the nature described is admissible in first degree murder cases on the issue of premeditation. Defendant argues that it should have been received at the trial on that issue. . . .

. . . For protection of society the law accepts the thesis that all men are invested with free will and capable of choosing between right and wrong. In the present state of scientific knowledge that thesis cannot be put aside in the administration of the criminal law. Criminal blameworthiness cannot be judged on a basis that negates free will and excuses the offense, wholly or partially, on opinion evidence that the offender's psychological processes or mechanisms were such that even though he knew right from wrong he was predetermined to act the way he did at that time because of unconscious influences set in motion by the emotional stresses then confronting him. In a world of reality such persons must be held responsible for their behavior.

*   *   *

Criminal responsibility must be judged at the level of the conscious. If a person thinks, plans and executes the plan at that level, the criminality of his act cannot be denied, wholly or partially, because, although he did not realize it, his conscious was influenced to think, to plan and to execute the plan by unconscious influences which were the product of his genes and his lifelong environment. So in the present case, criminal guilt cannot be denied or confined to second degree murder (when the killing was a "rational murder" and the product of thought and action), because Sikora was unaware that his decisions and conduct were mechanistically directed by unconscious influences bound to result from the tensions to which he was subjected at the time. If the law were to accept such a medical doctrine as a basis for a finding of second rather than first degree murder, the legal doctrine of *mens rea* would all but disappear from the law. Applying Dr. Galen's theory to crimes requiring specific intent to commit, such as robbery, larceny, rape, etc., it is difficult to imagine an individual who perpetrated the deed as having the mental capacity in the criminal law sense to conceive the intent to commit it. Criminal responsibility, as society now knows it, would vanish from the scene and some other basis for dealing with the offender would have to be found. At bottom, this would appear to be the ultimate aim of the psychodynamic psychiatrists.

*   *   *

[F]or purposes of administration of the criminal law in this State we cannot accept a thesis that responsibility in law for a criminal act perpetrated by a legally sane defendant, can be considered nonexistent or measured by the punishment established for a crime of lower degree, because his act was motivated by subconscious influences of which he was not aware, and which stemmed inevitably from his individual personality structure. A criminal act of that nature is nothing more than the consequence of an impulse that was not resisted.

In first degree murder cases psychiatric testimony of the type adduced here should be admitted but its probative function limited to the area of sentence or punishment. . . .

*   *   *

. . . Dr. Galen's testimony should have been admitted at the trial, and submitted to the jury for consideration solely on the issue of punishment—life imprisonment or death. But the error cannot be deemed prejudicial. The jury did in fact recommend life imprisonment as part of its verdict, and that sentence was imposed. Under the circumstances, there is no basis for a new trial and accordingly the judgment of conviction is affirmed.

*   *   *

WEINTRAUB, C. J. (concurring).

*   *   *

To put the subject in perspective, we must start with the common law's conception of crime. The common law required (1) an evil deed and (2) *mens rea*—a guilty mind. This conception emerged from man's then understanding of himself. It was felt to be unjust to stigmatize a man a criminal unless his evil deed was accompanied by an evil-meaning mind. Insanity was relevant only insofar as it denied the existence of an evil intent and thus disputed that critical element of the State's charge. It was assumed that all men were able to adhere to the right if they saw the right, and hence insanity was conceived to be such disease of the mind as prevented the accused from understanding the nature of his act and that it was wrong. The law thus separated the sick from the bad upon the basis of a man's capacity to know what was right. Any other imperfection or defect was deemed to be merely a bad trait of character or personality.

The law's conception, resting as it does upon an undemonstrable view of man, is of course vulnerable. But those who attack it cannot offer a view which is demonstrably more authentic. They can tear down the edifice but have nothing better to replace it.

The psychiatric view advanced by Dr. Galen seems quite scientific. It rests upon the elementary concept of cause and effect. The individual is deemed the product of many causes. As a matter of historical fact, he was not the author of any of the formative forces, nor of his capacity or lack of capacity to deal with them. In short, so far as we know, no man is his own maker. I say so far as we know, for man has yet to catch a glimpse of the ultimate truth. The concept of cause-and-effect, satisfying though it may be for most matters, is a dead-end approach to the mystery of our being.

Actually this psychiatric view of man is not new. It was centuries ago that an Englishman, seeing another taken to the place of execution, said of himself, "But for the grace of God there goes John Bradford." Wordsworth knew "The child is father of the man." What the psychiatrist has added is the detailed psychodynamics beneath an individual's objective behavior.

Abstractly, the cause-and-effect thesis could suggest a stultifying determinism whereunder every stroke of a man's pen was ordained when time first stirred. But the psychiatrist, awed by it all, wisely leaves that subject to the philosopher. Besides it is not easy for an inquiring mind to believe it is on a string stretching from infinity. Nonetheless the cause-and-effect thesis dominates the psychiatrist's view of his patient. He traces a man's every deed to some cause truly beyond the actor's own making, and says that although the man was aware of his action, he was unaware of assembled forces in his unconscious which decided his course. Thus the conscious is a puppet, and the unconscious the puppeteer.

And so, Dr. Galen, in expounding the psychodynamics of Sikora's murderous exploit, started with the premise that Sikora appreciated the nature of his act and knew it was wrong; that Sikora was aware of the events which indeed he recalled with great detail, but was unaware that his unconscious was so constituted that its reaction to his conscious experience had to be homicidal. The doctor added, as I understand him, that the unconscious probably decided on murder in order to avoid a complete disintegration of the personality.

Now this is interesting, and I will not quarrel with any of it. But the question is whether it has anything to do with the crime of murder. I think it does not.

The witness described Sikora's actions as wholly "automatic." While at times he spoke in other terms, such as that Sikora was really not "fully" conscious of what he was doing despite his "long . . . and rather clear history of what occurred," and although on cross-examination the doctor found himself differentiating between rational and irrational ways of committing murder (a most unscientific discourse, it seems to me), his professional theme remained that the conscious was the unwitting and unsuspecting puppet of the unconscious.

Further, "disease" has nothing to do with this automatic behavior. Although in obeisance to M'Naghten the witness said his "diagnosis" of a "personality disorder of a passive dependent type with aggressive features" describes "a mental disorder" listed in the Manual of the American Psychiatric Association, he denied the reality of such classifications. Rather he said mental disturbances or disorders are merely gradients in the range from "essentially normal" to "marked disturbance of the thinking mechanism." The point I stress is that the automatic thesis in nowise depends upon the existence of some "disorder" of the mind. Rather it accounts for all human behavior, whether it be a murder or the retaliatory action of the witness's doctor friend who cut off a motorist who had cut him off, or the raising of one's index finger rather than his pinky, to refer to still another example Dr. Galen gave of the dictatorial control of the unconscious.[1]

Under this psychiatric concept no man could be convicted of anything if the law were to accept the impulses of the unconscious as an excuse for conscious misbehavior. Although the specific question put to Dr. Galen was whether the defendant was capable of premeditating the murder, his answer would have to be the same if he were asked whether defendant was able to form an intent to do grievous bodily harm or any harm at all. His answer would have to be that the unconscious directed the killing in response to the stimulus of the events preceding the killing. The same explanation would account for the misbehavior of Dr. Galen's motoring friend if he were charged with a violation of the motor vehicle act.

What then shall we do with our fellow automaton

---

1. This automaton concept apparently differs from the "irresistible impulse" concept in that it proclaims the conscious is subservient to the unconscious in illness or in health, whereas the irresistible-impulse concept attempts to distinguish between impulses which were not resisted and impulses which could not be resisted because of mental illness.

whose unconscious directs such antisocial deeds? For one thing, we could say it makes no difference. We could say that in punishing an evil deed accompanied by an evil-meaning mind, the law is concerned only with the existence of a will to do the evil act and it does not matter precisely where within the mind the evil drive resides.

Or we could modify the law's concept of *mens rea* to require an evil-meaning unconscious. The possibilities here are rich. It would be quite a thing to identify the unconscious drive and then decide whether it is evil for the purpose of criminal liability. For example, if we somehow were satisfied that a man murdered another as an alternative to an unconscious demand for suicide or because the unconscious believed it had to kill to avoid a full-blown psychosis, shall we say there was or was not a good defense? Shall we indict for murder a motorist who kills another because, although objectively he was negligent at the worst, the psychoanalyst assures us that the conscious man acted automatically to fulfill an unconscious desire for self-destruction? All of this is fascinating but much too frothy to support a structure of criminal law.

Finally, we could amend our concept of criminal responsibility by eliminating the requirement of an evil-meaning mind. That is the true thrust of this psychiatric view of human behavior, for while our criminal law seeks to punish only those who act with a sense of wrongdoing and hence excuses those who because of sickness were bereft of that awareness, the psychiatrist rejects a distinction between the sick and the bad. To him no one is personally blameworthy for his make-up or for his acts. To him the law's distinction between a defect of the mind and a defect of character is an absurd invention. . . . [T]he psychiatric conception of man would lead the law to discard insanity as a defense and to think of *mens rea* as nothing more than a conscious intent, objectively-found, to do the forbidden act.

The subject of criminal blameworthiness is so obscure that there is an understandable disposition to let anything in for whatever use the jury may wish to make of it. But it will not do merely to receive testimony upon the automaton thesis, for the jury must be told what its legal effect may be. Specifically, the jury must be told whether a man is chargeable with his unconscious drives.

It seems clear to me that the psychiatric view expounded by Dr. Galen is simply irreconcilable with the basic thesis of our criminal law, for while the law requires proof of an evil-meaning mind, this psychiatric thesis denies there is any such thing. To grant a role in our existing structure to the theme that the conscious is just the innocent puppet of a nonculpable unconscious is to make a mishmash of the criminal law, permitting—indeed requiring—each trier of the facts to choose between the automaton thesis and the law's existing concept of criminal accountability. It would be absurd to decide criminal blameworthiness upon a psychiatric thesis which can find no basis for personal blame. So long as we adhere to criminal blameworthiness, *mens rea* must be sought and decided at the level of conscious behavior.

NOTES

NOTE 1

PEOPLE v. GORSHEN
51 Cal. App. 2d 716, 336 P. 2d 492 (1959)

SCHAUER, JUSTICE.

Defendant pleaded not guilty to a charge of murder. Trial by jury was waived . . . and the court . . . found defendant guilty of second-degree murder. Defendant appeals from the ensuing judgment. He urges that uncontradicted psychiatric testimony, accepted by the trial court, established that defendant did not intend to take human life or, at least, he did not act with malice aforethought, and that therefore he should be acquitted or, as a minimum of relief, that the offense should be reduced to manslaughter. . . .

Defendant, a longshoreman, shot and killed his foreman, Joseph O'Leary, at about 2:30 a.m. on March 9, 1957. The record discloses the following events leading up to the homicide: At 5 p.m. on March 8 defendant reported to the dispatching hall. Between 6 and 7 o'clock he and a fellow worker ate and consumed a fifth of a gallon of sloe gin. Defendant worked until 11 p.m. Between 11 and 12 o'clock defendant and the fellow worker ate and consumed a pint of sloe gin. Shortly after 12 midnight O'Leary saw defendant standing on the deck of the ship drinking a glass of coffee. O'Leary told defendant to go to work. Defendant threw the glass to the deck, exchanged "a few words" with O'Leary, and went to work. Thereafter O'Leary told defendant that he was drunk and was not doing his work properly and directed defendant to go home. They argued, defendant spat in O'Leary's face, and O'Leary knocked defendant down and kicked him. At the request of other workers O'Leary walked away from the defendant. Defendant threw a piece of dunnage and brandished a carton at O'Leary.

Paul Baker, a "walking boss," took defendant to a hospital. Defendant was bleeding and bruised; his left eye was swollen shut and a deep cut under it required five or six stitches. Defendant was discharged at 1:45 a.m. The hospital records bear the notation, "Alcoholic Breath." As Baker drove defendant back to the pier where they worked, defendant said "that he was going to go home and get a gun and kill this fellow."

When he reached the pier defendant said that he

wished to return to work but his superiors insisted that he go home. Defendant said, "I'll go home and get my gun. I'll come back and take care of him." Defendant drove to his home, got a .25 caliber automatic pistol which contained two bullets, fired one shot in his living room, put the gun in his apron, and drove back to the pier. He arrived there about thirty minutes after he had been sent home and went onto the ship looking for O'Leary.

O'Leary and Nelson, a union business agent, had followed defendant to his house and, when they saw defendant leave his house, had driven to a police station. Police officers went to the pier. They searched defendant but did not find his gun. Defendant told the officers that he "had a fight with Mr. O'Leary, and . . . that he couldn't forget about the eye that he had obtained during the fight." One of the officers described defendant as "angry," "almost tearsome," "emotional," but not incoherent or boisterous.

O'Leary and Nelson then appeared. Defendant said, "My buddy. Hah, my buddy," and produced the gun. O'Leary shouted, "Look out, he's got the gun." Defendant shot. The single bullet entered O'Leary's abdomen, killing him; it also wounded Nelson's arm. The officers subdued defendant after a brief struggle. Defendant told the authorities, shortly after the homicide, that O'Leary was "looking at me, smiling, so I just let him have it . . . Nelson was standing by; I had to take chance to hit him, because I had only one bullet."

Defendant had a very good reputation for peace and quiet and did not usually drink to excess. He testified as follows: During the fifteen years he had known O'Leary prior to the night of the homicide they had been friends and had had no trouble. Defendant's recollection of the events of that night was "kind of hazy." He considered it unfair of O'Leary to order him to go home but to retain the fellow worker with whom defendant had been drinking.

"The argument starts about he wants me to go home and I . . . tell him that I intend to wait until business agent comes in, so apparently he, he hit me and knocked me off, off the floor and when I jumped up, he got on and hit me again, and that's—then I tried to defend myself. I, I didn't hit him. . . .; he was apparently too fast for me or stronger, bigger." Defendant did not recall throwing a piece of dunnage or brandishing a carton or threatening to go home and get a gun. When he discharged the gun in his home, "I didn't know it was on the safety or not, I was shaky, I didn't know what I was doing." Defendant recalled little of his return to the pier, but did recall that the police searched him. Then he saw O'Leary "grinning, looking at me. I don't know what, what become of me. I just grabbed the gun and shot."

Dr. Bernard L. Diamond, a psychiatrist who examined defendant, testified. After described examin-ations and tests of defendant, he had concluded that defendant suffers from chronic paranoiac schizophrenia, a disintegration of mind and personality.[2] For twenty years defendant has had trances during which he hears voices and experiences visions, particularly of devils in disguise committing abnormal sexual acts, sometimes upon defendant. Defendant recognizes that these experiences are "not real" but believes that they are forced upon him by the devil. Apparently defendant, prior to his examination by Dr. Diamond, had not disclosed these experiences to anyone.

A year before the shooting, defendant (who was fifty-six years of age at the time of trial) became concerned about loss of sexual power. With this concern his sexual hallucinations occurred with increased frequency and his ability in his work became increasingly important to him as a proof of manhood.

On the night of the shooting, O'Leary's statement that defendant was drunk and should leave his work was to defendant the psychological equivalent of the statement that "You're not a man, you're impotent, . . . you're a sexual pervert." Then, according to defendant's statements to Dr. Diamond, O'Leary applied to defendant an epithet which indicated sexual perversion. At this point, according to Dr. Diamond's opinion, defendant was confronted with "the imminent possibility of complete loss of his sanity. [A]s an alternate to total disintegration . . . , it's possible for . . . an individual of this kind, to develop an obsessive murderous rage, an unappeasable anger. . . . The strength of this obsession is proportioned not to the reality danger but to the danger of the insanity. [F]or this man to go insane, means to be permanently in the world of these visions and under the influence of the devil. [A]n individual in this state of crisis will do anything to avoid the threatened insanity, and it's this element which lends strength to his compulsive behavior so that he could think of nothing else but to get O'Leary, so he went home and got the gun and shot him; and [as] is usually the case in this type of event, the shooting itself released the danger of [defendant's complete mental disintegration]."

Defendant told Dr. Diamond that from the time he was taken to the emergency hospital until the time of the shooting "That is all I was thinking about all of this time is to shoot O'Leary. I forgot about my family, I forgot about God's laws and human's laws and everything else. The only thing was to get that guy, get that guy, get that guy, like a hammer in the head."

In the opinion of the doctor, defendant acted almost as an automaton; "even the fact that policemen were right at his elbow and there was no pos-

---

2. It should be noted that no question of legal insanity is here involved.

sibility of getting away with this, still it couldn't stop the train of obsessive thoughts which resulted in the killing. [H]e did not have the mental state which is required for malice aforethought or premeditation or anything which implies intention, deliberation, or premeditation."

Dr. Diamond quoted section 188 of the Penal Code, which provides that the "malice aforethought" which is an essential element of murder "may be express or implied. It is express when there is manifested a deliberate intention unlawfully to take away the life of a fellow creature. It is implied, when no considerable provocation appears, or when the circumstances attending the killing show an abandoned and malignant heart." He then gave his opinion of the 'medical essence" of "malice aforethought"; i.e., "whether an individual performs an act as a result of his own free will or intentionality, or . . . whether the action is directly attributable to some abnormal compulsion or force, or symptom or diseased process from within the individual."[3]

The doctor further explained that in his opinion "actions, like the threat to kill, the going home to get the gun and so forth"—actions which "in an ordinary individual" would be evidence "that he intended to do what he did so, and that this was an act of free will and deliberation"—in defendant's case were, rather, "just as much symptoms of his mental illness as the visions and these trances that he goes into."

In cross-examining Dr. Diamond, the prosecuting attorney quoted the following statements from an article by the doctor entitled "With Malice Aforethought," (*Archives of Criminal Psycho-dynamics* 1957, Vol. 2, No. 1).[4]

The prosecuting attorney then asked, "you feel there is no such thing as free will?" The doctor replied, "I believe in what the philosophers call the posit of free will. A posit is a working assumption.

When I treat a patient, if I believed as a working assumption, that everything is predetermined or determined by forces outside of the patient's choice and consciousness, there would be no point in my doing psychotherapy or psychoanalysis; because obviously nobody would ever get better. I certainly proceed on the theory that I and our patients have something to say about what I do and about our choices. What I cannot tell you, because there is no scientific proof, is how much. . . . I know that individuals who are suffering from certain kinds of mental illnesses tend to have very little to say about many of the things that happen to them; other people have a great deal to say about it. . . . Now, whether or not it could be scientifically demonstrated that in no instance is there any free will, this is something I can't give you any answer to."

The trial court stated at some length the matters which it considered in reaching its decision. It said, "up till the time that Dr. Diamond testified in this case, there was no explanation of why this crime was committed. [The doctor is] the first person that has any reasonable explanation. Whether it's correct or not, I don't know. [I]f I would follow Diamond's testimony *in toto*, I should acquit this man. . . .

"I'm willing to go on the record, that in all probability his theories are correct . . . that he had no particular intent to commit this crime.

"I like to be advanced. But it seems to me that my hands are tied with the legal jurisprudence as it stands today, and that's why I'm saying this for the purposes of the record. The Appellate Court might say that my hands are not tied, but I think they are. [E]ven accepting in part the testimony of Dr. Diamond, I still feel that this man is guilty of second-degree murder."

In reply to defense counsel's assertion that "There is not one scintilla of malice," the court said, "it

---

3. The trial court correctly overruled the People's objection that by this testimony the doctor gave "a medical interpretation of a legal principle." The court did not permit the doctor to usurp the judicial function of interpreting legislative language; rather, it properly permitted him to explain what he meant by his opinion that defendant lacked malice aforethought.

4. The trial court considered the entire article, not merely the portions which the prosecuting attorney read aloud. The doctor's position can be better understood when the statements excerpted by the prosecuting attorney are read in their context, which is as follows:

"[T]he central issue [in a psychiatric evaluation of malice aforethought], that of the age-old philosophical abstraction of free will v. determinism, is itself undetermined. Freud, in 1904, brilliantly demonstrated by analysis of slips of the tongue, forgetting, and trains of association that what we call free will or voluntary choice is merely the conscious rationalization of a chain of unconsciously determined processes. Each act of will, each choice presumably made on a random basis, turns out to be as rigidly determined as any other physiological process of the human body. Yet all of us continue to live our lives, make our choices, exercise our free will, and

obey or disobey the law as if we actually had something to say about what we are doing. Criminal law could not exist were it not for this posit that each normal person intends to do the act which he does do and that such intention is based upon the exercise of free will.

"Medical psychology has embarrassingly few answers to this one question which the criminal law is most interested in. It does no good to proclaim to the jurist that scientific evidence proves that there is no such thing as free will. There is a subjective phenomenon which the normal individual experiences as free will. Illusory or not, free will remains the basis of all criminal law simply because free will is the basis of all normal social behavior.

"In truth, today, *we do not have a sufficient foundation of scientific knowledge about the ego functions of decision, choice, and determination of action to justify the formulation of any general principles which could be applied to the law. . . .*

"*The task then becomes to understand the motivations, intent, and actions of the individual who deviates from the common-sense posit of free will. This can be accomplished without specious generalizations which would attack the very structure of the law itself and would compel nonacceptance by the juridical mind. . . .*" (Italics added.)

all depends on how you view it. . . . Some other person or another Judge, might say, 'Malice, why, it's full of it. He planned it. He said he was going to do it, he went home, he had an hour.' "

Again defense counsel asked, "Does your Honor feel that there is malice here?" The court replied, "there was some intent. Now, whether you have free will or not free will, that's so advanced, we're not prepared for that. . . .

Dr. Diamond's testimony was properly received in accord with the holding of People v. Wells (1949), 33 Cal.2d 330, 346–357, 202 P.2d 53, that on the trial of the issues raised by a plea of not guilty to a charge of a crime which requires proof of a specific mental state, competent evidence that because of mental abnormality not amounting to legal insanity defendant did not possess the essential specific mental state is admissible. . . .

* * *

It would seem elementary that a plea of not guilty to a charge of murder puts in issue the existence of the particular mental states which are essential elements of the two degrees of murder and of manslaughter. . . . Accordingly, it appears only fair and reasonable that defendant should be allowed to show that in fact, subjectively, he did not possess the mental state or states in issue.

* * *

Defendant and *amici curiae* urge that in the present case statements of the trial court affirmatively show that it believed the expert testimony that defendant, because of the concurrence of mental disease and the objective circumstances with which he was confronted, in fact lacked intent to kill and malice aforethought, yet erroneously concluded that the law required it to find that those elements were present. Defendant would attribute to selected portions of the trial court's remarks the force of findings of fact and conclusions of law. But those remarks when read as a whole set forth reflections and reasoning pro and con, matters which tend to support the judgment and matters which tend to suggest a contrary conclusion, but all proper to be considered by the fair, impartial, conscientious, and able judge in resolving the several issues and reaching his ultimate conclusion.

* * *

[W]e conclude that the judgment of conviction reached by the trial court is based on a reasonable view of the evidence and a correct understanding and application of the law.

For the reasons above stated, the judgment is affirmed.

NOTE 2

FREUD, SIGMUND

The Loss of Reality in Neurosis and Psychosis (1924)*

[O]ne of the features which differentiate[s] a neurosis from a psychosis [is] the fact that in a neurosis the ego, in its dependence on reality, suppresses a piece of the id (of instinctual life), whereas in a psychosis, this same ego, in the service of the id, withdraws from a piece of reality. Thus for a neurosis the decisive factor would be the predominance of the influence of reality, whereas for a psychosis it would be the predominance of the id. In a psychosis, a loss of reality would necessarily be present, whereas in a neurosis, it would seem, this loss would be avoided.

But this does not all agree with the observation which all of us can make that every neurosis disturbs the patient's relation to reality in some way, that it serves him as a means of withdrawing from reality, and that, in its severe forms, it actually signifies a flight from real life. This contradiction seems a serious one; but it is easily resolved, and the explanation of it will in fact help us to understand neuroses.

For the contradiction exists only as long as we keep our eyes fixed on the situation at the *beginning* of the neurosis, in which the ego, in the service of reality, sets about the repression of an instinctual impulse. This, however, is not yet the neurosis itself. The neurosis consists rather in the processes which provide a compensation for the portion of the id that has been damaged—that is to say, in the reaction against the repression and in the failure of the repression. The loosening of the relation to reality is a consequence of this second step in the formation of a neurosis, and it ought not to surprise us if a detailed examination shows that the loss of reality affects precisely that piece of reality as a result of whose demands the instinctual repression ensued.

There is nothing new in our characterization of neurosis as the result of a repression that has failed. We have said this all along, and it is only because of the new context in which we are viewing the subject that it has been necessary to repeat it.

Incidentally, the same objection arises in a specially marked manner when we are dealing with a neurosis in which the exciting cause (the "traumatic scene") is known, and in which one can see how the person concerned turns away from the experience and consigns it to amnesia. Let me go back by way of example to a case analyzed a great many years ago, in which the patient, a young woman, was in love with her brother-in-law. Standing beside her sister's deathbed,

* Reprinted from: 19 *The Standard Edition of the Complete Psychological Works of Sigmund Freud*, James Strachey, ed. London: The Hogarth Press and the Institute of Psychoanalysis, 1961. (pp. 183–87). Reprinted by permission of Hogarth and Basic Books, Inc.

she was horrified at having the thought: "Now he is free and can marry me." This scene was instantly forgotten, and thus the process of regression, which led to her hysterical pains, was set in motion. It is instructive precisely in this case, moreover, to learn along what path the neurosis attempted to solve the conflict. It took away from the value of the change that had occurred in reality, by repressing the instinctual demand which had emerged—that is, her love for her brother-in-law. The *psychotic* reaction would have been a disavowal of the fact of her sister's death.

We might expect that when a psychosis comes into being, something analogous to the process in a neurosis occurs, though, of course, between different agencies of the mind; thus we might expect that in a psychosis, too, two steps could be discerned, of which the first would drag the ego away, this time from reality, while the second would try to make good the damage done and re-establish the subject's relations to reality at the expense of the id. And, in fact, some analogy of the sort can be observed in a psychosis. Here, too, there are two steps, the second of which has the character of a reparation. But beyond that the analogy gives way to a far more extensive similarity between the two processes. The second step of the psychosis is indeed intended to make good the loss of reality, not, however, at the expense of a restriction of the id—as happens in neurosis at the expense of the relation to reality—but in another, more autocratic manner, by the creation of a new reality which no longer raises the same objections as the old one that has been given up. The second step, therefore, both in neurosis and psychosis, is supported by the same trends. In both cases it serves the desire for power of the id, which will not allow itself to be dictated to by reality. Both neurosis and psychosis are thus the expression of a rebellion on the part of the id against the external world, of its unwillingness—or, if one prefers, its incapacity—to adapt itself to the exigencies of reality. . . . Neurosis and psychosis differ from each other far more in their first, introductory, reaction than in the attempt at reparation which follows it.

Accordingly, the initial difference is expressed thus in the final outcome: in neurosis a piece of reality is avoided by a sort of flight, whereas in psychosis it is remodeled. Or we might say: In psychosis, the initial flight is succeeded by an active phase of remodeling; in neurosis, the initial obedience is succeeded by a deferred attempt at flight. Or again, expressed in yet another way: neurosis does not disavow the reality, it only ignores it; psychosis disavows it and tries to replace it. We call behavior "normal" or "healthy," if it combines certain features of both reactions—if it disavows the reality as little as does a neurosis, but if it then exerts itself, as does a psychosis, to effect an alteration of that reality. Of course, this expedient, normal, behavior leads to work being carried out on the external world; it does not stop, as in psychosis, at effecting internal changes. . . .

In a psychosis, the transforming of reality is carried out upon the psychical precipitates of former relations to it—that is, upon the memory traces, ideas, and judgments which have been previously derived from reality and by which reality was represented in the mind. But this relation was never a closed one; it was continually being enriched and altered by fresh perceptions. Thus the psychosis is also faced with the task of procuring for itself perceptions of a kind which shall correspond to the new reality; and this is most radically effected by means of hallucination. The fact that, in so many forms and cases of psychosis, the paramnesias, the delusions, and the hallucinations that occur are of a most distressing character and are bound up with a generation of anxiety—this fact is without doubt a sign that the whole process of remodeling is carried through against forces which oppose it violently. We may construct the process on the model of a neurosis, with which we are more familiar. There we see that a reaction of anxiety sets in whenever the repressed instinct makes a thrust forward, and that the outcome of the conflict is only a compromise and does not provide complete satisfaction. Probably in a psychosis the rejected piece of reality constantly forces itself upon the mind, just as the repressed instinct does in a neurosis, and that is why in both cases the consequences too are the same. The elucidation of the various mechanisms which are designed, in the psychoses, to turn the subject away from reality and to reconstruct reality—this is a task for specialized psychiatric study which has not yet been taken in hand.

There is, therefore, a further analogy between a neurosis and a psychosis, in that both of them the task which is undertaken in the second step is partly unsuccessful. For the repressed instinct is unable to procure a full substitute (in neurosis); and the representation of reality cannot be remolded into satisfying forms (not, at least, in every species of mental illness). But the emphasis is different in the two cases. In a psychosis it falls entirely on the first step, which is pathological in itself and cannot but lead to illness. In a neurosis, on the other hand, it falls on the second step, on the failure of the repression, whereas the first step may succeed, and does succeed in innumerable instances without overstepping the bounds of health—even though it does so at a certain price and not without leaving behind traces of the psychical expenditure it has called for. These distinctions, and perhaps many others as well, are a result of the topographical difference in the initial situation of the pathogenic conflict—namely whether in it the ego yielded to its allegiance to the real world or to its dependence on the id.

A neurosis usually contents itself with avoiding the piece of reality in question and protecting itself against coming into contact with it. The sharp distinction between neurosis and psychosis, however, is weakened by the circumstance that in neurosis, too, there is no lack of attempts to replace a disagreeable reality by one which is more in keeping with the subject's wishes. This is made possible by the existence of a *world of fantasy*, of a domain which became separated from the real external world at the time of the introduction of the reality principle. This domain has since been kept free from the demands of the exigencies of life, like a kind of "reservation"; it is not inaccessible to the ego, but is only loosely attached to it. It is from this world of fantasy that the neurosis draws the material for its new wishful constructions, and it usually finds that material along the path of regression to a more satisfying real past.

It can hardly be doubted that the world of fantasy plays the same part in psychosis and that there, too, it is the storehouse from which the materials or the pattern for building the new reality are derived. But whereas the new, imaginary external world of a psychosis attempts to put itself in the place of external reality, that of a neurosis, on the contrary, is apt, like the play of children, to attach itself to a piece of reality—a different piece from the one against which it has to defend itself—and to lend that piece a special importance and a secret meaning which we (not always quite appropriately) call a *symbolic* one. Thus we see that both in neurosis and psychosis there comes into consideration the question not only of a *loss of reality* but also of a *substitute for reality*.

NOTE 3

MORISSETTE v. UNITED STATES
342 U.S. 246 (1952)

MR. JUSTICE JACKSON delivered the opinion of the Court.

*   *   *

The contention that an injury can amount to a crime only when inflicted by intention is no provincial or transient notion. It is as universal and persistent in mature systems of law as belief in freedom of the human will and a consequent ability and duty of the normal individual to choose between good and evil. A relation between some mental element and punishment for a harmful act is almost as instinctive as the child's familiar exculpatory "But I didn't mean to," and has afforded the rational basis for a tardy and unfinished substitution of deterrence and reformation in place of retaliation and vengeance as the motivation for public prosecution. Unqualified acceptance of this doctrine by English common law in the Eighteenth Century was indicated by Blackstone's sweeping statement that to constitute any crime there must first be a "vicious will." . . .

Crime, as a compound concept, generally constituted only from concurrence of an evil-meaning mind with an evil-doing hand, was congenial to an intense individualism and took deep and early root in American soil. As the states codified the common law of crimes, even if their enactments were silent on the subject, their courts assumed that the omission did not signify disapproval of the principle but merely recognized that intent was so inherent in the idea of the offense that it required no statutory affirmation. Courts, with little hesitation or division, found an implication of the requirement as to offenses that were taken over from the common law. The unanimity with which they have adhered to the central thought that wrongdoing must be conscious to be criminal is emphasized by the variety, disparity, and confusion of their definitions of the requisite but elusive mental element. However, courts of various jurisdictions, and for the purposes of different offenses, have devised working formulae, if not scientific ones, for the instruction of juries around such terms as "felonious intent," "criminal intent," "malice aforethought," "guilty knowledge," "fraudulent intent," "wilfulness," "*scienter*," to denote guilty knowledge, or "*mens rea*," to signify an evil purpose or mental culpability. By use or combination of these various tokens, they have sought to protect those who were not blameworthy in mind from conviction of infamous common-law crimes.

*   *   *

NOTE 4

KNIGHT, ROBERT P.

Determinism, "Freedom," and Psychotherapy*

*   *   *

Psychiatry, with its techniques of psychotherapy, is a discipline based on the science of medical psychology and therefore cannot be exempt from the rigorous determinism which is a prerequisite of all science and its applications. Yet psychiatry, and more especially psychotherapy, aims at—and is capable of achieving—the rescue of the patient from the causally determined psychopathological state which brought him to treatment. Thus the psychotherapist, recognizing, as he must, the deterministic factors and influences which inevitably produced the end product which is the psychiatrically ill patient, nevertheless expects to change this patient by releasing him from the grip of the causal factors which bind him to his illness. There is even the expectation that that patient will achieve, through successful psychotherapy, a subjective sense of "freedom," and, indeed, a real freedom, which is not merely an illusion, in his increased capacity to utilize his ener-

---

* 9 *Psychiatry*, 251–59 (1946). Reprinted by permission.

gies for constructive and gratifying achievement and thus to manage his life instead of being an automaton driven by hereditary and environmental influences in whose grip he is helpless. Is this not a paradox? From the viewpoint of the therapist, how can he be both a scientific psychologist who recognizes the rigorous determinism in the operation of the causal factors which have made his patients what they are, and yet a psychotherapist who expects them to change, and is often able to help them to change? And from the standpoint of the patient how can he escape from the fatalism apparently inherent in the insight into the causal factors which produced him—the very insight which is supposed to free him from the tight grip of those causal factors?

*   *   *

The first step in extricating ourselves from the confusion inherent in the determinism versus free will debate lies in clarifying the terms. Determinism in the physical world is no longer seriously questioned by scientists or philosophers. Its alternative, indeterminism—pure chance, accident, unpredictability—represents chaos. "Indeterminacy" in modern (post-Newtonian) physics, simply refers to the fact that human limits of perception and their intrusion into the field of the experimental measuring instruments make absolute precision impossible. Rigorous physical determinism is not contested by Heisenberg's principle of indeterminacy. In the psychological and philosophical realm there is also no real alternative to psychic determinism. To defend "free will" as an alternative is to be guilty of semantic confusion. Determinism refers to the complex of causal factors, hereditary and environmental, internal and external, past and present, conscious and unconscious, which combine to produce a certain resultant in a given individual. Determinism is thus a theoretical construct which fits the observed data, as demonstrated by predictions which were fulfilled, and which is essential to any psychology which claims to be scientific. The antithesis to this construct is the construct, indeterminism—pure chance, chaos. "Free will," on the other hand, is not on the same conceptual level as are these constructs. It refers to a subjective psychological experience, and to compare it to determinism is like comparing the enjoyment of flying to the law of gravity.

. . . A scrutiny of this matter of "choice" may lead us to further understanding. When such choices involve only trivial matters, the mentally healthy person has the subjective sense of complete freedom of choice, and hence feels that he has acted of his own free will. Indeed, were a person not to feel free to choose in trivial matters, but instead feel powerfully compelled toward a single course, and experience anxiety if prevented from completing his choice, we would suspect him of suffering from a compulsion

neurosis. Or if he were unable to choose quickly and lightheartedly—that is, with a sense of freedom of choice—in unimportant matters we would suspect the presence of obsessional doubt. In weightier matters, however, the healthy person has a combined feeling of freedom and of inner compulsion. He feels that his course is determined by standards, beliefs, knowledge, aspirations that are an integral part of himself and he can do no other; yet at the same time he feels free. A decision or course of action that is in harmony with his character seems to carry with it the reward of a pleasurable sense of freedom. It is not easy to analyze the sense of freedom as it is used in this context but it can be described more fully. In a negative sense it means absence of anxiety, of irrational doubt, and of those inhibitions and restrictions which paralyze both choice and action. In a positive sense it connotes feelings of well-being, of self-esteem, of confidence, of inner satisfaction based on successful use of one's energies for achievement that promotes the best interests of one's fellow men as well as one's own.

It is a part of the thesis of this essay that this kind of "freedom" is experienced only by emotionally mature, well-integrated persons; it is the goal sought for one's patients in psychotherapy; and this freedom has nothing whatever to do with free will as a principle governing human behavior, but is a subjective experience which is itself causally determined. This subjective experience, however, is subjective in a special sense, not in the one which equates "subjective" with "spurious." The behavior of a well-integrated, civilized person can be objectively assessed as "free." Observers see that such a person makes ego-syntonic choices, that his motives are "good," and that he is able to carry out what he wills to do.

There are, however, experiences of freedom which are illusions to the persons experiencing them. They are subjective in the sense of spuriousness. Critical examination of the nature of such varieties of the subjective experience of freedom, and objective assessment of their relationship to the actualities of life, distinguish them readily from the freedom defined above. There is, for example, the sense of freedom in children or immature adults which occurs with the removal of external pressure or with solitary flights of fantasy of being omnipotent. The release from inner checks and restraints that occurs in mania likewise conveys a sense of complete freedom. There is a spurious sense of freedom in those persons, who, unconsciously driven by intense defiance, carry out criminal acts, acts of libertinism, and acts of spurious independence and self-assertion. One of the first tasks in the psychotherapy of such persons is to show them that they are not free, as they have thought, but are enslaved and driven by their compulsion to defy others. There is also the spurious sense of freedom that accompanies the hypocritically righteous decision in a person who perceives that a nefarious purpose may be executed under the cloak of righteousness. In such persons closer scrutiny will reveal a complicated scheme of balances between well-rationalized, sadistically motivated acts of aggression and compulsive acts and rituals of penance. Many other examples could be cited to illustrate varieties of subjective freedom which are illusions to the subject, and are vulnerable to objective assessment.

The genuine freedom which is a mark of mental health and emotional maturity is best expressed by the following quotation, whose authorship I do not know: "That man is free who is conscious of being the author of the law that he obeys." This definition includes both the sense of freedom and the sense of inner compulsion which we have designated as inseparable subjective feelings in matters of real importance in life. It also includes the concept of integration of the personality, that is, the individual's energies and impulses are subject to conscious control but are capable of satisfying discharge according to standards which the ego accepts. If it is correct to assume that this linkage of subjective freedom with inner acceptable compulsion is a criterion of mental health and of emotional and intellectual maturity in human beings, and that other experiences of subjective freedom which do not meet the test of linkage with acceptable inner compulsion and of objective assessment are psychiatrically suspect, then we have narrowed down the problem of freedom by eliminating from further consideration the spurious varieties of subjective freedom. It is sufficient to say, then, that all of the subjective experiences of freedom are, like every other psychological datum, understandable as causally determined products of many factors—hereditary, experiential, biological, cultural, and so on. "Free will" is thus reduced from its presumptuous position as a real threat or alternative to determinism, and is demoted to the position of a variety of subjective experience—one which is itself causally determined.

*   *   *

Scientific psychology, and especially psychoanalytic findings and theories, have in recent decades tackled the problem of the relationship of freedom to law which philosophy has struggled with for centuries. Our ego psychology is far from complete, and its deficiencies are apparent in relation to many aspects of man's ambitions, aspirations, potentialities, strivings, limitations, and lack of psychological integration. However, dynamic psychology has been able to develop constructs which fit the observable clinical data, which provide a scientific theory based on the axiom of psychological determinism, and which supply a basis for constructing a scientific theory of psychotherapy.

The first construct is that there is an unconscious part of the self, the id, containing the instinctual forces which are rooted in biology, and molded by infantile emotional experience. These forces are aggressive, selfish, lustful, and seek immediate gratification. But their full satisfaction in each individual, were there no external or internal controls, would result in collision with the external laws and limitations of the physical world on the one hand, and with the attempts of other individuals to fulfill their instinctual strivings on the other hand. The result would be chaos. We are saved from such chaos in organized society by the inevitable operation of natural laws and by man-made restrictive rules (laws) under which unlimited freedom for each individual is sharply curtailed so that the interests of each person are protected. The aim of man-made laws is—or, at least, should be—to guarantee the maximum degree of gratification of individual needs which is consistent with the protection of the rights of others. Civilization thus sacrifices individual freedom of action to promote collective security.

The second construct of dynamic psychology is that out of the original infantile unorganized mass of instinctual wishes there develops an organized portion of the self, the ego, which is largely conscious. It co-ordinates the faculties of perception, intelligence, judgment, memory, discrimination, learning, and so on. The ego has the task of achieving what satisfactions it can of the instinctual drives of the id, while taking cognizance of the nature of the environment and its natural and man-made restrictions. The ego is the feeling, experiencing, aware portion of the personality.

The third construct is that there also develops, in early childhood, as an internalization of the restricting, frustrating, disciplining parents and their surrogates, a third portion of the psyche called the superego, or conscience, which is largely unconscious. It is an internal master to which the ego is subject, so that the ego's adjustive task becomes one of managing the instinctual drives from within against the limitations and frustrations of the outer world, while being compelled to obey also the forbidding directives of the superego.

The development and operation of each of these portions of the self, and thus of the total personality, is causally determined in accordance with the psychological laws governing the inherited endowment, biological drives, physiological and emotional experiences, and external, natural, cultural, and interpersonal pressures affecting each individual in the milieu in which he is reared. In the healthy person there is a harmonious interrelationship between the various parts of the self and with the environment, and one of the important by-products of such harmonious integration is a subjective sense of freedom. Viewed in this way, the feeling of freedom is also determined, and is possible to be experienced only to the extent that there exists within the individual a harmonious integration of his instinctual drives, his superego standards and restrictions, his ego perceptions and discriminative faculties, and the possibilities provided by the environment. Such a theoretically healthy, integrated person will then feel free, and, to some extent, will be "free." That is, his flexibility of adaptation will be greater than that of the neurotic person, and what behavior he "chooses" will conform to the laws and standards, internal and external, which he accepts, but his choices will *feel* free.

*   *   *

NOTE 5

KATZ, WILBER G.

Responsibility and Freedom*

*   *   *

. . . Dr. Robert P. Knight, in . . . "Determinism, 'Freedom,' and Psychotherapy" [summarized] the concern of the bar association . . . as follows:

> They fear that the deterministic view implies an encouragement to irresponsibility, and that crimes will go unpunished and criminals unconvicted if the culprits can be successfully defended on the basis that they could not help doing what they did. They wonder how it can be decided which human acts are "free" and therefore punishable, and which acts are "determined" and therefore unpunishable.

While conceding that this was a "genuine concern" on the part of the lawyers, Dr. Knight took the completely determinist position and expounded it at length. He frankly raised, however, the question as to how it is that freedom from psychic determinants may develop in the process of therapy. The therapist, of course, brings new determining influences to bear upon the patient, but Dr. Knight recognized that, in addition, "effort" on the part of the patient is necessary if therapy is to be successful. This seemed to me an admission that paradox is not avoided even by scientific psychology. After an argument on this subject with one of my colleagues, I laid a wager that Dr. Knight would admit that he had not quite eliminated the paradox of freedom. When I wrote to him, he replied:

> Yes, I puzzled quite a bit over the paradox of psychic determinism v. "effort," and have not yet reconciled it to my satisfaction. One can say that the effort itself is also determined—which seems to be something of a tour de force—or one can concede

that, especially in psychotherapy, one expects and mobilizes more effort than the amount which is yet "determined" by previous experience. Such factors as transference (in therapy), inspirational influences, and conceptions of one's self or of one's completed work, projected into the future, may be regarded as determining factors, but I still, at this stage of my thinking at least, feel there is something left over. Harry Emerson Fosdick . . . calls it a "personal rejoinder" to life experience.

He added, "I think you win your bet."

*   *   *

NOTE 6

LEWY, ERNST

Responsibility, Free Will, and Ego Psychology*

*   *   *

. . . D. Rapaport in a personal communication [stated]:

"Man has developed an anticipatory apparatus which is far more effective than any other animal's. This apparatus is very effective for outside events and fairly effective (anxiety and other affect signals) for internal events. These events play a causal role in behavior. But man himself (and every organism to some degree) is a source of causes. Man's anticipatory apparatus is a particularly effective mobilizer of man's own causal role. Man isn't freed from internal and external causes by means of his anticipatory apparatus, that is, by dint of his being also a source of causes. But he certainly can within limits avoid, evade, cushion, and counteract causes which would determine his behavior. Some of these causes he is less adept at avoiding or cushioning (instinctual drives)—but to the extent that he has a relatively autonomous ego, he can do even some of that. Instinctual drives are causes and motives; other causes of the same sort (neutralized to various degrees) he can cushion better. Nonmotivational causes he can yet easier evade or cushion, somatic ones less so than environmental ones.—So to the degree to which he is within these limits, he is a free agent. To this degree (and to the degree he fails to use this ability) he is responsible in the broadest sense."

In addition to the above . . . there is the question of how the acceptance of one's responsibility is achieved and transmitted. I submit that if responsibility of the individual for himself is considered traditionally and conventionally an established reality factor, this very fact acts as a sufficiently strong adaptive force to determine the individual's choice. Assuming the capacity of the ego to adapt its operations and reactions to the environment and its realities, we can expect that the ego can be purpose-

---

* Reprinted from the *Journal of Legal Education*, Vol. 5, No. 3, pp. 274–75 by permission of the Association of American Law Schools. Copyright 1953 by the Association.

* 42 *International Journal of Psychoanalysis*, 267–68, (1961). Reprinted by permission.

fully influenced by reality factors. Thus, specifically the reality fact that traditionally, conventionally, and tacitly every individual is considered to be responsible for his acts by the society in which he lives, and that this is inculcated in the child through the educational and rearing process, constitutes a powerful reality factor to which the ego has to adapt itself and is capable of adapting itself. The established standard provides the environmental setting to which the adaptable ego responds. I am referring to what Erikson calls our "institutionalized attitude." . . .

* * *

An important part of the dynamics of adaptation is played, of course, in particular in the course of growing up, by the process of the formation of the superego through identification with the authority figures, their introjection and the subsequent internalization of accepted standards. . . .

* * *

I should like to go further now and say: We not only can, we also must hold man responsible, in order to establish the necessary and correct environment. . . .

* * *

NOTE 7

KWOSEK v. STATE
8 Wis. 2d 640, 100 N.W. 2d 339 (1960)

* * *

HALLOWS, J. . . . The determinists and some psychoanalysts consider man's actions to be so influenced or controlled by urges, impulses, and the subconscious as to be caused or determined without any power within man to control or choose his course of conduct in any situation. Other psychiatrists believe that man is a highly complex, integrated personality with the power of self-choice and determination and whose mental process has a unit of perceiving, apprehending, judging, and willing which may be interfered with by a disease or defect of the mental order through no fault of his.

Criminal law and responsibility are based upon the fact that an individual human being is mentally free to exercise a choice between possible courses of conduct in respect to those acts condemned by the law and is therefore morally and legally responsible. A human being has inherently and within himself a free will—the power of self-control. In those situations when the volitional power is impaired to such a degree or is totally destroyed or the requisite psychological conditions are not present for the exercise of a free choice, because of mental disorder or defect responsibility for such act should not be imputed to that person. . . . Lacking either [knowledge and

reason] the will is not free. But there are other conditions of the mind which affect the freedom of choice. The mind does not function in departments but as an integrated whole. . . . .

NOTE 8

GREGG CARTAGE CO. v. UNITED STATES
316 U.S. 74, 79 (1942)

MR. JUSTICE JACKSON delivered the Opinion of the Court.

* * *

How far one by an exercise of free will may determine his general destiny or his course in a particular matter and how far he is the toy of circumstance has been debated through the ages by theologians, philosophers, and scientists. Whatever doubts they have entertained as to the matter, the practical business of government and administration of the law is obliged to proceed on more or less rough and ready judgments based on the assumption that mature and rational persons are in control of their own conduct. . . . The Bankruptcy Act states that even an involuntary adjudication results only from some "act of bankruptcy," defined upon the clear assumption that it is within the bankrupt's control. Whether or not this assumption squares with philosophical doctrine, or even with reality, is not for our determination. The Commission, and the courts too, must get on with the application of the federal statutes without waiting to settle the verity of the philosophical assumptions on which they rest.

* * *

NOTE 9

CULOMBE v. CONNECTICUT
367 U.S. 568 (1960)

FRANKFURTER, J.

* * *

The ultimate test [of whether a confession is admissible in a state court] remains that which has been the only clearly established test in Anglo-American courts for two hundred years: the test of voluntariness. Is the confession the product of an essentially free and unconstrained choice by its maker? If it is, if he has willed to confess, it may be used against him. If it is not, if his will has been overborne and his capacity for self-determination critically impaired, the use of his confession offends due process. The line of distinction is that at which governing self-direction is lost and compulsion, of whatever nature or however infused, propels or helps to propel the confession.

The inquiry whether, in a particular case, a confession was voluntarily or involuntarily made involves, at the least, a three-phased process. First, there is the business of finding the crude historical facts, the external, "phenomenological" occurrences and events surrounding the confession. Second, because the concept of "voluntariness" is one which concerns a mental state, there is the imaginative recreation, largely inferential, of internal, "psychological" fact. Third, there is the application to this psychological fact of standards for judgment informed by the larger legal conceptions ordinarily characterized as rules of law but which, also, comprehend both induction from, and anticipation of, factual circumstances.

In a case coming here from the highest court of a State in which review may be had, the first of these phases is definitely determined, normally, by that court. . . .

* * *

The second and third phases of the inquiry—determination of how the accused reacted to the external facts, and of the legal significance of how he reacted—although distinct as a matter of abstract analysis, become in practical operation inextricably interwoven. This is so, in part, because the concepts by which language expresses an otherwise unrepresentable mental reality are themselves generalizations importing preconceptions about the reality to be expressed. It is so, also, because the apprehension of mental states is almost invariably a matter of induction, more or less imprecise, and the margin of error which is thus introduced into the finding of "fact" must be accounted for in the formulation and application of the "rule" designed to cope with such classes of facts. The notion of "voluntariness" is itself an amphibian. It purports at once to describe an internal psychic state and to characterize that state for legal purposes. Since the characterization is the very issue "to review which this Court sits," the matter of description, too, is necessarily open here.

No more restricted scope of review would suffice adequately to protect federal constitutional rights. For the mental state of involuntariness upon which the due process question turns can never be affirmatively established other than circumstantially—that is, by inference; and it cannot be competent to the trier of fact to preclude our review simply by declining to draw inferences which the historical facts compel. Great weight, of course, is to be accorded to the inferences which are drawn by the state courts. In a dubious case, it is appropriate, with due regard to federal-state relations, that the state court's determination should control. But where, on the uncontested external happenings, coercive forces set in motion by state law enforcement officials are unmistakably in action; where these forces, under all the prevailing states of stress, are powerful enough to

draw forth a confession; where, in fact, the confession does come forth and is claimed by the defendant to have been extorted from him; and where he has acted as a man would act who is subjected to such an extracting process—where this is all that appears in the record—a State's judgment that the confession was voluntary cannot stand.

* * *

NOTE 10

UNITED STATES v. DRUMMOND
354 F2d 132 (2nd Cir. 1965)

* * *

KAUFMAN, Circuit Judge

Confessions are not suspect *per se*; it cannot be said that an individual who confesses has by that deed alone acted unreasonably or under compulsion. Our experience leads us to believe that often the conscience of an accused prods him to confess. Alternatively, expectation that independent investigation will lead to evidence sealing a conviction, or calculation of a *quid pro quo* in the form of a lenient sentence, can motivate a course of full disclosure. . . .

* * *

b.   UNITED STATES v. FLEMING
7 U.S.C.M.A. 543, 23 C.M.R. 7 (1957)

HOMER FERGUSON, Judge

The accused Army officer was tried by general court-martial. . . . He pleaded not guilty to all charges and specifications. . . . The accused was sentenced to total forfeitures, and to be dismissed from the service. [T]he two identical specifications of which the accused now stands convicted state as follows:

"that the accused, then Major and held as a prisoner of war by the enemy, did at or in the vicinity of Pyongyang, North Korea, between 1 February 1951 and 30 May 1951, willfully, unlawfully, and knowingly, collaborate, communicate, and hold intercourse directly with the enemy by joining with, participating in, and leading discussion groups and classes reflecting views and opinions that the United Nations and United States were illegal aggressors in the Korean conflict, . . . and by participating in the preparation and making communist propaganda recordings designed to promote disloyalty and disaffection among United States troops, by praising the enemy and attacking the war aims of the United States, which recordings were later broadcasted in English over the Pyongyang radio, to wit: A statement which was broadcasted on or about 13 April 1951, stating in effect that the Communists were treating prisoners of war in accordance with the principles of humanity and democracy, and that the

United States made a grave error in interferring [sic] in Korean internal affairs and should leave at once; an appeal to the 'Five Great Powers' (USSR, Peoples Republic of China, United Kingdom, United States, and France) broadcasted on or about 24 April 1951, urging them to sign a peace pact, and urging that any one of the powers which refused to attend conferences for that purpose be considered a government with aggressive intentions; an appeal to President Truman and General McArthur [sic] broadcasted on or about 24 April 1951, urging them to withdraw United Nations forces immediately from Korea; a surrender appeal broadcasted on or about 27 April 1951, inviting United Nations Troops to surrender and promising kind treatment by the Communists; and a round-table conference or panel of five prisoners of war broadcasted on or about 4 May 1951, urging support for the Communist sponsored Second World Peace Congress, in which he served as moderator; thereby giving aid and comfort to the enemy."

This Court granted the accused's petition for review, setting forth in pertinent part the following issues:

1. Whether the evidence is sufficient to support the findings of guilt.

2. Whether the law officer erred by instructing the Court that in order to excuse a criminal act on ground of coercion, compulsion, or necessity, one must have acted upon a well-grounded apprehension of immediate and impending death or of immediate serious bodily harm.

*   *   *

[There is] little dispute between the parties as to what happened. Basically the issue boils down not as much as to what the accused did or did not do, but rather to the justifications for his actions. As stated in the defense appellate brief, "the issues with which we are here concerned are not the acts of the accused but whether the affirmative defenses of these acts were rebutted by the prosecution evidence."

The accused was captured by the Chinese Communists near the Yalu River in the northern reaches of Korea. After his capture he was marched to different locations and ended up being interned in the Valley Camp for about two months and for a month at a camp near Pyoktong. At the Valley Camp an English-speaking North Korean officer, whom we will hereafter refer to as Colonel Kim or Kim, informed the accused that arrangements were being made to enable the prisoners to broadcast radio messages informing their families of their whereabouts. On January 29, 1951, Colonel Kim notified the accused, Lieutenant Colonel, then Major, Liles, and Major MacGhee, the three senior American officers in this particular prisoner of war group, that the time had arrived for the broadcast. The day following, these three officers, in company with seventeen other prisoners, departed by truck for Pyongyang. En

route, the party stopped at the badly damaged village of Tackchon. The populace was hostile and evinced a threatening attitude toward the prisoners. A People's Court or Town Meeting was called, attended by about eighty-five Korean civilians. Questions were asked by the villagers as to why the Americans had come to Korea. According to a number of witnesses at the trial, most of the questions were answered by the accused and Colonel Liles through Colonel Kim, who acted as interpreter. Captain Galing testified that the accused stated that South Korea was the aggressor; that the war was propagated at the instigation of the imperialistic war mongers of Wall Street; and that President Truman and General MacArthur were the tools of the Wall Street conspiracy. Major MacGhee could not recall the accused specifically answering any questions; however he did remember that the answers given were to the effect that the United States was the aggressor in Korea; that its forces had no business there, and that the war and slaughter should be ended. The accused admitted that in order to placate Kim and the hostile and threatening crowd, he *might* have used some "party line" phrases.

Upon arrival at Pyongyang on February 2, 1951, the accused was elected compound leader. Not only was he responsible for the discipline and organization of the prisoners but he was also the link between the prisoners and Colonel Kim. He transmitted the captors' orders to the prisoners of war, and, conversely, the complaints and requests of the group to their captors. The accused held the position of group leader until June 1, 1951, at which time Captain Allen succeeded him.

After arrival at Pyongyang, Kim informed the prisoners that they were to prepare radio scripts describing their capture and Korean experiences. The accused testified that up to this time his idea had been only to let his wife know he was alive. To that end the accused submitted a short script. This was returned and he was informed by Kim that his broadcast time had been lengthened to fifteen minutes. The script was written, rewritten, and revised some twenty or thirty times until finally broadcast. According to the accused he resisted the propaganda directed against President Truman along with demands that only United Nations troops be withdrawn from Korea. He testified that he succeeded in getting by with comments about the Roosevelt administration and a statement that *all* foreign armies—which of course included the Chinese—be withdrawn from Korea. Also included in the broadcast were statements that the prisoners were being treated according to the principles of democracy and humanity, and that the United States erred when it interferred in the internal affairs of Korea.

The accused testified that after the broadcast, Kim informed him that he was dissatisfied with the co-operation he had been receiving from the prisoners. They were insincere and, apparently to educate them, he was going to commence round-table discussions. The accused objected, but he was forced to pick four other prisoners to participate in a panel discussion, of which he was to act as moderator. Subsequently a month was spent in preparation of the script, after which time the panel discussion recording was made. The subject matter was the "Second World Peace Congress." The accused testified that Kim had inserted in the script as broadcast a number of his own Communist line phrases. A member of the panel, Lieutenant Wilson, testified that included among the points discussed were reduction of armaments and the outlawing of mass destruction weapons.

While the round-table script was being prepared, Kim read several "appeals" to the prisoners. The substance of these appeals is related in the specifications. In brief, they were for a Five Great Powers Peace Pact; for President Truman and General MacArthur to withdraw United Nations forces from Korea; and for the United Nations troops to lay down their arms and surrender, being assured of kind treatment by the Communists. Each appeal was reduced to writing on a separate sheet of paper. They were laid on a table and a blank sheet for signature was placed underneath. The accused testified that he wrote his name on two of the blank sheets of paper. However, blank sheets of paper, or not, he pointed out that it made little difference whether the prisoners did or did not sign the appeals, for the Communists had already obtained the prisoner's signatures and would simply superimpose any signature upon any publication or article they desired.

Toward the end of April 1951, the prisoners were taken to a Korean house, which had electricity, where the round-table discussion and the appeals were to be recorded. After the panel discussion was recorded, the appeals were read into the microphone. When an appeal was read, each prisoner by order of rank trooped to the front of the room and "voice signed" his name, rank, and serial number. The accused admitted voice signing the Five Great Powers Peace Conference Appeal. However, he and the other prisoners objected to signing a *demand* to President Truman and General MacArthur to withdraw United Nations troops from Korea. The prisoners finally prevailed in that the word "demand" was changed to "appeal." The accused then voice signed it. In addition he admitted voice signing the surrender appeal. After the accused and Colonel Liles had voice signed the latter appeal, dissension began to develop among the prisoners in the back of the room. This dissension grew into outright refusal to sign this appeal. The objections became so vehement that Kim thereafter abandoned any attempt to secure voice signatures to the surrender appeal.

To keep the picture in focus, it is advisable at this point to drop back and pick up the coercive circumstances leading up to the accused's surrender, and his participation in the propaganda broadcasts. The accused testified that just before his capture, while firing upon the enemy, he was rendered unconscious by a shell blast. The blast resulted in approximately fifteen superficial wounds in his back and legs. His first recollection after the blast was being kicked in the head by a Chinese soldier. He struggled to his feet and noticed a wounded fellow officer who had been his assistant as an advisor to a South Korean regiment. While prevented at bayonet point from rendering aid to this officer, another Communist soldier walked over to where he lay and killed him with a burp gun. The accused was marched south about seventy miles. He was questioned on numerous occasions and during one of the interrogations, when he continued to refuse to give more than his name, rank, and serial number, he was physically abused by being slapped, knocked down, kicked, and pushed around on the floor. For about ten days he was given practically no food and water. He was subsequently taken to the Valley Camp. By this time, due to wounds, mistreatment, malnutrition, and debilitation, he had lost approximately forty pounds. Conditions at the Valley Camp—not only according to the accused, but other prisoners as well—were extremely bad. Few of the captured soldiers had other than summer clothing. The accused in company with twelve other prisoners, occupied one small room. There was not enough space for all the prisoners to lie down at night and stretch out. Two cups of millet per day constituted the daily sustenance. Approximately 60 per cent of the prisoners were unable to walk and the mortality rate was so high that the dead were not buried for days, merely stacked up like cordwood outside in the freezing weather. The accused made numerous demands upon his captors for more food and for other necessities of life, such as medical attention and medical supplies for the sick and wounded. He felt that he was able to restore some type of discipline, organization, and the will to live among the prisoners. Toward the end of 1950 the prisoners were marched to another location. The accused testified that due to his intercessions, the sick and wounded were carried in ox carts, instead of being marched on foot, which would have resulted in death to a sizable number. The accused was himself so weak that he was unable to carry his own knapsack. Conditions at the new camp were as bad, if not worse than those at the original location. The accused continued his efforts to obtain better treatment from his captors.

After the twenty prisoners arrived at Pyongyang, the food and living conditions markedly improved.

Before making the broadcasts, the accused testified that he was constantly harangued and pressured by Colonel Kim. According to Kim, there were two kinds of people: Those for peace and those against peace. Those against peace were war criminals and not fit to live. If the accused fitted into that category he would be put in a "hole" and would never come out. But if he were for peace, he was a friend. His actions would indicate whether he was for or against peace. When the accused initially refused to do the acts to prove his "friendliness," he was asked if he wanted to return to the previous camp up north. The accused replied in the affirmative and Kim informed him that he could start walking the 150–200 mile distance. It was midwinter, the accused's shoes had been stolen, and he was wearing rags wrapped around his feet. These factors, plus his greatly weakened physical condition, led the accused to the conclusion that he would never reach the north camp alive. Thereafter, on each occasion when the accused objected to Kim's propaganda efforts, he was threatened with the walk north.

Colonel Liles testified that when Kim insisted on the manuscripts being prepared, the accused informed him that the prisoners could not comply unless more food was forthcoming. Kim promised to try to accomplish that objective, but subsequently returned and said he was unable to secure additional rations. In the meanwhile nothing more had been done on the manuscripts. Kim was angry and declared that any man who refused to make a radio recording would march back to Pyoktong on foot. After this threat, the writing commenced. Major Allen also testified to numerous threats to march the prisoners north to the Yalu River. In his opinion, none could have survived the march.

The accused ascribed as further reasons for lending support to the round-table panel and the appeals, the fact that due to his weakened physical condition and the constant psychological hammering of Colonel Kim, he was in a state of complete confusion, frustration, and hopelessness. Morale among the prisoners had reached bottom. The food was barely sufficient to sustain life, and during the arguments over the appeals Kim even threatened to cut that off.

Also Kim's subsequent threat of the caves made to the accused and the other prisoners of war unless they co-operated undoubtedly affected prisoner co-operation. After completion of the accused's broadcast at Pyongyang, the prisoners were moved to a location near the caves. The latter were recesses in the hillside. They were wet and muddy with little or no heating facilities. The prisoners lived in the muck and mire like animals. Primarily the caves were used for South Korean prisoners, but also some American and British soldiers were incarcerated there. Also a great many transient, sick, and wounded, and in some instances recalcitrant prisoners, resided in the caves. The mortality rate in the indescribable filth and privation of these holes in the ground was extremely high. The prisoners felt that a sentence to the caves was almost tantamount to a sentence of death. Of the prisoner group with whom the accused was associated at least eight were punished by being sent to the caves. Fortunately these eight survived, except that one officer died shortly after being taken out of the caves because of his weakened condition. Almost all who testified were of the opinion that had their confinement in the caves lasted much longer, they would have died. Major MacGhee, one of the officers sentenced to the caves, testified that all twenty-three Americans already there when he arrived died.

The accused testified that when he objected to a round-table discussion, Kim took him to see fourteen recently captured young American enlisted men huddled together in the filth of a small cave. They were sick, dirty, had no latrine, little water, and no hope. The accused tried to get them moved to his camp, and they pleaded with him to try to accomplish this objective. Kim kept the accused "dangling" with vague promises. According to the accused, whenever he balked on the propaganda, Kim reminded him of the Americans in the caves and again took him to see them. Each time marked fewer numbers. On the last trip only one American remained. He was lying in the mud, too sick to rise, and he informed the accused that all the rest had died, and that he too was dying.

Discussion groups were formed and classes were held in the prisoner of war camp. Initially, Mr. and Mrs. Suh came over in the evenings and discussed political matters. These discussions and subsequent developments will be related through the witnesses.

According to Captain Galing, after the twenty prisoners were taken to Pyongyang, Kim or his secretary, Suh, came to their rooms on a number of occasions and one- or two-hour discussions would be held with respect to who started, and who was responsible for the Korean war. Magazine articles were sometimes read, followed by questions. The accused responded to these questions and some of his statements were to the effect that South Korea was the aggressor; that Americans had no business interfering in a Korean civil war, and that Wall Street was backing the war for financial gain.

Major MacGhee testified that study classes were supervised by Suh or Colonel Kim. These classes were held in the evenings after Communist propaganda for study had been given to the accused for distribution to the prisoners during the day. During the study sessions one of the prisoners would be called upon to read a portion of the material and thereafter the group would discuss it. MacGhee recalled that on one such occasion, the accused made remarks with respect to business in America, which highlighted the decadence of capitalism. Quite often the Korean who had commenced the class would leave. When that happened, normally the accused or Colonel Liles led the discussion.

* * *

When the twenty prisoners, together with another group of fifteen prisoners who had joined them two weeks earlier, were moved to the new location near the caves—sometime in March 1951—two-hour indoctrination classes were held during the day followed by two-hour evening discussion periods. Sergeant Gardiner testified that the accused appeared to be in charge of these evening sessions. He could not recall that anything anti-American was stated by the accused. A number of witnesses testified that when the Korean monitors left the room, the accused would slant his discussion favorably to the United States.

John Narvin, formerly private first class, recalled being posted by the accused to watch for the Koreans during one of the discussions. Colonel Liles testified that when the captors were absent the accused attempted to point out flaws in the Communist system.

An article appearing in a North Korean magazine bore the accused's name and picture. It stated that United States forces should leave Korea. The accused testified that although he did not author the article it appeared to contain language similar to his first broadcast. He pointed out that it was an easy matter for the Communists to obtain one's picture and signature on any publication they desired. They frequently took pictures of the prisoners and had everyone's signature.

After June 1st, 1951, Captain Allen was elected group leader and the accused was made librarian. He was responsible for a considerable quantity of Communist propaganda. He did not let the prisoners use the material for toilet paper because it was inventoried and he was held responsible for the missing items.

The accused's policy with respect to co-operation with the enemy by the other prisoners was predicated upon his belief that every prisoner had to be guided by his own conscience. The record is clear that Fleming did make statements to that effect to a number of prisoners. But there is also testimony in the record that he urged some of the prisoners to complete propaganda writings and not hold back from involvement in the political activities or else Kim might make some changes. The accused's idea of his policy as to the propaganda activities can best be described by his own testimony. He testified:

"I know in my own mind that if I had taken the policy of saying to these men: Resist them; everybody resist them, that information would have gone to headquarters so fast that they would have known it about as fast as everybody else. And I had a pretty good idea of what would happen to me.

"Secondly, I then would be the individual responsible for any beatings, tortures, or deaths that may occur to any one of the men there.

"Another thing was that a policy like that was absolutely not practical because you have to take human nature into this thing. They wouldn't have done it.

"So it had to be one where the individual himself, in the final analysis, was going to be the one that said: 'I stop here regardless of what happens.'

"And I am firmly convinced in my own mind that the policy was right. It proved itself right when the flareup came during the recordings of the so-called appeals; when some of these people went to the end and stopped, and that was it.

"That is the only policy I could see that would have any practicability at all and be workable.

"By doing that we would resist in every way that we could think of as individuals. I resisted in every way that I could, and I know that every other individual resisted in every way that he could, and the resistance was different as the situations developed. Some of it was blunt resistance; some of it was passive; some of it took the turn, as I have mentioned so many times, of delay, double talk, sabotage, not understanding, everything we could think of to hold off.

* * *

"I felt this way, and this was certainly nothing new at Camp Twelve. It had started long before I had anything to do with Camp Twelve. The most futile thing in the world was a dead prisoner of war in North Korea. And I had determined a long time before this that I was going to do everything in my power to keep those people alive. By doing so I was, in some small way, defeating what the Communists were trying to do.

"As I said before, the best thing that could happen to the Communists was to have us all die. And, secondly, in a situation like that you have many thoughts of home. I thought, and everyone else thought—not only thoughts of just yourself getting home, but the thoughts of those people at home that are waiting for you to get home, the mothers, and the wives, and the fathers. And the way I feel about it personally is, and I think I am right, that for these men that came back that may have done things wrong over there, it means more to their mothers and their families than a little bit of Communist indoctrination. . . .

* * *

"I feel that there are innumerable officers and enlisted men that have had a long-time experience as prisoners of the Communist armies, that can give invaluable information to not only the American military establishment as to what can be done to better the situation if and when we fight the Communists again, for those that may be captured in the future; lessons that were learned by our mistakes, and by the suffering of the men that were over there. But also to show the American people our side of what Communism really is. And, believe me, the American people need to be shown."

There is evidence in the record that by virtue of the

accused's efforts more favorable conditions were obtained for the prisoners. A kitchen was set up with some degree of cleanliness, which helped reduce dysentery which was fatal to so many prisoners in Korea. Some semblance of discipline was restored and the prisoners were forced to exercise and follow a more or less military routine. They were not allowed, as Fleming testified, to merely lie down, give up, and die. On at least one occasion, the accused obtained hospitalization for two prisoners which possibly saved their lives. Also he was able to secure a certain amount of medical attention and supplies. He pushed some of his demands so forcefully that, according to his testimony, on at least two occasions Colonel Kim flew into a ranting rage, pulled out his pistol, and threatened to kill him. Other witnesses testified that they recalled one instance when the accused was forced to get up before the prisoner group and condemn himself for his persistent behavior.

To counterbalance the scale, there is evidence that a number of prisoners reached a point from which they refused to budge with regard to Communist propaganda. These prisoners unquestionably knew that their refusal would mean banishment to the caves. They nevertheless threw back the challenge to their Communist captors and refused to go any further. One British soldier, Sergeant O'Hara, refused from the inception to have anything to do with the Communist propaganda. A devoutly religious man, he was apparently able to withstand the Communist pressure. He eventually ended up in the caves but survived the war.

*   *   *

. . . For all practical purposes the accused admits that he committed the acts alleged but insists that under the circumstances he was justified in so doing. According to the accused the acts were committed (1) to protect the lives and well-being of the fellow prisoners of war; (2) under coercion and duress. . . .

There is considerable evidence in the record indicating that the accused was motivated—in part at least—by the well-being of his fellow prisoners of war. There is other evidence, however, which casts a doubt as to the accused's primary motivation. Major MacGhee testified that when he refused to make a recording, Fleming informed him that he, Fleming, would have to report to Colonel Kim that MacGhee had double crossed him. Within a short space of time thereafter MacGhee was transferred to the caves. According to Sergeant Gardiner, the accused informed him that if he didn't straighten out he would be "shipped to the caves." Lieutenant Van Orman recalled that the accused told him that Kim's "got his eye on some of the people laying down around here and trying to get by and not get involved in the political program." And "Kim is getting sick of

people hanging around here who are not producing, and is thinking about lowering the strength of the camp." Van Orman took the last statement to mean that if he didn't start co-operating, he would be transferred to the caves. But under the circumstances of this case, as it pertains to the issue now under discussion, we will assume that the motives of the accused were to "protect the lives and well-being of his fellow prisoners of war." However, good motives are not a defense to a crime.

In United States v. Batchelor, 7 USCMA 354, 22 CMR 144, the Court had before it the defense contention that under the law officer's instructions the members of the court-martial could convict the accused if they were satisfied that he had voluntarily and knowingly communicated with the enemy without proper authority "even though the accused believed his acts contributed to world peace and the best interests of his fellow prisoners and his country." The Court concluded that "the instruction is a good statement as to what the law is in this field," adding:

". . . The question then becomes one of whether what might be a laudable motive—in entirely different circumstances—will serve to exculpate a defendant charged with improper communication with the enemy.

"In Chandler v. United States, 171 F 2d 921 (CA 1st Cir) (1948), the accused, an American citizen, was charged with treason. It was argued that treason is a crime dependent upon the actor's motives, and that the jury should have been told that the defendant could not be found to have had an 'intent to betray' if they believed that he acted from patriotic motives upon a firm conviction that what he did was for the best interests of the United States. The Circuit Court rejected this argument, and we believe its language is appropriate here. Chief Judge Magruder, disposed of the matter as follows:

" '. . . if appellant's argument in this connection were sound, it would of course be applicable whatever might be the character of the overt acts of aid and comfort to the enemy. Suppose Chandler had obtained advance information of the Anglo-American plans for the invasion of North Africa and had passed the information on to the enemy. Would a treason prosecution fail if he could convince the jury that, in his fanatical and perhaps misguided way, he sincerely believed his country was on the wrong side of the war; that he sincerely believed his country's ultimate good would be served by an early withdrawal from the war; that he sincerely believed that the best, perhaps the only, way to accomplish this good end was to bring it about that the first major military operation of the United States should be a resounding fiasco, thereby stimulating such a revulsion among the American people that the perfidious administration would be forced to negotiate a peace? It is hardly necessary to state the answer to that question.

" 'When war breaks out, a citizen's obligation of allegiance puts definite limits upon his freedom to act on his private judgment. If he traffics with enemy agents, knowing them to be such, and being aware of their hostile mission intentionally gives them aid in steps essential to the execution of that mission, he has adhered to the enemies of his country, giving them aid and comfort within our definition of treason. He is guilty of treason, whatever his motive.'"

In United States v. Schniederman, 106 F Supp 906, 930 (S.D. Calif) (1952) . . . the court made the following observation:

"Intent and motive should never be confused. Motive is that which prompts a person to act. Intent refers only to the state of mind with which the act is done.

"Personal advancement and financial gain are two well-recognized motives for much of human conduct. These laudable motives may prompt one person to voluntary acts of good, another to voluntary acts of crime.

"*Good motive alone is never a defense where the act done is a crime.* If a person intentionally does an act which the law denounces as a crime, motive is immaterial except insofar as evidence of motive may aid determination of the issue as to intent." [Emphasis supplied.]

The evidence in the instant case is ample to support the conclusion that the accused intended to do the acts charged. Since, as we will hereafter discuss, the offenses here require no specific intent, the accused's motives are immaterial, except, of course, as they relate to the determination of an appropriate sentence.

The accused next argues that the evidence is insufficient because he was excused from the legal consequences of his actions by virtue of duress and coercion. In substance, the law officer instructed the court that in order to convict it had to find beyond a reasonable doubt that the accused *did not* act under a well-grounded apprehension of immediate and impending death, or of immediate serious bodily harm. The trial court did not so find. . . . The real issue then is whether the instructions on the claimed defense of duress and coercion were legally correct. . . . Since this Court cannot weigh the facts as to this, for the accused to prevail we would have to find as a matter of law that the accused's actions were committed under a well-grounded apprehension of *immediate* death or serious bodily harm. Although by civilized standards conditions in the prisoner of war camp were deplorable, we cannot conclude as a matter of law that the threat of duress or coercion was so immediate as to legally justify the accused's acts. Admittedly, lingering in the background at the camp was the threat of the caves. Moreover it appears that the accused was threatened with a 150–200 mile hike back north. At the time of this threat the accused was without shoes and he deduced that he would be

unable to successfully accomplish the trip alive. However, assuming this fact to be true, the court-martial did not find that the threat, standing alone, fell within the immediacy contemplated by the law. Perhaps they felt that accused should have determined by refusal what would have then happened; whether and under what conditions the threat would have been carried out. He might have been given shoes. He might have been called upon to make the march in stages that he could have endured. We note that as a matter of fact many threats were made by the Communists which were not carried out. Major MacGhee testified that after several months' captivity, he definitely concluded that his captors would not carry out their threats to the death. He thereafter refused to "co-operate" and although sent to the caves, he survived. Also, the court-martial could have found that daily life in the prisoner camp did not equate to fear of immediate death or great bodily harm. During the accused's tenure as group leader, not a single prisoner of war died. Many people who resided in the caves died; many did not. Of the eight prisoners in Colonel Fleming's group who eventually ended up in the caves, all survived. One, Lieutenant Crockett, died shortly after his release; however, he had long been seriously ill. At one time he had been hospitalized by his captors. The rigors of prison life eventually exacted their toll and this fine officer—like many others—died. Further, there is evidence in the record which indicates that the accused had already communicated and co-operated with his captors prior to his knowledge of the caves. He testified that he made his initial recording in Pyongyang and then moved to the new location near the caves. Before the move he had not been impressed with Kim's threats to put him into a "hole," and it was not until later that he was aware of the fact that the threat actually referred to the caves. But prior to that time he had made a recording allegedly stating that prisoners were being treated humanely and the United States had made a mistake in interfering in Korea. He had addressed the town meeting in Tackchon, purportedly declaring that the war was being fought at the behest of the Wall Street profiteers. He had also participated in some of the discussion groups. Finally, the fact finders could have concluded that the prisoners were not—with isolated exceptions—physically abused. A number of witnesses testified that they were not subjected to physical abuse and that they had never noticed marks of physical violence upon the accused.

After a careful study of the facts in this case, we cannot conclude that the court-martial erred as a matter of law in not finding that the threats of duress and coercion fell within the law officer's definition of immediacy, which would excuse the accused's conduct. Stated differently, the court on the evidence of record could have reasonably found that the accused acted *without any* well-grounded apprehension of immediate death or serious bodily harm.

*   *   *

The decision of the board of review is affirmed.

NOTES

NOTE 1

LIFTON, ROBERT J.

Thought Reform and the Psychology of Totalism*

One priest [said]:

> To resist . . . you must affirm your personality whenever there is the opportunity. . . . When I was obliged to speak my views about the government, I would each time begin, "I am a priest. I believe in religion." I said it strongly every time.

This statement was perhaps a retrospective exaggeration of his self-assertion, but there was no doubt that so personal a reminder served him well.

A European professor used a more creative approach. He somehow managed during moments when pressures were relatively relaxed to make a series of drawings representing precious moments in his past: A mother and baby, a boy before a Christmas tree, a university city, a young man on a romantic stroll with his fiancée. He also wrote a brief, idealized account of the incident in his life each drawing represented. He worked on both the drawings and the essays during moments when he was off by himself in a corner of the cell or with other Westerners; and they became so precious to him that he smuggled them out of the prison at great risk and proudly displayed them to me during our interviews. They reestablished for him the world in which he wished to exist: "I could escape the horrible world around me and move in a world whose values I agreed with."

NOTE 2

CODE OF CONDUCT FOR MEMBERS OF THE ARMED FORCES
EXECUTIVE ORDER 10631**

By virtue of the authority vested in me as President of the United States, and as Commander in Chief of the armed forces of the United States, I hereby prescribe the Code of Conduct for Members of the Armed Forces of the United States which is attached to this order and hereby made a part thereof.

Every member of the armed forces of the United States is expected to measure up to the standards embodied in this Code of Conduct while he is in

---

* New York: W. W. Norton & Co. (pp. 447–48). Reprinted by permission of Norton. Copyright 1961 by Robert Jay Lifton.

** 20 *Federal Registrar* XX, (1955), 6057.

combat or in captivity. To ensure achievement of these standards, each member of the armed forces liable to capture shall be provided with specific training and instruction designed to better equip him to counter and withstand all enemy efforts against him, and shall be fully instructed as to the behavior and obligations expected of him during combat or captivity.

The Secretary of Defense . . . shall take action as is deemed necessary to implement this order and to disseminate and make the said Code known to all members of the armed forces of the United States.

Dwight D. Eisenhower

THE WHITE HOUSE

August 17, 1955

*   *   *

CODE OF CONDUCT FOR MEMBERS OF THE UNITED STATES ARMED FORCES

[*I*]

I am an American fighting man. I serve in the forces which guard my country and our way of life. I am prepared to give my life in their defense.

[*II*]

I will never surrender of my own free will. If in command I will never surrender my men while they still have the means to resist.

[*III*]

If I am captured I will continue to resist by all means available. I will make every effort to escape and aid others to escape. I will accept neither parole nor special favors from the enemy.

[*IV*]

If I become a prisoner of war, I will keep faith with my fellow prisoners. I will give no information or take part in any action which might be harmful to my comrades. If I am senior, I will take command. If not, I will obey the lawful orders of those appointed over me and will back them up in every way.

[*V*]

When questioned, should I become a prisoner of war, I am bound to give only name, rank, service number, and date of birth. I will evade answering further questions to the utmost of my ability. I will make no oral or written statements disloyal to my country and its allies or harmful to their cause.

[*VI*]

I will never forget that I am an American fighting man, responsible for my actions, and dedicated to the principles which made my country free. I will trust in my God and in the United States of America.

NOTE 3

THE QUEEN v. DUDLEY and STEPHENS
14 Q.B. 273 (1884)

INDICTMENT for the murder of Richard Parker on the high seas within the jurisdiction of the Admiralty.

[T]he jury, at the suggestion of the learned judge, found the facts of the case in a special verdict which stated "that on July 5, 1884, the prisoners, Thomas Dudley and Edward Stephens, with one Brooks, all able-bodied English seamen, and the deceased also an English boy, between seventeen and eighteen years of age, the crew of an English yacht . . . were cast away in a storm on the high seas . . . and were compelled to put into an open boat belonging to the said yacht. That in this boat they had no supply of water and no supply of food, except two one-pound tins of turnips, and for three days they had nothing else to subsist upon. That on the fourth day they caught a small turtle, upon which they subsisted for a few days, and this was the only food they had up to the twentieth day when the act now in question was committed. That on the twelfth day the remains of the turtle were entirely consumed, and for the next eight days they had nothing to eat. That they had no fresh water, except such rain as they from time to time caught in their oilskin capes. That the boat was drifting on the ocean, and was probably more than 1,000 miles away from land. That on the eighteenth day, when they had been seven days without food and five without water, the prisoners spoke to Brooks as to what should be done if no succour came, and suggested that some one should be sacrificed to save the rest, but Brooks dissented, and the boy, to whom they were understood to refer, was not consulted. That on the 24th of July, the day before the act now in question, the prisoner Dudley proposed to Stephens and Brooks that lots should be cast who should be put to death to save the rest, but Brooks refused to consent, and it was not put to the boy, and in point of fact there was no drawing of lots. That on that day the prisoners spoke of their having families, and suggested it would be better to kill the boy that their lives should be saved, and Dudley proposed that if there was no vessel in sight by the morrow morning the boy should be killed. That next day, the 25th of July, no vessel appearing, Dudley told Brooks that he had better go and have a sleep, and made signs to Stephens and Brooks that the boy had better be killed. The prisoner Stephens agreed to the act, but Brooks dissented from it. That the boy was then lying at the bottom of the boat quite helpless, and extremely weakened by famine and by drinking sea water, and unable to make any resistance, nor did he ever assent to his being killed. The prisoner Dudley offered a prayer asking forgiveness for them all if either of them should be tempted to commit a rash act, and that their souls might be saved. That Dudley, with the assent of Stephens, went to the boy, and telling him that his time was come, put a knife into his throat and killed him then and there; that the three men fed upon the body and blood of the boy for four days; that on the fourth day after the act had been committed the boat was picked up by a passing vessel, and the prisoners were rescued, still alive, but in the lowest state of prostration. That they were carried to the port of Falmouth, and committed for trial at Exeter. That if the men had not fed upon the body of the boy they would probably not have survived to be so picked up and rescued, but would within the four days have died of famine. That the boy, being in a much weaker condition, was likely to have died before them. That at the time of the act in question there was no sail in sight, nor any reasonable prospect of relief. That under these circumstances there appeared to the prisoners every probability that unless they then fed or very soon fed upon the boy or one of themselves they would die of starvation. That there was no appreciable chance of saving life except by killing some one for the others to eat. That assuming any necessity to kill anybody, there was no greater necessity for killing the boy than any of the other three men. . . . But whether upon the whole matter by the jurors found the killing of Richard Parker by Dudley and Stephens be felony and murder the jurors are ignorant, and pray the advice of the Court thereupon, and if upon the whole matter the Court shall be of opinion that the killing of Richard Parker be felony and murder, then the jurors say that Dudley and Stephens were each guilty of felony and murder as alleged in the indictment."

*   *   *

LORD COLERIDGE, C. J.

. . . From these facts, stated with the cold precision of a special verdict, it appears sufficiently that the prisoners were subject to terrible temptation, to sufferings which might break down the bodily power of the strongest man, and try the conscience of the best. . . .

*   *   *

. . . To preserve one's life is generally speaking a duty, but it may be the plainest and the highest duty to sacrifice it. War is full of instances in which it is a man's duty not to live, but to die. The duty, in case of shipwreck, of a captain to his crew, of the crew to the passengers, of soldiers to women and children, as in the noble case of the Birkenhead; these duties impose on men the moral necessity, not of the preservation, but of the sacrifice of their lives for others, from which in no country, least of all, it is to be hoped, in England, will men ever shrink, as indeed, they have not shrunk. It is not correct, therefore, to say that there is any absolute or unqualified necessity to preserve one's life. [I]t is enough in a Christian country to remind ourselves of the Great Example whom we profess to follow. . . .

*   *   *

It must not be supposed that in refusing to admit temptation to be an excuse for crime it is forgotten how terrible the temptation was; how awful the suffering; how hard in such trials to keep the judgment straight and the conduct pure. We are often compelled to set up standards we cannot reach ourselves, and to lay down rules which we could not ourselves satisfy. But a man has no right to declare temptation to be an excuse, though he might himself have yielded to it, nor allow compassion for the criminal to change or weaken in any manner the legal definition of the crime. It is therefore our duty to declare that the prisoners' act in this case was wilful murder, that the facts as stated in the verdict are no legal justification of the homicide; and to say that in our unanimous opinion the prisoners are upon this special verdict guilty of murder.

THE COURT then proceeded to pass sentence of death upon the prisoners.[1]

NOTE 4

STATE v. RODRIGUEZ
25 Conn. Supp. 350 (1964)

BY THE DIVISION

*   *   *

On August 3, 1963, the defendant became involved in an altercation with a group of Puerto Ricans in the north-end section of Hartford where he lived. The altercation carried over into the next day and evening and reached the point where defendant went home and got a .22 caliber revolver and returned to the street. He was then cornered by the same gang in his own neighborhood. The gang went after him with clubs and a baseball bat. Defendant retreated some and then stood his ground and fired one shot into the ground. Someone in the gang shouted, "That gun is blank, don't wait any longer," and again they surged forward toward him, at which time defendant fired five more shots, one of which struck the victim.

*   *   *

At the time of sentencing, the State's attorney made the observation that in his experience with Puerto Ricans, he found that one of the things they never do is run; that you are not a man if you back off, you must face your enemy; that this is the cultural background or heritage that they have.

The defendant has no prior record and is twenty-one years of age. He is a native of Puerto Rico and

came to Hartford in May, 1960. He has an excellent work record and good reputation here as well as in Puerto Rico, where his family resides. He comes from an excellent family, and the Puerto Rican authorities speak highly of him. He presents a picture of a young man of better than average character, intelligence and ability.

. . . Certainly what the defendant did cannot be condoned. However, in view of his excellent record, his youth and apparent lack of judgment because of it, and his racial heritage, a modification of the sentence is warranted.

*   *   *

LOISELLE, J. (dissenting). . . . I cannot subscribe to the proposition that the cultural background or heritage of the accused that a person is not a man if he does not stand up and fight should be a determining factor in the modification of his sentence. The accused is twenty-one years old and is no child.

NOTE 5

FREUD, SIGMUND

Beyond the Pleasure Principle (1920)*

. . . "Fright," "fear," and "anxiety" are improperly used as synonymous expressions; they are in fact capable of clear distinction in their relation to danger. "Anxiety" describes a particular state of expecting the danger or preparing for it, even though it may be an unknown one. "Fear" requires a definite object of which to be afraid. "Fright," however, is the name we give to the state a person gets into when he has run into danger without being prepared for it; it emphasizes the factor of surprise. . . .

*   *   *

[W]hat *we* seek to understand are the effects produced on the organ of the mind by the breach in the shield against stimuli and by the problems that follow in its train. And we still attribute importance to the element of fright. It is caused by lack of any preparedness for anxiety, including lack of hypercathexis of the systems that would be the first to receive the stimulus. Owing to their low cathexis those systems are not in a good position for binding the inflowing amounts of excitation and the consequences of the breach in the protective shield follow all the more easily. It will be seen, then, that preparedness for anxiety and the hypercathexis of the receptive systems constitute the last line of defence of the shield against stimuli. In the case of quite a number of

---

1. This sentence was afterwards commuted by the Crown to six months' imprisonment.

* Reprinted from: 18 *The Standard Edition of the Complete Psychological Works of Sigmund Freud*, James Strachey, ed. London: The Hogarth Press and the Institute of Psychoanalysis, 1955. (pp. 12, 31–2). Reprinted by permission of Hogarth and Liveright Publishing Co.

traumas, the difference between systems that are unprepared and systems that are well-prepared through being hypercathected may be a decisive factor in determining the outcome; though where the strength of a trauma exceeds a certain limit this factor will no doubt cease to carry weight. . . .

c.

R. I. RECREATION CENTER v. AETNA C. & S. Co.
177 F 2d. 603 (1st Cir. 1949)

WOODBURY, CIRCUIT JUDGE

The plaintiff in an action brought to recover on a Comprehensive Dishonesty, Disappearance, and Destruction policy of insurance, has taken this appeal from a final judgment entered for the defendant on its motion for summary judgment under Rule 56, Federal Rules of Civil Procedure, 28 USCA.

The policy in suit, which it is conceded was in force when the plaintiff's admitted loss of $3,800 in currency occurred. . . . This agreement in pertinent part provides for payment up to the limit of the liability assumed ($4,000) for loss of "Money and Securities" occurring within the insured's premises "caused by the actual destruction, disappearance, or wrongful abstraction thereof," except "loss, damage, or destruction caused or contributed to by . . . any dishonest, fraudulent, or criminal act, . . . committed by any employee, director, or trustee of the assured, whether acting alone or in collusion with others."

*   *   *

The plaintiff's general manager and its manager, Joseph A. Sullivan and Edward H. Sullivan, respectively, are brothers. Edward as manager had custody of the plaintiff's funds which he kept in a safe on the premises of the corporation. Neither he nor his brother had authority to borrow corporate funds or to make any use of them for their personal needs or purposes.

About two o'clock in the morning of April 23, 1947, Edward received a telephone call from his brother Joseph's wife asking him to meet his brother in front of a hotel in Pawtucket. Edward complied and arriving at the hotel saw his brother's car parked in front of it. He drove up behind his brother's car and got out, whereupon he was confronted by an armed stranger in dark glasses who ordered him into the back seat of his brother's car. As he complied another armed stranger got in beside him from the opposite side, and the two searched him and then disclosed their plan. This was to drive him in his own car to the premises of the plaintiff corporation in Providence, where he was to enter, take all the money out of the safe, and turn it over to them. He was told that if he did not do as directed "they would take care of" his brother and his wife and "would not forget" him later on, and further "that they would take care of" his child also. During this conversation Joseph sat on the front seat with his wife and another armed stranger but did not speak and Edward was not allowed to speak to him. Apparently a fourth armed stranger was also present.

Following these events the two who had searched Edward and given him his orders, leaving Joseph and his wife with the other two unknowns in Joseph's car, drove Edward in his car to the corporation's place of business and there let him out and drove away. Edward then rapped on the window with his key to call one of the three employees of the corporation who were in the premises cleaning up, and one of them admitted him. He said nothing to this employee, or to either of the other two, but went directly to the office, where there was a telephone, unlocked the safe and removed all the money in bills from it leaving only some silver. He did not count the bills but putting them in a deposit bag he immediately left the office and walked along Main Street into Pawtucket as directed. After he had walked a mile or so the two strangers drove up in his car, ordered him into it, and drove off. They at once relieved Edward of the deposit bag in which he had placed the money and then drove around for a time, eventually meeting Joseph in his car with his wife and their two guards. The four unknowns then ordered Edward out, gave him the key to his brother's car, told him to wait five minutes while they escaped, and then drove off in his car after letting him know where he would find it later. Edward waited as directed, then went and found his car, and only after that reported the night's proceedings to the police.

The defendant contends that applying settled principles of law to the facts outlined above Edward could not be found to have been acting under coercion when he took the plaintiff's money out of its safe. Hence it says that although the plaintiff might have insured against its loss had it seen fit to broaden the scope of its coverage by taking out insurance under other insuring agreements in the policy, its loss was not covered by Insuring Agreement II since it was caused or contributed to by the criminal act of an employee. The plaintiff, on the other hand, takes the position that the agreed facts at least provide a basis for finding that when Edward took the money he was acting under coercion, as that term is defined in the law, and thus in doing so was but the innocent tool or instrumentality of the bandits. Hence it says, in the event of a finding of coercion, it would follow as a matter of law that Edward was innocent of any dishonest, fraudulent, or criminal act, with the result that its loss was clearly covered by Insuring Agreement II of the policy.

. . . It appears to be established, however, that although coercion or necessity will never excuse taking the life of an innocent person, it will excuse lesser crimes. But to provide an excuse the compulsion must be present, immediate, and impending, and of such a nature as to induce a well-founded fear of death or at least serious bodily injury. And there must be no reasonable opportunity to escape the compulsion without committing the crime. . . .

Literally applying the foregoing principles to the conceded facts there can be no doubt that the plaintiff has not established a factual basis for the finding that Edward was acting under coercion when he took the money. Obviously it did not suit the bandits' purposes to shoot the Sullivans down in the street in front of a hotel in a city of substantial size if they should prove recalcitrant for their only threat was of future reprisal. And a veiled threat of future unspecified harm, as the threat "to take care of," and "not to forget" is not the equivalent of an immediate threat of death or severe bodily injury. But perhaps the law of coercion developed in a tougher-minded age, and now-a-days its severity should be relaxed. . . . But however this may be, the fact remains that Edward did not take the money out of the plaintiff's safe under the muzzles of the bandits' guns. . . . He was left free while he was in the building to communicate his plight to the employee who had let him in, or to one or both of the other night workers there, and to enlist their aid, and he was free to telephone the police himself, and certainly while he was opening the safe, taking out the money and walking over a mile to his rendezvous with the bandits there was ample time for the police to provide him with protection. Under these circumstances we do not see how it could be found that Edward did not have full opportunity to avoid the criminal act without present danger to himself.

But, calling the bandit "gangsters," the plaintiff argues that Edward acted throughout in present and reasonable fear of reprisal should he fail to do as directed. This argument rests upon the presupposition that the local police would be powerless to protect him, his family, and his brother and his family, from such revenge as the bandits, if disappointed, might attempt to take. In the first place there is nothing to indicate the work of a "gang," as that term has come to be used in recent years. Indeed the crime is not typical of "gangsters," who ordinarily seek larger game by more subtle means, but of ordinary bandits. And in the second place there is no basis for the assumption that the police of Providence or Pawtucket, both populous civilized communities, would be unable to afford adequate protection against any revenge which persons of that ilk, or even "gangsters," would be likely to attempt or to accomplish. We think Edward's reputed fear of future reprisal, under the circumstances disclosed, cannot reasonably be said to have been well founded, and thus it is not the kind of fear necessary to establish the excuse of coercion.

Furthermore, however, the plaintiff argues that Edward was deterred from calling the police earlier than he did, not alone by fear of future reprisals upon himself and members of his family, but by fear that if he called for police protection while his brother and sister-in-law were still under guard, one or both of them might be killed or injured either by the bandits, or in a gun battle between the bandits and the police. Perhaps a well-grounded apprehension of death or serious bodily injury to another, particularly to a close relative, may constitute coercion. We are not prepared to hold otherwise. But we cannot see how it could be said that Edward's fear for the immediate safety of his brother and sister-in-law was well founded. As already pointed out, it did not suit the bandit's purposes to shoot in the public streets, and we do not see how Edward could have entertained a well founded fear that the bandits would murder his brother and sister-in-law in cold blood in a public place should he disappoint them. The remainder of the argument rests upon the presupposition that there would inevitably be a gun battle with the bandits should the police attempt to rescue Joseph and his wife from their custody. We do not see any adequate basis for this. Knowing the facts, it is certain that the police would not risk an open battle with the bandits in order to save their innocent captives, but instead would resort to safer and subtler means to attain their end. It seems to us abundantly clear that Edward had not only a reasonable but an ample opportunity to escape the bandits' compulsion without taking the plaintiff's money.

Therefore on the conceded evidentiary facts we fail to find any basis for the ultimate conclusion that Edward was acting under legal coercion when he took the money. Under these circumstances, should that evidence be submitted to a jury, the court below would have no alternative but to direct a verdict for the defendant. In this situation there is no genuine issue of material fact for trial and summary judgment is in order. . . .

*   *   *

MAGRUDER, CHIEF JUDGE

The opinion of the court assumes that, in respect of crimes like larceny, embezzlement, and other lesser offenses, the defense of coercion is available to an accused when he can show that he acted under compulsion of a well-grounded apprehension of death or serious bodily injury either to himself or to a near relative if he should refrain from committing the otherwise criminal act. As to fear for the bodily safety of a third person, even a close relative, there is a surprising dearth of authority; but if the question were ever presented under sufficiently strong, dramatic, and convincing circumstances, I am fairly sure the courts would sanction the defense of coercion. However that may be, the present is not a criminal case, but involves the application of language in an insurance policy. If Edward Sullivan took the money off his employer in compliance with the demand of the criminal gang, knowing that his brother had been abducted and was being held as a hostage by the gang, having a reasonable fear that his brother would be "done in" by the gangsters if the money were not forthcoming, and not daring to run the risks which would be involved in notifying the police, then I would say that the loss claimed here by the insured was not a loss "caused or contributed to by * * * any dishonest, fraudulent, or criminal act," committed by an employee, within the meaning of the insurance contract. Of course, the rather lurid tale recited in the depositions may have been only a cock-and-bull story, but its credibility was for the jury. My only doubt is whether the case should have been disposed of on summary judgment, instead of being submitted to the jury under appropriate instructions as to coercion. For present purposes, not only must the facts recited in the depositions be taken as true, but every reasonable inference therefrom must be taken in favor of the insured. When Edward Sullivan left to get the money, his brother and sister-in-law were being held captive at gun point. Edward had no assurance that the gangsters who held his brother would remain parked on a public street in front of a hotel. They might have driven off to a hide-out with their hostages, so far as Edward could have known when he entered the premises of the insured to get the money. It is not necessary to assume that if the gangsters should have had occasion to do violence to their hostages they would do so in a public place. A hostage abducted and held by an armed gang of desperadoes is under a present impending menace, I should say, not merely under apprehension of possible future harm. I would have been inclined to the view that it was for the jury to say, accepting the facts as stated in the depositions, whether the risks to the hostages involved in any alternative course of action Edward might have taken were so insubstantial as to make it unreasonable for Edward to comply with the demands of the criminal gang. But my brethren think otherwise on this point, and I do not feel strongly enough about it to register a dissent.

One side issue is perhaps worthy of mention. Even if Edward would not be liable criminally for taking his employer's money under the circumstances, it does not necessarily follow that he would not be liable civilly to his employer for the value of the property taken to remove a menace to his own bodily safety or that of his brother. If the insurance company were held liable to the insured for the loss here, it would of course be subrogated to any claim for reimbursement which the insured might have against Edward Sullivan.

NOTE

LYNUMN v. ILLINOIS
372 U.S. 528 (1963)

MR. JUSTICE STEWART delivered the opinion of the Court.

The petitioner was tried in the Criminal Court of Cook County, Illinois, on an indictment charging her with the unlawful possession and sale of marijuana. . . .

* * *

The officers testified to this oral confession at the petitioner's trial, and it is this testimony which, we now hold, fatally infected the petitioner's conviction. The petitioner testified at the trial that she had not in fact sold any marijuana. . . . She also testified, however, that she had told the officers on the day of her arrest that she had sold . . . marijuana, describing the circumstances under which this statement was made as follows:

"I told him [Officer Sims] I hadn't sold . . . I didn't know anything about narcotics and I had no source of supply. He kept insisting I had a source of supply and had been dealing in narcotics. I kept telling him I did not and that I knew nothing about it. Then he started telling me I could get ten years and the children could be taken away, and after I got out they would be taken away and strangers would have them, and if I could co-operate he would see they weren't; and he would recommend leniency and I had better do what they told me if I wanted to see my kids again. The two children are three and four years old. Their father is dead; they live with me. I love my children very much. I have never been arrested for anything in my whole life before. I did not know how much power a policeman had in a recommendation to the State's Attorney or to the Court. I did not know that a Court and a State's Attorney are not bound by a police officer's recommendations. I did not know anything about it. All the officers talked to me about my children and the time I could get for not co-operating. All three officers did. After that conversation I believed that if I co-operated with them and answered the questions the way they wanted me to answer, I believed that I would not be prosecuted. They had said I had better say what they wanted me to, or I would lose the kids. I said I would say anything they wanted me to say. I asked what I was to say. I was told to say 'You must admit you [sold marijuana] so I said, 'Yes. . . .'

". . . The only reason I had for admitting it to the police was the hope of saving myself from going to jail and being taken away from my children. The statement I made to the police after they promised that they would intercede for me, the statements admitting the crime, were false.

". . . My statement to the police officers that I sold the marijuana . . . was false. I lied to the police at that time. I lied because the police told me they were going to send me to jail for ten years and take my children, and I would never see them again; so I agreed to say whatever they wanted me to say."

The police officers did not deny that these were the circumstances under which the petitioner told them that she had sold marijuana. . . . To the contrary, their testimony largely corroborated the petitioner's testimony. Officer Sims testified:

*   *   *

". . . While I was talking to her in the bedroom, she told me that she had children and she had taken the children over to her mother-in-law, to keep her children.

"Q. Did you or anybody in your presence indicate or suggest or say to her that her children would be taken away from her if she didn't do what you asked her to do?

"Witness: I believe there was some mention of her children being taken away from her if she was arrested.

"The Court: By whom? Who made mention of it?

"The Witness: I believe Officer Bryson made that statement and I think I made the statement at some time during the course of our discussion that her children could be taken from her. We did not say if she co-operated they wouldn't be taken. I don't know whether Kobar said that to her or not. I don't recall if Kobar said that to her or not.

"I asked her who the clothing belonged to. She said they were her children's. I asked how many she had and she said two. I asked her where they were or who took care of them. She said the children were over at the mother's or mother-in-law's. I asked her how did she take care of herself and she said she was on ADC. I told her that if we took her into the station and charged her with the offense, that the ADC would probably be cut off and also that she would probably lose custody of her children. That was not before I said if she co-operated, it would go light on her. It was during the same conversation."

*   *   *

It is thus abundantly clear that the petitioner's oral confession was made only after the police had told her that state financial aid for her infant children would be cut off, and her children taken from her, if she did not "co-operate." These threats were made while she was encircled in her apartment by three police officers and a twice-convicted felon who had purportedly "set her up." There was no friend or adviser to whom she might turn. She had had no previous experience with the criminal law, and had no reason not to believe that the police had ample power to carry out their threats.

We think it clear that a confession made under such circumstances must be deemed not voluntary, but coerced. That is the teaching of our cases. We have said that the question in each case is whether the defendant's will was overborne at the time he confessed.

. . . If so, the confession cannot be deemed "the product of a rational intellect and a free will." *Blackburn* v. *Alabama*, 361 U.S. 199, 208. . . .

*   *   *

d.   PENNEKAMP v. FLORIDA
328 U.S. 331 (1946)

MR. JUSTICE REED delivered the opinion of the Court.

*   *   *

[P]etitioners were responsible for the publication of two editorials charged by the citation to be contemptuous of the Circuit Court and its judges in that they were unlawfully critical of the administration of criminal justice in certain cases then pending before the Court.

Certiorari was granted to review petitioners' contention that the editorials did not present "a clear and present danger of high imminence to the administration of justice by the court" or judges who were criticized and therefore the judgment of contempt was invalid as violative of the petitioners' right of free expression in the press. . . .

*   *   *

What is meant by clear and present danger to a fair administration of justice? No definition could give an answer. Certainly this criticism of the judges' inclinations or actions in these pending nonjury proceedings could not directly affect such administration. This criticism of their actions could not affect their ability to decide the issues. . . .

It is suggested, however, that even though his intellectual processes cannot be affected by reflections on his purposes, a judge may be influenced by a desire to placate the accusing newspaper to retain public esteem and secure re-election presumably at the cost of unfair rulings against an accused. In this case too many fine-drawn assumptions against the independence of judicial action must be made to call such a possibility a clear and present danger to justice. For this to follow, there must be a judge of less than ordinary fortitude without friends or support or a powerful and vindictive newspaper bent upon a rule or ruin policy, and a public unconcerned with or uninterested in the truth or the protection of their judicial institutions. . . .

. . . We conclude that the danger under this record to fair judicial administration has not the clearness and immediacy necessary to close the door of permissible public comment. When that door is closed, it closes all doors behind it.

Reversed.

*   *   *

MR. JUSTICE FRANKFURTER, concurring.

On the basis of two editorials and a cartoon, the Circuit Court of Florida for the County of Dade found the publisher of the Miami *Herald* and one of its editors guilty of contempt of court. . . .[1]

*   *   *

Without a free press there can be no free society. Freedom of the press, however, is not an end in itself but a means to the end of a free society. The scope and nature of the constitutional protection of freedom of speech must be viewed in that light and in that light applied. The independence of the judiciary is no less a means to the end of a free society, and the proper functioning of an independent judiciary puts the freedom of the press in its proper perspective. For the judiciary cannot function properly if what the press does is reasonably calculated to disturb the judicial judgment in its duty and capacity to act solely on the basis of what is before the court. A judiciary is not independent unless courts of justice are enabled to administer law by absence of pressure from without, whether exerted through the blandishments of reward or the menace of disfavor. In the noble words, penned by John Adams, of the First Constitution of Massachusetts: "It is essential to the preservation of the right of every individual, his life, liberty, property, and character, that there be an impartial interpretation of the laws, and administration of justice. It is the right of every citizen to be tried by judges as free, impartial, and independent as the lot of humanity will admit." A free press is not to be preferred to an independent judiciary, nor an independent judiciary to a free press. Neither has primacy over the other; both are indispensable to a free society. . . .

*   *   *

These are generalities. But they are generalities of the most practical importance in achieving a proper adjustment between a free press and an independent judiciary.

Especially in the administration of the criminal law—that most awesome aspect of government—society needs independent courts of justice. This means judges free from control by the executive, free from all ties with political interests, free from all fears of reprisal or hopes of reward. The safety of society and the security of the innocent alike depend upon wise and impartial criminal justice. Misuse of

its machinery may undermine the safety of the State; its misuse may deprive the individual of all that makes a free man's life dear.

Criticism therefore must not feel cramped, even criticism of the administration of criminal justice. Weak characters ought not to be judges, and the scope allowed to the press for society's sake may assume that they are not. No judge fit to be one is likely to be influenced consciously except by what he sees and hears in court and by what is judicially appropriate for his deliberations. However, judges are also human, and we know better than did our forbears how powerful is the pull of the unconscious and how treacherous the rational process. While the ramparts of reason have been found to be more fragile than the Age of Enlightenment had supposed, the means for arousing passion and confusing judgment have been reinforced. And since judges, however stalwart, are human, the delicate task of administering justice ought not to be made unduly difficult by irresponsible print.

The English bench is justly noted for its sturdiness, and it was no weak-kneed judge who recently analyzed the mischief of exposing even the hardiest nature to extraneous influence: " . . . I think it is a fallacy to say or to assume that the presiding judge is a person who cannot be affected by outside information. He is a human being, and while I do not suggest that it is likely that any judge, as the result of information which had been improperly conveyed to him, would give a decision which otherwise he would not have given, it is embarrassing to a judge that he should be informed of matters which he would much rather not hear and which make it much more difficult for him to do his duty. To repeat the words I have already read from the judgment of Wills J. in *Rex* v. *Parke* [(1903) 2 K.B. 432]. 'The reason why the publication of articles like those with which we have to deal is treated as a contempt of court is because their tendency and sometimes their object is to deprive the court of the power of doing that which is the end for which it exists—namely, to administer justice duly, impartially, and with reference solely to the facts judicially brought before it.' . . . I venture to think that no judge with long criminal experience will fail to be able to recall instances in which the publication of matters such as that to which I have referred has had the effect of making the task of a judge extremely difficult, and no one has the right to publish matter which will have that effect." Humphreys, J., in *Rex* v. *Davies*, [1945] 1 K.B. 435, 442–43. The observations of another judge in the same case bear quoting: " . . . jurors are not the only people whose minds can be affected by prejudice. One of the evils of inadmissible matter being disseminated is that no one can tell what effect a particular piece of information may have on his mind. Why, as my Lord has asked, and I can think of no better word, should a judge be

---

1. The judges who tried the contempt cases were the same judges who were criticized by the editorials. The words of caution of Mr. Chief Justice Taft became relevant: "The delicacy there is in the judge's deciding whether an attack upon his own judicial action is mere criticism or real obstruction, and the possibility that impulse may incline his view to personal vindication, are manifest." *Craig* v. *Hecht*, 263 U.S. 255, 279 (concurring). But the judges who tried petitioners were sensible of the delicacy of their position, and offered to retire from the case if petitioners felt they would prefer to be tried by another judge.

'embarrassed' by having matters put into his mind, the effect of which it is impossible to estimate or assess? As an illustration of this proposition, the Court of Criminal Appeal has expressed, not once but many times, its thorough disapproval of evidence which is sometimes given by police officers at the end of a case when a man has been convicted. On such occasions all sorts of allegations are frequently made against a man's character, sometimes in the nature of hearsay and sometimes not supported by evidence at all. What is the ground for the disapproval of the Court of Criminal Appeal regarding such statements? It can only be that the judge who, after hearing the statements, has to pronounce sentence, may, quite unconsciously, have his judgment influenced by matters which he has no right to consider. . . . Not all defamatory matter can amount to contempt of court. . . . Whether defamatory matter amounts to contempt in any particular case is a question in each case of fact, of degree and of circumstances." Oliver, J. in *Rex* v. *Davies, supra*, at 445–46. . . . To deny that bludgeoning or poisonous comment has power to influence, or at least to disturb, the task of judging is to play make-believe and to assume that men in gowns are angels. The psychological aspects of this problem become particularly pertinent in the case of elected judges with short tenure.

"Trial by newspaper," like all catch phrases, may be loosely used but it summarizes an evil influence upon the administration of criminal justice in this country. Its absence in England, at least its narrow confinement there, furnishes an illuminating commentary. It will hardly be claimed that the press is less free in England than in the United States. Nor will any informed person deny that the administration of criminal justice is more effective there than here. This is so despite the commonly accepted view that English standards of criminal justice are more civilized, or, at the least, that recognized standards of fair conduct in the prosecution of crime are better observed. Thus, "the third degree" is not unjustly called "the American method." This is not the occasion to enlarge upon the reasons for the greater effectiveness of English criminal justice but it may be confidently asserted that it is more effective partly because its standards are so civilized. . . .[2]

*   *   *

If men, including judges and journalists, were

angels, there would be no problems of contempt of court. Angelic judges would be undisturbed by extraneous influences and angelic journalists would not seek to influence them. The power to punish for contempt, as a means of safeguarding judges in deciding on behalf of the community as impartially as is given to the lot of men to decide, is not a privilege accorded to judges. The power to punish for contempt of court is a safeguard not for judges as persons but for the function which they exercise. It is a condition of that function—indispensable for a free society—that in a particular controversy pending before a court and awaiting judgment, human beings, however strong, should not be torn from their moorings of impartiality by the undertow of extraneous influence. In securing freedom of speech, the Constitution hardly meant to create the right to influence judges or juries. That is no more freedom of speech than stuffing a ballot box is an exercise of the right to vote.

*   *   *

NOTES

NOTE 1

CRAIG v. HARNEY
331 U.S. 367 (1946)

*   *   *

MR. JUSTICE JACKSON, dissenting.

*   *   *

[T]his Court appears to sponsor the myth that judges are not as other men are, and that therefore newspaper attacks on them are negligible because they do not penetrate the judicial armor. Says the opinion: "But the law of contempt is not made for

---

2. The recent ruling by the Speaker of the House of Commons regarding the limitation on the right to comment even in Parliament on the pending proceedings against the accused Nazis before the Nuremberg tribunal bears significantly on the attitude and controlling standards deemed appropriate in England in order to protect the judicial process from extraneous influences:

"The Rule to which the Noble Lord has drawn my attention that reflections cannot be made on judges of the High Court and certain other courts, except by way of a substantive motion, applies only to the courts of this country. In terms,

therefore, it only covers the two British members of this tribunal. I feel that it would be worse than individious—indeed improper—not to extend the same protection to their colleagues on this tribunal who represent the three other Allied Nations.

"There is, however, another of our Rules of Debate which is relevant to this case, the Rule that matters which are *sub judice* should not be the subject of discussion in this House. This Rule again, in terms, applies only to British courts. The court in Nuremberg is a court in which British judges participate, and we have the same interest in seeing that nothing is done here to disturb its judicial atmosphere as we have in the case of British courts—indeed, perhaps a greater interest, since the eyes of the world are upon this new and difficult procedure of international justice, and the consequences of ill-advised interference might be incalculably mischievous.

"I think that the intention of both the Rules to which I have referred, is to preserve the House from even the appearance of interfering in the administration of British justice—and this should include trials for which this country has some responsibility; and I rule, therefore, that all the members of the International Court are protected to the same extent as British judges, and that discussion of its proceedings is out of Order, in the same way as matters under adjudication in a British court of law." 416 *Parliamentary Debates* (Hansard) 599–600, November 22, 1945.

the protection of judges who may be sensitive to the winds of public opinion. Judges are supposed to be men of fortitude, able to thrive in a hardy climate." With due respect to those who think otherwise, to me this is an ill-founded opinion, and to inform the press that it may be irresponsible in attacking judges because they have so much fortitude is ill-advised, or worse. I do not know whether it is the view of the Court that a judge must be thick-skinned or just thick-headed, but nothing in my experience or observation confirms the idea that he is insensitive to publicity. Who does not prefer good to ill report of his work? And if fame—a good public name—is, as Milton said, the "last infirmity of noble mind," it is frequently the first infirmity of a mediocre one.

From our sheltered position, fortified by life tenure and other defenses to judical independence, it is easy to say that this local judge ought to have shown more fortitude in the face of criticism. But he had no such protection. He was an elective judge, who held for a short term. I do not take it that an ambition of a judge to remain a judge is either unusual or dishonorable. Moreover, he was not a lawyer, and I regard this as a matter of some consequence. A lawyer may gain courage to render a decision that temporarily is unpopular because he has confidence that his profession over the years will approve it, despite its unpopular reception, as has been the case with many great decisions. But this judge had no anchor in professional opinion. Of course, the blasts of these little papers in this small community do not jolt us, but I am not so confident that we would be indifferent if a news monopoly in our entire jurisdiction should perpetrate this kind of an attack on us.

It is doubtful if the press itself regards judges as so insulated from public opinion. In this very case the American Newspaper Publishers Association filed a brief *amicus curiae* on the merits after we granted certiorari. Of course, it does not cite a single authority that was not available to counsel for the publisher involved, and does not tell us a single new fact except this one: "This membership embraces more than 700 newspaper publishers whose publications represent in excess of eighty per cent of the total daily and Sunday circulation of newspapers published in this country. The Association is vitally interested in the issue presented in this case, namely, the right of newspapers to publish news stories and editorials on cases pending in the courts."

This might be a good occasion to demonstrate the fortitude of the judiciary.

NOTE 2

ESTES v. TEXAS
381 U.S. 532 (1965)

MR. JUSTICE CLARK.

The potential impact of television on the jurors is perhaps of the greatest significance. They are the nerve center of the fact-finding process. It is true that in States like Texas where they are required to be sequestered in trials of this nature the jurors will probably not see any of the proceedings as televised from the courtroom. But the inquiry cannot end there. From the moment the trial judge announces that a case will be televised it becomes a *cause célèbre*. The whole community, including prospective jurors, becomes interested in all the morbid details surrounding it. The approaching trial immediately assumes an important status in the public press and the accused is highly publicized along with the offense with which he is charged. Every juror carries with him into the jury box these solemn facts and thus increases the chance of prejudice that is present in every criminal case. And we must remember that realistically it is only the notorious trial which will be broadcast, because of the necessity for paid sponsorship. The conscious or unconscious effect that this may have on the juror's judgment cannot be evaluated, but experience indicates that it is not only possible but highly probable that it will have a direct bearing on his vote as to guilt or innocence. Where pretrial publicity of all kinds has created intense public feeling which is aggravated by the telecasting or picturing of the trial the televised jurors cannot help but feel the pressures of knowing that friends and neighbors have their eyes upon them. If the community be hostile to an accused a televised juror, realizing that he must return to neighbors who saw the trial themselves, may well be led "not to hold the balance nice, clear and true between the State and the accused. . . ."

Moreover, while it is practically impossible to assess the effect of television on jury attentiveness, those of us who know juries realize the problem of jury "distraction." The State argues this is *de minimis* since the physical disturbances have been eliminated. But we know that distractions are not caused solely by the physical presence of the camera and its telltale red lights. It is the awareness of the fact of telecasting that is felt by the juror throughout the trial. We are all self-conscious and uneasy when being televised. Human nature being what it is, not only a juror's eyes but his mind will often be on that fact rather than on the witness stand.

*   *   *

The quality of the testimony in criminal trials will often be impaired. The impact upon a witness of the knowledge that he is being viewed by a vast audience is simply incalculable. Some may be demoralized and frightened, some cocky and given to overstatement; memories may falter, as with anyone speaking publicly, and accuracy of statement may be severely undermined. Embarrassment may impede the search for the truth, as may a natural tendency toward overdramatization. Furthermore, inquisitive strangers and "cranks" might approach witnesses on the street with jibes, advice or demands for explanation of testimony. There is little wonder that the defendant cannot "prove" the existence of such factors. Yet we all know from experience that they exist.

* * *

Judges are human beings also and are subject to the same psychological reactions as laymen. Telecasting is particularly bad where the judge is elected, as is the case in all save a half dozen of our States. The telecasting of a trial becomes a political weapon, which along with other distractions inherent in broadcasting, diverts his attention from the task at hand—the fair trial of the accused.

But this is not all. There is the initial decision that must be made as to whether the use of television will be permitted. This is perhaps an even more crucial consideration. Our judges are high-minded men and women. But it is difficult to remain oblivious to the pressures that the news media can bring to bear on them both directly and through the shaping of public opinion. Moreover, where one judge in a district or even in a State permits telecasting, the requirement that the others do the same is almost mandatory. Especially is this true where the judge is selected at the ballot box.

Finally, we cannot ignore the impact of courtroom television on the defendant. Its presence is a form of mental—if not physical—harassment, resembling a police line-up or the third degree. The inevitable close-ups of his gestures and expressions during the ordeal of his trial might well transgress his personal sensibilities, his dignity, and his ability to concentrate on the proceedings before him—sometimes the difference between life and death—dispassionately, freely and without the distraction of wide public surveillance. A defendant on trial for a specific crime is entitled to his day in court, not in a stadium, or a city or nationwide arena. The heightened public clamor resulting from radio and television coverage will inevitably result in prejudice. Trial by television is, therefore, foreign to our system. Furthermore, telecasting may also deprive an accused of effective counsel. The distractions, intrusions into confidential attorney-client relationships and the temptation offered by television to play to the public audience might often have a direct effect not only upon the lawyers, but the judge, the jury and the witnesses.

The television camera is a powerful weapon. Intentionally or inadvertently it can destroy an accused and his case in the eyes of the public. While our telecasters are honorable men, they too are human. The necessity for sponsorship weighs heavily in favor of the televising of only notorious cases, such as this one, and invariably focuses the beam of the lens upon the unpopular or infamous accused. Such a selection is necessary in order to obtain a sponsor

willing to pay a sufficient fee to cover the costs and return a profit. We have already examined the ways in which public sentiment can affect the trial participants. To the extent that television shapes that sentiment, it can strip the accused of a fair trial.

The State would dispose of all these observations with the simple statement that they are for psychologists because they are purely hypothetical. But we cannot afford the luxury of saying that, because these factors are difficult of ascertainment in particular cases, they must be ignored. Nor are they "purely hypothetical." . . . They are effects that may, and in some combination almost certainly will, exist in any case in which television is injected into the trial process.

* * *

NOTE 3

GREEN v. MURPHY
259 F. 2d 591 (3d Cir. 1958)

KALODNER, CIRCUIT JUDGE (dissenting).

I would grant forthwith the writ directing Judge Murphy's withdrawal from participation in the Green case.

A judge should not preside at the criminal trial of one (1) whose sponsorship he sought and received in obtaining his judicial appointment and confirmation; (2) whose aid he importuned to procure a lucrative State office for a lifetime friend; (3) with whom he had enjoyed a close personal and political relationship beginning with their service as members of Congress; and (4) whose codefendant . . . is allegedly an intimate friend of the judge who gave material assistance in obtaining his judicial appointment, and as to whom the judge is alleged to be "prejudiced in favor of."

* * *

The sum of Green's "leaning backward" contention is that Judge Murphy, because of their longstanding prior friendship and association, will consciously or subconsciously, through the trial, be affected by its existence.

As Green put it in his brief here:

"If a motion for judgment of acquittal were to be made before the respondent judge, could he pass upon that issue without considering, consciously or subconsciously, whether he would be accused of doing a favor in return for his friend? * * *

"If the judge should grant a motion for acquittal, will the public think he is favoring an old friend? Must the judge deny a proper motion to forestall such criticism? Is the defendant, under the Constitution, required to take this risk? * * *

"Obviously, the facts of the relationship between the defendant and the respondent, and the relationship between the respondent and codefendent McGlinchey, present ample facts from which any mind might properly draw an inference of bias or prejudice."

The nub of Green's contention was well-stated by the concurring judges as follows:

"The sole complaint is that the judge may overcompensate for his inclination toward the accused by leaning backward."[1]

I think such complaint merits consideration.

Certainly it cannot be gainsaid that the detachment which is an indispensable ingredient of the judicial attitude does not exist where a judge presides at the trial of one who has been his long-time friend and benefactor.

As was stated in 48 C.J.S. Judges 72, p. 1039:

"The underlying principle of rules for disqualification of judges is that no judge should preside in a case in which he is not *wholly free*, disinterested, impartial, and independent." (Emphasis supplied.)

Can it be said that the trial judge here is "wholly free"?

Judges are human beings and not mechanical

machines dispensing undistilled justice on a push-button basis. They are not judicial Univacs or mechanized "brains."

NOTE 4

PHILLIPS, HARLAN B.

Felix Frankfurter Reminisces*

*　　*　　*

Some of the lads at the Harvard Law School occasionally—a Jewish lad who failed and then thought there might be reasons for that—were soon made to realize that I was not a Jewish professor at the Harvard Law School, but I was a Harvard Law School professor who happened to be a Jew. In fact, I know that I exacted higher standards from Jews than from other people, and perhaps that was on the whole a good thing for Jews who have any capacity.

NOTE 5

PUBLIC UTILITIES COMM'N. v. POLLAK
343 U.S. 451, 466 (1952)

MR. JUSTICE FRANKFURTER

The judicial process demands that a judge move within the framework of relevant legal rules and the covenanted modes of thought for ascertaining them. He must think dispassionately and submerge private feeling on every aspect of a case. There is a good deal of shallow talk that the judicial robe does not change the man within it. It does. The fact is that on the whole judges do lay aside private views in discharging their judicial functions. This is achieved through training, professional habits, self-discipline and that fortunate alchemy by which men are loyal to the obligation with which they are entrusted. But it is also true that reason cannot control the subconscious influence of feelings of which it is unaware. When there is ground for believing that such unconscious feelings may operate in the ultimate judgment, or may not unfairly lead others to believe they are operating, judges recuse themselves. They do not sit in judgment. They do this for a variety of reasons. The guiding consideration is that the administration of justice should reasonably appear to be disinterested as well as be so in fact.

This case for me presents such a situation. My feelings are so strongly engaged as a victim of the practice in controversy that I had better not participate in judicial judgment upon it. I am explicit as to the reason for my nonparticipation in this case because I have for some time been of the view that it is desirable to state why one takes himself out of a case.

---

1. [Defendant] filed an affidavit of prejudice and a motion for change of judge, alleging that he believed that the trial judge was "personally prejudiced against me by reason of the many favors I have done for him and the obligation he owes me and that by reason of his desire to prove his integrity, he will be unable to afford me a fair and impartial trial." The affidavit contained supporting factual allegations. Appended to the motion was the opinion of a psychiatrist indicating that gratitude for favors done under the circumstances alleged would result in subconscious bias and prejudice on the part of the judge against the defendant.

The hypothetical question asked of the psychiatrist was as follows: "Assuming the judge and the defendant are of the same racial and religious background; that they are members of the same political party; that they have served together in the United States Congress; that they have been close friends and political associates; that, while he was a member of Congress, the judge requested petitioner to assist him in obtaining an appointment to the bench; that since his elevation to the bench, the judge has requested personal and political favors from petitioner, who has performed such favors for the judge; and that defendant is accused of an offense arising out of his office as a Congressman; under these circumstances, will the judge be biased and prejudiced against the defendant?"

The answer given by the psychiatrist was: "There will be a tendency for any action to be made more difficult and more inappropriate in relation to a fair trial on the issues resulting from psychological prejudice."

An attached chart explained that the relations between judge and defendant would result in an overidentification with the defendant upon the part of the judge and both a subconscious sense of hostility and a feeling of gratitude for past favors. Since reciprocity for such favors would violate the judicial oath, there would be a subconscious overcompensation resulting in prejudice. [Forer, Lois G.: *Psychiatric Evidence In The Recusation of Judges*, 73 Harv. L. Rev. 1325 (1960). Copyright 1960 by The Harvard Law Review Association.]

---

* New York: Reynal and Co., 1960, (p. 37). Reprinted by permission.

NOTE 6

PETERSON v. CITY OF GREENVILLE
373 U.S. 244 (1963)

*   *   *

MR. CHIEF JUSTICE WARREN delivered the opinion of the Court.

The petitioners were convicted in the Recorder's Court of the City of Greenville, South Carolina, for violating the trespass statute of that State. . . .

The ten petitioners are Negro boys and girls who, on August 9, 1960, entered the S. H. Kress store in Greenville and seated themselves at the lunch counter for the purpose, as they testified, of being served. . . .

The manager of the store did not request the police to arrest petitioners; he asked them to leave because integrated service was "contrary to local customs" of segregation at lunch counters and in violation of [a] Greenville City ordinance required separation of the races in restaurants. . . .

*   *   *

It cannot be denied that here the City of Greenville, an agency of the State, has provided by its ordinance that the decision as to whether a restaurant facility is to be operated on a desegregated basis is to be reserved to it. When the State has commanded a particular result, it has saved to itself the power to determine that result and thereby "to a significant extent" has "become involved" in it, and, in fact, has removed that decision from the sphere of private choice. It has thus effectively determined that a person owning, managing, or controlling an eating place is left with no choice of his own but must segregate his white and Negro patrons. The Kress management, in deciding to exclude Negroes, did precisely what the city law required.

Consequently these convictions cannot stand, even assuming, as respondent contends, that the manager would have acted as he did independently of the existence of the ordinance. The State will not be heard to make this contention in support of the convictions. For the convictions had the effect, which the State cannot deny, of enforcing the ordinance passed by the City of Greenville, the agency of the State. When a state agency passes a law compelling persons to discriminate against other persons because of race, and the State's criminal processes are employed in a way which enforces the discrimination mandated by that law, such a palpable violation of the Fourteenth Amendment cannot be saved by attempting to separate the mental urges of the discriminators.

*   *   *

MR. JUSTICE HARLAN, concurring in the result. . . .

*   *   *

. . . The rationale [of the Court's opinion] is that the State, having compelled restaurateurs to segregate their establishments through this city ordinance, cannot be heard to say, in enforcing its trespass statute, that Kress' decision to segregate was in fact but the product of its own untrammeled choice. This is said to follow because the ordinance removes the operation of segregated or desegregated eating facilities "from the sphere of private choice" and because "the State's criminal processes are employed in a way which enforces" the ordinance.

This is an alluring, but, in my view, a fallacious proposition. Clearly Kress might have preferred for reasons entirely of its own not to serve meals to Negroes along with whites, and the dispositive question on the issue of state action thus becomes whether such was the case, or whether the ordinance played some part in the Kress decision to segregate. That is a question of fact.

*   *   *

It is suggested that requiring proof of the effect of such laws in individual instances would involve "attempting to separate the mental urges of the discriminators." But proof of state of mind is not a novel concept in the law of evidence, see 2 Wigmore, Evidence (3d ed. 1940), §§385–393, and such a requirement presents no special barriers in this situation. The mere showing of such an ordinance would, in my judgment, make out a *prima facie* case of invalid state action, casting on the State the burden of proving that the exclusion was in fact the product solely of private choice. In circumstances like these that burden is indeed a heavy one. This is the rule which, in my opinion, evenhanded constitutional doctrine and recognized evidentiary rules dictate. . . .

NOTE 7

S.E.C. v. CAPITAL GAINS BUREAU
375 U.S. 180 (1963)

MR. JUSTICE GOLDBERG delivered the opinion of the Court.

We are called upon in this case to decide whether under the Investment Advisers Act of 1940[1] the Securities and Exchange Commission may obtain an injunction compelling a registered investment adviser to disclose to his clients a practice of purchasing shares of a security for his own account shortly before recommending that security for long-term investment and then immediately selling the shares at a profit upon the rise in the market price following the recommendation. The answer to this question turns on whether the practice—known in the trade as "scalping"—"operates as a fraud or deceit upon any client or prospective client" within the meaning of the Act. . . .

---

1. 54 Stat. 847, as amended, 15 U.S.C. § 80b–1 *et seq.*

The Investment Advisers Act of 1940 was the last in a series of Acts designed to eliminate certain abuses in the securities industry, abuses which were found to have contributed to the stock market crash of 1929 and the depression of the 1930's. . . . A fundamental purpose, common to these statutes, was to substitute a philosophy of full disclosure for the philosophy of *caveat emptor* and thus to achieve a high standard of business ethics in the securities industry.

*   *   *

The report [which led to the passage of the act] reflects the attitude—shared by investment advisers and the Commission—that investment advisers could not "completely perform their basic function —furnishing to clients on a personal basis competent, unbiased, and continuous advice regarding the sound management of their investments—unless all conflicts of interest between the investment counsel and the client were removed." The report stressed that affiliations by investment advisers with investment bankers, or corporations might be "an impediment to a disinterested, objective, or critical attitude toward an investment by clients. . . ."

This concern was not limited to deliberate or conscious impediments to objectivity. Both the advisers and the Commission were well aware that whenever advice to a client might result in financial benefit to the adviser—other than the fee for his advice—"that advice to a client might in some way be tinged with that pecuniary interest [whether consciously or] subconsciously motivated. . . ." The report quoted one leading investment adviser who said that he "would put the emphasis . . . on subconscious" motivation in such situations. It quoted a member of the Commission staff who suggested that a significant part of the problem was not the existence of a "deliberate intent" to obtain a financial advantage, but rather the existence "subconsciously [of] a prejudice" in favor of one's own financial interests. The report incorporated the Code of Ethics and Standards of Practice of one of the leading investment counsel associations, which contained the following canon:

> "[An investment adviser] should continuously occupy an impartial and disinterested position, as free as humanly possible from the *subtle* influence of prejudice, *conscious or unconscious*; he should scrupulously avoid any affiliation, or any act, which subjects his position to challenge in this respect." (Emphasis added.)

Other canons appended to the report announced the following guiding principles: that compensation for investment advice "should consist exclusively of direct charges to clients for services rendered"; that the adviser should devote his time "exclusively to the performance" of his advisory function; that he should not "share in profits" of his clients; and that he should not "directly or indirectly engage in any activity which may jeopardize [his] ability to render unbiased investment advice." These canons were adopted "to the end that the quality of services to be rendered by investment counselors may measure up to the high standards which the public has a right to expect and to demand."

One activity specifically mentioned and condemned by investment advisers who testified before the Commission was "*trading by investment counselors for their own account in securities in which their clients were interested. . . .*"

*   *   *

An adviser who, like respondents, secretly trades on the market effect of his own recommendation may be motivated—consciously or unconsciously—to recommend a given security not because of its potential for long-run price increase (which would profit the client), but because of its potential for short-run price increase in response to anticipated activity from the recommendation (which would profit the adviser). An investor seeking the advice of a registered investment adviser must, if the legislative purpose is to be served, be permitted to evaluate such overlapping motivations, through appropriate disclosure, in deciding whether an adviser is serving "two masters" or only one, "especially . . . if one of the masters happens to be economic self-interest." *United States* v. *Mississippi Valley Co.*, 364 U.S. 520, 549.[2] Accordingly, we hold that the Investment Advisers Act of 1940 empowers the courts, upon a showing such as that made here, to require an adviser to make full and frank disclosure of his practice of trading on the effect of his recommendations.

*   *   *

Respondents argue, finally, that their advice was "honest" in the sense that they believed it was sound and did not offer it for the purpose of furthering personal pecuniary objectives. . . . It is the practice itself, however, with its potential for abuse, which "operates as a fraud or deceit" within the meaning of the Act when relevant information is suppressed. The Investment Advisers Act of 1940 was "directed not only at dishonor, but also at conduct that tempts dishonor." *United States* v. *Mississippi Valley Co.*, 364 U.S. 520, 549. Failure to disclose

---

2. This Court, in discussing conflicts of interest, has said: "The reason of the rule inhibiting a party who occupies confidential and fiduciary relations toward another from assuming antagonistic positions to his principal in matters involving the subject matter of the trust is sometimes said to rest in a sound public policy, but it also is justified in a recognition of the authoritative declaration that no man can serve two masters; and considering that human nature must be dealt with, the rule does not stop with actual violations of such trust relations, but includes within its purpose the removal of any temptation to violate them. . . .

material facts must be deemed fraud or deceit within its intended meaning, for, as the experience of the 1920's and 1930's amply reveals, the darkness and ignorance of commercial secrecy are the conditions upon which predatory practices best thrive. To impose upon the Securities and Exchange Commission the burden of showing deliberate dishonesty as a condition precedent to protecting investors through the prophylaxis of disclosure would effectively nullify the protective purposes of the statute. Reading the Act in light of its background we find no such requirement commanded. Neither the Commission nor the courts should be required "to separate the mental urges," *Peterson* v. *Greenville*, 373 U.S. 244, 248, of an investment adviser, for "[t]he motives of man are too complex . . . to separate. . . ." *Mosser* v. *Darrow*, 341 U.S. 267, 271. The statute, in recognition of the adviser's fiduciary relationship to his clients, requires that his advice be disinterested. To insure this it empowers the court to require disclosure of material facts. It misconceives the purpose of the statute to confine its application to "dishonest" as opposed to "honest" motives. As Dean Shulman said in discussing the nature of securities transactions, what is required is "a picture not simply of the show window, but of the entire store . . . not simply truth in the statements volunteered, but disclosure." The high standards of business morality exacted by our laws regulating the securities industry do not permit an investment adviser to trade on the market effect of his own recommendations without fully and fairly revealing his personal interests in these recommendations to his clients.

*   *   *

Reversed and remanded.

e.   [i] CRAIG, MAUDE M. and GLICK, SELMA J.

A Manual of Procedures for Application of the Glueck Prediction Table*

FOREWORD

It is becoming more and more evident that in any fundamental preventive attack on juvenile delinquency some reliable device is necessary which will "spot" potential delinquents sufficiently early in life to permit of timely intervention. In our work, *Unraveling Juvenile Delinquency* (published in 1950) we presented such an instrument based on certain factors in family life, especially parent–child relationships.

*   *   *

The Research Department of the New York City Youth Board has worked valiantly and intelligently

------

* New York City Youth Board, October 1964.

for some ten years to check on the usefulness of the predictive device of Unraveling, a table designed to discriminate, at the early age of five or six years, between those children in a school population who are very probably potential delinquents and those who are not, (and, among children already showing signs of deviant behavior, between those who are true potential delinquents and those who are only pseudodelinquents).

*   *   *

The relevant question is "why prediction?" Is it better for family life and for society generally, to allow delinquency inducing influences to take their toll in overt and persistent delinquency and crime than it is to detect such dangerous influences sufficiently early in life to permit of doing something constructive to deflect or counteract them?

In the final analysis, it is far better that endangered children be identified and aided in early life than they be permitted to stumble along until arrested by the police, brought into court, and packed off to institutions and thence to prisons. The best available opinion of psychiatrists and criminologists indicates that the early discovery and treatment of aberrant emotional and behavioral tendencies makes the task of rehabilitation easier.

*   *   *

Sheldon and Eleanor Glueck

*   *   *

The Youth Board adopted the definition of delinquency presented by the Gluecks in *Unraveling Juvenile Delinquency:*

> "Delinquency refers to repeated acts of a kind which, when committed by persons beyond the statutory juvenile court age of sixteen, are punishable as crimes (either felonies or misdemeanors)—except for a few instances of persistent stubbornness, truancy, running away, associating with immoral persons, and the like. Children who once or twice during the period of growing up steal a toy in a ten-cent store, sneak into a subway or motion picture theatre, play hooky, and the like and soon outgrow such peccadilloes are not true delinquents even though they have violated the law."

*   *   *

In constructing their table, the Gluecks studied 500 persistent delinquent boys and 500 nondelinquent boys who were matched by age, intelligence, ethnic derivation, and neighborhood conditions. They compared both groups according to 400 traits and factors. From this study 5 out of 120 social factors in the family backgrounds of the two groups were selected from among those factors that markedly differentiated delinquents from nondelinquents early in the life of a child. Other predictive devices were constructed from different traits. These five factors constituted the original social factor prediction table.

1. Discipline of boy by father
2. Supervision of boy by mother
3. Affection of father for boy
4. Affection of mother for boy
5. Cohesiveness of family

The 500 delinquents and 500 nondelinquents were rated on each of the five factors and the percentages of incidence of delinquency and nondelinquency were noted. For example, in the subcategory—Unsuitable Supervision of boy by mother (No. 2), 83.2 per cent of the total group in which supervision of boys by their mothers was unsuitable, were delinquents. This became the prediction score rating for that category. The sum of the highest percentage scores on the factors established the upper limit and the sum of the lowest percentage scores the lower limit of the score classes.

In 1952 The New York City Youth Board embarked upon the first follow up of young children to test the validity of the Glueck Social Prediction Table. . . .

The table which the Youth Board set out to validate was the Glueck five-factor table. During the ten years of the study however, refinements were made, various abbreviated combinations of factors were tested, and ultimately the table was reduced to three factors. This latter table based on discipline of boy by mother, supervision by mother, and family cohesiveness, is the one we are presently using.

*   *   *

The findings reported are based on the total sample of 301 boys. Each has been followed up for ten years and each has reached his seventeenth birthday.

Results of applying the three-factor table indicate that of the 33 boys predicted as delinquent, 28 are delinquents, in accordance with the Glueck definition of delinquency, an 84.8 per cent accuracy in predicting delinquency. Of the 243 cases predicted nondelinquents 236 or 97.1 per cent are, in fact, nondelinquents. Of the 25 boys who were predicted as having an almost even chance of becoming delinquent or remaining nondelinquent, 9 are delinquents and 16 remain nondelinquent.

*   *   *

DEFINITION OF FACTORS AND THEIR SUBCATEGORIES

*Supervision of Boy by Mother, Discipline of Boy
by Mother, Family Cohesiveness*

1. Supervision of Boy by Mother: (Suitable, Fair, Unsuitable)

The woman who plays the greatest role in the supervision of the child would be rated on this factor.

Usually it is the mother; in some cases it may be the grandmother or foster-mother. The person rated depends on the period in the boy's life for which she is responsible for his care, how much time she spends with the boy, and for how long a period of time she supervises the boy. If a relative such as a grandmother or aunt is totally responsible for the supervision of the boy, cares for him for the major portion of the day, and exerts a consistent influence upon the youngster, then she, rather than the mother, is to be rated:

(a) Suitable Supervision

This may include overprotection. There is concern for the boy and his activities. He is guarded and guided. The mother or mother substitute personally knows where the youngster is and with whom, at all times. She is aware of his leisure-time activities and the youngster's associates. She is able to establish effective routines, which are consistent. If the mother is ill or works outside the home, there is a responsible adult in charge who supervises the boy in the manner described above, including close watching of the child, setting limits and consistency in her handling of him.

EXAMPLE: Frank W.

Mrs. W. has never worked outside the home. She takes the boy to school in the morning and calls for him in the afternoon because he must cross two busy intersections on his way to and from school. After school, Frank changes his clothes and in good weather Mrs. W. takes him and his brothers to the park where they can skate or play ball with the other youngsters. If the weather is bad he comes home and plays with his toys or watches television. Mr. and Mrs. W. go out evenings occasionally. During their absence the children are cared for by their maternal grandmother. The children like staying with the grandmother because she has "lots of stories to tell them."

(b) Fair Supervision

The mother, although not working and not incapacitated, gives only partial supervision. She is not sufficiently concerned with her son's associates. She may not be able to set realistic goals and may not be too consistent; or if the boy has several "caretakers" this may result in conflicting or inconsistent supervision. Although she provides supervision in her absence, the person to whom this responsibility is relegated does not have the maturity or judgment to supervise the boy closely and intelligently.

EXAMPLE: Richie, B.

Richie goes to school by himself even though he has a five-block walk and some heavy traffic. His mother works outside the home and provides him with funds to have lunch at school.

The maternal grandmother does work at home and supposedly is at home when Richie comes home from school. However, on occasion she has been known to be downtown getting her work assignment. At these times she gives Richie the key and he comes to an empty home, has some milk and then goes downstairs to play.

Mrs. B. usually returns home from work at about six o'clock. She prepares dinner for the family. Occasionally she and the grandmother go shopping and leave the boy in the care of a fifteen-year-old nephew who is retarded.

(c) Unsuitable Supervision

Mother or mother substitute is careless in her supervision, leaving the boy to his own devices without guidance, or in the care of a wholly irresponsible or immature person who is not capable of supervising well.

EXAMPLE: Robert, H.

Robert is the fifth of seven children. His mother realizes that Robert does not get sufficient supervision. "It's hard to care for so many small children all by myself," she says.

Robert goes to school with his brother age eight and returns with his sister age nine. After school he is allowed to play in the street until six o'clock under the supervision of his eight-year-old brother. There is never an adult in charge and often he roams far from home. Mrs. H. remarked that Robert is like the proverbial bad penny, he is bound to return.

Mother does not feel too close to Robert and states that he plays alone or with his brothers and sisters without any supervision for hours.

2. Discipline of Boy by Mother: (Firm but kindly, erratic, overstrict, lax)

The methods of disciplining children may vary greatly in different cultures and this has to be taken into consideration. Regardless of the disciplinary measures used, a degree of affection and concern for the youngster is essential to good discipline. The discipline here refers to the usual or typical discipline of the boy by his mother or mother substitute:

(a) Firm, but Kindly Discipline

Discipline based on sound reason which the boy understands and accepts as fair. This may include physical punishment, deprivation of privileges and the myriad other disciplinary methods employed. The child does not unduly fear the mother. She sets reasonable limits to his behavior and adheres to them.

EXAMPLE: Peter, J.

Peter is the only child in the family. His parents came to America from Germany two years ago and settled in a congested area of the city.

Peter is much loved by both his parents. He is the center of attention and everyone makes a fuss over him. However, Peter must toe the line or he is sharply disciplined by his mother. Mrs. J's method of dis-

cipline is first to talk to the boy and explain what he does that is unacceptable. If this doesn't work, she takes away a privilege such as TV or a favorite toy. If he fails to listen, she spanks him. Peter is a very active child and the mother recognizes that he needs close and careful discipline and supervision.

(b) Erratic Discipline

Inconsistent, unreasonable, and vacillating. Such a mother may punish for disobedience at one time and overlook this conduct on another occasion. Discipline seems to depend on the mother's mood more than the boy's behavior. Included in this category too is a mother who may administer physical or verbal abuse without sound reason.

EXAMPLE: Jackie, N.

Discipline is left chiefly to the mother since the father is out much of the time. Jackie is more afraid of his mother. At the beginning of the interview Mrs. N. said, "I'm old fashioned, I hit him." Mrs. N. stated that she has a hot temper and on her bad days she will swat him at the slightest provocation, while on her good days he can "get away with murder."

Mrs. N. agreed that deprivation of privileges such as TV, going down to play, etc., is much more effective, but Jackie gets under her skin and her one "out" is to give him a good "swat." Mrs. N. said she hits Jackie anywhere, whatever part is nearest. She laughingly told of Jackie's recent trip to the barber in which Jackie asked the barber to cut off all his hair so that his mother couldn't pull it.

At first Mrs. N. said she hits Jackie only for serious things such as lying or stealing but when later, interviewer referred to this for details, Mrs. N. said Jackie doesn't lie or steal. As the interview progressed Mrs. N. freely indicated that she hits Jackie whenever she loses her temper regardless of whether he is bad or not.

(c) Overstrict Discipline

The mother is harsh, her expectations are too great and she severely punishes child for the slightest infraction of her orders.

EXAMPLE: Willie, G.

Willie is one of seven children. At the time of our interview his father had been confined to bed for two years as a result of a paralytic stroke. He was disabled prior to that time with a kidney condition and high blood pressure.

Willie's school hours are from eight to twelve. He then comes home, takes a nap, and must play at home with his younger brother. He is not permitted out of the house.

Mrs. G. presented herself as being a person who believes that too much affection spoils children. She believes children should obey every command of their parents or it's time to strike. There was no evidence of toys for the children and when Mrs. G. was questioned as to what the children play with she was at a complete loss. The mother confines Willie to a baby's position, restricting him to his home, making him take a nap in the afternoon and discouraging outside activities. She appeared stern and very much the disciplinarian.

When questioned about her disciplinary methods Mrs. G. said she strikes first and then if Willie doesn't know why he was hit she strikes again. When the interviewer asked Mrs. G. if Willie is afraid of her she answered, "He better be or else." It was apparent that Willie's obedience is related to his fear of his mother and her tirades when he misbehaves.

(d) Lax Discipline

The mother or mother substitute is negligent, indifferent, and does not mind what the boy does as long as he doesn't bother her. The mother sets no goals or controls and allows the boy to do very much as he pleases.

EXAMPLE: Donald, K.

Donald's mother works outside the home every day and the boy is left in the care of his maternal grandmother who resents being tied down to the home because of the youngster. The grandmother has very little patience with the boy and when he misbehaves she sends him out on the street to get him out of the way.

When Mrs. K. returns from work a long list of Donald's misdeeds are recited to her by the grandmother. Frequently, she will laugh them off saying "He's still a baby." There are a few occasions when she will talk to the boy about his misbehavior or in any way indicate that, for example, taking a toy from another child is not permissible.

Donald entered school this year and was as much a problem to his teachers as he was to his grandmother. He would walk around the classroom when he was supposed to be working, he was defiant to his teacher because she insisted that he be still and was a general nuisance in the classroom.

3. Cohesiveness of Family Unit: (Marked, Some, None)

Cohesiveness is characterized by an atmosphere of affection and wholesome interdependence and interaction involving parents and children alike. If the boy makes his home with relatives or lives in a foster home (and has lived with the same relative or in the same home the major portion of his life) it is the relative's household or the foster home that is rated. It is necessary for the rater to take into consideration the relationship within the home in the formative period in a boy's life (first six years), a time when it would have the greatest effect upon the personality of the youngster. The important aspect is how much meaning this has to the boy and whether the home offers him security and a sense of belonging. In general, the fabric of family relationship should be firm and supportive as far as the child is concerned. In assigning a score to this factor it is necessary to determine whether this type of behavior is normal or usual for this family.

(a) Marked Cohesion

A strong "we" feeling among members of the family, evidenced by co-operation, group interest, including social and recreational pursuits, pride in the home, mutual affection and concern. There is an accepting and protective attitude between parents and children offering a sense of security. The family enjoys being together, planning together and having fun together. A feeling of unity prevails.

A markedly cohesive family can exist even though a father or a father substitute is not a part of the family group. If the mother is a warm accepting person, concerned for her children, fosters group interest, has pride in the home and a relaxed atmosphere prevails, the home can be rated as cohesive.

EXAMPLE: Jerry, B. (Father in Home)

The B. family consisting of Mr. and Mrs. B. and their three children have lived at the same address for the past nine years. Mr. B. is employed as a postal worker and has been able to provide adequately for his family's needs. There appears to be no conflict between the parents.

The family has breakfast and dinner together and spend many evenings watching television or listening to hi-fi records, which they all enjoy. During the summer the family spends weekends going to the beach or on picnics. In the winter they visit with relatives. Both Mr. and Mrs. B. come from fairly large families and have many folks within the vicinity with whom they enjoy spending their time.

The parents and children enjoy being together. Mr. B. says that he looks forward to weekends and vacations, for the family have such a good time together. The interviewer indicates in her remarks that this family is a very stable unit.

EXAMPLE: Kenneth, W. (No Father in Home)

Miss W. and her five children (all born out-of-wedlock) live in a tumbled down dilapidated two-story frame building. The flat is sparsely furnished, four children sleeping in one large bed in one bedroom and the mother and the youngest child sleeping in another. The other rooms of the house likewise, are inadequately furnished. Kenneth is the oldest of the five children. He has never known his real father, but has known Mr. Jones, the father of the four other boys in the family. Kenneth sees Mr. Jones about twice a week. However, Mr. Jones has never been a stable factor in the family life of the W. children. His visits have mainly been at night and he devotes little, if any time, to the children. He never disciplines them; this is left solely to their mother. Since 1951 he has not been seen and the children never ask about him.

Miss W. is always with her children. She takes them to and from school and when they are on the street watches them from the window. She is a warm accepting person, cognizant of the needs of her children. She talks to Kenneth and the other children a good deal, tells them stories, and brings them cookies and candies from the store.

Kenneth tells his mother a good deal about his school activities. She is interested and delighted in all his achievements. She plays and sings with the children and often sits with them and listens to radio programs which they all enjoy. Meals are eaten together and grace is said before each meal. At night the family enjoy doing things together and Miss W. has tried hard to keep the family intact. Before bedtime the children all join with their mother in saying prayers and singing hymns.

In studying this situation it was decided that Mr. Jones is not a father substitute since he is not in the home for any length of time and he was never a stable factor in the family life of these children. The youngsters do not consider him their father and do not ask for him when he does not come around. Actually the children had never formed any meaningful relationship to this man and regard him more as a visitor who now and then plays with them and brings them toys.

According to the definition of cohesiveness of the family unit, this home without a father or a father substitute would still be rated as cohesive. The mother in this situation is warm and accepting with a good deal of affection for all her children. The family participate freely in all activities.

(b) Some Elements of Cohesion

This category implies that although the home may not be markedly cohesive, there are nevertheless some strengths, ties and security in the family's interpersonal relationships.

EXAMPLE: Robert, P.

Robert was born out-of-wedlock and never knew his father. The putative father severed his common-law relationship prior to the boy's birth. Miss P. has worked consistently throughout the boy's life and Robert is left in the care of his nineteen-year-old sister.

Miss P. is described as a religious zealot who uses her religion to inculcate terror and inhibition in the child. She is nervous and usually tired and can't take much noise or foolishness. On these occasions she uses the strap. Mother indicates that Lucy, the boy's sister, is easy going and tolerant with the youngster. Robert is left on his own a good deal, going to and from school alone despite the dangerous crossings. He is permitted to go to the movies by himself. Miss P. believes it is important to foster independence in the boy and grants him these privileges. The mother appears to have some affection for this child. Although she displays very little overt affection, she does help him with his school work and brings home candy and toys for the boy. She provides him with spending money. Lucy, his sister, shows him a good deal of affection.

This is a broken home, but any friction that may have occurred between the parents occurred prior to Robert's birth and thus did not affect him. However, this home environment does not offer much in the way of real security for the boy. He has faced real confusion as to who his parents are, for example; it was at about the age of five that he realized that Lucy

is not his mother, but his sister. He never did know his real father. There is no male figure in the home with whom he can identify and there is no family or group activities in which the entire family participates.

(c) Unintegrated Home

Self interest prevails. There is no feeling of unity within the family. Each member more or less shifts for himself. The atmosphere is tense and cold. This category is diametrically opposed to the markedly cohesive home.

EXAMPLE: Herman, P.

The interviewer reports a great deal of marital friction in the home. Mrs. P. intimates that her husband drinks especially on pay day when he frequents bars with his fellow workers. When drunk, he is abusive to both his wife and the children.

There are many other quarrels within the family and these revolve mainly around the children. Mrs. P. states that whenever her husband has an opportunity he will go out with his friends and come home late at night after the family is asleep. Mrs. P. is a highly nervous, irritable person who will swat the children for the slightest offense.

The family eats at odd hours. The children eat first whenever they come in from playing in the street; then the mother eats her meal; and if the father is around he eats by himself.

Mr. P. has no patience with Herman. The boy's constant restlessness, his fighting with the older children in the family and his many attention-seeking ways are disturbing to him. At times he either slaps the boy or locks him in the bedroom. At other times he just ignores him. If Herman asks a question while his father is reading the paper, Mr. P. becomes so enraged that he gives him a good "whack."

Mr. P. takes no interest in the family. He feels it is sufficient that he supports them. He has taken the family out once and the youngsters were so unruly that he swore he would never do it again. The home, the interviewer remarks, "is like a battleground." Certainly it does not give a feeling of security to any of the other children.

* * *

A question which needs careful study and evaluation concerns the criteria for placing a boy in the "delinquent" category. It is important when using the Social Prediction Table to differentiate between the acting out problem child and the boy who is a serious and/or persistent delinquent. It is possible that the former child might possibly become a delinquent or that this acting out behavior might change for the better due to environmental or situational changes and would soon subside.

The Gluecks in constructing the prediction table used for their sample of delinquents, boys from two institutions for delinquents. These boys were serious delinquents—their crimes being of such magnitude as to indicate that incarceration was the best method of treatment available. In a good many of these situations the pathology in the home was so severe that removal seemed to be the solution.

In the Youth Board study several brushes with the law did not necessarily mean that a boy was placed in the delinquent category if they were all of a minor nature. If these encounters with the police continued, indicating a boy's continual defiance of the law, then placement in the delinquent category was indicated. It must be kept in mind that the purpose of the prediction table is to indicate a boy's chances of becoming a serious delinquent. It does not take into account those boys whose problem behavior might be part of the growing up process and is short lived.

*   *   *

NOTES

NOTE 1

FREUD, ANNA

Child Observation and Prediction of Development— A Memorial Lecture in Honor of Ernst Kris*

*   *   *

I owe Ernst Kris an apology for the fact that it took me a long time to come to terms with the word "prediction" which he used to designate the aims of his research. . . .

Ernst Kris was well aware of the difficulties of diagnosis which beset the child analyst and of the manner in which we all founder, more or less helplessly, in the mass of childhood disturbances which come to our notice via parents, pediatricians, schools, child-guidance clinics, and analytic practice. He regretted, as we all do, that our assessments are inexact, that our diagnoses usually come too late, when the disturbance has become massive and ingrained already, and that the dividing line between normality and pathology is too easy to miss. He knew that our diagnostic categories had become all the more inadequate since the concept of an "infantile neurosis" had ceased gradually to serve us as a focal point. The new ego psychology had made us acquainted with a further number of variations and deviations of structure, had added the atypical and autistic developments to our list and played havoc with former seemingly secure distinctions such as those between emotional and intellectual disorders, the latter now merely appearing as an adjunct or a function of the former. Investigations into the first year of life and the consequences of the earliest mother–child relationship had revealed that much may be acquired by the infant that had been considered as innate

before, thus putting out of action some more of our basic diagnostic categories. No wonder that the result was a chaotic one and that child psychiatrists and analysts have difficulty in finding their way in a field which is crowded by manifestations such as disturbances of vital functions (sleeping, eating, learning); retardation of ego activities (motility, speech); failures of management (toilet training); fixations and regressions (especially affecting smooth transition in phase development)—all this in addition to the more familiar anxieties, inhibitions, defenses, neurotic, psychotic, and borderline appearances.

It was this situation which, I believe, Ernst Kris was trying to remedy by placing fact finding in observational research at the service of diagnosis. He was trying, to use his own words, "to predict from observational data that pathology exists in a given child." He wondered "how soon can we spot it from the child's behavior, from that of the family unit, or from the history of the child and mother." It became his ambition "to recognize . . . symptomatology before it becomes manifest, . . . to spot danger before it appears."

Naturally, I do not mean to imply that Ernst Kris deceived himself about the difficulties of clinical foresight, or that he took prediction lightly. . . . It was Ernst Kris himself who drew our attention to the hopelessness of such clinical foresight in what he had described as the first phase of psychoanalytic child psychology. While we knew no more of the predestined sequences of development than the libidinal phases and "some crucial conflicts and typical danger situations related to the maturational sequence," prediction was not possible. There were too many unknown factors which determined the outcome of the child's reactions to his experiences and their genetic, economic, and dynamic interrelations.

It is true that all this seemed to change in the second phase. It became possible, as Ernst Kris remarks, "to view the interaction of libidinal and aggressive drives in each of the typical danger situations of childhood"; to "take the states of ego and superego development into account" regarding them; to correlate, in a number of instances, at least, "the use of certain mechanisms of defense to certain situations and developmental phases." Further, we came to understand the extent to which conflict, danger, and defense are "essential and necessary concomitants of growing up," as well as "the adaptive function of defense." If we add to this the increasing insight into "the uniqueness of the mother in human life," i.e., into the preoedipal experiences of the infant, we have a large number of added factors which can be taken into account in our assessment of a child's immediate condition or its prospects for the future.

In spite of these advances (and I feel sure that Ernst Kris would agree with this qualifying statement), there remain a number of factors which make clinical

* 13 *The Psychoanalytic Study of the Child*, 92, 95–115 (1958). Reprinted by permission of International Universities Press, New York.

foresight, i.e., prediction, difficult and hazardous. I name three of them here. (1) There is no guarantee that the rate of maturational progress on the side of ego development and drive development will be an even one; and whenever one side of the structure outdistances the other in growth, a variety of unexpected and unpredictable deviations from the norm will follow. (2) There is still no way to approach the quantitative factor in drive development, nor to foresee it; but most of the conflict solutions within the personality will, in the last resort, be determined by quantitative rather than by qualitative factors. (3) The environmental happenings in a child's life will always remain unpredictable since they are not governed by any known laws. . . .

Ernst Kris himself testified to the presence of the unknown or unknowable forces at work in development in the following sentences: "The self-healing qualities of further development are little known." And we do not know how much "latency, prepuberty, or adolescence do to mitigate earlier deviation or to make the predisposition to . . . disturbances manifest."

* * *

. . . Ernst Kris envisaged that the integration of observational with reconstructive data will teach us more about typical sequences in child development and that, in turn, such additional knowledge will enable us to foresee and anticipate pathology, at least in typical cases.

If this comes true, it will, indeed, revolutionize the conditions for child analysis and any known form of analytic child therapy. Even where we stand now, we have ample evidence that the date at which we take therapeutic action is of extreme importance. With children, usually, the interval between the outbreak of trouble and the onset of treatment is comparatively long. In the past this was due to the parents' distrust and fear of analysis which caused them to experiment with every conceivable educational or medical device before turning, at last, and often too late, to analytic help. At present the causes are of the opposite kind, so many parents seeking help for their children that the waiting lists for treatment are unduly long. However that may be, experience has taught us that the beginning of therapy, immediately after the appearance of trouble, will shorten the duration of treatment by many months. This has been proved repeatedly in connection with disturbances such as sleeping and eating disorders, phobias, inhibitions, and sudden regressive moves in development, such as loss of active aggression, of phallic qualities, or—earlier—of speech. It is easier, therapeutically, to intervene in a process of symptom formation in the fluid state than to deal with hardened symptoms. There is no child analyst, I believe, who would not welcome the next step forward to a state of affairs which places thera-

peutic intervention even earlier, namely at a time before symptom formation has been resorted to at all.

* * *

The truth is that, as knowledge stands at present, it is difficult to draw the line between prediction of pathology based on authentic danger signals, and a diffuse and indiscriminate overanxiousness, all too easily aroused by every slight deviation from the optimal and from the norm.

What we need to decide the issue is the further systematic inquiry into the possibility and the limitations of clinical foresight. . . .

In the medicopsychological baby service . . . our pediatrician . . . periodically sees an infant (from the age of two months onwards) whose mother shows indications of an unsatisfactory attitude toward the child. There is an apparent lack of genuine warmth, no visible pride in the baby's appearance or clothing, a reluctance to fondle or to play with the child's body and a marked clumsiness in distinguishing between the child's needs (whether for nourishment, body comfort, company or entertainment). At the same time the baby is adequately and conscientiously cared for in bodily matters, and there is no question of neglect in its official sense. The mother's attitude to life is revealed, on inquiry, as a depressed and withdrawn one, although not to the degree on which psychiatric diagnoses are based. The baby's responses are predominantly normal, so far, although his social reactions (smiling responses, etc.) were at times somewhat below the age level.

This is where our quandary begins. Our feeling, based on knowledge of typical developments, indicates that subtle harm is being inflicted on this child, and that the consequences of it will become manifest at some future date. But is this foresight backed by sufficient evidence to justify intervention? Further: what are the criteria for choosing between different ways of intervening, such as treatment of the mother (which may be unwelcome to her), introduction of a second mother figure (which may prove impracticable), or, if it comes to an extreme, separation of mother and child (which may harm the mother)? Or is the answer that we may have to wait with interference in such cases until the relations between cause and effect in mental matters have become as firmly established and removed from doubt, as they are today on the physical side, for example where tubercular infection through the mother is in question?

* * *

The following are some instances to illustrate the difficulties of clinical discrimination. . . .

* * *

[A] boy of ten and three quarter years, [was]

taken into treatment as a borderline case in the Hampstead Child-Therapy Clinic. He had lived for several years in identification with an underground train and spent his days withdrawn from reality, either imitating the action of such trains or, actually, walking on underground lines, thereby endangering his life. His intellectual activity (which was somewhat below average) spent itself on reading maps and memorizing the names of stations, streets, etc.

I quote this case for the reason that even this threatening spread of pathology in a child contained some elements of sublimation and neutralization which proved important for prognosis. It is true that the displacement of interest from the cavities of the human body to the system of underground tunnels hardly deserved to be called a sublimation at the time of diagnosis; it is true, equally, that his preoccupation with maps and names at that period was wholly in the service of his obsession. Nevertheless the latter achieved some degree of neutralization; in an ego which otherwise functioned poorly, memorizing became a strong point, extending from street names to the names of people, etc. I found it interesting to read five years later, after treatment, a report given on him by a Vocational Guidance Department. By this time, many other manifestations of his deep-seated pathology had disappeared from the surface; but the industrial psychologist in his write-up remarked among other things that this boy had "a soft spot for maps" and he recommended (among other possibilities) "work in delivery or collection," thus treating the former obsession (of which he was ignorant, of course) as the basis of a neutralized, ego-directed activity.

Perhaps in time, we shall learn to spot such potentially helpful props for the ego and links with reality even where they appear in the midst and at the service of severe pathology.

[Another] boy first showed interest in *water* at the age of twelve months, when he began to do without napkins during daytime; he was occasionally found patting a pool of water he had made on the floor. "Little pools of rainwater also interested him, and he thoroughly enjoyed smacking the water in the bath or wash-hand basin. At fourteen months he was very interested in turning water-taps on and off. When taken to the water-closet he watched the rush of water with great interest. At two years of age he spent hours controlling water supplies, filling and emptying buckets, tins, jars, tea-pots, hot-water bottles. He wanted to know where the water came from to the water-closet bowl. When he was taken to a gentleman's lavatory outside, he always insisted on seeing the hole down which the water went, and the cistern which supplied the water. At two and a half years he was tracing every pipe he could see; water-supply pipes, drain pipes, rain-pipes, gas pipes. Hours were spent lighting and

turning out gas jets." Before he was three, the father had to take the cover off the water-closet cistern to satisfy his curiosity. "He spent about half an hour every day for a fortnight, standing on a ledge up at the cistern. . . . He filled the cistern to the overflow, and wanted to know the function of every detail of the mechanism." The father goes on to show how the child's interest spread from here to fire-plugs, fire engines, water pumps, the gas works and the sewage works. In nursery school, at the age of four and a half years when told the story of Moses in the Bulrushes and asked to draw a picture of Moses in his cradle, he supplied the cradle with a long line, representing "a drain pipe" leading away from it.

For the direct observer of children, a behavioral picture of this kind gives rise to a number of important questions. He will have no difficulty in diagnosing the underlying presence of powerful pregenital interests with special preponderance of curiosity directed toward the urinary function and the inside of the human body. He will feel less certain about the degree of desexualization of curiosity (i.e., neutralization) achieved by the child. Accordingly he will be unsure whether what he sees should be assessed as the beginning of a true sublimation which will enrich the ego, or as the beginning of a fixation to a primitive pregenital level which will restrict it and, sooner or later, lead to pathology. Is it the correct procedure to assist the boy in his researches (as his father has done) or should he be helped to detach himself from his overriding interest in the subject and develop toward further levels, as treatment would do in all probability?

In the case in question the answer has been supplied by the further life history of the boy. In the thirty years since the observation was made, he has developed into a physicist of unusual ability and standing, the recorded incidents representing evidently the first steps in the direction of this lasting sublimation. This, to my mind, does not signify that other, almost identical pictures, seen for diagnosis could not lead to opposite results. In spite of all theoretical advances concerning the subject of sublimation, we are still—with Ernst Kris—impressed by the fluidity and uncertainty of these developmental processes. Perhaps we shall learn that it is not the sublimatory process itself from which we can take our cue, identical states or forms of sublimation possibly leading to different results; rather, that we have to look for our evidence to accompanying circumstances and conditions in the total picture of the personality. For example persistent waterplay of the kind described above may acquire a different and less favorable aspect where it is accompanied by bed wetting, etc.

However that may be, correct assessment in the very young remains a difficult matter; so does the prognosis for the future and the appropriate handling of the child based on our judgments. As matters stand now, we are apt still to do too little for those children where fixations and pathological developments are in the making. On the other hand there is the danger also that we may interfere too much or too soon and thereby (as somebody expressed it jokingly in discussion) "nip future physicists in the bud."

There is room still to turn to a further (and for this paper last) area where prediction in Ernst Kris' use of the term might prove invaluable for our clinical concerns. I refer here to the traumatic experiences of early childhood and the assessment of their impact on development.

Ernst Kris alluded to this subject in his "Notes on the Development, etc." by discussing the differences between the data on life history gained by direct observation and those supplied by psychoanalytic reconstruction. He stressed the objective unselected character of the former and stated that in contrast "data obtained by psychoanalysis are naturally selective," "contain more precise information on areas of conflict involvement than on areas free of conflict" and "indicate what had been important in an etiological sense and when it had become important."

. . . [Kris] went so far as to state that the traumatic significance of an event is not laid down from the time of its occurrence but that "the further course of life seems to determine which experience may gain significance as a traumatic one."

It is useful to keep these statements in mind when we inquire into the etiology of a child's disturbance. The life history of a child patient, as supplied by the parents, is the result of external observation. At best, it contains objective facts; more often, of course, it is given subjectively, with omissions, distortions and selections of facts which are determined by the parent's own emotional needs and limitations. Therefore, the biographical material cannot (or should not) be used for guidance as to the pathogenic importance of past events. The material is "weighted" (to use a term of Ernst Kris) according to the parents' and not according to the child's internal stresses.

There is no difficulty in confirming this from clinical material. One mother, for example, dated her boy's disturbance from a car accident of the father which had been traumatic for both parents; the child's analysis, on the other hand, showed that in his mind this event was overshadowed completely by the departure of a beloved maid, which had occurred at the same time and had proved traumatic for him; in turn, this latter event had been dismissed from the mother's memory as unimportant. Many mothers cite the loss of a grandparent as a decisive event in the child's life; here, subsequent analysis shows usually that the child has ignored the death as such, but has reacted violently to the mother's mourning, depression and emotional withdrawal which followed the event. Where bodily illnesses are concerned, the mothers will report those as significant which were

dangerous objectively or aroused their own anxiety; the child, on his part, may react pathologically to any minor disturbance of health on the basis of pain, discomfort, anxiety, dietary and motor restrictions which are felt to be intolerable, enforced passivity, etc. A similar variance in evaluation exists concerning time: separations may seem short and therefore negligible by adult standards and still be interminable, and therefore traumatic for the child, etc.

On the whole, such comparisons between biographical and analytic material constitute an instructive object lesson with regard to the gap existing between external and internal (psychic) reality.

. . . I should like to add that we do not know either which aspect or element of a given experience will be selected for cathexis and emotional involvement.

*   *   *

The wish to use analytic insight not only for therapeutic but for preventive purposes has played its part since the beginnings of analysis. We used to think that prevention was served best by applying analytic knowledge to the principles of upbringing. But we have learned since that even the wisest handling of a child cannot prevent stress, conflicts, and occasional pathology, all of which are inseparable from the hazards of development; thus, we need the readiness for therapeutic action.

It is on this point where Ernst Kris's statements about "prediction of pathology" and early "spotting of danger" fall into place. Prediction will serve prevention if it teaches us (to use his own words) "which therapeutic steps are appropriate to each age level and its disturbance, or to each typical group of disturbances."

NOTE 2

FREUD, ANNA

Normality and Pathology in Childhood*

[There is] uncertainty regarding the age at which the term homosexuality can legitimately be used. There are similar links between the manifestations of homosexuality and normal developmental stages. There is also a similar difficulty in predicting adult homosexuality proper, i.e., in establishing reliable connections between certain preliminary stages which are visible in childhood and the final abnormal sexual outcome.

. . . The important distinction between manifest and latent homosexuality . . . applies to the sexual behavior of adults and cannot be maintained in the same manner when applied to mutual masturbation and other sex play between children or even adolescents. The distinction between passive and active

New York: International Universities Press, 1965. (pp. 184–197). Reprinted by permission.

homosexuality, or rather between passive and active underlying fantasies, refers to the positions of the partners in the sexual act itself, i.e., again to practices after adolescence. The whole extensive debate concerning reversibility also applies only to the adult for whom his homosexual way of life is either ego dystonic, and therefore accessible to analysis or ego syntonic, when treatment is avoided or sought only under external pressure.

On the other hand, there are a number of questions concerning homosexuality which . . . are of great relevance for the child analyst in the sense that he can extract clues from them for his assessments or contribute data to their solution from his own findings. These questions deal with three subjects: with the topic of *object choice*; with the *reconstructions* in adult analysis and their significance for the prognosis of homosexuality in childhood assessments; and with the general question of *causation* of homosexuality by weighing inborn against acquired elements.

That children of both sexes make libidinal attachments to love objects of both sexes is one of the basic propositions in the psychoanalytic theory of infantile sexuality. In each period of childhood object choice is governed by different rules, needs, and necessities, as descriptions which follow will show. Thus, ties to persons of the same sex are as normal as ties to the opposite sex and they cannot be considered as forerunners of later homosexuality.

Infants, at the beginning of life, choose their objects on the basis of function, not of sex. The mother is cathected with libido because she is the caretaking, need-fulfilling provider, the father as a symbol of power, protectiveness, ownership of the mother, etc. A "mother relationship" is often made to the male parent in cases where he takes over the need-fulfilling role, or a "father relationship" to the female parent in cases where she is the dominant power in the family. In this manner, the normal infant, whether male or female, has object attachments to both, male and female figures. Although in the strict sense of the term the infant is neither heterosexual nor homosexual, he can also be described as being both.

That the object's functions and not sex decide these relationships is borne out also by the transference in analytic treatment, where the sex of the analyst is no barrier against both mother and father relationships being displaced onto him.

Apart from this object choice of the anaclitic type, however, it is obvious that the *pregenital component trends* depend for their satisfactions not on the sexual apparatus of the partner but on other qualities and attitudes. If these are found in the mother and if on the strength of them she becomes the child's main love object, then the boy in the oral and anal phases is "heterosexual," the girl "homosexual"; if they are found in the father instead of in the mother, the position is reversed. In either case, a choice of object determined by the quality and aim of the dominant drive component is phase adequate and normal, irrespective of whether the resulting partnership is a heterosexual or homosexual one.

In contrast to the preceding stages, the sex of the object becomes of great importance in the *phallic phase*. The phase-adequate overestimation of the penis induces both boys and girls to choose partners who possess a penis, or at least are believed to do so (such as the phallic mother). Whatever course their instinctive trends have taken otherwise, they cannot disengage themselves "from a class of objects defined by a particular determinant."

The oedipus complex itself, both in its positive and negative form, is based on the recognition of sex differences, and within its framework the child makes his object choice in the adult manner on the basis of the partner's sex. The positive oedipus complex with the parent of the opposite sex as preferred love object corresponds as closely to adult heterosexuality as the negative oedipus complex with the tie to the parent of the same sex corresponds to adult homosexuality. So far as both manifestations are normal developmental occurrences, they are inconclusive for later pathology; they merely fulfill legitimate bisexual needs of the child. Nevertheless, in the individual child the emphasis may be either on the positive or on the negative oedipal attitudes and these quantitative differences can be taken as prognostic indicators for the future. They reveal important preferences for either one or the other sex which are rooted in preoedipal experiences. On the one hand, the personalities of the parents and their own success or failure in their sexual roles have left their mark via the identifications, which have followed object love. On the other hand, the fixations to aggressive-sadistic trends push the boy as firmly in the direction of the positive oedipus complex and later heterosexuality as the fixations to the passive oral and anal strivings force him toward the negative oedipus complex and, perhaps later, homosexuality.

Altogether, the child's behavior during the phallic oedipal period foreshadows more closely than at other times his future inclinations regarding sexual role and choice of sexual object.

When entry into the *latency period* is made, this particular aspect of the child's libidinal life disappears once more from view. There are, of course, at this time, unmodified remnants of the oedipus complex which determine the attachments, particularly of the neurotic children, who have been unable to solve, and dissolve, their oedipal relationships to the parents. But apart from these, there are also the phase-adequate aim-inhibited, displaced or sublimated tendencies for which the sexual identity of the partner becomes again a matter of comparative indifference. Evidence of the latter are the latency child's relationships to his teachers, who are loved, admired, disliked, or rejected not because they are men or women but because they are either helpful, appreciative, inspiring, or harsh, intolerant, anxiety-arousing figures.

The diagnostician's assessments at this period are further confused by the fact that object choice with regard to contemporaries proceeds on lines opposite to those usual in the adult. The boy who looks for exclusively male companionship and avoids and despises girls is not the future homosexual, whatever the similarity in manifest behavior. On the contrary, such clinging to the males and retreat from and contempt for the females can be considered as the hallmark of the normal masculine latency boy, i.e., the future heterosexual. At this age the future homosexual tendencies are betrayed, rather, by a preference for play with girls and appreciation and appropriation of their toys. This reversal of behavior is taken for granted in latency girls, who seek boyish company not if they are feminine but if they are "tomboys" themselves, i.e., on the basis of their penis envy and masculine wishes, not on the basis of feminine desires for relations with the opposite sex. What appears in overt behavior as homosexual leanings are, in fact, heterosexual ones and vice versa. What has to be remembered in this connection is that the choice of playmates in the latency period (i.e., object choice among contemporaries) is based on identification with the partner, not on object love proper, that is, on equality with them, which may or may not include equality of sex.

In *preadolescence* and in *adolescence*, finally, homosexual episodes are known to occur more or less regularly and to exist side by side with heterosexual ones without being in themselves reliable prognostic signs. These manifestations have to be understood in part as recurrences of the young child's pregenital, sexually indiscriminate object ties, which become valid once more in preadolescence together with the revival of many other pregenital and preoedipal attitudes. Homosexual object choice in adolescence is due also to the adolescent's regression from object cathexis to love for his own person and identification with the object. In this latter respect the adolescent's object represents in many cases not only the individual's real self, but his ideal of himself, a concept which invariably includes the adolescent's ideal notion of his sexual role. Adolescent partnerships formed on these grounds display all the outward signs of homosexual object love and are frequently accepted as true prestages of adult homosexuality. But metapsychologically they are narcissistic phenomena which as such belong to the varied schizoid symptomatology of adolescence, and they are more significant as pointers to the depth of regression than as prognostic indicators for the individual's future sexual role.

Compared with the small number of prognostic clues to be found when following the forward movement of the child's libido, there is a mass of relevant data reconstructed in the analysis of adult homosexuals which trace back the various manifestations of latent and overt homosexuality to their infantile roots. . . .

*   *   *

Notwithstanding . . . numerous and well-documented links between infantile past and adult present, the reasoning cannot be reversed and the reconstructed data cannot be used for the early spotting of homosexual development in children. The reason why this cannot be done becomes obvious whenever one of the homosexual types is examined in detail, such as, for example, the passive feminine male homosexual whose psychopathology has been particularly closely studied in many therapeutic analyses.

This type of homosexuality is characterized by being mother bound unwilling and unable to carry out sexual intercourse with women, and by sexual activity with men, usually of a socially inferior order, who are sought out because they possess crudely masculine bodily attributes such as great muscular strength, a hairy body, etc. When analyzed, this homosexual symptomatology can be traced back to a passionate attachment to the mother which dominated infancy and childhood, from the oral through the anal and beyond the phallic phase; to a horror of the female body, usually acquired traumatically after discovering the mother's or a sister's genitals; and to a period of fascinated admiration of the father's penis.

These elements, which undoubtedly are pathogenic influences in the past of the homosexual, can nevertheless not be used for the prognosis of homosexuality if they form part of the clinical picture of a child. Far from being abnormal or even unusual manifestations, they are, on the contrary, regular and indispensable parts of every boy's developmental equipment. The close tie to the mother, which devastates the future homosexual by increasing his fear of the rival father, by heightening his castration anxiety, and by enforcing his regression to anal and oral dependency, is also the well-known centerpiece of the positive oedipus complex and as such the normal prestage of adult heterosexuality. The shock which every boy experiences when he is confronted with the female genital for the first time, and which creates in the later homosexual a lasting aversion against any attractions by the female sex, is a usual event and unavoidable since he begins by believing that every human being has a penis like himself. Normally, the discovery of the difference between the sexes means no more to the boy than a temporary increase in castration anxiety; it may even act as a healthy strengthening of his defenses against his own feminine wishes and identifications, may reinforce his pride in his own possession of a penis and merely give rise to the pitying contempt for the castrated female, which is a truly masculine characteristic of the phallic boy. Finally, the admiration for the bigger man's penis, which dominates the love life of this type of passive homosexual to the exclusion of all else, is also a normal intermediary station in every boy's relationship to his father. The future homosexual remains fixed here and continues to endow his male objects with all the desirable signs of masculine strength and potency, while the normal boy outgrows the stage, identifies with the father as the possessor of the penis, and acquires his male characteristics and heterosexual attitudes for his own person and future sexual identity.

In other words, that certain childhood elements in given cases have led to a specific homosexual result does not exclude a different or even the opposite outcome in other instances. Obviously, what determines the direction of development are not the major infantile events and constellations in themselves but a multitude of accompanying circumstances, the consequences of which are difficult to judge both retrospectively in adult analysis and prognostically in the assessment of children. They include external and internal, qualitative and quantitative factors. Whether a boy's love for his mother is a first step on his road to manhood or whether it will cause him to repress his aggressive masculinity for her sake, depends not only on himself, i.e., on the healthy nature of his phallic strivings, the intensity of his castration fears and wishes, and on the amounts of libido left behind at earlier fixation points. The outcome also depends on the mother's personality and her actions, on the amounts of satisfaction and frustration which she administers to him orally and anally, during feeding and toilet training, on her own wish to keep him dependent on her, or her own pride in his achieving independence of her, and, last but not least, on her acceptance or rejection of pleasure in or intolerance for his phallic advances toward her. The castration shocks which no boy can escape, whether in the shape of threats, observations, operations, etc., depend primarily, as far as the intensity of their consequences is concerned, on the time when they occur and make themselves felt most when they coincide with the height of phallic masturbation, passive-feminine wishes toward the father, guilt feelings, etc. The castration fears and passive strivings in their turn are influenced by the father's repressive or seductive attitudes, his suitability or unsuitability for the role of masculine model, etc. Where the father is absent owing to divorce, desertion, death, there is the lack of a restraining oedipal rival, a circumstance which intensifies anxiety and guilt in the phallic phase and promotes unmanliness. In this situation, the boy's fantasy that the father has been removed by the mother as a punishment for his masculine aggression also acts as a disturbance to the boy's normal heterosexual wishes.

What has to be reckoned with, finally, and what may encourage development in one or the other sexual direction are the purely chance happenings such as accidents, seductions, illnesses, object losses through death, the ease or difficulty of finding a heterosexual object in adolescence, etc. Since such events are unpredictable and may alter the child's life at any date, they upset whatever prognostic calculations may have been made previously.

According to the previous arguments it seems preferable to think not in terms of infantile prestages of adult homosexuality but in terms of developmental influences which promote or prevent homosexual development. Such thinking is based on the assumption that during the child's growth homosexual leanings compete and regularly alternate with normal heterosexuality and that the two tendencies make use in turn of the various libidinal positions through which the child passes.

Considered from this point of view, homosexual development can be summed up as being favored by the following factors:

(1) the bisexual tendencies which are considered as part of the inborn constitution. They endow all individuals with psychological characteristics not only of their own but also of the opposite sex and enable them to take as love objects, or offer themselves as love objects, not only to the opposite but also to their own sex. This innate bisexuality is intensified in the preoedipal period by the identifications with both male and female parent and remains the constitutional basis for any homosexual inclinations which arise later.

(2) the individual's primary and secondary narcissism, i.e., the libidinal cathexis of his own self. So far as object choice in later childhood follows this original narcissistic pattern, partners are chosen to be as identical as possible with the self, including identity of sex. Such homosexual, or more strictly speaking narcissistic relationships are characteristic of the latency period and certain stages of preadolescence and adolescence.

(3) the anaclitic object attachment of the infant, for which sex is of secondary importance. This is of special significance for female homosexuality since the girl may become fixated to this stage as to a "homosexual" one.

(4) the libidinization of the anus and the usual passive tendencies of the anal stage which provide the normal bodily basis for the boy's feminine identification.

(5) penis envy which provides the normal basis for the girl's masculine identification.

(6) the overestimation of the penis in the phallic phase which makes it difficult or impossible for the boy to accept a "castrated" love object.

(7) the negative oedipus complex which represents a

normal "homosexual" phase in the life of both boys and girls.

In contrast to the factors enumerated above which urge an individual toward homosexuality, there are other influences at work which act in the opposite direction and protect a given person from adopting this particular sexual solution:

(1) Heterosexual and homosexual strivings compete with each other quantitatively during the whole of childhood. Whatever promotes heterosexuality checks homosexuality to a corresponding degree. For example, the increase in heterosexuality which is bound up with a boy's entry into the phallic phase and the positive oedipus complex automatically decreases any homosexual inclinations which are left over as residues from the period of anal passivity. The same decrease of homosexuality occurs in certain adolescent stages owing to the influx of genital masculinity which turns the boy toward heterosexual object choice.

(2) The very intensity of castration fear which causes some males to avoid women and to become homosexual acts in others as a counterforce against the negative oedipus complex and a barrier against homosexuality. Since the passive feminine wishes toward the father presuppose for their fulfillment the acceptance of castration, they are avoided by such boys at all costs. This often results in a pseudo masculinity, which is overemphasized as a reaction against castration anxiety, and in a sexual aggressiveness toward women, which denies the possibility of castration and the presence of any feminine wishes and consequently blocks the road to any overt homosexual manifestations.

(3) While undefended regression to anality promotes passive feminine homosexual attitudes in the male, the reaction formations against anality, especially disgust, effectively block the path to homosexuality, or at least to its manifest expression. In adult analysis such men appear as "homosexual manqués."

(4) Finally, the "tendency to complete development" and the "biological reasonableness" (Edward Bibring, 1936) which make individuals prefer normality to abnormality can be counted as factors weighing against homosexuality.

On the whole, the balance between heterosexuality and homosexuality during the whole period of childhood is so precarious, and the scales are so readily tipped in one direction or the other by a multitude of influences, that the opinion still holds good that "a person's final sexual attitude is not decided until after puberty."

NOTE 3

ERIKSON, ERIK H.
The Problem of Ego Identity*

*   *   *

[T]eachers, judges, and psychiatrists, who deal with youth, come to be significant representatives of that strategic act of "recognition" (the act through which society "identifies" its young members and thus contributes to their developing identity). . . . If, for simplicity's sake or in order to accommodate ingrown habits of law or psychiatry, they diagnose and treat as a criminal, as a constitutional misfit, as a derelict doomed by his upbringing, or—indeed—as a deranged patient, a young person who, for reasons of personal or social marginality, is close to choosing a negative identity, that young person may well put his energy into becoming exactly what the careless and fearful community expects him to be—and make a total job of it.

*   *   *

NOTE 4

JONES et al. v. COMMONWEALTH
185 Va. 335, 38 S.E. 2d 444, 447 (1946)

SPRATLEY, JUSTICE

*   *   *

The judgment against a youth that he is delinquent is a serious reflection upon his character and habits. The stain against him is not removed merely because the statute says no judgment in this particular proceeding shall be deemed a conviction for crime or so considered. The stigma of conviction will reflect upon him for life. It hurts his self-respect. It may, at some inopportune, unfortunate moment, rear its ugly head to destroy his opportunity for advancement, and blast his ambition to build up a character and reputation entitling him to the esteem and respect of his fellow man. . . .

*   *   *

[i]

The Case of Jean Drew**

STATEMENT OF JEAN DREW—MARCH 9, 1961

I, Jean Drew have been advised by the Deputy

---

* 4 *Journal American Psychoanalytic Association*, 1956. (p. 56). Reprinted by permission.

** This case has been taken from the records and with the permission of the Family Court Center, Toledo, Ohio. The names of the parties and other identifying features have been fictionalized. Reprinted from: *The Family and the Law*, by Joseph Goldstein and Jay Katz. New York: Free Press, 1965. (pp. 915–927).

Sheriff that I am not required to make a statement at all but may remain silent, and that any statement I make may be used as evidence against me in court.

Q. How old are you? A. Fifteen.

Q. Where do you live and with whom? A. 8 Barn Street with my mother.

Q. What school do you attend, and what grade are you in? A. Stevens High School and I am in the ninth grade.

Q. Have you ever been in trouble before? A. Yes.

Q. What for? A. Running away.

Q. What kind of trouble are you involved in? A. I broke a window in a gas station and stole some candy.

Q. At this time relate to me in your own words exactly what happened and who was with you on this B & E? A. Janet Pratt came over to my home Sunday evening, because she had got into a fight with her mother. She came over to my house with two (2) boys in a Ford. I had also been fighting with my mother, I believe all day. My mother said to Janet, "What happened to you?" She said this because Janet came in crying. Then Janet said something about drinking. My mother then said to her "How about you and me going out and getting drunk?" I don't know, but Janet and I just walked out of the house and we got in the car with these two guys. Then Janet said that she wanted to get some beer. We then found some place and got two six packs. This fellow by the name of Nelson bought the beer and he is only seventeen years old. I had three bottles and Janet had about a bottle and a half, but nobody got drunk. We rode around for a while and then the boys dropped us off near my house. We went into my house and my mother made some nasty remark to Janet. This burned me up, so I told Janet to come on let's go, she just wants to fight all night long. We walked over to a gas station. We bought some cigarettes and after that we started walking and we went down town. The two boys asked us if we wanted a ride. The two boys were in the front seat and we were in the rear seat. Then we got two more six packs. We then went over to this boy's house and drank it. After we got done with the beer one of the guys suggested that we go riding around. We were still in the rear seat and the guys were in the front seat. We went riding around. They then took us out in the country and dropped us off. We started walking around and it was raining. It seemed like we were walking for hours. We were soaking wet, and we seen this garage with a car in it. We went in there for a while until the rain stopped. After it stopped raining we then started walking again. We came to this gas station, I think it was. We came to this station and I think that I broke the window. Anyway my hand was bleeding. We got scared and started running. We then came to this other gas station. Then Janet broke the bathroom door down with her foot. We stayed in there for a while and got warm. We tore the towel from the towel rack so that I could wrap up my hand. We both wrapped our hands in this towel and then we left and went to the front of this station near this big window. Then Janet put her fist through first, and then I started hitting it. Then Janet crawled in and got about four boxes of candy and some gum. We then started running again and by this time it was getting light out. We then walked for a while and we came to this garage. We seen this car and crawled in because we were cold. This woman came out and wanted to know what we were doing in there. We told her we were cold and then we left. We started walking again and then this woman came by and took us to this gas station. We then tried to call Fred to take us home. There was a policeman in there. He became suspicious of us. We then got in touch with Fred and he said that he would pick us up. Then when he came the policeman told us that he wanted to talk to us. He then questioned us for a while and then he told us we could go. Fred then took us home. He dropped me off first and then he took Janet home. When I got home my mother started yaking again, so then I took some aspirins. In fact I will do it again if I get my hands on some. Then my mother saw the empty bottle and she made me take some soap and water so I could throw them up. I guess I threw some of them up. I then went to sleep. Then this policeman came and told my mother that he was sorry, but he had to take me to C.S.C. Then she asked him what for. Then I told her. As I started to the car, my mother told him that I had taken some aspirins and he said that I should go to the hospital and they called the ambulance. I guess they took me to Valley Hospital. That is all that I remember.

Q. Are you involved in any other trouble? A. No, that is all that I have done.

I have read the above statement and understand it. This statement is true to the best of my knowledge and belief and was made by me /s/ Jean Drew voluntarily. I was made no promises of reward or leniency and was not threatened, harmed, or in any manner put in fear.

* * *

PRELIMINARY HEARING—MARCH 13, 1961

Present at this preliminary hearing before Referee, Jane Parker were: Jean Drew; her mother, Mrs. Pulaski; Mrs. Sears CWB.

* * *

At the preliminary hearing on this date, Jean was almost noncommunitive in the presence of her mother. She indicated her home was "OK," she stated she didn't obey her mother all of the time, and she did not like Stevens High School or the kids in the neighborhood. The mother was willing to excuse Jean's behavior and indicated this was only a part of growing up. . . . The mother went into a terrible tirade regarding Stevens High School and complained because a man psychologist had talked to Jean regarding delicate things that she would not mention to anyone. It seems the irritating point was the teacher had suggested Jean buy a special kind of a bra, since her busts were so large. The mother further stated, she had called the school and advised them not to tell Jean she had called but immediately, Jean was called into the office and asked if she could not keep her mother from calling the school every day. Jean states she is not doing well in school but indicated she attended regularly.

Jean had been known to the Child Welfare Board for about two years as a dependent child and she was placed in the Children's Home and was not happy there.

The delinquency affidavit was filed by Mrs. Sears, Child Welfare Board, and the mother attempted to keep Jean from going to Child Study Center, but Jean broke away from her and ran to the CSI door and as she went up the stairs, she screamed "thank God, I'm not going home." The mother went to the window in referee's office and pretended like she would jump out the window if she had not been prevented from doing so because of the screen. After a little time, she became a little more calm and left the office with Mrs. Sears but she was almost out of her mind to realize Jean did not want to return home.

Later in the day, League of the Hard of Hearing called and advised Mrs. Pulaski had been there and talked for an hour and a half reciting her home life and the problems she is having with Jean and she expressed dislike for CWE. Mrs. Pulaski is a most difficult woman to work with and in the past, the referee has found she will respond to firm but kindly treatment. When she came to Jean's hearing, she was reading a book, which she stated was one of the "great book series" and that she belonged to a group that meets at the YWCA on a Sunday night. She says she doesn't do much reading any more and she wants to read good things and she takes the time to read these.

Later in the day, Jean was interviewed alone and seemed very quiet and calm and stated she absolutely did not want to return home.

At first, Jean suggested she would like to be in a foster home, like her brother, Stan, but she indicated she knew foster homes were hard to secure so she did not know what would be best for her. She feels her brother, Stan, is doing well and stated her mother was very upset because he will not have a thing to do with his family.

Delinquency affidavit filed by Mrs. Sears and Jean placed in Child Study Center pending further hearing.

REPORT OF PROBATION COUNSELOR—APRIL 25, 1961

There is a great deal of information in the family file concerning Mrs. Pulaski. She is an odd and bizarre looking woman. She reports having some brain injury, either prenatal or at birth, which has affected her eyes, her hearing, and motor coordination. Therefore, she considered herself partially disabled. She has a habit, apparently uncontrollable, of rolling her eyes constantly and not being able to concentrate on any one object for any length of time. She reports that she is somewhat hard of hearing. She keeps her hands in constant motion. Her thinking is at times disarmingly logical and at other times highly exaggerated and illogical. She laughs nervously, inappropriately, and constantly at certain times, particularly when she is telling an extremely painful story. She has told Jean that if she does not return home she will kill herself. At another time when Jean was first in C.S.C. she told her that she had not eaten since Jean left home and is intending to starve herself to death.

Her vocabulary is excellent, her sentence construction exceptionally good and she refers to good books and articles which she has read from time to time. Her moral standards seem to be high and she verbalizes excellent attitudes toward bringing up children. For example, she has said that one of the difficulties between her and Jean is Jean's choice of associates. She believes that children should have good associates of whom they can be proud and that it is the parents' job to help the children understand this and to control it whenever possible. She is very resentful toward the court for removing Stan from her home. She, in connection with this, says that she does not feel that people have the right to run away from their particular situation in life. That is the easy way. What people should do is to take life as it is and try to make the best of it.

Mrs. Pulaski is very bitter about all of the relationships with other people that she has had throughout her life. She says that her father was very cruel to her and from the time she was six years of age she can remember nothing but cruelty and abuse from her father. This has affected her whole life. She was married to Norman Drew in 1940, reportedly not because she loved him but because she wanted to get away from her father. She says this marriage was very unhappy and her husband mistreated her and so she divorced him. In 1950, she married Mr. Pulaski and the same pattern was repeated. He refused to provide a good home for her, he was mean and abusive, and she never received any affection or devotion from him. During these years she knew nothing but hardship and discouragement and rejection. The relationship was somewhat the same with the step children. She is very sorry for herself because she tried conscientiously to bring the step children and her own children up in the way that she knows is right, but she met nothing but criticism and persecution from her husband, from her neighbors, from the police, from Child Welfare Board, from any agency which she had anything to do with, and from the Court. And one after another the children were removed from her home. She does not feel that this was her fault. She feels that it is the fault of the community and of society and she is very bitter against them.

Mrs. Pulaski is very unhappy at the moment because things have not gone the way she planned. She has felt that after a long and hard and unhappy life she has finally gotten to the point where she ought to be able to enjoy it. She has a small job selling cosmetics from door to door, she lives in a very simple house, but it is all paid for, and up until now she has had Jean with her whom she professes to love very dearly. Now she feels that the court is taking Jean away from her as they did Jean's brother and that in spite of the fact that she has done her best and tried very hard to build up a happy life everyone is against her and is trying to tear down what she has built up. Mrs. Pulaski does sell Avon products from door to door and feels that this type of work is particularly suited for her. She does not drive a car so she has a little wire push cart that she carries her cosmetics around in. She appears at court hearings and for interviews in this counselor's office pushing her little cart which, of course, causes people to look at her and sometimes to even snicker, this she is aware of and resents very much. She feels she is doing the best that she knows how and feels that no one has any right to make fun of her. Apparently, in the neighborhood she drags the cosmetics around in a little wagon, a fact which causes the neighbors to ridicule her and causes Jean a great deal of embarrassment.

It is almost impossible to counsel or discuss any subject with Mrs. Pulaski. She talks constantly and very often her voice rises to such a pitch that she is shrieking and raving. She asks the question, "What makes people do this?" but refuses to stop long enough for an answer.

In 1953, Mrs. Pulaski along with her son, Stan, were seen on several occasions by the Mental Hygiene Clinic. Mental Hygiene Clinic felt that the mother was a paranoid schizophrenic and was not amenable to counseling. In 1954, Dr. Heinz held a consultation with Mrs. Pulaski. He concurred in Mental Hygiene's diagnosis and felt that although she probably should be committed to the State Hospital it was impractical and unfeasible to do this.

There are many references on the various police reports in the file of Mrs. Pulaski's physically abusing and assaulting Jean. Jean has very little to say about this although she does admit that she is afraid of her mother. When this is discussed with her mother, her mother laughs hysterically and says that Jean is not afraid of her, that she is really afraid of Jean, that it is Jean who is stronger than Mrs. Pulaski and that Jean is lying if she says that she is afraid of her. However, there are constant references on the police reports both in Stan's file and Jean's of the mother's hitting, beating, and threatening both of the children.

Family Adjustment—It may be seen from the foregoing, that the crux of Jean's difficulties lie in a complex and unpleasant and chaotic relationship in the home. Apparently Mrs. Pulaski did not get along with Jean's father, Mr. Drew, and they were divorced. There are constant reports of Mrs. Pulaski and her second husband having marital conflict between themselves, over Mr. Pulaski's drinking, over the discipline and handling of the children, and of their relationship in the community.

Jean in some ways it is felt is quite attached to her mother. During the several times that she has been in C.S.C., although she has nearly always presented herself because she was afraid to go home or did not want to be with her mother, she has always thought it over and felt sorry for her mother, pitied her, felt that her mother needed her, and eventually went home. This is somewhat the situation at this point with Jean. However, she is refusing to go home this time. She has feelings of guilt and remorse and pity and concern and loyalty toward her mother. She becomes very upset whenever an attempt is made to talk about her mother and simply hurls invectives such as, "I hate her," "I never want to see her again," or "She is a pig and she doesn't love me and I hate her." She certainly is mixed up about her feelings about her mother, she is fearful that her mother will do something to injure herself and that would be the motivating force if she ever should say that she was willing to go back home again.

Jean speaks wistfully of her brother, Stan, who is two years older than she. She says that she is very proud of him now because he lives in a nice home, he is doing well in school, he is driving a car, and everybody likes him. She feels that he would not know her if he met her on the street and this causes her a degree of sadness. In some ways she envies Stan and would like to be in a foster home, hoping that she might live the kind of life that Stan does at this moment. It is not definitely ascertained how Stan and Jean got along when they were living together as it is six or seven years since Stan has been removed from the home.

Living Conditions—Mrs. Pulaski's home is a very small, asphalt-shingled bungalow, almost a shack. This counselor has not been inside of the house but the outside looks badly cared for, in poor repair and neglected. Panes of glass have been broken and patched with paper and generally speaking it is probably the smallest and least substantial home on this street. There have been reports made by others who have been in the home that the housekeeping standards are very low and there is a good deal of dirt and untidiness. Jean admits that her mother does not work on a routine schedule and that a good deal of the time there is no food in the house until her mother chooses to go out and buy some.

Child's History, Developmental and Health—Jean is a large, mature looking girl for her age. She is fairly coarse looking and has several physical difficulties. Her eyes are very poor. She has just been fitted with glasses to correct this and at this writing she seems to be adjusting rather well and feels more comfortable with them. The optometrist said it was an extremely strong prescription, this upsets Jean because she feels that perhaps she is going blind, which is not true. One side of Jean's face has been paralyzed since she was a baby. This causes her tremendous amount of embarrassment and self-consciousness and when she smiles or talks with anybody she is quite apt to keep one side of her face covered. The story is that when she was a baby she fell on a pair of scissors in her crib which severed a nerve in her neck and this has caused paralysis. She says that the doctors say that she will outgrow this by the time she is twenty-one. She admits that even now she feels a tingling sensation at times in her face and she feels that she can move her mouth. She is more conscious of it than anyone else is as it is not a disfiguring thing, but Jean thinks that it is. She has many scars on her body, she has one very large indentation on her leg that came from falling on a spike when she was quite young.

Jean's childhood seems to be normal physically as far as can be ascertained. Jean certainly does not seem to be conscious of anything out of the ordinary in her childhood and the mother refuses to discuss it with counselor. She always changes the subject. Although she is just fifteen years of age she has very large bust development. This has caused her a great deal of embarrassment.

Because of her physical deformities she has terrific feelings of inferiority, self-consciousness, and feels that people are laughing at her and making fun of her all the time. Also she is very jealous. Counselor has had one girl besides Jean up at C.S.C. and it has been a most difficult situation. Jean wants the undivided attention of the counselor but rejects any particular attention counselor wants to show her. Jean admits to having a temper which flares up a great deal at home and has ultimate periods of depression.

However, in spite of her feelings about herself and the fact that she is not one of the most beautiful girls at C.S.C., she has really shown that she has a very nice personality in a great many ways. She is very fair and loyal and honest in all of her dealings both with the leaders and with the girls and with this counselor. She puts herself out to be nice to people and in general she is well liked on the floor. It seems that she is more critical of herself and makes more disparaging remarks about herself, her own looks, her personality, then anyone else does. It is believed that she is beginning to feel a little bit more sense of her own worth than she did when she first came to C.S.C.

School Attendance—At Lake School Jean was reported as having above average grades in the seventh grade and to have been doing better in the seventh grade than she had previously. In the sixth grade she ranked seventh in her class of twenty-two. The school reported that she was inclined to be rude, noisy, sassy, and argumentative. They felt that her home conditions were primarily responsible for any poor behavior on Jean's part, that there was constant quarrelling and friction in the home which arose from the mother's mental condition, that the mother was belligerent and fault finding and made a nuisance of herself by talking endlessly and calling the school on frequent occasions.

The dean and Jean's counselor at Stevens High School have taken a great deal of interest in Jean ever since she entered this school. Jean has been the butt of much teasing and commenting by both boys and girls at Stevens. The primary reason for this was because of Jean's extremely large bust—the children would pass by her and say "hello size 40." This made Jean unhappy, self-conscious, and increased her low opinion of herself. She retaliated by quarrelling and using bad language. The school felt this was not entirely Jean's fault and that she had been severely aggravated. The mother called the school and wanted it announced over the loudspeaker that the rest of the children in the school should stop teasing Jean; of course, the school did not carry through with this. They did counsel her at great length concerning her physical difficulties. During the counseling period it was discovered that she not only was self-conscious about the size of her bust but experienced much discomfort and pain at night and was unable to sleep at times because of the weight of her breasts. They recommended that she wear a garment at night and this seemed to help to a certain extent. The school offered to buy her a corrective bra. The mother at first acquiesced and gave her written consent. However, later she objected by saying that the teachers should mind their own business and that they were causing Jean to be self-conscious about herself. After Jean was in C.S.C. the school wanted to complete their plan of purchasing a corrective garment and that has been done. They also tried to help Jean to know how to choose suitable clothing. The school felt that Jean was very receptive to this; however, when the corrective garment had been purchased and some premature inquiries made as to surgery to correct her large bust Jean objected strenuously saying she did not mind being large, many girls were, and she wished people would stop trying to shrink her. This behavior is typical. Jean alternates between accepting and rejecting any and all ideas as well as the people who are working with her.

At the end of the first semester, Jean's freshman year at Stevens, her grades were:

English C	Civics C—	Chorus A
Algebra B—	General Science D	

The school officials felt that she could do better. On her school report from C.S.C. it was mentioned that Jean was too disturbed to concentrate although her attitude and effort and behavior were extremely good.

Jean says she does not like school, yet in some way she wants to finish, because she wants to be a physical education teacher. She knows she needs an education for this.

Leisure Activities and Interests—Jean is particularly fond of sports, primarily ice skating and swimming and diving. She wants to become a physical education teacher. In the past she has spent a great deal of her leisure time swimming at Wales Park and skating there in the winter. She does not like to read at all and does as little of this as necessary. She has not been very interested in Arts and Crafts until recently when she got her new glasses. She admits that this makes a difference now and she is able to do close work and enjoy it more. She is learning to crochet at C.S.C.

Child's Attitude and Counselor's Evaluation—Jean knows that running away from home, breaking and entering the gas station, and consuming a quantity of aspirin were wrong. She even said that it was stupid. Yet she maintains that she will be forced to do these things again if she goes back to her mother's home. She feels that she must get away from her mother. She has tried many times before but has always returned. This time she feels that she just cannot go back. She doesn't much care what happens to her as long as she does not have to go back with her mother.

Jean talks rather objectively and dispassionately about her future. She thinks at times she would like a foster home because of her brother, Stan's, success in his present one. But she is not sure that she could adjust satisfactorily to a foster home. She also says she does not think she would do too well at a school because she has trouble getting along with other people. Yet she is willing to go wherever the court places her, she says.

Jean has many good qualities. She seems to have high moral standards, certain ambitions for herself. She says if she stays home she knows she will eventually leave school, drift into trouble, and end up a "nobody." She wants to become a physical education teacher, she loves sports. She has an inferiority complex, a poor opinion of herself, and feels that she has no redeeming qualities. At times she even wonders if she is crazy. Apparently her mother has accused her of this in the past. All of these attitudes and conflicts make Jean moody, difficult to relate to, and at times very hard to work with.

Diagnosis—Jean is a large, strong, mature-looking girl for her fifteen years. This is her fourth referral to court. At all times she has come to court because of an inability to get along with her mother, who talks constantly, nags, and is herself a psychotic. One thing that one cannot help wondering in reading Jean's record and knowing the present and past situation in her home is why Jean is not far more delinquent and disturbed than she is. One wonders where she gets the ego strength to cope with the situation as long as she has without being completely overwhelmed by it. In spite of the fact that she is bewildered, mixed-up, and highly disturbed, she is able to evaluate her mother and her relationship with her mother pretty honestly and to assume her own responsibility in the case.

There are several areas of conflict in Jean's life. The first and most all encompassing one is her relationship with her mother. The home is in a chaotic state most of the time. Jean and her mother cannot agree on anything, the mother nags, talks constantly, embarrasses Jean by her peculiar actions, disapproves of Jean's friends, interferes with her school relationships. The mother has a feeling that everyone is against her, that if it weren't for the neighbours and for the courts, the police, and for laws in general everything would be all right. Therefore she lashes out against all of these and feels that she has no faults, that she is a good, fine, intelligent mother with the interest of her child at heart. Jean has reacted to this turbulent relationship with her mother by having temper outbursts, by running away repeatedly, staying out late at night.

Another area which has caused Jean a good deal of concern in the past is her very large and mature figure. This has caused the children at school to make fun of her and to torment her. Also her paralyzed face has made her feel that she is ugly and all in all she has a very low opinion of herself. She too withdraws a bit from social contacts and is sure that nobody likes her and that she cannot get along with people.

Also, Jean is moody and vacillates between fairly pleasant behavior and periods of severe depression when she is unwilling to communicate with anyone. She has difficulty in relating to other children and to adults. The greatest difficulty in thinking about placement of Jean is her mixed-up, ambivalent, and guilt-ridden relationship with her mother. It may well be that a foster home with warm and accepting and affectionate parental figures is the very placement that Jean needs most, yet because of her faulty and damaged relationship with her mother it may be the very placement that Jean will not be able to adjust to. Other factors stand in the way of foster home placement, Mrs. Pulaski will somehow find out where Jean is in spite of every effort to prevent this. This will disturb Jean and sabotage the placement. It is also doubtful that any foster parents could tolerate or handle Mrs. Pulaski. Then too, Jean is not an attractive girl or one who could relate warmly to foster parents. It would take unusual foster parents to accept Jean, to train her patiently, and not be discouraged with her lack of response, her moodiness, and her obvious feelings toward her own mother.

For these reasons it may be that an open and permissive school may be the best answer for Jean. The psychological study now being done will undoubtedly reveal many factors that will help make this decision easier. From counselor's dealings with Jean and from observing her in C.S.C., from talking to the dean of her school and from knowing Jean's background and the factors which have caused her to be the way she is it would seem that possibly some psychotherapy may be advisable. It is certainly true that Jean needs some help in learning to accept herself and to appreciate her own good qualities as well as her limitations.

Jean is certainly reacting to a turbulent, chaotic, and disturbed family (home) situation which must have existed ever since she was born. It has caused her to mistrust people, to have a disparaging attitude toward herself and an extremely dim view of family life in general. It is felt that Jean is not very delinquent and certainly does not wish to be and if placed in the proper environment with the proper help could become a rather fine girl.

Recommendations—Although a definite recommendation will not be given until the psychological study is completed, it is felt by this counselor that perhaps an open permissive school which could accept Jean as she is and help her to appreciate herself would be the best possible recommendation at this time. Perhaps this school experience could be preparatory to an eventual placement in a foster home after Jean has had a chance to work out some of her problems in human relationship.

JENSON
Probation Counselor

PSYCHOLOGICAL REPORT—APRIL 27, 1961

REFERRED BY: Bridget Jenson, probation counselor (approved by Pat O'Hare, casework supervisor).

Breaking and entering. Previous runaway and attempted suicide. Nagged by mother who raves and talks incessantly. Feels mother is mentally deranged. Mother threatens self-destruction if Jean refuses to come home. What are Jean's strengths and weaknesses, her abilities, and her true feelings about her mother and home? Is she neurotic as mother claims? What planning is best? How could she respond to counseling?

The Wechsler Intelligence Scale Form I indicates that Jean is functioning at a Dull Normal level of intelligence (IQ 83, Verbal 80, Performance 90) with Average ability in Arithmetic reasoning and in nonverbal tasks which deal with visual patterns and the manipulation of concrete objects. Her ability to learn new associations is also Average. She tends to be distractible but can concentrate when interested. She has a very poor common sense reasoning ability, has a limited vocabulary and little knowledge about the world in general, and she frequently misinterprets the meaning of what is going on in social situations.

Jean was given the California Mental Maturity Test (short form) in 1957 and earned a total IQ of 101 with an IQ of 96 in the Language area and IQ of 107 in the nonlanguage area. The higher scores on this test, in comparison with Wechsler Scale administered by the writer, may be due to the difference in the tests themselves but may also suggest that Jean is more disturbed emotionally than she was four years ago.

The Wide Range Achievement Test scores, rating Jean at the middle of the eighth grade in Reading and Spelling and beginning ninth grade in Arithmetic show that she has actually kept up pretty well with the average child in her grade. Her grades in Grade School would also indicate that this is true except for a D in History which suggests that she was beginning to have difficulties in school work. Although her first semester grades in High School were average, Jean feels that she is not doing as well as she used to particularly because she finds it difficult to understand General Science. She also has difficulty in Algebra, as attested to in the Wide Range Achievement Test, but she claims that she can do Algebra.

Jean's responses to the California Test of Personality show maladjustment in most areas both within herself and in her relationship with others although she does profess to have high social standards and good social skills. She seems to feel just barely capable of standing on her own two feet but she resents the many limitations put upon her behavior by her mother. Her family relationships are, of course, very poor as are also her school and community relationships which reflect a number of antisocial tendencies. She has very little feeling of belonging and so tends to withdraw and worry about her problems. She has numerous nervous symptoms which include twitching muscles, disturbances in attention, difficulty in going to sleep at night, and bad dreams.

Jean's responses to the Incomplete Sentences show much concern about her mother. Her ambivalence toward her mother is reflected in her concern about what will happen to her if Jean leaves home, in her guilt about wanting to leave home, her indecision as to whether doing this is right or wrong, and her desire to know what she does that makes her mother angry. She admits her need for a mother and would like to get along with her. She feels pretty helpless about succeeding in doing this at home. She feels that she suffers when she is around her mother, is annoyed by her constant talking which interferes with her ability to concentrate on her homework, and she admits that she has, at times, deceived her. Jean seems to be disturbed about coming into womanhood and seems to have more masculine interests, such as sports, than does the average girl her age. She is self-conscious about her bust, which draws crude comments from boys, but she insists that it is not too large for her build. She tries to give the impression that she is not different from other girls but she feels that people, generally, do not understand her. She claims that most girls, however, are understanding. She thinks that she likes a boy who is in the Army but she is not sure and she does not express much interest in dating or dancing. The writer feels, however, that this attitude is a defense. She feels that her poor vision and the partial paralysis of her face interfere with her attractiveness. She feels that she is not doing as well in school as she used to do in the lower grades but she stresses the point that she has never failed "yet." She tries to keep an optimistic outlook about the future. She seems to have very little feeling or knowledge about her father except that he has never supported her.

The Rorschach examination shows an individual who is willing to put forth a normal amount of effort but has ambitious goals beyond her capabilities. She seems willing enough to conform but has some difficulty in understanding what is expected of her. She becomes emotionally disturbed to the point that her reasoning is not logical and she is likely to "blow up." Her impulsivity is still of a childlike nature and her ambivalence is reflected in difficulty in making clear-cut decisions. While her first response to a situation may show misinterpretation of the facts of reality, her perception can be improved if she is encouraged to think about it more. There is evidence of marked disturbance in interpersonal relationships which cause her considerable anxiety. It appears that she is greatly concerned about sexual problems (although she does not admit this) and it is suggested that she would have preferred to have been a male. She is likely to deny emotional involvement when questioned about it directly although she does react emotionally toward her environment. She shows some potentiality for developing insight but as her sensitivity toward the environment increases, it appears that she may become more crude and sensuous.

Jean's drawings also reflect her desire to be a male and she seems to identify with the male particularly in her less desirable characteristics, e.g., he is not smart but strong and tends to push people around. He wants to be friends with people but does not know how and fears that they will not like him. He becomes angry when people will not do what he wants them to do and he tries to boss older people. He is self-conscious and feels that people may be looking at him but he is not sure. He runs around with kids like himself and prefers girls who have little self-respect. He has his first sex experience at seventeen or eighteen. He tries to look happy but he is sad inside. He quits school in the ninth grade but has ambitions which are beyond his realization. Jean's drawings also show that she has a conflict between her identification with a character of this sort and the nice girl that she should be.

The writer cannot say that Jean is neurotic as the mother claims; however, the latter may not mean neurotic, specifically, but rather emotionally disturbed. With this, the writer would agree as does the counselor. Undoubtedly the mother's mental disturbance, as reported elsewhere, is accountable for Jean's problems and conflicts. She certainly has not been the kind of mother with whom a girl would want to identify so this may account for Jean's conflict about identifying with the female sex. Apparently, it was easy for Jean to identify with the male sex in her earlier years and this was shown in her interest in sports, her active participation in them, and her desire to be a physical education teacher. However, as she developed into womanhood and developed such a mature womanly figure with a rather large bust, she has become very self-conscious of this which not only attracts the attention of other people but also is in conflict with her identification with the male sex and this is very upsetting to her because it practically pulls the props out from under her self-image. She will need a lot of help from an understanding person who can listen to her work out this conflict as she swings from one side to the other, not sure whether she wants to be a male or female, whether she should be ashamed of her bust or proud of it, and whether she has what it takes to be a female who is accepted by other females as a friend and by males as a love object. No one can answer these questions for her. She must work out the solutions herself and the Rorschach shows that her perception can be improved when she is encouraged to think it through. It is quite natural that much of her thinking revolves around sex, at the present time, but it is difficult for her to admit this and talk about it because this would interfere with her concept of the good girl which she should be and she fears that no adult is likely to understand and condone her thinking. Because of this, there is danger of her trying to work out her conflict, on a testing basis, with boys with, of course, the probability of pregnancy occurring. Her tendency in this direction is shown by the recent episode when she and her girl friend went off in a car with a couple of boys (known to them), drank beer, and rode around in the car with them. Note that, later, they were picked up by two boys whom they apparently did not know, drank more beer with them, and were dropped off by them in the country. This incident suggests that the boys expected to have sex relations with these girls and dropped them off because the girls would not agree. Jean denied that she has ever had any sex relations but the writer feels that this trend in running around with boys, riding in cars with them and drinking beer, which is likely to lower inhibitions, will lead to sexual intercourse.

In view of the above, the writer feels that it is important for Jean to be removed from these temptations to work out her sexual problems on an experience level and to be given an opportunity to work them out on a verbal level with a therapist or counselor in a boarding school setting. The writer feels that there should be a certain amount of security about the school, i.e., that it not be an open school in town or very close to town, but might be a fairly open school if it were far enough away from town to minimize the temptation to go to town to meet boys. On the other hand, associating with boys under supervision, even in a coeducational school, might be helpful to her.

A word might be said about Jean's IQ and her school achievement inasmuch as it appears that she has done better than her recent IQ of 83 might indicate. The subjects in which she has succeeded, however, must be taken into consideration. The test results showed that she can learn new associations, as she has done in the mechanics of Reading, Spelling, and Arithmetic, but when she has to deal with more complex processes which may involve abstract reasoning, she is not likely to succeed. Her muscular co-ordination, however, is quite good and she is able to manipulate concrete objects. Her ambition to be a physical education teacher is not likely to be realized because she would be unable to go successfully through college. She seems to have the ability to become a typist, if she could become so interested, and may be able to continue her interest in sports as an avocation.

The Rorschach warns that Jean is likely to express herself crudely and evidence of this was shown last year when she made vulgar statements to two children and their mother so the school should be prepared for this and not look upon it as personality deterioration unless it becomes extreme.

Placement in a boarding school, away from town, with an intramural school program and counseling available.

BETTY COMBS,
Psychologist

DECISION OF FAMILY COURT—APRIL 27, 1961

Court of Common Pleas
Division of Domestic Relations

FINDING OF FACTS: This is Jean's first referral to the Court, although she has been known as a dependant under the care of Child Welfare Board. On this occasion she ran away from home with a friend and codelinquent, and the girls broke into a gas station and stole some gum, candy, potato chips, etc. The preliminary hearing was stormy. Mrs. Pulaski, the mother, is severely disturbed mentally, and in 1958 Dr. Heinz classified her as psychotic, but possibly not commitable. Jean begged not to be sent back home again, she says she hates her mother, and of course the mother is always making a scene and embarrassing Jean. Mrs. Pulaski talks constantly, nags, scolds, disapproves of Jean's friends, interferes in her school relationships, etc. Because of the difficulties between the two, Mrs. Pulaski was not permitted to visit Jean at Child Study Center. Miss Combs did a psychological study on Jean and finds her quite a disturbed girl with many problems in the sex area. Both she and her counselor, Mrs. Jenson, recommend a private school placement for further protection for Jean, and to aid her in working through her many problems. Jean is quite accepting of this plan.

RECOMMENDATION: Finding of delinquency reaffirmed, Jean ordered committed temporarily to a private training school to be selected by the Court. County to pay for her care at stipulated rate and to be financially responsible for clothing, medical, dental, and all other necessary expenses. Mother notified by Citation sent by Certified Mail, and return receipt received signed "Bea Pulaski," but she came not.

I hereby certify that all parties present have been notified of this recommendation and there are no objections.

Signed: PAT O'HARE
Referee
Dated: 4-27-61

The Foregoing report received and examined. No timely objection having been made, recommendation is hereby adopted and made the order of the Court.

Judge Brooks

REPORT OF PROBATION COUNSELOR—DECEMBER 14, 1962

On 5-30-61, Jean was placed at Highland School. By the time Jean departed from home, the attitude toward placement was very good. She had some misgivings about her ability to succeed and whether she would be happy, but on the whole she was looking forward to the experience. Counselor took her out and bought her a great many clothes. They were attractive and becoming, and Jean appreciated them very much. Prior to her placement Jean had not seen her mother for several weeks. Her mother did not come to the hearing. Jean professed not to care and yet, as has been mentioned before, there is a close emotional tie between Jean and her mother, and Jean did, deep down within her heart, regret not being able to talk with her mother. It may be also noted that her mother had raised such a row and created so much confusion and unpleasantness on a visit to C.S.C. that Jean had been highly embarrassed and requested that she not be compelled to see her mother again.

When Jean arrived in Highland, during her intake interview, she stated that she did not wish to correspond with her mother for the time being. She felt that she ought to get adjusted and get her thoughts straightened out before she let her mother know where she was. She also stated that she was determined to do well and to make something of herself, and that she was well aware this was not possible at home. Jean seemed quite impressed with Highland and the housemother, a warm, outgoing gay person to whom it could be possible for Jean to relate if she so chose.

Jean's adjustment to Highland was good in nearly every area. A great deal can be learned about Jean's progress in her own thinking, in her feelings about herself, about her mother, and about the future, as well as her activities by reading the extensive correspondence in the family file. Jean wrote frequent long and excellent letters. She expressed moods of elation and of depression, which is quite characteristic of Jean's make-up. Always she has guilt feelings concerning her mother, about leaving her mother, about the bad feeling that there was between her and her mother, and Jean worried a great deal about her mother. It was not very long after Jean arrived at Highland that she began corresponding with her mother. Through these letters to this counselor Jean expressed an intense desire to finish school, to get some further education, and "to make something of herself." The letters show a high degree of insight into herself, a realistic evaluation of her home, and of her past, and a tenderness and affection and pity, toward her mother. In general, Jean likes Highland very much. There were times when she became discouraged and moody, yet the next letter would express a fondness and a happiness about her placement there. Jean received excellent grades for her sophomore year in high school. In fact she received all A's except one C in home economics. She studied very hard and reported that she put in several hours a day on her home work. The school authorities reported that Jean was "a very bright girl." It was interesting to note that the school reported that she was the best geometry student they had. This is particularly noteworthy in view of the fact that when Jean was at C.S.C. she simply could not master even the basic skills in algebra. When she was reminded of this, she said she guessed at that time she was too disturbed and perturbed to grasp it. Jean derived a tremendous amount of satisfaction from this success. Not only that, but she received a great deal of social acclaim, too. When Jean first went to Highland, she did not relate too well with her peers.

Jean used her physical difficulties as an excuse. However, the housemother refused to be impressed by this and gradually Jean reached out and has become one of the leaders on campus. She was captain of her cottage baseball team, which is a singular honor in that baseball is one of the main interests and projects of the school. She was also elected president of student government. Last summer, the school sent this counselor a small note saying that their new swimming pool had just been completed, and because Jean was one of the best swimmers in the school the school selected her to be the first one to dive in and christen the pool. Jean has taken understandable satisfaction from all of these events. She has written counselor that never had anything like this happened to her before and she knew that it would have been impossible had she remained home. She talked about some of the other girls who did not have goals in life and that she had very definite goals. These were to finish high school, to receive some further training, college if possible, and to work hard and make something of herself.

In the fall of 1962, Jean has not been quite so happy. Her mother has been in State Hospital since July (see paragraphs below). Jean took an extremely sensible and mature attitude toward this. She said that she had realized her mother needed this for many years, and that counselor could not conceive the bizarre and unappropriate behavior which her mother had evinced throughout the past ten or fifteen years. However, this placement in State Hospital aroused again many of Jean's guilt feelings. She felt that it was possibly because she left home that her mother finally gave up and had to seek help. She will also admit that she is so glad that her mother is getting the kind of help that she needs, and that she feels better to know that she is warm and well-cared for, and well fed, and yet she is still searching around for evidences of guilt on her own part. She has said that for some reason or other she has been very discouraged and low and moody this fall and has not been able to concentrate on her school work as well as she did last year. She felt that she was failing everything, particularly chemistry. As a matter of fact, at the end of the first grading period Jean ended up with all B's, with the exception of one C.

These next few weeks will undoubtedly be very crucial ones in Jean's life. She is worrying about a home visit, she has these guilt feelings, and she has a decided responsibility toward her mother. She will undoubtedly be subject to all kinds of pressures when she comes home, and all kinds of unpleasantness. She may even verbalize that she wants to stay home. On the other hand she may realize that it will do no good to stay home. Whatever the situation is there is no question that this will be a difficult time in Jean's life and she will probably experience some definite reactions.

Home Situation—Mrs. Pulaski, Jean's mother, has continued to be hostile toward the court and all authority figures, critical of Highland School, critical of Jean's attitude, and disparaging about practically everything in Jean's life. She wrote long, raving, incoherent letters to Jean. During this first year of Jean's residence at Highland, apparently Mrs. Pulaski's economic situation was very acute. She continued to sell Cert and Avon products, but she was so highly disorganized and angry that it is highly possible that she did not carry through with this job as well as she intended to. For a time she worked weekends as a cook.

At Christmas time (1961), Jean made a home visit. The visit was an extremely disturbing one to Jean. She spent part of the time at the Wilsons, where her mother was working during the holidays. It was the time at her own home that was particularly unhappy. Mrs. Pulaksi continued to downgrade the school, Jean, the court, other people's decisions and attitudes, and in general exhibited all her previous paranoid characteristics. She was highly disorganized and excitable, and even almost physically violent. Counselor talked with Jean on the day that Jean was supposed to return to Highland. The plan was for counselor to come out and pick up Jean and take her to the bus station. The mother objected to this and accused the counselor of talking about her behind her back, and did everything in her power to make it impossible for counselor to see Jean alone. However, counselor and Jean did have a long talk when counselor took Jean to the cleaners to pick up some clothes. Jean burst into tears at this time and said she never wanted to come home again, and she was highly embarrassed to think that counselor had to see her home in a state of dirt, untidiness, disorder, etc. She felt that her mother did not have to live like that, and she must like it that way and that Jean wanted no more to do with it. Jean stated that her mother wanted her to be a housemaid or cleaning woman, and if Jean should return home that is all she could look forward to in life. Mrs. Pulaski insisted upon coming to the bus station and counselor and Jean had to listen to her constant naggings all the way down town. However, a very serious episode occurred at the bus depot. There were some four to six girls waiting in a very crowded bus station for the bus to go back to Highland. When Jean introduced her mother to these other girls and to their parents Mrs. Pulaski began to rave and to cry and she prostrated herself on the floor in the bus depot begging Jean not to go back to school and declaring that Jean had persecuted her and the court had no feelings, etc., etc. This was a highly dramatic event and one which attracted the attention of nearly everyone at the bus station. Counselor was able to steer Mrs. Pulaski out of the bus station only to have her return again later. Jean

was embarrassed and crushed about this whole incident.

Jean has not been home since. However, in the summer her anxieties began to rise and as her housemother at Highland stated, every once in a while Jean had the need to punish herself so she figured that she ought to go home. This counselor tried to make contact with the mother, but by letter, telephone, and home visits it was impossible to reach her. When Jean found out about this she was completely satisfied to stay at the school and made no more overtures to the school about permitting her to have the home visit.

In the latter part of July, Counselor learned from Jean that her mother had committed herself to State Hospital. Counselor visited the Social Service Department out there and discovered that Mrs. Pulaski had committed herself, stating that Mr. Pulaski had been the cause of all her troubles because she had him committed to State Hospital, and then State Hospital released him without telling her. This created a great degree of trauma in the home and emotionally disturbed all of her children.

Therefore, this was the beginning of her problem and it was up to the State Hospital to help her figure it out. She was diagnosed as "manic-depressive" with the manic phase predominating, paranoid tendencies. Counselor had several conversations with Dr. Fleming, who states that Mrs. Pulaski is a very sick woman. If at all possible she is to be detained at State Hospital for some length of time.

Counselor visited Mrs. Pulaski at State Hospital. During this time Mrs. Pulaski ran the gamut with counselor of hate, accusations, anger to dependency and pathos. The visit ended up with a degree of pleasant relationship between counselor and Mrs. Pulaski for the first time. During this period, counselor had the opportunity to tell Mrs. Pulaski of Jean's good progress in school and of her desire to go ahead and take further training, college or otherwise, after she was graduated. The matter of finances was discussed, Mrs. Pulaski said that Jean had some kind of an inheritance from her grandfather and gave counselor permission to talk with Mr. Angel, Mrs. Pulaski's brother, who is executor for this trust fund.

Counselor did get in touch with Mrs. Pulaski's brother and he said that Jean has some $2,300 in a trust fund, but her grandfather's will is so written that money cannot be given to Jean until she is twenty-one. However, Stan Drew, Jean's brother, has an equal amount in this fund. He, too, cannot touch this until he is twenty-one. However, he needed some money for college and Mr. Angel had borrowed the money from the bank for Stan. The money will be paid back when Stan is of age and has access to this fund. Mr. Angel said that if Jean was at all willing and showed any interest he would be glad to help her out if she wanted to go to college too.

Since Jean has been very anxious to see her mother, the plan was devised that Jean could come for a Christmas visit and stay with her uncle and his wife. She would then be allowed to visit her mother in the hospital. This met with Dr. Fleming's approval and seemed all right with Jean. The school also approved of this. Counselor wrote Mrs. Pulaski about these plans.

However, apparently in the last few weeks Mr. Pulaski, Mrs. Pulaski's second husband whom she divorced some years ago, showed up and has been living in Mrs. Pulaski's home. He has been taking her out for an occasional visit and Mrs. Pulaski says that she is planning to marry him again. Now, Mrs. Pulaski (and Mr. Pulaski, too) are extremely angry and upset that Jean is going to stay with "that man" —meaning Mr. Angel. They feel that she should be with her mother at Christmas time and that since Mr. Pulaski is in the home and Mrs. Pulaski will be permitted to visit all day on Christmas day, that Jean should stay with them. According to Mr. Pulaski, Mrs. Pulaski is adament that Jean should not see her in the hospital. Therefore, there is general confusion at this writing about the success of any Christmas visit.

Mention should be made here that even if the court had known about Mr. Pulaski living in the home, and of Mrs. Pulaski making periodic visits there, it would not have been feasible that Jean stay there. Highland School felt from their contacts with Jean that she could not tolerate an extended visit with her mother. Dr. Fleming has felt that an hour's visit was certainly long enough. And the court knowing the mother's behavior (even though it is conceivably vastly improved) could not condone a lengthy visit with the mother with the situation as it is now.

Even spending the whole day on Christmas day would not be feasible, as the situation would not be fair to the Angels. Predictably, Mrs. Pulaski will be very hostile, will rant and rave at the court for its decision, but it is felt that for Jean's mental and emotional health the court should stand firm on the plans that it has already formulated for Jean's vacation—that is, (1) Jean should stay with her uncle, and (2) that she could visit her mother once or twice for a short period of time. If Mrs. Pulaski refuses to have Jean see her in the hospital consideration might be given to Jean going to the Pulaski home on Sunday, the day she arrives, or on Tuesday (Christmas day) *if* it is convenient to her uncle.

Even though Mrs. Pulaski may play hard on Jean's sympathies and urge her to stay home it is felt that Jean should almost definitely return to Highland and stay there as long as possible. Jean may even resist this, although intellectually she knows that being home is a poor plan and she will be miserable. Jean is so full of guilt, sympathy for her mother, that she

periodically has the need to punish herself. If Jean should return home now it would be impossible for her to finish school and there would certainly be no opportunity for education beyond and for Jean to realize some of her fine goals.

Therefore, it is recommended that even though it may be a difficult adjustment for awhile that Jean return to Highland School, and that this counselor continue to keep in as close touch with Jean as she already has, as this has proven a rather satisfactory channel for Jean's progress.

JENSON
Probation Counselor

NOTE

FREUD, ANNA

Jean Drew*

There are some lessons to be learned from Jean Drew's case, for the complexity of human development as well as for . . . law in various of its aspect.

1. *The Psychotic Parent.* Jean's mother is not a neglecting indifferent, immoral, i.e., a "bad" parent in the ordinary sense of the word. On the contrary, her "moral" standards seem to be high and she verbalizes excellent attitudes toward bringing up children. Her close tie to Jean is expressed in her wish for the girl's companionship; her bitter complaints that "Jean never wanted to go any place with her or do anything with her"; the fact that "she was almost out of her mind to realize Jean did not want to return home"; her threats to kill herself if Jean does not return home; the terrible scene at the bus stop when she prostrates herself on the floor of the depot begging Jean not to go to school; and finally her commitment of herself to a mental hospital after she has lost Jean's support. It belongs to the reverse side of this parental dependence and solicitude for the child that Mrs. Pulaski also nags Jean constantly, deprives her of the normal pleasures of life, accuses her of imagined acts of misbehavior, and punishes her unreasonably and unmercifully. Jean answers to this incomprehensible mixture of demandingness, love, hate, and overbearing injustice with an ambivalence in her own feelings. She is sorry for her mother, pities her, feels needed by her, is protective and responsible for her, reveals guilt, remorse, concern, and loyalty. At the same time she also hurls invectives at her such as "I hate her," "I never want to see her again," "She is a pig and she doesn't love me and I hate her." While her repeated running away reflects the negative side, her equally frequent willingness to return home expresses the positive side of her relationship to her mother.

* Reprinted from: *The Family and the Law* by Joseph Goldstein and Jay Katz. New York: Free Press, 1965. (pp. 960–62). Reprinted by permission of the authors.

For Jean, as for many other children who grow up with a parent diagnosed as paranoid schizophrenic, the bond of affection which ties them to the ill father or mother exerts an unholy influence on their development. They are frequently "the more tolerant and understanding" in the partnership, as Jean is described to be, thereby reversing the normal roles of parent and child. The ill parents whom they cannot help loving, nevertheless cannot be respected by them, nor can they wish to grow up like them as children do normally. The abnormality of the parent's behavior is perceived by them, first dimly, in time sharply. In either case they are frightened by it, as Jean admits to be when "her mother sticks her tongue out; starts scratching her head" and has a strange look in her eyes. Like Jean, such children are also invariably at odds with the neighbors against whom the parent raves and rants in the child's hearing, as Mrs. Pulaski does, and who retaliate as openly by branding her as crazy. Faced by a mother of whose bizarre behavior Jean is deeply ashamed, and by a community with which she cannot identify in loyalty to her mother, Jean and others like her are pushed into an unhealthy social isolation. This state of affairs is summed up expressively in a sentence contained in the Intake Sheet of the Juvenile Court at the preliminary hearing after Jean's first runaway escapade: "This mother is impossible to live with and Referee has never seen an unhappier child."

2. *The Timing of State Intervention before or after the Delinquent Act.* Under these external and internal circumstances Jean spends her early years with the results showing in feelings of self-denigration, self-consciousness, uncertain tempers, and difficult relationships to contemporaries and adults expressed by coarse language, rude, noisy, "sassy" manners, and argumentativeness. On the bodily side there are weak eyes, scars remaining after childhood accidents, and a one-sided facial paralysis.

What has been submitted to within the home in childhood becomes a matter for police attention with the approach of adolescence. At this time Jean first runs away from her mother, a reaction which is repeated on three other occasions in the same and following year. Significantly for her social orientation at this time, Jean runs for help to neighbors, even turns herself in to the police voluntarily. These escapades are no more than open bids for removal from a home which has become intolerable and from a tie which she cannot break by herself in spite of everything. When these appeals fail, then—and only then—follow a police complaint about Deportment, an incident of Breaking and Entering and an attempt at suicide. By then, Jean has collected a police record of impressive length with five charges listed; her attitude is described as worse than when the Sheriff's office first had contact with her; and Delinquency finding is reaffirmed in Court.

What can be traced in the story without difficulty is the "unhappy" child's further growth into an unstable dissocial adolescent. The intervention which was asked for by her at age thirteen as a protective and preventive measure is granted finally by the Court two years later but as the result of trial for a delinquent act which, without the delay, need never have occurred.

3. *Problems in Assessment and Prediction.* There are two reports before the Court each giving a completely different assessment of the subject under examination. The Probation Counsellor, who has probed extensively into Jean's past and present, and describes her many internal and external difficulties, sees her nevertheless as a "very nice personality in a great many ways," with "many good qualities," "high moral standards," "certain ambitions for herself," i.e., somebody who "with the proper help could become a rather fine girl." The psychologist on the other hand who approaches her with a battery of tests has little or no good to say about her functioning intelligence, her social adaptation, or her emotional relationships and gives a glowing outlook on probably increasing crudity and sensuous development. Luckily, the recommendations made by both agree on removal from home and placement in a good training school, although many schools might well have been discouraged in the efforts from the outset by the findings of the tests.

In the further course of events Jean Drew's reports from school do not confirm the current belief that standardized psychological tests provide more objective personality assessments of children and allow for more accurate predictions of their future development than ordinary unaided contacts with them. On the contrary, while Jean fulfills all the expectations of her Counsellor, the unfolding of her personality in school runs counter to almost the whole range of test results. According to report from school, within eighteen months, the girl of Dull Normal level of intelligence (IQ 83, Wechsler) becomes "a very bright girl," "the best geometry student." Her "poor community relationships" and "antisocial tendencies" (California Test of Personality) do not prevent her from becoming within the same time one of the leaders on campus, captain of her cottage baseball team, and elected president of student government. Findings on the same test (C.T.P.) that she feels "just barely capable of standing on her own two feet" and her "poor common sense reasoning ability" (Wechsler) contrast sharply with the reported "high degree of insight into herself, a realistic evaluation of her home and of her past" which her letters to her mother reveal a year later. The "ambitious goals beyond her capacity" (Rorschach) are actually nearing fulfilment in her school performance. Granted that the tests gave an accurate assessment of Jean's "maladjustment in most areas" (C.T.P.) at the time of trial, what testing obviously was not able to convey for the purpose of prediction was the degree to which her inner potentialities were held in check by external pressure.

That there is in Jean an almost automatic correspondence between intellectual performance and emotional upset is borne out by the events in her second school year, when her mother's placement in a State hospital arouses her worries and guilt feelings and consequently her excellent grades of all A's except one C drop to all B's with the exception of one C.

4. *The Role of Internal and External Factors in the Production of Abnormality*. There are many children in whom the influences and conflicts of their childhood produce either early pathology or a more or less complete blocking of healthy progressive development. By the time they have reached adolescence, the interactions between internal givens and environmental influences have become so entangled and ingrained in them, that we meet them as confirmed neurotics, or delinquents, or as individuals who function intellectually, emotionally, or morally on a substandard. In these instances, no change of environ-

mental circumstances by itself will bring about internal improvements and rehabilitation can be expected only from the patient, long-term analytic disentangling of the dynamic conflicts, compromises and inhibitions within the personality.

For the purpose of understanding Jean Drew's case, it is important to note that she does not belong in this category. In spite of the severity and potential harmfulness of her environmental conditions, her inner potentialities for warm emotionality, for intellectual achievements, and for moral and social adaptation have remained latent but unharmed and were ready to unfold as soon as external pressure was removed. We may take it as a sign of the present-day insufficiency of available social services that the removal of pressure happened so late in Jean's life and that she was allowed to go as far as she did on the road toward dissociality. If the delinquent escapade of Jean's had not occurred to alert the Court, there is little doubt that one more individual would have taken the path toward suicide, promiscuity, and intellectual malfunction without any inherent necessity to end up this way.

CHAPTER II

LAW AND
PSYCHIATRY

In the preceding Chapter we examined theories of man as perceived by psychoanalysis and law. We concluded that examination with a theoretical consideration of the limitations on predicting human behavior. In this Chapter we shift our primary focus from theory to process, namely the process of deciding who should be labelled and what consequences should flow from being labelled "mentally ill or healthy"; "of sound or unsound mind"; "normal" or "abnormal"; "competent" or "incompetent"; "compos or non compos mentis"; and "sane" or "insane." In this encounter between law and psychiatry, as in any legal process, decisions of legislator, court, counsel, and expert rest on many predictions, implicit more often than explicit, about the occurence of as yet unconsummated but feared events. These predictions are cloaked in such other labels as "dangerousness to self or others," "in need of care or custody," "treatable," "releasable on or without condition," and "competent to do or not to do a particular task." We analyze this multi-labeling process in terms of its predictive assumptions, procedures, consequences, and most importantly the values it seeks to implement.

We focus first on those decisions which result in admission/commitment to, or departure/ release from, "mental institutions" and then, after examining the role of various State agencies in supervising hospitals and doctors, we focus on those procedures which, although not involving institutionalization or deinstitutionalization, do result in the deprivation or restoration of, or the disqualification or qualification for, specific rights or opportunities. As we move along this continuum of state intervention—from total institutionalization to partial supervision—we juxtapose, for purposes of analysis, the criteria and procedures for attaching these labels and consequences with the criteria and procedures for removing them. We consider, therefore, the meanings and relevance of "dangerousness," "treatability," "availability of treatment," "competency to make decisions about the need for treatment," and "voluntariness and mental state" to decisions concerned with commitment and release, admission and departure, qualification and disqualification, and deprivation and restoration.

PART ONE

PROBLEMS FOR DECISION IN THE CIVIL COMMITMENT PROCESS—THE CASE OF BERTHA RADEK

Most jurisdictions throughout the world and through the ages have had a process for designating certain people "mentally ill" and subject to the care and/or custody of the State. We begin our study of the many facets of this process by focusing on the case of Bertha Radek which arose under the following statute then in force in the District of Columbia.

A.

The Legislature Decides

Chapter 3.—INSANE PERSONS INQUESTS

D.C. Code §21-301-333 (1939)

§ 21–301. *Estates of lunatics—Accounting—Compensation—Dower.* The equity court shall have full power and authority to superintend and direct the affairs of persons *noncompos mentis*, and to appoint a committee or trustees for such persons after hearing the nearest relatives of such person, or some of them if residing within the jurisdiction of the court, and to

make such orders and decrees for the care of their persons and the management and preservation of their estates, including the collection, sale, exchange, and reinvestment of their personal estate, as to the court may seem proper.

§ 21–302. *No committee to be appointed for more than five wards. . . .*

§ 21–306. *Proceedings by Commissioners to determine mental condition.* Proceedings instituted upon petition of the commissioners of the District of

423

Columbia to determine the mental condition of alleged indigent insane persons and persons alleged to be insane, with homicidal or otherwise dangerous tendencies shall be according to the provisions of the code of law for the District of Columbia relating to lunacy proceedings.

* * *

§ 21–308. *Commission on Mental Health.* There is hereby established a Commission on Mental Health (hereinafter referred to as the commission), which shall examine alleged insane persons, inquire into the affairs of such persons, and the affairs of those persons legally liable as hereinafter provided for the support of said alleged insane persons, and make reports and recommendations to the court as to the necessity of treatment, the commitment, and payment of the expense of maintenance and treatment of such insane persons. The said commission shall be drawn from a panel of nine, who shall be appointed by the judges of the United States District Court for the District of Columbia.

Eight members of said panel shall be physicians who have been practicing medicine in the District of Columbia, and who have had not less than five years' experience in the diagnosis and treatment of mental diseases, none of whom is financially interested in the hospital in which the alleged insane person is to be confined, and the ninth member shall be a member of the bar of the District Court of the United States for the District of Columbia who has been engaged in the general active practice of law in the District of Columbia for a period of at least five years prior to his appointment. Each physician member of the panel shall be assigned by the Chief Judge of the United States District Court for the District of Columbia to active service on the commission for three months in each calendar year, and the Chief Judge may change such assignments at any time at his discretion. The two physician members on active service and the lawyer member shall constitute the commission for the purposes of this section. . . . Physician members of the commission may practice their profession during their tenure of office. The lawyer member of the commission shall be chairman thereof, and it shall be his duty, and he shall have authority to direct the proceedings and hearings in such a manner as to insure dependable ascertainment of the facts, by relevant, competent, and material evidence, and so as to insure a fair and lawful conduct and disposition of the case. The lawyer member shall devote his entire time to the work of the commission. [A]ppointments shall be for four years each. . . .

. . . The court may compel, by subpoena, the appearance of alleged insane persons before the commission for examination, and may compel the attendance of witnesses before the commission. If it shall appear to the satisfaction of the commission that the appearance before it of any alleged insane person is prevented by reason of the mental or physical condition of such person, the commission may, in its discretion, examine such person at the hospital in which such person may be confined, or, with the consent of the relatives, or of the person with whom such person may reside, at the residence of the alleged insane person.

* * *

§ 21–310. *Insanity proceedings—Application for writ de lunatico inquirendo, and for observation.* Any person with whom an alleged insane person may reside, or at whose house he may be, or the father or mother, husband or wife, brother or sister, or the child of lawful age of any such person, or the nearest relative or friend available, or the committee of such person, or an officer of any charitable institution, home, or hospital in which such person may be, or any duly accredited officer or agent of the Board of Public Welfare, or any officer authorized to make arrests in the District of Columbia who has arrested any alleged insane person under the provisions of sections 21–326 to 21–331, may apply for a writ de lunatico inquirendo and an order of commitment, or either thereof, for any alleged insane person in the District of Columbia, by filing in the United States District Court for the District of Columbia a verified petition therefor, containing a statement of the facts upon which the allegation of insanity is based.

Any person believing he has, or is about to, become mentally ill may, upon his own written application, in the discretion of the chief psychiatrist of Gallinger Municipal Hospital, enter Gallinger Municipal Hospital for observation and place himself subject to examination and commitment as hereinafter provided.

§ 21–311. *Issuance of attachment—Examination.* Upon the filing with the court of a verified petition as hereinabove provided, accompanied by the affidavits of two or more responsible residents of the District of Columbia setting forth that they believe the person therein named to be insane or of unsound mind, the length of time they have known such person, that they believe such person to be incapable of managing his own affairs, and that such person is not fit to be at large or go unrestrained, and that if such person be permitted to remain at liberty the rights of persons and property will be jeopardized or the preservation of public peace imperiled or the commission of crime rendered probable, and that such person is a fit subject for treatment by reason of his or her mental condition, the court . . . may, in its . . . discretion, issue an attachment for the immediate apprehension and detention, for preliminary examination, of such person in Saint Elizabeths Hospital and, unless found by the staff of Saint Elizabeths Hospital to be of sound mind, therein for a period not exceeding thirty days. Any person so apprehended and detained shall be given an examination within five days of his admission into Saint Elizabeths Hospital by the staff of Saint Elizabeths Hospital. The Superintendent of Saint Elizabeths Hospital is hereby authorized to receive and detain such persons, at the expense of the District of Columbia.

If any person while a patient in Gallinger Municipal Hospital being observed for his or her mental condition can not be cared for or treated adequately in said hospital or if such person be in need of treatment which can not be given properly in said hospital, then the superintendent of Gallinger Municipal Hospital may effect the transfer and temporary commitment of such person to Saint Elizabeths Hospital. . . .

Persons arrested under the provisions of sections 21–326 to 21–331 shall be detained in Gallinger Municipal Hospital pending the filing of a petition as provided in section 21–310. Such petition shall be filed within forty-eight hours after such person shall have been admitted into Gallinger Municipal Hospital, or, if such forty-eight-hour period shall expire on a Sunday or legal holiday, then not later than noon of the next succeeding day which is not a Sunday or legal holiday. The court . . . may, upon being satisfied of the sufficiency of the petition, sign an order authorizing the continued detention of said person in Gallinger Municipal Hospital and, unless found by the staff of Gallinger Municipal Hospital to be of sound mind, in Saint Elizabeths Hospital for a period not exceeding thirty days from the time of his apprehension and detention. If such petition be not filed, and such order of court obtained within the aforementioned period, the person shall be discharged forthwith. If said staff shall find that such person is of unsound mind and suitable for treatment by reason of mental illness, the superintendent of said hospital may immediately transfer such person to Saint Elizabeths Hospital, and shall report the fact of such transfer to the commission. . . .

If as a result of examination, the staff of Gallinger Municipal Hospital or Saint Elizabeths Hospital shall find that any person detained . . . is of sound mind, he shall be discharged forthwith by said Gallinger Municipal Hospital or Saint Elizabeths Hospital, and the petition, if any, shall be dismissed.

Any petition filed in the equity court for a writ de lunatico inquirendo or for an order of commitment of any alleged insane person, shall be referred by the court to the commission for report and recommendation within such time as the court may designate, not exceeding seven days, which time may be extended by the court for good cause shown, and in such event the period of temporary commitment in Saint Elizabeths Hospital may be extended by the court for such additional time as the court shall deem necessary. The commission shall examine the alleged insane person and any other person, including any suggested by the alleged insane person, his relatives, friends, or representatives, whose testimony may be relevant, competent, and material upon the issue of insanity; and the commission shall afford opportunity for hearing to any alleged insane person, his relatives, friends, or representatives. At all hearings the alleged insane person shall have the right to be represented by counsel.

The commission is hereby authorized to conduct its examination and hearings of cases elsewhere than at the offices of said commission in its discretion, according to the circumstances of the case.

If in the determination of the commission he be found not to be sane, then it shall be the duty of the commission to apply to the court for a date for a hearing. In all cases before said hearing, the said commission shall cause to be served personally upon the patient a written notice of the time and place of final hearing at least five days before the date fixed. Five days' notice of the time and place of the hearing shall in all cases be mailed to or served upon the applicant, but in case the applicant is not the husband, wife, or nearest relative, the notice shall be mailed to or served upon the husband, wife, or nearest relative, if possible. The notice shall contain a statement that if the patient desires to oppose the application for a final order of commitment, he may appear personally or by attorney at the time and place fixed for the hearing. . . . The court may in its discretion appoint an attorney or guardian *ad litem* to represent the alleged insane person at any hearing before the commission court, or before the court and jury, and shall allow the attorney or guardian *ad litem* so appointed a reasonable fee for his services. Such fees may be charged against the estate or property, if any, of the alleged insane person.

If a demand is made for a jury trial, the superintendent of Gallinger Municipal Hospital or Saint Elizabeths Hospital shall see that the patient has been given opportunity to appear personally or by attorney at the hearing and assist him in communicating with his friends, relatives, or attorney. If the superintendent shall certify that in his opinion it would be prejudicial to the health of the patient or unsafe to produce the patient at the inquiry, then such patient shall not be required to be produced.

§ 21–312. *Report to be served—Demand for jury trial—Trial.* Upon the receipt of the report and recommendation of the commission, a copy shall be served personally upon the alleged insane person, his guardian *ad litem*, or his attorney, if he has one, together with notice that he has five days within which to demand a jury trial. A demand for hearing by the court, or a demand for jury trial for the purpose of determining the sanity or insanity of the alleged insane person or by anyone in his behalf, or a jury trial may be ordered by the court upon its own motion. If demand be made for a jury trial, or such trial be ordered by the court on its own motion, the case shall be calendared for trial not more than ten days after demand for hearing by the court for a jury trial, unless the time is extended by the court. The commission, or any of the members thereof, shall be competent and compellable witnesses at any trial or hearing of an alleged insane person. In any case in which a commitment at public expense, in whole or in part, is sought, the corporation counsel or one of his assistants shall represent the petitioner unless said petitioner shall be represented by counsel of his or her own choice.

* * *

§ 21–314. *Procedure if no jury trial demanded.* If no demand be made for a jury trial, the judge holding court shall determine the sanity or insanity of said alleged insane person, but such judge may, in his discretion, require other proofs, in addition to the petition and report of the commission, or such judge may order the temporary commitment of said alleged insane person for observation or treatment for an additional period of not more than thirty days. The judge may, in his discretion, dismiss the petition notwithstanding the recommendation of the commission. If the judge be satisfied that the alleged insane person is of sound mind, he shall forthwith discharge such person and dismiss the petition.

§ 21–315. *Commitment after trial.* If the judge be satisfied that the alleged insane person is insane, or if a jury shall so find, the judge may commit the insane person as he in his discretion shall find to be for the best interests of the public and of the insane person. In case of a temporary commitment, the court may make additional temporary commitments upon further examination by, and recommendation of, the commission.

* * *

§ 21–316. *Recommendations of commission.* Recommendations of the commission must be made by the unanimous recommendation of the three members acting upon the case. If the three members of the commission be unable to agree . . . the court shall hear and determine the case, unless the alleged insane person, or someone in his behalf, shall demand a jury trial. . . .

If the commission shall agree upon a recommendation, it shall file with the court a report setting forth its findings of fact and conclusions of law and its recommendation based thereon which recommendation shall be in one of the following forms:

(A) That the person is of sound mind and should be discharged forthwith and the petition dismissed.

(B) That the mental condition of the alleged insane person is such that a definite diagnosis can not be made without further study, or that the mental in-

capacity of said person will probably be of short duration, and that said person should be further detained and committed . . . for further observation or treatment for such period of time as the court may determine, during which said time the commission shall from time to time examine said person and make a recommendation to the court as to the final disposition of the case.

(C) That the person is of unsound mind and (1) should be committed to Saint Elizabeths Hospital, or any other hospital provided by section 21–329, (a) at public expense, or (b) at the expense of those persons who are required by law, or who will agree to pay for the maintenance and treatment of said insane person, or (c) that the relatives of said insane person, mentioned in section 21–321, are able to pay a specified sum per month toward the support and maintenance of said insane person; (2) is harmless and may safely be committed to the care of his relatives or friends (naming them) who are willing to accept the custody, care, and maintenance of said insane person under conditions specified by the commission; . . . *Provided,* That there shall be filed with the court or commission a certificate executed by said administrator or his duly authorized representative, showing said person is entitled to such care and treatment and that facilities therefor are available.

§ 21–317. *Transfer of nonresident insane—Confinement of residents—Custody of harmless insane.* If an insane person be found by the commission, subject to the review of the court, not to be a resident of the District of Columbia, he may be committed by the court to Saint Elizabeths Hospital as a District of Columbia patient until such time as his residence shall have been ascertained. Upon the ascertainment of such insane person's residence in some other jurisdiction, he shall be transferred to the state of such residence. The expense of transferring such patient, including the traveling expenses of necessary attendants to insure his safe transfer, shall be borne by the District of Columbia only if the patient be indigent.

Any insane person found by the commission to have been a resident of the District of Columbia for more than one year prior to the filing of the petition, and any person found within the District of Columbia whose residence can not be ascertained, who is not in confinement on a criminal charge, may be committed by the court to, and confined in, said Saint Elizabeths Hospital, or any other hospital in said District, which, in the judgment of the commission of said District, is properly constructed and equipped for the reception and care of such persons, and the official in charge of which, for the time being, is willing to receive such persons.

* * *

If it appears that a person found to be insane is harmless and his or her relatives or committee of his or her person are willing and able properly to care for such insane person at some place or institution other than Saint Elizabeths Hospital, the judge may order that such insane person be placed in the care and custody of such relatives or such committee upon their entering into an undertaking to provide for such insane person as the court may direct.

§ 21-318. *Liability of relatives for costs of maintenance and treatment.* The father, mother, husband, wife, and adult children of an insane person, if of sufficient ability, and the committee or guardian of his or her person and estate, if his or her estate is sufficient for the purpose, shall pay the cost to the District of Columbia of his or her maintenance, including treatment in Saint Elizabeths Hospital or in any other hospital to which the insane person may be committed. . . .

* * *

§ 21-319. *Insane persons having property—Inquiry by board—Charge for care.* Whenever it appears in the case of any insane person whose insanity commenced while he was a resident of the District of Columbia that he is able to defray a portion, but not the whole of the expenses of his support and treatment in Saint Elizabeths Hospital, the board of visitors of the hospital is authorized to inquire into the facts of the case; and if it appears to the board, upon such inquiry, that such insane person has property and no family, or has more property than is required for the support of his family, then, as a condition upon which such insane person, admitted or to be admitted upon the order of the Secretary of the Interior, shall receive or continue to receive the benefits of the hospital, there shall be paid . . . such portion of his expenses in the hospital as a majority of the board shall determine to be just and reasonable, under all the circumstances.

§ 21-320. *Hearing to restore status of paroled person—Petition—Trial—Decision.* Any insane person who has been committed to Saint Elizabeths Hospital or any other hospital, and who shall have been released from such hospital as improved, or who shall have been paroled from such hospital (but who shall not have been discharged as cured), and who shall have been absent from the hospital on release or parole for a period of six months or longer, shall have the right to appear before the United States District Court for the District of Columbia for a hearing to determine the sanity and right to restoration to the status of a person of sound mind of said insane person by filing a petition therefor with the court upon a form to be provided by the commission for that purpose. It shall be the duty of the commission to make an examination of the records of Saint Elizabeths Hospital of the insane person as may be necessary to determine such questions, and if necessary have the person examined by the members of the staff of Saint

Elizabeths Hospital and to make a report and recommendation to the court. In the event the commission shall find from the records and examination that the said person is of sound mind and shall recommend to the court the restoration of said person to the status of a person of sound mind such recommendation shall be sufficient to authorize the court to enter an order declaring such person to be restored to his or her former legal status as a person of sound mind. In the event the commission shall find such person to be of unsound mind, it shall report that finding to the court. Upon the filing by the commission of a report finding such person to be of unsound mind, the insane person shall have the right to a hearing by the court or by the court and a jury. For the purpose of making the examination and observations required by this section, the commission shall have the right to examine the records and to interrogate the physicians and attendants at Saint Elizabeths Hospital or any other hospital in which such patient shall have been confined, who have had the insane person under their care, and the commission may recommend to the court the temporary recommitment of such person for said purpose. At such trial by the court or by the court and jury, an adjudication shall be made as to whether the person is of sound mind or is still of unsound mind.

§ 21-322. *Undertaking.* The court in its discretion may require the petitioner to file an undertaking with surety to be approved by the court in such amount as the court may deem proper, conditioned to save harmless the respondent by reason of costs incurred, including attorneys' fees, if any, and damages suffered by the respondent as a result of any such action.

* * *

§ 21-324. *Penalty for false petition or affidavit.* Any person who executes a verified petition or affidavit . . . by which he or she secures or attempts to secure the apprehension, detention, or restraint of any other person in the District of Columbia without probable cause for believing such person to be insane or of unsound mind, or any physician who knowingly makes any false certificate or affidavit as to the sanity or insanity of any other person, shall, upon conviction thereof, be fined not more than $500 or imprisoned not more than three years, or both.

§ 21-325. *Existing remedies preserved.* Nothing [herein] shall deprive the alleged insane person of the benefit of existing remedies to secure his release or to prove his sanity, or of any other legal remedies he may have.

§ 21-326. *Apprehension and detention by police, without warrant, of insane persons found in public places.* Any member of the Metropolitan police . . . authorized to make arrests is authorized and empowered to apprehend and detain, without warrant, any insane person or person of unsound mind found on any street, avenue, alley, or other public highway, or found in any public building or other public place within the District of Columbia; and it shall be the duty of the policeman or officer so apprehending or detaining any such person to immediately file his affidavit with the major and superintendent of said Metropolitan police that he believes said person to be insane or of unsound mind, incapable of taking care of himself or herself or his or her property, and if permitted to remain at large or to go unrestrained in the District of Columbia the rights of persons and of property will be jeopardized or the preservation of public peace imperiled and the commission of crime rendered probable: *Provided, however*, that it shall be the duty of the major and superintendent of the said Metropolitan police to forthwith notify the husband or wife or some near relative or friend of the person so apprehended and detained whose address may be known to the said major and superintendent or whose address can by reasonable inquiry be ascertained by him.

§ 21–327. *Arrest at other than public places.* The major and superintendent of said Metropolitan police is authorized to order the apprehension and detention, without warrant, of any indigent person alleged to be insane or of unsound mind or any alleged insane person of homicidal or otherwise dangerous tendencies found elsewhere in the District of Columbia than in the places mentioned in section 21–326 whenever two or more responsible residents of the District of Columbia shall make and file affidavits with said major and superintendent of the Metropolitan police setting forth that they believe the person therein named to be insane or of unsound mind, the length of time they have known such person, that they believe such person to be incapable of managing his or her own affairs, and that such person is not fit to be at large or to go unrestrained, and if such person is permitted to remain at liberty in the District of Columbia the rights of persons and of property will be jeopardized or the preservation of public peace imperiled and the commission of crime rendered probable, and that such person is a fit subject for treatment on account of his or her mental condition: *Provided,*

however, that before the major and superintendent of the said Metropolitan police shall order the apprehension and detention of any person upon the affidavits of the aforesaid residents or in case of arrest as provided in section 21–326, he shall, in addition thereto, require the certificate of at least two physicians who shall certify that they have examined the person alleged to be insane or of unsound mind, and that such person should not be allowed to remain at liberty and go unrestrained, and that such person is a fit subject for treatment on account of his or her mental condition.

§ 21–330. *Certificate by physician as to sanity or insanity—Qualifications of physician.* For the purpose of this chapter no certificate as to the sanity or the insanity of any person shall be valid which has been issued (a) by a physician who has not been regularly licensed to practice medicine in the District of Columbia . . . or (b) by a physician who is related by blood or by marriage to the person whose mental condition is in question. No certificate alleging the insanity of any person shall be valid, which has been issued by a physician who is financially interested in the hospital or asylum in which the alleged insane person is to be confined; nor, except in the case of physicians employed by the United States or the District of Columbia, shall any such certificate be valid which has been issued by a physician who is professionally or officially connected with such hospital or asylum.

§ 21–322. *Discharge of patients on bond.* If any person will give bond with sufficient security, to be approved by the United States District Court for the District of Columbia, or by any judge thereof in vacation, payable to the United States, with condition to restrain and take care of any independent or indigent insane person not charged with a breach of the peace, whether in the hospital or not, until the insane person is restored to sanity, such court or judge thereof may deliver such insane person to the party giving such bond.

§ 21–333. *Insane persons not to be confined in jail.* No insane person not charged with any breach of the peace shall ever be confined in the United States jail in the District of Columbia.

B.

The Radek Case I*

1.

A LAW ENFORCEMENT OFFICER INVOKES THE PROCESS

PETITION—21 APRIL 1954

To the United States District Court for the District of Columbia

Your petitioner Mary Spencer respectfully represents to the Court as follows:

1. That she is an officer authorized to make arrests in the District of Columbia, and

2. That Bertha Radek was apprehended in the District of Columbia on the 21st day of April 1954 and has been detained at District of Columbia General Hospital, to be observed and examined for her mental health, for the reason that:

On April 21, 1954 the Women's Bureau, Metropolitan Police Department, received a call to investigate a woman acting in a peculiar manner at the Greyhound Bus Terminal. Petitioner responded to the call. Patient was at the Terminal. When questioned, she said that she was "Aero Contact Bertha" but could give no other information about herself. She was confused and appeared to be unable to take care of herself. For her own safety and welfare, the patient was taken to District of Columbia General Hospital, where she was admitted for mental observation.

3. Your petitioner is informed, and believes and therefore avers said patient is of unsound mind, incapable of managing her own affairs; and within the purview of the statute in that case made and provided, it is not desirable to permit her to go about unsupervised, and she is a proper subject for commitment to a hospital for treatment.

Wherefore, the premises considered, your petitioner prays:

1. That the proper writ, as provided by law, may issue, and the Commission on Mental Health be directed to examine said patient and report its findings and recommendations to the Court.

2. That said patient, if found to be of unsound mind, (1) be committed to Saint Elizabeths Hospital or other hospital, or (2) if harmless, committed to relatives or friends willing to accept the care, custody and maintenance of patient. . . .

3. That a Committee of the estate be appointed.

4. And for such other relief as the best interest of the patient may require, and to the Court seem just and proper.

/s/ *Mary Spencer*

2.

THE DISTRICT COURT AND THE COMMISSION ON MENTAL HEALTH ADMINISTER THE PROCESS

a. Court Order—21 April 1954

United States District Court for the District of Columbia

Upon consideration of the petition filed in the above-entitled case, it is

ORDERED, that the writ provided by law issue and the patient is directed to appear before the Commission on Mental Health at the time and place therein designated, and it is

ORDERED, that the petition filed herein be referred forthwith to the Commission on Mental Health, acting under direction of this Court, for a report within seven days hereof . . . and it is

ORDERED, that Bertha Radek be detained in District of Columbia General Hospital, for thirty days hereafter, unless meanwhile discharged therefrom or transferred to Saint Elizabeths Hospital, and pending further order of this Court.

Judge

b. Preliminary Report—25 April 1954

To the United States District for the District of Columbia:

The Commission on Mental Health reports that they have examined Bertha Radek, patient, and find her not to be sane, and recommend that the rule to show cause issue and the matter be set down for hearing before the Commission on Mental Health and the Court set a date therefor.

c. Court Order—25 April 1954

To the Commission on Mental Health:

The rule to show cause why the above-mentioned Bertha Radek should not be adjudged to be of unsound mind has issued and the above-entitled cause

---

* This is an actual case. The name of the patient and other identifying data have been fictionalized.

shall be set for hearing before the Commission on Mental Health on the 1st day of May 1954, at 10:00 AM, and the Commission shall report its findings and recommendations to this Court, on or before the 23rd day of May 1954.

d. Rule to Show Cause—25 April 1954

United States District Court for the District of Columbia

The President of the United States

To Bertha Radek, Greeting:

You are hereby summoned to be and appear before the Commission on Mental Health, acting under the direction of this court, on the 1st day of May, A.D. 1954, at 10:00 o'clock, AM, at District of Columbia General Hospital, Psychopathic Department-Administration Building to show cause why you should not be adjudged to be of unsound mind, and why, if necessary, a committee of your person and your estate should not be appointed, as prayed in the petition filed in the above-entitled cause.

Harry M. Hull, Clerk

e. Order Assigning Guardian Ad Litem—26 April 1954

Upon consideration of the petition filed in the above entitled cause, it is by the Court

ORDERED that Andy Scott be and hereby is assigned as Guardian ad litem for the patient, Bertha Radek, and is directed to appear at the hearing before the Commission on Mental Health, and file his report within five days thereafter.

Judge

f. Certificate of Condition of Mental Health—28 April 1954

We, the undersigned, physicians of the Staff of the District of Columbia General Hospital, . . . do hereby certify that we have made an examination of the mental condition of Bertha Radek and in our judgment said Bertha Radek is of unsound mind and is a proper subject for commitment to a hospital for treatment of her mental condition.

g. Report and Recommendations of Commission on Mental Health—2 May 1954

To the United States District Court for the District of Columbia:

The Commission on Mental Health, acting under the direction of this Court, has made an examination of the mental condition of Bertha Radek and has in-

quired into her affairs; having conducted a hearing on the 1st day of May 1954, and having examined the patient, relatives, friends, and witnesses upon the issue of her mental condition and their ability to pay the expenses of her maintenance and treatment in a hospital, and reports its findings to be:

1. That Bertha Radek is of unsound mind, suffering from Schizophrenia (Paranoid Type),[1] is incapable of managing her own affairs, and should be committed to a hospital for treatment of her mental condition.

2. That Bertha Radek is not a resident of the District of Columbia. . . .

3. That Bertha Radek is reported to have approximately Seventy Dollars ($70.) with the property Clerk at D. C. General Hospital.

4. Present at the hearing were: Mary Spencer, Womens Bureau, Metropolitan Police Department, who testified the patient was apprehended at the Greyhound Bus Station and because of her actions felt she needed hospitalization for her own protection and welfare, and Mrs. Singleton, Interstate Services, Department of Public Health, who testified the patient has no fixed address and is not a resident of the District of Columbia; that she has a history of previous hospitalization in a New Jersey mental hospital, and further effort will be made to ascertain the State of her residence and return her thereto. Andy Scott, Esquire, testified he is the Court appointed Guardian *ad litem* and testified he interviewed patient previous to the hearing and she claims to have a son, Igor Radek, residing with his father in New Jersey [and] a mother residing in Pennsylvania. The patient was informed that the doctors are of opinion she is mentally ill and should stay in the hospital; however if any of her relatives are able to make satisfactory arrangements for her care and supervision elsewhere, such a plan would be given consideration; meanwhile she will be transferred to Saint Elizabeths

---

1. "Schizophrenic Reactions—This term is synonymous with the formerly used term dementia praecox. It represents a group of psychotic reactions characterized by fundamental disturbances in reality relationships and concept formations, with effective, behavioral, and intellectual disturbances in varying degrees and mixtures. The disorders are marked by strong tendency to retreat from reality, by emotional disharmony, unpredictable disturbances in stream of thought, regressive behavior, and in some, by a tendency to "deterioration." The predominant symptomatology will be the determining factor in classifying such patients into types.

Schizophrenic Reaction, paranoid type—This type of reaction is characterized by autistic, unrealistic thinking, with mental content composed chiefly of delusions of persecution, and/or of grandeur, ideas of reference, and often hallucinations. It is often characterized by unpredictable behavior, with a fairly constant attitude of hostility and aggression. Excessive religiosity may be present with or without delusions of persecution. There may be an expansive delusional system of omnipotence, genius, or special ability." [American Psychiatric Association: *Diagnostic and Statistical Manual—Mental Disorders* (1952)].

Hospital where she may receive care and attention until the State of her residence is ascertained and she may be returned thereto.

WHEREFORE, The Commission on Mental Health recommends to the Court as follows:

1. That Bertha Radek be adjudged and decreed to be of unsound mind.

2. That Bertha Radek be committed to Saint Elizabeths Hospital for maintenance and treatment of her mental condition until such time as the State of her residence is ascertained and she may be returned thereto.

* * *

NOTICE

To *Bertha Radek*   Commission on Mental
Health

You have, or any one in your behalf has, FIVE days from the day of service of a copy of this Report and Recommendation of the Commission on Mental Health upon you, within which to demand a trial by jury or a hearing by the Court to determine the issue of your insanity.

3.

REPORT BY THE GUARDIAN FOR THE PATIENT—5 MAY 1954

I, Andy Scott, appointed by the Court as Guardian attended the hearing . . . and I do concur in the recommendation made by the Commission on Mental Health.

Report of Guardian Ad Litem

It is my opinion that the patient is in some way mentally unbalanced. This opinion is based on a two-hour interview with the patient. During our lengthy conversation, said patient told me that, for some time, she has been receiving telepathic messages from certain persons. This experience is denominated, in her language, "airings on Bertha." She has received "airings" from, among other people, President Eisenhower. Moreover, she talked at great length about her "scientific theory of color psychology." Pursuant to that "theory," the patient makes conclusions about people's emotions from the color which she sees in their faces—viz., an orange face means desire. Although I am untrained in the medical sciences, her "airings" and her "color psychology" evidence mental unbalance to me.

Were it not for the aforementioned irregularities, the patient might have appeared rational to me. However, she does exhibit some abnormal concern for her well-being in that, while she does not believe she is mentally ill, she "likes" the hospital and feels that it would be "better" if she were to stay there "for awhile."

The fact that none of her relatives have come forward to date is, perhaps, troublesome. I have sent a wire to her mother, to her stepfather, and to her former husband in an effort to determine their opinion in this matter.

I have had a telephone response from the present wife of Mr. Radek. She confirmed the fact that the patient has been in a Pennsylvania mental hospital on three different occasions in the past ten years; and that the patient has a 15-year-old son living with his father. I was also advised by the present Mrs. Radek that the patient has apparently been getting along extremely well since her last release from a Pennsylvania mental hospital in April, 1953, and that her present setback might be attributed to the fact that she was precipitously fired last month from her job with Public Finance Corp.

The patient's mother and stepfather have not contacted me as yet in response to my wires to them.

The patient advised me that she has a brother who is an officer in the U.S. Navy. . . .

In conclusion, it is my opinion that the patient needs psychiatric treatment and that her safety and well-being might be imperilled if she were left without care.

Andy Scott
Guardian ad litem

4.

DECREE OF ADJUDICATION AND COMMITMENT—9 MAY 1954

This matter coming on to be heard by the Court, considering the petition filed herein and the report and recommendations of the Commission on Mental Health, who, having made an examination of the mental condition of the patient, and having conducted a hearing, at which the patient, her relatives, friends and witnesses testified and were examined upon the issue of her mental condition and ability to pay the expense of maintenance and treatment in a hospital, found the patient to be of unsound mind and in need of treatment in a hospital for her mental condition; and no demand for a trial by a jury or further hearing by the Court having been filed within five days as provided by law; it is by the Court,

ADJUDGED and DECREED:

1. That Bertha Radek is of unsound mind and is hereby committed to Saint Elizabeths Hospital until such time as she may be safely discharged therefrom or returned to the State of her residence.

2. That the expense of the maintenance and treatment of Bertha Radek in Saint Elizabeths Hospital shall be borne in accordance with the provisions of Public Law 724.

Guardian ad litem: Judge

5.

A HOSPITAL ADMINISTERS THE COURT DECISION AND KEEPS ITSELF "INFORMED" OF WHAT AND WHY?

a. Admission Note—9 May 1954

This 36-year-old, divorced, white woman, Catholic, native of Pennsylvania, high school education, no definite occupation, was admitted to Saint Elizabeths Hospital on May 9, 1954 as a transfer from the District of Columbia General Hospital.

The patient indicates that in March of this year she was fired from her job. At that time she began to get "thoughts" and made an "aerial contact." These thoughts were poured on her by some machine done by her enemies. She went to the church and finally decided to come to Washington to see Congress about a new discovery of hers called "Psychological Face Coloring." According to this theory, people have color tints on their face and by these different tints one can gauge their characteristics. For example, orange means desire; white is force; beige is self-consciousness. She feels that this discovery will be a boon to mankind. She does not understand just quite how, but she is sure that Congress in their wise judgment can utilize it and can make a great contribution to mankind.

She gives a history of being in a Pennsylvania State Hospital two times. Once from February 1946 to October 1946 and the second time from December 1950 to April of 1953. She says that at this time she had been mentally disturbed due to her difficulties with her husband and she was quite depressed and even thought of suicide. She is now divorced from her husband, having been divorced since June of 1948. She has a son 15 years of age who lives with his father. She insists that the father has kidnapped the boy. She herself has been living with her mother since her discharge from the Pennsylvania State Hospital. There is no history of antisocial behavior or of excessive drinking. Her past history is negative for convulsions or any physical illness. Her last menstrual period was April 19 and it was a normal period.

Throughout the interview the patient was cooperative and pleasant. She had a kind of Christ-like look about her. Affect, would I assume, be described as flat, yet there was something warm and tender about her that led one to believe that her mission was real and that she was motivated by strong needs to help mankind. She expressed the above-described delusions. There is certainly no evidence of depression or suicidal preoccupation now. She is precisely oriented in all spheres. Her memory is excellent. In fact, she goes into great detail and tends to be circumstantial in her description of anything, giving precise dates, times, and places. She has no insight at all into the fact that she is mentally ill, although she does recognize that she has been mentally ill in the past.

Physical examination will follow.

Diagnostic Impression: Schizophrenic Reaction. Paranoid Type.

Letter should be sent to the Pennsylvania State Hospital for information.

b. Abstract from Pennsylvania State Hospital Record

Patient admitted to Pennsylvania State Hospital on December 25, 1950 on a regular order of certification. The reason for this admission was because of confusion and paranoid ideas. The history indicated a previous admission to this hospital from August 10, 1945 to September 22, 1945. She was released on convalescent status and returned February 22, 1946 to October 11, 1946. This patient's family history is negative for nervous and mental disorders. She was born March 30, 1917 in Pennsylvania. Completed high school at the age of 17 or 18 and did some college work in 1942, majoring in English. She married Igor Radek in 1937 and divorced in 1948. There was one son of this union. Patient was in an automobile accident in 1943 and although nothing could be found wrong with patient, the case was brought to court and lasted for two years, as the patient had numerous complaints, although no physical basis was found for these. Prior to her first admission here in 1945, patient made a suicidal attempt. Diagnosis was made of Manic Depressive Psychosis, Hypomanic Type.[2] She improved with ECT [Electroconvulsive treatments] symptomatically, was finally released on October 11, 1946 and discharged from our records October 11, 1947.

In the interim period patient apparently moved about the country aimlessly and had sixteen different addresses during the two years prior to her second admission. She expressed the idea that her husband and various lawyers were in "communist collusion" and made several attempts to regain the custody of her child who was with her husband. On admission she was overtalkative, circumstantial, had a flat affect

---

[2.] "Psychotic Disorders—These disorders are characterized by a varying degree of personality disintegration and failure to test and evaluate correctly external reality in various spheres. In addition, individuals with such disorders fail in their ability to relate themselves effectively to other people or to their own work.

Manic depressive reactions—These groups comprise the psychotic reactions which fundamentally are marked by severe mood swings, and a tendency to remission and recurrence. Various accessory symptoms such as illusions, delusions, and hallucinations may be added to the fundamental affective alteration.

Manic depressive reaction is synonymous with the term manic depressive psychosis. The reaction will be further classified into the appropriate one of the following types: manic, depressed, or other." [American Psychiatric Association: *Diagnostic and Statistical Manual—Mental Disorders* (1952)].

and talked in detail regarding her difficulties with her child and husband. She refused to eat and had to be tube fed for several days. She continued paranoid and expressed ideas of grandeur. She finally improved on Thorazine medication [a tranquilizer] and was allowed to leave the hospital on April 13, 1953. The diagnosis made during this admission was changed to Dementia Praecox, Mixed Type.[3] She was finally discharged from our records on July 13, 1953.

I. Rowan, M.D.

c. Doctors' and Nurses' Progress Notes—9 May 1954 to 11 April 1955

9 May 1954—36-year-old nonviolent Catholic who came to see Congress about her great finding. Patient very delusional, oriented, flat, pleasant. Has history of two previous long hospitalizations at Pennsylvania State Hospital. Impression: Paranoid Schizophrenic.

J. Kelly, M.D.

10 May 1954—Mrs. Radek rested well during the night, pleasant and co-operative on arising in AM. Neat in appearance and tidy in toilet habits. Urine specimen collected.

R. Babcock, R.N.

—Quiet, co-operative, appetite good, neat and tidy in appearance and habits, does not discuss her ideas.

L. Beck, R.N.

—Neat in appearance, tidy in habits, very pleasant. Co-operative with routine. Spends her evenings reading. Appetite good.

E. Wall. R.N.

15 May 1954—Very co-operative, pleasant, cares for own needs, neat in appearance, tidy in habits. Very seclusive, spends her evenings reading. Appetite good. Likes to go to other wards dancing. Sleeps well on this shift.

E. Wall, R.N.

17 May 1954—Extremely neat and tidy in appearance and habits. Keeps to herself. Does not socialize much with fellow patients. Appetite good.

L. Beck, R.N.

[3.] This is now called: "Schizophrenic reaction, chronic undifferentiated type—The chronic schizophrenic reactions exhibit a mixed symptomatology, and when the reactions cannot be classified in any of the more clearly defined types, it will be placed in this group. Patients presenting definite schizophrenic thought, affect, and behavior beyond that of the schizoid personality, but not classifiable as any other type of schizophrenic reaction, will also be placed in this group. This includes the so-called 'latent,' 'incipient,' and 'pre-psychotic' schizophrenic reactions."
[American Psychiatric Association: *Diagnostic and Statistical Manual—Mental Disorders* (1952)].

Competency Statement—19 May 1954

Physician in Charge, please complete and sign the statement in Part B concerning the competency of the payee to endorse the described check or money order drawn payable to

Bertha Radek
(Name of Patient)

Amount: $10.00

Name and address of drawer   Charles Maddox
(Gratuity from
John Bartok)

Name and location of Bank   First National Bank
Jersey City, N.J.

In my opinion the patient is medically competent to endorse the above described instrument.

Dr. Prentiss

24 May 1954—Mrs. Radek is neat in appearance, tidy in habits, appetite very good. Helps with ward cleaning, has very queer ideas of being Christ in disguise. Talks with other patients. Co-operative and pleasant.

M. Grove, R.N.

—Mrs. Radek sleeps well at night, slow on arising in AM. Cares for her personal needs. Neat in appearance and tidy in toilet habits. Co-operative with ward routines. Mingles well with fellow patients.

R. Babcock, R.N.

30 May 1954—Bertha is a charming paranoid girl of 36, separated, one child: intellectual type, very grandiose, wants to be president, preoccupied with telepathy and "face coloring"; gets more bizarre by the minute. Should be on Thorazine fairly soon; is in Jane Kelly's research project as a control. Start her whenever you feel indicated, however. Would withhold privileges until less pressure about getting to the president.

J. Smith, M.D.

—Co-operative, does not discuss her ideas, pleasant.

E. Jones, R.N.

—Mrs. Radek admitted to ward from Adm. suite. Very pleasant, co-operative with routine, ate very well, spent the evening reading and watching TV—offered no complaints.

E. Wall, R.N.

1 June 1954—Mrs. Radek remains very quiet and withdrawn—very pleasant to fellow patients and employees—co-operative with routine—appetite good—neat in appearance—tidy in habits. Spends her evenings reading or just watching TV. Does no work of any kind.

E. Wall, R.N.

—Mrs. Radek sleeps well at night—arises a little slow in AM pleasant and co-operative.

V. Stone, R.N.

8 June 1954—Mrs. Radek is a very quiet person who does not mix with the other patients. She cares for her personal hygiene and is very neat in appearance.

M. Grove, R.N.

—Mrs. Radek is very quiet and withdrawn but pleasant to fellow patients and employees—very neat in appearance and tidy in habits—appetite good—spends her evenings reading or watching TV. No visitors.

E. Wall, R.N.

—Mrs. Radek sleeps well at night, pleasant and co-operative on arising. Cares for her personal needs. Neat in appearance and tidy in toilet habits. Quiet and withdrawn.

R. Babcock, R.N.

15 June 1954—Very quiet and withdrawn. Cares well for her needs and helps clean the sun room in the mornings.

M. Grove, R.N.

—Mrs. Radek is tidy in habits and appearance—friendly with others—talks of her being president of U.S.A.—appetite good—sleeps well—has no visitors.

L. Beck, R.N.

—Mrs. Radek remains seclusive—pleasant when spoken to—sleeps well—neat in habits and appearance—co-operative with ward routine.

M. Louis, R.N.

29 June 1954—Mrs. Radek is very neat in appearance —tidy in habits, very quiet. Does not mix with fellow patients—walks the hall a lot—continues to say she wants to get out of here—appetite good—sleeps well —no visitors.

E. Wall, R.N.

—Sleeps well—slow on arising—quiet and co-operative.

V. Stone, R.N.

3 July 1954—Thorazine Therapy. This patient who entered on May 9, 1954 for a month was a subject in the recent psychological study and fell into the control group and hence received no ataractic [tranquilizing] therapy. She is obviously schizophrenic and at times mildly hostile. She has a well-systematized preoccupation having to do with a certain psychological system which she has invented. This has to do with the complexion on peoples' faces in which subtle changes in coloration have great meaning. She was placed on thorazine on June 24, 1954 and has reached the dosage of 200 milligrams t.i.d.

[Three times a day.] In the brief period since that time no significant change appears to have occurred.

Dr. Jones

3 July 1954—The following is a letter written by the patient to President Dwight D. Eisenhower, White House, Washington, D.C.:

> "St. Elizabeth's Hospital
> Washington, D.C.
> June 23, 1954
>
> Dear Ikey Kikey,
>   Hello and how are you? I've been in Washington, D.C. since April 20, 1954 and haven't been able to see you.
>   I am quite angry at you for not ever answering my letters from Pennsylvania now I'm in this hospital and want to get out.
>   You are really naughty for not at least inquiring about "Psychological Face Coloring" facts, now that I am here in Washington, D.C. I'd like to talk to you personally.
>   Will you please be nice and send a note and car for me?
>   I hope you are well and all is well with you.
>
> Sincerely,
> "Bertha"

Dr. Murphy

4 July 1954—Mrs. Radek has expressed ideas of giving up the thought of being "the first woman president"—she is going to try to get literature on abstract thinking and write a paper on speaking and music—seems to ponder over atomic energy—her son and her brother—expresses verbally her desire to leave hospital. Still wants to have an interview with President Eisenhower. Is drawn at times, but seems to express herself more now. Seems well adjusted to ward routine. Doesn't approve of taking medication. Eats well.

R. Main, R.N.

5 July 1954—Mrs. Radek neat in appearance and habits—pleasant and co-operative with routine—does not mix with fellow patients—takes no part in ward affairs—appetite good—sleeps well.

E. Wall, R.N.

—Mrs. Radek apparently sleeps well during the night, very quiet and seclusive on arising in the AM—cares for own needs—neat and tidy in habits and personal appearance.

L. White, R.N.

12 July 1954—Mrs. Radek is pleasant and co-operative with ward routines. Cares for her personal needs. Neat and tidy in appearance and habits. Appetite good.

R. Babcock, R.N.

—Mrs. Radek sleeps well—pleasant upon rising—tidy in habits—neat in appearance.

M. Grove, R.N.

13 July 1954—GROUND PRIVILEGES. In view of this patient's recent improvement, co-operative ward adjustment, and satisfactory behavior on accompanied privileges, as well as satisfactory indication of a reliable desire to co-operate with the regulations involved, five PM ground privileges are being granted, with later extension to nine PM, depending upon a satisfactory adjustment.

Dr. Murphy

17 July 1954—Mrs. Radek is very neat in appearance, caring for her own needs. She remains by herself most of the day. Uses her privilege card frequently and seems to enjoy being out on the grounds. Expresses herself quite freely in group therapy stating she doesn't understand why she is here and that she wants to write to her senator. Very friendly and free with conversation toward nursing personnel. Appetite good.

S. Nightingale, R.N.

19 July 1954—Mrs. Radek talks more freely with personnel—is neat in appearance and habits—stays very much to herself—has no visitors—eats well and retires very early.

E. Wall, R.N.

—Mrs. Radek is a very good sleeper—up in the AM—cares for her own needs—have no complaints at present.

M. Grove, R.N.

Psychiatric Case Study

Dr. Blum
July 20, 1954

This 36-year-old divorced white woman was admitted to Saint Elizabeths Hospital on May 9, 1954, by transfer from the District of Columbia General Hospital where she was admitted by the Women's Bureau on April 21, 1954.

Family History

The patient's father is John Bartok, who is now 63 years old and living in Jersey City where he is a "Social Secretary." Previously he had owned a tavern from 1930 to 1943. Her mother is 56 years old and lives with her third husband on a chicken farm in Pennsylvania. Her parents were divorced when she was quite young and her mother remarried when she was about ten. She has never been very close to her father but in recent years she has come to an understanding with him and now feels friendly toward him. She describes her mother as a domineering person, adding, "at least she dominates me. I can't think clearly and independently when I am with her." She

apparently got along well with her first stepfather who had a grocery or produce store in Philadelphia; however, she has had trouble with her second stepfather (to the point of fisticuffs) whom her mother married after the patient was grown. She has one stepbrother more than ten years her junior whom she brought up from the age of 9 until he was 17 and went to college. She is apparently quite close to him and calls him her "big boy." There is no history of alcoholism or mental illness in the family.

Personal History

The patient was born on April 30, 1918, in Philadelphia where she grew up. She states that she was a very large baby, weighing 12 pounds at birth and that she developed normally. She enjoyed school and got along well with the other children. She graduated from high school and then took a special course in electrolysis school. In 1942, after she was married, she attended college for a while at University of Pennsylvania, majoring in English. She has had many different jobs, such as cashier, waitress, hostess, sales clerk in a five-and-ten, and she ran her own electrolysis office in Nevada while she was getting her divorce. In general she likes restaurant work best. She gives as the reason for her frequent job changes "litigations." Her last job was as a cashier in a finance company in Boston last summer. She was fired from this job after about three months when she gave her supervisor her papers on "Psychological Face Coloring," and asked for a raise. She has apparently done a great deal of moving about in the past five or ten years and has a very involved story about these moves, how she had an apartment of her own, then she stored her furniture, moved to another city, tried to get her furniture back, lived with her mother for a while until she got into a fight with her stepfather, lived with friends, et cetera.

Her menstrual periods began when she was 12 and a half years old and are regular. She occasionally has cramps and at one time was told that she had a tumor on her womb for which her doctor treated her until it went away. She started dating when she was 15 years old and in 1937 when she was 19 or 20 she married Igor Radek, a textile colorist. They have one child, a boy now 15, who is living with his father and a stepmother. After her marriage while she was a student at University of Pennsylvania she had a love affair with one of her professors which lasted from 1943 to 1945. It was in her relationship with this professor that she learned about psychological face coloring. She was having marital difficulties at this time and these, together with the shock of her sudden knowledge about face coloring, was enough, as she says, "to throw me off my rocker." She was in Pennsylvania State Hospital for about a year and when she was discharged she began divorce proceedings against her husband. She states that she left him on July 16,

1947, their tenth wedding anniversary, adding, "I was being very dramatic." She moved to Nevada with her son where she obtained her divorce and she says was granted "entire influence and custody" over her son; however, her husband somehow kidnapped her son from her and she has been trying ever since without success to get him back.

Although the patient was brought up in the Catholic faith she now states that she is a Protestant and attends church frequently. She enjoys knitting and reading and would like to go back to college so that she could get her B.A. Degree. She does not use alcohol and has never been arrested. She describes herself as "nice," and says that she is not particularly shy and not particularly outgoing. She says she is a business woman and that she gets along well with people.

The patient has had two previous hospitalizations for mental illness. The first was from the end of 1945 until September of 1946, at the Pennsylvania State Hospital. The reasons that she gives for this hospitalization are noted above. Her second admission was from November 1950 until March 1953. She gives as the reason for her second hospitalization "litigations," explaining that a Jewish lawyer who had obtained her divorce for her now seemed to be in league with her husband against her. She deduced from this that the lawyer must be a Communist and because she had known other Jewish lawyers who had treated her rudely she concluded that all Jews were Communists. She went with this information to an official in the Justice Department in Pennsylvania and he had her hospitalized, although she thought at the time that she was being placed in the hospital so that they could help her to get her son back. Prior to her first hospitalization she was depressed and had made a suicidal attempt. She felt that she was mentally ill and that that hospitalization was justified but that the second hospitalization was entirely unjustified.

Present Illness

Last summer after her discharge from Pennsylvania State Hospital she lived for a while with her mother where she started to rewrite her papers on "Psychological Face Coloring," her first papers having been stolen from her by the President of the Foundation for Cultural Relations between Poland and the United States. After a fight with her stepfather she left her mother and moved to Boston where she had a job for three months with a finance company. When she lost her job she was not particularly concerned because she had just realized that she was in "aerial contact" with some source whose "tones" she was able to hear. She traveled to Hartford where she told a number of people about her ideas on psychological face coloring so that if her papers disappeared once more it could not be said that this was a Russian discovery. She thought that psychological face coloring would be of crucial importance in foreign diplomacy and so on April 20, she traveled by bus to Washington in order to present her ideas to Congress. When she got to Washington she discovered that her period had started and that the back of her dress was badly stained. She went to the Greyhound Bus Terminal in order to clean up and somehow could not decide what to do and so stayed at the terminal all day and into the night. Finally a colored policewoman came and took her to the District of Columbia General Hospital for reasons unknown to her.

At the District of Columbia General Hospital she stated that she had come to talk to Congressmen about something that she had come to definite conclusions about, namely that we should have world peace. She felt that she had some secret information which might be of help to people and that it was her duty as a citizen to inform Congress of it. Her facial expression was rigid.

Mental Examination

Course in Hospital

On the ward she has been co-operative and fairly pleasant but quite seclusive. At first she was rather impulsive in her behavior but this has improved since thorazine was started although she has lost none of her delusions.

Formal Mental Examination

General Appearance and Behavior: The patient is a very attractive woman who is neatly dressed and made up. She is very alert and talks excitedly but exhibits no unusual activity or mannerisms.

Speech: Her speech is clear, coherent, and relevant but under some pressure and she will not be diverted in her story in order to answer specific questions. She is very circumstantial, giving minute details and specific dates and addresses.

Emotional Reaction: The patient's affect is very bland with frequent smiling, both appropriate and inappropriate, and inappropriate laughter. She appears quite cheerful at the present time although she is eager to leave the hospital in order to carry out her plans.

Abnormal Mental Content or Trends: The patient is apparently auditorily hallucinated and is very delusional with grandiose ideas predominating but with some persecutory ideas too. The fact that she hears "tones" because of being in aerial contact with others has been mentioned above as well as her special knowledge of the science of psychological face coloring. She feels that she is especially blessed with this knowledge and because she feels that this knowledge is so important for world peace she believes that she should be President instead of Eisenhower. She states, "If there is ever going to be a woman President, I'm certainly the one for the job," and she is eager to leave so that she can start her campaign. She admits that to some this may seem like a fantastic or even "crazy" idea but it does not seem so to her. She believes that someone has stolen her notebook on Psychological Face Coloring and that it may be attributed to the Russians. She also thinks that her husband and various Jewish lawyers are in Communistic collusion against her; however, she seems remarkably unconcerned over these ideas.

Mental Grasp and Capacity: Attention and comprehension are good. Memory seems very good and she is precisely oriented. Intellectual functioning seems to be on a normal or superior level. Although she realizes that she has been mentally ill in the past she has absolutely no insight into her present condition and her judgment seems very poor.

26 July 1954—Mrs. Radek is neat in appearances—tidy in habits—appetite good—speech very clear—talks freely with patients and personnel—will help with ward cleaning now and then—sleeps well.

3 August 1954—37-year-old intelligent friendly paranoid schizophrenic—sick off and on since 1948 in hospitals in Pennsylvania—has theory of "psychological face coloring" and would like to start a class for the doctors here—also wants to be President. Patient has held ground pretty well and promises to make no attempt to contact the President. No relatives in D.C. but father is to visit this month. A-Z test (pregnancy) positive but patient denies possibility.

Dr. Blum

—Mrs. Radek is very neat in appearance, caring very well for her own needs. She is co-operative with ward routine and friendly with patients and personnel. Has 9:00 PM parole which she uses very wisely. She is a pleasant person, frequently asks questions pertaining to psychiatry. Still expresses some delusional ideas such as her "theory on psychological face coloring." Appetite good. Transferred to Ward 4.

S. Nightingale, R.N.

—Mrs. Radek is pleasant and agreeable, operated the patients elevator this PM.

A. Olds, R.N.

3 August 1954—

Admission Conference

PRESENT: DOCTORS SORELLINO and MADDOX

This is an attractive, divorced 36-year-old white female patient. In a calm manner she immediately begins discussing her case and there is considerable spontaneous production. She came to Washington from Hartford in order to talk to "Representatives in Congress about Psychological Face Coloring." She

states that she discovered that it is now, "An open secret—it is one of the scientific studies in the humanities. It concerned color reaction on the face of an individual. It all came to me when I was in love. I had a husband and a love affair at the same time." She wrote a paper on the subject and left it with Dr. Grant at D.C. General. She wants the physicians here to help her to get this paper in order that she may show it to the members of Congress and to the President of the United States. She thinks the President may like to use this as a secret weapon. She wants to be a "science" doctor and wants the physicians to help her to get an appropriation to study "Psychological Face Coloring" further. She has been receiving Thorazine therapy but the delusions she expressed on admission are still quite prominent. As it appears her illness will be a long one, she should be transferred out of the service.

DIAGNOSIS: 22.1 SCHIZOPHRENIC REACTION. HEBEPHRENIC TYPE.[4]

Dr. Lisanti

4 August 1954—Mrs. Radek seems to sleep well, pleasant and co-operative in AM.

L. White, R.N.

5 August 1954—Adjusting well to ward.

N. Creighton, R.N.

15 August 1954—Mrs. Radek is a very pleasant person, who is co-operative, and helps with ward routine—she forgets to come in for 3 PM medication at times but makes no complaint about her medication. She runs the elevator for the patients in the afternoon—goes to group therapy, has 9 PM privileges, likes to take walks around the grounds. She is neat, habits good, converses well and easy, like group conversations on the ward—offers no physical complaints, eating habits good, seems to have trouble getting to sleep at nights, walks around and around for an hour or so, goes willingly to bed when attendant says good night.

A. Olds, R.N.

—*TRANSFER.* Today, in accordance with appropriate recommendation, this patient was transferred to William A. White Service.

Dr. Harold

—Received on WAW-5 this AM—Mrs. Radek is pleasant, quiet and co-operative with our routine—anxious to talk with doctor.

E. Walters, R.N.

[4.] "Schizophrenic reaction, hebephrenic type. These reactions are characterized by shallow, inappropriate affect, unpredictable giggling, silly behavior and mannerisms, delusions, often of a somatic nature, hallucinations, and regressive behavior." [American Psychiatric Association: *Diagnostic and Statistical Manual—Mental Disorders* (1952)].

—Mrs. Radek restful—very pleasant this AM.

M. Lester, R.N.

16 August 1954—Mrs. Radek appears very pleasant —has been co-operative with ward routine. Converses freely with fellow patients and personnel. No complaints.

A. Davis, R.N.

19 August 1954—Patient's handbag was ransacked by Joan Robinson who took a pair of contact lenses and lost one of the lenses.

B. Jarecki, R.N.

21 August 1954—Mrs. Radek is very neat and clean in appearance and cares for her own needs. Her hair especially is kept looking nice. She has a charming and quiet-spoken personality and manner. She is co-operative with the ward routine, although she does not offer to assist with the ward cleaning. She seems to enjoy reading books especially and conversing at fairly long intervals occasionally with certain other patients. She has expressed a "let-down" feeling at being transferred from Dix building to this building and this ward. She uses her 9:00 PM parole frequently. She eats little here.

S. Caplan, R.N.

15 September 1954—Mrs. Radek has been very pleasant and usually co-operative. She likes to leave the ward before 9:00 AM and usually tries to. She takes her medications well and has a good appetite. Mrs. Radek is neat in appearance. She goes to group therapy and Psychodrama and frequently uses her parole (9:00 PM).

B. Norton, R.N.

28 September 1954—Mrs. Radek is very neat and cares for her own personal needs. She sometimes has to be reminded to make her bed and often slips off the ward before doing her AM chore of helping to clean the ward. Does not associate with other patients on ward—stays outside most of the day— states she is pleased with her new job in the employees cafeteria—enjoys group therapy, dance therapy and psychodrama. Offers no physical complaints, appetite good.

M. Baxter, R.N.

10 November 1954—Mrs. Radek—cares for own needs—pleasant and co-operative. Patient is off the ward most of the day.

E. Bartlett, R.N.

—Received on ward at 9:00 PM—pleasant and co-operative.

H. Campbell, R.N.

18 November 1954—Mrs. Radek—when she left the ward this AM she stated she was going in town—instead she went to the White House—was sent for by two employees and transferred to Ward 7. Order of Dr. Small.

L. Rowe, R.N.

—Received on WAW-7—quiet and co-operative at this time. States "I am O.K. but the president is very undemocratic, he refused to see me."

J. First, R.N.

—Transferred to WAW-5 by order of Dr. Small.

J. First, R.N.

—This patient, formerly on WAW-7, this morning had a pass to go shopping but instead went to the White House, engaged the man at the gate in conversation, stating she had come to see the President about "federalized education and face color." She was not disturbing. The Secret Service telephoned the Hospital asking if the patient would be able to come back by herself but instead we sent for her. The patient thanked the attendants for bringing her back because she did not want to come home in the rain. Interviewed later, she was smoothing over about what she had done, stating the President had not answered her letter in 1953 so she thought she would call on him and this was a particularly good time now that the Queen is here. After she had talked awhile, she admitted that a voice would pass through the right side of her head, over her ear, and say Ike, Ike, Ike. Apparently these hallucinations are not controlling in her immediate environment. The patient is overapologetic and at the end of the interview said "I'm sorry I hurt your feelings." She at first was on WAW-7 but is being transferred to WAW-5 and privileges are being withheld. The patient for several weeks has done very well working in the employees' cafeteria.

Contact was made by Sam Hammer, Special Agent, Protective Research Section, Secret Service.

Dr. Small

5 January 1955—Very neat and tidy. Goes to dance therapy to sew costumes. Talks to personnel. Likes to go to group therapy.

R. Caplan, R.N.

—Glad to be chairlady. Has a tendency to think everyone should do what she wants done now. Very neat and tidy. Enjoys being on committees. Went to town with friend to shop.

R. Caplan, R.N.

29 January 1955—

Recommendation for Return of Ground Privileges

This patient since having her ground privileges and city privileges removed November 18, 1954, has shown marked improvement in her condition. She works in the ward cafeteria, takes an active part in ward self-government and in the patients' building council, is well liked and has been made "patient of the month." She is correctly oriented at the present time, shows no evidence of delusions or hallucinations. She avers that she will never go near the White House again. No delusional content is present now. I believe the patient can continue to handle ground privileges and will not leave without permission or annoy Federal officials again. The patient's accent on her discovery about face coloring remains in the content but is beneath the surface and is not causing her to do anything unusual at the present time. I believe her condition warrants the return of ground privileges. A letter has been sent to the White House Secret Service stating our intention of returning ground privileges to this patient and asking if they have any objection.

DIAGNOSIS: 22.1 SCHIZOPHRENIC REACTION. HEBEPHRENIC TYPE

RECOMMENDATION: Return of ground privileges.

Dr. Small

4 February 1955—Likes helping Mrs. Ketch for the play. Is very neat and tidy. Appears on the surface to be quite independent of others. Does not seem to associate with other patients on ward very much. Thinks she will get her ground privileges back soon. Wished everyone a Happy New Year. Spends much time in dance therapy for the play. Works in cafeteria.

R. Caplan, R.N.

23 February 1955—Mrs. Radek is very neat in appearance and personal hygiene. Doesn't talk or mix much with other patients. Works in cafeteria at breakfast and dinner. Attends group therapies. Reads in the evenings. Is not on ward much during the day. Appetite good. Pleasant and co-operative.

R. Cole, R.N.

18 March 1955—Mrs. Radek not in at 9:00 PM—placed on elopement order.

R. Trenk, R.N.
B. Blair, R.N.

Investigation of Physician

I have fully investigated the circumstances of the above elopement and find that patient has not returned from 9:00 PM ground parole. Is listed as White House Case but not considered dangerous.

In my opinion there is no blame attached.

Action taken: Placed on elopement as of 11:00 PM —White House Secret Service notified. Note and letter dictated.

11:30 PM. March 18, 1955.   J. Lester, M.D.

Accident, Injury, and Escape Report

Name: Bertha Radek   Hour: 9:00 PM
Date: 18 March 1955

Give full account of accident, injury, escape, suicide, sudden death, etc. Name all witnesses. Pass Report to Supervisor at once.

Mrs. Bertha Radek has 9:00 PM parole. Did not come in at 9:00 PM. Placed on Elopement.

L. Ronan, R.N.

Investigation of Supervisor

I have fully investigated the circumstances of the above *escape* and have examined the patient and find that: Patient not in at 9:00 PM—has ground parole. Carried on elopement. Routine report made.

R. Trenk, R.N.

19 March 1955—

Recommendation for Discharge While on Elopement

This 36-year-old white female, whose diagnosis is Schizophrenic Reaction, Hebephrenic Type, a D.C. nonresident, left the Hospital grounds yesterday without permission and was placed on elopement status. She is thought to be a resident of the State of Pennsylvania and has a history of two previous mental hospitalizations in that state, the last being from 1950 until 1953. Attention is called to Dr. Small's note, dated January 29, 1955, returning her ground privileges. At that time she showed no hallucinatory or delusional content. On this date a letter postmarked yesterday was received from the patient indicating that she is returning to New Jersey. She also refers to her "theory" of "psychological face coloring," indicating that there is still some delusional abnormal content.

Information from Interstate Services indicates that negotiations for the return of this patient to Pennsylvania are still pending.

In view of the patient's indication that she does not plan to return to the Hospital and since she is carried on our rolls as a D.C. nonresident patient, it is recommended that she be discharged from the rolls while on absent without permission status. It is felt that she should be discharged as improved.

DIAGNOSIS: 22.1 SCHIZOPHRENIC REACTION. HEBEPHRENIC TYPE

RECOMMENDATION: Discharge from the Hospital rolls while on elopement status.

CONDITION ON DISCHARGE: IMPROVED

Dr. Ball

24 March 1955—**Closing Note**

In accordance with the foregoing recommendation which has been approved, by direction of the Clinical Director this patient was today discharged while on elopement. The patient and her father have been notified by letter of this action.

Dr. Ball

March 25, 1955

Mrs. Bertha Radek
c/o John Bartok
New Jersey

Dear Mrs. Radek:

This is to inform you that you were officially discharged from the patient rolls of Saint Elizabeths Hospital on March 24, 1955, while away from the Hospital without permission.

We hope that you will continue to improve and get along well at home.

Sincerely yours,

Barry Lord, M.D.
Assistant Superintendent

cc: Mr. John Bartok
    New Jersey

April 11, 1955

Miss (sic) Bertha Radek
c/o Mr. John Bartok
New Jersey

Dear Miss Radek:

We forward to you herewith one Social Security Card and one penknife, your property left at this hospital at the time of your discharge from care and treatment.

Kindly acknowledge receipt for the above items by signing and returning to us the enclosed copy of this letter.

Sincerely yours,

Barry Lord, M.D.
Assistant Superintendent

RECEIVED: Bertha Radek

Thank you very much and I'm glad I left. I have a pleasant life working as a cashier in a very nice restaurant.

B.R.

C.

The Radek Case II

1.

A LAW ENFORCEMENT OFFICER INVOKES THE PROCESS

PETITION—18 OCTOBER 1955

States District Court for the District of Columbia

Your petitioner, Peter Bachrach, respectfully represents to the Court as follows:

1. That he is an officer authorized to make arrests in the District of Columbia, and

2. That Bertha Radek was apprehended in the District of Columbia on the 17th day of October, 1955 and has been detained at District of Columbia General Hospital, to be observed and examined for his-her mental health, for the reason that:

> Patient appeared at the Northwest Gate at the White House and requested an appointment with the President. She stated that she was being persecuted by a technical machine which entered her body and disturbed her brain waves. She stated that she had come to Washington because she had been informed that the President was likewise afflicted and wished to confirm this fact and do what she could to improve his condition.

3. Your petitioner is informed, and believes and therefore avers said patient is of unsound mind, in-

capable of managing his-her own affairs; and within the purview of the statute in that case made and provided, it is not desirable to permit him-her to go about unsupervised, and he-she is a proper subject for commitment to a hospital for treatment.

Wherefore, the premises considered, your petitioner prays:

1. That the proper writ, as provided by law, may issue, and the Commission on Mental Health be directed to examine said patient and report its findings and recommendations to the Court.

2. That said patient, if found to be of unsound mind, (1) be committed to Saint Elizabeths Hospital or other hospital, or (2) if harmless, committed to relatives or friends willing to accept the care, custody, and maintenance of patient.

3. That a Committee of the estate be appointed.

4. And for such other relief as the best interest of the patient may require, and to the Court seem just and proper.

2.

THE DISTRICT COURT AND THE COMMISSION ON MENTAL HEALTH ADMINISTER THE PROCESS

As in Radek I, the petition triggered a substantially similar flow of documents, reports, and consequences.

A slight variation in the participation of the guardian *ad litem*, Emil Oz, is reflected in the following excerpt from his report of 29 October 1955 to the court:

"I do concur in the recommendation made by the Commission on Mental Health with respect to the patient. Although I represented this patient at the hearing, I was not appointed her guardian until after the proceeding. I had no opportunity to interview the patient prior to the hearing.

On 7 November 1955 Judge Andrews decreed that Bertha Radek "is of unsound mind and is hereby committed to Saint Elizabeths Hospital until such time as she may be safely discharged therefrom or returned to the State of her residence."

3.

THE ADMITTING HOSPITAL ADMINISTERS THE COURT DECISION AND KEEPS ITSELF INFORMED OF WHAT AND WHY?

a. Medical Certificate

We certify, that after a personal examination of the within-named person we find her to be in need of hospital treatment for mental disease. . . .

Do suicidal or homicidal tendencies exist; if so, how manifested? *Yes. She is dangerous to herself and others because of her mental condition.*

b. Admission Note—29 October 1955

The patient indicates that she left without permission on March 18, 1955 and went to New Jersey to live with a relative whose name and relationship she refused to communicate. She apparently worked there for a while as a cashier in a restaurant. In the middle of this month she decided to come to Washington because she felt that the President was too preoccupied with sex and that she should come here and take over his job and work as an acting President. The patient is quite delusional and quite rambling in her delusions. She talks about machines operating on her and that these machines work through radar on her organs. She states that the machine is apparently operated by the United States Government, it has been on her for many years, and it is ruining her life. She indicates that she actually went to the White House. The medical certificate that accompanied her did not state this. Her speech is quite rambling but coherent. She is oriented for time, place, and person. She admits to auditory hallucinations but will not speak of their content, but has a lot of delusional ideas about radar machines as the cause of her trouble. Her affect is flat. There is no evidence of any suicidal preoccupation. Her sensorium is clear. Although she seems at first resentful about being brought back to Saint Elizabeths Hospital, before long it is quite obvious that she is glad to be back and is looking forward to returning to her old ward.

Apparently she has been in good health since her elopement from the hospital. She apparently has not been in any kind of legal difficulty and has not used alcohol or drugs.

Diagnostic Impression: Schizophrenic Reaction, Paranoid Type.

Dr. Kronkite.

c. The Secret Service Designates This a "White House Case"—7 November 1955

This patient is known to and recorded by the United States Secret Service at the White House, and is therefore referred to there and here as A WHITE HOUSE CASE.

In the event of this patient's death or discharge, please immediately notify the Registrar, who will appropriately mark the "Pink Card" now in the correspondence folder and will forward it to the Secret Service.

In the event of elopement, the physician in charge is to immediately notify the United States Secret Service Supervising Agent, District 1–15, Telephone confirming the message by letter and forwarding a copy thereof to the Registrar for filing in the Commitment File.

Edward Winn
Assistant Registrar

Copy for: Physician in Charge
Supervisor
Clinical Folder
Correspondence Folder
Commitment File

d. Doctors' and Nurses' Progress Notes—29 October 1955 to 15 January 1956

Entries made by hospital staff during Bertha Radek's second confinement at St. Elizabeths' are of substantially the same kind, quality, and frequency as these recorded during her earlier incarceration. Therefore only the following few excerpts are reproduced here:

18 December 1955—Pleasant, well-oriented female who speaks clearly and under considerable pressure. Speaks of external forces influencing her—has many delusional ideas including a system of equations which will lead to a new Constitution. Dr. Small investigating.

M. Rolloff, M.D.

29 October 1955—Mrs. Radek very quiet—pleasant to talk with—spent the evening watching TV—ate well—no complaints.

E. Allan, R.N.

8 November 1955—Mrs. Radek is quiet on ward, does not participate in activities nor does she initiate conversation. Most of day is spent pacing hall or looking out of window. Her appearance is neat and she is co-operative in ward routines.

M. Grove, R.N.

11 November 1955—

Psychiatric Case Study

The patient states that she went to New Jersey to live with her stepfather and promptly obtained a job as cashier which she kept for five months, working steadily part-time. She states that she felt very well, entered into some activities, including the American Association for the United Nations, where she did voluntary work. Very soon after this the patient began to notice that there was the mechanism interfering with her thinking, similar to what she had noticed previously. She then began to feel that the Roman Catholics were working against her and states that she eventually lost her job because of the Roman Catholics' influence on her boss. In addition, she stated that she began wearing unusual-colored clothes and a pony tail instead of her usual rather sombre colors. Her boss apparently told her that she should not wear these types of clothing while working for him. She refused and was subsequently discharged. Apparently the patient made a brief visit to Washington on July 18 to visit the Central Intelligence Agency in order to pick up her story she had written previously concerning "psychological face coloring." She returned to Jersey City, at which time she lost her job, remained with her stepfather for another two months, during which time she says she went out in the street thinking with other people. Apparently this involved a complicated system of thought interchange without actually speaking.

The patient came to Washington October 13, 1955 in order to replace President Eisenhower. She went to the White House in order to see him because of her objections to his use of a mechanism which operated on her mind. It was at this time that she was transferred to the District of Columbia General Hospital, and subsequently to Saint Elizabeths Hospital.

Mental Examination

On Admission

The patient was overtalkative, giving a rambling, tangential, difficult-to-follow account of various persecutions she has encountered during her months away from hospital.

Course in Hospital

The patient was openly delusional while on the ward, talking about the mechanism affecting her brain. Otherwise she was quiet and co-operative and had no other complaints. She gets along well with fellow patients but takes very little interest in ward activities. Generally, the patient can be described as being seclusive and preoccupied. Present medication has been Thorazine 100 milligrams 4 times daily.

Formal Mental Examination

General Appearance and Behavior: The patient is a severe-looking, middle-aged, homely woman with swept-back hair in a braided bun. There is a tense expression to her face and she sits forward in her chair and seems under considerable pressure to tell the doctor her difficulties.

Speech: The patient talks rapidly and cannot be interrupted. When questioned about subjects away from her delusional system the patient gives coherent answers but as soon as the subject matter comes close to her various and sundry delusions the patient talks rapidly in a circumstantial manner which is extremely difficult to follow. She often talks as though the examiner should know automatically about everything that has preceded her description. At times she is in such a great hurry that she skips from one part of the story to another.

Emotional Reaction: Generally flattened, but one of mild irritation and concern.

Abnormal Mental Content or Trends: As mentioned above the patient has the impression that she came to Washington to become President of the United States. She refers repeatedly to ideas of influence, ideas of passivity, and referential thinking. She denies any hallucinations, but gives a jumbled up system of persecutions. Mixed in with the persecutions, however, is a definite element of grandiosity, as mentioned before, in which the patient feels that she has some special powers herself.

Mental Grasp and Capacity, Attention, Perception, and Comprehension: All appeared normal.

Orientation: Correct.

General Intelligence: Average or above average.

Memory: Correct.

Insight: Completely lacking.

Judgment: Judgment appears to be poor.

The patient is a 38-year-old readmission from the District of Columbia General Hospital on October 29, 1955. This is the patient's fourth mental hospital admission, the second to Saint Elizabeths Hospital. Original diagnosis was Manic Depressive Reaction, Hypomanic Type, but this subsequently was changed to Dementia Praecox, Mixed Type, and on admission here to Schizophrenic Reaction, Hebephrenic Type. On recent admissions the patient has presented a system of paranoid and somewhat grandiose delusions and has always improved on Thorazine therapy. She eloped from the hospital in March of this year but very shortly after began developing her previous delusions with ideas of reference, passivity, and influence. She again felt compelled to visit the White

House on October 13, 1955 and was sent to the District of Columbia General Hospital and subsequently to Saint Elizabeths.

On admission here the patient again was overtalkative, expounding a number of paranoid and grandiose delusions. Affect was again flattened. During her stay in the hospital she has been generally seclusive and on formal examination presents a similar picture to the last admission. The patient is again being treated with Thorazine. The physical examination is essentially negative and laboratory work including X-ray and VDRL are negative.

In summary, the patient is a Chronic Schizophrenic Reaction, Paranoid Type.

J. Ferguson, M.D.

Reno, Nevada
November 21, 1955

St. Elizabeth Hospital
Washington, D.C.

Dear Sir:

Several years ago we represented Mrs. Radek in an action in Nevada for a divorce. We have been hearing from her intermittently and we are enclosing our last letter from her which might be of some assistance to you in her treatment.

Yours very truly,

BATTLE & PETERS

W. M. Peters

November 9, 1955

Dear Mr. Peters:

This is to ask you to please take my case about being "The She" on the mechanism that has been operating over people.

I learned that people were using me on others for about 14 years. I understand that you were aware of it at the time of my divorce in 1948.

I have been used and abused and want to sue President Eisenhower, Government of Pennsylvania and Federal for being subversive with some people and against Americans.

I learned in Pennsylvania, April 10, 1955, that people were very frightened having words like "she," "milch," and "preach" come to their minds from somewhere. I taught them to think for themselves and not be terrorized by anyone, wanted the people to know that as Americans there was no need to be frightened. I had ideas that were tried out on me and on the people themselves.

When we have a war people are principled with so I thought to the people to principle with themselves on the mechanism . . .

I want $5,000,000. It can be obtained from President Eisenhower himself for he doesn't believe in being a millionaire president.

The many titles of a person that you may get will all be "Bertha Herself," "The She—Bertha Radek," a saint to some, saintship, Holy See, Ladyship, principled, the brain, leader, Miss Manhattan, etc. all on the mechanism.

I also wrote an amendment to the constitution to prevent a mechanism ever operating on people again. I believe the United States needs federalized schooling, the Jews to be a nation in Australia and the Australians to this country. The Negroes to have their own territory. They want Georgia, Mississippi, and Louisiana from TV. Irrigation for the dry states and no war. The army in awhile will be obsolete if we do not have any more Roman Catholics in this country. We the people know in ourselves that that institution is obsolete . . .

I have opposed a mechanism with myself and wanted it disposed of and thrown away. If it wasn't I would replace President Eisenhower as "Acting President, Actively." Many people believed it and my mettle was tried by not providing me with money. I arrived in Washington, D.C., October 14, 1955. It really was October 13 because the newspapers had been printing the papers a day ahead to be ahead of the thoughts and ideas on the mechanism.

As President Eisenhower can be constitutionally replaced I came to Washington, D.C., to replace him but one of the guards wouldn't let me through and some petty politicians brought me to D.C. General Hospital and then to Saint Elizabeth's.

* * *

Sex was being used against me to ruin my reputation and yet I used it for good reason. Love and science. I sincerely like the people and also established some facts.

I want to buy a home of my own in Nevada and live peacefully with my son, and have a place for my brother to "hang up his hat."

I've been shuttled about from pillar to post and I don't want any more of it. The nasty people responsible for it owe me and society a debt.

Please, Mr. Peters, do something that will be affirmative and constructive on my behalf. Because I thought I had a good divorce, and I believe I do, so I look to you to getting money for me, $5,000,000, and also my moving into Nevada. As you know, I have a son whom I want to have with me as soon as possible so I can live some kind of stable life . . .

Could you please get me out of here? The doctor, Dr. John Coolidge, can help you and no doubt give you a report.

Of course I expect everyone would be paid up in some way and learn to trust one another, helping one another.

I would like to compensate people with money because they can get what they need for themselves in the way of personal comforts.

I need money for personal self-defense and I expect you, Mr. Peters, to get more than $5,000,000. Please write or call Dr. White at D.C. General whom I am sure can be very helpful.

Some scientific facts have been established on me such as people from the cradle to the grave are to drink milk for the bones are as alive as are muscles and we need milk to keep our bones healthy. Also taking lemon juice helps prevent black and blue marks on the body.

So you can, Mr. Peters, come to the conclusion that I am a very deserving case for monetary compensation. Looking forward to some immediate hope for a bright future.

Very sincerely,

Bertha Radek

November 27, 1955

Dear Mr. Peters:

Thank you for your letter of November 21, 1955, and the enclosed letter from Mrs. Radek.

Sincerely yours,

Barry Lord, M.D.
Assistant Superintendent

November 27, 1955

Mr. James Flynn
Agent in Charge
United States Secret Service
Washington 4, D.C.

Dear Mr. Flynn:

Our patient, Bertha Radek, is a White House case. In recent weeks, she has shown a favorable response to treatment and is now believed to be quite reliable and able to handle ground privileges, to walk on the Hospital grounds, according to certain regulations. We would like to ask your permission for such a procedure to be carried out.

Sincerely yours,

Barry Lord, M.D.
Assistant Superintendent

November 30, 1955

Barry Lord, M.D.
Assistant Superintendent
St. Elizabeths Hospital
Washington 20, D.C.

Dear Sir:

We are in receipt of your letter of November 27, 1955, relative to the above-named patient.

We are pleased to hear of the improvement in her condition and this Service has no objection to the granting of the privileges as set forth in your letter.

Thank you very much for your co-operation in this matter.

James Flynn
Special Agent in Charge

Battle & Peters
Attorneys at Law

Reno, Nevada
January 15, 1956

St. Elizabeth's Hospital
Washington, D.C.

Dear Sir:

Enclosed herewith is another letter which we have received from Mrs. Radek.

Yours very truly,

W. M. Peters

St. Elizabeths Hospital
Washington, D.C.
November 30, 1955

Dear Mr. Peters:

Enclosed is a copy of the letter I'm sending to President Eisenhower. It goes through the office here, that's why I'm sending it, I don't know how soon he'll receive it. . . .

Please excuse my using pencil but it is all I have available to write to you with.

Best wishes and good luck to you, can you please let me know what course to follow. I want to sue for money!!

Sincerely,

Bertha Radek

St. Elizabeths Hospital
Washington, D.C.
November 30, 1955

Dear President Eisenhower:

I am not a complete stranger to you, if you keep mail on file, I sent you three long letters from Jersey City, spring 1952. It also was a mental hospital.

The reason I am "in" now is because of a trip to the White House at an unscheduled hour. It is no way to treat a conscientious American citizen.

I feel and know that you are at least aware of my existence. Why I never received an acknowledgement from the White House I don't know. Be that as it may, I at that time wrote you about Psychological Face Coloring since then I have written out a paper starting with "The brotherhood of man can once more be proven etc. etc." Now I am firmly convinced that my theory if handled wisely can be instrumental in furthering World Peace, (United Nations for World Peace is what we want).

We must have the courage to be honest in our daily life and present facts as they are.

You have a mechanism operating that Radar's waves on the people so that one another's thoughts are thus communicated—it is unconstitutional for in the second part of the Constitution Article IV people are to be "secure in person" and because of the mechanism they aren't "secure in person."

You are hereby proving to be a disability to the nation for you permitted Roman Catholics who forswear all way of life and have no respect for good government and honest business to terrorize and coerce good and honest citizens. For Priests and nuns have no rights as citizens they are subjects of the Church and you permitted them to think to people and force people to accept a Saint in this country. It's preposterous and is finished.

In Pennsylvania we proved outdoors that they were "she-ing" all over people men and women alike. That she is me "The She" Bertha Radek. It has been in existence for around 15 years and it has to stop.

Now I am a sensible intelligent person with a little instruction I can meet and talk to groups, why not present me to the Public with my Face Coloring theory it is an indisputable fact!!

I do want to be first Lady President of the United States!!!

Sincerely,

Bertha Radek

Reno 2, Nevada
December 10, 1955

St. Elizabeths Hospital
Washington, D.C.

Attention: Chief Psychiatrist

In re: Bertha Radek

Dear Sir:

On November 21st we sent you a letter from Mrs. Radek. You were very kind to reply. We are now enclosing another letter which we received on November 5th.

We have not replied to any of these letters, however if you wish us to do so and if it might help Mrs. Radek in her treatment, we would be pleased to write to her providing you would give us the line along which we should write. Of course, she has absolutely no claim. While the letters are rather amusing, they are also rather pitiful and I only hope they may be of some assistance to you in curing her mental illness.

Yours very truly,

W. M. Peters

December 16, 1955

Mr. W. M. Peters
Battle & Peters
Attorneys at Law
Reno 2, Nevada

Dear Mr. Peters:

In reply to your letter of December 10, 1955, containing an epistle to you from Bertha Radek, who is currently under our care, I cannot think of a useful reply at this point you can make, and suspect that one might bring an unanswerable flood.

Mrs. Radek writes to a number of people, including the President of the United States, and appears to have reached some improvement at this point. There is evidence of appreciation of your interest as relayed to her by her ward physician, but I think unless a marked change occurs in her content, your best future service to her would be simply to receive her letters.

Sincerely yours,

Barry Lord, M.D.
Assistant Superintendent

7 December 1955—

Ground Privileges

In view of this patient's recent improvement, co-operative ward adjustment, and satisfactory behavior on accompanied privileges, as well as satisfactory indication of a reliable desire to co-operate with the regulations involved, 5 PM ground privileges are being granted, with later extension to 9 PM, depending upon a satisfactory adjustment.

Secret Service has been notified and approved this privilege.

D. Madson, M.D.

12 December 1955—

Social Service Branch

Referral

This 38-year-old, single, white patient was referred to Social Service by Dr. Jones on December 6, 1955, for help in locating her suitcase and portfolio.

The Patient

I interviewed Mrs. Radek on the ward and although she was concerned about her belongings, she expressed some delusional material concerning the United States President. She informed me that she was staying at the Hotel Franklin at the time she was picked up by the police and taken to D.C. General Hospital. With her permission, I called the hotel and learned that she had a bill of $20 for three days room rent. An additional fee of $25 was charged for baggage storage. I learned the hotel will not relinquish the baggage until the bill is paid. The hotel management did say they would make some settlement on the baggage fee.

The patient stated she had no funds to pay the bill, as a result she is not able to get her clothing. She suggested that I write to her mother and explain her need for money. Her mother has remarried and the family operates a chicken farm. Although her father is not willing to help, her mother is. She feels her mother makes a fuss at first about helping her, but eventually does. The patient says her father is not well and unable to give her large sums of money. It was decided by the patient that I would write a letter to her mother explaining about her hotel bill in addition to those she had written to both her father and mother.

The patient did receive $5 from her father but she has not heard from her mother. Mrs. Radek, who is a nonresident, has expressed a desire to be transferred to New Jersey in order to be near her father.

At present, the patient seems content to wait until she hears from her mother. Social Service will continue to provide services to this patient as they are needed.

K. Novak
Psychiatric Social Worker

18 December 1955—

Admission Conference

PRESENT: DOCTORS SMALL and JONES, and
STUDENT NURSES

This readmitted 38-year-old white divorcee is now getting 100 milligrams of Thorazine and 2 milligrams of Artane q.i.d. On the ward she has been making a good adjustment although her content has suggested that she is quite psychotic. She is co-operative with ground privileges.

The patient is a vivacious, alert, and coyly seductive in her manner. She is direct in her attitude, meets one's gaze well, and shifts attention well during conversation. She is correctly oriented. As the conversation progresses and she becomes more comfortable she gets progressively more disjointed and away from reality in her content. She said she was in Philadelphia and learned that communication with the radio waves between people in Washington and foreign countries might concern the President so she decided to come to Washington and communicate with Eisenhower about it. She goes on and on about "ideas and principles make a good contribution which equals co-operation which equals in turn the democratic equation, etc." She then went on to speak about her ideas of face coloring; "orange color means desire, pink means affirmation, red means strong feeling, blue means esthetics, green means seasick, yellow means cowardly." [She said she] went to the United Nations and found out that "Cash and clash and people with silver spoon in mouth were influencing others." As to why others thought she had mental disorder, she said, "The Roman Catholics want to sink me because of my name. There is no St. Bertha and I'm Bertha." Despite all of this content, patient behaves very well and keeps a rather normal appearing demeanour. She denies having been suicidal over a long period of time but shows a small scar on her left wrist which she cut while "in the depth of despair in 1945." After she had found out she could be a "constitutional American" she would not try to harm herself any more. On the ward she spends her time "knitting and reading." She is knitting a scarf for her mother and brother. She states it's nicer here than in the hospitals in New Jersey and "at least" she has sense enough to come here when she is getting sick.

Interstate Services have been contacted about plans for repatriating this Patient. Pending her transfer to Jersey State *she is approved for transfer* to a chronic service.

DIAGNOSIS: 22.3 SCHIZOPHRENIC REACTION.
PARANOID TYPE

Dr. Small.

DEPARTMENT OF
HEALTH, EDUCATION, AND WELFARE
SAINT ELIZABETHS HOSPITAL
Washington 20, D.C.

Re: Bertha Radek
December 18, 1955

Mrs. Danielle Varner
R.D. #1
Monroe, Pennsylvania

Dear Mrs. Warner:

This is to inform you of the admission to this Hospital of the patient named below. If your name, address, and relationship as they appear below are not correct, you are requested to supply such data to us by mail as soon as possible and to report promptly in the same manner any change in your address. All inquiries concerning the patient's welfare should be directed to the Superintendent, Saint Elizabeths Hospital, Washington 20, D.C.

In order to study and treat this patient in a satisfactory manner, we need reliable information as to the family and personal history. We should appreciate a letter from you telling us if any members of the family ever suffered from nervous or mental disease. We should also like to have a statement concerning development through childhood, progress in school, ability to get along at work and in social contacts. As you look back over the patient's life, if you think of anything concerning behavior, disposition, or traits of character that now seem to you to have been unusual or different from other members of the family, we would like to know about them. If treatment has ever been received in other hospitals, we should like to know the names of such hospitals and the approximate dates of residence in them.

If you live in the city of Washington, D.C., or if you plan to visit the city in the near future, we wish that you would call at the Hospital, so that you may be interviewed by one of our physicians for the purpose of giving further information concerning our patient. If you are able to make such a visit within the next few days, you may prefer to give us the above-requested information orally. Visiting hours for the Hospital are from 2:00 to 4:00 PM daily except Monday, Wednesday, and Friday.

We thank you for your co-operation and assure you that we will do everything possible to restore this patient to good health.

Patient's Name: Bertha Radek

Date of Admission: October 29, 1955

Admitted from: D.C. General Hospital

Your Relationship: Mother

Very truly yours,

Barry Lord, M.D.
Assistant Superintendent

23 December 1955—Miss (sic) Radek did not come in for 11 AM medication, lunch or 3 PM medication. Failed to return for dinner. Placed on elopement at 2 PM by Dr. Madson.

Investigation of Physician

I have fully investigated the circumstances of the above elopement and find that she is a White House case previously diagnosed hebephrenic who had been on ground privileges for 2 weeks and gave no indication I can find why she left today.

In my opinion there is no blame attached.

Re: Bertha Radek
December 23, 1955

Mrs. Danielle Varner
Monroe, Pennsylvania

Dear Mrs. Varner:

We are writing to notify you that your daughter, Mrs. Bertha Radek, left the hospital without permission today. She had shown recent improvement, but we had not as yet completed her treatment and, consequently, would appreciate your notifying us should you learn of your daughter's whereabouts.

Please be assured of our continued interest in Mrs. Radek's comfort and welfare.

Sincerely yours,
Barry Lord, M.D.
Assistant Superintendent

23 December 1955—

Elopement Note

This patient, who had had ground privileges for about three weeks, with the approval of the United States Secret Service, did not come in today from 5:00 ground privileges. I had been somewhat concerned about her before that because I received a notice from the ward that she had not appeared for lunch, but this was not particularly unusual for her. She had made a co-operative adjustment, although she was continuing to express delusional content regarding face coloration. Her ward physician had talked with her this morning, and she seemed quite comfortable and was looking forward to the possibility of her being transferred to a hospital in New Jersey, which would be closer to her home. I, therefore, do not know why the patient did not come back today. The Clinical Director placed the patient on elopement. I notified Agent Rand of the United States Secret Service by telephone and am forwarding a letter to the patient's mother.

D. Madson, M.D.

c/o Bartok
Philadelphia, Pa.
December 30, 1955

Dear Dr. Madson:

I stayed at my mothers for a little while and re-established family relations. Mother had been ill when I arrived but improved. I was there for Thanksgiving and arrived in Philadelphia Saturday, December 29th to stay with my Dad.

I am going to look for a job Monday and expect to get one in a day or two.

Please doctor will you please sign an order for all my things to be sent here to the above address. Also I hope they can find some beaded jewelry I had in my purse.

There is a mechanism operating on people and it ought to stop, it's subversive.

It has ruined my life for I learned the Roman Catholics want to Saint my name on me. I think that is nonsense.

I believe we all ought to co-operate in the world as Constitutional Citizens for World Peace.

I wanted to live in Nevada but it isn't feasible and I'm still North. My son will soon be going to College and I'd like to help him if I possibly can.

I had my heart set on having an electrolysis office of my own in Nevada. And here I am at 38 a sales girl at 95c an hour.

A flop to my way of thinking for I believe in the American Way of Life and know it is good.

If left alone I would have managed well for myself for I did when I was married and I did not know anything about home life or marriage.

$5,000,000 will be fine to sue someone for as far as I'm concerned.

Very sincerely,
Bertha Radek

2 January 1956—

Recommendation For Discharge While on Elopement

She is a 38-year-old divorced cashier admitted to this hospital for the second time on October 29, 1955, and adjudicated as a nonresident. She was also listed as a White House case. She was seen at admission conference on December 18, 1955 and this note has not yet been returned to the duplicate chart. On December 23, 1955 the patient left the hospital without permission and the Secret Service was notified. Dr. Jones has now received a letter from the patient giving her address as c/o Bartok, Philadelphia, Pa. This letter indicated that the patient is making a comfortable adjustment in Pennsylvania and did not plan to return to the hospital. I have notified the Secret Service by telephone of the patient's present address and they have no objection to our discharging her from our rolls at this time since she is a nonresident of the District on elopement. Such is recommended.

DIAGNOSIS: 22.3 SCHIZOPHRENIC
                    REACTION. PARANOID
                    TYPE.

RECOMMENDATION: DISCHARGE WHILE ON
                    ELOPEMENT.

CONDITION ON DISCHARGE: IMPROVED.

D. Madson, M.D.

SAINT ELIZABETHS HOSPITAL
Washington 20, D.C.
January 2, 1956

Mrs. Bertha Radek
c/o Bartok
Philadelphia, Pa.

Dear Mrs. Radek:

Your letter of December 30, 1955, addressed to Dr. Madson, of our staff, has appropriately been referred to me for reply.

I expect that the hospital will determine in the near future that, since you are a nonresident patient and out of the District of Columbia, your discharge should be effected, and as soon as that is done the Property Office here will be asked to forward your belongings to the above address.

Please be assured of our best wishes for your future good health.

Sincerely yours,
Barry Lord, M.D.
Assistant Superintendent

January 8, 1956

Dear Dr. Lord:

Thank you for your letters, I appreciate your attention on my behalf.

It is good for me in a practical way that I did leave St. Elizabeths Hospital, but I'm very fond of some of the people there and miss some of them.

Everyone is very nice at St. Elizabeths and it bolstered my ego, but a week at my mother's has me in a state of tears about my private life.

I have made a number of attempts to establish a residence but with outer influences I was not successful.

I feel at this time frustrated for I had hopes of being in the White House for at least a while and looking over some "bills" that were on the President's desk. That's what we had thought out in Jersey City in the summer.

Now all is quieter except someone thinks to me and is waiting for my blues to wear off.

My first pay envelope will be this Thursday and I'll be able to see my son, take him out, and buy him a Christmas gift so you can understand it was worthwhile for me to leave.

I had my son because I wanted him, had plans of sending him to Prep School.

I sold my typewriter and radio to buy the ticket to Washington, D.C. and my understanding was it would be all taken care of.

Yes I was put in a mental hospital and now I've had such a let-down that I'm physically upset. I ache all over and I know it's a case of nerves. But it's surprising how ill one's spirits can make one. My body chemistry is completely out of kilter for I never felt this way in my life.

I expect to go either to a doctor or the hospital but I'm hoping I'll feel better in a week or two.

I eat at work and have a uniform and am paid 95¢ an hour, but I'll receive a little more so it's all promising once I have a few dollars and see some friends I'll probably cheer up. I really should be in good spirits but I'm starting again and I hope it lasts this time. Thank you so very much for your correspondence.

Sincerely,
Bertha Radek

12 January 1956—Mrs. Radek discharged while on elopement—condition improved.

F. Ireland, R.N.

Re: Bertha Radek
(Discharged)
January 15, 1956

Mrs. Bertha Radek
c/o Bartok
Philadelphia, Pa.

Dear Mrs. Radek:

This is to notify you that as of January 8, 1956, you have been discharged from Saint Elizabeths Hospital while on elopement status.

Please be assured of our best wishes for your continued good health.

Sincerely yours,
Barry Lord, M.D.
Assistant Superintendent

Monroe, Pennsylvania
February 26, 1957

Dear Doctor Rankin:

I had planned on visiting St. Elizabeths but circumstances prevented me from doing so, instead am writing to you to request a favor of you—as usual for me, with you!

Please return my papers on my "Psychological Face-Coloring" theory.

The last time I was in St. Elizabeths was from October, 1955 to December, 1955 and I want to tell you that you do a wonderful job there.

Good health, best wishes.

Sincerely,
Bertha Radek

Re: Bertha Radek
(Discharged)
April 11, 1956

Mrs. Bertha Radek
c/o Bartok
Philadelphia, Pa.

Dear Mrs. Radek:

An extensive search has been made in Dix Service to try and locate your papers on face coloring but without success. You may rest assured that in the event the papers are located at a later date they will be forwarded to you.

Please accept our best wishes for your continued improvement in your present environment.

Sincerely yours,
Barry Lord. M.D.
Assistant Superintendent

D.
The Radek Case III

1.

A LAW ENFORCEMENT OFFICER INVOKES THE PROCESS

PETITION—17 JANUARY 1960

To the United States District Court for the District of Columbia

Your petitioner Gerhart Green respectfully represents to the Court as follows:

1. That he is an officer authorized to make arrests in the District of Columbia, and

2. That Bertha Radek was apprehended in the District of Columbia on the 17th day of January, 1960 and has been detained at District of Columbia General Hospital, to be observed and examined for her mental health, for the reason that: she appeared at the Office of the Vice President of the United States on the afternoon of January 17, 1960, demanding that she see the Vice President, because she needed money. She stated that Washington was being run by an "electronic machine" and that she was to take the President's job. She further stated that she was going to let the Vice President be the President for a short period of time. Subject was highly nervous and upset, and it was felt for her own safety and welfare, she should be committed for observation.

3. Your petitioner is informed, and believes and therefore avers said patient is of unsound mind, incapable of managing her own affairs; and within the purview of the statute in that case made and provided, it is not desirable to permit her to go about unsupervised, and she is a proper subject for commitment to a hospital for treatment.

Wherefore, the premises considered, your petitioner prays:

1. That the proper writ, as provided by law, may issue, and the Commission on Mental Health be directed to examine said patient and report its findings and recommendations to the Court.

2. That said patient, if found to be of unsound mind, (1) be committed to Saint Elizabeths Hospital or other hospital, or (2) if harmless, committed to relatives or friends willing to accept the care, custody, and maintenance of patient.

3. That a Committee of the estate be appointed.

4. And for such other relief as the best interest of the patient may require, and to the Court seem just and proper.

Gerhart Green

Subscribed and sworn to before me, this 18th day of January, 1960.

2.

THE DISTRICT COURT AND THE COMMISSION ON MENTAL HEALTH ADMINISTER THE PROCESS

As in Radek I and II, the Commission on Mental Health recommended commitment, with the guardian ad litem (Edward E. O'Neill) concurring in the recommendation. But on February 18, 1960, the following entry was made in the docket of the District Court:

"The Commission on Mental Health, acting under the direction of this Court, reporting that the petition in the above-entitled cause was dismissed in open Court and [requested that] the patient, Bertha Radek, be readmitted under the prior commitment filed on November 7, 1955." This entry set in motion the following flow of ducuments:

a. Petition for Writ of Habeas Corpus—1 March 1960

To the Honorable, The District Court of the United States in and for the District of Columbia.

Comes now the Petitioner, Bertha Radek, by her Guardian ad litem, Edward E. O'Neill, and proceeding without prepayment of costs, respectfully presents to the Court as follows:

I. That Petitioner is presently illegally confined in custody of the Respondent in Saint Elizabeths Hospital in the District of Columbia;

* * *

V. That on February 18, 1960 upon motion of the Chairman, Commission on Mental Health, the court entered an Order dismissing the petition thereto filed in Mental Health No. 2454–62 and reconfined your Petitioner to the care and custody of the Respondent under a prior commitment order filed on November 7, 1955;

VI. That the Respondent's records show that your Petitioner was discharged while on unauthorized leave on January 8, 1956 and that your Petitioner's, " . . . mental condition at the time of her discharge was IMPROVED.";

VII. That with the "IMPROVED" discharge on January 8, 1956 and the " . . . petition . . . dismissed."

On February 18, 1960 the present detention of your Petitioner by said Respondent is without legal grounds.

WHEREFOR, Petitioner prays:

1. That a writ of Habeas Corpus issue directed to the Respondent commanding him to produce the body of your Petitioner forthwith before the Court, to the end that the cause of confinement of your Petitioner may be inquired into;

2. That upon hearing, the Court order that your Petitioner be forthwith discharged from custody of the Respondent, and

3. That your Petitioner have such other and further relief as under the facts and law may be warranted.

Respectfully,

Bertha Radek
By

/s/ Edward E. O'Neill
Guardian ad litem.

b. Return and Answer to Petition of Habeas Corpus—8 March 1960

The return and answer on behalf of Dr. Reginald Britain, Superintendent, Saint Elizabeths Hospital, respectfully represents to the court:

1. The respondent admits that the petitioner is confined in Saint Elizabeths Hospital but denies that such detention is illegal.

* * *

2. During this petitioner's period of confinement in Saint Elizabeths Hospital, she has been under the care and observation of members of the medical staff of Saint Elizabeths Hospital, skilled in the care, diagnosis, and treatment of nervous and mental disorders, who are of the opinion that she is suffering from Schizophrenic Reaction, Paranoid Type; that she is of unsound mind, to wit: the petitioner talked with much pressure about delusional and grandiose material, she felt that other people had deprived her of bringing up her son, had prevented her from going to college and had interfered with her jobs. She noted that she had come to Washington to see the Vice President about "the Interstate fund for orange, that's me." Then indicating that she meant she wished to change her name to orange and she wished to open public lounges and community centers where people could stay. She also related that people were employing an electronic machine, that her profession was that of an electrologist, for the removal of superfluous hair. It is considered that her judgment is extremely poor and insight nil; and that she is still in need of care and treatment in a mental hospital.

WHEREFORE, the premises considered, the respondent prays that the writ herein be discharged, the petition dismissed, and the petitioner remanded to the custody of the respondent.

/s/ Reginald Britain
Superintendent
Saint Elizabeths Hospital

c. Summary and Recommendation for Diagnosis—8 March 1960

. . . During her stay on Ward-8 she expressed marked delusional ideas and persecutory trends. She feels that other people have deprived her of bringing up her son, have prevented her from going to college, and have interfered with her jobs. She believes she is a genius and knows too much about electronic machines and has extra powers to influence people and many other grandiose ideas. She often projects her frustrations on other people accusing them of being nasty to her and destroying her plans. She was always in a good mood, happy, active, and ready to express her grandiose ideas. She was interested in working in O.T. and doing hand work. She did not bother other patients and personnel and was not a management problem. She would frequently request ground privileges.

. . . This patient was receiving Mellaril 250 milligrams t.i.d. which did not show any effect in this case. This patient was admitted as a White House case.

RECOMMENDED DIAGNOSIS: 22.3 SCHIZOPHRENIC REACTION. PARANOID TYPE.

Dr. A. Rezhevsky

d. Recommendation for Transfer of Service—16 March 1960

During hospitalization the patient has persisted with her delusional ideation, though for the most part been co-operative. Historically, it is quite apparent that the patient's illness has remained quite constant and at this point could be considered a rather rigid paranoid system. In view of the prospect of prolonged hospitalization either here or in Pennsylvania, if residence is established, transfer to a continued treatment service is deemed appropriate. She has received no privileges as it is noted that on both previous times here she has been discharged while on elopement and she is a White House case.

* * *

DIAGNOSIS: 22.3 SCHIZOPHRENIC REACTION. PARANOID TYPE.

RECOMMENDATION: TRANSFER OFF SERVICE.

O. N. Klein, M.D.

e. Radek v. Britain

TRANSCRIPT OF PROCEEDINGS
1 APRIL 1960

Before Judge William B. Jones

Dr. Donald Madson

being first duly sworn, was examined and testified as follows:

Direct Examination

Q. Are you Acting Superintendent of Saint Elizabeths Hospital? A. That is correct, I am a psychiatrist.

Q. And you have been at the hospital for how many years? A. Fourteen.

Q. Doctor, did you know the patient, Bertha Radek, who presently is at the Saint Elizabeths Hospital? A. I knew her on her first two admissions to the hospital.

Q. Do the records show that Mrs. Radek was discharged from the hospital? A. Yes. She left the hospital without permission on December 23, 1955; . . . and consequently we discharged her from the hospital roll on January 8, 1956, as "improved."

Q. And what was the meaning of that entry, "discharged as improved"? A. "Improved" means that we considered her to some degree better than she was when she first came into the hospital, but not legally restorable.

Q. In other words, you did not figure she had recovered sufficiently to be released pursuant to the meaning of the statute; or, as a psychiatrist, that she had reached that point where you felt she could go back into society? A. That is correct.

Q. Was it your opinion at the time of her escape from the hospital that she still needed further care and treatment inside the hospital? A. Yes, that was our opinion. We felt that she had not in any way completed her treatment with us; still needed further care.

Upon her leaving the hospital without permission we wrote to her family, told them that we felt that she needed to be back. As a matter of fact, she had also been under the surveillance of the Secret Service, and we notified them that she had left the hospital, and later notified them of her address in Pennsylvania.

Q. And if she had come back at that time, you certainly would have kept her committed in the hospital, at least for some time? A. That would have been our plan, yes.

BY MR. SCHWARTZ.

Q. You have explained what the meaning of this "discharged as improved" meant medically. Does that entry have any other meaning besides the medical

meaning? A. It may be helpful to explain this. We have four basic conditions on discharge from the hospital.

At the top is "recovered." "Recovered" means to us that if such a patient becomes ill again and requires hospitalization, this will be a new illness. This patient is certified to the United States District Court for restoration of civil rights.

Then the majority of our patients who are discharged from the hospital, in a co-operative fashion, are called "social recovery." This means that the patient still has, in our opinion, a nucleus of the illness remaining, but has sufficiently recovered that he is able to conduct his own responsibilities in life, not be dangerous, and is also certified to the United States District Court for restoration of civil rights.

Then the other two conditions are "improved" and "unimproved."

"Unimproved" means that as far as we can see the patient has shown no change since he came into the hospital. And often, if such a person leaves the hospital unimproved, if it is an escape, for instance, we might notify the police, in view of the fact that we assume that this person is dangerous, having been committed to the hospital.

The "improved" category refers to those patients who may leave the hospital without permission, or in the case of a patient who we think can benefit no longer from hospitalization but is not sufficiently well to be able to take care of his own responsibilities outside the hospital, in such a case as an elderly person who requires the continued assistance of a committee. The "improved" patient who is discharged is not certified for legal restoration.

Q. If a person escapes from the hospital, and is a nonresident, and you never hear further from that patient, what would be your entry, if any, on the books of the hospital? A. Well, after a period of time, usually sooner for nonresidents of the District, but after a period of time, if we have heard no further from a patient, we usually discharge this patient from the hospital in order to keep our records up to date and in order not to have a large collection of unclosed records.

Q. And that would have nothing to do with the patient's actual mental condition, but just a bookkeeping arrangement to clear your records? A. I think a fair implication in that circumstance is that we feel the patient has not been sufficiently treated, but at the same time is not considered a serious danger to the community.

Cross Examination

BY MR. O'NEILL.

Q. Doctor, on this discharge, in the first place, the patient here, Mrs. Radek, was not in the strict sense an escapee? She didn't jump the wall or anything, did she? She was on a ground privilege, and just walked out? Wasn't that correct? A. That is correct, Mr. O'Neill.

Q. [I]f it was your opinion, or the opinion of the staff, that this patient was so dangerous, that her psychiatric condition was so acute, that she was definitely in need of institutionalization, you could have discharged her as "unimproved"; isn't that correct?— because you have that "unimproved" discharge that you just explained. Isn't that correct? A. Well, I am not sure I understand your question. If we considered her dangerous, we would have notified the police and attempted to have her returned to the hospital.

Q. And you would not have noted on your hospital records that this patient was discharged as "improved"; is that correct? A. That is right. The question is the degree of improvement.

Q. That is right. So that in this discharge as improved, whether on unauthorized leave or on authorized leave, so to say, it is a showing from your record that at the time you enter that you are of the opinion that there is not the acute need of institutionalization of that patient; isn't that correct? A. I would certainly say that is a possible interpretation. It may or may not be the case on an individual basis.

THE COURT. Doctor, in this instance you did advise the FBI when you found out where Mrs. Radek was after she left in December of 1955?

THE WITNESS: The Secret Service.

THE COURT: The Secret Service. Why? Was she considered dangerous?

THE WITNESS: We have a certain number of patients, and I suppose we are unique in that we have I suppose a larger number of patients than any other hospital, of patients who come to Washington with the interest of seeing either the President or someone close to him. She had come to Washington for the purpose of seeing the President, because she wanted to discuss certain theories that she had with him. And any such patient who comes into the hospital becomes a part of the concern of the United States Secret Service; and we notify them whenever such a patient leaves the hospital. This is whether we consider such a patient dangerous or not. Any discharge from the hospital of a patient who is known to the Secret Service, we notify them. We did call them when she left the hospital without permission. They went over the file, and informally they indicated to me that they felt that since she was in Philadelphia they did not feel that this was so serious a matter.

THE COURT: In other words, your concern at that time was not so much her being dangerous to herself or to others, but as being one who wanted to see the President or some other high official of the Government which the Secret Service had an obligation to protect; is that correct?

THE WITNESS: Yes; we notify the Secret Service because of administrative responsibility, not because of our opinion of the patient's condition.

THE COURT: Doctor, you explained four categories. You have those who are well, and you petition for their restoration to legal status. You also have a social recovery discharge, where again you certify to the Court for restoration. Then you say you have the "unimproved," which is the dangerous type, I believe, where you advise the police. Is that correct?

THE WITNESS: Generally so, yes.

THE COURT: And then you have the "discharged as improved" . . . includes people who leave without permission, as well as others where no further hospital treatment can aid them, and you let them go out. But you do not certify them for legal restoration.

THE WITNESS: That is correct. Frankly, this is our attempt to separate the commitment to a hospital from the automatic incompetence decision. In the District, as I understand it, commitment to a hospital here automatically renders a patient legally incompetent. We feel that there are many patients in the hospital who are legally competent, and we feel that there are many patients who no longer need hospitalization who are legally incompetent. And this is our attempt to distinguish or to set the plan for the future to the patient's condition.

THE COURT: As I understand, so far as Mrs. Radek is concerned, when she left in 1955, in December, you would have kept her there for further treatment, because hospital treatment you felt would be helpful to her; is that correct?

THE WITNESS: That is correct.

THE COURT: What is this parole procedure? Is that included in what you speak of as the "improved" discharge but not certified for legal restoration?

THE WITNESS. In paroling a patient from the hospital, or sending the patient out on visits from the hospital, we convert the patient from an in-patient to an out-patient, and continue to see him through periodic visits on his return to the hospital. He is not dropped from the hospital roll, he is not discharged, until we complete this program.

Our understanding of our limitations at the hospital has been that once we discharge a patient from the hospital, we cannot treat him further. So that a patient who has been on parole from the hospital is kept on the hospital roll until such time as either he has made other arrangements for further treatment or we feel that his treatment is completed. And this may be for a period of a month, or for a period of six months, or a year, or three years.

THE COURT: . . . But the one who has been discharged as improved, although you do not certify that patient for legal restoration, he is off your rolls; is that correct?

THE WITNESS: Yes. And up until this time we have

felt that we had no right to have anything further to do with such a patient. As a matter of fact, it became quite difficult, because there would be patients whom we had discharged as improved, and not legally restorable, who wanted to come back to the hospital and be examined for certification because they felt that they had continued to improve and were now restorable. Up until now, we felt that we did not have the right to see such a patient, to even examine him.

We also had the problem of patients who were discharged from the hospital as improved, legally unrestored, who wished to return to the hospital on a voluntary basis, and could not get in because they were not legally competent to sign the contract with the District of Columbia. Now we feel that if this move is appropriate, that we can take such a patient into the hospital, making certain that he understands that this is on a basis of his previous adjudication, particularly if we feel that his illness is a continuation of his previous illness.

THE COURT: You say "if this is appropriate." What do you mean by that, Doctor? The problem we have before us today? Is that what you are referring to?

THE WITNESS: Yes, that is right.

THE COURT: Is this matter of "discharged as improved," and your present practice of not permitting such a patient to come back to the hospital, either voluntarily or by picking the patient up and returning that patient to the hospital, is that a matter of your administrative regulations?

THE WITNESS: It is primarily administrative, Your Honor. And Mr. Bly, who I think is here, was very much concerned about the possibility of our trying to resolve this confusion, legal confusion, by calling these patients "dropped from the active roll," instead of "discharged," because "discharged" has a certain finality about it.

We have decided that this probably would perhaps be less confusing to the Court, but it would be more confusing to us, in the fact that we are a member of a national organization of mental health statistics, and all other hospitals call this action "discharge." And if we start changing that, we are going to have our IBM machines getting confused. I don't like to compare the relative importance.

THE COURT: There is a great deal of relevance.

THE WITNESS: But I felt that you would be able to understand, Your Honor.

THE COURT: Doctor, the—and I don't mean to speak discourteously of anything—but isn't there an advantage to the hospital to discharge a patient from the rolls from the point of view of statistics, too, in the case like one who has walked off without permission? In other words, it is another patient for which the hospital is no longer responsible.

THE WITNESS: I think that interpretation is a possible one, and I think administratively yes, we are

under a certain amount of pressure to do this; and I think personally—and I may well be prejudiced—that we resist this. But on the other hand I think there is some benefit to the patient to be discharged from the hospital.

THE COURT: Even though it is an escapee?

THE WITNESS: Even though it is an escapee.

We, I am afraid, occasionally make a mistake and keep a patient too long in our hospital. And I personally am aware of a number of people who have taken it upon themselves to leave the hospital and have done well, and I would not have predicted that they would have done well.

In the case of Mrs. Radek, we knew and were pretty certain that she was ill. We felt she had been ill for a period of at least 10 years before this. She had gotten along out of the hospital with her illness. We felt that she had improved to some degree, but was still ill, was still showing some impairment of judgment. We felt she would still benefit from hospitalization. We tried to get her to come back by holding her property— and this isn't very nice. But we decided it was to her best interests if she had the responsibility of trying to continue her life as at least free of the possibility of being picked up and being returned to the hospital.

*   *   *

THE COURT: The fact that Mrs. Radek came back to the District of Columbia, went to the office of the Vice President of the United States and wanted to see him, and had some sort of an electronic machine that would straighten out some financial problems, does that in any way surprise you in her case? Would that be, perhaps I should say, would that be what you would consider a normal thing for this patient to do, in light of her history?

THE WITNESS: Well, I am not sure I do understand your question, Your Honor. I think it fits in with her previous history. I thought, when we discharged her before, that there was a good possibility that she would have learned sufficiently by experience that she would not have come back to Washington again, particularly on such a noteworthy mission.

THE COURT: You stated that when she left in 1955 —escaped—the hospital felt that she still needed further hospitalization. And the fact that she did come back and went to see the Vice President, is that indicative to you that this was a proper conclusion of the hospital that she did need further hospitalization in 1955?

THE WITNESS: I am not positive of how well she did between 1955 and when she returned.

THE COURT: It is too long a period of time.

THE WITNESS: But it is certainly consistent with her previous history. And it is provocative to interpret the possibility that she is able to get herself into the hospital when the need becomes apparent, but only through this rather crazy mechanism.

* * *

THE COURT: Thank you, Doctor.

(The witness, Dr. Madson, left the stand.)

MR. SCHWARTZ. I might say what is typed in the petition by the petitioner's attorney, that the Mental Health Commission when they examined her on this trip found that she was schizophrenic, with paranoid tendencies.

MR. O'NEILL. If Your Honor pleases, I object to that going into this record, on your ruling in the other case. This petition has been dismissed.

THE COURT: It will not affect my view, in any event, what was found at this time, because I am going to the basic legal problem as to whether or not this patient, having been adjudicated first in 1954— and I don't know whether the Doctor testified whether she had been restored—

MR. O'NEILL: No, she was not.

MR. SCHWARTZ. She escaped.

THE COURT: I think she escaped at that time. But again being in the hospital under adjudication of committal in 1958, and definitely this time she was not restored, it is that that I am limiting my thinking to. And I will hear argument now, if you desire. I think I know your views.

MR. O'NEILL: If Your Honor pleases, I have nothing further to offer in my argument, except from the testimony of the Doctor, that it was not absolutely necessary in 1955 that she stay institutionalized. He had the means whereby, and I submit that this, as he calls it, "administrative discharge as improved," is in fact a showing to him and to the staff that it was not necessary to have this party back inside the hospital again, and that before she should go back in, she is entitled to a full hearing on her present condition of the mind, not via a habeas corpus but via the original petition that has been heretofore dismissed.

f. Ruling of the District Court—1 April 1960

THE COURT: In my view, as long as [the patient] remains under a decree of adjudication and an order of commitment of this Court, she is under a legal disability, to say the least. And in this instance, since she needed, at the time she left, further hospitalization, there is every reason to think that the order of commitment should have continued at least until such time as the Hospital permitted her to leave, either on parole or discharged as improved.

That was not so in this case. The Hospital, according to Dr. Madson, the Acting Superintendent, felt that she needed continued hospitalization. The only reason they did not bring her back, as I understood the Doctor, was that she was a nonresident. She was out of the jurisdiction and they had no way of bringing her back. But they did advise the Secret Service, who are responsible for the safety and welfare of the President of the United States and the Vice President of the United States. She in 1955 had attempted to see President Eisenhower.

Under Section 21–320 of the District of Columbia Code provision is made for one who has been discharged as improved or, as the Code uses the words, "released from such hospital as improved," or one who has been paroled from the hospital, but in neither case has been discharged as cured. That patient may, while a parolee or once discharged, or again, as the Code uses the term, "released," petition for restoration. Unless that petition is granted, that particular patient remains under the decree of adjudication as being of unsound mind.

There is no provision in the Code, so far as I can find, about an escapee or one who leaves without permission. However, it seems to me that one who escapes from the hospital, one who leaves without permission, should not be in a better position than one who has been permitted to leave, by parole or released as improved; that since either he who has been released as improved or he who has been paroled, and who shall have been absent from the hospital on permissive release or parole for a period of six months or longer, has to file a petition for restoration to the status of a person of sound mind, then this patient, Bertha Radek, who was not so released or so paroled, but left without permission, would have to obtain legal restoration. Until that restoration, it is my opinion that this patient needs no further adjudication as being of unsound mind and is properly in Saint Elizabeths Hospital under the 1955 adjudication, if not the 1954. This is not to say she cannot petition for a writ of habeas corpus on the ground that she is no longer insane. But the writ should not issue on the point here asserted.

g. Letter from the Patient to the Superintendent— 2 May 1960

Dear Dr. Britain:

On January 17, 1960 I went to the Vice-President's office in all friendliness to discuss some political matters such as federalized schooling for the country. He was out and some young men and one blonde woman brought me to General D.C. insisting I had to go to St. Elizabeths.

Dear Doctor I took the whole situation calmly because I was curious to see what would be done with me or for me. Since January 17, 1960 to now May 2, 1960 I have been put through hospital routine. It is unfair and unjust to deprive me of my own way of life just because I wanted to be friendly and helpful to the Vice-President.

You people have been forced to assume responsibility for me which is unnecessary because I'm fully capable of taking care of myself and I sincerely want to take care of myself.

Doctor please inform Dr. Bornstein that I'm a stale case and to let me out or as you say "discharge" me.

My doctor has been nice to me and his group therapy is very good and a must for some people. He knows I can take care of myself and it's just that you doctors try to manufacture some kind of happiness for people that keeps me here.

Doctor Britain, I have to get a job and get money because I'm in serious need of clothes. I use one woolen skirt and worn-out shoes and change blouses but keep my things washed and take a shower bath every night.

Please Doctor telephone the Vice-President's office and tell them I was made your responsibility against my will and you want to relieve yourself of the responsibility and why should you hold someone in good condition when there are really ill people who need the care.

You doctors ought to stand up for your rights about patients or some politicians will be in trouble if you encourage the politicians to put visitors to their office in the mental hospital.

I am 43, 5 ft. 5¾ in. tall and a size 12 and have dark hair and am white and believe in doing right for myself. I really have a case on the Vice-President's office and keeping me away from family and friends only aggravates the situation.

So please Doctor Britain inform the Vice-President's office and then Dr. Bornstein of my discharge for I want to be responsible for myself. My home town is Jersey City and I as a divorced woman live there with my dad and can always get a job though I'm an electrolygist (the removal of superfluous hair) by profession. I discovered that the face changes color and "orange" means "desire." Even though I have a new discovery to discuss that does not mean that I should be treated as a mentally incompetent person. Instead of being glad about my discovery, when I sent the papers to the President he never answered my mail.

So I shall keep my ideas to myself and do for myself and my 21-year-old son for World Peace!

Thank you for your kind attention and please help me to "life, liberty and the pursuit of happiness."

Sincerely,
Bertha Radek

h. Doctors' Progress Note—29 August 1960

Since transferred from CT-4 to CT-5 Building this patient has been as usual, extremely insistent, follows the physician almost constantly and demands that she be allowed to go to the home of the man she usually calls her father. When questioned more in detail, however, she says that he is not her father but her stepfather. Since Mrs. Radek is here as a Secret Service case because of her attempt to discuss her invention with the Vice President she has to be treated a little differently. On the past two admissions she was given her parole of the grounds and left the hospital, and it does not seem logical to give her parole again at this time unless the hospital wants to do it with the full understanding that she will almost certainly leave again. She has been told time and time

again that if she gets away from the city by any means she should never come back to Washington again unless she wants to be rehospitalized and promises solemnly that she will never do so. When she is told that she promised that before she says, "No."

The Interstate Services of the Board of Public Welfare is still trying to establish her residence. The so-called stepfather has told the authorities that the patient is no kin to him and he does not want any responsibility in the matter. The patient was told this and says that he just does not want to sign up for any responsibility and would certainly take her in if she appears adding "I have a key to the apartment." There is also a son in Pennsylvania, and it may be that the residence could be established so that she could again be transferred to Pennsylvania. She was in a Pennsylvania State hospital on one occasion. The writer is not sure just how she came to be released.

As far as can be determined this patient never showed any violent tendencies but has a high nuisance value.

B. N. Blatt, M.D.

i. Correspondence between Patient's Parents and Hospital

[i] From Parent—1 September 1960

Nelson Service 4
St. Elizabeth Hospital
Washington, D.C.

RE: Bertha Radek, patient

Dear Sirs:

We have been in touch with the above-named patient and she has asked us to take her out of the hospital.

We would appreciate knowing what condition the patient and if it is possible to have her discharged.

Hoping to hear from you soon, I remain

Respectfully yours,
Danielle Varner

[ii] From Hospital—3 September 1960

Mrs. Danielle Varner
Monroe, Pennsylvania

Dear Mrs. Verner:

A letter of recent date which you addressed to Nelson Service, Saint Elizabeths Hospital has been received, and we note what you say about Mrs. Bertha Radek. I believe that Mrs. Danielle Varner is Mrs. Radek's mother, but we do not know how long it has been since you saw each other. We should like a little more information about your living arrangements and financial circumstances before any decision is made as to her going to make her home with you.

You probably know that Mrs. Radek has been admitted to this hospital on three separate occasions, each time being hospitalized because she was annoy-

ing public officials about her invention which has to
do with skin coloring. On the first two occasions she
was allowed to walk about the grounds and left the
hospital without permission, and we are hesitant to
make any such arrangement which might lead to her
fourth admission to this hospital. She now promises
that she will not return to Washington if she is allowed
to go to Pennsylvania, but we do not feel that she
could be depended upon in this matter. Her abnormal
ideas have not changed, but she is able to be up and
dressed daily, cares for her own needs, and has not
been involved in any serious behavior difficulty.

We should like your answers to the following questions before we can decide whether or not she should
make her home with you. Have you seen much of Mrs.
Radek in the last several years, and do you know of
any difficulty in which she has been involved? Are you
two able to assume full responsibility for her care,
paying all of her bills and giving her some supervision? Can you tell us when Mrs. Radek was last
able to support herself and what work she did?
Lastly, and possibly most important, is can you tell
us where she has lived during the twelve months before she was admitted to this hospital. Mrs. Radek is
not a resident of the District of Columbia and is probably a resident of Pennsylvania. If we can establish
her actual residence she can probably be transferred
to the hospital in that state and allowed to go out on
visits at a later date.

> Sincerely yours,
>
> *B. N. Blaine, M.D.*
> Physician in Charge
> Nelson Service

[iii] From Parent—5 September 1960

Nelson Service
St. Elizabeths Hospital
Washington, D.C. 20032

Dear Dr. Blaine:

Thank you very much for answering my letter so
soon. Please accept my apologies for not writing
sooner.

We, of course, are concerned about Mrs. Radek as
much as you are but are still afraid of what she might
do if she is released again.

As to the questions that you asked in your letter of
September 3, 1960 please be advised that we have not
seen Mrs. Radek any time during the past 5 years. As
to the difficulties that she has been involved in, we
knew about it only slightly. Being as we are both up in
years it would be extremely hard for us to take full
responsibility for her care. We do not know what kind
of work she can do or did before being admitted into
the Pennsylvania Hospital.

Please let us know if we can be of any more assistance to you.

Until we hear from you again, I remain

> Respectfully yours,
>
> *(Mrs.) Danielle Varner*

[iv] From Hospital—8 September 1960

Mrs. Danielle Varner
Rural Delivery 1
Monroe, Pennsylvania

Dear Mrs. Varner:

The letter of recent date concerning your daughter
Bertha Radek, has been received, and I thank you for
answering our inquiries so clearly.

You say that you have not seen Mrs. Radek within
the last five years and have little information concerning the difficulties into which she has been involved.
She has an abnormal idea which is undoubtedly the
result of her mental illness that she has invented
something which will influence skin coloring and is so
firmly convinced that this is worthwhile that she has
made three trips to Washington to see officials. As
far as we know she has never been dangerous in any
way but has brought herself to the attention of the
authorities who realized she was ill and transferred her
to a mental hospital here in Washington. She is not a
resident of this district, and we should like to have her
returned to a mental hospital in the state of her residence, but we cannot determine what this is. Do you
have the address where she stayed during 1958 and
1959? We understand that she stayed in New Jersey
for the last six months of that time, but we have not
been able to check her residence during the year before
that. We should also like to know if you know whether
she supported herself during those two years or
whether she was supported by public funds. If we
could establish her residence at Pennsylvania where
she apparently spent her time she could probably be
hospitalized there and allowed on short visits home
as her condition improved. On her two previous
admissions to this hospital she was allowed to walk
around the grounds by herself and on each occasion
left without permission. She now promises that she
will not do this, but we do not feel that we are justified
in allowing her to go on the grounds again.

Please be assured of our continued interest in the
welfare of your daughter. We will, of course, keep you
informed of any steps taken in regard to the disposition of her case.

> Sincerely yours,
>
> *B. N. Blaine, M.D.*
> Physician in Charge
> Nelson Service

[j] Correspondence between Hospital and Secret Service

[i] From Hospital—27 September 1960

Special Agent in Charge
U.S. Secret Service
Washington, D.C.

Dear Sir:

We are writing to bring to your attention the case
of Mrs. Bertha Radek. This is her third admission to
Saint Elizabeths Hospital, coming in each time as a
White House case, because of her efforts to contact
Government officials about an invention of hers. She

is not a resident of the District of Columbia and efforts to establish her residence elsewhere have been unsuccessful.

While her delusional ideas are unchanged, she has shown some improvement in her reaction toward them. As far as we can determine, she has never shown any dangerous tendencies and we feel that discharge at this time is justified. She would be escorted to the station and put on a through bus or train for Philadelphia. She promises that she will not return to Washington.

We would appreciate your letting us know whether or not you wish to interpose any objection to this action.

Sincerely yours,

B. N. Blaine, M.D.
Physician in Charge

[ii] From Secret Service—10 October 1960

Dr. B. N. Blaine
St. Elizabeths Hospital
Washington 20, D.C.

Dear Dr. Blaine:

This is in reply to your letter dated September 27, 1960, concerning Bertha Radek.

Since the proposal in your letter to discharge this patient involves medical and professional judgment as to the degree to which she has responded to treatment, we feel that your judgment should prevail and we do not wish to interpose any objection.

We would, however, appreciate being notified of the date of discharge by means of our Form 1609 which is presently on file at Saint Elizabeths Hospital.

Thank you for your continued co-operation in these matters.

Very truly yours,

B. F. Linden
Special Agent in Charge

3.

THE COURT OF APPEALS REVIEWS THE PROCESS

BERTHA RADEK, APPELLANT
v.
REGINALD BRITAIN, SUPERINTENDENT,
St. Elizabeths Hospital, APPELLEE

Appeal from the United States District Court
for the District of Columbia

Decided November 3, 1960

CIRCUIT JUDGE: On November 7, 1955, appellant was found of unsound mind and committed to St. Elizabeths Hospital, a public mental hospital in the District of Columbia. On December 23, 1955, she left the Hospital without permission and returned to her home in Pennsylvania. On January 8, 1955, while she was still in Pennsylvania, the Hospital recorded that appellant was discharged as "improved." Four years later, January 1960, she returned to the District of Columbia and called at the office of the Vice President of the United States. As a result of her behavior at that time civil commitment proceedings were again instituted against her. Before their completion, but after appellant had demanded a jury trial under the D.C. Code, the Commission on Mental Health moved to dismiss the proceedings on the ground that the previous civil commitment order of 1955 was still in effect and a legal basis for her present detention. The District Court granted the motion and appellant filed the instant habeas corpus petition alleging that her present detention is unlawful because the 1955 order is no longer in effect. After a hearing, the District Court dismissed the petition and this appeal followed.

The District Court's holding that appellant's present detention in St. Elizabeths Hospital is legal was based on two points. First, the court held that her discharge as "improved" in 1955 did not terminate the earlier commitment order. Second, the court held that appellant could be recommitted without further hearing because an adjudication of unsoundness of mind, entered at the same time as the 1955 commitment order, was still in effect. We shall discuss these points in order.

Discharge of patients under the classification "improved" is a generally accepted practice. The hospital attaches no conditions to the release of patients so discharged. Therefore a discharge as "improved" must be regarded as legally final. Consequently, as other jurisdictions have decided, a new commitment proceeding must be held to compel a patient's return to the hospital. . . .

Adoption of a contrary rule for this jurisdiction would be "quite out of keeping with the congressional policy that underlies the elaborate procedural precautions included in the civil commitment provisions [which seem intended] to insure that only those who need treatment and may be dangerous are confined."

A discharge as "improved" purports, on its face, to rest upon an expert medical judgment that the patient's condition has sufficiently improved so as not to require further hospitalization for the safety of the patient or the community. In the present case, however, the testimony was ambiguous as to whether, in fact, appellant's discharge was based upon such judgment or was merely a bookkeeping entry recorded for administrative convenience. At the very least, the testimony fails to show that appellant's discharge is not what it purports to be, namely, an unconditional discharge. Therefore she may not be recommitted under the 1955 commitment order, and her detention is legal only if the 1955 adjudication of unsoundness of mind affords an adequate basis.

We turn, therefore, to the District Court's ruling that, since appellant had then been declared to be "of unsound mind" and since she has not been legally restored, "this patient needs no further adjudication as being of unsound mind and is properly in Saint Elizabeths Hospital under the 1955 adjudication. . . ." We agree that the adjudication of unsoundness of mind is still in effect. But in our opinion it does not follow that her present detention is authorized. To hold otherwise would overlook the proper distinction between the standards which should be applicable to determining unsoundness of mind, on the one hand, and the need for commitment to a hospital on the other.

Although our law provides that only persons of unsound mind may be committed, it does not require the commitment of all persons of unsound mind. See D.C. Code § 21–316(C)(2). Nor does it provide that one who has been committed must be detained until he is legally declared of sound mind. To hold that it does, "would be to ignore the rule that although a person may be of unsound mind to the extent that he cannot contract, nevertheless he cannot lawfully be restrained unless his mental condition is such as to render it necessary that he be placed under restraint. [It] would be to hold that when a mentally ill patient has once been confined in a state hospital for treatment he cannot be discharged until he has been completely restored to reason." *Hatton v. State Board of Control*, 146 Tex. at 163–64, 204 S.W. 2d at 391. Since the law recognizes that not all persons adjudged of unsound mind need be hospitalized, it follows that once a patient has been discharged from the hospital, even though he remain under an adjudication of unsoundness of mind, he cannot on that account be recommitted without a *de novo* proceeding. Therefore the District Court erred in holding that appellant's failure to obtain restoration to legal competency rendered her subject to recommitment under the 1955 order.

We reverse the District Court and hold that appellant's present detention under the 1955 commitment order is illegal. If it now appears that appellant requires further hospitalization, additional commitment proceedings must be instituted.

This case suggests a problem which deserves comment. The legislative trend throughout the country is away from making commitment depend on an adjudication of incompetency. Those concerned to protect the rights of the mentally disordered are looking with increasing disfavor on judicial decrees which take away a collection of individual rights, without specific findings as to the need to do so in each individual instance. The law in the District of Columbia would seem to be particularly vulnerable to criticism on these grounds. Dr. Madson testified that "commitment to a hospital here automatically renders a patient legally incompetent. We feel that there are

many patients in the hospital who are legally competent. . . ." Yet in order for these patients to get the hospitalization they require, they are, under our statutory procedure adjudged "of unsound mind." The disadvantages of commitment being dependent on such an adjudication of general incompetency are compounded by the failure of the statute to specify the implications of the adjudication. The result is a rebuttable presumption of incompetency to engage in any activity for which the law requires one to be "of sound mind." Thus, without any inquiry or finding as to *actual* competence in the given area, a patient in St. Elizabeths Hospital, or a former patient who has not been legally restored to soundness of mind, may apparently be deprived of the right to vote, to drive an automobile, to enter into binding legal arrangements and to exercise other civil rights.

Reversed

CIRCUIT JUDGE, dissenting: While Congress has established judicial proceedings for restoration of status after a person has been civilly committed to a mental institution, this court now holds that, by the simple act of escaping, the patient can avoid adjudication of her status in the courts. Thus a dangerously insane patient may be committed to Saint Elizabeths Hospital on Monday, walk out on Friday (as it appears may easily be done), be held to be "improved" under the circumstances present here, and, by the escape, the legal proceedings before the Commission on Mental Health are *nullified*. As I understand the statutory scheme this holding completely undercuts the intent of Congress and I must, therefore, dissent.

The commitment order which placed appellant in the hospital is still in effect. Had she not fled the hospital it is clear that § 21–320 D.C. Code would compel her to apply to the District Court to effect her release by habeas corpus. The majority holding means that every time a patient escapes and becomes legally a fugitive her commitment becomes void and a new jury determination must be made of the patient's mental condition.

The bizarre conduct of appellant at the Vice President's office is pregnant with dangerous possibilities and confirms the views of the Saint Elizabeths Hospital staff that at the time of her escape she was still in need of treatment and should not be allowed at large.

The provisions of § 21–320 make it plain that every patient released on parole by the hospital must petition for restoration in order to set aside the original commitment order.

*   *   *

Appellant has never been restored to capacity through the statutory procedure authorized in § 21–32, D.C. Code and the mere entry on the record that she was discharged as "improved" certainly cannot operate as an adjudication that she is of sound mind. The entry is purely administrative.

The above cited section of the D.C. Code provides for a jury trial when a patient, paroled or released as improved, petitions for restoration and the Commission on Mental Health finds the patient of unsound mind. Appellant did not apply for such a trial, and it would seem fairly clear that had she done so, and had she been granted one, she would not have been discharged, in view of her mental condition.

The District Judge makes clear in his opinion that appellant, through her escape from Saint Elizabeths Hospital, is seeking to obtain a benefit unavailable to a patient who does not escape. As the 1955 commitment remains in full force and effect, it was incumbent upon appellant to convince the court, in view of her being held under that commitment, that she has recovered her sanity and is entitled to her release. This she has signally failed to do.

In sum, I think appellant, for her own safety and for the safety of public officials and others, and in accordance with law, should remain in Saint Elizabeths Hospital until she has been properly determined to be of sound mind.

For these reasons I dissent.

NOTES

NOTE 1

Letter From Hospital to Patient

November 14, 1960

Mrs. Bertha Radek
Saint Elizabeths Hospital
Washington, D.C. 20032

Dear Mrs. Radek:

This copy of the authorization for your return to Pennsylvania is being given to you to assist you in proving your residence in Pennsylvania if necessary. As we anticipate your discharge through court order, you will not be transferred to Pennsylvania State Hospital. However, we advise you to apply there for admission if you are in need of further psychiatric treatment.

Sincerely yours,
E. Bornstein, M.D.

NOTE 2

Doctor's Closing Summary— 22 November 1960

Today (November 22, 1960) the patient was dis-

charged by Court order in custody of her attorney Mr. Edward O'Neill.

During her present admission, she has consistently been dignified, good-humored, but thoroughly convinced of her delusions which have to do with electronics machines, Communists, and the fact that people's faces turn different colors thereby expressing different emotions or character traits. She received no privileges although her general conduct would have warranted them because it was felt that at the earliest opportunity she would again leave the Hospital without permission and would again bring herself to the attention of the Secret Service. After considerable effort on the part of Interstate Services with the full co-operation of the patient, her residence in Pennsylvania was established and her return to Pennsylvania State Hospital was authorized. Mrs. Radek was eager to return to New Jersey to live with the elderly man whom she considered her stepfather, or to visit her mother, who lived in Pennsylvania. However, her Court appointed attorney had taken her case to court and the final decision was that she had never been properly committed.

DIAGNOSIS: 22.3 SCHIZOPHRENIC REACTION. PARANOID TYPE

CONDITION ON DISCHARGE: IMPROVED

E. Bornstein, M.D.

NOTE 3

Bertha Radek—Four Years Later

When an informal request was made for the jury trial, the governmental authorities would not go forward and accordingly, on the 22nd of November, 1960, I obtained an order from the District Court releasing her "from the custody of St. Elizabeth's Hospital." I might add one additional extralegal fact. Upon her release, Bertha was without funds. I picked her up at the hospital, personally, purchased her bus fare to New Jersey, and placed her on the Greyhound bus, wishing her "well." I have, since October, 1960, been in correspondence with Bertha, and the correspondence has increased this Fall during the Presidential Campaign. [Letter from Guardian ad litem —December 16, 1964.]

E.

Congress Informs Itself About the Process

Cases like *Radek* v. *Britain* prompted the 87th Congress to conduct a series of hearings to inform itself about the administration of statutes relating to the mentally ill. Consider the extent to which the material presented to the committee is responsive to the questions you would raise and how and why this information would be relevant to any decision you might reach. Concerning this problem the Royal Commission on the Law Relating to Mental Illness and Mental Deficiency observed:

"The proper treatment of people suffering from disorders of the mind, and any restrictions on the liberty of individual citizens which this may involve, are matters of public interest which may at any time become of immediate personal importance to anyone living in this country. Many different sorts of people with different knowledge and experience are involved in operating the laws which govern these matters. These include the patients' relatives as well as doctors, magistrates, public officials and social workers. Ideally, a branch of the law which may affect the liberty of any one of us and in whose operation any one of us may have to take an active part should be as simple and easily intelligible as possible. But our present laws on these subjects are complicated and difficult to understand, and very few people have any general knowledge of what they contain or how they work in practice.

"Yet the questions with which this branch of the law sets out to deal are simple. What forms of care need to be provided for people who are suffering, temporarily or permanently, from various forms of mental illness or disability? Who should be responsible for administering these services? Are there circumstances in which some patients should be compelled to accept care against their will, or be subject to detention while under care, either for their own welfare or protection or for the protection of other people? If there are, how are we to ensure that powers of compulsion and detention provided for this purpose are not abused?"*

Would you pose these or different questions and why?

* Cmnd. 169 (1954–57) p.7. Reprinted by permission.

**CONSTITUTIONAL RIGHTS OF THE MENTALLY ILL
HEARINGS BEFORE THE SUBCOMMITTEE ON CONSTITUTIONAL RIGHTS OF THE COMMITTEE ON THE JUDICIARY, UNITED STATES SENATE**

87th Cong., 1st Sess. and 88th Cong., Ist Sess. (1961 and 1963)

SENATOR ERVIN

In recent years the American public has become increasingly aware of the problem of mental illness. At present, one-half of the hospital beds in this country are occupied by persons afflicted with mental disorders, and the medical profession informs us that 1 person in every 12 will, at some time in his life, be hospitalized for a mental condition.

Thus far, little attention has been devoted to the constitutional rights of the mentally ill. Concern has been largely in the realm of hospitalization procedures. There has been substantial disagreement about the use of judicial procedures for involuntary hospitalization. The alleged position of the medical profession is that mental illness is a health problem, and therefore physicians should be responsible for hospitalization. Attorneys, however, generally be-

lieve that since compulsory hospitalization involves loss of liberty, it is a function of the courts.

Hospitalization under judicial or nonjudicial procedures often results in an automatic determination of incompetency. When this occurs under the latter procedure, there is a question of denial of property rights without due process of law. Also, there appears to be some disagreement within both the medical and legal professions over the issue of whether a person who needs hospitalization is necessarily incapable of handling his own affairs.

Another facet of the problem involves the right to treatment once the patient has been admitted to a hospital. This is an especially important issue when the basis of the hospitalization has been the "need for treatment" rather than the fact that the patient is dangerous to himself or others. In our overcrowded and understaffed hospitals he may receive only custodial care.

One of the paramount questions confronting us today is whether society, which is unable or unwilling to provide treatment, has the right to deprive the patient of his liberty on the sole grounds that he is in need of care.

The lack of hospital personnel may also affect the patient's right to release as soon as the conditions justifying his involuntary hospitalization no longer exist. If there is no qualified staff to examine the patient, who is to know when he is ready for release? Should the patient's right to discharge be restricted by the unavailability of psychiatric personnel to ascertain his condition? Only one State has a law which provides for frequent and thorough examination of patients, and three-fourths of the States have no statutory provisions on the subject.

* * *

We are aware of the magnitude and difficulty of the task we are undertaking. This subject has been described as "the most neglected area in the law." It is our hope that these hearings will cast new light on the problem, and possibly provide the information necessary for an enlightened revision of the statutes governing the mentally ill.

* * *

SENATOR HRUSKA

* * *

[O]nce we decide that certain individuals are unable to determine what is best for themselves and delegate this choice to others, we have entered upon sacred ground.

As we know, it is particularly difficult to legislate in this area because the basic rights of the individual must be reconciled with medical considerations. The doctor and the lawyer approach the problem from different angles and often find themselves in disagreement as to what procedure will best serve the needs of the individual. This poses a formidable obstacle to sound, effective legislation, but surely it is possible to harmonize these interests so that the patient's constitutional rights can be protected without unduly hampering his medical needs.

1.

STATEMENT OF HON. ALEXANDER WILEY, UNITED STATES SENATOR FROM THE STATE OF WISCONSIN, AS PRESENTED BY NICHOLAS N. KITTRIE, LEGISLATIVE ASSISTANT TO SENATOR WILEY

MR. KITTRIE. . . .

* * *

Let me remind those present here that over 250,000 people are committed to mental institutions each year, three times as many as are sentenced to State and Federal prisons. About 800,000 patients are kept in mental institutions, more than four times the present prison population. These people are not criminals. Nevertheless in most cases they are held involuntarily and are deprived of civil rights by either law or circumstance.

At the present rate of commitment to mental insti-

tutions, one out of every three American families is destined to have its legal situation seriously disrupted by the commitment of one of its members. The law not only determines who should be committed and pursuant to what procedure, but also determines many related questions such as may a wife of a committed patient sue for divorce; may a mental patient see his clergyman, lawyer, and family; should he be allowed to vote, to write checks, to sue and be sued; should he be deprived of his driver's license or the license to practice his profession?

One out of every two beds in our hospitals is occupied by a mental patient. The statistics would be even higher if the laws providing for the commitment of alcoholics, epileptics, and drug addicts were fully utilized.

* * *

Most of the laws dealing with mentally ill people are State laws because the care of the mental patient is primarily a State function. . . .

It is to be remembered that the care of the mentally ill imposes a heavy burden on most States. In my own State of Wisconsin some 6 per cent of the total State budget, or more than $29 million annually, is spent on the care of mentally ill patients. The Wisconsin mental institutions hold some 20,000 patients and some 8,000 new patients are admitted each year.

* * *

SENATOR LONG. . . .

* * *

. . . There is no question but that the due-process clauses of the fifth and fourteenth amendments to the Constitution of the United States are as applicable to individuals suffering from mental illness, as to other members of our society. I am cognizant of the fact that most of our State statutes make provision for the protection of the basic rights of notice, counsel, hearing, etc., but I believe, . . . that enforcement of these provisions in many instances has been woefully inadequate.

* * *

2.

STATEMENT OF ADDISON M. DUVAL, M.D., DIRECTOR OF THE MISSOURI DIVISION OF MENTAL DISEASES

* * *

. . . I am Dr. Addison M. Duval, the first qualified psychiatrist and certified mental hospital administrator to become director of Missouri's mental health program under new legislation effected in 1957. I assumed my present duties after completing

30 years of Federal service—all at St. Elizabeths Hospital in Washington, D.C.—where I served as assistant superintendent for my last 6 years there.

* * *

. . . Only a few years ago it was thought necessary to place every newly admitted State hospital patient in a locked unit, where his personal clothing and effects were removed, he was given used hospital clothing to wear, all jewelry, eyeglasses, and dentures were removed for the sake of safety and often the patient was only given a spoon with which to eat. Unfortunately, a few State mental hospitals still follow this abominable practice and do so largely because of the erroneous concept that all mentally ill people are dangerous.

This idea of dangerousness is attributable most frequently to the legally committed patient rather than to the voluntary patient. The same idea even influences the psychiatrist in his determination of which patients are ready to leave the hospital for return home. He will usually permit the voluntary patient to leave the hospital much earlier than the committed patient, as he doesn't want "to take any chances."

Other matters which interfere with the return of the mentally ill patient to the community have to do with the many prejudices and misconceptions on the part of average citizens who firmly believe that almost no committed patients ever recover from their mental illness and, therefore, the hospital must be mistaken in saying that a certain patient is ready for discharge. One of the great needs in America to help overcome these misunderstandings is for the development of a modern community-centered mental health program which will provide early diagnosis and treatment for beginning illnesses, together with the necessary consultation services to the community-serving agencies, with a major effort given to prevention of illness and the promotion of mental health. . . .

In conclusion, it is my belief that we should make admission and discharge of patients to and from State mental institutions as easy and nonlegalistic as possible. I believe that in all but a very few instances, if we make treatment hospitals of our present insane asylums, we will have no difficulty with the average citizen's willingness to be admitted on voluntary application. Only in very rare cases would a patient have to be certified or committed by the court. . . .

* * *

3.

STATEMENT OF
WINFRED OVERHOLSER, M.D.,
SUPERINTENDENT, ST. ELIZABETHS
HOSPITAL

SENATOR ERVIN. . . .

* * *

The chair is particularly pleased to have the opportunity to recognize Dr. Winfred Overholser, . . . Superintendent of St. Elizabeths Hospital in the District of Columbia.

* * *

DR. OVERHOLSER

[T]he District of Columbia, the laws of which are enacted by the Congress of the United States, has, to my mind, one of the least desirable procedures of any jurisdiction in the Union. It is cumbersome, unduly legalistic, unnecessarily distressing to the patient, and tends to delay rather than facilitate early hospital care of those patients who need it.

The general objectives of a law relative to the admission of patients to mental hospitals were never more effectively stated than by Isaac Ray, the great American forensic psychiatrist, in 1869. He said:

> In the first place the law should put no hindrance in the way to the prompt use of those instrumentalities which are regarded as most effectual in promoting the comfort and restoration of the patient. Secondly, it should spare all unnecessary exposure of private troubles and all unnecessary conflict with popular prejudices. Thirdly, it should protect individuals from wrongful imprisonment. It would be objection enough to any legal provision that it failed to secure these objects in the completest possible manner.

The law was interested, until the beginning of the last century, only in confining those who were considered to be "furiously mad" or "manifestly dangerous." Such a law was passed by New York State in 1788 and by Massachusetts in 1797.

The attitude toward the mentally ill at that time may be gathered from the fact that the law of Massachusetts was enacted as an "act of suppressing rogues, vagabonds, common beggars, and other idle, disorderly, and lewd persons."

In those days, and indeed for a good many years subsequently, the jails were used to a considerable extent as receptacles for persons who were mentally ill. It was not, for example, until 1827 that New York forbade the detention of "lunatics," as they called them, in any prison, jail, or house of correction.

There was, then, a glimmering of the fact that these individuals were sick. In the 1860's, as a result of the activities of a Mrs. Packard who had been confined in an Illinois State hospital, there was a wave of laws demanding jury trial, placing the proposed patient thus in a category with criminals.

I am glad to say that today no State requires a jury trial for admission to a mental hospital although in a number of States such a trial is available upon the demand of the patient or someone in his behalf.

There is, of course, under the United States Constitution no right to a jury trial for this purpose. Until the time of Mrs. Packard's crusade, admission except of the "furiously mad" has been pretty much informal, just as is today admission to a general hospital, but since that time the process of admission has been hedged about with detailed legal provisions.

Dorothea Lynde Dix, the great reformer of the care of the mentally ill, beginning in 1843 and continuing until the eighties, emphasized to the public that the mentally ill were sick persons, and indeed this is today the generally accepted point of view. For that reason psychiatrists prefer as informal a proceeding as is possible. Indeed, some States, beginning with Massachusetts in 1881, have encouraged the voluntary admission of patients, and in several States a very considerable proportion of the admissions are of this character, the patient entering voluntarily and being at liberty to leave in the same manner.

All States have provisions of some sort governing admissions to mental hospitals and providing, among other things, for compulsory admission and detention for those patients who are too ill mentally to appreciate their need of hospital care and who represent in some way a danger to themselves or others.

In a discussion of the rights of the mentally ill, unfounded fears have been created regarding possible unlawful deprivation of liberty of the patient. Actually, the public mental hospitals, as instrumentalities of the State, may reasonably be expected to send patients back to the community as soon as their condition warrants, and always habeas corpus is available.

In the case of private hospitals, which appear to be the chief targets of the "railroading myth," there is no reason why they should not be, as they are in many States, licensed and supervised by the State so that any improper confinement can be avoided.

After 45 years in mental hospitals and their administration, I am convinced that the basis for the belief that persons are improperly sent to mental hospitals is, for practical purposes, entirely without foundation. Certainly it should be a criminal offense to conspire in an improper commitment. As Isaac Ray remarked, many years ago, "Legislation will not still all the public clamor. That will continue," he said, "as long as the wrongful imprisonment of sane persons is capable of adding to the interest of a novel or as long as the stories of the insane are received by prejudiced people as unqualified truths."

A right of the mentally ill, which is sometimes forgotten, is the right to early and efficient treatment, whether that be in a hospital, an out-patient department, or a community clinic. Burdensome formalities in connection with the admission make a family reluctant to send the patient to the hospital; they are painful to the patient himself, and tend to foster the stigma of mental illness.

Fortunately today there is a gradual extension of facilities to those who are in need of treatment. Particularly, may we mention the establishment of psychiatric services in general hospitals and the growing tendency for nonjudicial commitment. Mental disease is an illness and should be treated as much as possible as other illnesses are.

*   *   *

[U]ntil 1938, compulsory jury trial was the law in the District of Columbia. The patient had to be taken into a criminal courtroom and tried before a jury on the charge of being of unsound mind. Testimony was given in his presence. It was as if he were being prosecuted. A jury, a nonmedical jury may I emphasize, passed on whether or not he should be sent to St. Elizabeths.

Fortunately, in 1938 that law was changed somewhat for the better in that the compulsory jury trial was abolished. For the jury of twelve laymen, a jury so to speak of a lawyer and two psychiatrists was substituted. That was almost the only change. There still is formal notice. There is summoning of witnesses. The witnesses must testify in the presence of the patient, and this is an extremely traumatic thing both for the patient and for his family. It is one thing which, all by itself, tends to make families hesitate greatly about sending a patient or proceeding for his commitment.

Then he is invited . . . after the Commission on Mental Health has decided that he should be committed, to go down to court to ask the judge not to sign the commitment order. If the judge signs, then, of course, the patient or someone on his behalf has the right to demand a jury trial. This procedure then not only authorizes the detention of the patient in St. Elizabeths Hospital but it adjudicates him to be a person of unsound mind. This makes it extremely difficult when we are sending patients out on visits, and we send a great many. It is in their way because technically they are *non sui juris*, if I may as a mere psychiatrist use a legal term, and they are technically not at liberty even to sign a payroll, sign a check, or have a bank account.

*   *   *

MR. CREECH: Sir, with regard to your psychiatric staff, what is the ratio of psychiatrists to the patients at St. Elizabeths?

DR. OVERHOLSER: All together of physicians, some of whom are residents in training, we have better than one to a hundred, which is pretty good as mental hospitals go. I think we are considerably, indeed very much, above the average for the country.

*   *   *

MR. CREECH: Well, what percentage of the patients you have at St. Elizabeths are on active therapy?

DR. OVERHOLSER: There again, of course, the question of what constitutes therapy is a difficult one to answer. There is individual psychotherapy and, of course, the number under that is pretty small because that takes a lot of individual time. About 50 patients are being seen regularly in individual psychotherapeutic sessions.

We have a good many hundred—I can't say just how many—who are under group psychotherapy of one sort and another. We have, of course, a very considerable number who are under drug therapy of one kind or another, under tranquilizers particularly. We do a great deal with what is sometimes nowadays called milieu therapy, an attempt at having patients attempt self-help. In other words, we try to throw as much responsibility on the patient as possible with the idea of resocializing them, getting them back into the community.

Now all of those are forms of treatment. Treatment doesn't consist merely in taking a pill, you see, and I think that is to be borne in mind.

We are dealing now more in ward programs. We have a very active volunteer program which augments in some respects, you see, our employee quota. Only last evening I was at a ward party which is run by volunteers who come in once a week, and what they have done with those patients who were very, very regressed patients is quite remarkable. It goes to show what can be done for mental patients with even a moderate amount of personal attention.

I cannot say, all together, just how many are under treatment. We certainly have programs of one sort and another, very considerably over half, and, of course, one has to remember that we have a very considerable number of elderly and infirm patients who are confined either to their beds or to wheelchairs who cannot get around, and, of course, in their case they do enjoy television, and they do enjoy ward parties, and some of them even play cards and that sort of thing.

We do a lot with recreation and with occupational therapy, but there are some patients who are really not amenable to any sort of therapy. But that represents by far the small minority.

MR. CREECH: And how often are the patients examined by a psychiatrist?

DR. OVERHOLSER: . . . The patients are perhaps not given a formal psychiatric examination every 6 months or something like that, but they are being seen very frequently, and programs are being worked out for them. It is not that they are being neglected or not seen by a doctor. . . .

MR. CREECH: Doctor, do you believe that involuntary hospitalization should be limited to persons who are dangerous to themselves or to others, at least until the hospitals are able to provide treatment?

*   *   *

DR. OVERHOLSER: In a general way I think provided there is a fairly broad interpretation of what dangerous means, a fair number of patients may not be going about like a raging lion who are nevertheless potentially likely, who may be likely to commit sui-

cide, for example. Or once in a while we read about tragedies of one sort and another in which an individual had been showing mental symptoms but nothing had been done about them.

You have the problem sometimes of unwilling patients, patients who will not go to a mental hospital or to a psychiatrist as they would go to a surgeon or to a general practitioner if they felt ill physically. But there have to be somewhere along the line some provisions for the involuntary hospitalization. But the easier that can be made and the less formal, the less judicial, the less connected or related to anything savoring of court proceedings and possibly criminal proceedings, the better.

In other words, these are sick people, and we want to see them cared for as sick people deserve to be cared for and not treated in a way that makes them feel and makes their families and their neighbors feel that maybe there is something just a bit criminal about it.

MR. CREECH: Is it your view that it is more traumatic for the individual to suddenly find himself in a mental institution, without notice or hearing, especially if the individual feels that he should have had some opportunity to confront those people who are accusing him of being mentally ill?

DR. OVERHOLSER. There are some patients who look upon the world with a jaundiced eye, so to speak, who feel they are victims of a persecution, and in that case they demand to be confronted with their accusers, and there ought to be some provision if that is demanded. It is too bad, however, to subject some patients to this, patients who feel very unworthy or, feel that they have committed the unpardonable sin, and this just impresses upon them all the more that their ideas are correct.

*   *   *

MR. CREECH: What kind of mechanical restraints are used at St. Elizabeths?

*   *   *

DR. OVERHOLSER: . . .

As far as straitjackets are concerned, I have never seen one there, and I have been there 24 years, and they weren't used even in my predecessor's time.

We have no padded cells. Those went out long before the bustle even did. Occasionally it is necessary to place a patient in a single room for a time, sometimes for his own protection and sometimes for the protection of the other people in the ward.

*   *   *

SENATOR HRUSKA: Doctor, I would imagine there are instances of violent cases, are there not, which require confinement, and do they not sometimes become so violent that an ordinary room is not sufficient to restrain them?

DR. OVERHOLSER: Well, in such a case we probably would resort to make some sort of what might be termed chemical restraints. That is, we might give them some sort of a hypodermic of sedative effect, you see.

SENATOR HRUSKA: That cannot be continued too long, however, can it? That would be for a relatively short duration?

DR. OVERHOLSER: Most of those episodes of violence are short lived. But it might be that a patient who is subject to those might not be a desirable person to have around the other patients. It might be necessary to keep him in a room for a time. That is quite different, of course, from restraining him in the sense in which you use the word.

SENATOR HRUSKA: Yes. I didn't have reference to therapeutic treatment. I had reference to some stages of mental illness which are, after all, a little more violent in nature than the normal case.

DR. OVERHOLSER: But we don't see very many nowadays, strangely enough. I think styles change in mental manifestations just as they do in ladies' hats. We don't see some of the forms of major hysteria— that you read about in the old textbooks of 50 years ago. And, of course, the tranquilizers have brought about a revolution in the atmosphere of mental hospitals. We don't see very many patients of the type you have in mind, Senator Hruska, I am glad to say.

SENATOR HRUSKA: [W]hat are your space problems there? What is your population and how well can you accommodate those that you are required to house and look after?

DR. OVERHOLSER: Well, I may say that we would rather put a patient in a somewhat crowded space than to make that patient wait outside. In other words, we don't have a waiting list. We do have some pretty crowded areas.

I should say we are approximately at least 10 per cent overcrowded.

SENATOR HRUSKA: How many do you have at St. Elizabeths?

DR. OVERHOLSER: We have on the rolls slightly over 8,000. About a thousand of these are out in the community on either a prolonged or sometimes a brief visit. We have about 7,000 on the grounds of the institution.

*   *   *

MR. CREECH: . . .
What is the percentage of voluntary patients at St. Elizabeths?

*   *   *

DR. OVERHOLSER: We now have about 265 out of 7,000. Many of those, you will understand, go out rather promptly.

In other words, we have admitted a great many more than 200. Indeed, we admit about 200 each

year. They occasionally decide they don't want to stay and may leave the day after they come in, practically.

MR. CREECH: This is of their own volition?

DR. OVERHOLSER: Yes, sir, entirely.

. . . When they come in, they are informed we expect them to give us 3 days' written notice. We like to make some plans about letting a patient go out and make sure that he is going to be cared for.

But it might be that his family came and wanted to take him out, in which case we would say, fine, we would waive that 3 days, in other words.

*   *   *

MR. CREECH: . . . How often do you have occasion to commence involuntary proceedings to keep a patient who has decided that he wants to be released, one who came there originally as a voluntary admittee?

DR. OVERHOLSER: I can't think of more than one case in the last 12 or 13 years in which a patient who would come in as a voluntary patient had subsequently been committed by us. We like to play squarely with the patient.

*   *   *

4.

STATEMENT OF ALBERT DEUTSCH, AUTHOR AND JOURNALIST, WASHINGTON, D.C.

*   *   *

MR. DEUTSCH: About a dozen years ago I conducted a nationwide survey of mental hospital conditions in the United States. . . . Some physicians I interviewed frankly admitted that the animals of nearby piggeries were better housed, fed, and treated than many of the patients on their wards. I saw hundreds of sick people shackled, strapped, straitjacketed, and bound to their beds. I saw mental patients forced to eat meals with their hands because there were not enough spoons and other tableware to go around—not because they couldn't be trusted to eat like humans. I saw them crawl into beds jammed together, in dormitories filled to twice or three time their normal capacity. I saw them incarcerated in "seclusion rooms"—solitary isolation cells, really— for weeks and months at a time. I saw signs of medical neglect, with curable patients sinking into hopeless chronicity. I found evidence of physical brutality, but these paled into insignificance when compared with the excruciating suffering stemming from prolonged, enforced idleness, herdlike crowding, lack of privacy, depersonalization, and the overall atmosphere of neglect. The fault lay not with individual physicians, nurses or attendants—underpaid, undervalued, and overworked as they were—but with the general community that not only tolerated but enforced these subhuman conditions through financial penury, ignorance, fear, and indifference.

Conditions . . . have improved considerably since then. The advent of the tranquilizing drugs a few years ago reduced tremendously the resort to straitjackets and other mechanical restraints, which our British cousins proved unnecessary in the first place, more than a century ago. The "disturbed wards" are not the bedlams they were a decade ago. The application of the "therapeutic community" concept in a few hospitals—where patients, instead of being herded like animals and reduced to subhuman status, are given greater measures of freedom, participation, and responsibility—has tended to transform asylums to hospitals where it is adopted. So have other therapeutic devices. But these improvements, heartening though they be, must be measured soberly against the primitive level they proceeded from, the great distance we remain from achievable goals, and the continuing injustices and deprivations still inflicted on hundreds of thousands of our fellow citizens.

Let us trace, briefly, the via dolorosa of the typical mental patient from the time of admission to the time of discharge, keeping in mind that there are notable exceptions in some communities and some States:

Firstly, there are the consequence of our outmoded, often outrageously unjust, commitment laws in most States. The mental patient is "suspected" of being insane. He or she is "apprehended" or "arrested" by a sheriff or other law-enforcement official. In many instances, he is thrown into jail and lodged there like a criminal awaiting determination of his mental status.

A recent survey in Indiana revealed that hundreds of harmless mental patients were thus confined in jail, many for long periods, while awaiting commitment.

If adjudged insane, he is committed by court order much as a criminal is committed to prison. Although modern psychiatry has demonstrated that individual mental patients differ vastly in their capacities for responsibility, mental hospital commitment in most States automatically strips them en masse of specific civil rights—sometimes of all such rights, regardless of their individual capacity.

In most cases, the committed patient is transported to the hospital by a police officer, often in handcuffs or straitjackets, although he or she may be perfectly harmless.

In spite of recent reforms here and there, commitment procedures in most States remain unsound, archaic, and even vicious in their operation. The combination of police, jail, and court can do incalculable harm to the patient, gravely impeding his chances of recovery. It often reinforces the delusions of persecution in some and the morbid feelings of guilt in others. Psychiatrists generally are appalled by the cumbersome, callous, and sometimes brutal legal machinery that "processes" sick people as though they were criminals.

Current commitment procedures, as with the institutional process itself, reflect in great measure the outworn popular misconceptions of the mentally sick or insane as either raving maniacs, dangerous lunatics, or gibbering idiots. The fact is that the great majority of hospitalized mental patients are too passive, too silent, too fearful, too withdrawn. Yet, for every real or potentially dangerous mental patient, we penalize a thousand or more sick people, perfectly harmless to the public peace or safety. . . .

Now, let us follow the mental patient into the institution. It is estimated that about 90 per cent of all State hospital patients in this country are there on commitment, rather than on voluntary admission.

* * *

. . . We will see later how it compares with what the British and the Europeans have been doing in this same field. If we said 8 to 9 per cent on commitment, we would probably be roughly right.

* * *

[W]e send them to these institutions without their approval or against their will. We do so on the implicit or explicit premise or promise that they will be treated with a view toward aiding their recovery. But what happens?

Recent studies . . . attest to the continuance of the stripping of the patient, loss of his individuality, and dignity, depersonalization, and demoralization. The chronically acute shortage of physicians in most wards makes the term "psychotherapy" a hideous mockery for most patients. In most public mental hospitals, the average ward patient comes into person-to-person contact with a physician about 15 minutes every month—not a day or a week, but a month. The wonder is that so many patients achieve social recovery, under these dismal circumstances. The grim tragedy of it all is that reliable psychiatrists tell us that the recovery rate could be doubled in many mental hospitals if modern therapeutic procedures were put to optimum use.

In return for depriving the institutionalized mental patient of his civil rights, we promise him treatment for his illness. In failing to redeem this pledge, we not only do not aid his recovery; in many cases, we make him worse.

* * *

This is in spite of the overwhelming evidence, not only abroad but now in this country, that loss of liberty harms the mental patient and is unnecessary for the public safety. Indeed, it has been amply demonstrated that freedom is a therapeutic tool, that it speeds recovery and that it therefore is conducive to economy.

Here is what I found in Embreeville after 2 years of operation as a completely open hospital:

The discharge rate of patients had doubled. Thanks to the zooming discharge rate, the hospital population had been reduced in the face of a doubled monthly admission rate.

The relapse rate was cut almost in half.

There was a sharp drop in violence. Patients got along better with themselves and the staff. Staff morale was raised tremendously. Property damage by patients was reduced 75 per cent.

There had not been a single serious incident in the surrounding community involving a patient. There were no more escapes than before the doors were opened. Patients were expected to act like human beings, and acted like human beings.

* * *

MR. CREECH: . . . Do you feel that [involuntary hospitalization] should be limited to patients who are dangerous to themselves or to others? Do you feel that it should be deferred until the hospitals are able to provide such treatment?

MR. DEUTSCH: That is a tough question. The fact of the matter is that most of the States have on their statutes books a very pious statement that commitment shall be made when the person is dangerous to himself or to others, and the treatment angle was added later. But the whole problem hinges basically on who is dangerous.

Now, in England they have the same kind of crazy people that we have here. They have schizophrenics and manic depressives and paranoids, and all the range of neurotic people. Yet you go into one of their hospitals, like Warlingham Park or Nottingham, and the doors are open and the patients are going about and wandering through the parks together.

And I wish I could have gone into detail about this other deprivation of rights—the arbitrary separation of the sexes, in social commingling.

In many of our State hospitals—indeed in most of them, there is this arbitrary separation in one degree or another. And now—

SENATOR KEATING: May I interrupt? You mean the sexes commingle in England in the mental hospitals?

MR. DEUTSCH: Dr. T. P. Rees, the superintendent at the time, was showing me through Warlingham Park, which is about 30 miles out of London, and I saw a male and female patient walking toward the beautiful woods locked arm in arm, and I turned to my escort, Dr. Rees, and I cleared my throat.

I asked, "Dr. Rees, do you have a little accident here once in a while?"

And he said, quite cheerfully, "Oh, sure, just as they do in the outside community."

In this country we are so frightened by the prospect of one such accident or incident that we lock up tens of thousands of people and we are supposed to be socializing them or resocializing them, for their return to the normal community.

We desocialize them. We deprive them for months and years of the natural commingling of sexes. Most State hospitals will have a dance once a week where the patients come together and these dances often are awful sights to watch, because these people have lost the capacity of social contact. They are fearful, they are awkward. They are embarrassed in each other's presence, and these weekly dances quite often are pretty gruesome experiences.

Now, why can't we have day-to-day commingling of the sexes without necessarily encouraging sexual intercourse between them? And there are all kinds of ways. And some of our best hospitals have adopted this desegregation of the sexes.

* * *

MR. CREECH: Sir, with regard to treatment of the patients, do you know of patients who are required to do other than therapeutic labor in hospitals?

MR. DEUTSCH: Many times. Not as often today as, say, a decade ago, but I am convinced on the basis of my own observation and reading that many patients are, in a sense, industrial peons. There is no doubt in my mind that many patients who could be discharged to the community, who are carpenters, or good plumbers, or good workmen generally, are maintained beyond their period of discharge in some of our State hospitals because they represent valuable free labor.

* * *

5.

STATEMENT OF DR. JACK EWALT, REPRESENTATIVE, AMERICAN PSYCHIATRIC ASSOCIATION, PROFESSOR OF PSYCHIATRY, HARVARD UNIVERSITY

* * *

From a medical point of view, the worst features of the commitment laws of the past (and some of these features are still with us in some States) are such requirements as these: That the patient must be given "notice" that he is to be committed; the insistence that the patient appear personally in court with consequent exposure of his problems to the public; the frequent identification of mental illness with criminality as a result of court procedures; the acceptance of a lay judgment as to the degree of illness as occurs, for example, in a jury trial; frequent acceptance of commitment as tantamount to legal incompetence, thus depriving a mental patient of his civil rights; the use of archaic legal terminology such as "insane," "of unsound mind," "idiot," "feeble-minded," etc.—all of them conveying a legal, rather than a medical, meaning; and embarrassing inquiries into the patient's financial status at the time of his commitment.

*   *   *

In general, psychiatrists favor a simple commitment procedure entailing an application to the hospital by a close relative or friend, and a certification by two qualified physicians that they have examined the subject and found him to be mentally ill. If judicial procedures must be brought into play at all, the court should have discretionary power to eliminate notification to the patient and not to require the patient to be present in person at a hearing. The examination by court-appointed physicians may be properly conducted in a medical facility, or at the home of the patient, and informally and in a manner that will have the least traumatic effect on the patient. In short, any procedures used should eliminate all public exposure and eschew any appearance of a criminal procedure.

*   *   *

It is of great importance that laws should provide for emergency commitments for limited periods of time without involving any court procedure. Over 20 States now have streamlined procedures for emergencies whereby a hearing may be waived, or a single physician instead of two physicians may commit a patient for a limited period of time. In such States there is a growing tendency to use emergency commitments for obvious reasons. They are speedier than regular commitment procedures and make it relatively easy for the doctors and the family concerned to take the patient directly to a hospital without going through the routine of a formal hearing. It allows for a temporary period of observing the patient in a medical setting during which formal commitment procedures may be instituted if deemed necessary. . . .

*   *   *

With regard to "notification of the patient" in court proceedings, this is one of the most irritating procedures to the physician. A paranoid patient, for example, may flee following such "notification." A depressed patient might commit suicide. It is increasingly recognized that if, in medical opinion, such notification would be harmful to the patient in this sense, then his rights can be sufficiently protected by avoiding notification to him and making him appear in court, and, instead, having his interests represented by an attorney. Such provision is made in at least 10 States.

*   *   *

All but a handful of States now provide for voluntary admissions to mental hospitals. . . . Perhaps 10 to 20 per cent of admissions to United States mental hospitals are voluntary. That more are not so is probably due to such factors as lack of general public respect for the mental hospital as a treatment center; the fact that the hospitals are overcrowded and understaffed; and the lingering stigma associated with being a mental patient.

There can be no doubt, however, that the use of voluntary admission procedures is much to be encouraged—and the more so as the Nation hopefully rallies behind a renewed effort to turn the public mental hospital into a genuine treatment center. Clearly, voluntary admissions encourage early treatment and a co-operative attitude toward the hospital by the patient. All of this is auspicious for more effective treatment and early recovery.

Here, again, there is a lack of legal clarity about the status of a voluntary patient—with regard to his exercise of various civil rights, for example—which serves to discourage voluntary admissions and these confusions need clarification.

*   *   *

It is clearly of the greatest importance that in protecting the rights of the patient who is hospitalized without his consent, that some system of periodic re-examination of his case be instituted. Obviously, if a patient is well enough to be discharged, but no one examines him to determine the fact, then he is being deprived of his freedom illegally.

*   *   *

It must be clearly understood that the establishment of a mental illness does not, *ipso facto*, warrant a finding of incompetency. Throughout the legal history of mental illness there has been considerable confusion about the two concepts, and in many States commitment can act as an automatic determination of incompetency. From a medical point of view there is not, necessarily, any connection between the two, and in general, psychiatrists are much concerned that any mental patient within a hospital should exercise as many of his ordinary civil rights as he has the capacity to exercise, such capacity being determined by medical judgment. We have in mind such rights as signing checks, selling property, retaining an automobile license, making purchases, executing contracts, voting, making a will, and the like. He must also retain the right to communicate by sealed mail, to receive visitors, to the confidentiality of his case records, to habeas corpus, and the right to protest further hospitalization.

The confusion between determination of mental illness and competency, for example, is reflected in an Ohio law which provides that except for voluntary patients: "No patient in a hospital . . . shall be competent to execute a contract, deed, or other instrument unless it has been approved and allowed by the court committing him. . . ." From a medical point of view, of course, such provisions can only frustrate the patient and therefore hamper the course of treatment.

This matter of being able to exercise civil rights also of the greatest importance in rehabilitating the patient. After a patient has been medically adjudged as sufficiently recovered for return to society, one can imagine the effect upon him when he is not allowed to drive an automobile, or sign checks, or make a contract, etc.

* * *

We may well ask, Why is a commitment procedure necessary anyway? Why would a delusional or hallucinating patient refuse to recognize these symptoms as those of an illness and seek treatment for them voluntarily? To be sure there are psychological reasons for his resistance and perhaps there will always be a number of mentally sick people who will refuse to recognize their illness because of their distorted sense of satisfaction in the symptoms. Still, we must recognize that the delusional patient conjures his delusions against a background of hundreds of years of intolerant prejudice against the very symptoms from which he suffers. The mentally sick patient may be disoriented, but he is not a fool. He is quite as aware as most of us of the public exposure that faces him if he goes to a hospital. He is alert to the tough time he will have getting a job when he gets out, if he does get out. He has read the newspapers about how overcrowded and understaffed the hospitals are. He knows that there lurks in the minds of his former friends the suspicion that he is a dangerous fellow. He is sensitive that a mother may recoil in fright if he stops to give her child a friendly pat on the head. What motivation has he to admit of his illness?

We are told by public opinion survey experts that the prevailing public image of the seriously mentally ill person continues to be an image of a violent, unstable, unreliable, dirty, disturbed, dangerous sort of a fellow and quite possibly one with criminal intent. One cannot help but hypothesize that our laws governing the mentally ill have developed in response to this public image in some measure. The general idea appears to have prevailed that if the seriously ill person is indeed such a risky fellow, then it becomes a terribly serious matter to accuse him of being sick, no matter how self-evident the symptoms may be. Thus all manner of legal safeguards must be established to insure that he shall not be so adjudged until the fact has been established beyond all possible doubt. In this spirit, legal procedures have taken on the atmosphere of a criminal trial, even though no crime has been committed. Similarly, once a sick person has been relegated to the custody of a mental

hospital, the same spirit dictates that we shall not make it too easy for the patient to be discharged and returned to the community for rehabilitation with his civil rights intact.

To the extent that the hypothesis holds water, it is, from a physician's point of view, based on a distorted conception of what the typical mental patient really is like. It is not that the physician would plead that the typical mental patient is pleasant to deal with. He is a challenge from any social point of view, to be sure. That is why, at some stage in his illness, he may need to be protected from society and society from him in some in-patient facility. But, to put it mildly, this is something less than to charge him with being dangerous, criminally inclined, or habitually violent. Speaking of crime, there isn't a shred of evidence that the incidence of crime among ex-mental hospital patients is any higher than for the general population, and there is some evidence that it may be less. . . .

* * *

6.

STATEMENT OF MICHAEL V. DiSALLE, GOVERNOR OF THE STATE OF OHIO

* * *

Two years ago, I began a hospital-by-hospital visit in Ohio. We have 25 mental institutions. In my visits I was quite struck by the number of people over the age of 65 who had been committed to our institutions. Upon inquiry from the central office and an inventory and diagnosis of the patients, we found that 25 per cent of our patients were over the age of 65—9000 in number—and of this number, approximately half, or 4500, were not psychotic or mentally ill in the commonly accepted sense.

These people were there as a result of someone refusing to accept the responsibility of their care or not being able to assume the responsibility. In many cases local subdivisions found that committing these people to mental institutions would eliminate a local financial burden and they were perfectly willing to have the State assume it.

We have now begun a program of releasing these people to nursing or rest homes, transferring them to the welfare program where they rightfully belong. To date, we have transferred 1500, and we may very well reach a total of 3000 before we complete this project.

The significant thing to me was that, under the State commitment law, this was possible. We are recommending to this session of the legislature a change in commitment laws in order that the State mental health department may have a chance to observe the potential patient for a period of 30 to 60 days before commitment. . . .

* * *

7.

STATEMENT OF
MANFRED GUTTMACHER, M.D.,
CHIEF MEDICAL OFFICER,
SUPREME BENCH, BALTIMORE, MD.

*   *   *

DR. GUTTMACHER: [P]eople who were released against hospital advice made about as good an adjustment as the people who were released by the hospital. This impresses me as very interesting; there are many angles of this that deserve further study. But the adjustment rate is a rather complicated thing. It is not merely a question of not being rehospitalized but of being able to do a job or earn a living and so forth and so on.

*   *   *

MR. CREECH: . . .

[P]erhaps out-patient treatment should be extended over a period of years. Would this be in the nature, sir, of clinical treatment?

DR. GUTTMACHER: I think the reason that this is in my mind particularly is that we have had in Maryland in the last decade three murders carried out by former hospital patients. One man killed his wife, one woman killed her mother, and then another patient killed someone not related.

These were all people who were released from the State hospitals against medical advice. That is, the families went to the hospital and said: "Please let these people out of the hospital. We can look after them. They don't need to be here." And the hospital, as long as the family wasn't willing to support them in going ahead with court confinement, acquiesced and gave the patients over to their families.

*   *   *

[T]here should be a longer period of surveillance in cases of people who have been considered very ill. Of course, we can tell from clinical types of illnesses whether there is more likelihood of recurrence in one type of case than another. Surveillance should continue, particularly of people who have been released against the advice of the hospital.

Social workers should go to the homes of these discharged patients and have a better line on what kind of adjustment they are making.

MR. CREECH: By the same token, sir, would you favor shorter periods of probation where it was indicated that the patient was cured rather than adhering to the statutory requirement of 1 year?

DR. GUTTMACHER: I think this should be individualized. I can see merit in certain cases in making it a very short period, yes, particularly where you have families that are very co-operative.

*   *   *

MR. CREECH: [Are] drugs and electroshock treatments administered with the consent of the patient?

DR. GUTTMACHER: No. In order to give electroshock one gets some member of the patient's family to sign a permission, the nearest of kin. The blank specifies that the member of the family has been acquainted with the dangers and so forth. But as far as the giving of drugs is concerned, this is completely under the control of the medical staff and no kind of permission is necessary.

There is a large group of these new drugs on which there is some danger of toxicity, but the medical staff is well aware of this, and on the lookout for it, so that they really are not in any sense dangerous drugs.

Electroshock I think has developed to a point where the danger now is very minimal. The mortality rate is extremely low now, and the number of fractures has also been very greatly reduced by using relaxing drugs at the time the treatment is given. But it is a practice, I believe, generally, to still get permission when this is done.

. . . Certainly my own feeling is that no matter what you are going to do to a psychiatric patient and no matter how much doubt you might have about his ability to comprehend fully what you are telling him, that you ought to go to great pains to explain to him just what is going to happen.

*   *   *

8.

TESTIMONY OF HUGH A. ROSS,
CLEVELAND, OHIO

MR. CREECH: Mr. Chairman, Mr. Ross is a lawyer . . . He is a member of the faculty of Western Reserve University Law School in Cleveland, and teaches a seminar for law students and social work students entitled "The Mentally Disabled in the Law."

MR. ROSS. . . .

*   *   *

[T]he definition of mental illness in Ohio is vague and ambiguous. This is true in many States.

Is it possible to draft adequate standards? We do not know. We do not have the information required to answer this question.

As a practical matter, the standards seem to vary from one community to the next. The decision as to what level of mental illness will require hospitalization depends upon such variables as community tolerance of abnormal behavior and availability of treatment facilities and other resources.

Closely related to the question of standards is the question of communication of these standards between the various professions which are involved with the commitment process—law, psychiatry, psychology, and social work. The medical witness in a commitment case is apt to use labels which are not well understood by the other participants in the decision, and sometimes he makes policy decisions which are phrased in terms of a medical decision.

* * *

One of the specific examples of that is the fact that in Cuyahoga County one of the psychiatrists for many months—this was a psychiatrist testifying before the court—for many months was under the mistaken impression that whenever the judge asked him about the patient's competence to handle his affairs, he was really asking him about hospitalization. The whole aspect of guardianship had never occurred to this physician. He was simply not aware of it. This was a young staff physician at one of the hospitals.

* * *

9.

STATEMENT OF JAMES V. BENNETT, DIRECTOR, UNITED STATES BUREAU OF PRISONS

MR. BENNETT: . . .
[T]here seems to me to have been too much emphasis placed on distinguishing sharply between [persons charged with crime and those committed civilly.] Frequently it is chance alone that determines whether particular mentally ill individuals will be handled through civil or criminal processes. . . .

* * *

MR. CREECH: . . .
Is [mental] treatment time considered as other time for good behavior for federal prisoners.
MR. BENNETT: No, sir, as not giving him credit for that time.
MR. CREECH: In other words, if a patient spends as much as several years receiving treatment he receives no credit for good behavior during this time?
MR. BENNETT: That is correct, sir.

* * *

MR. CREECH: Do you consider a prisoner who is receiving psychiatric treatment to be acting in good conduct?
MR. BENNETT: Well, sometimes, yes; yes, indeed. For the most part, we do not apply the usual discipline to such a person.
MR. CREECH: If a patient is suffering from some other type illness, for instance an appendectomy, while in the hospital, does he receive credit?
MR. BENNETT: He does. . . . The rationale of the provision against eligibility for good time allowance to a defendant who is mentally incompetent must be that he lacks the capacity to conduct himself in such manner as to entitle him to the allowance. Absent the

capacity to intelligently observe the rules and regulations laid down as requirements for the credit, he ought not in good conscience be held responsible if he violates them. It would seem completely unrealistic to set up credits in such case and subsequently be compelled, in the interest of sound and uniform administration, to annul them for some misconduct, the import and seriousness of which he might be, and conceivably would be, unable to comprehend.

* * *

10.

STATEMENT OF THOMAS S. SZASZ, PROFESSOR OF PSYCHIATRY, UPSTATE MEDICAL CENTER, SYRACUSE, N.Y.

DR. SZASZ: . . .
I am a psychiatrist and a psychoanalyst. My official position is that of professor of psychiatry at the State University of New York, Upstate Medical Center, in Syracuse.
I have a part-time private practice of psychoanalysis. My interest in this field—that is, of law and psychiatry—is mainly theoretical. . . .
My interest in this field has been to examine what seemed to me an important common area in the interests of jurists, legislators, and psychiatrists. This common area comprises, as I see it, two items: One is human beings, and the other is words. By being interested in words, I mean examining seriously the words we use in our everyday life—in this case, such words as "sickness," "treatment," "mental illness," "commitment," "hospitalization," and so forth. I have tried to examine seriously, as best I know, what we mean when we use these words.

* * *

. . . I thought I would first like to convey my opinion to you on this subject by examining what sort of conflict, what sort of social problem, motivates civil commitment. How does this phenomenon come into being? Thus, we shall scrutinize the moral conflict underlying commitment, rather than follow the ordinary approach, which consists of assuming that some people are mentally ill and, therefore, have to be put in mental hospitals.
As I see it, the main ethical and psychosocial function of the law is to provide a code of values by which men may orient themselves in their daily lives. This means that the law must establish a hierarchy of values to define the order of precedence in case of value conflict. Illustrative is the supremacy which the Anglo-American law gives to personal privacy and protection against self-incrimination over ready access to information concerning illegal activities required for the public good.

* * *

I would like to suggest that it is against this background that we should examine the issue of civil commitment. What exactly is the value conflict which civil commitment seeks to settle, and which values are given precedence in making civil commitment a legal procedure rather than an illegal procedure? Briefly, the conflict is between individual liberty and personal autonomy versus the integrity of the family.

In the vast majority of cases, civil commitment is instigated by a family member, for the purpose of removing another member from the family circle. If the offending person were not removed by way of civil commitment, the family unit might disintegrate (for example, husband or wife might commit suicide or might divorce each other). Commitment thus saves the family unit (at least temporarily), at the expense, I submit, of depriving the committed person of some of his civil liberties. Hence, the ethical value of the family as a social unit, is given preference over the value of individual liberty.

This hierarchy of values, codified by civil commitment is, however, usually considered and discussed in terms of mental health and mental illness. Accordingly, nothing is said about such things as, for example, the right to be eccentric, or the right to be a spendthrift and thus fail to support one's wife adequately. Instead, the language of the statutes speaks of "mental illness," "treatment," and "cure," and of similar abstractions. This strikes me as being in sharp contrast to the directness of the Bill of Rights on such matters as personal privacy, due process, the rights of an accused person to speedy trial, and so forth.

Commitment laws speak of "mental illnesses," rather than of annoying, irritating, or destructive behavior. However, what constitutes mental illness is nowhere clearly defined, as crimes are. Rather, it is established by reference to expert professional opinion: Thus, mental illness is behavior certified as such by psychiatrists. In actual practice, this results in a state of affairs which, to my mind, is exceedingly similar to *ex post facto* laws. Illustrative—and I take this illustration from a story mentioned in the newspapers a few months ago—is the example of the young heiress who wishes to marry a poor man against parental opposition. Often the parents can find a psychiatrist who is willing to consider the young woman's behavior *prima facie* evidence of mental illness. If he so certifies, and unless she is successful in objecting, such certification defines, for this particular case at least, what constitutes mental illness.

[S]o often in discussions and deliberations of this sort, reference is made to mental illness and mental treatment, or so-called psychiatric treatment. However, what constitutes psychiatric treatment is very rarely defined, just as what constitutes mental illness is very rarely defined. Since the precise character of psychiatric treatment is so manifold, and since different types of treatments are often spoken of as if they were all more or less alike, let us at least keep clearly in mind the usual arrangement that prevails in psychiatric practice. In other words, what do psychiatrists and patients do with each other, in this country, at this time. . . . What is ordinary psychiatric practice, or more precisely ordinary private psychiatric practice, like? The main features that I want to emphasize are these: The patient comes into the psychiatrist's office of his own accord, not because somebody sends him. He makes an appointment, and goes to a psychiatrist, and tells the psychiatrist what troubles him; usually he has to pay for this, and, as the humorists are apt to point out, he has to pay for this a great deal of money.

Now, for all this effort and money, the patient expects help for himself. He is paying for it. He does not expect help for his mother-in-law, he does not expect help for his employer. He expects help for himself.

I am not here to adjudicate the moral values of this arrangement, but I do want to describe the treatment to you. This is the ordinary model of private psychiatric treatment. When we speak of psychiatric treatment in penal institutions, and in other institutions, we mean something completely different, even though we use the same terms. I think this merits emphasis.

In other words, the patient is invited, . . . to incriminate himself. Why should he do it? If the patient accepts this invitation he does so in the hope of getting help for himself, and with the expectation that the psychiatrist will be on his side in his struggle with family, society, and so forth.

Saying that the psychiatrist will be on the patient's side, does not mean that the psychiatrist will help him achieve aspirations that are opposed to the interests of his wife, employer, or the social order at large. Psychotherapy is not a conspiracy. What is meant, is that the psychiatrist will assist the patient to understand his aspirations and his strategies, and will, most emphatically, refrain from doing anything to interfere with them, even if they are harmful to other persons or to society as a whole. Should the psychiatrist feel that acting in this way would be harmful to the patient, to himself, or society, he has the option—and in my view the only option, under the Hippocratic oath and an ethic protecting a person from self-incrimination—of refusing to treat the patient. He can send him away. No psychiatrist is forced to treat a patient.

If this is true, and if it is granted, how can the psychiatric situation be used to curtail the patient's freedom? It can be done by taking the stand that under some circumstances—usually not specified in advance—the interests of other persons or of society should be protected even at the cost of depriving the patient of his right not to incriminate himself. For example, a person may be committed to a State hospital on the basis of information furnished by himself. This might happen if someone confides in a psychiatrist that he wants to kill himself or another person. Or, a mother may be deprived of the custody of her child, if she reveals in the course of psychotherapy that she is gravely mishandling him.

The crucial issue in all of these situations is whether the psychiatrist is to be considered the agent of the patient or of someone else. I would like to repeat this because this is one of the principal points I would like to make at this point. I would like to urge you to consider carefully whose agent the psychiatrist is.

In this connection, drawing an analogy between legal and psychiatric functions and performances may be helpful. Attorneys may play any number of social roles. A particular person with legal training and qualifications may be legislator, judge, prosecutor, or defense counsel. Obviously, these are four different roles. It is also obvious that no attorney can be prosecutor, defense counsel, and judge all at the same time.

Yet, I submit that such a confusion among conflicting roles is commonplace in contemporary psychiatry. We must constantly ask ourselves questions such as these: Is the psychiatrist the patient's agent, or is he society's agent? Is he a therapist or a custodian? Is he a "doctor," or is he a "warden" of an institution which, although it is called "hospital," functions as a prison, inasmuch as patients cannot leave it at will?

If he is the patient's agent, the ethical value of protecting the patient's interests (e.g., his privilege against self-incrimination) must take precedence over the ethical value of society's need to protect the safety of people generally, and of a child vis-à-vis his parent in particular. If the psychiatrist is society's agent, the psychiatric situation implies that, if need be, the patient's interests will be sacrificed in order to protect the common good. . . .

It is, of course, perfectly reasonable and proper for a psychiatrist to serve as society's agent. Indeed, doing so may serve just as high an ethical aim as the purely psychotherapeutic position sketched earlier. However, if the psychiatrist acts as society's agent, it would behoove him to caution his patient that certain types of incriminating information may be used against him (much as police officers arresting a suspect are enjoined to do), and that he discloses these to the psychiatrist at his own peril.

As it stands the law recognizes none of these basic facts of psychiatric life. On the contrary, it considers every psychiatrist as if he were a "therapist" to his patient, rather than his potential adversary. By adversary, I mean here simply that the psychiatrist acts in a way opposed to the patient's self-interest, as defined by the patient.

Thirdly, I would like to say a few words about a subject which I have entitled "The Right to Be Mentally Ill."

I would like to preface my comments, at this point, by saying that I have very serious doubts about the usefulness of the term "mental illness."

[E]ven if we grant the argument, first, that there is such a thing as "mental illness"—I hold there is not, and that this is a metaphorical expression denoting, usually, some sort of socially deviant or inappropriate behavior—and, second, that such illness can be "diagnosed" and "treated," we are still left with the questions: Does a person have the right to be "mentally ill"? And further: Does he have the right to be "mentally ill" and deliberately not seek treatment for it?

This, I would like to submit to you, raises some rather simple but basic questions, and I am disturbed by the fact they are not raised more often in deliberations of this kind.

It seems to me that here we must rely on our practices in related areas of social life. As far as ordinary bodily illnesses are concerned—for example, pneumonia or lung cancer—it is obvious that we have the right to be ill and also the right not to seek treatment. In a democracy, to receive medical treatment is basically an option, not a requirement. Usually, the recipient has to pay for it. If he wants to suffer without medical aid, he is free to do so.

Of course, the right to be ill is abrogated when the illness is contagious and presents a public health hazard. And I think this is entirely correct.

One has no right to be ill with bubonic plague or with leprosy. Certain other diseases are also classified as "reportable." Although basically reliance is placed upon the individual patient to seek treatment voluntarily, persons who do not can be coerced to submit to medical care.

Finally, and most importantly, insofar as patients with contagious diseases are isolated from others this is done expressly for the benefit of those who are not ill. The segregation and isolation itself is not claimed to be "therapy." In mental hospital practice it is. I think this is false and very misleading.

In addition to the right to be ill, the Bill of Rights implicitly guarantees the right to commit a crime. I believe I am stating something quite trivial when I say this. This may be inferred from the provisions guaranteeing a speedy trial, the right to confront witnesses, etc.—all of which means that a man has the right to protest against the law itself, if he is willing to risk the consequences.

The point of this argument is that, insofar as we regard certain types of personal conduct as mental illness, we are logically obligated to take another step. We must consider the following questions: Does the so-called mentally ill person suffer from an illness for which he need not seek treatment? Or, does his illness constitute a public health hazard which threatens society, and hence requires isolation and involuntary treatment?

I believe I am substantially correct in asserting that the vast majority of persons hospitalized today involuntarily do not threaten the public safety or health. They often do threaten the integrity of the family, as was mentioned earlier. They do annoy certain people in their proximity, but they do not threaten the public health in the ordinary sense of the word. Accordingly, to treat mental illness as if it constituted a major public health hazard is completely unwarranted.

Should it be deemed desirable to consider mental illness a major public health hazard—a position that seems to me factually incorrect, but logically quite tenable—this would require establishing objective, and by objective, I mean publicly verifiable criteria for diagnosing the presence or absence of this alleged disorder.

In other words, this could no longer be diagnosed simply by professional opinion. No satisfactory criteria for this exist at present.

Again, I would like to add in my opinion the likelihood of establishing such criteria is very doubtful.

What would the establishment of so-called objective criteria for mental illness mean? It would mean that mental illness would have to be considered a health hazard, irrespective of the social position of the patient. It is a psychiatric and social fact, however, that sometimes the civil commitment procedure is utilized far more often in the case of lower than of upper class persons. A person's lack of social power— for example, education, occupation, social position, wealth, and so forth—and the degree of his commitability are directly proportional. Hence, even if we would wish to regard mental illness as a public health problem, I think it would be extremely difficult to implement this position, that is to implement it seriously.

If a person has tuberculosis and is contagious, or if he is a typhoid carrier, these diagnoses can be established objectively, even in prominent persons. However, I maintain that it is often virtually impossible to establish the diagnosis of so-called "mental illness" in a prominent person. This is so not because prominent persons are immune, in some mysterious way, from human problems and unhappiness, but because our psychiatric diagnostic terms—and here again I would like to call attention to what follows—because our psychiatric diagnostic terms are not descriptive of biological conditions, as are medical diagnoses. They function rather as commands, ordering others to act in certain ways. . . . For example, the diagnosis of psychosis means: "Do something to this person. He should be hospitalized, something should be done to him. He should be isolated from his family. He should be fired from his job, and so forth."

So long as the descriptive and prescriptive (or promotive) aspects of psychiatric diagnoses remain combined and confused, as they are today, we need especially enlightened legislative vigilance to protect people from what I consider the police powers of psychiatrists.

*   *   *

First, I would like to suggest that concerted effort be exerted toward the elimination of involuntary mental hospitalization—that is, toward the abolition of virtually all laws of civil commitment. Having heard some of the preceding testimony, may I add that I would like to go on record as being strongly opposed to the broadening of the scope of civil commitment. . . .

The vast majority of so-called mental patients, especially when acutely troubled, will readily accept decent, humane help, when such help is offered with dignity and without threats.

In this regard, mental illness, although I do not think it is an illness, is no different from any other human predicament, whether it be ignorance, poverty, or bodily illness. If people are offered help for any of these they will gladly accept it. There is rarely a need to impose "help" involuntarily.

This is the basis for our entire medical care system. When a person is medically ill, say with pneumonia or appendicitis, he goes to the hospital because he knows he will be well cared for. There is no force brought upon him by the law to seek treatment.

Second, in-patient or hospital psychiatric aid (or "treatment") should be provided under legal regulations similar to those for out-patient or office psychiatric aid. Again I consider this very fundamental and very simple. We already have a system of legal regulations and a model for out-patient or office therapy in operation. And it works.

Office practice is fundamentally a voluntary enterprise. Patients who want to visit a psychiatrist do so; those who do not, stay away. All mental hospitalization should be entirely voluntary. All of the quasi-criminal features of mental hospitalization (e.g., commitment, locked doors, release by habeas corpus, fingerprinting, etc.) should be abolished.

Third, some provisions for involuntary hospitalization are necessary for the relatively rare instances when persons become disabled, disoriented, and unable to secure the help they require. Again, let me emphasize that, in my opinion, such cases comprise an extremely small fraction of the people subjected to commitment procedures. In this type of case, the mental symptoms are often the expressions of bodily illness or toxicity (e.g., hypoglycemia in diabetics, acute alcoholic intoxication, and similar conditions). Hospitalization should therefore be in general (medical) hospitals, not in mental hospitals. Moreover, this type of involuntary hospitalization, in contrast to commitment, should last no longer than 48 to 72 hours. It should never be for an indeterminate period as every commitment now is.

In general, the rules governing such involuntary hospitalization should be similar to those governing hospitalization of persons rendered temporarily unconscious in accidents. They may be treated only while they are incapable of giving consent to treatment (and while their relatives are unavailable). Once they are able to give or withhold consent, treating them without it constitutes "assault and battery."

For example, if a person sustains a fracture, and is taken to a hospital by an ambulance, he has the right to leave that hospital and go to his private physician or go home without having the fracture set against his will.

* * *

Psychiatrists, and physicians generally are paid for committing patients, because this is considered to be a regular psychiatric or medical service. This, I think, provides an economic incentive to comply with whatever demands exist for commitment. While I do not think patients are generally committed for this reason, I think this arrangement is undesirable.

There are no forces in society, other than their conscientious reluctance, to restrain psychiatrists from certifying patients for commitment.

Each of these pressures toward commitment must be counteracted, by providing alternate solutions for social problems, and by devising legal penalties for the unwarranted commitment of patients.

* * *

[I] do not believe that mental illness should be used as an excusing condition in criminal proceedings. There may be some rare exceptions to this, but as a general rule I believe that all persons should be held accountable, legally accountable, for their actions.

* * *

MR. CREECH: Doctor, with regard to the right to be mentally ill . . . doesn't the term "mentally ill" of itself imply a lack of capacity to make the determination of whether one wants to be mentally ill?

DR. SZASZ: . . .

There is, first of all the *a priori* assumption that mentally ill people somehow are different from people not mentally ill, and that they cannot make a decision whether or not they should be treated. They cannot make a decision whether or not they should go to a hospital. They cannot make a decision whether or not they should defend themselves in a trial or how they should assist in their own defense.

Now, my personal opinion is that, on the whole, all of these propositions are much more false than they are true. Usually they are completely false. While the term "mental illness" has, as I said, virtually an infinity of meanings, it can be confidently asserted

that in most instances in which it is used nowadays, especially when the so-called patient is legally entangled, the patient's alleged mental illness most assuredly does not mean that his capacity to decide about matters of concern to him is significantly impaired.

For example, if the person who is said to be mentally ill is also one who has committed an antisocial act, more often than not the label of mental illness is attached to him simply because of his antisocial act, rather than because some "disease" has been found in his head, so to speak.

* * *

MR. CREECH: I wonder if you would care to contrast the voluntary patient in this country who must give from 10 to 60 days' notice of his desire to leave— with the Irish system where he may give written notice and leave almost immediately.

DR. SZASZ: . . .

What is called voluntary admission is really not voluntary. It is perhaps quasi-voluntary. What we call voluntary admission to a mental hospital doesn't resemble voluntary admission to a medical hospital, for example for pneumonia. It is rather a kind of voluntary involuntary admission. This so-called voluntary admission to a mental hospital is a procedure, which, more often than not, could be paraphrased as follows. It is as if the patient were told: "If you don't go to the hospital by signing this piece of paper, then we'll get you in by having someone else sign another piece of paper."

It is the same for release. Voluntary release is really pseudo-voluntary, or sometimes results in no release at all. What happens when a patient signs a form requesting release depends on many circumstances, mostly on what kind of doctor he happens to be confronted with. I don't have the facts on this, and I doubt that anybody does. But, again, the fact is that the patient may be released after 10 or 60 days, or may be not. Often, while he is waiting for release, forms are made out for involuntary commitment— and the patient's status may thus be changed from voluntary admission to involuntary commitment. Usually, the patient isn't told about this, and if he is, he is as a rule helpless to do anything about it.

So this right to apply for discharge looks better on paper than I think it is in actuality. In practices, I believe that the patient is very inadequately protected.

MR. CREECH: . . .

We have received testimony . . . that it is much more of a traumatic experience for a person who is mentally disturbed to find himself to be served with notice, and participate in a hearing, than suddenly finding himself in a mental institution.

I wonder, sir, if you would care to comment on this point.

* * *

DR. SZASZ: . . . I believe it is possible that such a hearing is traumatic for a person, as it is alleged to be. However, I believe even more strongly that to be placed in an institution without explanations of how one got there, why one got there, and for how long one will be confined, is even more traumatic. The question is not simply whether a given person is "mentally ill" and whether a hearing is "traumatic" —but rather what are our choices as to how we might deal with this person. If in the name of their allegedly traumatic experience we do what we now do—that is, confuse the patient and deprive him of the opportunity to effectively resist the commitment procedure —then I am 100 per cent against it.

. . . It is not enough to talk about hearings. There are hearings, and there are hearings. There are investigations, and there are investigations. I think if a hearing is conducted with humanity and with sensitivity, I don't see anything traumatic about it.

MR. CREECH: That is the point I am trying to make. I gather from your statement here that you did not feel that notices and hearings are necessarily too traumatic an experience for a mentally ill person to encounter.

DR. SZASZ: [I] would go so far as to say that they might be highly therapeutic. What I mean is that it is very beneficial for a human being to be told why other people object to him. This is what the hearing is all about in my opinion. For example, a person might be told that he is not taking the garbage out, it is accumulating in the garage, and he had better do something about it. I think if such a person is going to become better, he had better be told. If he is going to be committed without a hearing, without proper explanation, that will only make it worse.

* * *

SENATOR ERVIN: [Y]our position is notwithstanding the fact that [a person] may suffer from delusions of persecution and by reason thereof be dangerous to others, that society should not step in and restrain him?

DR. SZASZ: That is correct. But, Senator, I think you are making this a little sweeping, if I may say so. It is my personal opinion that insofar as we divide human beings or populations into two large groups, one who never have and never will be mentally ill and another who have been or are now or will be— there is no evidence that the ones who are mentally ill are any more dangerous than the ones who are mentally healthy.

Nor do I think that any evidence will be found, or even could be found, to show that mentally ill people are more dangerous than others, unless mental illness were defined objectively and in advance of the behavior to which it is to be applied. If mental illness is defined *a posteriori*—for example, by asserting that every drunken driver is mentally ill—then of course the answer will be yes, mentally ill persons are dangerous. If we define every employer who behaves unreasonably and makes other people under him suffer, then yes, they are dangerous.

But if we define mental illness empirically, that is, in terms of actual observations, then the question is quite open. By empirical definitions of mental illness I mean such things as for example defining those inside of mental hospitals as mentally ill, and those outside as not; or those who go to psychiatrists for help as mentally ill, and those who do not as not ill. These may not be good definitions, but if we insist on talking about mental illness, we have got to have some measures for defining it. Now, if we define mental illness in some such ways as these, then I say that there is not a shred of evidence that the mentally ill are any more dangerous than the mentally healthy.

* * *

SENATOR ERVIN: Even though they may manifest homicidal tendencies or suicidal tendencies, society should do nothing about it until they either commit a homicide, commit suicide, or attempt to do one or the other?

DR. SZASZ: . . .
As far as homicide is concerned, there I think we are dealing similarly with a variant of a criminal problem and it seems to me there the problem is one of preventive jailing. How long do you wait until someone commits a crime. This is a problem for criminalists and is no different from the mentally ill or the healthy. I don't think one should wait too much.

SENATOR ERVIN: You would punish them both alike when they do it.

DR. SZASZ: Without any doubt because I think that everybody who commits an act is more or less responsible. This is one of my philosophical beliefs. I do not believe that mentally ill people are not responsible for what they do.

SENATOR ERVIN: Do you not believe it is possible for a psychiatrist to take a person who has threatened suicide and confine him and to investigate the causes of his suicidal tendency and assist him in ridding his mind of that desire?

DR. SZASZ: Well, Senator, certainly this is possible, but I think as a practical matter it is my experience that—and it is difficult to speak confidently in terms of proportions or statistics—that a large proportion of people who want to kill themselves—let me put it this way: A certain proportion of people who want to kill themselves do so. And while I certainly don't want to appear peculiar or callous about this, it seems to me that we must recognize that ability to kill oneself is one of the opportunities which one has in a free society and there is absolutely no way of eliminating this completely. We can only reduce it. So given the people who remain after those who have not killed themselves, a large proportion of those, if they can, do seek psychiatric help and many of those profit from it and do not kill themselves.

Again, the fleeting idea of destroying oneself I believe—and I think most of my colleagues would agree with this—is something that occurs to virtually everybody between the ages of 8 and 80. So that we really have to judge not the idea or the wish or the desire to commit suicide but the intensity of it and to what extent one is prepared to implement it, how much one is willing to act upon it, and I think this has certain merits and I personally do not think that involuntary restraint is a particularly useful maneuver for this, but as I indicated in my testimony, I would not completely eliminate it. I would be willing, quite willing to leave room as a practical measure, but in a very limited way. I certainly would not think it reason to restrain somebody for a long time just because he might kill himself.

SENATOR ERVIN: It would seem to me that society should be primarily interested in prevention and, therefore, if there is any reasonable prospect of turning a person from suicide, or from homicide, which are certainly not normal average desires, that society should step in and restrain the person to the extent necessary to prevent those purposes from being carried out.

*   *   *

11.

STATEMENT OF DR. MORTON BIRNBAUM, ATTORNEY, NEW YORK, N.Y.

*   *   *

DR. BIRNBAUM: . . .

Mr. Chairman, my name is Morton Birnbaum. I live and work in New York City. I am, and have been for the last 9 years, engaged in the general practice of law and I am, and have been for the last 3 years, engaged in the general practice of medicine.

*   *   *

If the right to treatment were to be recognized, our substantive constitutional law would then include the concepts that if a person is involuntarily institutionalized in a mental institution because he is sufficiently mentally ill to require institutionalization for care and treatment, he needs, and is entitled to, adequate medical treatment. . . .

If this proposed development is to be achieved, rather than only discussed, the courts must be prepared to hold that if an inmate is being kept in a mental institution against his will, he must be given proper medical treatment or else the inmate can obtain his release at will in spite of the existence or severity of his mental illness. If an inmate were to apply for a writ of habeas corpus to obtain his release, among

the issues that he could raise at the hearing could be the questions of whether or not the formal procedures necessary to institutionalize him were complied with, whether or not he is sufficiently mentally ill to require institutionalization, or whether or not he is being given adequate medical treatment for his mental illness. If the court decides that the necessary procedures were not complied with, that he is not sufficiently mentally ill, or that he is not being given proper medical treatment, he would be released.

*   *   *

Admittedly, the proposed method of enforcing the right to treatment would represent a radical innovation in our present legal thinking in the field of mental illness. To release a mentally ill person who requires further institutionalization, solely because he is not being given proper care and treatment, may endanger the health and welfare of many members of the community as well as the health and welfare of the sick person; however, it should always be remembered that the entire danger to, and from, the mentally ill that may occur by releasing them while they still require further institutionalization can be removed simply by our society treating these sick people properly.

12.

STATEMENT OF ROBERT F. KENNEDY, ATTORNEY GENERAL OF THE UNITED STATES

Primary responsibility and jurisdiction with respect to persons committed and treated in State mental institutions rests with the several States. The Department's jurisdiction in this connection is limited. It arises under the civil rights statute (18 U.S.C. 242), which provides criminal penalties in situations in which individuals are willfully deprived of rights protected by the Constitution and laws of the United States by persons acting under color of law.

Ordinarily, complaints to this Department assert that the individuals involved have been deprived of their liberty without due process of law contrary to the provisions of the 14th amendment to the Constitution. Specifically, the complaint may allege:

1. Illegal involuntary commitment to the institution;

2. Continued confinement after cure and eligibility for release; or

3. Brutal treatment, while confined, at the hands of some employees of the institution.

The Department considers that deprivation of liberty without due process in violation of the above statute is shown only if investigation reveals that the complainant has been committed in defiance of State law and with intent to take away his liberty, or he has, with similar intent, been detained after becoming eligible for release, or has been willfully subjected to brutality amounting to summary punishment.

The Department acts only upon the receipt of complaints; it makes no surveys or investigations of State mental institutions to determine general conditions therein. It has no authority with respect to the manner in which patients are admitted or in connection with the quality of care and treatment accorded them, Such matters are within the exclusive jurisdiction of the States.

* * *

13.

STATEMENT OF
HON. ALEXANDER HOLTZOFF,
U.S. DISTRICT JUDGE FOR THE DISTRICT
OF COLUMBIA

JUDGE HOLTZOFF: I believe that there should be liberal provisions for voluntary patients. . . .

On the other hand, we must be careful not to permit a person to be pushed into a hospital on the theory that he is coming there voluntarily.

The present statute relating to voluntary admissions is a little cumbersome, and I think one of the things that perhaps acts as a deterrent is a provision that if a patient . . . decides to leave the hospital he cannot do so except giving a certain number of days' notice and giving an opportunity to the hospital to start commitment proceedings.

So many patients are liable to feel, if I may use a figure of speech, that he is sticking his head in a noose.

* * *

MR. CREECH: [Is it] necessary for the judge to see the allegedly mentally ill person?

JUDGE HOLTZOFF: No . . . We feel rather strongly that this would be an intolerable burden on the judges. In a congested jurisdiction such as ours, with a very heavy docket and the judges continuously sitting from day to day, we do not feel that it would be necessary or helpful to the rights of the mentally ill patient, because he is personally seen by the members of the Commission on Mental Health. The chairman of the Commission is a lawyer. . . .

* * *

MR. CREECH: [T]he subcommittee has received testimony to the effect that in 1962 the Commission heard some 2,450 cases, and that frequently they would hear as many as 15 cases a day, and that in some instances cases are disposed of within a matter of 8 or 10 minutes.

Would you say this is an unfair statement?

JUDGE HOLTZOFF: I think it is necessary to bear in mind that the patient is examined by the Commission on a prior occasion a few days before the hearing, so that the Commission, as a matter of routine sees every patient twice. . . .

MR. CREECH: So, in your view, sir, each case can be given adequate consideration without becoming a matter of routine, notwithstanding the number of cases and the speed with which they are dispensed.

JUDGE HOLTZOFF: Oh, yes; I think so, because, as I say the Commission sees each person twice, and I think if a judge were required to conduct every such hearing he probably couldn't devote as much time as the Commission does. Of course, we have the final safeguard if the patient isn't satisfied, all he has to do is ask for a jury trial.

[E]ach patient [should] be orally apprised of his rights by a clerk or a deputy clerk of the court designated by the chief judge. The official so designated would go around to the hospital and explain to every patient his rights to demand a jury trial so that no patient would be in position to say, "I got some sort of a notice, maybe it says I am entitled to a jury trial and maybe I don't understand it."

* * *

MR. CREECH: Do you feel that it would be desirable to have periodic reports on the mental health of the patient?

* * *

JUDGE HOLTZOFF: Theoretically, I see no objection to it. I understand from the superintendent of St. Elizabeths Hospital that administratively he would consider it highly objectionable because—and I can sympathize with his position—there are several thousand patients in St. Elizabeths Hospital.

Suppose he had to submit a report to the court every 6 months on several thousand patients. That would be an intolerable administrative burden and would require a large appropriation for a staff to do nothing but to prepare those reports and when those reports are submitted to the court what would we do with them? They would just clutter up our files.

Now, under the present system any patient who wants to be released, who claims he is entitled to be released, all he has to do is to write a letter to the court, and we treat that letter as a petition for a writ of habeas corpus.

So, when we get one of those letters we look up and see how long since this patient has had a hearing. Suppose he hasn't had a hearing in 6 months, we issue a writ of habeas corpus, bring him up and give him a hearing.

Now, the hospital puts no obstacles in the way of any patient writing to the court, and in fact, sometimes, to show how much freedom the patients have in that respect we frequently get most irrational letters but the hospital puts no obstacle in the way of its reaching the court.

* * *

MR. CREECH: [Would you abolish] the physician-patient privilege[?]

* * *

JUDGE HOLTZOFF: . . .

I have great doubt to what extent such a privilege exists in these mental health proceedings but some psychiatrists have some hesitancy in testifying in such a proceeding even for the patient, if they had previously examined the patient.

So that the suggestion has been made from various sources to clarify the matter really for the benefit of the psychiatrists who really aren't sure what their rights are, to permit a person's physician to testify concerning his mental state.

For example, suppose a man's family hires a psychiatrist, and the psychiatrist, after an examination, advises the family that this person needs to be committed to a mental institution, he needs mental treatment.

A proper proceeding is brought, and he is called upon to testify. The doctor has a doubt as to whether he has the right to testify in view of the fact that he had examined the patient as his personal physician.

Now, if he is not allowed to testify, I think it would be a great handicap to the patient.

* * *

SENATOR ERVIN: [B]y having an examination which is in a sense private, followed by a hearing befor the Commission, you avoid, to a great degree, that which the psychiatrists call the psychological trauma which a patient undergoes as a result of a public hearing. At the same time the patient has the right to have a hearing before the court if he so desires.

This is a very good procedure for reconciling the legal requirements of due process with medical requirements of minimizing chances of traumatic shock to the patient.

I wonder if you have had experiences and observations similar to my own. For instance, a person is physically ill, the family calls a doctor immediately. But, unfortunately, the same is not true for mental illness. Often, the family never undertakes to seek aid for the mentally ill person until he has almost reached the extreme point of his illness because of a feeling that there is something disgraceful about mental illness. Is that also your observation?

JUDGE HOLTZOFF: Yes, sir; family feelings have to be considered here, and I think we have to respect them, because the average family feels, unfortunately, that mental illness is an embarrassment or humiliation, whereas physical illness is not so regarded. But I think the law has to have regard for people's feeling. After all the law has to express the mores of the community. And we have tried to have regards for that.

SENATOR ERVIN: I think that one of the greatest advancements that we can hope to make in this field is to get the patient's family and the general public to look upon mental illness in the same context as they view physical illness, and to make them realize that there is no more disgrace connected with mental illness than there is with physical illness. I feel that if we can achieve this, a number of problems in this field will be solved.

* * *

14.

STATEMENT OF JACK R. EWALT, M.D., PRESIDENT OF THE AMERICAN PSYCHIATRIC ASSOCIATION

[It has been suggested that if] the administrator determines that the patient is no longer mentally ill he shall order the immediate release of the patient. Does that mean within the next 5 minutes? I can assure you that a discharge of a patient is seldom a simple matter of opening the front door and wishing him well. Often rather elaborate plans, usually carried out by a social worker, have to be worked out before a patient can be summarily dispatched back to the community.

* * *

15.

STATEMENT OF V. TERRELL DAVIS, M.D., VICE PRESIDENT, THE NATIONAL ASSOCIATION OF STATE MENTAL HEALTH PROGRAM DIRECTORS

* * *

In many instances, a psychiatrist can confirm a presumption of the existence of a mental illness of varying degrees of severity on the basis of an examination of an individual, but he is often pushed into the field of crystal-ball gazing and speculation when he is expected to make a statement under oath that the individual will be dangerous to others. It was the thought of the Mental Health Commission in New Jersey that the physician should notify the court of the existence of a mental illness and he should attach to it his expressed belief that the illness may be of a nature which would imperil life of the patient or others if not hospitalized but that a period of examination and observation in an appropriate mental hospital facility is necessary to make this determination. In other words, the initial confinement is a period of quarantine.

16.

STATEMENT OF DR. DALE CAMERON, SUPERINTENDENT, ST. ELIZABETHS HOSPITAL

DR. CAMERON: . . .

* * *

. . . We believe involuntary emergency admission should be limited to those persons where there is a clear and evident danger of harm to themselves or to others. For judicial commitment, we suggest this test plus the ability to commit persons whose mental illness is of such severity as to impair their judgment to the degree that they are not capable of making a sound judgment for themselves in connection with their need for treatment. We do not mean by this the commitment of persons who simply would benefit from treatment, but who are still in a position to make a responsible judgment as to whether or not they wish to seek treatment.

* * *

If the judge must see the patient it need not necessarily be, in our opinion, at the formal hearing and, as a matter of fact, the judge could talk to the patient fairly extensively at the time he sees him, and thus give him an opportunity to talk directly with the judge without necessarily being forced to sit in on a hearing where someone is telling all of the unusual and strange things this man has done in the past. But we would let the patient be present at the hearing if he insists.

* * *

. . . We believe that it is important that a bill should provide for a convalescent leave status where a person could be released from the hospital, physically leave, but remain under the supervision of the hospital for a period while in the community, and then "discharged from the rolls of the hospital," if you will, after he has demonstrated his ability to get along satisfactorily in the community.

* * *

. . . We do have some patients at St. Elizabeths who have been in difficulty with the postal authorities for sending obscene materials through the mail or otherwise violating postal regulations, and we would suggest that the superintendent of a hospital caring for a mental patient be authorized to review outgoing mail when he has reason to believe that it might contain material in conflict with postal regulations.

We would also note that some patients, while acutely ill, write letters which they later seriously regret, or some patients write volumes of letters which are essentially nonsense-word salad.

We see no particular reason why the patient should have the "right" to mail all of this material which will only be a later embarrassment to him when he improves, therefore we suggest a little more leeway on this right of communication as far as examining incoming and outgoing material.

We would insist, however, with you that the patient have the right to communicate whenever he wishes by sealed mail or otherwise with his attorney, with the court, with the superintendent of the hospital, others of this sort.

[There has been testimony about] the right to care and treatment. With this objective we certainly agree, but believe that monthly reporting to the District Commissioners as provided in the bill will not necessarily secure this end. The important issue is whether or not a hospital has sufficient staff to provide for necessary treatment and care.

We believe that would be a case where there would be little point in sending all of these reports to the Commissioners, and if the hospital were required to do so, it would absorb an enormous amount of staff time which could be more constructively used for the treatment of patients.

* * *

[The staff in a memorandum took the position that a statute should go beyond authorizing commitment for persons found] "to be mentally ill to the extent that he is likely to injure himself or others if allowed to remain at liberty. . . .

"Few statutes circumscribe the commitable class so narrowly. The Draft Act [prepared by the Department of Health, Education and Welfare] included, as an alternative ground for indeterminate commitment, a finding that the respondent is a mentally ill person who 'is in need of custody, care, or treatment' in a mental hospital and, 'because of his illness, lacks sufficient insight or capacity to make responsible decisions' with respect to hospitalization. The gloss accompanying the Draft Act explains this test as turning, not on whether the person is making or capable of making a wise decision or agrees with medical judgment as to the nature of his illness or the need for hospital care, but rather on whether he is capable of making a responsible decision or, to look at the other side of the coin, is 'so confused as no longer to have the capacity to make a decision having any relation to the factors bearing on [the need for] his hospitalization.' In short, this ground in effect requires an adjudication of mental incompetency to make a judgment as to the need for hospitalization, in analogy to a judgment of incompetency as to a person's transactions. It in effect casts the State in the role of *parens patriae*, as to hospitalization, for those who are incapable of rationally pursuing their interests in this matter.

"[O]nly 5 of the 37 jurisdictions that provide some form of judicial hospitalization phrase the test solely in terms of whether the person is dangerous to himself or others; 12 jurisdictions state the individual's need for care and treatment as an alternative ground, 7 state the test solely in terms of the patient's need for hospital care or treatment, and 7 permit hospitalization when the patient's own 'welfare' or the 'welfare' of others requires such care or treatment. What the actual practice has been under these statutes the study does not say.

" . . . We do believe it important, however, not to exclude those 'harmless' persons who are mentally ill, can be treated effectively only in a hospital, and, while not likely to do violence to themselves, are because of that illness so far incapable of attending to their immediate needs or safety as to be in danger of serious personal harm unless hospitalized. While, hopefully, most people in this category will acquiesce in the kind of informal hospitalization we have recommended in lieu of section 3, some may not. . . ."

* * *

SENATOR ERVIN: . . . Dr. Terrell Davis, the New Jersey State Director of Mental Health, suggested . . . that it might be desirable to use somewhat milder terms with reference to the mental state of the person to be subjected to informal commitment. He suggested that on the petition of a member of the family or friend who would have a peculiar interest in the welfare of the person, and accompanied by a certificate of his family physician, or, for that matter, any other physician who had adequate opportunity to observe him personally, the court might well make an *ex parte* order, that is, an order in the absence of the patient, committing him temporarily for observation where it appeared from the petition and the certificate of the physician that there was reason to believe that the person was suffering from a mental illness, and that there was reason to believe that such mental illness might make him a peril to himself or to the public.

In other words, he advocated a system in which you would not have to make a final adjudication on either of those points. What do you think of a procedure of this nature?

DR. CAMERON: Actually, this suggestion highlights the fact that there are two types of patients we are talking about when we talk of informal admission. First of all, the patient whom the physician, when he presents himself, would have every reason to presume competent, if a question of competency were ever raised in the court.

Now, if the patient is presumably competent, I think it should be possible for him to be admitted on his own request, if you will, and without the necessity of signing a statement which says, "I agree to give 3 days' notice." This would be informal admission and this, I think, should be sufficient for that type of patient.

* * *

If, on the other hand, this is a nonprotesting patient, but one whom he might believe to be incompetent, this, I think, is probably the class that Dr. Davis was mentioning.

* * *

Now, turning to the person who was not protesting but whom you have reason to believe might be found incompetent if the question were raised in court, under the current circumstances, Senator Ervin, such a patient cannot be admitted as a voluntary patient. He can sign the statement, and we find ourselves in the rather remarkable situation of the physician, family physician, saying that he needs treatment, the family wanting him to be treated, the hospital physician agreeing that he needs treatment, and the patient not objecting, and we cannot do anything about it. We have to send him away to be committed and forced to do that which he was willing to do in the first place. So we believe this should be modified very drastically.

Personally, I think it is sufficient for the admitting physician to be left with the discretion as to whether or not the nonprotesting but presumably incompetent patient needs admission, and he would reject him if he thinks he does not.

* * *

MR. CREECH: In regard to the type of attention you are able to give the patients, what percentage of your patients are discharged, say, within 3 months, even on a temporary basis, or are given out-patient care?

DR. CAMERON: First of all, you must realize that the patients we get at St. Elizabeths Hospital are a bias sample. Most of the patients go first to D.C. General Hospital, and if it is a nice easy depression or something else that can be dealt with quite readily, we never see them. We get only those patients where it is presumed there will be a prolonged period of hospitalization, so we have a biased sample. Despite that we discharge back to the community from those admitted well over half of the patients admitted to the hospital within the first 6 to 8 months.

MR. CREECH: Do you have many repeaters—people whom you treat who come back?

DR. CAMERON: Yes, we do. We run somewhere around 30 per cent of those who are released having at a future time, and this is pretty close to the national average.

We consider that when a patient has to return it is not necessarily a failure. It is much more a failure to have retained the patient in hospitals throughout that period unnecessarily, and if the man can go out and make a successful adjustment for 2 years, and then has to be readmitted, fair enough.

Just as you might have a coronary, recover, go out and have another coronary. We do not consider that a treatment failure the first go-around.

17.

STATEMENT OF PROF. HENRY WEIHOFEN, DIRECTOR, MENTAL COMPETENCY STUDY, GEORGE WASHINGTON UNIVERSITY

PROFESSOR WEIHOFEN: . . .

*   *   *

I have only one suggestion in connection with voluntary admission. . . . [P]ersons under 21 may [sometimes] be admitted on the application of their parent, spouse, guardian, and so forth. It seems to me that 21 is too high for that purpose. We allow youngsters to assume a good many other responsibilities before that age, including fighting for their country, and there seems to be no reason why a 20-year-old young man can't apply for treatment in a hospital on his own.

There are safeguards here. The hospital isn't going to take him if he doesn't belong there. They have enough to do without taking in those for whom they can do nothing. It would be well to use a flexible kind of restraint on this by providing that the hospital to whom a minor applies may in its discretion require the consent of parent or spouse. I think that would be sufficient protection there.

If this young man of 20 can't get consent of his parents or any of the other parties mentioned, or is alone—and we are a mobile society today in which young people do go off to the city from the farm or from one State to another, there is [often] no way . . . for him to be voluntarily admitted.

*   *   *

Another idea that some States have adopted is a kind of temporary observational admission. The observation and temporary admission really are for separate purposes. One is to observe him; the other is for actual treatment. The two usually go together, so it is not improper to lump them together, I think. In some of the States this temporary kind of commitment may run for 30 days or 60 or 90. This is an interesting device, because with modern, intensive kinds of treatments, such as drug therapy, when people are sent to the hospital, the great majority of them are back home within less than a year—90 per cent within less than a year. And many of them can be restored within such a period as 90 or even 30 days.

. . . The Texas mental health code not only permits this temporary kind of commitment but requires it; there must always first be a temporary commitment and then, if you still want to hold him, you start the judicial proceedings.

I am informed that at Austin State Hospital about 75 per cent of those who are sent to the hospital on this temporary procedure are discharged and back home before the end of that 90-day period, and of those who remain the vast majority convert their stay into voluntary; that is, they sign an agreement that they want to remain. Apparently now that they are there and see that the place isn't as bad as they had conjured up, they decide that it is a good idea to stay there, and so they sign the voluntary admission.

*   *   *

SENATOR ERVIN: This would certainly tend to minimize the possibility of anybody being "railroaded" to use a term in popular usage in connection with this, if there is hospitalization for a limited period of time before there can be an indefinite commitment.

PROFESSOR WEIHOFEN: Yes; or if he is wrongly sent there for whatever reason, by mistake, or an error of judgment, which is more likely to happen than a malicious railroading. Also perhaps, this kind of device would reach some of [your objectives] . . . by requiring examination of the person after 3 months and every 6 months thereafter, and requiring the hospital to submit monthly statements of the therapy that has been given to each patient. Here you have an automatic kind of cutoff at the end of the period, and this necessarily will call upon the hospital to make a determination then whether to let him go or file a judicial proceeding.

*   *   *

MR. CREECH: Sir, do you believe that the psychiatrist-patient privilege should be retained in mental health proceedings or do you believe that it would be more beneficial to all parties concerned if this privilege were abolished?

PROFESSOR WEIHOFEN: . . .

*   *   *

You always have a policy question here. Granting that the privilege may do some harm, may obstruct our efforts to inquire into the facts and get the full picture, is it worth the cost? Promoting doctor-patient confidentiality is much more important for psychiatric patients and their psychiatrists than in the work of ordinary doctors.

*   *   *

[I]n psychiatric care, it takes a long time for a patient to open up. He is ridden with guilt. His trouble is in sinful, illegal things he has done, or imagines he has done, which bother him now, bother him very seriously and it is difficult even to say this to a psychiatrist. It isn't easy for a patient to open up and talk about his sexual dream fantasies or homosexual activities, perhaps, or all kinds of other things, or for a married woman to tell her psychiatrist that she is upset because she really is in love with another man or actually carrying on an affair with another man. These are very difficult things to get, and I think a lack of the privilege may have an effect on therapy, may keep people from going to psychiatrists or from telling all when they do go.

I say I think so, but that is a pure guess because we have no statistics, whether in the District or elsewhere, to show whether lack of the privilege has this effect or not. . . .

* * *

MR. CREECH: Sir, you have stated that the individual who needs treatment but is not dangerous, and who is incapable of making a decision to hospitalize himself, should be able to be hospitalized without his consent. Does this comport with the individual's rights insofar as the stated intent of this type of proceeding is not to commit him unless he poses a threat to society?

PROFESSOR WEIHOFEN: Of course, there is a conflict here and it again illustrates what lawmakers usually more than often than not, I suppose, have to do to balance one good purpose against another in a situation where they conflict.

When you have two objectives, both of which are right, and you have to choose, it becomes difficult. But I think it would be possible to work out a compromise by which you go a certain distance in protecting people who are incompetent to protect themselves, without interfering with the free choice of those who are able to exercise it.

SENATOR ERVIN: Certainly, society should have enough concern about the ability of the citizen to function in the proper manner, to justify society in saying that if the individual needs psychiatric treatment in order to function properly as a member of society, even though he doesn't directly become a violator of the criminal laws, society ought to have some powers to restrain him and see that he gets treatment.

PROFESSOR WEIHOFEN: You can add to the categories of the people who might be sent to the hospital in addition to those who are dangerous to themselves or to others, those who are not capable of making a decision, or you can go further and subject to court order anyone who needs hospital care and treatment, whether he is capable of deciding for himself or not. He may say, I am alert and I understand what you are saying and I choose not to go. The State could still say we know best what is good for you and we are going to give it to you. Now, there I think we would probably all agree that this goes too far. A man should have some right to exercise his own judgment about whether he wants care or not. But I think you maintain that distinction if you only add to those who are dangerous to themselves or others those who need care but are incapable of exercising judgment.

I don't think that interferes too far with personal liberty because in fact there is no liberty here that can be exercised. The man can't make up his own mind.

So in balancing these two considerations, I think we might very well say we are willing to do this much for people without their affirmative consent, but not more.

Let us suppose the case of an old man, a widower living on his little farm, who gets along very well, doesn't want much, doesn't need much; he raises what he needs and manages well, but he is subject to serious fits of depression because of mental illness. He has tried to commit suicide once in one of these fits and doctors have predicted that he will continue to have these depressions every few months, and that unless hospitalized it is highly likely that he is going to kill himself within not more than a couple of years. But if he is able when he is not depressed to say, yes, I understand, I believe you; but this is where I have lived my whole life and I would rather stay here and take a chance than go to the hospital, I think he should be allowed to make that choice even though it is against his own interests.

* * *

MR. WATERS: In connection with . . . personal injury case[s] where the doctor's privilege may become pertinent, I think you are probably aware this is covered in most States by the presumption that the privilege, which, after all, is that of the patient, has been waived by the filing of the lawsuit in which he specifically puts his physical condition in issue and therefore the doctor may be required to come in and testify as to his subjective and objective findings.

PROFESSOR WEIHOFEN: You are quite right. The States vary on this. Some say merely filing the action waives the privilege as to all doctors he has consulted. Others are a little narrower than that. They say if he himself introduces medical testimony, then the other side can bring in any other medical testimony, including other doctors that he had consulted.

* * *

MR. WATERS: [Y]ou state that—

A minimal requirement of any law is that it permit honest administration and not force doctors and others to stretch interpretations and procedures.

Are you suggesting by that that perhaps the laws are not broken, but perhaps bent a little bit in order to accomplish a good and even though it is not strictly legal?

PROFESSOR WEIHOFEN: I have no data on that, and therefore I shouldn't undertake to say. But my guess would be that it is, and I can see why. If hospitalization is possible only for those who are dangerous and if the doctor feels very strongly that this person belongs in the hospital, he may be able to stretch that concept to cover it. The illness may be "dangerous" to the patient in the sense that it will get worse. He may even sink into a hopeless condition. But that isn't the normal and certainly not the narrow definition of dangerous. But you are going to have cases where everybody feels this poor person ought to be in the hospital. It would be a shame if the law doesn't permit it, so we convince ourselves that the law does permit it if we interpret it broadly enough. That is how the law is "bent a little bit" to accomplish a good end.

* * *

18.

STATEMENT OF ELYCE H. ZENOFF, REPRESENTATIVE FOR THE AMERICAN CIVIL LIBERTIES UNION AND THE NATIONAL CAPITAL AREA CIVIL LIBERTIES UNIONS ...

* * *

MISS ZENOFF: ...
We are ... concerned [about allowing] the parent or guardian of a person under 21 to place a minor in a mental hospital as a "voluntary" patient. It is easy to envision situations in which a parent opposing a marriage might pursue this course. We recognize that the hospital would release any person who obviously did not require hospitalization. Nevertheless, we feel the rights of minors should be more fully safeguarded. We recommend that, if the patient is 16 or over, and is capable of expressing his own opinion, he should be asked whether he wishes to enter or leave the hospital. If he desires to leave, it is our view that he should be allowed to do so.

* * *

We are aware that some persons criticize use of juries in hospitalization cases, on the grounds that laymen are not qualified to judge technical medical issues. But the same objection may be leveled at participation in the commitment process by judges. Few judges have any expertise in psychiatric matters.

The recent American Bar Foundation study replied to the argument against use of juries in these words:

> The jury is not asked ... to diagnose the illness of the patient. It has only to decide, on the basis of the medical evidence submitted to it, for the most part by experts, whether the patient's illness is of such nature that the statue requires his hospitalization. (Lindman and McIntyre, Jr., "The Mentally Disabled and the Law," p. 28 (1961)).

We strongly urge that [any statute] retain the provision of the present law which makes a jury trial mandatory in any case where it is requested by the patient, or someone in his behalf.

In addition we recommend that there be some guarantee that jury trials be conducted in the same way as jury trials in other civil proceedings. There is sometimes a tendency to maintain only the form and not the substance of a jury trial in mental illness cases. Opening statements, cross-examination of witnesses, and so forth, are as important in this type of case as in any other and we believe that the function of a jury trial is not served if it is a mere formality.

... We think that statutory provision should be made for fair and reasonable compensation to a psychiatrist who has been retained by counsel for an indigent respondent.

... There may be circumstances in which a person, detained for emergency purposes, could safely be discharged during the pendency of judicial proceedings. [We would] allow the hospital authorities and the court as a matter of discretion to release the patient pending the outcome of a judicial proceeding.

* * *

MR. CREECH: Most witnesses have testified that the hearing should be as informal as possible. Do you think that your suggestion to maintain the rule of evidence in court hearings would be conducive to informality? Will it in any way hamper the objectives of the recommendations of these witnesses?

MISS ZENOFF: ...
I think the hearing should be informal. We are certainly in favor of the provisions that they do not have to be held in a courtroom. They can be held in the patient's home, or they can be in a hospital, and anybody can sit where they want to. We are not concerned about these kind of things but we are concerned with people having the opportunity to find out what this proceeding is based on.

* * *

19.

STATEMENT OF DAVID L. BAZELON, CHIEF JUDGE, UNITED STATES COURT OF APPEALS FOR THE DISTRICT OF COLUMBIA

[There is a general] assumption that mental illness is a disorder which can always and necessarily be regarded as separable from mental retardation. In the past, this assumption has resulted first in mental retardation being of principal public concern; then, with the swing of the pendulum, in mental illness becoming the object of major concern—almost to the exclusion of mental retardation. It is my understanding that bifurcated consideration of the two disorders is not medically justified. First, it seems, there are acute problems of diagnosis. We have all heard stories of children shut up for years in institutions for the retarded, who turned out to be of average and above average intelligence. These tales reflect what is well known in the field—that sometimes it is exceedingly difficult to distinguish mental retardation from some forms of mental illness. Second, even where mental retardation is correctly diagnosed, psychological problems of differing degrees of intensity may also be present and require attention.

To argue that the two conditions may be interrelated, and that both deserve our attention, is not to deny that, in practice, decisions frequently have to be made designating one condition or the other as primary. For instance, if institutional care and treatment are called for, the most appropriate residential facility will have to be chosen. But the very awareness of possible erroneous diagnosis and overlapping conditions should caution us to provide for frequent review and ease of transfer between those facilities which deal primarily with the mentally ill and those whose main concern is with the retarded.

The fact that the two handicapping conditions are less clearly separable than might at first appear does not mean, of course, that they can be regarded as synonymous. Although some mentally retarded persons may be afflicted with mental illness, the vast majority of persons diagnosed as mentally ill are obviously not retarded. Since the two conditions are not synonymous, it is understandable that the identical provisions and protections are not equally appropriate to both. For instance, the proposed legislation would be of particular value in encouraging the mentally ill to seek voluntary hospitalization. Yet we should beware of relying heavily on voluntary admission procedures for the mentally retarded, many of whom simply lack the basic intellectual endowment to make any voluntary decision of this nature. In deciding the protections necessary for each group we should also take into account such factors as the differing age groups involved. Hospitalization of the mentally ill will presumably occur mainly among adults, whereas the majority of initial commitments among the mentally retarded will be children and adolescents. In another area, your bill's detailed provisions for emergency hospitalization of the mentally ill are probably unnecessary for the mentally retarded, whose long-term affliction is unlikely to deteriorate rapidly so as to require emergency treatment, unless, of course, mental illness is also present. Similarly, the provisions . . . for frequent periodic review of those hospitalized under court order are probably inappropriate to the mentally retarded. Although some periodic review of the need for continued residential care for the retarded is vital, the chances of any significant change in condition occurring within 3 to 6 months are slight.

In short, I think it would be a mistake merely to include mental retardation within [any statutory] definition of mental illness. A careful analysis would have to be made as to which provisions of [any statute] would be applicable, and with what modification, to the mentally retarded. . . .

* * *

20.

STATEMENT OF HUGH J. McGEE, FORMER CHAIRMAN AND PRESENT MEMBER OF BAR ASSOCIATION COMMITTEE ON MENTAL HEALTH, AND FORMER ASSISTANT UNITED STATES ATTORNEY FOR THE DISTRICT OF COLUMBIA

* * *

SENATOR ERVIN: [I]t is your opinion that the present Commission system, with the right of each individual to subsequent appeal to the courts minimizes what the psychiatrists call traumatic shock, and at the same time protects the patient's constitutional rights?

MR. McGEE: Absolutely. It is as kind, as friendly, as warm a treatment, and some of the hearings have been so chummy that they do not have too much legal appearance. Those are the cases where the patient's condition is so obvious and a few questions are asked about residence and about ability to pay, and then the hearing is over. But the interest of these psychiatrists and the doctors in keeping it nontraumatic is really a fine thing. I cannot imagine any other system that would make it more folksy or more comfortable without depriving the individual of some rights that we feel he should be entitled to, that the Constitution guarantees him.

* * *

[L]et me say one thing about jury trials in general and jury trials with reference to mental health cases.

I was with the Commission on Mental Health for $3\frac{1}{2}$ years and while I was with them I attended the hearings regularly and we had two doctors who had served for 3 months and then two would serve for another 3 months. When there was a request for a jury trial, that meant that the two doctors had to come down and testify on a Wednesday, and they had to stay away from their office, which was a day that they usually had remunerative cases coming in.

So that when they would sit, the person, the degree of mental illness is never clear, I mean it is not a numerical rating that you can give to a mentally ill person, and it is not obvious.

But the person's certain conduct would be attributed to this individual, and he would say something a little silly or irrelevent, and they would say, "All right, we will recommend commitment" and he would say, "I demand a jury trial."

There would be some whispering immediately then there would be a discussion with him, then their questions would change. The questioning of the patient then would be to see if maybe he wasn't sane and maybe he couldn't go without requiring their coming down to testify against him. And in almost every—well, say, in many instances when a request for a jury trial was made they looked at it with a different perspective as to whether he should be committed.

The doctors don't think as we do. They say, "Here is a man who obviously has something wrong with him mentally and it couldn't hurt him to be committed." It couldn't hurt his mental condition but if he doesn't want to go that jury trial and his right to that jury trial is what stops him from going in if he has a mild mental condition. It is a real big safeguard.

It is the only real safeguard in this field, and the jurors are not lawyers and are not psychiatrists. These people in the District of Columbia have no difficulty whatsoever disregarding psychiatric testimony either in criminal cases or in civil cases.

If that person shows a minimal ability to adjust to society, maybe a little bit odd, maybe a little strange, maybe ultraconservative or ultraliberal in their mouthings, that jury is going to say, "He might be a little whacky but we don't have to put him over there," and this is something that must be protected I feel.

* * *

I think that the civil patient has a right not to be incarcerated with criminal patients, and I think that the criminal patient if he is not going to be treated has a right not to be kept with insane people.

* * *

MR. WATERS: Is it your opinion that there are some practical defects in the function of the present habeas corpus writ to release the individual who is institutionalized in a mental hospital?

* * *

As I understand it . . . , then a petitioner on a writ of habeas corpus who is indigent usually cannot get a psychiatrist to testify in his favor or is he able to carry the burden himself, having in mind the fact that the court has his case history before it and that psychiatrists are reluctant to state what is normal and consequently reluctant to state that this petitioner is normal since he is hospitalized usually by reason of some transgression, and would be reluctant to put their reputations on the line to indicate that he would not commit a crime in the future, the petitioner has a pretty strong burden to carry, hasn't he?

MR. MCGEE: Tremendous burden. No one is in the hospital unless he has committed some erratic conduct or unusual acts so that the doctor has an impossible task of suggesting, "Well, I can't say he won't do it again," nobody knows what an individual will do in the future. He has got to make a guess, and he has to extend himself to make that guess. The court has to, when the individual says, "I want out. I am well enough to be released, I am no longer insane." The easiest thing for the doctor to say is that he should

stay a little longer because the assumption is he would have been released if he was all right, or he wouldn't have to be seeking it.

Then the judge has only the hospital doctor there, if a person is indigent, the judge has only the hospital doctor, who must defend their position of keeping this person who has done something wrong or something odd in the past.

They do exercise this discretion frequently and very bravely, I think, but I can't emphasize enough how necessary a reasonable workable standard for release is for the District of Columbia.

* * *

NOTE

Royal Commission Report on the law relating to Mental Illness and Mental Deficiency*

* * *

Admission to hospital without using compulsory powers should also be possible for considerably more mentally ill patients than are at present admitted as voluntary patients. Most "non-volitional" patients of the type who are now admitted as temporary patients could be treated without powers of detention. It should also be possible to admit informally a considerable number of mentally ill and infirm patients who can at present be admitted to designated mental hospitals only as certified patients because they are not considered capable of signing a voluntary application form; these would include a high proportion of elderly patients, of the type for whom "long-stay annexes" are at present provided in some areas.

We therefore recommend that the law and its administration should be altered, in relation to all forms of mental disorder, by abandoning the assumption that compulsory powers must be used unless the patient can express a positive desire for treatment, and replacing this by the offer of care, without deprivation of liberty, to all who need it and are not unwilling to receive it. All hospitals providing psychiatric treatment should be free to admit patients for any length of time without any legal formality and without the power to detain. . . .

* * *

If a patient expresses a wish to leave the hospital before his doctor considers him fit to do so, he should be seen by the doctor who should try to persuade him to stay to complete his treatment. If he refuses, however, the hospital will have no power to detain him, and he must be allowed to leave, unless the circumstances are such that the doctor considers it necessary to take steps to obtain power to detain him

---

*Cmnd. 169 (1954-57) pp. 101-111. Reprinted by permission.

by using one of the emergency or other compulsory procedures . . . Such procedures could of course not be used except under conditions in which a patient's compulsory admission to hospital would be allowed if he were not already in hospital. It should not be necessary to use compulsory procedures in this way very frequently, but we must recognize the fact that it is sometimes necessary now with voluntary patients, and will probably continue to be necessary from time to time in future. . . .

* * *

There is a fairly wide but circumscribed range of circumstances in which our society recognizes a general need to restrict the personal liberty of individual citizens either for the person's own protection or for the protection of other individuals or of society in general. Restriction of liberty is usually accompanied by the provision of special forms of care, treatment, training or occupation for the person who is placed under detention or control. Sometimes need for special forms of treatment or training is itself an essential element in the grounds on which compulsory restriction of liberty is accepted as justified.

The criminal law is concerned with anti-social behavior which is held to justify the restriction of personal liberty primarily for the protection of other individuals or of society in general. Within the criminal law there are provisions to meet the special needs of juveniles and other young offenders, and corrective training or preventive detention may be prescribed for persistent offenders. Outside the criminal law, persons suffering from certain infectious diseases may in certain circumstances be compulsorily removed to and detained in hospital to protect others from infection. Compulsion which may involve some restriction of personal liberty but which is based primarily on the person's own need for protection or for some form of care, treatment or training is also applied to children and to others not capable of looking after their own interests. . . .

Some forms of mental disorder have long been accepted as requiring or justifiyng the restriction of personal liberty in special ways. . . . Several considerations seem relevant to the question whether the law should continue in future to provide forms of control, within stated limits, over people suffering from mental disorder which do not apply to other people:—

(i) When an illness or disability itself affects the patients power of judgment and appreciation of his own condition, there is a specially strong argument for saying that his own interests demand that the decision whether or not to accept medical examination, care or treatment should not be left entirely to his own distorted or defective judgment. Admission to hospital against the patient's wishes at the time may be the only way of providing him with the treatment or training which may restore his health or enable him to take his place as a self-supporting member of the community or to develop his limited capabilities to the greatest possible extent. The better the prospects are of treatment or training being successful, the more important this consideration becomes.

(ii) Some adult mentally disordered patients, especially those who are severely sub-normal, may need the same type of protection as children, in order to prevent their parents or relatives or other persons from neglecting or exploiting them or obstructing the provision of treatment or training which they may badly need and from which they are likely to benefit.

(iii) When mental disorder is known to make a person prone to violence or other forms of seriously anti-social behavior or to persistent petty crime and he is thought unlikely to respond to ordinary penal measures, special preventive control may be justified. In these and other cases in which an offender against the law is found to be suffering from mental disorder, imprisonment under ordinary conditions or other penal measures may not provide appropriate treatment, and the length of time needed for suitable medical or social treatment or training to have a useful effect may be either longer or shorter than the sentence of imprisonment or length of probation or supervision which courts would normally impose. In cases of severe mental disorder it may be repugnant even to subject the patient to the normal procedures of prosecution and trial.

(iv) The behavior of a person who is suffering from mental disorder may be so annoying to other people and so persistent that even if it is not criminal the protection of other people from such behavior may be a factor which, combined with the patient's own need for treatment, may justify the use of special compulsory powers.

(v) Against these considerations, all of which tend to support the case for some special compulsory powers, must be set the individual patient's right to personal liberty. We are not thinking here of the possibility that the liberty of other citizens might be in danger from the wrongful application to them of special compulsory powers which the law intends only for use in case of mental disorder; safeguards against abuse of that sort should be provided by the special procedures which must be used when the compulsory powers are invoked in any individual case. We are thinking rather of the liberty of the mentally disordered person himself. No form of mental disorder should be considered to be, by itself, a sufficient ground for depriving a person of his liberty. It is necessary to balance the possible benefits of treatment or training, the protection of the patient and the protection of other persons, on the one hand, against the patient's loss of liberty on the other. . . .

We start our consideration of the need for compulsory powers in present-day conditions by repeating that when a patient is thought to require some form of care, but he or his relatives object, every effort should be made to persuade him or them to agree to care being provided without the use of compulsion. . . .

But, because various forms of mental disorder do affect the patient's own reason and powers of judgment and his power to appreciate the effect on others of his own behaviour, there are likely always to be some who will refuse the offer of treatment or training in any form. No one disputes that there are some circumstances in which society must in the last resort be able to compel some patients to receive treatment or training in their own interests or for the protection of others, and that some may need to be protected against exploitation or neglect. Indeed, we would go further, and emphasize that when every effort has been made to overcome the unwillingness of the patient or his relatives by persuasion, doctors and others should not be too hesitant to use such compulsory powers as the law may provide, if this seems the only method of giving the patient the treatment or training which he badly needs and which is expected to cure or relieve his illness or to enable him to live a more happy and useful life.

We consider that the use of special compulsory powers on grounds of the patient's mental disorder is justifiable when:—

(a) there is reasonable certainty that the patient is suffering from a pathological mental disorder and requires hospital or community care; and

(b) suitable care cannot be provided without the use of compulsory powers; and

(c) if the patient himself is unwilling to receive the form of care which is considered necessary, there is at least a strong likelihood that his unwillingness is due to lack of appreciation of his own condition deriving from the mental disorder itself; and

(d) there is also either

  (i) good prospect of benefit to the patient from the treatment proposed—an expectation that it will either cure or alleviate his mental disorder or strengthen his ability to regulate his social behavior in spite of the underlying disorder, or bring him substantial benefit in the form of protection from neglect or exploitation by others; or

  (ii) a strong need to protect others from antisocial behavior by the patient.

F.

Congress Enacts a Statute to Protect the Constitutional Rights of the "Mentally Ill"

DISTRICT OF COLUMBIA HOSPITALIZATION OF THE MENTALLY ILL ACT*

*   *   *

Definitions

Sec. 2. As used in this Act—

1. the term "mental illness" means any psychosis or other disease which substantially impairs the mental health of an individual;

2. the term "mentally ill person" means any person who has a mental illness, but shall not include a person committed to a private or public hospital in the District of Columbia by order of the court in a criminal proceeding;

3. the term "physician" means . . .

4. the term "private hospital" means . . .

5. the term "public hospital" means . . .

6. the term "administrator" means . . .

7. the term "chief of service" means . . . .

Commission on Mental Health

Sec. 3. The United States District Court for the

* D.C. Code ch. 21, §§ 501-591 (1966).

District of Columbia (hereinafter referred to as the "court") is authorized to appoint a Commission on Mental Health, composed of nine members. [The composition and function of the Commission is essentially unchanged.]

Voluntary Hospitalization

Sec. 4. (a) Any individual may apply to any public or private hospital in the District of Columbia for admission to such hospital as a voluntary patient for the purposes of observation, diagnosis, and care and treatment of a mental illness. Upon the request of any such individual 18 years of age or over (or in the case of any individual under 18 years of age, upon a request made by his spouse, parent, or legal guardian), the administrator of a public hospital shall, if an examination by an admitting psychiatrist at such public hospital reveals the need for such hospitalization, and the administrator of a private hospital may, admit any such individual as a voluntary patient to such hospital for observation, diagnosis, and care and treatment of a mental illness in accordance with the provisions of this act.

(b) Any voluntary patient admitted to any hospital pursuant to this section shall, if he is 18 years of age or over, be entitled at any time to obtain his release from such hospital by filing a written request with the chief of service. The chief of service shall, within a period of 48 hours after the receipt of any such request (unless such period shall expire on a Saturday, Sunday, or legal holiday, then not later than noon of the next succeeding day which is not a Saturday, Sunday, or legal holiday), release the voluntary patient making such request. In the case of any voluntary patient under the age of 18 years, the chief of service shall release such patient, according to the provisions of this section, upon the written request of his spouse, parent, or legal guardian. The chief of service may release any voluntary patient hospitalized pursuant to this section whenever he determines that such patient has recovered or that his continued hospitalization is no longer beneficial to him or advisable.

Hospitalization of Nonprotesting Persons

Sec. 5. (a) A friend or relative of an individual believed to be suffering from a mental illness may make application on behalf of that individual to the admitting psychiatrist of any hospital by presenting the individual, together with a referral from a practicing physician. Such individual may be accepted for examination and treatment by any private hospital and shall be accepted for examination and treatment by any public hospital if, in the judgment of the admitting psychiatrist, the need for such is indicated on the basis of the individual's mental condition and such individual signs a statement at the time of such admission stating that he does not object to hospitalization. Such statement shall contain in simple, nontechnical language the fact that the individual is to be hospitalized and a description of the right to release set out in subsection (b) of the section. The admitting psychiatrist may admit such an individual without referral from a practicing physician if the need for an immediate admission is apparent to the admitting psychiatrist upon preliminary examination.

(b) Any person hospitalized under the provisions of subsection (a) of this section shall be immediately released upon his written request unless proceedings for hospitalization under court order pursuant to section 7 have been initiated.

Emergency Hospitalization

Sec. 6. (a) Any duly accredited officer or agent of the Department of Public Health of the District of Columbia, or any officer authorized to make arrests in the District of Columbia, or the family physician of the individual in question, who has reason to believe that an individual is mentally ill and, because of such illness, is likely to injure himself or others if he is not immediately detained may, without a warrant, take such individual into custody, transport him to a public or private hospital, and make application for his admission thereto for purposes of emergency observation and diagnosis. Such application shall reveal the circumstances under which the individual was taken into custody and the reasons therefor.

(b) Subject to the provisions of subsection (c) of this section, the administrator of any private hospital, may, and the administrator of any public hospital shall, admit and detain for purposes of emergency observation and diagnosis any individual with respect to whom such application is made, if such application is accompanied by a certificate of a psychiatrist on duty at such hospital stating that he has examined the individual and is of the opinion that he has symptoms of a mental illness and, as a result thereof, is likely to injure himself or others unless he is immediately hospitalized; not later than 24 hours after the admission pursuant to this section of any individual to a hospital, the administrator of such hospital shall serve notice of such admission, by registered mail, to the spouse, parent, or legal guardian of such individual and to the Commission on Mental Health.

(c) No individual admitted to any hospital under subsection (b) of this section shall be detained in such hospital for a period in excess of 48 hours from the time of his admission (unless such period shall expire on a Saturday, Sunday, or legal holiday, then not later than noon of the next succeeding day which is not a Saturday, Sunday, or legal holiday) unless the administrator of such hospital has, within such period, filed a written petition with the court for an order authorizing the continued hospitalization of such individual for emergency observation and diagnosis for a period not to exceed 7 days from the time such order is entered.

(d) The court shall, within a period of 24 hours after the receipt by it of such petition (unless such period shall expire on a Saturday, Sunday, or legal holiday, then not later than noon of the next succeeding day which is not a Saturday, Sunday, or legal holiday) either order the hospitalization of such individual for emergency observation and a diagnosis for a period of not to exceed 7 days from the time such order is entered, or order his immediate release. In making its determination, the court shall consider the written reports of the agent, officer, or physician who made the application under subsection (b) of this section, the certificate of the examining psychiatrist which accompanied it, and any other relevant information.

(e) Any individual whose continued hospitalization is ordered under subsection (d) of this section shall be entitled upon his request to a hearing before the court entering such order. Any such hearing so requested shall be held within a period of 24 hours after receipt of such request (unless such period shall expire on a Saturday, Sunday, or legal holiday, then not later than noon of the next succeeding day which is not a Saturday, Sunday, or legal holiday).

(f) The chief of service of any hospital in which an individual is hospitalized under a court order entered pursuant to subsection (d) of this section shall, within 48 hours after such order is entered, have such individual examined by a physician. If the physician, after his examination, certifies that in his opinion the individual is not mentally ill to the extent that he is likely to injure himself or others if not presently detained, the individual shall be immediately released. The chief of service shall, within 48 hours after such examination has been completed, send a copy of the results thereof by registered mail to the spouse, parents, attorney, legal guardian, or nearest known adult relative of the individual examined.

(g) Any physician or psychiatrist making application or conducting an examination under this act shall be a competent and compellable witness at any trail hearing or other proceeding conducted pursuant to this act and the physician-patient privilege shall not be applicable.

(h) Notwithstanding any other provision of this section, the administrator of any hospital in which an individual is hospitalized under this section may, if judicial proceedings for his hospitalization have been commenced under section 7 of this act, detain such individual therein during the course of such proceedings.

Hospitalization under Court Order

Sec. 7. (a) Proceedings for the judicial hospitalization of any individual in the District of Columbia may be commenced by the filing of a petition with the Mental Health Commission by his spouse, parent, or legal guardian, by any physician, duly accredited officer or agent of the Department of Public Health, or by any officer authorized to make arrest in the District of Columbia. Such petition shall be accompanied (1) by a certificate of a physician stating that he has examined the individual and is of the opinion that such individual is mentally ill, and because of such illness is likely to injure himself or others if allowed to remain at liberty, or (2) by a sworn written statement by the petitioner that (A) the petitioner has good reason to believe that such individual is mentally ill and, because of such illness, is likely to injure himself or others if allowed to remain at liberty, and (B) that such individual has refused to submit to examination by a physician.

(b) Within 3 days after the receipt by it of any petition filed under subsection (a) of this section, the Commission shall send a copy of such petition by registered mail to the individual with respect to whom it was filed.

(c) The Commission shall promptly examine any petition provided by subsection (a) of this section and shall thereafter promptly hold a hearing on the issue of his mental illness. Such hearing shall be conducted in as informal a manner as may be consistent with orderly procedure and in a physical setting not likely to have a harmful effect on the mental health of the individual named in such petition. In conducting such hearing, the Commission shall hear testimony of any person whose testimony may be relevant and shall receive all relevant evidence which may be offered. Any individual with respect to whom a hearing is held under this section shall be entitled, in his discretion, to be present at such hearing, to testify, and to present and cross-examine witnesses. The Commission shall also hold a hearing in order to determine liability under the provisions of subsection (g) of this section for the expenses of hospitalization of the alleged mentally ill person, if it is determined that he is mentally ill and should be hospitalized as provided under this act. Such hearing may be conducted separately, it may be conducted by the Chairman of the Commission alone.

(d) The alleged mentally ill person shall be represented by counsel in any proceeding before the Commission or the court, and if he fails or refuses to obtain counsel, the court shall appoint counsel to represent him. Any counsel so appointed shall be awarded compensation by the court for his services in an amount determined by it to be fair and reasonable. Such compensation shall be charged against the estate of the individual for whom such counsel was appointed, or against any unobligated funds of the Commission, as the court in its discretion may direct. The Commission or the court, as the case may be, shall, at the request of any counsel so appointed, grant a recess in such proceeding (but not for more than 5 days) to give such counsel an opportunity to prepare his case.

(e) If the Commission finds, after such hearing, that the individual with respect to whom such hearing was held is not mentally ill or if mentally ill, is not mentally ill to the extent that he is likely to injure himself or others if allowed to remain at liberty, the Commission shall immediately order his release and notify the court of that fact in writing. If the Commission finds, after such hearing, that the individual with respect to whom such hearing was held is mentally ill, and because of such illness is likely to injure himself or others if allowed to remain at liberty, the Commission shall promptly report such fact, in writing, to the United States District Court for the District of Columbia. Such reports shall contain the Commission's findings of fact, conclusions of law, and recommendations. Any alleged mentally ill person with respect to whom such report is made shall have the right to demand a jury trial and shall be advised of that right by the Commission orally individual alleged to be mentally ill after the filing of a and in writing. A copy of the report of the Commission shall be served personally on the alleged mentally ill person and his attorney.

(f) Upon the receipt by the court of any such report referred to in subsection (e), the court shall promptly set the matter for hearing and shall cause a written notice of the time and place of the final hearing to be served personally upon the individual with respect to whom such report was made and his attorney, together with notice that he has 5 days following the date on which he is so served within which to demand a jury trial. Any such demand may be made by such individual or by anyone in his behalf. If a jury trial is demanded within such 5-day period, it shall be accorded by the court with all reasonable speed. If no timely demand is made for such trial, the court shall determine such individual's mental condition on the basis of the report of the Commission, or on such further evidence in addition to such report as the court may require. If the court or jury (as the case may be) finds that such individual is not mentally ill, the court shall dismiss the petition and order his release. If the court or jury (as the case may be) finds that such individual is mentally ill and, because of that illness, is likely to injure himself or others if allowed to remain at liberty, the court may order his hospitalization for an indeterminate period, or order any other alternative courses of treatment which the court believes will be in the best interests of such individual or of the public. The Commission, or any member thereof, shall be competent and compellable witnesses at any hearing or jury trial held pursuant to this act. . . .

(g) The father, mother, husband, wife, and adult children of a mentally ill person, if of sufficient ability, and the estate of such mentally ill person, if such estate is sufficient for the purpose, shall pay the cost of the District of Columbia of such mentally ill person's maintenance, including treatment, in any hospital in which such person is hospitalized under this act. . . .

(h) No petition, application, or certificate authorized under sections 6(a) and 7(a) of this act may be considered if made by a physician who is related by blood or marriage to the alleged mentally ill person, or who is financially interested in the hospital in which the alleged mentally ill person is to be detained, or, except in the case of physicians employed by the United States or the District of Columbia, who are professionally or officially connected with such hospital. No such petition, application, or certificate of any physician shall be considered unless it is based on personal observation and examination of the alleged mentally ill person made by such physician not more than 72 hours prior to the making of the petition, application, or certificate. Such certificate shall set forth in detail the facts and reasons on which such physician based his opinions and conclusions.

Periodic Examination and Release

Sec. 8. (a) Any patient hospitalized pursuant to a court order obtained under section 7 of this act, or his attorney, legal guardian, spouse, parent, or other nearest adult relative, shall be entitled, upon the expiration of 90 days following such order and not more frequently than every 6 months thereafter, to request, in writing, the chief of service of the hospital in which the patient is hospitalized, to have a current examination of his mental condition made by one or more physicians. If the request is timely it shall be granted. The patient shall be entitled, at his own expense, to have any duly qualified physician participate in such examination. In the case of any such patient who is indigent, the Department of Public Health shall, upon the written request of such patient, assist him in obtaining a duly qualified physician to participate in such examination in the patient's behalf. Any such physician so obtained by such indigent patient shall be compensated for his services out of any unobligated funds of such Department in an amount determined by it to be fair and reasonable. If the chief of service, after considering the reports of the physicians conducting such examination, determines that the patient is no longer mentally ill to the extent that he is likely to injure himself or others if not hospitalized, the chief of service shall order the immediate release of the patient. However, if the chief of service, after considering such reports, determines that such patient continues to be mentally ill to the extent that he is likely to injure himself or others if not hospitalized, but one or more of the physicians participating in such examination reports that the patient is not mentally ill to such extent, the patient may petition the court for an order directing his release. Such petition shall be accompanied by the reports of the physicians who conducted the examination of the patient.

(b) In considering such petition, the court shall consider the testimony of the physicians who participated in the examination of such patient, and the reports of such physicians accompanying the petition. After considering such testimony and reports, the court shall either (1) reject the petition and order the continued hospitalization of the patient, or (2) order the chief of service to immediately release such patient. Any physician participating in such examination shall be a competent and compellable witness at any trial or hearing held pursuant to this act.

(c) The chief of service of a public or private hospital shall as often be practicable, but not less often than every 6 months, examine or cause to be examined each patient admitted to any such hospital pursuant to section 7 of this act, and if he determines on the basis of such examination that the conditions which justified the involuntary hospitalization of such patient no longer exist, the chief of service shall immediately release such patient.

(d) Nothing in this section shall be construed to prohibit any person from exercising any right presently available to him for obtaining release from confinement, including the right to petition for a writ of habeas corpus.

Right to Communication—
Exercise of Certain Rights

Sec. 9. (a) Any person hospitalized in a public or private hospital pursuant to this act shall be entitled (1) to communicate by sealed mail or otherwise with any individual or official agency inside or outside the hospital, and (2) to receive uncensored mail from his attorney or personal physician. All other incoming mail or communications may be read before being delivered to the patient, if the chief of service believes such action is necessary for the medical welfare of the patient who is the intended recipient. However, any mail or other communication which is not delivered to the patient for whom it is intended shall be immediately returned to the sender. But nothing in this section shall prevent the administrator from making reasonable rules regarding visitation hours and the use of telephone and telegraph facilities.

(b) Any person hospitalized in a public hospital for a mental illness shall, during his hospitalization, be entitled to medical and psychiatric care and treatment. The administrator of each public hospital shall keep records detailing all such care and treatment received by any such person and such records shall be made available, upon that person's written authorization, to his attorney or personal physician. Such records shall be preserved by the administrator until such person has been discharged from the hospital.

(c) No mechanical restraint shall be applied to any patient hospitalized in any public or private hospital for a mental illness unless the use of restraint is prescribed by a physician and, if so prescribed, such restraint shall be removed whenever the condition justifying its use no longer exists. Any use of a mechanical restraint, together with the reasons therefore, shall be made a part of the medical record of the patient.

(d) No patient hospitalized pursuant to this act shall, by reason of such hospitalization, be denied the right to dispose of property, execute instruments, make purchases, enter into contractual relationships, vote, and hold a driver's license, unless such patient has been adjudicated incompetent by a court of competent jurisdiction and has not been restored to legal capacity. If the chief of service of the public or private hospital in which any such patient is hospitalized is of the opinion that such patient is unable to exercise any of the aforementioned rights,

the chief of service shall immediately notify the patient and the patient's attorney, legal guardian, spouse, parents, or other nearest known adult relative, and the United States District Court for the District of Columbia, the Commission on Mental Health, and the Board of Commissioners of the District of Columbia of that fact.

(e) Any individual in the District of Columbia who, by reason of a judicial decree ordering his hospitalization entered prior to the date of the enactment of this act, is considered to be mentally incompetent and is denied the right to dispose of property, execute instruments, make purchases, enter into contractual relationships, vote, or hold a driver's license solely by reason of such decree, shall, upon the expiration of the 1 year period immediately following such date of enactment, be deemed to have been restored to legal capacity unless, within such 1-year period, affirmative action is commenced to have such individual adjudicated mentally incompetent by a court of competent jurisdiction.

(f) Any patient, and the patient's spouse, parents, or other nearest known adult relative, shall receive upon admission of the patient to the hospital, a written statement outlining in simple, nontechnical language all release procedures provided by this act, setting out all rights accorded to patients by this act, and describing procedures provided by law for adjudication of incompetency and appointment of trustees or committees for the hospitalized individual.

Penalties

Sec. 11. (a) Any individual who, (1) without probable cause for believing a person to be mentally ill, causes or conspires with or assists another to cause the hospitalization of any such person under this act, or (2) causes or conspires with or assists another to cause the denial to any person of any right accorded to him under this act, shall be punished by a fine not exceeding $5,000 or imprisonment not exceeding 3 years or both.

(b) Any individual who, without probable cause for believing a person to be mentally ill, executes a petition, application, or certificate pursuant to this act, by which such individual secures or attempts to secure the apprehension, hospitalization, detention, or restraint of any such person, or any physician or psychiatrist who knowingly makes any false certificate or application pursuant to this act as to the mental condition of any person, shall be punished by a fine not exceeding $5,000 or imprisonment not exceeding 3 years, or both.

Nonresident

Sec. 12. If an individual ordered committed to a public hospital by the court pursuant to subsection (f) of section 7 is found by the Commission, subject to a review by the court, not to be a resident of the District of Columbia, and to be a resident of another place, he shall be transferred to the State of his residence if an appropriate institution of that State is willing to accept him. If the person be an indigent, the expense of transferring him, including the traveling expenses of necessary attendants, shall be borne by the District of Columbia. . . .

* * *

Not to be Confined in Jail

Sec. 14. No person apprehended, detained, or hospitalized under any provision of this Act, shall be confined in jail or in any penal or correctional institution.

* * *

G.

The Statute Applied—Protecting the Rights of Bong Yol Yang?

IN MATTER OF BONG YOL YANG
TRIAL TRANSCRIPT U.S. DISTRICT COURT,
D.C. (NOV. 18, 1964)

THE COURT: You may call your first witness.

1.

THOMAS M. WHITE

a.   Direct Examination

BY MR. NUNZIO:

Q. [W]ould you state your name and occupation? A. My name is Thomas M. White. I am a Special Agent with the United States Secret Service. My duty station [has been] at the White House [for] about 23 years.

Q. Do you know the patient in this case, Mr. Bong Yol Yang? A. Yes, sir, I saw him on October 5. . . . He came to the northwest gate of the White House. . . . The White House police called my office and said the gentleman was out there and wanted to see either the President or some representative of the President.

Q. Did you have any conversation? A. Yes, I went out and introduced myself to him and took him in the little back room where we usually talk to people.

Q. How long did you talk to the patient, sir? A. About 15 minutes, I would say. . . . He said he was a painter and brought in a couple of crude paintings. He said he was out of work; he could not sell his paintings. The people were bothering him, harassing him all the time, revealing through his subconscious mind, and he thought—he was afraid of these people because they followed him all the time, that they were going to kill him, and he could not go on living this way.

I didn't know whether he was going to commit suicide or not, but I felt very definitely he needed hospitalization at the time for protection of himself and other people.

Q. Did the patient appear as though he had been drinking? A. No, sir.

Q. Did he appear as though he had been fooling? A. No sir.

Q. You are not trained in psychiatry, is that correct? A. Oh, no, sir.

Q. But based upon your conversation you felt that he was mentally sick, is that correct? A. Yes, I did.

Q. Did he say anything with respect to what these revelations were to him, sir? A. One thing I omitted, that he did tell me that he had been lynched three different times by these revelations.

Q. Did he explain that? A. Or revealings. I couldn't understand him well enough to know exactly what he meant.

Q. Did you attempt to find out what he did mean by this? A. I asked him but I never did understand exactly what he meant except he did say he had been lynched on three different occasions.

Q. Now, we know that Mr. Yang is a Korean— Was his unclearness due to the language barrier or was he coherent with respect to the language? A. Partially, I think the language barrier.

* * *

b.   Cross-Examination

* * *

BY MR. FRANKLIN:

Q. I take it he didn't come to the White House insisting that: I want to see only the President of the United States. A. No, sir.

Q. In other words, he would have been satisfied to talk to anyone? A. I believe so.

Q. Did he seem satisfied talking to you? A. Apparently.

Q. I imagine you investigated as to whether or not he had any type of weapon? A. Yes.

Q. Did you find any type of weapon? A. No, sir.

Q. In your talking to him did he indicate anything that would be of a threatening nature to the President? A. No, sir.

* * *

2.

DAN F. KEENEY, M.D.—

a. Direct Examination

BY MR. NUNZIO:

Q. For the record, sir, would you state your name and your occupation? A. Dr. Dan F. Keeney; I am a physician and a psychiatrist.

* * *

Q Now, Dr. Keeney, I understand you are a member of the Mental Health Commission, is that correct, sir? A. That is correct. . . . For two years.

* * *

Q. . . . Dr. Keeney, do you know the patient in this case, Mr. Bong Yol Yang? A. Yes, I do. . . . I have examined him on at least four occasions, two at D.C. General Hospital and two at Saint Elizabeths Hospital. . . . The most recent examination was yesterday.

Q. Now, based upon these examinations, Doctor, did you reach a medical diagnosis as to whether he is mentally ill or not mentally ill? A. Yes, I believe he is mentally ill. . . . I believe that he is suffering from a paranoid type of schizophrenia.

Q. Would you explain that in lay terms to the ladies and gentlemen of this jury? A. Schizophrenia is disintegration of the personality in which the individual loses his ability to differentiate between what is real and what is not real. He often has hallucinations and delusions, false beliefs, and he is unable to tell whether these are true or not.

A paranoid type of schizophrenia is characterized primarily by delusions of persecution, the idea that people are following him or doing something to him that is harmful.

Q. Now, applying the diagnosis and the symptoms as you have explained them to us, can you relate them to this patient, Mr. Yang. A. Mr. Yang states quite frankly that for the last 42 months, he is quite specific about this, people have been revealing his subconscious thoughts. They have been following him and broadcasting in some way, which is not very specific; but they are broadcasting his subconscious thoughts in a way which keeps him from getting a job, and in a way that keeps him from being able to make a living.

He has written many letters about this to various Government officials, at least fifty, he admits, and has complained in recent months to the immigration officials and to the Department of Justice and to the White House, trying to see the President about this, in order to get people to stop this revealing of his subconscious thoughts.

He relates this quite freely and becomes rather irritated and overactive and agitated at times when people question this or do not believe it or do not accept it.

To the best of my knowledge, he has never actually attacked anyone as a result of this agitation, but certainly it is my opinion that he is potentially dangerous and might at any time do so.

Q. Now, Dr. Keeney, did you talk to the patient concerning his visit to the White House this past October? A. Yes.

Q. Did he state why he went to the White House? A. He went to the White House in order to get the President to stop this revealing of his subconscious thoughts.

Q. Did he state what subconscious thoughts that he wanted stopped that were being revealed? A. It is difficult to elicit specific examples of this, but he describes it as a situation in which he will have a thought that he is going to go some place or to do something, and suddenly other people will know all about this before he has ever revealed it consciously to anyone or told anyone about it. They know in advance what he is going to do and what he is thinking.

Q. Now, as of this moment, Doctor, based upon your examination, is it your opinion that the patient is now suffering from a mental illness? A. Yes, it is. His condition has not changed perceptibly during the month that I have been in contact with him.

Q. Is the patient oriented as to time and place and circumstances, Doctor, suffering from schizophrenia, paranoid type? A. To the best of my knowledge, he is fully oriented as to time, place, and person, yes.

Q. Now, Dr. Keeney, can you tell us whether as a result of this illness, this mental illness, this person is likely to injure himself or others if he is allowed to remain at liberty? A. It is my opinion that he is.

Q. Can you explain it to us, sir, in what respect he would likely injure himself or others? A. His delusions that people are following him, that they are revealing his subconscious are so fixed and this has become so much of an obsession with him that he becomes preoccupied with trying to stop this and trying to get somebody else to stop it, and it is certainly my opinion that if his frustration from this becomes great enough, he may potentially attack somebody in an effort to stop this revealing. If he gets to believe that some specific person is doing this, he may very well attack them assumedly in self-defense.

Q. This is assuming that he is allowed to remain at liberty, is that correct, sir? A. Yes, that is correct. His preoccupation with trying to do something about this prevents him from being able to engage in any constructive plan for his own welfare or to get a job or to earn a living. . . . In this respect he is really dangerous to himself in that he is unable to care for himself and to earn a living and be a productive citizen.

BY MR. NUNZIO:

Q. Thank you, Doctor. Then it is your opinion, Doctor, that the patient belongs in a controlled environment? A. Yes, it is. I think he should be confined in a mental hospital until such time as he has recovered from this delusion.

MR. NUNZIO: No further questions, Your Honor.

b.   **Cross-Examination**

BY MR. FRANKLIN:

Q. Doctor, I would like to ask you a few more questions about schizophrenia. There are a lot of types of schizophrenia, isn't that correct? A. Yes, there are.

Q. That is a serious mental disease, is it not? A. It is a serious mental illness that usually requires hospitalization but not always.

Q. Well, in light of that, nowadays there are a lot more drugs, tranquilizing drugs, so that people with schizophrenia may be able to be under drugs and be able to stay at their homes rather than be in the hospital, is that correct? A. Yes, that is correct.

Q. As a matter of fact, you have a private practice, as do many psychiatrists have a private practice, is that correct? A. Yes, that is correct.

Q. Isn't it a fact that there are many patients who have been diagnosed as schizophrenic who come once a week or twice a week to a doctor's office for therapy, psychotherapy, and relate their story or whatever the type of session it may be, and at the same time they are at home, resting at home or going about their job, taking at certain times of the day pills of some type, tranquilizing drugs? A. That is correct. It depends upon the severity of the illness as to whether they need to be in a hospital.

Q. So that not all persons who have the diagnosis of schizophrenia need to be in the hospital? A. That is correct. It has to be judged in each individual case.

Q. Now, with respect to the Respondent in this case, you feel that if he were at liberty in the community, he would be dangerous, or do I remember from your testimony on direct examination you prefaced this with, if he becomes agitated or assuming this or assuming that? Upon what do you base the fact that he will be either dangerous to himself, likely to injure himself or likely to injure someone in the community? A. At D.C. General Hospital he was started off on a certain drug which is a tranquilizing drug, but at times there when people would question his delusions he would become agitated and disturbed to such an extent that it was necessary to increase this drug considerably.

It is my feeling that his control of his aggressive and hostile impulses in situations where the questioning of these delusions comes up is very thin, and that it might break through at any time and he might attack someone; although I must admit I do not have any direct knowledge of his ever having attacked anyone so far.

Q. So this is only in the realm of possibility rather than real certainty? A. It is a potential danger, yes.

Q. Potential or possible? A. I think it is a probable danger.

Q. Well, he would be able to get these medicines on the outside if he were at liberty, would he not? A. If he were willing to take them. But he has no insight or understanding into the fact that he is sick; and it is my opinion that it would be very unlikely that he would be willing to submit to treatment outside or would be willing or able to continue such treatment and to take medications regularly on the outside of the hospital.

Q. This is something we are not certain about, is that not so, just what he would do? A. I am certain he has no insight or understanding into his illness and does not believe that he is sick.

Q. In your interviewing of him, haven't you determined that he had the occupation of being a painter? A. That is correct.

Q. Do you know of your personal knowledge of any of his work or the quality of it or as to whether or not he has been able to make a living in the past? A. It is my understanding that he has studied art in several universities and that he has been able to make a living in the past, has painted pictures for a greeting card company, and it was while he was working in such a greeting card company that he became ill, 42 months ago. He said he had been working there about 6 weeks when all this began. And it was his feeling that the greeting card company was responsible for starting these revealings of his subconscious thoughts.

My own personal knowledge of his artistic ability was—might be illustrated by . . . a sketch that Mr. Yang had made of [his lawyer] during that time, which was a quite recognizable likeness.

Q. So he does have a talent? A. He does have a talent, no question about that.

Q. If such an individual with this type of talent were free of any mental illness, he should have very little difficulty in making a livelihood, is that true? A. That is correct, if he were free of mental illness. But the problem comes up when he tries to get along with other people in such an employment situation and believes they are persecuting him.

*   *   *

MR. NUNZIO: We have rested, Your Honor.

MR. FRANKLIN: May counsel approach the bench, Your Honor?

(Whereupon counsel approached the bench and the following proceedings were held:)

MR. FRANKLIN: Your Honor, at this time the Respondent respectfully moves the court to grant a directed verdict in his favor based partially upon the fact that the Government has failed in its burden particularly on the second part of the standard, namely, to show that the Respondent is likely to injure himself or another.

The Secret Service Agent particularly emphasized that when the Respondent came to the White House he had no weapon, he made no threat as to the President's life. In fact, he didn't even really insist on seeing the President. He would have been satisfied to see a representative of the President and was satisfied seeing the Secret Service Agent.

With respect to the testimony of the doctor, his testimony was very hazy, I believe: If this, if that. He even at one point conceded that the Respondent had never struck anybody, and if he does this when he is outside, if he is not on medication—I think the reason this recent act was passed was to strengthen and insure that there was a double standard. As the doctor admitted, many people in his own practice are schizophrenic and are controlled by tranquilizing drugs and able to go about their business.

I feel the Government has failed to make a prima facie case at this time.

THE COURT: I will deny your motion.

3.

BONG YOL YANG

*   *   *

a.   **Direct Examination**

BY MR. FRANKLIN:

*   *   *

Q. Where are you from, Mr. Yang? A. I came from Korea . . . in 1948.

Q. When were you born? A. January 20, 1923, in Korea.

*   *   *

Q. Incidentally, do you happen to recall who was the President of the United States at that time? A. President Harry Truman.

Q. And who is the President of the United States at the present time? A. President Lyndon Johnson.

Q. All right. Did we have an election recently? A. Yes, we did have.

Q. When was that? Do you recall when that was? A. November 3, on Tuesday.

Q. What do you do to make a living, Mr. Yang? A. I paint and sell my painting to the people.

Q. How long have you been painting? A. That is —when I came to Washington, D.C., I have done that. That is about—I have been doing this for about two and a half years.

Q. Right now you are in hospital, isn't that right? A. Yes, in the St. Elizabeths Hospital.

Q. The type of ward that you are on—do you know what I mean by the expression, "locked ward"? Do you know what I mean by that? A. Expression of—

Q. Do you know what I mean if I say locked ward? Do you know what I mean by that? A. Locked ward?

Q. Are you able to go in and out of the ward that you are on at the hospital? A. Yes. I would like to leave the hospital.

Q. You wish to leave the hospital? A. Yes.

Q. Do you feel that you would be able to leave the hospital? Will you be able to leave Saint Elizabeths Hospital? A. Yes, I feel I would be able to leave the hospital.

Q. If you left the hospital—what would you do if you left the hospital? A. I explain to the President Johnson, I would like to work for the Federal Commission, work in the creative art field; and I explain— I wrote many letters to the late President Kennedy and the present President Johnson, that I had much trouble and much lynchings in the private companies where I had worked before. Therefore, I would like to get some Federal help from the Federal Government.

Q. Mr. Yang, if you were outside and began to try to get help to get a job, would you have in your mind to go and see a doctor on the outside? A. Yes, I don't mind to see doctor, I would be willing to see doctor.

MR. FRANKLIN: I have no further questions.

b.   **Cross-Examination**

BY MR. NUNZIO:

*   *   *

Q. You stated that if you were allowed to go that you would see a doctor, you would see doctors. A. Yes, I would see doctors.

Q. Do you believe that you are sick at all, as the doctors have testified? A. I don't think I am sick at all, because of lynching, maybe such a thing, such a minor indication has developed in my mind or in my body. I don't think in my mind. When anyone's subconscious mind and outward actions are revealed and when he gets irritated, when the person get irritated, naturally, he get nervous.

Q. Well, then, you are saying that your mind is all right. Is that what you are telling the court? A. Yes, I think I am all right, yes.

Q. So you don't think that you would have to see a doctor for your mind, do you? A. Well but, however, the doctor at St. Elizabeths Hospital Mental Commissioners asked me to see a doctor, then I am willing to see that doctor.

Q. But you, yourself, don't think there is anything wrong with your mind? A. I don't think so.

Q. You said something about when your own revealings are disclosed to other people that would irritate you, is that correct? A. That is quite right. This happens to anyone, too.

Q. When did these revealings start, Mr. Yang? A. It started about middle part of April 1961.

Q. And what type of revealings are conveyed to other people? A. Everything comes to my mind, that means my subconscious thoughts and my outward action, my 24 hours daily activities.

Q. In other words, what you are going to do, people know what you are going to do ahead of time? A. Yes, that is quite right.

Q. And this makes you nervous? A. Yes, nervous and irritating.

Q. Have you been writing to anyone to try to— A. I wrote to the immigration office and one or two times to the Justice Department.

Q. To try to get them to stop— A. And many times to the late President Kennedy and many times to the President Johnson.

Q. How do you expect the Federal Government to stop this, sir? A. Because keeps on—company authorized by the Federal Government without my permission. Keep on. Company had never asked me whether they could reveal my subconscious thought and my outward actions. Without my permission they—the company was authorized.

So after I left, because of lynching I left the company, but still the company had not notified to the Federal Government that I had left that company. Therefore, I think the Federal Government still has not stopped. And final authority—Federal Government has final authority to stop.

So I wrote to the President Johnson and the President Kennedy in order to stop; otherwise there is no ending of it.

Q. Is it still going on? A. Yes.

Q. Your subconscious is being revealed to other people? A. Yes, still has been going on.

Q. And it still irritates you? A. Oh, yes, of course, it is much irritating me.

Q. Does it make you angry? A. Angry and irritate—for the revealings, to a certain extent, I have to control. When I want to control myself, a lot of tension, commotion that cause in my stomach. Then I get stomach ulcers, stomach ache because of the tension. Then take some kind medicine. Then that makes so much sense, as far as I am concerned. The revealing goes on and I get lynching and then I take medicine. These things going about 42 months, all these times.

Q. In other words, it builds up when you control your emotions? A. To a certain extent, yes, I have a control of my emotions.

Q. Well, suppose you were to leave the hospital today, where would you find employment, Mr. Yang? A. I paint, as I did it before, before I came to the D.C. General Hospital. I go around to the city and ask for the people photos, and from photo, I paint their portraits; and I sold to one painting for $10.00, which is not right now, but before I have done that, in order to survive. But when I go out, it is harder to present me to selling like that. I have to raise my price; and I have to sell those paintings to the people; and—I owe about $100 to my rooming house. I have to pay those back. And I have to do those things.

In the meantime I tell President Johnson I work on Federal Commission work on creative art field and I hope that I would get such kind of work from the Federal Government.

Q. But how long have you been trying to get into the Federal Commission of the art field? A. That I explained to the President Johnson all this time, but still the revealing has not stopped.

* * *

THE COURT: Do you gentlemen want to argue this to the jury?

MR. FRANKLIN: Yes, Your Honor.

* * *

MR. FRANKLIN: May it please Your Honor, ladies and gentlemen of the jury: This is a very important type of case. It is a very important type of case for the Respondent, Mr. Yang.

* * *

The evidence as to whether or not the Respondent is mentally ill and whether or not because of that mental illness he is likely to injure himself or others is to be determined by you as the finders of the fact from the evidence that has come from the witness stand.

* * *

Now, the first witness was the Secret Service Agent. I didn't ask him very many questions, but the questions that I asked were of the nature as to whether or not he had a weapon with him, whether or not he went and made some type of a threat to the President. Did he really specifically want to see the President?

I think the testimony was he didn't go there simply demanding: I want to see the President of the United States. I think the testimony from the Secret Service Agent, himself, was that he wanted to see the President or some representative of him.

The Secret Service Agent, I think, also admitted that Mr. Yang was willing to talk to him. Of course, it was just about a year ago at this time that this nation and the world suffered the severe tragedy with the assassination of President Kennedy. I am sure if there were any element of a question of a presidential threat that the Secret Service Agent who was here, an officer of the Secret Service, would have made it mighty clear to you. Instead the Secret Service Agent felt this was a case of mental illness and Mr. Yang was sent to D.C. General.

* * *

Now we come to the testimony of the doctor who testified. . . .

He talked about schizophrenia, and I asked him—mental illness is at a stage today where we recognize there is nothing to be ashamed of. A person is sick. This doesn't mean a person has done anything wrong. But there is a question of whether or not people need help. But the question is whether or not the help should come from the hospital or could be helped from outside. That is why I asked the doctor, did he not have patients in his own private practice whom he has diagnosed as being schizophrenic, who, nevertheless, after they have a session of therapy, go right back to their normal life, take pills, tranquilizers, and they are able to control themselves.

It is significant, I think, that Mr. Yang did testify if he were to leave the hospital that he would go out and seek employment but he would also be willing, he stated, to go and see a doctor. I think that this is very important.

Now most important, with respect to the testimony of the Government psychiatrist, is this question again, which I feel is the most important point to the whole case, the second point: Is this man likely—really, just take a look at him. Is this the type of man who is likely to injure himself or to injure another? There was absolutely no testimony, and if there had been, I am sure there would have been by the Government psychiatrist as to suicide tendency. I am sure if that existed, the doctor would have said so. He said he didn't know. He admitted that he didn't know of any case where he went to strike anybody or hit anybody.

A man gets upset, agitated. There is no person who at one time or another doesn't get upset, doesn't get agitated. I don't think the fact that someone has stomach ulcers constitutes mental illness by any stretch of the imagination. All of us in our daily routine get upset once in a while.

What you really have here is a case of whether or not an individual should be in a mental hospital. Mental hospitals do well and they help people. Just the same, by being in a mental hospital, being on a ward, you are subject to restraint. You have to go along with whatever the rules are. You are in a ward; you are thrown together with people who very often may be much more ill than the particular patient; and this is something, I think, that is very important to consider.

Many of the things that Mr. Yang testified to, I think, made a lot of sense. I think he said he is going to raise the price. From that standpoint, he might be a good businessman; may recognize he wasn't doing so well and charge more for his paintings.

On the other hand, we had an admission from the Government psychiatrist that such a man is talented. I think he said he, himself, had seen a picture Mr. Yang had drawn and such a person free from illness could be talented and could make a good livelihood.

I just feel that particularly with respect to the important element that the Government must prove to your satisfaction that there is just nothing here that indicates that this man is likely to injure himself or hurt somebody else.

There are many people who aren't able to take care of themselves, that have to struggle making a living, getting on the right foot, finding a place to live. But this isn't a reason, I don't feel, to have a man in a mental hospital.

*   *   *

I ask that you deliberate on this matter and that you return a verdict in favor of the Respondent, Mr. Yang. Thank you.

MR. NUNZIO: . . .

I agree this is an important case to the patient as well as to society.

Now, counsel points out that the Secret Service officer testified that there was no danger with respect to this man; he was quiet; he came to ask to see the President, or someone else. But what prompted this officer to take this man to the hospital first of all was this man said something to the effect that there was nothing he could do, his life was lost, so to speak.

The officer had a fear of suicide, and that is what prompted the officer to refer the case. So in that respect something did demonstrate itself to a Secret Service Agent that perhaps the man was a danger to himself, not to others.

Dr. Kenney, counsel points out, failed to show any danger to the patient, to himself or to any others; and yet let me remind you that, number one, the statute doesn't say will injure himself or others. It says, is likely to injure himself or others. So there is a broad prospective here with the word "likely."

Dr. Kenney testified that if the man was allowed to remain at liberty, these revealings not being responded to by the Federal Government, the Justice Department, as the patient, himself, testified to, may reach a point where he feels that he has to do more than just write about having the subconscious ideas of his stolen, so to speak, that he may move in a further field.

I refer to the testimony of the witness, the patient, himself. He said he gets nervous and agitated and that it boils up in his stomach. Combining the patient's own testimony with that of Dr. Kenney, and Dr. Kenney used the word, when pressed by counsel, probably would injure himself or others. So I feel that we have satisfied the factual situation in that respect.

Also, Dr. Kenney did testify that there is an immediate danger to the patient. He is injuring himself through physical neglect and inability to find some sort of employment, to work towards his own physical needs and, as a result, he is physically hurting himself.

So it is not only physical abuse through violence

that we are concerned with, but injury to oneself through neglect. Dr. Kenney did testify to that.

Counsel makes a point of the issue that this man is an artist, yet he seeks no regular employment. He has only told us he sold one painting.

The man went to the White House because he was destitute, he wanted a job with the Federal Government. He was trying to sell two paintings that he brought with him.

So I think the Government has proved the point that the man is likely to injure himself or others. Of course, this does not preclude the fact that you must also find that the man is mentally ill. I think the man's own testimony shows he is mentally ill.

I feel on the basis of these facts that you should find for the Government. Briefly, I am asking you to find that the patient is mentally ill and you then return your verdict that he is likely to injure himself or others.

Robert Burns, the poet, once wrote:

"Oh wad some power the giftie gie us
To see ourselves as others see us."

For the average human being, this is simple. To a man with a mental disorder, hospitalization is the only way the man, through the help of doctors, can see himself; and I am asking you in your verdict to give this man an opportunity to see himself through psychiatric care. As counsel points out, there is a restraint on this man, but you can let him roam through the four corners of this earth and as long as his mind is not free, he is not free. He is a prisoner of his own mind. Give him this opportunity to see himself by returning the verdict that he is mentally ill and likely to injure himself or others.

THE COURT: Members of the jury, this case has now reached the stage where it becomes my duty to charge you on the law, the law with respect to this case.

*   *   *

. . . The purpose of this hearing is simple. It is to determine two matters: One, whether the Respondent is mentally ill. That is your first question. Second, if so, because of that illness is the patient likely to injure himself or others if allowed to remain at liberty.

*   *   *

As to the first question, the term "mental illness" means *any psychosis or other disease which substantially impairs the mental health of an individual.* That is the definition of mental illness which is contained in the statute under which we are proceeding.

In order to find that the patient is mentally ill, it is not necessary for you to find him to be dangerous. That is a separate question. If you determine that the Respondent has a mental illness, you will then go on to consider whether because of that illness the

Respondent is likely to injure himself or others if allowed to remain at liberty. In other words, if you answer the first question in the affirmative, you will then determine whether the illness is such that the Respondent is likely to injure himself or others if permitted to remain at liberty. I repeat that language: That the Respondent is likely to injure himself or others if permitted to remain at liberty.

As to both of these questions, the burden of proof is on the District of Columbia. The District must prove by a preponderance of the evidence that the Respondent is mentally ill and that because of the illness he is likely to injure himself or others if allowed to remain at liberty.

*   *   *

In this case there has been a psychiatrist who testified as an expert and gave his opinion as to the issues before you. In that regard I should say to you that a person who by education, study, and experience has become an expert in any art, science, or profession, and who is called as a witness, may give his opinion as to any such matter in which he is versed and which is material to the case. You should give careful consideration to the opinion expressed in connection with other evidence in the case and you should weigh the reasons if any given for such opinion. You are not bound, however, by such an opinion. You may give it such weight as you deem it is entitled to receive, whether that be great or slight, and you may reject it if in your judgment the reasons given for it are unsound.

*   *   *

In this case you are called upon to answer two questions. . . . Is this Respondent or is he not mentally ill? That is your first question. Is he mentally ill or is he not mentally ill?

If your answer is that he is mentally ill, the next question you are called upon to answer is: Because of that illness is he likely to injure himself or others if allowed to remain at liberty?

*   *   *

THE CLERK: Mr. Foreman, has the jury agreed upon a verdict?

THE FOREMAN: Yes, we have.

THE CLERK: Do you find the patient, Bong Yol Yang, mentally ill or not mentally ill?

THE FOREMAN: We find him mentally ill.

THE CLERK: Because of his mental illness, is he likely to injure himself or others if allowed to remain at liberty?

THE FOREMAN: We all think so.

*   *   *

NOTES

NOTE 1

CALIFORNIA SUBCOMMITTEE ON COMMITMENT PROCEDURES FOR THE MENTALLY ILL*

A Report on Commitment Procedures

JUDGE CHRISTIAN: I would like to point to [an] undesirable consequence of the use of the commitment procedure as the basic means of access to the public facilities. That is that where so many patients come into the system upon findings that courts, I fear, are not always careful to distinguish between the finding of need for care and treatment and the existence of a condition that is dangerous to the patient or to the public, where so many hundreds and thousands of patients come in under findings that they are dangerous to themselves or others. It is easy to lose sight of the few patients who come into the system who are really in that condition; who really are dangerous to themselves or to others.

I have a feeling that this lack of accurate classification in the intake contributes to some of the cases that, perhaps, members of the committee are aware of that have occurred in recent years where discharges have occurred, where absences without leave have been followed by a discharge rather than an attempt to locate the patient, and then these incidents have been followed by harm to the patient or to others.

I have a feeling that these events are made more likely by our failure to distinguish at intake between a person who really is dangerous to himself or to others and, therefore, perhaps, should have an authoritative placement under a court procedure with all the trappings of due process, than a person who is merely sick and in need of treatment.

NOTE 2

REPORT OF THE PRESIDENT'S COMMISSION ON THE ASSASSINATION OF PRESIDENT KENNEDY**

A basic element of Presidential protection is the identification and elimination of possible sources of danger to the President before the danger becomes actual. The Secret Service has attempted to perform this function through the activities of its Protective Research Section and requests to other agencies, Federal and local, for useful information. The Commission has concluded that at the time of the assassination the arrangements relied upon by the Secret Service to perform this function were seriously deficient.

Adequacy of preventive intelligence operations of the

Secret Service.—The main job of the Protective Research Section (PRS) is to collect, process, and evaluate information about persons or groups who may be a danger to the President. . . .

Many persons call themselves to the attention of PRS by attempting to visit the President for bizarre reasons or by writing or in some other way attempting to communicate with him in a threatening or abusive manner or with undue persistence. Robert I. Bouck, special agent in charge of PRS, estimated that most of the material received by his office originated in this fashion or from the occasional investigations initiated by the Secret Service, while the balance was furnished to PRS by other Federal agencies, with primary source being the F.B.I. . . .

Before the assassination of President Kennedy, PRS expressed its interest in receiving information on suspects in very general terms. For example, PRS instructed the White House mailroom, a source of much PRS data, to refer all communications on identified existing cases and, in addition, any communication "that in any way indicates anyone may have possible intention of harming the President." Slightly more specific criteria were established for PRS personnel processing White House mail referred by the White House mailroom, but again the standards were very general. These instructions to PRS personnel appear to be the only instance where an effort was made to reduce the criteria to writing. When requested to provide a specific statement of the standards employed by PRS in deciding what information to seek and retain, the Secret Service responded:

> The criteria in effect prior to November 22, 1963, for determining whether to accept material for the PRS general files were broad and flexible. All material is and was desired, accepted, and filed if it indicated or tended to indicate that the safety of the President is or might be in danger, either at the present or in the future. * * * There are many actions, situations, and incidents that may indicate such potential danger. Some are specific, such as threats; danger may be implied from others, such as membership or activity in an organization which believes in assassination as a political weapon. All material received by PRS was separately screened and a determination made as to whether the information might indicate possible harm to the President. If the material was evaluated as indicating some potential danger to the President—no matter how small—it was indexed in the general PRS files under the name of the individual or group of individuals to whom that material related.
>
> * * *

When PRS learns of an individual whose conduct warrants scrutiny, it requests an investigation by the closest Secret Service field office, of which there are 65 throughout the country. If the field office determines that the case should be subject to continuing

---

*January (1965) p. 11.
**Washington: U.S. Government Printing Office (1964), pp. 429-31, 461-63, 468.

review, PRS establishes a file which requires a check-up at least every six months. This might involve a personal interview or interviews with members of the person's household. Wherever possible, the Secret Service arranges for the family and friends of the individual, and local law enforcement officials, to advise the field office if the subject displays signs of increased danger or plans to leave his home area. At the time of the assassination there were approximately 400 persons throughout the country who were subject to periodic reviews.

If PRS concludes after investigation that an individual presents a significant danger to the life of the President, his name is placed in a "trip index file" which is maintained on a geographical field office basis. At the time of the assassination the names of about 100 persons were in this index, all of whom were included in the group of 400 being reviewed regularly. PRS also maintains an album of photographs and descriptions of about 12 to 15 individuals who are regarded as clear risks to the President and who do not have a fixed place of residence. Members of the White House detail of the Secret Service have copies of this album.

Individuals who are regarded as dangerous to the President and who are in penal or hospital custody are listed only in the general files of PRS, but there is a system for the immediate notification of the Secret Service by the confining institution when a subject is released or escapes. PRS attempts to eliminate serious risks by hospitalization or, where necessary, the prosecution of persons who have committed an offense such as threatening the President. In June 1964 PRS had arrangements to be notified about the release or escape of approximately 1,000 persons.

* * *

Preventive Intelligence

In attempting to identify those individuals who might prove a danger to the President, the Secret Service has largely been the passive recipient of threatening communications to the President and reports from other agencies which independently evaluate their information for potential sources of danger. This was the consequence of the Service's lack of an adequate investigative staff, its inability to process large amounts of data, and its failure to provide specific descriptions of the kind of information it sought.

The Secret Service has embarked upon a complete overhaul of its research activities. . . .

Broader and more selective criteria.—Since the assassination, both the Secret Service and the FBI have recognized that the PRS files can no longer be limited largely to persons communicating actual threats to the President. On December 26, 1963, the FBI circulated additional instructions to all its agents, specifying criteria for information to be furnished to the Secret Service in addition to that covered by the former standard, which was the possibility of an attempt against the person or safety of the President. The new instructions require FBI agents to report immediately information concerning:

> Subversives, ultrarightists, racists and fascists (a) possessing emotional instability or irrational behavior, (b) who have made threats of bodily harm against officials or employees of Federal, state or local government or officials of a foreign government, (c) who express or have expressed strong or violent anti-U.S. sentiments and who have been involved in bombing or bomb-making or whose past conduct indicates tendencies toward violence, and (d) whose prior acts or statements depict propensity for violence and hatred against organized government.

Alan H. Belmont, Assistant to the Director of the FBI, testified that this revision was initiated by the FBI itself. The volume of references to the Secret Service has increased substantially since the new instructions went into effect; more than 5,000 names were referred to the Secret Service in the first four months of 1964. According to Chief Rowley, by mid-June, 1964, the Secret Service had received from the FBI some 9,000 reports on members of the Communist Party. The FBI now transmits information on all defectors, a category which would, of course, have included Oswald.

Both Director Hoover and Belmont expressed to the Commission the great concern of the FBI, which is shared by the Secret Service, that referrals to the Secret Service under the new criteria might, if not properly handled, result in some degree of interference with the personal liberty of those involved. They emphasized the necessity that the information now being furnished be handled with judgment and care. The Commission shares this concern. The problem is aggravated by the necessity that the Service obtain the assistance of local law enforcement officials in evaluating the information which it receives and in taking preventive steps.

In June, 1964, the Secret Service sent to a number of Federal law enforcement and intelligence agencies guidelines for an experimental program to develop more detailed criteria. The suggestions of Federal agencies for revision of these guidelines were solicited. The new tentative criteria are useful in making clear that the interest of the Secret Service goes beyond information on individuals or groups threatening to cause harm or embarrassment to the President. Information is requested also concerning individuals or groups who have demonstrated an interest in the President or "other high government officials in the nature of a complaint coupled with an expressed or implied determination to use a means, other than legal or peaceful, to satisfy any grievance, real or imagined." Under these criteria, whether the case should be referred to the Secret Service depends on the existence of a previous history of mental instability, propensity toward violent action, or some similar characteristic, coupled with some evaluation of the capability of the individual or group to further the intention to satisfy a grievance by unlawful means.

While these tentative criteria are a step in the right direction, they seem unduly restrictive in continuing to require some manifestation of animus against a Government official. It is questionable whether such criteria would have resulted in the referral of Oswald to the Secret Service. Chief Rowley believed that they would, because of Oswald's demonstrated hostility toward the Secretary of the Navy in his letter of January 30, 1962.

> I shall employ all means to right this gross mistake or injustice to a boni-fied U.S. citizen and ex-service man. The U.S. government has no charges or complaints against me. I ask you to look into this case and take the necessary steps to repair the damage done to me and my family.

Even with the advantage of hindsight, this letter does not appear to express or imply Oswald's "determination to use a means, other than legal or peaceful, to satisfy [his] grievance" within the meaning of the new criteria.

It is apparent that a good deal of further consideration and experimentation will be required before adequate criteria can be framed. The Commission recognizes that no set of meaningful criteria will yield the names of all potential assassins. Charles J. Guiteau, Leon F. Czolgosz, John Schrank, and Guiseppe Zangara—four assassins or would-be assassins —were all men who acted alone in their criminal acts against our leaders. None had a serious record of prior violence. Each of them was a failure in his work and in his relations with others, a victim of delusions and fancies which led to the conviction that society and its leaders had combined to thwart him. It will require every available resource of our Government to devise a practical system which has any reasonable possibility of revealing such malcontents.

* * *

CONCLUSION

This Commission can recommend no procedures for the future protection of our Presidents which will guarantee security. The demands on the President in the execution of his responsibilities in today's world are so varied and complex and the traditions of the office in a democracy such as ours are so deepseated as to preclude absolute security.

The Commission has, however, from its examination of the facts of President Kennedy's assassination made certain recommendations which it believes would, if adopted, materially improve upon the procedures in effect at the time of President Kennedy's assassination and result in a substantial lessening of the danger.

As has been pointed out, the Commission has not resolved all the proposals which could be made. The Commission nevertheless is confident that, with the active co-operation of the responsible agencies and with the understanding of the people of the United States in their demands upon their President, the recommendations we have here suggested would greatly advance the security of the office without any impairment of our fundamental liberties.

PART TWO

TO WHAT EXTENT AND WHY ARE "MENTAL ILLNESS," "DANGEROUSNESS," "NEED FOR TREATMENT," "TREATABILITY" AND "AVAILABILITY OF TREATMENT" RELEVANT TO DECISIONS CONCERNED WITH INSTITUTIONALIZATION AND DEINSTITUTIONALIZATION?

Many are the processes for institutionalizing persons suspected of or found to be "mentally ill." These processes include "voluntary," "nonprotesting," and "involuntary" commitments, as well as commitments resulting from findings of "incompetency to stand trial," "acquittal by reason of insanity," and "incompetency to serve sentence." Common to such procedures is a determination (or assumption) of the presence or absence of "mental illness, disease, or defect." Though such a conclusion, whatever its content, may be sufficient to authorize institutionalization or deinstitutionalization, other factors frequently are crucial to these decisions. Thus in addition to exploring the meaning and function of "mental illness, disease, or defect" we examine the meaning and function of such other criteria as "dangerousness to self," "dangerousness to others," "harmlessness," "likelihood of injury to self or others," "need for custody or treatment," "competency to make a decision about need for custody or treatment," "treatability," and "availability of treatment."

To illustrate the types of questions that might be posed in evaluating these commitment processes we set forth a series of questions which were developed to facilitate analysis of acquital-by-reason-of-insanity commitment. The questions posed rest on an assumption that the purpose of the insanity defense is "the restraint of persons who have *committed* a crime and are feared to be dangerous and/or felt to need care and destigmatization because of criminality coupled with a finding of mental sickness."* But with appropriate variations such questions are relevant to an appraisal of any procedure for institutionalizing or deinstitutionalizing the "mentally ill."

A. RESTRAINT IN WHAT KINDS OF INSTITUTIONS?

"1. If restraint is in response to the *fear of dangerousness*, are not institutions of the Department of Correction and of the Department of Mental Health equally satisfactory?

"2. If restraint is in response to the *need for care* cannot correctional and mental health institutions be equally satisfactory if they are both oriented toward rehabilitation? If the impact of the desire to neglect is to be minimized, should not restraint be conditioned on the availability of a therapeutic opportunity?

"3. If restraint is in response to the *need for destigmatization* are not correctional and mental health institutions equally unsatisfactory?

"4. If restraint in either the correctional or mental health systems are equally satisfactory, what values or policies should be weighed against the flexibility that might come with restraint in and easy transfer between both systems?

B. RESTRAINT FOR WHAT LENGTH OF TIME?

"1. If length of restraint is in response to the *fear of dangerousness* should restraint be authorized for an indeterminate period? If the impact of the need to neglect is to be minimized, should there be provision, in addition to *habeas corpus*, for the automatic review, annually or semi-annually, of each person restrained in terms of his present state of dangerousness? If the impact of the urge to punish is to be minimized, should length of restraint be limited to the maximum sentence authorized for the crime committed?

"2. If length of restraint is in response to the *need for care* should restraint be authorized for an indeterminate period? If the impact of the need for neglect is to be minimized should provision, in addition to *habeas corpus*, be made for the automatic annual review and report to all interested parties (judge, defense attorney, etc.,) of the continued availability and use of therapy? If the impact of the need for neglect is to be minimized should provision be made for establishing, reviewing, and revising standards for therapeutic care?

"3. If length of restraint is in response to the *need for destigmatization*, should there be any restraint? If the impact of the need to stigmatize is to be minimized can procedures be developed

---

* Goldstein, J. and Katz, J.: "*Abolish the 'Insanity Defense'—Why Not?*" Reprinted by permission of the Yale Law Journal Co. and Fred B. Rothman & Co. From the *Yale Law Journal*, vol. 72, no. 5, p. 873 (1963).

to create an expectation in the community that release means a person is ready to participate in the life of the community?

C. RESTRAINT FOR WHAT CONDUCT?

"1. If restraint is in response to the *fear of dangerousness*, should certain "less serious or less dangerous" offenses be excluded as a basis for such restraint? If the impact of the urge to punish is to be minimized, should not all crimes be included as the basis for such restraint?

"2. If restraint is in response to the *need for care*, should not all crimes be included as a basis for restraint? If the impact of the need to neglect is to be minimized, should not all crimes be included as a basis for restraint?

"3. If restraint is in response to the *need for destigmatization* and if the label of criminality added to the label of mental sickness increases stigma, should not all crimes be excluded as a basis for restraint? If, on the other hand, stigma is decreased by such an association should not all crimes be a basis for such restraint?

D. RESTRAINT FOR WHAT MENTAL SICKNESSES?

"1. If restraint is in response to the *fear of dangerousness* should certain "less dangerous" mental sicknesses as well as mental sicknesses currently unaccompanied by overt symptomatology be excluded as a basis for restraint? If the impact of the urge to punish is to be minimized should restraint be limited to only those whose mental sickness could subject them to civil commitment?

"2. If restraint is in response to the *need for care* should not all mental sicknesses be a basis for restraint? If the impact of the need to neglect or to punish is to be minimized should all non-treatable mental sicknesses as well as mental sicknesses currently unaccompanied by overt symptomatology be excluded as a basis for restraint?

"3. If restraint is in response to the *need for destigmatization* and if the label of mental sickness added to the label of criminality increases stigma, should not all mental sicknesses be a basis for restraint? If, on the other hand, stigma is decreased by such an association should not all crimes be a basis for such restraint?

*   *   *

"In responding to these questions lawmakers will be pouring meaning into *the fear of dangerousness, the need for care*, and *the need for destigmatization.* . . ."*

In preparing this Part we initially sought, for analytic purposes, to examine problems for decision separately in terms of "mental illness and dangerousness" and then of "mental illness and need for treatment, treatability, availability of treatment, and competency to make decisions about the need for treatment." But since judges, legislators, administrators, and physicians have generally lumped these concepts together, we found it impossible to focus, through separate decisions, on any one concept without too much distortion. Thus in evaluating these materials it becomes all the more important to sort out the functional significance of such concepts, however defined.

Before turning to these problems we pause to examine the meaning and function of psychiatry's nosological scheme for diagnosing and categorizing "mental disorders." We ask: Of what relevance is such a scheme to decisions in law?

---

* Goldstein, J., and Katz, J.: *Ibid.*, pp 873-76.

A.

In Establishing "Sanity"?—The Forms of Action in Psychiatry

1.

AMERICAN PSYCHIATRIC ASSOCIATION STANDARD NOMENCLATURE (1952)*

Introduction

[T]he psychiatric nomenclature attempts to provide a classification system consistent with the concepts of modern psychiatry and neurology. It recognizes the present-day descriptive nature of all psychiatric diagnoses and attempts to make possible the gathering of data for future clarification of ideas concerning etiology, pathology, prognosis, and treatment in mental disorders. It attempts to provide for inclusion of new ideas and advances yet to be made without radical revision of the system of nomenclature.

This nomenclature limits itself to the classification of the disturbances of mental functioning. It does not include neurologic diagnoses or diagnoses of intracranial pathology, per se. Such conditions should be diagnosed separately, whether or not a mental disturbance is associated with them. When an intercranial lesion is accompanied by a mental disorder, it is the mental disorder which is diagnosed in this present classification. Provision is made for contributory etiological factors to be stated as a part of the diagnosis, or as an additional diagnosis, as necessary. . . .

This diagnostic scheme employs the term "disorder" generically to designate a group of related psychiatric syndromes. Insofar as is possible, each group is further divided into more specific psychiatric conditions termed "reactions."

All mental disorders are divided into two major groups:

1. Those in which there is disturbance of mental function resulting from, or precipitated by, a primary impairment of the function of the brain, generally due to diffuse impairment of brain tissue; and

2. Those which are the result of a more general difficulty in adaptation of the individual, and in which any associated brain function disturbance is secondary to the psychiatric disorder.

* * *

Tabulating Scheme Based on Structure of New Nomenclature with Corresponding Standard Nomenclature and International List Numbers

---

ACUTE BRAIN DISORDERS[†]

* * *

CHRONIC BRAIN DISORDERS[†]

* * *

PSYCHOTIC DISORDERS

Involutional Psychotic Reaction
Affective Reactions
  Manic depressive reaction, manic type
  Manic depressive reaction, depressed type
  Manic depressive reaction, other
  Psychotic depressive reaction
Schizophrenic Reactions
  Schizophrenic reaction, simple type
  Schizophrenic reaction, hebephrenic type
  Schizophrenic reaction, catatonic type
  Schizophrenic reaction, paranoid type
  Schizophrenic reaction, acute undifferentiated type
  Schizophrenic reaction, chronic undifferentiated type
  Schizophrenic reaction, schizo-affective type
  Schizophrenic reaction, childhood type
  Schizophrenic reaction, residual type
  Other and unspecified
Paranoid Reactions
  Paranoia
  Paranoid state
Psychotic Reaction Without Clearly Defined Structural Change other than above

PSYCHOPHYSIOLOGIC AUTONOMIC AND VISCERAL DISORDERS

Psychophysiologic Skin Reaction
Psychophysiologic Musculoskeletal Reaction

* * *

PSYCHONEUROTIC DISORDERS

Psychoneurotic Reactions
  Anxiety reaction
  Dissociative reaction
  Conversion reaction
  Phobic reaction
  Obsessive compulsive reaction
  Depressive reaction
  Psychoneurotic reaction, other

---

* Washington, D.C. Reprinted with permission.

[†] Subclasses omitted.

*   *   *

DISORDERS CAUSED BY OR ASSOCIATED WITH IMPAIRMENT OF BRAIN TISSUE FUNCTION

These disorders are all characterized by a basic syndrome consisting of:

1. Impairment of orientation
2. Impairment of memory
3. Impairment of all intellectual functions (comprehension, calculation, knowledge, learning, etc.)
4. Impairment of judgment
5. Lability and shallowness of effect

This syndrome of organic brain disorder is a basic mental condition characteristic of diffuse impairment of brain tissue function from any cause. It may be mild, moderate, or severe, but most of the basic symptoms of the syndrome are generally present to a similar degree in any one patient at any one time. The severity of this basic syndrome is generally parallel to the severity of the impairment of brain-tissue function.

This syndrome may be the only mental disturbance present or it may be associated with psychotic manifestations, neurotic manifestations, or behavioral disturbance. These associated reactions are not necessarily related in severity to the degree of the organic brain disorder or to the degree of brain damage; they are determined by inherent personality patterns, current emotional conflicts, the immediate environmental situation, and the setting of interpersonal relations, as well as by the precipitating organic disorder. These associated reactions are to be looked upon as being released by the organic brain disorder and superimposed upon it. Since personality function depends greatly upon the integrity of brain function, various changes in personality reaction are to be expected with organic brain disorders.

The organic brain disorders are separated into acute and chronic, because of the marked differences between these two groups in regard to prognosis, treatment, and general course of illness. The terms, "acute" and "chronic," refer primarily to the reversibility of brain pathology and its accompanying organic brain syndrome; and not to the etiology, onset, or duration of the illness. Since the same etiology may produce either temporary or permanent brain damage, a brain disorder which appears reversible, hence acute, at its beginning, may prove later to have left permanent damage and a persistent organic brain syndrome, which will then be diagnosed as chronic.

ACUTE BRAIN DISORDERS

These are the organic brain syndromes from which the patient recovers. They are the result of temporary, reversible, diffuse impairment of brain tissue function such as is present in acute alcoholic intoxication or "acute delirium." The basic disturbance of the sensorium may release other disturbances such as hallucinations, poorly organized, transient delusions, and behavior disturbance of varying degree. . . .

These disorders are subclassified according to the cause of the impairment of brain tissue function.

*   *   *

CHRONIC BRAIN DISORDERS

The chronic organic brain syndromes result from relatively permanent, more or less irreversible, diffuse impairment of cerebral tissue function. While the underlying pathological process may partially subside, or respond to specific treatment, as in syphilis, there remains always a certain irreducible minimum of brain tissue destruction which cannot be reversed, even though the loss of function may be almost imperceptible clinically. The chronic brain syndrome may become milder, vary in degree, or progress, but some disturbance of memory, judgment, orientation, comprehension, and affect persists permanently.

Other mental disturbances of psychotic, neurotic, or behavioral type may be superimposed on the chronic brain syndrome; when clinically significant, these will be recognized by addition of the appropriate qualifying phrase to the diagnosis. . . .

*   *   *

MENTAL DEFICIENCY

Here will be classified those cases presenting primarily a defect of intelligence existing since birth, without demonstrated organic brain disease or known prenatal cause. This group will include only those cases formerly known as familial or "idiopathic" mental deficiencies. The degree of intelligence defect will be specified as *mild, moderate,* or *severe,* and the current I.Q. rating, with the name of the test used, will be added to the diagnosis. In general, *mild* refers to functional (vocational) impairment, as would be expected with I.Q.'s of approximately 70 to 85; *moderate* is used for functional impairment requiring special training and guidance, such as would be expected with I.Q.'s of about 50 to 70; *severe* refers to the functional impairment requiring custodial or complete protective care, as would be expected with I.Q.'s below 50. The degree of defect is estimated from other factors than merely psychological test scores, namely, consideration of cultural, physical, and emotional determinants, as well as school, vocational, and social effectiveness. The diagnosis may be modified by the appropriate qualifying phrase, when, in addition to the intellectual defects, there are significant psychotic, neurotic, or behavioral reactions.

DISORDERS OF PSYCHOGENIC ORIGIN OR WITHOUT CLEARLY DEFINED PHYSICAL CAUSE OF STRUCTURAL CHANGE IN THE BRAIN

PSYCHOTIC DISORDERS

These disorders are characterized by a varying degree of personality disintegration and failure to test and evaluate correctly external reality in various spheres. In addition, individuals with such disorders fail in their ability to relate themselves effectively to other people or to their own work.

Involutional Psychotic Reaction

In this category may be included psychotic reactions characterized most commonly by depression occurring in the involutional period, without previous history of manic depressive reaction, and usually in individuals of compulsive personality type. The reaction tends to have a prolonged course and may be manifested by worry, intractable insomnia, guilt, anxiety, agitation, delusional ideas, and somatic concerns. Some cases are characterized chiefly by depression and others chiefly by paranoid ideas. Often there are somatic preoccupations to a delusional degree.

Differentiation may be most difficult from other psychotic reactions with onset in the involutional period; reactions will not be included in this category merely because of their occurrence in this age group.

Affective Reactions

These psychotic reactions are characterized by a primary, severe, disorder of mood, with resultant disturbance of thought and behavior, in consonance with the affect.

Manic Depressive Reactions

These groups comprise the psychotic reactions which fundamentally are marked by severe mood swings, and a tendency to remission and recurrence. Various accessory symptoms such as illusions, delusions, and hallucinations may be added to the fundamental affective alteration.

Manic depressive reaction is synonymous with the term manic depressive psychosis. The reaction will be further classified into the appropriate one of the following types: manic, depressed, or other.

*   *   *

Psychotic Depressive Reaction

These patients are severely depressed and manifest evidence of gross misinterpretation of reality, including, at times, delusions, and hallucinations. This reaction differs from the manic depressive reaction, depressed type, principally in (1) absence of history of repeated depressions or of marked cyclothymic mood swings, (2) frequent presence of environmental precipitating factors. This diagnostic category will be used when a "reactive depression" is of such quality as to place it in the group of psychoses.

Schizophrenic Reactions

This term is synonymous with the formerly used term dementia praecox. It represents a group of psychotic reactions characterized by fundamental disturbances in reality relationships and concept formations, with affective, behavioral, and intellectual disturbances in varying degrees and mixtures. The disorders are marked by strong tendency to retreat from reality, by emotional disharmony, unpredictable disturbances in stream of thought, regressive behavior, and in some, by a tendency to "deterioration." The predominant symptomatology will be the determining factor in classifying such patients into types.

Schizophrenic Reaction, Simple Type

This type of reaction is characterized chiefly by reduction in external attachments and interests and by impoverishment of human relationships. It often involves adjustment on a lower psychobiological level of functioning, usually accompanied by apathy and indifference but rarely by conspicuous delusions or hallucinations. The simple type of schizophrenic reaction characteristically manifests an increase in the severity of symptoms over long periods, usually with apparent mental deterioration, in contrast to the schizoid personality, in which there is little if any change.

Schizophrenic Reaction, Hebephrenic Type

These reactions are characterized by shallow, inappropriate affect, unpredictable giggling, silly behavior and mannerisms, delusions, often of a somatic nature, hallucinations, and regressive behavior.

Schizophrenic Reaction, Catatonic Type

These reactions are characterized by conspicuous motor behavior, exhibiting either marked generalized inhibition (stupor, mutism, negativism, and waxy flexibility) or excessive motor activity and excitement. The individual may regress to a state of vegetation.

Schizophrenic Reaction, Paranoid Type

This type of reaction is characterized by autistic, unrealistic thinking, with mental content composed chiefly of delusions of persecution, and/or grandeur, ideas of reference, and often hallucinations. It is often characterized by unpredictable behavior, with a fairly constant attitude of hostility and aggression. Excessive religiosity may be present with or without delusions of persecution. There may be an expansive delusional system of omnipotence, genius, or special ability. The systematized paranoid hypochondriacal states are included in this group.

Schizophrenic Reaction, Acute Undifferentiated Type

This reaction includes cases exhibiting a wide variety of schizophrenic symptomatology, such as confusion of thinking and turmoil of emotion, manifested by perplexity, ideas of reference, fear and dream states, and dissociative phenomena. These symptoms appear acutely, often without apparent precipitating stress, but exhibiting historical evidence of prodromal symptoms. Very often the reaction is accompanied by a pronounced affective coloring of either exitement or depression. The symptons often clear in a matter of weeks, although there is a tendency for them to recur. Cases usually are grouped here in the first, or an early, attack. If the reaction subsequently progresses, it ordinarily crystallizes into one of the other definable reaction types.

Schizophrenic Reaction, Chronic Undifferentiated Type

The chronic schizophrenic reactions exhibit a mixed symptomatology, and when the reaction cannot be classified in any of the more clearly defined types, it will be placed in this group. Patients presenting definite schizophrenic thought, affect, and behavior beyond that of the schizoid personality, but not classifiable as any other type of schizophrenic reaction, will also be placed in this group. This includes the so-called "latent," "incipient," and "prepsychotic" schizophrenic reactions.

Schizophrenic Reaction, Schizo-affective Type

This category is intended for those cases showing significant admixtures of schizophrenic and affective reactions. The mental content may be predominantly schizophrenic, with pronounced elation or depression. Cases may show predominantly affective changes with schizophrenic-like thinking or bizarre behavior. The prepsychotic personality may be at variance, or inconsistent, with expectations based on the presenting psychotic symptomatology. On prolonged observation, such cases usually prove to be basically schizophrenic in nature.

Schizophrenic Reaction, Childhood Type

Here will be classified those schizophrenic reactions occurring before puberty. The clinical picture may differ from schizophrenic reactions occurring in other age periods because of the immaturity and plasticity of the patient at the time of onset of the reaction. Psychotic reactions in children, manifesting primarily autism, will be classified here. Special symptomatology may be added to the diagnosis as manifestations.

Schizophrenic Reaction, Residual Type

This term is to be applied to those patients who, after a definite psychotic, schizophrenic reaction, have improved sufficiently to be able to get along in the community, but who continue to show recognizable residual disturbance of thinking, affectivity, and/or behavior.

Paranoid Reactions

In this group are to be classified those cases showing persistent delusions, generally persecutory or grandiose, ordinarily without hallucinations. The emotional responses and behavior are consistent with the ideas held. Intelligence is well preserved. This category does not include those reactions properly classifiable under Schizophrenic reaction, paranoid type.

Paranoia

This type of psychotic disorder is extremely rare. It

is characterized by an intricate, complex, and slowly developing paranoid system, often logically elaborated after a false interpretation of an actual occurrence. Frequently, the patient considers himself endowed with superior or unique ability. The paranoid system is particularly isolated from much of the normal stream of consciousness, without hallucinations and with relative intactness and preservation of the remainder of the personality, in spite of a chronic and prolonged course.

Paranoid State

This type of paranoid disorder is characterized by paranoid delusions. It lacks the logical nature of systematization seen in paranoia; yet it does not manifest the bizarre fragmentation and deterioration of the schizophrenic reactions. It is likely to be of a relatively short duration, though it may be persistent and chronic.

* * *

PSYCHOPHYSIOLOGIC AUTONOMIC AND VISCERAL DISORDERS

This term is used in preference to "psychosomatic disorders," since the latter term refers to a point of view on the discipline of medicine as a whole rather than to certain specified conditions. It is preferred to the term "somatization reactions," which term implies that these disorders are simply another form of psychoneurotic reaction. These disorders are here given a separate grouping between psychotic and psychoneurotic reactions, to allow more accurate accumulation of data concerning their etiology, course, and relation to other mental disorders.

These reactions represent the visceral expression of affect which may be thereby largely prevented from being conscious. The symptoms are due to a chronic and exaggerated state of the normal physiological expression of emotion, with the feeling, or subjective part, repressed. Such long continued visceral states may eventually lead to structural changes.

This group includes the so-called "organ neuroses." It also includes some of the cases formerly classified under a wide variety of diagnostic terms, such as "anxiety state," "cardiac neurosis," "gastric neurosis," and so forth. Differentiation is made from conversion reactions by (1) involvement of organs and viscera innervated by the autonomic nervous system, hence not under full voluntary control or perception; (2) failure to alleviate anxiety; (3) physiological rather than symbolic origin of symptoms; (4) frequent production of structural changes which may threaten life. Differentiation is made from anxiety reactions primarily by predominant, persistent involvement of a single organ system.

* * *

PSYCHONEUROTIC DISORDERS

The chief characteristic of these disorders is "anxiety" which may be directly felt and expressed or which may be unconsciously and automatically controlled by the utilization of various psychological defense mechanisms (depression, conversion, displacement, etc.). In contrast to those with psychoses, patients with psychoneurotic disorders do not exhibit gross distortion or falsification of external reality (delusions, hallucinations, illusions) and they do not present gross disorganization of the personality. Longitudinal (lifelong) studies of individuals with such disorders usually present evidence of periodic or constant maladjustment of varying degree from early life. Special stress may bring about acute symptomatic expression of such disorders.

"Anxiety" in psychoneurotic disorders is a danger signal felt and perceived by the conscious portion of the personality. It is produced by a threat from within the personality (e.g., by supercharged repressed emotions, including such aggressive impulses as hostility and resentment), with or without stimulation from such external situations as loss of love, loss of prestige, or threat of injury. The various ways in which the patient attempts to handle this anxiety results in the various types of reactions listed below.

In recording such reactions the terms "traumatic neurosis," or "traumatic reaction" will not be used; instead, the particular psychiatric reaction will be specified. Likewise, the term "mixed reaction" will not be used; instead, the predominant type of reaction will be recorded, qualified by reference to other types of reactions as part of the symptomatology.

Anxiety Reaction

In this kind of reaction the anxiety is diffuse and not restricted to definite situations or objects, as in the case of phobic reactions. It is not controlled by any specific psychological defense mechanism as in other psychoneurotic reactions. This reaction is characterized by anxious expectation and frequently associated with somatic symptomatology. The condition is to be differentiated from normal apprehensiveness or fear. The term is synonymous with the former term "anxiety state."

Dissociative Reaction

This reaction represents a type of gross personality disorganization, the basis of which is a neurotic disturbance, although the diffuse dissociation seen in some cases may occasionally appear psychotic. The personality disorganization may result in aimless running or "freezing." The repressed impulse giving rise to the anxiety may be discharged by, or deflected into, various symptomatic expressions, such as depersonalization, dissociated personality, stupor, fugue, amnesia, dream state, somnambulism, etc. The diagnosis will specify symptomatic manifestations.

These reactions must be differentiated from schizoid personality, from schizophrenic reaction, and from analogous symptoms in some other types of neurotic reactions. Formerly, this reaction has been classified as a type of "conversion hysteria."

Conversion Reaction

Instead of being experienced consciously (either diffusely or displaced, as in phobias) the impulse causing the anxiety is "converted" into functional symptoms in organs or parts of the body, usually those that are mainly under voluntary control. The symptoms serve to lessen conscious (felt) anxiety and ordinarily are symbolic of the underlying mental conflict. Such reactions usually meet immediate needs of the patient and are, therefore, associated with more or less obvious "secondary gain." They are to be differentiated from psychophysiologic autonomic and visceral disorders. The term "conversion reaction" is synonymous with "conversion hysteria." Dissociative reactions are not included in this diagnosis.

In recording such reactions the symptomatic manifestations will be specified as anesthesia (anosmia, blindness, deafness), paralysis (paresis, aphonia, monoplegia, or hemiplegia), dyskinesis (tic, tremor, posturing, catalepsy).

Phobic Reaction

The anxiety of these patients becomes detached from a specific idea, object, or situation in the daily life and is displaced to some symbolic idea or situation in the form of a specific neurotic fear. The commonly observed forms of phobic reaction include fear of syphilis, dirt, closed places, high places, open places, animals, etc. The patient attempts to control his anxiety by avoiding the phobic object or situation.

In recording this diagnosis the manifestations will be indicated. The term is synonymous with the former term "phobia" and includes some of the cases formerly classified as "anxiety hysteria."

Obsessive Compulsive Reaction

In this reaction the anxiety is associated with the persistence of unwanted ideas and of repetitive impulses to perform acts which may be considered morbid by the patient. The patient himself may regard his ideas and behavior as unreasonable, but nevertheless is compelled to carry out his rituals.

The diagnosis will specify the symptomatic expression of such reactions as touching, counting, ceremonials, hand washing, or recurring thoughts (accompanied often by a compulsion to repetitive action). This category includes many cases formerly classified as "psychasthenia."

Depressive Reaction

The anxiety in this reaction is allayed, and hence partially relieved, by depression and self-depreciation.

The reaction is precipitated by a current situation, frequently by some loss sustained by the patient, and is often associated with a feeling of guilt for past failures or deeds. The degree of the reaction in such cases is dependent upon the intensity of the patient's ambivalent feeling toward his loss (love, possession) as well as upon the realistic circumstances of the loss.

The term is synonymous with "reactive depression" and is to be differentiated from the corresponding psychotic reaction. In this differentiation, points to be considered are (1) life history of patient, with special reference to mood swings (suggestive of psychotic reaction), to the personality structure (neurotic or cyclothymic) and to precipitating environmental factors and (2) absence of malignant symptoms (hypochondriacal preoccupation, agitation, delusions, particularly somatic, hallucinations, severe guilt feelings, intractable insomnia, suicidal ruminations, severe psychomotor retardation, profound retardation of thought, stupor).

Psychoneurotic Reaction, Other

Under this classification will come all reactions considered psychoneurotic and not elsewhere classified. (Psychoneurotic manic reactions, etc.) This category is designed also for the use of record librarians and statisticians dealing with incomplete diagnoses. It does not include "mixed" reactions, which are to be diagnosed according to the predominant reaction.

PERSONALITY DISORDERS

These disorders are characterized by developmental defects or pathological trends in the personality structure, with minimal subjective anxiety, and little or no sense of distress. In most instances, the disorder is manifested by a lifelong pattern of action or behavior, rather than by mental or emotional symptoms. Occasionally, organic diseases of the brain (epidemic encephalitis, head injury, Alzheimer's disease, etc.) will produce clinical pictures resembling a personality disorder. In such instances, the condition is properly diagnosed as a Chronic Brain Syndrome (of appropriate origin) with behavioral reaction.

The personality disorders are divided into three main groups with one additional grouping for flexibility in diagnosis (special symptom reactions). Although the groupings are largely descriptive, the division has been made partially on the basis of the dynamics of personality development. The personality pattern disturbances are considered deep seated disturbances, with little room for regression. Personality trait disturbances and sociopathic personality disturbances under stress may at times regress to a lower level of personality organization and function without development of psychosis.

Personality Pattern Disturbance

These are more or less cardinal personality types,

which can rarely if ever be altered in their inherent structure by any form of therapy. Their functioning may be improved by prolonged therapy, but basic change is seldom accomplished. In some, "constitutional" features are marked and obvious. The depth of psychopathology here allows these individuals little room to maneuver under conditions of stress, except into actual psychosis.

Inadequate Personality

Such individuals are characterized by inadequate response to intellectual, emotional, social, and physical demands. They are neither physically nor mentally grossly deficient on examination, but they do show inadaptability, ineptness, poor judgment, lack of physical and emotional stamina, and social incompatibility.

Schizoid Personality

Inherent traits in such personalities are (1) avoidance of close relations with others, (2) inability to express directly hostility or even ordinary aggressive feelings, and (3) autistic thinking. These qualities result early in coldness, aloofness, emotional detachment, fearfulness, avoidance of competition, and daydreams revolving around the need for omnipotence. As children, they are usually quiet, shy, obedient, sensitive and retiring. At puberty, they frequently become more withdrawn, then manifesting the aggregate of personality traits known as introversion, namely, quietness, seclusiveness, "shut-in-ness," and unsociability, often with eccentricity.

Cyclothymic Personality

Such individuals are characterized by an extratensive and outgoing adjustment to life situations, an apparent personal warmth, friendliness, and superficial generosity, an emotional reaching out to the environment, and a ready enthusiasm for competition. Characteristic are frequently alternating moods of elation and sadness, stimulated apparently by internal factors rather than by external events. The individual may occasionally be either persistently euphoric or depressed, without falsification or distortion of reality. The diagnosis in such cases should specify, if possible, whether hypomanic, depressed, or alternating.

Paranoid Personality

Such individuals are characterized by many traits of the schizoid personality, coupled with an exquisite sensitivity in interpersonal relations, and with a conspicuous tendency to utilize a projection mechanism, expressed by suspiciousness, envy, extreme jealousy, and stubbornness.

Personality Trait Disturbance

This category applies to individuals who are unable to maintain their emotional equilibrium and independence under minor or major stress because of disturbances in emotional development. Some individuals fall into this group because their personality pattern disturbance is related to fixation and exaggeration of certain character and behavior patterns; others, because their behavior is a regressive reaction due to environmental or endopsychic stress.

This classification will be applied only to cases of personality disorder in which the neurotic features (such as, anxiety, conversion, phobia, etc.) are relatively insignificant, and the basic personality maldevelopment is the crucial distinguishing factor. Evidence of physical immaturity may or may not be present.

Emotionally Unstable Personality

In such cases the individual reacts with excitability and ineffectiveness when confronted by minor stress. His judgment may be undependable under stress, and his relationship to other people is continuously fraught with fluctuating emotional attitudes, because of strong and poorly controlled hostility, guilt, and anxiety.

This term is synonymous with the former term "psychopathic personality with emotional instability."

Passive-aggressive Personality

Reactions in this group are of three types, as indicated below, and the diagnosis can be further elaborated, if desired, by adding the specific type of reaction observed. However, the three types of reaction are manifestation of the same underlying psychopathology, and frequently occur interchangeably in a given individual falling in this category. For these reasons, the reactions are classified together. The clinical picture in such cases often has, superimposed upon it, anxiety reaction which is typically psychoneurotic.

Passive-dependent type: This reaction is characterized by helplessness, indecisiveness, and a tendency to cling to others as a dependent child to a supporting parent.

Passive-aggressive type: The aggressiveness is expressed in these reactions by passive measures, such as pouting, stubbornness, procrastination, inefficiency, and passive obstructionism.

Aggressive type: A persistent reaction to frustration with irritability, temper tantrums, and destructive behavior is the dominant manifestation. A specific variety of this reaction is a morbid or pathological resentment. A deep dependency is usually evident in such cases. The term does not apply to cases more accurately classified as antisocial reaction.

Compulsive Personality

Such individuals are characterized by chronic, excessive, or obsessive concern with adherence to standards of conscience or of conformity. They may be over inhibited, overconscientious, and may have an inordinate capacity for work. Typically they are rigid and lack a normal capacity for relaxation. While their chronic tension may lead to neurotic illness, this is not an invariable consequence. The reaction may appear as a persistence of an adolescent pattern of behavior, or as a regression from more mature functioning as a result of stress.

Personality Trait Disturbance, Other

This category is included to permit greater latitude in diagnosis. Instances in which a personality trait is exaggerated as a means to life adjustment (as in the above diagnoses), not classifiable elsewhere, may be listed here.

This category is designed also for the use of record librarians and statisticians dealing with incomplete diagnoses. It is not intended for use with "mixed" states, which are to be properly diagnosed according to the predominant trait disturbance.

Sociopathic Personality Disturbance

Individuals to be placed in this category are ill primarily in terms of society and of conformity with the prevailing cultural milieu, and not only in terms of personal discomfort and relations with other individuals. However, sociopathic reactions are very often symptomatic of severe underlying personality disorder, neurosis, or psychosis, or occur as the result of organic brain injury or disease. Before a definitive diagnosis in this group is employed, strict attention must be paid to the possibility of the presence of a more primary personality disturbance; such underlying disturbance will be diagnosed when recognized. Reactions will be differentiated as defined below.

Antisocial Reaction

This term refers to chronically antisocial individuals who are always in trouble, profiting neither from experience nor punishment, and maintaining no real loyalties to any person, group or code. They are frequently callous and hedonistic, showing marked emotional immaturity, with lack of sense of responsibility, lack of judgment, and an ability to rationalize their behavior so that it appears warranted, reasonable, and justified.

The term includes cases previously classified as "constitutional psychopathic state" and "psychopathic personality." As defined here the term is more limited, as well as more specific in its application.

Dyssocial Reaction

This term applies to individuals who manifest disregard for the usual social codes, and often come in conflict with them, as the result of having lived all their lives in an abnormal moral environment. They may be capable of strong loyalties. These individuals typically do not show significant personality deviations other than those implied by adherence to the values or code of their own predatory, criminal, or other social group. The term includes such diagnoses as "pseudosocial personality" and "psychopathic personality with asocial and amoral trends."

Sexual Deviation

This diagnosis is reserved for deviant sexuality which is not symptomatic of more extensive syndromes, such as schizophrenic and obsessional reactions. The term includes most of the cases formerly classed as "psychopathic personality with pathologic sexuality." The diagnosis will specify the type of the pathologic behavior, such as homosexuality, transvestism, pedophilia, fetishism, and sexual sadism (including rape, sexual assault, mutilation).

Alcoholism

Included in this category will be cases in which there is well-established addiction to alcohol without recognizable underlying disorder. Simple drunkenness and acute poisoning due to alcohol are not included in this category.

Drug Addiction

Drug addiction is usually symptomatic of a personality disorder, and will be classified here while the individual is actually addicted; the proper personality classification is to be made as an additional diagnosis. Drug addictions symptomatic of organic brain disorders, psychotic disorders, psychophysiologic disorders, and psychoneurotic disorders are classified here as a secondary diagnosis.

Special Symptom Reactions

This category is useful in occasional situations where a specific symptom is the single outstanding expression of the psychopathology. This term will not be used as a diagnosis, however, when the symptoms are associated with, or are secondary to, organic illnesses and defects, or to other psychiatric disorders. Thus, for example, the diagnosis special symptom reaction, speech disturbance would be used for certain disturbances in speech in which there are insufficient other symptoms to justify any other definite diagnosis. This type of speech disturbance often develops in childhood. It would not be used for a speech impairment that was a temporary symptom of conversion hysteria or the result of any organic disease or defect.

The diagnosis should specify the particular "habit." Learning disturbance; Speech disturbance; Enuresis; Somnambulism; Other.

TRANSIENT SITUATIONAL PERSONALITY DISORDERS

This general classification should be restricted to reactions which are more or less transient in character and which appear to be an acute symptom response to a situation without apparent underlying personality disturbance.

The symptoms are the immediate means used by the individual in his struggle to adjust to an overwhelming situation. In the presence of good adaptive capacity, recession of symptoms generally occurs when the situational stress diminishes. Persistent failure to resolve will indicate a more severe underlying disturbance and will be classified elsewhere.

Transient Situational Personality Disturbance

Transient situational disorders which cannot be given a more definite diagnosis in the group, because of their fluidity, or because of the limitation of time permitted for their study, may be included in this general category. This category is designed also for the use of record librarians and statisticians dealing with incomplete diagnoses.

Gross Stress Reaction

Under conditions of great or unusual stress, a normal personality may utilize established patterns of reaction to deal with overwhelming fear. The patterns of such reactions differ from those of neurosis or psychosis chiefly with respect to clinical history, reversibility of reaction, and its transient character. When promptly and adequately treated, the condition may clear rapidly. It is also possible that the condition may progress to one of the neurotic reactions. If the reaction persists, this term is to be regarded as a temporary diagnosis to be used only until a more definitive diagnosis is established.

This diagnosis is justified only in situations in which the individual has been exposed to severe physical demands or extreme emotional stress, such as in combat or in civilian catastrophe (fire, earthquake, explosion, etc.). In many instances this diagnosis applies to previously more or less "normal" persons who have experienced intolerable stress.

The particular stress involved will be specified as (1) combat or (2) civilian catastrophe.

Adult Situational Reaction

This diagnosis is to be used when the clinical picture is primarily one of superficial maladjustment to a difficult situation or to newly experienced environmental factors, with no evidence of any serious underlying personality defects or chronic patterns. It may be manifested by anxiety, alcoholism, asthenia, poor efficiency, low morale, unconventional behavior, etc. If untreated or not relieved such reactions may, in some instances, progress into typical psychoneurotic reactions or personality disorders. This term will also include some cases formerly classified as "simple adult maladjustment."

Adjustment Reaction of Infancy

Under this term are to be classified those transient reactions in infants occurring on a psychogenic basis without organic disease. In most instances there will be outgrowths of the infant's interaction with significant persons in the environment or a response to the lack of such persons. Undue apathy, undue excitability, feeding and sleeping difficulties are common manifestations of such psychic disturbances in infants.

Adjustment Reaction of Childhood

Under this heading are included only the transient symptomatic reactions of children to some immediate situation or internal emotional conflict. The more prolonged and definitive disturbances will be classified elsewhere.

Although the symptomatic manifestations are usually mixed, one type of manifestation may predominate.

Adjustment Reaction of Adolescence

Under this diagnosis are to be included those transient reactions of the adolescent which are the expression of his emancipatory strivings and vacillations with reference to impulses and emotional tendencies. The superficial pattern of the behavior may resemble any of the personality or psychoneurotic disorders. Differentiation between transient adolescent reactions and deep-seated personality trait disorders or psychoneurotic reactions must be made.

Adjustment Reaction of Late Life

Under this diagnosis will be included those transient reactions of later life which are an expression of the problems of physiological, situational, and environmental readjustment. Involutional physiological changes, retirement from work, breaking up of families through death, or other life situation changes frequently precipitate transient undesirable personality disturbances, or accentuate previous personality disorders. Such disturbances are to be differentiated from other psychogenic reactions and from reactions associated with cerebral arteriosclerosis, presenile psychosis, and other organic disorders.

2.

CAMERON, NORMAN

Personality Development and Psychopathology*

Psychopathology is a multidimensional continuum. We have to break it up into groups of related phenomena in order to be able to handle it and particularly to discuss it. In working with a patient on his problems, it is often necessary to make a diagnosis and attach a label to what he presents. Often it is impossible to do either. When it comes to communicating with someone else, however, the formulation may be so vague and inclusive that it only communicates

* Boston: Houghton Mifflin Company, 1963 (pp. 17–24, 470–475, 516–518, 538–590, 638–652). Reprinted by permission.

confusion. This, too, is an old tale. About a century ago, experts working in this general area decided that classification was worse than useless. They lumped all psychopathology together and called it all by one name. It was not long before this solution proved vain. The groupings began again; and they have continued to evolve up to the present day.

In presenting clinical material to illustrate psychopathology, we shall in general follow the official classification of the American Psychiatric Association. Wherever we deviate from it, we shall note the deviation and explain it. Classifications of illness, in other fields as well as in psychopathology, are always somewhat arbitrary and in some respects unsatisfactory. This is inevitable. They are the products of committees appointed for the task, and made up of representatives of more than one school of thought and more than one generation. What comes out of such a committee is always a compromise between opposing points of view, the best compromise that could be worked out.

The Psychoses

A clear-cut distinction between neuroses and psychoses is not universally accepted. . . . Nevertheless, the official classification does make the distinction and we shall do the same. [W]hen psychoses are severe, reality is usually much distorted. Delusions and hallucinations represent attempts to deal with previously unconscious material, which invades preconscious and conscious organizations, as regression becomes widespread and ego boundaries begin to dissolve. It should be repeated that mild or "borderline" psychotic states may interfere little with normal life, and are not inconsistent with great talent at times. They are sometimes chronic and are not recognized under ordinary conditions. We shall begin with paranoid reactions because they seem often to be a combination of neurotic and psychotic mechanisms, and because the denial and projection used are similar to normal denial and projection, as, for example, in the universal practice of scapegoating.

PARANOID REACTIONS

Paranoid reactions are attempts to escape the effects of previously unconscious impulses and fantasies, which have erupted into preconscious and conscious organizations, by processes of denial and projection. The patient tries to remain in contact with external reality by reconstructing it in accordance with the impulses and fantasies which he can no longer keep unconscious. The delusional reconstructions are in this sense spontaneous attempts at self-cure. Sometimes the product is a *delusional pseudo-community* of persecutors, which includes real and fictitious persons with real and fictitious roles. Delusions in any of the psychoses may be creative in the same sense that dreams are. The projective mechanisms used relate paranoid reactions to the phobias;

but whereas the phobic patient agrees that his fears sound absurd, the paranoid patient believes in his delusions. Paranoid elements enter into all of the other psychoses to some extent.

. . . Their chief characteristic is the presence of persistent organized delusions, which are usually persecutory, but are sometimes jealous, grandiose, or erotic. The prevailing mood is in keeping with the dominant delusions, being hostile in delusions of persecution and of jealousy, erotic in erotic delusions, and exalted in delusions of grandeur. There is no general personality disorganization in the paranoid reaction such as we see in schizophrenia. Paranoid persons usually remain in relatively good contact with their environment, much better than most schizophrenics do, and better than do most manics and psychotic depressives. Because of this good contact, the paranoid reaction forms a bridge between the *neuroses* and the *psychoses*.

. . . Paranoid reactions also form a bridge between normal and delusional thinking. It is common knowledge that attitudes of belief, confidence, and expectation—or their reverse—are a part of the context of every normal person's thinking, just as they are in paranoid reactions. We are all continually acting in accordance with such attitudes, even in such simple matters as approaching a door to open it, waiting for the evening paper to arrive, or driving to work. We take a lot for granted in all such ordinary matters. We assume that the door will open, that the evening paper has been composed and printed, and that we are among those destined to receive it. We assume that when we drive to work the place will still be there and that our services will still be in demand. None of these assumptions is absolutely trustworthy. In short, we act most of the time upon anticipations which are based upon incomplete information.

In perception it is the same. We usually see only parts of things, the mere beginnings of some complex series, or only its end-product. From such fragments we continually make assumptions that enable us to act confidently, as though the whole thing or every step were there in front of us to see. We seldom have either the opportunity or the patience to wait until all the evidence is in before we act.

[T]his leads up to the question of distinguishing between *delusional* and *nondelusional thinking*. The way we all have of acting on the basis of fragmentary information, of interpreting signs and signals, of depending heavily upon hidden meanings and intuitions, of reconstructing what we "recall," and of being always subject to shifting emotional influences, makes a clear distinction exceedingly difficult to formulate. At the same time, such examples help us to recognize that delusional thinking has normal counterparts, and that paranoid reactions can best be understood if we bear this fact in mind.

. . . *Paranoid reactions are attempts to escape from tension and anxiety through processes of denial and projection, which result in more or less systematized delusions.* These delusions, we have said, are usually persecutory, but sometimes jealous, erotic or grandiose; and the emotional component is in keeping with the delusion.

The term *delusion* itself needs to be defined. *A delusion is a fixed belief which persists even though social reality contradicts it.* Delusions are characteristic of paranoid reactions; but they are found in other psychoses also. As we shall soon see, it is the delusions from which psychotically depressed and manic persons suffer that render them socially incompetent. The schizophrenias are also delusional disorders; but schizophrenic delusions are as a rule poorly systematized, and often they are extraordinarily bizarre.

It would not be difficult to make a case for the presence of delusions even among normal persons. The full acceptance of a belief, and its indefinite persistence, even though it contradicts all the objective evidence, is not uncommon in ordinary life. When this is true, however, the belief is one that is shared by others in the same culture. It is a belief that depends, not upon objective evidence, but upon group identification.

Paranoid reactions, even though psychotic, are more often adaptively successful than are other psychoses. They lack the desocialization and disorganization of schizophrenia, and they do not show the profound mood changes that we see in psychotic depressions and in manias. . . .

[P]aranoid reactions may be a combination of neurosis and psychosis. The psychotic element appears in the fixed, inflexible delusional development and in the distortion of social reality, the formation of a pseudocommunity, to rationalize the delusion. The neurotic elements appears in the good residual object relations which, in many cases, allow the patient to carry on a comparatively normal life as business man or woman, as professional person, or as wife and mother, in spite of the delusions.

PSYCHOTIC DEPRESSIVE REACTIONS

Psychotic depressions are mood disorders in which dejection, self-depreciation, and self-condemnation reach delusional proportions. An acutely conscious sense of worthlessness and guilt develops and persists. There is a sweeping regression which revives conflicts between an *infantile ego*, which speaks with an adult voice, and a *primitive superego*, which persecutes the patient. The patient identifies now with the regressive, helpless, remorseful ego, now with the harsh, punitive superego. Often he tries to project his self-hatred as the attitudes of others toward him; but usually he is less successful in this maneuver than paranoid or paranoid schizophrenic persons are. The danger of suicide is a grave one. Prospects for recovery, regardless of the form of therapy, are excellent.

When a person develops a severe psychotic depression he shuts out as much of his environment as possible and withdraws into deep preoccupation. He may do this suddenly or gradually. He becomes absorbed in some overwhelming conflict over guilt and unworthiness, to the virtual exclusion of everything else. . . . Rarely do relatives and friends take a severely depressed person's delusional statements at face value. . . . The commonest and most dangerous mistake they make is to underrate the murderous self-hate in depressions, and so to let suicide take them by surprise. Occasionally, in committing a suicide, a depressed person also kills loved ones. In spite of the rationalizations which he gives for this, in advance or in suicide notes, it is actually an extension of archaic superego hostility to include other persons, as well as the depressive ego.

It is not as easy to understand psychotic depressions as it is to understand neurotic depressions. This is because of the deep regression and the loss of interest in almost everything in the environment. Discouragement, dejection, and disillusionment are not only deeper in psychotic depressions. They are also much more fixed and rigid than in neurotic depressions. Complaints are not made to stimulate others to contradict superego attacks; they are made as statements of fact. Attempts at reassurance are met with stubborn and often angry rejection. Depression has reached a delusional level; it has replaced external reality with an overwhelming internal reality. . . . There we shall find that psychotic depression is closely related to normal mourning and realistic grief. In fact, one could say that normal mourning is a realistic form of psychotic depression, especially when the lost person is resented as well as loved.

[W]hen other people attempt to contradict and reassure the patient, they may deepen the depression rather than lessen it. This contrasts sharply with the neurotic depression, in which the patient stimulates others to contradict and reassure him so as to ward off his own superego attacks. The psychotic depressive is moved by contractions and reassurances to heap up further self-depreciation and self-recrimination which are more and more delusional. The deep-seated guilt relates psychotic depressions also to obsessive compulsive neuroses; but the guilt in psychotic depressions is acutely conscious and the depressed patient is interested in almost nothing else. Moreover, he is usually actively suicidal in his fantasies, which is not true of obsessive compulsives, and much less true of neurotic depressives. [T]his difference goes deeper than the symptoms. It involves regression to a phase where the sadistic superego seems to be stating facts, and there is little really adult ego operative to resist it.

. . . There is little of adaptive value in psychotic depressions. They involve such deep regression that the patient can make little use of his environment and, unlike the paranoid person, he does not project his internal hate and fear; or if he does, he considers his fate, as he imagines it, to be a well-deserved one. He takes an actively cruel attitude toward himself and, in those cases which expect torture and death at the hands of sadistic people, the torture and death are felt to be right and just. The superego attitude is one of hatred, cruelty, and gloating—not unlike that of some obsessive compulsives—and the ego response to the superego is a submissive one, even a welcoming one. Perhaps this submissive, receptive attitude helps to account for the fact that psychotic depression is commoner among women than among men. As we have said, the psychotic depressive patient does not make his self-depreciatory statements to stimulate others to contradict him, but only as statements of "fact." Therefore his complaints are neither defensive nor adaptive. The only sense in which the term *adaptive* can be used in psychotic depression is that the patient manages somehow to escape the fragmentation and the abyss of schizophrenia. This is probably related to his much better object relations, when he is well, and therefore to his better organized personality.

MANIC REACTIONS AND MANIC-DEPRESSIVE CYCLES

Manic reactions are psychotic excitements which are characterized by overactivity and delusional elation or self-assertion, but show relatively little disorganization. The behavior of manic patients is a caricature of joy and optimism, of self-assurance and self-assertion. Often the caricature is childish. In a small minority of patients manic attacks alternate with psychotic depressions. . . . Many look upon the manic reaction as primarily a defense against an imminent threat of a psychotic depression, that is, a denial of depressive trends and a reaction formation against them, in fantasy and action. It is not unusual for a manic patient to burst into tears, make depressive statements about himself, and then to become manic again.

Manic reactions are mood disorders, with delusions, which are usually exaggerations and distortions of normal elation or self-assertion. They are often mistaken at first for happiness. They resemble the changes that come over people after they have had an alcoholic drink or two, but the manic reaction lasts for weeks or months, not hours, and no sign of intoxication is present.

Manic patients seem at first glance to be in good contact with their human environment, and their talk, though rambling, seems to spread freely over a wide range of topics. A closer examination, however, always reveals that both impressions are mistaken. The manic patient's contact with others is shallow and fleeting. His talk is actually limited in scope as compared with that of a normal happy person. Mania is deeply regressive. Manic patients use their environment in the service of fantasies and conflicts which

are still more primitive than those of paranoid persons. Their defenses, as we shall see, relate them to psychotic depressions, in spite of the prevailing opposite mood. We shall find no general disintegration, such as one finds in a high proportion of schizophrenics, and there are no hallucinations in typical cases.

. . . There are real dangers in mania, the danger of self-injury, the danger of starvation and physical exhaustion, of financial and erotic adventures, and, strange to say, even of suicide. The pervasive sense of aggressive self-assertion or seeming joy is dampened little or not at all by what other people say and do. If there is any change because of attempts at outside control it is most likely to be a change to irritability and increased self-assertion. Genuine communication is next to impossible. The manic patient's overactivity is self-propelled. His thoughts and acts run away with him. His talk flits quickly and irrationally from one thing to another. It is full of puns, sound associations, and wit, the sure signs of primary process thinking, but there is no general disorganization, such as we often find in schizophrenics.

. . . There is little of adaptive value in mania. Regression is too deep, reality testing too severely impaired. The manic patient is like an overexcited child who is unable to quiet down and unable to make use of his environment in adult ways. He behaves as though there were every reason for his being madly playful and aggressively, insistently self-assertive. His expansive and often silly talk, his often dangerous lack of consideration for others, his inability to run his own life and cope with his own daily needs—all these seem to the patient right and normal.

The only sense in which mania can be considered adaptive is that it does deny a reality which is too painful to be faced, a reality which would justify a psychotic depression in anyone with such a personality organization. In this sense the manic reaction can be considered as a defense against psychotic depression, as a refusal or inability to accept the intolerably painful truths of a reality situation. . . .

SCHIZOPHRENIC REACTIONS

. . . They are attempts to escape tension and anxiety by abandoning interpersonal relations and replacing them with delusions and hallucinations, which reconstruct external reality for the patient, in accordance with the previously unconscious fantasies which have invaded preconscious and conscious organizations on a large scale. They are baffling to the normal observer because the patient who has not given up completely continues to operate at several different levels of regression. These represent his multiple points of immature fixation. He may shift from concrete, infantile thinking to adult metaphorical thinking and back again to concrete thinking, several times within the same hour, or even mix the two in the same statement.

To understand an active schizophrenic patient, the participant observer must be flexible enough, intuitive enough, and sufficiently free from anxiety himself, to be able to shift his own levels of interaction so as to coincide with the patient's shifts. Such flexibility, intuition, and freedom from anxiety, in the face of strange, primitive thinking, are uncommon. If, however, a therapist is able to exercise them, he not only brings help to the isolated patient, but he also gains insight into human thinking which no other experiences provide.

It has been recognized for at least half a century that the group of schizophrenias includes a rich variety of unrealistic experience and behavior. Attempts to organize the variety into subtypes have so far failed. Patients themselves shift in their predominant experience and behavior from one subtype to another. A person may enter a hospital, for example, in a rigid stupor, and within a few days become excited and overactive; or he may come out of the stupor, express frank delusions and hallucinations, and give every evidence that during the stuporous phase he was still acutely observant. Sudden unexpected recoveries are not unknown, without the intervention of special therapy. They are most likely to occur when interaction with therapists is available at whatever level of thought is possible for the patient at the time. The outlook for recovery is not good; but in a suitable environment about 50 per cent get well; and these may stay well for a lifetime if not subjected to unusual stress.

The current official classification appears to differentiate eight varieties of adult schizophrenia. Three of these, however, we can eliminate at once. The *acute undifferentiated type* and the *chronic undifferentiated type* are merely convenient labels for the cases that are difficult to classify. The same is true of the *residual type*. This leaves us with the four classical varieties, *simple*, *hebephrenic*, *catatonic*, and *paranoid schizophrenia*, plus a fifth, the *schizo-affective type*, which makes room for the inevitable compromise between schizophrenic and manic or depressive reactions actually encountered in practice.

Simple type. . . . In the simple type we emphasize today a slow, insidious onset and an undramatic downhill course. The whole process looks like a slow fading of the promise of childhood, a gradual arrest of personality growth, followed by a monotonous, inexorable decline. It should be noted, however, that in many of these cases the patient has never been particularly lively, spirited, or brilliant. It is interesting, and it may be of some dynamic significance, that in the simple type neither delusions nor hallucinations seem to play a part. Delusions and hallucinations are often active attempts to regain lost object relations and hold on to them.

After a steady downward course, the decline may come to a halt at some relatively low level of adapta-tion. Here the patient often lives an idle, ineffectual, and apparently meaningless life. If his level of adaptation is very low, or his behavior too unpredictable, he may require permanent institutional care. If not, he may lounge about the house or the neighborhood as an irresponsible idler, or wander aimlessly from place to place as a vagrant. . . .

Hebephrenic type. . . . The onset may be slow and insidious; but it may also be sudden, following quickly upon a personal loss or failure. Silly, disorganized behavior is common. Giggling, smiling, and laughter occur which seem empty and irrelevant to the observer. If, on the other hand, there is sadness it seems shallow, and if there is weeping it may appear inexplicable. There may be outbursts of anger.

* * *

With these emotional expressions go also gestures, postures, and mannerisms, which appear to be symbolic, but are usually strange, more or less fragmentary, and often bizarre. Speech becomes manneristic also, even to the point of being incoherent and including made-up words (*neologisms*). The delusions which develop are also likely to be bizarre and incoherent, including often weird notions of body change. Hallucinations are usually prominent, although if the patient is uncommunicative they may have to be inferred from the behavior.

With time, the hebephrenic often withdraws more and more into preoccupation with private fantasy until he becomes almost completely desocialized and inaccessible. He may even wet and soil like a baby. He may have to be helped to eat, or he eats greedily like a starved person. Occasionally a hebephrenic patient who has regressed almost to a vegetative level manages to reorganize and regain his lost object relations, with the help of an undaunted and gifted psychotherapist. As a rule, however, there is no complete return.

Catatonic type. The stress in this subtype of schizophrenia is laid upon motor disturbances. At one extreme a patient may be in a disorganized excitement; at the other extreme he may be mute and motionless, as though in a stupor. All kinds of combinations of such symptoms may appear in the same person. In catatonic excitement there may be the same degree of incessant activity that one sees in mania, the same inability to sleep, the same unwillingness to eat or drink. It differs from mania, however, in seeming weird, unrealistic, incoherent. In catatonic stupor the behavior seems constricted, sometimes negativistic and sometimes overcompliant. The patient may lie rigidly, eyes closed and with a masklike face, as though he were dramatizing his own death. Or he may sit or stand staring blankly ahead or at the floor, for hours at a time.

In both the excited and the immobile catatonic patient there are delusions, persecutory in character or mystical and miraculous. There are nearly always hallucinations also. These consist predominantly of terrifying visions, unintelligible apparitions, religious visitations, or voices and other sounds having fearsome or mysterious meanings. One can often learn something about the character of these delusions and hallucinations during relatively clear phases in the illness; but the chief source of information is the retrospective account which many patients are willing and able to give after partial recovery. Catatonic schizophrenia is more likely than the other types to come on suddenly and to clear up suddenly. This statement must, however, be tempered by the realization that pure types seldom appear.

Paranoid type. Delusions hold the spotlight in this group. The paranoid schizophrenic patient has usually been having serious interpersonal difficulties for many years before he becomes ill. He is characteristically tense, uneasy, and distrustful, with a tendency to read hostile and belittling meanings into other people's comments and to apply these to himself. He may have tried to compensate for his mistrust by keeping a watchful, suspicious eye on whatever goes on around him, so as to be ready for anything that happens. He may, instead, have remained for many years defensively aloof, asocial and withdrawn, so that nothing can touch him. His lifelong custom is to mull things over alone, looking for explanations which seem plausible to him. Naturally, his personal fears, needs, wishes and uncertainties will play a large part in such lonely brooding.

The onset of paranoid schizophrenia comes when a person begins to lose his grip on reality, substitutes his misinterpretations and fantasies for the realities of shared social operations, and acts upon these as though they were publicly accepted fact. When this happens, the paranoid schizophrenic person regresses more quickly and further than the person with a paranoid reaction. His delusions are likely to be vague, bizarre, and unconvincing. . . . Their structure varies all the way from a mere succession of disjoined fragments to the most florid, imaginative jungles. Some are full of contradictions, of condensations and displacements, and of archaic symbolism such as we find in ordinary dreaming. Persecutory delusions are common, as are also delusions of influence and of grandeur, with ideas of reference. There are admixtures of the magical, mystical, religious, and sexual, often in weird combination. Somatic delusions are characteristically bizarre. One finds sometimes vivid delusions of catastrophe, world destruction, salvation, and world reconstruction. . . .

Hallucinations are nearly always present, and in greater profusion than in any other major syndrome, with the exception of toxic and infectious states. The hallucinations usually support and enrich delusional beliefs. Auditory hallucinations are the most common; visual the next most common. Hallucinations of smell, taste, body equilibrium, and skin sensation may also appear as important expressions of the patient's dynamics.

Schizo-affective type. The schizo-affective type is exactly what the name implies, a mixture of schizophrenic symptoms with manic or depressive ones. It is nothing more than a necessary convenience in classification, although it may also have dynamic implications. Essentially the clinical picture is one of an elation or a depression, in which delusions are more weird, vaguer, and less well organized than usual. Hallucinations are common, as they are not in mania and depression. Estrangement, depersonalization and bizarre somatic delusions are common. On the other hand, the elated or depressive component is more stable, better organized, and deeper than in most other schizophrenic illnesses. The mode of onset, course, and outcome are as variable as in other types, but the chances for recovery are perhaps better. If there are recurrences, after recovery, the schizophrenic features grow more prominent and the chances for recovery grow poorer.

INVOLUTIONAL PSYCHOTIC REACTIONS

This designation has only historical precedent to justify it. In the official classification it is an obvious compromise between those who would like to preserve the old concept of involutional melancholia, which it includes, and those who would like to drop it altogether. The commonest syndromes now included in this grouping are psychotic depressions and paranoid reactions appearing for the first time in middle or late life. There is no doubt that depressive and paranoid reactions to signs of senescence are common; but they are no different from depressive and paranoid reactions to other crises. Even the tendency of the psychotic state to persist is hardly surprising, since senescence and senility persist. It is unlikely that this group will survive another revision of our classification.

Other Major Disorders

Under this general heading the official classification has made a heroic attempt to gather together under one large tent a number of miscellaneous disturbances. Many of them are highly important in behavior pathology. Unfortunately the result has been rather to confuse than to clarify.

The confusion becomes obvious the moment we look at the official descriptions of what are usually called *character disorders*, there divided between "personality trait disturbances," some of which are neurotic, others nonspecific, and "personality pattern disturbances," most of which are prepsychotic personalities. The overall definition of personality disorders states without qualification that patients experience "minimal subjective anxiety"; but descriptions of subgroups go on to ignore this important stipulation. Thus, patients with personality trait and pattern disturbances (character disorders) are called fearful, sensitive, elated, sad, suspicious, envious, and extremely jealous. Surely no one supposes that such characteristics reach pathological levels without strong anxiety." Another subgroup, with three subtypes, is described as frequently having anxiety reactions superimposed upon it.

When we turn to the *sociopathic personality disturbances* (the ones that used to be called psychopathic states and impulse disorders), we find no mention of anxiety or anxiety equivalents. Yet we know that careful clinical studies of *antisocial* and *dissocial* persons—who fight against or seem to disregard social sanctions—have revealed over the past fifty years that anxiety is a leading factor, even subjective anxiety, appearing in the midst of reactively hostile or defensively callous behavior. In *deviant sexuality*, *drug addiction* and *alcoholism*, also classified under personality disorders, it is well known . . . that intense objective and subjective anxiety appear as part of the behavior pathology. Yet minimal subjective anxiety still stands as the official description of the whole group of personality disorders, which includes these.

Finally, we come to a heterogeneous class called *transient situational personality disorders*. These are described as acute symptomatic reactions to overwhelming stress occurring temporarily in persons who seem not to have an underlying personality disturbance. They include responses to civilian catastrophe and military combat, certainly a timely topic today, and adaptive failures at various age levels from infancy to normal senility.

This last grouping is not without practical usefulness. In the case of military personnel, for example, experience has taught that, when diagnoses are made in terms of neurotic, psychotic, or psychosomatic reactions, such diagnoses may be interpreted outside of the medical corps in ways unnecessarily detrimental to the military patient. Transient situational personality disorder is a euphemism that avoids stigmatizing a patient in his own eyes and in the eyes of others. The grouping is also useful in emphasizing the vulnerability of everyone to personality disturbances when stress is great enough. . . . The crises in adaptation at different age levels are also universally recognized and are an integral part of our understanding of behavior pathology. Aside from these emphases and practical uses, there is no good reason for looking upon transient disturbances as fundamentally different from neurotic, psychotic and psychosomatic disorders. We have already described cases which last only a few days and seem to clear up without leaving permanent new defects. Even in a catastrophe or in combat the personality disturbances which appear always involve internal forces that are highly personal and by no means simply situational. Again, we point out that everyone is vulnerable to personality disorganization, given enough stress, and that his response to the threat or the actual beginnings of disorganization will depend upon what his defenses and coping mechanisms are and how well they function under the stress circumstances.

* * *

Character Disorders

In the *character disorders*—called "personality trait and pattern disturbances" in the official classification—some distortion of the personality develops early in life and persists as a person's style, as the characteristic way in which he copes with his environment and defends himself. A character disorder may never be experienced as something abnormal or intrusive, and may therefore never give rise to anxiety once it becomes established. It is the bent twig of childhood which distorts the form of the personality and gives rise to compensatory changes to offset the distortion. The end-result may be an adult who seems always inhibited in certain areas of function, or who shows exaggerations of certain personality characteristics, or who stands chronically apart from the affairs of the marketplace, or rushes impetuously into every quickening stream that passes near him. If such an adult and those who are close to him accept his peculiarities as simply as his nature he is not likely to find them disturbing or seek to change them. He may be proud of them and consider them, not incorrectly, as signs of his individuality.

It is only when a person with a character distortion realizes that something is wrong with him, with his attempts at adaptation, defense, mastery, and satisfaction, that he experiences his difficulties as ego-alien, usually without knowing precisely what they are or why he feels as he does. The realization often comes with repeated failures and dissatisfactions which a person cannot explain away. It may come because new circumstances force a person to compare himself with others, and the comparison raises self-doubt, dissatisfaction, and perhaps anxiety. He may even recognize that some of what he has regarded as his special virtue or his mark of individuality may be in fact a pathological need, fear, or incapacity. He may find, for example, that his vaunted firmness rests upon a rigidity which keeps him from changing even when a change is necessary, or that his widely known affability is actually a fear of displeasing anyone, or that his willingness to compromise stems from an inability to take a firm stand.

One of the simplest ways of illustrating how a character disorder may be mistaken for a virtue is to look into the motives and the methods of conforming. Every child learns to conform to what is expected of him. This is an integral part of growing up from babyhood through childhood and adolescence to adult-hood. It is also the basis of cross-cultural differences in adult personality. The child in each different society is provided with unique models for identification and with adult guidance in learning to conform to these models.

A child in any culture may learn to conform gladly and willingly, but still without achieving normal, effective adulthood. If, for example, a parent demands unquestioning conformity of a child, regardless of the circumstances and of the child's changing needs, the child is most likely to be what he is compelled to be, even if this means serious distortion in his personality or character organization. If a child receives love in return for self-effacement, and if no other significant adult counteracts this trend, he will grow to adulthood as a chronically self-effacing person who even seeks out a marital partner who will also reward his self-effacement. This may be an acceptable situation, satisfying to all concerned, but it is not a normal personality organization.

Neither is the personality organization normal that is built around the *masochistic acceptance of punishment or restraint as an inevitable part of parental love*, nor one built around *infantile dependence*. Nevertheless if a parent treats a child consistently with *sadistic affection*, the child is likely to develop a reciprocal *masochistic acceptance of sadistic affection* which may last into adult life, as we have seen in some of our neurotic and psychotic patients. If a parent keeps a child consistently in a state of *infantile dependence*, no matter how this is rationalized, the child may always seek out situations and persons that encourage his lifelong pattern.

The important point here is that unquestioning conformity, self-effacement, masochistic suffering, and infantile dependence are often acceptable and even sometimes highly valued by society. That is, persons who are themselves relatively free of character distortions often admire them in others, without stopping to consider why these others have them while they themselves do not. It is self-evident that persons who cannot be comfortable unless they are conforming, who enjoy self-effacement and masochistic suffering, or who live contentedly in infantile dependence, are not likely to get into trouble unless they carry their characterological needs to extremes. To avoid common misunderstandings, it is essential to state here that courage, integrity, dependability, normal self-sacrifice, and the ability to accept dependence upon others are not signs of character disorder. It is only when the seeming *qualities* turn out to be *demands*, upon a human environment which does not want them, and does not gain in warmth or understanding from them, that we call them disorders rather than virtues.

*   *   *

Sociopathic Personality Disturbances

This group corresponds to what used to be called *psychopathic personality* and is now called *sociopathic personality disturbance* in the official classification. . . . The sociopathic personality seems unable to learn, that is, to profit by his experiences, in certain areas of interpersonal relationship. He may be of average or superior intelligence. Yet he repeatedly acts out in such a way as to invite social ostracism and often legal prosecution, without being able to change his impulsive behavior. As a rule the sociopathic person cannot fully realize that what he does is socially wrong or dangerous, or that he has any responsibility to society to control his behavior.

3.

REDLICH, FREDERICK C.

The Concepts of Health in Psychiatry*

*   *   *

There are three points which need to be considered before any act may even tentatively be labeled normal or abnormal. The first is motivation. The difference between a washing compulsion and "normal" washing depends not merely on the frequency but on the conscious and unconscious motivation of the act.

The second point involves consideration of the context in which the act occurs. A man promenading in swimming trunks on a New England main street in January may be considered "abnormal," but the same act on a beach in summer will not call for such a judgment.

The third point has to do with the question—by whom is the judgment made? Is it made by experts—e.g., psychiatrists, who can claim a more thorough acquaintance with abnormal behavior—or by the general public? If there is agreement between expert and public, there will be little occasion to challenge expert judgment. If judgments are discrepant, they will be challenged by either fellow scientists or by the public. If the expert opinion is too much removed from the public's notions, it will be met with incredulity, ridicule, and criticism. As we do not possess a universal, rigorous science of man, many propositions on normality of behavior have a palpably low degree of validity and reliability and are apt to be challenged by a startled public, especially if scientific evidence for them is not particularly strong or runs counter to prevalent public opinion. . . .

*   *   *

* Reprinted from F. C. Redlich's "The Concept of Health in Psychiatry," Chapter V of *Explorations in Social Psychiatry*, 139–158, edited by Alexander H. Leighton, John A. Clansen and Robert N. Wilson, © 1957, by Basic Books, Inc., Publishers, New York. Reprinted by permission.

In defining normality, most psychiatrists and behavioral scientists, including psychoanalysts, have been satisfied with listing certain traits, capacities, relationships which they consider normal. Jones lists as criteria the intricate relationships between strivings for happiness and effectiveness and sensitive social relations. Glover describes normality as characterized by freedom from symptoms, being unhampered by conflict, and having the capacity to love other than oneself. A plea for a balanced and integrated approach is made by Hacker, who finds any single or simple criterion unacceptable and defines normality as a successful integration of the personality. Hartmann stresses the importance of balance of instinctual and ego forces. Menninger writes, in a much quoted statement: "Let us define mental health as the adjustment of human beings to the world and to each other with a maximum of effectiveness and happiness. Not just efficiency, or just contentment, or the grace of obeying the rules of the game cheerfully. It is all of these together. It is the ability to maintain an even temper, an alert intelligence, socially considerate behavior, and a happy disposition. This, I think is a healthy mind."

* * *

. . . According to Waelder, behavior is simultaneously serving the demands of the id, ego, and superego. Using this premise as a starting point for an integrative approach, behavior will approximate normality if it simultaneously gratifies and does not frustrate instinctual needs, leads to success rather than to failure, and produces social praise rather than punishment. Obviously, the conditions of satiation, mastery, and esteem will rarely and possibly never be fully met in life, but marked deviations from such an ideal may point to various degrees of abnormality. Appraisal of gratification, achievement, and social approval will depend on integrated and interrelated judgment of individual and society. In most of our psychiatric patients, we will be able to discern some dysfunction in all three spheres; in the antisocial character, the dysfunction will be primarily, though never exclusively, in the deviation from social and ethical standards; in the neurotic, the dysfunction will be expressed more in frustration and failure and self-punishment.

* * *

Most propositions about normal and abnormal behavior contain normative elements. [T]he question as to normal or abnormal usually turns out to be a question about good or bad. Some of the most quoted statements, such as the one by Menninger, are definitely value statements. It is by no means clear whether some of these statements refer to an ideal (usually unattainable) adjustment or to the modal range in which people have managed to work out a fairly livable adjustment. . . . It is obvious that normality, in the sense of freedom from mental disorder, is not identical with conformity to social norms. Certainly, conformity even to those social norms which may be considered dominant is not identical with clinical normality.

Cultural influences (as well as cultural judgments) in the area of mental disorders are as yet difficult to isolate and evaluate. In a society like ours, some of the most severe neurotics may be conformists and some of the most radical nonconformists may be relatively healthy. Patients with mental disorder are not necessarily morally weak or depraved and some of them have exhibited in their sufferings and in the solutions of their problems the highest virtues.

* * *

Lewis presents another argument differentiating abnormal from asocial or antisocial behavior, to the effect that, even in those societies in which suicide is socially and ethically acceptable, it may be a clinically abnormal act if carried out by a psychotic patient.

* * *

Although we do not know in clear scientific terms what normality is, we usually know quite well who should be treated by psychiatrists. Psychiatrists have some general guidelines for this, and they are usually able to decide whether or not a specific patient should receive treatment. I feel that the problem as to who should be treated, though not identical with the problem of normality, is an important practical problem on which social psychiatry can throw some light. . . .

Who should be treated is not identical with the question of who acquiesces to treatment or of who is being treated; both questions, however, are of significance in the exploration of who should be treated, as judged by psychiatrists and society. The question as to who should be treated is related in principle to other problems of selection and decision, such as who should or should not be drafted into the Armed Forces, who should be admitted to higher educational institutions, who should be promoted for certain positions, etc. For many of these assessments we have common sense and technical procedures, which essentially tell us, or pretend to tell us, who is or might be a problem or who might do particularly well in the Armed Service, in school, in jobs. Although psychiatrists have shown some interest in such problems, their central question remains and should remain: Who should and could be treated?

The problem of normality, as the author sees it, can be put in form of the questions "normal for what?" and "normal for whom?" A moderately inadequate person working in a position of little responsibility in an industrial plant may be a very small problem to anyone except himself. The situation is entirely different if the man with "problems" is an important executive. It is different if psychiatric help is, for geographic, cultural, and psychological reasons, unavailable or if such help can be readily obtained and is considered beneficial in problems of this sort. Actually, only if the latter is the case should we speak of "psychiatric" problems. Otherwise, it would be more appropriate just to speak of "problems." To what extent such problems can be tolerated by the people who suffer from them or whether professional groups—e.g., physicians, teachers, lawyers, ministers, welfare personnel, psychiatrists, etc.—who encounter them are ready to tackle them is another matter. The self-perception of the person with the problem and the role assignment of all actors involved will determine subsequent labeling (normal or abnormal with reference to certain tasks) and subsequent action.

Essentially, I propose to examine the interaction between psychiatrist, patient, and the society in which they function. In doing this there will be focus on the establishment of contact between psychiatrist and patient, on some of the social agreements implied in the treatment process, and on the termination and goals of treatment. It is hoped that these processes will be outlined with particular reference to norms, mores, laws, and social institutions which govern the conduct of the actors involved.

As a preliminary, I shall propose tentatively a dichotomy of the "abnormal" persons into a "severely abnormal" group and a "moderately abnormal" group. It is evident that the first group will not be rigidly delineated from the second group either by symptoms or etiology and course, and that the second group will blend equally into the so-called "normal" population. Sometimes a severe disorder may be camouflaged by a seemingly normal surface and the more severe conditions may rapidly or slowly develop out of the mild conditions. Recognition of such phenomena usually will require high diagnostic skill from the expert and often enough challenges the expert beyond his present capacities. Yet I feel that the severe group, which includes all the psychotics and the severe neurotics, can more often be clearly recognized not only by the expert but by lay persons with whom these abnormal persons are in contact. Recognition of the moderately disturbed group is usually much more difficult and in most instances requires the most skillful professional judgment. I propose the above dichotomy because I think that it will aid us in our scrutiny of the social interactions between psychiatrist, patient, and society. Such a scrutiny involves not only an observation of social consequences of mental illness but an attempt to understand action in terms of social theory.

The first point of inquiry is concerned with the contact between psychiatrist and patient. How does one become a patient? There is considerable clinical experience in this area, but little systematic knowledge.

The relationship between psychiatrist and patient is defined by folkways, mores, and laws; these are different in the two groups of severe and moderate disorders. One of the more striking differences is the degree of urgency for treatment, which is usually greater in the case of the severe illness as compared with the mild disorder; sometimes a situation is found in which there is acute danger for the life and safety of the patient or those who are in contact with him. Intervention is often demanded so urgently that treatment and usually hospitalization is mandatory. . . . The contact between psychiatrist and the severely ill patient is at times brought about forcibly. Cooperation from the patient in such a process is thought to be desirable but not necessary. There is the assumption that such a step is necessary both from the patient's and from society's point of view, even if patients are not capable of, or willing to, recognize it.

The mandate of society to the psychiatrist in those cases is clear: To segregate, detain, and treat the patient and prevent his discharge until it is safe for him and society. In furthering such a mandate, society will, if necessary, deprive the patient of his most important citizen's rights and force him into a relationship of care and treatment. This is done by strong social pressures, by family, friends, and professional persons, or, in most instances, particularly in the lower socio-economic group, by enacted laws. In the severe cases, psychiatric help is, theoretically at least, available to all who need it. When psychiatrists and psychiatric facilities do not exist, as in certain geographic areas, the lack of psychiatric help is felt as seriously as the lack of other medical personnel, facilities, and supplies. Ultimately, it is not the individual but society that decides upon intervention; the psychiatrist behaves according to the customs and enacted laws of his culture.

*   *   *

NOTES

NOTE 1

Hartmann, Heinz
Ego Psychology and the Problem
of Adaptation*

[T]he commonly used criteria of health are obviously colored by *Weltanschauung*, by "health-morality," by social and political goals. In the analysis of our patients we have become familiar with the psychological background for the various conceptions of health. I believe, therefore, that for the time being, we will have to forego the formulation of a definitive

* New York: International Universties Press, 1958. (pp. 80–81). Reprinted with permission.

and general theoretical concept of health, lest we unwittingly base the evaluation of our experience and the formation of the concept of our own subjective goals. Still another consideration should caution us against making hasty pronouncements about the attributes of "ideal" health (a concept formed mainly as an antithesis of neurosis): the recurrent observation that the very mechanisms which lead to obvious pathology can, under different conditions, serve adaptive reactions, and that the outcome often depends on a quantitative rather than a structural factor. A concept of health which is conceived solely as the negative of neurosis and disregards the state of the conflict-free sphere is too narrow, if only because without taking this sphere into account, the concepts of ego strength, rank order, and equilibrium cannot be satisfactorily delineated. Another reason why some theoretical concepts of health are too narrow is that they usually underestimate both the great variety of personality types which must, practically speaking, be considered healthy and the many personality types which are socially necessary. Thus at present we must limit our theory to the exploration of the concrete relationships of mental functions to adaptive and synthetic processes and achievements. But all this does not alter our practice, does not change the aims of psychoanalytic therapy (which, from the vantage point of a future theoretical concept of health, are tentative aims): to help men achieve a better functioning synthesis and relation to the environment. . . .

NOTE 2

Transcript of Hospital Staff Meeting in the Long Case*

*   *   *

Participating are Staff psychiatrists and psychologists.

[The patient's] emotional responses are greatly impaired and there is manneristic and impulsive escape for them indicating a degree of disintegration and splitting. He has obviously been a neurotic character from early childhood and I believe there are enough evidences of disintegration to warrant a diagnosis of schizophrenia, simple type, being made. He cannot logically be held responsible for his acts.

DR. GAU: I'm sorry I cannot agree with all that. To me he is just another psychopathic personality, markedly so. I think he could answer much different than he does. I think he is shrewd and following a definite pattern in his answers.

---

* Reprinted from: Reid, J. P.: "The Working of the New Hampshire Doctrine of Criminal Insanity," 15 *University of Miami Law Review*, 14, 44–49 (1960). State v. Long 4 A.2d 865 (1939), 6 A.2d 752 (1939). By permission.

DR. GAL: If you talked to him for an hour and still said he was shrewd—

DR. GAU: Shrewd enough to have gotten along fairly well—what was he doing up there—having a little business and getting along pretty good.

DR. GAL: For a while—fair. He had an income from his stepfather so he did not have to be too shrewd in his business and could get along without money in the business. In fact he got into several difficulties because he did not pay his bills for painting his store. He called in the executor of the estate to pay the bills.

DR. GAU: That also speaks for psychopathic—thinks he can get away with things the average individual has to do—paying bills, leading a straight life. He thinks he can do the contrary and get away with it. He got away with it many times. I fail to see any evidence of an out and out psychosis. I agree it is a character neurosis but what else can you call it besides psychopathic personality—and if there isn't any evidence of psychosis you have to face that and call him not insane and let him face punishment for his crime.

DR. WELLS: I am inadequate to discuss the case but I think a lot of his actions would go along with a low intellect. Whether a man of this type of character neurosis—whether he would get over sexual drives and be a normal person—it is what I'd like answered. He might go along to a certain age and develop a change of life or something and that's all there is to it—or whether they continue along that line.

DR. GAL: You can't let him go along indefinitely killing children.

DR. W: If he had sodomy and was satisfied—he evidently got along with it for some time and then had to take it up again and had the drive.

DR. D: Is there any record from the prison?

DR. GAL: Yes, but we don't have much. Most of it is repeating what the Boston Psychopathic said. Shall I read it?

DR. D: Yes.

DR. H: He has a definitely inadequate personality and it seems the continued acts he has had and his psychological tests seem sufficient to put him in the schizophrenic group.

DR. J: He is on the borderline to me. It is a difficult case. As you formulated it he is either a psychopathic personality with strong schizophrenic traits or a simple praecox. I really think it is more or less a toss-up. A strong case could be built up for either side, I think.

DR. B: It is very hard to tell whether he should go in the schizophrenic group or psychopathic. To me the most abnormal thing is his unusual fatalistic attitude—everything is predestined and you cannot help it. If you drive fast you just got to drive fast and if you assault and murder children, it is predestination. He apparently realizes that his conduct is considered asocial by the majority of people but yet he feels he just cannot avoid doing it. Whether that makes him definitely psychotic I can't say. I'd be inclined to call him a simple praecox in a psychopathic individual. I think he has always been psychopathic and perhaps has gone beyond the limits of even psychopathic now. He is a very dangerous man in the community and I think they made a serious mistake when he was let out in Massachusetts.

DR. D: What was the basis of letting him out?

DR. GAL: Judge Stone was executor of the estate. As far as I know, good behavior. Judge Stone was executor of the estate and made application for his release and a judge—I've forgotten his name—signed the order for release and he was put on parole for a year.

DR. D: He must have had some recommendation from the institution.

DR. GAL: There is nothing in the record to indicate it. They put it all on the court. They said he was ordered released by the court.

DR. B: It seems from the psychiatric and psychological standpoints these people who have had perversions with children repeat the offense if they have the opportunity and that is where the danger lies. If he is called psychotic he should be in an institution always.

MISS R: The psychiatrists did not want him to go out but the judge was anxious to get him out.

DR. O: I think he is a very sick man and although he does not know it, I think his attitude is somewhat right. He can't possibly be held responsible for his early conditioning and inadequate development of personality. I don't think just because his antisocial acts are of a sexual nature that it necessarily means that he has to be labeled a psychopathic. I think the whole personality picture is more of a simple schizophrenic. Of course because there isn't anything that can be done with him it does not make any difference whether he goes to prison or stays here. Do you think there is a possibility of his becoming suicidal?

DR. GAL: I think there is a possibility of his murdering an attendant. His aggression has never been directed against himself but it has been explosive manifestations against someone else.

DR. O: He is always going to be a dangerous man to handle.

DR. F: I usually prefer to emphasize the constitutional factors rather than conditioning. Both are prominent. I think his fatalistic attitude is one of the most important features here. It is very noteworthy. He is using it presumably to cover up his ideas of inadequacy. He is trying to explain, excuse, and forgive on that basis. It would be interesting to learn when he developed that attitude and what the circumstances were. I am almost inclined to a belief in lack of free will. There is much to be said for it. After all, we all have certain characteristics that make us do certain things. I may be a fast driver because I have those characteristics and someone else may be a cautious one because of the same characteristics. To a certain extent that is lack of free will. It is a very broad subject but there is something to be said.

DR. O: Don't you think he says it because of his fundamentally passive nature?

DR. F: To explain his inadequacy and excuse these things he has been doing. I definitely agree he is a dangerous element.

DR. RANGER: Without psychosis, psychopathic personality, emotional immaturity—pathological sexuality.

DR. D: I am so emotionally upset by the unanimity of opinion that the man is insane that I am thrown off balance and don't know what to do. I wonder if my judgment is defective. I can't see it in the same light you do.

DR. F: You have the concept of the court in mind too.

DR. D: As psychiatrists we have to have some reconciliation with the courts and if I think a man is insane regardless of what the court thinks I will so state. Question of whether he should be kept here or in prison is another question. I could say he was insane and the court could give him a life sentence in prison without any difficulty. The fact we say he is insane does not mean he has to come here. It has been done before. I reported a case once before as insane and the judge didn't pay any attention to it and sent the man to state prison. Another case I sent in the woman was not insane and the judge decided she was and sent her here, so the court reserves its own opinion regardless of any idea of the psychiatrists. As a rule they are satisfied to take our opinion and in the great majority we turn them back as not insane. This is a very outstanding case that will cause a lot of feeling in the way it is handled by the court. That is not really our problem either. Looking at the case purely as psychiatrists I feel about it the way Dr. Ranger does. I think his diagnosis fitted in with my mental conception of such cases. I don't take a lot of stock in what he says about everything being so predestined. I think if I discussed it with him more at length I think I could shake him down. When you put him in a corner with a bit of logic he runs to cover saying he does not understand, which helps him out. How many accidents did he get into driving his car?

DR. GAL: Five.

DR. D: Were they serious?

DR. GAL: Yes.

DR. D: I wonder how they kept allowing him to drive?

DR. GAL: He did have his license revoked for drunken driving. After he got out of the army it was renewed.

DR. D: Did he injure anyone?

DR. GAL: One woman very severely but most of it was smashing his car. He ran her down.

DR. D: Does he admit he intended to kill these children?

DR. GAL: No.

DR. D: It was just an aftermath—being frustrated?

DR. GAL: The first one of the children jumped out of the car.

DR. D: There was some question whether it was an accident, wasn't there? The few times I have seen him he does not present the picture of praecox. I think he is more emotionally upset over this than he admits. It has been my experience that praecoxes are not quite so aggressive and murderous as he is.

DR. F: Would he be held in first degree?

DR. D: Yes. They will charge him with the most serious type and then—if they make it any less and if it should develop that he did it with malice afore-thought they could not give him the extreme penalty. They can start at the top and work down but not at the bottom and work up. I feel he is a psychopath and strongly sexed—and undoubtedly of limited mentality. The psychologist says he is definitely deteriorated.

MISS R: Definitely inefficient—4.4.

DR. D: What does that mean?

MISS R: I'd not go so far as to say the inefficiency was permanent, which is what deterioration implies.

DR. GAL: There are many evidences of psychiatric deterioration which I have enumerated.

DR. GAU: Did he seem to try to answer questions?

MISS R: He co-operated very well.

DR. J: Could you consider that the murder of these people was a homosexual panic to a psychotic degree?

DR. GAL: I don't know. I hadn't thought of it in that way. I can't think of any reason for thinking so.

DR. B: Are they the result of frustration?

DR. GAL: Aggressive to a psychotic degree.

DR. RA: I think our analytical study gives conscious and unconscious motives but it does not remove the fact he did these things and socially it is important. I don't care why a fellow throws a stone at me but what is important is that he did it. I think people should be judged by what they do and not by how they rationalize.

DR. F: What chance do you think he has of getting off with less than life? We have to consider that.

DR. D: He can't get out of it for less than life. If they agree he is insane they could send him down here. I doubt if they would send him here. If I said he was insane they would probably send him to jail anyway. The question of punishment does not enter here. It is as much punishment for him to be sent to PIA for life as to prison for life, as far as punishment goes.

DR. O: Are his lawyers going to be able to get him free?

DR. D: No.

DR. O: They did before.

DR. F: He might serve five years or so.

DR. D: He was not charged with murder before.

DR. F: Don't life murderers get out after ten years or so?

DR. D: Some do but this one never will. Most of those that get out—it is an episode in their lives—followed by good behavior. This fellow of course now they find he has a terrible record—two children dead and the whole background of sexual misbehavior—so if they once get him locked up I think he will stay there.

DR. RA: Why not string him up and let the state protect itself?

DR. D: Society is just that sadistic. Society will delight in having this fellow hang. They say what's the matter if he is insane—why not string him up.

DR. D: I think one reason people are trying to find a psychosis is an attempt to be fair toward him. Personally we might like to see him hang but I feel we must be fair as psychiatrists.

B.

In Establishing "Sanity"?—Forms of Action in Commitment

1.

AN INTRODUCTION TO THE POINTS OF DECISION—THE CASES OF DALLAS WILLIAMS

a.   WILLIAMS v. UNITED STATES
250 F.2d 19 (D.C. Cir. 1957)

BAZELON, Circuit Judge.

Appellant, having waived jury trial, was convicted on May 4, 1956, of assault with a deadly weapon, on an indictment returned in November 1949 for a shooting on September 26, 1949. It was his fifth trial and third conviction for that offense. The case is here for the third time.

His first conviction was reversed when the Government confessed error. The second and third trials resulted in mistrials. The conviction resulting from his fourth trial was reversed by this court, sitting in banc, because the trial court had denied appellant's motion for an adjudication of his competency to stand trial . . . Between his first and second trials appellant was adjudicated incompetent and committed to St. Elizabeths Hospital. He was again adjudicated incompetent and committed to the hospital between his third and fourth trials and between his fourth and fifth trials. On his first conviction in February 1950, which was on three counts, appellant was sentenced to two to seven years on counts 1 and 2 and one year on count 3, all concurrent. The second conviction in December 1953 brought a sentence of three to nine years. The present sentence is one to three years. He has already been confined for a total of about seven years in the course of this long prosecution—about six years in jail and about a year in St. Elizabeths Hospital. With time off for good behavior, his present sentence will have been served by September of 1958.

The principal defense at the trial under review was insanity. Appellant claimed that his mental illness had started long before 1949 and that the crime was a product of the illness. The Government's theory was that appellant had not been mentally ill at the time of the crime, but had developed "prison psychosis" as a result of subsequent confinement.

The grounds of this appeal are (1) that Williams was denied the speedy trial required by the Sixth Amendment and (2) that the prosecution failed to sustain its burden of proving his sanity.

Whether long delay of prosecution requires dismissal of an indictment even if there is no showing that the delay prejudiced the accused need not be determined here. The question here is whether, when such delay does result in prejudice to the accused, it is just to try him. The Government states that it would have moved for a dismissal of this indictment, were it not for its concern with appellant's dangerous recidivism.[1] It seems, therefore, to have recognized that it is unjust to try an accused after long and prejudicial delay.

Undeniably the bulk of the seven-year delay in bringing appellant to the trial which resulted in his present conviction was a direct or indirect consequence of his mental incompetency. The accused's incompetency necessarily slows the judicial process. Such delay is inevitable. By the Government's construction of the facts, however, appellant's mental illness had not existed at the time of the crime or even at the time of the first trial, but was brought on by the pressure of imprisonment some time after his first conviction. If the judicial process could and should have been completed before appellant became ill, his eventual illness will not excuse a long-delayed prosecution.

Appellant's 1950 conviction was reversed on the Government's admission that it could not sustain it "because of the total lack of any instruction on the elements of the offense charged." The prosecution's recognition of its duty to confess error when error is clear is commendable. But the prosecution's confession came only after the lapse of more than two years. Except for this, there is no reason to believe that, if appellant was not ill at the time of the offense, a second trial could not have been completed before he became ill. Exactly when appellant's illness began, by the Government's theory, is not clear. The prison authorities noticed bizarre behavior on appellant's part some time in 1950, but it was not until June 28, 1951, that the Government filed the lunacy petition which led to appellant's incompetency adjudication on July 2, 1951. Instead of speedily admitting the invalidity of the first conviction and bringing appellant on for a second trial without delay, the Government postponed as long as possible the necessity of confessing error. . . . It was not until April 17, 1952, after appellant was discharged from St. Elizabeths Hospital to the jail and moved for release on bail, that the Government made its confession of error. In the circumstances of this case, I cannot hold that there was no more delay than was reasonably incident to the ordinary processes of justice.

Whether or not the Government unreasonably extended the delay, we are agreed that the delay in this case was beyond the ordinary and that the extraordinary delay resulted in serious prejudice to appellant.

When prosecution is delayed because of the accused's mental incapacity to stand trial, the difficulty of determining whether the accused was mentally responsible at the time of the crime is increased.
. . .

The preparation of the psychiatric evidence which is required to prove an individual's mental condition at some past date is a very difficult task. It is a task for which the accused generally lacks both financial[3] and intellectual capacity.[4] The facts required by way of psychiatric testimony are a "description and explanation of the origin, development, and manifestations of the alleged disease . . . how it occurred,

---

1. The prosecutor told the court, at the opening of the trial, "This man has the worst criminal record for violence I have ever seen." We are informed by the Government that he was convicted of attempted robbery in 1933; twice of assault and battery in 1934; of manslaughter in 1936; of assault and battery with intent to kill in 1940 and in 1941; of shooting with intent to kill in 1942; of assault with a pistol in 1944; of assault in 1945; of assault with intent to kill, assault with a dangerous weapon and carrying a dangerous weapon in 1949. In 1952, twelve days after he was released on bail to await his second trial for the present offense, he threatened someone with a pistol and was convicted of that offense. While on bail before his fifth trial in 1956, he committed another crime involving a pistol and was convicted of that crime a month after the present conviction. Williams told one of the court-appointed psychiatrists who examined him in 1953 that he had spent about 20 of his 39 years in jail.

3. As is almost invariably true in these cases, appellant is a pauper.
4. The Government concedes that appellant's intellect, as measured by tests at St. Elizabeths Hospital, is no better than "dull." Earlier tests taken at D.C. General Hospital had indicated that he was a moron.

developed, and affected the mental and emotional processes of the defendant. . . . " *Carter* v. *United States*, 101 U.S.App.D.C. ——, ——, 252 F.2d 608, 617. The examinations conducted by the psychiatrists must be of a character they deem sufficient for the purpose of determining the facts required. If brief jail interviews with the defendant are inadequate for the purpose, the defendant should be committed to a mental hospital where he can be examined under clinical conditions and for a long enough time to satisfy the psychiatrists. . . .

In the case at bar, the Government not only failed to take any steps to ascertain the facts which would determine appellant's mental condition as it bore upon guilt or innocence, but resisted every defense attempt to produce those facts. . . . When Williams was brought to trial for the third time, the doctors' testimony about his 1949 mental condition was concededly relevant. But too much time had already passed for the testimony to be useful. Dr. Perretti was unavailable and Dr. Gilbert had very little recollection of his early examinations of the defendant. He testified only to what had been recorded in his files about those examinations and he said the purpose of the examinations had been "to determine . . . was he sick enough to be in hospital, or was he well enough to remain in jail."

* * *

That the evidence produced by a proper and adequate investigation of the facts relating to the accused's mental condition at the time of the crime may prove that he was not mentally responsible will not, we assume, influence the Government in its pursuit of the facts—and, of course, it should not. Under our criminal jurisprudence, mentally responsible law breakers are sent to prison; those who are not mentally responsible are sent to hospitals. To that end the District Code makes possible a verdict of not guilty by reason of insanity, and directs that under such a verdict the defendant is to be confined in a hospital for the mentally ill until it is determined that he "has recovered his sanity . . . [and] will not in the reasonable future be dangerous to himself or others." Two policies underly the distinction in treatment between the responsible and the non-responsible: (1) It is both wrong and foolish to punish where there is no blame and where punishment cannot correct. (2) The community's security may be better protected by hospitalization under D.C.Code, § 24–301 than by imprisonment. If Williams' violent act in 1949 sprang from mental disorder—if, indeed, he has a mental illness which makes it likely that he will commit other violent acts when his sentence is served, imprisonment is not a remedy. Not only would it be wrong to imprison him, but imprisonment would not secure the community against repetitions of his violence. Hospitalization, on the other hand, would serve the dual purpose of giving him the treatment required for his illness and keeping him confined until it would be safe to release him. Society's great interest in the proper disposition of such cases would be disserved if the Government, in prosecuting them, adopted an attitude of passivity or resistance to the production of evidence.

In the light of the foregoing, we hold that appellant was denied a speedy trial. We reverse the conviction and remand the case to the District Court for dismissal of the indictment.

Appellant also contends that his conviction should be reversed because the evidence overwhelmingly establishes insanity at the time of the crime. Since the conviction is reversed on a different ground, we do not reach this contention. We may note, however, that if a judgment of acquittal by reason of insanity were entered, appellant would be committed to a mental hospital under D.C.Code, § 24–301, until it should be determined that he would not "in the reasonable future be dangerous to himself or others." Considering the pattern of violence characterizing appellant's behavior since his adolescence and the Government's justifiable concern with his criminal recidivism, commitment of the appellant to a mental hospital might well have been the wisest and most desirable disposition of this case. In his three previous commitments to St. Elizabeths Hospital, appellant received medical treatment only to the extent necessary to restore the cognitive powers thought to be required for trial competency. If he were committed under D.C.Code, § 24–301 after acquittal by reason of insanity, he would presumably receive more therapy than in any of his previous commitments. Release from such commitment, requiring a determination of safety, would provide some assurance that, as a result of the therapy administered to him, he would not be likely in the reasonable future to pursue his former violent course. The present disposition of the case sets the appellant free some months before he might go free if he completed the sentence we hold to be invalid. It is open to the Government, however, to proceed for a civil commitment under D.C.Code, § 21–326, if it considers that, with Williams at large in his present state, "the rights of persons and of property will be jeopardized or the preservation of public peace imperiled and the commission of crime rendered probable."

Reversed and remanded with instructions to dismiss the indictment.

b.   IN RE WILLIAMS
                157 F. Supp. 871 (D.D.C. 1958)

KEECH, District Judge.

This matter is before the court on a writ of habeas corpus seeking the discharge of the petitioner, Dallas O. Williams, from the custody of the Superintendent of Saint Elizabeths Hospital, to which he was committed by order of this Court in Mental Health No. 34–58, "pending the outcome of proceedings to be forthwith instituted by the Mental Health Commission."

At the time of the signing of the order of commitment, the petitioner was before the court for presentation of the certified copy of the judgment and opinion of the United States Court of Appeals for the District of Columbia Circuit, reversing his conviction in Criminal No. 1572–49 for lack of due process. The government requested that the court, before receiving the mandate of the Court of Appeals in the criminal case, consider the petition of the United States Attorney, on behalf of the Superintendent of the District of Columbia Jail, that the Mental Health Commission examine Williams and report its findings to the Court.

The petition, sworn to by the United States Attorney, recited:

"1. Dallas O. Williams, colored, male and about 43 years old, was charged with assault with a dangerous weapon in November, 1949. [T]he United States Court of Appeals for the District of Columbia Circuit has reversed and remanded with instructions to dismiss the indictment.

"2. *The staff of St. Elizabeth's Hospital advised that Dallas O. Williams at the present time shows no evidence of active mental illness but that he is potentially dangerous to others and if released is likely to repeat his patterns of criminal behavior, and might commit homicide.*

"3. This petition is filed pursuant to the opinion of the United States Court of Appeals wherein that Court stated: 'It is open to the Government, however, to proceed for a civil commitment under D.C.Code 21–326, if it considers that, with Williams at large in his present state, "the rights of persons and of property will be jeopardized or the preservation of public peace imperiled and the commission of crime rendered probable." ' " (Emphasis supplied.)

The petition then prayed that the Commission on Mental Health be directed to examine petitioner and report its findings to the Court and that he be committed to Saint Elizabeths Hospital pending determination of the need for his continued confinement in a mental institution. Attached to the petition were the unsworn statements of Doctors Cody and Platkin, two psychiatrists who had examined the petitioner on December 28, 1957, at the jail.[1]

---

1. Dr. Platkin's report concluded with the following paragraph:

"Summarizing the present examination: Mr. Williams appears to be a man of grossly average intelligence, *who at the present time shows no evidence of active mental illness.* However, in view of his history, as provided by himself, and the long-standing pattern of drinking, gambling, and fighting, with frequent arrests for carrying, possession of, and assault with dangerous weapons; the absence of any regular occupational adjustment, and persistent difficulties with the law;

The court granted this petition for commitment, "sitting as a court of equity." The order did not provide any definite term of temporary commitment. Thereafter a supplemental order was signed by the court, directing the Mental Health Commission to include certain specific findings in its report.[2]

The petition for a writ of habeas corpus followed. Issuance of the writ was granted, and a full hearing has now been had before this court upon the return to the writ. The sole issue in this proceeding is whether the petitioner is lawfully restrained by the respondent. At the outset, it should be pointed out that, inasmuch as there is no criminal charge now pending against petitioner, there is no contention that any provision of the criminal code authorized his commitment. The legality of his confinement must therefore be tested solely upon the civil authority of this Court.

* * *

Under no statute is the court authorized to commit any person for mental examination on a petition which fails to state facts upon which an allegation of present insanity is based.

Aside from the fact that the psychiatrists' statements were unsworn, they contained no allegation of present insanity. Although both doctors indicated that they anticipated further antisocial behavior by the petitioner upon his release to society and believed him to be a potential danger to others, neither stated

---

it would not seem realistic to expect that this man could re-enter the community without being a danger to it. His attitude of suspiciousness and resentment toward authority; his refusal to admit or accept responsibility for the numerous crimes of which he has been convicted; and his apparent lack of anxiety or remorse over his past pattern of antisocial behavior, would tend to emphasize the potential danger that this man might offer the community."

Dr. Cody's report contained the following opinion:

"*Summary:* This is a middle-aged Negro male with a long antisocial history including several charges of assault. Alcohol appears to be an important precipitating factor in his criminal behavior. *While he shows no evidence of psychotic thinking today, it is probable that he was mentally ill a few years ago. At present there are no symptoms, singly or in the aggregate, which would justify a hospital commitment for this man.* However, it should be kept in mind that he is potentially definitely dangerous to others, and once released is likely to repeat his patterns of criminal behavior, including homicide." (Emphasis supplied.)

2. "Ordered that in the report by the Mental Health Commission findings of fact will be made as follows:

"1. Is Dallas O. Williams presently suffering from any mental disease, defect or any type of insanity? If the answer is 'No,' state whether he previously has had any mental disease, defect or any type of insanity, and if so, state the extent of his recovery and whether the illness is likely to recur in the event of his release from hospitalization.

"2. In the event said Dallas O. Williams is permitted to be at large, will he likely be dangerous to himself or will the rights of persons or of property be jeopardized or the preservation of public peace imperiled and the commission of crime rendered probable? If your answer to the foregoing question is 'Yes,' state whether this is by reason of any present or likely future mental disease, defect, or form of insanity?"

that he believed, or that there was ground to believe, that petitioner is presently suffering from a mental illness or mental defect which requires treatment or restraint in a mental institution.

Conceding that there is a rebuttable presumption of continuing insanity where one had been adjudged insane, the last judicial determination of this petitioner's mental state was a finding of competency to stand trial; and even without such judicial determination, any presumption of continuing insanity would be rebutted by the statements of the psychiatrists upon which respondent relies.

* * *

While the closing statement in the Court of Appeals' opinion may be interpreted as giving color to the right to commit a person merely because he is a potential danger to the community, the quotation from § 21–326 is a mere fragment and must be read in context with the balance of the section. . . .

The transcript of the hearing preceding the signing of the order of commitment indicates that the court purported to act under an inherent equity jurisdiction to deal with insane persons. . . . Even if one concedes that there is a margin of authority remaining to the court which has not been restricted by the Code provisions, it is apparent from the recitations of the petition for commitment, the very terms of the court's supplemental order, and the transcript of the proceedings before the court on that petition, that there has been no finding or allegation of belief that the petitioner is presently insane.

However commendable was the court's purpose to protect the public from the release to society of a man "potentially dangerous to others," there is no District of Columbia statute or inherent equity power permitting commitment to any institution upon that showing alone. Many persons who are released to society upon completing the service of sentences in criminal cases are just as surely potential menaces to society as is this petitioner, having a similar pattern of anti-social behavior, lack of occupational adjustment, and absence of remorse or anxiety; yet the courts have no legal basis of ordering their continued confinement on mere apprehension of future unlawful acts, and must wait until another crime against society is committed or they are found insane in proper mental health proceedings before confinement may again be ordered.

The Court of Appeals, which by reversing petitioner's conviction necessitated his release from custody on criminal charges, without any finding as to his present mental state, did not, and could not, suggest that petitioner be committed to a mental institution, temporarily or permanently, via civil proceedings without compliance with the insanity statute and on a mere showing that he may reasonably be expected to commit further criminal offences. The procedural provisions of § 21–301 *et seq.* were enacted by the Congress for the protection of all persons alleged to be insane in civil proceedings, and the statutory safeguards were not withheld from those with criminal records.

It would indeed be anomalous if a person who, after arrest, indictment, plea of not guilty, defense of insanity, and conviction by jury of a felony, is ordered by the Court of Appeals to be released because of a lack of due process in his trial, could thereafter be incarcerated in civil insanity proceedings without due process.

This court is conscious, as was the United States Attorney, of the need for protection not only of the community but also of individuals in need of psychiatric care and treatment. But these laudable purposes, under our form of government, must be accomplished by procedures which are legal and not at the cost of disregarding constitutional safeguards by deprivation of liberty without due process of law. The mere fact that a commitment without due process is temporary and for the purpose of psychiatric examination renders it no less unlawful. As broad as the general equity jurisdiction of the judicial system is, it cannot be said to override specific statutory provisions or constitutional guarantees of personal liberty.

For the foregoing reasons, I am constrained to grant the petition of Dallas O. Williams for release from the custody of the respondent.

c.   WILLIAMS v. OVERHOLSER
    162 F. Supp. 514 (D.D.C. 1958)

PINE, District Judge.

* * *

. . . On February 3, 1958, petitioner was charged in the Municipal Court with being drunk or intoxicated on a public street. After a continuance, defendant pleaded guilty to the offense, and the Court ordered a mental examination. Subsequently the Chief Psychiatrist of the District of Columbia General Hospital made a report on the mental condition of defendant, and upon objection being made and after hearing the Municipal Court on its own motion, set aside the plea of guilty and entered an order finding petitioner to be of "unsound mind" and directing that he be confined in St. Elizabeths Hospital until released in accordance with Section 24–301, as amended, D.C.Code 1951.

This is the most recent of petitioner's encounters with the law. It follows an almost incredible record since 1933 of criminal charges and convictions, including manslaughter, assault and battery, assault with intent to kill, shooting with intent to kill, assault with a pistol, and other crimes of violence. Much of petitioner's adult life has been spent in penal and mental institutions. There is no doubt that he has been a turbulent, dangerous character, but that alone is not sufficient to incarcerate him in a mental institution unless committed there pursuant to law.

In his petition for the writ petitioner claims that his confinement is illegal on the following grounds:

(1) Lack of judicial determination of the competency of petitioner to stand trial, but only a finding of unsoundness of mind.

(2) A lack of substantial evidence to support the finding of unsoundness of mind, and

(3) A claim that petitioner is now competent to stand trial regardless of his mental condition at the time of the Municipal Court hearing.

*   *   *

The statute under which these proceedings are governed is Sec. 24–301, as amended, D.C.Code 1951, *supra*. It provides in brief that whenever a person is charged with an offense and prior to the imposition of sentence it shall appear to the Court that the accused is of unsound mind or is mentally incompetent so as to be unable to understand the proceedings against him or properly to assist in his own defense, the Court may order the accused committed to the District of Columbia General Hospital for examination and observation; and if after such examination and observation the Chief Psychiatrist of the District of Columbia General Hospital shall report that the accused is of unsound mind or mentally incompetent, such report shall be sufficient to authorize the Court to commit by order the accused to a hospital for the mentally ill, unless the accused or the Government objects, in which event the Court after hearing without a jury "shall make a judicial determination of the competency of the accused to stand trial." It further provides that, if the Court shall find the accused to be then of "unsound mind or mentally incompetent to stand trial, the court shall order the accused confined to a hospital for the mentally ill." And further, it provides that whenever an accused person so confined is restored to mental competency in the opinion of the Superintendent of the Hospital, the Superintendent shall certify such fact to the Clerk of the Court in which the indictment or information against the accused is pending, and that such certification shall be sufficient to authorize the Court to enter an order thereon adjudicating the accused to be competent to stand trial unless the accused or the Government objects, in which event the Court after hearing without a jury "shall make a judicial determination of the competency of the accused to stand trial," and that nothing in the statute shall preclude a person confined under its authority from establishing his eligibility for release under the provisions of this section by a writ of habeas corpus.

It will thus be noted that the statute makes a distinction between unsoundness of mind and mental incompetency to stand trial . . . The statute refers three times to these two mental conditions as follows: (1) when it authorizes the Court to order the accused committed for examination and observation to a mental hospital, the first procedural step in the statute; (2) when it refers to the report to the Court from such hospital on his mental condition, the second procedural step; and (3) when it refers to the finding to be made by the Court when objection to the report is made, the fourth procedural step. But the statute does not make the distinction in the two mental conditions when it refers to the judicial determination required to be made by the Court, but only refers to the mental competency of the accused to stand trial, which is the third procedural step, and does not make the distinction when it refers to the procedure to be followed and judicial determination to be made upon a claim of restoration of mental competency to stand trial.

Where the distinction is made in the two mental conditions, the statute is in the disjunctive and permits the Court to make a finding on either condition; but where no distinction is made, the statute is mandatory and requires the Court to make a judicial determination of the sole mental condition stated, namely competency to stand trial. It would therefore appear that the Court may or may not make a finding on whether the accused is of unsound mind, but must determine whether he is mentally competent to stand trial, when objection is made to the report from the Hospital and a hearing is held, as in this case. If he is found to be of unsound mind the statute requires the Court to commit the defendant to a mental hospital. If the Court also determines him to be incompetent to stand trial the statute requires the same commitment. But as above stated, the statute requires a judicial determination in the latter type of mental condition, but does not require a determination in the former.

In this case the Municipal Court has not made a determination on the latter point, namely competency to stand trial, to which the accused is entitled, bearing in mind that under the authoritative decisions of this Circuit he may be of unsound mind and yet competent to stand trial. This failure has resulted in a denial of a right given him by the statute as well as his right, if competent, to a speedy trial under the Constitution.

I, therefore, conclude that petitioner is illegally detained in the absence of a determination of competency to stand trial, and shall order that the writ of habeas corpus issue unless within 10 days from the date of the order signed pursuant to this opinion, or such extension thereof as may be granted for good cause shown, the Municipal Court determines petitioner's mental capacity to stand trial. If at that time he is found incompetent to stand trial he will be committed under the statute to a mental hospital. If he is found competent to stand trial, he will have his trial, and whether convicted or acquitted he will be returned to the mental hospital under the prior commitment on unsoundness of mind. If, then, he believes that he has been restored to soundness of mind he may establish his eligibility for release by a writ of habeas corpus, which is expressly provided for in this statute.

*   *   *

d.   WILLIAMS v. OVERHOLSER
259 F.2d 175 (D.C. Cir. 1958)

EDGERTON, Chief Judge.

*   *   *

[T]he District Court's order . . . determines that the appellant will be confined in a mental hospital, whether he is found competent or incompetent to stand trial.

The proceedings in the Municipal Court were ostensibly under § 24–301(a) of the D.C.Code, which provides that when the mental competency of a person accused of crime is in issue "the court, after hearing without a jury, shall make a judicial determination of the competency of the accused to stand trial. If the court shall find the accused to be then of unsound mind or mentally incompetent to stand trial, the court shall order the accused confined to a hospital for the mentally ill." The last sentence, as we read it in its context, comes only to this; the court shall order the accused confined in a mental hospital if it finds that because of unsoundness of mind or for any other reason he is mentally incompetent to stand trial.

*   *   *

Title 21, beginning with § 306, of the District of Columbia Code contains elaborate provisions for commitment of persons alleged to be insane. In general, the procedure includes a report and recommendation by the Commission on Mental Health, a jury's verdict if demanded, and an order of the District Court. In the present case, the Municipal Court and the District Court seem to have thought that when the person suspected of insanity is also accused of crime, Congress intends to bypass all those provisions and safeguards and to permit any trial court, including the Municipal Court, to commit the person to a mental hospital without benefit of a jury or of the Mental Health Commission, although he may be perfectly competent to stand trial. We think Congress had no such intention. Such an intention, if it were plainly expressed, would raise serious questions of due process of law and equal protection of the laws. . . . The purpose of § 24–301(a), we think, is simply to prescribe the procedure for determining whether an accused person can understand the proceedings against him and properly assist in his defense,

and to provide for his confinement in a hospital instead of a jail until he can.

The order of the District Court should be modified so as to provide, without prejudice to a prompt trial in the Municipal Court if appellant proves to be competent to stand trial, that the writ of habeas corpus shall issue unless within ten days either (1) the Municipal Court determines that he is mentally incompetent to stand trial and orders him confined on that ground or (2) "proper lunacy proceedings are instituted."

e.   IN RE WILLIAMS
165 F.Supp. 879 (D.D.C. 1958)

YOUNGDAHL, District Judge.

Petitioner has filed a writ of habeas corpus seeking release from St. Elizabeths Hospital. The facts giving rise to this present proceeding are as follows:

*   *   *

In accord with [Judge Edgerton's decision in *Williams* v. *Overholser* 259 F.2d 175] a hearing was held on July 18, 1958, to determine the petitoner's competency to stand trial. The Court then ruled "that as of this time he is mentally competent to understand the proceedings against him and to properly assist in his own defense." Petitioner volunteered a plea of guilty, which the Court refused to accept. The Court directed the entry of a plea of not guilty and put the Government to its proof.

Petitioner argues in his motion that once he has been adjudged competent to stand trial, the Court must accept his plea. However, this contention flies in the face of Rule 11 of the Federal Rules of Criminal Procedure, 18 U.S.C.A.,[1] and the psychiatric testimony adduced before the Court in this case.[2] The issues involved in the plea of guilty and the consequences which attach to a plea require a greater degree of awareness than the competency to stand trial. The Court may reasonably find, as it did in this case, that the latter competency may exist and still not feel justified in accepting a plea of guilty on the defendant's behalf.

After the trial court's ruling, the Government then placed on the stand its only witness, Officer William Booth, who testified that on the night of February 2, 1958, petitioner was "observed . . . in the middle of the street with his hands up in the air, screaming, and

---

1. " . . . The court may refuse to accept a plea of guilty, and shall not accept the plea without first determining that the plea is made voluntarily with understanding of the nature of the charge. . . ."

2. Dr. McAdoo testified that petitioner was capable of understanding the charges against him, but did not completely understand the nature of a guilty plea. Dr. Aloysius Miller testified that petitioner could comprehend the nature of the proceedings but might not be aware of the nature of the punishment to be meted out.

yelling. . . . He had an odor of alcohol on his breath.
. . . He appeared to be under the influence of alcohol
at first sight." Defendant did not cross-examine and
did not offer any testimony on his own behalf.

The Court found the defendant not guilty because
of insanity quite clearly because of the April 21 finding
of unsoundness of mind.

Petitioner contends in his motion for a writ of
habeas corpus that the use of the finding of April 21,
for any purpose other than to determine competency
to stand trial, is contrary to Sec. 24–301(a) as interpreted by the Court of Appeals and that he is, therefore, being held contrary to law. He further urges that
eliminating this April 21 finding, there was no testimony at the trial to form the basis for the Court's
verdict.

This Court is in accord with petitioner's contention
that under the Court of Appeals' decision any hearing
under Sec. 24–301(a) can be on the issue of competency to stand trial and nothing more. Consequently, the evidence of April 21 cannot be used to
sustain a finding of not guilty by reason of insanity.

Moreover, the Durham rule requires a finding of
causal relationship between the mental disease or
mental defect and the crime committed. This issue of
causal relationship was not even mentioned at the
hearing of April 21. Further, the standard involved
in competency to stand trial is far less demanding
than that of mental disease or mental defect. One
might very well be found competent to stand trial
and still be found not guilty by reason of insanity.[4]

There remains, then, the testimony admitted at
the trial itself—the testimony of police officer Booth.
From the Court's examination of the records of the
case it would appear that Officer Booth expressed no
opinion as to petitioner's mental health. However,
the evaluation of Officer Booth's testimony involves
consideration of the sufficiency of the evidence to
support the Court's judgment. The proper court to
determine this issue is the Municipal Court of Appeals
where petitioner's case is now pending. . . .

The Court notes further Dr. Overholser's affidavit
of August 1, 1958, appended to defendant's answer.
In that affidavit he states petitioner is suffering from
a mental disorder, a chronic brain syndrome with
behavioral reaction. He further attests that petitioner
is dangerous to himself and to others and should be
in a mental institution. This affidavit indicates that
there is now a basis for the commencement of new
proceedings under the civil commitment procedure
authorized by District of Columbia Code, Sec. 21–
306 *et seq.*

It is clear to this Court from the record and the
history of various proceedings involving this petitioner that he is dangerous to the community and is

afflicted with a mental illness which requires medical
attention and confinement in a mental hospital
rather than incarceration in a workhouse or other
penal institution. The deterioration in petitioner's
condition, as evidenced in the affidavit, eliminates the
obstacles which prevented his commitment this past
winter. The Court of Appeals has urged the District
to utilize the civil commitment procedure. This Court
would also recommend that avenue. Should it choose
to pursue this course, the District would accomplish
its results quickly and further appellate proceedings
would be unnecessary.

The motion for habeas corpus is denied.

f.   WILLIAMS v. DISTRICT OF COLUMBIA
147 A.2d 773 (Mun. Ct. App. 1959)

CAYTON, Acting Judge.

From a simple beginning as a charge of intoxication, this case before long became the subject of a
habeas corpus proceeding in the U.S. District Court;
an appeal therein to the U.S. Court of Appeals; a
sanity inquisition in the Municipal Court; and a
second habeas corpus proceeding in the District
Court.

The case is now before this court on defendant's
appeal from rulings of the Municipal Court refusing
to accept his plea of guilty, entering a not guilty plea
over protest of his counsel, putting him on trial as to
his sanity, adjudging him to be of unsound mind, and
ordering him committed to St. Elizabeths Hospital.

*   *   *

. . . Of various errors assigned we need discuss only
one: the sufficiency of the evidence to support the
finding of insanity. . . .

[T]here is no evidence in the case except that of the
police officer. And he really said nothing more than
that when arrested on February 3, 1958, Williams
seemed to be drunk and was acting strangely. He was
asked nothing, and said nothing, about his prisoner's
sanity. Plainly, it must be held that there was no
evidence to support the finding that defendant was
not guilty of intoxication because of insanity. That
finding must be reversed.

We have taken the time to deal most carefully with
this case in all its distressing ramifications and with
full awareness of our duty to the public as well as to
this defendant and others in the same situation. That
duty impels us to call attention, as other courts and
judges have done so plainly and even urgently, to
civil commitment procedure as the real solution of the
problems inherent in this case.

We are aware that one attempt in that direction
failed because of insufficient allegations in the petition. . . . But in the year which has elapsed stronger
reports and fuller information have been developed
and presented, and there should now be no difficulty in

---

4. Of course, this is the situation which is presented in every
case where an acquittal is had because of insanity.

preparing a petition which will meet statutory requirements.

Reversed with instructions to set aside order of commitment . . .

g.   WILLIAMS v. UNITED STATES
312 F.2d 862 (D.C. Cir. 1962) *Cert. den.* 374 U.S. 841 (1963)

WRIGHT, Circuit Judge.

On March 15, 1961, Dallas O. Williams shot and killed two men. He was committed to St. Elizabeths Hospital under 18 U.S.C. § 4244 for mental examination to determine whether he was competent to stand trial. That examination disclosed that he was competent and the District Judge so found. A seven-day trial followed, during which Williams relied primarily on the defense of insanity. Eleven psychiatrists, one psychologist, four lay witnesses and appellant himself testified on this issue. But the defense did not prevail. Williams was convicted on all counts[1] and sentenced to serve from 21 to 61 years in the penitentiary. He now appeals, asserting that a directed verdict of not guilty by reason of insanity should have been entered. . . .

[The history of this case] shows not only Williams' failure to adjust to society, but society's failure to find a satisfactory means of restraining offenders of his sort. It is a history which is, in a sense, the foundation for this appeal. Indeed, the argument here, between the Government and appellant, and between two groups of experts, is essentially whether Williams' criminal record, heavily drawn on at his trial, indicates that his latest crime is the product of a diseased mind.

The history shows that Williams is a confirmed criminal, a "recidivist" in the parlance of the penologists. But that fact alone does not require that he be committed to a hospital rather than the penitentiary. A long criminal record does not excuse crime. True, the record also shows that appellant was on several occasions found temporarily incompetent to stand trial. But, without long delay, he was, in each instance, later certified as competent. That is not, of course, equivalent to a finding that he was responsible for his crimes. However, there are other important facts disclosed by the public records.

The first is that not once in his many trials was Williams acquitted by a jury on the ground of insanity. One Municipal Judge so ruled, over appellant's strenuous objection, but that finding was subsequently vacated as made on no evidence. The other relevant point is that the Government, having once

been unable to even *allege* existence of mental disease, did not again attempt civil commitment of Williams, despite reiterated suggestion by this court, the District Court, and the Municipal Court of Appeals. We cannot assume the Government was insensitive to these proddings or indifferent to the obvious danger to the public in Williams' remaining at large. On the contrary, the only reasonable inference from official non-action in this direction is that the available evidence simply would not support the necessary allegation of insanity.

It is against this background that we must decide the prime issue in this case: Did the evidence, as a matter of law, fail to establish beyond a reasonable doubt that the offenses charged were not the product of mental disease or mental defect? If so, a directed verdict of acquittal by reason of insanity should have been entered by the trial court.

We pose the question in this way because it is clear beyond cavil that appellant's sanity was a legitimate issue in the case. Indeed, five psychiatrists testified that Williams was a "psychopath" or "sociopath" on the day of the killings and at least some of them thought this condition a "mental disease." Without any evidence relating the abnormality to the offenses, this was enough to raise the issue and require the Government to disprove the claim that the crimes were the product of mental disease or defect beyond a reasonable doubt. We conclude, however, that although the defendant's evidence relating to insanity was sufficient to make the issue, it was not so strong, when considered with the evidence offered by the Government, as to require a directed verdict of acquittal by reason thereof.

The psychiatric testimony . . . shows that while nine psychiatrists, many of them possibly influenced by appellant's long criminal career, labelled Williams a "sociopathic personality," or thought him otherwise mentally unbalanced on the crucial date, only six characterized his condition as a "mental disease or defect," and, of these six, only three could say the killings in question were the product of that disorder. The net of it is, then, that of eleven psychiatrists called, the great majority could not relate the offenses to a mental disease or mental defect. In the circumstances, we cannot say reasonable men must necessarily, and as a matter of law, have entertained a reasonable doubt as to appellant's legal responsibility for his acts. This conflict in medical evidence could only be resolved by the jury.

We conclude that appellant's trial was free of prejudicial error and that his conviction must be affirmed. In so doing, however, we do not foreclose the possibility of a further inquiry, by the proper authorities, whether his sentence should be served in the penitentiary or a mental hospital. Indeed, under the general law, 18 U.S.C. § 4241, and the District of Columbia Code, § 24–302, any prisoner found to be

---

1. Appellant was indicted in three counts, each of the first two charging first degree murder of one of the victims and the third charging the offense of carrying a dangerous weapon without a license. The jury returned a verdict of second degree murder on the first two counts. On the last count Williams was found guilty as charged.

"mentally ill" may be transferred to a mental hospital. It may well be that Williams is a proper candidate for such action.

Affirmed.

NOTES

NOTE 1

Dallas Williams—Four Years Later

[Williams] was sentenced on December 22, 1961, to a term of 20 to 61 years on two charges of Second Degree Murder. While still being handled by the District of Columbia Department of Corrections, he was placed at St. Elizabeths on three different occasions because of indication of mental instability. He was never certified psychotic, however. Our psychiatrist at Leavenworth describes him as a psychopathic personality with a history of chronic alcoholism and chronic brain syndrome.

Mr. Williams was transferred to Leavenworth from the District of Columbia system on September 15, 1965. On one occasion he incurred a disciplinary report for threatening the life of an officer but, for the most part, he has adjusted well. He has a good work record in the shoe shop and has voluntarily taken part in academic schooling. The Leavenworth report, moreover, indicates that there has been some change in Williams' attitude. He now appears to be friendly and cheerful and has a more wholesome outlook on life.

This man's conduct at Leavenworth has not occasioned attention from the psychiatrist except for evaluation purposes and he has not asked for treatment. While we would not anticipate Mr. Williams' involvement in intensive psychiatric treatment, he will be kept under observation and will be provided with appropriate care as the need arises. [Letter from Richard J. Heaney, Acting Assistant Director, Bureau of Prisons, U.S. Department of Justice, dated March 28, 1966.]

NOTE 2

District of Columbia Code: Insane Criminals §§ 24–301, 302 (1961)

§ 24–301.

(a) Whenever a person is arrested, indicted, charged by information, or is charged in the juvenile court of the District of Columbia, for or with an offense and, prior to the imposition of sentence or prior to the expiration of any period of probation, it shall appear to the court from the court's own observations, or from prima facie evidence submitted to the court, that the accused is of unsound mind or is mentally incompetent so as to be unable to understand the proceedings against him or properly to assist in his own defense, the court may order the accused committed to the District of Columbia General Hospital or other mental hospital designated by the court, for such reasonable period as the court may determine for examination and observation and for care and treatment if such is necessary by the psychiatric staff of said hospital, If, after such examination and observation, the superintendent of the hospital . . . shall report that in his opinion the accused is of unsound mind or mentally incompetent, such report shall be sufficient to authorize the court to commit by order the accused to a hospital for the mentally ill unless the accused or the Government objects, in which event, the court, after hearing without a jury, shall make a judicial determination of the competency of the accused to stand trial. If the court shall find the accused to be then of unsound mind or mentally incompetent to stand trial, the court shall order the accused confined to a hospital for the mentally ill.

(b) Whenever an accused person confined to a hospital for the mentally ill is restored to mental competency in the opinion of the superintendent of said hospital, the superintendent shall certify such fact to the clerk of the court in which the indictment, information, or charge against the accused is pending and such certification shall be sufficient to authorize the court to enter an order thereon adjudicating him to be competent to stand trial, unless the accused or the Government objects, in which event, the court, after hearing without a jury, shall make a judicial determination of the competency of the accused to stand trial.

* * *

(d) If any person tried upon an indictment or information for an offense, or tried in the juvenile court of the District of Columbia for an offense, is acquitted solely on the ground that he was insane at the time of its commission, the court shall order such person to be confined in a hospital for the mentally ill.

(e) Where any person has been confined in a hospital for the mentally ill pursuant to subsection (d) of this section, and the superintendent of such hospital certifies (1) that such person has recovered his sanity, (2) that, in the opinion of the superintendent, such person will not in the reasonable future be dangerous to himself or others, and (3) in the opinion of the superintendent, the person is entitled to his unconditional release from the hospital, and such certificate is filed with the clerk of the court in which the person was tried, and a copy thereof served on the United States Attorney or the Corporation Counsel of the District of Columbia, whichever office prosecuted the accused, such certificate shall be sufficient to authorize the court to order the unconditional release of the person so confined from further hospitalization at the expiration of fifteen days from the time said certificate was filed and served as above; but the court in its discretion may, or upon objection of the United States or the District of Columbia shall, after due notice, hold a hearing at which evidence as to the mental condition of the person so confined may be submitted, including the testimony of one or more psychiatrists from said hospital. The court shall weigh the evidence and, if the court finds that such person has recovered his sanity and will not in the reasonable future be dangerous to himself or others, the court shall order such person unconditionally released from further confinement in said hospital. If the court does not so find, the court shall order such person returned to said hospital. Where, in the judgment of the superintendent of such hospital, a person confined under subsection (d) above is not in such condition as to warrant his unconditional release, but is in a condition to be conditionally released under supervision, and such certificate is filed and served as above provided, such certificate shall be sufficient to authorize the court to order the release of such person under such conditions as the court shall see fit at the expiration of fifteen days from the time such certificate is filed and served pursuant to this section: *Provided*, That the provisions as to hearing prior to unconditional release shall also apply to conditional releases, and, if, after a hearing and weighing the evidence, the court shall find that the condition of such person warrants his conditional release, the court shall order his release under such conditions as the court shall see fit, or, if the court does not so find, the court shall order such person returned to such hospital.

*   *   *

§ 24–302.

Any person while serving sentence of any court of the District of Columbia for crime, in a District of Columbia penal institution, and who, in the opinion of the Director of the Department of Corrections of the District of Columbia, is mentally ill, shall be referred by such Director to the psychiatrist . . . and if such psychiatrist certifies that the person is mentally ill, this shall be sufficient to authorize the Director to transfer such person to a hospital for the mentally ill to receive care and treatment during the continuance of his mental illness. . . .

*   *   *

2.

CIVIL COMMITMENT

a.   DODD v. HUGHES
               398 P.2d 540 (Nev. 1965)

THOMPSON, JUSTICE.

By a habeas corpus application . . . Dodd sought

his release from the Nevada State Hospital. . . . He had been committed to that institution as a mentally ill person. . . . At the habeas hearing, the Superintendent of the Nevada State Hospital gave his opinion that Dodd, though a sociopath, was not psychotic, and therefore not "mentally ill" within the meaning of NRS 433.200. He suggested that Dodd be released from his confinement. Another doctor was of a different view. Though he agreed that Dodd was not psychotic, he believed that a sociopathic personality may be considered "mentally ill" as that term is used in the statute. Additionally, he stressed Dodd's high potential for homicidal activity. At the conclusion of the hearing, the court directed the superintendent to apply to the board of state prison commissioners for that board's consent to confine Dodd at the Nevada State Prison. The superintendent did as directed. The prison commissioners consented, and Dodd was delivered to the Nevada State Prison for confinement until further order of the court (NRS 433.310).[2] The hearing convinced the lower court that Dodd was and is mentally ill, a menace to public safety, and that the hospital facilities are inadequate for his safe confinement. Dodd has appealed from the order committing him to the state prison. . . .

The legislature did not define "mentally ill" when it passed the law governing the Nevada State Hospital. . . . Its failure to do so supplies the basis for Dodd's appeal. It is his position that a person must exhibit one of the psychotic reactions as classified by the American Psychiatric Association before he may be considered mentally ill. Absent a classified psychosis, one may not be committed and confined. A sociopath (defined in the testimony as a disorder of personality affecting the ethical and moral senses) like Dodd, (and all the evidence is in accord that Dodd is, indeed, a sociopath), does not fall within any of the classified psychotic reactions and, therefore, may not be institutionalized. So it is that we are urged to fashion a definition for the words "mentally ill" and thereby fill the void in the statutory hospital law. It is suggested that we confine mental illness to the psychotic reactions as classified by the American

---

2. NRS 433.310 provides:

"[1]. Whenever a person legally adjudged to be mentally ill is deemed by the court or the superintendent to be a menace to public safety, and the court is satisfied that the facilities at the hospital are inadequate to keep such mentally ill person safely confined, the court may, upon application of the superintendent, commit such person to the Nevada state prison. The person shall be confined in the Nevada state prison until the further order of the committing court either transferring him to the hospital or declaring him to be no longer mentally ill.

*   *   *

"[3]. All the provisions of law, so far as the same are applicable relating to the confinement of mentally ill persons in the hospital shall apply to confinement of mentally ill persons in the Nevada state prison."

Psychiatric Association. We are wholly unable to follow that suggestion. The record before us shows that the psychiatrists who testified do not agree on the statutory meaning of "mentally ill." Further, the record reflects that psychiatrists in general are at war over the propriety of the classifications of psychosis as specified by the American Psychiatric Association. We seriously doubt that the legislature ever intended medical classifications to be the sole guide for judicial commitment. The judicial inquiry is not to be limited so as to exclude the totality of circumstances involved in the particular case before the court. Recidivism, repeated acts of violence, the failure to respond to conventional penal and rehabilitative measures, and public safety, are additional and relevant considerations for the court in deciding whether a person is mentally ill. The assistance of medical examination and opinion is a necessary concomitant of the court hearing, but the court alone is invested with the power of decision. . . . That power is to be exercised within the permissible limits of judicial discretion.

Here the record demonstrates a combination of things which should, and did, unquestionably, influence the lower court to enter the order it did. Dodd, an 18 year old, was shown, by testing, to have the intelligence quotient of a high-grade moron. All agree that he is a sociopath almost devoid of moral sense. He has been proven, at least to date, wholly unresponsive to either penal or rehabilitative measures, nor does he give promise or response to available probation services or psychiatric treatment. He possesses homicidal tendencies, and is dangerous. Finally, one of the testifying psychiatrists stated that Dodd is mentally ill within the intendment of the statute. In these circumstances the lower court did not abuse its discretion in denying habeas relief and ordering that Dodd be transferred to the Nevada State Prison for confinement.

Affirmed.

NOTES

NOTE 1

EX PARTE PERRY
137 N.J.E. 161, 43 A.2d 885 (1945)

JAYNE, VICE CHANCELLOR.

*   *   *

On August 24, 1944, one Willard Parker Perry was adjudged to be an insane person and thereupon committed to the New Jersey State Hospital at Trenton, where he continues to be confined. A writ of habeas corpus has been allowed and testimony has been adduced relative to his existing mental state. . . . The statutory duty in such an inquisition is to "find and determine whether the person in whose behalf the writ was sued out, is sane or insane."

It is no less difficult to evolve a standard chart of behavior sufficient to justify the continued confinement of an alleged insane person than it is to precisely define insanity. Most of the attempts to define insanity are more sententious than definitive, sometimes leaving some shadowy margin between the perceptible boundaries of sanity and insanity.

Psychiatry lies within the field of the specialist. His opinions are influential and serviceable, but it does not follow that every type of psychosis has the legal implication of insanity under the statute applicable to the immediate inquiry.

Basically viewed, the power of the state to restrain insane persons and confine them in some asylum is an exercise of the police power deemed in its operation to be conducive to the public welfare. The motive supporting such legislation is the desire to protect the public or the person confined, or both. An unwarranted deprivation of personal liberty is more than unconscionable. The permanent incarceration of a sane person in such an environment without hope of release is probably little less punitive than a sentence of death.

Therefore, differently expressed, I suppose the purpose of this inquiry to be to ascertain whether or not the mental condition of the patient is at present such that a continuance of his confinement is reasonably necessary to obtain the objects of the statute. For that practical purpose it is not obligatory to declare what constitutes insanity in general, but rather to inquire wherein consists the alleged insanity of this particular individual.

This person is forty-eight years of age. He has and still does exhibit noticeable idiosyncracies. However, the insanity implied by the statute is not established by proof of mere eccentricities of mind and action manifested by occasional breaches of decorum. We observe amidst humanity an indescribable variety of whims, caprices, and eccentricities. Perry is undoubtedly emotional, and in matters in which he is naturally interested, he displays some inordinate vigor and acuteness. On the few occasions in the past when he is said to have resorted to violence, there were evidently some inducements, the elements of which have not been revealed with the attending circumstances, and so whether he then displayed an emotional instability due to a mental deficiency is indeterminate. He is loquacious, yet his conversation is in point and coherent. He had a propensity to ride in automobiles and somewhat habitually indulged in "hitch-hiking," which was probably in many instances importunate and exasperating to motorists. Incidentally, on one such occasion he stopped the clinical director of the State Hospital, who literally (not colloquially) "took him for a ride."

His aberrant deportment over a span of years has aroused several complaints, from most of which, I note, he has been discharged. His peculiar acts have doubtless caused the police some annoyance. From such circumstances usually sprout the idea and inclination to "put him away." His commitment resulted from the application of the Ewing Township Chief of Police. His freedom is sought to be obtained by his mother and sister.

Contemplating his own welfare, I learn that he is not receiving any therapeutic treatment at the institution. In actuality he is not a patient. He is a prisoner. He has been in custody and presumably under critical observation for more than a year, and yet only three incidents of his conduct are reported. It is said that he is frequently noisy and vociferates what he himself describes as a "hog call." One wonders what emotional outlet a neurotic but sane person so situated would choose to pursue. Then, it is stated that he has complained of a distressing sensation in his bowels and entertains the notion that there is a tapeworm in his intestine. If his diagnosis is unauthentic, I would hesitate to label such an error as an insane delusion. In psychiatry, I imagine it might be catalogued as a slight manifestation of pathopsychosis. Thirdly, he asserted that he had conceived a device that would be exceedingly useful to the government in war, yet he has persistently declined to divulge its nature or character. While seemingly incongruous, the falsity of his statement is not at present demonstrable. At the hearing he stated that he did not wish to reveal the nature of the contrivance until he had obtained the protection of a patent. A delusion, I conjecture, implies a false impression without any real or possible factual basis.

*   *   *

Supposing the evidence to reveal that this man manifests an unusual personality, eccentricities, perversity of conduct, and when aggravated or excited shows characteristics of emotional instability in the respects mentioned, should I adjudge him to be insane within the meaning of this statute? Does the public welfare or his own require his continued imprisonment? If liberated, is he likely to appreciably menace the safety of himself or that of the person or property of others? In the present posture of the proofs, I am inclined to think not. He retains a perception of right and wrong. I cannot regard him as an irresponsible being. I am not informed of any deplorable prognostic symptoms. A glimpse of the future can only be caught with the light of the present. Certainly with the right of liberty involved, a reasonable doubt of his insanity should be resolved in his favor. It is my conscientious judgment that although the mind of this man may be in some respects deficient superficially, it is not so substantially impaired in intellectual power as to necessitate his confinement. I shall therefore order his release.

NOTE 2

CARRAS v. DISTRICT OF COLUMBIA
183 A.2d 393 (D.C. Mun. Ct. App. 1962)

HOOD, CHIEF JUDGE.

Appellant was arrested for an indecent exposure in a local bus terminal. He pleaded guilty to the charge, and on a showing to the court that appellant had twice before been committed to St. Elizabeths Hospital for similar offenses and that he had been released from that institution only two months before the later offense, proceedings were had under our sexual psychopath statute. After a hearing he was found to be a sexual psychopath and committed to St. Elizabeths Hospital. On this appeal appellant's chief argument is that the evidence did not sustain the finding that he was a sexual psychopath within the statutory definition, which reads as follows:

"The term 'sexual psychopath' means a person, not insane, who by a course of repeated misconduct in sexual matters has evidenced such lack of power to control his sexual impulses as to be dangerous to other persons because he is likely to attack or otherwise inflict injury, loss, pain, or other evil on the objects of his desire." Code 1961, § 22–3503(1).

In the preliminary report the psychiatrists concluded that appellant was a sexual psychopath within the definition of the statute, but added: "Mr. Carras is not dangerous to others in spite of offensive inclinations. It is our recommendation that he receive ambulatory treatment (psychotherapy) for his condition."[1]

The psychiatrist who testified at the hearing stated that appellant was of sound mind but had a compulsion to expose himself which he could not resist. He further said he did not believe appellant was dangerous in that he would physically attack anyone in any manner. He conceded there could be possible psychological damage to a minor child or sensitive adult should such a person observe an indecent exposure, but he repeated that appellant would not physically harm other persons and would be helped by ambulatory treatment.

The gist of appellant's argument is that in order to come within the statutory definition of sexual psychopath, one must be dangerous to others, and that this means likely to inflict physical injury to another; and that, absent the likelihood of physical danger to others, one cannot be classified under the statute as a sexual psychopath, no matter how disgusting and offensive his conduct may be to others.

It is our opinion that the words of the statute, "likely to attack or otherwise inflict injury, loss, pain, or other evil," are not to be restricted to physical injury alone. In the common understanding of the

_____
1. Presumably "ambulatory treatment" means treatment, without confinement, at the hospital.

words, injury includes injury to the feelings, and pain includes mental suffering.[2] The psychiatrists conceded, and without that concession we would hold as a matter of common sense, an exhibition of the sort here described might result in a painful reaction on the part of the observer and might produce a psychological injury. Much, of course, would depend upon the age, sex, sensitivity and experience of the observer, but the statute requires only a likelihood and not a certainty. It is our conclusion that the evidence sustained the conviction.

Appellant next contends that the court should have explored various means of treatment short of commitment, especially in view of the psychiatrists' recommendation that he receive ambulatory psychotherapy. Under the statute the court had no choice but was required to order commitment to St. Elizabeths.

* * *

NOTE 3

OVERHOLSER v. RUSSELL
283 F.2d 195 (D.C. Cir. 1960)

PER CURIAM.

. . . We think the danger to the public need not be possible physical violence or a crime of violence. It is enough if there is competent evidence that he may commit any criminal act, for any such act will injure others and will expose the person to arrest, trial, and conviction. There is always the additional possible danger—not to be discounted even if remote—that a nonviolent criminal act may expose the perpetrator to violent retaliatory acts by the victim of the crime.

* * *

NOTE 4

STATE v. GREEN
388 P.2d 362 (Mon. Sup. Ct. 1964)

JOHN C. HARRISON, JUSTICE.

The defendant was tried and convicted of the crime of "Attempt to commit a lewd and lascivious act upon a child, together with two prior convictions of a felony." The district court sentenced him to fifty years. . . .

The facts giving rise to this appeal are as follows. On or about May 27, 1962, a ten-year-old girl and her two younger brothers were seated in their parent's car in front of a Great Falls bar. They had been left there by their parents who had entered the bar. The defendant was in this same bar and he admits being somewhat intoxicated. He left the bar and upon seeing the children in the car approached it and in-

formed the children that his name was Adam Green and that he knew their daddy very well. He then said to them: "I will offer each of you one dollar if you will come sit in my car." The offer was refused by the girl and her brothers and so the defendant returned to his own car, which was parked nearby. A few minutes later he returned to the children's car. On this occasion he attempted to shake hands with the two boys who were in the back seat. In attempting to do this he scratched the hand of one of the boys. He then climbed into the front seat of the car and rested his arm on the back of it. The palm of his hand was behind the little girl's head. His arm remained in this position for a couple of seconds and it touched her hair and shoulders. The defendant again asked the ten-year-old girl to shake his hand, which was answered by a request to leave the car. He then got out of the car and returned to his own car. . . .

The first witness called by the State was the complaining witness who told all about the incident. . . .

* * *

The State then called Dr. George Gelernter, [a psychiatrist]. . . . He testified as follows:

"A. I felt that Mr. Green was a sexual deviate; that he had poor control of his impulses; that he was subject to periods of heavy drinking and when drinking he was even under less control of his impulses; he was poorly motivated insofar as wanting help, he seemed to feel there should be some magic way to get free of this problem, he seemed to have very little idea as to what was involved to get help, and he had very little desire to get it; he had never sought help prior to this time.

"Q. Do you feel there is any chance for rehabilitation of this man based on your evaluation? A. I never like to say a man can't be rehabilitated; I felt the chance here was probably very small because of lack of motivation, his limited intelligence, and the poor facilities available.

"Q. Did you arrive at a conclusion as to his relationship with society? A. In my opinion he represented a threat to society because of his inability to control his impulses."

The essence of this doctor's testimony, it can be seen, went to the possibility of the defendant's ability to be rehabilitated. [T]here was no attempt on the part of the State to connect his "problem" with the events of May 27. The only thing that was discussed was his apparent mental illness.

The State next called the father of the little girl who testified . . . that he had met the defendant before, but that he was not intimately acquainted with him. . . .

* * *

The defendant took the stand in his own behalf and . . . stated that he knew the children and that he was merely attempting to shake their hands. On cross

---

2. Webster's New International Dictionary (2d ed.).

examination the defendant was questioned about a personal problem with small children. To which he replied that he had one to an extent. He stated, however, that on the day in question he was not bothered by this so called "problem." The State on cross examination attempted to question the defendant concerning incidents similar to the one in question, where he was picked up.

* * *

Sex offences . . . relating to lewd and lascivious acts upon children are viewed with abhorrence by the public. That is why we think that the language of this court in *State* v. *Keckonen*, 84 P. 2d 341, 346, is particularly *apropos*:

> "* * * Crimes against nature are naturally revolting to a normal person, and the subject is truly a loathsome one. In such cases, jurors are sometimes moved by abhorrence of the offense to convict upon slight evidence. * * * this fact alone should be enough to put a tribunal assiduously on guard against yielding to the dictates of such intense prejudice."

It is with this caution in mind that we have reviewed the proceedings in this appeal before us.

* * *

The record indicates that in its opening statement the prosecution stated that it would through medical testimony . . . prove the defendant's state of mind at the time he committed the act. Clearly this was not done. The testimony of [the doctor] transformed what had therefore been a criminal prosecution into a commitment proceeding. . . .

[N]o effort was made by the prosecution to use the testimony of the doctor to prove intent. . . . Never once [did he] describe exactly what the defendant's problem is or how it is apt to be manifested. It is impossible to tell, from a reading of [the] testimony, whether or not this problem of the defendant even related to little children. . . .

After hearing such testimony from the doctor, what jury would not feel that this man should be locked up? The opinion of [the doctor] could not have but helped overwhelm the jury into convicting this defendant, not because of what he had done, but because of what they thought he might do. In the final analysis, it appears that the defendant was convicted for being a sexual deviate. Whether he actually is or not, is immaterial because he could not be criminally charged with such an offense in Montana. Unlike many States, Montana does not have a "sexual psychopath" law, which provides for a determination, during a pending criminal action and after a thorough medical and psychiatric examination, of whether the individual involved is a "sexual psychopath or deviate" and further providing for civil commitment and treatment. The need for such legislation is a matter for the Legislature. . . . However, should a person pose a threat to society, in Montana, the public can protect itself by virtue of the provisions of Chapter 2 of Title 38, R.C.M. 1947, which provides for civil commitment of the mentally deranged.

For the foregoing reason, the judgment is reversed and the case remanded for a new trial or such other proceedings as the State deems necessary.

NOTE 5

WECHSLER, HERBERT, JONES, WILLIAM K., and KORN, HAROLD L.

The Treatment of Inchoate Crimes in the Model Penal Code of the American Law Institute: Attempt, Solicitation, and Conspiracy*

. . . The primary purpose of punishing attempts is to neutralize dangerous individuals and not to deter dangerous acts. Nonetheless, the dangerousness of the actor's conduct has some relation to the dangerousness of the actor's personality, and to the need for preventive arrest. . . .

The basic premise here is that the actor's mind is the best proving ground of his dangerousness.

* * *

NOTE 6

Commissioner's Committee on Police Arrests for Investigation, Report and Recommendations**

[A]rrests for "investigation" are often "preventive" arrests. A person trying front doors of stores, or peering into parked cars, in the early hours of the morning; a person "known" to the police as a pickpocket loitering at a crowded bus stop; a "known" Murphy game operator talking to a soldier or a sailor —such persons may be arrested for "investigation," not primarily for the purpose of interrogation, though some interrogation may occur, but largely in order to eliminate at least temporarily the occasion for any possible criminal activity. The principle upon which such arrests are made appears to be: If the individual is detained until 10 or 11 a.m. the following day, at least he will have committed no crime that night, and may be discouraged from attempting any similar crime on later occasions.

One eloquent advocate of greater arrest privileges for police is O. W. Wilson, Superintendent of Police in Chicago, Illinois, and earlier Professor of Police Administration at the University of California. In a recent article entitled *Police Arrest Privileges in a Free Society: A Plea for Modernization*,[1] he had this to say on the subject of "preventive" arrest:

> "People on the whole want protection from

---

* 61 Columbia L. Rev. 571, 579, 587 (1963). Reprinted by permission.
** District of Columbia, 1962 (pp. 18–19).
1. 51 J. Crim. L., C. & P.S. 395 (1960).

criminal attack; they want to feel secure in their homes and on the streets from disturbances and molestations. To meet this need, local communities in our free society have created uniformed bodies of police to prevent crimes and to bring to court those who commit them. Responsibility for the prevention of crime rests principally on city police forces, sheriffs' departments, and local detachments of state police."

"To prevent crime, the police must either stand guard at every point of possible attack, which is a physical and economic impossibility, or intercept the person with criminal intent before he robs, rapes, or kills. It is better to have an alert police force that prevents the crime than one that devotes its time to seeking to identify the assailant after the life has been taken, the daughter ravished, or the pedestrian slugged and robbed."

"The local police feel the restrictions imposed on arrest privileges more keenly than do the specialized police agencies whose principal responsibility is the gathering of evidence to identify and convict persons after they have committed a crime, rather than to prevent the act in the first instance. . . ."

One aspect of "preventive" arrests for investigation, often found in other communities, but apparently not in the District of Columbia, is the harassment of "undesirable" characters by repeated arrests until the person simply leaves town. The Committee has found no reason to believe that arrests for "investigation" are used for that purpose in the District of Columbia.

*   *   *

NOTE 7

EX PARTE STONE
87 Cal. App. 2d 777, 197 P.2d 847 (1948)

*   *   *

ADAMS, PRESIDING JUSTICE.

On July 12, 1940, an information was filed in the Superior Court of Shasta County, charging petitioner with a violation of section 288 of the Penal Code in that he had committed a lewd and lascivious act upon a girl ten years of age. Stone pleaded not guilty, and on August 20, 1940, his attorney filed a petition under sections 5500 and 5501 of the Welfare and Institutions Code seeking to have him declared a sexual psychopath. After a hearing the court adjudged him to be such a sexual psychopath, and on August 22 ordered that he be committed to the Mendocino State Hospital, and that proceedings on the criminal charge be suspended.

On December 12, 1941, Dr. Rapaport, the medical superintendent of said State Hospital, certified to the district attorney of Shasta County, by letter, that they had given Stone all the treatment possible, and while his physical condition had improved his mental attitude continued to be such that he would not, in their opinion, be improved by further care and treatment. He stated that he believed Stone to be so sexually ill and mentally deranged that, without supervision, treatment, care, or restraint he would be dangerous to himself or to other persons, and to society as a whole but he requested that the sheriff be directed to call for and return Stone to the superior court for further disposition pursuant to section 5502.5 of the Welfare and Institutions Code.

*   *   *

The court, however, readjudged Stone to be a sexual psychopath and ordered that he be returned to the Mendocino State Hospital to be held "as required by law."

*   *   *

[T]he applicable statutes do not authorize a court to continue the detention of a sexual psychopath indefinitely . . . or until he shall have recovered from his psychopathy. [S]ection 5502.5 specifically provides that when the medical superintendent concludes that such person will no longer benefit by hospitalization he may be returned to court "for further disposition of his case."

While the statute does not say, in so many words, that he shall be returned for trial on the original criminal charge, we are of the opinion that such was the intention of the legislature. Otherwise there would have been no logical reason for making such provision in the Act. The purpose of hospitalization under the sections of the code applicable to sexual psychopaths obviously is for treatment for the mental disease or disorder from which the psychopath is suffering; and they contemplate that in either of two contingencies such hospitalization shall cease, to wit, if the accused has recovered, or if he will no longer benefit by further care and treatment in the hospital. And where such person has been returned to court "for further disposition of his case" the conclusion seems to be obvious that by such language the legislature meant that he should then be tried for the criminal offense. While it may well be said that where by lapse of time it has become probable that as the result of such a trial the defendant will be acquitted and be entitled to be restored to his liberty while still a menace to society because of his sexual psychopathy, we cannot therefore hold that accused, without ever being granted a trial on the charge against him, and without the imposition of any sentence fixing a term of imprisonment, may be incarcerated for the remainder of his life because he is such a psychopath, or that he may be bounced from the court to the hospital and from the hospital back to the court *ad infinitum*. If the legislature had intended that a sexual psychopath might or should be, merely because of such condition, incarcerated in a hospital until cured, it would have so provided in the statute. It is not contended that one not accused of crime may be deprived of his liberty because of a sexual psychopathic condition, nor do we believe that merely because a sexual psychopath is accused of crime he may be held indefinitely in a hospital when he will not benefit from further treatment there, and never permitted to have the question of his guilt or innocence of such crime determined.

Statutes applicable to sexual psychopaths charged with crime differ from those applicable to the insane, for sexual psychopaths are not necessarily insane and are not by reason of their mental condition unable to defend themselves from criminal charges; and if they are convicted of crime, and cannot be benefited by hospitalization, the public is as well protected from them when they are committed to a prison; and if they are innocent of the crime they are entitled to their liberty until again charged with crime or committed as insane under proceedings brought for that purpose under the applicable statutes. The presumption of innocence still protects petitioner, and he is not to be dealt with as a lawbreaker unless and until so adjudicated.

*   *   *

May we suggest that if, because of lapse of time during which a sexual psychopath has been detained in a hospital it may become impracticable to bring him to trial when it has been determined that he will no longer benefit from hospitalization, section 5501 may well be amended to provide that proceedings for determining his condition as a sexual psychopath may be had only *after* adjudication of the criminal charge. . . . And if the protection of society from sexual psychopaths is the *sine qua non* of the statutory enactments regarding such persons, and their confinement in state hospitals *until their recovery is accomplished* is necessary for such persons, then the legislature should so provide in no uncertain language. This it has not done, but, on the contrary, it has provided that when in the opinion of the superintendent of the state hospital a sexual psychopath will not benefit by further treatment he may be returned to the court for further proceedings in his case. And when he has been so returned, as was Stone, . . . and there is no reason to believe that he will be benefited by further hospitalization, it must have been the intention of the legislature that he should then be tried upon the criminal charge. . . .

[W]e conclude that petitioner is entitled to his discharge from the custody of the said hospital; and it is so ordered.

NOTE 8

California Welfare and Institutions Code Sexual Psychopaths (1956)

§ 5501. . . . When a person is convicted of any criminal offense, whether or not a sex offense, the trial judge, on his own motion, or on motion of the prosecuting attorney, or on application by affidavit by or on behalf of the defendant, if it appears to the satisfaction of the court that there is probable cause for believing such person is a sexual psychopath within the meaning of this chapter, may adjourn the proceeding or suspend the sentence, as the case may be, and may certify the person for hearing and examination by the superior court of the county to determine whether the person is a sexual psychopath within the meaning of this chapter. . . .

*   *   *

§ 5517. . . . Whenever a person who is committed for an indeterminate period to the department for placement in a state hospital as a sexual psychopath (a) has recovered from his sexual psychopathy to such an extent that in the opinion of the superintendent the person is no longer a menace to the health and safety of others, or (b) has been treated to such an extent that in the opinion of the superintendent the person will not benefit by further care and treatment in the hospital and is not a menace to the health and safety of others, or (c) has not recovered from his sexual psychopathy, and in the opinion of the superintendent the person is still a menace to the health and safety of others, the superintendent of the hospital shall file with the Director of Mental Hygiene a certification of his opinion under (a), (b), or (c), as the case may be, including therein a report, diagnosis, and recommendation concerning the person's future care, supervision, or treatment. . . . If the opinion so certified is under (a) or (b), the committing court shall forthwith order the return of the person to said committing court and shall thereafter cause the person to be returned to the court in which the criminal charge was tried to await further action with reference to such criminal charge.

NOTE 9

PEOPLE v. LEVY
151 Cal. App. 2d 460, 311 P.2d 897 (1957)

PETERS, PRESIDING JUSTICE

*   *   *

[Appellant contends that a sexual psychopath] statutory procedure which permits a person convicted of a misdemeanor to be transferred from court to court, and from hospital to court to hospital to court as was appellant, is arbitrary and unreasonable, particularly when such procedure culminates in an indeterminate commitment to San Quentin. This argument is based on a misconception of the purposes of the statute. The main purpose of the Act is to protect society against the activities of sexual psychopaths. The secondary purpose is to rehabilitate the sexual psychopath. . . . In *People* v. *McCracken*, 39 Cal. 2d at page 346, 246 P.2d at page 918, the Supreme Court properly pointed out that "the sexual psychopath may be removed from society under the sexual psychopath law until he is cured or until he is no longer considered a menace to the safety of others." Thus, the place of commitment and the possibility of criminal punishment on the misdemeanor charge does not affect the validity of the objectives of the Act, which are admittedly proper.

The emphasis that appellant places on the fact that he was originally convicted of a misdemeanor, and now finds himself in San Quentin, possibly for life, is misplaced. This argument would be sound only were his confinement punishment. As we have already seen, the purpose of the confinement is to protect society and to try and cure the accused.

* * *

NOTE 10

R. v. HIGGINBOTHAM
[1961] 3 All E.R. 617

GLYN-JONES, J.

This appellant pleaded guilty [of having] taken and driven away . . . a motor vehicle in a manner dangerous to the public at Camberley. He was sentenced to twelve months' imprisonment [and] to eight years' preventive detention to be served concurrently with the sentence of twelve months' imprisonment. . . . He was also disqualified for holding a licence to drive a motor car for the rest of his life. He now appeals. . . .

His case is this. The maximum punishment for taking and driving away a motor car is twelve months. The maximum punishment for dangerous driving is two years. He says that the maximum sentence for the two offences would have been three years in all if consecutive sentences had been imposed, that it is an unjust and excessive sentence that he should be given eight years' preventive detention, and that the effect is that he is being punished again and again for his record. His counsel adds this argument. The appellant has a bad record, to which I shall have to refer in greater detail, but the offences of which he has been convicted in the past do not include the offence of driving a motor car dangerously or indeed any other form of bad driving. Counsel says that it is inappropriate that a sentence of preventive detention should be imposed for an offence which has been committed for the first time.

The appellant has an extremely bad record. He is forty-two years of age, and between 1931 and 1960 he has been convicted seventeen times. . . .

* * *

It seems to us that this appellant has amply demonstrated the fact that the public are not safe from his depredations in crime unless he is in a place of safety,

a place where he can be kept in safe custody. In other words, we think that this is a proper case for a sentence of preventive detention.

* * *

This appellant cannot get out of his head the idea that a sentence of preventive detention is imposed on him as a punishment not so much for the offence which he has just committed, which is the occasion for the award, but for the offences which he has previously committed and for which he has already been punished and, taking that view of the sentence of preventive detention it is understandable that he should feel aggrieved by it. He doubtless feels that having been punished once he ought not to be punished again. It is, I think, desirable that we should say that while in a sentence of preventive detention there is and must be a punitive element, the sentence normally is for a term which exceeds that which would be appropriate as a punishment even taking the past record of the offender into consideration, and the balance of a term of preventive detention beyond that part which is purely punitive is not imposed by way of punishment of the offender at all; it is imposed for the protection of the public against the depredations of the man who has demonstrated by his record that he cannot be trusted with his liberty without losing it. Whether he cannot help committing crime or does not want to stop committing crime, the public needs protection. It follows that in most cases the term of preventive detention awarded must necessarily exceed that which would be appropriate as a punishment if the punitive element alone were considered. . . .

* * *

. . . In this case the doctor at the hospital to which he was sent [from prison where he was serving a sentence under a prior conviction] examined him and, treating him as a patient, came to the conclusion that there was very little sign of mental illness about him. If the doctor is right, this man is not mentally unstable; *he is just wicked*, and the doctor, having come to the conclusion that there was no evidence of mental instability justifying his being kept in safe custody, left him at large to go about the hospital as he thought fit and to work in the grounds outside with no physical obstacle to his walking out of the gate of the hospital at any time he liked. In due course, that is exactly what he did, he walked out of the hospital and committed the crime for which he was rightly given, as we have found, eight years' preventive detention. It may be useful if we say that it is unsafe for courts to assume that the making of a hospital order coupled with a restrictive order under [the Mental Health Act] is sufficient by itself to ensure that the convicted person in respect of whom such orders are made will be kept in safe custody. As far as we can see, the only way in which that result can be achieved is for the court to ascertain first before making the order which mental hospital can receive the man, and that of course the court must do, and further than that to find out whether or not the mental hospital is one in which facilities exist for keeping patients in safe custody so that they will not have the opportunity to walk out and commit crime. There are such institutions, and if it be discovered that there is no vacancy in any institution in which the convicted person can be kept in safe custody, one must point out that the powers of the court to make a hospital order are permissive, not mandatory, and if the court thinks it necessary for the protection of the public that the accused man should be incarcerated, then the court should use its ordinary penal jurisdiction and order, if it thinks that a man needs medical treatment, that arrangements should be made in some place where he can be kept in safe custody and the kind of thing that happened in this case avoided.

Appeal dismissed.

NOTE 11

PAULSEN, MONRAD G.

Fairness to the Juvenile Offender*

A juvenile court judge may not make disposition of a child just because it seems like a good thing to do. The trial judge in *In re Coyle*[30] defended his adjudication by saying that "the court was simply making a determination as to whether or not the . . . appellant's future training, and the best interests of the State would be best served by taking him from his home and placing him where proper training was available." The appellate court did not agree. "Juvenile court procedure has not been so far socialized and individual rights so far diminished that a child may be taken from its parents and placed in a state institution simply because some court might think that to be in the best interests of the state. . . . Some specific act or conduct must be charged as constituting the delinquency and the truth of such charge must be determined in an adversary proceeding."

[U]nder the most frequently used provisions of juvenile court acts, a child comes within the power of the court if he violates any state law, federal law or municipal ordinance, if he is acting beyond the control of his parents, or if he is associating with persons probably leading him to a life of crime.

It can be seen that the statutes are very far ranging indeed. By these definitions, almost every child could be adjudicated a delinquent. What youngster grows up without violating a federal or state law, or a municipal ordinance? What child has not stolen an apple or filched a penny or played a harmful Halloween

prank? Yet the youngster is probably not more completely blanketed by the delinquency law than an adult by the criminal law. To some extent we are all law violators. Adults must rely on the good sense of law enforcement officers, prosecutors and judges. The prosecutor does not normally play the same sifting role in children's cases as he does in those concerning adults, so the young must depend upon good sense of intake services, and on the discretion of juvenile judges themselves, for protection from the tyranny of "over enforcement" of the law.

Some of the statutory language in juvenile court acts would be unconstitutionally vague if it were used as the basis for criminal prosecution. What does it mean to be "incorrigible," to "grow up in idleness or crime," to "so deport himself as to injure or endanger self or others," or "to engage in immoral or indecent conduct?" Without defending the specific formulations above against constitutional attack even in a juvenile case, we must admit that some juvenile cases do call for a *standard* rather than a single, specific law violation to measure the appropriateness of court intervention. There must be some way to deal with a boy of sixteen who spends a lot of his time visiting a home that has been turned into a school for sexual delinquency even though he himself did not participate.[37] If the treatment process is, in fact, rehabilitative and redemptive, it ought to be applied to cases in which the youngster's commission of an actual criminal act is just a matter of time. Fundamentally, any standard employed should suggest an inquiry into parental supervision and control. If that control is permitting criminality to develop or is seriously defective in other ways, the rest of us must take a hand. Unhappily, the standard cannot state with precision the circumstances under which the courts will act. Nevertheless, the only alternative would be to refrain from action which might salvage an obviously deteriorating life.

NOTE 12

ALLEN, FRANCIS A.

The Borderland of the Criminal Law: Problems of "Socializing" Criminal Justice*

*   *   *

It is important . . . to recognize that when, in an authoritative setting, we attempt to do something *for* a child "because of what he is and needs," we are also doing something *to* him. The semantics of "socialized justice" are a trap for the unwary. Whatever one's motivations, however elevated one's objectives, if the measures taken result in the com-

* 41 Minn. L. Rev. 547, 555 (1957). Reprinted with permission.

30 122 Ind. App. 217, 101 N.E.2d 192 (1951).

37. State v. Myers, 74 N.D. 297, 22 N.W.2d 199 (1946).

* 32 *Social Service Rev.* 107, 116–119 (1960). Reprinted with permission of The University of Chicago Press. Copyright 1958 by The University of Chicago.

pulsory loss of the child's liberty, the involuntary separation of a child from his family, or even the supervision of a child's activities by a probation worker, the impact on the affected individuals is essentially a punitive one. Good intentions and a flexible vocabulary do not alter this reality. This is particularly so when, as is often the case, the institution to which the child is committed is, in fact, a penal-custodial establishment. We shall escape much confusion here if we are willing to give candid recognition to the fact that the business of the juvenile court inevitably consists, to a considerable degree, in dispensing punishment. If this is true, we can no more avoid the problem of unjust punishment in the juvenile court than in the criminal court.

There is a second sort of confusion that stems from the distinction between doing something to and for a child. All too often it is forgotten that, for the purpose of determining what a child *is*, it may be highly important to know what he has actually done. For this reason, if for no other, we cannot afford to be careless in establishing the facts of his conduct. The point has broader application than to the procedures of the juvenile court. This interesting case is said to have occurred in California: A defendant was convicted of a sexual offense. Subsequently he was committed as a sexual psychopath following a psychiatric examination. In making their diagnosis the psychiatrists *assumed* that the defendant had committed the sexual act which provided the basis for the criminal conviction. The difficulty was that, as later established, the defendant had all along been the victim of misidentification. Thus, the mistake as to the facts not only resulted in an improper conviction but rendered invalid the psychiatric judgment of the defendant's personality and propensities. However advanced our techniques for determining what an individual *is*, we have not yet approached the point at which we may safely ignore what he has done. What he has done may often be the most revealing evidence of what he is.

NOTE 13

Supreme Court of the United States
KENT v. UNITED STATES
383 U.S. 541 (1966)

MR. JUSTICE FORTAS delivered the opinion of the Court.

* * *

The theory of the . . . Juvenile Court Act is rooted in social welfare philosophy rather than in the *corpus juris*. Its proceedings are designated as civil rather than criminal. The Juvenile Court is theoretically engaged in determining the needs of the child and of society rather than adjudicating criminal conduct. The objectives are to provide measures of guidance and rehabilitation for the child and protection for

society, not to fix criminal responsibility, guilt and punishment. The State is *parens patriae* rather than prosecuting attorney and judge. But the admonition to function in a "parental" relationship is not an invitation to procedural arbitrariness.

Because the State is supposed to proceed in respect of the child proceeding as *parens patriae* and not as adversary, courts have relied on the premise that the proceedings are "civil" in nature and not criminal, and have asserted that the child cannot complain of the deprivation of important rights available in criminal cases. It has been asserted that he can claim only the fundamental due process right to fair treatment. For example, it has been held that he is not entitled to bail; to indictment by grand jury; to a speedy and public trial; to trial by jury; to immunity against self-incrimination; to confrontation of his accusers; and in some jurisdictions that he is not entitled to counsel.

While there can be no doubt of the original laudable purpose of juvenile courts, studies and critiques in recent years raise serious questions as to whether actual performance measures, well enough against theoretical purpose to make tolerable the immunity of the process from the reach of constitutional guarantees applicable to adults. There is much evidence that some juvenile courts, including that of the District of Columbia, lack the personnel, facilities and techniques to perform adequately as representatives of the State in a *parens patriae* capacity, at least with respect to children charged with law violation. There is evidence, in fact, that there may be grounds for concern that the child receives the worst of both worlds: that he gets neither the protections accorded to adults nor the solicitous care and regenerative treatment postulated for children.

NOTE 14

STOUTENBURGH v. FRAZIER
16 D.C. App. 229 (1900)

MR. CHIEF JUSTICE ALLEY delivered the opinion of the Court.

* * *

By the information upon which the appellee was tried and convicted, . . . the appellee was charged in the police court, with being . . . *a suspicious person*, in and about the streets, avenues, alleys, roads and highways, to wit, Four-and-a-half street, southwest, contrary to and in violation of the act of Congress entitled "An act to amend for the preservation of the public peace and the protection of property in the District of Columbia," approved July 8, 1898.

* * *

. . . The suspicion of which he is the object is wholly undefined, and in no manner connected with any criminal act or conduct either of the past or that might occur in the future. By whom the suspicion is to be entertained does not appear,—whether it be by one policeman or by several, seems not to be regarded as material; or whether it be a suspicion entertained by one or more citizens is by no means certain. . . . General suspicion, without even reference to a propensity or intent to commit some particular crime or offense against the law or police of the Government, must be conceded to be wholly inoperative and without effect, as a definition of crime. Mere suspicion is no evidence of crime of any particular kind, and it forms no element in the constitution of crime. Suspicion may exist without even the knowledge of the party who is the object of the suspicion, as to the matter of which he is suspected. The suspicion may be generated in the mind of one or more persons without even colorable foundation of truth for the suspicion; and yet the party, the object of the suspicion, may, under the statute upon which the prosecution against the appellee was founded, be seized and imprisoned, tried and convicted, merely because some persons or police officer may have concluded (whether upon reasonable ground or not) that he was a *suspicious person*. Of what suspected? and what degree of suspicion exists? must always be the first thought that occurs upon such a charge as that made in this case. But here the party is charged, in an abstract way, of being a suspicious person merely; there being no act or conduct of his mentioned in the statute, to which the suspicion could relate. How is he to meet such charge? Suspicion, as a conception of the mind, is well defined as the imagination of the existence of something upon little or no evidence; doubt; mistrust; and so the adjective *suspicious*, descriptive of the quality or condition of a person, as well the party suspecting as the party suspected, is defined, as apt to imagine with little or no reason; distrustful; liable or open to suspicion; exciting suspicion; giving reasons or grounds to suspect or imagine ill.

*   *   *

. . . Under the Constitution of the United States, Articles IV and VIII of the Amendments, every person is intended to be secure in his person against unreasonable searches and seizures, and against cruel and unusual punishments; and it would clearly be a cruel and unnatural punishment to impose fine and imprisonment upon a party, because he might happen to be regarded by some persons as a *suspicious person*, without anything more.

NOTE 15

MOORE v. DRAPER
57 So.2d. 648 (Fla. Sup. Ct. 1952)

MATHEWS, JUSTICE.

The petitioner was confined in the Southwest Florida State Sanitarium at Tampa pursuant to a commitment issued by the County Judge of Dade County, under the provisions of Chapter 25241, Laws of 1949, . . .

The petitioner claims that the statute in question is unconstitutional and that his confinement thereunder is unlawful, a denial of due process of law . . .

*   *   *

Recent history of public health matters shows that tuberculosis was recognized as one of the most dreadful diseases and one of the greatest killers. The State has spent millions of dollars prior to 1949 in an attempt to minimize as far as possible the spread of this terrible disease. It had established a few hospitals and clinics and had carried on a program of detection, education, and advice. It was recognized that those afflicted with this disease were a menace to society. They walked the streets; went to public places such as theatres, hotels, and restaurants; they rode in common carriers; in their homes and other places they came in close contact with relatives and friends and the general public. They not only suffered themselves, but left disease, misery, sorrow, and death in their wake.

*   *   *

Vital statistics showed that tuberculosis was taking an awful toll. The death rate was startling. In 1949 it was recognized that the Legislature would probably levy sufficient taxes and appropriate sufficient money to erect suitable sanitaria where people suffering with tuberculosis could be confined and treated. This law was enacted by the Legislature in anticipation that sufficient facilities would be provided. The Cigarette Tax Law, F.S.A. § 210.01 *et seq.*, provided sufficient funds to carry on this work and some of the sanitaria have already been completed and others are nearing completion.

*   *   *

When the Petitioner feels that he has been cured or that his disease has been so arrested that he is not and will not be dangerous to others, the Courts of the State will be open to him and he should be afforded ample opportunity to obtain his release, if an examination, scientific tests, and other evidence justifies it.

*   *   *

NOTE 16

REX v. HALLIDAY
[1917] A.C. 260

LORD FINLAY, L.C.: My Lords, the appellant in this case is a naturalized British subject of German birth who has been interned by an order made by the Secretary of State under the powers of reg. 14B, which . . . is as follows:

"Where on the recommendation of a competent

naval or military authority or of one of the advisory committees hereinafter mentioned it appears to the Secretary of State that for securing the public safety or the defence of the realm it is expedient in view of the hostile origin or associations of any person that he shall be subjected to such obligations and restrictions as are hereinafter mentioned, the Secretary of State may by order require that person forthwith, or from time to time, either to remain in, or to proceed to and reside in, such place as may be specified in the order, and to comply with such directions as to reporting to the police, restriction of movement, and otherwise as may be specified in the order, or to be interned in such place as may be specified in the order.

* * *

The order complained of was made by the Home Secretary on October 15, 1915, and is as follows:

"Whereas, on the recommendation of a competent military authority . . . it appears to me that, for securing the public safety and the defence of the realm, it is expedient that Arthur Zadig . . . should, in view of his hostile origin and associations, be subjected to such obligations and restrictions as are hereinafter mentioned.

"I hereby order that the said Arthur Zadig shall be interned in the institution in Cornwallis Road, Islington, which is now used as a place of internment, and shall be subject to all the rules and conditions applicable to aliens there interned.

"If within seven days from the date on which this order is served on the said Arthur Zadig he shall submit to me any representations against the provisions of this order, such representations will be referred to the advisory committee appointed for the purpose of advising me with respect to the internment and deportation of aliens and presided over by a judge of the High Court, and will be duly considered by the committee. If I am satisfied by the report of the said committee that this order may be revoked or varied without injury to the public safety or the defence of the realm, I will revoke or vary the order by a further order in writing under my hand."

The truth of the recital that Zadig is a person of hostile origin and associations was not questioned, but it was insisted that Parliament had not conferred the power to make such an order in the interest of the public safety against such persons. . . .

* * *

The regulations are to be for preventive purposes as follows:

(*a*) The prevention of communication with the enemy or obtaining information for that purpose or any purpose calculated to jeopardize the operations of His Majesty's forces or those of his Allies or to assist the enemy;

(*b*) To secure the safety of His Majesty's forces and ships and the safety of any means of communication and of railways, ports, and harbours;

(*c*) To prevent the spread of false reports or reports likely to cause disaffection to His Majesty or to interfere with the success of His Majesty's forces or to prejudice His Majesty's relations with foreign Powers.

(*e*) Otherwise to prevent assistance being given to the enemy or the successful prosecution of the war being endangered.

One of the most obvious means of taking precautions against dangers such as are enumerated is to impose some restriction on the freedom of movement of persons whom there may be any reason to suspect of being disposed to help the enemy. It is to this that reg. 14B is directed. The measure is not punitive but precautionary. It was strongly urged that no such restraint should be imposed except as the result of a judicial inquiry, and indeed counsel for the appellant went so far as to contend that no regulation could be made forbidding access to the seashore by suspected persons. It seems obvious that no tribunal for investigating the question whether circumstances of suspicion exist warranting some restraint can be imagined less appropriate than a Court of law. No crime is charged. The question is whether there is ground for suspicion that a particular person may be disposed to help the enemy. The duty of deciding this question is by the order thrown upon the Secretary of State, and an advisory committee, presided over by a judge of the High Court, is provided to bring before him any grounds for thinking that the order may properly be revoked or varied.

The statute was passed at a time of supreme national danger, which still exists. The danger of espionage and of damage by secret agents to ships, railways, munition works, bridges, &c., had to be guarded against. The restraint imposed may be a necessary measure of precaution, and in the interests of the whole nation it may be regarded as expedient that such an order should be made in suitable cases.
. . .

* * *

LORD ATKINSON: Preventive justice, as it is styled, which consists in restraining a man from committing a crime he may commit but has not yet committed, or doing some act injurious to members of the community which he may do but has not yet done, is no new thing in the laws of England. . . . In the same way a dangerous lunatic may be committed to a lunatic asylum; if while at large, he might be a danger to the community. One of the most effective ways of preventing a man from communicating with the enemy . . . is to imprison or intern him. In that as in almost every case where preventive justice is put in force some suffering and inconvenience may be caused to the suspected person. That is inevitable. But the suffering is, under this statute, inflicted for something much more important than his liberty or convenience, namely, for securing the public safety and defence of the realm. . . .

. . . And as preventive justice proceeds upon the principle that a person should be restrained from doing something which, if free and unfettered, it is reasonably probable he would do, it must necessarily proceed in all cases, to some extent, on suspicion or anticipation as distinct from proof. . . .

* * *

LORD SHAW OF DUNFERMLINE. . . .

. . . The interpretation put upon this Government power to issue regulations for safety and defence is that of perfect generality. Is this generality limited? it was asked. Yes, replied the Crown; the limitations are two, and two only. In the first place, regulations can only be issued during the war—a limitation in time. In the second place, they can only be issued for the public safety and for the defence of the realm—a limitation of purpose. But who is to judge of that purpose? As to what acts of State are promotive or regardful of that purpose, can a Court of law arrest the hand of a responsible Executive? Extreme cases may be figured in which personal caprice and not public considerations might be imagined, but in everything, from the lighting of a room to the devastation of a province, no Court of law could dare to set up its judgment on the merits of an issue—a public and political issue—of safety or defence. So that this limitation, as a legal limitation, is illusory. . . .

[It is argued] that the provisions of the sub-section embrace two parts—namely, prevention and punishment; that these are two separate things; and that what has been done here is prevention and is not punishment. This last may sufficiently surprise those who are subjected to it; but "stone walls do not a prison make." Those interned are being cared for, watched over, prevented, not punished. Very different, and very properly different, from this was the view of Blackstone (Commentaries, i. 136): "The confinement of the person, in any wise, is an imprisonment. So that the keeping a man against his will in a private house, putting him in the stocks, arresting or forcibly detaining him in the street, is an imprisonment."

Further, my Lords, I am humbly of opinion that the attempted distinction fails; and that in no event could it have the slightest bearing upon the point of construction to be determined.

For it is when, and only when, the sub-section comes to categorize the heads and particulars of public safety and defence to which the regulations might be directed that the word "prevent" occurs. The regulations are for preventing certain things and for securing other things—for preventing (1.) communication with the enemy, (2.) spreading false reports, &c., and (3.) assisting the enemy; and for securing (1.) safety of forces, ships, railways, or har-

bours, (2.) navigation according to Admiralty direction. This is the distinction, if it be a distinction —namely, between preventing and securing. But, when punishment is dealt with, such a distinction no longer holds; and if there be disobedience to regulation upon all or any one of these heads and particulars, whether for preventing danger or securing safety, then punishment may follow. The statute is careful to prescribe punishment for all. Punishment is not distinguished from either preventing or securing; it applies to disobedience or offence under both the latter heads alike.

How then, I respectfully ask, how then can it be thought possible to construe the sub-section as meaning not only the grant of a power of prevention from doing certain things, which done shall be punishable, but the reserve of some other and super-eminent power of prevention, which is distinguished from punishment? There is no such reserve and no such distinction in the Act of Parliament. There might have been, but there is not; and the fact that this is so is a strong confirmation of the view that Parliament never intended the vesting of the Executive with arbitrary power, but gave power to set up a code of conduct and action and to reach the region of punishment when, and only when, that code was broken.

* * *

But does the principle, or does it not, embrace a power not over liberty alone but also over life? If the public safety and defence warrant the Government under the Act to incarcerate a citizen without trial, do they stop at that, or do they warrant his execution without trial? If there is a power to lock up a person of hostile origin and associations because the Government judges that course to be for public safety and defence, why, on the same principle and in exercise of the same power, may he not be shot out of hand? I put the point to the learned Attorney-General, and obtained from him no further answer than that the graver result seemed to be perfectly logical. I think it is. The cases are by no means hard to figure in which a Government in a time of unrest, and moved by a sense of duty, assisted, it may be, by a gust of popular fury, might issue a regulation applying, as here, to persons of hostile origin or association, saying, "Let such danger really be ended and done with; let such suspects be shot." The defence would be, I humbly think, exactly that principle, and no other, on which the judgments of the Courts below are founded—namely, that during the war this power to issue regulations is so vast that it covers all acts which, though they subvert the ordinary fundamental and constitutional rights, are in the Government's view directed towards the general aim of public safety or defence.

Under this the Government becomes a Committee of Public Safety. But its powers as such are far more arbitrary than those of the most famous Committee of Public Safety known to history. It preserved a form of trial, of evidence, of interrogations. And the very homage which it paid to law discovered the odium of its procedure to the world. But the so-called principle —the principle of prevention, the comprehensive principle—avoids the odium of that brutality of the Terror. The analogy is with a practice, more silent, more sinister—with the *lettres de cachet* of Louis Quatorze. No trial: proscription. The victim may be "regulated"—not in his course of conduct or of action, not as to what he should do or avoid doing. He may be regulated to prison or the scaffold. Suppose the appellant had been appointed for execution. Public outcry, public passion, public pity—these I can conceive; but I cannot conceive one argument upon the legal construction of this Act of Parliament that would have been different from the one which is now affirmed by Courts of law. It is this last matter with which these are concerned. In my humble opinion the construction is unsound. I think that if Parliament had intended to make this colossal delegation of power it would have done so plainly and courageously and not under cover of words about regulations for safety and defence. The expansions of such language into the inclusion of such a power appear to me to be unwarrantably strained.

The use of the Government itself as a Committee of Public Safety has its convenience, has its advantages. So had the Star Chamber. "The Star Chamber," says Maitland (Constitutional History of England, p. 263), "examining the accused, and making no use of the jury, probably succeeded in punishing many crimes which would otherwise have gone unpunished. But that it was a tyrannical court, that it became more and more tyrannical, and under Charles I. was guilty of great infamies, is still more indubitable." And then occur his memorable words: "It was a court of politicians enforcing a policy, not a court of judges administering the law."

There is the basic danger. And may I further emphatically observe that that danger is found in an especial degree whenever the law is not the same for all, but the selection of the victim is left to the plenary discretion whether of a tyrant, a committee, a bureaucracy or any other depository of despotic power. Whoever administers it, this power of selection of a class, and power of selection within a class is the negation of public safety or defence. It is poison to the commonwealth.

For within the range even of one regulation—say to affect "persons of hostile origin or association"—no one can say where the axe will fall. That description applies in all ranks and classes of society. That is why I feel constrained to dissent respectfully from the suggestion that in administering this power over liberty we ought to trust the Government. . . .

And once you have abandoned the line of safety which I have sketched—namely, confining regulations to rules of conduct to be obeyed with safety or punished after trial for the breach—once that is abandoned, how far may you not go? Once a discretion over all things and persons and rights and liberties, so as to secure public safety and defence, what regulations may issue? This one is founded on "hostile origin or associations." It enters the sphere of suspicion, founded not on conduct but on presumed opinions, beliefs, motives, or prepossessions arising from the land from which a person sprang. This is dangerous country; it has its dark reminders. It is the proscription, the arrest of suspects, at the will of men in power vested with a plenary discretion. If the power to issue regulations meant thus to warrant a passage from proof to suspicion and from the sphere of action to the sphere of motive or the mind, let us think how much this involves.

* * *

. . . I think that the judgment of the Courts below is erroneous, and is fraught with grave legal and constitutional danger. In my opinion the appeal should be allowed, the regulation challenged should be declared ultra vires, and the appellant should be set at liberty.

LORD WRENBURY. . . .

* * *

The appellant's counsel argue that an authority "to issue regulations for securing the public safety and the defence of the realm" does not authorize preventive detention, which is, they say, imprisonment without trial. They contend that there must be express words where the liberty of the subject is to be affected; that the general words of this statute are not enough. My Lords, I find no ground upon which this contention can be supported. For instance, the statute says in so many words that a regulation may prevent persons communicating with the enemy. What is the man to be tried for before he is so prevented? The very purpose is not to punish him for having done something, but to intercept him before he does it and to prevent him from doing it. What limit does the statute place upon the steps that may be taken so to prevent him? There is no limit. No doubt every statutory authority must be exercised honestly. There is, I conceive no other limit upon the acts that the regulations may authorize to achieve the defined object.

NOTE 17

EX PARTE ENDO
323 U.S. 283 (1944)

MR. JUSTICE DOUGLAS delivered the opinion of the Court.

* * *

Mitsuye Endo, hereinafter designated as the appellant, is an American citizen of Japanese ancestry. She was evacuated from Sacramento, California, in 1942, pursuant to certain military orders . . . and was removed to the Tule Lake War Relocation Center located at Newell, Modoc County, California. In July, 1942, she filed a petition for a writ of habeas corpus in the District Court of the United States for the Northern District of California, asking that she be discharged and restored to liberty. That petition was denied. . . .

The history of the evacuation of Japanese aliens and citizens of Japanese ancestry from the Pacific coastal regions, following the Japanese attack on our Naval Base at Pearl Harbor on December 7, 1941, and the declaration of war against Japan on December 8, 1941 . . . has been reviewed in *Hirabayashi* v. *United States*, 320 U.S. 81. . . .

*   *   *

A citizen who is concededly loyal presents no problem of espionage or sabotage. Loyalty is a matter of the heart and mind, not of race, creed, or color. He who is loyal is by definition not a spy or a saboteur. When the power to detain is derived from the power to protect the war effort against espionage and sabotage, detention which has no relationship to that objective is unauthorized.

Nor may the power to detain an admittedly loyal citizen or to grant him a conditional release be implied as a useful or convenient step in the evacuation program, whatever authority might be implied in case of those whose loyalty was not conceded or established. If we assume (as we do) that the original evacuation was justified, its lawful character was derived from the fact that it was an espionage and sabotage measure, not that there was community hostility to this group of American citizens. The evacuation program rested explicitly on the former ground not on the latter as the underlying legislation shows. The authority to detain a citizen or to grant him a conditional release as protection against espionage or sabotage is exhausted at least when his loyalty is conceded. If we held that the authority to detain continued thereafter, we would transform an espionage or sabotage measure into something else. . . . Detention which furthered the campaign against espionage and sabotage would be one thing. But detention which has no relationship to that campaign is of a distinct character. [We will not] assume that the Congress and the President intended that this discriminatory action should be taken against these wholly on account of their ancestry even though the government conceded their loyalty to this country. . . .

Mitsuye Endo is entitled to an unconditional release by the War Relocation Authority.

*   *   *

NOTE 18

ROSTOW, EUGENE V.

The Japanese American Cases—a Disaster*

*   *   *

Much was made in the Japanese American cases of the analogy of temporary preventive arrest or other restriction, approved for material witnesses, the protection of the public at fires, the detention of typhoid carriers, mentally ill persons, and so on. The analogy has little or no application to the problems presented in these cases, except perhaps for the curfew or conceivably the abstract issue of exclusion, as distinguished from detention. The restrictions involved here were not temporary emergency measures, justified by the breakdown of more orderly facilities for protecting society against espionage and sabotage. . . .

*   *   *

NOTE 19

INTERNAL SECURITY ACT,
50 U.S. C.A. (1959)

§ 811. Congressional finding of necessity.

As a result of evidence adduced before various committees of the Senate and the House of Representatives, the Congress finds that—

(1) There exists a world Communist movement which in its origins, its development, and its present practice, is a world-wide revolutionary movement whose purpose it is, by treachery, deceit, infiltration into other groups (governmental and otherwise), espionage, sabotage, terrorism, and any other means deemed necessary, to establish a Communist totalitarian dictatorship in all the countries of the world through the medium of a world-wide Communist organization.

*   *   *

(9) The agents of communism have devised clever and ruthless espionage and sabotage tactics which are carried out in many instances in form or manner successfully evasive of existing law, and which in this country are directed against the safety and peace of the United States.

(10) The experience of many countries in World War II and thereafter with so-called "fifth columns" which employed espionage and sabotage to weaken the internal security and defense of nations resisting totalitarian dictatorships demonstrated the grave dangers and fatal effectiveness of such internal espionage and sabotage.

* Reprinted by permission of the Yale Law Journal Co. and Fred B. Rothman & Co. from the *Yale Law Journal*, Vol. 54, p. 528.

(11) The security and safety of the territory and Constitution of the United States, and the successful prosecution of the common defense, especially in time of invasion, war, or insurrection in aid of a foreign enemy, require every reasonable and lawful protection against espionage, and against sabotage to national-defense material, premises, forces and utilities, including related facilities for mining, manufacturing, transportation, research, training, military and civilian supply, and other activities essential to national defense.

(12) Due to the wide distribution and complex interrelation of facilities which are essential to national defense and due to the increased effectiveness and technical development in espionage and sabotage activities, the free and unrestrained movement in such emergencies of members or agents of such organizations and of others associated in their espionage and sabotage operations would make adequate surveillance to prevent espionage and sabotage impossible and would therefore constitute a clear and present danger to the public peace and the safety of the United States.

* * *

(14) The detention of persons who there is reasonable ground to believe probably will commit or conspire with others to commit espionage or sabotage is, in a time of internal security emergency, essential to the common defense and to the safety and security of the territory, the people and the Constitution of the United States.

(15) It is also essential that such detention in an emergency involving the internal security of the Nation shall be so authorized, executed, restricted and reviewed as to prevent any interference with the constitutional rights and privileges of any persons, and at the same time shall be sufficiently effective to permit the performance by the Congress and the President of their constitutional duties to provide for the common defense, to wage war, and to preserve, protect and defend the Constitution, the Government and the people of the United States.

* * *

§ 812. **Declaration of "internal security emergency" by President; events warranting; period of existence.**

(a) In the event of any one of the following:

(1) Invasion of the territory of the United States or its possessions,

(2) Declaration of war by Congress, or

(3) Insurrection within the United States in aid of a foreign enemy,

and if, upon the occurrence of one or more of the above, the President shall find that the proclamation of an emergency pursuant to this section is essential to the preservation, protection and defense of the Constitution, and to the common defense and safety of the territory and people of the United States, the President is authorized to make public proclamation of the existence of an "Internal Security Emergency."

* * *

§ 813. **Detention during emergency; release.**

(a) Whenever there shall be in existence such an emergency, the President, acting through the Attorney General, is authorized to apprehend and by order detain, pursuant to the provisions of this subchapter, each person as to whom there is reasonable ground to believe that such person probably will engage in, or probably will conspire with others to engage in, acts of espionage or of sabotage.

* * *

§ 814. **(g)** . . .

No . . . regulation shall require or permit persons detained under the provisions of this subchapter to perform forced labor, or any tasks not reasonably associated with their own comfort and well-being, or to be confined in company with persons who are confined pursuant to the criminal laws of the United States or of any State.

* * *

§ 819. **(h) Evidentiary matters considered in deciding questions as to security risks.**

In deciding the question of the existence of reasonable ground to believe a person probably will engage in or conspire with others to engage in espionage or sabotage, the Attorney General, any preliminary hearing officer, and the Board of Detention Review are authorized to consider evidence of the following:

(1) Whether such person has knowledge of or has received or given instruction or assignment in the espionage, counterespionage, or sabotage service or procedures of a government or political party of a foreign country, or in the espionage, counterespionage, or sabotage service or procedures of the Communist Party of the United States or of any other organization or political party which seeks to overthrow or destroy by force and violence the Government of the United States. . . .

(2) Any past act or acts of espionage or sabotage committed by such person, or any past participation by such person in any attempt or conspiracy to commit any act of espionage or sabotage, against the United States . . .

(3) Activity in the espionage or sabotage operations of, or the holding at any time after January 1, 1949, of membership in, the Communist Party of the United States or any other organization or political party which seeks to overthrow or destroy by force and violence the Government of the United States or of any of its political subdivisions and the substitu-

tion therefor of a totalitarian dictatorship controlled by a foreign government.

(i) Necessity for reasonable ground for belief.

The authorization of the Attorney General and the Board of Detention Review to consider the evidence set forth in subsection (h) of this section shall not be construed as a direction to detain any person as to whom such evidence exists, but in each case the Attorney General or the Board of Detention Review shall decide whether, on all the evidence, there is reasonable ground to believe the detainee or possible detainee probably will engage in, or conspire with others to engage in, espionage or sabotage.

b.   LAKE v. CAMERON

[*i*]

331 F. 2d 771 (D.C. Cir. 1964)

PER CURIAM.

On October 11, 1962, appellant filed in the District Court an omnibus pleading—styled "Petition for a Writ of Habeas Corpus and Also a Writ of Prohibition"—naming as respondents the Superintendent of the District of Columbia General Hospital . . .

. . . When, as here, a petition for a writ of habeas corpus alleges an unlawful deprivation of liberty, the "judge entertaining an application for a writ . . . *shall forthwith* award the writ or issue an order directing the respondent to show cause why the writ should not be granted." 28 U.S.C. § 2243. . . . "The appropriate procedure in these circumstances is to require a return from the appellee, hold a hearing and thereafter make findings or file a memorandum adequate for appellate review." *Smith* v. *Anderson*, 115 U.S. App. D.C. 109, 317 F.2d 172 (1963). Since this required procedure was not followed here, the judgment below must be reversed and the case remanded to the District Court for further proceedings. And in the circumstances of this case we think it would be appropriate for the District Court to appoint counsel to assist the petitioner in such proceedings.

* * *

WILBUR K. MILLER, CIRCUIT JUDGE (dissenting).

The appellant's brief is incoherent to the point that it is plainly the work of a disturbed mentality. I do not think it presents a case worthy of consideration.

[*ii*]

From Transcript of Habeas Corpus Proceedings

* * *

ETHEL H. FRIEDMAN

a witness called by counsel for the Government, having been first duly sworn, was examined and testified as follows:

DIRECT EXAMINATION BY MR. JONES:

Q. [Y]ou are a physician at St. Elizabeths? A. I am on the staff of St. Elizabeths Hospital.

Q. Do you know the petitioner here, Mrs. Catherine Lake? A. I do.

Q. And has she been under your treatment as a patient? A. Yes, she has.

Q. For how long a period of time? A. About eleven months, I believe since May, 1963.

* * *

Q. Based on your own observations and also on the records to which you have had access, do you have a medical conclusion as to whether [Mrs. Lake] suffers from mental disease or defect? A. Yes . . . Her diagnosis is chronic brain syndrome, with arteriosclerosis . . .

Q. How does that manifest itself in Mrs. Lake's actions? A. Well, for probably a number of years, surely for the time she has been at St. Elizabeths Hospital, she has shown memory defect for remote and recent events. This memory defect varies, as it does frequently in this condition.

Q. Yes. A. For instance, she was unable to give me the date of the death of her sister, the date of the death of her son. She believed that her son died over in Normandy in 1947, when actually he died many years later at St. Elizabeths Hospital.

Then she could not give me the date of her husband's—nor when she was married for the second time. She is not sure when she came to St. Elizabeths Hospital, she thinks maybe a few months. She cannot give dates.

In addition, she has a general paranoid trend in that she feels that police officers have been following her, and together with various bureaus, as she talks about, Veterans Administration, Women's Bureaus, and others, have sort of worked together to keep her from having this, that she has this grievance and has been constantly going to the various Bureaus to get the money back.

She is not sure when this pension was stopped. She feels, also, her neighbors must have talked about her with the Police Officers and influenced each other against her.

She is given to wandering away, and evidently this happened a number of times before she was hospitalized this time. She was hospitalized in 1956 at the D.C. General and again in 1959 for apparently similar reasons.

When she was taken to D.C. General Hospital in 1962 according to the medical certificate she had been wandering the streets and had been preoccupied with getting her pension back.

When she came to the hospital, she was confused

and had poor memory and she was agitated for some time. But gradually, with treatment and medication, she became very comfortable.

Mrs. Lake was doing very nicely at the hospital, in a protective environment of the hospital, with all the assistance that she had been getting.

She actually is quite comfortable here. She has shown us this tendency of wandering away, too. She has wandered away a few times, and on one occasion, she wandered away and was missing for about 32 hours or a little more. She was away overnight, and the next day and the next evening, after midnight, when she was brought back by an officer who had found her wandering in the streets not too far from the hospital —when she was brought back, she thought she had been away just a few hours.

She could not give any information as to where she had been. She had a minor injury which she said was caused by someone being after her—some boys had been after her and caused the injury, a fall or something.

*　*　*

[When] she came to the hospital, [she] was poorly nourished and was anemic, and with all of the amount of care and medical attention, she improved a great deal. She has gained 65 pounds during the time she has been in the hospital, so that she is now overweight. And it is not good for her health, so she has been on a diet. . . .

*　*　*

Q. Now, doctor, . . . do you feel in her condition that she could re-enter the community, considering her medical and physical . . . needs? A. From my observation, I feel she needs considerable attention, that she needs help, that she surely could not take care of herself in the community; that she needs supervision.

*　*　*

Q. And does she create any physical danger to others? A. No, she does not.

Q. And she doesn't create any physical danger to herself either, then does she? A. The only danger is her exposure in wandering away and being out exposed at night or any time that she is out.

For instance, as I mentioned about her being away this period of time, she came back hungry and disheveled and evidently helpless. She was not able to find her way to her sister or husband during that period. Yet she could have, if she wanted to, if she could have known how.

Q. She would not do any harm to anyone intentionally or otherwise? A. No, she would not.

Q. Likewise she would not do herself intentional harm? A. No, she would not.

*　*　*

THE COURT: Doctor, as the Court understands from you, if there were facilities to properly provide for Mrs. Lake, so far as the wandering about is concerned, and also the medical attention, that she would be no problem to anyone?

THE WITNESS: No, if she has this supervision, she would be no problem.

THE COURT: You would have no objection?

THE WITNESS: No, if she were in a nursing home, or a place where there would be supervision.

*　*　*

[iii]

Opinion of The United States Court of Appeals—April 1, 1965

. . . Appellant was a patient in St. Elizabeths Hospital. The court found, on sufficient evidence, that "the petitioner is suffering from a mental illness with the diagnosis of chronic brain syndrome associated with cerebral arteriosclerosis"; that she "is in need of care and supervision, and that there is no member of the family able to give the petitioner the necessary care and supervision; and that the family is without sufficient funds to employ a competent person to do so"; that she "is a danger to herself in that she has a tendency to wander about the streets, and is not competent to care for herself." The court dismissed the petition "without prejudice to . . . [filing] a new petition at a time when the family of the petitioner is able to provide for her care and custody."

The District of Columbia Hospitalization of the Mentally Ill Act . . . provides for involuntary hospitalization of a person who "is mentally ill and, because of that illness, is likely to injure himself or others if allowed to remain at liberty." § 21–356(f); cf. § 21–357. The term "injure" in this context is not to be construed narrowly. Unless so construed, it applies to unintentional as well as to intentional injuries.

Affirmed.

[iv]

Order of The United States Court of Appeals— October 12, 1965

On consideration of appellant's petition for re-hearing *en banc*, it is

ORDERED by the court *en banc* that . . . the judgment and opinion entered herein on April 1, 1965, are vacated.

The court requests that within forty (40) days from the date of this order additional briefs be filed directed but not limited to the following issues:

1. The statutory commitment standards contained in the 1964 District of Columbia Hospitalization of the Mentally Ill Act and, in particular,

(a) whether the phrase "is likely to injure himself" should be interpreted to require a *substantial* likelihood of *imminent* injury;

(b) whether there is an additional implied prerequisite that one who is found "likely to injure himself" also be found to lack capacity to choose between the risks of freedom and the safety of hospitalization.

2. Whether there was adequate support in the record for the finding that petitioner is "likely to injure [her] self."

3. Even if petitioner may be involuntarily confined pursuant to the statutory standards, is her commitment to a mental hospital authorized? Is the District Court required to explore other community resources as an alternative to confinement in a mental hospital?

4. Is the District Court required to make explicit findings or otherwise articulate its reasons for concluding that commitment to a particular mental hospital is necessary where that institution has facilities for the custodial care required? What is the scope of the District Court's discretion and what is the scope of appellate review of the District Court's determination?

5. Is hospitalization in a mental hospital pursuant to civil commitment for mental illness restricted to those who need psychiatric care? Is it proper to confine in a mental hospital a person who does not need or cannot benefit by psychiatric care but who does suffer from mental infirmity and is likely to injure himself or expose himself to injury if no other, more appropriate public facilities are available?

6. Does it violate the constitutional command of equal protection of the laws to commit to a mental hospital a person who would be released into the care of his family if his family was financially able to provide adequate care and custody suitable to the particular form of mental condition involved?

The Clerk is directed to schedule this case for reargument before the court *en banc* on a day as soon after the briefs have been filed as the business of the court will permit.

Per Curiam.

NOTES

NOTE 1

WARNER, SILAS L., FLEMING, BURT, and BULLOCK, SAMUEL

The Philadelphia Program for Home Psychiatric Evaluations, Precare, and Involuntary Hospitalization*

*   *   *

Formerly, the decision to hospitalize a psychiatric patient was made by the clinical directors of the two public psychiatric hospitals serving Philadelphia. There was no uniform policy for admission and the directors were subject to pressures and bombarded

*52 *Am. J. Public Health*, pp. 29–36. Copyright 1962, by The American Public Health Association, Inc. Reprinted by permission.

by phone calls from well-meaning general practioners, city councilmen, clergymen, and others representing patients, constituents, parishioners, and friends who, for various reasons, wanted to hospitalize alleged psychiatric patients. When these patients were seen, some proved to be mentally ill; others, however, proved to have transient emotional upsets, or were mainly incompatible with members of their families. To standardize admission policy and to provide statistical control, the Commonwealth Mental Health Reception Center was created in 1957. The center has a staff of psychiatrists, psychiatric social workers, and psychologists, 25 overnight psychiatric beds, and has become the central funnel through which are screened all public psychiatric admissions in Philadelphia.

*   *   *

Four years of experience with psychiatric home evaluations have indicated to us certain special well defined community problems and needs. Many cases we see fall into one of the categories to be discussed, or exemplify certain typical problems we regularly encounter.

The Aged Patient

The problem of the aged psychiatric patient has many facets. From the psychiatric hospital's standpoint, there is a disinclination to fill too many hospital beds with aged patients, so their priority for admission is very low. Only custodial care has been available for most of the hospitalized aged patients, because by the time hospitalization is considered their condition has become chronic with increasingly severe organic brain changes. In addition, there are so many economic, medical, and social problems which create loneliness, malnutrition, chronic physical disability, and poverty that it is often hard to judge how much of the problem is primarily psychiatric and how much is secondary due to neglect in other areas. If possible, the Division of Mental Health tries to correct the patient's nonpsychiatric problems through other agencies and improve his mental status so hospitalization will not be necessary. . . .

A typical example of the aged patient whose problems stem from psychiatric illness is that of Mrs. T. G., a 72-year-old widow living alone on money received from several small trust funds. Help for her was requested by her landlady who felt Mrs. G.'s living habits were dangerous to her health and that her eccentric behavior with money might cause her to lose the little she had. For instance, Mrs. G. would take a fancy to a delivery boy, or a cab driver, or even a perfect stranger and hand him anywhere from a few to $50, seemingly on impulse and apparently limited only by the amount she had on hand.

When evaluated in her third-floor apartment, Mrs. G. was quite spry and loquacious, but rather suspicious of the nature of the visit. She lived in a state of filth with bundles of clothing scattered about. The furniture was ragged and disarranged and collections of bottles, empty food containers, assortments of trinkets, pictures, and letters were arrayed in her several small rooms as if it were necessary for her to have visible and available all the objects which now comprised her constricting world. The gas stove was lit although the burners were empty and a pile of clothing on an adjacent table was dangerously close. The rooms were dark and musty, the windows tightly sealed, although the weather outside was warm and clear. Mrs. G. wandered freely in her mental productions from the present to the past, often confusing the two, and was obviously disoriented in respect to her own position in time. She seemed to feel that her husband was still alive and would walk through the door momentarily—an obvious and pitiful attempt to cling to the security of the past. Her body was emaciated and evidently unbathed for weeks, possibly months or years. At times, Mrs. G. was paranoid toward her landlady or the officer who administered her trust fund and she voiced resentment of their interference in her affairs.

[I]t was evident that this elderly woman's existence was both disturbing to those around her and hazardous to her. The likelihood of a steady decline in her strength and general physical condition, due to grossly inadequate attention to her health and nutrition, was less immediate than the dangers of an accidental fall or fire, although no less certain in its disastrous outcome for her. This is not to mention her careless dissipation of the meager funds which were supposed to provide for her welfare. Prompt arrangements for her hospitalization were made. . . .

The Division of Mental Health has established an Adult Health and Recreation Center in Philadelphia to try to prevent the ever-increasing problem of the needy, neglected, aged patient who, if his condition is allowed to continue, may ultimately need psychiatric hospitalization. It provides psychiatric, medical, casework, vocational, and other services for the ambulatory older person before chronic and irreversible personality changes occur. If the patient mentioned above had had such a center available earlier in life, her later personality and physical deterioration might well have been prevented. There is not always a good correlation between organic brain changes and personality alteration; on autopsy some of the most psychotic aged patients have the least brain pathology and vice versa. Consequently, it would appear that the social milieu and psychological atmosphere play an important part in preventing psychiatric conditions in the aged.

The "Slow Suicides"

Another problem we run into occasionally in home evaluations is the nonpsychotic person who does not

care to live and refuses to go into the hospital. If the patient is obviously depressed, or if the family is cooperative, involuntary hospitalization can be arranged. If the family is unavailable or unwilling to hospitalize a patient, however, and the patient is adamant in his refusal to be hospitalized, an impasse is created. It raises the question of an individual's rights and self-determination as opposed to a government agency's power to force a probable lifesaving procedure upon him against his will.

One such situation involved a family in which the oldest daughter, a woman 37 years of age, lived at home with her mother and grandmother, had been in bed for seven months, and was refusing most food. The referral to our agency had been made by one of two younger sisters, both of whom were married and out of the home. The sister described a lifelong situation of excessive control and rejection of the patient by the mother. The patient had been unsuccessful in her attempts to become independent, which represented defiance of her mother's wishes.

On a home visit, a central portion of the family pathology was clearly shown. The patient was severely emaciated and malnourished, having lost weight from 115 to 70 pounds, and appeared to be in a terminal state. When the psychiatrist attempted to interview her, the mother and grandmother, who refused to leave the room, would answer the questions in unison. The mother declared, "After all, I am her mother and have a right to know how she feels." The patient was extremely angry at her mother and grandmother and stated, "I have taken care of them both all my life; now they can take care of me." She saw her inability to eat as just "nerves," and was convinced that she would soon be well. Although the seriousness of the patient's situation was clearly explained to her, she refused hospitalization. When the mother and grandmother were told that the patient would die if she did not receive medical care, their reponse was, "Well, if she doesn't want to go to the hospital or to see a doctor, there is nothing we can do." Four days after this home visit, the patient died. The autopsy findings showed only malnutrition.

We did not feel we could label this patient psychotic and remove her from the home against her wishes or against those of her relatives in the home.

Another case, which recently had an unhappy ending, illustrates more of these problems. L. E. was an attractive woman of 40 who lived with her parents. She had worked as a bacteriologist in a local hospital but quit because of "personality incompatibilities." She was unable to get another job because of increased hostility towards her parents and the outside world, and because she did not try wholeheartedly, since she felt her parents "owed her a living." She had diabetes and had an uncanny ability to "have it go out of control" at crucial times in her life so that she remained angrily unemployed and financially dependent on her parents. It was apparent, dynamically, that she was expressing her hostility to her parents by being dependent on them and by constantly complaining that they did not do enough for her. The father made the original referral to us and wanted to "put her in the hospital because she's ruining our lives."

A home psychiatric evaluation of L. E. showed her to be livid with rage toward her parents and unable to be objective in this area, but to be in good mental and emotional health in all other areas. There was an encapsulated paranoid type of thinking toward her parents, but her overall evaluation revealed no need for involuntary psychiatric hospitalization. She was unwilling to go voluntarily into a psychiatric hospital and it was hoped that the situation could be modified by interviews with her and her parents. A few interviews were held but there was no improvement in their relationships as both sides tended to blame everything on the other. L. E. was offered out-patient psychotherapy but would not accept it. Instead, she preferred to phone the evaluating psychiatrist at all hours during the week chiefly to complain to him about her parents. The case was periodically re-evaluated but it was felt that all parties concerned were sane, competent, and responsible and that it was essentially a domestic problem between parents and daughter. All of this was repeatedly explained to them but no change in attitude resulted.

The unfortunate ending occurred in August, 1960 (during the evaluating psychiatrist's vacation), when L. E. apparently went into a diabetic coma while smoking a cigarette and set fire to her room and was burned to death. Although this may not have been conscious and deliberate on her part, it seemed obvious that the neglect involved in this situation both by L. E. and her parents, plus L. E.'s desire to "make her parents pay for her misery," found its solution in what amounted to a suicidal act. It was speculated that, unconsciously, she felt martyred and exonerated by killing herself, whereas she hoped her parents would have to suffer with guilt over her death for the rest of their lives.

We asked ourselves after this tragic ending what we could have done to prevent it. One obvious answer would be to have put L. E. into a psychiatric hospital involuntarily. We are, however, only too aware of our responsibility both to society and to the individual. So that hospitalization never becomes a maneuver of convenience to the family, or a manifestation of our "superior wisdom," we have to guard preciously our right to incarcerate a person against his will—and then only when careful clinical study points up mental illness which requires such treatment. In another way, we are saying: If a person is legally sane, competent, and responsible he has a right to determine what he will do with his life. It is a difficult clinical problem to decide when our intervention is essential

and we try to keep re-evaluating cases to decide this. We also try to remind ourselves that for every such tragic ending there are probably dozens of cases which stay in the community successfully.

*   *   *

NOTE 2

CAPLAN, GERALD

Principles of Preventive Psychiatry*

*   *   *

[P]rimary prevention of mental disorders [includes] individual-focused methods to ensure that persons in crisis choose effective, reality-based ways of handling their crisis tasks so that they emerge from the period of upset with a lowered vulnerability to mental disorder. The mental health worker may achieve this goal in two main ways: (1) by intervening directly in the lives of individuals and their families during crisis and (2) by personal contact with care-giving professionals who in turn intervene in the crisis situations.

Direct Intervention by the Mental Health Specialist. In this type of preventive activity, the psychiatrist or one of his specialist colleagues gains access to a population of individuals in crisis, such as may be found in a prenatal clinic, a surgical ward, a divorce court, or a group of freshman students who have just come to college. He screens this population in order to identify those who seem to be having special difficulty dealing with the crisis or who show signs of beginning to choose such maladaptive and maladjustive coping responses as evasion of the crisis tasks, lack of activity in exploring the crisis situation, inability to express and to master negative feelings in consonance with the stress, or difficulty in obtaining help from others in handling feelings and in dealing with the crisis tasks. He identifies these cases himself by his observations of crisis behavior, or he communicates a knowledge of the signs of poor coping to the care-giving professionals, who are in a position to make the observations as part of their regular work. The psychiatrist makes contact with those who show maladaptive signs while the crisis is still in progress. He offers his help, which is likely to be acceptable at this stage of disequilibrium. Then, either on an individual or small-group basis, he influences those in crisis to choose healthy coping responses. He does this by enlarging their understanding of the situation; by supporting them in expressing their negative feelings; by pointing out avenues for useful exploration; by helping them to see what is happening in a reality-based frame of reference so that they can

* Reprinted by permission from *Principles of Preventive Psychiatry* by Gerald Caplan, copyright 1964 by Basic Books, Inc., Publishers, New York (pp. 82–84).

regain hope of influencing the outcome by their efforts; and by opening channels of communication to other helping figures among their relatives, friends, and professional care-givers. The psychiatrist supplements his assistance to the individual in crisis by discussing the problem with family, friends, and professionals; and he influences these to support the individual in the utilization of healthy coping responses.

*   *   *

Such an approach has proved effective when the mental health specialist has been able to gain ready access to people while they are experiencing their crises, which means that he must earlier have built collaborative relationships with the care-giving professionals with whom they are in regular contact. His intervention must be guided by specific knowledge of the particular crisis. This knowledge is derived from systematic studies which define the regularly occurring psychological tasks involved in the crisis, the signs of poor coping or poor accomplishment of these tasks, and the alternative healthy patterns of dealing with the crisis. The mental health specialist identifies those people whose behavior indicates that they are beginning to use ineffective coping methods, and he helps them work out more effective ways of dealing with the crisis.

*   *   *

This technique of preventive intervention by the mental health specialist during the crisis can be supplemented by a technique known as "anticipatory guidance," or "emotional inoculation." The preventive psychiatrist gains access to a population which he has reason to believe will shortly be exposed to hazardous circumstances that will provoke crisis in a significant proportion, such as a group of patients awaiting elective surgery, a group of children awaiting admission to kindergarten or college, a group of pregnant women before labor, or a group of Peace Corps volunteers preparing to go overseas. In small-group or individual discussions, the specialist then draws their attention to the details of the impending hazards and attempts to evoke ahead of time a vivid anticipation of the experience, with its associated feelings of anxiety, tension, depression, and deprivation. He then helps them begin to envisage possible ways of solving the problems, including mastery of their negative feelings. When the experience itself arrives, the hazards will be attenuated because they have been made familiar by being anticipated, and the individuals will already have been set on the path of healthy coping responses.

*   *   *

Just as with preventive intervention, anticipatory guidance can be more potent if the program is not restricted to the individuals awaiting crisis, but is also directed to their relatives, friends, and supporters who will help them when they are in need. . . .

However economical preventive intervention and anticipatory guidance may be, they do demand a good deal of specialist time and effort, and their community effect is therefore necessarily restricted. A preventive program which aims at community-wide coverage would therefore place considerable emphasis on achieving similar results through the efforts of professional care-givers, who will in any case be on the spot when their clients are in crisis.

In such a program, the knowledge and skills of the mental health specialists would be used to (1) study crises of various types and derive the necessary information about good and bad coping patterns and about how to influence people to cope more effectively, (2) communicate this knowledge to care-givers so that they could incorporate techniques of crisis intervention into their day-to-day functioning, and (3) support and "backstop" the care-giving professionals when they run into difficulties from time to time in carrying out this preventive work.

*   *   *

NOTE 3

California Welfare and Institutions Code: Mentally Ill Persons (1965)

§ 5567. If, after examination and certificate have been made, the judge believes that the person is either (a) of such mental condition that he is in need of supervision, treatment, care, or restraint, or (b) of such mental condition that he is dangerous to himself or to the person or property of others, and is in need of supervision, treatment, care, or restraint, the judge may adjudge the person to be mentally ill, and may . . . order.

(a) That the person be cared for and detained in a county psychopathic hospital, in a community mental health service . . . or a licensed sanitarium or hospital for the care of the mentally ill. . . .

§ 5568. If, on the examination as provided by law, the court finds a person to be mentally disordered and bordering on mental illness but not dangerously mentally ill, the court may commit him to the care and custody of the counselor in mental health and may allow him to remain in his home subject to the visitation of a counselor in mental health and subject to return to the court for further proceedings whenever such action appears necessary or desirable; or the court may commit him to be placed in a suitable home, sanitarium, or rest haven home, subject to the supervision of the counselor in mental health and the further order of the court.

NOTE 4

MATTER OF JOSIAH OAKES
8 Mass. Law Reporter 122 (1845)

*   *   *

SHAW, C. J. . . .

*   *   *

The right to restrain an insane person of his liberty, is found in that great law of humanity, which makes it necessary to confine those whose going at large would be dangerous to themselves or others. In the delirium of a fever, or in the case of a person seized with a fit, unless this were the law, no one could be restrained against his will. And the necessity which creates the law, creates the limitation of the law. . . . [I]f a man may be restrained in his own house, he may be restrained in a suitable asylum, under the same limitations and rules. Private institutions for the insane have been in use, and sanctioned by the courts; not established by any positive law, but by the great law of necessity and humanity. Their existence was known and acknowledged at the time the constitution was adopted. The provisions of the constitution in relation to this subject must be taken with such limitations, and must bear such construction, as arise out of the circumstances of the case. Besides, it is a principle of law that an insane person has no will of his own. In that case it becomes the duty of others to provide for his safety and their own. . . .

*   *   *

NOTE 5

IN THE MATTER OF HEUKELEKIAN
24 N.J. Super. 407 (1953)

BIGELOW, J. A. D. (dissenting). . . .

Until half a century ago, an insane asylum was no more than an institution in which the insane were housed and were prevented from injuring other persons or themselves. But nowadays an important function of a hospital like Marlboro is medical treatment and the attempt to cure those patients whose condition is not incurable. An insane person, like a child, is apt to be incapable of making a reasonable choice, either to undergo the treatment offered by the hospital, or to reject it. The State makes the decision for the child. . . . Can not the State also make the decision for an insane person? To warrant commitment to the Marlboro Hospital, I suggest that it was enough to show that the appellant, by reason of mental disease, lacked capacity to decide for herself, and that treatment in the hospital would probably be beneficial to her.

*   *   *

NOTE 6

CERTIFICATION OF ANONYMOUS NO. 1 TO ANONYMOUS NO. 12
138 N.Y.S. 2d 30 (1954)

BRENNER, JUSTICE.

*   *   *

[I] certified persons . . . "helpless due to old age but capable of self-harm." I had hoped that the state mental hospitals concerned would accept such certification in lieu of a certification of mental illness, thereby avoiding the unfair stigma placed upon the reputation of the elderly people and their respective families. In each such case the hospitals rejected the patients, insisting that the Mental Hygiene Law . . . prohibit the admission of any person in such hospitals unless certified to be mentally ill.

*   *   *

NOTE 7

IN RE BROOKS ESTATE
32 Ill. 2d 361, 205 N.E. 2d 435 (1965)

UNDERWOOD, JUSTICE.

This is an appeal from the probate division of the circuit court of Cook County which entered an order appointing a conservator of the person of Mrs. Bernice Brooks, and allowed the conservator's request to be authorized to consent, on behalf of Mrs. Brooks, to transfusions of whole blood to her. The transfusions were made, and appellants, Mrs. Brooks and her husband, now seek to have all orders in the conservatorship proceedings expunged, and the petition therein filed dismissed. . . .

On and sometime before May 7, 1964, Bernice Brooks was in the McNeal General Hospital, Chicago, suffering from a peptic ulcer. She was being attended by Dr. Gilbert Demange, and had informed him repeatedly during a two-year period prior thereto that her religious and medical convictions precluded her from receiving blood transfusions. Mrs. Brooks, her husband, and two adult children are all members of the religious sect commonly known as Jehovah's Witnesses. Among the religious beliefs adhered to by members of this group is the principle that blood transfusions are a violation of the law of God, and that transgressors will be punished by God. . . .

Mrs. Brooks and her husband had signed a document releasing Dr. Demange and the hospital from all civil liability that might result from the failure to administer blood transfusions to Mrs. Brooks. The patient was assured that there would thereafter be no further effort to persuade her to accept blood.

Notwithstanding these assurances, however, Dr. Demange, together with several assistant State's attorneys, and the attorney for the public guardian of

Cook County, Illinois, appeared before the probate division of the circuit court with a petition by the public guardian requesting appointment of that officer as conservator of the person of Bernice Brooks and further requesting an order authorizing such conservator to consent to the administration of whole blood to the patient. No notice of this proceeding was given any member of the Brooks family. Thereafter, the conservator of the person was appointed, consented to the administration of a blood transfusion, it was accomplished and apparently successfully so. . . .

* * *

[W]e should predicate our decision upon the fundamental issue posed by these facts, i.e.: When approaching death has so weakened the mental and physical faculties of a theretofore competent adult without minor children that she may properly be said to be incompetent, may she be judicially compelled to accept treatment of a nature which will probably preserve her life, but which is forbidden by her religious convictions, and which she has previously steadfastly refused to accept, knowing death would result from such refusal? So far as we have been advised or are aware, there is no reported decision in which this question has been squarely presented and decided.

* * *

Appellees argue that society has an overriding interest in protecting the lives of its citizens which justifies the action here taken. . . .

[The] cases are not determinative of the instant issue, and some are, in fact, supportive of a conclusion contrary to that urged by appellees. We believe the compulsory vaccination cases inapposite since society clearly can protect itself from the dangers of loathsome and contagious disease, a question with which we are not concerned; the polygamous marriage bans were upheld because the practice consisted of overt acts determined to be deleterious to public morals and welfare (no overt, immoral activity appears here); . . . the Georgetown College case was an altogether unique proceeding in which a single Federal Court of Appeals judge entered an order allowing a blood transfusion to an adult member of Jehovah's Witnesses. A doctor and hospital authorities had appeared originally before a Federal district judge and orally requested entry of an order permitting blood transfusions to be administered to a patient evidently *in extremis*. The request was denied. Later that same day, an "appeal" was taken to a single Court of Appeals judge, and the same order was requested of him. In reaching his determination, the judge went to the hospital and spoke with the patient and her husband. The husband said that while his wife was obliged to "abstain from blood," if the court ordered a transfusion, the matter would be out of his hands.

The patient stated that the transfusion would be against her will, but she also intimated that the court could take the matter from her hands. The judge then entered the order, determining to "act on the side of life."

. . . However, irrespective of the merits of that case, it is readily distinguishable from the instant one. There, the person alleged to be *in extremis* was the mother of minor children. The State might well have an overriding interest in the welfare of the mother in that situation, for if she expires, the children might become wards of the State. Such reasoning is inapplicable here since all members of the Brooks family are adults.

Similarly, the holding of the New Jersey Supreme Court . . . authorizing blood transfusions for a nonconsenting Jehovah's Witnesses member who was quick with child is not here persuasive since the court there held it unnecessary to determine whether the mother could be compelled to accept a transfusion to save her own life because it was so inextricably interwoven with that of the child as to render it impracticable to distinguish between them.

We believe Jefferson's fundamental concept that civil officers may intervene only when religious "principles break out into overt acts against peace and good order" has consistently prevailed. . . .

* * *

[W]e find a competent adult who has steadfastly maintained her belief that acceptance of a blood transfusion is a violation of the law of God. Knowing full well the hazards involved, she has firmly opposed acceptance of such transfusions, notifying the doctor and hospital of her convictions and desires, and executing documents releasing both the doctor and the hospital from any civil liability which might be thought to result from a failure on the part of either to administer such transfusions. No minor children are involved. No overt or affirmative act of appellants offers any clear and present danger to society—we have only a governmental agency compelling conduct offensive to appellant's religious principles. Even though we may consider appellant's beliefs unwise, foolish or ridiculous, in the absence of an overriding danger to society we may not permit interference therewith in the form of a conservatorship established in the waning hours of her life for the sole purpose of compelling her to accept medical treatment forbidden by her religious principles, and previously refused by her with full knowledge of the probable consequences. In the final analysis, what has happened here involves a judicial attempt to decide what course of action is best for a particular individual, notwithstanding that individual's contrary views based upon religious convictions. Such action cannot be constitutionally countenanced.

* * *

Accordingly, the orders of the probate division of the circuit court of Cook County are reversed.

NOTE 8

IN MEMORY OF MR. JUSTICE JACKSON
349 U.S. XXVII (1955)

* * *

MR. SOLICITOR GENERAL SOBELOFF addressed the Court as follows:

* * *

Associate Justice Robert Houghwout Jackson died suddenly of a heart attack on Saturday, October 9, 1954, at the age of sixty-two and at the height of his brilliant judicial career. . . .

* * *

Justice Jackson had suffered a previous attack in the spring of 1954. . . . His doctors gave him the choice between years of comparative inactivity or a continuation of his normal activity at the risk of death at any time. With characteristic fortitude he chose the second alternative. . . .

* * *

NOTE 9

MILL, JOHN S.

On Liberty (1859)*

* * *

The object of this Essay is to assert one very simple principle, as entitled to govern absolutely the dealings of society with the individual in the way of compulsion and control, whether the means used be physical force in the form of legal penalties, or the moral coercion of public opinion. That principle is, that the sole end for which mankind are warranted, individually or collectively, in interfering with the liberty of action of any of their number, is self-protection. That the only purpose for which power can be rightfully exercised over any member of a civilized community, against his will, is to prevent harm to others. His own good, either physical or moral, is not a sufficient warrant. He cannot rightfully be compelled to do or forbear because it will be better for him to do so, because it will make him happier, because, in the opinion of others, to do so would be wise, or even right. These are good reasons for remonstrating with him, or reasoning with him, or persuading him, or entreating him, but not for compelling him, or visiting him with any evil in case he do otherwise. To justify that, the conduct from which it is desired to deter him must be calculated to produce evil to some one else. The only part of the conduct of

* H. M. Coldwell Co., N.Y., 1898, (pp. 20-22).

any one, for which he is amenable to society, is that which concerns others. In that part which merely concerns himself, his independence is, of right, absolute. Over himself, over his mind and body the individual is sovereign.

It is, perhaps, hardly necessary to say that this doctrine is meant to apply only to human beings in the maturity of their faculties. We are not speaking of children, or of young persons below the age which the law may fix as that of manhood or womanhood. Those who are still in a state to require being taken care of by others, must be protected against their own actions as well as against external injury.

* * *

The only freedom which deserves the name, is that of pursuing our own good in our own way, so long as we do not attempt to deprive others of theirs, or impede their efforts to obtain it. Each is the proper guardian of his own health, whether bodily, *or* mental and spiritual. Mankind are greater gainers by suffering each other to live as seems good to themselves, than by compelling each to live as seems good to the rest.

* * *

NOTE 10

OLMSTEAD v. UNITED STATES
277 U.S. 438, 479 (1927)

BRANDEIS, J., dissenting.

* * *

. . . Experience should teach us to be most on our guard to protect liberty when the Government's purposes are beneficent. Men born to freedom are naturally alert to repel invasion of their liberty by evil-minded rulers. The greatest dangers to liberty lurk in insidious encroachment by men of zeal, well-meaning but without understanding.

* * *

c.   APPLICATION OF HOFMANN
      131 Cal. App. 2d 758, 281 P.2d 96 (1955)

PER CURIAM.

Upon petition one of the attorneys for Betty Short Hofmann representing that the latter is confined at Kimball Sanitarium in Los Angeles County as a mental patient under an order of commitment of the Superior Court, we issued a writ of habeas corpus to which return has been filed and upon which a hearing has been held. We conclude that the petitioner should be ordered released because of irregularities in the proceedings leading up to her commitment. . . . The proceedings may be outlined as follows. The son of petitioner filed an affidavit which set forth facts sufficient to warrant examination into the mental health and condition of the patient but failed to allege any facts showing necessity for the immediate apprehension of his mother, that is to say, no facts were alleged from which it would appear that the condition of Mrs. Hofmann was such that she was likely to injure herself or others if not placed under restraint. At the same time there was presented certificate of a physician that he had several times examined Mrs. Hofmann, the last time on February 4, and which stated: "It is my impression that she is in a state of paranoid reaction and that she should be observed in Psychiatric Unit No. 3 LACGH." Upon the basis of the affidavit and the certificate an order was made by a judge of the superior court which recited that Mrs. Hofmann was likely to injure herself or others if not immediately hospitalized and detained and which commanded that she be forthwith apprehended and detained for examination and hearing, pending the further order of the court. Mrs. Hofmann was taken from her home and immediately placed in the Psychiatric Unit of County General Hospital where she remained until February 9 when she was committed by order of court to the care and custody of the Counselor of Mental Health to be placed in Kimball Sanitarium, there to remain under the supervision of the Counselor of Mental Health until further order of the court. The order for the examination and detention of Mrs. Hofmann was on a printed form consisting of an entire page of closely typed material comprising several paragraphs and it contained what purported to be a notice to the person involved of a right to a hearing, to produce witnesses, and to be represented by counsel. The printed form was designed to be used in a number of different situations and if read as a whole it would be meaningless. If care was taken to delete the paragraphs and other statements inappropriate to the proceeding in hand, it could constitute an intelligible notice to the person addressed. Likewise, the notice of hearing and of the right to be represented by counsel, the latter of which is in small print at the bottom of the notice, would, if read by a person of intelligence and understanding, be sufficient to advise him of his rights. However, portions of the writing were stricken out by heavy pencil lines in a manner which rendered it impossible to determine what was intended to be stricken out and what to be retained. The portion containing the statement as to the right to notice, right to produce witnesses, and to be represented by counsel was so emasculated that it might well indicate that the whole thereof was intended to be stricken and rendered ineffective.

In no other manner nor at any other time was any attempt made to inform Mrs. Hofmann of her right to counsel. It appears from her affidavit attached to the petition that upon numerous occasions she requested of hospital attendants that she be given an oppor-

tunity to communicate with her attorneys; no attention was paid to these requests and she was unable to communicate with them.

On February 7, an order was made fixing 9:30 AM, February 9, 1955, for hearing and examination in department 54 of the court in the General Hospital and Mrs. Hofmann received notice thereof. At the time set for the hearing Mrs. Hofmann was in a room which had been assigned to her. There appeared at her room a judge of the superior court, two physicians, a person identified as a mental health counselor, the husband, and son of Mrs. Hofmann. It was not announced that a hearing was to take place. No witnesses were then sworn; statements of two physicians were received and taken by a court reporter. The physicians signed a certificate, the purport of their statements and certificates being that the patient was confused, illogical, suffering from a delusion she had special powers and evidenced a suspicious nature, all of which indicated a chronic brain syndrome for which treatment in a sanitarium was recommended. Mrs. Hofmann did not then request that she be allowed to have an attorney present but it is clear from the transcript of the proceedings that she at no time was advised and that she did not understand that a hearing was taking place or that there would not be a proceeding in court at a later time. She was not questioned in a manner that would have enabled the court to determine her apparent mental state and when she undertook to express herself was interrupted and prevented from making whatever statements or explanation she desired to make. Although Mr. Hofmann and the son were present they gave no testimony concerning the patient's mental condition. The hearing was terminated abruptly and petitioner was taken to the sanitarium. She was then given shock treatments over her objection, and although she again requested an opportunity to telephone her attorney, permission was refused until eight days after the hearing.

*   *   *

Under the circumstances of the case, and especially because Mrs. Hofmann did not realize that a hearing was taking place, we think the hearing in question was not in a courtroom, that Mrs. Hofmann did not waive notice of the hearing, and that there was a failure to observe the requirement for five days' notice prescribed by § 5052 of the Welf. & Inst. Code. As we read . . . the code, a patient shall be permitted to remain in his home or other place of domicile pending the examination in the absence of a showing that because of illness he is likely to injure himself or others if not immediately hospitalized or detained, which showing may be made either by certificate of a physician dated not more than three days prior to the presentation of the petition or by other affirmative evidence. There was no evidence before the court of the existence of facts which would have warranted the immediate hospitalization or detention of Mrs. Hofmann. She had a right to remain in her home pending the examination. Deprivation of this right affected adversely her interests in all the subsequent proceedings.

The authority of the court in such matters is statutory. . . . The right of the patient to remain at liberty with an opportunity to consult with relatives and friends, to receive legal advice, and in other ways prepare for the examination and hearing, is one that should be scrupulously observed by the authorities. The law not only specifies the conditions under which immediate detention is permitted, but provides that if such conditions are not shown to exist the patient may remain at home with family and friends. It is unnecessary to repeat the particulars in which Mrs. Hofmann's freedom of action was interfered with as a result of her confinement and her failure to comprehend what was going on. The statute recognizes the right to representation by counsel. Petitioner was deprived of that right. There was, in our opinion, not even substantial compliance with the prescribed procedure; we can only conclude that petitioner's present confinement is illegal.

It is ordered that Mrs. Hofmann be released from confinement.

NOTES

NOTE 1

STATE v. MULLINAX
369 Mo. 858, 269 S.W. 2d 72 (1954)

LEEDY, JUDGE.

*   *   *

Relatrix characterizes the nonjudicial procedures as the great innovation of the act, and section 6 as being perhaps the most important, in that they "permit friends or relatives of those suffering from mental illness to apply for and receive for them skilled medical treatment without undergoing the ignominy of an appearance in open court or without having to suffer the stigma of a permanent record of formal adjudication of insanity." If the constitutional rights of such unfortunates are sufficiently safeguarded so as to satisfy the requirements of due process, then, of course, these beneficent purposes may be achieved, and the scheme of the act given effect. The question raised by respondent in this connection is that the act, under sections 6, 7, and 8, permits citizens to be deprived of their liberty without notice, hearing, or opportunity to defend on the question of their insanity or mental illness, and for these reasons offends against the due-process guaranties of the federal and state constitutions.

Both sides recognize that the state, in the exercise of the police power, may provide for the summary apprehension of an alleged insane person, dangerous to self or to others, and his temporary detention (without notice or hearing) until the truth of the charges can be investigated. . . . Admittedly, under the procedures set up by sections 6, 7, and 8, no provision is made for notice, hearing, or an opportunity to defend. This omission is sought to be justified on the ground that the act authorizes only temporary detention in the absence of a judicial determination. This is asserted to be so because of the provisions of section 17 under which it is argued that to effect the release or secure a judicial determination of the mental condition of any patient hospitalized under sections 6, 7, or 8 "he or someone on his behalf, need only demand his freedom and he is immediately granted a full hearing."

Relatrix places her principal reliance upon a line of cases from other jurisdictions upholding the constitutionality of statutes which did not require notice or an opportunity to be heard in advance of commitment where a later hearing was afforded either by a special statutory proceeding (not unlike that referred to in section 17 as provided by section 9), or by resort to habeas corpus. . . .

. . . In State ex rel. *Kowats* v. *Arnold*, 356 Mo. 661, 673, 204 S.W.2d 254, 260, it was said: "The exercise of the power [to hold insanity inquisitions and issue commitments thereunder] may deprive the subject of precious constitutional rights, liberty and the enjoyment of property, which cannot be done without due process of law. *And it will not do to say in such a case that relief can be obtained afterwards by habeas corpus.*" (Emphasis supplied.)

*   *   *

Because of the constitutional infirmity of the act hereinabove pointed out, the respondent's action in refusing to admit the proposed patient was justified. . . .

*   *   *

NOTE 2

APPLICATION OF NEISLOSS
171 N.Y.S. 2d 875 (1957)

HAROLD T. GARRITY, JUDGE.

This court has become increasingly concerned with a situation fraught with danger to the freedom and rights of individuals. It is a particularly vital matter since the persons involved are usually incapable of asserting their rights and privileges in their own behalf.

I refer to what has become a practice of virtually wholesale commitments to mental institutions without, in my opinion, full assurances and safeguards that constitutional requirements have been met.

My records indicate that during the past year

approximately 50 to 60 petitions were presented to me each month for the commitment of allegedly mentally ill persons.

These petitions are printed forms and the information supplied is, to put it rather mildly, so meagre as to convey little real information concerning the patient. Neither the petitions nor the physicians' certifications are verified or acknowledged. Invariably the court is requested to dispense with personal service on the alleged incompetent for the stereotyped reason that "to do so would unduly disturb the patient."

These proceedings, based on section 74 of the Mental Hygiene Law, seek to confine such persons to a mental institution for a period of only 60 days. Under subdivision 7 of the said statute, however, the mere filing of a certificate in the County Clerk's office within 60 days of the order—and with no further court action or review—continues the confinement of a mentally ill person in such institution on a permanent basis.

Whether the commitment is permanent or for a period of 60 days—and most certainly where it is permanent—there should be true due process and judicial review. There is no other way in which the constitutional and legal rights of such persons can be adequately protected.

Incarceration, whether called hospitalization or by other euphemism, means depriving a person of liberty. No matter how sweetly disguised or delicate the language, involuntary confinement is a loss of freedom.

I use this occasion to advise both public and private institutions that henceforth, I shall not sign any order based upon an unverified petition or medical certification. Furthermore, unless the most compelling reasons are set forth, I shall not dispense with personal service upon the alleged incompetent or his next of kin.

It is my further firm conviction that no person should be placed in any such institution without an opportunity to be heard, or by someone in his behalf. I shall accordingly make myself available to conduct such hearings at the hospital if appearance by the patient in court is deemed inadvisable. Such hearings can be scheduled prior to the opening of court or after the close of the regular court day.

I do not believe it is imposing upon the court or others involved in such proceedings to devote the necessary time to prevent possible miscarriages of justice.

Lest it be thought that the court is exaggerating the problem, since I have been on the Bench, despite the hundreds who have been so confined, only one writ of habeas corpus on behalf of a mentally ill person has been presented. It is uncomfortably significant that in that single instance the writ was sustained and the patient discharged. The involuntary patient was an old man whose only difficulty was that he was hard

of hearing. This diagnosis was made in open court by an exceptionally well-qualified psychiatrist.

There is always the danger of allowing the judicial process to become a matter of rote and routine. We have perhaps reached that unhappy state in these proceedings; but it is not too late to call a halt.

That these changes may result in additional work and inconvenience to the court's personnel, those of the institutions as well as myself is of no importance whatever when weighed against the rights and dignities of persons who are under the protection of the courts and our laws. Our courts must zealously guard and preserve their vast powers. Speed is not necessarily synonymous with justice; nor is it desirable that our courts degenerate into assembly lines.

It is with reluctance that I grant the within petition; but I am constrained to do so having given no prior indication of my views and the new procedures I intend to follow. An amended proposed order, however, is to be submitted with the customary provision for automatic finality deleted and provision made therein for appropiate proceedings and notice prior to permanent commitment in accordance with the within opinion. Submit order.

Supplemental Opinion

* * *

With respect to the proposed order, I have spoken to an eminent psychiatrist who was retained by the patient's family. The doctor is of the firm opinion that his patient requires continued hospitalization and treatment. Furthermore, the patient's father retained an attorney to protect his son's legal rights. The said attorney has appeared but does not oppose the signing of the order. Order submitted pursuant to the Mental Hygiene Law signed and filed.

NOTE 3

IN RE CROSSWELL'S PETITION
28 R.I. 137, 66 A.55, 58 (1907)

DOUGLAS, C. J. This proceeding is a petition for a writ of habeas corpus and for discharge from custody of a patient confined against his will in the Butler Hospital.

* * *

The right of filing with a justice of the Supreme Court a petition for a commission to determine the question of sanity or insanity is given to the person confined, as well as to any one on his behalf, and he is also given the right to prosecute such petition in person. [It goes too far to go] to the length of demanding that a trial shall in all cases precede the apprehension and restraint of a person suspected to be insane. . . . It seems to us that much popular misapprehension of this subject grows out of the feeling that constraint of a person as insane is analogous to the punishment of a criminal, and carries with it some stigma; and to this may be added in some minds a repulsion to submitting one's self or one's friend to hospital treatment away from the continued supervision of family and personal friends. But insanity is a disease, and the State has the right to treat one who has the misfortune to suffer from it, as it does one who has a contagious malady. The exercise of this right of self-protection must be regulated by the circumstances of the case. If it is dangerous to the community that a citizen should go at large, whether because he is liable to spread contagion, or to commit some act of violence, public safety demands that he be immediately confined, either with or against his will, and the extent of his personal right can only be to test by judicial process, at a time when it may safely be done, the propriety of his restraint. We are of the opinion that the safeguards of this right provided by the statute are ample and just. The person confined has two methods at his command of invoking the action of the highest judicial authority, and severe penalties are imposed upon the managers and guards of the institution if they fail to bring the remedial provisions of the statute to his notice or impede his access to the remedies provided. In addition to this, careful supervision of such institutions is provided for by citizens of character and standing, and the system of operation is so regulated by law as to prevent abuses, or to insure the correction of them, as far as wise legislation can go. . . .

NOTE 4

CAMPBELL v. PEOPLE
190 Cal. App. 2d 253, 12 Cal. Rptr. 60 (1961)

KAUFMAN, P. J.

*   *   *

Appellant . . . is particularly concerned with the fact that he had received medication a few hours before the hearing was held. He argues that as a result of this fact, he was denied his right to participate in the hearing and defend himself. However, the validity of commitments cannot be made dependent upon the ability of a patient to participate in the hearing. Very often, drugs and medication are necessary. The requirements of the Welfare and Institutions Code include the consideration of the best interests and protection of the patient. Thus, if the prescribed statutory commitment procedure is followed, it must be left to the sound discretion of the trial court to determine what is a reasonable opportunity for the exercise of the patient's rights. . . .

*   *   *

NOTE 5

Opinions of the Attorney General of New York (1946)*

*   *   *

It is my opinion that, if the patient does not object . . . the Director of the institution may accept the patient . . . as the statute does not call for consent, but merely specifies a failure of objection on the part of the patient.

NOTE 6

APPLICATION FOR CERTIFICATION OF ———
172 N.Y.S. 2d 869 (1958)

BENJAMIN BRENNER, JUSTICE.

Voluntary transfer to a state mental institution upon a pink sheet form pursuant to section 73 of the Mental Hygiene Law was not requested of the aged senile as to whom this application is directed, apparently because he is ninety-six years of age. This was fortunate for the senile because it made a judicial hearing possible with the result that happily his daughter has now agreed to provide the custodial care that he requires.

The patient is described as having a happy mood with "gross memory impairment"—quite understandable for a man of his great age. The diagnosis is the usual one, namely, chronic brain syndrome associated with cerebral arteriosclerosis. The added phrase "with psychotic reaction, mild" is the diagnostic phrase currently used to insure qualification for admission to a state mental institution. Yet all that the senile concededly needs is custodial attention in a hospital for the aged which is unavailable because the State and local governments have thus far failed to adequately supply such facilities.

[T]he pink form is being increasingly used by the Department of Mental Hygiene for the transfer and admission to state mental institutions, without judicial consideration, of most of the senile aged who do not make *positive objection*, and that it accounted for more than 1000 such transfers within a period of nine months in 1957 from Kings County Hospital alone. [T]his is a development of recent date, conceived as a technique for circumventing judicial sanction, due to much criticism by judges and doctors alike of certification procedures of aged seniles to state mental institutions as being morally wrong. This newly used technique effectively shunts seniles into involuntary confinement without awareness by them of their plight and without their actual approval or judicial surveillance. These unwanted seniles may not even hope to escape factually involuntary confinement because the possibility of private care, often provided at a judicial hearing, is denied to them and, of course, they cannot thereafter effect their own release.

---

*1946 Report of the Attorney General 265.

Moreover, the denial of judicial hearing or sanction is based on a statute of questionable constitutionality because it is grounded on a fictitious consent given by one who concededly is confused and disoriented. Even if *positive objection* is not required by the Mental Hygiene Department, the consent thus extracted is dubious because the senile is not likely to understand that the admitting institution is a mental institution, even if he be told that it is. Often he is chagrined and humiliated following family rejection and has neither the will nor the capacity to object even if he be carefully advised. That he is aware of his right to object or of the significance of his failure to object is doubtful. In short, the pink sheet procedure, in my view, is little less than a ruse designed to circumvent the need for judicial consideration or review of the transfer of the senile to a mental institution. Thus unknowingly certified, without opportunity to secure private custodial care, we have assembly line incarceration, depriving the aged of their liberty of person and, as was said by Judge Garrity (Matter of Neisloss, 8 Misc.2d 912, 171 N.Y.S.2d 875, 876) "no matter how sweetly disguised or delicate the language, involuntary confinement is a loss of freedom."

According to the Department of Mental Hygiene, the pink form procedure is followed because it has received official sanction and is in accord with section 73 of the Mental Hygiene Law. It is contended by those who favor it that it is applied only where relatives of friends petition for certification. But generally relatives are all too eager to rid themselves of the senile, though at judicial hearings they frequently undergo a change of heart and agree to provide the needed care. It is further contended that patients admitted under section 73 are less emotionally disturbed when a court appearance is obviated. They say that a commitment is itself "fraught with stigma and the sound of doom to both patients and members of the family." Nothing can be further from the truth. Proceedings at the hospital are free of the courtroom atmosphere. No one is sworn to testify. The room in which the hearing is held has every appearance of easy informality. A psychiatrist and social workers are at hand to discuss the problem and to report findings. The aged person is excluded from the room if he is uncomfortable or physically unable to take part in the discussion and relatives and friends are put at their ease. If there are no relatives or friends willing to undertake custody or other custodial provision is not possible, the court certification follows and involves no greater stigma than does the certification by the doctors. But though certification to a mental hospital is wrong in either case, the aged person has at least had a hearing or judicial review of his personal disposition in the last days or years of his life.

* * *

The suggestion by the Mental Hygiene Department that judicial hearings are tantamount to criminal proceedings is outrageous. That Department readily admits that mental hospitals do not answer the need of seniles. To liken an informal and humane inquiry into the possibility of substituting home custodial care for that of custody in a mental institution to a criminal proceeding is an admission of ignorance about the actual nature of the proceeding. But no more reason exists for the summary bundling off of these seniles without hearing, court review, or at least court sanction, than exists for summary imprisonment without hearing of persons charged with crime. The aged are at least entitled to equal protection at a time when they are least capable of defending their right to personal freedom.

Private care having been assured to the senile involved, the petition has, on request by the court, been withdrawn.

NOTE 7

COMMITTEE OF THE ASSOCIATION OF THE BAR OF THE CITY OF NEW YORK

Mental Illness and Due Process*

. . . Ordinarily, no one represents the patient or outlines the possible alternatives to care in a state hospital. No one points out the factors and developments in his work or family life which may have created temporary emotional strain or which may now ease his return to normal life in the community. No one is charged with this responsibility.

To fill in these blank areas and to implement the changed methods of admission proposed by the committee in this report, we make the following recommendation:

Recommendation No. 1 (Mental Health Review Service). A new state-wide agency, called provisionally the Mental Health Review Service, shall be established as an agency independent of the hospitals and of the Department of Mental Hygiene and shall be responsible to the courts handling mental hospital admissions.

The Mental Health Review Service will have the duty of studying and reviewing the admission and retention of every nonvoluntary patient. It shall have two aims: (1) to explain to the patient and his family the procedures under which a patient enters and is retained in a mental hospital, and to inform them of the patient's right to a hearing before a judge, his right to be represented by a lawyer, and his right to seek an independent medical opinion, if desired; and (2) to provide the court with information on the patient's case to establish the need for his care and

* © 1962 by the Association of the Bar of the City of New York F   J, Inc. (pp. 20–21). Used by permission of Cornell University Press.

treatment in the hospital or his right to discharge. The Service will also recommend to the court, in all cases where the Service sees the need, the desirability of the patient's having legal representation or of his being examined by another psychiatrist.

Staffed by persons trained for this work, the Mental Health Review Service will have a primary duty to guarantee that patients know their rights and that the court has before it the facts necessary for deciding the question of the propriety of a patient's retention.

The Mental Health Review Service shall be available in state hospitals, in licensed private institutions, and in psychiatric receiving hospitals—in short, in all mental hospitals which any patients enter against their will.

Although the primary functions of the Service will relate to non-voluntary patients, it will also have the duty of explaining to voluntary patients who ask for its help.

* * *

NOTE 8

DENTON v. COMMONWEALTH
383 S.W. 2d 681 (Ky. 1964)

MOREMEN, JUDGE

* * *

[1] At the outset we should examine the nature of an inquest. We have held that a lunacy inquest is a special proceeding neither wholly civil nor wholly criminal. We have also recognized that the public is concerned in any trial which involves personal liberty. Therefore, an inquest has been regarded generally as a quasi criminal proceeding.

[2] Although lunacy inquests are not concerned with criminal intent or criminal acts they may result in depriving the defendant of his liberty and his property. This deprival should be obtained only by the due processes of law under constitutional guarantees. We have therefore concluded that when a proceeding may lead to the loss of personal liberty, the defendant in that proceeding should be afforded the same constitutional protection as is given to the accused in a criminal prosecution.

* * *

3.

INCOMPETENCY-TO-STAND-TRIAL COMMITMENT

a.   APONTE v. STATE
30 N.J. 441, 193 A. 2d 665 (1959)

* * *

WEINTRAUB, C. J.: Juan Rivera Aponte, a native of Puerto Rico, migrated to New Jersey in August 1953

and obtained work as a farm laborer at Vineland. Early in 1956, to improve himself, he wrote for an English-Spanish dictionary. In response, he received advertisements of books on black magic. He purchased them, and thus began a bizarre and macabre story.

He learned that if he prepared a magic circle he could summon the devil who would fulfill his wish. What he wanted was a woman who would be his alone. It is the Faustian theme. The vital ingredients of the magic circle, described by the author as "all these horrible and difficult to get objects," included "the cranium of a murderer." Aponte apparently understood that the skull of one who met a violent death would satisfy the text. He pondered how to obtain one. He explained that, being unaware of cemetery practices in the United States, he decided not to play the ghoul lest he become involved with the law. Instead, on October 13, 1956, he killed a 13-year-old boy, buried the body, and seven months later claimed the skull. Having thus acquired "the most important, the principal thing," he thought "I would be able to directly put myself into communication with the devil, person to person." He incanted the prescribed words, but nothing happened. He then tried to obtain "some sort of powder" of which he had read in one of the books, whereby "you gain the love of a woman but I never got to make it." He failed because the local pharmacy required a prescription. "I thought I would take it out in someone else's name but that I would get caught in some sort of mix-up, a crime, and I did not want to do that. I returned without my medicine. From there and from then on was born my loss of hope in what I was trying to gain."

Faithful to the book, Aponte throughout the period drank heavily of rum and wine. When his failure became evident he thrust aside the bottle and black magic, "and I was disgusted and I said to me, to myself, 'I am not going to gain anything by this. I am losing time and, who knows, my life.' " After two weeks of reflection, he returned to drink and decided to reveal the murder, but "I was afraid to go directly to the police and tell them I did it." Instead, he planned to have some trouble with his employer "and when the farmer calls the police I will tell the police everything." He precipitated the scene he contemplated, but instead of telling all, he charged he had seen his employer kill the boy. The employer and Aponte were arrested, and when the cries of the wife of the employer "entered my body like a spear," Aponte felt sorrow and his injustice to the employer. Two days later he confessed.

Aponte was indicted for murder. Upon his application, a hearing was held to determine his then sanity as well as his sanity at the time of the homicide. The jury found him sane on both critical dates. . . .

We merely sketch the psychiatric proof. Two experts on behalf of Aponte found him to be suffering from Schizophrenia, characterized by one as the catatonic paranoid form and by the other as paranoidal; committable because of homicidal and suicidal tendencies; and legally insane at the time of the murder. The testimony for the State, synthesized, was that Aponte is and was sane, medically and legally; that his faith in black magic is in kind indistinguishable from faith in the tenets of various cults or in horoscopy. The testimony was that the book was simply his "bible," and if he had had greater education (his schooling totalled four years), he probably would have rejected its thesis. The State's doctors found no delusions, since Aponte had merely through ignorance subscribed to an existing text. Reference will later be made to the testimony concerning capacity to stand trial.

*   *   *

"Insanity" has many meanings. A man may be insane for one purpose and sane for another. For present purposes, three concepts should be distinguished:

1. As a defense to crime, it must be proved that the accused was laboring under such a defect of reason, from disease of the mind, as not to know the nature and quality of the act, or if he did know it, that he did not know what he was doing was wrong. . . .

2. For the purpose of commitment to a mental institution, insanity usually comprehends any disease or disorder of the mind which renders its victim dangerous to himself or to others. . . .

3. As a test of ability to stand trial on a criminal charge, insanity means a mental illness or condition which prevents the accused from comprehending his position and from consulting intelligently with counsel in the preparation of his defense. . . .

*   *   *

. . . Counsel for Aponte presented an application [in civil commitment terms, i.e., "dangerous to himself or others"] but devoid of a suggestion of inability to stand trial. Indeed, in the examination of his experts he did not touch the subject of capacity for trial, nor did the prosecutor on cross-examination. It was the trial judge who interrogated Aponte's witnesses on that topic. Although the moving papers were framed as just stated, yet it is clear that the purpose of counsel was not to seek a civil commitment but rather to obtain a judgment that Aponte was mentally unfit to stand trial on the indictment. We can only surmise that it was believed that insanity justifying commitment would itself dispel capacity to defend against a criminal charge.

The fact that an accused may be committable civilly by reason of the suicidal or homicidal tendencies here claimed does not of itself establish inability to stand trial on an indictment. Thus in *State* v. *Noel* (102 N.J.L., at p. 671), the fact that the defendant had been committed to a mental institution did not bar the criminal trial, the court observing.

". . . The fact that a person has been adjudicated a lunatic does not mean that he is exempt from prosecution for the commission of a crime. Insane persons may be adjudicated insane and be committed for the protection of the public against violence, or for the care and cure of the person committed, or for the conservation and management of the lunatic's property. A regular inquisition is not conclusive. In cases of confinement where the confinement is made for the protection of the public or for the care of the individual, the commitment is evidential of nothing more than a condition justifying the confinement. A commitment adjudges no more than that it is necessary to confine the patient for the good of the public or himself, or both. The fact that a person has been committed as insane has no necessary relation to the question whether such a person can intelligently go to trial for a crime. Persons having some forms of insanity are as responsible for crimes committed by them as normal persons. It was not error to put the defendant to a trial merely because he had been committed to a hospital for the insane."

*   *   *

A further misconception seems to be that the existence of an issue as to capacity to defend should in the ordinary course lead to a common trial of that issue and the issue of legal insanity at the time of the offense. Such is not the legislative scheme. Prior to the revision of Title 2 in 1951, . . . [there was no] procedure for an inquiry into insanity at the time of the crime in the situation in which an accused was found unable to defend. By the revision of 1951, a procedure for that purpose was established . . . The reason for the proposal was that, when an accused is found unable to defend, he may be returned for trial on the indictment years later after much of the evidence pertinent to the issue of insanity at the time of the offense may have been lost. Hence it was recommended that discretionary authority exist for the trial of the latter issue in a preliminary proceeding under terms which would not prejudice the accused, i.e., a dismissal of the indictment if he is adjudged to have been insane at the time of the crime, and otherwise a right to re-try the issue under the indictment.

*   *   *

N.J.S. 2A:163–2 and 3 were not intended to permit an accused to by-pass the criminal trial if he is able to defend, or to entitle him to a trial run of his defense of insanity by the expedient of asserting incapacity to defend. Rather the purpose was to permit a termination of the criminal proceeding *if the accused is unfit for trial*. Nor does the statute require a trial of the defense of insanity at the time of the inquiry into ability to stand trial. . . . For that matter, the court need not order a trial of the defense at all. And if the accused is found to be fit for trial, the issue of insanity at the time of the crime should not be adjudged, and if both issues are tried together with a jury, the jury should be so instructed. This is especially true since, as pointed out in *Gibson* (15 N.J., at pp. 377-89) the proceeding under N.J.S. 2A:163-2 is deemed to be civil and determinable by the vote of ten jurors.

Hence, a court should not deal with the defense of insanity until after the incapacity of the accused to stand trial has been established, unless from the facts on hand it is virtually certain that incapacity to defend will be found. Rather, it should first try the issue of capacity for trial, and although both by our case law and the statute it may sit with a jury, we think it ordinarily more appropriate that that issue be tried by the court alone. If incapacity is found, then, in its discretion, the court may, alone or with a jury, inquire into the defense of insanity.

In the present case the proof at the trial was formidable on the issue of insanity at the time of the homicide. The proof, however, with respect to incapacity to stand trial was extremely meagre. As already stated, it was adduced on Aponte's case solely upon the instance of the trial court. The following was thereby revealed.

Dr. Brancale testified Aponte's illness has its peaks and valleys. He said "this man certainly knows his attorney, knows the psychiatrists that have examined him, and he remembers the date and knows he is on trial. But underneath all of this I do not think there is a real comprehension of the dilemma." He conceded that Aponte answered questions "at a reasonably intellectual level" and the answers were "responsive," although the witness added, "I think he was beginning to get irrelevant material in there." In answer to specific questions as to whether Aponte could intelligently consult with counsel and plan his defense, the witness said his opinion was "guarded," but he did not venture a negative answer.

Dr. Brunt, on the trial judge's interrogation, said Aponte "intellectually" comprehended his situation, but not "emotionally"; that his answers were "intelligently responsive," but "emotionally he is not involved in this in any way whatsoever"; that he could consult with counsel "In a limited way, or in the limited framework of intelligence." In summary, the doctor stated his "guarded" view was that "Intellectually, and as the Judge asked me, he can answer questions intelligently and at the same time his emotional disturbance is such that he would not give or be able to present an adequate defense or help his lawyer because his emotions would not allow him to do so."

The State's experts, as noted above, found no evidence of insanity, present or at the time of the crime, and hence no impairment of capacity to defend.

Aponte's testimony itself gives no evidence that he could not fairly stand trial. We find therein nothing to suggest that he is unaware of his position. His memory was precise with respect to the homicide and his conduct before and since. His testimony was vivid. He was responsive. There was some ambiguity as to whether years ago he drank Lysol by mistake or with intent to destroy himself, and Aponte did dispute most of the alleged record of legal involvements in Puerto Rico. The two items just mentioned, if attributable to mental illness, present no barrier to a full, fair, and impartial trial. The psychiatrists were evidently able to obtain the data they needed and Aponte's counsel was able to secure the full story of the homicide and a rather complete picture of his background.

Upon the dry record, we would incline to find Aponte able to stand trial, and upon that view we would affirm notwithstanding the errors found . . . above. We however hesitate to do so because we did not see the witness and do not have the benefit of the views of the trial judge who did. Hence we believe we should reverse and remand the matter. . . .

*   *   *

NOTES

NOTE 1

PATE v. ROBINSON
383 US. 375 (1966)

MR. JUSTICE CLARK delivered the opinion of the Court.

. . . We have concluded that Robinson was constitutionally entitled to a hearing on the issue of his competence to stand trial, Since we do not think there could be a meaningful hearing on that issue at this late date, we direct that the District Court, after affording the State another opportunity to put Robinson to trial on its charges within a reasonable time, order him discharged. . . .

The State concedes that the conviction of an accused person while he is legally incompetent violates due process . . . and that state procedures must be adequate to protect this right. . . .

*   *   *

The State insists that Robinson deliberately waived the defense of his competence to stand trial by failing to demand a sanity hearing as provided by Illinois law. But it is contradictory to argue that a defendant may be incompetent, and yet knowingly or intelligently "waive" his right to have the court determine his capacity to stand trial. In any event, the record shows that counsel throughout the proceedings insisted that Robinson's present sanity was very much in issue. He made a point to elicit Mrs. Robinson's opinion of Robinson's "present sanity." And in his argument to the judge, he asserted that Robinson "should be found not guilty and presently insane on the basis of the testimony that we have heard." . . .

We believe that the evidence introduced on Robinson's behalf entitled him to a hearing on this issue. The court's failure to make such inquiry thus deprived Robinson of his constitutional right to a fair trial. Illinois jealously guards this right. Where the evidence raises a "*bona fide* doubt" as to defendant's competence to stand trial, the judge on his own motion must impanel a jury and conduct a sanity hearing . . . The Supreme Court of Illinois held that the evidence here was not sufficient to require a hearing in light of the mental alertness and understanding displayed in Robinson's "colloquies" with the trial judge. But this reasoning offers no justification for ignoring the uncontradicted testimony of Robinson's history of pronounced irrational behavior. While Robinson's demeanor at trial might be relevant to the ultimate decision as to his sanity, it cannot be relied upon to dispense with a hearing on that very issue. . . .

*   *   *

The case is remanded to the District Court for action consistent with this opinion.

It is so ordered.

MR. JUSTICE HARLAN, whom MR. JUSTICE BLACK joins, dissenting.

*   *   *

Before turning to the facts, it is pertinent to consider the quality of the incompetence they are supposed to indicate. In federal courts—and I assume no more is asked of state courts—the test of incompetence that warrants postponing the trial is reasonably well settled. In language this Court adopted on the one occasion it faced the issue, "the 'test must be whether . . . [the defendant] has sufficient present ability to consult with his lawyer with a reasonable degree of rational understanding—and whether he has a rational as well as factual understanding of the proceedings against him.' " *Dusky* v. *United States*, 362 U.S. 402. In short, emphasis is on capacity to consult with counsel and to comprehend the proceedings, and lower courts have recognized that this is by no means the same test as those which determine criminal responsibility at the time of the crime. . . .

[T]here was evidence of a number of episodes of severe irrationality in Robinson's past. . . .

Whatever mild doubts this evidence may stir are surely allayed by positive indications of Robinson's competence at the trial. Foremost is his own behavior in the courtroom. The record reveals colloquies between Robinson and the trial judge which undoubtedly permitted a reasonable inference that Robinson was quite cognizant of the proceedings and able to assist counsel in his defense. . . . The conclusive factor is that Robinson's own lawyers, the two men who apparently had the closest contact with the

defendant during the proceedings, never suggested he was incompetent to stand trial and never moved to have him examined on incompetency grounds during trial. . . .

Thus, I cannot agree with the Court that the requirements of due process were violated by the failure of the trial judge, who had opportunities for personal observation of the defendant that we do not possess, to halt the trial and hold a competency hearing on his own motion. . . .

*   *   *

NOTE 2

UNITED STATES v. GUNDELFINGER
98 F.Supp. 630 (W.D. Pa. 1951)

STEWART, DISTRICT JUDGE.

*   *   *

. . . The courts have long recognized that the constitutional right of a defendant to a fair trial includes not only his right to be physically present and to assist in his own defense, but also embraces his right to be present mentally as well. This was well stated in *Ashley* v. *Pescor*, 3 Cir., 1945, 147 F.2d 318 at page 319 (D.Pa. 1951): "The defendant is entitled to be present at the time of trial so as to render assistance to his counsel, and if insane, while he may be physically present he is mentally absent, and his insanity may be of such a nature as to render him wholly unable to be of any assistance to his counsel."

The question for determination is not whether the defendant is insane so as to be criminally not responsible for his act. . . .

It was apparent to the Court that the psychiatrists who examined the defendant did not understand the purpose of the examination and the narrow issue to be determined by the Court. Both doctors obviously made extensive psychiatric examinations of the defendant and both agreed that he was insane. However, neither doctor testified regarding the ability of the defendant to understand the nature of the charges against him or to assist in his defense until specifically questioned in this regard by the Court. It seems apparent that when the examinations were made, the doctors did not have in mind this specific issue. At the close of his direct testimony, the Court asked Dr. Mayer the following question:

"Q. What would you say, Doctor, as to the ability of the defendant to understand the nature of the proceedings against him and as to whether he would be able to assist his attorneys in defending the charges against him? A. In my opinion he does not understand the nature and consequences of what he proposes, and therefore is unable to assist his attorneys. He is pathologically delusional and, therefore, cannot be changed into any other attitude."

This answer, while, we feel, not intentionally evasive, was none the less not wholly responsive to the question. Dr. Mayer did not say that the defendant was unable to understand the nature of the charges against him and only inferentially states that he is unable to assist his attorneys. . . .

The normal course would be to request the physicians to examine the defendant further with the specific questions for our determination in mind. However, we believe that this is unnecessary because of the fact that the defendant himself testified at length, and it seems clear to the Court that the defendant well understood the nature of the charges against him and was able to state with accuracy what they were. The only impediment the Court observed which would affect his ability to assist his counsel in his own defense was a slight impairment of hearing. . . .

It is concluded, therefore, that the defendant may properly be tried on the indictment pending against him, and the United States attorney is directed to place this case on the next Criminal Trial List.

NOTE 3

PEOPLE v. BERLING
115 Cal. App. 2d 281, 251 P.2d 1017 (1953)

DORAN, JUSTICE.

*   *   *

What may be denominated as appellant's main contention is that "A major part of the trial was conducted in the absence of the appellant," who, although physically present in the court room, was often unconscious or only semiconscious, and "mentally absent during much of the trial." Appellant's affidavit seeking a new trial recites that "her trial began January 3, 1951 . . .; she recalls the selection of the jury, the opening statement by Mr. Ted Sten, co-counsel for the People, and many of the witnesses who testified against her . . .".

Miss Berling "recalled wire-playing apparatus set up" on or about March 8, 1951; that thereafter she became unconscious and recalls only occasional happenings in the court room . . . until April 28, 1951, when she heard a woman scream, and thereafter heard the judge read something to the effect that the defendant was guilty of murder in the first degree, and heard him ask the jury if that was their verdict, at which time she again lapsed into unconsciousness . . . that she has no recollection of conferences with her attorney between March 8 and April 13; that she had desired to have Miguel Verdugo called as a witness on her behalf and was not aware of the fact that he had not been called; that she was unaware of the fact that she had fainted 11 times in the court room, twice on the witness stand," etc.

That during the latter part of the trial Miss Berling

was unwell is fully borne out by the record. According to appellant's count, there are 47 separate references to appellant's mental and physical condition between March 8 and April 12, 1951, including many (appellant's brief says 20) recesses granted for this reason, extending from a few minutes to five days. For example, on March 8, the trial court excused the jury, having observed that appellant appeared ill with "a severe tremor and she is sitting now at the counsel table with her head down and her eyes closed part of the time." To the Court's inquiry "She gave me no answer, which doesn't show an alertness that is necessary for a defendant in her position."

*   *   *

It was the physician's opinion that "her present condition is functional, that it is an emotional and nervous upset from strain. . . . Well, I believe she is capable of understanding a wire recording or understanding questions and answers. I think that with an emotional disturbance such as she has, some inattention to her surroundings is apt to result." The witness further stated that whether the trial might proceed without detriment to appellant's interests, "is largely up to her."

*   *   *

Frequent remarks by the trial judge to the effect that "the defendant gives evidence of not being in a condition to proceed," cannot but indicate that the Court entertained serious doubts as to whether appellant was conscious, semiconscious, or unconscious during various phases of the trial. It is well to note that in the present case there appears to be no charge that Miss Berling was malingering. Indeed, appellant's condition was readily observable, not only calling forth comment from the trial judge but also from the deputy district attorney who openly questioned the advisability of continuing with cross-examination. That the situation was of an especially serious nature seems to have been recognized by everyone connected with the case.

Article I, Section 13 of the California Constitution gives a defendant the right to appear and defend in person, and Section 1943 of the Penal Code provides that "If the prosecution be for a felony, the defendant *must* be personally present at the trial." (Italics added.) The rule is familiar and fundamental, "that the prisoner, in case of a felony, must be present during the *whole* of his trial," (Italics added), quoting from *People* v. *Kohler*, 5 Cal. 72. The same case states: "In favor of life, the strictest rule which has any sound reason to sustain it, will not be relaxed."

*   *   *

The real reason for continuing with the trial of the case is shown by the trial court's statement made at the argument of appellant's motion for a new trial: "It was our attempt to get this case ended so that we could have a conclusion of it one way or the other, and that's what we did." In other words, anxiety to finish the long and difficult trial was given priority over the more important question of the defendant's mental condition. . . .

*   *   *

. . . No court possesses any discretion whatsoever in reference to giving or withholding the fundamental rights and privileges of one accused of murder.

*   *   *

NOTE 4

STATE v. MURPHY
56 Wash. 2d 761, 355 P.2d 323 (1960)

FINLEY, JUDGE.

*   *   *

After consultation between appellant and his counsel, it was decided that appellant should participate in the trial as a witness in his own behalf. [P]rior to being conducted from the county jail to the courtroom, appellant complained of a severe cold to one Robert Gibson . . . a medical trusty under the supervision of the jail physician. Gibson gave appellant a pill containing equanil, a tranquilizing drug, at about 8:30 a.m., and saw appellant take the pill. At about 9:00 a.m., Gibson gave appellant two pills containing trancopal, another tranquilizing drug, and saw him take one of them. Although appellant was told that these latter two pills were tranquilizers, he had never taken a tranquilizer before and did not know their effect.

Thereafter, appellant was conducted to the courtroom. He took his place on the witness stand at about 10:00 a.m. In response to questions posed by Mr. Guterson, he first described in some detail the events of his life leading up to the commission of the crime charged. He then candidly testified with respect to his commission of the criminal act itself.

According to the undisputed testimony of Mr. Bianchi and Mr. Guterson, appellant's appearance, demeanor, and manner of speaking while on the witness stand were markedly different from what they had been during the numerous pretrial interrogations. [D]efense counsel's contention in the trial court and on this appeal is that, but for appellant's casual, cool, somewhat lackadaisical attitude, appearance and demeanor, induced by the tranquilizer drugs, the jury might not have imposed the death penalty. The trial judge's answer to this claim, as stated in his oral ruling denying the motion for new trial, was that

"* * * although I believe the tranquilizer relaxed him [the appellant], I feel that it did not affect the jury in their verdict."

The difficulty with this answer is that neither the trial judge nor the members of this court on appeal can know to what extent, if any, appellant's attitude and appearance as a witness influenced the jury with respect to the penalty to be imposed. . . .

Article I, § 22 (amendment 10) of our state constitution, declares that

"In criminal prosecutions, the accused shall have the right to appear and defend in person."

Of this right, this court, in *State* v. *Williams*, 1897, 18 Wash. 47, 50 P. 580, 581, 39 L.R.A. 821, stated:

"The right here declared is to appear with the use of not only his mental but his physical faculties unfettered."

We believe that this right is of particular significance in a case such as that now before us, where the matter of the life or death of the accused may well depend upon the attitude, demeanor and appearance he presents to the members of the jury, who are the ultimate determiners of his fate. In such a case, strong and compelling reasons manifestly exist for careful judicial scrutiny of every aspect of the trial afforded to the accused to the end that a new trial be granted in the event of a showing by the accused of a reasonable possibility that his attitude, appearance, and demeanor, as observed by the jury, have been substantially influenced or affected by circumstances over which he had no real control. We are satisfied that such a showing has been made in the instant case; i.e., it reasonably appears in the instant case that the attitude, appearance, and demeanor of the accused may have been influenced by the tranquilizer drugs, administered to him under at least a semblance of authority or approval from the public officers who had custody over him, and taken by the accused apparently without awareness of their probable effect upon him.

*   *   *

NOTE 5

PEOPLE v. GUILLORY
178 Cal. App. 2d 854, 3 Cal. Rptr. 415 (1960)

ASHBURN, JUSTICE.

*   *   *

It is a generally accepted rule that a trial judge should afford to a defendant who is handicapped by deafness, blindness, or other affliction, such reasonable facilities for confronting and cross-examining the witnesses as the circumstances will permit. But he cannot restore sight to the blind, hearing to the deaf, or speech to the mute. He need only give such aid to intelligent appreciation of the proceeding as a sound discretion may suggest. "If the accused is deaf or blind, so that on being confronted by the witnesses his physical infirmity will lessen his capacity to utilize his right, this will not prevent his being subject to trial. In the proper administration of justice, however, the court should give a person accused of crime a reasonable opportunity to obtain the benefit of this constitutional right. If he is deaf, such opportunity as may be necessary should be allowed for communication to him of the testimony of the witnesses to insure him a full and fair exercise of his legal rights. The exact manner in which this result should be arrived at must depend on the circumstances of the case and, to a considerable extent, be left to the sound discretion of the court." (14 Am. Jur., § 181, p. 892.)

*   *   *

b.   The Case of Anthony Giordello*

[i]

Indictment

The Grand Jurors of the State of New Jersey, for the County of Bergen, upon their oaths present that

ANTHONY GIORDELLO

on or about the 20th day of October, 1961, in the Borough of Fairview, county and jurisdiction aforesaid, with intent to defraud MULLER FUEL OIL COMPANY, a corporation of New Jersey, unlawfully did make, draw, utter, and deliver to the said MULLER FUEL OIL CO. a certain check . . . well knowing at the time of so doing that he had insufficient funds, in or credit with the bank aforesaid for the payment of such instrument in full upon its presentation. . . .

[ii]

Transcript of Proceedings

MR. FREIMAN: If Your Honor please, I represent the defendant, who is not here because he cannot physically or mentally make the trip from North Bergen, New Jersey, to Hackensack. . . .

THE COURT: What is the matter with him?

MR. FREIMAN: He has an absolute fear of traveling away from his home, and he cannot make the trip.

THE COURT: I will give you until one o'clock to get him. Otherwise I will revoke the bail and put him in jail, where he will not have to travel.

MR. FREIMAN: If Your Honor please—

THE COURT: This has been going on too long. This has been on for arraignment a number of times, and to me it sounds like a phony excuse. I am not ascribing this to you, Counsellor; I am talking about your client. He apparently did not have any phobia to get himself involved in fraud.

---

*This is an actual record. Defendant's name and other identifying features have been changed.

MR. FREIMAN: [I]f there is any question as to the validity of this case, we would be willing if this court would convene, say, anywhere in Fairview. . . .

THE COURT: If he can go to Fairview, he can come to Hackensack. I will not adjourn this case to any place except the court room, and I will not go out of my way as a County Judge to accommodate anyone charged with crime. . . . Is it true that he can go to Fairview?

MR. FREIMAN: Last night, he told me, he got as far as the Overpeek Creek and he couldn't go any further.

THE COURT: That does not appeal to me as a sound reason; that it is something, at the best, imaginary. I am concerned with the physical aspects of his ability to get here. There is no contention here that this man is physically disabled in some way, or ill in bed, or in a hospital, or anything of that sort. Although I know we live and learn and we always hear of something new, this is entirely new to me, that somebody has a phobia of some sort the nearer he gets to the Court House.

MR. FREIMAN: Well, if Your Honor please, the certificates are on file of two reputable medical men who certify to that.

THE COURT: I do not have them, and I do not have any certificate as to his condition today; and I am telling you now, Mr. Freiman, that I will give you until quarter to one. . . . If he is not here at that time to be arraigned, I will revoke the bail and order him arrested—order a bench warrant for his arrest. That is the only way to handle these things. I am not going to listen to any nonsense of that sort. We are getting to a point where it seems that the rest of the population exists for the so-called criminal population. As far as I am concerned, I am not going to accept that. . . . He is physically able to move, and he has got to be here. What you have to say might have a bearing in connection with what might happen to him either at the trial or if he should plead guilty; or if he is convicted, it might have a bearing on the sentence, but it has nothing to do with his appearance here to be arraigned.

MR. FREIMAN: I can say to Your Honor that his plea is not guilty, and that we will be willing to stand trial at any time.

THE COURT: The Court will not accept a plea of not guilty, or any other plea, without the presence of the defendant. He has to be here. He has not been processed, he has not been photographed. What is he? Some kind of a privileged character? . . . Is he suffering from illness, or are you talking about some mental quirk that makes it inadvisable for him, at least in his own estimation, to come to court?

MR. FREIMAN: I am not talking about a mental quirk. I am talking about what two doctors have certified to this court.

THE COURT: What did they certify?

MR. FREIMAN: They certified that he cannot, it is impossible for him to come to this court.

THE COURT: How do you reconcile that with your statement that he got as far as the Little Ferry Circle and then turned back, or that he is willing to go to Fairview if the court will convene in Fairview?

MR. FREIMAN: [T]he only way I can reconcile it is by producing the physicians; and if Your Honor wants me to produce Doctor Robert Weitz, he is an eminent neurologist and he is well known, I will try to produce him by quarter to one in the court.

THE COURT: I want the defendant here at quarter to one. If he is not here, you will be given an opportunity to present anything that might affect the situation; but don't bring some kind of— Well, I better not say it. I am getting a little tired hearing that everybody who does something wrong fell on his head when he was a child or something. I fell off a cherry tree, but I do not think it made me crazy. Maybe some defendants might think I am, I don't know.

MR. FREIMAN: Your Honor please, I happen to be personally acquainted with the facts in this case, and I say to your Honor that there is absolutely no basis upon which this man, by any stretch of the imagination, can be found guilty. As a matter of fact—

THE COURT: Don't let us get into the merits.

MR. FREIMAN: Your Honor has referred to him as a criminal.

THE COURT: No, I have not, and don't put words in my mouth. . . .

*   *   *

1:45 PM.

MR. FREIMAN: Your Honor please, I have here Doctor Weitz, who has been treating Mr. Giordello, and I ask Your Honor to take his testimony to explain medically why he cannot be here today.

THE COURT: All right.

*   *   *

Q. Doctor, will you tell the court what was the trouble with Anthony Giordello for which he had consulted you and for which you were treating him?

*   *   *

A. The man's trouble was a deep seated phobia. He could not travel. When I first saw him, he couldn't travel more than 10 blocks from his home in any direction. His work was right at the corner. This man would go into a panic. In attempting to treat this man, I actually went as far as getting into his car with him. He would be able to go up to a certain line, and then he would rather die than to move beyond that point. . . .

*   *   *

MR. FREIMAN: If Your Honor please, I think there is evidence before Your Honor now to at least give me the opportunity to bring in the treating physician. . . .

*   *   *

(The Court recessed until 2:00 PM)

MR. FREIMAN: If Your Honor pleases, during the lunch hour I tried to get hold of Doctor Katz. I reached him at his office. He is busily engaged and he cannot come in here. But based on what he told me and based on my own observation of the defendant, I make the representation to Your Honor, that it will be dangerous, from a point of view of mental health, for him to be brought here forcibly; and that if it is done, he may be in danger of winding up in a mental institution. I make this suggestion to Your Honor, if Your Honor will be willing to act on it. Let the court appoint a psychiatrist, for which we will pay, let the psychiatrist examine the defendant, and satisfy the court as to the truth of the representations that I am making today.

*   *   *

THE COURT: . . . What you are asking the court now is, that here is a person who has been indicted for fraud—I guess bad checks . . . and the case was sent down for arraignment I think as early as last June, and some representation was made to whoever was sitting at the time that the man was ill or unable to appear, and it has been adjourned from time to time, as far as I know. Whether or not there was more than one adjournment I do not know, but at any rate it was on the calendar for today for arraignment.

Now, there is no allegation that I know of that this man is mentally incompetent in the sense that I have indicated—

MR. FREIMAN: No, Your Honor, there is none, and I say—

THE COURT: There is no allegation that he is physically incapable of getting around—

MR. FREIMAN: There is an allegation that he is medically unable to get here.

THE COURT: Oh, no, there is not . . . You seem to be so awfully persistent in contending that this man cannot be here, in the face of your own statements, in the face of all the evidence that physically he can be here. He goes to work every day. He attempts to come here, from what you say, but then when he gets as far as Little Ferry, he has to turn around. You say that if I would convene court in the Borough of Fairview, some eight miles from here and presumably the reason he suggests Fairview is because it adjoins Hudson County—your client lives in North Bergen —then he could leave his house, come to Fairview, and he could be arraigned. I do not profess to know everything that goes on in the world of psychiatry or in the world of psychology, but it sounds a little bit crazy to me, and not in the sense that your man is crazy.

MR. FREIMAN: Your Honor please, that is the reason I suggested that an expert be chosen by this court at our expense to verify whether he is really crazy or whether it is really the truth.

* * *

What I am trying to say is this: That he is actually personally unable to get here under his own volition.

THE COURT: That is what he tells you.

MR. FREIMAN: That is right.

THE COURT: Suppose you, as his attorney might well believe him, and I choose not to believe that.

MR. FREIMAN: So I say to Your Honor, let us get an expert of Your Honor's choosing, at our expense. He will then tell Your Honor from an expert point of view, whether that is true or not. [W]e would be more than happy to have this case tried. We will even be satisfied to have the case tried without a jury. This is an open and shut case where there was no fraud, there was no bad check. As a matter of fact, the bank attorney called up the complaining witness' father and told him they made a mistake—

THE COURT: Don't go into the merits of it—

MR. FREIMAN: So it isn't a question of we don't want to try it. It is a question where the man's actual mental health is involved. This is not a felony, it is a run of the mill—

THE COURT: It involves a check of $1133.65. It is not so run of the mill.

MR. FREIMAN: I think Your Honor will be satisfied, if Your Honor hears it without a jury, that the case never should have been brought in.

THE COURT: Don't put me in the position of even attempting to pass on the merits, because I am certainly—

MR. FREIMAN: I am not asking that.

THE COURT: As far as this defendant is concerned, at this point he is presumed to be innocent, and that presumption is in his favor right up to the time that either a judge or a jury, as the case may be, would find him guilty; so that we have to assume that presumption of innocence. But that has nothing to do with his obligation to appear and answer to this charge by pleading to the indictment, and eventually, of course, appearing for trial.

I do not know what good purpose there would be to talk more and more about this. It is silly that a person can move around, go to work, go from North Bergen to the Little Ferry Circle—and my guess would be that is a good 6 or 7 miles—but when he comes within two miles of the Court House, he suddenly gets some kind of a phobia that he just cannot bear to get any closer. Well, he will have to try it—

MR. FREIMAN: May I say this, Your Honor—

THE COURT: And if he will not come unescorted, he is going to come escorted. . . . [I]f the Prosecutor moves for the issuance of a bench warrant, I will pass on it.

MR. DILTS: I so move.

THE COURT: All right. The motion is granted that a bench warrant will be issued for the arrest of Anthony Giordello . . . and I will revoke the bail.

* * *

[*iii*]

Appellate Decision

Before: Goldman, Foley and Leiws, J.J.

[I]t appearing that the trial court is to appoint a psychiatrist to examine the defendant, at the defendant's cost and expense, and will thereafter conduct a hearing with reference to the findings of said psychiatrist.

* * *

ORDERED that in the meantime the execution of the warrant and the revocation of bail herein be stayed until the further order of this court.

[*iv*]

Psychiatric Report

Guy W. Calissi, Esq.
Bergen County Prosecutor
Hackensack, N.J.

Dear Sir:

* * *

Recommendations: Because of the chronicity and severity of this psychoneurotic reaction it is recommended that whatever legal transactions must ensue as a result of this patient's offense be executed within his present range of activity imposed upon this patient by his emotional difficulty. It is my considered neuropsychiatric opinion that any attempt at coercion of this individual at the present time may precipitate a serious emotional and physical reaction. [T]his patient is consciously willing to co-operate and I am certain he will do his utmost to abide by the dictates of the court.

Thank you for the opportunity of examining this patient.

Very truly yours,

J. F. Zigarelli, M.D.

[*v*]

Transcript of Further Proceedings

MR. FREIMAN: Your Honor, on behalf of my client, who is present here today, I wish to express my appreciation for your humane decision to bring his case for trial in this hall in Fairview Borough, a place close enough to his home for him to appear without jeopardy to his mental health.

THE COURT: Thank you counsel. Your willingness to waive a jury trial greatly facilitated this decision.

* * *

MR. DILTS: If Your Honor please, in view of the bank auditor's testimony that he had made a mistake and charged two earlier checks to the wrong account, and that GIORDELLO had enough money in the bank to cover the $1,100 check, I move that the charge be dismissed.

THE COURT: Motion granted, case dismissed.

MR. FREIMAN: In America, every man gets his day in court, even if the court has to come to him.

THE COURT: I have no recollection of the court ever having been summoned to appear before the defendant before.*

c.   The Case of Louis Perroni**

Until May 5, 1955, Mr. Louis Perroni[1] operated a filling station in Glenview, a Syracuse suburb. . . .

* * *

Early in 1955, Perroni was informed that the lease on his filling station, which was to expire on July 1, was not going to be renewed. The station he had operated for approximately ten years was in an area that was to be razed in preparation for a new shopping center.

During the winter, Perroni was approached by agents of the real estate developer with a request that he vacate his premises early, preferably no later than May 1. Although offered compensation, Perroni refused.

As Mr. Peronni tells it, the real estate developer went to court and obtained permission to take possession of Perroni's filling station on May 1. Perroni was the last occupant on the property, and therefore the only obstacle in the way of proceeding with the building of the new shopping center. After urging Mr. Perroni to move and offering him bonuses for doing so, the agents of the real estate developer allegedly threatened him with court action. He, on the other hand, began to feel that he was being "pushed around," and resolved not to give an inch from what he considered his "legal rights."

On May 2, 1955, representatives of the real estate

developer erected a sign on what Mr. Perroni considered his gas station. He remonstrated with them and removed the sign. At last, when two men appeared on May 5 and proceeded to erect another sign, Mr. Perroni took a rifle from his station and fired a warning shot into the air. The men departed. Soon Mr. Perroni was arrested by the police.

This was Peronni's first brush with the law. . . .

Aided by his brothers, Perroni tried by every means possible, including an appeal to the United States Supreme Court, to secure his right to be tried. At long last, in June 1961—six years after Perroni was committed to the Matteawan State Hospital—a writ of habeas corpus was heard and sustained by the State Supreme Court judge in Dutchess County (where the hospital is located). Perroni was ordered to be tried or discharged. Nevertheless he was not immediately released. "The wheels of justice moved slowly," reported the Syracuse *Post-Standard*, "and only when officials of Matteawan State Hospital were faced with contempt charges did they send Perroni back to Onondaga County."

Perroni was returned to Syracuse on Thursday, August 31, and held incommunicado in the county jail. "His relatives," according to the newspaper, "have not been allowed to visit him." Perroni was to be arraigned in County Court, Tuesday, September 3. His arraignment was adjourned to the following day. On September 4, however, he was neither indicted nor released. Instead, he was ordered to submit to a fresh pretrial psychiatric examination.

A month later, on October 1, 1961, the Syracuse *Herald-Journal* reported that the court issued a new order for "mental tests" on Perroni. "For the fourth time since his arrest—and the second in less than a month—Louis Perroni, 46, former operator of a Glenview gasoline station, has been ordered to a hospital for mental tests. Perroni, who has been in and out of County Court more than a half dozen times since his arrest in 1955, was in court again yesterday, and again, County Judge Francis T. Kirby ordered mental tests."

In due course, Perroni was committed to the Oakville State Hospital near Syracuse to determine once more whether he was competent to stand trial.

In anticipation of the hearing to be held in Onondaga County Court concerning Mr. Perroni's fitness to stand trial, the defendant's family and his attorney, Mr. Jerome Gross, sought my help. They requested that I furnish psychiatric testimony to support the claim—shared by the defendant, his family, and his attorney—that Mr. Louis Perroni was mentally competent to stand trial. . . .

* * *

The hearing was held on April 12, 1962, in Onondaga County Court before a judge and without a jury. It lasted for two full days. The following excerpts

---

*This is a reconstruction based on a newspaper account of what took place at the final proceedings.

** Reprinted with permission of The Macmillan Co. from *Psychiatric Justice* by Thomas S. Szasz. Copyright by Thomas S. Szasz, 1965.

1. The dates and the names of persons, places, and institutions (except mine, the Onondaga County Court's, and the Matteawan State Hospital's) are fictitious; otherwise, the account is factual.

from the hearing are taken from the official records of the court stenographer. . . .

PROCEEDINGS BEFORE HONORABLE FRANCIS T. KIRBY, COUNTY COURT HOUSE, ON APRIL 12, 1962, AT 10 AM.

APPEARANCES:

FOR THE PEOPLE: Robert Jordan, Esq., Assistant District Attorney

FOR THE DEFENDANT: Jerome Gross, Esq.

*   *   *

JAMES B. ROSCOE, having been called and duly sworn, testified as follows:

DIRECT EXAMINATION BY MR. JORDAN

*   *   *

Q. [I]n what field are you engaged in at Oakville State Hospital?

A. I am engaged in the practice of psychiatry.

Q. And for how long, sir, have you been a psychiatrist?

A. I have been a psychiatrist for fifteen years [and] I have examined approximately 200 individuals under the Code of Criminal Procedure.

Q. Doctor, let me ask you, have you ever had occasion to talk or meet an individual by the name of Louis Perroni?

A. Yes, I have.

Q. Now, if you can recall, when was the first time you examined Mr. Perroni?

A. I examined Mr. Perroni on February 24, 1962.

Q. Now, can you tell us what your examination consisted of?

A. It consisted of an interview of an hour and a half's duration, proceeding in the usual form of a psychiatric interview in order to ascertain the individual's mental state. I determined his attitude and general behavior. I determined his stream of mental activity, his emotional reaction, his content of thought, and his sensorium.

Q. Now, Doctor, as a result of your examinations of Mr. Perroni were you able to form an opinion whether this patient was in such a state of idiocy, imbecility, or insanity as to be able to understand the nature of the charge against him and to make his defense?

A. It is my opinion that Mr. Perroni is in such a state of idiocy, imbecility, or insanity as to be unable to understand the charges against him, the procedures, or of aiding in his defense.

*   *   *

MR. JORDAN: You may inquire, Mr. Gross.

CROSS-EXAMINATION BY MR. GROSS

Q. Dr. Roscoe, can you tell us what Mr. Perroni is charged with—what the charge is?

A. I believe it is a charge under the Penal Law having to do with carrying a gun.

Q. Do you know whether or not he is charged with assault?

A. That I do not know.

Q. I see. And is he charged with anything else, Doctor?

A. To my knowledge, no.

Q. And do you know, Doctor, whether carrying a gun is a violation of law?

A. I do not know. I'm not a lawyer.

Q. I see. Doctor, in order to defend against a charge of carrying a gun what does a defendant have to know in order to aid his attorney in the trial of the case?

MR. JORDAN: I will object to that, if Your Honor please.

THE COURT: No, overruled.

MR. GROSS: It is the meat of the case, Your Honor. It is the very basis of it.

THE COURT: The witness may answer.

MR. JORDAN: I don't know if a proper foundation has been laid for the witness to be qualified to answer.

THE COURT: He may so state if he is not.

MR. GROSS: I will withdraw that question, Your Honor.

THE COURT: All right.

Q. Doctor, you have stated as a conclusion and as the result of your examination of this defendant Perroni under Court order, you have come to the conclusion that Perroni is not able to understand the charges or to assist with his defense. Now, Doctor, is it not true that in order to come to that conclusion, whether you be a psychiatrist or a man on the street, that it is first necessary to know what a defendant has to know in order to understand the charges against him and to aid his attorney? Is it not necessary first to know what capacity he must have in order to co-operate with his attorney?

A. I would say that he had to be capable of judgment, capable of sufficient thinking capacity to be able to co-operate.

Q. Is it not true, Doctor, that the defense of different charges would require different capacities for the purpose of defense?

A. I am not a lawyer. I don't believe I can answer that question.

Q. Doctor, I do not mean from a legal standpoint, but I mean from a layman's standpoint and a psychiatrist's standpoint.

A. From a psychiatric standpoint again a person must have demonstration of judgment, intelligence, contact with reality to be able to co-operate in defending any charge.

Q. Any charge? Would there be a different capacity required between defending a murder charge and a speeding charge?

A. From a psychiatric point of view, no.

Q. No difference at all? In other words, the simplicity of the charge and the simplicity of the defense makes absolutely no difference?

A. That would be my opinion.

Q. And is that a psychiatric conclusion, Doctor?

A. Yes.

* * *

Q. Now, you say he was evasive, Doctor. . . . In what way? Can you give us some specifics.

A. To my questions he answered with a response "That is a good question."

Q. Well, which question was it? Give us one question he answered that to.

A. I do not recall specifically.

Q. Well, Doctor, February twenty-fourth isn't long gone. It is just two months. Can't you remember a single solitary question that he so responded to with "That is a good question"?

A. I do not. There were a number of them on that occasion.

Q. But you cannot remember a single solitary question?

A. I cannot specifically remember a question.

Q. You didn't make a single note of any question you asked him?

A. I did not write up the results of this interview on a question-and-answer basis.

Q. And is there anything abnormal, Doctor, for any person to respond "That is a good question"—anything abnormal about that?

A. When this is a response to a number of different questions it has significance psychiatrically.

Q. How many times did he repeat that phrase, Doctor? How many times on February twenty-fourth did he use that phrase "That is a good question"?

A. At least half a dozen.

Q. At least half a dozen times in an hour and a half, is that right?

A. Yes.

Q. By your standards and your judgment you think the phrase "That is a good question" during an hour-and-a-half interrogation, that indicates in some fashion to you, does it, Doctor, that that is an abnormality?

A. It does.

* * *

Q. Now, Doctor, I understand you to say this man was untidy?

A. Yes.

Q. Can you describe in detail for me what that untidiness was?

A. On every occasion that I examined Mr. Perroni the upper button or two of his shirt was unbuttoned, his sleeves were not buttoned, and his shoelaces were untied.

* * *

Q. When you reported to Judge Kirby on March twenty-seventh, when you signed a written report that Mr. Perroni was in a state of insanity, that is not a medical conclusion, right?

A. It is a translation of a medical conclusion into accepted legal terminology.

Q. And what is the equivalent, Doctor, of insanity in medical terminology?

A. As close as I could come to it would be that of psychosis.

Q. What you are saying to the Court today is that Mr. Perroni is in a state of psychosis, is that right?

A. I am saying today that the last time I examined Mr. Peronni he was in such a state of imbecility, idiocy, or insanity as to be incapable of understanding the charges, procedures, or making his defense.

Q. Do you mean he was in a state of psychosis?

A. Yes.

Q. Do you have any conception, Dr. Roscoe, of what the defense of Mr. Perroni's case will entail?

A. Not being a lawyer, I am afraid I don't understand the full possibility.

MR. GROSS: That's all.

* * *

THOMAS S. SZASZ, having been called and duly sworn, testified as follows:

DIRECT EXAMINATION BY MR. GROSS

* * *

Q. . . . In your opinion, Doctor, is or is not Louis Perroni, the defendant here, in such a state of idiocy, imbecility, or insanity as to be incapable of understanding the charge against him, or the proceeding or of making his defense?

* * *

A. In my judgment Mr. Louis Perroni is not in such a state of idiocy, imbecility, or insanity as to be unable to understand the charges.

* * *

CROSS-EXAMINATION BY MR. JORDAN

* * *

Q. Now, . . . if you examined Mr. Perroni and, say, one hundred other people, would you ever come to the conclusion that any one of those people are mentally ill?

A. I was not hired to examine Mr. Perroni to determine whether he was mentally ill.

Q. Will you please answer my question, sir?

A. You have asked a hypothetical question. In my professional life I have gone out of my way to be sure I would not be put in the position of having to do what you are asking me to do, namely of having to pronounce somebody mentally ill—because this is like branding him a criminal without a trial in this day and age. I would not do this. I would not accept the position.

Q. Doctor, isn't it true that in the development of the law, that one of the great beauties of the law is that a mentally ill person is not responsible for his acts?

A. I consider this is one of the most catastrophic things in American law.

Q. Would you rather have it this way, that a person who would be called mentally ill at the time he killed somebody should be hung or sent to the electric chair?

A. I am also opposed to the death penalty.

Q. Given life sentence, Doctor?

A. I think that every person accused of crime should stand trial. This is my bias.

*   *   *

Q. What did your examination consist of, Doctor?

A. Conversation.

Q. Conversation? Would that take the form of a narrative or questions and answers?

A. A friendly conversation, questions and answers, but not a stoical "Did you do this?" or "Did you do that?"

Q. What questions did you ask him, Doctor?

A. I asked him about what happened when he was first apprehended. I told him to tell me only what he wanted to tell me because I may have to reveal in Court whatever he tells me.

THE COURT: Did he respond to that question?

A. He responded just as humanly as we are responding to each other, I would say. I also asked him about his marriage. I asked him about many of the things that were covered in the previous testimony.

*   *   *

Q. Can you diagnose schizophrenia as a result of a conversation with an individual?

A. This is a loaded question because I don't believe in the diagnosis—

Q. (Interrupting) You don't believe in diagnosis, Doctor?

A. No, I don't believe in diagnosis, I know how to make one. But I disbelieve in it.

Q. You don't believe such a thing as schizophrenia exists?

A. Not otherwise than as ink marks on a piece of paper. It is a name. But that the disease exists, no, I don't believe it.

*   *   *

If you came to me as a private patient—nobody knows about this—and if I say "You have schizophrenia. You should come and see me for interviews and maybe I can help you," this will not affect you directly, socially. If you want to come, you come. If

you don't, you don't. You will not lose your job, nothing dire will happen. But if I use the word *schizophrenia* outside of my office or in a courtroom it is a terrible thing. It is not the word—it is the context in which you say it that matters. . . . So these diagnostic terms have a tremendous social impact. To be called mentally ill is like being called a Negro in Alabama or a Jew in Nazi Germany—or to be called a schizophrenic in a courtroom. You are finished, unless somebody defends you. You can't stand trial, you have no rights, you can't get out of the hospital. Everybody is protecting you. Even the District Attorney is protecting you. Once this word gets out, particularly in the courtroom, you are finished. You have no more rights. Everybody all of a sudden wants to help, and you have no more enemies. Someone said "Protect me from my friends, and I will take care of my enemies." The so-called patient has no enemies; everybody wants to help. Has it occured to his friends that letting him stand trial would be good for him?

*   *   *

Q. Do you think everybody is against Mr. Perroni in this case?

A. On the contrary. I have just tried to explain that everybody is for him. You should be against him and then he could stand trial. This is my point. You shouldn't be for him; be against him. Let Mr. Gross be for him and me. Don't let Dr. Lipsky be for him, but let him be his adversary. I believe in the American adversary system of justice. It may be old-fashioned but I believe in it. But I don't believe that people opposed to the defendant should be allowed to retain a psychiatrist. I think this is gross misrepresentation.

Q. Didn't you hear the psychiatrists say who examined him as a result of the Court order that they had no disposition whatever, didn't you hear that?

A. No disposition? I am sorry.

Q. They didn't care one way or the other which way it went.

A. I heard it and I do not believe it for a moment. As a human being I believe, I know as surely as I am sitting here, that it is impossible to be impartial in a case like this. How can you be impartial? This case has been in the papers for seven years.

Q. Well, Doctor, you don't like a man being examined by a psychiatrist who you think is against him because they come out prejudiced, is that correct?

A. Correct.

Q. What about psychiatrists retained by the patient or his agents to examine him—do they come out prejudiced?

A. I have been trying to tell you about my prejudice for the last hour. I don't claim to be impartial. But I would say more. Not only do I not claim to be impartial, but it is my opinion that no psychiatrist is impartial in a case like this. I may be wrong. This is my opinion.

Q. You are of the opinion that this man was not insane before you even saw him, right?

A. No, that is not my opinion. In fact, I would like to tell you how I was retained in this case, if I may, because I think it is relevant at this point.

Q. Go ahead, Doctor.

A. I told Mr. Perroni's brother when he asked me to see Mr. Louis Perroni that I would not accept the case until I have had a chance to talk at sufficient length with Mr. Louis Perroni to see whether or not he is really out in left field—whether or not he thinks he is Jesus Christ, or that right is left, or day is night—or if he is completely disoriented.... So I said to Mr. Perroni's brother that I would like to talk to Mr. Louis Perroni, and if he seems to know what is going on then I would be glad to take his case. Otherwise, I would not—would have nothing to do with it. But you are quite right in one respect. In no circumstances would I be willing to examine him, take his money, then testify that he is mentally ill.

Q. Did you tell the brothers of Mr. Perroni that you will continue to treat him?

A. The subject never came up.

Q. So you aren't there to treat Mr. Perroni, are you, sir?

A. Certainly not.

Q. Just to examine him?

A. No, not to examine him. To give this testimony. The examination is just a preliminary. This was the point of my intervention, as I understood it. This was what I was hired for.

Q. To give testimony?

A. To give testimony.

Q. Not to examine him?

A. The examination was a preliminary, a necessity, in order for me to give rational, relevant, meaningful testimony.

*   *   *

Q. What do you look for, Doctor, in determining whether a man is able to stand trial or assist his counsel in defending the charges against him on a criminal charge?

A. Maybe to me psychiatry is simpler than to some people, but I just like to ascertain whether he can talk to me reasonably, like anybody else, whether he is mentally clear and rational.

Q. You came to the conclusion that Mr. Perroni did not have any mental illness, is that correct—that Mr. Perroni does not have any mental illness?

A. Oh, no. I didn't try to examine him for mental illness. I have already told you my reservations about mental illness.

Q. You came to the conclusion Mr. Perroni is not in such a state of insanity he couldn't prepare for his defense?

A. As I understand it.

*   *   *

(Witness excused)

THE COURT: All right. The evidence is closed. The Court will reserve decision.

*   *   *

Approximately six weeks after the hearing, Judge Kirby handed down his decision: he found Mr. Louis Perroni incompetent to stand trial. Mr. Perroni was thereupon transferred from the Cedar Street Jail in Syracuse to the Matteawan State Hospital in Beacon, N.Y. Appeals from the Court's ruling have failed. At the time of this writing (February 1965), Mr. Perroni remains confined at Matteawan. He has now been incarcerated for nearly ten years.

NOTE

PEOPLE v. WARDEN OF CITY PRISON
235 N.Y.S. 2d 531 (1962)

MATTHEW M. LEVY, JUSTICE.

The person on whose behalf this writ of habeas corpus was obtained appeared before a City Magistrate of the City of New York in the Manhattan Housing and Building Court as a defendant in a number of cases involving allegedly unlawful conditions in buildings owned by him....

The Magistrate heard argument by the tenants' attorney, to the effect that they had been forced to heat the buildings themselves for a time during the Winter, and that children living there had become ill....

During the presentation of statements of counsel, the defendant twice voluntarily interposed—once saying: "I don't feel well"; and, on the other, saying: "Please call a doctor. I don't feel well. Call a doctor." He said and did nothing else throughout the proceedings. No comment was made by court or counsel as to these remarks, but, after the defendant's attorney's final plea for the court's mercy, the Magistrate said to the defendant: "Now, Mr. Weinstein, I have been on the Bench here nearly eight years. I don't think I have ever had a defendant before me who was as cruel as you are, absolutely callous to the feelings of other people, little children, sick children. I don't believe anybody in his normal mind could do what you have done over the period of several years. You have forty-some-odd prior convictions. You pay no attention to the authorities, no attention to the courts, no attention to these inspectors. I think you are a cruel, vicious man and I don't think that you could possibly be normal—so therefore you are committed to Bellevue for examination. Bring him back to this court for sentence and the case must be before me."

*   *   *

[T]here is no jurisdiction in the court to order the

hospital commitment of the defendant for mental examination and observation unless "it shall appear . . . that there is reasonable ground to believe that such defendant is in such [mental] state . . . that he is incapable of understanding the charge or proceeding or of making his defense." . . .

*   *   *

I need not expand upon the fact that I sympathize with the magistrate's opinion that a landlord who, in the operation of his properties, has repeatedly violated the health code to the detriment of his tenants may well be cruel and callous. It is known that, in certain economic circles, some few selfish real estate owners pay no attention to violations placed upon their properties or to prosecutions for the commission of health code and similar offenses. Their cold and calculating theory is that the fines thereupon imposed are business expenses, as in the routine conduct of their affairs—and, if, perhaps, a jail sentence results in an aggravated case, that circumstance is a hazard, to be taken in one's stride, not to be wished but not always entirely unexpected.

However, being a scofflaw, even of that kind, is not —without more—an indication of mental inadequacy within the meaning of section 870 of the Code of Criminal Procedure. One may be fully able to present his defense and to understand court proceedings in which he is involved notwithstanding that he repeatedly violates the law. In holding otherwise the magistrate has imported into our law a socioeconomic theory of crime and punishment and of mental health that is not consistent with the accepted concept upon which legal responsbility for one's conduct is based. . . .

. . . Accordingly, the writ is sustained, and the defendant is released from the hospital commitment. He is remanded to the respondent warden to be produced before the appropriate court for sentence in pursuance of his plea of guilty to the offenses charged. . . .

*   *   *

d.   R. v. ROBERTS
          [1953] 2 All E.R. 340

TRIAL on an indictment for murder.

The defendant, on being arraigned, stood mute, and a jury was impanelled to try the issue whether he was mute by malice or by the visitation of God. Evidence, which was not contradicted, was called by the defence to show that he had been deaf and dumb from birth, and the jury found that he was mute by the visitation of God. Counsel for the Crown submitted that the evidence so far called raised a presumption of idiotism; that, prima facie, the accused was unfit to plead, and incapable of following the proceed-

ings, of instructing counsel for the defence, or of challenging a juror; and that on the authorities these matters (on which the Crown had further evidence to call) should be next tried. It was common ground that, if the accused were found unfit to plead, the learned judge must order his detention as a Broadmoor patient till Her Majesty's pleasure should be known. Counsel for the defence submitted that no presumption of idiotism arose, and that there was no precedent for trying the issue whether or not the defendant was fit to plead before the general issue on the application of the Crown, although such a course had been taken on an application by the defence. In reply to Devlin, J., he intimated that there was a defence on the facts, and that he desired that the jury should try the defendant on the general issue.

DEVLIN, J.: In this case the defendant has been found to be mute by the visitation of God on the verdict of a jury, and principle and authority direct that, unless there is some reason for taking some other course, that finding should be the basis of entering a plea of Not Guilty on behalf of the defendant and the trial against him must proceed. But whether the defendant is found mute of malice or mute by the visitation of God, a question often laid down clearly by the authorities that, if it be established that a man's mind is such that he would be incapable of understanding the nature of the proceedings, it would not be right that he should be put on his trial and convicted of the offence. Such a conviction could not stand. It is clear from the authorities that it is not merely defects of the mind which may bring about that result. Defects of the senses, whether or not combined with some defect of the mind, may do so, and the authorities are clear that, if there are no certain means of communication with the defendant so that there are no certain means of making sure that he will follow as much as it is necessary that he should follow of the proceedings at his trial, he should then be found unfit to plead.

In this case, the defendant being mute by the visitation of God, counsel on both sides are agreed, broadly speaking, that there are no certain means of communicating with him the procedure which takes place at this trial, and the question which has arisen is whether that is a matter which has to be determined by the jury in this case, as it is in most cases, at once, the jury being specially sworn for that purpose, or whether, in effect, it can be tried and determined by the jury together with the trial and determination of the general issue whether the defendant be Guilty or Not Guilty. Counsel for the defence wishes the general issue to be tried. He has not disclosed, as, of course, he is not bound to disclose, and, indeed, should not have disclosed, what the nature of his defence is. It may well be that the defence is that the prosecution witnesses do not make out a *prima facie* case, or it may be that the defence has other witnesses, not yet called, who, if believed, would destroy the case which the prosecution would otherwise have made out. Whatever it may be, it is a perfectly conceivable situation, though it never appears to have arisen in practice before, that counsel for the defence, although he cannot be instructed by the defendant, may say: "I do not think the prosecution can make any case against the defendant. If it can, then, of course, I am in no position to defend it with his aid because he cannot instruct me and cannot tell his story. But, as the prosecution can make out no case, I am not prepared to let the matter go merely on the issue whether he is fit or unfit to plead." If that issue is tried, and is tried alone, and a verdict is returned by the jury that the defendant is unfit to plead, the court has no power except to make one order, viz., that he should be detained as a criminal lunatic, or Broadmoor patient as it is now called, until Her Majesty's pleasure be made known, which means, of course, for an indefinite period.

Counsel for the defence cannot be forced to accept that course for his client if, on a true view of the facts, he thinks that he cannot obtain for his client properly a verdict of Not Guilty. Nor can he be forced to elect. He must be entitled to retain his right to say that the defendant is not in a position to give him instruction and, therefore, he cannot put the defendant in the witness box to tell his own story. He cannot be forced to say to himself: "Shall I play for safety and obtain a verdict whereby the defendant is detained as a criminal lunatic, or shall I, in effect, gamble on the chance of my being able to get him off altogether, with the knowledge that if my gamble fails he will be convicted of murder and there is only one sentence which the court can pass." Though, therefore, it does not appear to be a position which has ever arisen before, and counsel have told me that they have found no authority on the matter, it seems to me that there must be a procedure which would enable counsel for the defence to have the advantage of taking both points. There cannot be any doctrine in a criminal case which compels counsel to elect, and, if there was no such procedure, I think that it would be necessary to invent one, because to insist on the issue being tried of fitness to plead or not might result in the grave injustice of detaining as a criminal lunatic a man who was innocent, and, indeed, it might result in the public mischief that a person so detained would be assumed, in the eyes of the police and of the authorities, to have been the person responsible for the crime—whether he was or was not—and investigation which might have led to the apprehension of the true criminal would not take place.

[I]n *R.* v. *Berry* [1 Q.B.B.D. 447 (1856)] . . . it is plain . . . that, although a question arose whether or not the prisoner was fit to plead, that question was not submitted to the jury until the prosecution had proved their case, when it was submitted to them, they being asked for a special verdict in conjunction with the general issue. That case was also one where the jury had been sworn to ascertain whether the prisoner stood mute of malice or by the visitation of God, and they found that the prisoner was mute by the visitation of God. The trial proceeded because it was thought that a brother-in-law of the prisoner might be able to communicate with him by means of signs. The learned chairman of the quarter sessions then put two questions to the jury: (i) whether they found the prisoner Guilty or Not Guilty of the indictment, and (ii) whether, in their opinion, the prisoner was capable of understanding, and had understood, the nature of the proceedings. The verdict of the jury was:

> "We find the prisoner Guilty on the evidence; and we also find that he is not capable of understanding, and, as a fact, has not understood the nature of the proceedings."

. . . On that verdict the court held that the proper course was that he should be detained under the Criminal Lunatics Act 1800, s. 2, as the finding of the jury amounted in point of law to a finding of insanity.

*   *   *

[I]n *R.* v. *Stafford Prison* (*Governor*). *Ex p. Emery* [2 K.B. 81 (1909)] . . . an accused person, who had been found by a jury to be unfit to plead, was detained under the Criminal Lunatics Act, 1800, s. 2, and the validity of his detention was challenged by a writ of habeas corpus, the question which the court had to determine being whether deafness and inability to read and write and, therefore, to be communicated with, was equivalent, for the purposes of the wording of the act, to a finding of insanity, and they held that it was. . . .

*   *   *

In cases where the defence is not going to challenge that the prosecution has a *prima facie* case, and has no evidence which might induce a jury to reject the evidence for the prosecution, then the convenient course is to let the issue be tried at once. I can find no authority in the cases . . . which would prevent counsel for the defence, who wishes to do so, at the same time preserving all those rights which flow to the defence from the fact that the defendant is a person, if it be so established, who is incapable of being communicated with or from instructing counsel for his defence. Were it otherwise, I think that the gravest mischief and injustice might follow. The defence might wish to tender a witness who, if he was believed, could prove that the defendant was ten miles away at the time of the alleged crime. It cannot, I think, be our law that, by some formality of procedure, counsel for the defendant should be prevented from laying matters of that sort before the jury, and so achieving for his client, if he can, a verdict of Not Guilty.

In the course of giving this ruling, I have not concerned myself with the question whether it is right for the prosecution to begin such matters, i.e., whether the burden is on the prosecution or on the defence to establish unfitness to plead. That is a mere matter of presumption one way or the other. . . .

. . . I do not see why I should not leave the questions to the jury . . .

The indictment was then read, and a plea of Not Guilty entered by direction of the learned judge. Leading counsel for the defence did not desire any part of the proceedings to be interpreted to the defendant and Devlin, J., so directed, observing that, if there were no certain means of communicating with the defendant, there was no possible advantage in embarking on a doubtful means. The trial then proceeded. . . .

[The jury, by direction, found the defendant Not Guilty.]

*   *   *

NOTES

NOTE 1

United States v. Pound

Motion to Dismiss Indictment

Comes now Ezra Pound, defendant, through his committee, Mrs. Dorothy Shakespear Pound, and moves that the indictment in the above-entitled proceeding be dismissed.

And for grounds of the said motion, he respectfully represents:

1. On November 26, 1945, defendant was indicted on charges of treason relating to certain radio broadcasts made by defendant in Italy during World War II. On November 27, 1945, he stood mute on arraignment and plea of not guilty to that indictment was entered by the Court. . . . On December 14, 1945, in pursuance of an appointment by this Court, Drs. Winfred Overholser, Marion R. King, Joseph L. Gilbert, and Wendell Muncie submitted a joint written report to the court that they had thoroughly examined the defendant on several occasions between December 4 and December 13, 1945, that it was their unanimous opinion that defendant was suffering from a paranoid state which rendered him mentally unfit to advise properly with counsel or to participate intelligently and reasonably in his own defense, and that he was insane and mentally unfit for trial. . . . On February 13, 1946, the court held such formal inquisition at which the jury, after hearing the evidence, report and conclusions of Drs. Overholser, King, Gilbert, and Muncie, entered a formal verdict that

the defendant was of unsound mind. Following that verdict, the defendant was committed to the custody of the United States and confined in Saint Elizabeths Hospital.

2. The defendant has remained in confinement at Saint Elizabeths Hospital since that time, where he has been the subject of constant and intense psychiatric tests, examinations, observation, and study. As a result thereof, it is the opinion and conclusion of officials of Saint Elizabeths Hospital that defendant remains mentally unfit to advise properly with counsel or to participate intelligently and reasonably in his own defense and that he is insane and mentally unfit for trial, or to comprehend the nature of the charges against him.

3. Furthermore, it is the opinion and conclusion of these same officials that defendant's condition is permanent and incurable, that it cannot and will not respond to treatment and that trial on the charges against him will be forever impossible because of insanity.

4. Defendant is 72 years old. If the indictment against him is not dismissed he will die in Saint Elizabeths Hospital. He can never be brought to a state of mental competency or sanity sufficient to advise properly with counsel, to participate intelligently and reasonably in his own defense or to comprehend the nature of the charges against him. There can be no benefit to the United States in maintaining him indefinitely in custody as a public charge because that custody cannot contribute to his recovery and defendant's release would not prejudice the interests of the United States. The inevitable effect of failure to dismiss the indictment will be life imprisonment on account of alleged acts and events which can never be put to proof.

5. The primary alleged acts and events on which the indictment is based occurred prior to July 25, 1943. In the ensuing fifteen years memories have faded and direct evidence by the constitutionally-established minimum of two witnesses to each of the various alleged acts and events have inevitably dissipated. In all probability, therefore, the United States lacks sufficient evidence to warrant a prosecution at this time.

6. Suitable arrangements for defendant's custody and care are otherwise available. In the event that the indictment is dismissed, Mrs. Dorothy Shakespear Pound, committee proposes to apply for the delivery of the defendant from further confinement at Saint Elizabeths Hospital to her restraint and care with bond under such terms and conditions as will be appropriate to the public good and the best interests and peace of mind of the defendant in the remaining years of his life.

*   *   *

WHEREFORE, Ezra Pound, defendant, by his

committee, Mrs. Dorothy Shakespear Pound, respectfully moves that the indictment be dismissed.*

Respectfully submitted,

THURMAN ARNOLD
WILLIAM D. ROGERS

NOTE 2

UNITED STATES v. BARNES
175 F. Supp. 60 (S.D. Cal. 1959)

HALL, DISTRICT JUDGE.

On March 4, 1959, an Indictment was returned in this District charging that on or about June 10, 1949, within this District and Division, and in a place under the exclusive jurisdiction of the United States known as Branch United States Disciplinary Barracks, Camp Cooke, California, defendants murdered one Charlie W. Taylor, Jr.

The defendants have filed a Motion to dismiss the Indictment.

*   *   *

I conclude that the prosecution of defendants by court-martial under Article of War, Section 92, without jurisdiction therefor, was such a "deliberate choice" on the part of the government, under the facts in this case, as to amount to a denial of a speedy trial of the defendants by the civil authorities, in violation of their rights under the Sixth Amendment to the Constitution of the United States.

The Motion to dismiss was made on behalf of defendants Barnes, Coons, Lee and Spasoff.

Coons was brought here from the Medical Center for Federal Prisoners at Springfield, Missouri, to which place he was transferred as a mental patient with a mental illness diagnosed as "paranoid schizophrenia and sociopathic personality disturbance."

. . .

*   *   *

On the day of the hearing, in order to be sure that the defendants were satisfied that they had competent and effective counsel in Mr. Hannon, the Court interrogated each one of them. It became apparent to the Court that there was some doubt concerning the present mental competence of Coons, and the Court appointed Dr. Karl Von Hagen, a competent psychiatrist, to examine Coons. Dr. Von Hagen examined Coons at the County Jail, and reported that in his opinion Coons is presently insane and so mentally incompetent as to be unable to understand the proceedings against him, or to properly assist in his own defence.

---

*With the consent of the Government the Federal District Court dismissed the indictment returned against Mr. Pound [*The New York Times*, April 19, 1958].

While the case is to be dismissed on Constitutional grounds, and it seems there may be little that Coons could do to properly "assist" counsel in that regard, the Statute (18 U.S.C. § 4244) is cast in the alternative. If the accused is "presently insane *or* otherwise so mentally incompetent as to be unable to understand the proceedings against him, *or* properly to assist in his own defense," the court shall hold a hearing as to his then state of sanity, and may commit him under 18 U.S.C. § 4246.

*   *   *

It must not be forgotten that underlying Sections 4241–4248 is the concept of *some protection to society*, as well as the preservation of the rights of an accused person.

The Court finds, as a fact, from all the evidence, and adjudges, that Coons is presently insane and so mentally incompetent as to be unable to understand the proceedings against him, and hereby orders that defendant Coons be committed to the custody of the Attorney General of the United States, or his authorized representative, until he shall become mentally competent to stand trial, or until the pending charges in the instant case are disposed of as to him according to law.

As to the remaining defendants, Barnes, Lee and Spasoff,

It is Ordered, Adjudged and Decreed that the Motion to dismiss the Indictment in the instant case be, and the same is hereby granted.

NOTE 3

COMMONWEALTH v. FRANKLIN
172 Pa. Super. 152, 92 A. 2d 272 (1952)

JUDGE MILNER.

*   *   *

. . . Edward J. Franklin, the petitioner, was indicted for assault and battery and for unlawfully resisting arrest . . . The matter came on for trial before a judge and jury and the petitioner was found *not* guilty. The trial judge, nevertheless, thereupon ordered that the defendant be "held in $1,000.00 bail to keep the peace for a period of two (2) years. Defendant permitted to sign own bond," and the order was duly endorsed upon the bill of indictment upon which petitioner had been acquitted. . . .

*   *   *

Because we are aware that many judges in this state have exercised a similar power to that which we are now called upon to subject to inquiry, and because we regard the matter as involving fundamental civil rights, we shall undertake an extended review of the authority upon which the power to bind after acquittal is alleged to rest.

*   *   *

From our survey we have been unable to find any other state in our Union in which it is maintained that a defendant acquitted in a criminal trial can be held under bond to keep the peace. Yet the practice has persisted for many years in Philadelphia County. The Public Defender, in his excellent brief as amicus curiae, states that the Report of the Board of Inspectors of the Philadelphia County Prison for the years 1939 to 1949 indicates that in that period 478 men, after acquittal of criminal charges, were compelled to serve an aggregate of over 600 years in the Philadelphia County Prison in default of bonds aggregating $613,200. Hundreds of defendants, acquitted by juries of their peers, have been placed under the restriction of a bond to keep the peace and many who have been unable to furnish bond or have failed to enter their recognizance have languished in jail and some are now in jail as a result of this practice. . . .

*   *   *

We have concluded that there is no valid authority under the law as it exists today to place the petitioner under bond. He was acquitted of the charge lodged against him and he is entitled to his complete freedom, unfettered by any bond or restriction.

Because of the importance of this and the fact that the practice we condemn has apparently been accepted and followed without adequate examination into its legitimacy, we are obliged to re-examine the subject at some length.

The first reported Pennsylvania case which we have found which approved the requirement that defendants post bond after and despite their acquittal, was *Respublica* v. *Donagan*, 1729, 2 Yeates 437. In that case Patrick Donagan and Francis Cox, the defendants, were charged as accessories before the fact to murder and were found not guilty. The court ordered each to "give security to keep the peace, and be of good behavior to all the liege citizens of the United States, and in particular to Peter Shitz, for the term of fourteen years, each in the sum of 10,000 dollars and two good sureties in 10,000 dollars each."

The report states that "there was strong reason to believe that the prisoners had been concerned in a most horrid murder, though there was not sufficient evidence to convict them of the crime. The court directed them to give the above security, under the firm opinion that they were persons of most dangerous character, and not being able to give the security, they had remained in gaol."

On a motion for their enlargement it was contended that the orders operated as life sentences; that the constitution forbade requirement of excessive bail, imposition of excessive fines or imposition of cruel punishments. The motion was denied per curiam on the statement that "The court before whom the trial was had, under their general authority to preserve the peace, had a right to require such bail and for such

a length of time, as they judged would best answer the ends of public justice. No doubt can be entertained of it. And it would be highly improper for us to interfere, in a matter wherein they have exercised their legal discretion. Unsafe would the community be, if such characters could prowl at large through the country, without a sufficient tie on them." . . .

*   *   *

A note following the opinion states, "The prisoner afterwards broke gaol and escaped."

*   *   *

It is apparent that the sole authorities relied upon by our cases is the Statute of 34 Edw. III, c. 1, and certain English cases.

*   *   *

The Statute of 34 Edw. III, c. 1, enacted in 1360, is as follows:

*   *   *

1. "That in every County of England shall be assigned for the keeping of the peace, one Lord, and with him three or four of the most worthy in the County, with some learned in the law";
2. "And they shall have power to restrain the offenders, rioters, and all other barrators, and to pursue, arrest, take, and chastise them according to their trespass or offense";

*   *   *

6. "And take of all them that be, not of good fame, where they shall be found, sufficient surety and mainprise of their good behaviour towards the King and his People and the others duly to punish, to the intent that the people be not by such *rioters* or *rebels* troubled nor endangered, nor the peace blemished nor merchants nor others passing by the Highways of the realm *disturbed*, nor put in the peril which may happen of such offenders."

*   *   *

Counsel for the petitioner in his excellent brief has indicated at length the vast and significant differences in the world of 1360 and the world of 1952. We shall not undertake any extended historical review of those differences. Suffice it to note that that statute fell into a period of disorganization, riot, illness and death. [T]he reason for the statute was that, due to temporary peace, the soldiers of Edward III returned from years of plundering and pillaging in France, which practice they apparently continued in England. . . .

[T]he power which the judiciary has arrogated unto it itself is a crystalization of a judicial attitude that the jury is not to be fully and finally trusted with its function. The power to bind to good behavior after acquittal is and has been used when the trial judge is of the opinion that the jury erred in its verdict. [I]t should be sufficient to observe that the jury is more than just a juridical instrument, it is a *political* institution which should not be hastily infringed upon in particular and difficult cases lest the generality of freedom which it purports to represent be undermined without planned substitute. To the jury belongs the power to err, not alone in gullibility but also deliberately. . . .

Finally we may state of record that the essentially real basis for our decision is simply that we consider the practice under review to be wrong. We are of the firm conviction that the practice is fundamentally in conflict with any modern and enlightened view of individual civil rights; that it offends the spirit and instinct, and the very letter of due process. The practice of binding after acquittal, even if we were to assume a proper historical basis for it, which we do not, is an anachronism; it is a vestige of a social form which has passed and it cannot coexist with the modern concept of due process; it has been repealed by change. Our very jurisprudence is predicated upon rule by law as distinguished from rule by man. The evil of the practice we are considering is that it is in reality an effective power to punish in virtually unrestrained form. Suppositions of right to review are in practice unrealistic. The liberties of the people are not to be committed to such despotic power—be it executive, legislative or judicial; nor are these liberties to be diluted by pretense and supposition that such virtually unreviewable power will be wielded sparingly.

* * *

The practice we have reviewed is in reality not in any real sense a method of "preventive justice." When a person is committed for default of entry of security after acquittal he is simply being punished without trial. . . .

NOTE 4

BLACKSTONE, WILLIAM

Commentaries*

. . . And really it is an honor, and almost a singular one, to our English laws, that they furnish a title of this sort, since *preventive* justice is, upon every principle of reason, of humanity, and of sound policy, preferable in all respects to *punishing* justice, the execution of which, though necessary, and in its consequences a species of mercy to the commonwealth, is always attended with many harsh and disagreeable circumstances.

This preventive justice consists in obliging those persons whom there is a probable ground to suspect of future misbehavior to stipulate with and to give full assurance to the public that such offence as is

---

* Vol 4, Lewis' Edition, 1897, Rees & Welsh & Co., Philadelphia, pp. 1649-50.

apprehended shall not happen, by finding pledges or securities for keeping the peace, or for their good behavior. This requisition of sureties has been several times mentioned before as part of the penalty inflicted upon such as have been guilty of certain gross misdemeanors; but there also it must be understood rather as a caution against the repetition of the offence than any immediate pain or punishment. And, indeed, if we consider all human punishments in a large and extended view, we shall find them all rather calculated to prevent future crimes than to expiate the past; since . . . all punishments inflicted by temporal laws may be classed under three heads: such as tend to the amendment of the offender himself, or to deprive him of any power to do future mischief, or to deter others by his example; all of which conduce to one and the same end of preventing future crimes, whether that can be effected by amendment, disability, or example. But the caution which we speak of at present is such as is intended merely for prevention, without any crime actually committeed by the party, but arising only from a probable suspicion that some crime is intended or likely to happen; and consequently it is not meant as any degree of punishment, unless perhaps for a man's imprudence in giving just ground for apprehension.

NOTE 5

EX PARTE STATE
268 Ala. 524, 108 So. 2d 448 (1959)

COLEMAN, JUSTICE.

* * *

Silas Coma Garrett, III, hereinafter referred to as the defendant, was indicted by the Grand Jury of Russell County for murder in the first degree. . . .

* * *

In the case at bar, a controversy exists between the state and the defendant wherein the state contends that defendant should be delivered by the sheriff "to the Superintendent of the State hospitals," to remain in his custody "for such length of time as may in the judgment of the commission of lunacy be necessary to determine his mental condition," etc. The defendant says he cannot be confined lawfully in the State Hospitals, or elsewhere, so long as he is entitled to remain at large on bail.

* * *

If by a statute the legislature could require that a defendant, otherwise entitled to bail, should be committed to the State Hospitals and there confined while awaiting trial, that defendant would be denied bail as effectually as if he were confined in jail or elsewhere. If § 425, Title 15, requires that a defendant shall be confined on the report of the superintendent, the defendant would be denied bail by that report as effectually as by legislative act. The legislature cannot do indirectly that which it is forbidden to do directly.

* * *

NOTE 6

STATE v. SWAILS
223 La. 751, 66 So. 2d 796 (1953)

MCCALEB, JUSTICE.

Appellant, Roy C. Swails, was indicted on February 4, 1952, for [murder.] On March 18, 1952, he pleaded present insanity and insanity at the time of the commission of the crimes in each case and the court appointed a lunacy commission. . . .

* * *

. . . After hearing the evidence, the judge wrote an opinion in which he accepted the views voiced by Doctors Butler and Kerlin in their report and testimony, viz.—that appellant is able to understand the proceedings against him and to assist in his defense although he is afflicted with a brain syndrome (cerebral arteriosclerosis) which is presently in a state of remission, meaning "a diminution or abatement of the symptoms of his disease * * *." Nevertheless, the judge ruled that, in view of the further medical opinion that appellant, if released from the hospital, would very likely relapse into his prior unsound mental state and would become a menace to society and dangerous to the community . . . it was ordered that appellant be returned to the mental hospital. He has appealed from the adverse decision.

* * *

. . . The apprehension and even the predictions of some of the physicians that appellant may be a menace to society, if he is ever released, affords no basis whatever for holding him presently insane, within the meaning of the law, or for recommitting him to an institution. And to deny him a trial for such a speculative reason would, we think, infringe upon his fundamental right of due process of law and to be accorded a speedy public trial vouch-safed by . . . our Constitution and the Fourteenth Amendment to the Constitution of the United States.

* * *

. . . The statute is founded on the cardinal and humane concept that no person shall be tried for the commission of a crime when he is mentally incapable of understanding the proceedings against him and of making an intelligent defense. Protection of the public from possible harm from the accused is not envisioned by the law. . . .

* * *

[The] principal contention [of the State] on this appeal is that the trial judge erred in concluding that appellant was able to assist in his defense, in view of the report of the lunacy commission in which it is stated that "Mr. Swails claims that at present he recalls practically nothing for a period extending for a year or more before the time of the commission of the alleged crime until after he had been committed to the hospital for about two months, and that all that he knows about any such crime is what his wife has told him and what he later read in the papers, and with this statement we agree." It is argued by the district attorney that it is not enough that appellant is able to confer with his counsel intelligently; that, in order to be able to assist them in his defense, he must have such possession and control of his mental powers, including the faculty of memory, as will enable him to testify and inform his counsel of material facts bearing upon the criminal acts charged against him, which he cannot do in this case as he remembers nothing.

This contention would be very forceful and persuasive were this a prosecution in which the accused was pleading not guilty for, in such case, his inability to inform his counsel of any of the facts regarding his own movements in relation to the charges against him would materially affect him in his defense. But, here, appellant is pleading insanity at the time of the commission of the crimes. . . . His alleged amnesia as to the events occurring at, before and after the crimes were committed is not a factor which hampers his defense. On the contrary, the very fact that appellant does not remember anything concerning his alleged criminal acts may be of material aid to his counsel in their presentation of a case of insanity and his testimony, if he sees fit to take the stand, may have considerable weight with the jury.

The judgment appealed from is reversed. . . .

NOTE 7

FREED, DANIEL J.

Preventing Pretrial Release*

* * *

Bail today may be defined as serving two functions. Its lawful purpose is said to be to assure the presence of the defendant at trial, and for this purpose we tend to acknowledge that bail can be set high to prevent flight. This purpose is contrasted with the supposedly unlawful practice of preventive detention, under which high bail is set to protect the community against a risk of danger from the defendant's future crime. For the purpose of discussion I would like to suggest— (1) that this formulation of the contrast exaggerates

* Paper delivered at the Institute on the Operation of Pretrial Release Projects (1965). Reprinted with permission of the author who retains reprint rights.

the distinction between the two functions of bail;

(2) that the terminology "preventive detention" as applied to one but not the other is misleading and

(3) that history affords little support for the supposedly wide distinction between the use of bail to secure appearance and its use in protecting against danger.

Permit me, if you will, to rephrase the functions of bail. What happends today when a defendant is detained prior to his trial? When a court sets high bail to detain on grounds of flight risk, let us speak not of assuring appearance but rather of the court's prediction that, if released, the defendant may jump bail and run away. And when a court sets high bail to detain on grounds of risk of danger, let us speak not of protecting the community but rather of the court's prediction that, if released, the defendant may injure persons or property rights. So rephrased, we find that both forms of high bail involve

(a) a prediction of the defendant's future conduct on the basis of past events;

(b) a prediction that, if released, the defendant will do something illegal, i.e., jump bail or perform some unlawful act; and

(c) detention of a man who is presumed to be innocent of the present charge against him.

In other words, detention in both cases is grounded on a belief in future personal misbehavior—that the defendant will not conform his conduct to the requirements of law but will instead commit a crime if the court does not stop him.

Once we analyze the two forms of detention in these terms, we find, *first*, that neither kind of detention alters the presumption of innocence with respect to the crime charged. For both released and detained defendants, the traditional presumption of innocence operates with respect to the current charge as an element in allocating the burden of proof at trial. Detention prior to trial is not based on a determination of guilt. It is designed not to punish the defendant for past acts but to prevent him from engaging in future acts. *Second*, we see that both forms of detention equally violate the due process clause, or are equally irrelevant to due process, because each equally deprives a man of his liberty by imposing a prior restraint to guard against anticipated misconduct. *Third*, we discover that both forms of detention equally merit the description "preventive detention" because each equally restrains the accused's freedom in order to prevent misbehavior. And *fourth*, both forms of detention find strong support in history. This is evident from the fact that at the time of the Constitution, the right to bail was confined to noncapital cases but did not exist as to capital offenses which, as of 1790, embraced virtually every crime we worry about and call a felony today. In other words, history accorded a right to bail in misdemeanor cases but only a discretionary entitle-

ment to pretrial release for persons charged with many of the more serious offenses.

*   *   *

One hundred and seventy five years have seen profound changes in the classification called capital crimes. But these changes have come about not because the conduct they apply to is deemed less offensive or less to be feared by society, but rather because changing attitudes toward criminal behavior and corrections have evolved a more humane and individualized approach. In retrospect, the changes in classifying offenses for purposes of sentencing do not seem relevant to pretrial bail decisions, nor to have been designed to affect those decisions. I doubt, for instance, that the growing number of states which are today abolishing capital punishment intend thereby to establish for the first time an absolute right to bail in murder cases.

These reflections have caused me to wonder whether the bail system was really intended to develop as irrationally as it sounds when lawyers tell laymen that bail can be used to prevent flight but not crime. It is irrational, I think, to say that our system can detain a man who will interfere with court proceedings but that it must release a man whose harm to society can be predicted. It is irrational to say we are forced to release a father charged with incest but can with perfect propriety detain his daughter to protect her against the danger of repeated assaults. Even when speaking in the context of protecting court proceedings, it makes little sense to say that we have to release suspects even if we know they will pose great danger to victims and witnesses. Can we really find support in constitutional history for the proposition that the law is more readily able to safeguard the sanctity of court proceedings than the safety of streets and homes? . . .

This analysis suggests to me that perhaps the question of the right to bail is historically and logically more a subject of legislative classification than of constitutional status. If this is so, we would still be a long way from solving the problem of preventive detention. A number of thorny issues would remain to be faced by legislatures: E.g., which offenses ought to be bailable as of right? What criteria ought to be adopted for detention in cases involving offenses not bailable as of right? What procedures should be devised to fairly and speedily predict future misbehavior?

. . . Predicting future crime and predicting future flight are terribly difficult assessments for courts to make, and can result in seriously hampering an accused in his preparation for trial and his quest for equal justice. Abolishing detention based on inability to raise money bail, and replacing it by explicit authorization to detain on grounds of predicted danger, may well increase the risk that some judges will unfairly detain more accused persons in response to community pressures. But our hostility towards the notion of preventive detention ought not lead us to continuing the game of making believe that the practice does not exist. It ought not blind us to the fact that the practice is indulged in by criminal courts every day through the often unfair and often ineffective medium of excessive bail, without the candor that is needed to make it visible, controllable and susceptible to appellate review and constitutional testing.

. . . I would hope that much good could come from recognizing the similarity between the risk of flight and the risk of danger, since both involve predicting future behavior, both deal with concerns present in 1790, and both equally can be classified as preventive detention when they are used to prevent future misconduct. Considering the subject more openly will perhaps prevent us from continuing to detain ourselves in a doctrinal box which compels a result few today think is sensible when a violent recidivist makes high bail and goes free, and which certainly does not promote respect for law or the objectives of selective pretrial release.

NOTE 8

DERSHOWITZ, ALAN M.

The Role of Law in the Prediction and Prevention of Harmful Conduct*

It does not follow from the fact that preventive detention *is* surreptitiously "indulged in by criminal courts every day" that its continuation *should* be authorized. Its social benefits and costs should be articulated and balanced. If the former are thought to outweigh the latter, then perhaps some form of preventive detention should be authorized in appropriate situations. If not, then procedure should be devised to purge it from the system. If preventive detention is to be authorized, it should be candid, visible, controllable and subject to review. Moreover, it should not employ distorting variables—like money—which result in the detention of some people who are less dangerous than others who are released.

There is another distorting variable implicit in the recent suggestions for preventive detention of persons awaiting trial. If detention to prevent certain predicted harmful acts is a desirable goal, why should it be limited to instances where a person is charged with a crime (of which he is presumed innocent)? If the goal of preventive detention is to reduce the frequency of certain predictable patterns of behavior, then it should be authorized whenever such patterns are reliably predicted, without regard to whether the

* Paper delivered at the 43rd annual meeting of the American Orthopsychiatric Association (1966). Reprinted with permission of the author who retains reprint rights.

predicted law breaker is, or is not, awaiting trial.

[Likewise,] if the function of involuntary hospitalization is the preventive detention of dangerous people, then why should it matter whether such people are, or are not, "mentally ill." If a "mentally healthy" person is sufficiently dangerous, why should he not be confined? If a "mentally ill" person is not sufficiently dangerous, why should he be confined?

[T]he law should not authorize the detention of allegedly dangerous persons who are awaiting trial or who are mentally ill, unless we would also be willing to incarcerate equally dangerous persons who are neither awaiting trial nor mentally ill. This, of course, forces a confrontation of the critical question: Should the law authorize the preventive detention of persons solely on the basis of a prediction that they are likely to cause harm? To pour content into this broad question, we need: more precise definitions of "harm" and "likely"; more reliable information about the increasing accuracy of predictions; and more candid acknowledgement of the extent to which preventive detention is practiced today. But we must not fall into the trap of believing that precise definitions, reliable information, and candid acknowledgments will produce a system of preventive detention which does not entail the sacrifice of other important values. What it will produce is a clearer picture of how much sacrifice of which values will be required to assure what degree of safety. And this will help us strike a fair and intelligent balance between the safety of those individuals who would be harmed if preventive detention were not authorized, and the freedom of those individuals who would be confined on the basis of erroneous predictions if preventive detention were authorized.

NOTE 9

FOOTE, CALEB

The Coming Crisis in Bail*

[I]t will be useful to examine the concept of preventive detention on its possible merits as sound policy.

Such proposals have all the seductive appeal of the maxim that an ounce of prevention is worth a pound of cure, but the impropriety of the application of that maxim to a democratic system of criminal law should give one pause. Behind the proposals are certain assumptions:

(a) that the contingencies which are to justify detention are sufficiently narrow and precise to be capable of administration as meaningful legal standards;

(b) that we have the ability to predict the probability of occurrence of these contingencies in individual cases;

* 113 University of Pennsylvania *Law Review* 1125, 1165-1175 (1965). Reprinted by permission.

(c) that there is or will be an investigatory structure which can develop the facts necessary for decision;

(d) that there is or will be an adjudicatory system before a person competent to make the necessary prediction, with right to counsel, hearing, an opportunity to contest the facts and their application to law, and provision for appellate review;

(e) as time is of the essence in a process where even a day's delay is important and five or six weeks moots the entire issue, that the fact-finding, adjudication, and appellate review can all be accommplished with great dispatch.

In determining the substantive standards which might be proposed for preventive detention, lack of precision is as much a vice as is vagueness in the substantive criminal law. A standard which provides merely for detention if the accused is deemed a danger to the community[333] or if it would not be "proper"[334] to release him gives no guidance to trial judges, permits no effective appellate review and invites abuse by allowing the trial judge to indulge his own feelings and prejudices.

More specific grounds usually advanced as possible bases for preventive detention include the risk of nonappearance for trial, the danger that the accused will commit a crime while on pretrial release, the danger that he will intimidate witnesses, harm a complaining witness or attempt to influence a juror. . .

The risks of flight and criminality need further narrowing if they are to be used as standards. What kind of nonappearance for trial, for example, should warrant detention? . . . In view of the strength of the policy against detention, is bringing a gambler or a prostitute to trial of sufficient importance to warrant detention if there is a finding of a risk of nonappearance? Second, most nonappearance is temporary. In Philadelphia a common complaint was that defendants on bail did not appear on the day scheduled if they were slated to appear before a "hanging judge," but instead would show up soon thereafter. Such judge-jumping is a nuisance and complicates court calendars; is it enough to warrant detention? . . . Unless the standards are sufficiently narrow to require proof of particular circumstances which set the individual case apart from the general run of cases, there are no real limits on detention. . . .

* * *

Evaluation of the desirability of attempting to predict such criteria for determining pretrial detention as flight, anticipated serious criminal conduct, or intimidation of witnesses turns both on our underlying set of values and on whether or not we possess the knowledge which such predictions would require. This can best be illustrated if we taken an example.

[E]xisting data show a very low incidence of flight for the purpose of avoiding trial and that there is no reason to expect that this would be significantly increased by the release of indigents. Leaning over backwards to overstate the risk, I will assume that under present conditions the rate of absconding to avoid trial is one and one-half percent of bailed cases, and then I will double this rate to allow for any additional risk created by the release of all indigents. This leaves us with a pretrial defendant population of which we would expect three percent to try to avoid trial by flight.

In any situation in which the event to be predicted occurs so infrequently in the population concerned, any attempt to individualize prediction must start off against very heavy odds.[346] By the simple expedient of releasing every defendant pending trial, the implied prediction made as to each one that he would not flee would be right ninety-seven percent of the time. The only way in which individualized prediction could improve upon this success rate would be if individualization made less than three mistakes out of every one hundred cases. This is clearly impossible in dealing with the treacherous quicksand of future human conduct, and I will note below some of the reasons why this is so. Moreover, even if a slight improvement could be achieved, for example, a reduction to only two mistakes in a hundred instead of three, it is very questionable as a practical matter that so slight an improvement would be worth the cost of processing every case individually. Individual prediction, after all, is expensive for all concerned— for the state because it requires times for adjudication and assignment of counsel; for the accused because it delays the decision as to his right to be released promptly after arrest.

All of the criteria which might be used as standards for preventive detention share this characteristic of being statistically infrequent. Probably we know least about the degree of probability that a defendant during the period of pretrial release will commit a

333. *Rehman* v. *California*, 85 Sup. Ct. 5 (Douglas, Circuit Justice, 1964) (denying bail pending appeal where state court held appellant's enlargement would present "an immediate, clear and present danger imperiling, jeopardizing, and threatening the health, safety, and welfare of the community"); D.C. Cir R. 33(f), cited in *Hairston* v. *United States*, 343 F.2d 313, 316 n.13 (D.C. Cir. 1965) (*per curiam*) (Bazelon, C.J. dissenting) (providing for denial of bail pending appeal when "the safety of the community would be jeopardized").

334. Att'y Gen. Rep. 76.

346. See, e.g., Rosen, "Detection of Suicidal Patients: An Example of Some Limitations in the Prediction of Infrequent Events," 18 *J. Consulting Psychology* 397, 402 (1954)

The low incidence of suicide is in itself a major limitation in the development of an effective suicide detention device, for in the attempt to predict suicide or any other infrequent event, a large number of false positives are obtained (patients incorrectly classified as suicides). . . . A suicide detention device is not feasible until much more is learned about the differential characteristics of patients who commit suicide.

serious crime. Here we have no data at all, but it is inconceivable that the probability is higher than five percent and more likely it is considerably lower. The other criteria noted—that the defendant will intimidate witnesses or jurors or injure a complainant—are apparently very rare, statistically well below one percent.

The foregoing probability analysis rests on a value judgment: that all mistakes in prediction are equally bad, and that it is as unfortunate mistakenly to detain A because of our erroneous assumption that he would flee as it is mistakingly to release B only to find that he will abscond. I think this is the proper value judgment to apply, for it seems to me just as important for the administration of the criminal law not to lock up an accused unnecessarily as it is not to permit a defendant to escape trial by flight. But as it seems so obvious that proceeding upon the assumption of this value judgment leads to rejection of the claim for preventive detention, I am forced to the conclusion that the advocates of preventive detention must make a different underlying value judgment. It is worthwhile, then, to examine an alternative value hypothesis.

Let us suppose that the flight of one defendant to avoid trial is regarded as a more serious occurrence than the erroneous detention of one defendant who in fact would not have fled if released. We might paraphrase but reverse another old maxim and conclude that the prevention of one flight is ten times as important to society as the prevention of one unnecessary detention. We would have to devise a different method which would allow for this weighting in an evaluation of success or failure of prediction. This could be done by assigning a score of one point for each defendant who does not flee and ten points for each one who does. Thus in our sample of one hundred cases, a perfect score would be ninety-seven points for that many defendants correctly predicted not to flee plus thirty points for three defendants correctly predicted to flee, or a total of 127 points. Applying this measure to the method of automatic release of every defendant, we see that its success rate falls sharply: it earns ninety-seven points (one for each defendant who does not flee) out of the possible total of 127 points, or only about seventy-six and one-half per cent of perfection. Thus a competing system of preventive detention which tries to do better by predicting on an individualized, case-by-case method faces odds which, while still formidable, are no longer overwhelming. An example of the most favorable kind of result we could expect from individualized prevention under ideal conditions might come out as follows: Eighty-five defendants would be predicted not to flee, of whom one in fact does flee and eighty-four do not; and fifteen defendants would be predicted to flee, of whom in fact two flee and thirteen do not. The evaluation score for this result would be eighty-four (for those correctly predicted not to flee) plus twenty (for the two cases correctly predicted to flee), a rating of nearly eighty-two per cent of perfection (104 out of the possible 127 points). Thus although the method of individualized prevention has made fourteen mistakes against only three mistakes for automatic release, we might still prefer it if we make the hypothesized value judgment that one escape is ten times as serious as one unnecessary detention.

It may be objected that the example just given is not fair to the method of individualized prevention because we have assigned it too many mistakes. On the contrary, by assuming it would make eighty-six correct judgments in one hundred cases we have given it a success rate probably higher than anything to be expected. In all areas where prediction of future human conduct has been subjected to empirical validation the results have proved to be very modest indeed. The critical part of the foregoing sentence is subjection of *all* the results to empirical validation. When we use prediction today in the criminal law, as in imposing a prison sentence instead of probation or in granting or withholding parole because of anticipated future dangerousness, the validity of the predictions made are not subjected to scientific study; instead the system conceals most of its mistakes. Thus when a judge or a psychiatrist advising him concludes that a particular defendant poses too great a risk to be released on probation, the prison sentence which the judge imposes as a result of the prediction prevents any evaluation of its accuracy. The only errors which show up—and they are ones of which judges and parole boards are made painfully aware—is where a defendant given probation or parole turns out to be dangerous. The errors on the other side of the ledger—the cases of those sent to prison as bad risks but who in fact would not have proved to be bad risks—are never identified and therefore cannot be counted. But all experience with the scientific study of prediction shows that this back side of the moon is where most of the errors will in fact occur.[347]

---

347. See, for example, a very recent prediction study of problems closely analogous to those of pretrial preventive detention: Molof, *Prediction of Future Assaultive Behavior Among Youthful Offenders* (California Youth Authority, Research Rep. No. 41, 1965). An actuarial prediction instrument was applied to two samples of male first parole releases from California institutions, the first consisting of 2,060 cases and the second of 8,017. Those groups predicted to produce the highest proportions of assaultive offenders did so to a statistically significant degree, but the number of false predictions was so high that "the prediction instrument are neither accurate nor efficient." *Id.* at 58. For example, for the score category predicted to produce and which did produce the highest proportion of assaultive offenders, only 29 out of 128 offenders so classified in one sample, and 29 out of 334 in the other, actually turned out to be assaultive offenders; all the rest were false predictions. *Id.* at 56–57, Tables 13, 15. Molof's work uses actuarial or statistical prediction techniques. An

What causes this overprediction of a criterion, a phenomenon which has plagued all efforts at systematic prognosis of future conduct, can be better understood if we retrace our steps for a moment and put ourselves in the shoes of the judge who made the predictions of risk of flight in our last example. We hypothesized a sample of one hundred defendants and an average flight rate of three per cent. The judges' job, then, is to identify those three, and only those three. In this real and far from perfect world, the judge is faced at the outset by two fundamental limitations on his work: the inadequacy of the factual data available to him and the inadequacy of our knowledge—we simply do not know much about the human mechanics which cause three of our sample and only three, to decide upon the desperate and probably self-defeating expedient of flight. Perhaps seventy of our defendants will be relatively easy to classify as good risks—their records will not be as bad as the others and as to each there is no special reason to think they will abscond. Another fifteen or so will be borderline—they give us a lot of trouble, but they are not as bad as the worst. As a good judge will be keenly aware of the low incidence of flight, constantly reminding himself that only three out of the one hundred are actually likely to flee, he will give these fifteen the benefit of the doubt and also classify them as good risks. There is a substantial likelihood, however, that this group of eighty-five so far granted release from detention will contain one of the three who will actually flee, an error due either to the omission of critical information from the factual record submitted to the judge or to the vast unknowns in our knowledge of human conduct. There will remain, then, fifteen defendants who will be almost indistinguishable from one another according to any of the standards which the judge might reasonably guess (because we have little tested knowledge) to be relevant to an assessment of the risk of flight. All of these fifteen will have prior criminal records, inadequate ties to the community, a sketchy employment history, and the prospect of probable conviction and a probable substantial prison sentence. Application of such standards to this group, therefore, will not help the judge to distinguish the two or three who will flee from the twelve or thirteen who, despite their equally bad records, will not. This places the judge in a dilemma[348]—and this is the dilemma of preventive detention. If he decides to select only three for detention, because he knows from the statistical probabilities that only three will actually flee, he has no method for choosing these three from the other twelve better than using a pack of cards, although he may choose to call this process intuition or otherwise mask what he is doing behind some similar label. If he decides nonetheless to try picking just three, he would avoid the error of a high rate of unnecessary detention. The trouble with this, of course, is that he is more likely than not to miss both the two remaining cases of actual flight, while to identify them both would require luck of the order needed to draw a full house in poker. So I hypothesized instead that the most reasonable thing for the judge to do would be to detain all fifteen, which gave us the results noted above. At least the judge has identified and thereby prevented two out of the three flights— a modestly successful result. If the cost of this success is that he was wrong about thirteen of the fifteen bad risks whom he detained, this is unavoidable. The only way to reduce this error would also reduce his chances of identifying even as many as two-thirds of those who in fact will flee.

As the same analogy applies to other criteria of detention, it is again apparent that the critical threshold problem in an evaluation of preventive detention is the judgment of how much to weigh the mistake of allowing a defendant to flee (or commit a serious crime, or intimidate a witness) relative to the weight assigned to a mistake of unnecessary detention. Unless we choose to give the first kind of mistake much more weight, the case for preventive detention collapses and we need to proceed no further. Moreover, even if we make the alternative value judgment that unnecessary imprisonment of the untried is the much less serious error, it will be recalled that we postulated ideal conditions for our judge who, in our hypothetical, achieved eighty-two percent of perfection. In practice the judging function would be

---

analysis of the comparative efficacy of statistical and clinical methods of prediction in twenty-seven studies in which both methods were used showed that in seventeen the statistical method was superior, in ten they were about the same, and in none was clinical prediction superior. See Meehl, *Clinical v. Statistical Prediction* 82–128 (1954).

Predictions by psychiatrists attempting to assess the probability of future breakdown of army inductees show similar results on evaluation. For example, Berlien studied 248 World War II inductees who fell in a class usually rejected for service as risks of becoming psychiatric casualties but who in the instance studied had been inducted. One year later 209 were still in service, 32 had been discharged, five died and two were commissioned as officers. Berlien, "Psychiatric Aspects of Military Manpower Conservation, 111 *American J. Psychiatry* 91, 95, Table 4 (1954).

---

348. This problem has been beautifully analyzed by Freud: Even supposing that we thoroughly know the aetiological factors that decide a given result, still we know them only qualitatively, and not in their relative strength. Some of them are so weak as to become suppressed by others, and therefore do not affect the final result. But we never know beforehand which of the determining factors will prove the weaker or the stronger. We only say at the end that those which succeeded must have been the stronger. Hence it is always possible by analysis to recognize the causation with certainty, whereas a prediction of it by synthesis is impossible.

Freud, "The Psychogenesis of a Case of Homosexuality in a Woman," in 2 *Collected Papers* 227 (1959).

diffused, a process which could only reduce the effectiveness of prediction. . . .

* * *

. . . The addition of the label "preventive" does not cleanse detention of its vices: pretrial punishment and impairment of a fair trial. The overwhelming objection to such detention is that the kinds of precise prediction of future conduct which it requires cannot be made with significant reliability even under the best of fact finding and diagnostic circumstances. As it would have to be administered on a mass scale before the lowest level judiciary with no practical possibility of fast and effective appellate review, it would deteriorate into the worst kind of uncontrolled discretion.

The impossibility of individualized preventive prediction in this area and the statistical demonstration that the least number of mistakes will be made by releasing everyone is a convincing modern vindication of the wisdom of the absolute right to bail which has been an important part of our history since the Massachusetts Body of Liberties in 1641.

* * *

NOTE 10

WILLIAMSON v. UNITED STATES
184 F. 2d 280 (2nd. Cir. 1950)

MR. JUSTICE JACKSON, as Circuit Justice for the Second Circuit:

These Communist Party leaders were convicted for conspiring to advocate and teach the violent overthrow of the United States Government and to organize the Communist Party for that purpose. . . .

* * *

After the Court of Appeals affirmed the convictions, defendants expressed an intention to petition the Supreme Court to review their cases. The Prosecution asked that bail be revoked and defendants remanded to jail [on the ground] that defendants, while at large, *have pursued* and *will continue to pursue* a course of conduct and activity dangerous to the public welfare, safety and national security of the United States. . . .

To remain at large, under bond, after conviction and until the courts complete the process of settling substantial questions which underlie the determination of guilt cannot be demanded as a matter of right. It rests in sound judicial discretion. . . .

* * *

The Government's alternative contention is that defendants, by misbehavior after conviction, have forfeited their claim to bail. Grave public danger is said to result from what they may be expected to do,

in addition to what they have done since their conviction. If I assume that defendants are disposed to commit every opportune disloyal act helpful to Communist countries, it is still difficult to reconcile with traditional American law the jailing of persons by the courts because of anticipated but as yet uncommitted crimes.[1] Imprisonment to protect society from predicted but unconsummated offenses is so unprecedented in this country and so fraught with danger of excesses and injustice that I am loath to resort to it, even as a discretionary judicial technique to supplement conviction of such offenses as those of which defendants stand convicted.

* * *

NOTE 11

CARBO v. UNITED STATES
82 S. Ct. 662 (1962)

MR. JUSTICE DOUGLAS, Circuit Justice.

* * *

One convicted of rape or murder is not necessarily turned loose on bail pending review, even though substantial questions were presented in the appeal. If, for example, the safety of the community would be jeopardized, it would be irresponsible judicial action to grant bail. As stated in United States ex rel. *Estabrook* v. *Otis*, 8 Cir., 18 F. 2d 689, 690, "Bail should not be granted where the offense of which the defendant has been convicted is an atrocious one, and there is danger that if he is given his freedom he will commit another of like character."

* * *

NOTE 12

CROSBY v. POTTS
8 Ga. 463, 69 S.E. 582 (1910)

POWELL, J.

On September 1, 1910, during a term of the city court of Sylvester, the judge ordered from the bench that the plaintiff in error, Crosby, who had been subpoenaed as a witness for the state in a criminal case pending before the court, should be held for that purpose by the sheriff, and that he be committed to jail for the purpose of securing his presence at the trial, unless he would enter into bail in the sum of $200, conditioned for his appearance at the trial. This order was orally delivered, and the sheriff took Crosby into custody. He sued out habeas corpus.

---

1. There are ways of dealing with certain threats to commit crime. In these cases the law only imprisons in default of furnishing an undertaking, but the person held is released if he furnishes the required undertaking to abide the court's order and "keep the peace." . . .

[T]he court as an arm of the state has the right to impose hardship upon the citizen whenever the state's interests being administered in the court require the imposition. It is a hardship upon one, whose only connection with a case is that he happens to know some material fact in relation thereto, that he should be taken into control by the court and held in the custody of the jailer unless he gives bond (which, from poverty, he may be unable to give), conditioned that he will appear and testify; but the exigencies of particular instances do often require just such stringent methods in order to compel the performance of the duty of the witness appearing and testifying. There are many cases in which an ordinary subpoena would prove inadequate to secure the presence of the witness at the trial. The danger of punishment for contempt on account of a refusal to appear is sometimes too slight to deter the witness from absenting himself. Especially is this true where there are but few ties to hold the witness in the jurisdiction where the trial is to be held, and there are reasons why he desires not to testify; for, when once he has crossed the state line, he is beyond the grasp of any of the court's processes to bring him to the trial or to punish him for his refusal to answer to a subpoena. . . .

It is hardly necessary to say that the imprisoning of a witness to secure his attendance is a harsh remedy—one that should be very sparingly exercised. No court should ever order a witness to be imprisoned in default of bond, except from grave necessity. Unless his testimony is material and important, and unless there is strong likelihood that, if he is not restrained by confinement or bond, he will violate the mandates of the subpoena and flee the limits of the state, the power should not be exercised. This is a matter as to which every court, when it is presented, must exercise a broad, humane discretion, having in view the rights of the citizen, and the even higher rights of justice and of the state.

The present record does not disclose the grounds upon which the trial judge acted. We therefore presume that he acted upon sufficient grounds. . . .

* * *

Judgment Affirmed.

4.

INSANITY-DEFENSE COMMITMENT

a. OVERHOLSER v. LYNCH
288 F.2d 388 (D.C. Cir. 1961)

* * *

BASTIAN, CIRCUIT JUDGE

On November 6, 1959, appellee [defendant in the

trial court] came before the Municipal Court for the District of Columbia on informations charging two violations of the bad check law . . . Pursuant to § 24–301(a), D.C. Code, the trial judge ordered appellee committed to District of Columbia General Hospital for mental observation, and appellee entered that hospital the same day. A report from the hospital was received by the court on December 4, 1959, stating that appellee was at that time incompetent to stand trial. Under the provisions of § 24–301(a), the trial judge ordered that appellee remain at the hospital for treatment. On December 28, 1959, a second report was received from the hospital stating that appellee had improved and was then competent to stand trial. The psychiatrist who wrote the report went on to state that, in his opinion, appellee was a manic-depressive, manic type, and that this disease particularly affects financial judgment. He further stated that, in his opinion, appellee's crimes were the product of this mental disease or defect and that appellee required further treatment to insure against repetition of the offenses. . . .

On December 29, 1959, appellee was brought to trial and was represented by counsel. When his case was called, appellee sought to withdraw the not guilty plea which he had entered earlier and to enter a plea of guilty. The trial judge, having before him the report that appellee was not mentally competent when the acts were committed, refused to allow a change in the plea and proceeded to conduct a trial on the charges. During the course of this trial, the psychiatrist who had examined appellee testified,[1] over objection, as to appellee's mental condition at the time of the commission of the offenses. At the trial, it appears that appellee took the stand and denied essential elements of the crimes with which he was charged. At the conclusion of the case, the trial judge found appellee not guilty by reason of insanity and pursuant to § 24–301(d) D.C. Code, ordered him committed to St. Elizabeths Hospital. No appeal was taken.

On June 13, 1960, appellee filed a petition for a writ of habeas corpus in the District Court, to test the legality of his detention at St. Elizabeths. That court held that the Municipal Court was without jurisdiction to commit appellee in the manner described above and, on June 27, 1960, ordered that he be

1. In *Berger* v. *United States*, 1935, 295 U.S. 78, 88, the Supreme Court said:

"The United States Attorney is representative . . . of a sovereignty . . . whose interest . . . in a criminal prosecution is not that it shall win a case, but *that justice shall be done*. As such he is in a peculiar and very definite sense the servant of the law, the two-fold aim of which is that guilt shall not escape or innocence suffer. . . ." [Emphasis supplied.]

We think that the aim "that justice shall be done" applies at least equally to the courts. We therefore agree with the Government that it does not matter whether the psychiatrist was called by the court or by the Government; in either case, he was properly called.

released unless civil commitment proceedings were instituted within ten days of the date of the order.

* * *

... Rule 9, Mun. Ct. Crim., states:

"A defendant may plead not guilty, [or] guilty .... The court *may* refuse to accept a plea of guilty, and shall not accept the plea without first determining that the plea is made voluntarily with understanding of the nature of the charge. ..." [Emphasis supplied.]

Appellee contends that the "shall not" clause modifies the first clause of this rule, with the net effect that the only circumstance in which a plea of guilty is properly refused is that outlined in the second clause. We do not think this is the case. ...

* * *

... The permissive clause beginning with "may" indicates a general discretion in the court, while the mandatory clause beginning with "shall not" indicates one circumstance where the court has no discretion but must refuse to permit the guilty plea.

We turn now to the issue of whether the trial judge abused his discretion in refusing to permit the guilty plea.

[A]n examination conducted to determine a defendant's competency to stand trial must be broad enough to include an inquiry into his mental condition at the time the act in question was committed. ... Therefore, the psychiatrist's reports which were before the Municipal Court properly included evaluation of appellee's mental condition at the time the acts complained of were committed.

Perhaps we can not say that at that point the trial judge *knew* that appellee was not guilty of the crimes charged by reason of insanity but we certainly can say that he had every reason, at that point, to believe that there was grave doubt about appellee's criminal culpability and that the issue should be litigated. The preceding statement, of course, is based on the Davis rule,[2] that insanity is not strictly an affirmative defense and can be raised by either the court or the prosecution.

* * *

In Williams v. United States, 1957, 250 F.2d 19, 25–26, we clearly stated that imprisonment was *wrong* in the case of a mentally ill person, as well as a remedy which could not possibly secure the community against repetition of the offense. "Under our criminal jurisprudence, mentally responsible law breakers are sent to prison; those who are not mentally responsible are sent to hospitals. ... It is both wrong and foolish to punish where there is no blame. ... The community's security may be better protected by hospitalization ... than by imprisonment."

---

2. *Davis* v. *United States*, 1895, 160 U.S. 469.

The cases ... establish almost a positive duty on the part of the trial judge not to impose a criminal sentence on a mentally ill person. In this case appellee had never before been convicted of a criminal offense and had previously served honorably as a commissioned officer in the armed forces. We suggest it would have been a plain abuse of discretion for the trial judge, in these circumstances, to allow a plea by which society would brand such a person with a criminal record. Appellee argues that the plea of guilty had been carefully considered by competent counsel and by appellee, who had been judicially declared competent to stand trial and to assist in his own defense. We think that, for the reasons stated above, this decision was one which appellee and his counsel did not have an absolute right to make. We might add that the foregoing reasoning omits consideration of *Clark* v. *United States*, 1958, 259 F.2d 184 ... where we held that trial counsel had no right to concede his client's sanity; and *Plummer* v. *United States*, 1958, 260 F.2d 729, where we held, in effect, that failure of trial counsel to raise the defense of insanity was ineffective assistance of counsel. ... Society has a stake in seeing to it that a defendant who needs hospital care does not go to prison.

In the light of the previous discussion in this opinion, we are convinced that criminal insanity is a matter of grave public concern, particularly with respect to the problem of rehabilitation. Once it is established that the defendant did in fact commit the act charged but that he was insane at the time, then the problem is one of rehabilitation. In this context, the only issue is whether the defendant will go to jail for punishment or to a hospital for treatment. In either event he will be confined, deprived of his absolute liberty.

By its very nature, a jail sentence is for a specified period of time, while, by its very nature, hospitalization, to be effective, must be initially for an indeterminate period. This difference is not fatal because of the overriding interest of the community in protecting itself and its interest in rehabilitating the defendant himself. Certainly a man is not truly free if he has a sickness which results in his continual criminal activity, which, in turn, leads to a lifetime in jail with only short breaks between sentences. In the case before us, had Lynch not been treated, he might have been in and out of jail for the rest of his life on bad check charges. Now that he has received treatment, he is well on the way to unconditional release, without the probability of repeat offenses.

Therefore, once it is determined that a defendant is to be hospitalized for treatment of a mental disease or defect, further consideration of the criminal penalty provided by statute becomes irrelevant, for any and all purposes. The length of his hospitalization must depend solely on his need (or lack of it) for further treatment. It is true that he may be hospitalized for a longer time than the maximum jail sentence provided by statute. It is equally true that he may be released in a shorter time than the minimum sentence. Hospitalization, in this respect, bears no relation to a jail sentence. A jail sentence is punitive and is to be imposed by the judge within the limits set by the legislature. Hospitalization is remedial and its limits are determined by the condition to be treated. . . .

In *Overholser* v. *Russell*, 1960, 108 U.S. App. D.C. 400, 283 F.2d 195, we said that mandatory commitment under § 24–301(d) was proper even in the case of nonviolent crimes (coincidentally, bad check charges) because, even in the case of nonviolent crimes, society has a great interest in protecting itself.

Once a man has been committed to a hospital under § 24–301(d), we do not think, as did the District Judge, that the Government should thereafter be forced to prove his insanity as the price of continuing treatment. The remedy afforded by habeas corpus under present well settled law permits a person so confined to obtain his release through the courts by establishing that he has met the tests for such relief laid down in the governing statute.

*   *   *

[T]he order of the District Court is Reversed.

FAHY, CIRCUIT JUDGE, with whom EDGERTON and BAZELON, CIRCUIT JUDGES, join, dissenting.

*   *   *

I agree with [District] Judge McGarraghy as to the invalidity of the commitment. . . . Both the public and the private interests are protected by the course he directs: The individual concerned is held no longer by virtue of the invalid trial, and the public as well as the private interests are protected by conditioning the individual's release upon the outcome of future proceedings under our Code, 21 D.C. Code § 306 (1951), for the commitment of persons of unsound mind.

. . . The [Municipal] court refused to permit the guilty pleas, obviously believing there was a substantial question whether appellee was of sound mind when the checks were cashed. Thus a serious question arose involving the right of a person accused of a misdemeanor, who is competent to plead guilty and is represented by counsel, not to be compelled by the court to enter a plea of not guilty. I do not find it necessary to resolve this most difficult question, because even if it be assumed that the Municipal Court could compel this, and validly did so in this case, nevertheless I think the commitment which eventuated from the trial was invalid for other reasons.

Upon refusing the guilty plea the court then brought on the charges for trial over appellee's ob-

jection. We have no transcript of what occurred, and so we cannot accurately reconstruct the events.

. . . As near as we can make out from the data we have, the case was turned into an inquiry concerning appellee's sanity at the time the checks were cashed. The evidence consisted of the testimony of a psychiatrist that appellee was of unsound mind at that time. Appellee and his counsel were thus confronted with a serious situation affecting appellee, and the record does not show they were given a reasonable opportunity to cope with it by showing appellee was not of unsound mind when the checks were cashed. In the absence of that opportunity, there could be no valid finding that he was not guilty by reason of insanity. Such data as is before us supports the findings of Judge McGarraghy that the Municipal Court proceeding was not a valid trial but an invalid commitment proceeding. In the absence of a valid trial and acquittal by reason of insanity, there could be no valid commitment to St. Elizabeths under section 24–301(d).

*   *   *

I, of course, agree with the majority that a person of unsound mind who is charged with crime is not to be sent to prison if the alleged crime was due to his unsoundness of mind. Instead, he should be treated for his condition. . . . And I readily agree also that criminal insanity is a matter of grave public concern, particularly with respect to the problem of rehabilitation. But these sound general principles are not dispositive of the particular problem raised by the continued restraint imposed upon Lieutenant Colonel Lynch.

. . . Even if the Municipal Court trial were in all respects valid, followed by a valid mandatory commitment under section 301(d), appellee's detention would no longer be sustainable on the basis of that commitment.

Section 301(d)—the mandatory commitment provision—and section 301(e)—governing subsequent release—are part of a general plan and are to be read in relationship of one with the other. It is plain that Congress was concerned that an accused person might escape prison by reason of his defense of insanity and be immediately released upon the community, although he had engaged in dangerous conduct. This is what Congress sought to prevent. There is no reason to suppose Congress intended that a person not accused of any dangerous offense and not found to be of unsound mind should be held indefinitely against his will in a mental institution because believed to be a person of bad character; that is, Congress was not establishing a system of "protective" or "preventive" custody of persons neither dangerous nor found to be of unsound mind.

An important factor to be remembered in interpreting the valid scope of section 301(e) is that an acquittal by reason of insanity, which leads to commitment under section 301(d), is not an adjudication of insanity. It is well settled that such acquittal means only that sanity has not been established beyond a reasonable doubt. . . . One in appellee's position not only has not been charged with a dangerous offense, but has not been adjudged to be of unsound mind.

The dangerousness referred to in section 301(e), upon which continued restraint is conditioned, . . . is related to conduct comparable to the offense charged. The offenses charged to appellee, the cashing of two "bad checks" of $50 each, were not of a dangerous character within the meaning of section 301(e). Therefore the release conditions of that section do not apply in appellee's case and his continued restraint cannot be justified under the criteria of that section.

*   *   *

Whichever criteria are followed it remains true, I think, that Congress in section 301(e) is not concerned with persons who have engaged in any kind of unlawful conduct, however minor, but only with persons who have engaged in unlawful conduct of a dangerous character. The language used conveys the idea of physical danger to persons and, perhaps, to property. I do not attempt to delineate precisely the boundaries fixed by the language used, but obviously they do not encompass any and every minor conflict with the law of which a person has been acquitted because of a doubt about his sanity. Had Congress intended such a broad coverage, it would have used broader language such as "likely to engage in unlawful conduct," rather than the narrow language of section 301(e), "dangerous to himself or others."

Our jurisprudence knows no such thing in times of peace as "preventive" or "protective" custody of persons not guilty of crime and not found to be of unsound mind. Congress, of course, was aware of this and did not cloud its enactment with grave constitutional doubts by requiring a person of sound mind to be held under restraint in a mental institution on the theory he had done an act having the elements of a minor and nondangerous offense. The most serious constitutional doubts are avoided by giving the provisions of section 301(e) their natural meaning which excludes nondangerous conduct. It follows that valid restraint of appellee depends upon a finding, never yet made, that he is of unsound mind and not upon meeting the conditions for release applicable to persons committed under section 301 (d). On the issue of his present soundness of mind, appellee's prior conduct, as well as his present condition, may of course, be considered insofar as relevant.

I would affirm the judgment of the District Court.

b.   LYNCH v. OVERHOLSER
369 U.S. 705 (1962)

MR. JUSTICE HARLAN delivered the opinion of the Court.

*   *   *

[W]e conclude that to construe § 24–301(d) as applying only to criminal defendants who have interposed a defense of insanity[6] is more consistent with the general pattern of laws governing the confinement of the mentally ill in the District of Columbia, and with the congressional policy that impelled the enactment of this mandatory commitment provision, than would be a literal reading of the section. That construction finds further support in the rule that a statute should be interpreted, if fairly possible, in such a way as to free it from not insubstantial constitutional doubts. . . Such doubts might arise in this case were the Government's construction of § 24–301(d) to be accepted.

To construe § 24–301(d) as requiring a court, without further proceedings, automatically to commit a defendant who, as in the present case, has competently and advisedly not tendered a defense of insanity to the crime charged and has not been found incompetent at the time of commitment is out of harmony with the awareness that Congress has otherwise shown for safeguarding those suspected of mental incapacity against improvident confinement.

*   *   *

. . . This is the more so when there is kept in mind the contrast between the nature of an acquittal by reason of insanity and the finding of insanity required in other kinds of commitment proceedings. [T]he trial judge or jury must reach a judgment or verdict of not guilty by reason of insanity even if the evidence as to mental responsibility at the time the offense was committed raises no more than a reasonable doubt of sanity. . . .

*   *   *

Moreover, the literal construction urged here by the Government is quite out of keeping with the congressional policy that underlies the elaborate procedural precautions included in the civil commitment provisions. It seems to have been Congress' intention to insure that only those who need treatment and may be dangerous are confined; committing a crimi-

---

6. The defense of insanity need not, of course, be asserted by means of a formal plea. [A] defense of insanity in a criminal proceeding in the District of Columbia may be established under a general plea of not guilty. We read § 24–301(d) as making commitment mandatory whenever the defendant successfully relies, in any affirmative way, on a claim that he was insane at the time of commission of the crime of which he is accused.

nal defendant who denies the existence of any mental abnormality merely on the basis of a reasonable doubt as to his condition at some earlier time is surely at odds with this policy.

The criminal defendant who chooses to claim that he was mentally irresponsible when his offense was committed is in quite a different position. It is true that he may avoid the ordinary criminal penalty merely by submitting enough evidence of an abnormal mental condition to raise a reasonable doubt of his responsibility at the time of committing the offense. Congress might have thought, however, that having successfully claimed insanity to avoid punishment, the accused should then bear the burden of proving that he is no longer subject to the same mental abnormality which produced his criminal acts. Alternatively, Congress might have considered it appropriate to provide compulsory commitment for those who successfully invoke an insanity defense in order to discourage false pleas of insanity. We need go no further here than to say that such differentiating considerations are pertinent to ascertaining the intended reach of this statutory provision.

The enactment of § 24–301(d) in 1955 was the direct result of the change in the standard of criminal responsibility in the District of Columbia wrought by *Durham* v. *United States*, 214 F.2d 862. That decision provoked a congressional re-examination of the laws governing commitment of the criminally insane. . . . The [congressional] Committee noted that while under the then existing discretionary commitment statute[9] it had been customary for the court and the appropriate executive official to order the confinement of all those who had been found not guilty solely by reason of insanity, more assurance should be given the public that those so acquitted would not be allowed to be at large until their recovery from past mental illness had been definitely established.

*   *   *

Nor is it necessary to read § 24–301(d) as an assurance that an accused who requires medical treatment will be hospitalized rather than be confined to jail. Simultaneously with the mandatory commitment provision, Congress enacted the present § 24–302, which permits transfers of mentally ill convicts from penal institutions to hospitals. Consequently, if an accused who pleads guilty is found to be in need of psychiatric assistance, he may be transferred to a hospital following sentence.

---

9. The statute then in effect provided:
"If the jury shall find the accused to be then insane, or if an accused person shall be acquitted by the jury solely on the ground of insanity, the court *may* certify the fact to the Federal Security Administrator, who *may* order such person to be confined in the hospital for the insane, and said person and his estate shall be charged with the expense of his support in the said hospital." 59 Stat. 311. (Emphasis added.)

Finally, it is not necessary to accept the Government's literal reading of § 24–301(d) in order to effectuate Congress' basic concern, in passing this legislation, of reassuring the public. Section 24–301 (a) provides a procedure for confining an accused who, though found competent to stand trial, is nonetheless committable as a person of unsound mind. That section permits the trial judge to act "prior to the imposition of sentence or prior to the expiration of any period of probation," if he has reason to believe that the accused "is of unsound mind *or* is mentally incompetent so as to be unable to understand the proceedings against him." (Emphasis added.) The statute provides for a preliminary examination by a hospital staff, and then "if the court shall find the accused to be then of unsound mind *or* mentally incompetent to stand trial, the court shall order the accused confined to a hospital for the mentally ill." (Emphasis added.) This inquiry, therefore, is not limited to the accused's competence to stand trial; the judge may consider, as well, whether the accused is presently committable as a person of unsound mind. Since this inquiry may be undertaken at any time "prior to the imposition of sentence," it appears to be as available after the jury returns a verdict of not guilty by reason of insanity as before trial.

In light of the foregoing considerations we conclude that it was not Congress' purpose to make commitment compulsory when, as here, an accused disclaims reliance on a defense of mental irresponsibility. This does not mean, of course, that a criminal defendant has an absolute right to have his guilty plea accepted by the court. [T]he trial judge may refuse to accept such a plea and enter a plea of not guilty on behalf of the accused. We decide in this case only that if this is done and the defendant, despite his own assertions of sanity, is found not guilty by reason of insanity, § 24–301(d) does not apply. If commitment is then considered warranted, it must be accomplished either by resorting to § 24–301(a) or by recourse to the civil commitment provisions in Title 21 of the D.C. Code.

The judgment of the Court of Appeals is reversed and the case is remanded to the District Court for further proceedings consistent with this opinion.

*   *   *

MR. JUSTICE CLARK, dissenting.

*   *   *

It is well to point out first what is not involved here. First, this is not a civil commitment case, although this court attempts to force one upon the parties. In providing the safeguards of D.C. Code § 21–310 as to the ordinary civil commitment of persons claimed to be insane the Congress clearly acted in protection of those who were not charged with criminal offenses or who had never exhibited any criminal proclivities. In protecting the public from the criminally incompetent it could with reason act with less caution. . . . In criminal cases the person could be held in custody in any event and humanitarian principles require his hospitalization where needed. Nor are the procedures for release involved here. Petitioner has not sought his release under the statute. The procedure, however, is simple and effective, i.e., a doctor's certificate recommending release filed with the court is sufficient. If the doctor refuses such certificate, the inmate may seek to prove his sanity on habeas corpus. Here, however, no claim of sanity has been made.

* * *

Finally, the fallacy in the court's position is clearly apparent when in an attempt to justify its holding on practical grounds it says that an accused who pleads guilty and is sentenced may thereafter be transferred from the prison to a hospital and the assurances of hospitalization provided by § 24–301(d) thus afforded. The short of this is that if the accused pleads guilty and is sentenced he then may suffer in addition to his conviction the same fate as petitioner suffers here. With due deference, this is a most cruel position. The accused, though innocent of the crime because of insanity, pleads guilty in hopes of a short jail sentence. He then has the stigma of criminal conviction permanently on his record. During or after sentence he is transferred to the hospital where he *may* be released at the end of his sentence but if found not cured at that time may still be subject to further custody and treatment.

It has long been generally acknowledged that justice does not permit punishing persons with certain mental disorders for committing acts offending against the public peace and order. But insane offenders are no less a menace to society for being held irresponsible, and reluctance to impose blame on such individuals does not require their release. The community has an interest in protecting the public from antisocial acts whether committed by sane or by insane persons. We have long recognized that persons who because of mental illness are dangerous to themselves or to others may be retrained against their will in the interest of public safety and to seek their rehabilitation, even if they have done nothing prescribed by the criminal law. The insane who have committed acts otherwise criminal are a still greater object of concern, as they have demonstrated their risk to society. . . .

* * *

This is not to say, however, that the sole purpose of § 24–301(d) is commitment as a protection to the public. The policy of the law also includes assurance of rehabilitation for those so committed. . . . There can be no question that the interest of a free society is better served by commitment to hospitals than by imprisonment of the criminally incompetent. While, as the court points out, transfer after confinement permits treatment during sentence, it is not mandatory, and it may be interrupted before completion and the patient set free. Almost every newspaper reports depredations of the criminally insane who unfortunately for themselves and the safety of others have been released on the public. It was the purpose of the statute to prevent this occurrence whether or not the accused pleads not guilty because of insanity. A defendant's plea neither proves nor affects his guilt or his sanity. To make the commitment procedure effective only on the defendant's option limits the statute's protection of the public, forces an unfortunate choice on attorneys appointed to represent defendants, convicts those who are innocent by reason of insanity and deprives them of the treatment afforded by a humanitarian public policy. . . . The requirement that the petitioner here go free unless civil commitment proceedings be filed and he be adjudged insane creates a serious risk that petitioner will again be turned loose on an unsuspecting public to carry on his check-writing proclivities and perhaps much worse. . . .

* * *

[P]etitioner has no constitutional right to choose jail confinement instead of hospitalization. It is said that automatic hospitalization without a finding of present insanity renders the statute invalid but, as I see it, Congress may reasonably prefer the safety of compulsory hospitalization subject to the release procedures offered by the statute and through habeas corpus. It is said that these release procedures are too strict, placing the burden on the petitioner. But it appears reasonable once a jury or a judge has found a reasonable doubt as to the sanity of a man who has admittedly passed bad checks to require a doctor's certificate to authorize release, and failing such to require proof of the doctor's error in refusing to issue it. There is no reason to believe that the doctors or, for that matter, the judge would be improperly motivated. Release is by no means illusory. In the past six years over 25 per cent of those committed have been released. . . .

In any event, petitioner does not claim that he is now sane. He has made no effort to secure his release on the ground of being cured. Surely he should be required to make such an effort before asking the court to strike down the statute on that ground. Moreover, if the burden is too heavy, rather than opening the hospital doors to all persons committed under the statute, it would be more fitting to rewrite the release procedures by shifting the burden to the hospital authorities to prove the necessity for further hospitalization. . . .

NOTES

NOTE 1

ARENS, RICHARD

Due Process and the Rights of the Mentally Ill*

Far from assuring Frederick Lynch's release, the Supreme Court's decision of his case precipitated active consideration by the office of the public prosecutor of further committment proceedings against him.[125]

Still upon the premises of St. Elizabeths Hospital, still without treatment meeting the standards of the American Psychiatric Association, still without hope of early release, and still the target of legal proceedings, Frederick Lynch committed suicide.[126]

*   *   *

NOTE 2

DIAMOND, BERNARD L.

The Simulation of Sanity**

There is very considerable literature on the subject of malingering, particularly the simulation of mental disease. Yet very little has been written about the simulation of sanity even though the pretense of mental health would seem to be a much more frequent and more important problem than is malingering.

*   *   *

. . . Because the burden of proof of insanity lies

---

*13 *Catholic University L. Rev.*, 37–8 (1964). Reprinted by permission.

125. Disposed initially to proceed under § 24–301(a), the prosecutor's office subsequently indicated that it was preparing to proceed under the Civil Commitment Law.

126. In a letter dated January 22, 1962, Frederick Lynch wrote:

"Frankly, the conditions here are almost more than anyone can bear . . . the monotony—78 cents per day per patient food budget, no laundry, and above all no treatment. This hospital . . . is a human warehouse.

*   *   *

"Even if the Court does rule in my favor, it is kind of a case where the operation was a success but the patient died."

A news item, dated August 24, 1962, in the local press reported the denouement in the strange case of Frederick Lynch:

"Frederick C. Lynch, who charged an insanity defense was forced upon him in a Municipal Court trial, yesterday threw himself under the wheels of a slow-moving truck on the grounds of St. Elizabeths Hospital, police said.

"The apparent suicide of the 45-year-old Air Force Lieutenant Colonel came on the eve of a new court hearing today in which the Government, which lost the case before the Supreme Court, sought a civil hospital commitment.

"The Government had its fingers crossed in the Lynch case, because for a while it appeared that he might not be sick enough to qualify for a civil commitment." *Evening Star*, August 24, 1962, p. B–2.

** 2 *Journal of Social Therapy* (1956). Reprinted by permission.

---

with the defendant, if the defendant chooses not to reveal mental illness a grave miscarriage of justice may result. It seems to me that the forensic psychiatrist has a heavy responsibility in this type of case. If there is any possibility of mental unsoundness existing, it should be his responsibility to uncover it, and he should be prepared to use all of his technical skill as well as auxiliary aids, like the Rorschach and the Thematic Apperception tests, to follow up any clues that might lead to an uncovering of major psychopathology. Too often the examining psychiatrist conducts a brief interview under unfavorable circumstances with haste and lack of privacy. He obtains little or no intimate information from the patient, yet he doesn't hesitate to report the patient as sane and mentally responsible. I realize that the law views this matter differently, but I think that anyone who commits a serious crime, particularly murder, is very apt to be suffering from serious mental abnormalities. Before giving a decision that a patient is mentally responsible, one should be absolutely certain that one has penetrated through the rationalizations and surface defenses and has been able to appraise properly the true mental state of the accused individual. I do not wish to imply that all major criminals are insane. But a major criminal action does, in my opinion, carry a heavy medical, even though not legal, presumption of mental illness, and the examiner must be exceedingly cautious in assuming that a defendant is telling the whole story of his thoughts, feelings, and inner life.

All of us like to believe that our actions are the result of our own free will, and we are reluctant to admit that much of what we do is the result of unconscious compulsions rationalized by *ex post facto* intellectualizations. The paranoid schizophrenic is especially averse to admitting that his actions are due to mental disease and will insist, even in the face of the threat of the death punishment, that his criminal actions were intentional. To conceal his delusions he will confabulate logical reasons for his crime and resist all attempts of the psychiatrist to discover his psychopathology. Such schizophrenics pretend to be mentally healthy because to admit mental illness would destroy their self-esteem and break down the remnants of their contact with reality. Often, too, their delusions and hallucinations involve highly secretive material of a supernatural or sexual nature that must not be communicated to another person. So they would far rather go to prison or even to the gas chamber than to violate the dictates of their delusional systems.

[T]he failure to properly diagnose mental illness in a defendant accused of a minor crime will often result in his release after a short jail or prison sentence, with the imminent possibility of his committing a much more serious crime later. For practical as well as humanitarian reasons, it is very much to society's advantage that all who are dangerously mentally ill be so diagnosed and hospitalized until such time as they have recovered and all danger of aggressive acts has passed.

NOTE 3

FRENCH v. DISTRICT COURT, DIVISION 9
153 Colo. 10, 384 P. 2d 268 (1963)

MOORE, JUSTICE

*   *   *

"Can a defendant who enters a plea of not guilty by reason of insanity at the time of the alleged commission of the crime, but who thereafter wilfully refuses to co-operate and permit an examination of himself by physicians as prescribed by law, when said defendant is capable of co-operating in said examination, nevertheless maintain that plea and have a jury determination thereof?"

Facts raising this question are set forth . . . as follows:

After the plea of not guilty by reason of insanity was entered, French was committed to the Colorado Psychopathic Hospital for observation as required by statute. The examining psychiatrists reported by letters addressed to the trial court that French refused to co-operate with them and that co-operation would be necessary to determine his mental condition. August 22, 1962, a hearing was had at which the court ordered that French withdraw his plea of insanity or co-operate with the examining psychiatrists, and he was ordered returned to the hospital for a thirty-day period for a psychiatric evaluation. The examiners notified the trial court by letters that a determination of sanity or insanity could not be reached as French "again would not furnish the examiner with any information about himself." A further continuance was ordered, at the expiration of which three additional letters had been received by the trial court from the examining physicians, all of which indicated that the petitioner refused to "co-operate" with them. With reference to this refusal we quote from one of these letters the following:

"... of his own volition and he was in my opinion, at the time of my examination, capable of such discussion."

Thereupon the trial court upon oral motion of the district attorney ordered the plea of not guilty by reason of insanity stricken, and further ordered that the case be tried, at a day fixed, on the merits of the plea of not guilty.

*   *   *

... A number of compelling reasons come to mind which require a holding that the trial court erred in striking the insanity plea. We need mention but one. The Constitution of Colorado provides . . . "No person shall be compelled to testify against himself in a criminal case. . . ." The statute . . . provides in substance that any statements made by the defendant to examining psychiatrists cannot be used as evidence against him *in a trial on the issue of guilt of the crime charged.* However it is also provided that such evidence may be received "on the trial of the issue of guilt of a murder charge to rebut evidence of insanity offered by the defendant to reduce the degree of murder. . . ."

*   *   *

A person accused of a crime who enters a plea of not guilty by reason of insanity, cannot be compelled to carry on conversations against his will under the penalty of forfeiture of the defense for failure to respond to questions, or for a refusal to "co-operate" with persons appointed to examine him. The statute which prescribes the procedures to be followed upon the entry of a plea of not guilty by reason of insanity cannot operate to destroy the constitutional safeguards against self-incrimination.

*   *   *

NOTE 4

DURHAM v. UNITED STATES
214 F.2d 862 (D.C. Cir. 1954)

BAZELON, CIRCUIT JUDGE.

*   *   *

It has been ably argued by counsel for Durham that the existing tests in the District of Columbia for determining criminal responsibility, i.e., the so-called right-wrong test supplemented by the irresistible impulse test, are not satisfactory criteria for determining criminal responsibility. . . .

. . . The right-wrong test has its roots in England. There, by the first quarter of the eighteenth century, an accused escaped punishment if he could not distinguish "good and evil," i.e., if he "does not know what he is doing, no more than . . . a wild beast." Later in the same century, the "wild beast" test was abandoned and "right and wrong" was substituted for "good and evil". And toward the middle of the nineteenth century, the House of Lords, in the famous M'Naghten case restated what had become the accepted "right-wrong" test in a form which has since been followed, not only in England but in most American jurisdictions as an exclusive test of criminal responsibility:

"... the jurors ought to be told in all cases that every man is to be presumed to be sane, and to possess a sufficient degree of reason to be responsible for his crimes, until the contrary be proved to their satisfaction; and that, to establish a defense on the ground of insanity, it must be clearly proved that at the time of the committing of the act, the party accused was labouring under such a defect of reason, from disease of the mind, as not to know the nature and quality of the act he was doing, or, if he did know it, that he did not know he was doing what was wrong."

*   *   *

Nine years ago we said [that]: "[t]he modern science of psychology . . . does not conceive that there is a separate little man in the top of one's head called reason whose function it is to guide another unruly little man called instinct, emotion, or impulse in the way he should go."

By its misleading emphasis on the cognitive, the right-wrong test requires court and jury to rely upon what is, scientifically speaking, inadequate, and most often, invalid and irrelevant testimony in determining criminal responsibility.

The fundamental objection to the right-wrong test, however, is not that criminal irresponsibility is made to rest upon an inadequate, invalid, or indeterminable symptom or manifestation, but that it is made to rest upon *any* particular symptom. In attempting to define insanity in terms of a symptom, the courts have assumed an impossible role, not merely one for which they have no special competence. As the Royal Commission emphasizes, it is dangerous "to abstract particular mental faculties, and to lay it down that unless these particular faculties are destroyed or gravely impaired, an accused person, whatever the nature of his mental disease, must be held to be criminally responsible. . . ." In this field of law as in others, the fact finder should be free to consider all information advanced by relevant scientific disciplines.

*   *   *

We find that as an exclusive criterion the right-wrong test is inadequate in that (a) it does not take sufficient account of psychic realities and scientific knowledge, and (b) it is based upon one symptom and so cannot validly be applied in all circumstances. We find that the "irresistible impulse" test is also inadequate in that it gives no recognition to mental illness characterized by brooding and reflection and so relegates acts caused by such illness to the application of the inadequate right-wrong test. We conclude that a broader test should be adopted.

*   *   *

The rule we now hold must be applied on the retrial of this case and in future cases is . . . simply that an accused is not criminally responsible if his unlawful act was the product of mental disease or mental defect.

We use "disease" in the sense of a condition which is considered capable of either improving or deteriorating. We use "defect" in the sense of a condition which is not considered capable of either improving or deteriorating and which may be either congenital, or the result of injury or the residual effect of a physical or mental disease.

*   *   *

NOTE 5

BRISCOE v. UNITED STATES
243 F.2d 640 (D.C. Cir. 1957)

BAZELON, CIRCUIT JUDGE.

*   *   *

. . . The reports of the psychiatrists do not reveal the basis for their conclusions and there is no way of knowing whether they used the terms "sound mind" or "mental disease" or "mental defect" in their legal or medical sense. At a trial, however, whether petitioner was suffering from such "mental disease" or "mental defect," when he lit the fire, as to discharge him of criminal responsibility, would be determined by the trier of the facts, not by the psychiatric witnesses. The witnesses' role would be to supply to the trier of the facts the data upon which the determination can be made. If, by testimony that the accused either was or was not suffering from a "mental disease" or a "mental defect," a psychiatrist would be expressing a judgment that the accused should or should not be acquitted, that would be a legal rather than medical judgment and would usurp the function of the trier of the facts. While the state of the accused's mental health is a proper subject of medical opinion, no purpose is served by giving the fact trier a doctor's version of a legal opinion. To that end, if the psychiatrists were to testify in terms embodying legal conclusions, the lawyers, by examination and cross-examination, would seek to bring out the medical facts. The same is true if the psychiatrists were to testify in such ambiguities as "sound mind" or "unsound mind."

The statements of the psychiatrists . . . that petitioner was free from "mental disease" could have been intended to mean that he was of normal mental health—a medical judgment within the witnesses' competence and useful to the fact trier. They could also have been intended to mean that petitioner's illness, not being a psychosis, was not such a "disease" as discharges of guilt—a legal judgment not within the witnesses' competence and of no use to the fact trier. With the ordinary trial processes unavailable for elucidating the psychiatrists' conclusory statements, the District Court had no way of knowing what meaning was intended. The court's conclusion that the psychiatrists' statements amounted to no "showing of sufficient facts as would constitute a legal defense of insanity" is meaningful, therefore, only on the unacceptable theory that the burden of proving sanity is upon the accused.

*   *   *

NOTE 6

LYLES v. UNITED STATES
254 F.2d 725 (D.C. Cir. 1957)

Transcript of Proceedings

THE COURT: Doctor, from a layman's point of view, isn't the difference this, that psychosis is insanity and neurosis is just a nervous state?

THE WITNESS. [Dr. Perretti]: That is right.

THE COURT: Is that it?

THE WITNESS: If I just can explain in my own way?

THE COURT: Yes.

THE WITNESS: A psychotic person, a person who has a psychosis, is insane. A person who has a neurosis is not insane.

Q. BY MR. DWYER: A psychosis is a brain disease, isn't it? A. BY DR. PERRETTI: Well, we don't use the word "brain" disease. We use the word "mental" disease.

Q. What diagnosis was it? A. Sociopathic personality.

*   *   *

THE COURT: Is that the same thing as psychopathic personality?

THE WITNESS: That is right. It is the same thing as a psychopathic personality.

THE COURT: And that is not a form of insanity, is it?

THE WITNESS: Sociopathic personality is not a psychosis, and it is not insanity.

Q. BY MR. DWYER: It is a neurosis, isn't it? A. No. It is a form of personality disorder.

NOTE 7

BLOCKER v. UNITED STATES
274 F.2d 572 (D.C. Cir. 1959)

WILBUR K. MILLER, CIRCUIT JUDGE (dissenting).

*   *   *

...I think...the testimony of Dr. Addison Duval in the Leach case of November 18, 1957, has been erroneously construed as being that on that day St. Elizabeths Hospital adopted a new policy which required its psychiatrists to testify that sociopathic personality disturbance is a mental disease. I quote from the evidence of Dr. Duval:

> Q. Tell me, Doctor, has there been any determination by your institution as to whether or not persons with merely sociopathic personality disturbance are with or without mental disorder?
>
> *   *   *
>
> A. Late in 1954, after the Durham decision, we had a staff meeting at which the psychiatrists discussed what should be the uniform, if possible, type of name which we would give to this particular group of cases, known as sociopathic personality disturbance, namely, whether we would report them as with mental disorder or without mental disorder.

This is a difficult medical question which I would be glad to discuss, if you might wish me to do it.

The decision at that time was that in the agreed-upon consensus of our psychiatric staff this group of individuals so classified would be considered without mental disorder.

*   *   *

> ... [I]t was the policy of the hospital to insert the words "without mental disorder" after the diagnosis of sociopathic personality disturbance in our records.

Dr. Duval said the *Diagnostic and Statistical Manual on Mental Disorders*, published in 1952 by the American Psychiatric Association, refers to sociopathic personality disturbance as a disease. He then added, " ... [A]s of today we are, the superintendent and I have both agreed that hereafter we will eliminate from our records the words 'without mental disorder,' where the diagnosis of this particular group of personality disorders is made. And we will hereafter *let the diagnosis stand on its own feet*." (My emphasis.)

*   *   *

NOTE 8

CARTER v. UNITED STATES
252 F. 2d 608 (D.C. Cir. 1957)

PRETTYMAN, CIRCUIT JUDGE.

*   *   *

The simple fact that a person has a mental disease or defect is not enough to relieve him of responsibility for a crime. There must be a relationship between the disease and the criminal act; and the relationship must be such as to justify a reasonable inference that the act would not have been committed if the person had not been suffering from the disease.

*   *   *

When we say the defense of insanity requires that the act be a "product of" a disease, we mean that the facts on the record are such that the trier of the facts is enabled to draw a reasonable inference that the accused would not have committed the act he did commit if he had not been diseased as he was. There must be a relationship between the disease and the act, and that relationship, whatever it may be in degree, must be, as we have already said, critical in its effect in respect to the act. By "critical" we mean decisive, determinative, causal; we mean to convey the idea inherent in the phrases "because of," "except for," "without which," "but for," "effect of," "result of," "causative factor"; the disease made the effective or decisive difference between doing and not doing the act. The short phrases "product of" and "casual connection" are not intended to be precise, as though they were chemical formulae. They mean that the facts concerning [the disease and the facts concerning] the act are such as to justify reasonably the conclusion that "But for this disease the act would not have been committed."

NOTE 9

McDONALD v. UNITED STATES
312 F.2d 847 (D.C. Cir. 1962)

PER CURIAM.

*   *   *

Our eight-year experience under *Durham* suggests a *judicial* definition, however broad and general, of what is included in the terms "disease" and "defect." In *Durham*, rather than define either term, we simply sought to distinguish disease from defect. Our purpose now is to make it very clear that neither the court nor the jury is bound by *ad hoc* definitions or conclusions as to what experts state is a disease or defect. What psychiatrists may consider a "mental disease or defect" for clinical purposes, where their concern is treatment, may or may not be the same as mental disease or defect for the jury's purpose in determining criminal responsibility. Consequently, for that purpose the jury should be told that a mental disease or defect includes any abnormal condition of the mind which substantially affects mental or emotional processes and substantially impairs behavior controls. Thus the jury would consider testimony concerning the development, adaptation and functioning of these processes and controls.

*   *   *

c.   **Rouse v. Cameron**

Transcript of Proceedings (D.C. September 13, 1965)

MR. EHRLICH: [A]s I remember the facts, this boy was acquitted on the ground of insanity some, approximately, three years ago. He has been confined to St. Elizabeths as a result of that acquittal on the ground of insanity and I am informed that he has received very little, if any, treatment, and we have witnesses to show that he is not of unsound mind and he ought not to be kept in St. Elizabeths Hospital, at least John Howard Pavilion, under maximum security confinement. And, of course, if the Government wants to proceed against him civilly, nobody can stop them from doing that. But as far as treatment is concerned, he is receiving none. He has received very little, if any, and he has served three years, and the offense [carrying a deadly weapon] for which he was acquitted, I think the maximum penalty was one year.

THE COURT: I have urged lawyers, for a number of years, not to plead insanity as a defense in cases where the maximum possible sentence could be short. It is one thing to plead insanity in a murder case or in a case where a person could get a fifteen-year sentence, but I think many lawyers render bad service to their clients by pleading insanity in petty cases and find their clients in a mental institution for a much longer period than they would have been in jail. Of course, they say, well, they save their clients from the stigma of a criminal conviction. As a practical matter, I think it is easier for an ex-convict to get a job than an ex-inmate of a mental institution because people are afraid of ex-inmates.

MR. EHRLICH: I agree fully with the Court. I have found that from practical experience in practicing law.

THE COURT: My jurisdiction is limited to determining whether he has recovered his sanity. I don't think I have a right to consider whether he is getting enough treatment or not enough treatment because, after all, treatment of a mental disease ordinarily is only talking to a person. That is what treatment consists of, you know. Also, I cannot determine whether he should be in one pavilion rather than in another.

MR. EHRLICH: I am not going to ask the Court to determine that. I am saying that failure to accord this accused any treatment at all is a violation of his constitutional rights in keeping him there.

*   *   *

STRATY H. ECONOMON, called as a witness by the Respondent and, having been first duly sworn, was examined and testified as follows:

DIRECT EXAMINATION BY MR. SILBERT:

Q. What is your occupation?

A. I am a Staff Psychiatrist at St. Elizabeths Hospital, assigned to the Maximum Security Division.

*   *   *

Q. Are you personally familiar with the patient in this case, Charles C. Rouse?

A. Yes, I am.

Q. For how long a period of time have you known him?

A. I have been Mr. Rouse's ward administrator since July 16, 1964.

Q. Doctor, what is your opinion as to his present mental condition?

A. In my opinion, Mr. Rouse suffers from an anti-social reaction, has been mentally ill and presently is mentally ill. The diagnosis is anti-social reaction.

THE COURT: What does that mean? Is that a personality disorder?

THE WITNESS: Yes, Your Honor, it is.

BY MR. SILBERT:

Q. What are the symptoms of this illness as they are manifested in this patient?

A. Anti-social reaction is a recognized mental illness and it is a disorder of the character of the personality. Individuals suffering from this condition in a quantitative sense—

THE COURT: What do you mean by in a quantitative sense?

THE WITNESS: Amount, quantitative. They show a preponderance of symptoms which prevent them from making an adequate adjustment in normal living.

THE COURT: No, Doctor, this is just words. What does he do or what does he say that distinguishes him from normal human beings?

THE WITNESS: A person suffering from an anti-social reaction repeatedly manifests anti-social acts, which may be legal or illegal.

THE COURT: What does it mean? Tell me what he does or says, specifically.

THE WITNESS: In the case of Mr. Rouse, he has been involved in criminal acts.

THE COURT: You mean he committed criminal acts?

THE WITNESS: Yes, Your Honor.

THE COURT: What criminal acts?

THE WITNESS: Specifically, the criminal acts with which he was charged and which occurred several years ago, were carrying a deadly weapon. For example, he had on his possession a .45 caliber gun, approximately five or six hundred rounds of ammunition, and several tools, some of which may be interpreted to be burglar's tools.

It is illegal and also, in my opinion, anti-social to carry a weapon unlicensed and 500 rounds of cartridges.

THE COURT: [T]hat is not a symptom of insanity, Doctor, because many sane people do those things.

Now, will you tell us what things he has done or what he has said which indicates mental abnormality?

THE WITNESS: Yes, Your Honor. He reveals very little insight or awareness into himself as a person and to his functioning—

THE COURT: Those are just words. Tell me what he does or says. In other words, how do you reach those conclusions? You must have heard him say, or seen him do something which leads you to these conclusions. Now, what are they?

*   *   *

THE WITNESS: Mr. Rouse's problem is not that he does not have anxiety, all human beings have, but he cannot tolerate a normal amount of anxiety. He must take it and discharge it immediately. Generally, he discharges it in anti-social acts.

THE COURT: What do you mean? Just what does he do? To say anti-social doesn't mean anything because it might mean any one of a hundred things. What does he do?

THE WITNESS: Mr. Rouse, in the past, has been involved in difficulties with the law.

Anti-social implies against society. Society consists of people.

THE COURT: You don't mean to say just because a man commits a crime or a series of crimes, that therefore that is a sign of a mental abnormality?

THE WITNESS: It could or could not be, Your Honor.

THE COURT: You know, we just couldn't accept any psychiatric testimony or theory to the effect that the commission of a crime is a sign of mental disease because if we accepted that our whole system of criminal law would have to break down and have to be abrogated.

THE WITNESS: That is correct, Your Honor.

THE COURT: Are you one of those psychiatrists who believes that every dishonest man is necessarily insane?

THE WITNESS: Not at all.

THE COURT: Or that dishonesty, itself, or criminality is a symptom of a mental illness?

THE WITNESS: Not at all, Your Honor. I do believe, however, that a given individual, and in this instance, Mr. Rouse, can commit anti-social acts, which I have already indicated can be either legal or illegal, and be suffering from a mental illness.

THE COURT: Let's leave out the words "anti-social acts" because that term is too general and might mean any one of a hundred things. I think you have got to come to grips with specific things.

THE WITNESS: Yes. I would like to define it: An anti-social act literally is an act against society.

THE COURT: I know as much about the dictionary, I presume, as the average person. I say to you that the words "anti-social acts" is so general that it does not help anybody. You have got to tell us concretely what specific things he says and does that differentiate him from a normal person.

THE WITNESS: Yes, Your Honor.

THE COURT: That is the trouble we have, Mr. Silbert, in all these cases where there is no psychosis and where the only mental abnormality is a personality disorder. I am going to leave it to you; it is your function to bring concrete testimony.

I am not going to keep anybody deprived of his liberty on adjectives and generalities, it has got to be verbs and nouns, something that a person does or says that differentiates him from normal people and makes him dangerous.

MR. SILBERT: Very well, Your Honor.

THE COURT: Liberty is too precious to leave it merely with the opinions of psychiatrists.

MR. SILBERT: I understand that, Your Honor.

THE COURT: I have a very high regard for the science of medicine, of which psychiatry is a branch, but matters like these are, in the ultimate analysis, for the Court to determine.

MR. SILBERT: I agree with that, Your Honor.

*   *   *

BY MR. SILBERT:

Q. Doctor, what does Mr. Rouse do, what has he

done in the recent past, what does he say and what has he said in the recent past? In other words, specific actions, whether they be actions or words, that have led you to your present conclusion as to his mental condition?

A. Mr. Rouse has several times been offered by me the opportunity to be recommended for transfer off service, beginning with being transferred from the very tightest and most secure ward to the most open ward in the building and then being transferred off service on the grounds of St. Elizabeths Hospital. He has refused this, seeking other ways, if I may say, by litigation or by legal procedures, to get out of the building. This has been extant for one year.

I think he has exercised poor judgment and does not reveal any insight into what is going on within himself. In other words, he was offered out. He refused it. I think this is mentally ill.

Q. Are there any other examples of which you can think with respect to his receptivity to treatment and with respect to his actions involving other patients in the hospital where he has stayed?

A. Mr. Rouse was offered something which is quite rare, group psychotherapy in the John Howard Pavilion. We have approximately 400 patients. Surely, they cannot all be in group psychotherapy or in individual therapy. He rather likely, and in a very cavalier manner, in my opinion, voluntarily left this therapy. I think this shows poor judgment. I think he lacks insight. I think he is mentally ill.

Mr. Rouse is a constant and consistent manipulator on the ward in terms of agitating his fellow patients and he spends much more time doing this than he does in seeking something for himself. I think this is poor judgment. Again I think he lacks insight. I conclude that he is mentally ill.

Q. Can you be more specific as to the type, when you used the word agitation, agitating other patients, can you be more specific in that, explain to the Judge how he does that, in what way other patients are affected?

*   *   *

A. Over and over and over again I have pleaded with him to make attempts to be more comfortable in a downstairs ward, where he will have more privileges, to get involved with people. He does not get involved with people. Rather, he stays unto himself basically and is semi-secluded voluntarily. And because he does not get together with people I conclude that he is anti-social, anti-social since he cannot tolerate the anxiety that comes with having relationships with people.

*   *   *

Q. Doctor, as a result of his mental illness, what is your opinion as to whether or not he would be likely to be dangerous to himself or others in the reasonably foreseeable future if placed at liberty?

A. In my opinion, if Mr. Rouse were placed at liberty at the present time it would be a precipitous thing to do and he would be dangerous to himself and to other people by virtue of this mental illness. I think he needs supervision over the long haul.

THE COURT: Specifically, in what respect would he be dangerous to others or might he be dangerous to others?

THE WITNESS: He might be dangerous to others, Your Honor, in terms of anti-social acts, which might include acts of violence, criminal acts.

THE COURT: Suppose you be more specific.

THE WITNESS: Getting a gun and some ammunition.

THE COURT: And then?

THE WITNESS: And being at large in the public.

THE COURT: And shooting somebody?

THE WITNESS: This is what guns do. Yes, he could shoot someone, perhaps.

THE COURT: You have to be concrete in these matters; you can't just be general. You say that he has committed a lot of criminal acts. What type of acts, what type of criminal acts, does your file show?

THE WITNESS: I can look at the FBI record.

THE COURT: Yes, surely.

(Pause)

THE WITNESS: On August 10, 1962, he was arrested in Arlington County, Virginia, by the Arlington Police, charged with three counts of grand larceny by checks; on September 7, 1962, he was arrested by the Police Department in Washington, D.C. They were investigating a robbery, the possibility of suitcase containing guns and ammunition, and on that same day he was charged with carrying a deadly weapon. . . . Mr. Rouse has, as he put it to me about three or four weeks ago, he said, "Doc, writing with a pen is the easiest thing in the world," and he told me of how easy it is to forge someone's name on a check. And joshing with him I signed my own signature, which is, as most signatures are, rather unique and singular. He said, "This is too difficult for me to reproduce by hand," but then he explained to me how with a system of mirrors he could reproduce it exactly. And he said that once you have used a pen you never want to go back to anything else because it's so easy. And he failed to see something very basic. We are still under the Calvinistic idea of work is good, work has dignity and meaning and work gives growth and stability. He fails to see that.

THE COURT: Have you ever asked him why he carried the gun out of which this commitment arose?

THE WITNESS: He couldn't give an adequate explanation.

THE COURT: Have you asked him?

THE WITNESS: Yes, Your Honor. But he did say that there were some people that might possibly be after him, he was involved in running around with a dangerous crowd and he had friends in the underworld, and things like this, a rather grandiose presentation of his social relationships.

THE COURT: But they weren't sufficient to justify a diagnosis of psychosis, were they?

THE WITNESS: No—

THE COURT: Or delusions of grandeur?

THE WITNESS: No, I would not call them delusions, Your Honor, simply because he was and is in touch with reality, but it is the manner in which he speaks. He shows the same grandiosity that one would have after a few drinks in which he says, set them up for everyone in the house, failing to realize that this statement will cost him $100 because there are that many people in this restaurant. His grandiosity is that of a person who doesn't really see himself in terms of a reality setting and he has to pretend almost that he is some one bigger and mightier than he truly is. . . .

CROSS-EXAMINATION BY MR. EHRLICH:

Q. Doctor, in answer to Judge Holtzoff's number of questions to you about the crimes, you kept using the word crimes that this boy has committed. Is it true now that the only offense with which he was charged in court is this carrying a dangerous weapon case?

A. I would have to refer to the U.S. Attorney's letter.

Q. Please do, Doctor.

(Pause)

A. Yes.

Q. Now, the check charge that you told Judge Holtzoff about, isn't it true that he was arrested for over-drawing his own bank account and there were small checks and he made them good? Isn't that true?

A. I don't know. I was merely reading the FBI record.

Q. Don't you have the history in the case?

THE WITNESS: I cannot answer that question with any certainty. The most I can say is this, that to the examining physicians at the time of admission Mr. Rouse had stated that he had been in difficulties with the law since the age of 14, that he had had numerous charges on safe-cracking, housebreaking. None of these have ever been substantiated in terms of having been arrested for this.

BY MR. EHRLICH:

Q. I am asking you about the facts themselves.

A. I cannot tell you if this is a fact, sir, as you state. I can only tell you he was arrested for that reason.

*   *   *

Q. I think you testified on direct examination that poor judgment is a basis for your conclusion that the petitioner is suffering from a mental illness, is that correct?

A. It is one of them.

Q. Well, isn't it true, Doctor, that many people exercise poor judgment many times and most people sometimes?

A. I would say that all human beings exercise poor judgment at one time or another.

Q. Now, is it the poor judgment that you have indicated that he exercised by leaving this group therapy after eight months, the basis for your statement that he is dangerous to himself and to others?

A. It is one of the bases.

*   *   *

Q. Now, Doctor, you testified further, in answer to one of Judge Holtzoff's questions, that another reason that you arrived at a conclusion that the petitioner would be dangerous to himself and to others, is because he exhibited anti-social tendencies, is that correct?

A. Mr. Rouse does not exhibit anti-social tendencies. He exhibits frank overt anti-social behavior.

Q. What anti-social behavior have you ever observed him commit?

A. As I have already indicated, one example which comes to my mind at this point is Mr. Rouse's statement that once you have used a pen to forge checks, you wouldn't want to do anything else because it's so easy. I think this is extremely anti-social.

Q. You mean you have taken some statement that you recall and you have characterized it yourself as anti-social behavior; isn't that what you have done, Doctor?

A. Yes, I am giving it as my opinion.

THE COURT: Doctor, suppose a forger makes a statement to you that it is so easy to keep on forging. You wouldn't treat that as a symptom of insanity, would you? Because there are forgers who might be called professional forgers.

MR. EHRLICH: I represent a few, if the Court please.

THE WITNESS: Your Honor, in and of itself, one data signifies nothing. I think one has to consider data, tendencies, propensities and preponderance of quantitative data. Taken out of context, one cannot answer yes, or no, to anything.

THE COURT: You practically ask us to take your opinion for the sum total of the tendencies and all the data, instead of enumerating the data so that we could test the conclusion that you reach.

Well, proceed, Mr. Ehrlich.

BY MR. EHRLICH:

Q. Doctor, you would call this psychotherapy group treatment, wouldn't you?

A. Yes, I would.

Q. Other than that, has the petitioner received any sort of treatment in the three years that he has been in St. Elizabeths Hospital?

A. Yes, he has.

Q. Consisting of what, Doctor?

A. The basic therapy that is available to the general patient in John Howard Pavilion and, of course, also to Mr. Rouse, is environmental therapy. Specifically, this is a therapeutic environment, controlled, structured and predictable. It is not the environment of the world outside. We have external controls on the people that are within the building. By and large, for many reasons, these people do not, themselves, display internal controls. Mr. Rouse certainly has indicated this in his past behavior.

*   *   *

Environmental therapy is a situation in which a person recognizes that he is sick and, because everyone who works there is a therapeutic person, he can seek means on his own of understanding himself and of getting better. This was something that came about simply because no one can carry one doctor, one nurse, and one psychiatrist in his hip pocket. There aren't that many people. And it did work. People do not get sick in a vacuum, they get sick in a certain setting, in the role of a member of a family, in the role of a person at work or in school. This is not a vacuum. They got sick amongst human beings. Now, for various reasons, these external human forces may work and be conducive to mental illness in a given individual.

I think it is always wise that when a person decompensates, gets sick enough, that he be labeled sick, that he should be removed from the so-called sick environment or the environment in which he became ill, and placed in an environment which is different, which is also therapeutic.

This is environmental therapy. He has had the benefit of this for a long time now. I think that he has not always made use of this as much as he could. He has not responded as well to this as perhaps he might have. But I must also add that he has not made an effort, a sincere effort to respond to this and, indeed, to the group therapy that he had for fifty sessions.

Q. Doctor, do I understand you to mean by that lengthy statement that environmental therapy is the same as being locked up in that John Howard Pavilion? Is that environmental therapy that you are talking about?

A. No, sir, it is not. And I take sincere issue with his statement, Your Honor.

Q. Well, I am asking you a question. What do you mean by environmental therapy? I don't think I understood you.

A. Shall I repeat what I just said?

Q. No, don't repeat all of that.

THE COURT: No. Suppose you tell us in a sentence or two. I had a little difficulty in following it. I rather concluded that you meant that the very presence in that environment is a form of treatment, is that it? Do I correctly understand that?

MR. EHRLICH: That is what I understood him to say.

THE WITNESS: This is one way of putting it.

BY MR. EHRLICH:

Q. All right, sir, you have answered the question, Doctor.

Now, also on direct examination, in answer to one of the questions propounded to you by the prosecutor—

MR. SILBERT: I object to that classification. I am not a prosecutor in this case and this person is not an accused.

MR. EHRLICH: Well, I meant no offense.

THE COURT: Of course you meant no offense. It is just one of those slips of the tongue. This is not a criminal prosecution. I think it is better to refer to Mr. Silbert as counsel for the respondent or counsel for the government.

*   *   *

REDIRECT EXAMINATION BY MR. SILBERT:

Q. On cross-examination, Doctor, you were asked by counsel for the petitioner whether or not all people in the United States exercise, at one time or another, poor judgment, and I believe your answer to that question was yes, is that right?

A. That is correct.

Q. Would you explain, for the benefit of the Court, why it is you believe that the poor judgment that you have said is exercised by this petitioner in some way or another separates him from most of the people in the United States?

*   *   *

THE WITNESS: The phrase "poor judgment" is a qualitative statement. It is a statement of quality. He has poor judgment or he exercises poor judgment. It makes no statement about the quantitative aspects of it.

For example, if someone were to say to me that Mr. Rouse were carrying a loaded pistol in his hip pocket and he was going to rob a store, I don't think that I would say poor judgment in that very brief respect. However, if someone were to say to me that he had on his possession a suitcase containing an automatic pistol and five or six hundred rounds of ammunition, I would say this is poor judgment, and the reason I say this is because, why is this necessary? This exceeds something already.

He reveals poor judgment qualitatively, as all human beings do at one time or another, but in my experience with him he has revealed poor judgment consistently in many of my dealings with him, in many of the dealings of the ward staffs with him.

THE COURT: Could you give us some examples?

THE WITNESS: It looms large in my mind that the offer to transfer him downstairs and off service has been denied by him.

THE COURT: Anything else? You have told us that.

THE WITNESS: Well, I think that is enough, Your Honor.

THE COURT: Very well.

MR. SILBERT: That completes the Government's case, Your Honor.

THE COURT: Very well. You may proceed, then. Thereupon,

ALBERT E. MARLAND, called as a witness by the petitioner and, having been first duly sworn, was examined and testified as follows:

DIRECT EXAMINATION BY MR. EHRLICH:

Q. Doctor, do you know the petitioner, Charles Rouse?

A. Yes, I have examined him a number of times.

Q. Where have your examinations taken place?

A. All of them at John Howard Pavilion, St. Elizabeths Hospital.

*   *   *

Q. Doctor, would you say he is suffering from any mental disease?

A. Not in my sense of the term. I agree that he suffers from a personality disorder, but I do not think that this constitutes mental disease simply because it is in the Diagnostic Manual and since 1950 because by fiat, as it were, St. Elizabeths declares it is. . . .

Q. Doctor, as a qualified psychiatrist would you take the responsibility of having this young man released? Would you take that responsibility as a doctor?

A. Providing he was released conditionally, I would supervise him.

I am doing that for a number of other cases. So far I have had good luck. I am making no predictions.

He can get into difficulties and I would not like to take it unless it was a conditional, implied ability to report back to the Court whenever necessary.

THE COURT: In other words, you recommend a conditional release, not an unconditional release?

THE WITNESS: Precisely.

THE COURT: When you asked him why he carried a gun, did he explain to you why he carried 500 rounds of ammunition?

THE WITNESS: No, he didn't explain that. He just liked guns and he admitted that there wasn't any particular reason for it that he knew about.

As far as I know, there was no particular crime that he had in mind.

THE COURT: How did he come to be arrested? Do counsel know how he came to be arrested under this charge?

MR. SILBERT: No, Your Honor.

THE COURT: I venture to suggest, Mr. Silbert, that in these cases that arise out of a criminal proceeding it would be useful to know the facts of the crime in every case, even if you have to dig them up from the files of the Municipal Court, because I have to protect the public. That is the principal thing that I have to consider. I would consider myself derelict in my duty if I released him and then a few weeks later he shot somebody with a .45 Colt automatic. That is why I want to know how he came to be arrested for carrying a gun. He must have done something to call the attention of the police to the fact that he had a gun. The police don't just stop anybody on the street and say, have you got a gun.

*   *   *

There is a big difference between releasing a man, say, who overdrew his bank account and releasing a man who had a gun. If you release a man who overdrew his bank account, the worst that can happen, he might do it again; but when you release a man who has been carrying a .45 automatic, that is a pretty serious matter.

*   *   *

BY MR. EHRLICH:

Q. Doctor, you heard the previous psychiatrist testify that in his opinion the petitioner was suffering from a personality disorder and among the things that caused him to arrive at that conclusion was that he showed poor judgment. Would you agree with that?

A. Well, he has shown poor judgment, of course, in getting into difficulties and in that sense I agree. But the major problem that has been caused has been this refusal to leave the upper ward and go down to the lower ward. I was puzzled by that, myself, for awhile, until June, through information that I had received, I discussed it with him, and there was a certain man, Greeley, who is not particularly literate, who has forced him to keep books for him and has threatened him every time he left. He showed me a bruise which either Greeley or some of his cohorts had inflicted on him.

*   *   *

BY MR. EHRLICH:

Q. Doctor, in your opinion, is continued confinement in John Howard Pavilion good or bad for the petitioner?

A. I—

MR. SILBERT: I object to that. I don't think that is a relevant and material question.

THE COURT: I am going to allow that. In these proceedings I allow both the Government and the Petitioner wide leeway. We don't enforce the rules of evidence strictly. There is no jury here. In one sense, although a writ of habeas corpus is a legal writ, we treat these as equitable proceedings.

THE WITNESS: No, I don't see that he is getting any particular advantage from being incarcerated. Call it environmental treatment, what you want, it is still incarceration. It is still as rigid as that of a jail, particularly under conditions he is thrown with others. One of the reasons he doesn't want to leave this ward, it is quieter. It is more rigidly controlled. Although he hasn't been bothered by homosexuals, a couple of them are up there, there is more on some of the other wards.

He does have a penchant for reading. I agree that much of his reading is superficial, but he does have an ambition or intent, at least, to take up the study of electronics. He has the brains to do it, if he would get down and study, but he is going to need a good deal of supervision to see that this is done.

BY MR. EHRLICH:

Q. Will you tell us what your opinion is as to whether or not, if placed upon conditional release, whether he would be dangerous to himself and to others in the foreseeable future?

A. I don't think he is going to be dangerous to himself unless a penchant for getting into trouble might show itself.

THE COURT: How about dangerous to others?

THE WITNESS: Frankly, he has shown no idea of violence. This gun is a solitary incident, out of context with every other problem that he has had. He has done stupid things, but there has been no crime of violence shown.

THE COURT: I believe you said that he said to you he likes guns?

THE WITNESS: He told me that he rather liked to collect them. Now, what he is doing with the ammunition, I don't know.

*   *   *

From the standpoint of a mental disease, I don't think he is a menace to himself or to others.

THE COURT: Do you think he is likely to get a gun and shoot somebody?

THE WITNESS: Frankly, I don't.

BY MR. EHRLICH:

Q. Now, it is true that people who are not alleged to have any mental disease go out and shoot people, don't they?

A. I can't predict that, but from the standpoint of a mental disease, I don't think there is any tendency in that direction.

*   *   *

THE COURT: [Y]our point was that if he shoots somebody it won't be because of any mental disease.

MR. EHRLICH: That is right.

MR. SILBERT: Your Honor, may I inform Your Honor that after you asked me as to whether or not we had any facts as to the origin of his arrest, Dr. Economon found in the file of St. Elizabeths Hospital, a statement of facts as to the basis for the offense, that is, the police statement of facts. . . . This is the police statement of facts:

"About 1:45 a.m., the above subject was observed loitering by the arresting officer at the corner of 14th and Harvard Streets, Northwest. He had in his possession a suitcase and when asked by the officer what it contained, he opened it and the contents were as follows: One .45 caliber Colt automatic pistol loaded with seven rounds of ammunition. Also in the suitcase was an additional hundred rounds of .45 caliber ammunition and 500 rounds of .22 caliber ammunition, two electric drills, hacksaw blades, hacksaw, and miscellaneous tools."

*   *   *

BY MR. SILBERT:

Q. [H]as he ever told you why he terminated the group therapy that was offered to him by the hospital?

A. He got rather tired of it. For a while he felt that he was getting some benefit and then it got a bit repetitious and he didn't think it was worth the time and effort spent. That is his opinion. I don't know exactly what the group therapy consisted of, discussion among the various people, and he may have felt that it was not worthwhile.

*   *   *

Q. Let me ask you this, Doctor: Don't you believe that it would be better for him to graduate, as to the amount of supervision he receives, from the most secure ward in John Howard Pavilion to a less secure ward in John Howard Pavilion, and then, perhaps, if he improves enough, to the detached service, West Side Service, or some other service? Don't you think that would be a better mode of recovery for him to follow, rather than be released outright into the community at this stage?

A. In his case, no. In the first place, I don't believe he belongs in John Howard. I don't think he belonged there any time.

In the second place, if he commits crime he can go to jail, and that is probably the best place for him if he did.

But with this atmosphere of fear of St. Elizabeths, I think he belongs out. And I do think if he does commit anti-social acts, if he commits crime, in other words, he should be reported to the Court immediately.

THE COURT: Do I infer correctly from what you said that he should have been sent to jail instead of St. Elizabeths Hospital for carrying a .45?

THE WITNESS: If he was guilty, he should have been.

THE COURT: Well, he must have been guilty because he was acquitted on the ground of insanity and an acquittal on the ground of insanity by necessary implication contains a finding that the person committed the act, the criminal act with which he was charged.

BY MR. SILBERT:

Q. Doctor, do you believe that if he were released he might again charge an over-draft to a checking account?

A. I don't know what he might do. I can't predict what he would do.

THE COURT: I am not too much impressed by this

over-draft aspect of the matter. I am more impressed with the gun and the burglar's tools and ammunition.

*　　*　　*

BY MR. SILBERT:

Q. Let me ask you this, Doctor: As I understand your testimony, if this man were to go out, were to be released by His Honor and were to commit a criminal act and then you were called to testify, your testimony would be that the act he committed was not the product of any mental disease, is that right?

A. Precisely, and if he is guilty, he ought to go to jail.

Q. Even though you would agree that the act would be a product of an anti-social reaction?

A. No, I wouldn't necessarily agree to that. I mean, after all, I can't separate a man's personality from— it's true that that has its influence, but in the sense it's the product of mental disease, no. I believe in free will. I think he has the ability to make a choice. Maybe there is some diminution in this ability to choose the right and adhere to it; that I will agree.

THE COURT: Unfortunately, Doctor, there are some psychiatrists who no longer believe in free will, which is very unfortunate. I am glad to hear that you do.

REDIRECT EXAMINATION BY MR. EHRLICH:

Q. Doctor, I think you suggested to the Court that as a juvenile the petitioner had taken somebody's car without permission. Isn't it true, Doctor, that the car he took was his mother's car? Didn't he tell you that?

A. He didn't tell me. He was charged with it. I knew that there was a charge, but he didn't mention that, no.

Q. Didn't he tell you, Doctor, that his mother took him before a Judge named Dudley over in Virginia, in which jurisdiction the procedure is a little bit different from the District of Columbia, and had Judge Dudley give him a talking to? Didn't he tell you that?

A. No, he didn't actually do that.

MR. EHRLICH: I see. I can put his mother on the stand.

*　　*　　*

THE COURT: We are dealing here with a young man who was arrested quarter after two in the morning, in a criminal neighborhood, carrying a .45 Colt automatic, a large number of rounds of ammunition, and tools that might be used as burglar's tools. Now, there is no explanation as to why he was there, what he was doing with all that paraphernalia.

Now, both Dr. Marland and Dr. Economon agree that this petitioner is suffering from a personality disorder known as anti-social reaction. There is a difference of opinion between them as to whether this personality disorder amounts to a mental disease.

Unfortunately, there is that cleavage in the psychiatric profession, and, certainly, the Courts cannot

determine when the medical profession disagrees among itself.

Dr. Marland does not recommend an unconditional release, although Dr. Marland was retained in behalf of the petitioner.

In view of the fact that the original arrest involved a dangerous weapon, an extremely dangerous weapon, with a great deal of ammunition, the Court is not going to undertake to release him unconditionally and would have great hesitancy in releasing him even conditionally.

The Court is willing to do this, if the parties will request that the Court do it, the Court would be willing to obtain the advisory opinion of the Commission on Mental Health in this case. I will be glad to refer the matter for their advisory opinion.

*　　*　　*

November 1, 1965.

The above cause came on for further hearing before the HONORABLE ALEXANDER HOLTZOFF, United States District Judge.

THE COURT: The Court has before it the report of the Commission on Mental Health.

Is this the case in which the petitioner was arrested in possession of a .45 caliber revolver?

MR. SILBERT: With 600 rounds of ammunition, too. This was at 1:45 in the morning at 14th and Harvard Streets, Northwest.

THE COURT: The Court has before it the report of the Commission on Mental Health, and it says this:

> "It is the considered opinion of the Commission, after examination of Charles C. Rouse, that he has recovered from the mental illness for which he was committed in 1963 and is not mentally ill at this time. For the past 18 months he has exhibited no anti-social behavior, confusion, or grandiose ideas. He is aloof from most other patients, but during his stay in the hospital he has had several buddies. He tends to choose an environment that provides no social conflict for him.
> "It is the opinion of the Commission on Mental Health that further hospitalization of this man will stifle his future development and that he should be discharged. He has arrangements to see a psychiatrist upon discharge to aid in his rehabilitation."

Now, I am a little bit troubled by this report because if he is free of mental disease he doesn't need a psychiatrist.

*　　*　　*

Opinion of the Court

THE COURT: There is no doubt in the mind of the Court that this patient has improved and that he is continuing to progress. The only question is whether he has reached a point at which he should be released.

The staff of St. Elizabeths Hospital say no and they support their views by a showing that he refuses to accept opportunities for a greater degree of freedom within the hospital than he has today and that that hampers and handicaps the staff of St. Elizabeths Hospital in determining or reaching a conclusion that it is safe to release him. I think in that sense he is his own worst enemy.

I was very much impressed by . . . the fact that Dr. Marland, who testified in behalf of the petitioner, did not recommend an unconditional release. He recommended a conditional release. In other words, the physician who testified in his behalf would hesitate to express the opinion that it is safe to release him unconditionally.

I think that the petitioner should take advantage, first, of the opportunities of greater freedom in the hospital and, if he shows that he is capable of making use of those opportunities, it may well be that the hospital will admit him to conditional release; but even if it does not, the Court would consider a renewal of the application with a view to possibly granting a conditional release. But I do think that he should first co-operate with the hospital and take advantage of the opportunities which they are willing to accord to him for greater freedom within its walls.

Writ discharged and petition dismissed, with leave to renew after a reasonable time.

d.   HOUGH v. UNITED STATES
                271 F.2d 458 (D.C. Cir. 1959)

BAZELON, CIRCUIT JUDGE: . . .

Appellant was indicted on June 17, 1957, for a murder. . . . The trial, held on July 10, 1958, culminated in a judgment of acquittal by reason of insanity and appellant was committed to St. Elizabeths Hospital as required by D.C. Code § 24–301(d).

On October 20, 1958, when appellant had been under treatment for about sixteen months, the Superintendent of St. Elizabeths Hospital filed in the District Court a certificate stating in pertinent part:

> "Miss Hough has now recovered sufficiently to be granted her conditional release from Saint Elizabeths Hospital pursuant to section 927(e) of Public Law 313.
>
> "The plan under which we recommend that the conditional release be granted is that in accordance with the continuation of a total plan of rehabilitation Miss Hough be permitted to leave Saint Elizabeths Hospital to go to the city of Washington, D.C., unaccompanied in an effort to obtain employment. It is recommended that this plan be carried out under very close hospital supervision and that she be subject at all times during the period of her conditional release to the supervision of the Social Service Department of Saint Elizabeths Hospital and that she report to Saint Elizabeths Hospital for examinations at such times as are designated by the authorities of Saint Elizabeths Hospital."

Release of persons who have been committed to a mental hospital after acquittal by reason of insanity is governed by D.C. Code § 24–301(e). *Unconditional* release is authorized fifteen days after certification by the hospital superintendent "(1) that such person has recovered his sanity, (2) that, in the opinion of the superintendent, such person will not in the reasonable future be dangerous to himself or others, and (3) in the opinion of the superintendent, the person is entitled to his unconditional release from the hospital. . . ." But upon objection by the prosecutor's office, the court is required to—or, upon its own initiative, may—hold a hearing and determine from evidence presented therein whether "such person has recovered his sanity and will not in the reasonable future be dangerous to himself or others. . . ."

Conditional release is authorized upon the certificate of the superintendent that the individual "is not in such condition as to warrant his *unconditional* release, but is in a condition to be *conditionally* released under supervision. . . ." (Emphasis supplied.) For "such certificate" the procedural hearing provisions for unconditional release are applicable: ". . . and, if, after a hearing and weighing the evidence, the court shall find that the condition of such person warrants his conditional release, the court shall order his release *under such conditions as the court shall see fit,* or, if the court does not so find, the court shall order such person returned to such hospital." (Emphasis supplied.)

The release here proposed for appellant was a conditional release. The United States Attorney objected to it and the District Court held a hearing. Testifying at the hearing in support of his proposal to release appellant conditionally, Dr. Overholser, the Superintendent of St. Elizabeths Hospital, stated that he would require appellant to report to the hospital once a week under a plan of close supervision and treatment. To show that she had demonstrated her readiness for release under such conditions without danger to the community, the doctor cited the hospital's successful experience with appellant in a treatment and rehabilitation program under which appellant had been allowed to leave the hospital grounds for several hours a day, accompanied only by her seventy-five-year-old mother, returning every evening; that as appellant improved this was allowed with increasing frequency until after October 15, 1958, appellant was away from the hospital grounds under similar circumstances almost every day; that, in the opinion of the hospital authorities, she had progressed sufficiently to do this without danger to the community.

*   *   *

[A]ppellant seeks review denying conditional release. Her points are (1) that the order is contrary to the weight of the evidence and (2) that the court below erred in its interpretation of the statute with respect to the standard to be applied for conditional release.

This is the first appeal involving construction of the conditional release provisions of § 24–301(e). *Overholser* v. *Leach*, 103 U.S. App. D.C. 289, 257 F.2d 667 (1958), a habeas corpus proceeding, involved construction of the finding required for *unconditional* release: "that such person has recovered his sanity and will not in the reasonable future be dangerous to himself or others. . . ." There we rejected the contention that recovery of sanity was sufficient for release. We construed the statute to require "freedom from such abnormal mental conditions as would make the individual dangerous to himself or the community in the foreseeable future."

But for conditional release the statute is less specific: It requires the court to "find that the condition of such person warrants his conditional release, . . ." whereupon he shall order his release "under such conditions as the court shall see fit [to impose]. . . ."[1] We must construe this provision in light of the basic policy underlying the statute. That policy, as we read the legislative history, is to provide treatment and cure for the individual in a manner which affords reasonable assurance for the public safety. Accordingly, we think that to order conditional release upon a challenged certification the court must conclude that the individual has recovered sufficiently so that under the proposed conditions—or under conditions which the statute empowers the court to impose "as [it] shall see fit,"[2]—"such person will not in the reasonable future be dangerous to himself or others." This gives effect to the legislative distinction between conditional and unconditional release without diluting the statute's grant of judicial power to protect the public safety.

In an oral opinion denying conditional release in this case, the District Court cited the agreement of the psychiatrists that appellant was still suffering from schizophrenia of the paranoid type, the seriousness of her offense, the doctor's testimony that she lacked insight concerning the seriousness of the offense, the short period which had elapsed since her trial, and the need of punishment for crime. The court also filed formal findings of fact and conclusions of law. It found that appellant had not recovered her sanity and that "it had not been shown that [she] will not in the reasonable future be dangerous to herself or others." The conclusions of law stated that "it has not been shown by a preponderance of the evidence that [appellant] should be released conditionally. . .; that the Government has shown by a preponderance of the evidence that [she] should not. . . ."

We cannot discern from either the court's oral opinion or its findings of fact and conclusions of law what distinction, if any, it drew between the statutory requirements for conditional release and those for unconditional release. The District Court did not have the benefit of our present construction of the statute, made now for the first time. Sound judicial administration dictates that we refrain from review of the evidence and allow the trial court to evaluate it in the first instance in light of the principles we now hold applicable. Accordingly we reverse the appealed order and remand the case to the District Court with directions to afford the parties an opportunity to reconsider the case in the light of this opinion, with leave to supplement the record if the court or the parties are so advised.

*   *   *

WILBUR K. MILLER, CIRCUIT JUDGE, dissenting. . . . On May 30, 1957, Zurab Abdusheli called on the appellant, Edith L. Hough, at her apartment in The Woodner, a large apartment hotel in the District of Columbia, to express his sympathy over the recent death of her father. She said later that Abdusheli became "psychologically aggressive," so she wrapped her pistol in a towel and shot him several times. As he lay moaning on the day bed where he had fallen, the appellant placed the pistol close to his temple and shot again, "to put him out of his misery." Then she telephoned the police. In due course, she was indicted for first degree murder . . . and was found not guilty by reason of insanity. Thereupon, . . . the court ordered her to be confined in a hospital for the mentally ill. Her malady was diagnosed as high-grade schizophrenia, paranoid type—a condition which was present before and during the trial and which, according to all the psychiatrists, still exists.

*   *   *

I dissent from this reversal and remand because I think the order of denial was justified and indeed required by the evidence. It seems to me the District Judge demonstrated that he was quite familiar with the statute, which after all is not difficult to understand, and that he employed the correct standards in reaching his decision. . . .

*   *   *

It seems clear to me that a confined insane person "is in a condition to be conditionally released under supervision" only when he will not in the reasonable future be dangerous to himself or others. In deciding this it is of course important for the court to know what sort of supervision is proposed. In the present case, there is no suggestion of any physical, restraint supervision, or control, the only supervision suggested by the superintendent is that the patient report perhaps once a week for an interview. Otherwise she is

---

1. D.C. Code § 24–301(e).
2. Clearly the court is not bound to an all-or-nothing acceptance or rejection of the conditions recommended by the hospital superintendent.

to be entirely on her own, free of any sort of actual day-to-day supervision by hospital authorities and attendants.

Obviously, conditional release is more difficult to justify than is unconditional release. For, with respect to conditional release, the certificate is that the confined person is still insane, but that the superintendent thinks it would be safe to release him under supervision. It is, of course, much easier to believe that a sane person will not in the reasonable future be dangerous to himself or others than to believe that an insane person will not be. The court should be even more careful in examining the evidence as to the danger involved in conditional release of an insane person, than with respect to the unconditional release of a person who has recovered his sanity.

* * *

. . . Dr. Overholser did not certify, as he should have done, that the appellant is still insane. That he was of that opinion, however, clearly appears from his testimony, a pertinent part of which appears in the margin.[3] These excerpts also show that, although Dr. Overholser had proposed conditional release, he was not convincing in his effort to justify it.

---

3. Excerpt from Dr. Overholser's testimony:

"Q. And after the verdict, when you had occasion to examine her, was your opinion the same; namely, she was suffering from a major mental disease? A. Yes, although she had shown considerable improvement as far as her adjustment to the other patients on the ward, for example, was concerned.

"Q. What symptoms did she evidence in June of '57, if I might go back for a moment to that first time you saw her? A. One of the features that was rather striking, I think, was that she saw nothing unusual in what she had done. She saw no reason why your office, Mr. Flannery [the Assistant United States Attorney], should have done anything about it, should have obtained an indictment, or why the police should have made any arrest.

"Q. And is it not a fact also that she didn't think that she should have even been charged? A. Yes, that is correct. She showed a general aloofness, I may say, too. She stayed pretty much away from the other patients; stayed by herself pretty much.

* * *

"Q. Now then, would you say that this unusual attitude she had about the act she had committed was due to the fact she was mentally ill? A. I take it so in this case, yes.

"Q. Now, as of this moment, doesn't she still feel that she did no wrong in killing the deceased in this case? A. I think so.

"Q. So she hasn't changed in that regard? A. In that regard no. Her behavior has changed considerably, of course, for the better.

"Q. Up until this moment, has she shown any remorse for having killed Zurab Abdusheli? A. I can't say that I had gone into it enough for that. I assume it would follow there wouldn't be much remorse if she thought she had done nothing wrong.

"Q. And doesn't she still feel today that she was justified in doing what she did and that she was protecting her soul? A. I believe she has made that statement—not to me.

The testimony of Dr. Karpman was particularly illuminating. He had been a friend and associate of appellant's deceased father (who had also been a psychiatrist) and had known and observed Miss Hough for many years. Because he was a family friend, he was a reluctant witness. As early as 1945, Dr. Karpman had been apprehensive as to what might happen. He said:

"I urged the father to hospitalize her; and of course he wouldn't do it. I predicted, I told him personally, that we never can tell what measures or what a person of this type of psychosis might do. It may be something very drastic. But I didn't think of murder, because I am not an astrologer and I couldn't predict in advance; but I said something drastic might happen.

"Q. You thought she had a psychosis at that time? A. Yes.

Q. What psychosis? A. Paranoid schizophrenia.

* * *

"Q. In your opinion is Edith L. Hough the aggressive type of paranoid? A. Yes, she is the aggressive type—as evidenced by the fact that she took measures of her own in killing the man. That is aggressiveness.

"Q. In your opinion is an aggressive paranoid

"Q. And today she still can't understand why criminal charges were placed against her in this case, can she? A. I think, from what she said, that is her general attitude, yes.

"Q. She can't exercise objective reasoning in regard to that, can she? A. I suppose not. Many people have difficulty in objective reasoning.

* * *

"Q. Now, doctor, the present diagnosis is schizophrenic reaction, paranoid type; is it not? A. That is correct.

"Q. So the diagnosis hasn't changed from what it was originally? A. That's right.

"Q. In other words, she is still suffering from a major mental disease known as schizophrenia, paranoid type? A. Yes.

"Q. However, although she still has a major mental disease, you have certified that she should have a conditional release? A. I have.

"Q. Very well, now if she were given a conditional release, what protection would be afforded to the public under your plan, if you do have a plan? A. Yes, we do have a plan to keep in touch with her through our social service, to have her return to the hospital at fairly frequent intervals for interview, but it seems to me, at this stage of the proceedings, she has had enough opportunity that we have given her to show that she is no substantial menace to the community.

"Q. And you say that despite the fact that just less than 18 months ago she killed someone under very violent circumstances? A. Yes, and under great stress. Other factors were involved as well as the man; the fact her father had just died and so on.

"Q. Now, if this woman, who had this major mental disease, were released conditionally into the community and met a great number of frustrations in adjusting herself in getting along, isn't there a probability or possibility that she might explode, so to speak, and even do harm to herself or to others? A. Well, there is that possibility with a great many people, some of whom have never been in mental hospitals. I can't make any guarantee about permanence, or even about the conduct."

potentially dangerous? A. It is conceded universally an aggressive paranoid is dangerous. I would even say that universally we think that any paranoid schizophrenic is potentially dangerous, because one can never tell when the meekness and submissiveness may suddenly turn around and become aggressive.

"Q. Would you say Edith L. Hough at this time is potentially dangerous because she has schizophrenia, paranoid type? A. I would rather not answer this question directly. Ask me whether a paranoid schizophrenic is potentially dangerous, and I would say yes.

*   *   *

"Q. And you know that the hospital diagnosis in this case is that she at the present time is a schizophrenia, paranoid type? A. Well, that is about the same thing."

This woman is suffering from schizophrenia of the paranoid type. That she is aggressive, as testified to by Dr. Karpman, is readily apparent from her action in coolly killing her caller. She fell far short of showing she is entitled to conditional release. The Government showed, rather conclusively I think, that her condition is such that she might well harm herself or others were she released and permitted to go about without restraint. I think the District Judge was fully justified in refusing to grant conditional release, and that he understood and accurately applied the statute when he did so. Accordingly, I would affirm his order.

*   *   *

NOTES

NOTE 1

GOLDSTEIN, JOSEPH and KATZ, JAY

Dangerousness and Mental Illness
Some Observations on the Decision to Release
Persons Acquitted by Reason of Insanity*

*   *   *

[N]o criteria for "dangerousness" have been precisely articulated. The major problem is to identify criteria for evaluating the appropriateness of the many possible responses to the question posed: Assuming mental illness requiring some form of treatment or care, what behavior should be classified dangerous enough to authorize deprivation of liberty by continued detention in a mental institution or by release under supervision? Dangerous behavior might be construed to include: (1) only the crime for which the insanity defense was successfully raised; (2) all crimes; (3) only felonious crimes (as opposed to misdemeanors); (4) only crimes for which a given

_____
* Reprinted by permission of the Yale Law Journal Co. and Fred B. Rothman & Co. From the *Yale Law Journal*, vol. 70, p. 225. (1960).

maximum sentence or more is authorized; (5) only crimes categorized as violent; (6) only crimes categorized as harmful, physical or psychological, reparable or irreparable, to the victim; (7) any conduct, even if not labeled criminal, categorized as violent, harmful, or threatening; (8) any conduct which may provoke violent retaliatory acts; (9) any physical violence toward oneself; (10) any combination of these. More or other than the kind of offense for which the defense was raised was intended, for the statute specifically adds dangerousness to self as a basis for confinement. However, the D.C. court has not been challenged to further sort out the kinds of behavior to be classified as "dangerous" or to identify the values to be minimized and maximized. But it has already recognized the existence of these problems and has registered concern, for example, about the possible need for handling differently a patient with homicidal tendencies and one with a potential for forging checks. In the absence of court-created standards, the psychiatrist, it might be argued, is in an intolerable position. Actually the opposite is true, for he is presently free to apply for a patient's release on what has been called "his own best judgment." The psychiatrist, trained to seek release as soon as there is thereapeutic indication for such a decision, can face the court with release applications involving a wide variety of behavioral pathology and thus prompt a series of decisions giving substantive content to "dangerousness." Coupled with patient challenges to denials for release by psychiatrists, these applications will permit court and psychiatrist to examine the values operative in their decisions. This in turn will permit the psychiatrist to more easily differentiate those aspects of his decision primarily determined by his expertise from those determined by his value preferences. In sharing with the court those aspects of decision in which community values are at stake the psychiatrist need neither be apologetic for having values, nor be misled into feeling that his role as expert is being usurped.

*   *   *

NOTE 2

OVERHOLSER v. LEACH
257 F.2d 667 (D. C. Cir. 1957)

WASHINGTON, CIRCUIT JUDGE.

This case deals with the standards to be applied when a person—in this case the appellee Leach—has been accused of crime, has been found not guilty by reason of insanity, and subsequently seeks release from the mental institution to which he was committed after his criminal trial. The issue was raised here in a habeas corpus proceeding brought by Leach against Dr. Overholser, the Superintendent of St. Elizabeths Hospital, where Leach is presently confined pursuant to the Act of August 7, 1955, discussed below. The District Court after a lengthy hearing, ordered Leach's discharge. Dr. Overholser appealed to this court, and moved for summary reversal. . . .

* * *

The test of this statute is not whether a particular individual, engaged in the ordinary pursuits of life, is committable to a mental institution under the law governing civil commitments. Those laws do not apply here. This statute applies to an exceptional class of people—people who have committed acts forbidden by law, who have obtained verdicts of "not guilty by reason of insanity," and who have been committed to a mental institution pursuant to the Code. People in that category are treated by Congress in a different fashion from persons who have somewhat similar mental conditions, but who have not committed offenses or obtained verdicts of not guilty by reason of insanity at criminal trials. The phrase "establishing his eligibility for release," as applied to the special class of which Leach is a member, means something different from having one or more psychiatrists say simply that the individual is "sane." There must be freedom from such abnormal mental condition[1] as would make the individual dangerous to himself or the community in the reasonably foreseeable future.

The order of discharge will accordingly be Reversed.

NOTE 3

OVERHOLSER v. O'BEIRNE
302 F.2d 852 (D.C. Cir. 1962)

BURGER, CIRCUIT JUDGE.

[I]t may be useful to recall the reasons for confinement of persons found not guilty by reason of insanity. While the statute making such confinement mandatory is recent, its antecedents go back more than a century. As early as Hadfield's case, and ever since then, courts acting under their inherent powers or under statutes have ordered hospital confinement of persons who were relieved of criminal responsibility because of their mental condition when the criminal act was done. This was not for punishment since the very purpose of providing such a verdict was to excuse the act and relieve the actor from penalties. In its earliest development, confinement was primarily for the protection of society, but as medical knowledge increased and rehabilitation therapy developed more and more emphasis has been placed on the restoration of the subject to normal life free from the stigma of a criminal record. Roughly

one third of those committed to St. Elizabeths Hospital since 1954 under this statute have been released, including eight who had committed homicide. . . .

The *twofold* purpose of the mandatory hospital confinement must never be overlooked, first, recovery of the patient and second, protection of society and the patient. To ignore the need for both protections or to equate this "protective" hospitalization with punishment confuses the issue and does a grave disservice to the broad social purposes of the statute, as well as the objectives of our rule on criminal responsibility. That the available hospitals may have too few psychiatrists or inadequate facilities or that they may not use the appropriate techniques, or that some may consider mental institutions worse than prisons, or that it is thought by some that civil commitment standards . . . should be used—all of these factors are the business of the legislative, not the judicial branch of government if the statute is valid. . . .

Inherent in the statutory scheme, whether we like it or not, is the proposition that one who is "incurably insane" *and* "incurably dangerous"—if there are such—may be hospitalized indefinitely.

* * *

The issue is not whether O'Beirne now has a "mental disease" but whether he has an "abnormal mental condition" which will cause him to be dangerous to himself or others if released. The difficulty is partly one of semantics and "labels" but it is also deeper than that. . . .

[I]t must be presumed, and certainly hoped, that a confinement in St. Elizabeths after a verdict of not guilty by reason of insanity, will bring about an improvement and recovery of the individual so he can resume a place in society without danger to himself or the public. [R]ecovery from mental ills does not come overnight; we are not dealing here with an affliction like a diseased appendix where a surgical operation and a brief convalescence are almost invariably followed by a recovery. Recovery from behavior disorders or mental ills, by whatever names or labels we use, is slow and dubious at best and is rarely as predictable as the course of a physical disease. Judge Washington's choice of words "abnormal mental condition" in Leach was not casual or thoughtless, but studied and calculated. That concept means that a patient like O'Beirne may progress from a true and undisputed "mental disease" such as a psychosis, which he formerly had, to his present undisputed state of "sociopathic personality disturbance, antisocial reaction." But that result does not qualify him for release; he cannot be released until the process of recovery reaches the point that his release will not expose him or others to danger. . . .

* * *

---

1. Thus even, though Leach's mental health may have mproved, if there remains an abnormal mental condition which is certified as a source of potential danger, he is to be retained in custody under Section 24–301.

The dissenting opinion* does not meet the central issue in the case but rather asserts in essence that $3\frac{1}{2}$ years in St. Elizabeths Hospital constitutes too much confinement for a one-year offense. This approach strikes at the very heart of the effort to rehabilitate the maladjusted offender. The purpose of the standard of criminal responsibility, adopted for this jurisdiction in 1954, did more than broaden the area of exculpation from criminal responsibility; it also contemplated rehabilitation in a *medical* rather than penal context. . . .

It is fundamentally wrong, we think, to measure the treatment needs of a sick person by the length of the penal sentence he would have received had he not been excused from punishment, for in the eyes of the law such a person has committed no *crime*. Statutes tell us how long a sentence should be but neither statutes nor medical books can tell us how much hospitalization is needed to effect rehabilitation. The dissenting opinion seems to regard O'Beirne as "paying his debt to society" by his stay in St. Elizabeths Hospital when the truth is that this is in no sense a "punishment." If any debt is being paid, it is precisely the reverse of this; it would be more nearly correct to say society is discharging an obligation to O'Beirne in the procedure established by Congress to assure him psychiatric care at public expense.

The dissenting opinion also seeks to introduce into the process civil standards of committability by the Mental Health Commission in direct conflict with the plain congressional intent expressed in § 24–301. It is one thing to argue that confinement after a verdict of not guilty by reason of insanity, without a special and contemporaneous hearing, is a violation of due process; it is quite another proposition to say that as soon as the hospital confinement exceeds the maximum sentence for a guilty person, we will review the problem and shift into a civil proceeding not designed, as the Leach opinion pointed out, to deal with persons who have committed dangerous acts. The civil commitment process while available for some kinds of aberrant conduct was not established to deal with persons whose dangerous propensities and mental illnesses come into focus and relevancy when they commit what otherwise would be criminal acts.

*   *   *

In *Taylor* v. *United States*, 1955, 95 U.S. App. D.C. 373, 379, 222 F.2d 398, 404, we held that the jury must be told what becomes of an accused who is found not guilty by reason of insanity and Judge Edgerton, speaking for the court, said:

"... we think that when an accused person has pleaded insanity, counsel may and the judge should

_____
*Not reprinted here.

inform the jury that if he is acquitted by reason of insanity *he will be presumed to be insane* and may be confined in a 'hospital for the insane' as long as 'the public safety and . . . [his] welfare' require. Though this fact has no theoretical bearing on the jury's verdict it may have a *practical* bearing." (Emphasis added.) (Footnotes omitted.)

It seems reasonably clear that the "practical bearing" Judge Edgerton referred to in the context of the issues of the Taylor case was the greater likelihood that a jury would accept the claim of insanity if they knew the accused would not be set free without some medical attention being given him because of his claimed abnormal mental condition. . . .

The position expressed by Judge Edgerton in his dissent is, of course, sharply at odds with his position in the Taylor . . . case. Were we to adopt his present position it would be incumbent upon the trial judges to explain to the jury that "within a reasonable period of time which will vary from case to case" continued hospital confinement under § 24–301 would require a civil proceeding under the Mental Health Act, D.C. Code 1951, § 21–301 *et seq.* It is at least arguable that as a "practical" matter such an enlarged cautionary instruction could well cause jurors to be less willing to reach a verdict of not guilty by reason of insanity. The underlying purposes of § 24–301 and the instruction called for by the Taylor [and Lyles] cases would thus be thwarted if the jurors should render a guilty verdict on an accused who in fact should be held not responsible because of insanity. . . .

*   *   *

The suggestion that civil mental health commitment procedures, with their "greater procedural safeguards," are a more appropriate remedy seems to rest on the idea that O'Beirne committed a "nondangerous offense." But to describe the theft of watches and jewelry as "nondangerous" is to confuse danger with violence. Larceny is usually less violent than murder or assault, but in terms of public policy the purpose of the statute is the same as to both. Larceny, assault, and murder are all dangerous; they are simply different areas of prohibited conduct. Hence unless we are to ignore the objectives and policies of the statute in question, the release provisions must apply in the same way and with the same force to larceny without violence as to a crime of violence until Congress speaks otherwise. Of course the Superintendent of St. Elizabeths might well take into account, in making his appraisal of potential danger, the quality of the patient's abnormal mental condition as well as the history of conduct. . . .

In the face of the opinions of psychiatrists on both sides that O'Beirne probably is not now committable under the civil procedures, the argument that he should not be held longer without a civil commitment is the familiar contention of those who "want to have it both ways." To yield to that view would mean that sociopathic personality disturbance constitutes a valid defense to a criminal charge but is not a basis for hospital confinement under § 24–301. . . .

*   *   *

NOTE 4

RAGSDALE v. OVERHOLSER
281 F.2d 943 (D.C. Cir. 1960)

FAHY, CIRCUIT JUDGE (concurring).

*   *   *

. . . I agree that there is a rational relationship between mandatory commitment . . . and an acquittal by reason of insanity. . . . But this mandatory commitment provision rests upon a supposition, namely, the necessity for treatment of the mental condition which led to the acquittal by reason of insanity. And this necessity for treatment presupposes in turn that treatment will be accorded.

Since an accused is entitled to be acquitted on the ground of insanity although the evidence may merely have led the jury to entertain a reasonable doubt as to his sanity when the offense occurred, the validity of continued confinement under the mandatory commitment provisions . . . may require that, unless within a reasonable time he progresses toward becoming not dangerous to self or community, the person committed can be held only by a separate civil adjudication of unsoundness. . . . It is by no means clear that society can continue to deprive a person of liberty by attributing to a jury's doubt about his mental condition, which led to his acquittal and mandatory commitment, any and all evil or criminal propensities he may be thought to have, and to keep him in confinement because of them. This would transform the hospital into a penitentiary where one could be held indefinitely for no convicted offense, and this even though the offense of which he was previously acquitted because of doubt as to his sanity might not have been one of the more serious felonies.

*   *   *

NOTE 5

PEOPLE v. MISEVIC
32 Ill.2d 11, 203 N.E. 2d 393 (1964)
Cert. Denied 380 U.S. 963 (1965)

DAILY, JUSTICE.

This is an appeal from an order of the circuit court of Cook County quashing a writ of *habeas corpus*. . . .

In June, 1954, Paul Pauling was indicted and tried in the criminal court of Cook County for the crime of attempted murder, but a jury found him not guilty by reason of insanity when the offense was com-

mitted. At the same time, in conformity with section 12 of division II of the Criminal Code then in effect, (Ill. Rev. Stat. 1953, chap. 38, par. 592) the jury made a further finding that he had not "entirely and permanently recovered from such insanity."[1] The trial court . . . thereupon entered an order transferring relator to the custody of the Public Welfare Department and directing his confinement in a security hospital until such time as "in a subsequent hearing before a jury, the said Paul Pauling shall be determined by a verdict to have entirely recovered from such insanity." Since that time relator has been confined in State hospitals, and it is undisputed that he was afflicted with schizophrenia, a form of insanity.

Nearly ten years later, in February, 1964, a brother of the relator filed a petition for writ of *habeas corpus* in his behalf, alleging that relator is not now insane and praying for his release from confinement. In addition, it was alleged that relator had been examined by a licensed psychiatrist in November, 1963, and that the doctor reported: (1) that relator was no longer a source of danger to himself, his family or the community; and (2) that his continued confinement in a State hospital would bring no further benefit to the relator or society. A synopsis of the doctor's interview and his findings, attached to the petition as an exhibit, disclosed that relator has become blind during his confinement. Further, it is the reasonable intendment of the entire record that relator's brother, who resides on a farm, is willing to assume the burden of relator's care and custody.

A writ issued, returnable February 18, 1964, and on such date relator appeared in court with his counsel. However, after hearing arguments and permitting a State psychiatrist to testify that relator had not recovered his sanity and that he was still in need of 24-hour observation and treatment, the trial court quashed the writ and remanded relator to the custody of respondent. The precise basis for the order was

---

1. The relevant Illinois statutes read as follows: 592. Insanity. §12. An insane person without lucid intervals, shall not be found guilty of any crime or misdemeanor with which he may be charged: Provided, the act so charged as criminal shall have been committed in the condition of insanity. If, upon the trial of a person charged with crime, it shall appear from the evidence that the act was committed as charged, but that, at the time of committing the same, the person so charged was insane, the jury shall so find by their verdict, and by their verdict shall further find whether such person has or has not entirely and permanently recovered from such insanity; and in case the jury shall find such person has not entirely and permanently recovered from such insanity, the court shall commit such person to the Department of Public Welfare. But in case the jury shall find by their verdict that such person has entirely and permanently recovered from such insanity, he shall be discharged from custody. If after commitment such person in a subsequent hearing before a jury shall be determined by verdict to have entirely and permanently recovered from such insanity, he shall likewise be discharged from custody. . . .

*   *   *

that the petition was insufficient because it did not allege relator was "entirely and permanently" recovered as provided in the statute under which he was committed. In such regard, relator's counsel has admitted, both below and in the briefs filed in this court, that schizophrenia is a mental disease from which one never entirely recovers.

At issue here is that portion of the statute which states: "If after commitment such person in a subsequent hearing before a jury shall be determined by verdict to have *entirely and permanently* recovered from such insanity, he shall likewise be discharged from custody." (Ill. Rev. Stat. 1953, chap. 38, par. 592, emphasis ours.) Due to the circumstance that schizophrenics never fully recover, relator concedes that he cannot meet the criteria of "entire" recovery, or "permanent" recovery. . . . What he asks is that this court either except schizophrenics from the operation of the statute, or that we construe the statute as reflecting a legislative intent that the confinement it directs should not continue once the insane person has become blind and harmless to himself and others. To sustain his first alternative relator points out that a schizophrenic can never be released from confinement within the contemplation of the statute, and brings to our attention medical opinion that prolonged confinement is in fact a detriment to one suffering from schizophrenia; as to the second alternative it is argued that ethics, morals, and good conscience require such a construction.

We are sympathetic to relator's position and pleas, and we are likewise aware that the statute under which he is confined antedates new insights into the problem of mental illness and its treatment and control. These considerations, however, afford no basis for the judiciary to invade the province of the legislative arm of our government. The State, as *parens patriae*, exercises the same control over insane persons as was formerly exercised in England by its king, and under our form of government the power is exercised by the courts only through legislative enactments. . . .

In plain and unambiguous terms our legislature has provided that persons who escape the consequences of criminal acts by reason of insanity must, if the insanity continues at the time of trial, be given to the custody of the Public Welfare Department and confined in a security hospital until such time as they have entirely and permanently recovered from such condition. . . . Based upon these principles, we conclude here that the concession that relator had not entirely and permanently recovered from the condition which led to his confinement left the trial court with no alternative other than to quash the writ, and that any relief to relator from the operation of the statute must come from the legislature rather than the courts.

*   *   *

Order affirmed.

NOTE 6

WATSON v. CAMERON
312 F.2d 878 (D.C. Cir. 1962)

BURGER, CIRCUIT JUDGE.

Appellant [seeking release from St. Elizabeths Hospital to which he had been committed after being found not guilty by reason of insanity] claimed in the District Court that he was entitled as a matter of right to examination by an independent expert such as a member of the Mental Health Commission.

Heretofore we have considered that the allowance of such examination by an outside expert was within the sound discretion of the District Judge but in this particular context—release from confinement under § 24–301 D.C. Code Ann. (1961)—we have laid down no guidelines. Indeed on this record we could not say that discretion was abused, partly because no standards for its exercise exist.

In these circumstances we conclude that the ends of justice and its efficient administration will be best served by prescribing that an independent examination by an expert appointed by the District Court shall be granted as a matter of right (a) where no such examination has previously been granted, and (b) where the movant has been confined in the hospital for a substantial period such as here where the confinement has been more than one year. We do not decide whether appointment of an outside expert is required in every case on demand, nor do we suggest these criteria must always be present to warrant such an appointment. We hold only where, as here, a person is confined for more than one year without such an examination he is entitled, as a matter of right, to an independent examination to test the findings and conclusions of the hospital staff where he is confined.

*   *   *

e.   GOLDSTEIN, JOSEPH and KATZ, JAY

Abolish the "Insanity Defense"—Why Not?*

*   *   *

To demonstrate the kind of analysis we think essential to a meaningful examination of insanity as a defense, we first analyze the concept of the defense of self-defense. If a person intentionally kills another human being, the criminal law, in support of a basic community objective—the protection of human life—defines such conduct as a crime and authorizes as the sanction life imprisonment of the offender.[7] Few would disagree about the ultimate

*Reprinted by permission of the Yale Law Journal Co. and Fred B. Rothman & Co., from the *Yale Law Journal*, vol. 72, pp. 855–871, (1963).

7. We exclude from our analysis of self-defense the death penalty which may accompany a finding of murder in the first degree, for feelings about that sanction are likely to distort the already complex issues to be unravelled . . .

objective of protecting life and about the elements of the crime, but there may be little or no consensus about the sanction or its purposes. The imposition of life imprisonment rests on a variety of oft-conflicting and mutually inclusive assumptions shared by legislature, court and community about deprivation of liberty and its psychological significance. As *punishment*, life imprisonment is assumed to satisfy and channel the community's need to express feelings of vengeance or desires to effect rehabilitation of the offender. As *restraint*, it is assumed to remove from circulation a person who is believed likely to kill again, to provide a structure for satisfying community vengeance or to offer an institutional opportunity for care and rehabilitation. As *rehabilitation*, it is assumed to reduce the likelihood that he who has killed once will kill again, to increase the likelihood of returning a life to the community or to provide a basis for rationalizing community vengeance. As a *deterrent of others*, it is assumed to reinforce internal controls over the urge to kill through external threats of punishment, restraint, rehabilitation and the accompanying stigma.[11] Thus, via a variety of assumptions which may or may not be related to an actual impact on any one offender or on other members of the community, life imprisonment becomes the sanction for one who kills another intentionally.

Intentional killing in defense of self, however, is an exception which denies the State authority to impose the sanction authorized for intentional killings. This

exception "rests upon the necessity of allowing a person to protect himself from . . . [lethal] harm in cases where there is no time to resort to the law for protection."[12] Thus under circumstances where, by definition, one of two must die, the law seeks a solution least incompatible with its overall objective of protecting life by preferring the life of the "law-abiding" citizen. He is the man whose inner controls reinforced by the threat of external sanction hold in check his urge to kill except when his own life is jeopardized by someone not so deterred. The law thereby recognizes that the sanction for intentional killings is drained of any deterrent strength when external reality's system for protecting life fails and in turn releases internal reality's instinct for self-preservation. Conceptualized another way, authorizing the potential victim to kill his assailant constitutes a sanction which may be assumed to fulfill punitive, restraining, and deterrent functions in the service of the community's objective to safeguard human life. To generalize, when a situation is identified in which the application of the authorized sanction would conflict with basic criminal law objectives, a rational system of law would seek first to articulate why such an application is inappropriate and then to formulate the exception to accord with those objectives.

Having articulated the reasons for an exception to liability for intentional killings in defense of self, it becomes possible to evaluate such competing formulations as for example, (a) the actor's "right to stand his ground" and meet force with force, or (b) the actor's duty to "do everything reasonably possible to escape [without resorting] to the use of deadly force." Formulation (a) subordinates the value of safeguarding human life whenever possible to the values of safeguarding a threatened man's right to protect his interest in property as well as his right to be free from the stigma or uneasiness associated with cowardice. Formulation (b) prefers the value of safeguarding human life whenever possible. Conceptually, and probably in practice, the second formulation would best serve to protect both lives. Its application would restrict to a minimum the number of instances where reality leaves no choice and forces favoring one life over another. The sanction authorized for intentional killings, therefore, remains operative except in those situations where the choice is between one of two lives, not between, for example, life and an interest in property, price or reputation.

With this framework for identifying a need for an exception to criminal liability and for evaluating formulations to meet such a need, we turn to an examination of the "insanity defense."

Like self-defense, the insanity defense applies, theoretically at least, only to persons against whom

---

11. "Psycho-analysts have drawn attention to three main motives in our attitude towards law-breakers and criminals that operate in addition to the conscious reasons that are more readily recognized. . . . In the first place, the criminal provides an outlet for our (moralized) aggression. In this respect he plays the same role as do our enemies in war and our political scapegoats in time of peace. That some very real satisfaction is to be found in this way is shown by the vast crowds that attended public executions. . . . In the second place, the criminal by his flouting of law and moral rule constitutes a temptation to the id; it is as though we said to ourselves, 'if he does it, why should not we?' This stirring of criminal impulses within ourselves calls for an answering effort on the part of the super-ego, which can best achieve its object by showing that 'crime doesn't pay.' This in turn can be done most conveniently and completely by a demonstration on the person of the criminal. By punishing him we are not only showing him that he can't 'get away with it' but holding him up as a terrifying example to our own tempted and rebellious selves. Thirdly . . . is the danger with which our whole notion of justice is threatened when we observe that a criminal has gone unpunished. The primitive foundation of this notion . . . lies in an equilibrium of pleasures and pains, of indulgence and punishment. This equilibrium is disturbed, either if the moral rewards of good conduct are not forthcoming . . . or if the normal punishments of crime are absent or uncertain. . . . It is to prevent disturbance of the latter kind that we insist that those who have broken the law shall be duly punished. Through their punishment the equilibrium is re-established, without it (so we dimly feel) the whole psychological and social structure on which morality depends is imperilled." Flugel, *Man, Morals and Society*, pp. 169–70 (1945).

12. 5 *Wis. Legislative Council, Judiciary Committee Report on the Criminal Code* 44 (1953).

each of the elements of the offense charged could be established. Like defense of self, the defense of insanity, if successfully pleaded, results in "acquittal." But unlike the acquittal of self-defense which means liberty, the acquittal of the insanity defense means deprivation of liberty for an indefinite term in a "mental institution." And unlike the purpose of self-defense, the purpose of the insanity defense either has been assumed to be so obvious as not to require articulation or has been expressed in such vague generalizations as to afford no basis for evaluating the multitude of formulae.

Neither legislative report, nor judicial opinion, nor scholarly comment criticizing or proposing formulations of the insanity defense has faced the crucial questions: "What is the purpose of the defense in the criminal process?" or "What need for an exception to criminal liability is being met and what objectives of the criminal law are being reinforced by the defense?"

The Royal Commission on Capital Punishment (1953) [p. 98] disposed of this issue with apodictic assurance by asserting:

> We make one fundamental assumption, which we should hardly have thought it necessary to state explicitly. . . . It has for centuries been recognized that, if a person was, at the time of his unlawful act, mentally so disordered that it would be unreasonable to impute guilt to him, he ought not to be held liable to conviction and punishment under the criminal law. Views have changed and opinions have differed, as they differ now, about the standards to be applied in deciding whether an individual should be exempted from criminal responsibility for this reason; but the principle has been accepted without question. . . .

Thus the Royal Commission reiterated the well-rounded proposition that "if a person was . . . mentally so disordered that it would be unreasonable to impute guilt to him, he ought not to be held [guilty, i.e.] liable to conviction and punishment." The Commission neither sought to identify the purposes of not imputing guilt to "individuals whose conduct would otherwise be criminal," nor did it ask why and when does the imputation of guilt for being "mentally so disordered" become "unreasonable." The Commission had no basis for evaluating the changing views and opinions "about the standards to be applied," and the principle "accepted without question" remained without meaning.

A century earlier the pattern had been firmly set of accepting an insanity defense without asking: "Why an insanity defense?" or more appropriately, "What objective of the criminal law suggests the need for an exception to the law's general application—an exception which would require taking into account the mental health of the offender?" In *M'Naghten's* Case (1843), the House of Lords, acting in their judicial, not legislative capacity, asked only what is the law respecting alleged crimes committed by persons afflicted with "insane delusions." And the innovating court in *Durham* (1954), after promulgating a new formulation gave no guide to evaluating its adequacy beyond noting:

> Our collective conscience does not allow punishment where it cannot impose blame. . . .
>
> The legal and moral traditions of the western world require that those who, of their own free will and with evil intent (sometimes called *mens rea*), commit acts which violate the law, shall be criminally responsible for those acts. Our traditions also require that where such acts stem from and are the product of a mental disease or defect . . . moral blame shall not attach, and hence there will not be criminal responsibility. . . .[25]

The court leaves without definition and without identification of purpose such ambiguous words as "punishment," and "blame," and thus in effect only says "he who is punishable is blameworthy and he who is blameworthy is punishable." Never established is the relevance of these words to a defense which would compel supposedly different dispositions of persons involved in activity labeled "criminal." Moreover, the court, though not blinded by precedent, left unasked and therefore unanswered: "What underlies the 'legal and moral traditions' in 'our collective conscience' which prevents us from inquiring why a rule is required?"

Likewise, the American Law Institute (1956–1962) provides no basis for evaluating its formula for a defense of insanity. With focus on consequences, it "explains," echoing the Royal Commission and *Durham*, that the purpose of the insanity defense is "to discriminate between the cases where a *punitive-correctional* disposition is appropriate and those in which a *medical-custodial* disposition is the only kind that the law should allow." Once "*punitive*" is substituted for "*custodial*" and "*correctional*" for "*medical*," or however the terms are juxtaposed in the ALI statement, the "distinctions" seem to disappear. Moreover, criteria for evaluating what constitutes an "appropriate" disposition for either category remain unarticulate. Thus those characteristics which determine who is to fit into which category remain unidentified. This may be because the distinctions between alternative responses are never clarified. Finally, a Committee of distinguished doctors, lawyers and religious leaders, appointed by the Governor of New York (1958) to improve the defense of insanity, pronounced before formulating their rule:

> We are unanimously of the view that there are compelling practical, ethical and religious reasons for maintaining the insanity defense; . . . We believe . . . that it is entirely feasible to cast a formulation

---

25. *Durham* v. *United States*, 214 F.2d 862, 876 (D.C. Cir. 1954).

which . . . will sufficiently improve the statute to meet working standards of *good morals*, *good science*, and *good law*.[30]

Never identified are the reasons labeled "practical," "ethical," and "religious," or the standards labeled "good morals," "good science" and "good law."

In enunciating yet another formula for insanity, the Court of Appeals for the Third Circuit in *United States* v. *Currens* (1961) contaminates its thinking by confusing and merging the inherently incompatible concepts of "insanity" as a defense to a crime with "insanity" as evidence to cast doubt on a material element of an offense. It suggests, as did the court in *Durham*, that some relationship exists between the insanity defense and *mens rea*, a material element of every major crime. In *Currens*, *mens rea* (guilty mind) is used to mean that criminal liability rests

> . . . on the assumption that a person has a capacity to control his behavior and to choose between alternative courses of conduct. . . . When a person possessing capacity for choice and control, nevertheless breaches a duty . . . he is subjected to . . . sanctions not because of the act alone, but because of his failure to exercise his capacity to control. . . . For example, an act of homicide will create no liability, only civil liability or varying criminal liability depending on the nature of the mental concomitant of the act. Generally the greater the defendant's capacity for control of his conduct and the more clearly it appears that he exercised his power of choice in acting, the more severe is the penalty imposed by society.[31]

And the court criticized the *Durham* and *M'Naghten* formulae because:

> They do not take account of the fact that an "insane" defendant commits the *crime* not because his mental illness causes him to do a certain prohibited act but because the totality of his personality is such, because of mental illness, that he has lost the capacity to control his acts in the way that the normal individual can and does control them. If this effect has taken place he must be found not to possess the guilty mind, the *mens rea*, necessary to constitute his prohibited act a *crime*.[32]

At this point the court by the force of its own reasoning *should* have been led to say:

> *Without the essential element of mens rea, there is no crime from which to relieve the defendant of liability and consequently, since no crime has been committed, there is no need for formulating an insanity defense.*

But instead the court actually concludes:

> We are of the opinion that the following [insanity] formula most nearly fulfills the objectives just discussed. . . .[34]

The court uses the word "crime" first to mean "dangerous conduct" and then, without alerting itself to the shift, to mean technically the establishment beyond doubt of each material element of an offense. With this sleight of thought the court shifts focus from "insanity" as a *defense* to conduct "otherwise criminal" to insanity as *evidence* to negate an element essential to categorizing the accused's conduct "criminal."

In announcing a new formula for the insanity defense, the court fails to recognize that there is no need for such a defense to remove criminal liability since it has concluded that no crime is established once mental illness (however defined) has cast doubt on *mens rea* (however defined). Conceptually, at least, outright acquittal would result and instructions to the jury would reflect a time, pre-*M'Naghten*, when evidence of mental condition, like any other relevant evidence, was used to cast doubt on a material element of the crime.

In our efforts to understand the suggested relationship between "insanity" and "*mens rea*" there emerges a purpose for the "insanity defense" which, though there to be seen, has remained of extremely low visibility. That purpose seems to be obscured because thinking about such a relationship has generally been blocked by unquestioning and disarming references to our collective conscience and our religious and moral traditions. Assuming the existence of the suggested relationship between "insanity" and "*mens rea*," the defense is not to absolve of criminal responsibility "sick" persons who would otherwise be subject to criminal sanction. Rather, its real function is to authorize the state to hold those "who must be found not to possess the guilty mind *mens rea*," even though the criminal law demands that no person be held criminally responsible if doubt is cast on any material element of the offense charged. This, in some jurisdictions, is found directly reflected in evidentiary rules making inadmissible testimony on mental health to disprove a state of mind necessary to constitute the crime charged. A more dramatic expression of abandoning the rule of proof of each element beyond a reasonable doubt has slipped into those instructions to the jury which advise the ordering of deliberations:

> If you find the defendant not guilty by reason of

---

30. *Report of the Governors Committee on the Defense of Insanity* 140 *N.Y.L.J.* No. 88, p. 4 (Nov. 5, 1958), No. 89, p. 4 (Nov. 6, 1958) (emphasis supplied).

31. *United States* v. *Currens*, 290 F.2d 751, 773 (3d Cir. 1961).

32. *Id.* at 774 (emphasis supplied).

34. 290 F.2d at 774. For its test the court proposed:
The jury must be satisfied that at the time of committing the prohibited act the defendant, as a result of mental disease or defect, lacked substantial capacity to conform his conduct to the requirements of the law which he is alleged to have violated.

insanity, you will render a verdict of not guilty by reason of insanity.

If you do not so find, then you will proceed to determine whether he is guilty or innocent of one or both of the offenses charged on the basis of the same act.

[T]here are two principle issues for you to determine. The *first* is his mental condition and the *second* is whether he committed the offenses charged or whether he is innocent of them. . . .

Now, on the issue of guilt or innocence of the offenses charged, the essential elements of the first count or the housebreaking count, *if you do not find the defendant not guilty by reason of insanity*, are as follows:

First, that the defendant broke and entered or entered without breaking . . . the place described in the indictment;

Second, that the place entered was occupied or belonged to the complaining witness; and,

Third, that he *intended* to steal or commit the offense of larceny. . . .[39]

Yet, since a verdict of not guilty results in outright release and a verdict of not guilty by reason of insanity results in incarceration, jury instructions must require *first* a determination of innocence or guilt and *second* a consideration of the insanity issue *only* after a determination that guilt can be established.

What this discussion indicates, then, is that the insanity defense is not designed, as is the defense of self-defense, to define an exception to criminal liability, but rather to define for sanction an exception from among those who would be free of liability. It is as if the insanity defense were prompted by an affirmative answer to the silently posed question: "Does *mens rea* or any essential element of an offense exclude from liability a group of persons whom the community wishes to restrain?" If the suggested relationship between *mens rea* and "insanity" means that "insanity" precludes proof beyond doubt of *mens rea* then the "defense" is designed to authorize the holding of persons who have committed no crime. So conceived, the problem really facing the criminal process has been how to obtain authority to sanction the "insane" who would be excluded from liability by an overall application of the general principles of the criminal law.

Furthermore, even if the relationship between insanity and "*mens rea*" is rejected, this same purpose re-emerges when we try to understand why the consequence of this defense, unlike other defenses, is restraint, not release. Even though each of the elements of an offense may be established, release will follow acquittal or dismissal if, for example, entrapment, self-defense, or the statute of limitations are successfully pleaded. Assuming, then, that all elements of an offense are to be established before the insanity

defense becomes operative, the question remains: "Why restrain rather than release?" Restraint cannot be attributed to potential "dangerousness" associated with the crime charged, no matter how serious, for that kind of "dangerousness" is characteristic of defendants whose defenses prevail. The crucial variable leading to restraint seems to be the "insanity at the time of the offense," i.e., a fear of danger seen in the combination of "mental sickness" and "crime." This fear of freedom for those acquitted by reason of insanity comes sharply into focus at the close of the *Currens* decision. The court, uncertain of the consequences of such an acquittal for federal offenses outside of the District of Columbia, warns, in reversing the judgment of conviction: "[W]e are concerned with the disposition of Currens should he be found not guilty by reason of insanity. . . . In any event [in the light of doubt about the appropriate federal procedure for commitment] should Currens be acquitted at his new trial, the federal authorities should bring him and his condition to the attention of State authorities to the end that he may not remain in a position in which he may be a danger to himself or to the public."[45] That mandatory commitment, not release, generally follows the insanity defense becomes then particularly striking since, to the extent "insanity at

---

39. *Durham* v. *United States*, Record on Retrial under the new rule—reprinted Donnelly, J. Goldstein and Schwartz, *Criminal Law* at 775–76 (emphasis supplied).

45. *United States* v. *Currens*, 290 F.2d 757, 776 (3d Cir. 1961):

Courts of appeal have differed in their views as to available procedure in the event that a person is found not guilty of a federal criminal charge by reason of insanity. See *Pollard* v. *United States*, 6 Cir. 282, F.2d 450, 464, Order of Issuance of New Mandate, 6 Cir. 1960, 285 F.2d 81 . . . but compare *Sauer* v. *United States*, 9 Cir. 1957, 241 F.2d 640, 651–52 n. 32. . . .

Earlier in its opinion the court quotes with approval from *Biggs, The Guilty Mind* 144–45 (1955):

[T]he mental competence of recidivists should be questioned by realistic means at the earliest possible stage. So long as courts judge criminal responsibility by the test of knowledge of right and wrong, psychotics who have served prison terms or are granted probations are released to commit increasingly serious crimes, repeating crime and incarceration and release until murder is committed. Instead of being treated as ordinary criminals, they should be confined to institutions for the insane at the first offense and not be released until or unless cured.

Id. at 767.

Similarly this fear coupled with the possibility of an ironic twist prompts Judge Hastie in his dissent in *Currens* to note:

If we should affirm the judgment below, as I think we conscientiously can, the result of appellant's conviction and the consequent invocation of the Youth Correction Act would be his confinement for an appropriate period in a psychiatric institution for such treatment and supervision as are best calculated, in the light of our present medical knowledge, to accomplish his rehabilitation and cure. On the record this result would be good for the appellant and good for society. On the other hand, as the majority opinion recognizes, it is doubtful whether the federal authorities could require the restraint and psychiatric treatment of the appellant if he should be retried and, by reason of his mental illness, found not guilty. I think we need not and, therefore, should not thus

the time of the offense" is related to "mental health at the time of acquittal," the State is authorized to select from the mentally ill those who require civil restraint for custody and care. Thus the insanity defense is not a defense, it is a device for triggering indeterminate restraint.

The real problem which continues to face legislators, judges, jurors, and commentators is how to restrain persons who are somehow feared as both crazed and criminal. This oft-unconscious fear has precluded thinking about "insanity" in terms of traditional principles of law, whether that "insanity" is conceptualized as doubt-casting evidence or as an independent defense. Though unpleasant to acknowledge, the insanity defense is an expression of uneasiness, conscious or unconscious, either about the adequacy of such material elements of an offense as "*mens rea*" and "voluntariness" as bases for singling out those who ought to be held criminally responsible, or it is an expression of concern about the adequacy of civil commitment procedures to single out from

among the "not guilty by reason of insanity" those who are mentally ill and in need of restraint.

The problem of "whether there should be an insanity defense" or "how to formulate it" must continue unresolved as long as largely unconscious feelings of apprehension, awe, and anger toward the "sick," particularly if associated with "criminality," are hidden by the more acceptable conscious desire to protect the "sick from criminal liability." What must be recognized is the enormous ambivalence toward the "sick" reflected in conflicting wishes to exculpate and to blame; to sanction and not to sanction; to degrade and to elevate; to stigmatize and not to stigmatize; to care and to reject; to treat and to mistreat; to protect and to destroy. Such ambivalence finds expression in legislative proposals that persons acquitted by reason of insanity be "committed to the custody of the commissioner of correction [not mental health] to be placed in an appropriate institution of the department of correction [not mental health] for custody, care, and treatment."[48] And such

---

risk the release of one found to be a criminal psychopath when restraint and treatment seem desirable both medically and socially.

For these reasons I would affirm the conviction and commitment of the appellant. . . .

[A] person who has been shown to have committed an act resulting in serious harm to a member of the community, and who is also shown to be irresponsible by reason of mental disorder, ought to be the object of an even more thoroughgoing inquiry as to his risk to society than the responsible offender. This is so, of course, because by definition such a person lacks the capacity for individual self-control that is ultimately society's most secure protection.

State of California, *Special Commissions on Insanity and Criminal Offenders, First Report* 31 (July 7, 1962).

This report comes close to verbalizing the fears and concerns of the community and attempts to resolve or gives the appearance of resolving the conflict between relieving a person of criminal liability and compulsorily holding him for care and custody as a mentally ill person in a maximum security unit of the correctional system by separating, as if they were clearly separable, a finding of no criminal responsibility from its consequences, which is a special hearing for such acquittals, not all acquittals, to determine present dangerousness. It suggests

that the defendant alleged to be mentally ill presents two questions: First, whether he ought to be condemned by a criminal conviction, and second, whether he is such a substantial risk to the public safety that he must be securely confined.

Id. at 20.

Since the question of criminal responsibility is a legal question, the ultimate decision in a particular case is properly to be made by the judicial system and not by the medical profession.

Id. at 21.

Upon finding that a defendant is not criminally responsible for the act with which he is charged, an inquiry immediately ought to be made whether he is a substantial present risk to the safety of the public. The inquiry should be squarely directed to the question of whether the defendant is dangerous. This is a different question than whether he is "insane" within the meaning of the rules defining his

accountability under the criminal law. If he appears to be dangerous, he should be committed to secure custody. And he should be so committed without regard to whether he is "psychotic," whether he "knows right from wrong" or, indeed, whether he is effectively treatable by presently developed therapeutic techniques. The point is that he is dangerous and should not be let loose on society.

Id. at 31.

Similarly,

The only proper verdict is one which ensures that the person who suffers from the disease is kept secure in a hospital so as not to be a danger to himself or others. That is, a verdict of guilty but insane.

Bratty v. *Att'y-Gen. for N. Ireland*, [1961] 3 All E.R. 523, 533 (H.L.).

For the purposes of the criminal law there are two categories of mental irresponsibility, one where the disorder is due to disease and the other where it is not. The distinction is not an arbitrary one. If disease is not the cause, if there is some temporary loss of consciousness arising accidentally, it is reasonable to hope that it will not be repeated and that it is safe to let an acquitted man go entirely free. But if disease is present the same thing may happen again, and therefore, since 1800, the law has provided that persons acquitted on this ground should be subject to restraint. The acquittal is now given in the illogical and disagreeable form of the verdict, "Guilty, but insane" . . .

Hill v. *Baxter*, [1958] 1 Q.B. 277, 285–86 (1957) (CA). . . .

---

48. *Report of the Governor's Committee on the Defense of Insanity*, 140 N.Y.L.J. 4 (Nov. 5, 6, 1958).

In extreme cases, such as that of the homicidal offender, the security required must exceed that required for even the most dangerous convict. . . . [W]e recommend that the dangerous offender who has been acquitted by reason of mental disorder should be placed in the custody of the Department of Corrections at one of its medical facilities.

State of California "Special Commission on Insanity and Criminal Offenders, First Report" 34 (July 7, 1962). See also "Model Penal Code" § 4.08 (Tent. Draft No. 4) providing commitment of persons acquitted by reason of insanity "to the custody of the Commissioner of Correction" or alternatively to the Commissioner of Mental Hygiene or Public

ambivalence has blinded lawmakers to their tampering via the insanity defense, with fundamental principles on which their authority to impose criminal liability presently rests. By obfuscating the function of the defense in terms of the ethical and religious values of western civilization to care for the "sick," lawmakers have not only misled themselves but psychiatrists as well who, confused by their own ambivalence, have willingly, defiantly, unquestioningly, or with misgivings, joined in these deliberations. Psychiatrists have participated in the process without identifying the role they must play and without forcing the process to clarify that role. The plea to care for the "sick" muffles the call to segregate the "dangerous" whom the criminal law can not hold. With the real problem so disguised, the fruitless and frequent searches for new formulae and the frustrating and fighting exchanges between law and psychiatry become somewhat understandable. Thus, another low visibility purpose of the insanity defense emerges. That purpose is to keep sufficiently ambiguous the consequences of the defense, whatever the formula, so as to prevent at least conscious recognition that the prerequisites of criminal liability have been abandoned.

Lawmakers could decide to implement any or all of these now visible purposes. Provisions could be drafted to restrain: (1) persons *charged* with a crime who are feared to be dangerous and/or felt to need care and destigmatization because of a suspicion of criminality coupled with a finding of mental sickness;

Health. The official draft eliminates commitment to the Commissioner of Correction. "Model Penal Code" § 4.08 (Proposed Official Draft 1962).

> Label the judical process as one will, no resort to subtlety can refute the fact that the power to imprison is a criminal sanction. To view otherwise is self-delusion. Courts should not, ostrichlike, bury their heads in the sand.

City of Canon City v. *Merris*, 137 Colo. 169, 174, 323 P.2d 614, 617 (1958).

Report of Commissioners Appointed Under a Resolve of the Legislature of Massachusetts, to Superintend the Erection of a Lunatic Hospital at Worcester and to Report a System of Discipline and Government for the Same. *Sen. Doc.* No. 2, Jan. 4, 1832, pp. 22, 23:

> [The insane] . . . should be treated, not with a sole regard to the security of others, but with special reference also to their own misfortunes, and in a manner to shorten their duration, or where that is impossible, at least to mitigate their severity.
> . . . reprinted in Donnelly, J. Goldstein and Schwartz *Criminal Law* at 266.

On the situation in Massachusetts 125 years later so far as it concerns special custodial facilities for the "criminally insane" or the "insane criminal" who have been found incompetent to stand trial or who have been relieved of criminal liability see "Commonwealth of Massachusetts, Governor's Committee to Study the Massachusetts Correctional System, Second Report 47 (1956):

> The level of care is so low . . . that one is forced to conclude that Massachusetts is willing to abandon almost 1000 persons who would, if not criminal or difficult to handle, be receiving the best medical care the Commonwealth can provide.

(2) persons *acquitted outright* of a crime who are feared to be dangerous and/or felt to need care and destigmatization because of criminality coupled with a finding of mental sickness; and (3) persons who have *committed* a crime and are feared to be dangerous and/or felt to need care and destigmatization because of criminality coupled with a finding of mental sickness. In promulgating such provisions, answers are required to a series of questions [set forth at page 504 *supra*] which must be consciously posed about *restraint*—restraint in what kind of an institution and for how long; restraint for what crimes and for what mental illnesses; and restraint at whose initiative and at what stage in the process. In responding to these questions lawmakers will be pouring meaning into "the fear of dangerousness," "the need for care," and the "need for destigmatization." And if obfuscating developments are to be avoided, lawmakers not only must acknowledge wishes to neglect, stigmatize, punish, and destroy, but they must also consider the extent to which these wishes are to be realized through *restraint*. Awareness that such wishes constantly press for satisfaction in conflict with preferred goals should stimulate the development of formulations and procedures designed to maximize consciously thought-through preferences and to deflect those conflicting and otherwise unconscious wishes which might gain satisfaction under cover of these preferences. The operational significance of key phrases in any formulation will thus be shaped and joined by the values to be preferred.

NOTES

NOTE 1

UNITED STATES v. FREEMAN
357 F. 2d 606 (2nd Cir. 1966)

KAUFMAN, CIRCUIT JUDGE.

*   *   *

. . . Because M'Naghten focuses only on the cognitive aspect of the personality, i.e., the ability to know right from wrong, we are told by eminent medical scholars that it does not permit the jury to identify those who can distinguish between good and evil but who cannot control their behavior. The result is that instead of being treated at appropriate mental institutions[35] for a sufficiently long period to bring about a cure or sufficient improvement so that the accused may return with relative safety to himself and

---

35. We recognize our inability to determine at this point whether society possesses sufficient hospital facilities and doctors to deal with criminals who are found to be incompetent. But our function as judges requires us to interpret the law in the best interest of society as a whole. We therefore suggest that if there are inadequate facilities and personnel in this area, Congress, the state legislatures and federal and state executive departments should promptly consider bridging the gap.

the community, he is ordinarily sentenced to a prison term as if criminally responsible and then released as a potential recidivist with society at his mercy. To the extent that these individuals continue to be released from prison because of the narrow scope of M'Naghten, that test poses a serious danger to society's welfare.

*   *   *

[I]n order to avoid any misapprehension as to the thrust of our opinion some mention should be made of the treatment to be afforded individuals found to lack criminal responsibility under the [American Law Institute] test we adopt. There is no question but that the security of the community must be the paramount interest. Society withholds criminal sanctions in cases of incompetence out of a sense of compassion and understanding. It would be obviously intolerable if those suffering from a mental disease or defect of such a nature as to relieve them from criminal responsibility were to be set free to continue to pose a threat to life and property.

A verdict of "not guilty by reason of incompetency" has, in the past, been equivalent in the federal judicial system to a simple "not guilty" verdict because of the existing void in provisions for commitment and treatment. As a result of the comparatively recent adoption by various federal courts of more enlightened tests of responsibility, we trust that Congress will explore its power to authorize commitment of those acquitted on these grounds. . . . Pending Congressional action, however, we are confident that the several states will continue to step into the breach as they have in the past. Accordingly, we suggest that those adjudged criminally irresponsible promptly be turned over to state officials for commitment pursuant to state procedures.

Effective procedures for institutionalization and treatment of the criminally irresponsible are vital as an implementation to today's decision.[60] Through-

out our opinion, we have not viewed the choice as one between imprisonment and immediate release. Rather, we believe the true choice to be between different forms of institutionalization—between the prison and the mental hospital. Underlying today's decision is our belief that treatment of the truly incompetent in mental institutions would better serve the interests of society as well as the defendant's.

*   *   *

NOTE 2

DRIVER v. HINNANT
356 F.2d 761 (4th Cir. 1966)

ALBERT V. BRYAN, CIRCUIT JUDGE:

The question is whether a chronic alcoholic, as appellant Joe B. Driver has been proved and confesses to be, can Constitutionally be criminally convicted and sentenced, as he was, for public drunkenness.

*   *   *.

Driver was 59 years old. His first conviction for public intoxication occurred at 24. Since then he has been convicted of this offense more than 200 times. For nearly two-thirds of his life he has been incarcerated for these infractions. Indeed, while discharged on bail pending determination of this appeal, he has been twice convicted for like violations.

. . . The World Health Organization recognizes alcoholism "as a chronic illness that manifests itself as a *disorder of behavior.*" It is known that alcohol can be addicting, and it is the addict—the involuntary drinker—on whom our decision is now made. Hence we exclude the merely excessive—steady or spree—voluntary drinker.

This addiction—chronic alcoholism—is now almost universally accepted medically as a disease. The symptoms, as already noted, may appear as "disorder of behavior." Obviously, this includes appearances in public, as here, unwilled and ungovernable by the victim. When that is the conduct for which he is criminally accused, there can be no judgment of criminal conviction passed upon him. To do so would affront the Eighth Amendment, as cruel and unusual punishment in branding him a criminal, irrespective of consequent detention or fine.

Although his misdoing objectively comprises the physical elements of a crime, nevertheless no crime has been perpetrated because the conduct was neither actuated by an evil intent nor accompanied with a consciousness of wrongdoing, indispensable ingredients of a crime. . . . Nor can his misbehavior be penalized as a transgression of a police regulation—*malum prohibitum*—necessitating no intent to do what it punishes. The alcoholic's presence in public is not his act, for he did not will it. It may be likened to the movements of an imbecile or a person in a

---

60. As Professor Wechsler observed, commitment after a verdict of "not guilty by reason of criminal incompetency" is not only desirable but necessary in the sound administration of justice: " . . . I also believe that it is part of any proper system that when a defendant in a criminal case asks for exemption from conviction and condemnation on the ground of irresponsibility, that it is appropriate that there should be as a requirement of law a civil commitment if that defense is sustained. And that, as a matter of fact, is now the law of New York as a result of a statute [N.Y. Code Crim. Proc. §454] passed two or three years ago. Now, how long should the detention last? Well, it certainly ought to last long enough to allow a full diagnostic study and a determination as to whether it is safe to release the offender from his own point of view and from the point of view of others. The New York statute justified detention on grounds of public danger so long as that danger endures." Remarks, *op cit. supra* note 39 at 398.

We believe that such institutionalization will deter "normal" defendants from choosing to defend on the ground of irresponsibility. The prospect of commitment to a mental institution for an indeterminate period is much less desirable than a fixed term in prison.

delirium of a fever. None of them by attendance in the forbidden place defy the forbiddance.

*   *   *

. . . The California statute [declared unconstitutional in *Robinson* v. *California* 370 U.S. 660] criminally punished a "status"—drug addiction—involuntarily assumed; the North Carolina Act criminally punishes an involuntary symptom of a status—public intoxication. In declaring the former violative of the Eighth Amendment, we think *pari ratione*, the *Robinson* decision condemns the North Carolina law when applied to one in the circumstances of appellant Driver. . . .

The Constitutional premise of *Robinson*, and so apt here, is found in the opinion, 370 U.S. at 666:

"It is unlikely that any State at this moment in history would attempt to make it a criminal offense for a person to be mentally ill, or a leper, or to be afflicted with a venereal disease. A State might determine that the general health and welfare require that the victims of these and other human afflictions be dealt with by compulsory treatment, involving quarantine, confinement, or sequestration. But, in the light of contemporary human knowledge, a law which made a criminal offense of such a disease would doubtless be universally thought to be an infliction of cruel and unusual punishment in violation of the Eighth and Fourteenth Amendments. . . ."

*   *   *

We do not annul the North Carolina statute. It is well within the State's power and right to deter and punish public drunkenness, especially to secure others against its annoyances and intrusions. . . . To this end any intoxicated person found in the street or other public areas may be taken into custody for inquiry or prosecution. But the Constitution intercedes when on arraignment the accused's helplessness comes to light. Then it is that no *criminal* conviction may follow.

The upshot of our decision is that the State cannot stamp an unpretending chronic alcoholic as a criminal if his drunken public display is involuntary as the result of disease. However, nothing we have said precludes appropriate detention of him for treatment and rehabilitation so long as he is not marked a criminal.

The judgment denying appellant's petition for habeas corpus will be vacated, and the case returned to the District Court with directions to order Driver's release from the impending detention by North Carolina unless, within ten days, the State be advised to take him into civil remedial custody.

NOTE 3

LEWIS, C. S.

The Humanitarian Theory of Punishment*

. . . Those who hold [the Humanitarian theory]

---

* *Res Judicatae*, VI (1953), p. 224. Reprinted with permission of Melbourne University Law Review.

think that it is mild and merciful. In this I believe that they are seriously mistaken. I believe that the "Humanity" which it claims is a dangerous illusion and disguises the possibility of cruelty and injustice without end. I urge a return to the traditional or retributive theory not solely, not even primarily, in the interests of society, but in the interests of the criminal.

According to the Humanitarian theory, to punish a man because he deserves it, and as much as he deserves, is mere revenge, and therefore, barbarous and immoral. It is maintained that the only legitimate motives for punishing are the desire to deter others by example or to mend the criminal. When this theory is combined, as frequently happens, with the belief that all crime is more or less pathological, the idea of mending tails off into that of healing or curing and punishment becomes therapeutic. Thus it appears at first sight that we have passed from the harsh and self-righteous notion of giving the wicked their deserts to the charitable and enlightened one of tending the psychologically sick. What could be more amiable? One little point which is taken for granted in this theory needs, however, to be made explicit. The things done to the criminal, even if they are called cures, will be just as compulsory as they were in the old days when we called them punishments. If a tendency to steal can be cured by psychotherapy, the thief will no doubt be forced to undergo the treatment. Otherwise, society cannot continue.

My contention is that this doctrine, merciful though it appears, really means that each one of us, from the moment he breaks the law, is deprived of the rights of a human being.

The reason is this. The Humanitarian theory removes from Punishment the concept of Desert. But the concept of Desert is the only connecting link between punishment and justice. It is only as deserved or undeserved that a sentence can be just or unjust. I do not here contend that the question "Is it deserved?" is the only one we can reasonably ask about a punishment. We may very properly ask whether it is likely to deter others and to reform the criminal. But neither of these two last questions is a question about justice. There is no sense in talking about a "just deterrent" or a "just cure." We demand of a deterrent not whether it is just but whether it will deter. We demand of a cure not whether it is just but whether it succeeds. Thus when we cease to consider what the criminal deserves and consider only what will cure him or deter others, we have tacitly removed him from the sphere of justice altogether; instead of a person, a subject of rights, we now have a mere object, a patient, a "case."

The distinction will become clearer if we ask who will be qualified to determine sentences when sentences are no longer held to derive their propriety from the criminals' deservings. On the old view the problem of fixing the right sentence was a moral problem. [T]he code was never in principle, and not always in fact, beyond the control of the conscience of the society. And when (say, in eighteenth-century England) actual punishments conflicted too violently with the moral sense of the community, juries refused to convict and reform was finally brought about. This was possible because, so long as we are thinking in terms of Desert, the propriety of the penal code, being a moral question, is a question on which every man has the right to an opinion, not because he follows this or that profession, but because he is simply a man, a rational animal enjoying the Natural Light. But all this is changed when we drop the concept of Desert. The only two questions we may now ask about a punishment are whether it deters and whether it cures. But these are not questions on which anyone is entitled to have an opinion simply because he is a man. He is not entitled to an opinion even if, in addition to being a man, he should happen also to be a jurist, a Christian, and a moral theologian. For they are not questions about principle but about matter of fact; . . . Only the expert "penologist" (let barbarous things have barbarous names), in the light of previous experiment, can tell us what is likely to deter; only the psychotherapist can tell us what is likely to cure. It will be in vain for the rest of us, speaking simply as men, to say, "but this punishment is hideously unjust, hideously disproportionate to the criminal's deserts." The experts with perfect logic will reply "but nobody was talking about deserts. No one was talking about *punishment* in your archaic vindictive sense of the word. Here are the statistics proving that this treatment deters. Here are the statistics proving that this other treatment cures. What is your trouble?"

. The Humanitarian theory, then, removes sentences from the hands of jurists whom the public conscience is entitled to criticize and places them in the hands of technical experts whose special sciences do not even employ such categories as rights or justice. It might be argued that since this transference results from an abandonment of the old idea of punishment, and therefore, of all vindictive motives, it will be safe to leave our criminals in such hands. I will not pause to comment on the simple-minded view of fallen human nature which such a belief implies. Let us rather remember that the "cure" of criminals is to be compulsory; and let us then watch how the theory actually works in the mind of the Humanitarian. The immediate starting point of this article was a letter I read in one of our Leftist weeklies. The author was pleading that a certain sin, now treated by our laws as a crime, should henceforward be treated as a disease. And he complained that under the present system the offender, after a term in gaol, was simply let out to return to his original environment where he would probably relapse. What he complained of was not the shutting up but the letting out. On his remedial view of punishment the offender should of course,

be detained until he was cured. And of course the official straighteners are the only people who can say when that is. The first result of the Humanitarian theory is, therefore, to substitute for a definite sentence (reflecting to some extent the community's moral judgment on the degree of ill-desert involved) an indefinite sentence terminable only by the word of those experts—and they are not experts in moral theology nor even in the Law of Nature—who inflict it. Which of us, if he stood in the dock, would not prefer to be tried by the old system?

*   *   *

It is indeed, important to notice that my argument so far supposes no evil intentions on the part of the Humanitarian and considers only what is involved in the logic of his position. My contention is that good men (not bad men) consistently acting upon that position would act as cruelly and unjustly as the greatest tyrants. They might in some respects act even worse. Of all tyrannies a tyranny sincerely exercised for the good of its victims may be the most oppressive. It may be better to live under robber barons than under omnipotent moral busybodies. The robber baron's cruelty may sometimes sleep, his cupidity may at some point be satiated; but those who torment us for our own good will torment us without end for they do so with the approval of their own conscience. They may be more likely to go to Heaven yet at the same time likelier to make a Hell of earth. Their very kindness stings with intolerable insult. To be "cured" against one's will and cured of states which we may not regard as disease is to be put on a level with those who have not yet reached the age of reason or those who never will; to be classed with infants, imbeciles, and domestic animals. But to be punished, however severely, because we have deserved it, because we "ought to have known better," is to be treated as a human person made in God's image.

[I]f crime and disease are to be regarded as the same thing, it follows that any state of mind which our masters choose to call "disease" can be treated as crime; and compulsorily cured. It will be vain to plead that states of mind which displease government need not always involve moral turpitude and do not therefore always deserve forfeiture of liberty. For our masters will not be using the concepts of Desert and Punishment but those of disease and cure. . . . Even if the treatment is painful, even if it is lifelong, even if it is fatal, that will be only a regrettable accident; the intention was purely therapeutic. Even in ordinary medicine there were painful operations and fatal operations; so in this. But because they are "treatment," not punishment, they can be criticized only by fellow experts and on technical grounds, never by men as men and on grounds of justice.

[T]he Humanitarian theory wants simply to abolish Justice and substitute Mercy for it. This means that you start being "kind" to people before you have considered their rights, and then force upon them supposed kindnesses which they in fact had a right to refuse, and finally kindnesses which no one but you will recognize as kindnesses and which the recipient will feel as abominable cruelties. You have overshot the mark. Mercy, detached from Justice, grows unmerciful. That is the important paradox. . . .

*   *   *

NOTE 4

WAELDER, ROBERT

Psychiatry and the Problem of Criminal Responsibility*

*   *   *

. . . The seemingly factual question of whether or not a person *is* (or *was*) mentally ill, or *was* acting under an irresistible impulse, covers a question of morality and public policy: whether he *should* be punished or subjected to some other disposition or be allowed to leave the courtroom a free man. It would not be too difficult to agree that the "normal" offender (e.g., the racketeer who miscalculated his risks) should face the penalty and that the manifestly insane should be committed to a mental institution. But what should be done with a large group of offenders who do not fit into either of these two extreme categories? How should we deal with psychopaths, borderline schizoids, or perverts? They have not made calculations of gain and risk like the racketeer; nor are they insane. They do not seem to be deterrable, but the man on the street does not feel them to be too different from himself and would look askance at their remaining unpunished.

The exhibitionist is a case in point. He has been in and out of jail for the better part of his life. Or perhaps he has not been apprehended as yet, but jeopardizes a respectable position in life and puts himself at the mercy of a stranger each time he exhibits himself. He has made good resolutions many times over and tried to fight against his temptations; time and again the flesh has proved weak. As a matter of experience one can call him undeterrable. It may well be that he would not exhibit himself were the policeman present at the right moment, but short of this he cannot be deterred by the threat of any punishment that morally can be applied and that will not be so brutal as to be worse than the offense it is meant to forestall. He is certainly not psychotic. The man on the street does not feel this type of offender to be sufficiently different from himself so that he can let him off without danger to his own morale—except after such an offender has been in trouble many times and has continued his perverse practices nonetheless.

Behind the apparent problem of defining criteria of criminal responsibility, there is the real problem of how to deal with the large group of offenders who do not fit into the marginal categories of "normality" and insanity—the group of psychopathies, primary behavior disorders and perversions. This is not a factual question, to be decided on the basis of expert testimony—e.g., whether or not the offender "knew" that what he did was "wrong," or whether or not his particular mental make-up should be properly termed a "disease of the mind," or whether or not his impulse was "irresistible." Rather it is a question of legal policy to be decided by all of us as citizens, guided by prevailing standards of morality and by the social interests at stake. In trying to arrive at a policy in this matter, we have to take advice from experts —psychiatrists among them—as to the facts and as to the probable consequences of any policy on which we may embark. But the decision—and the responsibility—is ours as citizens. We cannot pass it on to the expert witness by asking him questions which appear to be questions of fact but are actually questions of what we ought to do.

Whenever the existing line of approach does not seem to lead to a satisfactory solution, a fresh beginning may be tried. I am a layman in jurisprudence— a shortcoming which must necessarily detract from the validity of my reasoning but may hold some compensation. I may venture into speculation about a desirable solution without regard for the realities of existing law, leaving it to lawyers to decide how much, if any, of such speculation can be used either within the existing legal framework or after such changes of the statutory law as reasonably can be attempted.

*   *   *

It seems advisable, first of all, to reformulate our laws in such a way that they are no longer focused on punishment as the normal consequence of crime, with other dispositions taking their place as exceptions from the rule; and to allow for three alternate dispositions of the criminal, principally of equal penological rank, *viz.*, punishment, custody and therapy (medical or educational). In such a system the court, after determining the facts of the case, would proceed to the consideration of the way in which the offender should best be dealt with from the point of view of the merits of the case, the requirements of public morality and public safety and the chances of the offender's rehabilitation; and would dispose of each case by punishment, custody or treatment, or by a combination of these, or by release, as seems best fitted to the total situation.

In this system, the psychiatrist could make a major contribution to the court's decision. He would not be forced to relinquish what insight psychiatry actually has gained into human behavior in favor of a testi-

---

* 101 University of Pennsylvania Law Review, 378, 385–390 (1952). Reprinted by permission.

mony on issues of doubtful meaning and questionable relevance but could bring the resources of his knowledge to an evaluation of the consequences of the various rival dispositions in the case. Instead of the M'Naughten questions, the psychiatrist could be asked three questions which are equally meaningful to him and to an appropriate disposition of the case and which he frequently will be able to answer with reasonable estimates: *is the lawbreaker dangerous*, i.e., how likely is he to commit the same or another crime again; *is he deterrable*, is the motivation of his unlawful behavior such that anticipation of consequences can decisively influence his behavior; and *is he treatable* by medical or educational methods?

The psychiatrist could try to answer these questions without *sacrificium intellectus* and without fear that the implications of his words may carry a jury of laymen in a direction which does not seem warranted in terms of the actual scientific meaning of his words. His answers could substantially assist the court in arriving at a reasonable decision about the disposition of the case through punishment, custody, or treatment, as illustrated in the following scale:

Symbol	Diagnostic Characterization	Disposition
1, 1, 1	Dangerous Deterrable Treatable	Punishment and Treatment
1, 1, 2	Dangerous Deterrable Not treatable	Punishment
1, 2, 1	Dangerous Not deterrable Treatable	Preventive Custody and Treatment
1, 2, 2	Dangerous Not deterrable Not treatable	Preventive Custody
2, 1, 1	Not dangerous Deterrable Treatable	Punishment with Probationary Period and Treatment
2, 1, 2	Not dangerous Deterrable Not treatable	Punishment, perhaps with Probationary Period
2, 2, 1	Not dangerous Not deterrable Treatable	Treatment
2, 2, 2	Not dangerous Not deterrable Not treatable	Release

5.

COMPETENCY-TO-SERVE-A-SENTENCE COMMITMENT

Statement of Governor Edmund G. Brown upon Commutation of Sentence of Edwin M. Walker, March 28, 1961

I have decided to grant a commutation of sentence from death to life imprisonment without possibility of parole to Edwin M. Walker, San Quentin, now an inmate of the California Medical Facility at Vacaville, who was convicted in Los Angeles County in June, 1947, of murder, first degree, and of two counts of attempted murder. His sentence was fixed at death and he was scheduled to be executed on Good Friday, April 15, 1949. He suffered a mental breakdown in prison and on the morning of his execution day, was declared insane, and the execution was called off. In May, 1949, a Marin County jury pronounced him legally insane and he was ordered committed to a State hospital.

For twelve years Walker has been confined as a mental patient in California hospitals, undergoing treatment to which he has slowly responded. On March 1, 1961, the Marin County Superior Court found that he has recovered the ability to comprehend his status as a prisoner awaiting death, and is therefore legally sane. On March 28, 1961, I conducted an executive clemency hearing at which the entire matter was carefully reviewed.

The evidence presented to me is as follows:

Walker, an ordinary youth, was born and raised in Southern California. He did well in school, was athletic, well-liked, but shy and retreating. After a year in college he was employed as a radio dispatcher for the Glendale Police Department. He was remembered as alert, kind, gentle with children, respected, completely law abiding. He entered military service in World War II and served for three years in forward combat areas of the South Pacific. He was commissioned as an officer and detailed to serve with a radar maintenance group attached to amphibious invasion forces. Here too, he was known as a considerate and dependable soldier, liked and looked up to by his men.

Without dispute the record shows that he was subjected to a series of traumatic experiences which, in the opinion of the psychiatrists who have worked with him for many years, exerted powerful and disintegrating affects upon his personality and conduct. These included severe aerial bombardment, parachute invasions, wholesale death and destruction, climaxed by a surprise attack which decimated his group during his absence. And though no blame in fact attached to him, he blamed himself for not having averted this tragedy.

From these events his troubles appeared to have stemmed. His personality and conduct changed so markedly as to indicate a complete character breakdown. He became morose, withdrawn, suspicious, detached, sullen. At his own request he was returned to the United States. There, during the several months he remained in military service in California, and during his terminal leave period, he descended steadily into the violent criminal conduct which led him eventually in 1947 to a sentence of death.

In inexplicable conflict with his former quiet and

law-abiding personality, he embarked upon a series of robberies, burglaries, and other antisocial conduct. Eventually he fell into a trap set by the Los Angeles Police, but escaped after wounding two officers. In the final explosion of violence he was halted by California Highway Patrolman Loren Roosevelt while attempting a burglary. In the ensuing struggle, Officer Roosevelt was killed. Walker, who was captured shortly afterwards, was convicted of the two assaults and the murder.

Through the long months of Walker's intervening insanity constant efforts have been made to find an explanation to this drastic reversal of character.

In the background of this abnormal conduct and undoubtedly of strong causal influence, the experts found a strain of insanity running through five generations. From his paternal great great great grandfather, who had been committed to Stockton State Hospital, and from his maternal great great grandfather, each succeeding generation has exhibited actually diagnosed insanity, melancholia, hallucination, self-destruction, and suicidal tendencies. His own father, who himself saw military service as a captain, was discharged as psychotic and committed suicide in 1947. The dismal count reveals fifteen of his immediate family as obviously totally insane, mentally defective, or borderline psychotics.

At his trial, Walker's only defense was the plea of not guilty by reason of insanity. He was pronounced legally sane and sent to death row. But gradually Warden Clinton Duffy and his prison staff noted a further and marked deterioration in his mentality. He attempted unsuccessfully to take his own life the day before his scheduled execution. And finally, one hour before his appointed time with death on April 15, 1949, the strands of sanity broke. A panel of seven psychiatrists, hastily convened, reported that he was catatonic, broken off from reality, and insane. Warden Duffy halted the execution. . . .

*   *   *

On March 30, 1961, an executive clemency hearing was held in this office. . . .

Dr. Schmidt and other experts have stated that although Walker now is legally sane—in the sense of understanding the object and purpose of punishment—he is still seriously mentally ill with the diagnosis of chronic undifferentiated schizophrenia, and will remain so for a long time yet to come.

That the medical resources of this State and the devotion to duty and skill of psychiatrists have combined to restore in such large measure Walker's health and mind, is a real tribute to the advance of science and the level of institutional care of California. We are justly proud of the mending process which we have so far accomplished.

In my term as Governor I have never before stayed the execution of one convicted of slaying a peace officer. And were it not for the overwhelming evidence of mental illness and the fuller light cast upon his behavior over these many years, I would be loath to intervene now. But I cannot, after a painstaking review of this record, find it possible to believe that California, after investing twelve years, thousands of hours of expert therapy, and incalculable reserves of scientific resources in restoring this broken mind has done so only that it may be thrust into the cell for execution.

Rather, I believe it proper that the victory which our science has achieved in overcoming the stigmata of 90 years of hovering mental sickness requires and demands that we exercise the conscience and common sense of California in the limited form of commutation of sentence from death to life imprisonment without possibility of parole.

*   *   *

NOTE

SOLESBEE v. BALKCOM
339 U.S. 9 (1950)

MR. JUSTICE BLACK delivered the opinion of the court.

Petitioner was convicted of murder in a Georgia state court. His sentence was death by electrocution. Subsequently he asked the Governor to postpone execution on the ground that after conviction and sentence he had become insane. Acting under authority granted by § 27–2602 of the Georgia Code[1] the Governor appointed three physicians who examined petitioner and declared him sane. Petitioner then filed this habeas corpus proceeding again alleging his insanity. He contended that the due process clause of the Fourteenth Amendment required that this claim of insanity after sentence be originally determined by a judicial or administrative tribunal after notice and hearings in which he could be represented by counsel, cross-examine witnesses, and offer evidence. . . .

In affirming, the State Supreme Court held that a person legally convicted and sentenced to death had no statutory or constitutional right to a judicially conducted or supervised "inquisition or trial" on the

---

1. "Disposition of insane convicts. . . . Upon satisfactory evidence being offered to the Governor that the person convicted of a capital offense has become insane subsequent to his conviction, the Governor may, within his discretion, have said person examined by such expert physicians as the Governor may choose; and said physicians shall report to the Governor the result of their investigation; and the Governor may, if he shall determine that the person convicted has become insane, have the power of committing him to the Milledgeville State Hospital until his sanity shall have been restored, as determined by laws now in force. . . ." Ga. Code Ann. § 27–2602 (1074 P.C.); Acts 1903, p. 77.

question of insanity subsequent to sentence. It viewed the Georgia statutory procedure for determination of this question as motivated solely by a sense of "public propriety and decency"—an "act of grace" which could be "bestowed or withheld by the State at will" and therefore not subject to due process requirements of notice and hearing. . . .

*   *   *

Postponement of execution because of insanity bears a close affinity not to trial for a crime but rather to reprieve of sentences in general. The power to reprieve has usually sprung from the same source as the power to pardon. . . .

We are unable to say that it offends due process for a state to deem its Governor an "apt and special tribunal" to pass upon a question so closely related to powers that from the beginning have been entrusted to governors. And here the governor had the aid of physicians specially trained in appraising the elusive and often deceptive symptoms of insanity. It is true that governors and physicians might make errors of judgment. But the search for truth in this field is always beset by difficulties that may beget error. . . .

*   *   *

. . . There is no indication that either the Governor or the physicians who acted on petitioner's application violated the humanitarian policy of Georgia against execution of the insane. We hold that the Georgia statute as applied is not a denial of due process of law.

Affirmed.

*   *   *

MR. JUSTICE FRANKFURTER, Dissenting.

In the history of murder, the onset of insanity while awaiting execution of a death sentence is not a rare phenomenon. The legal problems which such supervening insanity raises happily do not involve explorations of the pathological processes which give rise to the conflict between so called legal and medical insanity. . . .

*   *   *

That it offends our historic heritage to kill a man who has become insane while awaiting sentence cannot be gainsaid. This limitation on the power of the State to take life has been part of our law for centuries, recognized during periods of English history when feelings were more barbarous and men recoiled less from brutal action than we like to think is true of our time. . . .

"It was further provided by the said Act of 33 H. 8. that if a man attainted of treason became mad, that notwithstanding he should be executed; which cruel and inhumane law lived not long, but was repealed,

for in that point also it was against the common law, because by intendment of law the execution of the offender is for example, *ut poena ad paucos, metus ad omnes perveniat*, as before is said: but so it is not when a mad man is executed, but should be a miserable spectacle, both against law, and of extreme inhumanity and cruelty, and can be no example to others." Coke, Third Institutes 6 (1644).

*   *   *

[I]t is inconsistent with Religion, as being against Christian Charity to send a great Offender quick, as it is stil'd, into another World, when he is not of a capacity to fit himself for it. But whatever the reason of the Law is, it is plain the law is so. . . ." Remarks on the Tryal of Charles Bateman by Sir John Hawles, Solicitor-General in the reign of King William III. 3 State-Tryals 651, 652–53 (1719).

"If a man in his sound memory commits a capital offense, and before his arraignment he becomes absolutely mad, he ought not by law to be arraigned during such his phrenzy, but be remitted to prison until that incapacity be removed; the reason is, because he cannot advisedly plead to the indictment. . . . And if such person after his plea, and before his trial, become of *non sane memory*, he shall not be tried; or, if after his trial he become of *non sane memory*, he shall not receive judgment; or, if after judgment he become of *non sane memory*, his execution shall be spared; for were he of sound memory, he might allege somewhat in stay of judgment or execution." 1 Hale, *The History of the Pleas of the Crown* 34–35 (1736).

*   *   *

However quaint some of these ancient authorities of our law may sound to our ears, the twentieth century has not so far progressed as to outmode their reasoning. We should not be less humane than were Englishmen in the centuries that preceded this Republic. And the practical considerations are not less relevant today. . . . If a man has gone insane, is he still himself? Is he still the man who was convicted? In any event "were he of sound memory, he might allege somewhat" to save himself from doom. It is not an idle fancy that one under sentence of death ought not, by becoming *non compos*, be denied the means to "allege somewhat" that might free him. Such an opportunity may save life, as the last minute applications to this Court from time to time and not always without success amply attest.

*   *   *

[The] impressive body of State legislation [requiring some sort of hearing procedure] signifies more than the historic continuity of our repulsion against killing an insane man even though he be under sentence of death. The vindication of this concern turns on the ascertainment of what is called a fact, but which in the present state of the mental sciences is at best a hazardous guess however conscientious. If the deeply rooted principle in our society against killing an insane man is to be respected, at least the minimum provision for assuring a fair application of the principle is inherent in the principle itself. And the minimum assurance that the life-and-death guess will be a truly informed guess requires respect for the basic ingredient of due process,

namely, an opportunity to be allowed to substantiate a claim before it is rejected.

* * *

To deny all opportunity to make the claim that was here made on behalf of the petitioner is in my view a denial of due process of law.

PART THREE

TO WHAT EXTENT AND BY WHAT MEANS SHOULD THE STATE SUPERVISE INSTITUTIONS AND STAFF IN THE ADMINISTRATION OF MENTAL HOSPITALS?

In the previous part, we dealt with the criteria for admission to and release from State custody via a number of different processes. In this part, we consider the responsibility, if any, of various agencies of government in supervising the administration of the "patient" in custody. Although we have not divided the material in terms of the processes and criteria for custody, the question should be asked: should an administrative response depend on the process selected for determining custody? Nor have we divided the materials in terms of causes of action (e.g., tort, injunction, or habeas corpus) or agencies of government (court, legislature or administrative agency) through which the State supervises the administration of the "patient" in custody. Instead, we have divided the materials primarily in terms of the intended impact of state supervision on various functions of the custodial institutions to determine: the appropriateness of settings for custody and/or treatment; the appropriateness of treatment techniques and facilities for what purposes within such settings; how to finance custody and treatment; and how to design procedures for uncovering and remedying errors inevitable in any bureaucratic structure.

In seeking guides for delineating the role of the State for supervising the administration of "patients" in custody, consider the following suggestion made to the Royal Commission on Mental Illness:

"... because all mentally disordered patients are in some degree helpless and may need protection against ill-treatment special legislation is required to ensure proper standards of care through a special system of inspection of hospitals and other procedures different from those which apply to other ill or disabled people. ..." *

* Cmnd. 169, 1957 (p. 38).

A.

An Introduction to the Problems for Decision—The Case of Tony Savarese*

May 22, 1923:

Danvers State Hospital   Name: Tony Savarese:

Revere police who were called in during family row were unable to state if patient used razor or threatened his family with one. They saw no evidence of it. They took a razor from his vest pocket but they attached no importance to this on account of patient's being a barber and barbers frequently carry their tools about with them. The party was considerably under the influence of Italian wine. They removed a large hunting gun. Mrs. Venezia, sister of patient, says that patient did have a knife and not only brandished it about and threatened to cut anyone who came near him but that he slashed his brother John's arm. When she was told by worker that the brother John had been visited and said that he did not see a razor and did not believe that patient had drawn one, she then stated that she was sure that at least patient had cut John's sleeve with a razor.

Police think the quarrel was started mostly on account of money matters. Patient has been anxious in this since his marriage to have his wife made guardian and his sister who is mercenary was unwilling to give up the guardianship.... The sympathy of the police is very strong with the patient, whom they think was aroused to a fit of rage because he felt he was being imposed upon. Patient has lived in the neighborhood about 11 months and they have always thought well of him. According to John, brother of patient and a man of good reputation, honest and reliable, Mrs. Venezia's word is not to be relied upon as she is an excitable, nervous woman who would not hestitate to fabricate in order to convince others of her story. In the past she has frequently told conflict-

* This is an actual record of substantially every entry (1923–1956) in the "hospital" folder of a "patient," whose name has been fictionalized. This material was collected with the generous support of a grant by The Russell Sage Foundation (1955–56) by J. Goldstein.

ing stories and she and her husband have always shown greed for money to the point of being unscrupulous.

July 10, 1924:

INDICTMENT: Suffolk Superior Court, Grand Jury: "The jurors of the Commonwealth of Massachusetts on their oath present that Tony Savarese on the twenty-first day of June in the year of our Lord one thousand nine hundred and twenty-four did assault and beat Theresa Savarese, with intent to murder her by shooting her with a shotgun, and by such assault and beating and shooting did kill and murder the said Theresa Savarese.

And the jurors do further say that the defendant is guilty of murder in the second degree and not in the first degree.

July 11, 1924:

FORM NO. 14, MEDICAL CERTIFICATE: Observation by A. W. S. and C. B. S. "Within five days prior to my signing and making oath to this certificate, namely on the third and ninth days of July, A.D. 1924, I the subscriber, personally examined with care and diligence Tony Savarese now in Boston, County of Suffolk in the Commonwealth of Massachusetts and as a result of such examination find and hereby certify, that in my opinion he is in such mental condition that his commitment to a hospital for the insane is necessary for his proper care or observation pending the determination of his insanity, under the provision of Sec. 77, Chapter 123, General Laws.

"3. That I have formed the above opinion from (a) facts observed by me (here record what the patient said and describe his appearance and behavior).

"He appears retarded and confused—he gives a history of fits—which has been confirmed by the hospital attendant—fears he is going to die—says he has heard voices telling him to go to church—also sees and hears his wife—"

July 11, 1924:

WARRANT TO REMOVE TONY SAVARESE, A PRISONER IN JAIL TO BRIDGEWATER STATE HOSPITAL . . . : It has been brought to the attention of said court that Tony Savarese, a prisoner held in the common jail in Boston in said County of Suffolk, upon indictment wherein he is charged with the crime of murder in the second degree is insane and his removal to a hospital has become expedient, and whereas said court had employed C. B. S., M.D. and A. W. S., M.D., experts upon insanity, to examine said Savarese in said jail and whereas said experts have made report to said court in writing that said Savarese is insane, and said court, after a hearing on the 11th day of July, A.D. 1924, finds said Savarese insane and in such mental condition that his commitment to a hospital for the insane is necessary and orders that said Savarese be removed from jail to the Bridgewater State Hospital in said Bridgewater, there to be detained in the opinion of the trustees and superintendent of said hospital, he may be returned to said jail restored to sanity."

July 11, 1924:

ADMISSION NOTE, Dr. S.: Patient is underdeveloped. Appears somewhat depressed, leans forward and looks down much of the time and answers questions in a barely audible voice. Many of the answers aren't intelligible. Usually responses are somewhat delayed and are given very slowly. Appears emotionally weak and tears frequently appear in his eyes without apparent cause. Many of his replies are hesitating and uncertain. Patient first gives the month as June, then says "July 4 this month, I see fireworks." Finally after a pause says, "Today the eighth." Gives the day of the week as Monday (Friday), and the year as 1923 or 1924. Cannot give the names of the officers who brought him but states that he has not seen them before today. Understands their official position. Understands that he has come to Bridgewater but has not heard the name of this institution. States that he came from Charles River (he has been in Charles Street Jail, from there he was able to obtain a view of the Charles River). Signed mailing card willingly and went to the ward quietly in charge of Supervisor Mr. Stone.

July 11, 1924:

MENTAL STATUS — ATTITUDE AND MANNER: In the ward has been at all times quiet and well behaved. Keeps by himself, somewhat seclusive. Has done no work. Is fairly neat in personal appearance, is tidy in habits. At all times appears exceedingly timid.

During the examination is quiet and well behaved. Gives fair attention and is fairly direct and coherent in many of his statements. Frequently however he is contradictory. Appears to co-operate as well as he is able but gives the impression that he is not telling the entire story.

ORIENTATION: Well oriented for place and time but partly disoriented for person. Cannot give the name of anyone here.

Q. What day is this? A. Tuesday.

Q. What day of the month? A. July 15.

Q. What year? A. 1924. . . .

Q. What place is this? A. The Bridgewater State Hospital.

Q. For what kind of people? A. Crazy people.

Q. Do you think that people here are crazy? A. Yes, crazy, nervous . . .

MEMORY: For recent and remote occurrences as shown by answers to set questions is fair for the main events, however, is somewhat poor for details. His statements occasionally are contradictory. For example, first says that he began to use intoxicants one year ago. Later says it was four months ago and still later says two months ago. . . .

STREAM OF THOUGHT: Production directly or through the interpreter is direct and coherent, somewhat circumstantial. At times is rather voluble. At times contradictory. Gives fair attention.

ANALYSIS OF DELUSIONS AND HALLUCINATIONS: Presents auditory and visual hallucinations of at least three years' duration. God first appeared and spoke to him three years ago. States that he has seen God perhaps two dozen times, the last three nights ago. During the last two or three weeks patient's wife has appeared and spoken to him every night. His story that for some time his wife had been living a life of ill fame under the direction of an Italian named Tony and in connection with a gang may constitute a paranoid system of delusions. This, however, would depend upon the degree of actual truth in his belief.

July 29, 1924:

STAFF MEETING. (Dr. S.): (Present, Drs. H., M., S., and B.). Patient is somewhat careless in personal appearance. Sits quietly in his chair, looks about with a somewhat dazed expression. He, however, gives fair attention and answers many simple questions in a direct and coherent manner. His statements, however, frequently are contradictory. He tells the story already in his record, to the effect that God has appeared to him several times within the last two or three years and has spoken to him. During the last two or three weeks, with wife, has appeared in patient's room and has spoken with him. Later in the interview states that his wife and God are in his head. Tells the same general story previously given, to the effect that an Italian named "Tony" had been going about with his wife and in effect had acted as her manager in a house of ill fame. When patient returned home late one evening, he heard his wife crying in the back yard and found her there upon the ground with a bullet wound in her leg. His gun was lying near by. Asserts that he himself had nothing to do with this injury, but that his wife told him, in the presence of the police and hospital attendants, that she had been shot by "Tony." Later in the interview, when questioned again regarding the circumstances, denies that his gun was lying nearby. When questioned again, says his wife did not die, but a minute later gives a description of the surroundings in the hospital, and says that she did die there. Apparently does not notice the discrepancies in his own statements. Is emotionally weak. When speaking of his own arrest, is on the verge of tears, also when speaking of his wife. In answer to direct questions, states that he may have been "crazy in the head." Patient at first denies absolutely the fairly well authenticated report that he threatened his wife and her relatives with a razor and also threatened to shoot them. Later in the interview, however, admits that he threatened to cut them, but that he was flourishing a comb and did not have a razor in his hand at any time. Still continues to deny threatening anyone with his gun.

The staff agree that auditory and visual hallucinations have been present for two or three years and that his ideas in regard to the loose character of his wife and her relations with the man "Tony" are suggestive of systematized delusions, although positive conclusions in this respect would depend on what part of these ideas are based upon actual fact.

DISCUSSION: Dr. H. notes that there is evidently more trouble than appears upon the surface. There is reason to believe there are religious ideas about which he will not talk. He knows enough to endeavor to conceal what he did, but in the end, makes some admissions. For example, at first says that his wife is not dead, but later speaks of "my wife who is dead," and so forth. Probably he always has been a psychopathic personality. Probably his experience during the war acted as the exciting cause. He shows delusions of sight and hearing. Dr. H. believes that the evidence indicates paranoid praecox. Dr. M. notes that the psychosis is of considerable duration and that patient is smart enough to know that he should not admit his crime. Staff agree upon the diagnosis of dementia praecox, paranoid form, and that it is of several years duration.

September 3, 1924:

(Dr. S.): . . . Tells the story previously given to the effect that his wife had been unfaithful for a considerable time, that among other things she was in an improper relationship with a man named Tony, whose last name or present address patient cannot give, and through his agency she was frequently in a house of ill fame where she was associated with other men. Now denies that God actually appeared or talked to

him or that he has heard his wife talking to him since her death. He states that at the time he believed these things but thinks it was his imagination. Continues to assert that "Tony" shot his wife and that he himself knows nothing about it. Shows himself to have a fair grasp upon his surroundings, stating that this place is Bridgewater and for the "crazy." Knows the name of his questioner. Does not believe himself to be insane but thinks the judge may have thought so. States that he is here because the judge decided to send him to this place. Is emotionally weak, talks in a plaintive voice. Is frequently on the verge of tears when talking of his wife and his past experiences.

November 14, 1924:

(Dr. S.): . . . Shows no evidence of new delusions or hallucinations. Adheres to the story given in the previous interview and states that God and his wife do not really talk to him or appear to him; that it was "imaginary." Continues to state that Tony shot his wife and that his wife was unfaithful and frequented a house of ill fame where Tony acted as her boss or manager. . . .

December 29, 1924:

(Dr. M.): Patient invited patient Sam Alberts to play a few games of checkers this afternoon. Alberts agreed and they played several games. All went well and Savarese won. Savarese suggested that they now play for one cigarette. Savarese lost and began cheating. Alberts very quietly called his attention to the fact and in a second Savarese became a violent, desperate, maddened man. He jumped to his feet, grabbing the wooden checker board, scattering the checkers over the day hall floor and raising the board above his head screamed, "I'll beat your brains out." He would have struck Alberts had it not been for the timely arrival of Mr. McDonald. Savarese then said, "I'll beat your brains out, you s— of a b—" using various other foul names. "If I met you on the outside, I will kill you."

January 27, 1925:

(Dr. S.): Has been getting along in a very comfortable manner since his trouble on December 29, 1924. Continues to believe that his wife was unfaithful. . . . Is inclined to minimize his trouble on December 29, 1924: now stating that the checkers fell upon the floor simply because he accidently moved the chair and the board fell from the edge. Denies that he screamed or threatened Alberts or that there was any dispute whatever. Shows no evidence of hallucinations at this time. Physical condition apparently satisfactory.

March 17, 1925:

(Dr. S.): Shows no important change. . . . Continues to deny that he himself had anything to do with the shooting of his wife which he lays to Tony. . . .

May 19, 1925:

(Dr. B.): This patient is pleasant and co-operative. Is oriented for time and place. Says this is the hospital for the insane, there are a good many of them here. He was sick when he first came here and did not know anything. "Just like a kid, that's all." Is all right now. Asked if he has been insane at any time, says he doesn't think so. Hallucinations of hearing not elicited. Says he has no enemies; there seem to be some vague ideas of persecution. Thinks his wife was an unfaithful woman and that she told him before she died that Tony shot her. She told this in the hospital. Eats and sleeps fairly well. . . .

July 27, 1925:

(Dr. B.): This patient is pleasant and answers questions readily, but may be evasive. He is oriented for time and place. Denies that he has heard voices. Doesn't remember saying that he heard the voice of God or that of his wife. Says all he knows is that he is all right now. Thinks his wife was a bad woman and her friend Tony is the one who shot his wife. He will not admit ideas of persecution. . . .

November 14, 1926:

(Dr. M.): This morning patient was very much excited. Got into trouble with the attendants and threatened to hit them. It was necessary to place him in a room. Examination of his room showed that he had a piece of tin, from a tobacco can, made into a saw and also another piece of tin sharpened to a very cutting edge. These were taken from him.

November 7, 1927:

(Dr. B.): This patient is oriented for time and place. Thinks he is all right now, mentally, but may have been unbalanced a little when he came here; now feels fine, could not feel better. Says he is under guardianship and cannot be tried; they should let him go home and he should leave this country, would not stay in the United States if they were to give him a thousand dollars a minute. No hallucinations of hearing now, and never had as far as he can remember. Claims he knows nothing about the murder of his wife; asked if he was drunk and didn't know what he was doing at the time, says, "I don't know." Wants to be a good man and says they will never see him get into trouble, never in his life again, everyone can be sick. Was arrested for the crime of first degree murder, not tried; and says if a man is insane he cannot be tried. Seems to be evasive about the trouble with his sister, brother-in-law, and wife; admits he did have a little trouble with the brother-in-law, that the latter owed him money and paid him part of it and the rest he will think nothing more about.

October 24, 1929:

(Dr. S.): . . . He is well oriented in all three spheres. Thinks he came here June 26, 1924 (came July 11, 1924). Says he was born May 3, 1892, according to the record he was born May 19, 1892. His memory for recent events seems to be fairly good. Remote events are not too good probably due to his inadequate schooling and lack of information. No hallucinations of sight or hearing could be elicited. Denies any hallucinations in the past. There seems to be a trend of persecutory delusions. Maintains he was framed up. Claims that he is entirely innocent of the crime he committed. Minimizes the family disputes which caused his commitment to the Danvers State Hospital. Minimizes also the violent episode during the checker game of December 29, 1924. Maintains that there is no evidence to point that he killed his wife. Says that his wife had a lover who killed her. Wants examiner to show him in what respect he is insane. Pleas for help with tears in his eyes. Is emotionally very unstable. His facial expression is dull and he appears to be mentally fairly bright. Seems to be evasive. He is co-operative and well behaved. His physical condition is good.

March 25, 1930:

(Pink Slip): Patient had a fight with Albert Pierce and received two slight cuts on the left hand, where he claims Pierce bit him. Pierce was not hurt.

June 5, 1930:

(Dr. S.): He is oriented in all three spheres. His memory is fairly good. No hallucinations of sight or hearing were elicited. Maintains some persecutory ideas. Thinks he was framed up and minimizes most of the troubles he has had in the past. There is no apparent change in his mental condition from the previous note. He is depressed at times. He is well behaved and co-operative. At times becomes somewhat evasive.

August 29, 1930:

(Pink Slip): This patient struck Tim Reardon and was confined in his room.

March 18, 1931:

(Dr. F.): There is no noticeable change in patient's condition. He is fairly well nourished, clean and tidy about personal appearance, quiet, attentive, and co-operative. He is dull, somewhat depressed and indifferent. Says he feels depressed because he does not like to stay here. He wants his liberty. He is well oriented in all spheres. No hallucinations or delusions were elicited. Memory is fairly well preserved. Denies he is guilty. He is quite evasive when questioned concerning his crime.

Heart and lungs essentially negative.

April 16, 1931:

(Dr. M.): Today patient got mad when some of his own food was not served him just when he thought it should be. He took a dry cell and smashed it on his door breaking the door. He was transferred to Ward F. (Patient remained in Ward F until May 8, 1931.)

June 19, 1931:

(Pink Slip): Patient struck Walter Rousseau on the face inflicting a cut requiring three stitches by Dr. M. Rousseau was sitting on a bench at the time, in the yard. Patient became enraged over a ring which Rousseau was wearing, which patient claimed belonged to him.

Dr. M. investigated and found conditions as stated.

July 27, 1931:

(Pink Slip): While engaged in a card game in the yard at 3 PM today, Vincent Rossi struck patient fracturing his lip. Rossi was removed from the yard by attendants McDermott and Mann and placed in seclusion.

August 30, 1932:

(Dr. L.): . . . He is oriented for time, place, and person. Grasp of general information and memory satisfactory. No hallucinations or delusions were elicited. Says he believes he is perfectly sane but cannot be released until the doctors say he is all right. He believes the doctors are acting in good faith. Denies murdering his wife. Says he was told she was unfaithful to him but he did not believe it, never having seen for himself. If released he would go at once to Italy

August 6, 1933:

(Pink Slip): Patient and Peter Menetta, another patient, got into an argument and came to blows. They were separated by Jenkins and Nelson. Each patient was taken in from the yard and placed in their rooms. Patient's left . . . was bruised.

September 5, 1933:

(Dr. L.): . . . He is oriented in all three spheres. Grasp of general information is fair; memory is satisfactory save for period involving crime of which patient is accused. He believes he was mentally upset when he came here, remembers having hallucinations and feeling everyone was against him. No hallucinations or delusions elicited at present. Patient has occasional upsets. Appears emotionally unstable. Does not believe that he was framed in being sent here, believes all was done in good faith.

May 24, 1934:

(Dr. L.): . . . He is oriented in all three spheres. Memory is satisfactory. No definite hallucinations nor delusions could be elicited. Denies committing the crime with which he is charged. Does not believe he was insane when he first came here; no history of hallucinations or delusions can be obtained at present. Patient appears to be of unstable emotional makeup, has occasional upsets. He has spells of excitement when he thinks everybody is against him. He has been found to show sugar in his urine; has been put on insulin regime.

June 17, 1934:

(Pink Slip): Patient was struck by another patient but does not know his name. . . .

January 14, 1935:

(Dr. L.): . . . He is oriented in all spheres. Memory appears satisfactory. No hallucinations or delusions can be elicited at present. Patient appears to show emotional instability and has occasional upsets.

October 29, 1935:

(Pink Slip): During a quarrel with Joseph Sparros, patient received a slight cut over his right eye.

Patient claims Sparros came into his room talking and singing and when patient told him to stop it, Sparros struck at patient with his shoe.

Sparros claims that he was passing patient's room, patient called him insulting names and Sparros told him to stop, but patient would not so Sparros picked up patient's pants and struck him, the button hitting him.

Dr. M. investigated and found conditions as stated.

March 23, 1936:

(Dr. S.): . . . He is oriented in all three spheres. Memory is good. No hallucinations of any kind were elicited. Claims he is entirely innocent of the crime for which he was arrested. No delusions were determined but there seems to be a persecutory trend to his ideas. He is emotionally very unstable. Has frequent periods of excitement. Thinks that everybody is against him. There has been no particular change in his mental condition from description in previous notes. He is in good contact with his surroundings and shows fair insight but his judgment is defective.

December 10, 1936:

(Dr. M.): Patient is very unstable emotionally. Sometimes he will go along for months in a quiet, comfortable condition and then with little or no warning will have an emotional outbreak and go on a violent temper tantrum and threaten to kill someone. He has now gone about a year without having one of these outbreaks. No delusions or hallucinations can be elicited at the present time but he has a mild paranoid trend. At present he has a very pleasant attitude. Memory and orientation are good. He is being given insulin every day for his diabetes.

December 30, 1937:

(Dr. C.): . . . He is correctly oriented in all spheres. Memory is very good both for recent and remote recall. No hallucinations were elicited. Patient denies the crime for which he was committed and says he never murdered his wife. Patient at present is very sociable and good natured, but at times becomes highly excited and is very unstable emotionally. He has periodic or occasional emotional outbreaks when he exhibits violent temper spells and is quite voluble and explosive. Of late however, he has been quite well behaved. He is on Ward I where he is being treated for diabetes and receives insulin daily.

November 12, 1938:

(Pink Slip): Patient attacked attendant Hopkins, slightly wounded him after Mr. Hopkins checked him, about yelling in the yard, and waking the night men who were sleeping in the adjoining building. Mr. Hopkins said Savarese first called him names and then scratched him with a nail or something sharp.

Dr. S. investigated and found conditions as stated.

January 10, 1939:

(Dr. M.) There has been no change in patient's condition during the past year. Most of the time he is quiet and pleasant in his attitude but he is very unstable emotionally and has occasional outbursts of violent temper and during such spells he is dangerous and homicidal. Memory and orientation are good and he is in good contact with his surroundings. No definite delusions or hallucinations can be elicited but he is so unstable in his emotional relations that he is distinctly abnormal. . . .

August 6, 1939:

(Pink Slip): Patient was fighting with George Osher, patient, and when asked to let Osher alone he continued to hit him and began to swear and talk out loud. I asked him to keep quiet for the nightmen were sleeping and still he kept on saying that he didn't care about the nightmen, he was going to report me for using my hands on him. I only pushed him away from Osher. (Signed: A. T.).

(Dr. M. investigated and found conditions as stated.)

July 3, 1940:

(Dr. M.): . . . He presents an intelligent, calm face. Is in good humour and can discuss sensibly in conversation. He claims that he has not been feeling too well for the last month. He has a heavy morning cough and much sputa. . . . Patient is oriented as to time but denies date of birth. He says it is May 3, 1891 (record, May 19, 1892). Oriented as to place and person. Memory for recent events is fair. Remote memory is not good. He admits he is not interested in events or reading since he declares, he will "never get out." He denies all hallucinations and delusions. His emotional tone is quite flat. He is slightly apathetic and discouraged over his incarceration but seems resigned to it. Patient is in contact with his surroundings but is quite uninterested about it all. He denies he killed his wife. Says he was always happy at home.

April 8, 1941

Medical Director
State Farm, Massachusetts

Dear Dr. H.:

Thank you for your letter of April 7. There is a considerable discrepancy in the matter of the number of visits which John Savarese made to Tony Savarese during 1940. According to the records which he has in the book he kept for the Veterans' Administration, John made six visits to the hospital, taking along food each time.

He claims that he made a visit in February, March, and April and May, in October, in December, whereas you only have him there in March, October and December.

I note that you saw in your letter that Mr. Savarese always brings something for the patient, and I wonder if it can be possible that some of my client's visits have not been noted down in the record.

After the experience which he had in the probate court last year, as a result of which my client has been ordered to pay back $800 for the costs of visits and food which he did not furnish or make, it is very disconcerting to strike this situation for the 1940 account.

My client is a poor tailor and has a hard time to get along and raise his family. He has been, to be sure, rather lax in his bookkeeping, but he swears by all that is good and holy that he made those six visits last year. He even has slips showing the purchase of the food stuffs which he took out to Bridgewater on the dates of the visits, and receipts from persons who drove him out there in an automobile.

I wonder if you would be willing to tell me if it is possible for him to come out there to visit his brother without having a record made of it. Thanking you in advance, I am very truly yours,

Alfred W. I.

April 14, 1941

Alfred W. I.
Attorney-at-Law
Boston, Mass.

Dear Sir:

I am sorry that our accounts do not seem to agree with your client's, John Savarese, but a record is made of every visit to patients at this institution. This is one rule that is strictly adhered to.

Very truly yours,

John H. W., M.D.
Medical Director

July 20, 1941:

(Pink Slip): Patient was creating a disturbance and using unnecessary language. When he was told to stop, he turned and spit into Attendant Leving's face. He was taken to his room and locked in. Dr. S. investigated and found conditions as stated.

December 4, 1941:

(Dr. C.): There has been no change in the patient's mental condition since last note. . . . He is correctly oriented for time, place, and person. He knows his age, date of admission, and the number of years he has been here. His memory for recent and remote recall is quite good. He is, however, moronic in intelligence; he is emotionally dull. He has resigned himself to his fate. Says he is here for life, will never get out. He denies hallucinations and delusions nor were any elicited. His insight is rather poor and his judgment defective.

November 27, 1942:

(Dr. H.): Patient struck patient Basili Geomillo in the left eye. No officer heard the argument or saw the patient strike Geomillo. (Dr. H. investigated and found that patient Geomillo had swollen cheek, eyeball cut, hemorrhage of the eyeball. Necessary to enucleate the eye.)

November 27, 1942:

(Dr. G.): Patient isolated. Reason: assault.

Attendant stays about 9:45 AM and for no apparent reason and without provocation Tony Savarese approached and assaulted another patient, causing the assaulted patient to lose complete vision in the left eye. The assaulted patient was removed to dispensary for examination and treatment. The assaultee was isolated.

When interviewed this AM the patient was calm, responded quietly to questions, and appeared indifferent as to the seriousness of the incident. States that he is sorry but does not know how it could have happened and expresses great remorse. Denies having malicious intent and insists that the striking of another patient was merely a playful gesture. Statements as to whether or not he actually held a knife in his fist at the time of the assault are inconsistent. Does admit that he did have a knife in his possession which was later found by an attendant.

April 17, 1944:

(Pink Slip): The above patient was locked in his room by Officer Holmes for being threatening and abusive. I have put up with this for a week. This morning when I told him to keep still and go to his room, he refused and when I took hold of his arm, he struggled and tried to hit me. Also kept threatening to get me the first time he gets a chance. (Dr. G. investigated and found conditions as stated.)

November 5, 1945:

(Dr. G.): He is usually of cheerful disposition and of pleasant attitude. However, he shows considerable emotional instability and at times becomes quite excited. In his rage, he is liable to do most anything and cannot be reasoned with. He is of homicidal make-up and has but little regard for the rights of others.

At this interview no frank delusions or hallucinations can be brought out although he does express numerous mild persecutional paranoid ideas. He seems clearly oriented and has a good grasp of his surroundings. Memory shows no gross defects.

General impression is that of a small, well-developed, middle-aged male who occasionally displays severe temper tantrums which assume homicidal proportions.

May 21, 1948:

(Dr. S.): Patient interviewed today. Patient smiles pleasantly during the entire interview. No history of attacks since his admission here.

August 12, 1948:

To: Director, Disability Insurance Claims Service, Washington 25, D. C.

From: A. W. S., Medical Director

"He has shown no marked improvement in his mental condition and is still psychotic. He is diagnosed as dementia praecox, paranoid.

It is doubtful whether or not this patient will ever recover sufficiently to be released from this hospital."

January 5, 1950

Mr. Paul A. Dever [Governor]

Sir:

I am writing for my wife in regards to Tony Savarese who has been confined to the State Farm, Bridgewater, Mass. for 25 years last May. Please advise me if you can do anything about his release or what is the procedure.

I have quarters at this address for him. I own my own home, also my wife is related to him by marriage. He is her uncle.

The story I get is this. He came home one day and found this man in bed with his wife and through a fit of temper he grabbed a shot gun and killed his wife. The courts at the time declared him insane at the time. After 25 years, 8 months, could you find out if he is still insane or not. If not, who do I see for help? We're trying to get him out if possible. He has a guardian for all these years because he draws money from the government. . . . I have found out that the guardian gets his fee and the rest is turned into government bonds.

Will you please advise me what to do and how will I go about it to get some action if possible on this case. Edward Morley who is judge in Pemberton Square Courthouse is a very close friend of mine. He lives in Manchester, Mass. and I always see his mother and him when I go down there. I went to school with him and worked for his father. Could he help me in any way. Please answer. I thank you.

H. L.

Commonwealth of Massachusetts
Department of Mental Health

January 13, 1950

Medical Director
Bridgewater State Hospital

Dear Dr. S.:

I am enclosing copy of a letter written by Tony Savarese's nephew and sent to the Governor's office. May I have an abstract of this case and your comments in order that I may reply to the Governor.

Very truly yours,

Peter B. H., M.D.
Assistant Commissioner

January 18, 1950:

(Dr. K.): . . . Patient today stated that he would not take any more insulin because he wants to die. Said he had some words with another patient and made up his mind about this because he is mistreated.

This individual is the most unco-operative person to deal with. Threatens to write to his guardian to say that he is not given any more treatment here. Says it's up to himself, that if he wishes treatment or not and he is going to see to it that he does not get any more here.

Assistant Commissioner
Department of Mental Health
Boston, Massachusetts

Dear Dr. H.:

Your letter of January 13 was received regarding Tony Savarese, patient at the Bridgewater State Hospital. He was admitted here on July 11, 1924 from the Suffolk Superior Court and his legal status at this institution is Court 100.

Though he is usually well conducted there are times that he is quite irritable and hard to manage. In regard to his mental condition, I do not feel that he shows sufficient improvement to be returned to court to stand trial at the present time.

Very truly yours,

A. W. S.
Medical Director

Abstract of Case History

Tony Savarese   B.S.H. No. 3036

Tony Savarese was admitted to the Bridgewater State Hospital on July 11, 1924 from the Suffolk Superior Court where he was waiting trial for the crime of murder, second degree with which he had been charged. He was admitted to this hospital for a period of mental observation under section 100. As there was no change in his mental condition, he was

therefore regularly committed to this institution on April 16, 1934 under section Ct. 100.

Prior to his admission here, he had two other admissions to state hospitals, the first being the Boston Psychopathic Hospital to which he was admitted on April, 17 1923 and diagnosed on April 16, 1923. At that hospital he was given the diagnosis of: dementia praecox. He was transferred to the Danvers State Hospital on April 26, 1923, condition improved.

The patient was admitted to the Danvers State Hospital on April 26, 1923 as a transfer patient from the Boston Psychopathic Hospital. He was discharged on May 23, 1923. On admission to the Danvers State Hospital he was oriented, cheerful, and talkative. He did not cause any trouble while there and was fairly industrious, working on his ward. At this hospital he was given the diagnosis of psychopathic personality.

Previous to these mentioned admissions, he had been a patient at the United States Veterans Hospital at West Roxbury, Massachusetts. He was admitted there on January 4, 1922 and discharged on May 20, 1922. Condition—unimproved, absent without leave for 7 days. Diagnosis at the Veterans Hospital was dementia praecox—paranoid type.

He has also had an admission to the Chelsea Marine Hospital, where he remained for 3 months.

Tony Savarese was born on May 3, 1891, in Italy, is the son of Mike and Fellie Savarese who were also born in Italy. He arrived in the United States on September 16, 1905, we believe. He had a few years of schooling, can read and write a little. His religion is that of a Catholic. His occupation was that of barber. It is believed that in 1923 he married a Theresa Massina.

Patient did not have any previous criminal record; the only arrest was the one for murder for which he was committed to this institution.

He is a veteran of World War I, having enlisted on May 3, 1918, being sent to Camp Devens, 151 ST. Depot Brigade, where he remained until his discharge on January 15, 1919.

On admission to this hospital, patient was underdeveloped, appeared depressed, and answers to questions were barely audible. Response was delayed and slow and unintelligible. He appeared emotionally weak and tears frequently appeared in his eyes without apparent cause. Patient, however, did not cause any trouble and went to his receiving ward.

His attitude and manner were that of seclusiveness. However, he was quiet and well behaved during interviews and was co-operative to the best of his ability, although it was felt he was not telling the entire story. He was oriented for place and time but partly disoriented for person. His memory for recent and remote appearances was fair. Emotionally, he appeared somewhat weak. He also presented auditory and visual hallucinations of at least three years duration. He did not have insight, as he thought that at the time, he was not mentally ill; his judgment was defective.

On May 24, 1934 urinalysis test was given him and it was found that there was sugar in his urine, therefore he was put on an insulin regime which consisted of 5 units in the morning. . . . At the present time he is receiving treatment for diabetes.

There has been no considerable change in his mental condition. Most of the time he is quiet and pleasant in his atitude, but he is very unstable emotionally and has occasionally loud bursts of violent temper and during such spells he is dangerous and homicidal. Memory and orientation are good and he is in good contact with his surroundings. He presents no definite delusions or hallucinations but is unstable in his emotional reactions and is distinctly abnormal.

In September, 1949, patient appeared to have lost some weight, his face appeared pale and haggard. . . . He refuses to eat what is given to him and is reluctant to co-operate.

In January, 1950, the patient was put on 40 units . . . insulin. Patient stated he would not take any more insulin because he wants to die. This individual is most unco-operative person to deal with. He says it is up to himself whether or not he shall receive further treatments.

January 2, 1951:

Staff meeting: Patient has had no fits for years and is getting along fine.

Assistant Commissioner
Department of Mental Health
Boston, Massachusetts

Dear Dr. H.:

Your letter requesting information as to the present legal status and whether or not charges are pending against Tony Savarese, BSH No. 3036, was received.

Please be informed that patient was admitted here July 11, 1924 from the Suffolk Superior Court where he is charged with the crime of murder, and his legal status in this institution is Ct. 100. Charges are still pending against this patient.

With regard to his mental condition, I do not feel that he shows sufficient improvement to be returned to court to stand trial.

Very truly yours,

A. Warren S., M.D.
Medical Director

August 11, 1951:

(Dr. K.): Patient was seen to assess his present mental condition. He was asked to give an account of his history leading up to the crime from the time of his army discharge.

"Upon discharge, I was weak and shaky, I was a little sick."

That's why he was under guardianship, because of his nervousness. He worked as watchman at the army base, South Boston. After two or three months, the Major asked him "do you want to go home and get $80 a month or do you want to continue working here. I said I want to go home instead of working for $100 a month. Besides I could make a little extra at work."

Upon discharge from army he was treated for six months in West Roxbury Veterans Hospital. He spent nine to ten months in the army, Camp Devens, Ayer, Massachusetts.

Says he was drinking moonshine which made him sick. "I tell you the truth, I drink a little too much." He does not remember experiencing hallucinations.

Says he married his wife after his discharge from the army. He had known her for a year.

Says he was getting along pretty good "getting his $80" compensation, in addition to which he made money barbering and selling eggs.

Says a man named Tony came to his home one day and said "Tony, I want to talk to you. I told him to sit down. He asked me for $500. He said, Tony, I want $500. I asked him for what. Why do I have to give you $500, for what. He said he gave my wife a $500 diamond ring before I married her. At that time he said he was courting her and she was his sweetheart.

"I told him, you wait for my wife to come. My wife worked in the chocolate factory and she came about 5:35 PM from work. He waited.

"My wife told him, 'If you don't get out of here I'll call a cop.' This man, he go, say you gonna pay for that." Patient says he never saw the ring. Maybe she sold it, he doesn't know. Says his wife was too smart for him. She told him to mind his own business. Four or five months later, "I come back from my sister's house, it was 9:15 PM. I see my wife in the garden, she holler, help, help! I told my wife, what's the matter, you afraid of rats? I go closer and she said, 'somebody shoot me.' " He called his next door neighbor to help him take her to the bedroom. He noticed five buckshot wounds in her leg. Says he told the neighbor to sit with her and he went to telephone the police. "Me and the police took my wife to the Massachusetts General Hospital." Says he was questioned the next day and was asked whose gun it was, found at the scene of the crime. He admitted it was his and that he had a permit. Says the police threatened him with arrest if he didn't tell them who "done" it and he was arrested on suspicion. Says he told the police to take him before his wife at the Massachusetts General Hospital. "She tell you who did it." Says he asked his wife to tell the police who did it. Says she told him in front of two doctors and three nurses that he did not shoot her, but in spite of this he was arrested.

He was kept at Charles Street Jail for three days and then transferred here. "I've been here ever since. I come here and am not guilty and do life for nothing, that's the whole story."

He is sure if he went to court he would be released as there is no existing evidence to convict him.

He has a past history of admission for observation

at Danvers State Hospital about 29 years ago. "My sister put me in there, she tell the police 'I don't think he's all right because I want to move away.' She had four kids and make too much noise. I was all right. After two weeks the doctors sent me home."

Admits his belief that his wife was prostituting. But says, "what chance have I got. It's all crooked. The man belonged to a gang, the police, sheriff, and mayor played ball with them. I cannot say too much. If I do they say I am crazy."

When asked why did the doctors hold him here so many years, he replied, "I don't know. Some of the doctors promised me a return to court, pretty soon, pretty soon, but I never got to court."

Says he is indicted for murder and he wants to clear himself as he is not guilty of the crime. But first the doctors have to clear him.

Says, "nobody framed me up. I got charged by the court. I am a court case. I'm going to fight my case." After he is cleared up as not insane.

Patient talks sensibly at this interview. He insists he is not guilty. He says he is a court case, and upon a clearance of his mental condition by the doctors and being returned to court, he feels he will be a free man.

He admitted repeatedly that his wife was prostituting for Tony who was doing the pimping. He was afraid to start anything with her as he was under a guardianship and could quickly be sent to a mental hospital as a troublesome character in the community. This has been considered a paranoid delusion but deserves investigation in order to substantiate it as fact or imagination. To date, no investigation has been made and the record contains none.

He has been a difficult patient at times throughout his hospitalization and he is demanding and often unreasonable. He is a diabetic and has on occasion used this as a lever with which to gain his end by either refusing to eat or refusing his insulin. Otherwise, he is clean, neat, busy on the farm with his garden project and no particular problem.

August 11, 1951:

He may be a paranoid condition. More work-up is needed from the investigative aspect.

The record indicates the presence of hallucinations of visual and auditory types, early in his abnormal mental history.

September 2, 1951:

(Pink Slip, Dr. L.): The above-named patient was seen gambling and when asked for his money he ran into the dormitory and fell on the floor in a seizure yelling, "I might commit suicide," all the officers and Superintendents were all against him and they all bothered him. Superintendent Smith was notified; patient transferred to H-3. Condition as reported. Signed: Dr. L.

September 13, 1951:

Staff meeting: See again. Still somewhat excitable.

May 2, 1952:

(Dr. G.): Patient is an elderly man who has been here for many years. At the present time he shows no evidence of his psychosis; is clearly oriented in all spheres; has a good grasp of his surroundings; vigorously denies hallucinations of all forms; no frank delusions can be demonstrated. From time to time he becomes somewhat irritable, but requires no special supervision.

January 9, 1953:

To: Disability Claims Division, Veterans Administration, Washington, D.C.

From: M. K.

"His (Tony Savarese) diagnosis was dementia praecox, paranoid type. Diagnosis remains the same. His mental condition is essentially unchanged."

August 10, 1954:

(Dr. W.): Patient was called for a routine interview. He is a 64-year-old white male, small in stature, who had a good grasp of his surroundings and who was anxious to discuss his case to the minutest detail as he emphatically denies having murdered his wife.

It was interesting to note that although orientation pertaining to time was defective (he thought this was the year 1924), he did know that he is incarcerated in Bridgewater for 30 years (correct). He readily recalled having been in the army at the time of World War I and that he did not go overseas, and on the other hand was unable to recall the date 1917 nor the name of the President at the time (Woodrow Wilson), having absolutely no idea what year it may have been at that time.

Another remarkable feature of this interview was his ability to recall almost in detail the entire story he gave, which is written up in the lengthy note of August 11, 1951. While he thought that the crime occurred in 1921 (correct date 1924), nevertheless was otherwise coherent and relevant throughout and he could not be confused concerning the principal aspects of his case. He did not know who is now President but he pleaded that he took neither interest in dates nor in politics as he stated that he was unconcerned in these matters. He appeared to be a good-natured individual with no peculiar mannerisms who is otherwise oriented for prison, and he showed no good memory for names of various relatives mentioned in the charge. He denied hallucinations and no delusions could be elicited. The examiners were under the impression that he may have been malingering concerning his confusion of dates.

May 12, 1955:

Veterans Administration
Regional Office

Superintendent
State Farm

Dear Sir:

... For your own information and in the event that it might be of some assistance in helping the patient you are advised that the veteran's guardian, Charles Savarese, has submitted four guardian's accounts to the Suffolk Probate Court, the fourth account having an ending date of November 8, 1954, at which time he had in his possession $14,339.23 of the veteran's personal funds. The veteran's estate is protected by a $14,000 surety company bond with the Maryland Casualty Company as surety. The corpus of the estate consists of $6,009.23 in the East Boston Savings Bank with the Maryland Casualty Company having joint control. The remainder of the estate consists of United States bonds which are held in the custody of the Maryland Casualty Company.

The disbursements during the accounting periods have been nominal considering the value of the veteran's estate.

Very truly yours,
George N. W.
Chief Attorney

August 3, 1955:

Seen by Dr. G., Department of Mental Health.

August 3, 1955:

Staff meeting: (Dr. K; Present: Dr. A. Warren S., Consultant, Drs. K. and A., Social Worker L., S. and P., Psychologists Willey and Robb): No entry.

August 10, 1955:

A. Warren S., M.D.
Billerica, Massachusetts

August 10, 1955

Medical Director
Bridgewater State Hospital

Dear Dr. K.:

Concerning Tony Savarese whom I saw in consultation with you on August 3, I have known this man for some time and have seen him off and on. In my opinion he is psychotic and although he shows few active symptoms at the present time, I doubt whether he has recovered.

Sincerely yours,
A. W. S.

November 14, 1955:

(Dr. A.): ... Is oriented in all spheres and his replies are coherent and relevant. Expressed no

deluded ideas but still believes his guardian is holding money on him. Is well adjusted and gets along well, except at times gets excited to obtain his wishes.

November 17, 1955:

Patient seen today by Dr. M., Department of Mental Health.

April 6, 1956:

(Dr. K.): This patient's history is of an abnormal individual who manifested extreme instability with gross psychotic symptoms for which he had several state hospital admissions in his early 30's. In the interim, between these hospitalizations, he threatened to drive a knife into one of his relatives during a party at which he was drinking.

1. Following his last hospital sojourn as a civilian, he was arrested for the murder of his wife. At the time of his arrest he was psychotic, according to medical opinion.

2. Throughout his hospitalization at Bridgewater he has proved to be a most unstable person who is unable to get along with other patients, and was suspected of influencing a disturbed patient to blind the eye of another patient while he remained in the background. He has always been demanding, complaining, argumentative, fault finding and unco-operative. He has always been extremely rebellious or ingratiating. In recent years he has had several mild hysterical seizures of short duration whenever he was determined to gain some advantage. Being a diabetic he has on several occasions refused his insulin and refused to eat unless he obtained what he wanted.

3. In recent years he has been distrusting his nephew who is his guardian, and has repeatedly accused him of lying to him about his financial status. This attitude toward his nephew persists with tones of unfriendliness and even hostility which he covers. Presently he accused him of wanting his money for himself and waiting for him to die. Other relatives of his are living. He has a sister whom he accuses of having stolen $2,000 from him when she was his former guardian.

4. He has an explosive temper and when angered becomes unreasonable to the extreme so that he is difficult to pacify.

5. Because of his childish patterns of behavior, his insistence on having his own way, his strong paranoid trends, marked emotional instability, immature judgment and still no appreciation or evidence of proper feeling over the alleged offense which he denies, his account indicating distortion of reality, he is considered to be of vicious tendencies of insufficient mental and emotional soundness to be returned to stand trial, despite the absence of deluded ideas and his denial of hallucinations.

April 13, 1956:

Bridgewater State Hospital
South Bridgewater, Mass.

April 13, 1956

Acting Assistant Commissioner
Department of Mental Health
Boston, Massachusetts

Dear Dr. H.:

Re: Tony Savarese, No. 50–3036

On December 7, 1955 a letter received from your office recommended the return of the above patient to court to be tried for the crime of murder. After considerable thought and for the following reasons, I feel that this individual is not a well man.

His history is of an abnormal individual who manifested extreme instability and with gross psychotic symptoms for which he had several state hospital admissions in his early 30's. In the interim, between these hospitalizations, he threatened to drive a knife into one of his relatives during a party, at which he was drinking.

[The remainder of the letter contains paragraphs 1–5 of above letter.]

Very truly yours,

Morris K., M.D.
Medical Director

April 17, 1956:

The Commonwealth of Massachusetts
Department of Mental Health
Boston

April 17, 1956

Medical Director
Bridgewater State Hospital

Dear Dr. K.:

Your letter concerning Tony Savarese, No. 50–3036, has been received. Dr. M. examined this patient November 18, 1955 and states that he does not believe the man is psychotic nor has been for many years. In reviewing this, I talked the situation over with the Commissioner; and, in view of Dr. M.'s examination, it would seem that he should be returned to court. However, having received your letter, I believe one of the other psychiatrists from the Department should see this patient before any action is taken, so kindly destroy my letter of December 7, 1955.

Very truly yours,

William M. A. H., M.D.
Acting Assistant Commissioner

April 26, 1956:

Patient interviewed today by Dr. G., Department of Mental Health.

May 16, 1956:

(Dr. C., consultant): Subject is friendly, quiet, agreeable, relevant, and coherent in speech. He is a barber by trade. Neat and clean. Said to be subject to hysterical episodes. Veteran of World War I.

A wrinkled, furrowed, elderly appearing individual, but alert, spontaneous in speech, who is anxious to obtain his freedom. He is free of complaints, offers none and acknowledges none. Feels well and is able to work and contribute to his future happiness and betterment.

Hallucinations denied. Orientation and memory correct. Partial insight; superficial judgment.

A 65-year-old white male who is charged with second degree murder. He has a history of several state hospital admissions in the past. According to the records he threatened to drive a knife into one of his relatives during a party.

This patient has been examined by Dr. S. and Dr. K., both of whom feel that he is not suitable for release. Dr. G. and Dr. M. hold contrary opinions.

Patient adopted a general attitude of innocence and denial.

According to medical opinion, he was psychotic at the time of his arrest. At Bridgewater, he has been rather unstable in his adjustment. He is being treated for diabetes.

He is described as annoying, agitating, demanding, quarrelous, fault-finding, negativistic, argumentative, antagonistic, and disputatious. There is the suggestion of hysterical episodes motivated by the factor of secondary gain. He also is distrustful of his nephew, his guardian, relative to the handling of his funds. There is an undertone of hostility directed toward the latter. He charges his sister took between $1,000 and $2,000 from him.

He has long been an immature, unstable individual, a problem in management, detached and childish in his point of view with much evidence of distortion of truth and reality.

This patient is basically schizoid in make-up. He has long been an unstable personality with easily traumatized ego. He is given to rationalizing in inaccuracies with distortion of the truth and with a poor social perception, and with little feeling or sense of responsibility regarding his alleged crime. He was complacent, approval-seeking, and submissive on examination. He adopts a defensive facade and has a bewildering capacity to becloud issues. He lacks a social consciousness or a guilty conscience. In short, he has psychopathic traits of long standing and he is unable to stand off from himself and look objectively and without partisanship at himself. Patient allows his feelings to act as uncensored guides to action and though intellectually aware, he refuses to accept any adult responsibilities and direct his energy in activity along paths laid down by social needs. Writer feels that those symptoms are not especially alive, he is basically a calculated risk for extramural living.

May 16, 1956:

Mass. Correctional Institution
Bridgewater, Mass.

May 16, 1956

District Attorney
Suffolk County Court House
Boston, Massachusetts

Re: Tony Savarese

Dear Sir:

The above patient was arrested on 6/28/24 for the crime of murder by the police department of the city of Chelsea. Subsequent to his arrest he was brought before the grand jury, indicted, and prior to trial committed to this hospital under the provisions of section 100. He has been regularly committed since then and considered to be mentally ill.

In reviewing his record, we have attempted to secure an official version of the offense for the evaluation of the medical staff and in order to complete our case records. Upon inquiring of the Suffolk Superior Court, the probation department, we received reply that the files on his case had been destroyed. We have also attempted to secure the official version from the arresting police department and have not met with success yet.

We are wondering if your office has any information that might assist us in obtaining this official version in order to complete our records.

Very truly yours,
Morris K., M.D.

May 16, 1956:

Police Department
City of Chelsea

May 16, 1956

Bridgewater State Hospital
Bridgewater, Massachusetts

Dear Sir:

I was notified by the Desk Sergeant of your call this day regarding Tony Savarese. I recall a communication received at this office on the above subject and also a letter sent by me stating that there are no records of this man's arrest in the department.

I also mention that this is a Revere Police Department case. If you communicate with Chief Gillis of the Revere Police, you may receive the desired information.

Very truly yours,
John J. K.
Chief of Police

May 17, 1956:

Social Service Note, May 17, 1956, by D. L.

Following receipt of a negative reply from the Chelsea police concerning the case of the above patient, a phone call was made to the Revere Police and I spoke to a Sergeant Paterson. He informed me that previous inquiries had been made on the case and there was no information recorded on the case in his book. He added that a retired police officer by the name of Sweeny had made the arrest and that they are trying to contact him to secure more accurate information. He also suggested that the District Attorney of Suffolk County be contacted for some assistance. To date it appears that there is no information concerning the official version of the offense available.

May 17, 1956:

(Dr. C., consultant): The above patient was examined by writer May 16, 1956. In view of the complexity of the case and the divergence of psychiatric opinion, a supplementary examination was undertaken to pick up some of the loose ends and reach an opinion based on more conclusive data if possible. The matter of the ring, which entered into the crime, was discussed. Patient's wife was killed according to patient, by her old sweetheart. He claims he arrived 20 minutes after the crime and called police immediately. He claims a certain Tony had given Mrs. Savarese a ring prior to her marriage. It seems he demanded the ring back but was told it was lost. Thereupon he demanded $500 in place of the ring and when the money was not forthcoming he threatened reprisal on the wife.

Veteran also discloses that he has drawn a pension of $120 a month from the United States Government for 34 years. He figures he should now have $58,000 but instead has only $14,000. He claims that if outside he would hire a lawyer and investigate the discrepancy in the amount of money. He claims 100 per cent disability for "little nervousness" (total disability). He is rather suspicious about his loss of money and is determined to obtain redress.

On examination he was restless, tense, with an attitude of injured innocence and self-pity. This patient does not find the slightest subjective interest in anything outside of himself. His emotional reactions are diffuse and spurious, his orientation defensive. He continually expresses a desire to go to Italy on the grounds that he is getting old, that he would be free and rid of all his present problems, even at the risk of losing his pension.

He carries on an involved conversation and is quite ambivalent about many things. He paints himself as a friendly, quiet, agreeable, likeable person, without enemies, and liked by everyone. Speech is relevant and coherent but has a tendency to overproductiveness and garrulousness. Hallucinations again denied in a vague matter. Again there is the suggestion that he is covering up as he has a strong tendency to avoid concrete answers and changes the subject, especially when questioned regarding hallucinations or any topic that touches on the matter of psychiatric symptoms.

Patient is charged with the crime of murder and

wants to clear himself as he contends he is not guilty of the crime. Patient is a diabetic, the records show, who has been unstable, demanding, and unreasonable. The records indicate visual and auditory hallucinations previously. He is well oriented. He has excuses and rationalizations for about everything.

Patient has a good grasp of his surroundings. His orientation is correct. However, he cannot recall accurately the year that the crime was committed and in general shows some confusion in dates. There is a history of hospitalization at Danvers about 33 years ago.

In general, this patient has been and continues to be an unstable personality, rebellious, given to hysterical manifestations for secondary gain. He remains a suspicious, distrustful, muddled personality with definite paranoid trends. He believes his sister stole his money.

Patient has long demonstrated a tendency to explosiveness and childish patterns of behavior. He insists on the reality of his ideas. His judgment strikes one as definitely immature and by and large shows a lack of capacity for the successful refashioning of his environment.

I am of the opinion that he still retains underlying psychotic trends. He shows little capacity for checking on the validity of his interpretation. His ideas are vague and inaccurate. He tends to disregard logic. He is inept at self-observation. He employs circumlocution, evasiveness and obscurity. Paranoid ideas seem to be in the background though not openly expressed at times. He effects an air of humility. He is pulled apart, unhappy, at odds with the world. At all times, did he lean over backwards to impress examiner and arouse sympathy.

Diagnosis: Paranoid conditon, chronic.

Disposition: Further observation and suggest psychological testing, that is, Roshack and thematic apperception tests as adjuncts to clinical examination.

Recommend the return to court be postponed.

May 17, 1956:

Mass. Correctional Institution
Bridgewater, Mass.

May 17, 1956

Revere Police Department
Revere, Massachusetts

Dear Sir:

Pursuant to our telephone conversation this morning on the above patient, I am sending you the information you have requested.

This patient, to the best of our knowledge, was arrested on or about 6/28/24 for the crime of murder. In reconstructing the offense, it would seem that the above patient was brought to the Chelsea police station by a Revere police officer.

Following his arrest, he was indicted for the crime by the Suffolk Grand Jury and prior to trial was committed to this hospital as insane. He has remained hospitalized to date.

It would be appreciated if you could send us all the information you may have on this case.

Very truly yours,
David L.
Psychiatric Social Worker

May 28, 1956:

COMMONWEALTH OF MASSACHUSETTS
District Attorney
Boston, Massachusetts

May 28, 1956

Medical Director
Massachusetts Correctional Institution
Bridgewater, Massachusetts

Dear Doctor:

Receipt of your recent communication relative to information concerning the above name is acknowledged.

Please be advised that a diligent search for the records in this office reveals that our Suffolk County Grand Jury notes are not available for the dates prior to 1929. An exhaustive search of all probation records was conducted but reveals nothing. Indictments #4285 and 4324 pertaining to Mr. Savarese indicate that he was indicted in Suffolk County in the month of July, 1924. He was defended during all stages of the proceedings by Raymor M. Gardner and Walter H. Watson, who gave as their professional address, 16A Ashborn Place, Boston, Massachusetts.

Before the trial Savarese or Savarici as his name is spelled on one indictment, was examined by Dr. A. Warren S. and Dr. Charles B. S., and was found to be insane. Based on this recommendation, the defendant was committed.

I trust that the shreds of information contained herein may prove of some assistance to you and if you desire this office to assist further, we should be happy to oblige.

Very truly yours,
Garrett H. B.

June 6, 1956:

The following copy of entries in the Revere Police Journal of June, 1924:

Friday, June 20, 1924, 10.30 PM
Telephone from unknown party that some person was shot in a house on Lincoln Street. Sent McChristl with wagon.—*Lt. Chainey*
10:30 PM
Went to Lincoln Street and took Mrs. Savarese to the Massachusetts General Hospital who had been shot in the leg, near the groin. Her husband said she did it. When I got to the hospital I telephoned to Lt. Chainey to have her husband arrested as her face was also cut, and I asked her if her husband did it and she shook her head as if to say yes. I returned to the house coming from the hospital, Officer Sweeney had been

there and arrested him. I took the keys to the house to the station.—*McChristl*

11:20 PM

Officer McChristl phoned from Massachusetts General Hospital. He had taken woman there from Lincoln Street who was shot and to arrest her husband.

11:30 PM

Officer Daniel Sweeney brought Savarese to the station. Sgt. Blythe, Officer Sweeney and Ciaccia went to hospital with Savarese to get antimortem statement.

Saturday, June 21, 1924, 12:15 AM

Sgt. Blythe phoned woman was on operating table and he would stay awaiting developments.

12:30 AM

Sgt. Blythe phoned woman would not come out of ether before 4 or 5 AM, told to bring Savarese to station.

Friday, June 20, 1924, 11:30 PM

Sent from the station to Oakland Street on the corner of Griffin Street in response to a telephone call. The shooting already had taken place and when I arrived there I found a man, a Tony Savarese, age 31, there with his face covered with blood and blood spots over his coat and also the bed. Said his wife shot herself and an ambulance had taken her to the hospital. I found a shotgun broken in halves on the floor near the bed and empty shells in gun and a bunch of long hair caught in the trigger of gun. Savarese then told me another story that his wife was unfaithful to him and that he told her so and she then said "I'll shoot myself" and she then picked up the gun and shot herself in the leg. He told two more stories in regards to shooting. With Officers Church and Hanagan I went back to the house and 50 feet from the rear steps we found there was a mark of a struggle and lots of blood on the ground and also found the broken butt of the gun.

Officer Church talked to the witness who heard the shot and helped to carry the woman into the house.—*Daniel T. Sweeney*

11:45 PM

Warned Tony Savarese of his right that anything that he said to me would be for or against him. I asked him how did his wife get shot and he said his wife was drunk. He said to his wife I heard you aren't true to me, and you go around with other men. She then said she was going to shoot herself and she took the gun and shot herself in the leg.

I asked him how could she shoot herself in the leg, and he said she fell downstairs and the gun went off. I asked him how did the gun break and he said when she fell downstairs and the hair on the gun got there when he took her in the house with the gun. I told him to tell the truth, to tell me how it happened. He said he would not say anything until tomorrow. He did not know that one of her boiler-makers shot her. I talked with Gorenzo Belmonti living next to him. He said he heard "come in the house or I'll shoot you," and then he heard a shot and a woman screaming for help. He then came out and saw Savarese with a gun in his hand and his wife on the ground.

Savarese asked Belmonti to help him. He would not go out because Savarese had the gun in his hand. He then took the gun in the house and came out again and Belmonti helped Savarese take his wife to the house.—*D. Ciaccia*

June 21, 1924, 9:10 AM

Notified by the hospital that Mrs. Savarese just died.—*The Chief*

9:15 AM

Notified her folks Venasie of the death.—*Captain Tappan*

NOTES

NOTE 1

HALE v. SAVARESE
Mass. (1960)

WILLIAMS, JUSTICE.

This is a petition by an attorney to the Probate Court that it fix and determine his compensation for services rendered to one Tony Savarese, an insane person under guardianship, determine his expenses in connection therewith, and direct payment from "the estate generally or as the court may determine." . . .

The material facts are reported by the judge. In 1924 Tony Savarese was indicted for murder of his wife. Before arraignment he was committed to Bridgewater State Hospital as an insane person and remained there until August, 1958. At the time of his commitment he was placed under guardianship by the Suffolk County Probate Court. "[N]o constructive effort was made by successive guardians or members of his family to obtain his release," although in recent years two attorneys, at his request, investigated his case and reported that they were unable to help him.

In January, 1957, he sought help from Mr. Hale, the petitioner, a competent attorney of considerable experience in criminal matters. Mr. Hale examined the records in the case and consulted Dr. Stearns, a well-known psychiatrist, who had been one of the panel that had examined the ward prior to his commitment. A petition to expend money from the guardianship estate to pay for a psychiatric examination was opposed by the guardian as "fruitless" and was denied by the Probate Court. Dr. Stearns, however, made the examination and gave an opinion that the ward was sane.

In April, 1957, Mr. Hale filed his appearance for the defendant in the murder case and petitioned for a writ of habeas corpus. There were two hearings on the petition, in the second of which four psychiatrists testified and the medical director of Bridgewater State Hospital gave his opinion that the ward was then sane. After commitment for thirty-five days to the Boston State Hospital for further observation, the ward was certified as sane and ordered to stand trial on the murder indictment. He was arraigned on

August 4, 1958, and pending trial was released on $1,000 bail. Mr. Hale prepared the case for trial and conferred with the district attorney, who recommended that a plea of *nolo contendere* be accepted. The court approved its acceptance and the defendant was placed on probation for two years from October 22, 1958.

In his petition Mr. Hale asks to be paid $7,026.30 for counsel fees and expenses which amount includes a fee of $1,750 for services from March, 1957, through August, 1958; a fee of $5,000 for services "rendered on second degree murder indictment"; and a claim for reimbursement of $200 paid to Dr. Stearns.

* * *

Both claims for services related to matters plainly material to the welfare of the ward. Those pertaining to the adjudication of the ward's sanity and the obtaining of his release from the insane hospital were rendered directly to the ward for his benefit and advantage and were properly chargeable to his estate. G.L. c. 201, § 37. Payment by the guardian would be allowable in his account. The services in connection with the murder indictment were apparently contracted by the guardian and he became personally liable for their payment. . . . As he would be entitled to reimbursement for such payment from the estate by equitable substitution the petitioner could obtain an order for payment directly from the guardianship funds. . . .

As to the charge of $1,750 for accomplishing a determination of the ward's sanity and his consequent release from the hospital, we have no question that the award of the judge for that amount should stand. The services of Mr. Hale were unusual in character performed with pertinacity and skill in the face of opposition by the guardian and resulted in great benefit to the ward. That an attorney is entitled to be compensated for such services, although employed by a person who is legally incapable of entering into a contract, was decided in *Hallett* v. *Oakes*, 1 Cust. 296. . . .

As to the charge of $5,000 for services rendered in defence of the murder indictment, we think that it is too high. . . . Mr. Hale entered his appearance for the defendant and prepared the case for trial. He arranged with the district attorney for a favorable disposal of the indictment and within a short time brought the prosecution to an end. We are not disposed to minimize the value of these services, but experience leads us to doubt whether in the circumstances great difficulty was encountered in prevailing upon the district attorney to conclude the prosecution. It does not appear whether in fact the murder could then have been proved. Having in mind that the maximum compensation allowed an attorney who is assigned to defend a first degree case is $1,000 (Rule

95 of the Superior Court [1954] and considering the financial condition of the ward, we think that the award for defending against the indictment for second degree murder should be not more than $3,000. The decree should therefore be modified as to amount to provide for a total award of $5,026.30.

* * *

NOTE 2

General Laws of Massachusetts, Chapter 123

Section 100. Commitment to State Hospitals of Persons under Indictment.—If a person under complaint or indictment for any crime is, at the time appointed for trial or sentence, or at any time prior thereto, found by the court to be insane or in such mental condition that his commitment to an institution for the insane is necessary for his proper care or observation pending the determination of his insanity, the court may commit him to a state hospital or to the Bridgewater state hospital under such limitations, . . . as it may order. The court may in its discretion employ one or more experts in insanity, or other physicians qualified as provided in section fifty-three, to examine the defendant, and all reasonable expenses incurred shall be audited and paid as in the case of other court expenses. A copy of the complaint or indictment and of the medical certificates attested by the clerk shall be delivered with such person . . .

Section 100A. Investigation of Mental Condition of Certain Persons Held for Trial: Notice; Fees; Penalty.—Whenever a person is indicted by a grand jury for a capital offense or whenever a person, who is known to have been indicted for any other offense more than once or to have been previously convicted of a felony, is indicted by a grand jury or bound over for trial in the superior court, the clerk of the court in which the indictment is returned, or the clerk of the district court, as the case may be, shall give notice to the department, which shall cause such person to be examined with a view to determine his mental condition and the existence of any mental disease or defect which would affect his criminal responsibility. . . .

Section 105. Reconveyance of Prisoners Restored to Sanity, Not Dangerously Insane, etc.—When, in the opinion of the superintendent of the state hospital to which a prisoner has been committed or removed . . . the mental condition of the prisoner is such that he should be returned to custody or to the penal institution from which he was taken, he or they shall so certify[t.] such penal institution, who shall thereupon cause the prisoner to be reconveyed to such custodian, or to such penal institution, there to remain pursuant to the original sentence if committed or removed under section one hundred and three or one hundred and four, computing the time of his detention or confinement in the said hospital as part of the term of his imprisonment under such sentence; provided, that a prisoner committed or removed to a state hospital under section one hundred, one hundred and three, or one hundred and four for his proper care or observation pending the determination of his insanity shall, unless found to be insane as hereinafter provided, be returned in the manner hereinbefore provided to the penal institution or custody whence so taken, not later than thirty-five days thereafter, but such prisoner shall in all other respects be subject to the provisions of this section. If a prisoner committed as insane under section one hundred, who has not been restored to sanity, is returned as aforesaid because in the opinion of the superintendent, or of the commissioner and said medical director, as the case may be, neither the public interest nor the welfare of the prisoner will be promoted by his further retention in the hospital, he or they shall so certify upon the warrant or commitment and shall append thereto a report relative to the prisoner's mental condition as affecting his criminal responsibility and the advis-

ability of his discharge or temporary release from the penal institution or custody to which he is returned.

If a prisoner under complaint or indictment is committed in accordance with section one hundred, and such complaint or indictment is dismissed or nol prossed, or if a prisoner is committed in accordance with sections one hundred and three or one hundred and four, and his sentence has expired, the superintendent of the institution to which commitment was made or said medical director and the commissioner, in case of commitment to the Bridgewater state hospital, as the case may be, may permit such prisoner temporarily to leave such institution in accordance with sections eighty-eight and ninety or may discharge such prisoner in accordance with section eighty-nine. The word "prisoner" as used in this section shall include all persons committed under section one hundred, whether or not in custody when so committed; and in construing this section a maximum and minimum sentence shall be held to have expired at the end of the minimum term, and an indeterminate sentence, at the end of the maximum period fixed by law.

B.

Some Guides for Decision

1.

CONCERNING INSTITUTIONS

GOFFMAN, ERVING

Characteristics of Total Institutions*

Social Establishments—institutions in the everyday sense of that term—are buildings or plants in which activity of a particular kind regularly goes on. In sociology we do not have an apt way of classifying them. Some, like Grand Central Station, are open to anyone who is decently behaved. Others, like the Union League Club of New York or the laboratories at Los Alamos, are felt to be somewhat "snippy" about the matter of whom they let in. Some institutions, like shops and post offices, are the locus of a continuous flow of service relationships. Others, like homes and factories, provide a less changing set of persons with whom the member can relate. Some institutions provide the place for what is felt to be the kind of pursuits from which the individual draws his social status, however enjoyable or lax these pursuits may be. Other institutions, in contrast, provide a home for associations in which membership is felt to

*Reprinted from: Stein, *et al*, eds, *Identity and Anxiety*, 449, (1960). Reprinted with permission of the Walter Reed Army Institute of Research, Washington, D.C.

be elective and unserious, calling for a contribution of time that is fitted in to more serious demands.

In this paper another category of institutions is recommended and claimed as a natural and fruitful one because its members appear to have so much in common—so much, in fact, that if you would learn about one of these institutions you would be well advised to look at the others. My own special purpose in examining these institutions is to find a natural frame of reference for studying the social experience of patients in mental hospitals. Whatever else psychiatry and medicine tell us, their happy way of sometimes viewing an insane asylum as if it were a treatment hospital does not help us very much in determining just what these places are and just what goes on in them.

Every institution captures something of the time and interest of its members and provides something of a world for them; in brief, every institution has encompassing tendencies. When we review the different institutions in our western society we find a class of them which seems to be encompassing to a degree discontinuously greater than the ones next in line. Their encompassing or total character is symbolized by the barrier to social intercourse with the outside that is often built right into the physical plant: locked doors, high walls, barbed wire, cliffs and water, open terrain, and so forth. These I am calling total institutions, and it is their general characteristics I want to explore. This exploration will be phrased as if securely based on findings, but will in fact be speculative.

The total institutions of our society can be listed for convenience in five rough groupings. *First*, there are institutions established to care for persons thought to be both incapable and harmless; these are the homes for the blind, the aged, the orphaned, and the indigent. *Second*, there are places established to care for persons thought to be at once incapable of looking after themselves and a threat to the community, albeit an unintended one: TB sanitoriums, mental hospitals, and leprosoriums. *Third*, another type of total institution is organized to protect the community against what are thought to be intentional dangers to it; here the welfare of the persons thus sequestered is not the immediate issue. Examples are: jails, penitentiaries, POW camps, and concentration camps. *Fourth*, we find institutions purportedly established the better to pursue some technical task and justifying themselves only on these instrumental grounds: army barracks, shops, boarding schools, work camps, colonial compounds, large mansions from the point of view of those who live in the servants' quarters, and so forth. *Finally*, there are those establishments designed as retreats from the world or as training stations for the religious: abbeys, monasteries, convents, and other cloisters. This sublisting of total institutions is neither neat nor exhaustive, but the listing itself provides an empirical starting point for a purely denotative definition of the category. By anchoring the initial definition of total institutions in this way, I hope to be able to discuss the general characteristics of the type without becoming tautological.

Before attempting to extract a general profile from this list of establishments, one conceptual peculiarity must be mentioned. None of the elements I will extract seems entirely exclusive to total institutions, and none seems shared by every one of them. What is shared and unique about total institutions is that each exhibits many items in this family of attributes to an intense degree. In speaking of "common characteristics," then, I will be using this phrase in a weakened, but I think logically defensible, way.

A basic social arrangement in modern society is that we tend to sleep, play, and work in different places, in each case with a different set of coparticipants, under a different authority, and without an overall rational plan. The central feature of total institutions can be described as a breakdown of the kinds of barriers ordinarily separating these three spheres of life. *First*, all aspects of life are conducted in the same place and under the same single authority. *Second*, each phase of the member's daily activity will be carried out in the immediate company of a large batch of others, all of whom are treated alike and required to do the same thing together. *Third*, all phases of the day's activities are tightly scheduled, with one activity leading at a prearranged time into the next, the whole circle of activities being imposed from above through a system of explicit formal rulings and a body of officials. *Finally*, the contents of the various enforced activities are brought together as parts of a single overall rational plan purportedly designed to fulfill the official aims of the institution.

* * *

The handling of many human needs by the bureaucratic organization of whole blocks of people—whether or not this is a necessary or effective means of social organization in the circumstances—can be taken, then, as the key fact of total institutions. From this, certain important implications can be drawn.

Given the fact that blocks of people are caused to move in time, it becomes possible to use a relatively small number of supervisory personnel where the central relationship is not guidance or periodic checking, as in many employer-employee relations, but rather surveillance—a seeing to it that everyone does what he has been clearly told is required of him, and this under conditions where one person's infraction is likely to stand out in relief against the visible, constantly examined, compliance of the others. Which comes first, the large block of managed people or the small supervisory staff, is not here at issue; the point is that each is made for the other.

In total institutions, as we would then suspect, there is a basic split between a large class of individuals who live in and who have restricted contact with the world outside the walls, conveniently called *inmates*, and the small class that supervises them, conveniently called *staff*, who often operate on an eight-hour day and are socially integrated into the outside world. Each grouping tends to conceive of members of the other in terms of narrow hostile stereotypes, staff often seeing inmates as bitter, secretive, and untrustworthy, while inmates often see staff as condescending, highhanded, and mean, Staff tends to feel superior and righteous; inmates tend, in some ways at least, to feel inferior, weak, blameworthy, and guilty. Social mobility between the two strata is grossly restricted; social distance is typically great and often formally prescribed; even talk across the boundaries may be conducted in a special tone of voice. These restrictions on contact presumably help to maintain the antagonistic stereotypes. In any case, two different social and cultural worlds develop, tending to jog along beside each other, with points of official contact but little mutual penetration. It is important to add that the institutional plant and name comes to be identified by both staff and inmates as somehow belonging to staff, so that when either grouping refers to the views or interests of "the institution," by implication they are referring (as I shall also) to the views and concerns of the staff.

The staff-inmate split is one major implication of the central features of total institutions; a second one pertains to work. In the ordinary arrangements of living in our society, the authority of the workplace stops with the worker's receipt of a money payment; the spending of this in a domestic and recreational setting is at the discretion of the worker and is the mechanism through which the authority of the workplace is kept within strict bounds. However, to say that inmates in total institutions have their full day scheduled for them is to say that some version of all basic needs will have to be planned for, too. In other words, total institutions take over "responsibility" for the inmate and must guarantee to have everything that is defined as essential "layed on." It follows, then, that whatever incentive is given for work, this will not have the structural significance it has on the outside. Different attitudes and incentives regarding this central feature of our life will have to prevail.

Here, then, is one basic adjustment required of those who work in total institutions and of those who must induce these people to work. In some cases, no work or little is required, and inmates, untrained often in leisurely ways of life, suffer extremes of boredom. In other cases, some work is required but is carried on at an extremely slow pace, being geared in to a system of minor, often ceremonial payments, as in the case of weekly tobacco ration and annual Christmas presents, which cause some mental patients to stay on their job. In some total institutions, such as logging camps and merchant ships, something of the usual relation to the world that money can buy is obtained through the practice of "forced saving"; all needs are organized by the institution, and payment is given only after a work season is over and the men leave the premises. And in some total institutions, of course, more than a full day's work is required and is induced not by reward, but by threat of dire punishment. In all such cases, the work-oriented individual may tend to become somewhat demoralized by the system.

In addition to the fact that total institutions are incompatible with the basic work-payment structure of our society, it must be seen that these establishments are also incompatible with another crucial element of our society, the family. The family is sometimes contrasted to solitary living, but in fact the more pertinent contrast to family life might be with batch living. For it seems that those who eat and sleep at work, with a group of fellow workers, can hardly sustain a meaningful domestic existence. Correspondingly, the extent to which a staff retains its integration in the outside community and escapes the encompassing tendencies of total institutions is often linked up with the maintenance of a family off the grounds.

Whether a particular total institution acts as a good or bad force in civil society, force it may well have, and this will depend on the suppression of a whole circle of actual or potential households. Conversely, the formation of households provides a structural guarantee that total institutions will not arise. The incompatibility between these two forms of social organization should tell us, then, something about the wider social functions of them both.

Total institutions, then, are social hybrids, part residential community, part formal organization, and therein lies their special sociological interest. There are other reasons, alas, for being interested in them, too. These establishments are the forcing houses for changing persons in our society. Each is a natural experiment, typically harsh, on what can be done to the self.

*　　*　　*

The Inmate World

It is characteristic of inmates that they come to the institution as members, already full-fledged, of a *home world*, that is, a way of life and a round of activities taken for granted up to the point of admission to the institution. It is useful to look at this culture that the recruit brings with him to the institution's door—his *presenting culture*, to modify a psychiatric phrase—in terms especially designed to highlight what it is the total institution will do to him. Whatever the stability of his personal organization, we can assume it was part of a wider supporting framework lodged in his current social environment, a round of experience that somewhat confirms a conception of self that is somewhat acceptable to him and a set of defensive maneuvers exercisable at his own discretion as a means of coping with conflicts, discreditings, and failures.

Now it appears that total institutions do not substitute their own unique culture for something already formed. We do not deal with acculturation or assimilation but with something more restricted than these. In a sense, total institutions do not look for cultural victory. They effectively create and sustain a particular kind of tension between the home world and the institutional world and use this persistent tension as strategic leverage in the management of men. The full meaning for the inmate of being "in" or "on the inside" does not exist apart from the special meaning to him of "getting out" or "getting on the outside."

The recruit comes into the institution with a self and with attachments to support which had allowed this self to survive. Upon entrance, he is immediately stripped of his wonted supports, and his self is systematically, if often unintentionally, mortified. In the accurate language of some of our oldest total institutions, he is led into a series of abasements, degradations, humiliations, and profanations of self. He begins, in other words, some radical shifts in his *moral career*, a career laying out the progressive changes that occur in the beliefs that he has concerning himself and significant others.

The *stripping processes* through which *mortification of the self* occurs are fairly standard in our total institutions. Personal identity equipment is removed, as well as other possessions with which the inmate may have identified himself, there typically being a system of nonaccessible storage from which the inmate can only reobtain his effects should he leave the institution. As a substitute for what has been taken away, institutional issue is provided, but this will be the same for large categories of inmates and will be regularly repossessed by the institution. In brief, standardized defacement will occur. In addition, ego-invested separateness from fellow inmates is significantly diminished in many areas of activity, and tasks are prescribed that are *infra dignitatem*. Family, occupational, and educational career lines are chopped off, and a stigmatized status is submitted. Sources of fantasy materials which had meant momentary releases from stress in the home world are denied. Areas of autonomous decision are eliminated through the process of collective scheduling of daily activity. Many channels of communication with the outside are restricted or closed off completely. Verbal discreditings occur in many forms as a matter of course. Expressive signs of respect for the staff are coercively and continuously demanded. And the effect of each of these conditions is multiplied by having to witness the mortification of one's fellow inmates.

We must expect to find different official reasons given for these assaults upon the self. In mental hospitals there is the matter of protecting the patient from himself and from other patients. In jails there is the issue of "security" and frank punishment. In religious institutions we may find sociologically sophisticated theories about the soul's need for purification and penance through disciplining of the flesh. What all of these rationales share is the extent to which they are merely rationalizations, for the underlying force in many cases is unwittingly generated by efforts to manage the daily activity of a large number of persons in a small space with a small expenditure of resources.

In the background of the sociological stripping process, we find a characteristic authority system with three distinctive elements, each basic to total institutions.

First, to a degree, authority is of the *echelon* kind. Any member of the staff class has certain rights to discipline any member of the inmate class. . . .

Second, the authority of corrective sanctions is directed to a great multitude of items of conduct of the kind that are constantly occurring and constantly coming up for judgment, in brief, authority is directed to matters of dress, deportment, social intercourse,

manners, and the like. In prisons these regulations regarding situational proprieties may even extend to a point where silence during mealtime is enforced, while in some convents explicit demands may be made concerning the custody of the eyes during prayer.

The third feature of authority in total institutions is that misbehaviors in one sphere of life are held against one's standing in other spheres. Thus, an individual who fails to participate with proper enthusiasm in sports may be brought to the attention of the person who determines where he will sleep and what kind of work task will be accorded to him.

When we combine these three aspects of authority in total institutions, we see that the inmate cannot easily escape from the press of judgmental officials and from the enveloping tissue of constraint. The system of authority undermines the basis for control that adults in our society expect to exert over their interpersonal environment and may produce the terror of feeling that one is being radically demoted in the age-grading system. On the outside, rules are sufficiently lax and the individual sufficiently agreeable to required self-discipline to insure that others will rarely have cause for pouncing on him. He need not constantly look over his shoulder to see if criticism and other sanctions are coming. On the inside, however, rulings are abundant, novel, and closely enforced so that, quite characteristically, inmates live with chronic anxiety about breaking the rules and chronic worry about the consequences of breaking them. The desire to "stay out of trouble" in a total institution is likely to require persistent conscious effort and may lead the inmate to abjure certain levels of sociability with his fellows in order to avoid the incidents that may occur in these circumstances.

It should be noted finally that the mortifications to be suffered by the inmate may be purposely brought home to him in an exaggerated way during the first few days after entrance, in a form of initiation that has been called *the welcome*. Both staff and fellow inmates may go out of their way to give the neophyte a clear notion of where he stands. As part of this *rite de passage*, he may find himself called by a term such as "fish," "swab," etc., through which older inmates tell him that he is not only merely an inmate but that even within this lowly group he has a low status.

While the process of mortification is in progress, the inmate begins to receive formal and informal instruction in what will here be called the *privilege system*. Insofar as the inmate's self has been unsettled a little by the stripping action of the institution, it is largely around this framework that pressures are exerted, making for a reorganization of self. Three basic elements of the system may be mentioned.

First, there are the *house rules*, a relatively explicit and formal set of prescriptions and proscriptions which lay out the main requirements of inmate conduct. These regulations spell out the austere round of life in which the inmate will operate. Thus, the admission procedures through which the recruit is initially stripped of his self-supporting context can be seen as the institution's way of getting him in the position to start living by the house rules.

Second, against the stark background, a small number of clearly defined *rewards or privileges* are held out in exchange for obedience to staff in action and spirit. It is important to see that these potential gratifications are not unique to the institution but rather are ones carved out of the flow of support that the inmate previously had quite taken for granted. On the outside, for example, the inmate was likely to be able to unthinkingly exercise autonomy by deciding how much sugar and milk he wanted in his coffee, if any, or when to light up a cigarette; on the inside, this right may become quite problematic and a matter of a great deal of conscious concern. Held up to the inmate as possibilities, these few recapturings seem to have a reintegrative effect, re-establishing relationships with the whole lost world and assuaging withdrawal symptoms from it and from one's lost self.

The inmate's run of attention, then, especially at first, comes to be fixated on these supplies and obsessed with them. In the most fanatic way, he can spend the day in devoted thoughts concerning the possibility of acquiring these gratifications or the approach of the hour at which they are scheduled to be granted. The building of a world around these minor privileges is perhaps the most important feature of inmate culture and yet is something that cannot easily be appreciated by an outsider, even one who has lived through the experience himself. This situation sometimes leads to generous sharing and almost always to a willingness to beg for things such as cigarettes, candy, and newspapers. It will be understandable, then, that a constant feature of inmate discussion is the *release binge fantasy*, namely, recitals of what one will do during leave or upon release from the institution.

House rules and privileges provide the functional requirements of the third element in the privilege system: *punishments*. These are designated as the consequence of breaking the rules. One set of these punishments consists of the temporary or permanent withdrawal of privileges or abrogation of the right to try to earn them. In general, the punishments meted out in total institutions are of an order more severe than anything encountered by the inmate in his home world. An institutional arrangement which causes a small number of easily controlled privileges to have a massive significance is the same arrangement which lends a terrible significance to their withdrawal.

There are some special features of the privilege system which should be noted.

First, punishments and privileges are themselves modes of organization peculiar to total institutions. Whatever their severity, punishments are largely known in the inmate's home world as something applied to animals and children. For adults this conditioning, behavioristic model is actually not widely applied, since failure to maintain required standards typically leads to indirect disadvantageous consequences and not to specific immediate punishment at all. And privileges, it should be emphasized, are not the same as prerequisites, indulgences, or values, but merely the absence of deprivations one ordinarily expects one would not have to sustain. The very notions, then, of punishments and privileges are not ones that are cut from civilian cloth.

Second, it is important to see that the question of release from the total institution is elaborated into the privilege system. Some acts will become known as ones that mean an increase or no decrease in length of stay, while others become known as means for lessening the sentence.

Third, we should also note that punishments and privileges come to be geared into a residential work system. Places to work and places to sleep become clearly defined as places where certain kinds and levels of privilege obtain, and inmates are shifted very rapidly and visibly from one place to another as the mechanisms for giving them the punishment or privilege their co-operativeness has warranted. The inmates are moved, the system is not.

This, then, is the privilege system: a relatively few components put together with some rational intent and clearly proclaimed to the participants. The overall consequence is that co-operativeness is obtained from persons who often have cause to be unco-operative. A typical illustration of this model universe may be taken from a recent study of a State mental hospital:

> The authority of the attendant in the person of his control system is backed up by both positive and negative power. This power is an essential element in his control of the ward. He can give the patient privileges, and he can punish the patient. The privileges consist of having the best job, better rooms and beds, minor luxuries like coffee on the ward, a little more privacy than the average patient, going outside the ward without supervision, having more access than the average patient to the attendant's companionship or to professional personnel like the physicians, and enjoying such intangible but vital things as being treated with personal kindness and respect.
>
> The punishments which can be applied by the ward attendant are suspension of all privileges, psychological mistreatment, locking up the patient in an isolated room, denial or distortion of access to the professional personnel, threatening to put or putting the patient on the list for electroshock therapy, transfer of the patient to undesirable wards, and regular assignment of the patient to unpleasant tasks such as cleaning up after the soilers.

Immediately associated with the privilege system we find some standard social processes important in the life of total institutions.

We find that an *institutional lingo* develops through which inmates express the events that are crucial in their particular world. . . .

Also found among staff and inmates will be a clear awareness of the phenomenon of *messing up*, so called in mental hospitals, prisons, and barracks. This involves a complex process of engaging in forbidden activity, getting caught doing so, and receiving something like the full punishment accorded this. . . . Informally, inmates and staff may understand, for example, that a given messing up is a way for inmates to show resentment against a current situation felt to be unjust in terms of the informal agreements between staff and inmates, or a way of postponing release without having to admit to one's fellow inmates that one really does not want to go.

In total institutions there will also be a system of what might be called *secondary adjustments*, namely, techniques which do not directly challenge staff management but which allow inmates to obtain disallowed satisfactions or allowed ones by disallowed means. These practices are variously referred to as: the angles, knowing the ropes, conniving, gimmicks, deals, ins, etc. Such adaptations apparently reach their finest flower in prisons, but of course other total institutions are overrun with them too. It seems apparent that an important aspect of secondary adjustments is that they provide the inmate with some evidence that he is still, as it were, his own man and still has come protective distance, under his own control, between himself and the institution. In some cases, then, a secondary adjustment becomes almost a kind of lodgment for the self, a churinga in which the soul is felt to reside.

The occurrence of secondary adjustments correctly allows us to assume that the inmate group will have some kind of a *code* and some means of informal social control evolved to prevent one inmate from informing staff about the secondary adjustments of another. On the same grounds we can expect that one dimension of social typing among inmates will turn upon this question of security, leading to persons defined as "squealers," "finks," or "stoolies" on one hand, and persons defined as "right guys" on the other. It should be added that where new inmates can play a role in the system of secondary adjustments, as in providing new faction members or new sexual objects, then their "welcome" may indeed be a sequence of initial indulgences and enticements, instead of exaggerated deprivations. Because of secondary adjustments we also find *kitchen strata*, namely, a kind of rudimentary, largely informal, stratification of inmates on the basis of each one's differential access to disposable illicit commodities; so also we find social typing to designate the powerful persons in the informal market system.

*   *   *

The mortifying processes that have been discussed and the privilege system represent the conditions that the inmate must adapt to in some way, but however pressing, these conditions allow for different ways of meeting them. We find, in fact, that the same inmate will employ different lines of adaptation or tacks at different phases in his moral career and may even fluctuate between different tacks at the same time.

First, there is the process of *situational withdrawal*. The inmate withdraws apparent attention from everything except events immediately around his body and sees these in a perspective not employed by others present. This drastic curtailment of involvement in interactional events is best known, of course, in mental hospitals, under the title of "regression." . . .

Second, there is the *rebellious line*. The inmate intentionally challenges the institution by flagrantly refusing to co-operate with staff in almost any way. The result is a constantly communicated intransigency and sometimes high rebel morale. Most large mental hospitals, for example, seem to have wards where this spirit strongly prevails. Interestingly enough, there are many circumstances in which sustained rejection of a total institution requires sustained orientation to its formal organization and hence, paradoxically, a deep kind of commitment to the establishment. Similarly, when total institutions take the line (as they sometimes do in the case of mental hospitals prescribing lobotomy or army barracks prescribing the stockade) that the recalcitrant inmate must be broken, then, in their way, they must show as much special devotion to the rebel as he has shown them. It should be added, finally, that while prisoners of war have been known staunchly to take a rebeillious stance throughout their incarceration, this stance is typically a temporary and initial phase of reaction, emerging from this to situational withdrawal or some other line of adaptation.

Third, another standard alignment in the institutional world takes the form of a kind of *colonization*. The sampling of the outside world provided by the establishment is taken by the inmate as the whole, and a stable, relatively contented existence is built up out of the maximum satisfactions procurable within the institution. Experience of the outside world is used as a point of reference to demonstrate the desirability of life on the inside; and the usual tension between the two worlds collapses, thwarting the social arrangements based upon this felt discrepancy. Characteristically, the individual who too obviously takes this line may be accused by his fellow inmates of "having found a home" or of "never having had it so good." Staff itself may become vaguely embarrassed by this use that is being made of the institution, sensing that the benign possibilities in the situation are somehow being misused. Colonizers themselves may feel obliged to deny their satisfaction with the institution, if only in the interest of sustaining the countermoves supporting inmate solidarity. They may find it necessary to mess up just prior to their slated discharge, thereby allowing themselves to present involuntary reasons for continued incarceration. It should be incidentally noted that any humanistic effort to make life in total institutions more bearable must face the possibility that doing so may increase the attractiveness and likelihood of colonization.

Fourth, one mode of adaptation to the setting of a total institution is that of *conversion*. The inmate appears to take over completely the official or staff view of himself and tries to act out the role of the perfect inmate. While the colonized inmate builds as much of a free community as possible for himself by using the limited facilities available, the convert takes a more disciplined, moralistic, monochromatic line, presenting himself as someone whose institutional enthusiasm is always at the disposal of the staff. In Chinese POW camps, we find Americans who became "pros" and fully espoused the Communist view of the world. In army barracks there are enlisted men who give the impression that they are always "sucking around" and always "bucking for promotion." In prison there are "square johns." In German concentration camps, longtime prisoners sometimes came to adapt the vocabulary, recreation, posture, expressions of aggression, and clothing style of the Gestapo, executing their role of straw-boss with military strictness. Some mental hospitals have the distinction of providing two quite different conversion possibilities—one for the new admission who can see the light after an appropriate struggle and adapt the psychiatric view of himself, and another for the chronic ward patient who adopts the manner and dress of attendants while helping them to manage the other ward patients with a stringency excelling that of the attendants themselves.

Here, it should be noted, is a significant way in which total institutions differ. Many, like progressive mental hospitals, merchant ships, TB sanitariums, and brainwashing camps, offer the inmate an opportunity to live up to a model of conduct that is at once ideal and staff-sponsored-anodel felt by its advocates to be in the supreme interests of the very persons to whom it is applied. Other total institutions, like some concentration camps and some prisons, do not officially sponsor an ideal that the inmate is expected to incorporate as a means of judging himself.

*   *   *

First, in the inmate group of many total institutions there is a strong feeling that time spent in the establishment is time wasted or destroyed or taken from one's life; it is time that must be written off. . . . As such, this time is something that its doers have bracketed off for constant conscious consideration in a way not quite found on the outside. And as a result, the inmate tends to feel that for the duration of his required stay—his

sentence—he has been totally exiled from living. It is in this context that we can appreciate something of the demoralizing influence of an indefinite sentence or a very long one. We should also note that however hard the conditions of life may become in total institutions, harshness alone cannot account for this quality of life wasted. Rather we must look to the social disconnections caused by entrance and to the usual failure to acquire within the institution gains that can be transferred to outside life—gains such as money earned, or marital relations formed, or certified training received.

Second, it seems that in many total institutions a peculiar kind and level of self-concern is engendered. The low position of inmates relative to their station on the outside, as established initially through the mortifying processes, seems to make for a milieu of personal failure and a round of life in which one's fall from grace is continuously pressed home. In response, the inmate tends to develop a story, a line, a sad tale—a kind of lamentation and apologia—which he constantly tells to his fellows as a means of creditably accounting for his present low estate. While staff constantly discredit these lines, inmate audiences tend to employ tact, suppressing at least some of the disbelief and boredom engendered by these recitations. In consequence, the inmate's own self may become even more of a focus for his conversation than it does on the outside.

Perhaps the high level of ruminative self-concern found among inmates in total institutions is a way of handling the sense of wasted time that prevails in these places. . . .

*   *   *

In this discussion of the inmate world, I have commented on the mortification processes, the reorganizing influences, the lines of response taken by inmates under these circumstances, and the cultural milieu that develops. A concluding word must be added about the long-range consequences of membership.

Total institutions frequently claim to be concerned with rehabilitation, that is, with resetting the inmate's self-regulatory mechanisms so that he will maintain the standards of the establishment of his own accord after he leaves the setting. In fact, it seems this claim is seldom realized and even when permanent alteration occurs, these changes are often not of the kind intended by the staff. . . .

But what the ex-inmate does retain of his institutional experience tells us important things about total institutions. Often entrance will mean for the recruit that he has taken on what might be called a *proactive status*. Not only is his relative social position within the walls radically different from what it was on the outside, but, as he comes to learn, if and when he gets out, his social position on the outside will never again be quite what it was prior to entrance. Where the proactive status is a relatively favorable one, as it is for those who graduate from officers' training schools, elite boarding schools, ranking monasteries, etc., then the permanent alteration will be favorable, and jubilant official reunions announcing pride in one's "school" can be expected. When, as seems usually the case, the proactive status is unfavorable, as it is for those in prisons or mental hospitals, we popularly employ the term "stigmatization" and expect that the ex-inmate may make an effort to conceal his past and try to "pass."

The Staff World

Most total institutions, most of the time, seem to function merely as storage dumps for inmates, but as previously suggested, they usually present themselves to the public as rational organizations designed consciously, through and through, as effective machines for producing a few officially avowed and officially approved ends. It was also suggested that one frequent official objective is the reformation of inmates in the direction of some ideal standard. This contradiction, then, between what the institution does and what its officials must say that it does, forms the central context of the staff's daily activity.

Within this context, perhaps the first thing to say about staff is that their work, and hence their world, has uniquely to do with people. This people-work is not quite like personnel work nor the work of those involved in service relationships. Staffs, after all, have objects and products to work upon, not relationships, but these objects and products are people.

As material upon which to work, people involve some of the considerations characteristic of inanimate objects. Just as an article being processed through an industrial plant must be followed by a paper shadow showing what has been done by whom, what is to be done, and who last had responsibility for it, so human objects moving, say, through a mental hospital system must be followed by a chain of informative receipts detailing what has been done to and by the patient and who has most recent responsibility for him. In his career from admission suite to burial plot, many different kinds of staff will add their official note to his case file as he temporarily passes under their jurisdiction, and long after he has died physically his marked remains will survive as an actionable entity in the hospital's bureaucratic system. Even the presence or absence of a particular patient at a given meal or for a given night may have to be recorded so that cost-accounting can be maintained and appropriate adjustments rendered in billing.

Other similarities between people-work and object-work are obvious. Just as tin mines or paint factories or chemical plants may involve special work hazards for employees, so (staffs believe at least) there are special dangers to some kinds of people-work. In mental hospitals, staffs believe that patients may strike out "for no reason" and injure an official. In army prisons, staff "is ever haunted by the spectre of riot, revolt or mutiny. . . ." In TB sanitariums and in leprosoriums, staff feel they are being specially exposed to dangerous diseases.

While these similarties between people—and object—work exist, it is, I think, the unique aspects of people as material to work upon that we must look to for the crucial determinants of the work-world of staff.

Given the physiological characteristics of the human organism, it is obvious that certain requirements must be met if any continued use is to be made of people. But this, of course, is the case with inanimate objects, too; the temperature of any storehouse must be regulated regardless of whether people or things are stored. However, persons are almost always considered to be ends in themselves, as reflected in the broad moral principles of a total institution's environing society. Almost always, then, we find that some technically unnecessary standards of handling must be maintained with human materials. This maintenance of what we call humane standards comes to be defined as one part of the "responsibility" of the institution and presumably is one of the things the institution guarantees the inmate in exchange for his liberty. Thus, prison officials are obliged to thwart suicidal efforts of the prisoner and to give him full medical attention even though in some cases this may require postponement of his date of execution. Something similar has been reported in German concentration camps, where inmates were sometimes given medical attention to tidy them up into a healthier shape for the gas chamber.

A second special contingency in the work-world of staff is the fact that inmates typically have statuses and relationships in the outside world that must be taken into consideration. (This consideration, of course, is related to the previously mentioned fact that the institution must respect some of the rights of inmates *qua* persons.) Even in the case of the committed mental patient whose civil rights are largely taken from him, a tremendous amount of mere paper work will be involved. Of course, the rights that are denied a mental patient are usually transferred to a relation, to a committee, or to the superintendent of the hospital itself, who then becomes the legal person whose authorization must be obtained for many matters. Many issues originating outside the institution will arise: Social Security benefits, income taxes, upkeep of properties, insurance payments, old age pension, stock dividends, dental bills, legal obligations incurred prior to commitment, permission to release psychiatric case records to insurance companies or attorneys, permission for special visits from persons other than next of kin, etc. All of these issues have to be dealt with by the institution, even if only to pass the decisions on to those legally empowered to make them.

It should be noted that staff is reminded of its obligations in these matters of standards and rights, not only by its own internal superordinates, by various watchdog agencies in the wider society, and by the material itself, but also by persons on the outside who have kin ties to inmates. The latter group presents a special problem because, while inmates can be educated about the price they will pay for making demands on their own behalf, relations receive less tutoring in this regard and rush in with requests for inmates that inmates would blush to make for themselves.

The multiplicity of ways in which inmates must be considered ends in themselves and the multiplicity of inmates themselves forces upon staff some of the classic dilemmas that must be faced by those who govern men. Since a total institution functions somewhat as a State, its staff must suffer somewhat from the tribulations that beset governors.

In the case of any single inmate, the assurance that certain standards will be maintained in his own interests may require sacrifice of other standards, and implied in this is a difficult weighing of ends. For example, if a suicidal inmate is to be kept alive, staff may feel it necessary to keep him under constant deprivatizing surveillance or even tied to a chair in a small locked room. If a mental patient is to be kept from tearing at grossly irritated sores and repeating time and again a cycle of curing and disorder, staff may feel it necessary to curtail the freedom of his hands. Another patient who refuses to eat may have to be humiliated by forced feeding. If inmates of TB sanitariums are to be given an opportunity to recover, it will be necessary to curtail freedom of recreation.

The standard of treatment that one inmate has a right to expect may conflict, of course, with the standards desired by another, giving rise to another set of governmental problems. Thus, in mental hospitals, if the grounds gate is to be kept open out of respect for those with town parole, then some other patients who otherwise could have been trusted on the grounds may have to be kept on locked wards. And if a canteen and mailbox are to be freely available to those on the grounds, then patients on a strict diet or those who write threatening and obscene letters will have to be denied liberty on the grounds.

The obligation of staff to maintain certain humane standards of treatment for inmates represents problems in itself, as suggested above, but a further set of characteristic problems is found in the constant conflict between humane standards on one hand and institutional efficiency on the other. I will cite only one main example. The personal possessions of an individual are an important part of the materials out of which he builds a self, but as an inmate, the ease with which he can be managed by staff is likely to increase with the degree to which he is dispossessed. Thus, the remarkable efficiency with which a mental hospital ward can adjust to a daily shift in number of resident patients is related to the fact that the comers and leavers do not come or leave with any properties but themselves and do not have any right to choose where they will be located. Further, the efficiency with which the clothes of these patients can be kept clean and fresh is related to the fact that everyone's soiled clothing can be indiscriminately placed in one bundle, and laundered clothing can be redistributed not according to ownership but according to rough size. Similarly, the quickest assurance that patients going on the grounds will be warmly dressed is to march them in file past a pile of the ward's allotment of coats, requiring them for the same purposes of health to throw off these collectivized garments on returning to the ward.

Just as personal possessions may interfere with the smooth running of an institutional operation and be removed for this reason, so parts of the body itself may conflict with efficient management and the conflict resolved in favor of efficiency. If the heads of inmates are to be kept clean and the possessor easily identified, then a complete head shave is efficacious, regardless of the damage this does to appearance. On similar grounds, some mental hospitals have found it useful to extract the teeth of "biters," give hysterectomies to promiscuous female patients, and perform lobotomies on chronic fighters. . . .

*   *   *

While human materials can never be as refractory as inanimate ones, their very capacity to perceive and to follow out the plans of staff insures that they can hinder the staff more effectively than inanimate objects can. Inanimate objects cannot purposely and intelligently thwart our plans, regardless of the fact that we may momentarily react to them as if they had this capacity. Hence, in prison and on "better" wards of mental hospitals, guards have to be ready for organized efforts at escape and must constantly deal with attempts to bait them, "frame" them, and otherwise get them into trouble. This leads to a state of anxiety in the guard that is not alleviated by knowledge that the inmate may be acting thus merely as a means of gaining self-respect or relieving boredom. Even an old, weak, mental patient has tremendous power in this regard; for example, by the simple expedient of locking his thumbs in his trouser pockets he can remarkably frustrate the efforts of an attendant to undress him.

A third general way in which human materials are different from other kinds and hence present unique problems is that, however distant staff manages to stay from them, they can become objects of fellow-feeling and even affection. Always there is the danger that an inmate will appear human. If what are felt to be hardships must be inflicted on the inmate, then sympathetic staff will suffer. And on the other hand, if an inmate breaks a rule, staff's conceiving of him as a human being may increase their sense that injury has been done to their moral world. Expecting a "reasonable" response from a reasonable creature, staff may feel incensed, affronted, and challenged when this does not occur. Staff thus finds it must maintain face not only before those who examine the product of work but before these very products themselves.

*   *   *

When we combine together the fact that staff is obliged to maintain certain standards of humane treatment for inmates and may come to view inmates as reasonable, responsible creatures who are fitting objects for emotional involvement, we have the background for some of the quite special difficulties of people-work. In mental hospitals, for example, there always seem to be some patients who dramatically act against their own obvious self-interest. They drink water they have themselves first polluted; they rush against the wall with their heads; they tear out their own sutures after a minor operation; they flush false teeth down the toilet, without which they cannot eat and which take months to obtain; or smash glasses, without which they cannot see. In an effort to frustrate these visible self-destructive acts, staff may find itself forced to manhandle these patients. Staff then is forced to create an image of itself as harsh and coercive, just at the moment that it is attempting to prevent someone from doing to himself what no human being is expected to do to anyone. At such times it is extremely difficult for staff members to keep their own emotions in control, and understandably so.

*   *   *

NOTES

NOTE 1

COMMITTEE OF PATIENTS AND STAFF

A Description of the Yale Psychiatric Institute*

The Yale Psychiatric Institute is a 46-bed intensive treatment hospital staffed by faculty and selected advanced resident psychiatrists of the University's Department of Psychiatry. Each patient's treatment program includes individual and group psychotherapy with the resident staff and participation in a closely structured therapeutic milieu. There are both open and locked ward facilities for men and women. Because of the hospital's intensive emphasis, there tends to be a large proportion of patients in teens and twenties.

Treatment

The treatment program may be divided into two parts: (a) Intensive psychotherapy: and (b) the Therapeutic Community.

---

*Reprinted with permission.

A. Each patient participates in individual psychotherapy for about three hours per week, and in group therapy for two hours.

B. The Therapeutic Community, as practiced at Yale, involves:

1. The concept of patients and staff forming a community united in the common goal of helping all patients overcome their emotional problems.
2. The open discussion of any problems which affect the community as a whole.
3. The concept that patients have a responsibility to each other and are largely responsible for the atmosphere that will prevail on the wards.
4. The encouraging of patient participation in the running of the hospital, including the acceptance of many patient-originated ideas, a Patient-Staff Advisory Committee which makes recommendations to the staff, Patient-Government, an Activities Committee to plan recreational activities, and a Refreshment Committee which buys and prepares special refreshments.
5. A tendency toward greater openness on the staff's part in explaining reasons for decisions and how they come about, including frank admission that staff members often disagree, and that the concept of a single, one-minded staff is inaccurate.
6. An attempt to remove from the staff as much as possible the necessity of "policing," leaving them free to concentrate on constructive help, with patients exerting a measure of social control to prevent destructive behavior.
7. A general awareness that all relations and situations that exist within the community affect its members, so that efforts are made to maximize the beneficial aspects of all parts of hospital life.

C. In addition, tranquilizing drugs are sometimes used, particularly early in treatment.

D. A program of activities, athletics, OT, music instruction, education and work is available according to the needs of the individual patient.

E. All patients of high school age who do not attend local schools are expected to attend the Cedarhurst high school classes held within the hospital. This school is run and accredited by the New Haven School system. The purpose of this program is to permit the student to continue his studies in a normal classroom environment.

F. Ward rounds are made every week by the Medical Director, the Assistant Medical Director, and the Chief Resident.

Patient-Staff Meeting

One of the most important developments in this hospital is the Patient-Staff Meeting, begun in September, 1956. It meets for one hour three times a week and is attended by the entire patient and staff population—patients, senior and resident doctors, nurses, social workers, psychologists, student nurses, aides, and occupational therapist. Relatives sometimes visit. Anyone at the meeting may bring up whatever he wishes, making for a wide range of topics discussed. Some examples of subjects which come up are:

A. Open and realistic discussion of a patient's and staff's action, how they affect others (both patients and staff), an attempt to understand them, and, when necessary, recommendations for dealing with them.

B. Attitudes of patients and staff toward each other.

*   *   *

The guiding principle of these meetings is that each individual's behavior affects and is affected by every other member of the hospital community so that all bear the responsibility of voicing their opinions. The attitude that discussion of a specific individual would indicate lack of friendship or betrayal of confidence is discouraged. An opportunity is given to everyone to talk about issues that concern him. Differences of opinion among staff members are frequently expressed.

The purpose of the meeting is to promote discussion among all members of the community, both patients and staff, of all decisions, issues, grievances and behavior which affect the group. Although Patient-Staff Meetings are impossible to define and many meetings have periods of silence and leave the participants disappointed, the general helpfulness of the meeting is widely felt.

Patient Government

Patient Government is the meeting at which patients transact business and elect committees. It is attended by all patients; also present in an advisory capacity are the social group worker, a nurse, and at times the doctor on call. Chairman and secretary are elected for four weeks and conduct the meetings according to parliamentary rules. The business, rather than therapeutic, nature of the meeting is stressed. Typical topics include: maintenance items, purchasing equipment, ward management problems, reports of Activities and Advisory committees and specialing.

Patient-Staff Advisory

Patient-Staff Advisory Committee is composed of six patients elected for staggered terms of three months each; plus the secretary or chairman of Patient Government, the Chief Resident, two chief nurses, and the Social Group Workers, meeting for one hour twice a week. That patients take this committee seriously is seen in the consistent election of the better integrated patients for these positions.

The committee was formed because it was felt that patients living together had an understanding of one another which could be usefully shared with the staff. By doing this, the patients share the responsibility of making decisions with the staff.

This committee makes frequent recommendations on room and floor assignments and brings to the staff's attention potential difficulties, and speaks with other patients who present problem behavior, when the patient contact is felt to be more beneficial.

When the occasion arises, the committee is called into an emergency meeting to deal with sudden ward disturbances which necessitate immediate action.

Minutes of the meetings are read in Patient-Staff Meetings, posted on bulletin boards and given to the Social Group Worker and Chief Resident.

Adult Education and Cedarhurst High School representatives are appointed from the advisory membership to report to advisory; attendance, behavioral problems, etc. The committee assumes responsibility for enforcing regular attendance and seeks to deal with these behavioral problems.

Furthermore, there is a sponsorship representative appointed to oversee the program which assists in orienting new patients to the hospital.

Activities

Patients participate in the planning and conducting of the program. The activities committee of six patients elected for staggered terms of eight weeks meets weekly with the Social Group Worker and Assistant Activities Worker to plan the program. Patients are encouraged to develop leadership, potential, and to demonstrate ability in their activities.

Each floor is equipped with a music room containing a piano, two lounges, and a dining room in which activities are held. Patients have access to a tennis court and squash courts and a very small gymnasium. There is also a small terrace. Among the handicaps of being in a city is the limitation of space—there is no single indoor recreation area, nor any grounds. On the other hand, we take advantage of the facilities of the community—the many Yale University facilities, YMCA, etc.

Some of the planned activities are:

A. *In-Hospital:* Social dancing, cooking, volleyball, talent shows, folk and square dances, Monte Carlo nights, barbecues, tournaments (ping pong, checkers, pool, etc.).

B. *Community:* Theater, concerts, movies, swimming (at Yale and public beach), picnics, bowling, skating, and softball, and trips to places of interest such as New York City and Mystic.

The following activities are of a regular nature and do not require weekly planning:

A. Movie in the hospital (weekly).

B. Calisthenics.

C. Adult Education Program. This presently consists of two classes History and World Politics, each of which meets for one hour a week and is taught by members of the Yale University faculty. Other courses, from which the patient community selects twice a year, are available. This program is administered by the hospital, which employs instructors from the university faculty. This means that these courses are not part of the Yale University curriculum. In addition, there are special courses available for those desiring lessons in introductory electronics, stenography, and typing.

All patients except those excused by the Advisory Committee are required to take at least one course and may take more. The classes are conducted along the lines of a seminar with participation encouraged. Readings and preparation are necessary in some courses. In a hospital where so many patients are of student age the opportunity to add to one's education in an informal situation with few of the usual school stresses has proved most valuable and has contributed to several patients' interest in resuming studies on the outside.

D. Many patients from both floors resume their studies in the high schools and universities of the area while they are still full-time in-patients; a variety of volunteer jobs are available in the general hospital across the street; and some remunerative work within the university and in the community is often available for the patient who is ready to undertake it. This includes patients from the locked floor and most of the patients from the open floor.

E. Music and drama instruction: A music instructor is available for individual sessions with interested beginners and experienced musicians in piano; instrumental and vocal accompaniment is also available. A drama instructor is available for any interested group.

F. Occupational Therapy: The OT shop at the Institute is an integral part of the therapeutic community. Staffed by a registered occupational therapist, an OT aide, and three special teachers, the shop is open approximately twenty hours a week. Crafts and arts predominate, but individual hobbies are also encouraged. An atmosphere of freedom and creativeness prevails, and for many patients the OT shop is simply a place to sit, relax, and socialize.

Attendance at the shop is not compulsory except in rare instances where the doctor feels active participation therapeutic. The time spent there depends on individual schedules. Many patients attend for the full twenty hours each week.

Patients are not charged for use of materials, with the exception of such crafts as copper-enameling. Encouragement is given to patients with special interests.

*   *   *

A yearly Art Show is held by the OT shop in which both staff and patients participate. This includes a tea prepared by the patients, as well as getting the material together and arranging the exhibits. Weather permitting, this show is held on the first floor terrace.

Group Therapy

Shortly after admission each patient is included in a therapy group. An attempt is made to balance groups in relation to the number of male and female members, proportion to the communicative and non-communicative patients, etc. Groups, numbering about six patients, meet twice weekly with a therapist. (At times a nurse and/or a social worker is a co-therapist.) Attendance is mandatory. Patients do not have the same resident in both individual therapy and group. All residents meet once a week under the supervision of the Assistant Medical Director to discuss problems and progress in their respective groups.

The following is a presentation of some of the problems involved in group therapy, as seen by one patient:

"It is hoped that patients will discuss problems common to members of the group, using their own experience and understanding to help one another with their difficulties; this type of interaction, however, does not originate spontaneously when a group is formed or a new member is added. A great deal of co-operation is necessary and is only gradually developed.

"On the one hand, there is sometimes benefit from interacting on the most obviously inoffensive of topics. At other times it helps the patient's understanding when he hears another's interpretation of real problems. Some group members seem to find that the way they interact in 'group' is the way they interact on a larger scale. Others discover that group makes interaction easier than in larger groups. Behavior not purposely 'anti-social' (e.g.), but subtly disturbing, is sometimes discussed and contributes to patients realizing how they affect and are affected by others.

"On the other hand, the ideals of the group therapy are seldom attained. Several factors seem to inhibit open discussion of vital problems. Often these factors are exploited by group members and used as convenient rationalization to avoid facing basic problems of social anxiety. Perhaps most valid, fear of social ostracism and ridicule is always present. Yale Psychiatric Institute is a small closed society whose members must live in almost constant contact with one another. Under these circumstances it often seems more important than ever to maintain the respectable facade of normalcy. Topics such as personal sexual problems and psychosomatic symptoms are rarely discussed. Excessive teasing, rudeness, physical isolation, widely diffused anger, and other overtly disturbing ward behavior are convenient subjects, and, despite their often evasive quality, sometimes their consideration leads to improvement on the part of the 'accused.' Speculation about length of hospitalization, recollection of 'flipped-out' behavior, tale-telling, and patients and people outside the group, are generally regarded as inoffensive topics.

"Various other reasons limiting depth of group conversation are suggested by patients. Yale Psychiatric Institute treats diverse types of mental illnesses, many of which are characterized by extreme lack of verbal ability. The existence of non-verbal members in a group often provides other patients with an excuse for reluctance to communicate.

"Fear of loss of privileges is quoted as a reason for lack of frankness and expression of sincere feeling.

"Yale Psychiatric Institute offers its patients frequent sessions of intensive individual therapy. Patients, therefore, can rationalize that psychic and verbal energy are expended and diffused in private therapy. Consequently, it can be claimed that there is very little left for group. Staff observation seems to contradict this view. Generally, patients who 'do well' and produce in private therapy tend to do the same in group.

"Because of the extremely potent quality of such inhibiting factors, the group therapist at the outset often indicates to the patients that these problems must be explored and, if possible, overcome. If problems of social criticism, fear of restriction, etc., are not worked through, patients and therapists can sometimes expect lengthy discussions of trivia and escape topics."

Staff Meetings

There are two meetings a week attended by doctors, nurses, social workers, the social group worker, psychologist, and aides; here there is an exchange of information and a give and take between staff members. Staff decisions are arrived at without the need of voting.

On Monday and Friday right after the Patient-Staff meeting, the staff meets to examine and learn from what took place during the Patient-Staff meeting.

Nurses have meetings with the doctors and with the nursing director and assistant nursing director.

The residents meet twice a week with the Chief-Resident, have seminars and case presentations, and discuss their therapies with supervising psychiatrists. The Medical Director and Assistant Medical Director meet with each resident, the Nursing Director, and the Chief Social Worker.

The aides meet for two hours with the Chief Resident once a week: the first hour is a Seminar within the curriculum of the Divinity School; the second hour the aides meet with the Social Group Worker and a nurse to discuss interactions with patients, ward issues, and hospital routines.

The social workers meet individually once a week with the Chief Social Worker to discuss their contacts with the patients' families and the patients. In addition, social workers meet with the patients' therapist.

Case Presentation

Each patient, about six weeks after admission, meets with the Staff to evaluate his or her treatment plans.

Roles in the Hospital Community

A. *Patients:* The hospital accepts a wide variety of patients, including neurotics, psychotics, character disorders, alcoholics, etc.; mildly disturbed as well as acutely disturbed and suicidal patients. (While diagnostic labels are not used within the hospital, they may be useful in this context.) Patients come from fairly high socio-economic groups, and most are of student age.

B. *Doctors:* Most of the individual therapy is conducted by six second and third year residents supervised by senior doctors; residents act as administrators for those patients who have outside doctors. In addition, there are a Chief Resident and an Assistant Director. The Director is Doctor Daniel Schwartz and the Assistant Director is Doctor David Carlson.

Outside Doctors: A number of Patients at Yale Psychiatric Institute have therapists other than residents, including psychiatrists practicing in the community who are selected by the staff. These patients are assigned administrators who are residents on the staff. The administrator, who has an opportunity to attend staff meetings and is in a position to observe his patients in the hospital environment, sees the patient briefly two or three times a week. He deals with the patient only within the area of hospital matters, e.g., visiting privileges, medication, work or school, etc.

Communication between therapist and administrator is often extremely limited, with each working independently of the other. Clear definition of the distinction between therapist's and administrator's roles, plus the outside doctors' familiarity with the hospital's way of operating, tend to minimize the friction between the two groups. In some cases, the administrator also acts as the patient's caseworker and sees the family once a week.

The Director and Assistant Director, and at times the clinical psychologist, may act as therapists, and because they do not have an opportunity of attending all staff meetings, an administrator is assigned for their patients.

An outside doctor is sometimes selected where it is anticipated that a patient will leave the hospital in the foreseeable future and will settle in the immediate vicinity. The purpose of this is that it is felt that an easier transition is made possible at the time of the patient's leaving the hospital.

C. *Nurses and Ward Personnel:* There are 15 registered nurses in addition to the Nursing Director and Assistant Nursing Director, providing a 3:1

patient-nurse ratio. Many of the nurses have considerable experience while positions are held open each year for qualified nurses, inexperienced in this work, who are interested in receiving in-service training.

The role of the nurse is very important, especially on the locked floor. Their main function is to help the patients in their social interaction and to provide a stable personal contact, giving control, support, or sympathy according to the needs of the patient, with special attention to isolated or withdrawn patients. Uniforms today are optional.

Approximately two student nurses each month add an important influence to the wards, being closer to the ages of most of the patients.

An important addition is the use of 15 students from the Yale Divinity School as aides, the School giving them field-work credit. This is the equivalent of an additional eight full-time personnel, of a caliber usually out of reach of any hospital. In addition, there are three part-time male attendants trained at the Veteran's Hospital.

D. *Social Service:* The hospital maintains contact with each patient's family, usually through a Psychiatric Case Worker, but sometimes through an administrative doctor. Contact between therapist and the family is purposely limited. The social worker:

1. Learns pertinent facts concerning the family situation.
2. Helps the family understand the meaning of the patient's hospitalization.
3. Often helps the family members with their own problems in order to improve the environment to which the patient will some day return.
4. Family groups conducted by social workers are available for families living near the hospital. They facilitate family understanding of their own as well as the patients' problems.

Social workers usually arrange regular appointments with the relatives.

There is a full-time Social Group Worker with a part-time assistant, advising in the activities program.

E. *Psychologists:* The psychology section consists of three staff and one or two advanced student psychologists. While their major function in the hospital (they have additional teaching and research duties) is to administer psychological tests to all patients and interpret them to the staff, psychologists are involved in other functions. They attend patient-staff meetings; and one of them is a co-therapist in a group.

* * *

Security Measures

Security measures are necessary for the safety and reassurance of certain patients. Close observation of the patient is felt to be more effective than making lists of objects which patients may not have; and

nurses and doctors rely more on their own judgment than on specific rules. Nurses and aides check to see what each patient is doing every fifteen minutes on the locked ward and every half hour on the open ward, and verbal communication is made every ten minutes with patients in seclusion. Patients and Staff members each take their turn to accompany another patient on the locked floor when he is acutely disturbed.

Acutely disturbed and suicidal patients are sometimes confined to a seclusion area; but an attempt is made to keep such patients active on the ward by providing constant accompaniment by another patient or by a staff member. This is called "specialing."

On occasion, patient conduct necessitates the separation of the male and female wards on the locked floor.

While the degree of responsibility assumed by the patients fluctuates greatly, the following are examples of responsibility assumed:

A. Patients give the staff information they have about potential destructive behavior, e.g., suicide attempts, possession of matches, potential run-aways; and the staff advises patients concerning patients needing closer attention. The stigma of "tattling" has largely been overcome.

B. Patients frequently intercede to prevent destructive behavior until a staff member can arrive, and keep an eye on patients who are not feeling well.

C. Disturbed patients are often dissuaded by their fellows from acting out, and escapees are at times brought back by other patients.

D. Patient Advisory Committee holds emergency meetings to deal with ward problems and assigns members to help patients overcome anti-social behavior.

E. Ward meetings are frequently held on the initiative of patients.

F. Patients frequently take responsibility for each other when going outside the hospital, obviating the need for staff accompaniment.

In addition, frequent explanations of the need for locks, locked razors, and the prohibitions of carrying matches, as protecting the few who might get hurt, tend to mitigate patients' resentment toward these measures.

* * *

"Privileges" and Restrictions

The new patient entering the locked ward at times may not be permitted visitors or use of the phone; his outgoing mail at times may be read by his doctor, and he may not leave the floor. As the doctor gets to know him, he receives those responsibilities or "privileges" which seem to the doctor to be indicated. Because of the intensive treatment used here, the staff proceeds more slowly and cautiously than may be the case in shorter term hospitals; and there is tremendous variation in the speed at which patients are given responsibilities. Responsibilities often given include:

A. Individual accompaniment by a staff member.

B. Accompaniment in a group of patients by a staff member.

C. Staying with other patient(s) without any staff member.

D. Completely unaccompanied.

These privileges apply both to visiting the unlocked ward and to going out of the hospital; these are given in no set order but according to how helpful they may be and are irrespective of the patient's being on a locked or unlocked ward; and can be altered in a wide variety of ways to fit individual needs. Well-defined limits are often more helpful to a patient than excessive permissiveness, and, when needed, four seclusion rooms are available for agitated patients for their own well-being as well as for that of the Hospital.

While "privileges" and restrictions are not viewed by the staff as rewards and punishments, patients sometimes see them that way. Restrictions are sometimes used for disciplinary purposes, e.g., to assure attendance at the compulsory activities of calisthenics, Adult Education, and Cedarhurst (high school).

While the use of rules merely as guideposts leads to some irritation when different nurses apply them differently, the great degree of flexibility and discretionary powers available allow patients to get really individualized care.

* * *

NOTE 2

BLOOMBERG, W.

A Proposal for a Community-based Hospital as a Branch of a State Hospital*

On any given day there are, in the publicly supported hospitals for mental diseases of this country, between 600,000 and 700,000 patients. An enormous number of these patients have been hospitalized for many years. There is repetitive evidence that once a patient has remained in a large mental hospital for two years or more, he is quite unlikely to leave except by death. He becomes one of the large mass of so-called "chronic" patients.

If one believes, as I do, that this "chronicity" in mental illness is a reflection, not of the nature of the disease, but of the attitudes of family and community, and later, of the structure of the hospital and the methods by which we are for such patients, one is confronted with a problem which many of us as psychiatrists have refused to face realistically. . . .

*116 *American Journal of Psychiatry* 814–817, (1960). Reprinted by permission.

[W]e are unrealistic in our approach to this problem because we have not given sufficient thought to the next 600,000 patients who will be admitted to our hospitals. We cannot, of course, ignore our responsibility for the care and the treatment, so far as we know how to administer it, of the patients we already have. I suggest that we have an even greater responsibility to the patients who will be coming to us in the next few years to use all the knowledge that we already have to prevent them from becoming a second group of "chronic" patients numbering 600,000 to 700,000.

Even as psychiatrists we have suffered from the limitation of tradition. We were so convinced that schizophrenia is a long-term chronic illness that when we began to see, during the war, large numbers of acute schizophrenics evacuated from theaters of operations and apparently recovered by the time they reached the zone of the interior, we decided they were not really "schizophrenia." Instead of realizing that this, too, might be schizophrenia, seen in an acute phase because patients were under observation early, were exposed to exaggerated stresses, and could not be carried along for many months by indulgent families, we decided that this must be a different kind of disease because it wasn't chronic. We refused to draw conclusions about schizophrenia as a disease from the things that we were seeing.

It has been shown over and over again, in many different and disparate places, that with proper staffing and proper facilities, 85 and even 90 per cent of first admissions for mental illness can be returned to their homes and their communities in 4 to 6 months. As a matter of fact, when we look at the situation clearly in the light of our overall medical knowledge, we should be proud, as psychiatrists, to be able to point out that of all the so-called long-term chronic illnesses, the mental diseases seem to be the most reversible. Our internist colleagues have not yet discovered how to replace the damaged kidney cells in a chronic nephritis, or the damaged liver cells in a cirrhosis of the liver. They are quite content with their accomplishments if they can, by drugs, keep a hypertension down within certain clinical limits and have not yet told us how to reverse whatever process that it is that causes hypertension. Physicians have even been content, in recent years, to produce symptomatic relief of hypertension by carrying out enormously extensive operations on the sympathetic nervous system. No surgeon I know believes that he can cure *all* patients with cancer.

Yet, for many of our psychotic patients, within a comparatively short time, an adequate and at least apparent complete reversal to normality can be obtained. I think we must concentrate more of our efforts, therefore, on these problems of the acute psychosis at a time when it has still all the likelihood of reversibility and before any of our iatrogenic operations force it into the mode of "chronicity."

Our typical public mental hospitals are over large, their social standards are artificial and total, they are isolated, they perpetuate ostracism of patients and personnel. I submit that we need to get our hospitals back to the communities from which the patients derive. A hospital built in the community would be more like a general hospital in the attitude of the community toward it. It seems to me we must begin to recognize that hospitalization for mental illness is only part of the total range of services which we can offer to our patients. In the average physical illness a patient sees his family physician in his office or if he is too ill to get out of bed, the family physician comes to his home. Treatment is started ordinarily either at home or in office visits. Early diagnostic and laboratory tests are carried out on this basis. It is only when the tests become too complex or when the illness of the patient becomes too severe that hospitalization is made use of. And clearly, in this instance, hospitalization is for as brief a period as is necessary to accomplish the elimination of the specific factors which require it; and not for definitive treatment of the disease. As soon as the need for bed care and specialized nursing techniques or the need to carry out special laboratory procedures which can only be done in a hospital is over, the patient is again returned to his home and the treatment is continued at home or in the doctor's office on the basis of the information gained during the brief hospitalization.

I submit that we must begin to treat our mentally ill patients in the same way. Because the State has for so long a time accepted the responsibility for the care of the mentally ill, it is probable that most such patients will be treated in out-patient departments of state hospitals rather than in private psychiatrists' offices. Then, too, as we all know, there are an insufficient number of private psychiatrists for the need. However, whether in an out-patient department of a state hospital or under the care of a private psychiatrist, the situation should obtain that treatment can be started and diagnosis established insofar as possible without hospitalization until such time as a brief hospitalization becomes necessary. This hospitalization should be merely an incident in the overall care of the patient, and should be available to the patient whether the physician carrying out the out-patient treatment is a state employee or a private psychiatrist. On release from a hospital the patient should go back, either to the out-patient department or to his private physician or psychiatrist.

Because of the nature of psychiatric treatment with its need to manipulate the patient's total activities rather than just to see him briefly to prescribe a pill or even for a somewhat longer period for a session of intensive psychotherapy the logical development for the mental hospital after the out-patient department is the day care center. Only when a patient is unable to be handled on an out-patient level plus a day care level, should 24-hour hospitalization be sought.

All of these things can take place much more effectively if isolation of the patient can be avoided and he can be treated in the community in which he lives. Day care becomes easier if the patient does not need to be transported 14 to 40 miles from his home to the hospital every morning and then brought back every night. Families can visit patients when they are hospitalized in a community-based hospital, clergymen can keep track of their flocks, local family doctors can follow their psychiatrically ill patients just as they follow their medically or surgically ill patients who are admitted to a hospital. One of the not inconsiderable gains. I think, of this technique might well be that a family would find it harder to change the family constellation and close up the space left by the hospitalization of one member of it if that hospitalization occurred in the community and the family was visiting frequently. We are all aware of how often the remaining family closes ranks after a patient is hospitalized at a distant place in a state hospital; and even when he is ready for discharge there is no longer any place for him in the family constellation. . . . [I]t appears that 40 per cent at least, of patients who have been hospitalized in state hospitals two years or longer never have a visit from a member of the family.

*   *   *

NOTE 3

KNIGHT, ROBERT P.

Management and Psychotherapy of the Borderline Patient*

*   *   *

One primary purpose of the comprehensive evaluation of the patient's total ego functioning is to determine whether or not he can be treated in an office, the alternative being usually regarded as referral to a psychiatric hospital, with the implications of confinement on a closed ward, possible commitment, and associated feelings in the patient and family of stigma. This is an unfortunate alternative for the borderline schizophrenic patient. He usually needs more organized support between treatment hours than living at home provides, but a closed hospital may, in attempting to provide complete support, actually accomplish the opposite. It is not so much that his experiences with sicker patients will be antitherapeutic for him, although this does happen occasionally. It is more that external controls are forced upon him as a substitute for his own inner controls, that

*Reprinted with permission from the *Bulletin of the Menninger Clinic*, Vol. 17, pp. 139–150, copyright 1953 by the Menninger Foundation.

customary channels of ego activity are taken from him, and that the necessary closed hospital routines and procedures carry an implication of mistrust. If he is still fighting for his integration, he will rebel against restrictions and try to regain his freedom, while if he cannot muster the energy to fight, he will tend to regress. In either event some ground, possibly crucial ground, will have been lost. The answer to this dilemma would seem to lie in a therapeutic setting such as an open sanitarium, or day hospital arrangement, where quantitative flexibility of support can be provided as needed, but where essentially the patient is encouraged and permitted to remain in charge of himself. I would like to emphasize the therapeutic desirability of such open facilities for voluntary residential treatment of the borderline schizophrenic.

Granting the availability of the open hospital or sanitarium setting, in addition to the alternatives of outpatient therapy and closed hospital therapy, there are a number of relevant factors to be taken into account in making the decision as to what to recommend for the patient. One group of factors relates to the patient's level of ego functioning, and the other to his home or environment. These factors are summarized for convenience of the reader in Table I.

The closed hospital indications are, for the most part, self-evident. Regardless of fine distinctions and possible disadvantages of confinement, closed hospital care obviously must be recommended when the patient shows a "clear and present" danger to

Table I

OUT-PATIENT	OPEN HOSPITAL	CLOSED HOSPITAL
	Ego	
Patient aware of being ill	Patient aware of being ill	Patient insufficiently aware or unaware of being ill
Patient sufficiently motivated to co-operate in psychotherapy	Patient sufficiently motivated to become voluntary in-patient and co-operate	Patient usually unwilling to be hospitalized and unable to co-operate fully
No special supervision or observation required	Some degree of supervision and observation desirable	Close supervision and observation essential
Danger to self or others highly unlikely	Danger to self or others unlikely, but calculated risks taken	Danger to self or others likely or possible. Risk taking unwise
Patient able to continue activities in usual environment on reduced basis	Activities rather severely reduced in usual environment. Reclaimable in protected setting	Life activities invaded and contaminated by psychosis or psychopathy
Behavior within normal limits, or queerness concealed by isolation, discretion, or nature of environment	Behavior somewhat beyond normal limits but controllable by effort or group pressure, or tolerable to tolerant group	Behavior abnormal and uncontrollable. Containment necessary
Taking distance from self possible in usual environment	Taking distance from self severely handicapped or impossible in usual environment. Possible away	Taking distance from self almost absent wherever patient is
	ENVIRONMENT	
Home environment favorable or neutral	Home environment unfavorable	Home environment unfavorable, or this factor irrelevant
Patient "unseparatable"	Patient "separatable"	Patient "separatable" or this factor irrelevant
Patient "nondisposable"	Patient "disposable"	Patient "disposable" or this factor irrelevant
Group atmosphere or pressure adequate or necessary	Group atmosphere or pressure desirable as therapy aid	Group atmosphere or pressure desirable or this factor irrelevant

himself or others and/or severely abnormal and uncontrollable behavior. Even for the borderline schizophrenic, closed hospital care—or rather care in a psychiatric hospital which has closed and open facilities, with flexibility of placement of the patient—may be indicated, if a thorough appraisal shows that severely disturbed episodes are likely to occur during the course of therapy.

. . . A patient is separatable from his home environment if his family can manage somehow without him for a time—manage economically, emotionally, and practically with regard to household responsibilities. For example, a housewife whose psychoneurotic or borderline psychotic illness should, according to all other criteria, be treated in an open hospital, might nevertheless be vitally necessary to the household, handicapped in her functioning though she might be, and thus be regarded as "unseparatable." Either she would have to be treated as an out-patient, with all the disadvantages of this arrangement, or environmental arrangements would have to be made through social service to make her separatable. In the latter event, the separatability problem might not even then be solved if her overconscientiousness regarding the family acted as a block to her therapeutic accessibility. Of course if the patient is so sick as to make closed hospitalization imperative, then the criterion of separatability is overshadowed and has to be ignored.

"Disposability" as an environmental factor must be thought of before admission to inpatient open hospital treatment, even though it operates later, at the time discharge might take place. It connotes the "welcome back" into some kind of liavble, social, economic, and emotional context. The state hospitals are, of course, loaded with such nondisposable patients—elderly, without interested relatives or friends, unloved, unwanted, and unable to support themselves economically—for whom the hospital has become the only home they know. Disposability thus becomes entwined with secondary gain from illness considerations, and is especially operative with free or low pay patients. It can be, nevertheless, an important consideration with patients paying full rates also.

The remaining two environmental criteria may be considered together. Outpatient treatment is, of course, aided enormously if the significant persons in the home and job provide sufficient emotional support and encouragement, and out-patient treatment may be carried on with some patients even if this environmental support is only a neutral factor. If the home environment is definitely unfavorable, and other social contexts of the patient are similarly non-supportive or deleterious, then this factor alone may make successful out-patient treatment impossible. Furthermore, especially in the borderline schizophrenics, not only is the home environment often

ipso facto antitherapeutic, but also a favorable group atmosphere is an imperatively needed supplement to individual psychotherapy.

*   *   *

NOTE 4

DUNHAM, H. WARREN

Community Psychiatry*

The proposal to add community psychiatry to the ever-widening list of psychiatric specialists deserves a critical examination. . . .

*   *   *

A pattern concerned with maximizing treatment potential for the mentally ill is gradually taking shape. This newest emphasis points to a declining role of the traditional state hospital and the rise of the community mental health center with all of the attendant auxiliary services essential for the treatment of the mentally ill. In its ideal form the community mental health center would provide psychiatric services, both diagnostic and treatment, for all age groups and for both in-patients and out-patients in a particular community. In addition, the center would have attached closely to it day and night hospitals, convalescent homes, rehabilitative programs or, for that matter, any service that helps toward the maximizing of treatment potential with respect to the characteristics of the population that it is designed to serve. Also attached to this center would be several kinds of research activities aimed at evaluating and experimenting with old and new therapeutic procedures. In the background would still be the state hospital which would, in all likelihood, become the recipient for those patients who seemingly defy all efforts with available therapeutic techniques to fit them back into family and community with an assurance of safety to themselves and others. This reorganization of psychiatric facilities as a community mental health program also implies an increased and workable coordination of the diverse social agencies in the community toward the end of detecting and referring those persons who need psychiatric help.

*   *   *

. . . In reviewing the limited literature it is all too clear that different conceptions abound as to what community psychiatry is and while these conceptions are not always inconsistent they nevertheless attest to the fact that the dimensions of the proposed new subspecialty are by no means clear-cut. These conceptions range all the way from the idea that community psychiatry means bringing psychiatric tech-

---

*12 *Archives General Psychiatry*, 303–306, (1965). Reprinted by permission.

niques and treatments to the indigent persons in the community to the notion that community psychiatry should involve the education of policemen, teachers, public health nurses, politicians, and junior executives in mental hygiene principles. A mere listing of some of the conceptions of what has been placed under the community psychiatry umbrella will give a further notion of this uncertainty. Community psychiatry has been regarded as encompassing (1) the community base mental hospital, (2) short-term mental hospitalization, (3) attempts to move the chronically hospitalized patient and return him to the community, (4) the integration of various community health services, (5) psychiatric counselling and services to non-psychiatric institutions such as schools, police departments, industries, and the like, (6) the development of devices for maintaining mental patients in the community, (7) reorganization and administration of community mental health programs, and finally (8) the establishment of auxiliary services to community mental hospitals, such as out-patient clinics, day hospitals, night hospitals, home psychiatric visits, and the utilization of auxiliary psychiatric personnel in treatment programs.

*   *   *

There is no clearer support for this conception than Leonard Duhl's paper where he discusses the training problems for community psychiatry. In this paper he speaks of three contacts that the psychiatrist has, the traditional one with the patient, the more infrequent one with the family, and still more infrequent one with the community. In connection with his community contact, the psychiatrist states, according to Duhl, "I will try to lower the rate of illness and maximize the health of this population." Duhl continues, and I quote, because the direction is most significant.

> In preparing psychiatrists for these broadened contacts, a new set of skills must be communicated. For example, he must learn how to be consultant to a community, an institution, or a group without being patient-oriented. Rather, he must have the community's needs in central focus. He must be prepared for situations where he is expected to contribute to planning for services and programs, both in his field and in others, that are related: what information is needed; how it is gathered; what resources are available, and so forth. Epidemiology, survey research, and planning skills must be passed on to him. He must be prepared to find that people in other fields, such as the legislature, often affect a program more than his profession does. He must find himself at home in the world of economics, political science, politics, planning, and all forms of social action.

. . . In this conception of the community psychiatrist as a person skilled in the techniques of social action there lie so many uncertainties, unresolved issues, and hidden assumptions that it is difficult to determine where it will be most effective to start the analysis, with the role of the psychiatrist or with the nature of the community. . . .

[I]t seems that those leaders of psychiatry who are proposing this new subspecialty imply several things at the same time and are vague about all of them. They seem to be saying, in one form or another, the following:

1. We, psychiatrists, must know the community and learn how to work with the various groups and social strata composing it so that we can help to secure and organize the necessary psychiatric facilities that will serve to maximize the treatment potential for the mentally ill.

2. We must know the community because the community is composed of families which, through the interaction of their members, evolve those events and processes that in a given context have a pathic effect upon some of the persons who compose them.

3. We must know the community in order to develop more effective methods of treatment at the "collective level," to eliminate mentally disorganizing social relationships, and to achieve a type of community organization that is most conductive to the preservation of mental health.

4. We must know the community if we are ever to make any headway in the prevention of mental illness. For we hold that in the multiple groups, families, and social institutions which compose the community, there are numerous unhealthy inter-personal relationships, pathological attitudes and beliefs, cultural conflicts and tensions, and unhealthy child training practices that make for the development of mental and emotional disturbances in the person.

An analysis of our first implication shows that no new burden is placed upon the psychiatrist but it merely emphasizes his role as a citizen—a role that, like any person in the society, he always has had. It merely emphasizes that the psychiatrist will take a more active part in working with other professionals in the community such as lawyers, teachers, social workers, ministers, labor leaders, and businessmen in achieving an organization of psychiatric facilities that will maximize the therapeutic potential in a given community. To be sure it means that in working with such persons and groups, he will contribute his own professional knowledge and insights in the attempt to obtain and to organize the psychiatric facilities in such a manner as to achieve a maximum therapeutic potential. Thus, this is hardly a new role for the psychiatrist. It only becomes sharper at this moment in history when a social change in the care and treatment of the mentally ill is impending, namely, a shift from a situation that emphasized the removal of the mental patient from the community to one that attempts to deal with him in the community and family setting and to keep active and intact his ties with these social structures.

The second implication is routine in the light of the orientation of much of contempory psychiatry. Here, attention is merely called to the theory that stresses the atypical qualities of the family drama for providing an etiological push for the development of the several psychoneuroses, character disorders, adult behavior disturbances, and, in certain instances, psychotic reactions. Thus, it follows that to change or correct the condition found in the person, some attention must be paid to the family as a collectivity, in order to grasp and then modify those attitudes, behavior patterns, identifications, and emotional attachments that supposedly have a pathogenic effect on the family members. From the focus on the family the concern then extends to the larger community in an attempt to discover the degree to which the family is integrated in or alienated from it.

However, it is in the third application that many probing questions arise. For here the conception is implicit that the community is the patient and consequently, the necessity arises to develop techniques that can be used in treating the community toward the end of supplementing the traditional one-to-one psychiatric relationship. This position also implies a certain etiological view, namely, that within the texture of those institutional arrangements that make up the community there exist dysfunctional processes, subcultures with unhealthy value complexes, specific institutional tensions, various ideological conflicts along age, sex, ethnic, racial, and political axes, occasional cultural crises, and an increasing tempo of social change that in their functional interrelationships provide a pathogenic social environment. Thus, when these elements are incorporated into the experience of the persons, especially during their early and adolescent years, they emerge as abnormal forms of traits, attitudes, thought processes, and behavior patterns. . . .

These issues point to some very pressing queries. What are the possible techniques that can be developed to treat the "collectivity"? Why do psychiatrists think that it is possible to treat the "collectivity" when there still exists a marked uncertainty with respect to the treatment and cure of the individual case? What causes the psychiatrist to think that if he advances certain techniques for treating the "collectivity," they will have community acceptance? If he begins to "treat" a group through discussions in order to develop personal insights, what assurances does he have that the results will be psychologically beneficial to the persons? Does the psychiatrist know how to organize a community along mentally hygienic lines and if he does, what evidence does he have that such an organization will be an improvement over the existing organization? In what institutional setting or in what cultural milieu would the psychiatrist ex-

pect to begin in order to move toward more healthy social relationships in the community? These are serious questions and I raise them with reference to the notion that the community is the patient.

If a psychiatrist thinks that he can organize the community to move it toward a more healthy state I suggest that he run for some public office. This would certainly add to his experience and give him some conception as to whether or not the community is ready to be moved in the direction that he regards as mentally hygienic. If he should decide on such a step he will be successful to the extent that he jokingly refers to himself as a "head shrinker" and that he becomes acceptable as "one of the boys." But if he does, he functions as an independent citizen, in harmony with our democratic ethos, bringing his professional knowledge to bear on the goal he has set for himself and his constituents. However, successful or not, he will certainly achieve a new insight concerning the complexity involved in treating the community as the patient.

* * *

2.

CONCERNING THERAPY AND THERAPISTS

a.   GILL, MERTON M.

Psychoanalysis and Exploratory Psychotherapy*

My general topic is a comparison of psychoanalysis with psychotherapy as methods of treatment. . . .

* * *

. . . The word "psychotherapy" is used in two main senses, first as a broad term to include all types of therapy by psychological means, under which psychoanalysis is included, and second in a narrow sense to designate methods of psychological therapy which are not psychoanalysis, even if they are grounded in the theory of psychoanalysis. The latter restricted sense is the one generally employed if it is not further specified, and it is the one we are using here.

Methods of psychotherapy, using the term now in the broader sense, are primarily supportive or primarily exploratory, with all grades in between. Here I am considering the difference between psychoanalysis and exploratory psychotherapy, using the term now in the narrower sense. Exploratory psychotherapy may be brief or it may be long, even longer than the usual psychoanalysis, and indeed it is this sort of indication of the range of activity for which the term psychotherapy is used which makes it desirable for us to distinguish among some of the

---

*2 *Journal of the American Psychoanalytic Association*, 771–797, (1954). Reprinted by permission.

major foci of discussion and contention in the field, distinctions which I will then use in the rest of this paper.

* * *

... There are those who feel that, however valuable psychotherapy may be, it cannot do what psychoanalysis can do, that it cannot produce intrapsychic or structural ego modifications, can only operate by way of persistent transference effects or by rechannelization of various techniques of defense, and can be understood only by comparison and contrast with psychoanalysis. On the other hand there are those who feel that, to quote one of the adherents of this point of view . . . ". . . psychodynamic psychotherapy is an approach as strong or stronger than classical psychoanalysis, has increasingly greater range of applicability than classical psychoanalysis, is more inclusive theoretically, and classical psychoanalysis may turn out to be a special procedure of limited but significant usefulness in certain cases." As will become clear in what follows, my opinion is much closer to the first point of view than the second, though it is significantly different from either.

One more important distinction before I embark on the subject matter proper. I believe that an important source of confusion is that psychotherapy is often discussed without clearly defining whether one is talking about cases in which psychoanalysis would have been theoretically applicable, but could not be used because of external reasons such as lack of time or money so that psychotherapy with lesser goals is employed, and those in which psychoanalysis is regarded as contraindicated whether because of temporary reasons, like an acute reality crisis, or more permanent reasons, such as a psychotic ego, so that psychotherapy with or without a reduction of goals is employed. The distinction, it is generally agreed, rests on the degree of ego modification or distortion, with the correlated ability or disability on the patient's part to enter and maintain the analytic compact. In what follows I shall almost always attempt to split my discussion on psychotherapy into two parts in terms of these two classes of cases. Incidentally, this leads to a terminological problem which I believe may be profitably mentioned. Some people seem to feel that the best kind of psychological therapy possible in any particular kind of disorder ought to be called psychoanalysis, however much it differs from the classical technique. I feel that this can only becloud matters and that we must be content to admit, with Freud, that psychoanalysis has its undeniable limitations as a therapeutic technique. Eissler suggests calling this best therapy "psychoanalytic," but this can too easily be confused with "psychoanalysis."

Indeed Freud's position on this particular matter is unequivocal: "The possibility of analytic influence rests upon quite definite preconditions which can be summed up under the term 'analytic situation'; it requires the development of certain psychical structures and a particular attitude to the analyst. Where these are lacking—as in the case of children, of juvenile delinquents, and, as a rule, of impulsive criminals—something other than analysis must be employed, though something which will be at one with analysis in its *purpose*." . . .

We will turn now to a discussion of the techniques of psychoanalysis, for the present principally characterizing psychotherapy negatively by saying it does not employ this technique. Many people have tried to state the essence of the psychoanalytic technique, and the task is not an easy one. One thing seems clear to me. It is useless and even foolish to try to define the technique by such quantitative matters as how often the patient comes, or by such matters of physical arrangement, such as the recumbent position and inability to see the analyst. These features are important but they are important only as auxiliary devices to enable the application of certain technical principles, and to call these auxiliary devices technical principles is to run the risk of losing the usefulness of the work technique. . . .

[I] believe that the essence of the psychoanalytic technique is stated in the following formula: *Psychoanalysis is that technique which, employed by a neutral analyst, results in the development of a regressive transference neurosis and the ultimate resolution of this neurosis by techniques of interpretation alone.*

I will now amplify the separate parts of this definition.

It is said that the analyst is *neutral*. Admittedly this is to some extent an ideal. It is now generally agreed that the analyst cannot be a mirror. There is a vast difference, however, between attempting to maintain a position of neutrality by engaging in the regular self-analysis of countertransference which is part of the work of any analyst and deciding that since perfect neutrality cannot be maintained anyhow, we might as well plunge into emotional participation with the patient. . . .

Of course, it is true that the analyst has his own value system and that this will influence his conduct in the analysis; nor will he be able to refrain from emotional responses, but again it is his attitude toward them which is important. If these are too strong or persist despite his efforts to understand his countertransference, he should relinquish the case. Neutrality does not mean that the analyst is a stick of wood without spontaneity. It does not mean that he may not laugh at a joke, or make one, or show irritation, or find tears in his eyes when the patient relates a moving incident. This neutrality is not contradicted by the analyst's feeling a general benevolent friendliness toward his patient. Indeed without such an attitude on the analyst's part, an analysis is bound to fail. Such friendliness is not countertransference but the realistically desirable attitude of the therapist to the suffering patient. But neutrality does mean that the analyst is on the alert for the development of *patterns* of emotional response in himself to the patient, and that he always remains neutral in the basic sense of never trying to mold the patient in his own image. . . .

* * *

The next part of our definition is that there is the development of a *regressive* transference neurosis. That the development of a transference neurosis is an essential part of psychoanalytic technique is generally accepted, but that this transference neurosis must become intensive and regressive is less generally emphasized and accepted. . . . Many of the technical adjuncts, including what we have called above the "trappings" of analysis, have as their purpose the acceleration and deepening of the regression of the transference neurosis. To list a few of the most important: the recumbancy and inability to see the analyst who sits and may look, with the inevitable accompanying sense of being inferior; the frustration by silence and through other techniques; the awakening of strong needs without gratification; the absence of reality cues from the analyst; the general atmosphere of timelessness, with the relative disregard of symptoms and the taking of the whole personality as the relevant province of activity; free association, bringing into the field of consciousness the thoughts and feelings ordinarily excluded from the usual interpersonal relationship; the emphasis on fantasy; and last but not least the frequency of visits which, metaphorically speaking, we may regard as the constant irritation necessary to keep open the wounds into the unconscious, and indeed as a general strong invitation to become dependent, to regress, and to feel safe enough to do so because there is time enough and stability and frequency. The reproduction of the infantile neurosis in the transference can only mean a regressive transference. . . .

I shall not deal much with the question of why a regressive transference is an essential part of psychoanalytic technique. Clearly it is related to the ambitious goal of psychoanalysis, to the need to actualize latent conflict, and the more particularly because in psychoanalysis we are dealing with a relatively strong ego whose defenses and adaptations are working well enough so that, if we do not enforce a regression, we shall not be able to come to grips with the deeper problems. Indeed there is a clear correlation between the regressive transference produced by the psychoanalytic technique and the fact that the ego must be relatively strong to be suitable for the analytic technique. The patient must be capable of transitorily regressing more or less only during the analytic hour. . . .

Emphasis on the regressive character of the analytic transference makes clearer some of the contraindications to the analytic technique. A major contraindication is the presence of severe regressive features or the dangers that such may develop. The instances of rather sudden onset of psychosis shortly after beginning psychoanalysis are to be attributed to the regressive pressure of the technique per se on a precariously balanced personality.

* * *

This leads us then to the last part of our definition of the technique of psychoanalysis—that the transference must be resolved by techniques of interpretation alone. "By techniques of interpretation alone" means "and not by any other techniques of interpersonal behavior." This is not meant to deny that unceasing processes of affective nonverbal communication go on between analyst and patient but that the goal of analysis is not to rest until these affective interchanges have been converted into explicit verbalizations and have been encompassed by interpretation. . . . I think there is little doubt that . . . by overt behavior toward the patient one can more quickly get him to change some aspects of his behavior. But what is the meaning of such a change? It is an adaptation to this particular interpersonal relationship—as it exists between patient and analyst. But this is not the goal of analysis. The goal of analysis is an intrapsychic modification in the patient, so that for example his dependent behavior is given up not because he has learned that if he acts too dependent he will be punished by a loss of therapy hours, but because despite the invitation to regress and the maintenance of the frequency of his hours he has come to feel and understand his dependency in such a way that he no longer needs it or wants it—and that is a conclusion valid not simply for this particular interpersonal relationship but has more general applicability, in short has the status of an intrapsychic change.

In a sense the phrase that the transference neurosis must be resolved by techniques of interpretation alone is a redundancy, since there is no other way in which it *can* be resolved. Any other kind of interpersonal interaction can only complicate and maintain the transference relationship.

It is clear that an ego which can respond to interpretation alone, which is after all symbolic behavior, and an ego for which the symbolized behavior embodied in the interpretation will have an effect as forceful on the patient as overt behavior, must be a relatively strong ego. But this is the kind of ego, we have agreed, which the psychoanalytic technique demands.

* * *

Having now presented a statement of the essence of psychoanalytic technique with interlarded remarks on how psychotherapy differs, we may attempt to summarize features of exploratory psychotherapeutic technique, as it is usually practiced. . . .

First we will discuss psychotherapy in the general class of cases in which the ego structure is theoretically amenable to psychoanalysis but where psychoanalysis cannot be done for external reasons.

The therapist engages in various kinds of activity. He is not neutral, but is willing to take a definite hand in decisions and values, though he usually tries to avoid being too active in these areas if he can. He does not foster a regressive transference neurosis, since he does not employ the devices which would lead to this, but on the contrary actively discourages the development of such a transference by conducting the interview more like a social interchange of equals, by avoiding free association, by emphasizing reality rather than fantasy, by creating an atmosphere of temporariness, and similar measures. He observes various elements of transference developing anyhow —which he correctly calls transferences rather than a transference neurosis—and he may or may not interpret these. If they become obtrusive and seem to be hindering the treatment, or if he sees an opportunity to make a valuable point by interpreting a piece of transference, he will do so. But if the transference is reasonably positive and desirable behavioral changes are occurring, or if evidences of hostile transference seem too hot to handle, he will remain silent about it and permit the transference to persist unresolved. He will also engage in various kinds of behavior to foster particular feelings in the patient toward him, and these feelings in the patient will be a blend of reality reactions to the therapist's behavior and transference reactions. The therapist will not try to disentangle these. In contrast to our analyst then, the psychotherapist is willing to permit many transference manifestations to remain unresolved on the one hand and on the other to behave in ways which would make it more difficult to resolve if he were to attempt it.

In the weak egos, a somewhat similar situation prevails. The difference lies in the fact that these patients are more regressed with the danger of further regression, so that regression is not only discouraged but active techniques of interpersonal interaction are even more extensively employed. But the spontaneous development of strong and regressive transference manifestations can often not be ignored, so that transference interpretations may come to play a large role in the treatment. It is concerning these patients that Freud's early statement distinguishing them from the so-called transference neurosis has been revised. It is not that these patients do not develop a transference. Rather, that transference is florid, wild, and fluctuating. What they are able to

develop only with great difficulty is a stable object relationship within which the transference can become a usuable therapeutic instrument. As far as frequency is concerned, such patients may be seen as frequently as patients in analysis, if not more frequently. But here the frequency is not to promote intensity of involvement and regression. The intensity of involvement and regression are already there. It is designed rather to provide support and continuity to the failing, if not disintegrating, ego.

[W]e shall [now] take up the goals of the various therapies.

The goals of psychoanalysis have been clearly stated . . . by Freud.

> It may be laid down that the aim of the treatment is to remove the patient's resistances and to pass his repressions in review and thus to bring about the most far-reaching unification and strengthening of his ego, to enable him to save the mental energy which he is expending upon internal conflicts, to make the best of him that his inherited capacities will allow and so to make him as efficient and as capable of enjoyment as is possible. The removal of the symptoms of his illness is not specifically arrived at, but is achieved, as it were, as a by-product if the analysis is properly carried through.

*   *   *

The goals of psychotherapy extend over a very wide range. To take first the goals in psychotherapy with a relatively strong ego. The goal may be a resolution of a crisis, assistance through a troubled period, or symptom amelioration. The more limited the goal and the more acute the situation, the more likely is the therapy to veer toward the supportive rather than the exploratory end of the continuum and the more active is the therapist likely to be. But goals may range up to much more ambitious aims in cases where there is no pressing problem, but where psychoanalysis is impossible or not used for external reasons. Such are the patients who are seen for example once or twice a week over a period of a year or more, in whom the goals are much more ambitious than in palliative psychotherapy, and in whom, as I hope to show later, more important results are achieved than I believe is often admitted.

The goals of exploratory psychotherapy with patients whose egos are theoretically unsuitable for psychoanalysis likewise extend over a very wide range. Here too there are emergency situations such as panics in psychotic characters, and again the treatment is likely to be supportive rather than exploratory and the therapist to be more interactive. But ambitious attempts at reconstruction can be undertaken with patients whose egos are unsuitable for psychoanalysis, such as the psychotic and the delinquent. Here it must be remembered that the ultimate goal may long remain in doubt, the therapist planning to go as far as he can get. We will return to this point again in considering the results achievable in various kinds of psychological therapy.

Now to the remarks which I promised about suggestions for psychotherapeutic technique. I have one major point to make. I believe we have failed to carry over into our psychotherapy enough of the non-directive spirit of our analyses. I do not refer to the emergency situations where active intervention seems unavoidable and where the essential goal is supportive, but to the less urgent problems seen over longer periods of time with more ambitious goals. I think it may even be that where the ego is relatively strong the resolution of an acute crisis may require no more support than that implicit support without which, as Knight says, a therapy would be a poor therapy indeed. . . . I think that together with a diminution of our degree of directiveness in psychotherapy there may take place some change in our view of the results achieved and achievable in the various therapies, to which I now turn.

First as to psychoanalysis. It is generally the more experienced analysts who are not so optimistic about the sweeping character changes often hoped for from psychoanalysis. And there is no doubt that we can still recognize our friends and colleagues, even after they have been analyzed. In "Analysis Terminable and Interminable," Freud quotes wryly the observation that "Every advance is only half as great as it looks at first." In this essay Freud feels that he cannot come to a conclusion as to whether analysis can actually change the personality in such a way that increases in the strength of an instinctual demand; cannot reawaken an old conflict. He says that sometimes it does so succeed, but that "sometimes its effect is simply to raise the power of the resistance put up by inhibitions, so that after analysis they are equal to a much heavier strain than before the analysis took place or if it had never taken place at all." Almost throughout the essay he emphasizes that in our search for qualitative alterations we have neglected the quantitative factor. My stress on this point arises from my feeling that discussion of therapeutic results in psychoanalysis and psychotherapy too often views them as qualitative polar opposites, with psychoanalysis regarded as producing structural changes, and psychotherapy as unable to produce any significant intrapsychic change, but only altering techniques of adjustment through transference effects or shifts in defensive techniques.

*   *   *

. . . I would raise the question . . . as to whether there is not more to be said on results and mechanisms in prolonged psychotherapy with more ambitious goals by a relatively inactive therapist and in intensive psychotherapy with ego structures inaccessible, at least to begin with, to the psychoanalytic technique.

. . . I would like to present a number of reasons to try to buttress this possibility:

First: Psychological methods of therapy as employed by analysts have until fairly recently actually *been* at opposite poles. A patient was either analyzed, or else he was treated by an active brief psychotherapy. This is the kind of psychotherapy practiced in out-patient clinics where the goal is a rapid resolution of the presenting problem so that the patient can be soon discharged and yield his place to the next one on the waiting list.

What we might call more intermediate types of psychotherapy are relatively recent. This is the psychotherapy done by people analytically oriented or trained where goals are intermediate between rapid symptom resolution and character change, where techniques are in a sense intermediate—for example, relative neutrality and inactivity; transference dealt with, though not a full regressive transference neurosis; interpretation the principal vehicle of therapist behavior—and I suggest, where results are likewise intermediate.

Second: I believe that to some extent these conclusions are a reaction to the glib claims of enthusiastic innovators who seem to value so lightly the hard-won insights of psychoanalysis and by whom, to quote Eissler, "The question of 'at what cost to and limitation of the ego' is no longer asked; instead pride in the alleged superiority of the contemporary analysts' knowledge makes many authors believe that Freud's safeguards against the effect of the therapist's personality—in situations where a structural change, induced by the analytic process, ought to take place—have become superfluous." I am in general agreement with this point of view, but I think it may act to retard somewhat the more positive description of what can actually take place in intensive psychotherapy of what I have called the intermediate kind.

I think that current positions on this problem may be illuminated by a glance at their history, because they are an outgrowth of a long struggle. Psychoanalysis was born out of hypnosis—the technique which, as then employed, maximally used suggestion. Freud's first understanding of transference came, he tells us, when he saw apparently secure therapeutic results blown away by a change in the patient's feelings about him. Ever since, analysis has struggled to develop a treatment technique which will be free of the influence of suggestion. A major milestone in this development was Freud's recognition that suggestion operates all through the therapeutic process, but that it can be employed to further the therapeutic work, and be ultimately more or less resolved rather than remain as the precarious underpinning of the therapeutic result. . . . The use of transference to further the exploration of unconscious material, for example, is a technical device, while the resolution of transference by its interpretation is a therapeutic device. The essential difference between psycho-analysis and other psychotherapies has long been seen as consisting precisely in this—that psycho-analysis alone of the psychotherapies attempts to resolve the suggestive influence of the therapist on the patient. Until recently any innovation introduced into psychoanalytic technique was scrutinized from this point of view—was it introducing a suggestive factor into the treatment?

* * *

And this leads me to my third point. I think there has been so far a relative underemphasis in psycho-analytic theory on the positive aspects of adaptation, an understanding of which would enable us better to describe the mechanisms in psychotherapy and in normal functioning. . . . To some extent I think this underemphasis is also a reaction to the glib claims of those who measure the therapeutic results in terms of symptoms and adjustment and again overlook "at what cost to and limitation of the ego." Particularly is this true in these times of emphasis on social con-formity so that by some writers psychoanalysis is re-ferred to as the last stronghold of individualism. Again my agreement is with those who are struggling against permitting psychoanalysis to be caught up in the opportunistic, anti-intellectual reactionary tide, but again I feel this has retarded the amalgamation into our theory and practice of such insights as Erikson's on the role of ego identity in adaptation. I think it should be possible to retain our emphasis on structural and intrapsychic change and still develop an understanding of adaptation, value system, and social role in their positive aspects as well as in their meaning in terms of shifts in defensive techniques. I think there is some truth in the assertion that there has been in psychoanalysis a relative preoccupation with intrapsychic structure and a relative lack of emphasis on reality adjustment and social role, and a general emphasis on pathology rather than the mechanisms of effective functioning.

Fourth: I believe the progress of ego psychology should lead us to re-examine some of our views about id-ego relationships and symptom formation. The technical implications of ego psychology for psycho-analysis—let alone psychotherapy—have been rela-tively little systematized. The fact of relative lack of correlation between ego structure and symptom—the existence of similar symptomatic pictures in very different ego structures—is one of the important problems needing more study. The earlier view held a very close relationship between id-ego conflict and ego functioning. In particular this conflict was viewed as ever raging afresh, so that ego functioning was viewed as the more or less direct and immediate result of the interaction of libidinal and aggressive energies with mechanisms of defense. This view is giving way to one of a psychic structure in which

hierarchical organization plays a more prominent role, in which the outcome of id-ego struggles has become crystallized in structuralized, relatively en-during, relatively autonomous ego organizations which operate with energy that has been relatively neutralized as compared with its original libidinal or aggressive state. In particular, as especially empha-sized by Hartmann, analytic theory is expanding to include an intrasystemic as well as an intersystemic point of view. In this connection, this suggests that intraego mechanisms, the study of the relationship of organizations within the ego system, the manner for example in which areas of ego functioning pass in and out of the conflict-free sphere of the ego, need to be included in our theory of therapy. What I am suggesting here is that such study may enable us to describe in more positive and detailed terms the alterations in ego structures which psychotherapy—and for that matter psychoanalysis—can bring about.

* * *

NOTES

NOTE 1

KNIGHT, ROBERT P.

A Critique of the Present Status of Psychotherapies*

* * *

Freudian psychoanalysis—and psychoanalysis ac-tually implies "Freudian"—is a major, time-consum-ing, and therefore expensive, type of psychotherapy. It is by no means a panacea, and its most competent practitioners would readily concede that as a method of therapy it has limited application in the vast field of human psychological distress. (As a dynamic psy-chology and as a method of investigation it is, of course, invaluable, and possesses almost unlimited applicability.) Its limitations as a method of therapy do not depend merely on such factors as its duration (twelve to eighteen months as a minimum; four to five years as a maximum), its cost to the patient, and the availability of analysts (approximately five hundred in the United States, with one fourth of these in New York City). There is also a considerable list of special indications and contraindications, as, for example:

1. The patient should be of at least bright normal intelligence on the Bellevue-Wechsler scale (115 to 120 IQ).

2. The suitable age range for adults is about 20 to 50, with certain exceptions to be made at either end of this range.

3. There must be some capacity for introspection, and some awareness of nuances of feeling in himself and in others.

*25 Bulletin New York Academy of Medicine 100 (1949). Reprinted by permission.

4. There must be sufficient motivation in terms of distress and strong desire to change.

5. The patient must possess sufficient intactness of personality so that this intact portion may become allied with the analyst in the analytic work.

6. In general patients with unalterable physical handicaps are not suitable subjects for psychoanalysis.

7. The general field for psychoanalytic therapy includes the psychoneuroses, character disorders, some of the perversions, neurotic depressions, anxiety states, and some of the psychoses. Patients in the midst of acute external turmoil should not begin psychoanalysis as such until their life situations are more stable.

With all of its limitations, however, psychoanalytic therapy is, in well trained hands, a highly effective procedure for achieving in patients a profound alteration in their neurotic personality structure and developing otherwise latent potentialities for achievement and responsible living.

The Freudian school of psychoanalysis is the main stream of the psychoanalytic movement. There have, in the past, been several split-offs from the main stream which resulted in transient and minor developments of non-Freudian schools. The school of the late Alfred Adler took one aspect of psychoanalysis, namely, the methods of the ego in dealing with external forces, and attempted to develop it into a system called individual psychology. The central theme of this psychology was that of inferiority feelings and the drive for power. This psychology and system of therapy is still in existence, but plays a minor role in psychiatry today. Carl Jung, also an early pupil and associate of Freud, split with him and developed a school of "analytical psychology" which emphasized symbolism and religious beliefs and which explained mental disorders, especially those of middle life and after, in terms of regressions to a collective unconscious, or racial heritage. His school still persists, with headquarters in Zurich, Switzerland. The late Otto Rank, also an early pupil of Freud's, developed a system of therapy which emphasized the transference and the uncovering and working through of birth anxiety in a three months' period of treatment. There were many short Rankian analyses in the 1920's, but this system is now practically extinct. The late Wilhelm Stekel, a remarkably intuitive man and a prolific writer, attracted a few followers to his technique of rapid and early deep interpretations of symbolic and unconscious meanings. His influence has now become almost nil. Karen Horney, originally a Freudian with many fine contributions to the literature, has led a movement in the last decade to eliminate a number of the fundamental concepts of psychoanalysis and to focus attention on current cultural conflicts as the main source of personality disorders. She rejects the libido theory, the significance of early psychosexual development, and in general takes a stand against genetic psychology in favour of culturalism.

There are other deviations from orthodox psychoanalytic techniques which are not represented by their practitioners nor regarded by others as separate dissident schools of psychoanalysis, but which are modifications of technique to meet the therapeutic problems in patients who are too ill to co-operate in the usual analytic procedure. These modifications are used chiefly with psychotics and involve approaches by the analyst which actively cultivate a treatment relationship, communication with the sick patient being established on whatever level is possible in the individual case. The success of such attempts depends on the resourcefulness of the analyst in coping with the patient's inaccessibility and his capacity for enpathy and intuition in understanding what is communicated by the patient's verbalizations, behavior, and attitudes. Long periods of careful therapeutic work are required but the results are often very rewarding. As the patient improves the treatment may emerge into a more regular psychoanalytic procedure.

* * *

In order to shorten the duration of therapy many attempts have been made. . . . Chief among these techniques have been the use of hypnosis and certain sedative drugs. Under hypnosis or narcosis (also mild elation or light anesthesia) some patients are able to gain access to and to verbalize with effect otherwise unconscious memories, and to profit from the ventilation and abreaction and the interpretations of the therapist associated with this therapeutic experience. During World War II there was widespread use of intravenous sodium amytal and sodium pentothal as well as of hypnosis to produce dissolution of the resistance barriers against recalling overwhelming traumatic experiences, with associated assimilation of the overstressful event and great diminution or relief of the symptoms. It was found that early treatment was essential, delay resulting in the building of stronger barriers against recall and fixing of the symptomatology, to which was then added the exploitation of secondary gains. These psychotherapeutic procedures had enormous significance in military psychiatry, but as sole treatment attempts have proved to be disappointing in civilian psychiatry except with early traumatic neuroses in civil life. Such techniques of reducing resistance through hypnosis or narcosis do not constitute separate systems of psychotherapy, so that it is incorrect to speak of narcoanalysis, narcosynthesis, hypnotherapy, and hypnoanalysis as psychotherapies. They are adjuvant techniques, to be used as a preliminary step in overcoming an initial impasse, or as devices to be introduced during psychotherapy when strong resistance blocks further progress.

* * *

In the last analysis there is only one psychotherapy, with many techniques. This one psychotherapy must rest on a basic science of dynamic psychology, and those techniques should be used which are clinically indicated for each individual patient—certain appropriate techniques for the initial stages, and others later as the continuous clinical evaluation proceeds *pari passu* with therapy, and the goals and potentialities for the patient become more clearly delineated through his responses to therapy. And, finally, it is important to recognize that techniques as such are hardly separable from the individual who uses them. Psychotherapy is an enormously complex intercommunication and emotional interaction between two individuals, one of whom seeks help from the other. What is done and said by the one who tries to give help is inevitably his personal version of technique. Beyond all knowledge a dynamic psychology and training in techniques is his own individual personality, with its inevitable variables as to sex, physical appearance, depth of understanding, ability to communicate ideas, tone of voice, set of values, and all of the other highly individual elements which differentiate one therapist from another. The utmost impersonality and analytic incognito cannot exclude the effect of such individual elements. Hence we may say that in addition to a critique of psychotherapy one must also make a critique of the psychotherapist.

NOTE 2

FREUD, SIGMUND

Lines of Advance in
Psycho-Analytic Therapy (1919)*

. . . You know that our therapeutic activities are not very far reaching. There are only a handful of us, and even by working very hard each one can devote himself in a year to only a small number of patients. Compared to the vast amount of neurotic misery which there is in the world, and perhaps need not be, the quantity we can do away with is almost negligible. Besides this, the necessities of our existence limit our work to the well-to-do classes, who are accustomed to choose their own physicians and whose choice is diverted away from psychoanalysis by all kinds of prejudices. At present we can do nothing for the wider social strata, who suffer extremely seriously from neuroses.

Now let us assume that by some kind of organization we succeeded in increasing our numbers to an extent sufficient for treating a considerable mass of the population. On the other hand, it is possible to

*Reprinted from: 17 *The Standard Edition of the Complete Psychological Works of Sigmund Freud*, James Strachey, ed. London: The Hogarth Press and The Institute of Psychoanalysis, 1955 (pp. 166–168) and 2 *Collected Papers of Sigmund Freud*. Reprinted by permission of Hogarth and Basic Books, Inc.

foresee that at some time or other the conscience of society will awake and remind it that the poor man should have just as much right to assistance for his mind as he now has to the life-saving help offered by surgery; and that the neuroses threaten public health no less than tuberculosis, and can be left as little as the latter to the impotent care of individual members of the community. When this happens, institutions or out-patient clinics will be started, to which analytically-trained physicians will be appointed, so that men who would otherwise give way to drink, women who have nearly succumbed under their burden of privations, children for whom there is no choice but between running wild or neurosis, may be made capable, by analysis, of resistance and of efficient work. Such treatments will be free. It may be a long time before the State comes to see these duties as urgent. Present conditions may delay its arrival even longer. Probably these institutions will first be started by private charity. Some time or other, however, it must come to this.

We shall then be faced by the task of adapting our technique to the new conditions. I have no doubt that the validity of our psychological assumptions will make its impression on the uneducated too, but we shall need to look for the simplest and most easily intelligible ways of expressing our theoretical doctrines. We shall probably discover that the poor are even less ready to part with their neuroses than the rich, because the hard life that awaits them if they recover offers them no attraction, and illness gives them one more claim to social help. Often, perhaps, we may only be able to achieve anything by combining mental assistance with some material support, in the manner of the Emperor Joseph. It is very probable, too, that the large-scale application of our therapy will compel us to alloy the pure gold of analysis freely with the copper of direct suggestion; and hypnotic influence, too, might find a place in it again, as it has in the treatment of war neuroses. But, whatever form this psychotherapy for the people may take, whatever the elements out of which it is compounded, its most effective and most important ingredients will assuredly remain those borrowed from strict and untendentious psychoanalysis.

NOTE 3

HOLLINGSHEAD, AUGUST B. and
REDLICH, FREDERICK C.

Social Class and Mental Illness*

*   *   *

Two distinctly different therapeutic orientations are represented by the 30 practitioners who live in the community. We divide these practitioners into those

*New York: John Wiley and Sons, 1958 (pp. 155–61). Reprinted by permission.

who have an analytic and psychological orientation (referred to as A–P group) and into those who have a directive and organic (D–O group) orientation. At first, we referred to the D–O group—following common usage—as eclectics. However, most of these practitioners are not real eclectics. One psychiatrist who falls into the D–O group once declared, "To help a patient I would do anything, even stand on my head if necessary." He might do that, but he would not practice psychoanalytic therapy for two reasons: He is opposed to it, and he has never learned the technique. There are a few outstanding specialists, particularly in the psychosomatic field, who master all available methods, true eclectics—we prefer to call them individualists—but today most practitioners, including psychiatrists in university centers and other institutions, fall into one group or the other. We recognize that this division, like any other, is somewhat arbitrary, and there are considerable variations. We also hope that this division will not last forever, and that *one* scientific psychiatry will emerge. In this particular community, the University psychiatrists belong largely to the A–P group, and the public hospital psychiatrists largely to the D–O group.

Our division is based on two criteria: the principal method of therapy and training for such therapy. We find that there is a definite division in theory and practice between the analytic-psychological approach and the directive-organic approach. The analytic approach consists essentially of analyzing behavior, relationships, and conscious and unconscious motivations according to psychoanalytic theories. The classical psychoanalytic approach consists of analyzing symptoms and defenses, transference, and resistance, with the purpose of strengthening the ego through insight into unconscious forces, particularly into those which are apt to produce psychopathology. The so-called dynamic psychotherapeutic approach follows this general line with less rigor and greater flexibility. The emphasis is on gaining insight and applying insight and not on manipulation or direction unless this is absolutely necessary because of a weak ego; whenever directions are given they must at least be based on analytic insights of the therapist. The approach is almost entirely psychological; organic methods of diagnosis and treatment are extraneous to it and are rarely employed by its practitioners.

The directive approach consists of changing attitudes, opinions, and behavior of the patient by means of directive and supportive methods such as assertion, suggestion, reassurance, advice, manipulation, and even coercion. It is usually not based on analytic insight but on the therapist's judgment and what is called clinical experience and evaluation of the patient's problems and situation. Depending on the therapist and the patient, the therapist may try to buck up the patient's low esteem, convert him to the therapist's own philosophy of life, give him a stern lecture, friendly advice, tell him to go to a resort, to take it easy or work harder, to treat his wife kindly or get a divorce. The success of any of these maneuvers, and they can be quite successful, depends on the wisdom and strength of the therapist rather than on his technical knowledge and also on the suggestibility and the ego strength of the patient. The directive approach requires, besides clinical experience, and even more urgently than technical knowledge, broad human experience and a willingness to assume authority.

Directive techniques are often combined with organic medical techniques, both diagnostic and therapeutic. D–O practitioners are likely to do medical and neurological examinations, carry out laboratory tests, prescribe drugs, administer shock treatments, and refer their patients to neurosurgeons or even carry out, themselves, "minor" neurosurgical procedures, like transorbital lobotomies. Many of their explanations, to themselves and to their patients, are couched in medical or pseudomedical terms. Although D–O practitioners have a general interest in psychology and the social sciences, their knowledge of these disciplines is, in practice and theory, weaker than that of the A–P group. What interest and knowledge they have are overshadowed by their stronger biological and medical interests. Hence, we refer to one as psychological and to the other as organic. Another basic difference is that the A–P group holds the expressed belief that the etiology of most mental illnesses, with the possible exception of a few organic disorders, is primarily psychological and that treatment, too, should be psychological.

The training of the two groups is different; the A–P group goes through full or partial psychoanalytic training and orientation; their set of axioms stems from Freud's theories and recommendations. Their postgraduate training in the basic biological and clinical sciences tends to be secondary and minimal: Little neurology, for instance, at one time psychiatry's fraternal twin, is known and learned by the average member of the A–P group. The D–O group has a strong affinity to the organic medical approach and is more apt to be trained in neurology and its basic biological sciences.

The A–P group includes those psychiatrists who are fully trained psychoanalysts, among them some of the leaders in the field, as well as those who had some psychoanalytic orientation in their residence training, for instance, or therapeutic experience by way of their own psychoanalysis or intensive psychotherapy. Members of the group not fully trained usually consider the trained analysts as persons of higher professional status and consider themselves as second-class citizens in the hierarchy. Among the A–P group, the members of the American Psychoanalytic Association usually point with pride to their intensive training in the field and consider themselves as the outstanding representatives of classical psychoanalysis; when the discussion turns in that direction they look down their classical analytical noses at their colleagues who have a Jungian, Horneyan, or Sullivanian orientation.

Those we call the D–O group also represent a spectrum. At one end are those who employ psychotherapeutic methods such as reassurance, persuasion, suggestion, advice, and support, based on insights mixed with their personal philosophies. Treatment among these men varies from patient to patient and depends largely on attempts of the therapist to teach the patient to look at problems in the therapist's way. A certain measure of organic treatment may be used by these therapists, as, for example, the prescription of tranquillizing drugs. On the other end of the spectrum are those who prescribe an almost exclusively organic therapy, such as drugs, shock therapy, and psychosurgery.

Although there are minor differences among individuals in each therapeutic orientation, for present purposes we will group the A–P practitioners in one category and the D–O practitioners in a second category. As we compare and contrast the two groups, we will not differentiate within a group unless there is a particular point to emphasize.

The A–P psychoanalyst works regular hours, mornings and afternoons, and sometimes evenings; he does not make house calls. The D–O therapist makes house calls, works uneven hours, and accepts emergencies as part of each day's work. The psychoanalyst charges from $20 to $35 for each visit; a few patients pay less, and some pay $40. The D–O practitioner uniformly charges from $10 to $20 per visit. The analytic practitioner sees his patients longer and more frequently than the D–O practitioner. Patients in psychoanalytic treatment are seen for a "50-minute hour" four or five times a week. The D–O therapist sees his patients for 15 to 30 minutes once a week, perhaps only once a month, or as one practitioner stated, "when they drop in for a pill and a little advice." Another "external" mark of difference is this: The D–O practitioner generally wears a white coat in the office and hospital; the A–P psychoanalyst wears a business suit in his work.

The analytic practitioner may sit behind his patient who lies on a couch; the D–O practitioner never does. "One almost needs a special license to have a couch," one D–O practitioner sighed. The A–P analyst listens to the patient's free associations and is relatively less active than the D–O therapist; his main job is to "analyze" with his patient the patient's unconscious conflicts, resistances, and transferences. The D–O practitioner may get involved in Socratic dialogues, actively advise, suggest, and prescribe. At times he prescribes and administers drugs and electroshock

treatments to his patients either in his office or in the hospital where he has privileges to treat. The analysts and the analytically oriented practitioners, as we mentioned before, almost never make physical and neurological examinations; among D–O practitioners such medical examinations are the rule. They perform medical procedures such as venous and lumbar punctures, whereas the analyst refers a patient who needs such an examination to an internist or neurologist.

The local Psychoanalytic Institute is the polar attraction for analytically oriented practitioners and for most university psychiatrists from the senior men to the newest residents. Instruction in the Institute is in great demand among psychiatrists who want to become psychoanalysts or get experience in the field to become better practitioners, teachers, and investigators. Membership in the Institute is a coveted honor, both among the younger men and those who are fully trained. The Institute is rigidly organized; each student is brought under the professional influence of the senior instructors for several years. Few schools have such strong impact on and control over their disciples. The most important figures in the Institute are the senior training analysts. To be a training analyst is considered a high distinction by all analytically oriented psychiatrists. Most of the patients of the training analysts are psychiatrists-in-training; thus, the training analysts exercises a decisive influence on their disciples and a strong indirect influence on the profession.

The analytically oriented psychiatrists have a local Psychoanalytic Society that is more inclusive in its membership than the psychoanalytic institute, but privileges of membership in this society are still very strict and primarily based on complete and proper analytic training except for a few "friends" of analysis who are "extraordinary" members. At one meeting of the Psychoanalytic Society, the question of inviting the D–O group to a joint meeting of the two groups was raised, but it was coolly received and nothing was done. Most of the members of the Psychoanalytic Society belong to the American Psychiatric Association and to the State Medical Society, but the local Psychoanalytic Society is probably as "exclusive" as any professional organization can be. The D–O practitioners belong to local medical societies and the State Society for Psychiatry and Neurology which is a branch of its national organization. The analysts rarely attend medical society meetings, and most of them are little interested in the Mental Health Society of the state and the local psychiatric society. The analysts barely know the D–O practitioners; only a few meet socially and then on rare occasions when circumstances happen to bring individuals together.

Psychiatrists with an analytic orientation read

markedly different journals from those with a directive-organic orientation. The analysts read primarily professional analytic journals; the D–O group read journals with an organic orientation such as the State Medical Journal, the Journal of the American Medical Association, and the neurological journals. Both groups read the American Journal of Psychiatry, the trade journal of the profession. Neither the A–P group nor the D–O group read, as a rule, psychological, sociological, and general scientific publications.

The analytic group impress us as being more "inner-oriented," introspective, and psychologically sensitive than their D–O colleagues. The A–P group believe they were impelled to become psychiatrists by their childhood and adolescent experiences. For example, one fully trained psychoanalyst stated that his interest in psychiatry developed from an attempt to solve a hateful or, at best, ambivalent relationship with his father. Another believes his choice of profession was determined largely by a wish to help his mother solve her neurotic problem. We think motivations in the D–O group are hardly different, but the D–O practitioners do not appear to be aware of them or state them in such frank ways. The D–O practitioners are inclined to attribute their occupational choices to factors such as "fine opportunities in a new field," or a "chance to help where help is badly needed." They stress therapeutic needs of other persons rather than their own impulses and identify more with the acknowledged tasks of the medical profession.

When the respondents discussed their professional satisfactions with the interviewer, the analytically oriented physicians emphasized the personal gratifications they gained from understanding the complexities of human behavior; the directive-organic physicians stressed the opportunities their training and ability opened to them to help other people. In the area of professional disappointments, the analysts regret how little they know about individual motivation of behavior; this did not bother the D–O group. They are more concerned with the administrative tasks of their practice and the economic obstacles their patients face when they try to obtain psychiatric care. In short, the analysts stress the unsolved theoretical problems; the D–O practitioners stress practical obstacles which need to be overcome.

Differences in theoretical orientations and practices are accompanied by professional jealousy and a certain hostility between the two groups. Moreover, each group is keenly aware of the other's shortcomings and weaknesses. The D–O practitioners reproach the A–P group for their "doctrinaire" and "unmedical" attitudes and, when tempers rise, "quackery." The analysts view the directive-organic group as "ignorant," "low-brow," and, when they use predominantly organic methods, as "shock artists." A screen of "professional" dignity usually covers such differences of opinion, attitudes, and facts; the public seldom gets a glimpse of these "border wars" within the profession. These feuds and splits may become milder as our knowledge of the nature of mental illness advances; they may even disappear, but they are prominent, if publicly well-masked, elements in the practice of psychiatry today.

All private practitioners have completed work for the degree of Doctor of Medicine in approved medical schools, and most have served general internships in hospitals. In addition, most of them have had residency training required by the Specialty Board in Psychiatry; more than half of them have been certified by the Board. If psychiatry were compared with other medical specialties, it probably would be found to be essentially similar in training, accomplishments, and internal organization. Psychiatrists, as members of a new specialty, tend to be self-conscious and defensive about their work and its difficulties and possibilities. Both the A–P and D–O groups believe in the importance of their work and think that, although psychiatrists are not the most revered specialists in the medical profession, they have the broadest background and are the most intellectual members. They point with pride to the impressive growth of the specialty in the last thirty years.

Very few psychiatrists extend "professional courtesy" for prolonged treatment to colleagues in psychiatry and other branches of medicine and their families. Psychiatrists may reduce their fees in the case of professional patients, but very few are treated free of charge for any length of time. When psychiatrists are asked by their colleagues to justify this position, they point out two factors: First, their income would be drastically reduced especially when their practice consists of a large percentage of professional persons who are in long-term therapy, and second, many psychiatrists, particularly analysts, claim that patients must bring a "financial" sacrifice for their treatment or it will not be successful. The reluctance of psychiatrists to participate in the widespread medical folkway of "professional courtesy" generates intense feeling among the other medical specialists who participate in the etiquette of the profession toward psychiatrists. In our opinion, there is no evidence that psychiatrists are "greedier" than anybody else. They are hardworking professionals who more than anyone else, including the complaint office of the department store, have to face a relentless barrage of hostility, dependence, and raw impulses; this is hard to take and requires defenses and rewards of its own.

* * *

b.   WILL, OTTO A.

Process, Psychotherapy and Schizophrenia*

*   *   *

At the onset it is of importance to me to specify that which I shall *not* attempt to do:

I shall not claim that I "know" just what schizophrenia is, or precisely what its origins are.

I shall not insist that individual psychotherapy, as we now know it, is the only useful therapeutic approach (recognizing its difficulties, expenses in money and time, and limitation of facilities).

I shall not deal with group or multiple therapy or with characteristics of the therapeutic social milieu, noting only that each of these approaches, although characterized as psychological, is concerned with the totality of the organism's behavior.

I do not propose that the fragments of therapeutic intervention upon which I shall comment are necessarily examples of "what to do," or of particular skill in human relationships; they are intended as evidence of the interpersonal aspects of the disorder and one form of its treatment.

In speaking as a therapist I am not identified adequately by the terms *psychiatrist* and *psychoanalyst*, as we so entitled are not cast from a single mold, but differ in our life experiences and retain much of our individual views despite shared aspects of our training. The therapeutic process is furthered through the recognition of two aspects of living: (1) the common qualities of men (including patients)—those patterns of behavior whereby past experience can be extended to a greater comprehension of the present, predictions made and foresight developed, and technical operations refined, tested, and demonstrated for use by others; and (2) the unique qualities of men, contributing to the elusive and ever altering complexity of the interpersonal field and resisting control by any mechanistic, reductionistic theory, or any therapy designed to "discover all" about human motivation.

The social field in which I play the role of therapist is influenced by my personality and by my views of myself, my fellows, and my profession. Because certain of these notions are relevant to a comprehension of my attitude regarding patients and therapy, and influence (as well as being influenced by) my clinical work, I shall summarize them at this point, recognizing that some distortion may occur through their necessary condensation.

I do not think of people as "schizophrenics" (or as "diabetics" or "tuberculars," for that matter). I suggest that the human being is to some extent the ruler of his own destiny and is able to make certain choices (unconscious or otherwise) about the course of his living, once he is enabled to accept his identity. The individual need not lose his identity to a "sickness," and my use of the appellation "a schizophrenic" may indicate that I concur with such identity loss and declare either my greater interest in disorder than person or my fear of the person in my turning to the more impersonal concept of disease.

I am not content currently with thinking of schizophrenia as a disease entity. As a physician (and a member of the American culture—in the general meaning of that term) I have grown accustomed to think in terms of dichotomies—of person and object, inner and outer, body and mind (or soul), biological and cultural, organic and emotional, good and evil, past and present, present and future—and emphasize boundaries and distinctions without recognition on occasion of the possible artificialities of separation, and of the intermingling of one concept with others. I may think of a disease which *infects* or *invades* a person, who thereupon sickens and manifests *signs*, *symptoms*, and evidences pathological alterations, justifying the giving of a treatment with the hope that the illness will be driven from him, leaving him *well*— to the pleasure of his friends and the regret of his foes. Such concepts regarding a barrier between person and environment have demonstrable utility, but may limit our comprehension of schizophrenic behavior. The undue emphasis on such a dichotomy can lead to man's becoming the object—being depersonalized and losing this identity—and even becoming an object to himself in states of alienation and "detachment from the world."

I think of schizophrenia as being a dynamic process rather than a clearly circumscribed entity. Each "case" has an existence of his own, views the world in his own way, and must be dealt with somewhat uniquely for his own greater realization.

*   *   *

Miss X was the oldest of two children, and was "always" known as bright, affectionate, and "good." In her first college year she lived at home, and one night surprised her parents by entering their room unexpectedly, awakening them, accusing them of wishing to harm her, and striking her mother. When she was asked to explain herself she shouted that she had been aroused from sleep by her father's voice telling her that she was no good, and that she believed that her mother wished to kill her by poisoning her food and that she had spread derogatory stories about her in the community. Her parents denied this, asked where she had gotten such wild ideas, and suggested that she pull herself together and behave in her more usual fashion. The girl's response was another violent attack on the mother, complicated by the father's efforts at conciliation and control, and ending with the daughter running from the house to that of a

---

* Reprinted from: *Psychotherapy of the Psychoses*, edited by Arthur Burton, © 1961, by Basic Books, Inc., Publishers, New York.

neighbor, where she arrived weeping, disarrayed, frightened, and markedly confused. She locked herself in the neighbor's bathroom, swallowed several barbiturate capsules, broke the window (cutting her arms superficially), and finally subsided on the floor in the corner, mute and stuporous. She was taken to a hospital. Her mild drug intoxication and wounds were treated, and she remained there withdrawn and silent for five days during which time she seemingly paid no attention to anyone and was fed by tube. On the fifth day she became disturbed, attacked her nurse, screamed, broke furniture, attempted to run out of the room, and acted as if she were terrified. Upon being restrained she fought briefly, but again became mute and withdrawn, lying on her back on her bed, or curled up on the floor beneath it. Two days lager she was transferred to a psychiatric hospital, diagnosed as dementia praecox (schizophrenia), catatonic type.

Miss X remained in the mental hospital for eighteen months, during which time she was treated with insulin (sixty-five comas) and electroshock (fifty convulsions). For weeks at a time she was mute and unresponsive, her withdrawal being interrupted by transient episodes of assaultiveness and destructiveness. She showed some improvement during the shock therapy, for several seven-to-ten-day periods dressing conventionally, eating, talking somewhat guardedly, and preferring to stay by herself rather than to join in group activities. When questioned about her difficulties she became tense, said that there was nothing wrong with her, and asked to be discharged from the hospital. She would say nothing about the events that preceded hospitalization and refused to visit with her parents. The quiet periods were soon followed by disturbance, and shock treatment was discontinued after the first year. During the last six months in the hospital Miss X spent the greater portion of each day in a single room because of her assaultiveness and her apparent fear of others. She would wear no clothing other than an old dressing gown, resisted bathing, frequently burned herself with cigarettes, and was apparently hallucinating. Through these months the approaches of staff members were repeatedly rebuffed, and toward the end of her stay there was very little optimism about the prospects of her betterment. Miss X became increasingly isolated, and any ideas that she had about being unapproachable and hopeless were confirmed and matched by those of the personnel. It was in a state of discouragement, low morale, withdrawal, bitter resentment, and a feeling of personal destructiveness that this woman of twenty came to the hospital where we first met.

*   *   *

When I first met Miss X she displayed no great enthusiasm for me, psychiatrists in general (or anything psychiatric), having found little in her life so far that reassured her about the benefits of human contacts, professional or otherwise. When I entered her room she was crouched in a corner behind the head of the bed, and drew away as I introduced myself. I spoke quietly, said that I would stay for a while, and seated myself in a chair across the room from her. Miss X kept her back turned to me, and after about ten minutes of silence I said that I knew a little about her previous hospitalization, having read the record, but that I wanted to hear from her what her experiences had been. She suddenly turned toward me, spat on the floor, and told me to get out. I did not leave, but said that I should remain for about half an hour, and should return for several such meetings each week on a regular schedule. Miss X then said that she was no good, and that no one could help her. I suggested that there might be a certain extravagance in such statements, and that all I could guarantee was that I should attempt to get some clarity about what had happened to her and what went on between us. For a moment she seemed to be more relaxed, but then became frightened, pointed at her head, and said, "I know what you'll do." "No," I said, "we'll do nothing but meet and talk together. There's no insulin or electric treatment here."[9]

"I don't believe you," was the reply, but her tenseness subsided a little.

Without going into further detail regarding this particular interview, I shall outline certain things which I wish to accomplish in my first meeting with a patient. I do not always realize these goals, but I keep them in mind and try to discover what may lead me to fail in their attainment.

1. I make some simple concise statement regarding what I know about the patient's difficulties.

2. I briefly identify myself, answering directly any questions directed to me, and suggest that since I am a therapist and the patient is supposedly someone with difficulties in living, there is professional reason for our meeting.

3. If possible, I obtain some account from the patient about his life and his concept of his problems.

4. I attempt to act in such a fashion that excessive anxiety is not roused in the patient, and do not "push" at any topic when I observe a marked increase of discomfort.

5. I am not restrictive beyond setting limits to behavior that might be hurtful to the patient, to me, or to others.

---

9. I do not make use of somatic procedures (insulin and electroshock) in the psychotherapy of schizophrenia. The difficulties encountered in treatment are to be dealt with by an investigation of, and an appropriate modification of, movements in the interpersonal field and not by maneuvers which, in my experience, jeopardize rather than improve the therapeutic relationship. Beyond the occasional use of mild sedatives I have not had experience with attempts to modify the course of therapy by chemical means (use of ataractic drugs, for example).

6. If there is evident some marked distortion in the patient's perception of the current field, I comment on this and suggest other possibilities of interpretation.

7. I outline my plan for seeing the patient, give him a schedule of my appointments with him, and indicate without undue pressure that I shall continue to see him, and that I shall not be driven away by fear of him or his behavior.

It was my opinion that Miss X would do well in intensive psychotherapy. This view was based on the following observations:

1. Her intelligence was superior and she had demonstrated ability as a student; she was obviously well equipped to deal with abstract symbol operations and their verbalization.

2. Although she had encountered difficulties in her living she had also had successes—as a member of her family, as a student, and as a participant in social activities. Self-esteem is not so fragile if there are some tangible, socially recognized and approved accomplishments in one's life.

3. Miss X had had some experience with a friend in early adolescence. Such a contact with intimacy, imperfect though it may have been, ties one to human relatedness, and is a useful background to the development of a therapeutic relationship.

4. Although Miss X was discouraged she had not yet succumbed to the demoralizing experience of prolonged hospitalization, and clearly hebephrenic or paranoid changes had not occurred.

5. Miss X showed organization of the ego despite her obvious great vulnerability to anxiety, and displayed a reactivity indicating that the despair which she often experienced had not been replaced by the apathy and detachment of chronic withdrawal.

The Therapist

I don't know just what kind of a person is best suited for work with a schizophrenic patient. I have observed that various people with contrasting personalities do well as therapists, which leads me to think that the schizophrenic person has considerable ability to form a relationship in which growth is possible providing that the therapist (or other) has patience as well as a fair degree of liking and respect for his fellow man. There are certain qualities which seem to me to be of importance in a therapist.

1. He should be able to participate in, as well as observe, the reciprocal action of the therapeutic field as there will be many times during which he cannot be the detached onlooker.

2. He often will be required to deal with rapidly shifting events, the mode of communication and action altering with little preliminary notice. He must also endure the discouragement and frustration arising during long periods in which no progress is evident and in which he may become the target of

hostility and despair, and the participant in painful loneliness.

3. He should have some interest in, and facility with, nonverbal communication.

4. If the therapist has a great need to organize speech and behavior in logical, rational sequences, he will be disturbed by the frequency with which the treatment is marked by the illogical, by time distortions, by seeming inconsistencies, and a quality of the odd. In brief, he must feel some comfort with the primary process.

5. The unduly conventional therapist may find it necessary to "fit" his patient into a conventional mold, not permitting the patient to develop in a different, and possibly more suitable, fashion. Such conventionality may hinder therapy.

6. The therapist should be able to participate in a relationship marked at times by great intensity and structured so that mutual growth can occur, dependence can be experienced and independence fostered, appropriate limits set, and eventual separation made possible.

7. The therapist will experience strong feelings during the work, and must maintain a curiosity about his own behavior and motivations. At times he will find it useful to discuss the course of therapy and his participation in it with a colleague, and on occasion he may seek further clarity about his actions in the therapeutic sessions by talking about them with his patient. By this last I do not mean that I favor burdening the patient with my own reactions, but I do suggest that there may be times when patient and therapist may collaborate in seeking the explanation for a troublesome aspect of behavior exhibited by either of them.

8. Unless the therapist has had some personal experience of the distress of anxiety he may be insensitive to his patient. In any case he will experience at times considerable anxiety in his work, and this he must attempt to understand and endure, without seeking to eliminate it entirely.

9. The relationship with the schizophrenic person (and with many others not so entitled) is marked by recurrent approach and withdrawal. The patient, having developed the need for relationship, responds to its persistent and understanding offer with some acceptance and improved communication. Having experienced much anxiety with humans, he is wary of relationship and tends to withdraw from it, the mounting anxiety disturbing communication. In the moves toward closeness the person finds the needed relatedness and identification with another; in the withdrawal (often marked by negativism) he finds the separateness which favors his feeling of being distinct and self-identified. Such recurrent movements are components of growth and self-realization. They may be thought of as promise and disappointment, and as acceptance and rejection. The therapist

must be able to tolerate these characteristics of the field without becoming unduly anxious or feeling rejected himself.

Course of Therapy

Miss X and I worked in therapy for four and a half years, the first eighteen months of which she lived in the hospital. During the first two years we met five to seven days each week, usually spending an hour together; but on some occasions the session was extended to two hours or longer. I frequently (usually each day) discussed the course of treatment with the nurses and others concerned with the patient's care, and the collaborative nature of this work deserves much greater attention than I am able to devote to it here. Although I had a regular schedule for my meetings with Miss X, I also saw her at unscheduled times at her request, or because she was disturbed, or because I thought that therapy would be advanced by so doing. In the last three years of treatment we met regularly three to four hours weekly.

In the first few months of therapy Miss X was frequently disturbed, and I made an effort to be consistent in my attitudes, to present a clear picture of myself, to avoid making verbal statements that conflicted with my nonverbal operations, and to set clear-cut and firm limits to any destructive behavior. During this period I usually met Miss X in her room because she was too frightened and unpredictably violent to come to my office. I emphasized tangible aspects of the situation available to observation by both of us, avoid "pushing" for information about obviously distressing subjects, and did not attempt to interpret the content of dreams and hallucinations, although I listened to her accounts of these as I did to any other communication—without excessive interest or surprise. One of my goals during this time was to identify a need of the patient, respond to it quickly when possible, help her recognize her own need and express it more clearly, and encourage her to accept the help of others in meeting her needs as well as to discover ways of more effectively meeting them herself.

During the first year Miss X's anxiety subsided somewhat. I was more acceptable to her; we were consistently identified as therapist and patient (although she was frequently anything but in agreement with many of my ideas); hallucinations appeared only at times of intense anxiety; and we were able to meet in my office.

After the reduction of the major disturbance Miss X spoke of me as a therapist, but made many observations about me that I did not attempt to interpret but observed as slowly forming a picture of me not entirely in keeping with the usual view of myself. I was described as some twenty years older than my actual age, harsh, cold, unsympathetic, controlling, and seductive, and she feared that my only concern with her would be to satisfy my own ambitions. With the experience of much anxiety and recurrent bursts of rage Miss X noted that in her description of me she was telling me about her attitudes towards her father and men in general, and something of life in her home. We were able to discriminate realistic and accurate (sometimes painfully so) observations of me from those that were more exaggerated and to a greater extent influenced by her past.

With increasing clarification of her relationship to her father Miss X seemed more at ease, and for a couple of months she talked with relative freedom about many current and past events, but had very little to say of her mother. The sessions then became marked by increasing anxiety, the source of which we could not at first identify. Miss X became more suspicious of me and her anger increased, with the result that she would suddenly attack me. I was now described as something loathsome, filthy, disgusting, and essentially evil that would destroy the young woman. Any interpretations I made were met with denial, silence, or increases of anxiety, and I realized that I was being dealt with by Miss X in terms of experience that possibly had occurred early in life, had been dissociated, and could not be expressed readily in words. When her anxiety was very intense and her behavior unpredictable she would be admitted to the hospital for periods of one to three or four days. During this time of the recurrent intense anxiety accompanying the coming into awareness of symbols of very troublesome aspects of important interpersonal experiences, we slowly learned something of her relationship with her mother. I personally felt considerable anxiety while we worked on these problems, and was disturbed by the intensity of the patient's emotions, by my own anger and fear aroused in response to them, and by the vagueness and lack of organization that characterized the communication. At times I found myself strongly moved by feelings whose origins I could not at first discover; but later I noted that they were apparently in response to the multitude of nonverbal cues presented by the patient, not clearly observed in my awareness, but nonetheless reacted to by me in an empathic fashion.

With increased comprehension of Miss X's relationship to her mother, anxiety again was reduced. She visited her parents (which she had not wished to do for about two years), and the therapy continued in a more conventional manner. We sat in chairs about six feet apart, and I listened while she attempted to note and express verbally whatever "came to mind." Evidences of psychosis were no longer present and for the last two years we explored her current and past relationships (including the one between us), and she took part in activities which she had previously avoided. Her physical symptoms— fatigue, diarrhea, vomitting—were increased at intervals during the first three years of therapy, but subsided without our attempting to "explain" their possible connection to obscure referents. She took pride in her obviously increasing attractiveness, gained tolerance of competitive situations, began to date with young men, and completed her college studies. We terminated our work together when she was well on the way to gaining increased satisfaction in her living, related to people without excessive anxiety, had a reasonably accurate and confirmable view of herself (and of me), and was no longer so fearful of her self-identity.

*   *   *

In the course of my days I do not see a large number of patients, and not all of those whom I do see will be significantly bettered through my therapeutic efforts. I have not discovered in myself any unusual characteristics which particularly qualify me for this work. I am often baffled by the behavior of others (and sometimes by my own), and not infrequently experience anxiety, anger, and discouragement in the course of treatment. I do not think that intensive psychotherapy can be provided for every schizophrenic patient and, even if this were done, the results of such a human enterprise could not be guaranteed.

*   *   *

NOTES

NOTE 1

ARIETI, SIVANO

Interpretation of Schizophrenia *

*   *   *

[S]hock therapy is only a symptomatic treatment. The patient may lose his overt symptomatology, but the basic psychopathological factors remain unchanged, unless the treatment is accompanied by psychotherapy, or by changes in the environment of the patient. Fortunately, environmental changes may occur, since the drastic nature of shock treatment often acts as a catalyst on the emotional attitudes of the relatives toward the patient. The majority of cases which after shock therapy are discharged from hospitals as cured, are in reality only freed of symptoms. The fact that patients have lost delusions and hallucinations and other apparent symptoms does not mean that they are cured. If these patients who are discharged were to be probed by more psychodynamically oriented procedures (a measure which I do not recommend unless sustained by regular prolonged psychotherapy), the incompleteness and fragility of their improvement would manifest themselves.

_____

* © 1955 by Robert Brunner, Basic Books, Inc., Publishers, New York (p. 480).

In spite of these negative aspects shock treatment should by no means be removed from our armamentarium. It is still useful in several cases. The reasons for my apparently inconsistent attitude are simple ones which must be faced with equanimity and in a realistic spirit by those who advocate psychotherapeutic methods as I do:

1. Psychotherapy, even at the present stage of psychiatric development, can be available only to an infinitesimal minority of patients.

2. Psychotherapy, even in the hands of the most experienced, does not work in every case.

3. There are cases which are extremely urgent on account of the concomitant occurrence of a physical illness. In these cases some results have to be quickly effected, and one cannot afford to wait for the long, time-consuming therapeutic procedure.

4. Symptomatic treatment cannot be condemned when something better is not available. For example, x-ray treatment may be an unsatisfactory, symptomatic treatment for malignant neoplasms, but in many instances it is the only treatment which may be given.

Another point which should be considered, because it has been a subject of concern for many who advocate the exclusive use of psychotherapeutic methods, is the question of whether shock treatment can hurt the patient physically or psychologically. _Primum non nocere_ has been one of the first therapeutic concepts since ancient times. It seems to me that this concern has been exaggerated. Complications such as fractures are no more common than complications, let us say, after general surgery. The treatment, however, does produce a change on the nervous system. Some writers have found severe histologic alterations, especially in the case of insulin treatment, . . . while instead, others have found irreversible cell damage _only_ when the animals died in coma, or when unusually high doses of units were injected over a long period of time. . . .

As far as the convulsive treatment is concerned, both metrazol and electric, the works of many authors . . . seem to have made evident that the produced changes are all _reversible_, unless an unusual quantity of treatment is given for a prolonged period of time. From the histologic studies, it is to be deduced that the nervous tissue returns to a normal condition not too long after treatment.

If physical hazards do not exist or are minimal when proper therapy is given, then the objections of many authors must concern possible psychological harm. Eissler speaks of "the great danger" he saw in shock therapy, and of his great efforts to save patients from it. Many psychiatrists . . . go so far as to feel that the practice of shock treatment is the expression of some hostility of the therapist, or of the desire to get rid of the patient, or a remnant of the medieval concept which held that it was good to punish the "possessed" mental patient. These feelings and ideas to me seem far-fetched and unduly dramatic. I do admit that therapists who do not succeed with psychotherapy, may have the desire to remove the patient from the psychotherapeutic situation, and refer him to shock therapy. With a few exceptions, which involve personal problems of the therapist, I do not feel that patients recommended for shock therapy are being punished. This may actually be the concept of the patients. There is no more hostility or desire to punish in instituting shock therapy than there is in doing surgery on a patient who needs it. I feel, as a rule, that the selection of shock treatment is the expression, not of hostility, but of the organic learning of the psychiatrist. This learning may be valid or not, but it need not be an expression or a rationalization of hostility.

But let us go back to the psychological harm that the treatment may produce. Usually it is assumed that the patient feels that finally he has been punished or "castrated." From the cases of schizophrenia which I have treated psychotherapeutically after shock treatment, I cannot reach that conclusion. The feeling of having been punished is more frequently encountered in manic-depressive or involutional patients who have been treated with convulsive therapies.

The other psychological objection is based on the fact that the shock treatment does not eradicate the causes but represses them. This statement about shock treatment is correct; it was implicit in the statement that this therapy is only symptomatic. But if, in many patients, it is impossible to eradicate the causes of the disorder, it is of some value at least to repress the asocial and antisocial symptoms. Incidentally, even certain forms of psychotherapy, like that of Federn, aim at a symptomatic repression of the id.

Generally, after shock therapy, the patient is able to return to society; he will no longer be a public charge, and although his functions may be curtailed, he may be able to live some kind of limited social life. In many fortunate cases, where the dramatic succession of events (acute attack—hospitalization—institution of shock treatment) have acted as catalytic agents on the environmental forces, the results may be much more than a removal of the immediate symptoms.

How is shock treatment capable of producing its symptomatic therapeutic effects? Here the field is still open to the realm of speculation. Gordon, in an interesting short paper, lists no less than fifty theories which have been advanced to explain the effect of shock treatment. Twenty-seven of them are somatogenic theories and twenty-three are psychogenic. At the present stage of our knowledge it is difficult to ascertain which one or which combination of them is valid. In spite of the fact that shock treatment acts as a psychological catalyst on the relatives of the patient, and in spite of the fact that I consider schizo-phrenia a psychogenic condition, I am inclined to believe that shock treatment has a predominantly physiological action, not a psychological one. Although the improvement may be partially due to the fact that the patient receives some kind of care, obviously it cannot be due only to the fact of being treated, irrespectively of the nature of the treatment. Past physical treatments, like hormone therapy, did not produce any effect on schizophrenics. The symptomatic improvement is also not due to the fact that patients become more accessible to psychotherapy. Although it is true that they become more accessible to psychotherapy, I have seen hundreds of patients, discharged from hospitals after shock treatment free of overt symptoms, even though they did not receive any kind of psychotherapy.

*   *   *

. . . The shock treatment is successful if the patient, with the help of others, can manage to reach some kind of solid integration before the conflicts come back; so that he will be able then to repress them or to find some kind of modus vivendi with them. . . .

*   *   *

NOTE 2

WINKELMAN, N. WILLIAM

A Long-term Investigation of Chlorpromazine*

*   *   *

. . . It has been our main thesis for the last 3 years that optimum results with the neuroleptic drugs can be achieved only by understanding the patient's personality structure. Accordingly, intelligent treatment must be individually determined, not only from the personality at the onset of treatment, but from an informed evaluation of the changes that are constantly taking place. . . .

Our present conception of the psychologic action of chlorpromazine, that is, the action on psychological functions secondary to the actions on certain brain centers, we explain by using the concept of psychic energetics. Every psychic act is invested with psychic energy which is freely mobile and shifts from one psychic element to another. When this energy charges or cathects an unconscious instinctual drive, the drive presses for immediate discharge in affects and in motility. This characterizes unconscious or primary process activity. The ego may or may not be able to accept cathected contents of the unconscious that are pressing for discharge, such as fantasies, drives, wishes, sensations, and feelings. Thus, conflicts develop. Handling of the conflict can be either by complete repression and a decathexis of

*116 *American Journal of Psychiatry*, 865–869, (1960). Reprinted by permission.

the instinctual drive or by acceptance of the drive by the ego as it becomes fully conscious. Each of these two methods of handling a conflict can be utilized and elaborated into a scientifically organized method of psychiatric treatment. Probing of the unconscious with acceptance of the drive, is accomplished by psychotherapy, and convulsive therapy is an example of suppressive therapy.

We feel that the phenothiazines can be utilized for either of these two basic methods of treatment. In the literature, for the most part, phenothiazine therapy means suppressive therapy and utilizes moderately large or large doses with a rapid buildup to the optimum therapeutic dosage, which in suppressive therapy is much higher than the dosage used in the uncovering techniques. . . . Ego functions are, without doubt, also affected at this dosage, but comparatively far less than the knocking out of the abnormal primary process activity with the result that symptomatology is markedly altered. Whenever there is a reduction in dosage below a point that is constantly varying according to the status of the ego-id conflict, the inhibition of the cathexis ceases, and symptomatology bursts forth. . . .

If it is clinically desirable to treat a patient by a technique of probing the unconscious with acceptance of the drive and development of insight, there is an entirely different approach. . . . We feel that mild to moderate dosages of chloropromazine produce an alteration of psychic energy and its distribution, which in turn affects many aspects of intrapsychic dynamics. There is alteration in the energy directed into the various psychic-structural components which can be studied by very careful observation. When the carefully determined optimum therapeutic dose is achieved, the following changes may occur which we repeatedly observed in studying patients for 3 hours per week over 3 years with alternating drug and non-drug months. There is lessening of primary process drives. There is lessening of super ego strength. There is minimal diminution of ego functioning. There results from these changes a relative increase in ego strength. Defenses need be less strongly cathected. However, since the energy of the instinctual need is reduced, the defenses are relatively stronger. With unimpairment of the ego, there is improved reality testing. There also results an unusual emotion, indifference to painful internal and external stimuli. There appears to be a decrease in symbolizing ability with a lessening of displacement, so people are seen more realistically. Owing to this and the increase in ego strength, "acting out" is markedly reduced. Interpersonal relationships are much improved.

*   *   *

. . . We feel more and more strongly that the entire treatment philosophy should be oriented towards an understanding of the status of the ego and adjusting the dosage accordingly. In the acute psychotic patient, we first use large doses to subdue the pathological id drives. In so doing, we hope that the ego will eventually be strong enough to take more control. In the psychoneurotic and chronic psychotic patient, we treat while carefully watching the status of the ego, always endeavoring to strengthen that structure. We feel that these drugs have great value in the psychoneurotic patient when administered with knowledge and above all, understanding.

*   *   *

. . . Cessation of the drug treatment brings on a return of original symptomatology in three quarters of the patients. We felt that the more successful the psychotherapy or living experiences during the drug treatment the less likely was there to be a return of symptoms. The more generally successful the treatment of a psychiatric patient, the more likely will the patient remain asymptomatic when the dosage of drug ultimately is decreased or stopped completely. We observed unequivocally that the patients who received only drug treatment also had a quick return of symptomatology upon drug withdrawal, whereas those in well-oriented long-term psychotherapy either did not have a return of symptoms or only a partial return. Furthermore, they could go longer without the drug before any symptoms developed. We feel that the amount of drug needed to maintain the patient free of symptoms is an excellent indication of the degree of recovery from the abnormal intrapsychic process.

It is concluded that long-term chlorpromazine therapy is an extremely valuable and sensitive treatment, not only in the unapproachable psychotic as a suppressive therapy, but also in the approachable chronic psychotic and more approachable psychoneurotic, where it can be used as a constructive force furthering the psychotherapeutic process. Without psychotherapy, many good results are seen where successful living was combined with the drug. It is believed that in general the effectiveness of treatment is directly related to the orientation of the treating physician, how well he understands his patient, and how he applies this knowledge not only in the pharmacologic treatment but in the total treatment of his patients.

NOTE 3

EDITORIAL

Peace of Mind*

*   *   *

If we take the easy way and merely "tranquilize" our patients with new or old drugs, we may seduce them into a bogus health, but it will weaken their

* 113 *American Journal Psychiatry*, 663–664 (1957). Reprinted by permission.

adaptive capacities. Our patients will lose some of the keenness needed to live in this accelerated world; there may be more traffic accidents and the cult of relaxation may degrade our morale. If we psychiatrists surrender to this easy kind of therapy, and give up the careful study of our patient's problems, we might as well let the manufacturers of the "tranquilizers" contact with the municipalities to put tons of drugs into the reservoirs of drinking water. Then everybody will relax.

No psychiatrist would subscribe to such a ridiculous notion. Our aim is to make patients responsible and at peace with themselves. For those patients capable of adaptation there are no cheap, wholesale shortcuts. Lasting peace of mind can be bought only dearly, by self-knowledge.

C.

Some Problems for Decision

1.

WHAT THERAPEUTIC RESPONSES ARE APPROPRIATE FOR WHAT PURPOSES?

a. The Case of Bernard Goldfine
Transcript of Habeas Corpus Hearing (December 9, 1960, D.D.C)

Before

HONORABLE GEORGE L. HART, JR.

* * *

MR. EDWARD BENNETT WILLIAMS: . . .

[O]n October 3rd, when the income tax evasion case in which this petitioner is the defendant came on for trial in the United States District Court for the District of Massachusetts, the question was raised with respect to the petitioner's competency to stand trial.

Chief Judge Sweeney of the United States District Court *sui sponti* ordered a . . . mental examination, under Section 4244 of Title 18 of the United States Code. The petitioner was remanded to St. Elizabeths Hospital in Boston for purpose of that examination, and three psychiatrists were appointed by the court to conduct it.

On October 10th those psychiatrists unanimously reported to the Court, via a letter which they each signed, that the petitioner was incompetent to stand trial.

At the request of the United States Attorney for Massachusetts a hearing was held on that subject under the provisions of Section 4244, and a decision was rendered by the judge in Massachusetts that the defendant was in fact incompetent to stand trial.

At that time he was . . . sent to St. Elizabeths Hospital in Washington, D.C., where he has been since October 18th.

Now, if the Court please, we have no quarrel with the action of Judge Sweeney in the District Court in Massachusetts in exercising his discretion to place the petitioner in the custody of the Attorney General pusuant to Section 4244 of Title 18.

Our contention is that the Attorney General is now flagrantly abusing his custodial function, which is designed to bring about the return to competency of this defendant so that he can stand trial and face the indictment under which he is charged in Massachusetts.

It is our contention . . . that the manner in which the Attorney General has exercised his custodial function has been to bring about a situation where the defendant will never be able to face trial because the custodial function which he has been exercising has been detrimental to the petitioner's mental health, and has the effect of causing further deterioration of his mental health, and that he can be restored to mental health only if a different form of custody is exercised over him.

I think under the authorities we are clearly entitled to test this, if the court please, under a petition for writ of habeas corpus.

* * *

THE COURT: Well, now, let me get your contention correctly: If you test only whether the method of confinement is such as to deprive him of his constitutional rights, it certainly could not test whether in the matter of discretion he should be treated one way or treated another way.

* * *

MR. WILLIAMS: Of course not. Of course, this proceeding . . . is designed to test the exercise of custody by the Attorney General by confinement in this case, because we expect to show through testimony offered here today before Your Honor that confinement is not the proper way to treat this sick petitioner, and that it will not bring about his restoration to competency, if that be possible. That the most effective method of treating him is in a method other than by confinement at the hospital where he is now confined.

* * *

THE COURT: Are you . . . prepared to show that he is financially able to get out-patient treatment?

MR. WILLIAMS: We are prepared to show that he is financially able to provide his needed psychiatric help.

THE COURT: All right, then you may present your testimony.

*   *   *

David J. Owens

was called as a witness by the petitioner . . .

DIRECT EXAMINATION BY MR. WILLIAMS.

*   *   *

Q. Are you presently a physician specializing in psychiatry attached to St. Elizabeths Hospital here in Washington, D.C.?   A. Yes, sir, I am.

*   *   *

Q. As a result of your interviews with Mr. Goldfine and your observations of Mr. Goldfine while he has been at St. Elizabeth's Hospital, did you come to any conclusions with respect to his mental health? A. Yes, I did.

*   *   *

In my opinion, he is suffering from an organic disease of the central nervous system, specifically classified as a chronic brain syndrome associated with cerebral arterio-sclerosis, which is hardening of the arteries of the central nervous system or the brain, and as a result of this illness he is incompetent to stand trial.

*   *   *

Q. Now, when you use the term "chronic brain syndrome" would you state for the court and for the record precisely what you mean? A. Well, by chronic I mean that the condition shows chronicity, it is progressive, it is irreversible. A brain syndrome is a group or a syndrome of symptoms that are more or less characteristic of this particular condition, such as impaired judgment, disorientation, bad memory, the lability of affect, and in general intellectual impairment.

Q. Now, when you say that the disability is organic in nature, what do you mean, Doctor? A. That there is actual damage of an irreversible nature within the brain itself or in the vessels of the brain.

*   *   *

Q. What was the collective opinion of the doctors with respect to his prospects for improvement? A. As mentioned before, his prospects for improving and becoming competent are poor if he remains in the hospital environment.

[H]e should be treated on an out-patient basis.

*   *   *

BY THE COURT.

Q. Now, Doctor, you say . . . that his prospects for improving and becoming competent are poor if he remains in the hospital environment.

Do you all mean by that in St. Elizabeths' environment or any hospital environment? A. Well, my understanding, my impression is that any type of rather rigid confinement.

Q. Whether in your hospital or any other? A. That is correct, sir.

BY MR. WILLIAMS:

Q. Doctor, when you concluded that the patient had a better chance of regaining competency on an out-patient treatment basis, what do you have in mind as a method of treatment for this man? A. I would say under some supervision, that is, psychiatrically and medically speaking. That is supervision to the extent that a psychiatrist would see the patient once or twice a week depending on his needs, to observe the patient for any change in his mood or behavior; or he certainly needs an internist to follow him medically speaking because of some heart disease that he has had a history of having had; and some supervision for the individual.

*   *   *

Q. Now, what is your diagnosis with respect to his chance to regain competency if he is continued in the hospitalization program which he is now undergoing? A. Extremely poor.

*   *   *

Mr. Goldfine has become more agitated, more anxious, and more tense. Since he has been at the hospital, the depression has improved somewhat in his condition in that he does not weep or cry as frequently as he did.

However, I feel that the symptoms of arteriosclerosis have become, shall we say, more aggravated, or at least more pronounced since he has been hospitalized; and I attribute some of this to the external stress and pressures that have been on him since he has been at the hospital.

Q. Have you had discussions with various members of his family? A. Yes, I have.

Q. Is it your conclusion, Doctor, that he would have a better chance for recovery with his family and with out-patient psychiatric treatment? A. I think that he would.

Q. Why do you say that, sir? A. Well, I think at the present time there is considerable friction in the family, a tremendous amount which has certainly been accentuated since he has been hospitalized at St. Elizabeths. My own opinion is that if he is treated on an out-patient basis that this friction will be alleviated to a considerable extent once he reappears at home.

* * *

Q. Doctor, in your opinion, from your observations of the petitioner, is he potentially harmful to himself or to others? A. I do not think that he would be.

Q. Is he potentially harmful to property or officers of the United States. A. I do not think that he would be.

* * *

He is making plans and hopes for the future, hoping to get back into his business and his home. Even though some of his plans may be unrealistic, at least the thought of making plans for the future, as though things are going to be much better than the possibility that they are going to be, this is not indicative of someone who is a suicidal risk.

He holds no animosity toward anyone else, and he feels that he has been well treated. There is no real complaint about others, so I don't think he would have any homicidal tendencies toward anyone else.

* * *

CROSS-EXAMINATION BY MR. GASCH:

* * *

Q. Now, from what you have observed of Mr. Goldfine, would you believe that he was competent to handle his business affairs? A. Well, I don't know enough about his business affairs to make that decision. I think that certainly he would be able to go to a grocery store and purchase groceries, or such as, minor chores such as this, but I don't think to engage in a big concern or big type of business. . . .

* * *

I don't think that in his present condition he could resume full-time work the same as he was doing ten years ago. I don't think he could manage it adequately or, I would say, as adequately as he has done previously.

* * *

Q. Would you find it desirable to see to it that everyone who wanted to see him was prevented from seeing him, in other words, limit the number of those who saw him? A. I think that certainly not everyone who wanted to see him should see him, no. But I think he has ability to decide if he wants to see someone, and wants to be visited by them, I think that he should make this decision, that he should have a right to have a visit with his wife, or any friend or attorney, if he so desires.

Q. The hospital has not limited those whom he has wanted to see, has it? A. Yes, we have.

* * *

Mauris Platkin

was called as a witness by the petitioner . . .

* * *

CROSS-EXAMINATION BY MR. GASCH:

* * *

Q. Was he able to transact business in the hospital? A. Well, he did, as was indicated, meet with a number of, some business associates, a fair number of attorneys, and the nature and the character of the transactions which took place, I don't know anything about. I do think some of them were in the nature of business transactions.

Q. You feel that he should be permitted to continue to engage in business? A. To a limited extent, yes.

Q. How would you limit it, Doctor? A. Well, to begin with, I think that this man should be placed under . . . the care of a doctor who should be made fully acquainted with his history at St. Elizabeths Hospital in Washington, his previous hospitalizations.

BY THE COURT:

Q. What type of doctor, Doctor? A. This might be an internist, it might be a psychiatrist; perhaps it should be both, who can evaluate both his physical condition as well as his psychiatric changes.

BY MR. GASCH:

Q. Once or twice a week? A. This I think should be left to the judgment of the doctors in question.

Q. Do you think that would be adequate?

* * *

A. I don't see why not if he were—

Q. Would that be better than the type of treatment that you give him at St. Elizabeths? A. I think—it is not better; it is different because we do a little more than simply confine him.

Q. Now when he calls for a doctor under the circumstances that you mention at St. Elizabeths, eventually he sees one, doesn't he? A. Sometimes he does; other times he doesn't.

Q. You gentlemen are there, are you not? A. Well, we have other matters; we have other patients; we have other commitments. We are not always available.

Q. Do you see him once a day at least, either you or Dr. Owens? A. Or one of the other staff physicians manage, generally manage to see him about once a day.

Q. But if he were home and saw a psychiatrist once a week, he wouldn't have access to the psychiatrist, would he? A. Well, he would certainly have access to him if he wanted to see him.

What he wants to see us about in those cases is

simply to transmit to us some of the problems that he wants to deal with, because he is confined, and he has no way, and knowing that either Dr. Owens or I are in the best position to grant certain requests, he wants to see us very frequently for those reasons, rather than for treatment in the conventional sense.

*   *   *

Q. Would an individual who was in the condition that you have found Mr. Goldfine to be, be likely to dissipate assets if he were allowed to manage his affairs? Would you feel that his business judgment was 100 per cent? A. Oh, I don't feel his business judgment is 100 per cent.

Q. If he were allowed to manage his affairs, might he not dissipate his assets? A. This is a question I can't answer with any degree of certainty.

*   *   *

THE COURT: Will counsel approach the bench?

*   *   *

. . . We are taking testimony on this rule, and, of course, the petitioner is entitled to be here if he wishes to be.

Now, you have not requested that the petitioner be here, so I take it you do not want him here.

MR. WILLIAMS: Yes. All I want to say, Your Honor, is that it was from the medical point of view better that he not hear this testimony concerning his own state of mental health.

THE COURT: I agree with you, but I wanted to get it on the record, if you want him to be here, because he is entitled to be here.

*   *   *

MR. WILLIAMS: Well, I took this position in Boston also, with the Judge's indulgence, that it would be better from a medical point of view and from a humanitarian point of view that he do not hear the testimony.

THE COURT: I am sure of that too.[*]

(Thereupon counsel resumed their places in the courtroom and the following occurred:)

*   *   *

---

[*] [T]he process of the trial in itself was a punishment for Jack Ruby far beyond what the jury decreed or what he deserved. Although Oswald may have died, undisturbed, with whatever illusions led him to his deed, Jack Ruby, before a crowded courtroom and the press of the world, was stripped of both his self-respect and his illusions. He heard himself analyzed by his psychiatrist as a latent homosexual with a compulsive desire to be liked and respected, described by his own lawyer as the village clown, damningly quoted—untruthfully, he felt—by members of the police department in whose reflected prestige he had been happy to bask, and forced to sit as a passive witness while the attorneys, the judge and the jury fought over and decided his fate. As one of the newsmen, Edward Linn, put it, "It would have been kinder to stone him to

Winfred Overholser

was called as a witness by the respondent . . .

DIRECT EXAMINATION BY MR. GASCH:

*   *   *

Q. What is your present position? A. I am Superintendent of St. Elizabeths Hospital.

*   *   *

Q. Now, what is your conclusion about whether Mr. Goldfine is making progress in your hospital since his admission? A. Well, I have seen no great change in him. In fact, in some ways, perhaps due to the fact that he is receiving a tranquillizing drug, he has seemed somewhat less anxious than he did . . . when I saw him first.

I do not see that there has been any marked deterioration. I think he is approximately the same as when he came in.

*   *   *

Q. How about his anxieties? How do you feel about that? A. Well, I don't know to what extent, of course, the tranquillizing drugs that he has had have affected his anxiety. He certainly has some. He did have a good bit apparently when he came in and, of course, there was a certain amount of justification for it. It is a realistic situation in part.

Q. Do you find that persons committed to the hospital, locked up, are generally depressed by that at the outset? A. Rather likely to be at the start until they become somewhat reconciled to it, perhaps, yes. It is not unusual.

Q. Have you seen evidence of reconciliation to that condition on his part? A. He seems moderately so. He doesn't like to be confined. He says that, and I think it is perfectly understandable, and we recognize it.

Q. Isn't that true of most of your patients, Doctor? A. I should say so. . . . I think we all like our liberty.

*   *   *

CROSS-EXAMINATION BY MR. WILLIAMS:

*   *   *

Q. Now, Doctor, it was your decision to permit persons who had been part of Mr. Goldfine's previous surroundings to come and communicate with him? A. Yes.

---

death." And most of this was unnecessary; Ruby himself was only an exhibit at his own trial and not a very important one at that. There is no reason in law or humanity that he could not have been excused from the courtroom during the more painful episodes. The apparent deterioration in Ruby's mental condition after the trial may be due not so much to the impending death sentence as to the trial itself. The sorry consequence might have been avoided had anyone thought of it—and cared enough to act. [Kaplan J. and Waltz, J. R.: *The Trial of Jack Ruby*. New York: Macmillan Co. 1965 p. 370)].

Q. Isn't that so? A. That is correct.

Q. And that was contrary to Mr. Bennett's desires in the matter, was it not? A. Well, I should say that in general, of course, it is not the policy of the Bureau of Prisons to have communications very free. But, after all, I had in mind Mr. Goldfine as a patient at our hospital, and we didn't intend to treat him any better or any worse than any other patient under the circumstances.

* * *

Q. Isn't it possible, Doctor, to provide controls for treatment in this case by out-patient means? A. Well, conceivably. It might involve turning a home into a hospital, and it would seem to me that he could be much better supervised if he were in a hospital, where a certain amount of latitude of occasional visits, and longer visits, and so on, might be arranged, rather than leaving the thing wholly up, essentially, to the patient.

* * *

BY THE COURT:

* * *

. . . Do you think his continued confinement in St. Elizabeths Hospital is likely to adversely affect his chances of recovery of his mental competency to stand trial, considering the fact that his home and his business connections are in Boston, and so on? A. Well, of course, in conditions of this sort, Your Honor, there is a large emotional element, and situations which are likely to evoke worry and anxiety certainly don't do the patient any good.

* * *

Q. Would you have an opinion, one, as to whether or not if Mr. Goldfine were confined in, say, a civilian hospital in Boston, that the chances of his recovery of his competence to stand trial would be better than if he remained in St. Elizabeths Hospital? A. I think they might be, yes.

Q. Let me put the same question to you: If he were permitted to be at home under proper supervision, and I don't know at this point what proper supervision would be, but, say, under such supervision and therapy as you might recommend, then do you think under that circumstance that chances of recovery of his competency to stand trial would be improved? A. We might guess that they would not be quite so good. I think he would be better off where he had a certain amount of control, but a certain amount too of freedom.

Q. Well now, would you care, or would you make a suggestion, and as to this, I won't insist if you would rather not, but if he were going to be placed or permitted to go to his home in Boston, what supervision and therapy would you recommend? A. I am afraid

I would like to know a good deal more about the home and the home situation, and what his reaction to any supervision or control would be. He has never been used to having much control or supervision exercised over him.

Q. In other words, I take it, then, that you don't feel that you can answer the question. A. No, sir.

* * *

William G. Cushard

was called as a witness by the respondent . . .

DIRECT EXAMINATION BY MR. GASCH:

* * *

Q. Could Mr. Goldfine be treated on an out-patient basis, for instance, at St. Elizabeths Hospital? A. If you mean by on an out-patient basis, permitted to leave the hospital grounds, we would have to have special permission from the court because we are not permitted to allow a patient under charges, under any criminal charges to leave the hospital.

He could have—we do have the right to give them privileges within the hospital reservation, but not to permit them to leave the hospital grounds.

So it would be on an out-patient basis only to the extent that he would have to remain on the hospital reservation.

Q. Now, if the court were to change its order, he could be given out-patient treatment at St. Elizabeths Hospital, could he not? A. If the court specifically stated that he could leave the hospital reservation, of course, then we would not be legally bound to keep him on the reservation, yes, sir.

Q. So by out-patient treatment you do not necessarily mean that the individual be sent home? A. No, not necessarily.

Q. Now, in connection with Mr. Goldfine, do you think it would be desirable from a medical standpoint to send him home as an out-patient? A. I think he would be more comfortable and more at ease at home. So purely from his own standpoint, I do think he would be more comfortable and probably—or certainly happier.

Q. Are there influences at his home that would not necessarily be conductive to his recovery? A. Well, first may I say, I would not expect his recovery either in or out of the hospital in the ordinary course of events.

From what I have been able to learn about the home situation, there are certain factors operating there which lead to a good deal of conflict within the family constellation.

* * *

THE COURT: . . .

Doctor Overholser . . . If the petitioner in this case is going to be permitted to live for some time in the immediate future, without giving any length of time, in a more normal home environment, would you be able to recommend what degree or degrees of frequency of out-patient treatment would be indicated in this case? In other words, if he were under the treatment of an outside psychiatrist, should he see the psychiatrist once a week, twice a week, or can you give any opinion on this?

*   *   *

DOCTOR OVERHOLSER: I think at the start, Your Honor, it ought to be not less than twice a week, until the doctors become more familiar with the case.

THE COURT: Would you feel that more than one doctor would be required or that it would be better at least at the start to use one doctor?

DOCTOR OVERHOLSER: I think it might be well to have, even perhaps two, one representing possibly the Government, one selected by the Government, and one selected by the family.

THE COURT: All right. Thank you.

Now, Mr. Williams, would the petitioner be willing to pay for treatment by two outside psychiatrists, one to be chosen by the petitioner and one to be chosen by the Government?

MR. WILLIAMS: Yes, sir.

THE COURT: All right.

Is Solomon Goldfine in Court? Will you come forward . . . ?

*   *   *

[Mr. Goldfine] would you be willing until such time as the court in Boston might make other arrangements, to provide a home for your father in Boston and take care of him and furnish him a home environment there?

MR. S. GOLDFINE: Yes, Your Honor.

*   *   *

THE COURT: You have children, do you not?

MR. S. GOLDFINE: I have three children, Your Honor, and my wife is here with me today too. Actually, by car we are not that far from Boston, and I am only three and a half hours, right near the Connecticut line in New York, but, of course, I would like to have him stay with us at our home, but that would have to be up to the court.

THE COURT: No, I think not.

*   *   *

Opinion of the Court

THE COURT: This court finds the following facts as of this time, today:

That the petitioner is presently incompetent to stand trial; that as of now his condition so far as it affects his competency to stand trial, is not improving at St. Elizabeths Hospital, where he is confined, and

he is not likely to improve so long as he is under confinement;

That the probabilities of his recovering competence are less in confinement that if he is permitted to return to a normal environment with out-patient psychiatric and medical treatment;

That he is not presently dangerous to himself or to others; that he is able economically to maintain himself in a home environment and to pay for private psychiatric and medical treatment.

The court will order the petitioner returned to Boston, Massachusetts, under the following conditions:

One, that he remain within the jurisdiction of the United States District Court for the District of Massachusetts;

Two, that he have a proper place to live in Boston with his son, Solomon Goldfine;

Three, that initially he undergo out-patient treatment by one psychiatrist to be designated by the Government and one psychiatrist to be designated by the petitioner, that that treatment be not less than twice a week, until such time as the psychiatrists themselves determine a different frequency of treatment; that the fees of those psychiatrists shall be paid by the petitioner;

*   *   *

Mr. Williams, do you have any suggestions to make as to the conditions I have not covered?

MR. WILLIAMS: I have two questions, Your Honor. First of all, may his son take him back to Boston?

THE COURT: Yes.

MR. WILLIAMS: . . . I am not sure whether Your Honor meant that he should see each psychiatrist twice a week or each one once a week for a total of two psychiatric visits a week.

THE COURT: Doctor Overholser, what would be your feeling about that?

DOCTOR OVERHOLSER: I think, Your Honor, at the start that they ought to be joint interviews. Perhaps later on some other arrangement could be made.

THE COURT: Well, I will follow Doctor Overholser's suggestion that initially they be joint treatments with the two psychiatrists until such time as they determine otherwise.

Now, what about reports from those psychiatrists? Would it be feasible, Doctor Overholser, for those psychiatrists to make a report once a week?

DOCTOR OVERHOLSER: I should think at the start again. Presumably after that, after a week or two or three perhaps, the period could be lengthened, depending on what the court may desire.

*   *   *

MR. GASCH: There are two questions raised, Your Honor. Do these psychiatrists, or to take the one to be designated by the Government, have any authority over the person of the petitioner, or are they simply to make reports to the court, and to Mr. Williams, and I don't understand what Mr. Bennett's status would be. He seems to have no authority over the man at the present time. Is that all up in the air?

THE COURT: What do you mean by, what authority does the Government psychiatrist have?

MR. GASCH: Suppose he feels that the petitioner, for instance, is doing things that he thinks are detrimental to the petitioner. Can he say anything to him about those instances?

THE COURT: Yes, he can say something to him about it, and reommend that if he doesn't do it, he can put it in his report, which will go to the court in Massachusetts, and to Mr. Bennett, and then an application, if it is indicated, can be made to Judge Sweeney to do whatever may be necessary.

*   *   *

NOTE

UNITED STATES v. KLEIN
325 F.2d 283 (2d Cir. 1963)

KAUFMAN, CIRCUIT JUDGE.

Herman Klein appeals from a judgment and order of commitment, entered pursuant to 18 U.S.C. § 4246. In April of 1962, Klein was indicted for income tax evasion. After four separate hearings and extensive examinations by three different psychiatrists, he was found mentally incompetent to stand trial under 18 U.S.C. § 4244. Although the psychiatrist who had treated him for more than thirty years insisted that institutionalization would prove "catastrophic," Kelin was committed to the custody of the Attorney General until "he shall be mentally competent to stand trial, or until the charges in the indictment pending against him are disposed of according to law."

Certain essential facts are not in dispute. Klein is said to be suffering from a manic-depressive psychosis, and has been so afflicted for the better part of his sixty years. His father committed suicide when Klein was an adolescent, and pronounced suicidal tendencies have been discovered in appellant. The medical reports further revealed that Klein is a diabetic, suffering from high blood pressure and is presently recuperating from a major rectal operation.

At the final competency hearing, the inquiry was directed toward selecting that method of treatment most likely to ameliorate Klein's admittedly deteriorating condition. Dr. Dudley Schoenfeld, the appellant's treating psychiatrist, testified in response to questions by the court that Klein's physical ailments would preclude the extensive pharmacological treatment or shock therapy recommended by one of the government's psychiatrists. Relying on his more than thirty years of close observation of the appellant, he

emphasized the dangers of disrupting Klein's normal way of life, and urged that he not be summarily removed from his home environment and a familiar pattern of therapy. Dr. Shoenfeld insisted that to a manic depressive with suicidal tendencies, the impact of institutionalization could be drastic; he warned that commitment would be "tantamount to signing Klein's death warrant."

Dr. Donald B. Douglas, a psychiatrist appointed by the court who had examined Klein on three occasions, disagreed. Disassociating himself from Dr. Shoenfeld's "psychoanalytic" approach, Dr. Douglas persisted in his opinion that immediate institutionalization would be beneficial. Disparaging the drastic consequences cited by Dr. Shoenfeld, Dr. Douglas asserted that the appellant would respond well and promptly to both pharmacological and shock treatment. Relying on these assurances, the court signed the order appealed from and suggested that Klein be confined in the Medical Center of the Bureau of Prisons, located at Springfield, Missouri.

Despite the government's argument to the contrary, we find the order of commitment clearly appealable. In view of the dire consequences predicted as a result of Klein's institutionalization and the indefinite period of his commitment, we feel that appellant is plainly entitled to review of the judgment at this juncture.

Although recognizing the discretion afforded the District Court by § 4246, we feel that the record does not furnish sufficient grounds for commitment. There is no issue here as to Klein's mental disorder; the only controversy concerns treatment. This is not a case in which a defendant is charged with malingering or suddenly finds himself incompetent for trial in the aftermath of an indictment; Klein, to the contrary, has been treated for his ailment all of his adult life. Accordingly, where a defendant such as Klein is receiving extensive psychiatric care and there is no question as to the integrity and high professional competence of his personal psychiatrist, we do not consider 18 U.S.C. § 4246 as intended to compel the District Court to determine which of two equally reputable methods of psychiatric treatment would prove most efficacious in a particular case.[3]

We understand and sympathize with the conscientious efforts of the court below, so clearly reflected in the record, to find a solution to the problems which flowed from appellant's serious mental and physical difficulties. Although the indictment was more than a year old, there had been no arraignment. Despite four

---

3. We note, moreover, that the court could not be assured that the Medical Center in Springfield, to which Klein was committed, would follow the course of treatment recommended by Dr. Douglas and apparently accepted by the court. Good medical practice would require that the Medical Center conduct their own "work-up" of the case, and form an independent appraisal of the proper treatment.

competency hearings and extensive psychiatric examinations, the date at which the appellant would be sufficiently competent to plead to the indictment was still unforeseeable. As a result, we can understand the sense of frustration which led the judge to search for a treatment for Klein's psychosis which would promise more immediate and tangible benefits and accordingly accelerate the date of trial.[4]

Mental disorders being what they are, it is nor surprising that eminent psychiatrists differ as to methods of treatment. Here, Dr. Shoenfeld believed that Klein would respond to a psychoanalytic form of therapy; Dr. Douglas, by his own testimony, favored a more physiological approach.[5] Courts of law, unschooled in the intricacies of what may be the most perplexing of medical sciences, are ill-equipped to choose among such divergent but responsible views. In a case such as this, where a man's life may literally hang in the balance, a judge ought not undertake the hazardous venture of changing the course of psychiatric treatment without, at the least, a much fuller hearing and a far greater preponderance of expert testimony than existed here.

Once more we emphasize that we are not faced with the determination commonly required by the statute as to whether a defendant is incompetent to stand trial; all agree that he is. Rather, the trial judge was asked to determine which of several recognized methods of therapy would be most beneficial, or to make a judgment as to methods of treatment in a field of medicine renowned for its responsible differences of opinion. The court felt called upon to resolve its dilemma by prying the appellant away from a course of treatment which had enabled him, during his periods of remission, to conduct a business and maintain social intercourse without the necessity of institutionalization. With the possibility of disaster lurking in the background and with a new form of treatment and its effectiveness here an unknown quantity, we do not consider a determination whether the appellant should now be committed to a distant and unfamiliar institution to be a decision which courts should be called upon to render.

We have already indicated our realization that vexing problems were presented to the district judge to resolve. However, the condition which temporarily prevents the appellant from conferring with counsel in order to prepare his defense is according to medical testimony subject to change. His present inabilities should not create a situation tantamount to dismissal of the indictment. The indictment remains outstanding and inquiry should be made from time to time as to appellant's condition. Perhaps it would be most helpful to take advantage of the flexibility afforded by informal conferences in which all interested parties—government, defense, psychiatrists and court—might together seek the proper road to their common objective, the amelioration of Klein's condition. [It] is not at all unlikely that such informal discussions, conducted with intelligence and compassion, could result in a solution acceptable to all concerned.

The judgment is reversed, without prejudice to further proceedings.

b.   UNITED STATES v. McNEILL
294 F.2d 117 (2d Cir. 1961)

WATERMAN, CIRCUIT JUDGE.

From September 26, 1950 to date the appellant, John Carroll, has been held in custody in Matteawan State Hospital (Matteawan), a New York State "hospital for insane criminals" located within the Southern District of New York.

*   *   *

In 1934 petitioner was convicted in the New York Courts of the crime of robbery, second degree. He was sentenced to serve from two to four years in prison. He served his sentence and was discharged on March 17, 1938. Fifteen years after this conviction, on January 7, 1949, pursuant to an order of certification of a Justice of the New York State Supreme Court, . . . appellant was committed to Pilgrim State Hospital (Pilgrim), one of several New York State hospitals existing for the care and treatment of the mentally ill of the State, an institution under the governance of the State Department of Mental Hygiene. Appellant does not challenge the propriety of this commitment order, or his continued detention thereafter at Pilgrim pursuant to a certificate of need of continued care and treatment. . . . On December 21, 1949, appellant escaped from Pilgrim. The following day, December 22, 1949, the Senior Director of Pilgrim addressed a letter to the Commissioner of Mental Hygiene requesting that appellant be transferred to Matteawan . . .

*   *   *

The director's letter, to which a copy of appellant's clinical summary was attached, referred to appellant's prior conviction and prison record and contained a statement that in the course of his escape from Pilgrim appellant had assaulted a hospital attendant and fractured his skull. . . .

*   *   *

---

4. We feel it significant that the District Judge himself expressed uneasiness over commitment to an institution in Springfield, Missouri, over 1,000 miles from appellant's home and family.

5. While Dr. Douglas did assert that proper dosages of medication could lift appellant from the depths of a depression, nowhere in the record is it claimed that Klein's psychosis may be "cured." As we understand the situation, the course of treatment urged by the government is at best intended to induce a prolonged period of remission during which Klein, though still a manic-depressive, could intelligently plead to and defend the charges against him.

Section 85 provides for detailed judicial proceedings leading to a court certification that the mentally ill patient is dangerous and that the safety of the institutional environment requires his transfer to Matteawan. It provides that a commission of three disinterested persons shall examine the patient and report findings to the court. The patient is entitled to be represented by counsel during the proceedings. However, under New York Correction Law, section 412 these usual procedural safeguards are denied to a mentally ill patient who has been previously sentenced to a term of imprisonment in a correctional institution even though the determination that he is mentally ill is made after the completion of his criminal sentence. Such a patient, as appellant, may be transferred, summarily, without any hearing whatsoever, to Matteawan pursuant to section 412.

We are of the opinion that the denial of a judical transfer procedure arbitrarily discriminates against those patients who have fully served prior sentences for crimes and have subsequently been admitted by civil process to a state institution of the type of Pilgrim, and denies to this class of patients the equal protection of the laws guaranteed to them by the Fourteenth Amendment.

During the hearing before the district judge, and during the argument on appeal, counsel for petitioner made efforts to distinguish the purpose of the two institutions. He correctly pointed out that Matteawan is denominated as a "hospital for insane criminals" and that Matteawan expressly does not deal with mentally ill persons committed into state custody by civil process, with the exception of those transferred from other institutions pursuant to the New York Mental Hygiene Law. . . . Counsel attempted through witnesses to show that Matteawan partook more of the character of a jail than a hospital, and, among other claimed differences, sought to prove that the treatment accorded the mentally ill at Pilgrim was far superior to that offered at Matteawan. The state, however, introduced evidence which tended to prove that the treatment of the inmates at both institutions was similar, and that the only administrative difference between the two was the standard of security enforced at Matteawan. After weighing the evidence the district judge concluded that "Matteawan Hospital is a security institution but it is undoubtedly a hospital and not a jail." Although we may well have reached a contrary result if the original decision had been ours, we may not set aside this finding of fact based upon all the evidence, for the finding is not a "clearly erroneous" one. . . .

However, the issue as to whether Matteawan is a hospital or a jail is not dispositive of the constitutional issue presented for our determination. The state argues that Matteawan is a hospital, and therefore is indistinguishable from any other mental hospital that is a part of the complex of New York state mental hospitals, and assuming, of course, that a patient initially has been legally committed, a transfer of that patient from one institution to another within that complex is merely an unreviewable administrative decision. But the statutes of the State of New York do not support the state's argument. As pointed out above, Matteawan, unlike Pilgrim and similar hospitals, is under the governance of the State Department of Correction and not the State Department of Hygiene, and is an institution existing for the purpose of caring for and having custody of insane criminals. It is of obvious importance in this connection to note that whereas no judicial procedures need be observed when a civilly committed patient is transferred from one state hospital for the mentally ill to another like hospital, New York has provided by a specific statute a specific detailed procedure to be followed when a civilly committed patient is transferred from one of these state hospitals to Matteawan. If Matteawan were not different from the other hospitals no such procedure would be necessary or prescribed. . . .

A state may, of course, in the interest of effectuating its valid governmental policies, make reasonable classifications among its citizens whereby those in one class may be treated differently from those in another. . . . However, in so doing, a state must guard against classifications which are so arbitrary that they are repugnant to the equal protection clause of the Fourteenth Amendment. . . . The State of New York has not attempted to justify its discrimination under Correction Law, section 412 against ex-convicts. . . . We have attempted to find a possible reasonable basis for this discrimination and we find none. We find nothing to demonstrate that ex-convicts who, after expiration of their sentences, become mentally ill, are inherently more dangerous than those mentally ill who are not ex-convicts. In fact there are many "criminal tendencies" that are in no way violent tendencies just as there are many convicts and ex-convicts whose crimes were nonviolent crimes. Nor, even if such an ex-convict should become dangerously insane, does there appear to be any justification for more hastily transferring him to Matteawan after his commission of a dangerous act at an ordinary mental hospital than in transferring any other patient who has committed such an act at such a hospital but whose transfer is nevertheless delayed until after he shall have had a judicial hearing.

*   *   *

We reverse the district court, grant the writ, and direct that the petitioner be discharged from Matteawan and returned to Pilgrim State Hospital, until the procedure set forth in New York Mental Hygiene Law, section 85 shall have been followed.

NOTES

NOTE 1

ASSOCIATION FOR IMPROVEMENT OF MENTAL HEALTH, INC.

The Case of the Matteawan 57*

On behalf of the State of New York the Attorney General's office appealed the decision of the Court of Appeals to the United States Supreme Court. While that appeal was pending, the patient, Carroll, died. This made the case moot and therefore the United States Supreme Court dismissed the appeal and vacated the orders of all the lower Federal Courts. [369 U.S. 149.]

In support of his appeal to the United States Supreme Court, contesting the finding of the United States Court of Appeals in the case of John J. Carroll, the Attorney General filed a "Jurisdictional Statement" in October, 1961 which contained the following:

> "The decision of the United States Court of Appeals, holding Correction Law Section 412 unconstitutional, affects the status of fifty-seven patients currently at Matteawan State Hospital."

It has been agreed by all parties concerned that the 57 patients, only three of whom have been identified by name, were transferred to Matteawan for "having exhibited criminal tendencies," and that these criminal tendencies were *presumed* on the basis of patients' previous conviction on a criminal charge. No hearings were given these patients; they did not have the opportunity to have legal counsel, and they did not have the opportunity to confront the witnesses accusing them.

If the patient Carroll had lived, a decision of the United States Supreme Court would have been determinative of the rights of the 57 patients referred to in this "Jurisdictional Statement." If the United States Supreme Court had affirmed in the Carroll case, the 57 patients would have been returned to the state hospitals from which they had been transferred.

However, the patients in question remained at Matteawan, still without the benefit of judicial hearing.

After the ruling of unconstitutionality of Section 412 by the Federal Court of Appeals in July, 1961, the AIMH asked Governor Rockefeller to retransfer all patients who had been sent to Matteawan under state law. The Governor refused to act, he said, because the State had appealed the Carroll case to the United States Supreme Court.

The sudden termination of the Carroll case left the fate of the 57 patients in limbo. As an organization interested in protecting the civil rights of mental health patients, AIMH felt an obligation to continue

---

*AIMH, 420 Lexington Ave., New York 17, N.Y. (1964).

to try and help the unfortunate 57. The Association was convinced that the 57 had been transferred illegally under a statute which an eminent court and many members of the New York Bar considered unconstitutional.

*   *   *

The AIMH authorized its counsel, David N. Fields, to institute a new action in the New York Supreme Court. This action, entitled: *People of the State of New York ex rel Aronson* v. *McNeill*, was started in the Supreme Court of Dutchess County in February, 1962. It was filed by Zola Aronson, law partner of the general counsel of the AIMH, with the latter arguing the case. "McNeill" was John F. McNeill, Superintendent of Matteawan State Hospital. The case was filed in behalf of the 57 patients in Matteawan, all of whose names were then unknown.

The AIMH counsel proceeded on the theory that in a habeas corpus proceeding the interest of unlawfully detained persons was so great that even a person, who did not know the names of the detained, had a right to start suit under existing statutes.

The case was lost in the Trial Court because the Trial Court Judge held that section 412 was not unconstitutional. He did not make any ruling that the action by Aronson on behalf of unknown patients was improper.

The decision was then appealed to the New York Supreme Court Appellate Division, Second Department. The Appellate Division affirmed the decision of the lower court, but the judges made it perfectly plain that they did so solely because of the fact that there was an existing and prior court decision which they felt was binding upon them. In their decision, however, they made it clear that while they were affirming the decision of the court below, they regarded section 412 as a statute which denied patients equal protection of the laws and possibly due process of law. Again, no issue was raised about the propriety of Aronson suing on behalf of unknown persons.

An appeal from the decision of the Appellate Division was taken to the New York Court of Appeals. However, it was never heard by that Court on the merits. At that point, the New York State Solicitor General, Paxton Blair, made a motion to dismiss the appeal on the ground that Mr. Aronson was not a party aggrieved and therefore had no standing to prosecute the appeal. The New York Court of Appeals, after vigorous opposition, upheld the position of the Solicitor General and dismissed the appeal on the technicality that Mr. Aronson was not a party aggrieved. [The United States Supreme Court denied cert. 377 U.S. 977 (1963).]

*   *   *

AIMH believes that Matteawan is a maximum security institution no different from a jail. There is no freedom of movement. Patients are always under strict supervision. They are confined to wards which are locked; they have no access to the outside. They are not permitted to visit their homes. They cannot look forward to convalescent care. They cannot telephone to their families. *They are permitted to write one letter a week.*

In civil mental hospitals, very few patients are in locked wards. Most have complete freedom of the grounds, virtually unlimited freedom to phone and write their families, and it is recognized they receive better therapeutic care. The emphasis at the civil hospitals is to try and help the patients get well so they can return to normal living outside the institution. The emphasis at Matteawan is on total confinement.

At Matteawan there is one physician for each 192 patients.

At Hudson River State Hospital, a typical civil mental institution, there is one physician for each 98 patients.

*   *   *

NOTE 2

BAXSTROM v. HEROLD
383 U.S. 107 (1966)

MR. CHIEF JUSTICE WARREN delivered the opinion of the Court.

We granted certiorari in this case to consider the constitutional validity of the statutory procedure under which petitioner was committed to a mental institution at the expiration of his criminal sentence in a state prison.

Petitioner, Johnnie K. Baxstrom, was convicted of second degree assault in April 1959 and was sentenced to a term of two and one-half to three years in a New York prison. On June 1, 1961, he was certified as insane by a prison physician. He was then transferred from prison to Dannemora State Hospital, an institution under the jurisdiction and control of the New York Department of Correction and used for the purpose of confining and caring for male prisoners declared mentally ill while serving a criminal sentence. In November 1961, the director of Dannemora filed a petition in the Surrogate's Court of Clinton County stating that Baxstrom's penal sentence was about to terminate and requesting that he be civilly committed pursuant to § 384 of New York Correction Law.

On December 6, 1961, a proceeding was held in the Surrogate's chambers. Medical certificates were submitted by the State which stated that, in the opinion of two of its examining physicians, Baxstrom was still mentally ill and in need of hospital and institutional care. Respondent, then assistant director at Dannemora, testified that in his opinion Baxstrom was still mentally ill. Baxstrom, appearing alone, was accorded a brief opportunity to ask questions.[1] Respondent and the Surrogate both stated that they had no objection to his being transferred from Dannemora to a civil hospital under the jurisdiction of the Department of Mental Hygiene. But the Surrogate pointed out that he had no jurisdiction to determine that question—that under § 384 the decision was entirely up to the Department of Mental Hygiene. The Surrogate then signed a certificate which indicated he was satisfied that Baxstrom "may require mental care and treatment" in an institution for the mentally ill. The Department of Mental Hygiene had already determined *ex parte* that Baxstrom was not suitable for care in a civil hospital. Thus, on December 18, 1961, the date upon which Baxstrom's penal sentence expired, custody over him shifted from the Department of Correction to the Department of Mental Hygiene, but he was retained at Dannemora and has remained there to this date.

Thereafter, Baxstrom sought a writ of habeas corpus in a state court. An examination by an independent psychiatrist was ordered and a hearing held at which the examining psychiatrist testified that, in his opinion, Baxstrom was still mentally ill. The writ was dismissed. In 1963, Baxstrom applied again for a writ of habeas corpus, alleging that his constitutional rights had been violated and that he was then sane, or if insane, he should be transferred to a civil mental hospital. Due to his indigence and his incarceration in Dannemora, Baxstrom could not produce psychiatric testimony to disprove the testimony adduced at the prior hearing. The writ was therefore dismissed. Baxstrom's alternative request for transfer to a civil mental hospital was again denied as being beyond the power of the court despite a statement by the State's attorney that he wished that Baxstrom would be transferred to a civil mental hospital. . . .

We hold that petitioner was denied equal protection of the laws by the statutory procedure under which a person may be civilly committed at the expiration of his penal sentence without the jury review available to all other persons civilly committed in New York. Petitioner was further denied equal protection of the laws by his civil commitment to an institution maintained by the Department of Correction beyond the expiration of his prison term without a judicial determination that he is dangerously mentally ill such as that afforded to all so committed except those, like Baxstrom, nearing the expiration of a penal sentence.

Section 384 of New York Correction Law prescribes the procedure for civil commitment upon the

---

1. The State apparently permits counsel to be retained in such proceedings where the person can afford to hire his own attorney despite the fact that § 384 makes no provision for counsel to be present. Baxstrom is indigent, however, and had no counsel at this hearing.

expiration of the prison term of a mentally ill person confined in Dannemora.[2] Similar procedures are prescribed for civil commitment of all other allegedly mentally ill persons. All persons civilly committed, however, other than those committed at the expiration of a penal term, are expressly granted the right to *de novo* review by jury trial of the question of their sanity . . . Under this procedure any person dissatisfied with an order certifying him as mentally ill may demand full review by a jury of the prior determination as to his competency. If the jury returns a verdict that the person is sane, he must be immediately discharged. It follows that the State, having made this substantial review proceeding generally available on this issue, may not, consistent with the Equal Protection Clause of the Fourteenth Amendment, arbitrarily withhold it from some.

The Director contends that the State has created a reasonable classification differentiating the civilly insane from the "criminally insane," which he defines as those with dangerous or criminal propensities. Equal protection does not require that all persons be dealt with identically, but it does require that a distinction made have some relevance to the purpose for which the classification is made. Classification of mentally ill persons as either insane or dangerously insane of course may be a reasonable distinction for purposes of determining the type of custodial or medical care to be given, but it has no relevance whatever in the context of the opportunity to show whether a person is mentally ill *at all*. For purposes of granting judicial review before a jury of the question whether a person is mentally ill and in need of institutionalization, there is no conceivable basis for distinguishing the commitment of a person who is nearing the end of a penal term from all other civil commitments.

The statutory procedure provided in § 384 of New York Correction Law denied Baxstrom the equal protection of the laws in another respect as well. Under § 384 the judge need only satisfy himself that the person "may require care and treatment in an institution for the mentally ill." Having made such a finding, the decision whether to commit that person to

a hospital maintained by the Department of Correction or to a civil hospital is completely in the hands of administrative officials. Except for persons committed to Dannemora upon expiration of sentence under § 384, all others civilly committed to hospitals maintained by the Department of Correction are committed only after judicial proceedings have been held in which it is determined that the person is so dangerously mentally ill that his presence in a civil hospital is dangerous to the safety of other patients or employees, or to the community.[4]

This statutory classification cannot be justified by the contention that Dannemora is substantially similar to other mental hospitals in the State and that commitment to one hospital or another is simply an administrative matter affecting no fundamental rights. The parties have described various characteristics of Dannemora to show its similarities and dissimilarities to civil hospitals in New York. As striking as the dissimilarities are, we need not make any factual determination as to the nature of Dannemora; the New York State Legislature has already made that determination. By statute, the hospital is under the jurisdiction of the Department of Correction and is used for the purpose of confining and caring for insane prisoners and persons, like Baxstrom, committed at the expiration of a penal term. Civil mental hospitals in New York, on the other hand, are under the jurisdiction and control of the Department of Mental Hygiene. Certain privileges of patients at Dannemora are restricted by statute. Moreover, as has been noted, specialized statutory procedures are prescribed for commitment to hospitals under the jurisdiction of the Department of Correction. While we may assume that transfer among like mental hospitals is a purely administrative function, where, as here, the State has created functionally distinct institutions, classification of patients for involuntary commitment to one of these institutions may not be wholly arbitrary.

The Director argues that it is reasonable to classify persons in Baxstrom's class together with those found to be dangerously insane since such persons are not only insane but have proven criminal tendencies as shown by their past criminal record. . . .

We find this contention untenable. Where the State has provided for a judicial proceeding to determine the dangerous propensities of all others civilly committed

---

2. As it appeared when applied to petitioner in 1961, N.Y. Correction Law § 384 provided in part:

"1. Within thirty days prior to the expiration of the term of a prisoner confined in the Dannemora State Hospital, when in the opinion of the director such prisoner continues insane, the director shall apply to a judge of a court of record for the certification of such person as provided in the mental hygiene law for the certification of a person not in confinement on a criminal charge. The court in which such proceedings are instituted shall, if satisfied that such person may require care and treatment in an institution for the mentally ill, issue an order directing that such person be committed to the custody of the commissioner of mental hygiene to be placed in an appropriate state institution of the department of mental hygiene or of the department of correction as may be designated for the custody of such person by agreement between the heads of the two departments."

4. . . . Former § 412 of Correction Law, permitting commitment to Matteawan State Hospital of any patient who had previously been sentenced to a term of imprisonment, without the benefit of the proceeding accorded others under § 85 of Mental Hygiene Law, was held unconstitutional as a denial of equal protection in *United States ex rel. Carroll v. McNeill*, 294 F. 2d 117 (C.A. 2d Cir. 1961), probable jurisdiction noted, 368 U.S. 951, vacated and dismissed as moot, 369 U.S. 149, and was repealed by N.Y. Laws 1965, c. 524. Even that provision required a showing that the person still manifested criminal tendencies.

to an institution of the Department of Correction, it may not deny this right to a person in Baxstrom's position solely on the ground that he was nearing the expiration of a prison term.[5] It may or may not be that Baxstrom is presently mentally ill and such a danger to others that the strict security of a Department of Correction hospital is warranted. All others receive a judicial hearing on this issue. Equal protection demands that Baxstrom receive the same.

The capriciousness of the classification employed by the State is thrown sharply into focus by the fact that the full benefit of a judicial hearing to determine dangerous tendencies is withheld only in the case of civil commitment of one awaiting expiration of penal sentence. A person with a past criminal record is presently entitled to a hearing on the question whether he is dangerously mentally ill so long as he is not in prison at the time civil commitment proceedings are instituted. Given this distinction, all semblance of rationality of the classification, purportedly based upon criminal propensities, disappears.

In order to accord to petitioner the equal protection of the laws, he was and is entitled to a review of the determination as to his sanity in conformity with proceedings granted all others civilly committed . . . He is also entitled to a hearing under the procedure granted all others . . . to determine whether he is so dangerously mentally ill that he must remain in a hospital maintained by the Department of Correction. . . .

It is so ordered.

NOTE 3

High Court Upsets Law on Prisoners*

*   *   *

Today's decision [in the Baxstrom case] will make about 460 of the inmates of Dannemora—or about half of the total—eligible for jury trials. They had been detained there after their terms expired under the procedure held unconstitutional. State officials say many of them are potentially dangerous.

_____

5. In oral argument, counsel for respondent suggested that the determination by the Department of Mental Hygiene to retain a person in Dannemora must be based not only on his past criminal record, but also on evidence that he is currently dangerous. Far from supporting the validity of the procedure, this only serves to further accent the arbitrary nature of the classification. Under this procedure, all civil commitments to an institution under the control of the Department of Correction require a determination that the person is presently dangerous; all persons so committed are entitled to a judicial proceeding to determine this fact except those awaiting expiration of sentence. Their fate is decided by unreviewable determinations of the Department of Mental Hygiene.

*The New York Times, Feb. 24, 1966, c. 7, p. 25. © 1966 by the New York Times Co. Reprinted by permission.

NOTE 4

TULLY v. TRAMBURG
57 N.J. Super. 377 (1959)

HANEMAN, J. A. D.: Appellant, Eugene Tully, protests the action of the Commissioner of Institutions of the State of New Jersey in transferring him from Greystone Park State Hospital to State Prison and in refusing his request for retransfer.

Tully was convicted of the crime of assault with intent to rape. [H]e was examined at the State Diagnostic Center at Menlo Park on January 23, 1957. On recommendation of the Commissioner of Institutions, . . . appellant was committed to Greystone Park Hospital on February 21, 1957, where he was given a psychiatric examination which resulted in a diagnosis of "Sociopathic Personality Disturbance, Dissocial Reaction." The following information was elicited from Tully during his examination: He was 22 years of age; the offense for which he was convicted involved a 16-year-old girl; he admitted that he overindulges in alcoholic beverages and has a preoccupation with movies and stories that depict crimes and violence; he served in the Marines for four years and saw combat duty in Korea; he got "a big thrill" out of killing enemy soldiers; he described various homosexual activities; while in the fifth grade at school he set a girl's hair on fire by flipping a match on her head; he had very strong and sometimes uncontrollable sadistic impulses which have been acted out not only in the present offense but in previous sexual attempts as well. It was concluded that Tully represented a threat to his community and to himself.

While the original investigation report suggested that appellant's problem was predominantly psychiatric, this theory was later abandoned. When . . . he received first consideration on July 16, 1957 by a review board for possible release on parole, it was reported that "No psychotic material has been detected. . . ." In his request to the Commissioner of Institutions on June 2, 1958 to transfer appellant to the State Prison, Dr. W. H. Longley, Clinical Director of Greystone Park Hospital, stated: "There is no psychosis present in this patient and he knows exactly what he is doing. . . . Request is made for his transfer to a penal institution as not amenable to rehabilitation by psychiatric means."

The following facts concerning Tully's behavior while a patient at the hospital are significant: He associated with the discontents of the ward in an attempt to create dissatisfaction; he gave the attendants back talk and refused to comply with hospital regulations; he had intercourse a few times with his fiancee on the hospital grounds; he tried to sabotage the laundry by having the special cases manning it slow down in their work and stay off-duty for sick call, with only flimsy excuses; he tried to organize a sit-down strike among the laundry workers; at times he has broken up group therapy sessions by shouting abuse at the doctor.

Tully was found to be brimming with hostility. He admitted that if he had a weapon he would have killed the girls who accused him and he would have shot up the courtroom when he was arraigned. Dr. Longley reported that: "We feel he is antisocial rather than insane and certainly not suitably motivated for therapy." The doctor continued by stating that Tully exploited the system that was trying to help him, and frustrated the hospital's main function of restoration and social rehabilitation for a great number of its patients by his example of urging misbehavior. The time was ripe, urged the doctor, "to rescue the hospital and its community function from his marasmic influence." . . .

*   *   *

Transfer of appellant was made on June 11, 1958.

*   *   *

Appellant contends that the Commissioner's decision to transfer him to State Prison, as well as his subsequent denial of appellant's request for retransfer were erroneous and should be reversed. It is alleged that the Commissioner's decisions were not based upon adequate considerations pursuant to the standards set by N.J.S. 2A:164–7, which reads as follows:

> "The commissioner of the department of institutions and agencies, upon commitment of such person, shall thereupon arrange for his treatment in one of the institutions under the jurisdiction of the department which, in the judgment of the commissioner, is best suited to care for the needs of such person. The commissioner, in his discretion, is hereby authorized . . . to arrange for transfer of such person to or from any institution within the jurisdiction of the department for the purpose of providing for the needs and requirements of such person according to the individual circumstances of the case."

Appellant argues that the reason for the transfer lay in the Commissioner's interest in the welfare of Greystone and its inmates rather than in appellant's welfare, which is not a legitimate consideration under the statute. He contends that it is his needs and requirements which must be subserved and not the needs and requirements of other patients or the public.

The State Prison is one of the institutions "within the jurisdiction of the department." . . . The statutory transfer power vested in the Commissioner is highly discretionary, and courts will not ordinarily interfere with its exercise. This power is not unlimited, however, and if a defendant who has been committed to a hospital for treatment under the terms of the Sex Offender Act makes an affirmative showing that his transfer to State Prison was arbitrary and in conflict with the purposes underlying his sentence, he may obtain judicial relief. . . . Undoubtedly, the Commissioner's broad transfer authority should be exercised with extreme caution. Nevertheless, there may well be compelling situations where the Commissioner has little or no practical alternative but to transfer a sex offender from a hospital to State Prison where he will receive the available psychiatric and medical attention suitable "to the individual circumstances of the case."

Greystone Park State Hospital is an institution for the treatment of persons suffering from mental disorders. Present overcrowding at the institution approximates 1,000 patients. No special facilities have been provided for the treatment of sex offenders, and other mental patients without criminal records are thereby obliged to mingle with them. In the light of the numerous facts set out above, we cannot conclude that the Commissioner abused his discretion in this instance. To the contrary, he had no alternative. This is certainly not to say that the Commissioner has unlimited discretion, which would amount to an unconstitutional delegation of legislative power. The Commissioner is confined by the wording of N.J.S. 2A:164–7, which limits his transfer discretion to the institution which, in his judgment, "is best suited to care for the needs of such person . . . according to the individual circumstances of the case." . . .

*   *   *

Affirmed.

NOTE 5

Brief of Donald McEwan, Petitioner Pro Se

By means of the following chart the petitioner proposes to show in detail the penal nature of his confinement [at Bridgewater Treatment Center]. Any one item taken separately is trivial, but together they reflect an attitude, so difficult to represent in any other way, which is even more punitive than that of the administration of the state prison at Walpole.

Though institutional officials may allege otherwise, the only rationale behind the more restrictive rules and regulations of the treatment center is punishment —punishment of those persons whom the commonwealth has declared to be sick. Such treatment is totally destructive of the supposed rehabilitative purpose of the statute.

COMPARISON OF PUNITIVE MEASURES

Item	Treatment Center	State Prison at Walpole
Personal clothing	Limited to 3 pairs white underwear, 6 pairs white or gray socks, 1 pair shoes without steel shank. May be ordered only at specified times.	Allowed any color underwear, socks, sweatshirts, bathrobe, pajamas, slippers, shoes without regard to shank, black or blue sweater. No limit, many items available in canteen.
Institutional clothing	Always wrinkled, usually ill-fitting, frequently worn out. All marked by messy stencil with "T.C." and name. Can change only at specified times and places. Cannot have institutional underwear if have personal.	One pair pressed each week; proper size; replaced when worn-out. Shirt only marked, neatly, with name. Change as required in own cell. Underwear issued to everyone.
Punishment (lock-up)	No semblance of trial. Any guard may order.	Only disciplinary Board (composed of deputy supt., a guard, and a civilian employee).
Rules and procedures	Different for night and day.	Same all the time.
Free time	Required to be either in yard or rec. room (no choice) or locked in cell.	Choice of yard, TV rooms, gym, chapel, own cell (which is open), other cell-block rec. areas.
Avocational area (free time)	Can enter and leave shops at only one specified time each night.	Can enter and leave whenever shops are open.
Library	Cannot browse; no catalog available.	Open daily for browsing; catalog available.
Visiting	1 hour once a week across table with wire fence underneath.	All morning or afternoon ($2\frac{1}{2}$ hours) twice a week, in chairs side by side.
Lawyer visit	In presence of guard.	Private.
Guards	Always "standing over your shoulder," causing tension. Harassment common.	Discreetly apart. Leave well-behaved inmates alone.
Rules	Continually being added.	Infrequent changes.
State job	Assigned arbitrarily; just work under threat; little variety.	Inmate's preference consulted in assignment and job changes. Greater variety of jobs.
Pay	More than 50% make lowest wages. Little opportunity for increase.	Only 25% make lowest wage. Easy to move to better paying job.
Marching	To work, evening recreation, church, entertainments, meals.	Only to meals and entertainments.
Entertainments	Sometimes forced to attend.	Always optional.
Common medications (aspirin, cold pills, etc.)	Handed out a dose at a time.	3 days supply or more given at once.
Food and menu	Frequently insipid and unimaginative.	Good quality, good preparation and imagination.
Time to eat	Frequently rushed at night.	Can remain until finished.
Meal schedule	Too close for digestion. (18 hour fast at night.)	Well spaced. (13 hour fast at night.)
Silverware	Frequently only a spoon. Always counted.	Always have appropriate utensils. Not counted.

Item	Treatment Center	State Prison at Walpole
Cells	No lockers; no control of light from inside; no lamps allowed. No smoking. Arrangements of furniture, blankets, etc. specified in detail. No glass objects or food allowed.	Wall locker provided; light switch inside; lamps allowed. Smoking allowed. No specification on arrangement. Glass objects and food allowed.
Institutional radio	None.	Two stations on earphone in cell.
Sleep at night	Frequently disturbed by guards.	Rarely disturbed.
Corridors	No smoking (though guards may).	Smoking allowed.
Personal safety razor	Not allowed.	Issued by institution and available in canteen.
Personal appearance	Told when to get haircut, shave. No beards allowed.	Left to individual. Beards allowed.
Canteen orders	Must be made 4 days in advance. One order per week.	Six times a week by order (same day delivery). A summer canteen in yard daily for purchases in person.
Canteen	Operated by civilians. High prices, low profits.	Operated by inmates. Low prices, high profits.
Cigarette lighters, nail clippers, metal ballpoint refills, stingers	Not allowed.	Available for purchase in canteen.
National slick magazines (Life, Newsweek, etc.)	Censored and sometimes mutilated.	Not censored; delivered intact.
Sanitary facilities	Primitive, no running water in cell; showers available only at specified times; frequently only 1 toilet for entire population (100+).	Modern toilet and basin in cell; showers available any free time.
Minimum security section	None.	Yes.
Trustee status	None.	Opportunities to work outside the wall. Special passes inside.
Mail	Frequently delayed by being passed to various persons. Outgoing certified mail may take weeks. Supt. includes apology in all mail to public officials. Censor stamp used on all mail.	Prompt delivery both incoming and outgoing. No unauthorized missives enclosed. Censor stamp not ordinarily used.
Inmate Council	Appointed by staff.	Elected by inmates.

NOTE 6

Memorandum[*]

TO: Superintendents, Clinical Directors, and Directors of Nurses

SUBJECT: Report of a Court Hearing

The Department was represented recently at a court hearing held at the request of a patient who had

*Dated February 10, 1965.

been transferred to the Bridgewater State Hospital on an emergency basis. The patient, who had no funds to hire counsel and no known relatives, was represented by court-appointed counsel. The Department and the hospital involved were represented by an Assistant Attorney General. The hearing occupied several hours on each of two days and required the testimony of a large number of people.

The judge ruled at the outset that the Department must establish, first, that there had been an emergency, and second, that the patient had actually in fact been on escape from the hospital or had actually been dangerous to others. The court would not permit the patient's record to be entered into evidence, and would not hear testimony from a representative of the Department, since, although he had personally interviewed the patient before the transfer, he had only second-hand knowledge of the alleged escapes or dangerous behavior.

In order to establish that the patient had been on escape, the testimony of five nurses and attendants and two physicians from the hospital's staff was heard. Each of these persons stated that the patient had been improperly absent from his bed and from the ward on certain occasions, and one attendant even testified that he had seen the patient rush out of the building and had seen him outside the building through the window. None of this testimony was sufficient, however, since it did not prove that the patient had actually left the grounds. On some occasions, the patient had been returned to the hospital by the police, but the police themselves were not there to testify, and the court would not permit the attendants to testify as to where the police had said they had apprehended the patient. It was finally necessary to call a brief recess while one of the physicians made contact with a bartender, who reluctantly agreed to come to the court house. The bartender testified that he had seen the patient in his bar on three occasions; since these three dates coincided with dates that he had been absent from the ward without permission, it was, therefore, established at last that the patient had actually been on escape.

The attendants and the physicians also testified to the patient's violent behavior, but they were subjected to very detailed cross-examination about these events. The patient also testified, and denied all allegations.

The judge's decision, rendered after fairly lengthy summations by both counsel, was that the transfer was indeed justified and that the patient should remain at Bridgewater.

The foregoing summary of this hearing is being circulated because it illustrates several points that are worthy of mention. First, because of the ruling of the United States Supreme Court in the Gideon case, patients involved in court action are likely to request that legal counsel be provided, and courts are likely to insist that patients appearing before them be represented by counsel. In an effort to protect the rights of his client, an attorney may demand that the Department and its hospitals provide detailed documentation of its allegations, and may insist that the rules of evidence be observed meticulously. Hearsay, opinions, and conjecture may be ruled inadmissible, and all testimony may be subject to lengthy cross-examination.

Second, court hearings involving patients may require the testimony of a number of hospital personnel and ward nurses and attendants may be frequently asked to testify; it is possible that superintendents will appear in court less frequently, except when they have direct personal knowledge of pertinent facts. In the foregoing case, seven hospital staff members spent nearly four hours in court, plus travel time to and from court and time spent in reviewing the case with the Assistant Attorney General. (Since the court had impounded the patient's record, the hospital personnel had to come to the courthouse prior to the hearing to review the record and to determine the dates on which the patient was recorded as being on escape.)

A third, and less important observation, is that the hospital personnel were, as might be expected, unfamiliar with the rules of evidence, and had to be cautioned repeatedly to avoid reporting hearsay and to confine themselves to facts rather than conclusions drawn from the facts. They could report that they had seen the patient digging with a spoon at the walls of his seclusion room, but they were not permitted to conclude from this that he was trying to escape. A few of those testifying were irritated by the repeated objections of the patient's counsel, and, having lost their composure, became less effective witnesses.

The following recommendations may be in order. If it is anticipated that a patient's transfer to Bridgewater may be requested, or if there is other reason to expect that a court hearing may be held, hospital personnel should be instructed to keep careful records of pertinent events, such as escapes and incidents involving violence. In particular, when a patient is returned from escape, those receiving him should note on the escape report the full names of the police officers or other persons who have returned him so that these persons can testify, if necessary, that the patient had actually been apprehended off the hospital grounds. Furthermore, if the police arrest a person for some kind of disturbance and later learn that he is an escapee, they do not usually file any formal charges against him; the hospital should, therefore, note on the escape report the nature of the disturbance along with the officer's name, so that he can be called, if necessary, to testify about the patient's behavior leading to his arrest and return to the hospital. How the facts are obtained and recorded is a matter for each hospital to decide; each hospital should, however, have in hand substantiated facts as well as a list of competent witnesses before it requests the Department to transfer a patient to Bridgewater.

It is further suggested that hospital personnel who are scheduled to testify in court be provided, when possible, with brief advice and instruction about courtroom procedures.

/s/Robert F. Moore
Director, Division
of Hospital Inspection

NOTE 7

GOFFMAN, ERVING

Asylums*

[*S*]*econdary adjustments*, defining these as any habitual arrangement by which a member of an organization employs unauthorized means, or obtains unauthorized ends, or both, thus getting around the organization's assumptions as to what he should do and get and hence what he should be. Secondary adjustments represent ways in which the individual stands apart from the role and the self that were taken for granted for him by the institution. . . .

*   *   *

. . . In what follows I want to consider some of the main themes that occur in the secondary adjustments I recorded in a year's participant observation study of patient life in a public mental hospital of over 7,000 patients, hereafter called "Central Hospital."

*   *   *

From the point of view of psychiatric doctrine, apparently, there are no secondary adjustments possible for inmates: Everything a patient is caused to do can be described as a part of his treatment or of custodial management; everything a patient does on his own can be defined as symptomatic of his disorder or of his convalescence. A criminal who "cops a plea" and elects to serve his time in a mental hospital instead of a jail can thus be thought to be really, underneath it all, in search of therapy, just as a malingerer in the army who affects mental symptoms can be thought to be genuinely ill, even though not ill with the particular disorder he is affecting. Similarly, a patient who settles down in the hospital, making a good thing of it, may be felt not to be abusing a place of treatment but to be really still ill since he elects this adaptation.

In the main, state mental hospitals do not function on the basis of psychiatric doctrine, but in terms of a "ward system." Drastically reduced living conditions are allocated through punishments and rewards, expressed more or less in the language of penal institutions. This framework of actions and words is the one employed almost entirely by attendants and to a considerable degree by higher staff, especially in connection with the day-to-day problems of running the hospital. The disciplinary frame of reference lays out a relatively full set of means and ends that patients can legitimately obtain, and against the background of this authoritative but not quite official system, a great

*From the book *Asylums*, 1961. (pp. 188–226, 286–320). Reprinted by permission of Doubleday & Co., Inc. [From the Preface: "I would like to acknowledge . . . the support I was given by the sponsoring agencies . . . to study St. Elizabeths . . . (Washington, D.C.)]

number of patient activities effectively become illicit or not permissible. So emptied is the effectively authorized life given some patients on some wards that almost any moves they make is likely to add an unplanned-for satisfaction.

*   *   *

I turn now to consider the sources of materials that patients employ in their secondary adjustments. The first thing to note is the prevalence of make-do's. In every social establishment participants use available artifacts in a manner and for an end not officially intended, thereby modifying the conditions of life programmed for these individuals. A physical re-working of the artifact may be involved, or merely an illegitimate context of use. . . .

In Central Hospital many simple make-do's were tacitly tolerated. For example, inmates widely used freestanding radiators to dry personal clothing that they had washed, on their own, in the bathroom sink, thus performing a private laundry cycle that was officially only the institution's concern. On hard-bench wards, patients sometimes carried around rolled-up newspapers to place between their necks and the wooden benches when lying down. Rolled-up coats and towels were used in the same way. Patients with experience in other imprisoning institutions employed an even more effective artifact in this context, a shoe. In transferring from one ward to another, patients would sometimes carry their belongings in a pillow slip knotted at the top, a practice which is semi-official in some jails. The few aging patients fortunate enough to have a private sleeping room would sometimes leave a towel underneath their room washstand, transforming the stand into a reading desk and the towel into a rug to protect their feet from the cold floor. Older patients who were disinclined or unable to move around sometimes employed strategies to avoid the task of going to the toilet: On the ward, the hot steam radiator could be urinated on without leaving too many long-lasting signs; during twice-weekly shaving visits to the basement barber shop, the bin reserved for used towels was used for a urinal when the attendants were not looking. Backward patients of all ages sometimes carried around paper drinking cups to serve as portable spittoons and ashtrays, since attendants were sometimes more concerned about keeping their floors clean than they were in suppressing spitting or smoking.[57]

*   *   *

57. In Central Hospital many patients remained entirely mute, were incontinent, hallucinated, and practised other classic symptoms. However, very few patients, as far as I could see, had the temerity purposely and persistently to drop ashes on the linoleum floor, just as few declined to line up for food, take their shower, go to bed, or get up on time. Behind a ward show of frank psychosis was a basic ward routine that was quite fully adhered to.

Timing was important in other means of working the hospital. For example, old magazines and pocket books donated through the Red Cross were delivered once a week by truck to the recreation building located on the hospital grounds, from the library of which these reading materials would be distributed to individual patients and to wards. A few avid readers knew the truck's exact routine and would await its coming in order to have first choice. A few patients who knew the timing of the underground food runs between one of the central kitchens and a chronic service would sometimes pause near ground-level points of the tracks, hoping to snag a portion of food from the mobile vats. Another example has to do with obtaining information. The meals served in one of the large patient cafeterias were first served to a ward-bound group of old men. Ambulatory patients who wanted to know whether to go to the cafeteria or to buy sandwiches from the patients' canteen would regularly look through the window of this ward at the right moment to learn what was on the menu.

Another hospital example of working the system was scavenging. A few patients made the rounds of the refuse dumps near their service just prior to collection time. They poked through the top layers of garbage collected in the large wooden storage boxes, searching for food, magazines, newspapers, or other oddments that were made meaningful to these collectors by short supply and by the necessity of humbly asking an attendant or other official for them, the means by which these materials could be obtained in a legitimate way. . . .

*   *   *

Perhaps the most important way in which patients worked the system in Central Hospital was by obtaining a "workable" assignment, that is, some special work, recreation, therapy, or ward assignment that alone could make available certain secondary adjustments—and often a whole set of them. . . .

*   *   *

As might be expected, many assignments gave patients a chance to make contact with members of the relevant sex, a secondary adjustment that is exploited and partly legitimized by many recreational and religious organizations in civil society. Similarly, some assignments made it possible for two persons, cut off by the internal residential segregation of the hospital, to consummate "a meet." For example, patients would come a little early to the movies and the charity performances in the auditorium building, engage in some cross-sex banter, and then attempt to arrange seating in the auditorium, or, if not seating, then communication channels, so as to carry on this activity during the performance. Leave-taking was also an occasion for these communications, giving to the evening the air of a small-town social function.

Meetings on hospital grounds of Alcoholics Anonymous seemed to function in a similar way, providing a means by which patients, now friends, whose drinking escapades had gotten them locked up, could get together once every two weeks to exchange gossip and renew ties. Athletics was similarly used. During the interservice volleyball tournament, it was not surprising to see a player rush over to the side lines whenever time was called in order to hold hands with his girl friend, who, in turn, having been let off her ward supposedly to watch the game, had in fact come to hold hands.

One of the distinctive mental-hospital assignments worked for purposes of sociable contact with one's fellow patients and for purposes of "making a meet" was therapy. In Central Hospital the chief forms of psychotherapy were group therapy, dance therapy, and psychodrama. All were conducted in a relatively indulgent atmosphere and tended to recruit the kinds of patients who were interested in contact with the opposite sex. Psychodrama was especially workable because lights would be turned low during a performance; dance therapy was especially workable because it often involved periods of ballroom dancing with a person of one's choice.

*   *   *

In Central Hospital there were two basic official types of organization in which the patient was located. One of these was the "ward system," consisting of place of residence, the supervision received there, and relations to other and differentiated wards from which the patient came and to which he might be sent. The other was the "assignment system" through which a patient left the ward and for all or part of the day came under the supervision of the staff person for whom he was working or from whom he was receiving one of the various kinds of therapies.

[H]ospital theory was that since the establishment cared for all the needs of the patients there was no reason for patients to be paid for the hospital work that they did. Willingness to work for nothing for the hospital was in fact defined as a sign of convalescence, a sign of interest in socially constructive activity, just as work itself was defined as therapeutic. But whether from a desire to act according to civilian standards, or in order to achieve discipline and motivation, staff persons to whom patients were seconded did feel obliged to "show their appreciation" of "their" patients. And a functionary who did not show this kind of regard for his clients might have to report at the end of the year a declining number of patients engaged in his activity.

The chief indulgence provided to those who worked was the right to leave the ward each day for the period of time worked—from one half to six hours—and the right of occasional time off during working hours to go to the canteen or to recreation-building socials. The traditional rule in the hospital was that ground parole was given only to those who paid for it by work. (At the time of the study this rule was changing—much to the displeasure of some functionaries who felt they would no longer be able to discipline their charges. Admission service patients seemed to be able to obtain ground parole without having to engage in any but token labor, and chronic service patients were increasingly managing to stay on parole without a hospital job.)

*   *   *

. . . One issue in Central Hospital, as in other such institutions, was that in according an attendant the selfless obligation physically to constrain and coerce patients who were deemed a danger to themselves or others, a convenient cover was provided for private coercion. Economic and social payments also came to cover arrangements nominally foreign to both. When one patient bought the service of a small errand from another by means of a cigarette or a "drag," the buyer occasionally handled the transaction in an imperious way, giving the appearance of getting more pleasure from making the other patient perform a menial act than from the service itself. Paternalistic old-line attendants on back wards, in getting ready to give a patient sweets bought with the patient's canteen funds, would sometimes teasingly hold off granting the indulgence until the patient had made some abject begging signs or affirmed that he did indeed want what the attendant was about to give him. Butt-giving, by both attendants and patients, was also sometimes used to humble the recipient. . . .

*   *   *

Inmate control of staff in total institutions takes traditional forms, for example: arranging for "accidents" to occur to a staff person, or the massed rejection of a particular item of food, or the slowing-down of work production, or the sabotaging of plumbing, lighting, and communication systems, all of which are readily vulnerable to inmate action. Other inmate sanctions of staff may take the form of "collective" or individual teasing and more subtle forms of ritual insubordination, such as the military technique of saluting a troublesome officer from too great a distance, or with too much precision, or with too slow a tempo. A staff threat to the whole system of undercover arrangements may be answered with extreme action such as strikes or riots.

*   *   *

The mental hospital represents a peculiar instance of those establishments in which underlife is likely to proliferate. Mental patients are persons who caused the kind of trouble on the outside that led someone physically, if not socially, close to them to take psychiatric action against them. Often this trouble was associated with the "prepatient" having indulged in

situational improprieties of some kind, conduct out of place in the setting. It is just such misconduct that conveys a moral rejection of the communities, establishments, and relationships that have a claim to one's attachment.

Stigmatization as mentally ill and involuntary hospitalization are the means by which we answer these offenses against propriety. The individual's persistence in manifesting symptoms after entering the hospital, and his tendency to develop additional symptoms during his initial response to the hospital, can now no longer serve him well as expressions of disaffection. From the patient's point of view, to decline to exchange a word with the staff or with his fellow patients may be ample evidence of rejecting the institution's view of what and who he is; yet higher management may construe this alienative expression as just the sort of symptomatology the institution was established to deal with and as the best kind of evidence that the patient properly belongs where he now finds himself. In short, mental hospitalization outmaneuvers the patient, tending to rob him of the common expressions through which people hold off the embrace of organizations—insolence, silence, *sotto voce* remarks, unco-operativeness, malicious destruction of interior decorations, and so forth; these signs of disaffiliation are now read as signs of their maker's proper affiliation. Under these conditions all adjustments are primary.

Furthermore, there is a vicious-circle process at work. Persons who are lodged on "bad" wards find that very little equipment of any kind is given them—clothes may be taken from them each night, recreational materials may be withheld, and only heavy wooden chairs and benches provided for furniture. Acts of hostility against the institution have to rely on limited, ill-designed devices, such as banging a chair against the floor or striking a sheet of newspaper sharply so as to make an annoying explosive sound. And the more inadequate this equipment is to convey rejection of the hospital, the more the act appears as a psychotic symptom, and the more likely it is that management feels justified in assigning the patient to a bad ward. When a patient finds himself in seclusion, naked and without visible means of expression, he may have to rely on tearing up his mattress, if he can, or writing with feces on the wall—actions management takes to be in keeping with the kind of person who warrants seclusion.

We can also see this circular process at work in the small, illicit, talisman-like possessions that inmates use as symbolic devices for separating themselves from the position they are supposed to be in. What I think is a typical example may be cited from prison literature:

> Prison clothing is anonymous. One's possessions are limited to toothbrush, comb, upper or lower cot, half the space upon a narrow table, a razor. As in

jail, the urge to collect possessions is carried to preposterous extents. Rocks, string, knives—anything made by man and forbidden in man's institution—anything, a red comb, a different kind of toothbrush, a belt—these things are assiduously gathered, jealously hidden or triumphantly displayed.

But when a patient, whose clothes are taken from him each night, fills his pockets with bits of string and rolled up paper, and when he fights to keep these possessions in spite of the consequent inconvenience to those who must regularly go through his pockets, he is usually seen as engaging in symptomatic behavior befitting a very sick patient, not as someone who is attempting to stand apart from the place accorded him.

Official psychiatric doctrine tends to define alienative acts as psychotic ones—this view being reinforced by the circular processes that lead the patient to exhibit alienation in a more and more bizarre form—but the hospital cannot be run according to this doctrine. The hospital cannot decline to demand from its members exactly what other organizations must insist on; psychiatric doctrine is supple enough to do this, but institutions are not. Given the standards of the institution's environing society, there have to be at least the minimum routines connected with feeding, washing, dressing, bedding the patients, and protecting them from physical harm. Given these routines, there have to be inducements and exhortations to get patients to follow them. Demands must be made, and disappointment is shown when a patient does not live up to what is expected of him. Interest in seeing psychiatric "movement" or "improvement" after an initial stay on the wards leads the staff to encourage "proper" conduct and to express disappointment when a patient backslides into "psychosis." The patient is thus re-established as someone whom others are depending on, someone who ought to know enough to act correctly. Some improprieties, especially ones like muteness and apathy that do not obstruct and even ease ward routines, may continue to be perceived naturalistically as symptoms, but on the whole the hospital operates semiofficially on the assumption that the patient ought to act in a manageable way and be respectful of psychiatry, and that he who does will be rewarded by improvement in life conditions and he who doesn't will be punished by a reduction of amenities. Within this semiofficial reinstatement of ordinary organizational practices, the patient finds that many of the traditional ways of taking leave of a place without moving from it have retained their validity; secondary adjustments are therefore possible.

*   *   *

If a function of secondary adjustments is to place a barrier between the individual and the social unit in which he is supposed to be participating, we should expect some secondary adjustments to be empty of intrinsic gain and to function solely to express unauthorized distance—a self-preserving "rejection of one's rejectors." This seems to happen with the very common forms of ritual insubordination, for example, griping or bitching, where this behavior is not realistically expected to bring about change. Through direct insolence that does not meet with immediate correction, or remarks passed half out of hearing of authority, or gestures performed behind the back of authority, subordinates express some detachment from the place officially accorded them. . . .

*   *   *

It would be easy to account for the development of secondary adjustment by assuming that the individual possessed an array of needs, native or cultivated, and that when lodged in a milieu that denied these needs the individual simply responded by developing makeshift means of satisfaction. I think this explanation fails to do justice to the importance of these undercover adaptations for the structure of the self.

The practice of reserving something of oneself from the clutch of an institution is very visible in mental hospitals and prisons but can be found in more benign and less totalistic institutions, too. I want to argue that this recalcitrance is not an incidental mechanism of defense but rather an essential constituent of the self.

*   *   *

c.   HOUGH v. UNITED STATES
            271 F.2d 458 (D.C. Cir. 1959)

BAZELON, CIRCUIT JUDGE.

*   *   *

[This appeal] . . . presents the question whether an individual who has been committed to a mental hospital after acquittal of a crime by reason of insanity may, without judicial approval, be permitted by the hospital authorities to leave the hospital grounds without a guard or attendant.

Dr. Overholser, the Superintendent of St. Elizabeths Hospital, testified that a course of periodic absences from the hospital without a guard or attendant is a necessary step in the process of rehabilitating the patient so that he can be restored to his place in the community without danger to himself or others. The District Court, on the other hand, suggested that an individual under such a commitment is supposed to be "a prisoner."

The statute under which appellant was committed is silent as to the conditions of confinement or treatment. It provides no specific test whereby one can determine whether rehabilitative therapy, which is clearly the province of the hospital alone, amounts to conditional release, which is the province of the court as well. So here, as with the criteria for conditional release, we must interpret the general language used in light of the legislative purpose.

In the light of that purpose, we must reject the District Court's suggestion that appellant is a "prisoner." Nothing in the history of the statute—and nothing in its language—indicates that an individual committed to a mental hospital after acquittal of a crime by reason of insanity is other than a patient. The individual is confined in the hospital for the purpose of treatment, not punishment; and the length of confinement is governed solely by considerations of his condition and the public safety. Any preoccupation by the District Court with the need of punishment for crime is out of place in dealing with an individual who has been acquitted of the crime charged.

It does not follow, however, that the hospital authorities are free to allow such a patient to leave the hospital without supervision. We readily grant that periodic freedom may be valuable therapy. So, we suppose, may outright release sometimes be. But the statute makes one in appellant's situation a member of "an exceptional class of people." *Overholser v. Leach, supra,* 103 U.S.App.D.C. at 291, 257 F.2d at 669. It provides, generally, that the District Court have a voice in any termination of her confinement, whether unconditional or conditional.

Although the statute does not speak of temporary leaves from the hospital, its purpose, as we read it, is to assure that members of the "exceptional class" to which appellant belongs be kept under hospital restraint until the District Court, in the exercise of a discretion, reviewable by this court, approves a relaxation of that restraint. We read "conditional release" as used in the present statute to include the kind of temporary freedom which has been given this appellant. We do not, of course, lose sight of the hospital's view that such temporary freedom is often an essential part of the therapeutic process and, therefore, must not be prevented. But calling it a conditional release does not prevent it. It simply requires the hospital authorities, when they decide that a patient has reached the stage where such freedom is necessary and proper, to certify that fact to the District Court and obtain an appropriate order, reviewable by this court. It should not be anticipated that the District Court would arbitrarily prevent the hospital authorities from utilizing temporary leaves for therapy in proper cases. The court would simply fulfil its statutory role by deciding whether or not the evidence supports the hospital's determination that in all reasonable likelihood the patient's temporary absence from the hospital under specified conditions will not endanger others.

The order . . . is accordingly affirmed.

NOTES

NOTE 1

DARNELL v. CAMERON
348 F.2d 64 (D.C. Cir. 1965)

BAZELON, CHIEF JUDGE.

Appellant is presently confined in St. Elizabeths Hospital. He appeals the District Court's dismissal of his petition for habeas corpus. At a hearing below, the court found the following facts. In 1959, appellant was charged in the District of Columbia Court of General Sessions with indecent exposure, found not guilty by reason of insanity and committed to St. Elizabeths Hospital under the mandatory provisions of D.C. Code § 24–301(d). In 1961, the Court of General Sessions approved appellant's conditional release, at the hospital's recommendation, permitting appellant to "live in the city, reporting to the hospital for [periodic] examination . . . ." In February, 1963, appellant was arrested in Arlington, Virginia, on an indecent exposure charge. Although appellant was never tried on that charge, the hospital superintendent averred that "after a lengthy discussion with a detective of the Arlington County Police Department, it was agreed that we would accept [appellant] if he was returned to this hospital. He was subsequently returned to our custody." The hospital made no application at that time to the Court of General Sessions for revocation of appellant's conditional release. In May, 1963, appellant escaped from the hospital and he was returned in October, 1963.

On September 29, 1964, this petition for habeas corpus was filed in the District Court. On October 8, 1964, the hospital requested the Court of General Sessions to revoke appellant's conditional release because of the May, 1963 "unauthorized leave from the hospital." This request did not mention appellant's Arlington arrest or explain the reason that appellant was in the hospital's custody in May, 1963.[1] On October 21, 1964, the Court of General Sessions revoked the conditional release on the ground that appellant "left Saint Elizabeths Hospital without authorization" in May 1963. This revocation was granted without a hearing and without the presence of appellant or his counsel. Appellant's counsel in this appeal says that no notice was given regarding this revocation proceeding, and that he discovered the revocation order only while inspecting the Court of General Sessions' records in preparing for the District Court habeas corpus hearing, which took place October 26, 1964.

The order for conditional release could be revoked

---

1. The hospital alleges it sent a letter to the Court of General Sessions on June 21, 1963, requesting revocation of appellant's conditional release solely on the ground of his May, 1963, "unauthorized leave from the hospital." According to court records, however, that letter was never received.

only by the court which granted it and only after full hearing. "The part of the court in the release procedure is not *pro forma* or merely technical; it is the performance of judicial acts, dependent solely upon the evidence and the judicial judgment of the court."[2] Release can only be granted by "the court in which the person was tried."[3] And we think the court also has an independent judicial role in any revocation of release. The hospital's recommendation for revocation "must be supported by *reasons*. . . . [Appellant] cannot properly be kept in confinement indefinitely on the bare opinion, conclusion or certificate of the superintendent. . . . [Appellant] is entitled to test that conclusion by familiar processes of adversary proceedings."[4]

In this case, the apparent ground for the hospital's "revocation" of appellant's release in February, 1963, was his Arlington arrest. But the adequacy of this ground was never tested "by the familiar processes of adversary proceedings" in the Court of General Sessions. The ground for that court's revocation of appellant's release—that he wrongfully left the hospital in May, 1963—was patently inadequate since no reason appeared why he was then in custody. The hospital now argues that the habeas corpus hearing in the District Court was adequate substitute for a hearing in the Court of General Sessions. But since only the latter court had jurisdiction to revoke appellant's release, the factual basis for revocation must be found by that court. Moreover, there was no inquiry at the habeas corpus hearing into the facts underlying appellant's Arlington arrest.[5]

The hospital's recommitment of appellant in February, 1963, without resort to the courts and solely on the basis of untested allegations by the Arlington police reveals an utter disregard for the procedural requirements which protect liberty. This action and the hospital's misleading request for revocation to the Court of General Sessions give unfortunate credence to charges that hospital authorities act lawlessly toward the mentally disabled. Such charges may not arise from conduct which is wilfully improper, but rather from hospital authorities' views of the requirements of administrative efficiency or from their beliefs that "papa knows best." . . .

We hold that appellant's conditional release has

never been validly revoked and his present confinement is unlawful. We remand this case to the District Court with instructions to hold it in abeyance for no more than ten days, to permit appellee to institute proceedings in the Court of General Sessions regarding the revocation of appellant's conditional release. If no such proceedings are instituted within that time, the rule shall be made absolute and the appellant discharged pursuant to the conditional release.

Another matter deserves mention. Appellant has been confined in St. Elizabeths Hospital for more than four years following his acquittal by insanity of an indecent exposure charge. The criminal penalty for conviction of that charge was a 90-day-to-one-year prison term. This disparity in confinement terms is not in itself a ground for appellant's release. But mandatory confinement in a mental hospital under D.C. Code § 24–301 "rests upon a supposition, namely, the necessity for treatment of the mental condition which led to the acquittal by reason of insanity. And this necessity for treatment presupposes in turn that treatment will be accorded."[9] Appellant's testimony casts doubt on whether he is receiving any treatment:

Q. Do you know the name of the doctor who is in charge of your case? A. Dr. Economon . . . He just started working over at John Howard [Pavilion] three months ago, maybe.

Q. And do you see him occasionally in the course of your present stay at the hospital? A. You mean, to talk to him?

Q. Yes. A. I think I have talked to him about three times since he has been there.

Q. Now, are you participating in any other kind of treatment at the hospital? A. No.

Q. Any group meetings, talk to any other psychiatrists? A. No, he is the only one.

Q. Do you do any work at the hospital? A. Oh, I work in the clothing room, passing out clothing.

Q. How often do you do that? A. Twice a week.

Q. For how long each time? A. Twenty minutes.

Q. Then is it fair to say that you have really very little to do in the hospital? A. There is not hardly anything to do up there.

The hospital introduced no evidence to show what treatment, if any, appellant was receiving. And the court made no findings of fact or conclusions of law on this question. Our disposition of this case does not bar appellant from raising this question again in habeas corpus proceedings if the Court of General Sessions does revoke his release. We are constrained to note this question here because the District Court did not recognize that the alleged absence of treatment might draw into question "the constitutionality of the mandatory commitment section" as applied to

---

2. *Isaac* v. *United States*, 109 U.S.App.D.C. 34, 38, 284 F.2d 168, 172 (1960).

3. D.C. Code § 24–301(e) . . .

4. *Ragsdale* v. *Overholser*, 108 U.S.App.D.C. 308, 314, 281 F.2d 943, 949 (1960) (emphasis in original).

5. Appellant argues that since the conditional release required only that he report to the hospital for periodic examinations, the sole ground for revocation could be failure to observe this condition. But we think the conditional release order reasonably implied the possibility of revocation on other grounds. Whether the alleged arrest is sufficient ground for revocation here is a question in the first instance for the Court of General Sessions, if revocation is sought.

9. Judge Fahy, concurring in Ragsdale v. Overholser, 108 U.S. App. D.C. at 315, 281 F. 2d at 950.

appellant. This question may be explored if raised in subsequent proceedings.

*   *   *

NOTE 2

SMART v. UNITED STATES
207 F.2d 841 (10th Cir. 1953)

HUXMAN, CIRCUIT JUDGE.

This was an action under the Federal Tort Claims Act for injuries sustained by appellant at the hands of one Ralph Edward Dungan, a mentally incompetent veteran, shortly after his release from a Veterans' Administration Hospital at Marion, Indiana, on a trial visit to his home.

*   *   *

The complaint . . . alleged that the Government's agents and employees in charge of the hospital were negligent in releasing Dungan from custody and that such negligence was the proximate cause of appellant's injuries.

The undisputed facts are these. Dungan was admitted to the veterans' hospital as a mental patient. Under treatment his condition improved. In a few months he was quartered in an open building and allowed the freedom of the grounds. On May 2, 1951, his physicians, after a staff conference, recommended his release on a 90-day trial visit to his home. Before his release became effective, his condition changed and he became violent and was transferred from an open building to a ward. When his proposed visit was cancelled, the staff advised his parents of his relapse and that he would be unable to come home on a trial visit.

By August 8, 1951, he had improved to the extent that he was allowed ground privileges. On October 14, 1951, the veteran's father wrote, requesting his release and stating that a job would be waiting for him in Phoenix, Arizona. By reply the authorities advised that his condition had improved and that a trial visit would be arranged. The father executed and returned to the hospital a Veteran's Administration Form 2832, formalizing his request for a trial visit, assuming responsibility for the patient's care, treatment, and conduct while in his custody, and agreeing to return him to the hospital at the end of the visit. Upon execution of this form, Dungan was released, given $141.23, and sent unaccompanied on a 90-day trial visit to his home in Pheonix, Arizona. While on the journey there, he stole an automobile in Oklahoma City and, while driving recklessly, injured appellant.

[T]he Government will be liable for the negligent or wrongful act of its employees, if a private person would be liable for similar acts by its or his employees, with certain exceptions, among which is that the Government will not be liable for any claim based upon the exercise or performance, or the failure to exercise or perform, a discretionary function or duty on the part of a federal agency or an employee of the Government, whether or not the discretion involved was abused.

. . . Regulation 6159 provides that when a request is made for the release of a psychotic patient not held under commitment he will be released, if mentally competent at the time, but if he is not mentally competent, he may be permitted a trial visit, if such is adjudged advisable. Regulation 6167(d) (1) provides that trial visits are to be encouraged. If the patient is found to be competent, he is entitled to be released. If he is not competent, then he is entitled to be released for such a visit if in the judgment of the hospital authorities it is deemed advisable. Whether such visits shall be permitted, when requested, of necessity involves the exercise of judgment and discretion. Before granting the request, it is necessary for the hospital authorities to consider the patient's case and determine whether in their judgment such a visit might be beneficial to him and whether authority therefor could be granted with safety to the public.

In *United States* v. *Gray*, 10 Cir., 199 F.2d 239, we held that the determination whether a wife of a veteran was to be admitted to a hospital involved the exercise of discretion. By analogy the determination whether a veteran shall be released for a trial visit likewise involves the exercise of discretion.

Appellant contends that, assuming that the decision to release Dungan involved discretion, the Government's agents were negligent in the manner in which they carried out his release, by failing to make full disclosure of his condition to the party who was to assume control of him while out on a trial visit. The record is clear that the hospital authorities fully advised Dungan's parents as to their conclusions with respect to his condition and gave it as their opinion that he could be released safely for the trial visit. Whether the patient could be safely released and permitted to go on his way without an attendant likewise involved the exercise of discretion.

We think the judgment of the trial court and the reasons assigned therefor are correct and it is, therefore,

Affirmed.

d.   LAKE v. CAMERON
— F.2d — (D.C. Cir. 1966)

BAZELON, CHIEF JUDGE: Appellant is confined in Saint Elizabeths Hospital as an insane person and appeals from denial of release in habeas corpus. . . . [The proceedings leading up to this decision appear on pages 552–553.]

*   *   *

Appellant contends in written and oral argument that remand to the District Court is required for a consideration of suitable alternatives to confinement in Saint Elizabeths Hospital in light of the new District of Columbia Hospitalization of the Mentally Ill Act, which came into effect after the hearing in the District Court. Indeed, her counsel appointed by this court, who had interviewed appellant, made clear in answer to a question from the bench on oral argument that although appellant's formal *pro se* pleading requests outright release, her real complaint is total confinement in a mental institution; that she would rather be in another institution or hospital, if available, or at home, even though under some form of restraint.

Habeas corpus challenges not only the fact of confinement but also the place of confinement. And the court is required to "dispose of the matter . . . as law and justice require." 28 U.S.C. § 2243. The court is not restricted to the alternative of returning appellant to Saint Elizabeths or unconditionally releasing her.

We are not called upon to consider what action we would have taken in the absence of the new Act, because we think the interest of justice and furtherance of the congressional objective require the application to the pending proceeding of the principles adopted in that Act. It provides that if the court or jury finds that a "person is mentally ill and, because of that illness, is likely to injure himself or other persons if allowed to remain at liberty, the court may order his hospitalization for an indeterminate period, or order any other alternative course of treatment which the court believes will be in the best interests of the person or of the public." D.C. Code § 21–545(b) (Supp. V, 1966). This confirms the view of the Department of Health, Education and Welfare that "the entire spectrum of services should be made available, including outpatient treatment, foster care, halfway houses, day hospitals, nursing homes, etc."[5] The alternative course of treatment or care should be fashioned as the interests of the person and of the public require in the particular case. Deprivations of liberty solely because of dangers to the ill persons themselves should not go beyond what is necessary for their protection.

The court's duty to explore alternatives in such a case as this is related also to the obligation of the state to bear the burden of exploration of possible alternatives an indigent cannot bear. This appellant, as appears from the record, would not be confined in Saint Elizabeths if her family were able to care for her or pay for the care she needs. Though she cannot be given such care as only the wealthy can afford, an earnest effort should be made to review and exhaust the available resources of the community in order to provide care reasonably suited to her needs.

At the habeas corpus hearing, the psychiatrist testified that appellant did not need "constant medical supervision," but only "attention"; that the psychiatrist would have no objection if appellant "were in a nursing home, or a place where there would be supervision." At the commitment hearing one psychiatrist testified that "Mrs. Lake needs care, whether it be in the hospital or out of the hospital," and did not specify what, if any, *psychiatric* care she needs. The second psychiatrist testified that she "needs close watching. She could wander off. She could get hurt and she certainly needs someone to see that her body is adequately cared for. . . . [She] needs care and kindness. . . ." It does not appear from this testimony that appellant's illness required the complete deprivation of liberty that results from commitment to Saint Elizabeths as a person of "unsound mind."

Appellant may not be required to carry the burden of showing the availability of alternatives. Proceedings involving the care and treatment of the mentally ill are not strictly adversary proceedings. Moreover, appellant plainly does not know and lacks the means to ascertain what alternatives, if any, are available, but the government knows or has the means of knowing and should therefore assist the court in acquiring such information.

We remand the case to the District Court for an inquiry into "other alternative courses of treatment." The court may consider, *e.g.*, whether the appellant and the public would be sufficiently protected if she were required to carry an identification card on her person so that the police or others could take her home if she should wander, or whether she should be required to accept public health nursing care, community mental health and day care services, foster care, home health aide services, or whether available welfare payments might finance adequate private care. Every effort should be made to find a course of treatment which appellant might be willing to accept.[14]

* * *

---

5. S. Rep. No. 925, 88th Cong., 2d Sess. 31 (1964). The Committee said: "The original bill did not provide for court order of any course of treatment besides indeterminate hospitalization. This provision was included to cover those cases where such treatment as placement in halfway houses or outpatient care may be indicated." S. Rep. No. 925 at 19.

14. "Care and services should be provided in such a way as to be most satisfying to the person concerned. This will usually, although not necessarily, imply keeping the person in his own home if possible; otherwise arranging for his care in surroundings which take into consideration not only his physical and mental health but also his usual and preferred mode of life." *The National Council on the Aging, supra,* note 11 at 5.

We express no opinion on questions that would arise if on remand the court should find no available alternative to confinement in Saint Elizabeths.[19]

Remanded for further proceedings in accordance with this opinion.

*   *   *

WRIGHT, CIRCUIT JUDGE, concurring: I concur in the court's opinion, but wish to make clear my position that, while the District of Columbia may be able to make some provision for Mrs. Lake's safety under our statute, the permissible alternatives, on the record before us, do not include full-time involuntary confinement. The record shows only that Mrs. Lake is somewhat senile; that she has a poor memory, has wandered on a few occasions, and is unable to care for herself at all times. This evidence makes out a need for custodial care of some sort, but I cannot accept the proposition that this showing automatically entitles the Government to compel Mrs. Lake to accept its help at the price of her freedom.

BURGER, CIRCUIT JUDGE, with whom DANAHER and TAMM, CIRCUIT JUDGES, join, dissenting: We disagree with remanding the case to require the District Court to carry out an investigation of alternatives for which appellant has never indicated any desire. The only issue before us is the legality of Mrs. Lake's confinement in Saint Elizabeths Hospital and the only relief she herself has requested is immediate unconditional release.[1] The majority does not intimate that Appellant's present confinement as a patient at Saint Elizabeths Hospital is illegal,[2] or that there is anything wrong with it except that she does not like it and wishes to get out of any confinement. Nevertheless, this Court now orders the District Court to perform functions normally reserved to social agencies by commanding search for a judicially approved course of treatment or custodial care for this mentally ill person who is plainly unable to care for herself. Neither this Court nor the District Court is equipped to carry out the broad geriatric inquiry proposed or to resolve the social and economic issues involved. . . .

Although proceedings for commitment of mentally ill persons are not strictly adversary, a United States court in our legal system is not set up to initiate inquiries and direct studies of social welfare facilities or other social problems. This Court exists to decide questions put before it by parties to litigation on the basis of issues raised by them in pleadings and facts adduced by those parties. D.C. Code § 21–545 (Supp. 1966) does not transmute the United States District Court for the District of Columbia into an administrative agency for proceedings involving the mentally ill. . . .

*   *   *

To show that Appellant really does object to the *place* of her confinement, the majority is forced to rely on the response of her appointed counsel to a question from the bench at oral argument. Counsel said that Appellant's major objection was that she was confined in a mental institution, and he intimated that possibly she might not be so unhappy with confinement in some other institution. This indicates that a large part of what troubles both Appellant and the majority is the fact that she is being confined in a *mental* institution and not some type of home for the aged which would provide essentially the same care but would not have attached to it the "onus" of being associated with a mental institution.

If Appellant were to receive precisely the same care she is presently receiving in the geriatrics ward of St. Elizabeths at an institution elsewhere with a name like Columbia Rest Haven, it does not appear that there would be much disagreement over the propriety of her confinement. However, a person's freedom is no less arrested, nor is the effect on him significantly different, if he is confined in a rest home with a euphemistic name rather than at St. Elizabeths Hospital. The cases the majority cites to support the proposition that habeas corpus is available to challenge the place of custody all involved the quite different situation of challenges based on the nature rather than simply the name of the place of custody. Any conceivable relevance of those cases to the contentions made in the present case is eliminated by the fact that no one denies that Appellant is mentally ill.

We can all agree in principle that a series of graded institutions with various kinds of homes for the aged and infirm would be a happier solution to the problem than confining harmless senile ladies in St. Elizabeths Hospital with approximately 8000 patients, maintained at a great public expense. But it would be a piece of unmitigated folly to turn this appellant loose on the streets with or without an identity tag; and I am sure for my part that no District Judge will order such a solution. This city is hardly a safe place for able-bodied men, to say nothing of an infirm, senile, and disoriented woman to wander about with no protection except an identity tag advising police where to take her. The record shows that in her past wanderings she has been molested, and should she

---

19. Such questions might be whether so complete a deprivation of appellant's liberty basically because of her poverty could be reconciled with due process of law and the equal protection of the laws.

1. The question of alternative treatment was never raised until this court requested counsel to discuss it in their briefs and arguments on rehearing *en banc.*

2. Undisputed medical testimony was that Appellant "surely could not take care of herself in the community; . . . she needs supervision."

be allowed to wander again all of her problems might well be rendered moot either by natural causes or violence.

*   *   *

2.

WHAT THERAPY, UNDER WHAT CIRCUMSTANCES IS APPROPRIATE FOR WHAT PURPOSES?

OPINION OF THE ATTORNEY GENERAL
SHOCK THERAPY IN STATE HOSPITAL
64 Pa. D. & C. 14 (1948)

WOODWARD, DEPUTY ATTORNEY GENERAL, May 18, 1948.—The Department of Justice is in receipt of your request for an opinion regarding the legality of State mental hospital superintendents proceeding with certain specific psychiatric therapies on patients committed to their custody, without first obtaining properly witnessed written permissions from the patients' nearest responsible relatives. In support of your request, you furnish the following information, stated substantially in the language of your request.

The specific therapies referred to are the so-called "shock" treatments of various types. . . .

The "shock" therapies came into prominence more than 15 years ago, when the use of insulin was introduced to produce coma in certain mental diseases. Other types of shock treatments were rapidly developed, but are becoming obsolete, except for the extensive more practical use of electro-shock therapy, which has been widely recognized in the past 10 years. These so-called shock treatments produce unconsciousness, and are frequently associated with convulsions. The electroshock is now accepted as specific for mental illnesses showing extreme agitation and mental depression. The insulin coma treatment has a place in certain types of dementia praecox or schizophrenia. Fatalities in shock therapies are practically unknown, and complications, such as fractures, have been reduced to less than $\frac{1}{2}$ of 1 per cent incidence.

Although relatives are routinely advised regarding the nature and implications of the treatment, difficulties sometimes ensue, in that there may be a delay of weeks or months required for relatives to investigate to their own satisfaction before signing such a permit. Furthermore, uninformed lay advice, ignorance, and general prejudice, especially from unco-operative families, may deprive a patient of a definite chance for improvement or recovery.

Consequently, months and even years of additional care, at the expense of the Commonwealth, have resulted for large groups of patients to whom specific treatments were denied. Depression cases have committed suicide, disturbed cases have continued with unnecessary violence, and among such untreated patients, there has been a definite contribution toward the secondary problems of overcrowding and difficult management.

*   *   *

We understand that shock treatments have been used by the State mental hospitals of this Commonwealth since 1939, and that during this time, there have been no deaths from the use of these treatments. There is at present a patient population in State mental hospitals of about 35,000; depression cases in which shock treatment is indicated amount to about one third of the above total.

Mental patients are generally legally, mentally, and medically incapable of giving consents to methods of treatment or other matters relating to their care and maintenance; therefore, it may be necessary to attempt resort to friends or relatives, who may prove unavailable, or unwilling to co-operate.

There is an indeterminate minimum of about 5 per cent of patients with whom difficulty is experienced in obtaining consents. Obviously, it is desirable to avoid the necessity of obtaining such consents, if possible, especially since such consents are generally considered unnecessary, because the treatments now constitute a recognized established procedure.

There are many other forms of treatment in use in the State mental hospitals in which consents are not considered necessary as follows: Infra red rays, ultra violet rays, insulin, drugs—orally and by needles, and hydrotherapy—wet packs, tubs, etc.

If written consent is necessary in any form of treatment, where is the line to be drawn?

*   *   *

Treatment of mental diseases by artificially inducing convulsions with electricity began in Italy in 1938; since then it has accomplished remarkable results, and has proved to be so satisfactory that it is now generally used. This treatment is discussed in an article entitled "Shock Therapy Saves Minds," in *Hygeia* . . . July 1947, at pages 516–517, wherein it is stated, *inter alia*, as follows:

> "The presently accepted procedure for shock therapy involves the passing of about 115 volts of alternating electric current through the patient's head for a period of about three-tenths of a second. The machine by which this shock is administered is designed to prevent the delivering of more than one ampere of current and to shut off automatically as soon as the current has passed for the desired length of time. Thus it is impossible for the patient to receive such a heavy shock as to endanger his life.

*   *   *

> "The first effect on the patient, as the current passes through his brain, is to cause him to lose consciousness. Thus the patient is entirely unaware of the con-

vulsion through which he passes and retains no memory of the treatment."

And at pages 550–552:

"One psychiatrist has already administered 35,000 shock treatments with only one death and this death was the direct result of coronary disease.

"The overall mortality rate from shock therapy during the few years it has been in use in the United States averages about one death for every two thousand cases treated. In view of the fact that many cases have received numerous individual treatments, this mortality rate is surprisingly low. In fact, it is even lower than in many types of surgery.

"The violent muscle contraction which occurs as soon as the current passes through a patient's brain has been, in some cases, the means of causing an injury to the patient's bones. Recent improvements in technique have materially reduced the number of such complications. Furthermore, the seriousness of these skeletal injuries is minimal compared with the psychic benefits to be derived from electric shock therapy.

*   *   *

"To date, it is the most effective, the most beneficial, and the most easily administered therapeutic agent for the functional psychoses. It is not a cure-all but in properly selected cases and in competent hands it benefits about 80 per cent of the cases, producing a practical cure in approximately half of these. . . ."

From the foregoing article, two facts are noticeable: One, that the mortality rate from shock therapy during the years it has been in use in the United States averages about one death for every 2,000 cases treated, which is a surprisingly low mortality rate, even lower than in many types of surgery; and the other, that it is the most effective, the most beneficial, and the most easily administered therapeutic agent for the functional psychoses.

*   *   *

[A]n essential characteristic of "mental illness" is the necessity for control of the patient; and that the "care" of mental patients is predicated largely upon custody, detention and discipline; therefore, the rules and practices for the care and treatment of mental patients must not be confused with those governing the voluntary confinement of patients in medical and surgical hospitals.

This situation is reflected in section 303 of The Mental Health Act of 1923 . . . which provides in part as follows:

"The superintendent of said hospital shall receive the said patient, and may *detain him therein until said patient shall have recovered or shall be removed according to law.*" (Italics supplied.)

This section clearly precludes the patient's exercising any voluntary control over his confinement in a mental hospital.

While an examination of the foregoing statutes fails to reveal any express authority for the use of shock treatments, or other specific forms of treatments, that authority may be implied from the quoted definitions of mental illness, care, etc., and the inherent concepts of custody, control, detention, etc., to be exercised "until said patient shall have recovered or shall be removed according to the law."

*   *   *

There is nothing in the form of the foregoing commitments, which gives a mental patient, or his friends, relatives, guardian, or other person, the right to determine what methods of treatment, either with or without written consent thereto, may be administered in his particular case, during his detention in a mental hospital. Ordinarily, except in cases of guardians of the persons of minors, there is no authority vested in a patient's friends, relatives, guardian, or other persons which entitled such persons to give such consent on behalf of such patient, which would be binding upon the patient and protecting to the Commonwealth and its officials, except possibly by estoppel.

*   *   *

[T]he board of trustees of each State institution has general direction and control of the property and management of such institution; . . . the superintendent of the institution, subject to the authority of the board, shall administer the institution in all its departments; and . . . subject to the approval of the Secretary of Welfare, the board has the power to make bylaws, rules, and regulations for the management of the institution.

Under the foregoing provisions, either the superintendent, or the board of trustees, of a State mental hospital has the implied authority, in the first instance, to determine the policy and procedure of the institution in the care and treatment of mental patients, including the treatment by electric shock therapy, or other treatment, and whether such treatments may be given without the consent of the patients, his friends, relatives, or others. The care and treatment of patients must be within the sound discretion of the duly appointed authorities of the institution.

That the Department of Welfare has the implied authority to determine whether or not the within mentioned therapies may be used in State mental hospitals, and without express written permission therefor, appears from section 2307 of The Administrative Code . . . which is as follows:

"*The Department of Welfare shall have the power*, and its duty shall be, from time to time, *to recommend* and bring to the attention of the officers or other persons having the management of the State and supervised institutions *such standards and methods as may be helpful* in the government and administration of such institutions and *for the betterment of the inmates* therein, whereupon it shall be the duty of such officers or other persons to adopt and put into practice such standards and methods." (Italics supplied.)

* * *

There is nothing in the [law], either expressed or implied, which gives to a mental patient the right to, or places the duty upon the Commonwealth to secure, the consent of the patient or of someone legally authorized go give it for him, before proceeding with any specific methods of treatment; accordingly, it may be inferred that the mental patient does not have such a right; and that, therefore, the Commonwealth is not required to obtain such consents.

"An insane person has no constitutional or statutory right of liberty in the ordinary and conventional sense of that term. Accordingly, the right to restrain an insane person is not precluded by the general law which provides that no one shall be deprived of life, liberty, or property, without due process of law. It is not disputed that *the commitment of insane persons to appropriate institutions for confinement and care, when reasonably necessary for the protection of the public or of the person so afflicted, is a proper exercise of the police power of the state*": 28 Am. Jur. 672, 673 § 26. (Italics supplied.)

"*Insane persons are considered as wards of the state; and the state as parens patriae may make provisions for their protection*, provided they are not in contravention of constitutional provisions. *Statutes to this effect are liberally construed to the end that their purpose may be effectuated*": 32 C. J. 627 § 162. (Italics supplied.)

It must be borne in mind that the care, treatment, and maintenance of mental patients is a governmental function, and that the basic consideration in this function is to serve the best welfare of the patient, and that this function is best carried out by the authorized agencies of the Commonwealth, uncontrolled by the dictates of the patient, his friends, relatives, or others.

* * *

We are of the opinion . . . and you are accordingly advised that the superintendents of State mental hospitals, in their sound discretion, may administer to patients of State mental hospitals, electric shock and such other treatments, which in the exercise of reasonable skill and judgment, are indicated, after observation and diagnosis, as being necessary and proper for the patients' best welfare, without first obtaining written permission for such treatments from such patients, their friends, relatives, guardians, or other persons who may be legally entitled to give such consent on behalf of such patients; while such consent may be desirable in some cases, it is not essential under the laws of this Commonwealth.

NOTES

NOTE 1

NATANSON v. KLINE
186 Kan. 393, 350 P. 2d 1093 (1960)

* * *

The conclusion to be drawn from the . . . cases is that where the physician or surgeon has affirmatively misrepresented the nature of the operation or has failed to point out the probable consequences of the course of treatment, he may be subjected to a claim of unauthorized treatment. But this does not mean that a doctor is under an obligation to describe in detail all of the possible consequences of treatment. It might be argued, . . . that to make a complete disclosure of all facts, diagnoses, and alternatives or possibilities which may occur to the doctor could so alarm the patient that it would, in fact, constitute bad medical practice. There is probably a privilege, on therapeutic grounds, to withhold the specific diagnosis where the disclosure of cancer or some other dread disease would seriously jeopardize the recovery of an unstable, temperamental, or severely depressed patient. But in the ordinary case there would appear to be no such warrant for suppressing facts and the physician should make a substantial disclosure to the patient prior to the treatment or risk liability in tort.

Anglo-American law starts with the premise of thoroughgoing self-determination. It follows that each man is considered to be master of his own body, and he may, if he be of sound mind, expressly prohibit the performance of life-saving surgery, or other medical treatment. A doctor might well believe that an operation or form of treatment is desirable or necessary but the law does not permit him to substitute his own judgment for that of the patient by any form of artifice or deception.

The mean between the two extremes of absolute silence on the part of the physician relative to the treatment of a patient and exhaustive discussion by the physician explaining in detail all possible risks and dangers was well stated by the California District Court of Appeal in *Salgo* v. *Leland Stanford, Etc. Bd. Trustees*, 1957, 154 Cal. App. 2d 560, 317 P. 2d 170. . . .

". . . A physician violates his duty to his patient and subjects himself to liability if he withholds any facts which are necessary to form the basis of an intelligent consent by the patient to the proposed treatment. Likewise the physician may not minimize the known dangers of a procedure or operation in order to induce his patient's consent. At the same time, the physician must place the welfare of his patient above all else and this very fact places him in a position in which he sometimes must choose between two alternative courses of action. One is to explain to the patient every risk attendant upon any surgical procedure or operation, no matter how remote; this may well result in alarming a patient who is already unduly apprehensive and who may as a result refuse to undertake surgery in which there is in fact minimal risk; it may also result in actually increasing the risks by reason of the physiological results of the apprehension itself. The other is to recognize that each patient presents a separate problem, that the patient's mental and emotional condition is important and in certain cases may be crucial, and that in discussing the element of risk a certain amount of discretion must be employed consistent with the full disclosure of facts necessary to an informed consent. . . .

*   *   *

NOTE 2

IRVIN, WILLIAM P.

"Now, Mrs. Blair, about the Complications . . ."*

*   *   *

Mrs. Blair entered, sat down, and lit a cigarette. Then she said calmly: "Well, here I am, Doctor. My husband was a little upset until I told him you said it was just a fibroid tumor, just a simple hysterectomy, and there wasn't much to it."

Dr. Jones winced. What his lawyer had told him made him sorry he'd used those words. "Now, Mrs. Blair, I didn't exactly mean it that way, You see . . ."

"Doctor, what is it? Do I have cancer?"

"No, still fibroids, Mrs. Blair. But a hysterectomy —well, frankly, there are some things that can go wrong. Not often, of course. But I should tell you of the possibilities."

"Oh, I'm not worried, Doctor. But if it'll make you feel better, go ahead and tell me."

"Well, after you're admitted to the hospital, they'll shave you. And occasionally they may nick the skin a little. . . . No, I realize that's not so bad. . . . Yes, I realize you're not the type to get upset over little things. . . . Well, then they'll draw your water. Sometimes this can cause a little inflammation of the bladder. . . . That's right—like you had with your last pregnancy. . . . Well, I know it took four months, but usually we can cure it much faster. We'd use some of the newer drugs because they don't cause as many reactions. . . . A reaction? Well, you break out in a rash and itch and . . . That's right—like your cousin, John, after he got penicillin. . . . He died? Oh, I didn't know. Mrs. Blair, you're shaking ashes all over my rug.

"Next they'll draw some blood from your arm for tests. . . . Yes, I know you've had it done before. But sometimes you can get a virus infection that

causes a little liver reaction. . . . Your friend's husband died, too? Well, most people get better. Of course, it takes years sometimes, and—well, anyway it doesn't happen often. Mrs. Blair, you look pale, Here, take this pill. That's better.

"Now at bedtime, they'll give you some drugs to help you rest. . . . Yes, I guess you could get a drug reaction from them, but usually . . . No, I don't mean that would be your second drug reaction. I mean, you probably wouldn't have any reaction. . . . Yes, I know what I said about the bladder.

"You'll also get a little enema at bedtime. . . . Mrs. Blair, what happened to your cousin in Omaha has nothing to do with this case. They won't punch a hole in *your* intestine. . . . Of course, I don't guarantee it. . . . Peritonitis? Well, yes, a hole in the intestine can cause it, but nobody will punch a hole in your intestine. . . . No, I wasn't aware that your brother is a lawyer.

"Well, let's see. Early the next day they'll take you to the operating room, which brings us to the anesthetic. Occasionally, it can cause a little problem. . . . Well, the heart might stop working. . . . Oh, yes, we can start it again. Usually. If we can get it going, it usually keeps on working O.K. Of course, if the brain had been damaged, the patient might not be too bright after surgery. . . . Yes, an idiot, you might say— but really, that doesn't happen often.

"Next, we open the abdomen and remove the uterus. Of course, once in a while—not often, you understand—but sometimes . . . Mrs. Blair, just because your grandmother said you were born under an unlucky star. . . . Now stop shaking. Here, take another pill. . . . No, it won't cause a drug reaction— I don't think.

"Now, in removing the uterus, we might—on very rare occasions, you understand—get into the bowel. . . . I mean we might cut a small hole in the bowel. Sort of like the enema thing, yes. . . . Well, what we do is just sew it up. . . . Yes, peritonitis is possible.

"If all goes well, and we haven't nicked the ureter . . . Oh, the tube that goes to the bladder. . . . Well, it might cause a fistula and—let's talk about that later. . . . Yes, your insurance would cover it.

"Now the uterus is out, and the incision is closed. . . . No, we won't sew the bowel up too tight. I mean, we won't touch the bowel. . . . Yes, I know what I said before. . . . No, I'm not contradicting myself. Now please relax. . . . After the surgery you'll be given some fluids through a needle in your vein. . . . Well, yes, I guess so. That old virus and the liver again. . . . Yes, you mentioned that he died.

"If the wound doesn't break open . . . Well, all your intestines would spill out. . . . Oh sure, we'd put them back. . . . No, that wouldn't cause idiocy.

"There's only one more thing. Of course, it doesn't happen often. We call it a staph infection. . . . Oh, you've read about it in the papers? . . . They all died?

**R.I.S.S.*, (March, 1964) pp. 48–52. Copyright © 1963 by Medical Economics, Inc., Oradell, N.J. Reprinted by permission.

But that was in a nursery. . . . Well, yes, grownups can die from it, but we have drugs, and . . . Well, a drug reaction isn't usually as bad as a staph infection.

"To sum it all up, Mrs. Blair, a hysterectomy really isn't so simple. Now if you'll just sign this paper that says I've informed you of these little complica—Mrs. Blair. We're not through. Where are you going? Come back, Mrs. Blair."

NOTE 3

MIMS v. BOLAND
110 Ga.477, 138 S.E. 2d 902 (1964)

BELL, PRESIDING JUDGE.

*   *   *

With respect to consent this case presents . . . an . . . unusual question for consideration, i.e., whether after treatment or examination has begun, the patient's consent previously given may be withdrawn so as to subject the doctor to liability for assault and battery if the treatment or examination is continued. After exhaustive research we have found no reported precedent in this or any other jurisdiction to guide us in this area.

In the interest of the individual's right of freedom from unwanted contacts and invasions upon his body, we can not go so far as to say that once the examination or treatment has begun with the patient's consent the patient can in no event and by no means withdraw his approval. On the contrary even after the treatment or examination is underway we wish to emphasize that consent once given can be withdrawn sufficiently to subject a doctor to suit for assault and battery if he continues the contact, provided however the physician's withdrawal under the medical circumstances then existing would not endanger the life or health of the patient. This presents a medical question.

It is difficult to set a standard to govern the doctor's conduct where the patient protests in the midst of treatment or examination. If the doctor should desist in midstream, so to speak, it might forfeit the patient's life or well-being and might result in the doctor's liability for malpractice or indictment for some criminal offense or might bring upon him the reproach and condemnation of his own profession. These possibilities of accusal should not be left to chance so a standard must be devised to regulate conduct in this scope of activity.

To constitute an effective withdrawal of consent as a matter of law after treatment or examination is in progress commensurate to subject medical practitioners to liability for assault and battery if treatment or examination is continued, two distinct things are required: (1) The patient must act or use language which can be subject to no other inference and which must be unquestioned responses from a clear and rational mind. These actions and utterances of the patient must be such as to leave no room for doubt in the minds of reasonable men that in view of all the circumstances consent was actually withdrawn. (2) When medical treatments or examinations occurring with the patient's consent are proceeding in a manner requiring bodily contact by the physician with the patient and consent to the contact is revoked, it must be medically feasible for the doctor to desist in the treatment or examination at that point without the cessation being detrimental to the patient's health or life from a medical viewpoint.

The burden of proving each of these essential conditions is upon the plaintiff, and with regard to the second condition, it can only be proved by medical evidence as medical questions are involved.

To permit a lesser standard would be to subject the medical profession to an endless possibility of harassment and would place upon them a potential of punishment in every case where their examination or treatment results in less than complete success. The possibility of irresponsible harassment is something the medical profession should not be called upon to bear, dealing as it does with human life and human frailty.

*   *   *

NOTE 4

FIELD, ELLEN

The White Shirts*

This document will outlaw at all times and places for the rest of my life use of any so-called therapy by any physician against my will. I am at time of writing of sound mind.

If I should fall ill, as a result of which I should be in a coma or near-coma (as for instance as a result of injuries received in an accident, or any illness which might affect the soundness of my judgment), then Dr. . . . . of . . . . should be notified. If Dr. . . . . should be unavailable at the time, then the following alternative Drs. should be contacted. These alternative Doctors' names are attached at end of this will. Dr. . . . . and all of these alternative Drs. in signing their names to this document agree to care for me as my temporary guardian until such time as my mind is normal. This does not mean that they are authorized to use any therapy they may see fit. It means that if surgery be used, it should be used only if death or serious consequences should threaten my physical body as a result of injuries or acute serious illness. No type of therapy such as psychosurgery, electric shock or insulin shock or admini-

---

*© 1964 by M. E. Redfield (pp. 15–16). Reprinted by permission.

stration of drugs coming under the category of therapy for mental illness, or in fact of any drugs coming under any category, except as anesthesia in case of post-accident surgery, or acute illness surgery, and that only, as aforesaid, if my life is in danger without their use. No tranquillizers or sedatives are to be used. This shall include not only all known forms of mental-illness treatments but also treatments perhaps not yet invented at the time of this writing.

If established by *due process* that I require detention, then let this be carried out under direction as to place of this detention by Dr.....................
This document will render invalid any commitment which might have taken place in ignorance of it. However, if there is reluctance on the part of these detainers to respect this document, then it is understood that the Drs. and lawyers undersigned will file appeal petitions until my release from these detainers is secured.

Dr.................... and alternatives, also lawyers undersigned agree to abide by prohibitions and rules set herein and also they obligate themselves to visit and consult with me at my request. If I should request to see them in Bombay, or some distant point, they are not excused but must refer me to local care adhering to all rules, with the understanding that as soon as I am able to travel, the local people will release me to their care. They are obligated to inform the local people that I cannot legally be subjected to any therapies which are outlawed in the foregoing, or to any drastic therapy of any imaginable kind. In other words, they would be able to control what the local authorities did and did not do, because the care would be considered as their own, the local Dr. acting as their agent only.

Any permission I may sign for treatments when in an abnormal state of mind, or under drugs shall be invalidated by this Will. This Will is my declaration of NO FAITH in Psychiatry, past, present or future. I prefer to remain untreated for any real or alleged mental illness. I prefer my own mind, though mad, to a mind conditioned by devices employed by others against MY OWN VOLITION. This includes hypnotic or psychological techniques deliberately imposed to alter my mental processes. It does not include psychotherapy which invites but does not impose itself upon my consciousness. In other words, if healers there be and if the methods used by these healers is to heal by inviting my own participation, they are welcome. What is to be prohibited is alteration of the mind without my conscious consent, from the outside, as it were. Or by prohibited unnatural methods of gaining my consent. In short, no conditioning from the outside may take place. I hold it to be self-evident that an individual's mind is his own; not subject to treatment by any other individual or society itself. If society, by due process, can declare me

to be so mentally ill that I must be confined, that confinement cannot extend beyond my physical body, and enter the sacred regions of mind and soul. A mind that is subject to other minds is less free though he may roam the earth, sea and air, than a mind that is not subject to any other mind, though confined within a prison. I hereby declare myself in favor of my own folly to the enforced so-called wisdom of outside parties. This is my faith and my philosophy.

The Drs., lawyers, and other parties listed at end of this WILL, and signing are to be legally authorized to be temporary guardians of my person and property, so that any necessary expense in carrying out the terms of this Will may be insured. Their privilege and obligation is to secure immediate remedial legal aid should I fall under care, domination or treatment by persons publicly or privately known as Drs. or psychiatrists, but whose practices are alien to the conditions set herein. May be cancelled by myself or signers except at time of crisis.

NOTE 5

HAYNES v. HARRIS
344 F.2d 463 (8th Cir. 1965)

REGISTER, DISTRICT JUDGE.

Petitioner is serving an indeterminate sentence at the Medical Center for Federal Prisoners, Springfield, Missouri, having been sentenced pursuant to the provisions of the Federal Youth Corrections Act . . . following said Petitioner's plea of guilty to charges involving interstate transportation of forged securities. . . .

On July 27, 1964, Petitioner filed a petition for writ of habeas corpus in the United States District Court . . . This appeal is from the order dismissing said petition.

In substance the alleged grounds upon which Petitioner bases his petition are:

(a) That the offense to which he pleaded guilty and of which he stands convicted is not punishable by corporal punishment, and that certain medical treatment administered to him, without his consent, constitutes corporal punishment;

*   *   *

(c) That, as a result of his conviction, he has not lost his United States citizenship, and therefore it is still his prerogative to determine whether to accept or decline medical treatment, so long as no other persons are endangered by his actions.

*   *   *

Nowhere in his petition does the Petitioner assert that the conditions of his incarceration and treatment he is receiving at the institution amount to "cruel and inhuman" punishment. The facts, as revealed by the record before us, would not substantiate such an assertion. However, Petitioner argues in effect that he, and he alone, should determine whether he should receive certain medical treatment, and that "forced medical treatment is corporal punishment and cannot be legally inflicted upon anyone confined under a sentence that calls for less than capital punishment." This contention is obviously without merit. One of the paramount purposes for which a defendant is committed to the Medical Center is that he have the benefit of receiving from trained and qualified personnel proper examination, diagnosis, and all necessary and available treatment.

*   *   *

b.   JOBSON v. HENNE
         355 F. 2d 129 (2d Cir. 1966)

WATERMAN, CIRCUIT JUDGE:

The plaintiff-appellant, Warren Jobson, was an inmate of the New York State Newark State School for Mental Defectives most of his life. He was first committed to it on August 27, 1935, when he was twelve years old. There he remained until he was placed on home convalescent care status in 1953. He was finally discharged on May 16, 1956, and shortly thereafter he apparently became associated with a group of boys who were engaged in various unlawful activities. He was soon arrested, was indicted, and pleaded guilty to the crimes of petty larceny and burglary in the third degree. Prior to sentence the charges were dropped, and twenty days after his discharge on June 5, 1956, the appellant was recertified to the Newark State School, where he remained until late in the year 1963.[1]

On November 18, 1963, the appellant filed a complaint in the United States District Court for the Western District of New York, naming the director of the Newark State School, two assistant directors, and the school's supervising psychiatrist as parties defendant. The complaint sought a judgment for money damages, totaling $100,000, alleging, *inter alia*, that "the defendants for a period of many months last past have wilfully intentionally and maliciously held the plaintiff in and to involuntary servitude, peonage and/or slavery in and in the vicinity of the Newark State School . . ." in violation of 42 U.S.C. § 1983, which reads as follows:

§ 1983. Civil action for deprivation of rights
    Every person who, under color of any statute, ordinance, regulation, custom, or usage, of any State or Territory, subjects, or causes to be subjected, any citizen of the United States or other person within the jurisdiction thereof to the deprivation of any

rights, privileges, or immunities secured by the Constitution and laws, shall be liable to the party injured in an action at law, suit in equity, or other proper proceeding for redress.

[T]he lower court decided the defendants were entitled to judgment as a matter of law because they were state officials and entitled to invoke traditional judge-made doctrines of official immunity[2] in a suit brought against subordinate state officials to enforce the tort liability created by 42 U.S.C. § 1983.

At the outset it should be noted that what we say in this case on the subject of the protection afforded by the Thirteenth Amendment has no bearing on the legality of the imprisonment of persons duly convicted of a crime; such persons are explicitly excepted from the Amendment's coverage.

*   *   *

. . . We assume that even though the purpose of the Thirteenth Amendment was to proscribe conditions of "enforced compulsory service of one to another," *Hodges* v. *United States*, 203 U.S. 1 (1906), the states are not thereby foreclosed from requiring that a lawfully committed inmate perform without compensation certain chores designed to reduce the finanical burden placed on a state by its program of treatment for the mentally retarded, if the chores are reasonably related to a therapeutic program, or if not directly so related, chores of a normal housekeeping type and kind.[3] Proceeding on this assumption it would seem to follow that those in control of institutions for the mentally retarded may subject inmates to a wide variety of programs with both therapeutic

---

1. In the reply brief for the plaintiff-appellant it is stated that the plaintiff no longer resides in a mental institution.

2. For a general discussion of the development and scope of common law notions of official immunity from actions for damages see Hart & Wechsler, *The Federal Courts and the Federal System*, 1215–1224 (1953).

3. It seems established that compulsory commitment of mentally ill individuals who may be harmful to themselves or to society if allowed to remain at large does not violate the Thirteenth Amendment if the commitment procedures contain sufficient procedural safeguards. One can still argue, however, that to require inmates to perform cost saving (as distinguished from therapeutic) labor contravenes the Thirteenth Amendment. Indeed, one court apparently has so held. *Stone* v. *City of Paducah*, 120 Ky. 322, 86 S.W. 531 (Ky. Ct. App. 1905). Nevertheless, many states do administer programs that are designed to supply institutional needs as well as provide therapy, see Note, 110 U. Pa. L. Rev. 78, 89 (1961), and we assume that mental institutions can constitutionally require inmate particpation in these programs to the extent that the programs have a therapeutic purpose, or are reasonably related to the inmate's housekeeping or personal hygienic needs. Therefore, whether an institution's required program in any given case constitutes involuntary servitude would seem to depend on the nature of the tasks that are required of the inmate. If a court can conclude that the chores are reasonably related to a therapeutic program or to the inmate's personal needs, the fact that the performance of the chores also assists in defraying the operating costs of the institution should not constitute involuntary servitude, even if inmates are required to engage in this activity. On the other hand, it would seem that the Thirteenth Amendment may be violated if a mental

and cost saving purposes without violating the Thirteenth Amendment. Nevertheless, there may be some mandatory programs so ruthless in the amount of work demanded, and in the conditions under which the work must be performed, and thus so devoid of therapeutic purpose, that a court justifiably could conclude that the inmate had been subjected to involuntary servitude. In the present case the appellant's supporting affidavits state that for long periods of time he was forced to work in the Newark State School's boiler house eight hours a night, six nights a week, while working eight hours a day at assigned jobs in the village of Newark.[5]

As we cannot say that any such work program would not go beyond the bounds permitted by the Thirteenth Amendment, the complaint states a claim under § 1983. We must therefore reverse the district court's grant of the motion for summary judgment unless we can conclude that the lower court correctly applied the defense of official immunity. [T]he purpose of § 1983 as well as the other Civil Rights provisions is to provide a federal remedy for the deprivation of federally guaranteed rights in order to enforce more perfectly federal limitations on unconstitutional state action. To hold all state officers immune from suit would very largely frustrate the salutary purpose of this provision. We conclude the defense of official immunity should be applied sparingly in suits brought under § 1983.

. . . We hold that in [these] circumstances the defendants are liable to suit under § 1983 even though they are state administrative officials.

Reversed and remanded for trial.

MOORE, CIRCUIT JUDGE (dissenting):

*   *   *

In the present case, defendants assert the state interest in being free to experiment in the therapeutic treatment of mental defectives; plaintiff asserts the need for some judicial review. Although to hold state psychiatrists absolutely immune from suit upon any state-of facts might leave persons in the position of plaintiff without any means of securing judicial review, in the case now before us the allegations of the complaint and the affidavits on defendants' motion for summary judgment show clearly that

defendants were acting within their discretion in their assignment of work to the plaintiff. In support of their motion for summary judgment, defendants submitted expert opinions indicating that the work was beneficial to plaintiff and had therapeutic value; in opposition to defendant's motion, plaintiff produced expert opinions that the work assignments were without therapeutic value. I would uphold the dismissal, interpreting Judge Henderson's decision not as holding that state psychiatrists are absolutely immune from suit under § 1983, but as holding that, as a matter of law, in light of the need to permit considerable flexibility in state treatment of mental defectives, plaintiff has failed to allege or show facts sufficient to constitute a cause of action under § 1983.

*   *   *

The reluctance of the courts to entertain actions of this sort is understandable. State psychiatrists need scope in their attempts to treat mental defectives, and courts have enough to do without practicing psychiatry. Only when a course of treatment is prescribed which cannot reasonably be defended as therapeutic should a suit of this type be able to withstand a defense motion for summary judgment. This is not such a case. I would affirm.

*   *   *

c.   HAMMER v. ROSEN
         App. Div. 2d 216, 181 N.Y.S. 2d 805 (1959)

*   *   *

MEMORANDUM DECISION.

The jury's finding that the defendant, a psychiatrist, had not undertaken to contract to warrant a cure for the plaintiff incompetent of schizophrenia within a few months is entirely justified by the record. The cause of action for fraud, which is closely dependent upon the contract cause, was properly dismissed by the court and is in any event not supported by proof. Plaintiffs did not establish *prima facie* a cause of action for malpractice. It is not shown that the treatment given by defendant was not consistent with good standards of professional judgment addressed to the patient's psychiatric problem. Before defendant undertook the case of this patient at the persistent solicitation of her parents, she had undergone radical psychiatric care, including over 150 electric shock treatments without improvement. It is not disputed that defendant's "direct analysis" treatment, making no use of shock or surgery, initially improved the patient's condition. That the improvement was not permanent seems to have had a complex causation. We see no basis in the record to justify a finding of malpractice.

The judgment should be affirmed, with costs.

*   *   *

---

institution requires inmates to perform chores which have no therapeutic purpose or are not personally related, but are required to be performed solely in order to assist in the defraying of institutional costs, and it would appear that this would be so even if the inmates were compensated for their labor, for the mere payment of a compensation, unless the receipt of the compensation induces consent to the performance of the work, cannot serve to justify forced labor.

5. In the brief for the plaintiff-appellant and in the supporting affidavit it is stated that the plaintiff was paid one cent an hour for his work in the boiler house and between thirty-seven and one-half cents and fifty cents an hour for the work he performed in the village of Newark, N.Y.

MCNALLY, JUSTICE (dissenting in part).

It is conceded that at the conclusion of defendant's treatment between 1948 and 1955, involving expenditures of over $55,000, the condition of the plaintiff had not improved. The lack of improvement despite the time lapse establishes regression rather than stabilization of her condition. Prior to 1948 the patient had been treated extensively and intensively by various psychiatrists and at institutions specializing in the treatment of neurotics and psychotics. Said treatments included a minimum of 200 shock treatments.

Defendant was licensed to practice medicine in the State of New York in 1928; he commenced the practice of the specialty of psychiatry in or about 1945, about three years prior to the time he was retained to treat the patient. Preliminary to his specialization in psychiatry, the defendant had been a resident of Brooklyn State Hospital for six months and a resident of New York Psychiatric Institute and Hospital for a period of $1\frac{1}{2}$ years. It was brought to the attention of the patient's family that the defendant made claims to dramatic successes in the treatment of schizophrenic patients. The defendant was sought out, requested to, and did agree to treat the patient.

Nurse H. Louise Wong, who attended the patient for 12 days during September, 1948, testified that on two occasions she took the patient to the defendant for treatment. On the first occasion she requested the defendant to permit her to be present. Defendant, stating that he did not allow anyone to be present during his treatment of the patient, refused, excluded Nurse Wong from his office, locked the door and directed her to return at the end of an hour. Within 15 minutes thereafter Nurse Wong heard screams which she identified as those of the patient emanating from the defendant's office. She returned, attempted to gain access to defendant's office but was again excluded by defendant. After the completion of the treatment on the first occasion, Nurse Wong observed that the patient's body was covered with bruises, and her clothes were torn and disheveled. There was no one in defendant's office except the patient and the defendant. Testimony regarding conversations between Nurse Wong and the defendant was erroneously excluded.

Apart from the testimony of Nurse Wong, there was ample evidence in the record of defendant's assaults of the patient on various occasions in the course of his treatments. Mrs. Hammer testified that after treatments she observed her daughter was "beaten up" and had "blue eyes"; that her daughter returned from treatments "black and blue." Mrs. Hammer also testified to conversations with the defendant wherein he stated that the assaults complained of were part of the treatment. In addition, Emma Reitz, a maid in the employ of the Hammers,

testified to circumstances establishing that the defendant slapped the patient without justification during the summer of 1950 at Bolton Landing, N.Y.

Defendant's brief concedes that any mode of treatment of a schizophrenic which involves assaults of the patient is fantastic. It is doubtful that defendant can or will attempt to justify the assaults as a constituent element of a recognized method of therapy. Where, as here, common sense suggests the incompatibility of physical assaults of the patient on the part of the treating physician with the proper medical treatment of a schizophrenic, expert medical opinion is not required to establish malpractice *prima facie*. Moreover, on this record, defendant's method of treatment of the patient is not clear. There is much suggesting the unorthodox and, apart from his own self-serving conclusory claims and the hearsay approval of others, nothing to establish that defendant's method of treatment was in accordance with recognized and established medical and psychiatric procedures. Defendant suggests and attempts to argue that if the assaults took place, they were justified as a matter of self-defense. The short answer to this is that the record does not establish such a defense and, in any event, it was an issue for the jury and not a ground for the dismissal of the cause of action.

... Defendant does not contend that assaulting the patient was part of the treatment. He seems to contend otherwise. Furthermore, Mrs. Hammer's statement is not binding upon her daughter and obviously was made on the assumption that defendant was pursuing a recognized method of treatment.

NOTES

NOTE 1

ROSEN, JOHN N.

Direct Analysis*

... *Handling Aggression.* One can predict that with the beginning of the return to reality, the patient whenever possible will get into violent, sometimes physical altercations with members of his family. If I see this tendency developing, I take a firm hand as follows: "*If you ever again lay a hand on your mother, father, husband, wife, child, sibling* [whoever was put in jeopardy by the patient] *I will give you worse by far than you ever thought of doing to them. I forbid you to make any physical attack on a member of your family. If you feel you have to hit someone, hit me.*" On rare occasions, patients have struck me or scratched me, but not seriously. ... I must concede that the patient has plenty of justification for the rage and hostility directed against the parental figure who has been so

---

*Grune and Stratton; New York, 1953. (pp. 16 and 26). Reprinted by permission.

traumatic. This may involve a great danger to treatment. . . .

*   *   *

The range of aggression is wide. You are frequently called upon to engage in an encounter which may require no more than that you out-glare the patient or stand your ground firmly as he assumes an angry, threatening attitude toward you, or you may actually be the victim of as much of a physical assault as the patient's strength makes possible. . . . Ordinarily interpreting the aggression neutralizes these situations. Sometimes you have to match and overcome physical violence with physical strength.

*   *   *

NOTE 2

LANDAU v. WERNER
105 Sol. J. 257 (1961)

A psychiatrist of repute undertook in 1949 the treatment of an intelligent middle-aged woman in an anxiety state. For some months she saw him in his consultation room and wrote to him copiously as part of the therapeutic process, giving or sending him the letters which he later returned to her and which she preserved. She developed toward him deep feelings of love, obsession, and bondage, which he explained to her as being part of the process of "transference," and he advised her to continue the treatment, as she was making progress. After six months it was decided that the treatment should cease as the woman was better, though feeling herself to be deeply in love with the doctor. He, taking the view that a sudden withdrawal might cause a relapse, decided on a series of innocent and friendly social contacts with her which continued over some months*; but he gradually withdrew from the relationship; and the patient, being by that time emotionally and sexually aroused and distressed, attempted suicide at his home. The doctor thereupon resumed the treatment in a final effort to resolve the transference, but brought it to an end when it has no effect. The woman's mental condition deteriorated to such an extent that she became wholly incapable of work. She decided on proceedings against the doctor, alleging that her illness was caused by his wilful misconduct and professional negligence; but for various reasons those proceedings were delayed for ten years. The doctor denied the charges.

BARRY, J., said that he entirely absolved the doctor

---

*"The doctor . . . took her out to tea and dinner in restaurants on a number of occasions and visited her once in her bed-sitting room; there were also conversations between them about spending a holiday together." [*Landau* v. *Werner*, 105 Sol. J. 1008 (1961)].

from any charge of misconduct; but the decision to embark on social contacts was admittedly a departure from standard practice in this special branch of medicine. A psychiatrist had explosive forces under his control and if a mistake were made the consequences might be disastrous and irrevocable. This doctor had said that his decision was justified by exceptional circumstances; but with the best intentions in the world he had made a tragic mistake. The departure from the recognized standard had resulted in gross deterioration in the patient's health, and on the evidence it would also amount to negligence in treatment. His lordship was not laying down as law that no psychiatrist could in any case take a patient out; but having regard to the state of this patient, he was not satisfied that there was any body of opinion which would have thought it desirable to bring this highly sexed emotional woman, already deeply in love with her doctor, into the kind of intercourse that occurred here. Negligence had been established and there must be judgment for the plaintiff for 6,000 pounds damages. Judgment for the plaintiff.

NOTE 3

LAUDAU v. WERNER
105 Sol J. 1008 (1961)

*   *   *

SELLERS, L.J., said that . . . a doctor might not be negligent if he tried a new technique but if he did he must justify it before the court. If his novel or exceptional treatment had failed disastrously he could not complain if it was held that he went beyond the bounds of due care and skill as recognized generally. Success was the best justification for unusual and unestablished treatment. Here the medical evidence was all one way in condemning social contacts and the doctor had failed to convince the judge that his departure from standard practice was justified and was a reasonable development in this young science. The judge was justified in his view that this unwise treatment had led to the grave deterioration in the plaintiff's health. It was negligent and in breach of the duty of the doctor to his patient. . . .

*   *   *

NOTE 4

SCHAFER, ROY

On the Nature of the Therapeutic Relationship*

I would like to mention that many of the issues to be touched on concern the practice of psychotherapy in general as well as psychoanalysis in particular;

---

* Goldstein, J. and Katz, J., *The Family and the Law* New York: The Free Press, 1963, (p. 171). Reprinted by permission of the Author who retains All Rights.

however, in the interest of conciseness I will restrict my remarks almost entirely to psychoanalysis.

Psychoanalysts have long recognized that the nature of their work exposes them to emotional stimulation of every variety and intensity—from the patient's irritation to his fury, from trepidation to terror, from liking to sexual passion, from moodiness to profound despair, from the maudlin to sheer tragedy, and from the excitement of discovery to the distress of sheer confusion. And so forth. Accordingly, it is not always easy for the analyst to maintain sufficient neutrality to be consistently able to help the patient understand what he is experiencing, why he is experiencing it and what its consequences are. He may then become defensive. It is his responsibility, however, to maintain *that* sufficient degree of neutrality and he does the best he can. It is his work ideal to do so. Without that neutrality—which should not be confused with cold aloofness and indifference—he cannot do his job well. If he gets swept up in the patient's emotional currents, he cannot maintain that balance of patience, curiosity, empathy, tolerance, perspective, and mobility of thinking that he needs in order to be a help rather than a hindrance to his patient.

What helps the analyst maintain an adequate degree of neutrality and balance? I do not pretend to offer a complete answer to this question but mention only a handful of salient factors. There is his intelligence and especially his common sense about people that enable him to appreciate the complexity of human experience and to keep his bearings in the face of it. There is his capacity for sublimated interest in the emotional lives of other persons. There is his belief in the unconscious which enables him to take strong emotions as partial and often direct expressions of processes going on beneath the surface. There is his personal analysis which increases his understanding of himself and fortifies his emotional stability so that he is not vulnerable to every passing reaction to him and not itching to form transferences of his own. Then there is the factor of his leading a personal life of his own that is sufficiently satisfying that he is not dependent on his patients for direct, nonprofessional gratifications. Also, his experience with patients teaches him that much of the time the feelings they have about him have little objective foundation and may change drastically even from one moment to the next. His formal training is another help, for he learns from it, among other things, how to recognize, investigate and understand emotions directed at his person or behavior as analyst. Finally there are his ethical sense and his ideals which are expressed in his respecting his patient and his keeping a watchful eye on his own frailties and self-indulgent tendencies.

My piling up of these characteristics may give the effect of portraying the analyst as a paragon of mental-health virtues, but if you were to review the list you would find that this is not so. Or it may seem to present an ideal of emotional indifference and non-participation, and this too is not implied for it is well-established in psychoanalysis, as in psychotherapy generally, that the analyst's empathy is an essential ingredient of the treatment process—and there can be no empathy without subjective participation in the patient's emotional experience. Any properly accredited graduate analyst more or less approximates the description I have given, and, with the exception of the factors specific to psychoanalytic training, so does any competent practitioner of dynamic psychotherapy.

My understanding of transference and its analysis are as follows—and I am confident that in its essentials it is the prevalent understanding in Freudian psychoanalysis. In the course of analysis, the patient has thoughts and feelings about his analyst. Some of these thoughts and feelings refer to observable characteristics of the analyst and how he goes about analyzing; some refer to information or misinformation about the analyst picked up outside the analysis; and some, as the patient himself may spontaneously recognize, center around pure fantasy. With the exception of countertransference, the analyst is not primarily concerned with whether the patient's thoughts and feelings refer to something real or not, though he does, of course, take account of that difference. Primarily, he is concerned with *what* the patient selects to say and feel about him, *when* and *how* the patient brings it up, *which* expressive or defensive function his bringing it up is meant to serve, *what* the background is in the patient's present life situation and past history that would predispose him to be concerned with this matter and to be concerned with it in the way that he is, and which unconscious and archaic fantasy systems concerning basic drives, body functions, and personal relations lie behind the immediate reaction. In other words, in the interest of helping the patient define, understand, and master his own experience, the analyst uses the thoughts and feelings concerning himself as an opening into the patient's unconscious conflicts.

What is essential is that the behavior relative to the analyst has a long and individually characteristic history in the patient's previous experience with significant persons in his life, especially his experience during his early formative years and thus especially with respect to his parents. And considering the scope and power of infantile fantasy, even the child's early experiences with his parents may have striking unreal elements.

Suppose, for example, that the psychoanalyst is actually somewhat stiff in his behavior. His patients will react to this trait soon enough. But one patient may find it forbiddingly aloof, the next reassuringly controlled, and a third an indication of anxious suppression of sexual excitement. Further, even in the instance of one patient, he may move from one of these reactions to the other and back again many times in the course of the analysis. These interpersonal and intrapersonal variations are matters to be investigated. The reality of the analyst's behavior does not explain them; it simply provides an occasion for the patient's unconscious wishes and defenses to express themselves. It may be harder to analyze transference when it is hung on a peg in reality but in principle the reality peg does not preclude or contradict such analysis.

And this is the way it is in analyzing the patient's relations with persons other than the analyst. For example, a husband is, in fact, a husband but unconsciously he may also be a father, a mother, a son, or some combination of these. The patient, even, is himself, of course, but unconsciously may be, through identification his spouse or parent or long-lost love. It is with transference within reality that we deal in such instances, the degree of transference varying from one relation to the next and often from one time to the next.

NOTE 5

Utah Code Mental Health (1961)

26–17–7. Mental health services authorized. . . . It shall be a felony to give psychiatric treatment, non-vocational mental health counseling, case-finding testing, psychoanalysis, drugs, shock treatment, lobotomy, or surgery to any individual for the purpose of changing his concept of, belief about, or faith in God.

NOTE 6

Missouri Revised Statutes
Public Health and Welfare 202.807 (1959)

*   *   *

No person who is being treated by prayer in the practice of the religion of any church which teaches reliance on spiritual means alone for healing, may be ordered detained or committed . . . unless substantial evidence is produced upon which the court finds in addition to the other findings required . . . that he is or would likely become dangerous to himself, or to the person or property of others, or unless he or his legal guardian, if any, consents to such detention or commitment. Sections 202.780 to 202.870 do not authorize any form of compulsory medical treatment of any person who is being treated by prayer in the practice of the religion of any church which teaches reliance on spiritual means alone for healing.

*   *   *

d.   TAYLOR v. UNITED STATES
            222 F.2d 398 (D.C. Cir. 1955)

EDGERTON, CIRCUIT JUDGE.

The appellant was indicted in December 1952 for robbery, housebreaking and grand larceny . . . Before trial, in proceedings under 18 U.S.C.A. § 4244, he was found in March 1953 to be "presently insane and so mentally incompetent as to be unable to understand the proceedings against him, or properly to assist in his own defense." He was committed to St. Elizabeths Hospital "until he is mentally competent to stand trial. . . ." In October 1953 the Superintendent of the Hospital certified that the appellant was mentally competent to stand trial, and in November 1953 he was tried.

His only defense was insanity. A psychiatrist, Dr. Joseph L. Gilbert, who examined him five times in January and February 1953, at the District Jail, on order of the court, testified in support of this defense. In Dr. Gilbert's opinion the appellant, at the time of the alleged offenses, was of unsound mind, suffering from dementia praecox, with symptoms that included confusion, memory failures, hostility, hallucinations and delusions. Dr. Gilbert also testified that appellant could not in a major way, or in any major activity, distinguish between right and wrong.

The prosecution called Dr. Leon Joseph Epstein, a staff psychiatrist and attending physician in the ward in which appellant was confined at St. Elizabeths from March to October 1953. Dr. Epstein promptly suggested that what he had learned from his patient was privileged. The court ruled it was not. Dr. Epstein then testified that appellant told him he had not suffered from hallucinations or delusions, but had been "going along with a gag" in describing such episodes. In Dr. Epstein's opinion the appellant, when he saw him could distinguish between right and wrong. He could not say whether appellant was able to do so at the time of the alleged offenses. He said appellant suffered from a "sociopathic personality disturbance with an antisocial reaction" and had a psychopathic personality, but was not psychotic or insane.

The appellant was convicted and sentenced to imprisonment for 5 to 15 years.

*   *   *

"In the courts of the District of Columbia no physician or surgeon shall be permitted, without the consent of the person afflicted, or of his legal representative, to disclose any information, confidential in its nature, which he shall have acquired in attending a patient in a professional capacity and which was necessary to enable him to act in that capacity . . . ." D.C. Code 1951 § 14–308. . . .

In regard to mental patients, the policy behind such a statute is particularly clear and strong. Many physical ailments might be treated with some degree of effectiveness by a doctor whom the patient did not trust, but a psychiatrist must have his patient's confidence or he cannot help him. "The psychiatric patient confides more utterly than anyone else in the world. He exposes to the therapist not only what his words directly express; he lays bare his entire self, his dreams, his fantasies, his sins, and his shame. Most patients who undergo psychotherapy know that this is what will be expected of them, and that they cannot get help except on that condition. . . . It would be too much to expect them to do so if they knew that all they say—and all that the psychiatrist learns from what they say—may be revealed to the whole world from a witness stand."[2]

"Presumably all of the patients in any good mental hospital are receiving psychiatric treatment. That is true of persons whether they are sent to St. Elizabeths Hospital as civil insane, as criminal insane, or as 'sexual psychopaths.'"[3]

Dr. Epstein testified that his work at St. Elizabeths was "entirely in the field of the treatment of patients that are mentally ill." In reply to a question whether he functioned at the hospital as he would in private practice he said only: "There is an essential difference . . . by the very nature of the fact that most of the patients whom we see at St. Elizabeths are psychotic patients. In private practice the patients whom I see in my office are overwhelmingly psychoneurotic and they may be treated on an out-patient basis."

Dr. Epstein treated the appellant about seven months. He testified: "In checking my notes I found five recorded interviews with him. However, I make daily rounds in the part of the hospital where he was a patient and had occasion to see him many other times." Dr. Epstein was asked, "Did you as the attending physician of that ward look at the admittance record to see what diagnosis is placed on his chart as to his mental ailment?" He replied, "I did."

Obviously Dr. Epstein attended Taylor "in a professional capacity." Obviously he succeeded in getting his patient's confidence. He tried to respect it as the District of Columbia statute requires. The court erred in requiring him to violate it.

The cases on which the government relies do not support its position. They hold that a doctor who does not treat a prisoner, but only examines him in order to testify about his condition, may testify about it. Of course he may. Examination for testimonial purposes only has nothing to do with treatment. A doctor who makes such an examination is not "attending a patient." There is no confidential relation be-

tween them. Instead of implying that confidence will be respected, the circumstances imply the contrary. It is a far cry from such cases to the government's contention that a psychiatrist who treats a patient charged with crime may expose the man's secrets to a jury despite a statute that expressly excludes information "acquired in attending a patient." The statute does not say or imply that the privilege it creates may be withheld from patients who have been committed to a public mental hospital. Most courts that have considered the matter hold, as we do, that such patients are entitled to the protection of such a statute.

*   *   *

Taylor did not consent to the violation of his privilege. He made no effort to consent. No effort he might have made would have been effective. Since it had been judicially determined that he was incompetent to stand trial, he could not validly consent to a trial or any part of a trial. In the course of a civil trial, perhaps an incompetent's committee might consent to the admission of privileged testimony. But this was not a civil trial and Taylor had no committee. . . .

What we have said relates only to the privilege of the accused when he is brought to trial. Exclusion of Dr. Epstein's testimony in Taylor's criminal trial does not mean that his testimony is to be excluded from consideration by the trial judge when he decides . . . the preliminary question whether Taylor is competent to stand trial. The judge may receive and consider, on that issue, any relevant testimony from Dr. Epstein. . . .

*   *   *

The judgment is reversed. . . .

PRETTYMAN, CIRCUIT JUDGE (dissenting).

*   *   *

The court indicates that Taylor's consent cannot be accepted, because he is now alleged to have been incompetent at the time and so could not either consent or authorize his legal representative to do so. But Taylor had been reported competent, and in the eyes of the law at the time he was competent; otherwise he would not then have been undergoing trial. My view is that if he was competent to stand trial he was competent to consent to this evidence. . . .

[I] think this testimony was not privileged. When pursuant to the dictates of criminal justice a person is confined by order of a court in a state institution for the mentally ill, the relationship between him and the doctor on the staff at that institution is not the ordinary relationship between physician and patient contemplated and treated by the statute which confers the doctor-patient privilege. Under such circumstances the Government, as a matter of public concern, is entitled to the benefit of the testimony of those

2. Guttmacher and Weihofen, *Psychiatry and the Law*, (1952), p. 272.

3. Winfred Overholser, Superintendent of St. Elizabeths, "Some Problems of the 'Criminal Insane' at Saint Elizabeths Hospital," *Medical Annual of District of Columbia*, Vol. XXII, p. 349, July 1953.

doctors, whether as to diagnosis, treatment or observation. It is contrary to the interests of justice to give such an accused person power to close the mouths of those doctors.

* * *

[T]his decision cuts off use of the testimony of all the Government doctors in these cases where an indicted man is in a Government hospital undergoing compulsory treatment as a result of which it is anticipated he will return to the authorities for trial. That is, it cuts off that testimony unless the accused consents, which in practical effect means unless it is favorable to him. It seems to me that this decision will badly handicap and confuse the handling of those cases in which persons accused of crime are committed to Government institutions because of incapacity to stand trial.

[I]t is clear enough that the relationship between Taylor and Dr. Epstein was not the ordinary one of doctor and patient. Nothing was voluntary about it on either's part. And certainly nothing was confidential about Taylor's admissions; they were made before a conference of several physicians. He was a person in custody under authority of the criminal law. Dr. Epstein was acting in the capacity of a Government officer, not as a personal physician. It seems to me the rationale of the rule relating to examinations by Government officers, rather than that of the rule relating to physician-patient relationships, applies to the present problem.

* * *

NOTES

NOTE 1

ANONYMOUS

Psychoanalyst Subpoenaed*

When I was subpoenaed to give evidence in the High Court about someone who was alleged to be a former patient of mine, I was placed between two conflicting moral obligations. I had to decide whether to obey the Law or to abide by the rules of professional conduct. I complied with the subpoena by attending Court, but I decided I could not answer any questions about the "patient," and I made all arrangements, including having a barrister to plead in mitigation of sentence, for the possibility that I should be sent to prison for contempt of court. In the event, although my silence probably did constitute a contempt, the judge declared he would not sentence me, saying it was obviously a matter of conscience. In this he was acting within the discretion the Law allows him.

Though I had no legal privilege, I was in effect given the same freedom to remain silent usually allowed to priests for the secrets of the confessional. It is possible that the judge was partly moved by the idea that any evidence I could give might only be of marginal relevance to the case.

The grounds for my decision were individual, but though some other psychoanalysts might not refuse to divulge whether they had treated a person, I think it likely that in all other aspects they would feel as I did. These grounds were partly explained in the statement I made when called to the witness box. I said that it was essential to my work as a psychoanalyst and psychotherapist that people should feel free to discuss with me everything that concerns them, including matters of great intimacy which they would not be able to reveal if there were any doubt about my trustworthiness. Indeed, one of these secrets could be the very fact that they had come to me for help. For me the need to retain secrecy was not just a moral imperative such as might exist, for example, for a general practitioner who was treating a patient for pneumonia. If such a doctor were to talk indiscreetly about his patient, he might not be behaving ethically, but he might still have treated the pneumonia adequately. But if I were to speak indiscreetly about a patient, I should not only be behaving unethically, but I should also be destroying the very fabric of my therapy. For people to be able to speak freely, and only then could I help them, I must supply a setting within which this could happen, and this setting was an essential part of the treatment. I had a quiet comfortable consulting-room; and when people kept their appointments I must not fail to be there; I must start and finish at the times agreed on. While they were with me there must be no interruption of the treatment; I did not talk on the phone, nor did anything besides the therapeutic task I had undertaken. I had to be completely reliable in all my dealings with my patients, and this included keeping their secrets under all circumstances. Failure to maintain any part of this essential setting would be malpractice of the same order as if the general practitioner had advised his pneumonia patient to get out of bed with a temperature of $105°$ and come to the surgery for treatment. My professional code applies whenever I receive anyone as a patient, whether it was someone who had attended regularly for years, or someone who had come only once, perhaps just to see what a psychoanalyst looks like.

To the judge's query whether I would still object if "the patient" gave permission, I answered with an example: Suppose a patient had been in treatment for some time and was going through a temporary phase of admiring and depending on me; he might therefore feel it necessary to sacrifice himself and give permission, but it might not be proper for me to act on this.

---

*The Lancet, October 16, 1965 (pp. 785–86). Reprinted by permission.

This example involves a vital principle. Some of the United States have a law prohibiting psychiatrists from giving evidence about a patient without the patient's written permission, but this honorable attempt to protect the patient misses the essential point that he may not be aware of unconscious motives impelling him to give permission. It may take months or years to understand things said or done during analysis, and until this is achieved it would belie all our knowledge of the workings of the unconscious mind if we treated any attitude arising in the analytic situation as if it were part of ordinary social interchange. If we allow and help people to say things with the ultimate aim of helping them to understand the real meanings underlying what may well be a temporary attitude engendered by the transference, it would be the crassest dishonor and dishonesty to permit unwarranted advantage to be taken of their willingness to avail themselves of the therapeutic situation. It would be as if a physician invited a patient to undress to be examined, and then allowed the Law to see him naked and to arrest him for exhibiting himself. Where no permission has been given, the rule to maintain discretion is, of course, similarly inviolable. Patients attend us on the implicit understanding that anything they reveal is subject to a special protection. Unless we explicitly state that this is not so, we are parties to a tacit agreement, and any betrayal of it only dishonors us. That the agreement may not be explicit is no excuse. Part of our work is to put into words things that are not being said. We are the responsible parties in the relationship, so surely it is we who should pay, if there is any price to be paid, because something has not been said clearly.

But should there by any price to pay? Was I arrogating to myself an unwarrantable freedom from the ordinary responsibilties of a citizen by refusing to give evidence? Was it not rather that the attitude of responsibility towards patients was also one of responsibility towards the Law? The fact that in theory people having analysis "tell everything" should not give rise to the misleading idea that we analysts are necessarily the repositories of secrets that could help the Courts if only we would divulge them. The concern of psychoanalysis is with the ever-developing unravelling of the unconscious conflicts of our patients. We know that these can affect the patient's perceptions and judgments while they are operative, hence the advice sometimes given to avoid major decisions during analysis. We are not seeking the "objective reality" the Courts want, and generally we are not in a position to give it to them. Over the years we may hear a number of different versions of the same event, each completely sincere, but varying with the changing emotional focus of the analysis and, each version being a clue to another level of unconscious conflict. To report on whichever is momentarily in the ascendant could mislead a Court as, for example, a report on an applicant's blood-pressure after a night of vomiting could mislead an insurance company. I would suggest that in principle there may be less conflict between our moral obligations to the Law and to the rules of professional conduct than would appear at first sight. If a psychoanalyst or psychotherapist wished to offer a patient's description of an event as objective evidence, it would be necessary to produce every version of the event, explaining the differences by detailing all the known underlying meanings; with the misleading probable result of the Court's either accepting one version unequivocally, or discrediting therapist or patient as unreliable. Justice, as well as our ethic, is likely to be served best by silence.

NOTE 2

Privileged Communications Between Psychiatrist and Patient
52 Conn. Stat. 146 (1961)

As used in this section, "patient" means a person who, for the purpose of securing diagnosis or treatment of his mental condition, consults a psychiatrist; "psychiatrist" means a person licensed to practice medicine who devotes a substantial portion of his time to the practice of psychiatry, or a person reasonably believed by the patient to be so qualified; "authorized representative" means a person empowered by the patient to assert the privilege granted by this section and, until given permission by the patient to make disclosure, any person whose communications are made privileged by this section. Except as hereinafter provided, in civil and criminal cases, in proceedings preliminary thereto, and in legislative and administrative proceedings, a patient, or his authorized representative, has a privilege to refuse to disclose, and to prevent a witness from disclosing, communications relating to diagnosis or treatment of the patient's mental condition between patient and psychiatrist, or between any of the foregoing and such persons who participate, under the supervision of the psychiatrist, in the accomplishment of the objectives of diagnosis or treatment. There shall be no privilege for any relevant communications under this section: (a) When a psychiatrist, in the course of diagnosis or treatment of the patient, determines that the patient is in need of care and treatment in a hospital for mental illness;[*] (b) if a judge finds that the patient, after having been informed that the communications would not be privileged, has made communications to a psychiatrist in the course of a psychiatric examination ordered by the court, provided that such communica-

---

[*] "An alternative and perhaps more desirable formulation of this exception might be as follows: '(a) in a proceeding for commitment of the patient to a mental hospital'" Goldstein, A. and Katz, J., *Psychiatrist-Patient Privilege*, 36 Conn. Bar Journal 175, 187 (1962).

tions shall be admissible only on issues involving the patient's mental condition; (c) in a civil proceeding in which the patient introduces his mental condition as an element of his claim or defense, or, after the patient's death, when such condition is introduced by any party claiming or defending through or as a beneficiary of the patient, and the judge finds that it is more important to the interests of justice that the communication be disclosed than that the relationship between the patient and psychiatrist be protected.

e.   KARDAS v. STATE
44 Misc. 2d 239, 253 N.Y.S. 2d 470 (1964)

DOROTHEA E. DONALDSON, JUDGE.

This is an action for damages for wrongful death and for antecedent pain and suffering. The cause is prosecuted here by the intestate's widow . . .

The evidence at trial indicated that Andrew Kardas, a retired employee of the Metropolitan Life Insurance Company, died by his own hand on August 28, 1960. The deceased had a long history of mental illness, consideration of which is essential in determining if there was liability on the part of the State.

*   *   *

Three issues were . . . presented to the court. First, were the State and its representatives chargeable with negligent conduct in not classifying the decedent a suicidal risk and placing him under appropriate restraint? Second, were the State and its representatives negligent in permitting the elopement of a patient who, while not having exhibited such tendencies theretofore, had been placed under close observation? Third, even though the State and its representatives were to be found to have acted negligently, could such conduct be construed to be the proximate cause of the death complained of?

In considering the first question posed, the court observes that the State preserved a continuing objection to admission of that part of the medical record of the Institute which it deemed multiple hearsay. Decision was reserved. It is well settled that entries in hospital records are within the "business entry" statute. . . . The hearsay exceptions extends to recorded information obtained by observation by all persons under a duty so to report. . . . The problem arises when statements by outsiders not under a duty to report are incorporated in the hospital records and are then offered as entries . . . when, in other words, hearsay is piled upon hearsay. . . . For such an entry to be admissible the report, itself, must, if hearsay in character, come in under a recognized exception and, also, it must be the business of the recorder to set down such statement. . . . In the case at bar, the principal objections by the Attorney General were directed toward that portion of the Admissions Certificate of August 10, 1960 which stated that

"[I]t was felt by observers in the Clinic that he presented a definite suicidal risk . . ."

The reference is to the Vanderbilt Clinic, a facility of the Columbia Presbyterian Medical Center. It appears from the record that the residents and staff of the Clinic are on the staff of the Psychiatric Institute as well and, indeed, rotate. The question then is raised whether the identity of personnel is such as to create an organizational entity. . . . If this is so, the Clinic members certainly being under an obligation to impart belief of potential suicidal tendencies and the Institute being under an equal duty to receive and record such impressions, the entry would be admissible. On the evidence adduced, the court finds that a sufficient identity existed and receives the entry.

However, the determination of the existence and gravity of suicidal tendency calls for a purely professional judgment on the part of the examining physician. While he no doubt is under a medical duty to consider all available evidence in reaching his diagnosis, the final responsibility is his, and in the absence of proof that there was a want of requisite knowledge or skill or an omission to use reasonable care or a failure to use his best judgment, the diagnosing physician or, derivatively, the State cannot be held liable for what, in retrospect, proved to be an error in judgment.

Proceeding to the second of the questions posed, the court finds that notwithstanding the failure to term the deceased suicidally inclined and so insure for him a more thorough and extensive control, action was taken to place Mr. Kardas "under close observation." Whether this "close observation" was for purposes of observing the patient's need for and reaction to various therapies or whether it was to serve as a device for protecting the deceased from himself or some combination of the two does not satisfactorily appear from the record. While it may be assumed that the diagnosis of mental disorder without specific suicidal tendencies was within the bounds of a reasonable professional judgment, the court finds that the Institute had notice of an alleged prior suicidal attempt by Mr. Kardas and notice of the Vanderbilt Clinic's current opinion that he was suicidally inclined. The medical staff was, as we have held, under no compulsion to establish its diagnosis upon this foundation, but certainly actual notice existed of the possibility of suicide.

The State urges that the claimant's intestate had never manifested escapist proclivities and that, therefore, the elopement was a risk not reasonably to be perceived. If we adopt the classic phrase of Chief Judge Cardozo that the "risk reasonably to be perceived defines the duty to be obeyed" . . . we find that the duty here has been defined by the direction that the decedent was to be kept under close observation. Manifestly, this was not accomplished. The State's breach of its duty to use reasonable care did not arise out of a misapprehension of the risk involved in not placing the decedent under suicidal observation but rather, having made a diagnosis and having determined upon a course of therapy, then negligently failing to fulfil that course. The record is clear that Andrew Kardas was to be permitted to leave the immediate area of the ward only upon "accompanied walks" in the presence of staff personnel. The ward was under continuous observation. The stairwells were locked. The only other method of egress, the elevator, was under control of operators who were forbidden to transport a patient in the absence of a nurse. The court finds that the supervision given this patient was faulty and answers the second question posed in the affirmative.

Even though negligence is thus found there remains the question of proximate causation. For the State to be compelled to respond in damages, the act or omission complained of must be causally related to the suicide. The State has argued that the record reflected no reasonable likelihood of danger as a consequence of the act complained of, to wit, permitting the elopement. The court disagrees. The mere fact that the decedent was classified other than as a potential suicide does not, under the circumstances, rule out or even render unlikely an act of self-destruction. It was apparent from the hospital records that Mr. Kardas had become increasingly agitated prior to his escape. This, coupled with the notice that existed of his prior suicidal tendencies, was sufficient or should have been sufficient to alert the Institute to the possible consequences of an elopement, i.e., a suicide.

The court therefore finds that the State, through its officers and employees, is chargeable with negligent conduct and that such conduct was a competent producing cause of the death of claimant's intestate. The State's motion to dismiss made at the conclusion of claimant's direct case and at the conclusion of the trial, decision upon which was reserved, are denied.

There remains to be considered the quantum of damages. The court finds that the decedent had a life expectancy of approximately twelve years according to statistics of the United States Department of Health, Education and Welfare. Mr. Kardas was receiving at the time of his death $113.34 per month from the Metropolitan Life Insurance Company, payments which were to continue until his death. He was also receiving Social Security payments of $105 per month, again to continue until his death. However, it is a fair assumption from the decedent's age and physical and mental condition that he never would have been able to earn any further sums and indeed, in all probability, would have had to be institutionalized for the remainder of his life. Normally, the rule is that where evidence sustains a finding that a patient in a State hospital is incurable and that no reasonable basis exists for hope for his ultimate cure and release, the only damages recoverable for his wrongful death apply from any possible cause of action for conscious pain and suffering or for funeral expenses incurred. . . . An apparent exception exists, however, where income to a next of kin results from disability payments. . . . The case at bar is analogous since the payments under Metropolitan's retirement program and under Social Security are dependent only upon the continued life of the insured and not upon his potentialities as a breadwinner. Furthermore, it appears . . . that these payments were not required to reimburse the Institute for Mr. Kardas' care.

While the proof under the conscious pain and suffering cause of action was minimal, the cause was properly before the court and an award will be made therefor.

The court determines that the claimant is entitled to damages in the amount of $20,616.00 for the wrongful death of Andrew Kardas, with interest thereon from August 28, 1960, to date of entry of judgment and the claimant, as administratrix of decedent's estate, is entitled to damages in the amount of $1,500.00 for conscious pain and suffering. The sum first named includes $616.00 as an adjusted amount representing reasonable funeral expenses.

NOTES

NOTE 1

KARDAS v. NEW YORK
24 App. Div. 2d 789, 263 N.Y.S. 2d 727 (1965)

PER CURIAM.

* * *

. . . Had the decedent's condition worsened because of negligence of the attendants in failing to carry out the orders, a case would have been presented for holding the State liable for deterioration of the decedent's condition. However, as the diagnosis was that the decedent's condition did not present a risk of suicide, the diagnosing and treating physicians were under no duty, for purposes of preventing suicide, to require close observation and confinement to the ward as precautions against suicide and hence the State, having through its physicians, made a diagnosis of no suicidal tendency, was under no duty to guard against suicide and, having been under no duty, may not be held liable in negligence for the decedent's death.

Judgment reversed . . . and claim dismissed. . . .

NOTE 2

HIRSH v. STATE
8 N.Y. 2d 125, 168 N.E. 2d 372 (1960)

VAN VOORHIS, JUDGE.

The State appeals from an affirmance of a judgment against it . . . based on alleged negligence in failing to prevent plaintiff's intestate from committing suicide while he was a patient at the Brooklyn State Hospital. He had a previous history of mental illness at other hospitals where he had made two suicidal attempts, one with phenobarbitol and the other by hanging. This time he succeeded in accomplishing his aim. . . . Death was caused by swallowing about a dozen capsules of seconal at night.

Nobody knew where or how this drug was obtained by him nor where he had kept or accumulated these capsules in his room. It was not medicine that was ordinarily used at the Brooklyn State Hospital at this time. He had been assigned to a ward for suicidal patients. Eighty-five patients were in this ward. Decedent was given his meals in the ward where he was confined, which he left only for treatment or for interviews with a psychiatrist. On these occasions he was accompanied by an attendant or a nurse. When medication of any kind was required on this ward, the nurse would unlock and relock the door upon departure, relocking it after her return with the drugs. These medications—not seconal—would be brought to the ward in such amounts as were used immediately, even though this meant repeating the procedure every four hours. Visits from family or friends were supervized, and gifts brought into the ward were checked by an attendant. Patients were allowed a monetary allowance of less than $1 at a time, enough to send for cigarettes or gum but insufficient to bribe anyone to get drugs. Decedent has not recently drawn upon this small allowance. When this patient was admitted to the State hospital, he was completely examined, his clothes removed and he was furnished with State clothing. The regular practice was for the night shift attendants to put the patient to bed after examining his clothing and bed. He had been put to bed wearing only a pair of shorts so as to prevent his secreting anything potentially dangerous. The regular routine included removal of the mattress and inspection under the bed by the attendants.

. . . The State could not have provided an employee to watch every move made by this unfortunate man during 24 hours of the day. We are not persuaded that it is evidence of negligence that he was not repeatedly wakened and his bed searched during the night. If institutions for the mentally ill are required to take all of the precautions contended for in this case, and are to be held liable for such delicate mistakes in judgment, patients would be kept in strait jackets or some other form of strict confinement which would hardly be conducive to recovery. No reason is asserted that decedent was not given suitable electric shock treatments, tranquilizers, or other treatment designed to mitigate mental depression and self-destructive tendencies. Reasonable care is required to protect such patients against themselves . . . but no evidence of lack of it has been shown in this case. An ingenious patient

harboring a steady purpose to take his own life cannot always be thwarted.

The judgment appealed from should be reversed and the claim dismissed. . . .

FROESSEL, JUDGE (dissenting).

* * *

The standard of care, or procedures, commensurate with the risk to be perceived, which should have been followed by the hospital authorities in this case, were outlined by plaintiff's expert witness at the trial. In view of decedent's "mental history," he stated that proper standards required a "search of personal effects and the immediate surroundings" frequently each day: "I would have instructed my attendants to search Irving from head to foot before they put him to sleep, and to search him several times during the day to examine him several times during the day and to examine his person and every part of his personal effects, and because of these suicidal tendencies I would have reminded and especially alerted the personnel and also the fact that he was a potentially barbiturate suicide, and if I may say so, counsel, I would have alerted them to the fact that they can't be sure that they have checked carefully unless they had searched him repeatedly, and unless they did a thorough, and I mean a thorough searching by means of palpating every part of his body and all of his clothing and—"

* * *

. . . Had the staff properly palpated his body, checked his clothing, bed and environs as they were duty-bound to do, the seconal would have been uncovered. . . .

* * *

Such "reasonable and necessary precautions" were not taken by the hospital authorities or staff in this case. It is stated in the majority opinion of this court that it was the regular practice for the *night* shift attendants to put the patient to bed after examining his clothing and bed, which included the removal of the mattress and inspection under the bed by the attendant, although these attendants did not report for duty until midnight. However, the record in this case discloses only the *duties* of the hospital staff as outlined earlier in this opinion—*not that they were in fact performed*. Indeed, there is absolutely no evidence in this record that these duties were performed or any practice of custom carried out on the morning, afternoon, evening or night of September 3, 1953, the day immediately preceding the fatal early morning hours of September 4 when Hirsh expired from barbituric acid poisoning. . . .

* * *

NOTE 3

WHITE v. UNITED STATES
317 F.2d 13 (4th Cir. 1963)

J. SPENCER BELL, CIRCUIT JUDGE.

Suit under the Tort Claims Act for death of plaintiff's intestate, one Donald E. Meeks, a veteran who died after being hit by a train while under treatment for mental illness at the Roanoke Veterans Administration Hospital at Salem, Virginia. Invoking the Virginia Wrongful Death Act, the Administrator charges that employees at the hospital failed to exercise the degree of care for the veteran's safety appropriate for his mental condition. . . .

* * *

The Roanoke Veterans Hospital is devoted predominantly to the care of psychiatric cases. It handles approximately 1,900 cases under the care of twenty-five doctors. Mental patients at the hospital are classified with respect to their freedom of movement in four categories: (1) privileged, (2) partially privileged, (3) locked ward, and (4) locked ward, observation status. Privileged patients are granted free access of the hospital grounds. Except for a ward visit in the morning, a bed check at night, meals, and certain work assignments, they are free to come and go as they please. Partially privileged patients are allowed to be "on their own" during certain periods of the day. Locked ward patients are confined to their wards. Locked ward, observation status patients are in addition kept in sight of hospital aides or nurses at all times. Upon admission to the hospital patients are placed in locked ward status until classified by staff doctors after consultation. However, a patient may be transferred from privileged status to locked ward or locked ward, observation status at any time by any staff physician acting pursuant to his own decision if the doctor is concerned that the patient might harm himself or injure others.

The policy expressed in the Veterans Administration regulations is to allow each psychiatric patient the maximum independence that his condition permits. On April 22, 1959, plaintiff's intestate was hospitalized for the fifth time since July of 1948. On August 10, 1959, he was released for a trial visit to his brother's home but he became disturbed and was admitted to Kecoughtan Hospital, Kecoughtan, Virginia. On August 27, 1959, he was transferred to the Roanoke hospital. No suicidal tendencies were observed in him by the admitting physician, but two days after his arrival, while still in locked ward status, he made remarks which a nurse interpreted to mean that he might harm himself, and he himself requested that he be anchored to his bed and placed in restraining cuffs. The physician on duty ordered him placed in observation status, where he remained until September 10.

On September 15 he was transferred to privileged status following a decision by a two man panel of doctors.

Many years before his current hospitalization Meeks had displayed suicidal tendencies. At the age of seventeen he had attempted to commit suicide in the presence of his brother. During his military service he made three other suicide gestures, once by taking an overdose of aspirin, once by jumping over the side of a ship, and once by an attempt with a firearm. There appears to be some professional doubt as to whether these acts were gestures or real attempts at suicide. At the time he was killed Meeks had been under treatment in privileged status for three weeks. He was receiving Thorazine, a tranquilizer. The day before, Friday, October 9, Meeks called upon Dr. Parks, the staff physician in charge of his ward, complaining that he felt tense and uneasy and expressing fears that he might be drifting back into the condition that he was in when he came to the hospital —the condition which caused him to request that he be anchored to the bed and placed in restraining cuffs. It was admitted by Dr. Parks that he was not then familiar with Meeks' suicidal attempts before his hospitalization or with the fact that Meeks had requested that he be restrained during the previous August. The doctor testified that Meeks did not in his opinion exhibit suicidal tendencies and that he did not feel it necessary to cancel his privileged status; instead he prescribed an additional dose of tranquilizer.

The last physician to see Meeks alive was Dr. Crowgey, who, though not a psychiatrist, was serving as officer of the day at the hospital on that Saturday, October 10. That morning Meeks again complained of apprehension and nervousness. After talking with him Dr. Crowgey enlarged the tranquilizer dose Meeks was receiving. Meeks did not appear to the doctor to exhibit suicidal tendencies. Later that day upon the basis of a report by a nurse that Meeks was still nervous, the doctor ordered administration of sodium luminal, a sedative. Apparently, neither Dr. Parks nor Dr. Crowgey was familiar with the details of the patient's medical record which was in the hospital files. Meeks was found outside the grounds on the railroad tracks later that day, dead from injuries suffered when he was struck by a train.

* * *

The Government contends that the decision as to the degree of freedom allowed Meeks was a discretionary function, in the exercise of which it is exempted from tort liability and it seeks to bring this case within the aegis of those cases holding that the decision to extend or terminate medical services to an individual is a discretionary function and, therefore, exempt. With this contention we cannot agree.

While the policy embodied in the Veterans Administration Regulations that patients should be allowed the maximum of freedom warranted by their condition is a discretionary decision, the application of that policy to an individual case is not within the category of policy decisions exempted by the statute. The application of that policy to the individual case is an administrative decision at the operational level which if negligently done will make the Government liable—whether it involves substandard professional conduct (malpractice) or simple negligence in custodial care. . . .

*   *   *

[O]nce having exercised the discretion to extend the service the Government is liable for negligent treatment of the patient as well as for injuries caused by a patient who has been negligently released from treatment.

*   *   *

Reversed and remanded.

NOTE 4

FROMM-REICHMANN, FRIEDA

Problems of Therapeutic Management in a Psychoanalytic Hospital*

*   *   *

The psychoanalyst who works with psychotics in a psychoanalytic hospital realizes more than do his colleagues in other mental hospitals that undue curtailment of the patients' freedom—i.e., misuse of authority by previous authoritative figures, especially by the parents in the patients' childhood and by their later representatives in society—is most frequent among the reasons for the rise of mental disturbance. Therefore, he is inclined to give the patients as much freedom and as many privileges as possible, and he will try to force on them the least number of regulations and restrictions. However, the hospitalized psychotic's conception of need and desire for freedom are not identical with those of the healthy person. How, then, can the hospital reduce a freedom which the psychotic is incapable of utilizing judiciously, without repeating the old traumatic authoritarianism? In other words, how does the psychiatrist succeed in granting to the psychotic the right amount of privileges for the time of his hospitalization?

The psychotic patient who needs hospitalization has not been capable of living without guidance and help; thus, admission to an institution is frequently a great relief from the unbearable burden of managing independently and of making decisions.

*16 *Psychoanalytic Quarterly*, No. 3, (1947). Reprinted by permission.

The psychoanalyst is aware that, in our culture, all his patients have had imposed overauthoritative restrictions of their freedom by at least one parent, if not both, or other important adults in their childhood. Many patients have subsequently been forced to submit to similar authoritative pressure from later parental surrogates in school, college, or work or by society at large. The latter may be the interpretation which those who have been severely thwarted in their early lives cannot help giving to their later interpersonal experiences. The therapist may therefore be inclined to counteract such traumatic influences by giving them the gift of more freedom than the psychotic patient can handle. While it is most undesirable for the psychiatrist to create additional frustrations in a thwarted psychotic's life, he cannot undo the evil consequences of the past merely by safeguarding against their repetition. The evil influences of the past have to be counteracted by recollection, "working through," re-evaluation, and integration of what happened in early life in terms of the present. The psychotherapist's attitude alone will not accomplish this.

The psychotherapist's conception of "freedom and independence," which he may cherish for himself, may not seem at all desirable to his psychotic patient, who may sense that the psychoanalyst or other staff members expect him to be desirous of the type of freedom that they want for themselves. If the psychotic is protected from developing wishes for freedom which are of the psychiatrist's making, he will ask less frequently for privileges which he cannot handle and be spared the frustration of being granted privileges and having them withdrawn; also, the psychiatrist will make fewer errors in handling the patient's privileges.

The psychiatrist should, of course, not be overconcerned with the conveniences of hospital routine or with his own prestige when conducting a patient's therapeutic management. He should not lack the courage to give the psychotic a chance when he believes that the patient is ready to derive therapeutic benefit from it, even if a repeal of these privileges may become necessary later on. This may or may not reflect unfavorably on the therapist's judgment in the eyes of the patients or of the staff which is inconvenienced by it.

I remember two patients who were temporarily more upset after they were taken for a shopping trip and to the movies than they had been during a long period of hospitalization without privileges. The administrative psychotherapists and the other staff members thought that a great mistake had been made. In the course of the further treatment of both patients, however, it became apparent that these trips, disturbing as they had been at the time, had, in the long run, meant a great, legitimate encouragement to the patients. This subsequently facilitated and speeded their collaboration in psychoanalytic therapy. I also remember the three or four patients who misused their privileges, ran way, and discontinued treatment. The psychoanalytic hospital has such patients, as does any hospital.

The newcomer on the staff of a psychoanalytic hospital will find himself easily misled in the evaluation of a patient's ability to handle town privileges, for the reason that even a very disturbed, delusional, or hallucinated paranoid or disoriented patient may, on the surface, appear rather well composed and rational as compared with an equally disturbed patient in another type of mental hospital. This is due to the consistent interpersonal exchange and rational, verbalized contacts which are offered to the patients by all the staff members of the psychoanalytic hospital and particularly by the psychoanalytic therapist.

*   *   *

NOTE 5

A.A. v. STATE
43 Misc. 2d 1004, 252 N.Y.S. 2d 800 (1964)

HENRY W. LENGYEL, JUDGE.

This is a claim against the State of New York based on the alleged negligence of the State of New York and its employees, arising out of an assault committed on October 20, 1959, against the claimant, "A. A.," an inmate of Rockland State Hospital, by another inmate of said hospital.

Rockland State Hospital, located at Orangeburg, New York, is owned and operated by the State of New York for the observation, treatment and care of the mentally ill.

Claimant, "A. A.," was admitted from Bellevue Hospital in New York City to Rockland State Hospital on August 13, 1959, and was given a tentative diagnosis of "Primary Behavior Disorders in Children, Conduct Disturbance." At the time of admission claimant was 12 years of age. After admission said claimant was placed in a children's ward but because of his violent exceptions to being placed with children he was transferred to wards which contained older patients. It is of interest to read the statement contained in the copy of said claimant's hospital record (Exhibit 6, page 22):

> "This boy has been a constant trial and tribulation since the hour of his admission. Review of the ward notes indicates that the boy has been transferred and lodged out from one ward to another, constantly because he created a rumpus each time near nightfall, at which time he was to be bedded down with his peers of his own age. He protests violently against residing on a ward with children of his own age and cannot ever explain correctly the reason why he feels this way. . . . Remarkably enough, the boy has continually pleaded to be placed on solitary confinement, or on a disturbed ward without giving any valid reason for his desires. . . ."

Eventually, several weeks before October 20, 1959, said claimant was lodged in and remained in Ward 5 which is located in the building known as "Male Reception." The "Male Reception" building contained 12 wards and was under the supervision of Dr. Chlenoff who was the State's principal witness during the course of the trial. Dr. Chlenoff testified that except for a specific ward for children in "Male Reception" and another for old or senile patients, all of the other wards, including Ward 5, received all patients indiscriminately. Apparently no distinction was made for age, prior history, diagnosis, propensity, prognosis nor degree or character of psychotic involvement. During cross-examination, Dr. Chlenoff stated in response to questions about the patient composition of Ward 5, the following:

"Q. But all other patients might be found in that room; is that correct, Doctor?

"A. Up to a certain age.

"Q. What age is that?

"A. I certainly wouldn't place there any youngster of—let us say—ten, eleven years old.

"Q. Did you have a separate ward for children of that age?

"A. At that time we had.

"Q. What ward was that?

"A. That was Ward 6.

"Q. What ages went into Ward 6?

"A. We were rather flexible, but at times we would keep people there 14 and younger."

When asked on re-direct examination why said claimant was placed in Ward 5, Dr. Chlenoff stated that although there was a ward for younger patients claimant was a bit too tall for his age and that knowing he didn't get along with younger people and as he was too tall, his physician decided to lodge him in Ward 5.

We are cognizant of the severe administrative burdens placed upon our hospitals for the mentally ill. However, no matter what the administrative problems, the State has accepted the responsibility for the care of such patients. We do not believe the State has fairly met its responsibilities when it permits a 12-year-old patient to be lodged in a ward with varied types of mentally ill patients, some admittedly violent, because that 12-year-old is tall for his age and had violent tantrums when placed in a children's ward. . . . We do not think the age of 12 marks such a growth to maturity as would justify placement in an adult ward. In fact we consider the distinction between a 10, 11, or 12-year-old to be so slight that the statement of Dr. Chlenoff that he wouldn't place a 10 or 11-year-old in that ward was tantamount to an admission that it would be an improper standard of supervision and medical treatment to place a 12-year-old in that ward. In so doing, the State obviously was playing with psychic dynamite and when it was, we believe expectably, exploded, the State must be held liable no matter what the direction or form of the blast. . . .

[I]t was established to our satisfaction that there were many beds available in Ward 6 for said claimant, not only on the day of the assault but also prior thereto. There was no problem of overcrowding which forced assignment of said claimant to Ward 5.

There was no justification in law or fact, legally or morally, or medically to house said claimant in Ward 5.

If the above had been the only action by the State preceding the assault, we would have found liability on the part of the State. However, the record shows further acts on the part of the State which strengthen a finding of liability.

Approximately a week before the assault in question, the said claimant stated that he, with other patients and a ward attendant, witnessed and watched one younger male patient commit an act of sodomy (buggery) with another male patient. He was cross-examined competently and strongly on this testimony but other than minor discrepancies his testimony stood up. The State did not offer any proof to contradict this testimony by the claimant and the court believes and finds this activity took place. The hospital officials permitted this 12-year-old to remain in the ward when it should have been obvious that a child might be subject to such acts of degeneracy.

*   *   *

It was stated in *Gould* v. *State of New York*, 181 Misc. 884, 46 N.Y.S.2d 313, 316:

> "Insufficiency of attendants in a mental institution is an act of negligence, on the part of the State.
> "The State is duty bound to furnish inmates of its hospitals for mental defectives with every reasonable precaution to protect them from injury, either self inflicted or otherwise."

In the case at hand the evidence discloses that Ward 5 was in the shape of an "L." The long end of the "L" was approximately 150 feet in length and contained the entrance to the ward, the day room and approximately 21 small individual rooms on the left side of the ward when one stands in the entrance looking to the rear of the ward and the clothing closet, several utility rooms and the ward office on the right side. The short end of the "L" contains five dormitory type wards and a utility room. This ward on the night in question contained 43 patients and yet it was under the control of but one attendant, Mr. Williams. The record shows that the State knew of the assaultive disposition of many of the inmates of this ward. Leaving such a ward under the care of one attendant was negligence on the part of the State.

It is our opinion and we find that the State was negligent . . .

*   *   *

Having determined liability against the State, we now come to the question as to the effect of the assault of October 20, 1959 upon the infant claimant. There is no question that said infant was suffering from a psychological disorder prior to the assault. The record clearly shows his difficulties at home which led to his commitment to Bellevue Hospital and thence to Rockland State Hospital. The fundamental question to be determined is whether or not his admittedly pre-existing mental disturbance was so aggravated and exacerbated by the assault as to become a much more severe mental disturbance, one less susceptible of improvement through psychiatric assistance.

*   *   *

We have not discovered many guidelines in the New York cases which assisted in the evaluation of damages. Apparently there have not been many cases where slight, albeit odious, physical impact has produced what is essentially and only severe physic pain and suffering. Certainly we are more accustomed to evaluating physical injury. However, in what we like to believe is an enlightened age, is not damage to the mental integrity of the individual to be considered at least as serious as severe physical injury?

We find that the infant claimant is entitled to an award in the sum of $90,000 and render judgment against the State of New York in that amount.

NOTE 6

WEINGAST v. STATE
44 Misc. 2d 824, 254 N.Y.S. 2d 952 (1964)

DOROTHEA E. DONALDSON, JUDGE.

This is an action for damages for mental suffering which is alleged to have been inflicted on the claimants as a result of a reversal of identity which occurred between two patients at Pilgrim State Hospital.

The facts are not in dispute. On September 28, 1959, a patient known to the hospital authorities as Elizabeth Gambardella died. Steps were taken to inform Mrs. Gambardella's family; they responded by authorizing the desired autopsy and requesting burial within the hospital cemetery. This was accomplished, the body apparently receiving the rites of the Roman Catholic Church with interment in grounds consecrated to such use for communicants of that faith. There is no indication in the record that any of the family viewed the remains. Nothing further occurred in this matter until April 16, 1961, when Rose Weingast, the sister of another patient at the hospital, received a telegram stating, "Tillie Reifer critically ill advise immediate visit." The message was signed by Hyman S. Barahal, M.D., the hospital's Acting Director. The following day a brother, Isaac Weingast, and another sister, Nettie Alberger, who are the claimants herein, made arrangements to visit the hospital. They were conducted to the bedside of a woman under an oxygen tent whose features were obscured thereby. They were informed that the woman was their sister and had suffered a heart attack. The patient remained asleep throughout their visit of a half hour or so and they then departed, having no reason to question the identity of the patient before whom they had been taken. The following day a telephoned inquiry by Mrs. Alberger elicited the opinion of the hospital staff that the patient's condition was improved. Two weeks later four members of the family traveled by automobile to the hospital where they were directed to the woman, now no longer on oxygen therapy. All four visitors agreed the patient was not Tillie Reifer.

The four duly apprised the hospital authorities who thereupon established through investigation that Tillie Reifer had, in fact, died on September 28, 1959, had been buried under the name of Elizabeth Gambardellas as heretofore described, and that the true Elizabeth Gambardella was continuing a masquerade that the two had begun for some unknown reason probably beginning at the time of an intra-hospital transfer on or about July 9, 1959. On that date the two patients were sent along with seven others from Building 12 to Building 14. In the investigation which the hospital made in April 1961, attendants who had known both patients were examined and positively identified the living woman as Mrs. Gambardella.

*   *   *

The Court holds as a matter of law that the supervision exercised over these inmates whereby they were successfully able to exchange identities was faulty and that the State's negligent conduct is thereby established. . . .

The damages recoverable are those stemming from injury to the feelings of the relatives and their mental suffering resulting directly or approximately from the wrongful act of deprivation and may be recovered though no actual or pecuniary damages be proven. In ascertaining the damages sustained by the claimants, the Court will be guided by the following circumstances, among others:

1. The body of the deceased up to and including the day of trial, remains in the Roman Catholic section of the hospital's cemetery although the Court finds that it is, in fact, the remains of Tillie Reifer;

2. No attempt has been made to exhume the body and reinter the remains in the family burial plot or, perhaps more in keeping with the practices of the Jewish faith, determining the location of the remains of Mrs. Reifer's husband which is now apparently unknown to any of the parties, and reburying the body therewith;

3. One claimant testified that he last saw the deceased in 1957 or 1958; the other testified that she last saw the deceased in 1957; there was, therefore, a period of at least two and one-third years during which time the deceased was, if not ignored, unvisited.

The Court finds that the claimants have been damaged each in the amount of $600.00 and awards judgment against the State of New York therefor in the amount of $1,200.00.

*   *   *

3.

WHAT PROCEDURES SHOULD BE DESIGNED TO UNCOVER AND REMEDY INSTITUTIONAL ERRORS?

a.   EGAN v. UNITED STATES
          158 F. Supp. 377 (Ct. Cl. 1958)

LITTLETON, JUDGE.

*   *   *

This is an unusual case of mistaken identity and almost incredible negligence, as a result of which plaintiff, an officer in the United States Marine Corps Reserve, was denied his promotion to captain on March 1, 1943, was illegally and erroneously released to inactive duty on October 28, 1943, and was illegally discharged from the Marine Corps Reserve on April 11, 1944. Plaintiff sues to recover the active duty pay and allowances which he claims were due to him and were wrongfully withheld from the date of his promotion to captain on March 1, 1943, to April 7, 1948, when plaintiff was finally given a legal and valid honorable discharge from the Marine Corps.

*   *   *

While serving overseas in Samoa, plaintiff, on February 12, 1943, was taken to a field hospital for treatment for an attack of bronchitis. Shortly after his admission to the hospital for treatment, another patient in plaintiff's ward made a violent attempt with a dangerous weapon upon the life of a Naval physician. Plaintiff, who was not seriously ill, intervened and disarmed the violent patient. In the course of an investigation following that incident, the witnesses to what happened, who were patients in the hospital at the time, denied that anything of the sort had occurred. It was later fully established that these witnesses lied. Plaintiff was also questioned by hospital doctors concerning two previous injuries which he had mentioned but which were not noted on his hospital medical record. Plaintiff had actually suffered the two injuries, had been treated for them by Army doctors, and had reported the injuries to the admitting physician of the hospital but, unaccountably, no record was made of this matter. The investigating physicians in the hospital made up their minds that plaintiff had imagined the ward encounter with the violent hospital patient and has also imagined the two injuries he claimed to have incurred. At about this time, plaintiff learned that his battalion had been ordered into combat. Plaintiff had recovered completely from the attack of bronchitis and asked to be discharged from the hospital to permit him to join his battalion. Hospital authorities refused to discharge plaintiff and his reaction was, naturally enough, quite violent. On February 17, 1943, the hospital physicians erroneously diagnosed plaintiff as insane and he was confined to the locked ward of the hospital.

On March 1, 1943, while plaintiff was in the locked ward under an improper diagnosis of insanity, he was given a temporary appointment as captain, subject to conditions and procedure specified in ALNAV 142 in part as follows:

> ". . . upon receipt notification of appointment in any form commanding officer direct appointee report for examination by at least one medical officer to determine physical fitness to perform duties of the rank to which appointed. Submit completed form yoke to Bureau of Naval Personnel with notation thereon 'for temporary promotion or appointment as appropriate,' making reference to appointment authority. If physical defects of a Naval reserve officer have been waived previously by the Department and upon physical examination for temporary promotion are found to be essentially the same, such defects will not be considered disqualifying. If found physically qualified and if in opinion commanding officer appointee is mentally, morally, and professionally qualified and not involved disciplinary action, appointee will be informed of his appointment. . . ."

Plaintiff's appointment as captain . . . was illegally withheld for the stated reason, which was erroneous, that "he was sick in the United States Naval Hospital." There is no indication that the promotion was withheld for any reason other than that plaintiff was then in hospital and confined to a locked ward under an erroneous diagnosis of insanity. His previous attack of bronchitis was not a factor in this. Under the conditions prescribed in ALNAV 142, plaintiff was, in the circumstances, erroneously and illegally deemed neither physically nor mentally qualified to accept the appointment. Plaintiff was in fact neither ill nor insane.

On March 15, 1943, plaintiff was transferred from the locked ward of the naval hospital in Samoa to the locked ward of a ship, the U.S.S. *Wright*, and transported back to the United States. On March 28, 1943, plaintiff was transferred to the locked ward of the United States Naval Hospital, Mare Island, California. On May 28, 1943, plaintiff was released from the Naval Hospital at Mare Island and ordered to proceed, *without escort*, to the Naval Medical Center, Bethesda, Maryland. Upon his arrival in Bethesda on June 7, 1943, plaintiff was placed in the locked

ward of that hospital. On June 17, 1943, plaintiff was transferred to Saint Elizabeths Hospital for the Insane, Washington, D.C.

During the five months of plaintiff's confinements in locked wards as an insane person, he attempted in every conceivable way to persuade the medical officers that he was not insane. His growing sense of frustration and his occasionally vehement protests only served to confirm the medical authorities in their opinion that plaintiff was insane. Throughout plaintiff's confinements no technical tests administered to him by doctors resulted in the manifestation of any symptom of a psychiatric origin, or of any physical condition of a psychogenic origin.

Not long after plaintiff's admission to Saint Elizabeths Hospital, he escaped and later returned armed with reports of several medical examinations attesting to his sanity. Plaintiff then appeared before a group of psychiatrists at Saint Elizabeths and told them that if he was held at the hospital he would seek a writ of habeas corpus. He was finally permitted to leave the hospital on October 30, 1943.

In the meantime, on July 30, 1943, a Board of Medical Survey convened at Saint Elizabeths Hospital and rendered a report which contained the following statement of so-called *facts:*

> "On admission to this hospital the patient was obviously making an effort to be as pleasant as possible but failed to conceal very definite tension, speaking very rapidly and lighting one cigarette from the other. He was intent upon establishing that he had no mental disorder and that he had been mistreated. He presented his case with considerable circumstantiality and detail, and made an especial effort to smooth over his past behavior difficulties, giving explanatory and personal versions *of a paranoid nature.*[3] Since then he has shown improvement. He is still however, preoccupied with explaining his psychiatric difficulties on the basis of errors on the part of the physicians, who have handled his case. He needs further hospital care. His physical condition is good.
>
> "*Verified history reveals* that this patient was discharged from the United States Army on March 3, 1942, because of a mental illness diagnosed, 'Psychoneurosis, Anxiety, Neurosis, with Schizoid Features.' In the opinion of this Board the origin of the patient's present disability existed prior to appointment and has not been aggravated by service conditions." [Italics supplied.]

The "verified history" reported in the statement of facts of the Board of Medical Survey was the service and medical history of *another* John J. Egan, not this plaintiff, who had indeed been discharged from the Army on March 3, 1942 as an insane person. Despite

---

3. It is interesting to note in this connection that plaintiff's personal versions of what had happened turned out to be the correct versions.

the asserted verification referred to, this other Egan had a service serial number different from the serial number of plaintiff, and his discharge from the Army antedated plaintiff's by several months. . . .

On the basis of the remarkable and untrue findings of fact quoted above, the Board of Medical Survey, without further inquiry into the matter, recommended that plaintiff appear before a United States Marine Corps Retiring Board "in order that his best interests be fully protected," inasmuch as he was deemed to be permanently "unfit for service" by reason of an unclassified psychosis which had existed prior to his Marine Corps service and had not been aggravated by such service. . . .

On September 24, 1943, a Marine Corps Retiring Board was convened pursuant to the incorrect and erroneous recommendation of the Board of Medical Survey. On October 25, 1943, the Commandant of the Marine Corps notified plaintiff that as of October 28, 1943, he would be relieved from active duty and be assigned to the Third Reserve District; that upon his discharge from treatment at Saint Elizabeths Hospital, he should proceed to his home in Connecticut. On October 28, 1943, plaintiff was relieved from active duty and his pay and allowances were discontinued. On October 30, 1943, plaintiff was discharged from treatment at Saint Elizabeths Hospital.

On November 27, 1943, plaintiff was advised by the Commandant of the Marine Corps that:

> "In view of the recommendation of the Board of Medical Survey convened in your case, which was approved by the Chief of the Bureau of Medicine and Surgery, it is the intention of the Commandant, United States Marine Corps, to recommend to the proper authority that you be discharged as an officer of the Marine Corps Reserve."

*   *   *

On December 5, 1943, plaintiff submitted a statement protesting the proposed discharge from the Marine Corps Reserve. . . .

*   *   *

On April 11, 1944, the plaintiff was notified by the Commandant of the Marine Corps, that effective that date, he was, by direction of the President, discharged from the Marine Corps Reserve under honorable conditions, having been found not physically qualified for active duty. On the same date the Secretary of the Navy issued to plaintiff a Certificate of Satisfactory Service.

*   *   *

In the meantime, plaintiff, a perfectly healthy and normal man, had, on December 13, 1943, secured employment in the Office of Price Administration in Hartford, Connecticut, and was employed thereafter in that and other civilian positions, including his employment with the Veterans Administration which was involved in plaintiff's claim in the first count of his petition. After hearing about the creation by Congress of the Board for the Correction of Naval Records . . . plaintiff, on December 27, 1947, applied to that Board to correct the errors and injustices resulting from the erroneous and careless medical diagnosis of his physical condition by the Navy, and the consequent erroneous and illegal discharge of plaintiff as unqualified for active service by reason of permanent psychosis. Following diligent efforts by plaintiff and a long investigation and an oral hearing, the Board on March 17, 1948, made findings of fact, conclusions, and a decision. The Correction Board concluded that plaintiff had at no time been mentally defective, nor had he ever suffered from any incapacity, physical or mental, which would have prevented him from performing active duty as an officer in the Marine Corps; that the many diagnoses of insanity rendered by the various medical officers and boards were all completely in error and had been based on numerous false premises, including the mistaken reports from Samoa that plaintiff had imagined two minor injuries prior to his hospitalization for bronchitis in Samoa, and that he had also imagined the encounter with the violent patient in the medical ward in the hospital in Samoa. The Board found that plaintiff's accounts of those incidents, consistently disbelieved by the Naval physicians and officials, had been completely accurate. The Board also found that the Adjutant General of the Army and the Bureau of Medicine and Surgery of the Marine Corps had confused plaintiff's Army records with the Army records of another former Army officer whose name was "Egan"; that on the basis of the Army medical records of the other Egan, Marine Corps officials were convinced that plaintiff had been found insane while serving in the Army and had been discharged from the Army as an insane person prior to his entry into the Marine Corps. In its decision, the Correction Board, after having carefully considered the true facts, concluded that plaintiff had never been insane; that all diagnoses of insanity had been negligently made and in error, that plaintiff had at all times been mentally and physically capable of performing active service as an officer in the Marine Corps; that the discharge in 1944 of plaintiff because of mental incapacity for service was clearly erroneous and should be changed to an honorable discarge without any reference therein to such nonexistent incapacity. The Commandant of the Marine Corps was ordered to cancel the previous illegal discharge and to issue to plaintiff a new honorable discharge in substitution therefor without any reference to physical or mental incapacity, together with a Certificate of Satisfactory Service. The Chief of the Bureau of Medicine and Surgery was directed by the Correction Board to add to plaintiff's medical records a certified copy of the

Board's conclusion and decision as the last and final official entry in plaintiff's medical records. . . .

* * *

On February 12, 1951, plaintiff filed his petition in the instant case claiming . . . that he was entitled to recover (1) the difference between the active duty pay of a captain and that of a first lieutenant from March 1, 1943, the date on which his promotion to captain was illegally withheld on the ground that he was insane, to October 28, 1943, the date on which he was illegally released to inactive duty; (2) the active duty pay and allowances of a captain from October 28, 1943 to April 7, 1948, the date on which his illegal and erroneous discharge for physical incapacity was vacated and a new honorable discharge was issued. . . .

* * *

[P]laintiff is entitled to recover active duty pay from October 28, 1943 to April 7, 1948, as claimed in his petition.

There remains for consideration the question of whether the withholding of plaintiff's promotion to captain was illegal in the circumstances of this case so that his active duty pay from the effective date of his promotion should have been that of a captain.

* * *

While, as urged by defendant, plaintiff's commanding officer could, in a proper case, have withheld plaintiff's promotion to captain for the reason that, in the opinion of such commanding officer, plaintiff's performance of his duties had not been satisfactory, there is no indication in the entire record in this case that the promotion would have been withheld for that reason if, on the effective date of the promotion, plaintiff had not been confined in the hospital under an erroneous diagnosis of insanity.

However, in our opinion, the most conclusive ground for holding that the three fitness reports (covering a period of three months) should not be deemed a valid reason for denying plaintiff the pay of a captain from the effective date of his promotion to that rank, is that on two occasions, subsequent to March 1, 1943, plaintiff received from no less a person than the Secretary of the Navy, formal certificates of Satisfactory Service covering his *entire* Marine Corps Service. . . .

* * *

Presumably, a Certificate of Satisfactory Service means what its name implies, i.e., that for the period covered thereby, the services of the recipient were satisfactorily performed. It therefore appears to us that when the services of this plaintiff were officially and advisedly certified by the Secretary of the Navy as satisfactory on two separate occasions, notwithstanding the Secretary's knowledge of the three unsatis-

factory fitness reports, those fitness reports must be deemed to have been superseded and negatived as a matter of law. As a matter of fact, it seems obvious that the Correction Board and the Secretary of the Navy inquired into and knew the facts and circumstances under which the fitness reports were made and they did not concur in those reports . . . The record justifies the conclusion that the reports were prejudiced and unwarranted basically.

On November 25, 1955, the Board for the Correction of Naval Records found that plaintiff had been nominated on March 1, 1943, for promotion to captain, but that his promotion had been withheld for the sole reason that he was then in the hospital under an erroneous diagnosis of insanity. The Board found that it was apparent from plaintiff's record that his temporary promotion to captain would otherwise have been effective and "that he would have served satisfactorily in that rank." The Board also found that plaintiff had received a Certificate of Satisfactory Service on April 11, 1944, and again on April 7, 1948, and concluded that plaintiff had suffered an injustice because of the failure of the naval authorities to promote him to the grade of captain as of March 1, 1943. The Board then found that plaintiff *was* promoted to captain on March 1, 1943, that he *was qualified* therefore in all respects, and that he did not decline the appointment. The Board recommended that the Secretary of the Navy determine that the highest grade and rank in which plaintiff performed satisfactory service was that of captain, and that the Certificate of Satisfactory Service originally issued in the grade of 1st lieutenant be corrected accordingly, *and that the Navy pay to plaintiff all monies lawfully found to be due as a result of that corrective action.*

* * *

Plaintiff is entitled to recover the difference between the active duty pay and allowances of a captain and the active duty pay and allowances of a first lieutenant from March 1, 1943 to October 28, 1943, and to recover the active duty pay and allowances of a captain from October 29, 1943 to April 7, 1948, less his earnings from civilian employment during the latter period. . . .

* * *

NOTES

NOTE 1

Testimony of John J. Egan—13 January, 1948

. . . I went absent without leave from St. Elizabeths Hospital for the express purpose of securing disinterested medical opinions, which I did and which are incorporated in the records and which give me a clean bill. I reported by whereabouts to the Navy Department and to St. Elizabeths and told them I did not intend to return unless they would either give me a discharge or send me back to duty as I did not intend to go back to that hospital. My records will show that my status was changed from "absent without leave" to "absent with leave" without any further hospitalization at that institution. They said, "If you will report back here on August 31, we will take action and you will not be confined to the hospital." I walked into the conference room that morning, and they discharged me to live at home and said that they were recommending that I appear before a retiring board, to give them my address, and they would notify me as to when I was to appear.

. . . I secured federal employment and have a personnel record which was sufficient to grant me three raises and a permanent civil service status and then a suspension and removal because I allegedly falsified an application for marking "no" in the X column to the question, "Have you ever had a nervous breakdown."

Now, I was suspended from that job.

MR. SULLIVAN: What were you doing?

MR. EGAN: I have a copy of my duties. I was a contact representative for the Veterans Administration.

MR. SCHUYLER: You are no longer so employed?

MR. EGAN: No, sir. I am not employed. I have had three jobs since then. I told the truth in my application. The question was, "Why did you leave previous employment," and I answered, "Because I was suspended and fired." Normally a personnel officer will say to you, "We don't care what happened to you in the past." Their curiosity gets the best of them after you have been there a week of two and they said, "Why were you suspended?" "Because I falsified an application for employment." And the first thing they do then is go back to their own application and one agency says, "You didn't falsify ours. What did you do on theirs?" I said, "At one time I said I wasn't in a mental institution." That's the last straw there. Three jobs I have lost there. Fortunately the thing has developed into such a series of events that have gone on in the past that it's actually at the top level of two other agencies besides this, and I didn't know anything about this Board until recently and that's why I filed an appeal to present my side of this story so I might get this thing off my record. I maintain there is no psychosis and there has never been a psychosis.

Now, I don't know what your reaction would be, whether you would physically fight an incarceration in a mental institution, but if you have been incarcerated you will find that you can't even get the information outside and that's the only recourse you have, because it's apparent that the psychiatrists in my case have just taken every argument and every time I have stated that I never had a mental disability as a different manifestation of the same disability.

NOTE 2

BLITZ v. BOOG
328 F. 2d 596 (2d Cir. 1964)

MARSHALL, CIRCUIT JUDGE.

* * *

[W]e affirm the judgment of the district court that Dr. Boog enjoyed immunity from suit for false imprisonment by virtue of the fact that her decision to transfer appellant to Bellevue Hospital was made in pursuance of her official duties in what reasonably appeared to her to be an emergency situation. Her actions fall clearly within the language of Judge Learned Hand in Gregoire v. Biddle, 177 F.2d 579, 581 (2 Cir. 1949), cert. denied, 339 U.S. 949 (1950):

"Again and again the public interest calls for action which may turn out to be founded on a mistake, in the face of which an official may later find himself hard put to it to satisfy a jury of his good faith. There must indeed be means of punishing public officers who have been truant to their duties; but that is quite another matter from exposing such as have been honestly mistaken to suit by anyone who has suffered from their errors. As is so often the case, the answer must be found in a balance between evils inevitable in either alternative. In this instance it has been thought in the end better to leave unredressed the wrongs done by dishonest officers than to subject those who try to do their duty to the constant dread of retaliation. Judged as res nova, we should not hesitate to follow the path laid down in the books."

The rationale of Gregoire is by no means limited to high-ranking officers. . . . Indeed, in Taylor v. Glotfelty, 201 F.2d 51 (6 Cir. 1952), the court held that a government psychiatrist who had made a report stating that plaintiff was insane could not be sued for libel. In our view, it is at least as important for a government psychiatrist to be able to arrange for care of a patient without fear of liability for false imprisonment as it is for him to be able to make diagnoses without fear of liability for libel. . . .

b. PEOPLE ex rel. ROGERS v. STANLEY
17 N.Y. 2d 256, 217 N.E. 2d 636 (1966)

Order reversed and the matter remitted to the Supreme Court, Rockland County, for further proceedings in accordance with the following memorandum: In our view, the principle of *Baxstrom* v. *Herold*, 383 U.S. 107; *Gideon* v. *Wainwright*, 372 U.S. 335; *Douglas* v. *California*, 372 U.S. 353; *Lane* v. *Brown*, 372 U.S. 477; *Griffin* v. *Illinois*, 351 U.S. 12, and of similar cases, demonstrates that an indigent mental patient, who is committed to an institution, is entitled, in a habeas corpus proceeding, (brought to establish his sanity), to the assignment of counsel as a matter of constitutional right. No opinion.

BERGAN, J. (dissenting):

The effect of the decision now being made is that it will become the mandatory duty of a judge before whom it is returnable a writ of habeas corpus sued out by a patient in a State hospital for the mentally ill to assign counsel to prosecute the writ. Presently such assignment of counsel is a discretionary matter with the judge; and it should remain that way.

There are some adversary trials with counsel now in cases where it is indicated to be necessary; but the new rule will greatly enlarge their number.

There is no possible hope that any good can be accomplished by the procedural innovation now being fashioned. The legal profession will be burdened by a frustrating and futile extension of its responsibilities in attempting to review by many new adversary trials current medical judgments of psychiatrists; the physicians themselves will be interrupted in their heavy schedules to prepare running forensic justification in a court for their medical judgments; and no one could pretend that a mentally ill patient could be helped by all this or that it would be conducive to good hospital management.

The view has been expressed in some intraprofessional legal discussions that every patient should be represented by counsel in judicial inquiries that test his need for new or continued medical treatment . . .

The basic concept in these contentions is that a mental hospital is equated to a prison. The two ought not be equated. They are totally different. The fact that a temporary deprivation of freedom exists in both does not make them alike.

A man is put in prison to punish him. A patient is in a hospital to help him. He is there to treat his illness because in the present state of science no better way to treat him has been discovered.

He is there because the people of New York at an operational cost to themselves in the 1965–1966 budget of $293 million and an additional $94 million for new facilities are interested in helping him get well.

Adversary trials have played a vital role in the preservation of our liberties and in the effective administration of justice; but they are not a cure-all for every social or public problem and their usefulness in prodding competent medical staffs into better diagnoses of mental illness or more effective releases from hospital care of patients able to be released is illusory.

The published records of the Department of Mental Hygiene demonstrate the present average stay of the newly admitted mentally ill patient in State hospitals is four months.[1] In the ten years from 1955 to 1965

this has been cut in half. In 1955 the average stay was eight months.

Mental hospitals, working under quite the same pressures and for quite the same reasons as general medical and surgical hospitals, have been trying consistently to reduce the time of hospitalization.

Even though there has been an increase in total admissions in the 10 years from 1955 to 1965, there has been a consistent reduction in the number of "resident patients" (those in hospitals) in the 10-year period. In June, 1955 there were 93,550 resident patients; March 31, 1965 there were 84,637 or a reduction of 8,913. During this period the annual rate of admissions increased by 58 per cent but releases increased 118 per cent.

The Department's comment on this is of direct relevancy to the question on hand: "The continuing growth in admissions is due not to a rise in the incidence of mental illness but rather to increasing longevity, increasing general population, increasing demand for psychiatric care, and increasing public confidence in state hospitals and in the effectiveness of their therapeutic programs. The essential element in the falling population trend is a reduction in the average length of hospitalization . . . the higher release rate is a direct result of vast improvements in the therapeutic program including large scale use of the tranquilizing drugs, intensive treatment for newly-admitted patients, the development of milieu therapy, and the establishment of the open ward policy in which New York State led the nation." (*State Programs for the Mentally Ill and Mentally Retarded*, N.Y. State Dept. of Mental Hygiene.)

The reduction in the number of resident patients is accompanied by increases in out-patient treatment in various facilities not requiring resident hospitalization.

. . . This and other material make it obvious that a prime objective of good hospital treatment is to get the patient out—not to keep him in.

*   *   *

There are, of course, borderline cases where conservative medical judgment foresees some danger in releasing a patient. The present appellant, who had shown assaultive tendencies against his mother and who is obviously still mentally ill, seems to present such a case. Public opinion has not been notably tolerant of mistaken predictions by psychiatrists of the future course of mental disease by a person who has been released on medical recommendation.

And judges, looking with the benefit of hindsight at mistakes in diagnosis and treatment, have had a tendency to keep psychiatrists well on the safe side of recommendations. One might look, for example, at the effect of *Collins* v. *State of New York* (17 N.Y. 2d 542) which imposed a State liability for a mistaken

---

1. The statistical and other statements are from *Annual Report of the Department of Mental Hygiene for 1961* (N.Y. Legis. Doc., 1961, No. 117); *1964 Statistics of State Mental Hospitals*, N.Y. State Dept. of Mental Hygiene; and the current edition of *State Programs for the Mentally Ill and Mentally Retarded*, promulgated by the Department of Mental Hygiene.

psychiatric judgment on the degree of protective special care against suicide needed by the patient.

It is unlikely, to say the least, if judges undertake on an enlarged scale, as the result of adversary trials, to supervise the current diagnosis of psychiatric staffs affecting risks to be taken in the future, as distinguished from looking back at and making value judgments on past psychiatric mistakes, that they will improve things or visibly affect the liberties of patients.

If a reputable psychiatrist has a reservation about a patient who may in the future do damage to himself or kill his nearest friend, it will not be often that a judge will take the risk because there is psychiatric proof before him the other way in a contested trial.

Thus the adversary trial of medical issues implicit in the universal and compulsory assignment of counsel in every habeas corpus proceeding by a patient in a mental hospital seems at once unwise and injudicious.

As the Department of Mental Hygiene itself notes, the revised New York statute (L. 1964, ch. 738, effective September 1, 1965) provides for "periodic court reexamination of the retention of involuntary patients" and this is regarded by the Department as a "significant" change accomplished by the new statute.

. . . Also significant, as the Department sees it, is the "establishment of a mental health information service, as an arm of the judiciary, to gather information for the court and to advise patients and their relatives of their rights under the law."

Thus the legal problem raised by the continuance of hospital care is placed in the sound discretion of experienced and conscientious judges and is a subject of periodic review. This kind of judicial inquiry is a marked improvement over the uneven and haphazard chance of patients making applications for writs of habeas corpus. There may be times when it will be appropriate for judges to assign counsel; it is quite inappropriate to hold they must always do so.

The nature of the lawyer's duty on assignment is essentially unsuited for on-going medical diagnosis. The lawyer, upon his assignment, must make out the best legal case he can for the discharge of the patient. The long tradition of the legal profession and its highest demands of duty require him to prosecute the writ with his best legal skill and ability.

He does not have a medical responsibility for the over-all good of the patient—his professional legal responsibility is toward sustaining the writ. And, of course, some, perhaps many, psychiatric estimations of future prognosis are arguable, but the lawyer is bound to advance that view which releases the patient from hospital care. This would regularly overrule the responsible medical staff judgment related to the kind of treatment needed. The possibilities of disservice to mentally ill patients in the enlargement of litigation could be significant.

The order should be affirmed.

NOTE 1

HOFF v. STATE
279 N.Y. 490, 18 N.E. 2d 671 (1939)

LEHMAN, JUDGE.

The claimant on March 6, 1936, while confined to Tonawanda State Hospital under an order of the court, signed and verified a petition for a writ of habeas corpus and placed it in a stamped envelope addressed to his attorney, A. Stanley Copeland. The claimant had been adjudged insane. It is the duty of an employee of the hospital, acting under the direction of the superintendent, to examine all the mail of patients confined in the hospital before the mail is sent out. The claimant, believing that he was sane, had written to many men in public life asking their assistance. The claimant's wife had been annoyed by inquiries from persons who have received such letters. She requested that all letters written by the claimant should be sent to her. The superintendent of the hospital acceded to her request and, by his directions, all mail including the letter addressed to the claimant's attorney and containing the petition for the writ of habeas corpus, was forwarded to claimant's wife, who suppressed the letter. On March 25th Copeland presented a new petition verified by himself to the County Judge of Erie county.

The writ was made returnable on March 30th before a jury. On April 2, 1936, the claimant was discharged from custody after the jury had determined that he was sane. Our constitutional guaranties of liberty are merely empty words unless a person imprisoned or detained against his will may challenge the legality of his imprisonment and detention. The writ of habeas corpus is the process devised centuries ago for the protection of free men. It has been cherished by generations of free men who had learned by experience that it furnished the only reliable protection of their freedom. The right of persons, deprived of liberty, to challenge in the courts the legality of their detention is safeguarded by the Constitution of the United States and by the Constitution of the State. The Legislature could not deprive any person within the State of the privilege of a writ of habeas corpus. (N.Y. Const. article 1, section 4.) The superintendent of the hospital by diverting to claimant's wife the letter and petition for a writ of habeas corpus obstructed the claimant's right to test the legality of his imprisonment. Doubtless the superintendent acted in the honest belief that the claimant was insane. Nevertheless, his act delayed for a time a test of the claimant's sanity which, when made, resulted in his discharge.

* * *

The right of the superintendent in the exercise of a reasonable discretion to censor the ordinary mail written by a patient who has been adjudged insane is not challenged. . . .

*   *   *

The act of the superintendent was an act of misfeasance, and the State may be held liable for any damages caused by that act. . . . In this case the damages were probably very small but there can be no doubt that the claimant's challenge, ultimately succesful, was delayed for approximately two weeks. There is finding "that the mental condition of claimant was substantially the same on March 6th, 1936, as it was upon March 30th, 1936, when brought into Erie County Court and on April 2nd, 1936, when discharged from custody." The determination of the jury on April 2nd is a conclusive adjudication that at that time the claimant was sane. We must assume that if his condition was the same earlier, a trial, whether before judge or jury, would have resulted in the same way, and there is evidence, which has not been substantially challenged, which supports the finding of the court.

*   *   *

NOTE 2

HANSON v. BIDDLE
116 P. & C. 639 (1911)

BURCH, J. The plaintiff is an attorney at law. The defendants are, respectively, the superintendent of the State hospital for the insane, at Topeka, and the members of the State Board of Control. The plaintiff alleges in his petition that in the regular practice of law he has received word from certain inmates of the hospital, who are confined there as insane patients, that they desire plaintiff to secure their discharge on the ground that they are not insane; that the defendants refuse to allow the plaintiff to see and talk with such inmates, and to inspect the hospital records relating to their confinement; and that, therefore, the plaintiff's rights are violated, and particularly his rights under section 8481, General Statutes 1909, which provides that every patient admitted to a public hospital for the insane shall have all reasonable opportunities for communicating with his or her friends. The prayer of the petition is that an alternative writ of mandamus issue, requiring the defendants to allow the plantiff the right he claims to possess.

The plaintiff has no legal right to see and talk with the patients in the hospital to whom he has been denied access. He does not pretend that he ever knew, or saw, or heard, of them before, and he has no interest in them, except as an attorney. The hospital is maintained for the benefit of persons afflicted with brain sickness, rendering them incapable of caring for themselves. To open the doors of the institution to the idle and curious, or to busybodies and persons with mercenary designs, would be to destroy discipline among the inmates, and to retard their restoration to mental health. Therefore the Legislature limits the right of communication with them to friends. The friends contemplated by the statute are relatives and former associates and acquaintances who, from sentiments of affection, esteem, or kindly regard, are interested in them and in their welfare. Attorneys who seek to invade the hospital in a merely professional capacity, for the purpose of promoting business, are not recognized.

If an inmate of the hospital have no friends in fact of the character described, the State of Kansas stands toward him in that relation. The welfare of the patient, who, because of his disability, is unable to make use of his normal liberties, is the matter of primary consideration in every case of detention at the hospital, and it is a subject of the deepest concern to all the authorities that no one who is fit to be discharged shall be detained. Private communication between patients and the Board of Control is secured by law. Ample provision is made for discharge and for parole when, in the judgment of the board or of the superintendent of the hospital, such course is proper, and for establishing the fact of sanity or restoration to reason in an orderly way, even in opposition to the judgment of those officials. It will not be assumed that power which is exercised with the kindest intention and for the most benevolent purposes is being abused, and small room should be allowed for the intervention of individuals to whom patients may smuggle communications, stating that they are of sound mind, and want to be released, and who are therefore intruders and disturbers.

The writ of mandamus is denied.

NOTE 3

ROSARIO v. STATE
42 Misc. 2d 699, 248 N.Y.S. 2d 734 (1964)

ALEXANDER DEL GIORNO, JUDGE.

*   *   *

The claim alleges the State was negligent "in the unlawful and wrongful detention, the false imprisonment, and the unjust and wrongful diagnosis of the sanity of the claimant at Matteawan State Hospital"; that claimant's imprisonment and incarceration were "based upon an improper, wrongful, cursory, sketchy, flimsy and negligent examination and diagnosis"; that the imprisonment was wrongful and that claimant should have been released therefrom had the State "used proper diligence, proper facilities and investigative means" at its disposal; that claimant was confined to the hospital on October 9, 1958 and was released on September 17, 1962; that the

State failed to provide claimant with qualified psychiatrists, proper and adequate facilities, Spanish-speaking interpreters and other personnel required so as properly to examine and diagnose the mental illness of claimant; that the State psychiatrists were guilty of malpractice in failing properly to diagnose claimant's mental condition and in being grossly negligent. Damages are claimed in the sum of $1,000,000.00.

Claimant had been arraigned in the Court of Special Sessions on July 15, 1958 on the charges of assault and violation of the Penal Law, Section 1897, and was committed to Bellevue Hospital for examination and report. Two qualified psychiatrists having reported that claimant was mentally incompetent, he was commited to Matteawan State Hospital until such time as he might become mentally competent. . . .

A writ of habeas corpus . . . was granted on May 5, 1961. . . . The return to this writ . . . stated that it was the opinion of John F. McNeil, M.D., Superintendent of the hospital, that claimant was then in such a state of insanity, idiocy or imbecility as to be unable to understand the nature of the charge pending against him and to make his defense thereto. [T]he writ was dismissed. . . .

A second writ of habeas corpus . . . was granted on June 22, 1961. . . . The return to this writ . . . indicated that the opinion of John F. McNeil, M.D. as to the mental incompetence of claimant was the same as it had been at the time of the return to the first writ. [T]he writ was dismissed. . . .

A further writ of habeas corpus . . . was granted on October 5, 1961. . . . The return . . . alleged that, in the opinion of the Superintendent of the hospital, claimant was still in a state of insanity. [T]he writ was dismissed. . . .

The claimant was not represented by counsel at any of the three habeas corpus proceedings. The present attorneys were retained by claimant's family on or about June 19, 1962. Counsel interviewed claimant at the hospital on June 26, 1962. . . . At the time of his interview with counsel, claimant related what counsel describes as a "seemingly strange and bizarre story." He had lived with one Carmen Ortiz in a common law relationship for about seven years, two children having been born of the union. Sometime prior to 1958, claimant brought an acquaintance, Roberto Castro to live with them. Castro alienated the affections of Carmen, and upon being ordered to leave the household, did so, but took Carmen with him. Shortly before this time, Castro had taunted claimant about his lack of masculinity. Castro then cut a blood vessel in his own arm, allowed the blood to flow into a glass of beer, then drank the combination, simultaneously boasting of his virility. Despondent over the turn events had taken, claimant engaged in an altercation with Castro and Carmen, was accused of assaulting Carmen and jailed. Upon his release, he went back and was accused by Carmen of another assault, was arrested and sent to Bellevue.

To the doctors at Bellevue, he related the same story in essence, denying his guilt of the pending charges.

After the contested sanity hearing in October, 1958, claimant was committed to Matteawan, to be returned to the jurisdiction of the Court upon the recovery of his sanity.

At the time of visiting the hospital, counsel discussed with the Assistant Director of the hospital the mental condition of claimant. The doctor stated that although claimant was well-behaved and rational, the story he had told indicated a paranoid personality. Counsel then contacted Carmen Ortiz. . . . She verifies the truth of the story told by claimant. In August 1962, counsel was informed by the Superintendent of the hospital that claimant's delusional ideas must prevent his release. In September, 1962, claimant was released from the hospital.

Claimant . . . contends . . . that the substance of his claim rests upon malpractice and negligence subsequent to his commitment to the hospital, and that once the story told by claimant to the authorities was verified by Carmen Ortiz, in August, 1962, there no longer existed a basis for a finding of incompetency by the psychiatrists.

Where a mentally ill person is committed, his detention is authorized only during the continuance of the condition. If he recovers while under lawful commitment, he may apply for a writ of habeas corpus to secure his release. If he establishes his mental soundness he will be released. . . . His release will be refused, however, where the evidence indicates that the relator requires further care and treatment. . . . The presumption of fact is that the condition of insanity continues to the present time, with the result that the burden of proving sanity is upon the person seeking release by habeas corpus after commitment to a state hospital for the criminally insane. Commitment for an indefinite time is legal where the statute makes provision for the mentally ill person to contest, by proof of his sanity, the legality of his confinement after admission. . . .

The purpose of the institution by the claimant in person of the three habeas corpus proceedings was to obtain a judicial determination on the return days of the sanity of claimant at such times. In each instance the Court found that claimant had not recovered his sanity. On this motion, the Court holds that as of October 23, 1961, the date of the order made after the third habeas corpus proceeding, there was an existing final judgment or decree of a court of competent jurisdiction rendered on the merits, determining the same cause of action between the parties but only on the issue of the then sanity of claimant up to such time. Questions as to the medical, rehabilitative and custodial care given claimant while an inmate of the hospital, however, were not and could not properly have been within the scope of the habeas corpus proceedings, and the orders entered in such proceedings were not necessarily determinative of such matters. These remain questions of fact which can be decided only upon a trial of the claim. It follows, therefore, that the orders in the habeas corpus proceedings constitute a bar to the present claim only so far as they determine, up to October 23, 1961, that the claimant was then mentally incompetent. The basic issue of sanity at such time is the same in the present claim as it was in the habeas corpus proceedings. . . . This issue, having been adjudicated in the former proceedings, may not be relitigated in the instant claim. . . .

Further, the incarceration of claimant continued from October 23, 1961, the date of the order in the final habeas corpus proceeding, through September 17, 1962, at which time he was released from the hospital. Claimant is entitled to a trial on the allegations of his claim for this period.

NOTE 4

HOLMES v. UNITED STATES
353 F.2d 785 (D.C. Cir. 1966)

BAZELON, CHIEF JUDGE: This is an appeal from the District Court's denial, after hearing, of appellant's post-conviction motion under 28 U.S.C. § 2255 to vacate his sentence for robbery and impersonating an officer. The motion alleged that counsel rendered ineffective assistance by failing to invoke the insanity defense at trial.

Before trial, counsel obtained a report from Dr. Hyman Shapiro, a psychiatrist who had treated appellant on several occasions, stating that appellant was suffering from a mental disease, "psychoneurosis with anxiety and depression, chronic, superimposed upon the schizoid personality makeup." At the hearing on the present motion Dr. Shapiro testified that the acts "were definitely a product of his long standing mental disorder"; but it appears that counsel did not pursue that question with Dr. Shapiro before or at trial, or seek examination by others.

Trial counsel testified that appellant vehemently objected to raising the insanity defense. Appellant stated that he would not have objected had he been apprised of Dr. Shapiro's report. Trial counsel stated that he did apprise him. This conflict was not resolved.

However, as the government concedes, counsel's prime concern was the threat of prejudice. He testified:

> I would find, as a practitioner with some experience involving defenses of insanity, it would be a most impractical approach or request to make of a jury.
> I would say, coupled with that defense of insanity, if you also attempted to have a defense on the merits,

you would jeopardize the defendant's position as regards both defenses . . . and I would have found great difficulty without first admitting to the jury that the defendant Holmes was guilty of all counts before interjecting a defense of insanity.

This view is entirely reasonable and could not, of course, render counsel's assistance "ineffective." This court has recognized that substantial prejudice may result from the simultaneous trial on the pleas of insanity and "not guilty." The former requires testimony that the crime charged was the product of the accused's mental illness. Ordinarily, this testimony will tend to make the jury believe that he did the act. Also, evidence of past anti-social behavior and present anti-social propensities, which tend to support a defense of insanity is highly prejudicial with respect to other defenses. Moreover, evidence that the defendant has a dangerous mental illness invites the jury to resolve doubts concerning commission of the act by finding him not guilty by reason of insanity, instead of acquitting him, so as to assure his confinement in a mental hospital. It appears that such doubts may have existed here since the jury found appellant not guilty on the charge of assault with intent to rape and the court dismissed a second charge of impersonating an officer.

Although trial counsel's appraisal of the prejudicial effect of the insanity defense on the defense of not guilty was entirely reasonable, it does not follow that the insanity defense had to be abandoned. He could have made a motion, like that made by able counsel in another case recently before us, that the District Court avoid the prejudice by exercising its discretion to first submit to the jury issues raised by the not guilty plea before the introduction of evidence on insanity. The power of courts to control the order of criminal trial and submission of issues to the jury has its roots in the common law, and is in no way inconsistent with the Federal Rules of Criminal Procedure. . . . Federal Courts in civil cases are specifically authorized to order the separate trial of any issue "to avoid prejudice." The need to avoid prejudice in criminal trials is even greater.

Relevant considerations upon a request for bifurcation include the substantiality of appellant's insanity defense and its prejudicial effect on other defenses. The court not only has a broad discretion in considering bifurcation, but also in prescribing its procedure, the form of the charge and submission of the questions to the jury, the admissibility of evidence in each stage, and even the impaneling of a second jury to hear the second stage if this appears necessary to eliminate prejudice.

* * *

[A]ppellant's claim is not such as to warrant retrospective application of this remedy, to judgments that have already become final, through a motion under 28 U.S.C. § 2255. Accordingly, the judgment is affirmed.

So ordered.

NOTE 5

DENNISON v. NEW YORK
49 Misc. 2d 933, 267 N.Y.S. 2d 920 (1966)

HELLER, J.

This is an action for false imprisonment based upon the allegedly unlawful confinement of the Claimant at Dannemora State Hospital from September 17, 1936 to December 16, 1960.

The illegality of the Claimant's confinement for the period indicated and the State's liability for any damages arising out of such confinement is unquestionable. . . .

[T]he United States Supreme Court has, since the trial of this claim, held that the statutory procedure utilized by the State in coninuing Claimant's confinement is unconstitutional. *Baxstrom v. Herold.*

The sole question to be decided by the Court, therefore, is what, if any, compensable damage Claimant suffered as a result of his confinement. Damages, of course, would be minimal if he were, in fact, dangerously insane and a fit subject for retention at or commitment to Dannemora.

* * *

Although relatively easy to state, the issues are extremely difficult to resolve. A considerable amount of speculation is necessarily involved in attempting to reach a satisfactory conclusion with respect to a person's potentialities or capacities. That psychiatry and psychology are not exact sciences becomes painfully clear to anyone charged with a fact finder's responsibility in cases such as that before the Court.

On October 6, 1925, the Claimant, then sixteen years old, pled guilty to an indictment charging him with burglary, third degree, and specifying that he had broken into a roadside stand and stolen about $5.00 worth of candy. Although he was given a suspended sentence, he violated his terms of probation by failing to report monthly to a minister in his home town, and on August 14, 1926 he was sentenced "to be confined in New York State Reformatory at Elmira, New York, until discharged by due process of law."

At Elmira, after observation and psychological testing, he was classified as a low grade moron, and on September 15, 1927 he was transferred to the Institution for Male Defective Delinquents at Napanoch. Except for a brief and unsuccessful release on parole, he was confined at Napanoch until March 3, 1936. On that date he was transferred to Dannemora State Hospital on the basis of a "Certificate of Lunacy," which certified him as insane and attributed the insanity to "constitutional defects."

Although his criminal sentence would have expired on September 17, 1936, shortly after he arrived at Dannemora, he was at that time still regarded as insane by the prison authorities and was retained at Dannemora. . . . Finally Claimant's half-brother, convinced by correspondence from him that Claimant was not insane, set the wheels in motion for the habeas corpus proceeding which resulted in his discharge.

Independent tests administered by three highly qualified psychologists subsequent to Claimant's discharge from Dannemora conclusively established that the Claimant possessed average intelligence and that he could not possibly have been a low grade moron at some other point in his life. In addition, it was obvious that had the Claimant not been subjected to the deadening atmosphere of Napanoch and Dannemora for a period of more than thirty years, his performance on the tests administered would have been much better.

It was conceded by Claimant's attorney that the initial ten year criminal sentence was valid. In addition, the evidence established that during his stay at Napanoch, he exhibited psychotic tendencies and was, in fact, insane for a period of time. The Court has concluded, however, that at the time his criminal sentence expired, he had recovered from his insanity in the sense that overtly psychotic behavior had ceased.

What the Claimant might have accomplished or what status he might have achieved had he been released after ten years depended upon the cause and nature of his insanity and the extent to which he would have continued to be disabled by the same. Prior to his conviction, he was unquestionably a maladjusted youth from a broken family, the product of an atmosphere of cultural poverty. In addition, he may have appeared dull, but it was brought out at the trial that a major reason for his so appearing was a purely physical condition which caused his eyelids to droop and which was related in no way to his mental capacity.

Through a tragic error, he was classified as a low grade moron and shipped to Napanoch which, at least during Claimant's years there, was a repository for unfortunates of varying degrees of imbecility, idiocy and moronity. In *People ex rel. Cirrone v. Hoffmann*, 255 A.D. 404, 8 N.Y.S. 2d 83, the Third Department took judicial notice of the character of that institution during Claimant's confinement there and regarded it as obvious that a person's "fundamental rights would be infringed . . . were he to be confined with mental defectives whose appearance, speech, and personal habits are abhorrent, as clearly as would be the case if he were required to live in a madhouse, or in fear of injury by untrained or unmanageable animals, if he were constantly subjected to offensive odors, or if confined for long periods to a dungeon or solitary confinement."

When the Claimant finally cracked and lost touch

with reality, such as it was, he was transferred to Dannemora, which, although called a "hospital", was essentially a prison with facilities for controlling psychotic convicts. His new home may have been a slight improvement, and the record indicates that after his transfer, his condition improved markedly.

The State repeatedly called attention to the fact that the hospital records repeatedly described Claimant's behavior as paranoid, or in lay terms, that he had delusions of persecution. If a person is, in fact, being treated unjustly or unfairly, the fact that he perceives, resents and reacts to the inequity could hardly be regarded as competent and conclusive evidence of paranoia or paranoid tendencies.

From the testimony and exhibits, there emerged a picture of a man full of despair and defeat, who had been condemned by society and confined for what are ordinarily the most productive years of a person's life. For more than thirty-four years, he remained in custody—first among idiots and imbeciles and then among men living without hope, sitting day in and day out in a big room looking at each other. He was exposed to indignities and degradation which are difficult, if not impossible, to imagine.

That despair might be reasonable under the circumstances is clear. The theft of $5.00 worth of candy precipitated a nightmare lasting for more than thirty-four years.

The conclusion is inescapable that, although the Claimant did become psychotic after several years at Napanoch, the psychosis or the appearance of psychotic symptoms was caused by the nature of his confinement. In a sense, society labeled him as sub-human, placed him in a cage with genuine sub-humans, drove him insane, and then used the insanity as an excuse for holding him indefinitely in an institution with few, if any, facilities for genuine treatment and rehabilitation of the mentally ill.

Although society may have been responsible for whatever disability resulted from Claimant's erroneous classification as a mental defective, there was no evidence that the psychological tests resulting in such classification were not administered or interpreted in accordance with the then accepted standards in the evaluation of mental capacity. The most reasonable assumption is that the tests that were used at that time were almost entirely verbal and that an individual lacking in verbal skills because of a poor educational or family background would almost inevitably tend to do poorly.

Legitimate reasons existed for the segregation of mental defectives, and the Claimant was a victim of the inability of science to devise methods or devices for accurately measuring the traits upon which such segregation had to be based. Thus, although Claimant's rights were obviously violated by being confined at Napanoch, the guilt rests not with the State of New York, but with society in general.

The State is responsible, however, for retaining the Claimant at Dannemora, and the proof not only justifies but compels the conclusion that if the Claimant had been transferred to a civil mental hospital upon the expiration of his sentence or during the four year period commencing in 1936, his chances of leading a productive and satisfactory life would have been good. Instead, however, he was forced to spend twenty-four more years in an institution devoted not to rehabilitation or to curing personality disorders, but to controlling the unfortunates suffering from them. It is precisely this orientation toward control rather than cure which gave rise to whatever compensable damage Claimant suffered.

Statistics were presented with respect to the average wages earned by production employees during the period of Claimant's wrongful imprisonment. The objective yardstick which such statistics might appear to provide must be tempered as far as any purely economic loss is concerned by the fact that even in 1936 Claimant's adjustment to "straight" society would have been difficult. On the other hand, a purely economic approach would not reflect the years of degradation, humiliation and frustration which the Claimant experienced.

The Court believes that no sum of money would be adequate to compensate the Claimant for the injuries he suffered and the scars which he obviously bears. A figure must be set, however, and the Court has concluded that the Claimant is entitled to recover from the State of New York the sum of One Hundred Fifteen Thousand Dollars ($115,000.00).

c.   ST. GEORGE v. STATE
203 Misc. 490, 118 N.Y.S. 2d 596 (1953)

SYLVESTER, JUDGE.

On March 1, 1950, one William Jones, then 19 years of age, was discharged as "recovered" from the Matteawan State Hospital for the Criminal Insane. On March 5, 1950, four days later, he brutally stabbed seven persons, none of whom he had ever seen before of whom four were killed, including Frank St. George. Charging negligence in the release of Jones from Matteawan, this claim is brought by the widow of St. George, as administratrix of his estate, to recover damages for his wrongful death. Jones was admitted to Matteawan on December 23, 1948, having been committed to that institution from the New York State Vocational Institution at Coxsackie, New York, where he had been serving a three-year indeterminate sentence as a Wayward Minor, charged with assault and attempted robbery. The reason for his commitment to Matteawan appears from the following summary of his mental condition which was made at Coxsackie on December 22, 1948, by the prison psychiatrist:

"Began imagining his name was called and that the inmates were making fun of him. Suspicious powder was blown at him. Fought imagined persecutors and threatened to kill an inmate. Change of behavior past three days; quiet, depressed, preoccupied. Strange behavior. Suspicious. Thinks people regard him as going crazy."

The Psychiatric Report prepared at that time contained the following additional comment on Jones' condition:

"Diagnostic summary: Psychosis with psychopathic personality. Paranoid episode.
"Prognosis: Poor. Will likely recover from present paranoid episode although it cannot be said with certainty he may not become schizophrenic.
"Recommendations: Commitment to mental hospital. Too dangerous to others and self to maintain in New York State Vocational Institute at this time."

The Coxsackie records amply substantiated the dangerous nature of Jones' condition. On one occasion, he attacked another inmate and held him by the throat against the wall; on another, when he was refused a minor request, he slammed a window with such force as to break a pane of glass; he started a fight with another inmate because "he looked at me and I didn't like it"; he started still another fight because an inmate "gave him the evil eye"; he repeatedly threatened to kill other inmates; and on one occasion, he was found standing on the top of his bed by a guard, whereupon he got down and with a "wild stare in his eyes," started to pace up and down, "swinging his arms wildly."

* * *

These evidences of psychosis are among the most common indicia of mental disorders accompanied by aggressive and violent behavior. The prison superintendent at Matteawan agreed that frequent assaults "motivated by delusional formation" would have a serious effect in the consideration of the discharge of an inmate. It has been said that "crimes of violence have followed the taunts, the insults, and the threats of the hallucinations of hearing, and one sees in the asylums all kinds of emotional and volitional responses to hallucinations, from cringing fear to desperate anger, from loud and obscene replies to the most belligerent conduct." . . . The "evil eye" is particularly common. "The idea of persecution, of hostility on the part of one's fellows, either in organized groups or as unorganized individuals, appears most conspicuously. In its lesser form it is the delusion of reference—people watch me and talk about me, sneer and laugh at me, slander and revile me." . . .

* * *

No contemporaneous record was made as to the specific circumstances surrounding each of these assaults or instances of disturbed behavior or as to their motivation, though the prison superintendent and head psychiatrist frankly admitted that assaultive behavior must be carefully investigated and analyzed to determine whether it is the result "of a delusional formation" which would indicate a condition of dementia praecox or schizophrenia, as modern psychiatry prefers to denominate this condition. It is to be kept in mind that Jones was subsequently released precisely because it was determined that his assaultive and disturbed behavior was not "of a delusional nature." Yet, many of the assaults which have been referred to were not described as to their character or motivation in the patient's case history. This record is admittedly of fundamental importance in the evaluation of his condition. There was ample psychiatric evidence that a proper evaluation of a patient's mental condition requires that there be available to the psychiatrist a complete record of the patient's prior history and background, including, more importantly, incidents of assaultive or disturbed behavior. . . . Curiously enough, the only entries made at Matteawan concerning Jones assaultive behavior were, with few exceptions, made by attendants in a record referred to as the "ward book" which was not customarily examined by the prison psychiatrists and which was not available to the psychiatrists at staff meetings when the patient was presented for diagnosis. For example, on April 20, 1949, Jones was interviewed by one of the prison psychiatrists who was primarily engaged in administrative work. Based merely upon this interview and a conversation which he had with the attendants, the diagnosis than arrived at was:

"The long antisocial history beginning at an early age, without evidence of mental deficiency or organic pathology, would suggest a psychopathic personality. The alleged hallucinatory experience has been too brief and too limited to assume a schizophrenic basis. It might have merely been misinterpretation and could also have been actual experience. Although he shows a personality make-up which might later develop into a malignant paranoid reaction, the present findings would seem merely to indicate episodes of emotional instability in a psychopathic personality and the diagnosis offered for consideration is psychosis with Psychopathic Personality, Episodes of Emotional Instability."

This diagnosis was approved at a staff meeting held on May 12, 1949. At this meeting, the ward book entries referring to the specific assaults and acts of violence which Jones had committed were not submitted to the physicians. They relied entirely upon the presentation made by the administrative psychiatrist who had interviewed Jones on April 20th and upon the questioning then conducted of Jones who was present at the meeting.
Between May and August 1949, Jones was con-

fined to camisole on at least four separate occasions for fighting or for assaultive behavior. The psychiatrist who had Jones in charge at this time, could not have been familiar with these incidents, since on August 9th, 1949, he included the following memorandum in the patient's case history:

"Since last noted the patient has been pleasant and agreeable with one exception."

The exception referred to in the memorandum, moreover, related to an incident which is not reflected in the ward book. Upon the trial, this psychiatrist, confronted by the entries in the ward book, admitted that his memorandum was in error. He said as to this: "Apparently I have an error here" which he agreed "was carelessly made." On August 30th, 1949, Jones was again presented at a staff meeting and was pronounced recovered. This finding, at least in part, was based upon the concededly erroneous case history.

The prison psychiatrists sought to support their finding of recovery on August 30th by testimony that some of the assaults committed by Jones were, in fact, investigated and were found not to be "motivated by delusional thinking." This testimony, however, was not convincing. The prison psychiatrist who was in charge of Jones at this time testified that Jones "might" have been assaultive because "someone may have called him a name or someone may have been teasing him." What might have happened is, of course, pure speculation. Good caution would seem to have required a more serious appraisement of the circumstance in view of a history punctuated by assaults and disturbed behavior.

Even when a specific assault by Jones was investigated, it appears that no diligent effort was made to probe into its motivation. On June 10, 1948, the "charge attendant" reported to Dr. Proctor that Jones stabbed another patient on the arm with a mechanical pencil. Jones complained that the other patient "would not let him alone." The psychiatrist testified that he could get no information from the other patient and that was the end of the investigation. Moreover, no reference whatsoever was made to this significant incident in the patient's case history. On September 13, 1949, Jones was transferred to another ward under the care of a different psychiatrist. Strangely enough, this psychiatrist did not even read Jones' case history until November 17, 1949, more than two months after Jones was transferred to his care. On at least six occasions in October 1949, entries were made in the ward book reflecting that Jones was disturbed and that on at least one occasion he had to be placed in seclusion because he committed an assault on another inmate. The psychiatrist in charge insisted that he had investigated this assault but nevertheless admitted that his investigation did not include an examination of Jones' case history, a procedure which should have been followed

as testified to by a State expert, who said that in investigating an assault, he would first examine into the inmate's hospital history and study his record. On November 17, 1949, this psychiatrist found that Jones "had been working in a satisfactory manner in the dormitory and has been sociable and co-operative on the ward." No mention or reference was recorded concerning Jones' assaultive behavior in October. On November 27, 1949, Jones committed an assault on an inmate in the wash room. The psychiatrist in charge testified that he was "probably" told about this incident but "it made no impression on him." The ward book indicates that Jones was "disturbed" on ten successive days between January 6th and January 15th, 1950. On January 18th, he was "assaultive" and put in seclusion; on January 19th, he was placed in seclusion as being "assaultive and disturbed"; on January 20th, he committed an assault on another inmate and was put in seclusion; on January 21st, he was put in seclusion as being "disturbed." On January 22nd, he was again put in seclusion. Despite these ward book entries, a memorandum prepared on January 21st by the psychiatrist in charge of his ward and included in the case history, stated:

"He has been sociable with other patients and has carried out the orders of the attendants."

Upon the trial, the prison psychiatrist in charge of Jones, confronted by the ward book entries, admitted that during the month of January, Jones was one of the three most "disturbed" patients in his ward and the most "assaultive."

The inference is inescapable from the record that the prison psychiatrists were never actually aware of the extent and nature of Jones' assaultive and disturbed behavior and that consequently, no substantial effort was made at any time to ascertain delusional motivation for his assaultive conduct. A psychiatrist called by the State testified to the importance of entering in the case record every indication of abnormal behavior. But at Matteawan, the question as to whether a particular act of misbehavior should be entered was left to the discretion of a lay attendant, so that it was conceded that not every assault or disturbance was actually entered even in the ward books. And, admittedly, the entries which were made were not always examined by the psychiatrists in charge.

A State expert unequivocally emphasized the fundamental importance of diligently investigating every assault, whether or not delusionally motivated. He stressed the necessity of a regular examination of the ward books particularly when the patient's release was being considered, at which time these ward books, with their detailed entries relating to the patients' behavior should definitely be available.

The reason for this inattention and neglect is at hand. Provision was made at Matteawan for ten psychiatrists, including the prison superintendent. Of these positions, four were vacant. Furthermore, between December 1948 and March 1st, 1950, the population of the institution ranged from 1650 to 1700, when the capacity of the institution was 1423. According to the testimony of the superintendent of the prison, two psychiatrists were doing the work of six. "The doctors were overworked and the institution was understaffed." It was his opinion that at least two and possibly three psychiatrists should have been assigned to the 500 patients who were under the care of the single psychiatrist who was in charge of Jones. One of the psychiatrists, admitting that he did not look at the ward books, said "he did not have the time to do it."

It was the opinion of experts called by the State, that every conceivable psychiatric precaution was taken in the release of Jones. Claimant's psychiatrists, on the other hand, testified that no diagnosis other than schizophrenia could have been made upon the basis of the records and that Jones should not have been released.

There was, in this case, psychiatric evidence that if delusions cannot be elicited even upon thorough investigation, a constant pattern of assaults is significant, particularly where the patient is the aggressor. This would signify that the patient is laboring from a delusion which is deep-rooted and which he is concealing. "Even patients who are almost incessantly occupied with their hallucinations and are influenced by them, consequently cannot even with the best of intentions give any account of them when they are questioned about them." (Bleuler, *Textbook on Psychiatry*, pages 389, 390.)

It is true that there were periods of time at Matteawan during which Jones was comparatively well behaved. But there was ample psychiatric evidence that remissions must not be confused with recovery, particularly where a period of good behavior is followed by further outbreaks of violence and aggression. As is pointed out in Jelliffe and White, *Diseases of the Nervous System*, "remissions are quite the rule. Often patients get along very well in an institution, but become upset shortly after going back to the conditions under which the conflict developed." Here, as has been noted, brief periods of remission were followed by further outbreaks of violence. A psychiatrist, called by the State, candidly admitted that if Jones were in fact disturbed day after day, and engaged in assaults as the aggressor, "he would be glad to change the testimony" which he had given to the effect that every psychiatric precaution had been taken in releasing Jones.

The evidence in this case clearly establishes that Jones was disturbed and assaultive on numerous occasions throughout his stay at Matteawan; that many of these incidents were not entered in the ward book; that even those incidents which were entered in the ward book were not examined by the psychiatrist in charge, and were not reflected in the patient's case history; that the determination made on August 30, 1949, that Jones was recovered, was based at least in part upon a concededly erroneous case history; that no substantial effort was ever made at any time to inquire into the motivation for the assaultive behavior of Jones; that admittedly, if Jones' assaultive and disturbed behavior was characterized by delusions, he would have been found psychotic and would not have been released; that the pattern of behavior shown by Jones throughout his stay at Matteawan was strikingly similar to that revealed at Coxsackie, upon the basis of which Jones had been committed to Matteawan as being too dangerous to himself and to the other inmates to be kept even at a prison institution; and that the psychiatrists who determined that Jones could be released never had the opportunity or the facilities to properly inquire into Jones' mental condition in order properly to evaluate his condition.

It was admitted by the superintendent of Matteawan that the diagnosis ultimately arrived at was erroneous and should have been "schizophrenia" of the paranoid type. He claims that the mistake could not have been avoided. The record proves the contrary. Had there been adequate facilities, had two psychiatrists not been doing the work of six, had entries been made in the ward books of each assault and incident of disturbed behavior, had the ward books been present at staff meetings, and had the psychiatrist in charge had the time and opportunity to investigate each incident of assault and disturbed behavior, the existence of delusions and hallucinations would have been ascertained and it is reasonable to believe that Jones' condition would then have been diagnosed either as psychosis with psychopathic personality or as schizophrenia, and in either event Jones would not have been released.

The deplorable condition of overcrowding and understaffing that prevailed at the institution makes it obvious from all the evidence that the institution's psychiatrists were simply unable to adequately administer their responsibilities and make sound clinical judgments due to the indicated handicaps. Thus, there was a failure of proper supervision and care by reason of the fact that the institution's psychiatrists were not afforded a reasonable opportunity to keep themselves informed of the true condition of Jones; and that they in fact failed and omitted to exercise the usual and approved techniques and procedures of the psychiatric therapeutist in the care and treatment of Jones and in determining the propriety of his discharge, all of which ultimated in the negligent discharge of Jones and the killing of the decedent.

The public is entitled to protection against dangerous psychotics. The State, having assumed to care for and treat a mental incompetent confined to its care on the basis of a psychiatric finding that he was too dangerous to himself and to others to be maintained even in a penal institution, was obliged to exercise a reasonable degree of care and attention in the proper treatment and psychiatric evaluation of the patient.

In *Flaherty* v. *State of New York*, 73 N.E. 2d 543, 544, it was said, per Fuld, J.:

> "The law is clear; it is only in its application that difficulty is encountered. The State—just as any other party . . . is responsible, in the operation and management of its schools, hospitals, and other institutions, only for hazards reasonably to be foreseen, only for risks reasonably to be perceived. . . ."

*   *   *

The overcrowding of state institutions and the inadequacy of supervisory personnel have frequently been held to establish negligence against the State. . . . In this case, the State had ample warning of Jones' pre-disposition to violence. The duty of the State being thus clearly defined, its failure to institute and carry out the procedure dictated by accepted psychiatric practice rendered the State liable for the resulting injury.

*   *   *

NOTES

NOTE 1

ST. GEORGE v. STATE
283 App. Div. 245, 127 N.Y.S. 2d 147 (1954)

COON, JUSTICE:

*   *   *

There is no claim or suggestion that the staff doctors who had Jones in charge at Matteawan were incompetent or unqualified. Claimant urges that Matteawan was overcrowded and understaffed, and that the diagnosis of Jones' condition was made upon inadequate observation and information. There is a contention that some incidents in his behavior were not recorded, and that some things that were recorded were not presented at the staff meetings. The record discloses, however, that a great deal of attention was given to Jones. He was personally interviewed and examined by the Superintendent about ten times during his stay there. Voluminous reports by attendants and doctors recording even minor incidents were presented to the staff meetings, his history at Coxsackie was before the staff, and his case was considered at considerable length at several staff meetings during his stay there of about fourteen months. If any incident affecting Jones was omitted it was of the same nature and part of the same pattern as the voluminous material before the staff meetings. The record

discloses entirely adequate material in the case record of Jones for purposes of diagnosis, and one of claimant's experts so testified.

About the last of August, 1949, according to the testimony, the staff had reached a conclusion that Jones had sufficiently recovered to be considered for release except that his sentence had not expired. The doctors did not consider it for his best interest to return him to Coxsackie so he was continued at Matteawan until his term expired on March 1, 1950. In the interval the record indicates that his condition was closely observed, and despite some incidents, the doctors felt he was improving. It is impractical and unnecessary to set forth in detail the case record of Jones at Matteawan. At times it shows him to be quiet and co-operative, engaging in sports and getting along well with others. At times it shows an assaultive disposition with numerous instances of disobedience, quarrels, scuffles, and altercations with other inmates, at least many of which were provoked by the other inmates. The record does not disclose that in any of these occurrences was any injury inflicted upon any one, and most of the difficulties would appear to be petty and such as might occur among any group of boys confined together, even normal ones, and, of course, Jones concededly was not normal, nor were his fellow inmates.

The diagnosis of mental cases is not an exact science. As yet the mind cannot be X-rayed like a bone fracture. Diagnosis with absolute precision and certainty is impossible. One of claimant's experts readily admits having made mistakes in diagnoses, yet says of the Matteawan doctors "They made a mistake." It has been recognized that insanity is difficult of detection, and frequently is cunningly concealed. . . . Of necessity it must be a matter of judgment by those qualified to pass judgments. It was the duty of the staff doctors at Matteawan to treat Jones and to use every effort to improve his condition, not just to confine him. The modern concept of handling cases of mental illness is treatment, not simply incarceration. The objective is to return the patient to society, which should be done as soon as, in the judgment of properly qualified doctors and psychiatrists, it is likely to be safe for others and helpful to the patient. Believing as they did, after observing Jones, discussing his case, and reading voluminous reports from attendants, the doctors could not have justified his detention had he sought habeas corpus on March 1, 1950. As indicated above, there is no suggestion that the staff doctors were not competent and qualified and properly educated and trained, and there is no suggestion in the record that they were not sincere and conscientious in making their diagnosis.

Thus the issue is narrowed to this: Are the doctors, or is the State which employs them, legally responsible in damages for an honest error of professional judgment made by qualified and competent persons?

We think this question must be answered in the negative. It has been so held in malpractice cases of all types for years. . . . Future human behavior is unpredictable, and it would place an unreasonable and unfair burden upon the State if it were to be held responsible in damages for everything that a person does after he has been discharged or released from one of its State institutions, even though the release was through an error of judgment, unless there is something more present than is contained in this record.

* * *

The "escape" cases . . . are readily distinguishable. In those cases it was *known* that the patient was suffering from a type of insanity requiring confinement and should not be at large and might do harm. The negligence lay in permitting the escape.

In considering this case it is difficult to free the mind from the events of March 5, 1950, subsequent to Jones' release, and "second guessing" is easy, but the diagnosis in question here was made before those events occurred and with no reasonable basis for anticipating that they ever would occur. Likewise, the case presents a strong sympathetic appeal. An innocent person was killed for no reason at all, yet that is one of the risks of living in modern society. Many innocent people lose their lives or are injured by insane persons who have never been committed to an institution; by criminals, and by accidents of all sorts and descriptions for which they were in no way responsible.

To sustain this judgment would have a more far reaching effect than the money damages. In its practical aspects it would mean that the State could release no one from any State mental institution without being under the risk of liability for whatever he did thereafter, and the result would necessarily be reluctance to release and the unnecessary confinement of persons who would benefit by release. . . .

* * *

NOTE 2

FAHEY v. UNITED STATES
153 F. Supp. 878 (S.D. N.Y. 1957)

* * *

LEVET, DISTRICT JUDGE:

This action, tried by this court without a jury, was brought under the Federal Tort Claims Act. . . . The plaintiffs' intestate, Eileen Fahey, a young woman of some 18 years, was shot and killed on July 14, 1952, by one Baynard P. Peakes, a demented war veteran. As a result of this tragic death, the administrators have sued the United States of America on the ground that its alleged negligence in permitting Peakes to be at large permitted the happening of the unfortunate occurrence.

* * *

The plaintiffs in effect are contending that since Peakes once served in the United States Army, the Federal government should thereafter be responsible to the public for failure to commit him irrespective of the cause of his disability. The Federal government has no consitutional or inherent power to commit. . . . Indeed, no authority seems to exist whereby any government, Federal or State, or any individual has been held liable for *failure to commit*. Many cases have held hospitals responsible for acts of *patients* who had escaped custody or committed improper acts while in custody. . . .

* * *

4.

WHO SHOULD BE RESPONSIBLE FOR FINANCING CUSTODY AND TREATMENT?

DEPARTMENT OF MENTAL HYGIENE v.
KIRCHNER*
60 Cal. 2d 716, 36 Cal. Rep. 6201, 388 P.2d 720 (1964)

SCHAUER, JUSTICE:

Defendant administratrix appeals from a judgment on the pleadings, in the sum of $7,554.22, entered against her in an action by the Department of Mental Hygiene of the State of California to recover the alleged cost of care, support, maintenance, and medical attention supplied to Auguste Schaeche, mother of defendant's intestate, as a committed inmate of a state institution for the mentally ill. As will appear, we have concluded that the statute upon which the judgment is based violates the basic constitutional guaranty of equal protection of the law, and that the judgment should be reversed.

Plaintiff in its complaint alleges in substance that in January 1953 the mother, Mrs. Schaeche, was adjudged mentally ill and by the court committed to Agnews State Hospital where she had remained under confinement to the date the complaint was filed in April 1961; that the decedent, Elinor Vance, was Mrs. Schaeche's daughter "and as such was legally responsible" for her committed mother's care and maintenance at Agnews; that pursuant to section 6651 of the Welfare and Institutions Code the Director of Mental Hygiene determined the rate for such care and maintenance, and "said charges were made continuously for every month" Mrs. Schaeche was a "patient" at Agnews; that for the period of August 25, 1956, through August 24, 1960, such charges totaled $7,554.22, none of which had been paid; that the daughter died on August 25, 1960, and in November 1960 plaintiff filed against the daughter's estate its creditor's claim for $7,554.22, which was rejected, and which sum plaintiff now seeks to recover.

_____

*Vocated 380 U.S. 194 (1965). For subsequent disposition by California Supreme Court sec: 43 Cal. Rep. 329, 400 P.2d 321 (1965).

[D]efendant directly challenges the right of a state to statutorily impose liability upon, and collect from, one adult for the cost of supporting another adult whom the state has committed to one of its hospitals for the mentally ill or insane. . . .

In support of the judgment plaintiff department relies upon the declaration in section 6650 of the Welfare and Institutions Code that "The husband, wife, father, mother, or *children* of a mentally ill person or inebriate . . . shall be liable for his care, support, and maintenance in a state institution of which he is an inmate . . ." (Italics added.)

. . . In Thrasher [234 P.2d 230, 235–236 (1951) it was held] that the husband of an incompetent committed to a state mental hospital was under the duty to support her therein even though she had estate of her own. That case is of small help to plaintiff here; manifestly, the basic obligation and relevant status of the husband arose from the marriage contract to which he was a consenting party and no consideration was given to the question as to whether imposing liability upon one spouse for support of the other in a state institution denies equal protection of the law to the servient spouse. . . .

Recently in *Department of Mental Hygiene* v. *Hawley* (1963) 59 . . . 379 P.2d 22, the department, relying upon this same section 6650, attempted to collect from a father for the cost of care, support, and maintenance in a state hospital for the mentally ill or insane of his son who had been charged with crime, but before trial of the criminal issue (and obviously without adjudication of that issue) had been found by the court to be insane and committed to such state hospital. We there held . . . that "The enactment and administration of laws providing for sequestration and treatment of persons in appropriate state institutions—subject of course, to the constitutional guaranties—who would endanger themselves or others if at large is a proper state function; being so, it follows that the expense of providing, operating, and maintaining such institutions should (subject to reasonable exceptions *against the inmate or his estate*) be borne by the state." (Italics added.) We further held that recovery could not constitutionally be had against the father of the committed patient. This holding is dispositive of the issue before us. Whether the commitment is incidental to an alleged violation of a penal statute, as in Hawley, or is essentially a civil commitment as in the instant case, the purposes of confinement and treatment or care in either case encompass the protection of society from the confined person, and his own protection and possible reclamation as a productive member of the body politic. Hence the cost of maintaining the state institution, including provision of adequate care of its inmates, cannot be arbitrarily charged to one class in the society; such assessment violates the equal protection clause.

Although numerous cases can be cited wherein so-called support statutes have been sustained against various attacks, research has disclosed no cases which squarely faced, considered, discussed and sustained such statutes in the light of the basic question as to equal protection of the law in a case wherein it was sought to impose liability upon one person for the support of another in a state institution. . . .

*   *   *

[I]n resolving the issue now before us, we need not blind ourselves to the social evolution which has been developed during the past half century; it has brought expanded recognition of the *parens patriae* principle . . . and other social responsibilities, including the California Rehabilitation Center Act (added Stats. 1961, ch. 850, p. 2228) and divers other public welfare programs to which all citizens are contributing through presumptively duly apportioned taxes. From all of this it appears that former concepts which have been suggested to uphold the imposition of support liability upon a person selected by an administrative agent from classes of relatives designated by the Legislature may well be re-examined. Illustrative of California's acceptance of this principle is the provision of section 6655 of the Welfare and Institutions Code that payment for the case and support of a patient at a state hospital "shall not be exacted . . . if there is likelihood of the patient's recovery or release from the hospital and payment will reduce his estate to such an extent that he is likely to become a burden on the community in the event of his discharge from the hospital." Thus, the state evidences concern that its committed patient shall not "become a burden on the community in the event of his discharge from the hospital," but at the same time its advocacy of the case at bench would seem to indicate that it cares not at all that relatives of the patient, selected by a department head, be denuded of *their* assets in order to reimburse the state for its maintenance of the patient in a tax supported institution. Section 6650 by its terms imposes absolute liability upon, and does not even purport to vest in, the servient relatives any right of control over, or to recoup from, the assets of the patient. A statute obviously violates the equal protection clause if it selects one particular class of persons for a species of taxation and no rational basis supports such classification. . . . Such a concept for the state's taking of a free man's property manifestly denies him equal protection of the law.

*   *   *

The judgment is reversed and the cause is remanded with directions to enter judgment for defendant.

*   *   *

PART FOUR

TO WHAT EXTENT AND WHY IS MENTAL HEALTH RELEVANT TO DECISIONS CONCERNING COMPETENCY?

In this Part the focus shifts from decisions concerning commitment, custody, care, treatment, and release of the "mentally ill" to decisions concerning the competency of individuals to perform various functions. Put another way, thus far primary emphasis has been on the general competency of individuals to be at large in the community; here, primary emphasis is on the specific competency of individuals to engage in certain activities, to qualify for particular exemptions, or to attain special status. Congress has recognized the desirability of distinguishing between decisions concerning institutionalization and those concerning competence for more specific purposes. The District of Columbia Hospitalization of the Mentally Ill Act provides:

> "No patient hospitalized pursuant to this act shall, by reason of such hospitalization, be denied the right to dispose of property, execute instruments, make purchases, enter into contractual relationships, vote, and hold a driver's license, unless such patient has been adjudicated incompetent by a court of competent jurisdiction and has not been restored to legal capacity. . . ."*

As "the problem of normality . . . can be put in the form of the question . . . 'normal for what?',† so the question of competency must be put, 'competency for what purpose?'" Thus we ask: To what extent and why should such determination as "mentally ill," "dangerous," "insane," "commitable" or "incompetent" be relevant to decisions concerning an individual's qualific-

---

*D.C. Code § 21–564 (Supp. 1966).
†See Redlich, F. C., p. 522, supra.

753

ations to exercise a variety of rights and privileges associated with citizenship, to hold a variety of jobs, or to be subject to a variety of liabilities?

In posing these questions we first examine some problems regarding an individual's qualifications to assume responsibility for the well-being of others and then to an individual's qualifications to assume responsibility for his own welfare.

A.

To Assume Responsibility for the Well-being of Others

1.

AS A GUARDIAN OF NATIONAL SECURITY

DEPARTMENT OF THE AIR FORCE

Guidance for Implementing the Human Reliability Program*

1. *Introduction.* [T]he objectives of the Human Reliability Program are to reduce, so far as possible, the occurrence of acts which could lead to an unauthorized detonation or launch. The term "prevention" is used in this manual only in a general sense, since strictly speaking it is impossible to prevent *all* unauthorized destructive acts. The goal of this program is to reduce by continuing research, education, selection, and screening the human potential for such acts.

* * *

3. *Avoiding Nuclear Accidents.* Modern weapons and weapon systems are intricate and complex. This situation requires that individuals who control the weapons, have access to, or control access must be continually alert and able to perform full duty. This duty, especially in the time of "cold war," imposes conditions of continuing stress which have never before existed. The destructiveness of nuclear weapons is so great that an unauthorized explosion would create untold havoc and extreme political repercussions. This manual provides information to assist in insuring and maintaining a high level of human reliability as one of the prime means of avoiding such a nuclear accident.

* * *

5. *The Unreliable.* There is no place in our nuclear weapons program for the easily bored, impulsive, neurotic, or psychotic individual. An airman or officer so assigned has a high responsibility to his country. Individuals who by reason of emotional disorder, personality make-up, character deficit, or

*AFM 16U–SS, 1962, (pp. 1-20).

habit are unable to consistently perform at a high level of efficiency have no place in this program. In many cases these persons can be discovered by careful selection before they are assigned. Others already in the program can be screened out only by continuing evaluation. This is necessary to locate and eliminate the possibly unreliable who have given some indication in their way of life that they are not capable of dealing with the tremendous stresses involved in such an assignment.

6. *Stress Factor.* Stress is a burden to all and a continuing load of stress can eventually wear down a good man. It has been clearly shown in war that flyers perform better when specific end points are established. An example of this is the clear definition of the number of missions in a rotation program. In the present "cold war" situation it is difficult to set limits on stress. Long periods of waiting and boredom are not conducive to alertness. Even periodic alerts and "dry-runs" only partially serve to stimulate motivation and tend over months and years to become boring and commonplace. Yet each man must remain aware that constant readiness is required. This is a difficult and stressful state for the human personality to maintain.

7. *Worry Factor.* Any external cause may produce a situation in which a normal individual responds by tension, insomnia, worry, etc. A man who is worried about his wife's fidelity or spending habits may become so upset he is unable to function in his usual manner. He might also be worried about his own excessive drinking, gambling, spending, or extramarital activity. Under these conditions tension arises which lowers reliability.

* * *

12. *Selection Requirements.* Optimum Personnel Selection Requirements for the Human Reliability Program are as follows:

a. The minimal recommended educational level is high school graduation. This requirement is not used as an index of academic achievement, but is based on experience and research which clearly establishes that high school graduates better adapt themselves to arduous routines, have a better capacity for remaining mentally alert under situations which produce boredom, and can conform to discipline with less impulsive activity than those who do not complete high school. Non-high school graduates generally reflect a greater inability to withstand stress to the necessary degree required for performing weapons duties. . . .

b. When the physical profile rating is available, it must include an S1 (Stability). This indicates that the individual has never had a recognizable personality or emotional disorder. Since a history of such disorders are disqualifying, the reason for this requirement is obvious. In officers, where no physical profile is available, the physical and mental examination for selection should in all cases be detailed enough to determine that the individual has no history of personality or emotional disorder.

c. The Mental Hygiene Clinic at Lackland Air Force Base examines and provides the final clearance for those airmen to be trained in the nuclear maintenance field. If a person who has been previously granted an S1 profile shows, when interviewed, some evidence or history of emotional disturbance, marked immaturity, or impulsive behavior, he is not cleared by the Mental Hygiene Clinic.

* * *

e. When available, an inquiry by the OSI into the family and developmental history as part of the background investigation, would provide the commander and medical officer with important data about the individual. Research to provide an expanded Background Investigation is currently being conducted.

f. Officers are required to meet high physical standards when commissioned. This work-up includes a thorough physical examination, a review of personal history and data on educational background, and general interviews. . . .

g. When selecting personnel for assignment, it should be noted that the commander's and physician's interviews and the review of all records (personal and medical), may give a clue to some hidden problem. Whenever medical records are available on members of an applicant's family, particularly his spouse, they should also be reviewed by the medical officer. A wife who has a long involved medical record of treatment for minor medical or emotional problems may place much stress on her husband and lower his effectiveness. Family medical records may give clues which point to stress. Families with long records of treatment for minor medical or emotional illnesses may be having problems which are more personal than medical. Many symptoms are due to worry over problems in living, and an interview may define the problem so the individual can do something about it. In this sensitive area gossip and rumors

must be clearly evaluated. Personal knowledge of infidelity or alcoholism on the part of the spouse are matters that call for tact, judgment, and action by the commander, but they do not necessarily come under the scope of Human Reliability Program.

* * *

16. *Introduction.* The following discussion is presented to give all personnel involved in the Human Reliability Program a better understanding of the kind of persons who should not be included in our nuclear weapon programs. In many cases the individual will appear to some physicians or commanders to be "normal." The following description of groups prone to unreliability will help evaluate the "in between" cases as to their elimination or retention.

17. *Identifying the More Apparent Disorders.* It is not usually difficult to identify by thoughtful interview and records review the prospective assignee whose social, educational, and occupational behavior indicates any of the following traits:

a. Hostility towards his country.

b. Evidence of accident proneness.

c. Evidence of repeated failure to perceive or understand directions or orders.

d. History of serious mental disorder.

e. Gross and continuing forms of mental illness are usually obvious to medical history and pre-assignment interview.

18. *Concealed Mental Disorders.* More important, and certainly much more difficult to detect, are the concealed but latent mental disorders. Aberrant thinking may be experienced in awareness while being consciously denied, or it may be quite out of awareness and yet active as a potential for aberrant behavior.

19. *Dominant Causative Factors.* Three general categories of mental disorder, SUSPICIOUS, IMPULSIVE, and SEMICONSCIOUS, are relevant to unauthorized destructive acts as possible dominant causative factors. Section B, C, and D deal with these three categories, and describe the early signs in observable behavior that strongly suggest the possibility of present or emerging mental disorder. These clues are useful also in detecting personality types inconsistent with sensitive job assignment. The information is intended to help the responsible superior directly observe such behavior and critically evaluate indirect reports as they come to his attention.

20. *Early Identification.* In the majority of instances these signs will predominately relate to and indicate the emergence of one of three disorders. Any individual whose potential for reliability of performance is decreasing may show various signs or clues described under any of the three categories. It must also be clearly understood that there will always be a certain incidence of malicious or "accidental" destructive acts for which no warning signs are pres-

ent, or have been noticed. The practical goal of early identification is to reduce the number of such unauthorized destructive acts, granted that their total elimination is not yet humanly possible.

21. *The Paranoid Group.* The first of these large groups is the paranoid thinking group. This group is, by far, the most potentially dangerous and is believed responsible for the highest incidence of senseless destructive acts.

22. *Cases of Paranoid Condition in Assassination Attempts.* Of the seven assassination attempts on the lives of the Presidents of the United States, the assassin in six instances was clearly a paranoid personality or paranoid schizophrenic. None was previously known as a criminal. After the assassination or attempted assassination, people who had known each of the six commented on their previous peculiarities and eccentricities. None of the six had been hospitalized for mental illness. In six instances, the individual acted alone and with considerable planning, foresight, and intent. In the unsuccessful attempt on President Truman's life, which involved two men, subsequent study showed no clear evidence of mental disorder. The paranoid condition, even to the practiced observer, may not be clearly apparent for years before it does become overt. It must be remembered that an unauthorized destructive act is a rare event even among the paranoid group.

23. *Paranoid Traits.* The following clues, seen in the behavior of the paranoid group of reactions are not of themselves in any single instance diagnostic, since many of the traits enumerated are sometimes seen in normal everyday behavior. Observing several of these traits in a single individual should arouse the interest of the responsible supervisor or superior.

a. Arrogance—wherein the individual assumes or presumes the possession of superior, unique or bizarre abilities, ideas, or theories.

b. Lack of humor—especially the inability to laugh at onself, one's mistakes, or weaknesses.

c. Constant jealousy, suspicion, and envy.

d. Inflexibility—especially in accepting new ideas originating among others.

e. Preoccupation with one or more ideas, to the relative exclusion of almost all other thoughts, so that relationships with others are strained and range of interests severely narrowed.

f. Sensitivity related to status where the individual is overly concerned with being left out, ignored, ridiculed, or talked about.

g. The tendency to develop and hold grudges and inability to overlook or forget unimportant differences of opinion.

h. Overalertness to real or fancied personal slights or departures by others from codes or regulations.

i. Preoccupation with historical, factual references relating to the individual's intense belief in his special competence or capability.

j. Exaggerated tendency to argue—often accompanied by the development of a personal logic to support a view usually not held by others.

k. Hypochondriasis and resultant disagreement with doctors who are pictured as not understanding. Such bodily concerns are often intensified and may be bizarre.

l. Legal or quasi-legal controversy about pay, time, accidents, unsatisfactory purchases, or matter of authority. This is often seen in conjunction with "letters to the editor" or "to the president of the company."

m. Common factors to all the above are poorly controlled chronic hostility and suspicion which may or may not be easily discerned. In military (war) situations, this chronic hostility may be drained off by reason of the military assignment, but there are not such opportunities in peacetime.

24. *Transition from Latent to Overt Paranoid Psychosis.* Symptoms of the transitional period from latent to overt paranoid psychosis occur almost always with progress from feelings of being slighted or overlooked to feelings of being ignored, and thence to ideas of being watched, slandered, attacked, or in some ways become the object of hostile action or intent on the part of others. *Fortunately, few people who are latently paranoid develop a paranoid psychosis and of those that do, fewer still commit violent acts.*

25. *Additional Signs of Paranoid Tendencies.* Muscular tension and rigidity, preoccupation with bodily functions, bodily complaints, and (almost invariably) serious insomnia are additional signs of paranoid tendencies. Lack of sleep from outside influences such as overtime work and emergencies may result in a fatigue state with transient irritability and feelings of being imposed upon. If not relieved by adequate rest this may progress to actual paranoid behavior.

26. *Transient Neurosis and Psychosis.* There is recent evidence that social isolation and prolonged boredom tend to make some normal individuals neurotic, at least transiently, and to make others transiently psychotic. Physiological or drug-induced changes which also alter consciousness and emotional reactions are: severe physical illness, head injury, alcoholic or drug intoxication, serious lack of water, near starvation, or existence in an atmosphere of lowered oxygen content.

27. *Predisposing Factors.* Among the most important predisposing psychological factors which lead from a latent to an overt paranoid state are significant changes in the personal status of the individual as they relate to prestige, and the assumption of or release from responsibility. These factors range from marriage to divorce or bereavement, becoming engaged or breaking an engagement, becoming a parent; and in academic, occupational, or military service, the fact of promotion or demotion. Being

placed under investigation is a particularly potent stress for the latently paranoid individual.

28. *The Paranoid Schizophrenic.* Unfortunately, the paranoid schizophrenic with his delusions of grandeur and need for omnipotence becomes a much greater potential hazard in space and thermonuclear age in which a single psychotic destructive act may endanger the lives of millions of people. The psychotic thinking accompanying such an act may evolve from the desire to seek fame or recognition even at the cost of the individual's own life, or a delusion of being divinely or supernaturally chosen to carry out a "mission" in defiance of established authority.

* * *

30. *Descriptive Terms.* The second large group of disorders, while difficult to differentiate technically, is not difficult to describe. Lack of control of those impulses which endanger the individual and alarm and endanger others is the main characteristic. Some of the common psychiatric descriptive terms for this group are as follows: constitutional psychopathic inferior, psychopath, sociopath, perverse personality, impulsive personality, neurotic character, infantile character, kleptomaniac (pathological stealing), pyromaniac (fire bug). The "Handbook of Standard Nomenclature," prepared by the American Psychiatric Association for the American Medical Association uses the following terms: antisocial reaction, emotional instability reaction, passive-aggressive personality-aggressive type, personality trait disturbance-infantile personality. The Army uses, in addition, the terms "pathological personality" and "immature personality." These terms are listed only to underscore the technical difficulty of differentiating these conditions.

31. *Some Characteristics.* Unlike the paranoid, the impulse-ridden individual does not plan his destructive acts over a period of time but acts on sudden impulse. A possible exception is the pyromaniac or fire bug, but even in this instance, while the desire or impulse to start a fire may be present, the precise site is not generally planned in advance. This situation is different from arson, where the goal is financial gain or criminal sabotage. The arsonist group includes, for example, a group of angry employees or enemy agents firing a mill or industrial plant. Only a close study of the individual's life history—developmental, academic and occupational—can indicate proneness to impulsive destruction.

32. *Self-Destructive Acts.* The many instances in the military service of those who pull the grenade pin to see what will happen and who play Russian roulette speak for themselves. Such seemingly foolish, if not stupid, acts are well known to the military. In almost all such instances, the individual in question has been repeatedly trained, instructed, and warned that such an act is self-destructive and is punishable by military law.

33. *Impulsive Theft.* Another comparable and publicized act is the take-off of an aircraft, civilian or military, by an unauthorized or untrained individual. In civilian life there is the discouragingly high incidence of impulsive theft of automobiles by impulse-ridden adolescent boys. It is psychiatrically significant that such impulsive acts as automobile thefts and fire setting are committed almost exclusively by young males. The hypothesis that there must be an inherent sexual conflict represented in these aberrant impulsive acts is based on statistical facts and the obvious sexual connotations in many carefully studied instances.

34. *Other Kinds of Impulsive Behavior.* Impulsive destructive behavior may not result in personal injury but, nevertheless, act to the serious detriment of the individual. For example, an Air Force general found two huge initials scratched on the door of the immaculately maintained aircraft he was scheduled to use. The initials were immediately found to be those of the Air Force policemen who, the previous night, had been responsible for sentry duty at this site. Of a different sort are the impulsive acts which constitute vengeful or meaningless sabotage, as when a handful of washers were thrown into the air intakes of a number of jet fighters staked down on a military airfield.

35. *Motivation.* The motivation of these acts is most perplexing. In the instances of personal self-destruction, as represented by "Russian Roulette" or grenade pin-pulling, there is evidence of intense childish braggadocio and the need to demonstrate fearlessness. The individual's personal need to demonstrate fearlessness or self-assertiveness must logically be in proportion to an equal or greater sense of personal inadequacy. Resentment toward superiors and authority figures may lead to destructive acts of malicious firesetting. But when long-range planning is involved, the indication is away from the impulse-ridden and toward the paranoid group characterized by the presence of delusions.

36. *Identifying the Impulse-Ridden Individual.* The clues that identify the impulse-ridden personality are mainly historical. A careful academic, occupational, and service history should indicate impulsive tendencies. In military services such behavior and immaturity of judgment will ordinarily be seen in basic training, especially in reaction to discipline, regular routine, and competitive performance situations. More important in the interest of good reliability management is the identification of those impulse-ridden individuals who escape *early* detection and identify themselves only after long observation or the ocurrence of a flagrant violation. There are certain common clues. Not uniquely diagnostic in one or two instances, the clues gain in significance as the incidence increases. These indicators are:

a. History of impulsive behavior in childhood such

as theft, running away, vandalism, and switch-blade fighting.

b. Unusually quick recovery from apparent anxiety, depression, or stress, which indicates only a shallow emotional involvement and a quick response to the environment.

c. Easy casual friendships in contradistinction to the paranoid. The impulsive person seeks friends and is superficially very friendly while the paranoid is withdrawn and suspicious.

d. Bursts of anger, sulking, or pouting over small things.

e. Glib explanations for personal errors.

f. Deceptive readiness to acknowledge failure or error.

g. Persistent boyishness or infectious "charm."

h. Playing a role of naivete or innocence, usually calculated to impress colleagues or superiors with one's sincerity.

i. Morbid eagerness to gossip with excitement about disasters, catastrophes, acts of violence, or destruction.

j. Attempts to play off one group against another, or attempting too obviously or eagerly to align oneself on the side of authority or the majority group.

k. Shallow loyalties to friends, shifting constantly toward symbols of power or wealth, with rarely solid, continuing, mature, shared respect for others as in a "buddy" relationship.

l. Frequent job changes or requests for such, attended by brief bursts of enthusiasm which lapse into poor performance, followed by another burst of enthusiasm and request for a new job assignment.

m. Sullen irritability, boredom, and restless behavior, with or without outspoken wishes for changes and excitement.

n. The tendency to "show off," with resentment of others who may be temporarily the principal focus of the group's attention. It should be noted that under exceptional circumstances, such as great general excitement, peril, or imminent catastrophe, these individuals may function temporarily well or even heroically. This is *not* to say all heroes are impulse-ridden individuals.

37. *Assignments Appealing to the Impulsive.* Impulse-ridden individuals often seek jobs as firemen or policemen which offer useful and socially acceptable means of satisfying impulsive needs. Again, this is *not* to say that all policemen, firemen, etc. are impulse-ridden persons. Dangerous weapons, explosives, or fires, have special appeal to the impulsive. Elaborate safety precautions may be carried out while under observation, but when unobserved by superiors impulsive persons may act in a foolhardy fashion.

38. *Situations Precipitating Breakdown.* As in a paranoid state, the following situations may precipitate a temporary but perhaps fatal breakdown in impulse control:

a. Prolonged lack of sleep due to imsomnia or lack of opportunity to sleep during emergency situations and overtime job assignments.

b. Clouding of consciousness by any of the common physiologic causes—severe physical illness, head injury, prolonged water or food deprivation. Perhaps the most important is alcohol intoxication. Witness the innumerable (normal?) impulsive destructive acts committed by college boys after football games or the furniture breaking and brawling of the manual laborer on a Saturday night spree.

c. Social isolation, prolonged boredom, and lack of changes in immediate experience have a debilitating effect upon both impulse control and alertness. Research into this problem, generally referred to as "sensory deprivation" research, has shown that normal men may become disoriented, have hallucinations, and even become delusional if kept too long at boring tasks in isolation.

d. Changes in personal responsibility or rank, especially as in demotion, may trigger impulsive destructive acts. Loss of favor with a powerful authority may act in the same way. The sullen response to disappointment and the sometimes excess exhuberance following promotion contain some danger of impulsive behavior.

e. Group taunts, skepticism, or admiration may cause an impulse-ridden individual to attempt or carry out destructive acts as a method of proving himself.

39. *Disorders Included in This Group.* The third general group of disorders which might lead to unauthorized destructive action, includes some forms of epilepsy, pathological intoxication (crazy drunk), and a collection of emotional reactions characterized by clouding of consciousness (for example, amnesia, wandering, change of identity, fugue state). *Any individual in the presence of overwhelming anxiety or panic may have impaired awareness. These situations can hardly be anticipated. Normal people recover full awareness when such an emergency is over.*

40. *Epilepsy.* Petit mal epilepsy is the name for frequent brief trance-like states in which the person is momentarily speechless or briefly stops his work and appears out of contact with his surroundings. Another uncommon epileptic form is the continuous blind rage, the epileptic furor, which is seen only in chronic epileptics. Psychomotor epilepsy (or epileptic equivalent), is not the typical epileptic fit characterized by a fall, rigidity, and convulsion. In this state the individual bursts into rages or automatically continues an activity without memory, even though the external situations would indicate stopping or shifting to another activity. (The incidence of psychomotor epilepsy is only one per 20,000 enlisted men.) Epilepsy in all its forms is usually revealed in a candid medical history or background investigations. Since epilepsy,

as described, rarely begins in adult years, a first fit or convulsion in the adult is usually a sign of disease of the brain. This may be caused by infection, intoxication with alcohol or drugs, or the result of a brain tumor.

41. *Pathological Alcohol Intoxication (Crazy Drunk)*. This somewhat uncommon form of mental disorder constitutes a reason for nonemployment based on emotional unsuitability. In these instances, the individual seems to be specifically "allergic" to alcohol. Even with a single drink, large or small, he will suddenly become enraged or extremely excited, confused, agitated, or act like a sleepwalker. The behavior of the individual up to the time of the sudden appearance of such an abnormal reaction appears quite usual. History of one well-documented incident of pathological intoxication is strongly suggestive of the likelihood of subsequent attacks. Some authorities have used test doses of alcohol to verify the diagnosis. Fortunately, the illness is quite uncommon. Psychiatric opinion is that pathological intoxication or "allergy to alcohol" does not actually represent a hypersensitivity of the individual to the chemical alcohol, but rather a sudden release of unconscious hostility in a potentially aggressive individual under the influence of relatively small (symbolic) drinks. Impulse control is lost and destructive acts or aggressions against others occur.

42. *Other Impairment of Judgment Situations.* Other possible situations leading to an impairment of judgment include covert or secret drugging of one individual by another (for example, "knock-out drops" secretly introduced into an alcoholic beverage). It is claimed that the excessive use of tranquilizers may lower an individual's will power and increase suggestibility. As a group, chronic alcoholics tend to deterioration of both moral and general judgment with associated diminution of personal integrity and dependability.

43. *Chronic Organic Diseases*. Such diseases as cerebral arteriosclerosis, brain tumors, and brain atrophy (shrinking brain without arteriosclerosis), are characterized by stupid behavior, forgetfulness, and exaggerated or inappropriate sentimentality. The picture is that of senility but is seen in those not chronologically old.

44. *Fugue State*. Emotional reactions with clouding of consciousness and some degree of unawareness of what is actually going on are called fugue states. They occur in dramatic (hysterical) personalities trying to defend themselves against great unconscious emotional conflict. These individuals, failing to defend themselves from the conflict, develop reactions of aimless running or walking, repetitive actions, or amnesia. An example is the individual who takes a train, plane, or bus trip to another city and cannot remember his name when picked up by the police in a strange city. Sleepwalking is probably a closely related phenomenon. A known predilection to fugue state or psychomotor epilepsy or any other condition of lessened awareness is incompatible with sensitive assignments.

45. *Careful Selection of Personnel.* In the prevention of unauthorized destructive acts due primarily to emotional disorders, the paranoid group has the greatest potential for bringing about a catastrophic unauthorized destructive act. The impulse disorder group, as in civil life, might contribute more incidence of all unauthorized destructive acts, but because of the latter being less deliberate and less planned the total destructiveness would probably be less. To avoid unauthorized destructive incidents, only those individuals whose past history and present performance show no evidence of such patterns of behavior should be used in all those nuclear occupations which require complex, smoothly organized patterns of thought as well as digital dexterity and controlled bodily movement.

46. *General Rules.* Prevention of unauthorized destructive acts is best accomplished by keeping in mind the following:

a. Routine, rigorous, screening procedures including a records review and a continuing evaluation of all such individuals by discerning and informed superiors. This is not only to check individuals but also to prevent and alter those situations, environmental or personal, which seem to precipitate deranged behavior.

b. The development of group spirit, morale, and goal orientation toward success will lessen the likelihood of individual failure. An individual who lacks the potential for full healthy group membership becomes much more obvious in a highly successful unit.

c. Impaired judgment may well result if a person is preoccupied with situations of blackmail, extortion, or fears disclosure of facts regarding sexual abnormality, drug addiction, or past criminal behavior. This is true of other situations of personal stress as in investigations, trials, or hearings.

d. Some of the common stressful human situations that may touch off emotional disorders include recent bereavement, first pregnancy of the wife, birth of the first child, severe illness of a close relative, demotion, or failure of an expected promotion.

47. *Additional Clues of Stress.* The following additional clues are common signals of individual distress:

a. Preoccupation with thoughts, day dreaming, etc.

b. Change in behavior patterns related to speech, such as a talkative person becoming quiet or vice versa.

c. A tendency to talk at length about personal activities or habits, such as drinking, gambling, and the like.

d. Changes in daily routine. For example, a gambler trying to recoup may be calling his bookie every day at the same time; or a sudden influx of unopened personal mail or telephone calls may indicate trouble with creditors or collection agencies.

e. The depressed individual contemplating suicide will generally tell someone of his plans or feelings. This may be anyone he knows—family, friend, or supervisor. The opinion held that individuals never mention serious suicidal preoccupation has been proved erroneous.

f. Changes in mood, from elation to depression or back again, with little or no apparent reason or frequent changes of mood in the same day. Marked mood changes without external cause should be investigated.

g. Complaints of sore back, vague abdominal pain, severe insomnia, and tremor of the hands all suggest an emotional disturbance and may call for medical and a psychiatric examination.

*   *   *

NOTES

NOTE 1

88TH CONGRESS—FIRST SESSION

Joint Resolution Proposing Constitutional Amendment re Succession to the Presidency and Vice Presidency (1963)*

Proposing an amendment to the Constitution of the United States relating to succession to the Presidency and Vice Presidency and to cases where the President is unable to discharge the powers and duties of his office.

*   *   *

"SEC. 3. If the President shall declare in writing that he is unable to discharge the powers and duties of his office, such powers and duties shall be discharged by the Vice President as Acting President.

"SEC. 4. If the President does not so declare, the Vice President, if satisfied that such inability exists, shall, upon the written approval of a majority of the heads of the executive departments in office, assume the discharge of the powers and duties of the office as Acting President.

"SEC. 5. Whenever the President makes public announcement in writing that his inability has terminated, he shall resume the discharge of the powers and duties of his office on the seventh day after making such announcement, or at such earlier time after such announcement as he and the Vice President may determine. But if the Vice President, with the written approval of a majority of the heads of executive departments in office at the time of such announcement,

---

*S.J. Res. 139, (December 12, 1963).

transmits to the Congress his written declaration that in his opinion the President's inability has not terminated, the Congress shall thereupon consider the issue. If the Congress is not then in session, it shall assemble in special session on the call of the Vice President. If the Congress determines by concurrent resolution, adopted with the approval of two-thirds of the Members present in each House, that the inability of the President has not terminated, thereupon, notwithstanding any further announcement by the President, the Vice President shall discharge such powers and duties as Acting President until the occurrence of the earliest of the following events: (1) the Acting President proclaims that the President's inability has ended, (2) the Congress determines by concurrent resolution, adopted with the approval of a majority of the Members present in each House, that the President's inability has ended, or (3) the President's term ends.

*   *   *

NOTE 2

LERNER, MAX

A Sick Chief*

*   *   *

The new amendment says that if a President is too sick, physically or mentally, to give way to the Vice President, the decision that he is unable to continue can be made only by the Vice President with a majority of the Cabinet; that it will take the same group to override a President seeking to resume his office, and —on a showdown—that it will need two-thirds of Congress as well. In a complex problem this strikes me as a procedure preserving an effective succession while guarding against a possible usurping cabal. To those who fear that it opens the door to a revolution by a Latin American junta, the role of the two-thirds Congressional majority should be an adequate answer.

The doubts remaining in my mind don't involve the amendment, but the problem itself, which has become almost an insoluble one. We know the high incidence of mental breakdown in modern urban uprooted cultures under today's tensions. We know that the ordinary tensions are multiplied in the White House. We know that in an age of overkill weapons, the head-of-state, whether in Russia, America, France, and presently China, has immense power for destructiveness. . . .

We know these things, but there remains the question of when a man is ill enough to be dangerous to the nation and the world. Many of us are neurotic in one way or other, but when can a President be

---

*Excerpts from Max Lerner column. Reprinted by permission of New York Post. © 1965, N.Y. Post Corp.

adjudged psychotic? The amendment is based on the theory that the people working most closely with him—the Vice President and Cabinet—would be most likely to sense dangerous changes in him. But can even they detect the line between a willful and even arbitrary chief and a really sick chief—a truly deranged one? And then there is the question . . . about a character disorder, not clear insanity, which may lead him to destructive policies as with Hitler and Stalin.

*   *   *

Presidents then are not only mortal: They are also human, living under human tensions, often strengthened by them, sometimes damaged. If it is true that a man's breakdown is in part related to the tensions of his work, then I suppose one possible contingency for the Presidential office would be paranoia. . . .

. . . The difficult part of it is that even the mooted proposals for full disclosure of the health of all Presidential candidates, both physical and mental, do not meet the problem. For the predictive power of psychiatry today is still too rudimentary to be relied upon. In the end, using whatever psychiatric light we can obtain, it is the political intuitions of the people that must serve as the shield of the republic from (as Lyndon Johnson has put it in his message to Congress) a President's "illness, senility, or other affliction."

NOTE 3

UNITED STATES SUBCOMMITTEE ON CONSTITUTIONAL RIGHTS

Monthly Staff Report on Rights of Federal Employees*

In its investigation of the use of psychological and psychiatric testing of government employees, the Subcommittee [on Constitutional Rights] found that in one example of such testing, the Department of State subjected a woman employee applying for Foreign Service to an extensive test on matters relating to her family, her sex life, her religion, her personal habits, and other matters. One phase of the test involved 570 questions to which she was to respond rapidly "quickly and without any thinking or deliberation." Included were such true-false questions as:

> "Christ performed miracles."
> "I believe there is a devil and hell in after life."
> "Once in a while I think of things too bad to talk about."
> "I believe in a life hereafter."
> "I feel sure there is only one true religion."
> "Many of my dreams are about sex matters."
> "I pray several times a week."

---

*December 1, 1964.

She had to indicate whether she was troubled, and to what extent, by matters including:

> "Deciding whether I'm really in love."   ·
> "Being too inhibited in sex matters."
> "Confused in my religious beliefs."
> "Differing from my family in religious beliefs."

Other questions in these categories were even more shocking.

She was given 225 questions consisting of "pairs of statements about things that you may or may not like," and directed to "choose the one that is more applicable to you. If you like both, choose one you like best. If you like neither choose one you like least." Included were the following choices:

> A. I feel depressed by my own inability to handle various situations.
> B. I like to read books and plays in which sex plays a major part.
>
> A. I feel like blaming others when things go wrong for me.
> B. I feel I am inferior in most respects.
>
> A. I like to listen to or tell jokes in which sex plays a major part.
> B. I feel like getting revenge when someone has insulted me.

The Subcommittee Chairman asked the Department of State for a report on the type of information gained from these tests which would justify such an invasion of privacy, a description of the circumstances that would require such tests, and the individuals who make the determination of their need. In its reply, the Department states that "There are at least three types of situations, and possibly others, in which such testing is necessary in order to provide suitable help to the individual and to protect the interests of the United States Government." The three situations described involved:

> 1. Foreign Service employees who have been overseas and have begun to have an emotional breakdown due to the stresses of the post to which they have been assigned.
> 2. Security matters, where psychiatric consultation and psychological testing may be necessary to fulfill responsibilities under Executive Order 10450.
> 3. An employee or a dependant who has an emotional problem which requires treatment.

"Psychological tests are not resorted to by the State Department unless in the opinion of a psychiatrist they are needed to evaluate more objectively an employee or the dependents of an employee," according to the Department. Although it is recommended by the Medical Division, it is carried out by a private consulting psychologist, in his private office, using only "professionally recognized" tests. The detailed answers remain as part of his records, and the

Medical Division receives only the conclusions of the testing.

In another instance, the Labor Department asked applicants for the Department's Youth Opportunity Program questions concerning such widely diverging subjects as whether they believed there was only one true religion, liked poetry, or hardly ever became "excited or thrilled."

*   *   *

NOTE 4

ERVIN, SAM J. JR.

Why Senate Hearings on Psychological Tests in Government?*

Psychology has achieved a pre-eminent position among medical practitioners and laymen alike in this century. In less than 100 years it has risen from a dubious cult to almost unqualified acceptance. Today its tenets are relied upon by many in explaining most phenomena of human existence.

Although the science of psychology began as an adjunct to the treatment of mental illness, today more and more Government administrators look to its doctrines when making personnel decisions. In this connection, departmental medical divisions, together with resident or consulting psychiatrists and psychologists, are being increasingly called upon to contribute to these decisions. The role of the medical man and the Government psychologist is thus being increased beyond the traditional treatment of individual patients.

Investigation by the Constitutional Rights Subcommittee disclosed that psychological test scores and psychiatric evaluations are frequently relied upon by a number of Federal Government departments and agencies in employment situations which radically affect the lives of the individuals involved. We have received numerous complaints that some of the questions contained in the personality inventories relating to sex, religion, family relationships, and many personal aspects of the employee's life constitute an unjustified invasion of privacy. Furthermore, the charge has been made that aside from the invasion of privacy, the procedures surrounding the testing and the use made of the test results present serious due process questions.

As a result the Sub-committee held hearings June 7–10 to examine (a) the content of psychological tests administered by the Government and the extent to which the questions asked constituted an unjustified invasion of the individual's psyche and private life, (b) whether the tests were scientifically valid, and (c) the procedural and due process issues

involved in the administration of the tests, including the employee's right to confront his accusers when his emotional stability and mental competency are questioned.

It is clearly not the intention of the Sub-committee to question the validity of psychological tests in therapeutic situations. However, the Sub-committee is concerned with the questions competent experts have raised concerning the validity, reliability, and accuracy of some of these tests as methods for determining the fitness and suitability of applicants or employees for their jobs.

If psychological tests have low reliability, and must be supported by outside data, then this would detract from the argument of some Government administrators that possible invasions of privacy must be balanced against the Government's need to obtain a psychological profile of its employees. Also, it would seem that principles of due process demand that if an individual's employment with the Government depends on his scores on psychological tests, then the tests must be of proven and demonstrable validity. In addition, due process demands that the employee and his attorney and private physician be allowed to examine the psychological reports and data which may adversely affect his employment. Otherwise, the employee is unable to confront the evidence against him, and is therefore unable effectively to present contradictory evidence in his own behalf.

Even apart from the issue of reliability of psychological interrogations, there are certain areas of our personal life and habits which the Government should not inquire about in its routine employment procedures. For example, the safeguards in our form of Government against official intrusion into the citizen's private life demand that the State strictly limit its inquiries into the sexual practices and re-religious beliefs of its employees. Clearly, the Government should not send out an investigator to peer through an employee's or applicant's bedroom window. Neither should the Government ask, through subtle psychological questioning, what a person does and thinks after he draws the curtains.

*   *   *

NOTE 5

Appeal of John F. Torrence*

This is an appeal from action of Allegheny County Board of Assistance, Department of Public Welfare, by which John F. Torrence was removed from his position as Caseworker II by letter dated August 3, 1965.

The record shows that the reason given for removal of appellant was "that he refused to have a psy-

---

*Monthly Staff Report to the Senate Sub-committee on Constitutional Rights, December 2, 1965.

* Commonwealth of Pennsylvania State Civil Service Commission Appeal No. 784.

chiatric examination to verify that he is both physically and mentally capable of continuing on the job." The results of such examination were to be discussed with the appointing authority. It is our considered opinion that removal should not be predicated on such a reason. There appears to be no authority in the Civil Service Act to demand a psychiatric examination and discussion of the same with the examiner as a prerequisite to retaining employment. Requiring an employee to get psychiatric help is proper. However, it is in error to insist upon discussion of such reports and diagnosis. Considerable evidence that would appear to be of substantial value was offered to show the deterioration in performance, and inability of appellant to do his job. We cannot pass judgment on such matters now, as such charges were not specifically delineated in the letter of removal. If the appointing authority should wish to remove the appellant for just cause based upon specific and definite charges, this hearing or adjudication would not foreclose or bar such further action. . . . [I]t is our determination that there was no prejudice toward appellant, but the reason for removal is a nonmerit factor, and not just cause. Therefore, on the basis of the foregoing findings of fact, we enter as

CONCLUSION OF LAW

The appellant was not removed for just cause under Section 807 of the Civil Service Act. . . .

NOTE 6

DEW v. HALABY
317 F.2d 582 (D.C. Cir. 1963)

WASHINGTON, CIRCUIT JUDGE:

. . . Appellant is a discharged Government employee, who seeks a declaratory judgment that his discharge was invalid, and reinstatement to his former position or one of like grade and tenure. . . .

. . . Appellant served in the United States Air Force in 1951–55. . . . He obtained employment thereafter in the Central Intelligence Agency as a file clerk handling coded data. In order to obtain the "secret" security clearance needed, he was required to take a lie detector test. Appellant admitted committing at least four unnatural sex acts with males, some of them for pay, in 1950, when he was 18 or 19 years of age. He also admitted smoking marijuana cigarettes on at least five occasions in 1951 and 1952 during his service in the Air Force. The officials of the Central Intelligence Agency thereupon offered to allow appellant to resign his post, and he did so.

He then applied to the Civil Aeronautics Authority for employment, and on September 17, 1956, was given an appointment as an Airways Operations Specialist, subject to a probationary period of one

year, and "subject to investigation." Appellant thereafter served for some twenty months as an air traffic controller in Denver, Colorado, receiving one promotion and on July 3, 1957, receiving a performance rating of satisfactory. On May 14, 1958, the agency, having just come into possession of the information above mentioned, notified him that his removal was proposed. . . .

*   *   *

. . . Appellant repeated his admissions as to the incidents, and was allowed to file a "psychiatric evaluation." The psychiatrist concluded that appellant was functioning normally, and that he did not believe him to have a "homosexual personality disorder."[3] The agency notified appellant, on February 16, 1960, that it had reviewed the materials submitted, and that the charges were sustained.

*   *   *

. . . Common sense tells us that in many situations the Government must have authority to separate employees because of misconduct occurring prior to their Government employment. . . .

*   *   *

Whether such a conclusion would be universally valid is not something we need pass upon here. But it seems to us to be rational and valid in the present case.[10]

*   *   *

3. "In short, it is my impression that Mr. Dew mentally and emotionally is functioning at this time entirely within the normal range, and I do not doubt that he has been doing so for at least a period of several years. He appears to be happily married and has assumed the responsibilities of parenthood without evidence of regression or emotional instability. He seems to be adjusting in his job. And I do not know what more one could ask.

"Furthermore, I decidedly do not believe him to have a homosexual personality disorder. I believe that the several incidents which he gave a history of having engaged in while age 18 and a freshman in college were isolated incidents primarily the result of his curiosity. I do not believe they have been repeated. Furthermore, at that age I do not feel that isolated episodes of homosexual behavior can be considered abnormal or perverted, but rather a process of normal sexual investigation and curiosity. There is considerable evidence in the psychiatric literature that this allegation is true."

10. The Appeals Examiner, at an earlier stage, had made this finding:

"While it is possible that Mr. Dew's admitted homosexual acts might have no relation to his competence and ability to perform the duties of his position it does not follow that employment of a person with such a background would not adversely affect the efficiency of the Federal service. Despite the Kinsey report which was offered in evidence by Counsel for the appellant to show the incidence of homosexual behavior in America such conduct still violates existing laws and morals of our society. To require employees to work with persons who have committed acts that are repugnant to the established and accepted standards of decency and morality

In considering whether the removal was arbitrary and capricious we cannot ignore the nature of appellant's duties. He was acting as an airport traffic controller. His duties were to regulate the flow of air traffic, issue clearances for the take-off and landing of planes, and maintain the proper separation of planes on the ground and in the air. His job thus gave him control over safeguarding the lives of passengers, crews, and persons on the ground. That such a position requires skill, alertness, and above all responsibility requires no demonstration. . . .

* * *

. . . We certainly are in no position to say that retention of the appellant, demonstrated to have evidenced a lack of good character in the past, would promote, or would not have a derogatory effect on, the efficiency of the service. The choice of personnel to direct the Nation's air traffic is for the Federal Aviation Agency, and not the courts. For these reasons, the order of the District Court will be Affirmed.

NOTE 7

Piedmont Airlines, Douglas DC-3, N 55V, on Bucks Elbow Mountain, near Charlottesville, Virginia, October 30, 1959*

About 2040, October 30, 1959, Piedmont Airlines Flight 349 crashed on Bucks Elbow Mountain located about 13 miles west of the Charlottesville-Albermarle County, Virginia, Airport. The crew of 3 and 23 of 24 passengers were killed; the sole survivor was seriously injured. The aircraft, a DC-3, N 55V, was demolished by impact.

* * *

The Board concludes that the lateral error resulted from a navigational omission . . .

* * *

During the course of the investigation the aeronautical history of Captain Lavrinc was reviewed. His training, qualifications, and proficiency reports were satisfactory. His history showed that he had progressed normally to captain and had served in that capacity since May 1957. It also showed that he had flown in and out of Charlottesville and over the route involved for several years on a regular basis. Captain Lavrinc had flown a total of 5,101 hours, of which 4,771 were in DC-3 aircraft.

To the Board there were numerous factors which

can only have a disrupting effect upon the morals and efficiency of any organization. Therefore, the fact that Mr. Dew had engaged in homosexual acts and smoked marijuana cigarettes prior to his employment does have a bearing upon and relate to the efficiency of the Federal service, and is not an arbitrary or capricious reason for removing a Federal employee."

* C.A.B. Aircraft Accident Report No. 1–0065 (April 18, 1961).

were obviously inconsistent with Captain Lavrinc's record. Some were: The apparent navigational omission, a non-adherence to precise tracking procedures, and a descent below the authorized procedure turn altitude. Others were: The failure to note that the time for station passage was in excess of that commensurate with a close-in position, and that ADF indications were not compatible with the normal procedure turn presentation. Still others were a failure to request the latest Charlottesville weather when the communicator did not furnish it, and not using the altimeter setting given in response to the inrange report. The Board believes these factors were not only inconsistent with Captain Lavrinc's reputation as an exacting pilot but were indicative of a serious departure from the high standard and quality of performance expected during an instrument operation. Because of these factors a comprehensive investigation was made into the personal background of Captain Lavrinc. This was done to search for reasons which could seriously impair his normal piloting ability. During this work reasons were found which could result in his preoccupation.

Captain Lavrinc had, for several years, been under severe emotional strain. The Board considers that disclosure of detailed information relating thereto would adversely affect the interests of certain persons and is not required in the interest of the public. A resume of the Board's significant findings and certain recommendations, however, are in the public interest and are set forth below.

Captain Lavrinc received psychotherapy in 1953–1954; he obtained further psychiatric counseling in 1957; intensive psychotherapy was resumed in May 1959, which he underwent several times a week thereafter; his last appointment was the night before the accident. This latter treatment involved the services of two psychiatrists. In the course of this treatment the first psychiatrist prescribed certain psychotropic drugs. After trials on Compazine, Prozine, Sparine, and Thorazine, Prozine was prescribed in August 1959 in a dosage of three of four times daily and was re-issued on September 18, 1959. This prescription specified an amount which, if taken as directed, would have been sufficient to last until two days before the accident.

On September 23, 1959, however, Captain Lavrinc commenced psychotherapy under the second psychiatrist who prescribed no drugs. The Board has been unable to determine whether or not Captain Lavrinc continued to take the medicine in the prescribed manner during the latter treatments, although there is evidence that he took the earlier trial prescriptions.

The Board has evaluated the background and history of Captain Lavrinc, including data set forth above. In addition, it submitted all the available information covering Captain Lavrinc to particularly qualified medical experts for evaluation as to its significance with respect to this accident.

The consensus is that Captain Lavrinc was so heavily burdened with mental and emotional problems that he should have been relieved of the strain of flight duty while undergoing treatment for his condition. This condition was such that pre-occupation with his problems could well have lowered his standard of performance during instrument flight. Furthermore, with respect to this accident the consensus is that the emotional and mental problems were of far greater importance in causing the preoccupation than would have the use of psychotropic medication.

The Board believes that the facts disclosed by this investigation demonstrate the adverse effects of serious emotional and mental stress on airman proficiency and performance. It further believes that the early recognition and correction of such conditions which might tend to impair an airman's proficiency and performance would be beneficial to flight safety. Accordingly, the Board recommends that the Federal Aviation Agency, appropriate segments of the aviation industry, and the medical profession initiate exploratory studies in this field.

The Board also considers that the investigation of this accident demonstrates the need for re-examination of the use of drugs which may affect the faculties of a flight crew member in any manner contrary to safety.

Since World War II there have been great advances in pharmacology and whole new families of drugs have become easily available to the public, either over the counter or by prescription. Since 1953–1954 one of the most significant advances has been in the field of psychopharmacology. There has been a proliferation of drugs which influence the state of mind, are employed in the treatment of mental disorders, or are used as psychic energizers. Within this group of drugs the so-called tranquilizers are being widely used by the public.

The basic question which the Board believes must be resolved, therefore, is how does the use of these drugs relate to the safety of flight. For example, within the framework of the present Civil Air Regulation covering the use of drugs, should these drugs be classified as ". . . drug which affects his (crew member) faculties in any manner contrary to safety. . . ." The Board is of the opinion that the answer to the question is a qualified "yes." In great part this decision is reached from review of military research into the relationship of drugs to the flying profession. The basic conclusion derived from this research can be stated quite simply: If a flight crew member's personal situation demands tranquilizers he should be removed from flying status while on the drugs.

*　　*　　*

2.

AS A GUARDIAN OF THE LEGAL PROCESS

IN RE SHERMAN
404 P.2d 978 (Wash. 1965)

HILL, JUDGE.

Different facets of this disciplinary proceeding, which began November 20, 1958, have been before this court. Two opinions have been written,[1] the substance of which was to hold that Arthur Eber Sherman, Jr., was entitled to a hearing on his defense of mental irresponsibility.

As a consequence of the hearings held on that issue, both the special trial committee and the Board of Governors of the Washington State Bar Association have concluded that Mr. Sherman has sustained the burden of establishing his mental irresponsibility at the time of the commission of the offenses with which he was charged in this proceeding.[2] The Board says that his "conduct was the result and consequence of his mental incompetency," while the special trial committee said that his offensive acts "were the product and the result" of his mental disorder. We accept these findings, and that is, of course, decisive of the question of whether Mr. Sherman should be disbarred or disciplined for that conduct.

The issue now becomes, on the basis of his present mental condition: Should we disbar Mr. Sherman, suspend him pending further developments, or permit him to continue practicing law.

No one is suggesting that Mr. Sherman should be disbarred because of his present mental condition. The Board of Governors has recommended that he be suspended from the practice of law until such time as he shall prove that the mental condition which was responsible for his misconduct "has been cured so completely that there is little or no likelihood of a recurrence of the condition."

The special trial committee was unanimously of the opinion that Mr. Sherman was not presently incapacitated from practicing law, and that he should be neither disbarred nor suspended, but permitted to practice law. However, two members of the committee attached a condition of voluntary psychiatric aid and consultation for a three-year period.[3] The other member of the committee, while believing that the

---

1. 58 Wash. 2d 1 and 7, 354 P.2d 888, and 363 P.2d 390.

2. Making a false statement in his application for admission to practice law (December 5, 1956), filing two petitions for rehearing with the Supreme Court of Oregon (December 4, 1957), and sending a letter to a trial judge in Oregon (February 28, 1958), all of which were insulting and contemptuous (copies of the letter were also sent to other parties).

3. The following is a portion of the findings of two members of the special trial committee:

"The Trial Committee believes and finds that at the time of committing the offensive acts listed in the complaint, Mr. Sherman was suffering from a form of mental or personality disorder (the testifying psychiatrists variously branded it as

psychiatric aid would be beneficial, did not believe it should be made a condition of Mr. Sherman's continuing in the practice of the law.

We are in accord with the conclusion of the special trial committee. The best evidence that Mr. Sherman is not presently incapacitated from practicing law is that he has been practicing . . . since September, 1958. . . .

* * *

[T]he Bar Association relies on the somewhat conflicting views of the psychiatrists, coupled with—and to some extent based upon—four incidents referred to as the Melendy, the Snowball, the McCoy, and the Duree episodes.[5] In each of these episodes, Mr. Sherman is said to have lost control of himself and demonstrated emotional instability.

It is interesting to note that Mr. Melendy and Mr. Duree both say that, notwithstanding the episodes in which they were involved, they still regard Mr. Sherman as a capable lawyer. Mr. Duree appeared as *amicus curiae* to urge that Mr. Sherman be permitted to continue to practice law. It is apparent that none of these incidents constitute any failure to protect the interests of a client, or reflect directly upon his conduct as a member of the bar.

The special trial committee seems to have regarded these incidents as of little significance in determining whether Mr. Sherman was presently capable of practicing law. However, the Board of Governors has made each one of them the basis of a lengthy finding of fact to support its conclusion that Mr. Sherman has failed to establish that the mental condition,

which was responsible for his misconduct, has been cured so completely that there is little or no likelihood of a recurrence of the condition.

* * *

If it be conceded that Mr. Sherman had failed to sustain that burden, the Board of Governors was "locked in" by our opinion; it could only disbar or conditionally suspend.

We will concede for our present purposes, that, based on the testimony of the psychiatrists,[8] Mr. Sherman did fail to sustain that burden and that the Board of Governors has recommended exactly the action which we said should be taken.

However, after studying the testimony of the psychiatrists, we are satisfied that our opinion of July 6, 1961, set up an almost impossible standard from a psychiatric standpoint, in requiring proof that there is little or no likelihood of a recurrence.[9]

* * *

'paranoia,' 'paranoid trend,' and 'paranoid personality'), and such offensive acts were the product and result of that disorder. We further find that Mr. Sherman is not yet so fully cured or rehabilitated as to render improbable some future manifestation of that disorder, although one cannot predict the gravity, seriousness or exact form of such future manifestation. Nevertheless, we find that Mr. Sherman has made progress and adjustment; that except for several minor emotional flareups he has been functioning as a lawyer and a citizen without complaint since moving to South Bend in 1958; . . . In other words, the Committee believes that Mr. Sherman's mental illness still exists, but not to a *presently incapacitating degree*—that the existing attitudes of defensiveness and persecution, though present, are essentially quiescent now, and that with help, Mr. Sherman can properly function. Absent such help, if subjected to extreme personal setbacks and disappointments, it is quite probable that he will be unable to maintain a realistic and balanced perspective and will be unable to creditably function as a lawyer." (Italics ours.)

5. He used force to take from Mr. Melendy, and retain, a plat which he had prepared as an engineer. (Mr. Sherman is qualified to do civil engineering and he holds a bachelor and master's degree in forestry from the University of Michigan.) He used force and threatening language (the extent of the force and the character of the language is in dispute) toward some teen-age boys who he thought had thrown a snowball at his car. He slammed a door on leaving Mr. McCoy's office, after he thought Mr. McCoy had ignored him. He wrote a letter discharging Mr. Duree as his attorney because he thought Mr. Duree was protecting interests other than his own.

8. Dr. Ralph M. Stolzheise (called by the Bar Association, and who had not had the opportunity of examining Mr. Sherman), when questioned on the probability of a recurrence of the condition which caused the conduct upon which this disciplinary proceeding was predicated (see note 2) testified: "As to a likelihood or probability, I can't say, but there is a strong possibility."

Asked about the likelihood of sending petitions and a letter, such as those referred to in note 2, he said: "Time tends to dissipate that pattern but there is too much submerged emotion here in this man's general thinking and feeling to have confidence he would keep it submerged."

He said that Mr. Sherman had not been cured—"It has been fluctuating with periods of exacerbations" (referring primarily to the four episodes previously mentioned). He testified that Mr. Sherman would never be cured "unless he goes through diagnostic work in order to properly understand the origin of these feelings and practices in that understanding a new attitude toward himself and toward life around him. This sort of illness does not get well by itself."

He did express the view that with treatment Mr. Sherman could be helped, and "with sufficient treatment (3 years of a sustained therapy program) he could probably achieve a recovered status."

Dr. Lawrence H. Schwarz (called by Mr. Sherman, and who had examined him) was reluctant to give an opinion about the likelihood of a recurrence of the condition existing when Mr. Sherman committed the acts on which the disciplinary proceedings were based (see note 2). He testified: "I would say . . . there is less likelihood of a recurrence than ever before in his life, but predictability in psychiatric matters is notoriously poor, especially in cases like this." Then he added: "If I can enlarge, the reason predictability is so poor is that there is such an enormous variety of circumstances which will press upon the individual in his life and which will test his stability or lack of stability—if life is fairly smooth or if problems don't arise, he may go along the rest of his life without an acute episode."

Dr. Schwarz, too, stressed the importance of treatment, saying, "that with treatment there would be less likelihood of a recurrence of an acute illness."

He discussed "treatment" in terms of "psychotherapy aimed toward helping him to find and understand his problems. This could be done by any qualified therapist, it might not have to be a psychiatrist, but someone skilled to deal with such problems."

9. A personal note: The writer of this opinion also wrote

We appreciate that the Board of Governors in its recommendation felt obligated to follow literally, and was following, our prior statement. We are conscious, too, that if Mr. Sherman had told the truth in his application for admission to practice that the application would not have been granted. However, all are now in accord with the proposition that his false answer and other misconduct "was the result and consequence of his mental incompetence." We are now of the view that the special trial committee concerned itself with the really relevant criteria, i.e., (1) Is Mr. Sherman presently able capably and competently to represent his clients; to so conduct himself as to reflect no discredit upon his profession, and to maintain its standards; and (2) If so, is the probability of a recurrence of the condition, existing at the time of his misconduct, so great that he should presently be deprived of his right to practice his profession.

The record sustains an affirmative answer to (1) and a negative answer to (2). We agree with the special trial committee that Mr. Sherman should not be suspended or disbarred and that he should be permitted to continue to practice law, conditional upon his complying with the recommendation made by the special trial committee for voluntary treatment. The details of the treatment program will be the subject of a special order prepared by counsel for Mr. Sherman and counsel for the Washington State Bar Association.

We make this disposition of the case in reliance upon the assurance of his counsel that Mr. Sherman will voluntarily conform with the recommendation of the special trial committee.

ROSELLINI, CHIEF JUSTICE (dissenting).

In the proceeding before this court, there was definitely no showing that the respondent's mental illness (paranoid personality) has been cured. Insofar as the record shows, no cure has been attempted. Although this proceeding has been pending since 1958, and the respondent defends his highly reprehensible actions in falsifying his application for admission to practice and in making unseemly attacks upon the courts of Oregon with an assertion that he was a victim of mental illness, he has not sought psychiatric help. He merely promises to do so if he is not disbarred or suspended.

the other two opinions in 58 Wash.2d 1 and 7, 354 P.2d 888, 363 P.2d 390: I admit, frankly, that the standard laid down in the second opinion was psychiatrically inappropriate. Conscientious experts in the psychiatric field concede that there are too many imponderables in such cases and too much of the unpredictable to warrant a flat statement that there is "little or no likelihood of a recurrence."

I would point out, too, that the further suggestion that a person be disbarred (with its definite connotation of misconduct) because he is incurably mentally ill is not defensible. We would not disbar a lawyer because of incapability caused by any other illness, why should we disbar a person for mental illness?

During the time that the respondent has been practicing law, it appears that he has committed no major offense of the type which paranoia induces, at least none that were brought to the attention of the trial committee. But "secretiveness" is a characteristic of paranoia, and we do not know what falsifications may have occurred and been concealed. It can be seen, from the record before us, in my opinion, that the respondent has not rid himself of all of his feelings of persecution or his tendency to duplicity.

For example, there is the matter of the appointment of an attorney to represent him in this proceeding. [H]e insisted that an attorney be appointed to represent him. He discharged the attorney who was appointed and who did represent him well and in evident good faith, protesting that he did not feel the attorney could represent him while he was also representing undesignated "conflicting" interests.

The respondent also insisted that a member of the trial committee was prejudiced against him, although he was not able to point to any evidence of such prejudice on the part of the committee member.

I have examined the record closely and find it devoid of any indication that the respondent realizes the seriousness of his offenses, that he truly regrets his action in falsifying his application, or that he feels now that it was unjustified. The respondent's appearances before the trial committee were, to my mind, characterized by a lack of candor consistent with the finding of the board of governors that his paranoia has not been cured. . . .

. . . I cannot believe that a doctor suffering with palsy would be allowed by the medical profession to practice surgery. By the same token a man afflicted with a mental or emotional disease which compels him to perform dishonest acts and warps his judgment, should not be allowed to practice law.

I would either vacate the order of admission or adopt the recommendation of the board of governors and order a suspension until such time as the respondent can produce satisfactory medical testimony that the disease has been treated and cured.

NOTES

NOTE 1

CHURCH v. CAPITAL FREIGHT LINES
171 Cal. App. 2d 246, 262 P.2d 563 (1956)

PEEK, JUSTICE.

*   *   *

[T]here can be no question but that the right to a trial before mentally competent jurors is as fundamental as the right to trial before unbiased and unprejudiced jurors which our courts have held to be an "inseparable and inalienable part of the right to a trial by jury guaranteed by the Constitution." In amplification of this constitutional right, the Legislature by statute has determined who are competent, Code of Civ. Proc. § 198, and who are not competent, Code of Civ. Proc. § 199, to act as jurors. By such statutory provisions a person not in "possession of his natural faculties" may be disqualified to serve as a juror. . . .

NOTE 2

SMITH v. BALDI
344 U.S. 561 (1953)

FRANKFURTER, J., dissenting.

* * *

But I am of the view that there is another reason, which in itself is for me conclusive, why this court should not affirm the judgment below. It is that a new decisive factor, which was introduced for the first time here, requires reconsideration of the disposition below. After the case left the Court of Appeals it came to the knowledge of petitioner's counsel that the court-appointed expert, the professional witness on the issue of insanity on whose testimony the Pennsylvania courts relied, had himself been committed, as of January 12, 1952, because of an incurable mental disease which had deprived him of "any judgment or insight." This fact was brought to the notice of this court in an affidavit not challenged by the respondent, which also averred that "this intellectual deterioration was evidenced even on a clinical level in January, 1951." The expert's report on Smith's sanity was made to the sentencing court on November 5, 1948. His disability was not known either to the District Court or the Court of Appeals in February and October, 1951, when they respectively ruled against the petitioner. Even uninformed judges may know that this kind of mental illness does not set in overnight but is the culmination of a long process. Indeed, the medical history, sketchy as it is, revealed by the affidavit filed here demonstrates the gradual manner in which the mental illness in question developed. The extent to which this affidavit vitiates the worth of the expert testimony taken by the sentencing court should not be made à matter of judicial notice. But to allow the victim of this testimony, which, in any event, has been brought into doubt, to go to his death without an opportunity for reassessment, by either State or federal court, of the basis for the rejection of his plea of insanity would constitute a denial of due process no less gross than if the sentence had been imposed without any hearing at all on the issue of sanity.

* * *

NOTE 3

PEOPLE v. HILL
9 App. Div. 2d 451, 195 N.Y.S. 2d 295 (1959)

WENZEL, J. . . . .

* * *

[W]here the *coram nobis* proceeding is grounded on a claim that the applicant was mentally incapacitated during the time limited by law for the taking of an appeal from a judgment of conviction and that the incapacity prevented him from taking an appeal within that limited time, and where the claim is properly and sufficiently presented in the papers in support of the application, a hearing should be accorded the applicant for the purpose of exploring the propriety of giving him appropriate relief. . . .

Our view that relief should be accorded to one who has been deprived of an equal opportunity to appeal because of his mental condition, finds support in legislation which has recognized the need to give appropriate protection to such persons against the operation of other time-limiting statutes, viz., our Legislature has given insane persons extensions of time to commence civil actions (Civ. Prac. Act, §§ 43, 60) and has given the court power to extend their time to serve a notice of intention to sue a municipality (General Municipal Law, § 59–e, subd. 5) and to extend their time to appeal if the attorney for the party who would appeal becomes mentally or physically incapacitated within the time limited for the taking of the appeal (Civ. Prac. Act, § 99, subd. 3). In other jurisdictions there are statutes which accord an extension of time within which to appeal for persons under a disability. . . .

A sufficient factual showing has been made in the papers herein to make applicable the above view that a hearing should be directed as to appellant's mental condition during the period allowed by statute for the taking of an appeal from the judgment of conviction, in view of the fact that the allegation in the petition that appellant was insane "after trial" is undenied, and in view of appellant's history of mental illness and the March 2, 1951 diagnosis of insanity by the Sing Sing Prison psychiatrist with his opinion that that particular siege of insanity began six months previously. . . .

The order should be reversed upon the law and the facts, and the application should be granted to the extent of directing that a hearing be held to determine the facts with respect to appellant's mental condition during the time limited by statute for the taking of an appeal from the judgment of conviction, and to determine the relief to which appellant would be entitled, if any.

* * *

NOTE 4

CARR v. NEW ORLEANS POLICE DEPARTMENT
144 So. 2d 452 (La. 1962)

RENE H. HIMEL, JUDGE AD HOC.

This is an appeal from a ruling of the Civil Service Commission dismissing plaintiff from the police department.

The reason for his dismissal was given to him by the superintendent of Police stating the report about his mental condition and "to declare you unfit for the police service."

*   *   *

. . . The mere fact that a civil employee has disagreements with fellow workers, is unpleasant to work with, experiences difficulty in adjusting to change, lacks adaptability and demonstrates inability to work with others is not sufficient cause for removal.

*   *   *

Appellant was given a full hearing by the Commission. He was represented by able counsel, who made the same argument there as here. His contention is that the testimony does not show that appellant was at the time of his dismissal unable to perform his duties. The doctors who testified that appellant suffers from schizophrenia with paranoid tendencies and ideas of persecution, and is unable to perform satisfactorily all duties required of him, admitted that he is in a state of remission. But the record shows that it cannot be predicted when an attack will happen or what will occur when it does, and that stress and strain to which he may be subjected makes it difficult for the mental balance to be maintained.

*   *   *

Appellant does not deny that he is suffering from schizophrenia with paranoid tendencies and ideas of persecution. He argues that, just because the doctors admit that he is presently in a state of remission, he should be restored to active duty. There is ample evidence that it is not safe to take the chance that, in a case of stress and strain and sudden, serious emergency, he will not be able to maintain his mental balance.

We must say that the Commission was justified in holding that it would be seriously detrimental to the appellant, the police service, and the community to put a man with that mental handicap in a uniform and arm him with a dangerous weapon. We hold that he is unable and unfit to continue to hold the position and that it would be greatly prejudicial to the service to let him do so.

*   *   *

NOTE 5

A Bill to Amend the Civil Rights Law, in Relation to the Amnesty of First Offenders*

Section 1. Declaration and purposes. The legislature hereby finds and declares that:

The lifetime impact of a criminal record, produc-

*New York Intro. 3368, January 29, 1964.

tive of an unceasing burden of socio-legal restraints and inequities affecting career, livelihood and personal welfare, is a major contributing factor of criminality and recidivism.

The permanent criminalization of every convicted offender is fundamentally inconsistent with and repugnant to the ideal correctional goal of total rehabilitation; the lifelong stigma attendant upon every criminal conviction is an insurmountable barrier to the regained self-respect, dignity, and esteem of millions of our citizens and their families, and as such, gravely undermines the essential values, attributes, and foundations of our democratic society.

The lifetime impugnment of veracity in the courts of law, attendant upon every party or witness previously convicted of a crime, has wrought grave consequences to the fair and impartial administration of justice; the indiscriminate deployment of a criminal record to impeach the credibility of the former offender has tended to destroy his effectiveness even as a disinterested truthful witness and to discourage him from further willing participation on the witness stand in the quest for truth, with resulting gross miscarriage of justice and with countless cost to all litigants, in civil and criminal proceedings alike.

The legislature further finds and declares, that:

It is the first offender who stands as society's prime hope for successful correctional redirection at its most crucial stage.

A person who has run afoul of the law should not be written off as socially incurable; to hold that a person who had once been guilty of an offense is for life to be discredited would be to declare that repentance and reformation were impossible, and at the same time take away one of the strongest motives for reformation.

Persons who have been convicted of an offense and served the sentence imposed should not be condemned as outcasts or permanently barred from normal intercourse with society; the legislature did not ever intend to close the door to reformation, repentance, or a new try at life.

Particularly as to the first offender, there can be no meaningful purpose of rehabilitation or reform unless society tenders him a genuine second chance to obliterate the fact and moral discredit of his single past transgression, and gives him an unqualified chance to make a fresh start in life, with full opportunity to undo the stigma, adversities, and handicaps of his criminal record after his sentence has been served.

The legislature further finds and declares that a legislative grant of automatic amnesty to first offenders—conditioned on the passage of a reasonable probationary interval after the sentence shall have been completed—would chart a wholly new course to peno-correctional reform, based upon a significant concept of total forgiveness of the first offense, generating a powerful incentive for re-habilitation-from-within. It may well yield an effective answer to the growing incidence of crime and to the high rate of recidivism, and to the massive strengthening of our democratic fabric by removing the hurtful stigma now attaching to a considerable number of first offenders in this country and in this state.

* * *

NOTE 6

ROCKEFELLER, NELSON A.

Veto Memorandum*

[U]nder the bill, the murderer, rapist, non-addict narcotics seller, briber or extortionist would be treated the same, for the purpose of qualifying for amnesty, as the burglar or larcenist. Persons remaining or never subject to parole or probation supervision would be equated to those who have successfully completed parole or probation. The test of "rehabilitation" would be determined solely by the offender's statement that he does not have a subsequent criminal record, not as a result of an inquiry into his actual behavior or good conduct. The offender given amnesty under these conditions would be entitled to hold *any* public office—in the Legislative, Judicial or Executive Branch of Government—irrespective of the nature of his prior crime. A convicted embezzler would be entitled lawfully to deny his conviction upon application for a position in a bank, a sex offender would be free to deny his conviction when seeking employment as a teacher, and a convicted perjurer would be entitled to deny his conviction while testifying, as a witness in a criminal case, that he saw the defendant commit a serious crime.

* * *

Finally, the bill would provide that an offender who has been granted amnesty has the right to reinstatement of any professional license previously suspended or revoked because of his conviction. In this regard, the language of the bill is mandatory. Under it a lawyer who has been convicted of embezzling his client's funds or a physician who has been convicted of abortion would be entitled to the restoration of his license after the passage of five years.

* * *

The bill is disapproved.

NOTE 7

TOLCHIN, MARTIN

United States Jobs Offered Ex-mental Patients**

The Federal Government, which pioneered in

finding jobs in the Civil Service for the physically handicapped, has undertaken a similar program to employ persons with a history of mental illness.

* * *

The Government believes the mentally rehabilitated are sometimes better suited than the population at large to certain types of work. The restoration of such persons to the working populace is considered a double fiscal gain since they cease being wards of the Government and become taxpaying citizens.

* * *

Some of the more dramatic placements include:

A man in his late 30's who spent 19 years in a Government mental institution, mostly in a state of extreme withdrawal. He was hired last year as a librarian by a Government agency that regards his performance as excellent.

A woman in her 40's who was placed after spending 10 years in a mental hospital. Hired as a clerk-typist, she was quickly promoted to a secretary and recently won an agency award for superior accomplishment.

A chronic schizophrenic in his 40's whose residual symptoms are a desire for solitude and noncommunication. This man works alone from midnight to dawn in a semideserted building on a job that requires high security clearance.

Although persons with a history of mental illness are ordinarily ineligible for security jobs, this man was considered by a Government placement specialist to be "the ultimate in selective placement."

Selective placement was also behind the employment of a number of obsessive-compulsive neurotics to jobs that required meticulous attention to detail. Unable to tolerate discrepancies, they were considered ideally suited for their jobs.

* * *

The psychiatric criteria for Federal employment are the applicant's current mental health and the probability of his continued well-being.

The duration and severity of his illness are not considered dependable predictors of future health, according to Dr. Melvin T. Johnson, medical director of the United States Civil Service Commission. The absence of residual symptoms and the stability of his social relationships are considered more important, Dr. Johnson said.

The same criteria apply to employees who become mentally ill in the course of Government employment. Of those requiring hospitalization, 60 per cent are returned to the Federal rolls.

However, the vast majority of those who experience emotional problems do not require hospitalization, the commission reports. Many are able to continue working while undergoing treatment, or return to the job after brief periods of hospitalization.

---

*Filed with Assembly Bill, Introductory Number 233 Senate Print Number 5363, July 21, 1965.
**The New York Times, November 11, 1962 (pp. 1 and 81).
© 1962 by The New York Times Company. Reprinted by permission.

Persons with a history of mental illness are sometimes better psychiatric risks than those without such a history, Dr. Johnson said. They have often developed insights and techniques that stand them in good stead, he said.

"There's no guarantee of the stability of an individual who has not had a psychiatric history," the physician said.

Nevertheless, the employment of the mentally rehabilitated raises some practical questions. Emotional problems are by definition problems in interpersonal relationships.

Can such persons work effectively with others? Do they tend to become overdependent and feel rejected if rebuffed? Is the tension and anxiety associated with some emotional ills contagious? Would such a person set an entire office on edge? Can they handle positions of authority?

No one really knows. . . .

* * *

Although some persons are reluctant to disclose their previous condition to their co-workers, the Civil Service Commission considers a willingness to do so a sign of improved mental health.

The co-workers are prepared for the arrival of such persons in informal discussions on the nature of mental illness, advances in the treatment of the illness, contributions of the mentally rehabilitated in the Civil Service, and a discussion of their role in helping such persons return to the working world.

The fact that persons in Government cannot "melt" into their jobs without divulging a history of mental illness, on penalty of *law*, is to the advantage of the former patients, in the opinion of Bernard Posner of the *ad hoc* committee.

"Instead of living in the shadows of a dark secret, they know that they are accepted and appreciated for the contributions of which they are capable," . . .

* * *

NOTE 8

GOLDSTEIN, JOSEPH

Police Discretion Not to Invoke the Criminal Process. Low-Visibility Decisions in the Administration of Justice*

The criminal process, from arrest through release, is comprised of a series of "status degradation

*Reprinted by permission of the Yale Law Journal Co. and Fred B. Rothman & Co. From the *Yale Law Journal*, vol. 69, No. 4, pp. 590–91. (1960).

ceremonies." A status degradation ceremony is "any communicative work between persons whereby the public identity of an actor is transformed into something looked on as lower in the local scheme of social types." Garfinkel, *Conditions of Successful Degradation Ceremonies*, 61 Am. J. Sociology 420 (1956). As a result of the redefinition of individual status which accompanies being labeled "accused," "convict," or "ex-convict," many releasees pay the penalty for their offenses and suspected offenses on a never ending installment plan.

> Many men on their release carry their prison about with them into the air, and hide it as a secret disgrace in their hearts, and at length, like poor poisoned things, creep into some hole and die. It is wretched that they should have to do so. . . . Society takes upon itself the right to inflict appalling punishment on the individual, but it also has the supreme vice of shallowness, and fails to realize what it has done. When a man's punishment is over, it leaves him to himself; that is to say, it abandons him at the very moment when its highest duty towards him begins. It is really ashamed of its own actions, and shuns those whom it has punished, as people shun a creditor whose debt they cannot pay, or one on whom they have inflicted an irreparable, an irredeemable wrong.

Wilde, De Profundis 26–27 (1905). Employers are reluctant to hire persons with arrest or conviction records.

* * *

One of the crucial problems facing the administration of criminal justice is how to establish release procedures which in practice become *status-elevation* ceremonies. Discharge from parole or from prison should carry with it, in appropriate situations, the kinds of redefinitions upward that are associated, for example, with graduation from high school or college, honorable discharge from the armed services, successful completion of apprenticeship in a trade or admission to a profession. Some ceremony or series of ceremonies must be devised to redefine the social status of releases to that the public will begin to entertain a presumption that a person honorably discharged (as opposed to neutrally discharged or possibly even dishonorably discharged) from the correctional service is ready to take his place as a law-abiding citizen in the community. Were such a ceremony or ceremonies created, effective pressure might be placed on correctional authorities to test and carry out rehabilitation programs and to develop a meaningful system of communication with the public.

* * *

B.

To Assume Responsibility for the Well-being of Self

1.

MORRIS v. UNITED STATES
217 F. Supp. 220 (N.D. Tex. 1963)

BREWSTER, DISTRICT JUDGE.

This controversy had its source in the fact that the wife and the sweetheart of Sgt. Olen R. Morris, the insured under a $10,000 National Service Life Insurance Policy, were not one and the same person, and in the further fact that his attempt to support two major vices was too much for him. The last one brought about his suicide, and the first one furnished the parties for the argument over the proceeds of the policy.

The sweetheart, Lucille Robertson, was the named beneficiary at the time of his death. Willie Morris, his estranged wife, was the beneficiary at the time of the change to Lucille Robertson. Mrs. Morris seeks to recover the proceeds of the policy on the ground that the insured was mentally incompetent to make the change. . . .

*   *   *

[G]enerally the standard for determining mental capacity in this kind of case is "the same as that necessary to execute a valid will, deed, or contract." 113 F. Supp. at p. 148. More specifically stated, the test is:

> "To be capable of effecting a valid change of beneficiary a person should have clearness of mind and memory sufficient to know the nature of the property for which he is about to name a beneficiary, the nature of the act which he is about to perform, the names and identities of those who are the natural objects of his bounty; his relationship toward them, and the consequences of his act, uninfluenced by any material delusions. . . .

*   *   *

This case presents a sordid state of fact, with little on either side to appeal to a sense of equity.

*   *   *

The insured was a Staff Sergeant stationed at Chenault Air Force Base, Lake Charles, Louisiana, when he committed suicide on April 1, 1961, at the age of forty-one. He had completed nineteen years of military service at the time, and would have been eligible for retirement at the end of his twentieth year. His closest surviving relatives consisted of his widow,

an eighty-six-year-old father, and some brothers and sisters.

Sgt. Morris and the plaintiff, whom he called "Billie," were married on March 1, 1954. The ceremony was certainly no amateur performance. It was hope prevailing over experience. He had been theretofore married and divorced three times. Matrimonially, she was also a three-time loser. At least one of her former divorces had been obtained by the husband. There was no child of any of the seven marriages involving the Sergeant or Billie. It is not clear from the evidence whether they solemnized their happy (?) event in a church, after a march down the aisle to the altar to the accompaniment of some well-known wedding hymn, or in the office of a justice of the peace to the tune of the less melodious noises usually heard around a county court house. However, from all the evidence and from observation of the plaintiff, there is little question that, as the time approached, there was uppermost in her mind: "Aisle-altar-hymn." The marriage was undoubtedly a happy thought, but nothing came of it except trouble.

Billie was in her middle forties, and eight years older than the Sergeant, when she married him in 1954. The evidence in this case and her demeanor during the trial left the impression that her main goal in life was to have some man for a meal ticket. Her marriage appeared to be, not for better or worse, but for more or less. As might have been expected from their disparity of age as she passed the half-century mark, he finally decided that he liked the smell of perfume better than that of liniment, and life came between them. He did not have to search far. Lucille, a tall brunet about the same age as the Sergeant, lived only two blocks from him. She had every appearance of being gay; and she could and did help him "whoop it up," to use her words, on festive occasions such as Christmas and New Year's Eve, and possibly at other times when he yielded excessively to his addiction to alcohol. She had only six handicaps: a husband, Johnny, and five minor children. Johnny was a cook, or as she put it, "in the food service," at the Air Force Base.

The romance began to ripen in May, 1960. On June 11 following, the Sergeant took Billie to the home of her parents in Parker County, Texas. He told her later that before his return to the Air Base, he filed a suit for divorce in Clay County, where he maintained his legal residence. . . .

*   *   *

On January 3, 1961, the Sergeant went to the office

of the Military Affairs Counselor, Personal Affairs Section, on the Air Base, and asked advice of Sgt. Henry M. Gay about changing the beneficiary in his National Service Life Insurance Policy. He was in the proper office talking to the right man to get the information. He explained that he was separated from his wife and did not want her to get the proceeds of his insurance. He inquired whether he had to designate a relative as beneficiary. Sgt. Gay explained to him that while the law required that his nearest relative get his survivor's benefits, he could name a person not related to him as beneficiary under his National Service Life Insurance Policy. Under Sgt. Gay's supervision, he signed the change of beneficiary on the regular form so as to name Lucille. Sgt. Morris was sober and mentally competent when he executed the change of beneficiary.

*   *   *

As if he did not have enough troubles, he acquired some more in March, 1961, the last month of his life. His letter of March 5 said that he was working on the night shift at the shop and at the bowling alley in the daytime. On March 17, he wrote that Johnny had got judgment that day in his suit for legal separation, and that Lucille had received practically nothing in the property settlement. That meant that the Sergeant was faced with the responsibility of having contributed to depriving five little children of the security of a home, or of trying to furnish one for them when he could not make just a fair living for himself. Billie had shown no signs of being willing to go back to him, and yet she was opposed to his getting a divorce. Lucille had begun to give up on him and was having dates with other men. On March 26, only five days before he shot himself, he wrote, "I am just sobering up from a week drunk, all because I was so stupid as to let her worry me." He was drunk again on March 31 when he went to Lucille's house. When she made him leave, he went to a tavern and called her from a pay telephone booth. It was during that conversation that he took action to relieve himself of his apparently insurmountable problems by committing suicide. He shot himself in the head while he still had Lucille on the telephone, and the wound brought about his tragic end on the following day.

In his position as Sergeant, the insured had a responsibility not only for himself, but for others under him. There is no evidence that he was ever mentally incapable of meeting, or that he ever failed to meet, those responsibilities at any time except when he was under the influence of intoxicants.

On January 3, 1961, Sergeant Morris had sufficient clearness of mind and memory to know the nature of the property for which he was about to name Lucille beneficiary. He fully realized that he was making a change of beneficiary that would transfer the right to the proceeds of the policy from Billie to Lucille. He knew the natural objects of his bounty and his relationship toward them. A person has the legal right to dispose of his property as he may wish, "regardless of the ties of nature or relationship" . . . . There was nothing unnatural about changing the beneficiary from his estranged wife. The only strange thing about it in this case is why he waited from June to January to do it. That kind of matter is one that is usually called to a spouse's attention by his lawyer at the time the decision is made to file a divorce suit. Under the circumstances, Lucille was a natural object of the Sergeant's bounty on January 3, 1961. He was in love with her. Apparently, she was the only woman who showed any interest in him. . . .

The remaining matter to be determined in applying the test outlined in the Taylor case is whether the change of beneficiary was the product of any insane delusion. [T]he standard of mental capacity required in cases involving change of beneficiaries is the same as that necessary to execute a valid will, deed, or contract. . . .

"... 'But to avoid a will because the testator entertained a delusion, the delusion must be an insane delusion, and the will must be the product thereof. . . .

"... 'The essence of an insane delusion is that it has no basis in reason, cannot be dispelled by reason, and can be accounted for only as the product of mental disorder. . . .

"...'To constitute a delusion sufficient to invalidate a will, the subject matter must have no foundation in fact, for there is no such thing as a delusion founded upon facts. . . .'

*   *   *

"Obviously, a testator need not always be right in his deductions in order to avoid being classed as insanely deluded. . . . One cannot be said to act under an insane delusion if his condition of mind results from an inference or a process of reasoning, however illogical, from facts which are shown to exist."

It is doubtful if the evidence is sufficient to establish any kind of delusion. The plaintiff did offer lay testimony to the effect that for a while the Sergeant feared that Lucille's husband was going to kill him. The Sergeant's sister said that he told her that the reason he could not come home during the 1960 Christmas holidays was because he was afraid that Johnny would kill him if he got off the Air Base. That apprehension on the part of the Sergeant was certainly not an insane delusion. It did not meet the test that it had "no basis in reason." There was some foundation in fact for it under the circumstances of this case. Even the two expert witnesses offered by the plaintiff did not regard that belief as a delusion.

The decision that there was no insane delusion could well rest on what is said above; but the Sergeant's fear will be better understood if the situation is viewed in the light of what is known about his background.

He was born in Montague County, Texas, and grew up in Clay County, immediately adjoining on the west. He left to join the Army when he was about twenty-two years old. Clay County is in the edge of the "big ranch" country which extends from there westward to the New Mexico border. Although attitudes in his home State have mellowed considerably in the almost two decades since he left it, during the period when he was growing up in Clay County, there existed in the ranch country of Texas what was known as the "unwritten law." Every young man understood it just as well as he knew what the meat course was going to be at ranch headquarters while calves were being "worked" during a roundup. The effect of the "unwritten law" was to make a bad insurance risk out of a man who broke up another man's home and deprived him of the daily association of his wife and children. He usually died suddenly of lead poisonin'. That was a disease contracted the first time the outraged husband and father came in gunshot range of the homebreaker. The husband himself was never plagued with the disease, but he was an almost certain carrier of it. He was usually equipped to give six doses of lead in rapid succession if necessary to produce fatal results. In some cases, the husband was not even indicted; but he was usually brought to trial so that his justification could be made public. The standard story was that the husband armed himself upon a-learnin' of the situation and sought out the other man for an explanation; that the deceased saw him a-comin' and reached for his pistol pocket as if to pull a gun; that in self-defense the husband had to draw, throw down on his "assailant," start a-fannin' his six shooter and keep a-fannin' it until, as the cases said, "all semblance of danger, real or apparent, viewed from the defendant's standpoint, had completely disappeared." It made no difference in the outcome of the case if it developed that the deceased was unarmed. During their deliberations, the juries usually found that the law given them in the charge was inadequate to what they thought was equity. To supply that deficiency, they resorted to the "unwritten law" of the purpose not only of acquitting the husband, but also of endorsing his conduct, of recognizing that it was open season on homebreakers, and of serving notice on each one of them, actual or potential, to stay in his own back yard.

*   *   *

When all the facts are taken into consideration in connection with the Sergeant's background, it cannot be said that his fear for his life had no foundation in reason, or even that his reasoning was defective, whether he thought that Johnny ought to shoot him, or that Johnny was going to shoot him, or both. A judge who was born and reared in West Texas and who, during the early years of his practice had experience both in prosecuting and in defending

"unwritten law" cases, by relating that experience to conditions as they existed in the Sergeant's home country when he grew into young manhood, has no difficulty in understanding the Sergeant's feeling that he had to ride low in the saddle until Johnny accepted the situation "peaceful-like."

*   *   *

NOTES

NOTE 1

DAVIS v. COLORADO KENWORTH CORP.
Colo. 396 P.2d 958 (1964)

DAY, JUSTICE.

Davis, a mental incompetent, filed suit through his wife as next friend. [He] alleged that he entered into a contract to sell [certain] "equipment" to Ben. A. Lucero and Dolores M. Lucero, and prayed for rescission and nullification of that contract.

*   *   *

Davis admits that his right to recovery depends upon the interpretation of the provisions of C.R.S. '53, 71-1-21, which provides, in material part:

> "All contracts, agreements, and credits with or to any insane person, shall be absolutely void as against such person, his heirs, or personal representatives; but persons making such contracts or agreements with any insane person shall be bound thereby at the election of his conservators. . . ."

Davis contends that he comes within the purview and meaning of the statute because on the October, 1951, date he was found not guilty by reason of insanity in a criminal proceeding wherein he had been charged with the crime of larceny. He argues that for the purpose of the statute there is no distinction between his insanity adjudication in the criminal proceeding and a similar adjudication in the county court under the mental health laws.

*   *   *

The Hanks case [114 Colo 578, 168 P.2d 256] is authority for the proposition that one may be insane on some subjects and still have the capacity to contract. The inability to form criminal intent is therefore not determinative in this case. That Davis had the capacity to know and understand his transactions is clearly demonstrated by the fact that he had borrowed $10,000.00 from a bank to start his trucking business and had opened an account in the name of Davis Trucking. With a portion of the $10,000.00 he purchased the equipment heretofore described. He entered into a lease arrangement with Ringsby Truck Lines, and for a period of a year he engaged in the trucking business.

NOTE 2

PIONEER TRUST COMPANY v. CURRIN
210 Ore 354, 311 P.2d 445 (1957)

WARNER, JUSTICE.

* * *

[W]e have consistently held that a deed of a person afflicted with a paranoid form of schizophrenia is void unless executed during a lucid interval.

* * *

Those moments when the mentally ill recoup for the time being a mental capacity sufficient to comprehend the nature of the business or other matters in which they are then engaged, even though they shortly thereafter relapse to a status of incomprehension caused by their mental disorder, are known to both medicine and the law as "lucid intervals." It is in these temporary moments of emergence from mental darkness to the light of rational understanding, be they of long or short duration, when the mentally ill attain a competency sufficient to execute a valid instrument. Deeds or other conveyances and contracts made by insane persons during such lucid interval are valid and enforceable.

Lucid interval, as we use it, is defined in 44 C.J.S. Insane Persons § 2, p. 36 as follows:

> "A lucid interval, as used in speaking of lucid intervals of insane persons, is not merely a cessation of the violent symptoms of the disorder, but a restoration of the faculties of the mind sufficiently to enable the person soundly to judge of the act; such a full return of the mind to sanity as places the person in possession of the powers of his mind, enabling him to understand and transact his affairs as usual. The term does not necessarily mean complete or perfect restoration of the mental faculties to their original condition; and it is sufficient if there is such restoration that the person is able to comprehend and to do the act with such reason, memory, and judgment as to make it a legal act; . . . "

* * *

NOTE 3

FABER v. SWEET STYLE MFG. CORP.
242 N.Y.S.2d 763 (1964)

BERNARD S. MEYER, J.

* * *

The standards by which competence to contract is measured were, apparently, developed without relation to the effects of particular mental diseases or disorders and prior to recognition of manic-depressive psychosis as a distinct form of mental illness. . . . Primarily they are concerned with capacity to understand: (*Aldrich* v. *Bailey*, 132 N.Y. 85, 87–88) "so

deprived of his mental faculties as to be wholly, absolutely and completely unable to understand or comprehend the nature of the transaction"; (*Paine* v. *Aldrich*, 133 N.Y. 544, 546) "such mental capacity at the time of the execution of the deed that he could collect in his mind without prompting all the elements of the transaction, and retain them for a sufficient length of time to perceive their obvious relations to each other, and to form a rational judgment in regard to them"; *Matter of Delinousha* v. *National Biscuit Co.*, 248 N.Y. 93, 95. "A contract may be avoided only if a party is so affected as to be unable to see things in their true relations and to form correct conclusions in regard thereto." . . . If cognitive capacity is the sole criterion used, the manic must be held competent . . . for manic-depressive psychosis affects motivation rather than ability to understand.

The law does, however, recognize stages of incompetence other than total lack of understanding. Thus it will invalidate a transaction when a contracting party is suffering from delusions if there is "some such connection between the insane delusions and the making of the deed as will compel the inference that the insanity induced the grantor to perform an act, the purport and effect of which he could not understand, and which he would not have performed if thoroughly sane" *Moritz* v. *Moritz*, 153 App. Div. 147, 152. . . . Moreover, it holds that understanding of the physical nature and consequences of an act of suicide does not render the suicide voluntary within the meaning of a life insurance contract if the insured "acted under the control of an insane impulse caused by disease, and derangement of his intellect, which deprived him of the capacity of governing his own conduct in accordance with reason." *Newton* v. *Mutual Benefit Life Ins. Co.*, 76 N.Y. 426, 429. . . . Finally, [we] consider not only ability to understand but also capacity to form "a rational judgment" or "correct conclusions." Thus, capacity to understand is not, in fact, the sole criterion. Incompetence to contract also exists when a contract is entered into under the compulsion of a mental disease or disorder but for which the contract would not have been made.

* * *

NOTE 4

IN RE NITSCHKE'S GUARDIANSHIP
113 Ohio App. 243, 177 N.E.2d 628 (1961)

BRYANT, PRESIDING JUDGE.

* * *

[W]hen an application for restoration to competency is made, the test is whether the ward has made substantial progress and whether he is at present competent to manage his affairs, both personal and financial. Should the condition recur at some future time, it will be sufficient at that time to bring a new proceeding and cause a new examination to be made. We feel that it is entirely too speculative to hold that, because there might be future marital difficulties or because there might be a return to the excessive use of alcohol or the excessive use of a drug, which might cause the condition to reappear, the restoration to competency should be indefinitely postponed and delayed.

NOTE 5

OLSHEN v. KAUFMAN
235 Ore. 423, 385 P.2d 161 (1963)
LUSK, JUSTICE.

The question is whether, under the statute of this state providing for the appointment of guardians for spendthrifts, recovery may be had on the contract of a spendthrift when his guardian has repudiated the obligation.

*   *   *

ORS 126. 005, in effect at the applicable time, provided:
"As used in this chapter:

"(1) 'Spendthrift' includes every person who, by excessive drinking, idleness, gaming or debauchery of any kind, shall spend or lessen his estate so as to expose or likely to expose himself or his family, to want or suffering, or to cause the county to be charged for the expense of the support of himself and his family."

*   *   *

The purpose of the appointment of a guardian of the estate of a spendthrift is to protect the ward in his property against his wasteful and vicious habits which expose him or are likely to expose him or his family to want or suffering or to cause any public authority to be charged for any expense for his support or that of his family. . . . It would seem to be fairly obvious that for the fulfilment of that purpose the responsibility of declaring void a contract entered into by the ward naturally devolves upon the guardian, along with his other duties. . . .

*   *   *

NOTE 6

WARD v. BOOTH
197 F.2d 963 (9th Cir. 1952)

POPE,   CIRCUIT JUDGE.

*   *   *

[T]he appellants have brought this appeal asserting . . . that under the requirements of the Fifth and Seventh Amendments, the appellants and the alleged incompetent [were] entitled to a jury trial upon the issues presented by the original petition for the appointment of a guardian.

*   *   *

It is argued that a jury trial was required here because of the requirement of the Seventh Amendment that "In Suits at common law, where the value in controversy shall exceed twenty dollars, the right of trial by jury shall be preserved. . . ." We agree with the conclusion arrived at by the Supreme Court of the Territory, and ably expounded in its opinion, that the proceedings here in question bear no resemblance to the "Suits at common law" referred to in the Seventh Amendment.

It has been pointed out that prior to the adoption of the Constitution and under the ancient English practice, the Lord Chancellor, as the delegate of the King to conduct insanity proceedings, was wont to issue a writ *de lunatico inquirendo* under which a jury was summoned to determine the question of sanity. . . . Our attention is called to a number of decisions by state courts holding that under the provisions of some state constitutions the question of a person's insanity must be tried to a jury. . . .

But there is a substantial difference between such state constitutional provisions and the Seventh Amendment, for the latter has application only to. . . . "Suits at common law, where the value in controversy shall exceed twenty dollars", etc. In a proceeding such as the one here involved, it cannot strictly be said that there is any value in controversy. The matter in controversy is the question of the competence or incompetence of the person named, and while the result of such a determination may affect extensive property holdings, it cannot be said that the issue to be tried is one where there is any "value in controversy."

*   *   *

NOTE 7

Designation of Person to Act as Committee in Event of Future Incompetence*

Persons of sound mind who fear that they may be unable to manage their affairs in the future are at present unable to make an effective provision for such an eventuality. They are not able to pre-select the committee who will be appointed in an incompetency proceeding; a power of attorney provides no solution because it ceases to be effective when the principal becomes legally incompetent. The [Law Revision] Commission is convinced that individuals should be permitted to designate the person whom they desire to be appointed as their committee in the event of future incompetency. Accordingly, it is recommending the enactment of a bill which allows a competent

---

*N.Y. State Bar Ass'n. Legislation Letter, Jan. 1966. (S. Int. 1434, Pr. 1459 Speno, Mental Hygiene.)

person of the age of eighteen or over to designate a person to be his committee. Such designation must be executed, and may be revoked, in the same manner as a will. The court is expected to accept this nomination if this is in the best interests of the incompetent.

2.

McGUIRE v. ALMY
297 Mass. 323, 8 N.E.2d 760 (1937)

QUA, JUSTICE.

This is an action of tort for assault and battery. The only question of law reported is whether the judge should have directed a verdict for the defendant.

The following facts are established by the plaintiff's own evidence: In August, 1930, the plaintiff was employed to take care of the defendant. The plaintiff was a registered nurse and was a graduate of a training school for nurses. The defendant was an insane person. Before the plaintiff was hired she learned that the defendant was a "mental case and was in good physical condition," and that for some time two nurses had been taking care of her. The plaintiff was on "24-hour duty." The plaintiff slept in the room next to the defendant's room. Except when the plaintiff was with the defendant, the plaintiff kept the defendant locked in the defendant's room. There was a wire grating over the outside of the window of that room. During the period of "fourteen months or so" while the plaintiff cared for the defendant, the defendant "had a few odd spells" when she showed some hostility to the plaintiff and said that "she would like to try and do something to her." The defendant had been violent at times and had broken dishes "and things like that," and on one or two occasions the plaintiff had to have help to subdue the defendant.

On April 19, 1932, the defendant, while locked in her room, had a violent attack. The plaintiff heard a crashing of furniture and then knew that the defendant was ugly, violent, and dangerous. The defendant told the plaintiff and a Miss Maroney, "the maid," who was with the plaintiff in the adjoining room, that if they came into the defendant's room, she would kill them. The plaintiff and Miss Maroney looked into the defendant's room, "saw what the defendant had done," and "thought it best to take the broken stuff away before she did any harm to herself with it." They sent for a Mr. Emerton, the defendant's brother-in-law. When he arrived the defendant was in the middle of her room about ten feet from the door, holding upraised the leg of a low-boy as if she were going to strike. The plaintiff stepped into the room and walked toward the defendant, while Mr. Emerton and Miss Maroney remained in the doorway. As the plaintiff approached the defendant and tried to take hold of the defendant's hand which held the leg, the defendant struck the plaintiff's head with

it, causing the injuries for which the action was brought.

The extent to which an insane person is liable for torts has not been fully defined in this Commonwealth. . . . In *Lawton* v. *Sun Mutual Ins. Co.*, 2 Cush. 500, at page 516, it is said that one "bereft of reason and judgment, and the use of his moral powers and intellectual faculties . . . is no longer a responsible being . . . and his acts must be considered as pure accidents." In *Brown* v. *Howe*, 9 Gray, 84, 69 Am.Dec. 276, it was held that the guardian of a lunatic cannot credit himself in his probate account with a sum intended to represent his personal loss from the negligent burning of his house by his ward. Here it seems to have been assumed that an action at law might lie. In *Morain* v. *Devlin*, 132 Mass. 87, at page 88, 42 Am.Rep. 423, this court said, through Chief Justice Gray, "By the common law, as generally stated in the books, a lunatic is civilly liable to make compensation in damages to persons injured by his acts, although, being incapable of criminal intent, he is not liable to indictment and punishment," . . . But the actual decision went no further than to hold the lunatic as a landowner receiving the benefits of ownership, liable for the defective condition of his premises. . . . These accident . . . cases are not controlling in the present case, for here the question is not one of causation, but is a question as to how far the subjective standard is admissible as governing the obligations of an insane person to others.

Turning to authorities elsewhere, we find that courts in this country almost invariably say in the broadest terms that an insane person is liable for his torts. As a rule no distinction is made between those torts which would ordinarily be classed as intentional and those which would ordinarily be classed as negligent, nor do the courts discuss the effect of different kinds of insanity or of varying degrees of capacity as bearing upon the ability of the defendant to understand the particular act in question or to make a reasoned decision with respect to it, although it is sometimes said that an insane person is not liable for torts requiring malice of which he is incapable. Defamation and malicious prosecution are the torts more commonly mentioned in this connection. . . . These decisions are rested more upon grounds of public policy and upon what might be called a popular view of the requirements of essential justice than upon any attempt to apply logically the underlying principles of civil liability to the special instance of the mentally deranged. Thus it is said that a rule imposing liability tends to make more watchful those persons who have charge of the defendant and who may be supposed to have some interest in preserving his property; that as an insane person he must pay for his support, if he is financially able, so he ought also to pay for the damage which he does; that an insane person with abundant wealth ought not to continue in unimpaired enjoyment of the comfort which it brings while his victim bears the burden unaided; and there is also a suggestion that courts are loath to introduce into the great body of civil litigation the difficulties in determining mental capacity which it has been found impossible to avoid in the criminal field.

The rule established in these cases has been criticized severely by certain eminent text writers both in this country and in England, principally on the ground that it is an archaic survival of the rigid and formal mediaeval conception of liability for acts done, without regard to fault, as opposed to what is said to be the general modern theory that liability in tort should rest upon fault. Notwithstanding these criticisms, we think, that as a practical matter, there is strong force in the reasons underlying these decisions. . . . Fault is by no means at the present day a universal prerequisite to liability, and the theory that it should be such has been obliged very recently to yield at several points to what have been thought to be paramount considerations of public good. Finally, it would be difficult not to recognize the persuasive weight of so much authority so widely extended.

But the present occasion does not require us either to accept or to reject the prevailing doctrine in its entirety. For this case it is enough to say that where an insane person by his act does intentional damage to the person or property of another he is liable for that damage in the same circumstances in which a normal person would be liable. This means that in so far as a particular intent would be necessary in order to render a normal person liable, the insane person, in order to be liable, must have been capable of entertaining that same intent and must have entertained it in fact. But the law will not inquire further into his peculiar mental condition with a view to excusing him if it should appear that delusion or other consequence of his affliction has caused him to entertain that intent or that a normal person would not have entertained it.

We do not suggest that this is necessarily a logical stopping point. If public policy demands that a mentally affected person be subjected to the external standard for intentional wrongs, it may well be that public policy also demands that he should be subjected to the external standard for wrongs which are commonly classified as negligent, in accordance with what now seems to be the prevailing view. We stop here for the present, because we are not required to go further in order to decide this case, because of deference to the difficulty of the subject, because full and adequate discussion is lacking in most of the cases decided up to the present time, and because by far the greater number of those cases, however broad their statement of the principle, are in fact cases of intentional rather than of negligent injury.

* * *

The defendant further argues that she is not liable because the plaintiff, by undertaking to care for the defendant with knowledge of the defendant's condition and by walking into the room in spite of the defendant's threat under the circumstances shown, consented to the injury, or, as the defendant puts it, assumed the risk, both contractually and voluntarily. Without considering to what extent consent is in general a defence to an assault . . . we think the defendant was not entitled to a directed verdict on this ground. Although the plaintiff knew when she was employed that the defendant was a mental case, and despite some show of hostility and some violent and unruly conduct, there was no evidence of any previous attack or even of any serious threat against anyone. The plaintiff had taken care of the defendant for "fourteen months or so." We think that the danger of actual physical injury was not, as matter of law, plain and obvious up to the time when the plaintiff entered the room on the occasion of the assault. But by that time an emergency had been created. The defendant was breaking up the furniture, and it could have been found that the plaintiff reasonably feared that the defendant would do harm to herself. Something had to be done about it. The plaintiff had assumed the duty of caring for the defendant. We think that a reasonable attempt on her part to perform that duty under the peculiar circumstances brought about by the defendant's own act did not necessarily indicate a voluntary consent to be injured. Consent does not always follow from the intentional incurring of risk. . . .

* * *

3.

SENATE COMMITTEE OF THE JUDICIARY REPORT TO ACCOMPANY A SPECIAL BILL— DEMETRIOS DOUSOPOULOS*

* * *

The purpose of the bill . . . is to waive the excluding provision of existing law relating to one who has suffered a prior attack of insanity in behalf of the brother of a United States citizen. The bill provides for the posting of a bond as a guaranty that the beneficiary will not become a public charge. . . .

The beneficiary of the bill is a 42-year-old native and citizen of Greece, who presently resides in that country with his wife and minor son. The family is eligible to nonquota status . . . but the beneficiary has been found ineligible to receive a visa because of an attack of insanity suffered in 1948, while he was serving with the Greek National Army. He was hospitalized for 20 days and has been physically and mentally well since that time. . . .

* * *

*Rep. No. 924, 88th Congress, 2nd Session (1964).

Hon. EMANUEL CELIER,
Chairman, Committee on the Judiciary,
House of Representatives.

DEAR MR. CHAIRMAN: . . .

*   *   *

The beneficiary has had three years of high school education and is a graduate of the Conservatory of Thessaloniki holding a diploma in vocal music issued to him in June 1961. He is an opera singer and is a member of the State Chorus of Northern Greece. Mr. Dousopoulos is also a shoemaker with eight years' experience in the profession. He served in the Greek National Army for an aggregate period of 18 months, from April 1946 to March 1948. He served during a critical period when the Greek Government was fighting the Communist guerrillas. He received a medical discharge as a schizophrenic because of a nervous and mental condition developed during a battle against the Communists, for which he was hospitalized for 20 days. The mental condition occurred when he found himself with a dead soldier and was suddenly seized with a fear that he too might die. Upon his discharge from the army, he returned home and worked as a shoemaker. In the meantime he began taking lessons in vocal music and graduated from the conservatory. The beneficiary stated that he has had no mental disorders or symptoms of psychosis since his discharge from the military hospital in 1948, and that his past mental condition has had no effect on his employment or his living with others.

*   *   *

The beneficiary received a complete medical examination on June 11, 1963, the results of which were negative, except for the finding of his ineligibility because of a previous attack of insanity. . . .

*   *   *

A recent security investigation conducted in the beneficiary's case revealed no adverse information. Sincerely yours,

FREDERICK G. DUTTON,
Assistant Secretary.

*   *   *

The committee, after consideration of all the facts in the case, is of the opinion that the bill (H.R. 7533), as amended, should be enacted.

NOTE

Entry of Insane Troubles Israel*

Officials of the Ministry of the Interior have been drafting amendments to legislation that now requires

---

*New York Times, January 17, 1965 (p. 14). © 1965 by the New York Times Co. Reprinted by permission.

---

the Government to admit Jews and grant them automatic citizenship even if they are insane.

The only persons the Government is lawfully able to bar are those "likely to endanger public health or the security of the state" or "with a criminal past which is likely to endanger public peace."

*   *   *

Dr. Joseph Goldin-Zahavi, Deputy Director for Immigration and Registration [said] in an interview in Jerusalem that the liberality of the legislation had been abused by Jews embarrassed by mental illness in their families.

*   *   *

A United States official familiar with the problem said American families who send their sick here are not unscrupulous but believe "that it would be a better place for their mentally ill kin than the cold non-Jewish society in the United States."

Many of those sent here receive monthly checks from their families or Social Security payments. Usually the money is insufficient.

*   *   *

United States policy has been to communicate with relatives in cases where such persons seek assistance from the consulate here and to recommend their return home.

Israel is seriously short of hospital beds. However, no one has ever been returned to the United States against his wishes or those of his family.

[T]he proposed amendment to the 1950 Law of the Return would empower the Minister of the Interior to exclude "mentally ill persons endangering public peace or likely to become a burden on the community."

He said it was also proposed to amend the Nationality Act that accords Jewish immigrants Israeli citizenship on arrival. By making six months or a year's residence a requirement, the authorities will have a chance to detect undesirables and expel them before they acquire the protection of citizenship, he added.

*   *   *

4.

THE DISGUISED OPPRESSION OF INVOLUNTARY GUARDIANSHIP: HAVE THE ELDERLY FREEDOM TO SPEND?*

By imposing an involuntary guardianship in the name of help and protection, a court suspends almost entirely an adult's power to create legal relations

---

**Reprinted by permission of the Yale Law Journal Co. and Fred B. Rothman & Co. From the *Yale Law Journal,* Vol. 73, No. 4, pp. 676–692 (1964).

with other persons. While the ward remains uncon-
fined, and may be left to make many of the non-legal
decisions of his daily existence, he may not direct the
disposal or use of his own property, enter valid
contracts, marry, change his domicile or choose
agents—doctor, lawyer or guardian. Probably he will
be unable to write a valid will and possibly, he will be
denied the right to vote. Involuntary guardianship is
imposed upon any adult found to be mentally incompetent. In difficult cases, where mental impairment is not so severe as to make the adult's inability to
care for himself or his property patent, a finding of
incompetency depends upon a showing of inability
to manage property as well as some slight mental
weakness or deterioration. Despite the severe incursions of an involuntary guardianship upon individual
freedom, courts use non-adversary procedures in
adjudicating competency and do not hesitate to impose a guardianship in even doubtful cases. Non-
adversary hearings are justified on the ground that
only the individual's best interests are at stake, in
theory, there is no one before the court who has an
interest adverse to that of the potential ward. But, in
fact, there will often be interests quite opposite to
those of the potential ward. Relatives, creditors and
potential heirs may have reasons to wish wardship
imposed. The possibility of conflict and the weaknesses of a non-adversary hearing may best be seen in
the treatment of the aged. An elderly individual,
having collected considerable funds over a lifetime
of savings, may begin to show signs of senility, the
inevitable deterioration of old age, as well as a change
in consumption patterns. Relatives interested in
receiving inheritances may then be able to secure their
expectations of inheritance by obtaining the imposition of involuntary guardianship, curtailing the aged's
ability to spend what he has amassed. The effectiveness of guardianship for their purposes of estate conservation is enhanced by procedures which favor
family interests and offer little real protection to the
individual seeking to avoid the imposition of
guardianship upon himself.

[An] Ohio case, *In re Tyrell*,[7] is illustrative. Walter
Tyrell, 85, had assured his personal security by
contracting with a rest home for his care until death;
his burial expenses were pre-paid. He had neither
living issue nor spouse. In the space of two years, he
spent $9,000, almost half his remaining estate; two
thousand of those dollars were given to a Mrs. Wise,
a widowed lady whom he felt "needed it." What was
left was $12,000 of bank stock, snugly bailed to his
sister-in-law. It was apparently she who, when return
of the stock was demanded, instigated the involuntary
guardianship proceedings against Mr. Tyrell. The
hearing which followed was brief. No independent

7. No. 20467, P. Ct., Preble County, Ohio, *aff'd.*, No. 42,
Ct. App., Preble County, Ohio, Oct. 31, 1962, *appeal dismissed*,
174 Ohio St. 554 (1963).

inquiry by court-appointed physicians preceded a
finding that Mr. Tyrell was incompetent. Instead the
court relied upon the testimony of petitioner's
physicians, who had given Mr. Tyrell a fifteen minute
examination in the jury room before the hearing.
Their evaluation, they admitted, was based on hearsay
as well as on their own inquiry. Although the court
recognized that Mr. Tyrell had a good memory and
an exceptionally keen, alert mind, it added its own
piece of demeanor evidence concerning him: "his
smile is at times not normal; his eyes do not focus
properly at all times; his gait and reflexes are not
normal; and . . . he is not laying his cane aside but
dropping it." Despite his customary generosity to
friends, and his careful planning for his own security,
Mr. Tyrell's expenditure of the previous two years
were found conclusive evidence of incapacity to
manage property. Since Mr. Tyrell had already
provided for his own personal care, the only real
function of the court-appointed guardian—another
relative, Helen Harshman—will be to conserve the
estate, thereby insuring a sizeable inheritance. This
result seems to contradict the premises of a doctrine
couched solely in terms of benefit to the ward.

Involuntary guardianships have developed, historically, as an almost necessary concomitant to commitment proceedings. In a society unaware of the
many forms of mental illness, guardians were appointed only for the "wildman" who required commitment and restraint. Once an adult was committed,
some method of caring for his property became
necessary. Early English law permitted the King to
appropriate the entire estate, under the theory of
parens patriae; only the profits in excess of an alloca-
tion for the support of the ward and his family were
conserved for the ward's possible recovery. Since
commitment was then used only in cases of extreme
mental disturbance, there was little danger of im-
pinging on freedom to handle property. The impulse
for paternal state care was strong. In this country,
statutes offered similar protection to lunatics, imbeciles or idiots, and to the society they endangered.
Only recently have the procedures of commitment
and the appointment of involuntary guardians been
at all separated, with the courts willing to appoint
guardians for those possessing more than a "spark of
intelligence."

Awareness of the breadth and complexity of the
problem of mental illness has wrought many changes:
the stigmatized terms of "lunacy, imbecility or
idiocy" have been removed from the statutes, and the
broader "mentally ill" or "mentally unsound" substituted. Confinement, a total remedy, is largely
reserved for extreme cases; but an adult need no
longer be a "gibbering, slobbering, lemon-headed
wildman" to be adjudicated mentally incompetent.
Modern statutes, sweeping a considerably broader
proportion of the population than the early statutes

within the disabled class, lay down a *Durham* test of civil responsibility: they define a mental incompetent as any person, who by reason of mental illness, mental deficiency, mental infirmities of old age, or any other cause, is unable to manage his own affairs or property or is likely to become the victim of designing persons. Since persons unable to manage personal affairs will often qualify for confinement, the principal expansion in the statutory standards has been their inclusion of persons who lack capacity only in property management.

In theory, then, mental illness has remained central. By refusing to appoint guardians for those clearly sane, despite evidence of "dissipation," wholesale involvement in the wisdom of private expenditures is avoided. Mental illness is used as the justification for the substantial deprivations of liberty involved in imposing guardianship. In practical administration of the statutory rule, however, courts have rendered virtually meaningless inquiry into the causation of erratic conduct. Psychiatrists rarely testify at guardianship hearings. And courts, once presented with any evidence of mental weakness in any realm of endeavour, immediately turn to evaluate decisions made in the management of property. If they reach a conclusion of mis-management, it is assumed to be the result of the weakness elsewhere discovered, however difficult the connection between the manifested mental unsoundness and the choices made concerning property management. Property mismanagement thus tends to reinforce and become itself evidence of mental weakness. The requirement of mental illness, then, serves as a stop-gap against involving the "clearly sane" in the process of guardianship rather than as a recognition of the specificity of some mental disabilities.

The result of this development is a greater risk that courts will restrain individuals in their freedom to make legally binding decisions. For the young and middle-aged, the effect of this expansion may not be too great. Because of realistic hopes of recovery from psychological disturbances, courts will hesitate to impose such a restraint. Evidence of mental disability is usually less available, and fewer hovering relatives will seek involuntary guardianship in expectation of personal benefit. For the aged, the possibility of involuntary guardianship imposed for reasons of property mis-management is more troublesome. Given the inevitable and irreversible character of senility, the mental deterioration of old age, evidence of mental illness will virtually always be available....

* * *

The problem of using property management as the test of mental incompetency for the aged is complicated by the change in the type of decision an individual makes concerning the expenditure of his estate at the end of his productive years. The aged rarely have legal dependents, their children being past minority and their spouse perhaps deceased. Without these responsibilities, and facing the prospect of a very short future, they may be more likely, as a matter of conscious decision, to consume at a higher rate while saving less. They may feel free to spend their entire estate; in anticipation of the disposition of their estate, they may begin to make *inter vivos* gifts with greater frequency, seeking to distribute their estate while they can still enjoy the gratitude of their beneficiaries and the tax advantages of early dispersal. Yet judges and juries are likely to measure the aged person's behavior against the norms of middle-aged consumption patterns. The middle-aged adult is still the mainstay of his dependent family, a member of the working force, a saver and a planner for the future. His decisions in business, personal consumption and savings are motivated by his present and probable future needs—a consideration no longer pressing for many of the aged, especially if some functional equivalent of annuity has been reserved from their estates. Ironically, the result of care and foresight in planning for retirement may render the guardian's only substantial duty the preservation for relatives of what was from the start intended as a "spendthrift fund" for carefree years.

* * *

All these dangers sharpen the problems involved in having nonadversary proceedings, for such proceedings are especially vulnerable to abuse by those who seek guardianship for essentially self-interested, adversary reasons. True, some recognition of the drastic consequences of becoming an adjudicated incompetent is inherent in a presumption of competency which attaches to every adult. But, in fact, the very structure of the proceedings—as well as judicial adherence to the view that guardianship serves the ward's best interest and lack of sympathy for the unproductive elderly—may encourage a finding of incompetency.

The protection of a burden of proof may not be very significant in proceedings denominated nonadversary. The proceedings, usually held in county or probate courts, may begin by a petition, which in many states need not be verified by affidavit or medical certificate. If medical certification of the petition is required, that certification may become *prima facie* evidence of the allegations, shifting the burden of proof at the start. Once a petition is filed, notice is served to the alleged incompetent; supplemental notice, intended to guarantee against the possibility that the adult will not comprehend notice sent him, is sent to relatives or an official. But this attempt to assure that there will be some party in court to represent the adult's interests will fail, where, as is often true in the case of the aged, relatives' expectations of near-immediate testamentary benefit may overcome their sympathy for the testator.

The proceedings are vulnerable to the possible self-interest of the subject's relatives in other ways. If the alleged incompetent is bed-ridden or easily disturbed emotionally, they may be able to convince the court to waive presence. Despite the practical adversity of the proceedings and the importance of the rights at stake, it is not clear that the alleged incompetent has any assurance of representation. Few states do more than permit appointment of a guardian *ad litem*; others explicitly deny the need for such appointment. Even should the alleged incompetent hire a lawyer to defend him, he may be prejudiced by the nature of the case to be made against him. Evidence at the hearing need not be medical or expert. Though such evidence is frequently admitted, the court has broad discretion whether to appoint its own examiners or to accept evidence presented by the medical experts called by petitioners or the alleged incompetent. The courts may rely on their own questioning and observation of the alleged incompetent, or upon the testimony of lay witnesses.

The appointment of a guardian virtually insures preservation of the estate for the family of the ward and effectively precludes realization of the ward's possible goals of expenditure and gift of his property. The ward is given no preference in selecting his guardian; in fact, the nomination of the relatives will usually prevail. Courts were once suspicious that the next of kin, because of their expectations of inheritance, might not respect their fiduciary duties or might be over-zealous in conserving the ward's estate. But the family is now presumed to be the most concerned with the ward's well-being, and relatives—even when petitioners—are often appointed guardian, despite their expectations of inheritance. Even where the guardian is disinterested, the very nature of his responsibility is likely to lead him to favor savings over the consumption pattern which the aged might well be expected to prefer. Based on a presumption that the ward will recover, the statutes focus on protection of property and impose strict fiduciary requirements upon the guardian, encouraging him to preserve the ward's property until that event. For expenses beyond the basic necessities, some statutes require the guardian to petition for court approval. And the guardian is discouraged by court practice from applying to the court for authorization for any such "extraordinary" expenditures. Using conservative estimates of how long the ward is likely to live, guardians get carried away by a "zeal for fiscal efficiency," providing only the clearest necessities of food, shelter and medicine.

The manner in which guardianship fails to carry through the expressed preference for the welfare of the ward is further seen in the fact that guardianship, concentrating primarily on conservation of property, neglects the personal care of the ward. Guardianship is relevant only for those aged who have some accumulated savings, and therefore already possess a degree of financial security. For these aged, the truly pressing need may be for adequate personal attention. . . .

* * *

. . . Of course, court favoritism for family interests could be defended as an attempt to preserve the integrity of the ward's intent. The ward would not want to act "foolishly" and the court aids him in fulfilling his desire. Such a defense is often used in analyzing court questions of testamentary capacity. Here also, courts protect those who would ordinarily be heirs but they disavow this function under the guise of sanctifying the integrity and freedom of testator's intent. A decedent will be said to have had testamentary capacity at the time he wrote his will, if he was able to comprehend the extent of his property and was aware of those who were the "natural objects of his bounty." Since the testator is necessarily absent from the courtroom the focus of court inquiry is even more sharply on the character of his disposition. When the disposition is "unnatural," i.e., when it goes to a taker other than relatives, the testator is often deemed mentally incapable of having drawn a valid will. Yet if the testator's intent is presumed always to involve adherence to the societal norm of dispositions within the family, express statements that he is free to dispose of his property as he wishes must be disbelieved. Freedom to neglect family expectations necessarily implies ability to depart from the norm. If each deviation from the norm is construed as evidence of non-intent, clearly freedom to dispose of property is curtailed in favor of the protection of the family. The argument that the judicial attitudes are defensible as an attempt to preserve the ward's intent, then, fails.

The consistency with which these family interests are favored suggests that there may be some reason to consider inheritance expectations as worthy of protection. True, these interests have been characterized as "mere" expectations, a "bright hope" underserving of legal recognition. But such characterizations have arisen more out of distate for negotiation and assignment of inheritances than out of respect for testamentary freedom, In fact, such expectations are protected both explicitly, as in the widow's elective share, and tacitly, as in the area of testamentary capacity, through standards which favor intestate succession whenever "unworthies" appear to be takers. A similar result is achieved in the imposition of involuntary guardianship where the existence of "dissipation" is tested by the "worthiness" of the taker. Antipathy to avaricious young ladies is not the sole cause for family preference. Much of the aged individual's property may have been secured by the joint efforts of family members, or inherited from common ancestors. It is not entirely accurate to say that what the individual owns, he owns entirely by his own initiative; many will have participated directly in the creation of his property. As against his claim to do with what is his as he will, these persons—in more-or-less accurate statistical shorthand, his family—have a claim that the property is not entirely his. It may be rational to favor the family, at least whenever the individual can be shown incapable of exercising his will. This is the effect of the law of involuntary guardianship as well as that of testamentary capacity.

If such a balance of interests is to be struck, it should be struck openly, so that courts can reason and express their results in terms of the family as well as the individual interests involved. It might then appear relevant whether the relatives who would benefit by the guardianship were so close to the individual that it could be said fairly that they had shared, in some way, in the creation of his estate, or had justifiable expectations about the flow of property from some common ancestor. And the present court practice of using neglect of family interests to prove the need for their protection would properly be restricted by a straightforward recognition by the courts that they are resolving a balance of adverse interests. Such a balance ought strongly to favor the individual in every case: freedom to deviate from norms of societal behavior is too important an aspect of our societal structure to be sacrificed to any but the most pressing of demands or the most clear evidence of mental incapacity. This is particularly the case with involuntary guardianship. Unlike a conclusion of testamentary incapacity, imposition of a guardianship results in an immediate and significant loss of freedom and dignity for the individual subject to its consequences.

Societal interests in involuntary guardianship, as distinct from family or personal interests, are of limited scope. If the goal is to protect society from dangerous individuals, confinement rather than involuntary guardianship would be the only satisfactory solution. If society is to be protected against bearing the welfare costs of persons who destitute themselves by dissipating their savings, this goal may be accomplished without the substantial incursions on individual freedoms represented by guardianship. Enforced savings programs such as social security may be used to assure steady sources of income for all the aged. Many aged . . . will already have provided for necessary security, and will not require the State's assistance. Society's interest in this respect, moreover, applies equally to all those who might become destitute—not only the mentally weak—and ceases once destitution is shown to have been avoided. It thus fails to explain the stringencies of involuntary guardianship upon private property control. Society

does use involuntary guardianship to further certain moral judgments and social norms. The very preference for family and the characterization of who is an "unworthy" taker are expressions of general community attitudes. A perference for youth or an intolerance of the aged and their burdensome and "eccentric" behavior may also be implicit in the imposition of involuntary guardianship. But if faced squarely with the question whether these implicit preferences or intolerances were to be enforced through explicit recognition of involuntary guardianship proceedings as adverse to the individual, it seems unlikely that courts or legislatures would often choose against the individual.

If involuntary guardianship should only be imposed in the interests of the ward, inability to manage property should not be sufficient grounds for imposition. Without a suggestion of mental weakness, there is no justification for protecting adults who can not manage property. Prevailing values allow an adult freedom to dispose of property as he wishes, and if he should choose to beggar himself or simply persist in bumbling through life, the law does not intervene paternally. Instead, society has chosen to retain a wide arena of unfettered freedom of decision despite the costs of mistakes and mismanagement. So long as evidence of property mismanagement is treated as sufficient for a finding of mental illness, preference for individual freedom and decision-making will be defeated.

The aged do have some interest in financial security, and, possibly, they are more easily defrauded. But financial security may be assured while allowing the individual a maximum of integrity and freedom. General savings plans, enforced for all members of society, as social security, insure at least some income for all the aged. A court order requiring purchase of an annuity or the establishment of a personal trust fund would insure security without deprivation of the adult's legal rights. The adult would be free to dispose of the insured income and whatever excess assets he retained. If there was strong suspicion that the annuitant was mentally ill, his conduct in disposing of the income might be final evidence of incompetence *vel non*. If he failed to use the income for his own welfare, his shelter, food and medicine, a court might order more drastic interference. As far as fraud is concerned, it seems too drastic to prevent inchoate schemes by imposing a total disability from dealing with any people. The alternative approach, to take action against persons guilty of fraud, though perhaps less effective, seems preferable in its respect for individual freedom.

As applied to adults truly incapable of making any decisions, the structure of guardianship should be amended to insure protection of the ward's real needs. An important need, presently unstressed by the law, is the need for personal care. Geriatric facilities are presently insufficient. An individual should be able to volunteer his need for personal help and to refuse it when he was already blessed with sufficient nurses, housemaids and doctors, likewise, where the need is for assistance in property management. Legal interference would be superfluous and officious. What the elderly need is a comfortable level of existence, not the preservation of the estate for the event of their recovery. Thus, the guardian of the estate should not be a possible heir with an interest adverse to expenditure. And he should be permitted to pay out for more than basic necessities, free from rigorous fiduciary standards.

The reforms suggested require considerable reworking of the institution of guardianship. To maximize the possibilities for personal care and financial supervision sensitive to the aged ward's needs, it would be wise, where possible, to appoint separate guardians of the person and of the estate. The family will often prove the most fruitful source of a guardian for the ward's personal needs, but not for his financial needs. Periodic medical examinations or visits by a social worker might be required to supervise the ward's personal care. Furthermore, improvements should be made in the hearing procedure. Medical testimony by impartial, preferably court appointed, physicians should be ordered before concluding that the adult cannot care for himself. Adversity should be recognized partly by making sure the potential ward is represented by counsel—court appointed, if necessary. It will be recognized that all these conclusions, like many reached above, apply with like force at whatever age level guardianship is applied, for at all levels the institution represents similar dangers. In the particular case of the aged, the court must be sensitive to the role of guardianship as but one part of an overall concern for their welfare. As specialized facilities such as cottage communities and geriatric nursing homes become increasingly available, commitment, allowing ambulatory freedom but providing personal care, will become a more effective institution for the aged. As commitment may become more prevalent, guardianship, once historically linked to commitment, may again become an integral part of such procedures. Commitment may become the means of assuring personal care of the aged ward, while guardianship, as a supplement, could fill the function it best serves, the management of property.

NOTE

WILKIE v. O'CONNOR
261 App. Div. 373, 25 N.Y.S. 2d 617 (1941)

CROSBY, PRESIDING JUSTICE.

The appellant, by petition dated March 29, 1940, commenced this proceeding . . . to show cause why the Commissioner of Public Welfare of Seneca County should not deliver to petitioner a check for $24.50, being the amount of "old age assistance," under Public Welfare Law, which petitioner had been receiving for some time.

The Commissioner's answer alleges that petitioner, despite all efforts to dissuade him, insists upon his right to sleep under an old barn, in a nest of rags to which he has to crawl upon his hands and knees. The answer further alleges that petitioner has been offered suitable living quarters and an increase in pension sufficient to enable him to maintain a so-called civilized standard of living.

The record discloses that the justice in Special Term made a personal inspection of petitioner's sleeping quarters before denying the prayer of his petition.

*   *   *

An appeal from the determination of the Commissioner of Public Welfare to the State Department of Public Welfare is specifically provided for in the Public Welfare Law (Section 124-d). Section 124-e provides that: "All grants of assistance under this article shall be reconsidered from time to time," and "it shall be within the power of the public welfare official at any time to cancel and revoke assistance for cause, and he may for cause suspend payments thereof for such periods as he may deem proper, subject to review by the State department, as provided in section 124-d."

*   *   *

. . . One of appellant's arguments, gathered from his brief, is that after the local welfare officer has once granted the petitioner a pension he has no control over the matter, and that his only duty is to pay the pension regularly, and that his power is limited to the performance of that duty. The Public Welfare Law clearly negatives that argument. Appellant also argues that he has a right to live as he pleases while being supported by public charity. One would admire his independence if he were not so dependent, but he has no right to defy the standards and conventions of civilized society while being supported at public expense. This is true even though some of those conventions may be somewhat artificial. One is impressed with appellant's argument that he enjoys the life he lives in his humble "home" as he calls it. It may possibly be true, as he says, that his health is not threatened by the way he lives. After all he should not demand that the public, at its expense, allow him to experiment with a manner of living which is likely to endanger his health so that he will become a still greater expense to the public.

It is true, as appellant argues, that the hardy pioneers of our country slept in beds not better than the one he has chosen. But, unlike the appellant, they did it from necessity, and unlike the appellant, they did not call upon the public to support them, while doing it.

Another of appellant's arguments is entirely fallacious. In his brief he says that to a man who has "lived a good life for sixty-five years . . . this old age assistance statute should be viewed in the light of a reward." There is nothing in the record to show that appellant has lived a "good life." In any case his old age pension is not given as a reward, it is given to satisfy a human need regardless of the kind of a life the man has lived, and, in accepting charity, the appellant has consented to the provisions of the law under which charity is bestowed. There is nothing in the record to show that the welfare law has, in this case, been improperly administered.

* * *

Order affirmed without costs. . . .

Table of Cases

Table of Authors

Table of Books, Articles, and Other Sources

Subject Index